LABOR RELATIONS LAW IN THE PUBLIC SECTOR

CONTEMPORARY
LEGAL EDUCATION SERIES

LABOR RELATIONS LAW IN THE PUBLIC SECTOR

Cases and Materials

FOURTH EDITION

Harry T. Edwards
Circuit Judge
United States Court of Appeals
for the District of Columbia Circuit

R. Theodore Clark, Jr.
Partner
Seyfarth, Shaw, Fairweather & Geraldson
Chicago, Illinois

Charles B. Craver
Professor of Law
George Washington University

THE MICHIE COMPANY
Law Publishers
CHARLOTTESVILLE, VIRGINIA

Preface to the Fourth Edition

The aim of this revision is to bring Labor Relations Law in the Public Sector up-to-date as of approximately January 1, 1991. We have retained the basic organizational structure of the casebook, since this has proved to constitute a logical and practical arrangement of the material. We plan to continue our practice of publishing annual supplements, so that the book will be current at the beginning of each academic year.

This casebook contains more material than would normally be covered in a two- or even three-hour course. We believe that each teacher should have the opportunity for personal selection. One may consider the initial development of the collective bargaining obligation to be of primary importance, while another may wish to concentrate upon the rights and duties which exist after a bargaining representative has been selected. Both should find ample material to satisfy their pedagogical objectives.

We are pleased to express our appreciation to Joy Axelrad, who provided invaluable research assistance during the preparation of this revision.

Washington, D.C.   *Harry T. Edwards*
Chicago, Illinois   *R. Theodore Clark, Jr.*
Washington, D.C.   *Charles B. Craver*
March 1991

Preface to the First Edition

Several premises underlie the preparation and offering of the materials contained in this volume. The first is that public sector "unionization" and collective bargaining represent the most important development in "labor relations" since the post-Wagner Act period of the 1930s and 1940s. This significance derives both from the sheer magnitude and success of organizing efforts in the public sector and from its major impacts on the management of governmental affairs and public employees at all levels of government — federal, state and local.

During the past decade, dramatic changes have occurred in the body of relevant public sector law, as was true in the private sector in the earlier era. These changes have both contributed to and resulted from public sector unionization. While labor relations law in the public sector has naturally drawn heavily on private sector precepts the models, it has also involved major departures, in response to numerous problems peculiar to the public sector. These are not only substantive. In contrast with the preemptive "federalization" in the private sector, the most important body of public sector labor relations law is state and local. Thus, there are wide variations, resting on differing judgmental evaluations and determinations of public policy. Indeed, the states have proven to be "laboratories" for socio-political experimentation in the development of the law in this area.

In our judgment, a law school curriculum is incomplete which does not afford students the opportunity to examine in some depth the parameters, important variations and problems of public policy embodied in this area of the law. The traditional law school Labor Law curriculum has given primary attention to the private sector, and the typical Labor Law "casebook" reflects this fact. It is quite apparent now, however, that adequate treatment of both private and public sectors is not feasible in a single volume. Hence a basic objective has been to provide a separate set of teaching materials for use in law schools and in other educational contexts. We have also sought to achieve a kind of approach and treatment of the relevant materials which will be of interest and value to those directly concerned on a working basis with public sector labor relations (lawyers, administrators, officials of labor organizations and public employees).

We have not sought to treat many of the obviously important problems relating to collective bargaining techniques, substantive collective bargaining provisions or the numerous practical aspects of labor relations, except to the extent these matters are affected or influenced by the applicable legal structure or rule. In many of these areas, the law does have significant relevance. But it has not seemed to us to be feasible to attempt to deal fully, in a single volume, with the process of collective bargaining or with the more practical aspects of administering labor agreements. In dealing with collective bargaining, therefore, we concentrate on the legal framework and not on specific techniques of collective negotiations or contract administration.

Although the body of "law" in the public sector is now substantial, it is still in the formative stage. As a consequence, we have sought to supplement the judicial decisions reported herein with numerous excerpts from other publications and with substantial text and note material written by the editors. It is our hope that this textual material, much of which has been written by some of the outstanding scholars and practitioners in the field, will raise significant policy questions for consideration in connection with the proper course of the development of labor relations law in the public sector.

The original footnote numbers from judicial opinions have been retained and bracketed. The editors' footnotes are numbered consecutively within each chapter. For the future, we plan to provide annual softbound supplements so that the work will be up-to-date at the start of each school year.

Our thanks to the following students who served as research assistants during the preparation of this volume: Donald Anderson, Zachary Fasman. Dianne Fraser, and Richard Moon. We are also especially indebted to Miss Patt Alfs and Miss Ruth Iverson, who toiled tirelessly to type the final manuscript.

Mr. Clark wishes to thank his wife, Sandy, and children, David, Sarah and Steven; Professor Edwards wishes to thank his wife Becky, and children, Brent and Michelle; and Professor Smith wishes to thank his wife, Berta — their patience, faith and encouragement helped to make possible the contribution of each of us.

<table>
<tr><td>Chicago, Illinois</td><td>R. Theodore Clark, Jr.</td></tr>
<tr><td>Ann Arbor, Michigan</td><td>Harry T. Edwards</td></tr>
<tr><td>Ann Arbor, Michigan</td><td>Russell A. Smith</td></tr>
<tr><td>June 1973</td><td></td></tr>
</table>

Summary Table of Contents

Table of Contents

Chapter 1

PUBLIC SECTOR UNIONISM — ORIGINS AND PERSPECTIVES

A. A HISTORICAL SURVEY

1. GENERALLY

PROJECT: COLLECTIVE BARGAINING AND POLITICS IN PUBLIC EMPLOYMENT, 19 UCLA L. Rev. 887, 893-96 (1972)*

Unionism among government employees began in the 1830's, when mechanics, carpenters and other craftsmen employed by the federal government joined craft unions which already existed to serve those employed by private industry. The natural affinity among skilled craftsmen overcame the differences between public and private employ, and encouraged public employees to join the unions.[1] Within ten years, the embryonic public employee movement began to assert itself, presenting employers across the country with demands for a shorter work day.[2] Private trade unions had already adopted this demand, encouraging their public sector brethren to follow suit.[3] Private sector employers had agreed to a ten hour work day in 1835, and ultimately public employers also acquiesced, not necessarily because they sanctioned union-type activity on the part of their employees, but rather because they competed with private industry for the same workers, and thus had to ensure the availability of their labor supply. Undoubtedly, however, union activities by public employees had some effect in gaining concessions by the government. Moreover, private sector employees, having won their own battle, assisted public employees in applying pressure on local governmental units,[4] and in most cases these combined efforts contributed to the change in policy by the public employers.[5]

While state and local government employees found relative success in union activity, workers in federal employ had less favorable results. Their employers were department heads who were divorced from popular pressure. Moreover, most of the federal artisans and craftsmen were employed by the War and Navy

---

*Copyright 1972 by the Regents of the University of California. Reprinted by permission.

[1]See M. Moskow, Collective Bargaining in Public Employment 29-30 (1969).... According to Moskow, the reasons for the affinity among craftsmen were that they "received the same training, associated socially and moved interchangeably between public and private sector jobs." *Id.*

[2]S. Spero, Government as Employer 77 (1948) [hereinafter cited as Spero].

[3]*Id.*

[4]In Philadelphia, for example, the ten-hour work day was adopted by the city council after a large demonstration involving privately employed artisans who were joined by a great number of public workers. See 6 J.R. Commons, Documentary History of American Industrial Society 41-42 (1918).

[5]Spero, *supra* note 2, at 77. Most strike and pressure activity engaged in during this period was by private sector unions acting on behalf of their government-employed members. Public employees did not have their own union, nor was the right of public employees to organize officially recognized by public officials. Thus, where the ten-hour work day movement was unsuccessful in private industry, the public officials of the same area were able to maintain their own resistance. *Id.*

Departments, which were run by military officers whose jobs were unaffected by public opinion. In the face of unalterable resistance by their employers, the federal workers resorted to the strike; in 1836, workers at the Washington, D.C. Naval Shipyard walked off the job. The strike continued for several weeks without any sign of ending, until finally, as had occurred many times at the local level the previous year, a mass demonstration involving strikers and their comrades from private sector organizations confronted President Jackson. The President yielded, establishing the shorter work day for federal employees.

In succeeding years, public employees maintained their status as secondary characters in the struggles of the labor movement. Any benefits secured by these employees generally resulted from the fact that the private sector labor union in their particular industry had already secured such benefits. Public employees benefitted from the fact that public employers adopted the policy of making pay rates and labor standards conform to those prevailing in private employment in the surrounding area.[6]

Until the 1880's, there were few organizations primarily for public employees; indeed, the trade union movement as a whole was just recovering from the Great Panic of 1873. However, with the return of prosperity, a substantial number of public employee organizations were formed. These organizations, which were called associations, were formed primarily for benevolent purposes, and thus they did not join in the renewed militancy of the labor movement which occurred in the late 1800's.[7] One result of the relatively docile attitude of these associations, was that the great labor activities of the two decades preceding the twentieth century, which brought labor in the United States to a position of great importance, occurred virtually without the participation of government workers. Perhaps the alienation of government workers from the mainstream of the labor movement resulted from the fact that militant activity in government employment was not essential, since public employers usually followed private industry job standards; if improvements secured by private sector unions would be granted to public employees without any effort on the part of their own unions, there was virtually no need for a strong, independent bargaining organization.

This situation remained static until well into the twentieth century. However, with the inflationary trend that preceded World War I, state and local government employees began to show an interest in affiliating with the private sector union movement. Significant progress in organizing public employees was stopped, however, in 1919, when the Boston police strike occurred. The great public opposition which resulted from that incident wiped out the progress of

---

[6]See, e.g., Act of July 16, 1862, ch. 184, 12 Stat. 587, amending Act of December 21, 1861, ch. 1, § 8, 12 Stat. 330: "[T]he hours of labor and the rates of wages of the employees in the navy yards shall conform as nearly as is consistent with the public interest with those of private establishments in the immediate vicinity of the respective yards...." This policy of making government employment standards conform with those in private industry was reversed by President Van Buren. Under his direction the foundation was laid for a government employment policy which later became the leader in setting labor standards that were followed by private employers; rather than vice versa. Spero, *supra* note 2, at 83-84.

[7]... "Benevolent" purposes included such goals as the upkeep of morale through association-sponsored social functions. Sometimes associations were formed primarily to take advantage of group insurance benefits.... In any event, activity was generally restrained and little, if any, pressure was exerted on public employers by the associations on their members' behalf.

public employee unionization for several years; only in the great labor upsurge of the 1930's did public employees begin to take renewed interest in labor organizations.

In 1936, the American Federation of Labor (AFL) founded the first national union for state and local government employees — the American Federation of State, County and Municipal Employees (AFSCME).[8] At the same time, all types of government employees began joining organizations comprised principally of workers of their own occupation; teachers, firemen and policemen being among the first to organize. But despite these developments unionization in the public sector progressed slowly, and not until the 1960's did organized public employees become a prominent national labor force....

NOTES

1. Although widescale organization of public employees is a relatively recent phenomenon, some groups of public employees have been organized for decades. For example, the Illinois Supreme Court in *Fursman v. Chicago,* 278 Ill. 318, 116 N.E. 158 (1917), noted that of the

> more than 7,000 teachers employed by the board of education of the city of Chicago ... more than 3,500 of these teachers have been and are members of the Chicago Teachers' Federation, which is affiliated with a federation of trade unions; that the Chicago Teachers' Federation is a corporation not for profit organized on April 9, 1898 ... ; that in November, 1902, the Chicago Teachers' Federation became and has since continued to be affiliated with the Chicago Federation of Labor; ... that in 1914 members of the Chicago Teachers' Federation affiliated with the American Federation of Labor.

2. Among the many useful books and articles examining the history of public sector unionism are S. Spero, Government as Employer (1948); Klaus, The Right of Public Employees to Organize — In Theory and in Practice (New York City Dep't of Labor Serial No. L.R. 1, March 1955).

The history of collective bargaining in New York City has been the subject of several books and articles. See generally Cook, *Public Employee Bargaining in New York City,* 9 Ind. Rel. 246 (1970); Russo, *Management's View of the New York City Experience,* in Acad. Pol. Sci. Proc., vol. 30 at 81 (1970); R. Horton, Municipal Labor Relations in New York City: Lessons of the Lindsay-Wagner Years (1973). For a critical review of the latter book by the Executive Director of District Council 37 of the American Federation of the State, County, and Municipal Employees, see Gotbaum, *Book Review,* The New Leader, May 14, 1973, at 21.

---

[8]... By this time, the federal service was already well-organized — particularly the Post Office Department. The first national union composed solely of government employees to receive an AFL charter was the National Federation of Post Office Clerks, founded in 1906. Unionism outside the Post Office was also well established with the foundation of the National Federation of Federal Employees in 1917 and, later, the American Federation of Government Employees, chartered by the AFL when the NFFE withdrew from the parent organization in 1935.

DEVELOPMENTS IN THE LAW — PUBLIC EMPLOYMENT, 97 Harv. L. Rev. 1611, 1614-16, 1676-82 (1984)*

Legal control of the public employment relationship is a subject of growing importance. Millions of Americans are employed by the federal, state, and local governments; the lives of these citizens are profoundly affected by the judicial, legislative, and administrative decisions that shape the law of public employment. The performance of public employees determines the quality of vital government services, and the government payroll has a major and direct impact on the public fisc....

The growth of government as an employer[3] is one sign of the significance of the law of public employment. Projections indicate a total of 15,707,000 public employees in 1984, composing 17% of the nonagricultural civilian work force. The federal government will employ 2,760,000 people, and state and local governments will employ 12,947,000.[5] Growth in public sector employment has outpaced growth in the private sector over the past forty years. In 1940, 4,202,000 Americans were on government payrolls. By 1960, that number had increased to 8,353,000; by 1980, it had peaked at 16,241,000. The fourfold increase in public employment from 1940 to 1980 compares with a threefold increase in the private sector. More recently, however, there has been a significant drop in the level of public employment; the number of public employees has fallen by nearly half a million since 1980.

Over the past few decades, government employees have played an increasingly vital role in the labor movement. Union membership has grown much more rapidly among public employees than among workers in the private sector. In 1956, there were 16,575,000 union members in the private sector as compared to 915,000 in the public sector. By 1978, private sector union membership had grown less than 1%, to 16,613,000, whereas public sector membership had grown by 296%, to 3,625,000.[9] Many public sector labor organizations

---

*Copyright © 1984 by the Harvard Law Review Association. Reprinted by permission.

[3]More than 82,000 governmental units are public employers. *See* Bureau of the Census, U.S. Dep't of Commerce, 1982 Census of Governments: Governmental Organization, at vi table A (1983). The number of governmental units in the United States has declined by 8,896 units from 91,237 units in 1962. See *id.* The 1982 Census of Governments is still incomplete; for the last complete tabulation, see Bureau of the Census, U.S. Dep't of Commerce, 1972 Census of Governments (1972-1975).

[5]See Employment and Earnings, *supra* note 4, at 45 table B-1. Local education employed 5,211,000 Americans in January 1983; state education accounted for 1,445,000 public sector jobs. Local government administration employed 2,764,000 government employees; state administration engaged another 1,065,000 persons. Medical care is another major source of public employment: in January 1983, hospitals provided 638,000 local, 492,000 state, and 236,000 federal public sector jobs. On the federal level, other major employers include the Department of Defense, which employed 940,000 civilians in 1983, and the Postal Service, which employed 660,000 workers. See Employment and Earnings, *supra* note 4, at 53-54 table B-2. Similar statistics are compiled by the Bureau of the Census. According to its figures, of the 10,314,000 state and local employees in 1980, 4,844,000 were employed in education, 526,000 in highway-related jobs, 1,007,000 in hospitals, 793,000 in police and fire protection, and 361,000 in public welfare. See Bureau of the Census, U.S. Dep't of Commerce, Statistical Abstract of the United States 1982-83, at 412 table 686 (103d ed. 1982).

[9]See *id.* The Bureau of the Census reports that in 1980, 5,031,000 state and local employees — 48.8% of all state and local workers — belonged to employee organizations. See Bureau of the Census, U.S. Dep't of Commerce & Labor-Management Servs. Admin., Labor-Management Relations in State and Local Governments: 1980, at 1 (1981) [hereinafter cited as Bureau of the Census, Labor-Management Relations]; Bureau of the Census, *supra* note 5, at 412 table 686. School dis-

have attracted sizeable followings: the National Education Association, with 1,684,000 members in 1980, was the nation's second largest labor organization; other prominent public sector labor organizations include the American Federation of Teachers, the American Federation of Government Employees, the American Postal Workers, the National Association of Letter Carriers, the American Federation of State, County, and Municipal Employees, and the National Association of Government Employees.

In 1980, 14,302 state and local governmental units, 17.9% of the total, reported having a labor relations policy. Employee bargaining units existed in 13,408 state and local government bodies; negotiations led to the signing of 27,274 contractual agreements and 7,477 memoranda of understanding. State and local governments experienced 502 work stoppages between October 1979 and October 1980; these strikes involved 233,095 employees and resulted in the loss of 2,406,708 work days. In the federal sector, 1,234,256 employees, or 61% of those surveyed, belonged to 2,463 recognized exclusive bargaining units in 1980. The federal government was party to 1,696 collective bargaining agreements covering 57% of all federal employees....

Collective bargaining came to the public sector much later than to the private workplace. In part, limitations on public employees' collective bargaining rights and right to strike stem from the notion that the government as sovereign stands in a different relation to civil servants than does the private sector employer to its employees. In contrast, the constitutional protections afforded government employees against their employers are not extended to private sector employees against their employers....

When Congress enacted the National Labor Relations Act (NLRA) in 1935, it exempted public employers — governments and their agencies — from the obligation to engage in collective bargaining. For several decades thereafter, the federal and state governments continued to resist public sector bargaining on the largely unquestioned assumption that granting bargaining rights to "public servants" would endanger the public good. Opponents of public sector bargaining argued that requiring the public employer to bargain with its employees would impair its political sovereignty and would amount to an illegal delegation of governmental powers. Moreover, it was feared, public employee unions would exploit their bargaining rights to win excessive economic concessions and would disrupt essential public services by exercising the right to strike.

Beginning in the 1960's, as public employee organizations grew in number and strength, Congress and several state legislatures enacted laws granting bargaining rights to public employees. To some extent, the trend reflected a renewed confidence in collective bargaining as a means of reducing labor-management strife, regardless of the employer's identity. The adoption of bargaining statutes was also spurred by a perception that public employers in many respects resemble private employers and that the total denial of bargaining rights to public employees is therefore unjustifiable. This perception may have been reinforced by the fact that it is sometimes difficult to discern whether an

tricts are the most heavily organized governmental units, with 60.2% membership, and county governments are the least organized, with 34.9% membership. See Bureau of the Census, Labor-Management Relations, *supra*, at 1 table B. Fire protection is the most heavily organized area of government employment with 70.6% membership. See *id.* at 2 table C.

employer is public or private. Moreover, increasing experience with public sector bargaining allayed legislatures' earlier fears that public employee unions would hold government and the public hostage to their demands....

In the late 1950's, Minnesota and Wisconsin became the first states to enact statutes extending some bargaining rights to public employees. [President Kennedy] followed suit by granting rights to federal employees in 1962[15] but did not address the rights of state, county, or municipal employees. In the absence of federal regulation, a number of states empaneled special advisory committees to study the desirability of public sector bargaining; following the committee recommendations, the states began to adopt bargaining statutes to supplement their existing civil service systems.

Today, collective bargaining in one form or another is — at least formally — a reality for public employees of the federal government and most state governments. Federal employees exercise bargaining rights under title VII of the Civil Service Reform Act of 1978.[18] The vast majority of public employees in over thirty states — as well as such specific groups of employees as police officers, firefighters, and teachers in a number of other states — now enjoy statutory bargaining rights. Even in states that either lack statutes authorizing public sector bargaining[21] or prohibit such bargaining as a violation of public policy,[22] collective negotiation is often an accepted practice.

Nevertheless, the particulars of the public employer's obligation to bargain vary widely from jurisdiction to jurisdiction. Most states have adopted a "collective negotiations" approach modeled on the NLRA. This approach requires the public employer to bargain in good faith about employment conditions and to make efforts to conclude binding contracts with employees' representatives. A number of other states, however, cling to the belief that it is inappropriate to require a public employer to bargain. In these states, employees are entitled only to "meet and confer" with the public employer about employment conditions; the employer need do no more than "hear the unions out and thank them for coming."

Even among states that require public employers to bargain, there persists an ambivalence toward public sector bargaining — an ambivalence reflected in the use of the NLRA as both a model and a foil for the framework of negotiations. Many statutes draw heavily on the NLRA in their definitions not only of such rights as the right of exclusive union representation, but also of election and union certification procedures and of unfair labor practices. With regard to other aspects of the bargaining relationship, however, many states have rejected the private sector model and have strictly limited the dimensions of public sector bargaining on the theory that public employers require greater protec-

---

[15] See Exec. Order No. 10,988, 3 C.F.R. 521 (1962), reprinted in 5 U.S.C. § 631 (1964). Executive Order No. 11,491, 3 C.F.R. 254 (1969), reprinted in 5 U.S.C. § 7301 app. at 576-81 (1976), replaced the earlier order in October 1969 and has since been amended twice, Exec. Order No. 11,838, 3 C.F.R. 957 (1975); Exec. Order No. 11,616, 3 C.F.R. 605 (1971). See Rosenblum & Steinbach, *Federal Employee Labor Relations: From the "Gag Rule" to Executive Order 11491,* 59 Ky. L.J. 833 (1971).

[18] 5 U.S.C. §§ 7101-7135 (1978). See generally S. Levitan & A. Noden, Working for the Sovereign (1983) (discussing development of collective bargaining rights for federal employees).

[21] Such states include Arizona, Arkansas, Colorado, Louisiana, Mississippi, and Utah.

[22] See N.C. Gen. Stat. § 95-98 (1981); Tex. Rev. Civ. Stat. Ann. art. 5154c-1 (Vernon 1971 & Supp. 1982).

tion than do private employers. The nearly universal denial to government workers of the right to strike is the prime example of the legislatures' continuing misgivings about public sector bargaining.

Whether the NLRA model is emulated or rejected, however, the preoccupation with the private sector system is unfortunate. Simply to import the private sector bargaining regime into the public sector would be to neglect the special role of the public employer as representative of the public interest....

Fortunately, the dominance of the NLRA model of collective bargaining is giving way to a number of imaginative approaches that attempt to respond to the duality of government's identity as both employer and governor. What has been characterized as a "crazy quilt-work pattern of law" among the different states can be reconceived as a laboratory for experimenting with novel ways of structuring public sector bargaining. Ironically, public sector bargaining law, which for so long took its cue from private sector practices, may prove a source of innovation and rejuvenation for collective bargaining in the private sector....

LEVITAN & GALLO, CAN EMPLOYEE ASSOCIATIONS NEGOTIATE NEW GROWTH?, Monthly Labor Rev., July 1989, at 5-13

The evolution of Government employee associations into virtual unions and the absorption of associations by established unions have played a major role in the growth of public-sector unionization. For many years now, most of the growth experienced by unions has come through the latter route of absorption. This article examines the ways in which the Government employee associations have flourished and briefly traces their history and interaction with unions throughout the 20th century, concluding that further unionization of Government employees by absorption is unlikely.

Two broad types of Government employee associations had evolved by the mid-20th century. Single-profession associations like the National Education Association, Fraternal Order of Police, and American Association of University Professors originated in the latter half of the 19th or early 20th century. Associations that served members united by a common employer (for example, the Federal Government or a State or local government) without regard to occupation were founded in the 1940's and 1950's. Generally, both varieties of association began with limited agendas and sometimes existed only to pool members in order to purchase insurance or organize social events. Even *bona fide* Government unions often behaved like associations before the 1960's, because public workers had no legal right to bargain collectively.

Until 1960, relatively little change occurred in either type of association. Thereafter, however, their character changed dramatically. To retain their independence in the face of union competition, associations of single professions became much more like unions themselves. Among common-employer organizations, many State and local associations were unsuccessful in their bid to resist raiding campaigns and merged with established unions.

Post-1960 Changes

The enactment of public-sector bargaining laws by most States, together with competition from established unions, was chiefly what drove public employee associations to adopt collective bargaining. The contributory economic, legal, attitudinal, and political factors are interrelated: unions and associations, of course, require political and sometimes economic clout to enact laws, but statutory power is also often necessary to overcome management opposition to organizing campaigns.

Public-sector bargaining laws were instrumental, if not critical, to the transformation of Government employee associations and their embrace of collective action. In 1959, Wisconsin enacted the first State public-sector bargaining law, and more than 30 States followed during the 1960's and early 1970's. Today, only 10 States remain outside the pale of such laws. These States, with 15 percent of State and local government employees, are almost all in the South and do not sanction bargaining rights for any group of public employees. According to Al Bilik, president of the AFL-CIO Public Employee Department, unions have abandoned efforts to enact public-sector bargaining laws in them. Because it is not usually explicitly forbidden, limited bargaining does occur in these States. However, the AFL-CIO reports that in 1982 (the latest data available) an estimated 71 percent of nonmanagerial Government workers were organized in States which legally permitted the majority of their employees to bargain, but only 14 percent were organized in the remaining States. In several instances, the enactment of a public-sector bargaining law has affected associations directly and visibly. For example, in Ohio and California, new laws precipitated negotiations that ended in unions absorbing several associations. And in Illinois and, again, in Ohio, following the enactment of bargaining laws in 1984, bargaining representation for nonmanagerial Government employees jumped sharply.

Membership drives by established unions have in most cases been the immediate catalyst prompting associations to engage in collective bargaining. Public-sector associations with very limited agendas coexisted for decades with weak Government unions before the unions successfully began to attract larger numbers of Government workers in the 1960's. Larger associations adopted collective bargaining both in response to member demands and to ensure their continued independence. Relatively smaller associations were in many cases unable to beat the unions at their own game and were consequently absorbed.

The changing public climate in the 1960's and 1970's was another catalyst that drove associations of Government employees to resort to collective action. As challenges to authority became fashionable, unions took advantage of the changing attitudes by appealing to Government employees and their associations. Other incentives to collective bargaining were an expanding Government role in societal affairs, increased educational levels attained by public employees, and race and gender discrimination, accepted earlier but proscribed in the 1960's and 1970's. Government employee unions seized these opportunities to expand their membership.

To avoid the onslaught of unions and to respond to member demands, some major associations adopted union tactics and retained their independent status, rather than merge with an existing union. The National Education Association and the Fraternal Order of Police are the most prominent examples of associations employing this strategy; the American Association of University Professors and a number of Federal employee associations also moved in this direction, albeit more slowly. In general, we can distinguish five public-sector employee associations: Public elementary and secondary schoolteachers, college and university professors, police employees, Federal employees, and social workers.

Public Schoolteachers

For over a century after its founding in 1857, the National Education Association (NEA) concerned itself with the state of education rather than the status of educators. To influence educational policy, the NEA functioned mainly as a national educational research institution at a time when Federal, State, and local governments performed virtually no educational research. The association advocated larger educational budgets, but expended only limited efforts to improve the working conditions of teachers, relying on a "trickle down" approach in the hope that increased educational investments would benefit teachers.

By the time the NEA celebrated its centennial, more than half of all public schoolteachers paid dues to the national organization or its State affiliates, but only 10 of NEA's first 97 presidents had been classroom teachers. School administrators and principals constituted only a fraction of NEA's membership, but they ruled the organization. In fact, school administrators commonly required teachers who worked in schools that were under their authority to join the NEA. But by the early 1970's, the dominance of school superintendents and principals over NEA policies was history. The 1971 NEA convention voted to allow administrators to retain their membership, but teachers controlled all elective and appointive NEA bodies. In effect, administrators could be seen but not heard. Having lost their clout, school administrators in 1976 founded the American Federation of School Administrators, currently with 10,000 members. Administrators are now more welcome in the NEA, probably because the preeminent position of the rank and file is secure, but ironically, the administrators' federation is affiliated with the more blue-collar AFL-CIO.

A major impetus to the transformation of the NEA was the American Federation of Teachers (AFT). Upon its founding in 1916, the AFT affiliated with the American Federation of Labor, but until the 1960's, the NEA could easily afford to ignore its weak rival. Before that time, the AFT's advocacy of union principles indirectly helped the NEA to maintain its conservative posture, by providing a haven for dissatisfied NEA members who favored more militant tactics to improve the status of teachers. Were there no AFT, these members might have organized factions challenging the entrenched NEA establishment. In 1961, however, the AFT became a threat to the NEA by garnering 44,000 New York City teachers in one stroke, increasing its membership by more than a third. Then, after winning the representation election, the AFT waged a successful strike in 1962 to break an impasse at the bargaining table. The AFT's organizing approach following the New York victory was simple but potent: union organizers displayed the New York contract to NEA members in other cities, saying, "Look, you can have that, too."

Gradually, the NEA moved to meet the new threat. In 1962, Executive Secretary William Carr acknowledged that the organization faced a crisis that could destroy it, and urged locals to secure written agreements with school administrators. As a result, at its 1962 convention, the NEA defeated a no-strike resolution and endorsed the use of ambiguously defined "professional sanctions."

Internal surveys showed that the association's teachers overwhelmingly favored collective bargaining, and even more telling was the fact that between 1963 and 1966 the smaller AFT matched NEA's vote totals in union representation elections. Reacting to these challenges, the NEA by 1968 explicitly endorsed both collective bargaining and the right to strike.

Table 1 presents the membership of the NEA and AFT in selected years, as well as the number of public elementary and secondary schoolteachers, from 1955 to 1987. The figures are approximations because the two organizations have not always disaggregated teacher from nonteacher members.

Table 1. Membership in public elementary and
secondary schoolteachers' associations,
selected years, 1955-87

[In thousands]

Year	Public elementary and secondary schoolteachers	National Education Association	American Federation of Teachers
1955 . . .	1,141	613	47
1960 . . .	1,408	714	59
1965 . . .	1,710	944	111
1970 . . .	2,055	1,100	205
1975 . . .	2,196	1,685	454
1980 . . .	2,184	1,681	551
1985 . . .	2,207	1,688	604
1987 . . .	2,276	1,829	651

The AFT was not the only catalyst prompting NEA's adoption of collective bargaining: changes in NEA leadership, the law, demographics, and professional qualifications were also important factors. Educational and societal changes radically altered the teaching profession in the 20th century. By 1920, women accounted for six of seven public elementary and secondary schoolteachers, but because many female teachers left their jobs upon marrying, teaching did not represent a career. Even if newlywed teachers continued working, they were commonly required to quit upon becoming pregnant. Following World War II, however, women were increasingly likely to stay in the labor force, giving female teachers a potential lifetime stake in the profession. Moreover, between 1950 and 1970, the proportion of male teachers in the public schools rose from 21 to 32 percent (most of these employed in secondary schools), and the figure remains at a third today. The number of public schoolteachers increased from about 900,000 in 1950 to more than 2 million by 1969. Most of these new teachers were younger, better educated, and more inclined than their predecessors to demand higher pay and enhanced status.

The public school system became increasingly bureaucratized, and administrators interposed themselves between teachers and both students and the community. Improved transportation made it feasible to centralize school facilities.

Despite swelling enrollments, the number of secondary schools remained relatively stable, and the number of elementary schools dropped from 160,000 at the end of the war to 66,000 a quarter century later. The once ubiquitous one-room schoolhouse nearly disappeared.

The market responded to the increasing demand for teachers and their demands for better pay. Concern over Soviet competition — in particular, seeming advances in Soviet space technology in the late 1950's — also spurred Federal investment in education. The ratio of teacher salaries to that of the average full-time worker increased from .88 at the war's end to 1.21 in 1970. Yet teachers wanted more, and they organized to get it.

During the 1970's, teachers lost ground. Unionization could not counteract the effect of a teacher glut as the baby bust replaced the baby boom and enrollment in public schools dropped by 11 percent. In the 1980's, teacher pay has again risen relative to that of other full-time workers as well as professional employees, although enrollment continued to drop during the first half of the decade. The rise in pay is attributable to a movement to improve school performance, which generated increased public support for making teaching salaries more attractive.

The National Labor Relations Act of 1935 did not protect public school-teachers. Consequently, although the first teacher contract was signed in 1944, few more were negotiated until the 1960's. The reason for the increase during that time was the enactment in 1959 of the first State law permitting or requiring bargaining. Between that law's enactment and 1975, 30 States extended the right to bargain to teachers, but only 5 more have subsequently done so.

More than two-thirds of public schoolteachers belong to unions, making the profession the most unionized in the public sector other than postal workers and firefighters. One-fourth of all teachers work in private (mostly church-affiliated) schools, are outside the union movement, and remain unlikely targets for the NEA or AFT because these unions vigorously oppose tuition tax credits or any other means of extending Government financing to private schools. In addition to teachers, the NEA now includes over 100,000 educational support personnel, the AFT, some 95,000. An additional 125,000 support workers have been recruited by the American Federation of State, County and Municipal Employees, and roughly 100,000 by the Service Employees International Union. Both organizations are making a concerted effort to enlist a greater share of the million public school support personnel.

Although the NEA and AFT acknowledge in principle that a single organization to represent teachers would be preferable, relations between the two unions remain contentious. A merger has been tentatively explored on several occasions, coming closest to fruition in 1973. Merger talks between the two organizations' California affiliates are now under way, but officials of both unions categorize these discussions as likely to lead nowhere. Questions of leadership, political differences, and the reluctance of the NEA to affiliate with the AFL-CIO have proved the most stubborn impediments to a national merger.

College and University Professors

The American Association of University Professors (AAUP), founded in 1915, concerned itself primarily with academic freedom during its first half century, but it also emphasized job security under the rubric of tenure. The association briefly debated the merits of pursuing collective bargaining after the enactment of the National Labor Relations Act in 1935, but chose to maintain the status quo. The NEA and AFT challenged this limited agenda in 1969 when they won representation rights for separate groups of faculty at the City University of New York, whereupon the AAUP, perceiving the situation as a threat, changed its policy toward collective bargaining.

In the early 1970's, 19 States enacted legislation permitting faculty bargaining, and a National Labor Relations Board ruling in 1970 extended its jurisdiction to faculty in private, nonprofit colleges and universities. These developments encouraged encroachments by the NEA and AFT on AAUP's turf. By 1988, 30 States granted faculty the right to organize and bargain. In the remaining 20 States, bargaining is spotty or nonexistent.

The number of unionized faculty leaped from 14,000 in 1968 to 84,000 in 1972, when the AAUP voted to embrace collective bargaining. Unlike the NEA membership, which overwhelmingly favored collective action to improve working conditions, the new policy generated conflict within the AAUP. Membership actually declined by a third within 2 years, from a peak of 91,000 in the early 1970's. Today, it stands at 45,000. In 1987, almost a third of faculty members were represented by collective bargaining agreements, mostly by the AFT or NEA. A breakdown, by union, follows:

Total faculty represented:
Number 213,700
Percent 100.0
   American Federation of Teachers 34.5
   National Education Association 27.5
   American Association of University Professors 10.0
   Coalitions 20.0
      AAUP/NEA 10.4
      AAUP/AFT 7.3
      Others 2.3
   Independent unions 4.5
   Other national unions 3.5

Because of its established and respected role in setting professional standards for academic freedom and tenure, the AAUP continues to play an important part in labor relations. The association also has greater familiarity and involvement with the traditional system of faculty governance than do the other unions. Accordingly, the NEA and AFT both solicit the AAUP's partnership in joint organizational drives. The AAUP lends greater respectability and acceptability to organizing efforts, especially at large research universities. As AFT president Albert Shanker notes, "AAUP has a very good name — it's like the Good Housekeeping seal of approval."

Despite these efforts at cooperation, coalitions between the AAUP and the other two teachers' unions have proven very unstable, due to the divergent interests of the partners. The AAUP's general secretary, Ernst Benjamin, describes his organization's relationship with NEA and AFT as one of courtship and competition, of "fight and talk, fight and talk." Joint ventures have created friction within the AAUP, to the extent that several have been abandoned since 1984 and others are in a precarious condition. In the remaining coalitions, the AAUP is clearly the junior partner. For example, at the University of Hawaii and the City University of New York, the AFT does the bargaining, maintaining only a formal partnership with the AAUP.

Postsecondary educational institutions have undergone numerous changes in the past few decades. Following dramatic growth, the number of full-time faculty has stabilized at about 700,000 since 1977. The prospective increase in the college-age population in the late 1990's and rising adult enrollments are likely to generate demands for additional faculty. Tenure-track positions have been cut, as the proportion of faculty working part time has increased from 22 percent in 1970 to 36 percent in 1986, and the share laboring at community colleges has risen from 19 percent to 30 percent over the same period. Real average annual earnings for full-time instructional faculty in 1985 were 8 percent less than the peak of $35,200 reached in the early 1970's, and did not even keep pace with inflation in the following 2 years while the real earnings of all workers stabilized. Declining salaries are partly attributable to the increasing number of community colleges and the increased reliance upon part-time instructors, dubbed the serfs of the academic establishment.

Probably reflecting attitudes in the rest of society, declining pay has not driven academics to embrace unionization. Despite increased dissatisfaction with higher education administration, fewer faculty favored collective bargaining in 1984 than in 1975. The proportion that rejected it increased from 30 to 39 percent, those who felt that unionization would improve compensation dropped from 76 to 61 percent, and those who condoned strikes under some circumstances declined from 61 to 51 percent.

A 1980 Supreme Court decision (*NLRB and Yeshiva University Faculty Association v. Yeshiva University*) exacerbated organizing difficulties by ruling that when faculties at private higher education institutions are substantially involved in the governance of the school, they are part of management. Accordingly, the court found that, for collective bargaining purposes, such university faculties are not protected by the National Labor Relations Act. Not only has the court ruling halted organizing at private colleges; it has actually resulted in the decertification of unions at several institutions. Following the decision, the number of private colleges and universities engaged in collective bargaining dropped from 89 to 74, and in eight cases the NLRB declared that faculty members were managerial employees.

The failure to secure public-sector higher education bargaining rights in 20 States, the *Yeshiva* decision, and more negative faculty attitudes toward bargaining have stymied campus organizing efforts. Although a high of 213,700 faculty members (29.6 percent of all faculty) was recorded as being under contract to some professional union or association in 1987, more careful data collection probably accounts for much of the increase over previous years' figures. (See table 2.) In addition, about 5 percent of the individuals covered by faculty contracts are not faculty members. For example, in the University of California system, 5,000 nurses are under faculty contract. Because of both stronger resistance in the private sector and the *Yeshiva* decision, only 5 percent of the faculty in private institutions — fewer than 10,000 professionals — are organized, compared with 40 percent of faculty in public colleges. AAUP represents the largest share of private-sector faculty; however, two of three faculty members work for Government institutions.

Table 2. Proportion of faculty under union
or association contract, selected
years, 1970-87

Year	Number (thousands)	Percent		
		Total	At four-year colleges	At two-year colleges
1970 . . .	47.3	10.0	6.1	26.0
1975 . . .	102.3	16.3	14.4	21.7
1980 . . .	148.9	21.7	17.6	32.3
1987 . . .	213.7	29.6	26.4	37.6

Adjunct faculty and nonteaching personnel appear to be relatively promising targets for membership drives, although the AAUP, NEA, and AFT have so far had little success with these groups. Just under 10,000 adjunct faculty (part-time, temporary, and non-tenure-track professors) bargain collectively, most having been organized by the NEA and AFT during the 1980's. The American Federation of State, County and Municipal Employees and the Service Employees International Union have organized most of the 60,000 clerical workers who bargain at the largest public and private universities. Thus, the AFT and NEA together represent only 7 percent of organized clericals at large institutions, and the AAUP does not represent any. Plainly, clerical employees are choosing to align themselves with the unions representing workers in similar occupations, rather than with the educational associations.

Police

An unsuccessful 1919 Boston police strike, which helped Massachusetts Governor Calvin Coolidge, who broke the strike, attain the White House, provoked a public backlash against police unions that lasted nearly half a century. Consequently, the police organized themselves into employee associations.

Although only 30 States have enacted laws explicitly authorizing police officers to bargain, they are currently one of the more highly unionized public employee groups, with more than 200,000, or about 40 percent, of the 515,000 police officers in 1986 belonging to a union. By far the largest of these is the Fraternal Order of Police, with 170,000 members. The 1987 median weekly full-time officer salary was $513, slightly more than that of teachers and nurses.

Given the relatively high level of unionization in States allowing bargaining by police officers, further growth depends upon the enactment of bargaining laws in the remaining 20 States or at the Federal level. Because there has been little movement in that direction during the past 15 years, further expansion of collective bargaining by police associations is unlikely in the short term. Furthermore, many unorganized police employees work in towns with small police forces, making them both difficult to unionize and a questionable investment for unions.

Federal Employees

The passage of the Pendleton Act in 1883 was the first important step leading to the establishment of the Federal Civil Service Merit System. Formerly, the Federal work force turned over almost completely upon the accession of a new president. Employees often obtained jobs because of their political connections, with little regard to occupational qualifications, a practice which still applies to top Federal policymakers and managers.

Over time, Federal employees formed associations, but except for postal workers, these were generally powerless to influence labor-management relations. In 1962, President Kennedy established the right of Federal employees to form and join unions. As a result of Kennedy's executive order and later actions by President Nixon, the proportion of nonpostal Federal employees represented by unions climbed from 13 percent in 1961 to 60 percent in the mid-1970's, about where it remains today. However, because the law requires Federal unions to represent workers in organized agencies whether they belong to the union or not, only a third of the workers who are represented by unions are members. The four major unions representing Federal employees are the American Federation of Government Employees (affiliated with the AFL-CIO), with 180,000 members and representing 700,000 employees; National Federation of Federal Employees (45,000 and 152,000, respectively); National Treasury Employees Union (65,000 and 146,000); and National Association of Government Employees (50,000 members), which was absorbed by the Service Employees International Union in 1982. In addition, the AFL-CIO Metal Trades Council and the International Association of Machinists claim to represent 100,000 Federal employees.

Legal restrictions prevent Federal unions from conducting direct bargaining over wages and benefits, from striking, and from engaging in a variety of political activities as an alternative to bargaining. The 1978 Civil Service Reform Act widened the scope of bargaining somewhat, but retained the prohibition on agency shops (which require employees to pay a fee to the union even if they choose not to join) and left the nature of Federal labor-management relations basically unchanged. Federal unions, however, are not completely without clout. While formally they can negotiate only over minor points, innovative leaders can expand the scope of collective bargaining by negotiating over the procedures used to implement management decisions, and this has permitted unions to influence the decisions themselves.

Prevented from bargaining with the direct employers of their members, Federal unions have access to the 535-member "board of directors" — the Congress — and to the White House. During the 1980's, however, their influence diminished with the Congress and they were rarely welcome at the White House. The statutory liabilities faced by Federal unions were underscored when President Reagan fired striking air traffic controllers in 1981, destroying their union. The action served as an effective warning to other Federal workers who might have been inclined to aggressively pursue their interests, and further weakened whatever influence Federal unions previously wielded. Partly as a result, membership declined.

The American Federation of Government Employees (AFGE) is currently in serious and perhaps terminal financial difficulty. In December 1987, the AFL-CIO organized a $1.5 million financial rescue package to keep the union going. The AFGE voted a dollar increase in national dues at its August 1988 convention, but the union is close to bankruptcy and may well have to merge with another public employee union, most likely the American Federation of State, County and Municipal Employees. On top of these financial woes, the National Treasury Employees Union has mounted a raid to capture 12,000 Social Security Administration workers currently represented by the AFGE. Thus, unless circumstances turn around, the future of Federal unions remains bleak.

Social Workers

With 500,000 practitioners, social work is by far the largest, and one of the fastest growing, of the "helping" professions. Social work is a relatively new and extremely broad profession. The first social work school opened its doors in 1898, and the establishment of professional associations took several more decades. As a rule, a professional degree is not required for entry into the field, and half of all social workers do not possess a college degree in social work.

The National Association of Social Workers (NASW) is the major organization of the profession, with 115,000 members. The NASW is the only major association in a profession that, although dominated by Government workers, does not bargain collectively. This aberration is probably due to the character of the association's membership. In contrast to the profession as a whole, NASW represents primarily social workers with advanced degrees in social work. Fifteen percent of NASW members are in private practice, and the remainder are split about evenly between Government and private-sector employers. Minorities constitute less than a tenth of the membership.

In line with the practice of several other professional organizations, including those for sociologists, economists, and political scientists, the NASW has eschewed involvement in labor relations and working conditions, but it has supported collective bargaining for its members since the 1940's. The current standards state that "participation in a strike by a member of NASW does not in itself constitute a violation of the Code of Ethics." Some members have argued that the association should pursue bargaining, but the NASW has rejected the option on the grounds that both sides of the bargaining table belong to NASW.

The first major successful organizing efforts in the profession occurred among social workers in welfare agencies during the 1960's. In addition to factors that have motivated many Government workers to establish unions, social workers faced welfare caseloads that burgeoned far more rapidly than did the number of caseworkers. Strikes occurred in New York, Chicago, and other cities. The American Federation of State, County and Municipal Employees, the Service Employees International Union, and the National Union of Hospital and Health Care Employees stepped in to fill the void left by the NASW in organizing social workers. Data based on a small sample indicate that roughly a quarter to a third of social workers now bargain collectively.

Social workers are ripe targets for further unionization. Nearly two-thirds are Government employees, 65 percent are women, and 25 percent are members of minority groups. Not surprisingly, the occupation is the lowest paid of the major professions, with 1987 median weekly earnings for full-time workers of $413, nearly $70 less than public schoolteachers. Real earnings have not grown during the past decade. Salaries for NASW members, the profession's elite, peak at under $30,000 on average. Most association members work at large institutions such as social service agencies and hospitals, where organizing efforts are relatively cost effective. Future organizing efforts will probably emanate from those unions which have had some experience with this group. The NASW is likely to remain aloof in any labor-management conflicts.

Union Absorption of Associations

While some associations have adopted union tactics, but retained their independent status, others have affiliated with existing labor unions. The American Federation of State, County and Municipal Employees and the Service Employees International Union have been the two most active and successful unions in absorbing associations. Largely because of their incorporation of associations, AFSCME and SEIU have been the two fastest growing unions during the past two decades. The Teamsters, Communications Workers of America, and American Federation of Teachers have pursued mergers with fewer gains. Unions have been successful in absorbing mostly smaller associations; the larger organizations — with some notable exceptions — have been able to fend off raids. Associations of State and local government workers have accounted for most of the affiliations with established unions, in many cases after they had already embraced collective bargaining. Few private-sector professional organizations have been caught in union nets.

Since the 1950's, union and association mergers have become increasingly common, although the pace has slowed, at least temporarily, in the late 1980's. In most cases, the affiliation of associations with unions has been the product of union raids on association membership. The AFL-CIO constitution bars member unions from raiding each other, making external associations targets for expanding membership. State laws sanctioning public-sector unionization spurred employee interest in collective bargaining, but many associations lacked resources and experience or were slow to capitalize on the new opportunities. This made the associations vulnerable to union raids and their members responsive to union appeals. The motivation driving the unions to absorb associations is that incorporation augments union size and power at a fraction of the cost of enlisting members in the old-fashioned way of organizing the unorganized.

However, most of the major State association trophies have already been bagged. Because of union absorption, independent association membership has been declining since the mid-1970's. In fact, the merger movement has been so successful that the Assembly of Governmental Employees, a loose federation of State employee associations, disbanded because its ranks had been decimated by union raids. Altogether, the membership of State employee associations of general government workers today numbers less than 200,000, and State associations of school employees total only slightly more than 100,000.

Local government employee associations usually have fewer members than State associations, although in the aggregate they probably outnumber them. The most recent Government census (1982) counted 3.8 million local union and association members, accounting for 41 percent of local government employees. Excluding members of national unions, local government association members probably number no more than 500,000. Local organizations are often so small that union competition over them is too costly to be worth the trouble.

Effects and Prospects of Bargaining

Absent the adoption of collective bargaining by associations of Government employees, union representation rates would have declined for more precipitously than they have during the past generation. Most of the increase in unionization of Government employees occurred because associations began bargaining rather than because unions recruited the unorganized. The proportion of full-time State and local employees belonging to either unions or associations (whether or not the association bargained) remained at roughly half between 1972 and 1982, the earliest and most recent years available. However, between 1974 and 1982, the proportion of full- and part-time State and local employees in bargaining units rose steadily from 31 to 40 percent.

The association movement has also had a strong impact upon the unionization of professional workers, who in 1988 were more likely to be represented by unions than nonprofessionals (26.8 percent of all professionals versus 17.8 percent of all nonprofessionals). Collective bargaining by professionals is highly concentrated among Government employees: four-fifths of those represented work in the public sector. Professionals are also much more likely to work for the Government than nonprofessionals, which also boosts representation rates among professionals.

The distinction between unions and associations has not always been sharp. For example, although in existence since the 1930's, the American Federation of State, County and Municipal Employees did not focus on bread-and-butter issues until the 1960's. During the past three decades, the contrast between unions and associations has continued to blur. Indeed, in emphasizing professional issues, such as teaching techniques and educational standards, the AFT has to some extent traded places with the NEA, which concentrates on bread-and-butter issues.

The adoption of collective bargaining by associations has taken place at widely varying paces. Once the process began, the National Education Association and the Fraternal Order of Police embraced bargaining within a few years. The American Association of University Professors and the Federal employee associations, despite a history of bargaining dating at least since the early 1970's, are still in many ways in midstream. Limited statutory bargaining rights have hampered Federal employee groups, while the AAUP in some respect faces the opposite problem. A unique system of faculty governance has long existed which gives professors more influence over their working conditions than most other groups of employees. This degree of influence, combined with light teaching loads, lengthy summer vacations, and relatively good pay, naturally diminishes the attractiveness of collective bargaining. Finally, the National Association of Social Workers shows no interest in bargaining for its members, partly because it represents the elite of the profession.

For associations that have merged with existing labor unions, often under the duress of raids, it is important to assess whether the membership has benefited from the absorption. Virtually no research exists on this question, but the possibilities of economies of scale in large organizations would enable them to offer potentially more effective representation.

With the association well running dry, future Government unionization is now much more dependent upon the old-fashioned campaign of organizing the unorganized. However, the prospects of organized labor meeting this challenge are not promising. For example, the States without bargaining laws are mostly Southern and Mountain States, where even successful enactment would have limited effects, if the experience in the private sector is any indication. The proportion of Government workers represented by unions or associations that have adopted collective bargaining dropped from a peak of 45.5 percent in 1983 to 42.5 percent in 1987, before rising slightly to 43.6 percent in 1988. Thus, there is even a possibility that public-sector unionization may be beginning a decline similar to what has been happening in the private sector for over three decades.

NOTES

1. The reasons why unionization in the public sector occurred much later than it did in the private sector have been the subject of much discussion. In addition to the legal and judicial impediments discussed above, some commentators have suggested that there were pragmatic reasons as well. Consider, for example, the following observations:

More practical considerations also delayed the advent of public employee unionism in the United States. The private sector unions and their international federations were fully occupied in trying to increase the extent of organization in the private sector. They had neither the money nor energy to turn to the public sector until the 1960's. Equally or more importantly, public employees were not generally dissatisfied with their terms and conditions of employment and therefore, except in isolated cases, did not press for collective bargaining rights. Though the wages and salaries of public employees in the United States had traditionally lagged slightly behind comparable private sector salaries, the greater fringe benefits and job security associated with public employment were traditionally thought to be adequate compensation.

By the late 1950's and early 1960's several of these practical considerations which had delayed public employee unionism had disappeared. Moreover, new factors came into play that are difficult to assess as to sequence or relative importance, but in total added to a new militancy. Change increasingly became endemic in American society as more and more groups, including public employees, found it commonplace to challenge the established order. Some public employees were made less secure by organizational and technological changes as government came under pressure to reduce tax increases and therefore turned to devices to increase efficiency and lower unit labor costs. Public employee wages and salaries began to lag further behind those in the unionized private sector as the post-war inflationary spiral continued. The private sector international unions saw the large and growing employment in the non-union public sector as a fertile alternative which might substitute for their failure after 1956 to increase membership steadily in the private sector. Finally, many observers of public employment both in and out of government began strongly and publicly to question the logic behind governmentally-protected collective bargaining in the private sector and government's complete failure to grant similar privileges and protections in the public sector.

By the 1960's these practical challenges to the traditional arguments of sovereignty and illegal delegation of powers came to be seen as overriding in a number of government jurisdictions.

Rehmus, *Labor Relations in the Public Sector,* prepared for the 3d World Congress, International Industrial Relations Association, London, England (Sept. 3-7, 1973).

2. In recommending that federal employees be affirmatively granted the right to join and participate in employee organizations and to bargain collectively, President Kennedy's Task Force referred to the following statement in ABA Section of Labor Law, Report of the Committee on Labor Relations of Governmental Employees 89, 90 (1955):

A government which imposes upon other employers certain obligations in dealing with their employees may not in good faith refuse to deal with its own public servants on a reasonably similar favorable basis, modified, of course, to meet the exigencies of the public service. It should set the example for industry by being perhaps more considerate than the law requires of private enterprise.

STERN, UNIONISM IN THE PUBLIC SECTOR, in Public-Sector Bargaining 52-53, 58, 62, 64-67, 69-73, 75-86 (B. Aaron, J. Grodin & J. Stern eds. 1988)*

At the outset it should be noted that with the exception of the federal sector, public-sector union decision making is decentralized. Bargaining leaders are usually representatives of municipal or state councils rather than national union representatives. This is contrary to the pattern found in the bargaining of major manufacturing units, for example, and gives rise to a situation in which the role of the national union president of the public-sector union is relatively less important than that of his private-sector counterpart. Analysis of unions that are active at the municipal and state levels is complicated, therefore, by this decentralized decision-making structure and the various patterns of public-sector unionism that have emerged in many cities and states.

Just the fact that labor relations legislation may be unique to one group of employees provides sufficient grounds for differences in the way the union conducts itself in a particular locality. Clearly, in jurisdictions where unions have not secured legal bargaining rights, their priorities will differ somewhat from union activities emphasized in localities where this goal has been achieved. And the union structure, even its finances, and the role of the union leader will be affected.

Another problem complicating the analysis of public-sector unions is the entrance into this field of what Jack Stieber identified as the "mixed unions" — those primarily private-sector unions which are now organizing public-sector

---

*Reprinted by permission of the Industrial Relations Research Association.

employees. Several of the latter unions, such as the Teamsters, the Laborers, and the Service Employees (SEIU), have become important public-sector unions in some localities but represent no public-sector employees in others. The reader is warned, therefore, that generalizations about public-sector unions are advanced with more than the usual reservations about exceptions to general practices....

The Postal Unions

The major postal unions — the National Association of Letter Carriers (NALC) and the American Postal Workers Union (APWU) — date back to the turn of the century and are among the older American trade unions. The APWU is a 1971 amalgamation of the postal clerks union, three smaller craft unions, and one breakaway industrial union of clerks and carriers....

Both the APWU and NALC are AFL-CIO unions with memberships of approximately one-quarter million.... The only non-AFL-CIO union holding national exclusive bargaining rights in 1986 for a significant number of employees is the National Rural Letter Carriers' Association (NRLCA), with about 40,000 members. Although it cooperates with the AFL-CIO in national negotiations about basic economic matters, it negotiates its own national craft agreement. The Mail Handlers Division of the Laborers Union also negotiates its own national agreement. The major and key bargaining process, however, is the joint negotiations of the APWC and NALC with the Postal Service....

The membership of the APWU is now nearly 50 percent female and, although there is no woman on the executive board, there are four female national business agents. One woman ran for the third top office, secretary-treasurer, in 1986 and was defeated by the male incumbent by only 7,000 votes. The APWU women's group, called POWER (Post Office Women for Equal Rights), is established under the APWU constitution and encourages women to be active in the union.

A growing number of Hispanics have been hired by the U.S. Postal Service and are expected to gain greater representation in the APWU structure in the future. In 1986, a Hispanic candidate from Texas for the national office of organization director defeated a long-term incumbent from New York, and a New York Hispanic was elected to the post of Northeast Regional Coordinator in a four-way contest. As of 1986, there were no Hispanics or women on the executive board, but five of the 14 board members, including the executive vice president, were black. In broad terms, APWU political developments seem to parallel those that are observed on the national scene, i.e., increased influence of minority groups and women, particularly in geographic areas where population is expanding faster than the average....

Unlike the APWU, the NALC has not opposed employee-involvement programs and signed an agreement with the Postal Service in March 1982 to introduce these programs on a trial basis. At a conference in August 1983, representatives of management and union gave favorable reports on the progress of the program. The NALC, a single craft union, is more homogeneous than the multicrafted APWU and appears to have the greater sense of solidarity needed to participate in the "trust me" style of labor relations that is a feature of the program. Also, minority groups seem content with the current union leaders and, although the percent of female letter carriers doubled between 1974 and 1982, only about 10 percent of the letter carriers are women.

The Federal Executive-Branch Unions

Without the postal unions, it is doubtful whether Presidents Kennedy and Nixon would have issued the famous executive orders creating and revising a labor-management framework for federal executive-branch employees. The slowness of the unions in this sector to take advantage of their opportunities after the first executive order was issued reflects primarily the poor position from which these unions started. In 1962, unions of federal employees — with the exceptions of the long-established International Association of Machinists (IAM) and AFL-CIO Metal Trades Council (MTC) units in shipyards and other industrial-type establishments — were underfinanced, understaffed, and relatively inactive. For the most part they were loosely affiliated locals in various federal agencies which supported a small national office in Washington to pursue their goals through the traditional political paths.

The major unions in the federal service and their approximate estimated membership as of 1983 are: American Federation of Government Employees (AFGE), AFL-CIO, 218,000 members; National Federation of Federal Employees (NFFE), independent, 34,000 members; and National Treasury Employees Union (NTEU), independent, 47,000 members. Each of the unions is discussed separately in this section of the chapter. Analysis of the annual report of the Civil Service Commission shows that these three unions represent approximately 75 percent of the federal employees covered by labor agreements. On the assumption that the ratio of the number of members to number of employees covered by agreements held by the three is a reasonable proxy for the relationship of membership to agreement-coverage among all federal unions, the 300,000 estimated membership of the three unions generates an estimate of 400,000 union members covered by the executive order.

This 400,000 estimate is somewhat higher than the Office of Personnel Management's estimate of 331,000 employees for whom union dues were being deducted. It should be emphasized, as is explained subsequently, that membership statistics and representation data in the federal sector differ significantly from those found in the private sector. Unions in the federal sector have won elections entitling them to represent 1.24 million employees, about 60 percent of those covered by the Civil Service Reform Act. The estimates suggest, however, that no more than one third of these employees are union members.

In addition to the three unions representing the largest number of federal employees, another 80 unions hold recognition rights, including the formerly independent National Association of Government Employees (NAGE) which is strong in New England and which in recent years has organized workers in local government and in private firms doing government business. In 1982, NAGE (which in 1985 represented about 67,000 employees) merged with the Service Employees International Union (SEIU), a union with which it had been competing in elections involving state and local government employees in New England. The merger put NAGE under the umbrella of the AFL-CIO "no raid" agreement and thereby reduced the efforts of AFGE to take over NAGE's federal employees as well as those of SEIU and American Federation of State, County and Municipal Employees to take over its local government employees.

Two other AFL-CIO groups representing a substantial number of federal employees are the IAM and MTC, representing approximately 34,000 and 67,000 federal employees, respectively — primarily wage-board employees in shipyards and other industrial-type situations. Of the 373,000 wage-board employees, 88 percent were represented by unions in 1985, compared to 53 percent of the general-schedule employees. Organization of the general-schedule employees (white-collar workers) followed the organization of the wage-board employees (blue-collar workers) and in recent years has plateaued at slightly over the 50 percent mark.

In addition to the employees covered by the Civil Service Reform Act (CSRA), there are several groups of federal employees which have organized under separate legislative arrangements. Employees of the Tennessee Valley Authority are well organized by a variety of unions. State Department employees are represented by an independent union.

The American Federation of Government Employees (AFGE), AFL-CIO

The American Federation of Government Employees was founded in 1932 by the AFL after the existing union, the National Federation of Federal Employees (NFFE), withdrew from the AFL because of jurisdictional disputes and policy differences with AFL unions representing blue-collar craft workers. AFGE is the major union representing federal employees and in 1985 represented about 690,000 of the 1.25 million employees in bargaining units. The union started with a membership of less than a thousand members in 34 locals, mainly located in the Washington, D.C., area. By 1961, its membership (based on AFL-CIO average per capita payments) had increased to 68,000 and, in the following decade under the impetus of the executive order, experienced its most rapid growth to almost 290,000 members. Since that date, although the number of employees it represents has continued to increase, its membership has declined significantly and was reported to be about 200,000 in 1983.

The "free rider" problem of AFGE and other federal unions seems to be much greater than the problem faced by private-sector unions and unions of state and municipal employees. To some extent, of course, the federal prohibition on compulsory payment of union dues could be cited as the obvious cause of the problem. Employees may vote for union representation and then be unwilling to pay dues voluntarily. But this explanation is not sufficient to account for the variations in the gap between membership and representation among the different unions which operate under a legal framework prohibiting compulsory payment of dues or service fees. Membership in the postal unions is probably as close to the number of employees represented as is found in private-sector union-shop situations, despite the legal prohibition against compulsory union membership.

A second factor that may shed further light on this question is the relatively low number of employees who bother to vote in union representation elections. From 1971 to 1975, 57 percent of eligible voters participated in elections under the executive order as compared to 88 percent of the eligibles in NLRB private-sector elections and a similar figure for postal-system elections. It seems quite possible that the membership figures of many federal unions reflect the number of employees who voted for the union in the representation election, and the gap between membership and representation consists of those employees who did not vote and those who voted against the union.

Although the elimination of the prohibition against agency shops may be a necessary step if membership figures are to approach representation figures, it should be kept in mind that the possibility of compulsory payment of union dues or a service fee may tend to bring out many voters who will vote against the union in order to avoid the possibility of being obliged to pay dues in the future. AFGE might find it more difficult to win representation elections in such a situation. In any event, this large gap between membership and representation figures is an unusual aspect of industrial relations in the federal sector....

The National Federation of Federal Employees (NFFE), Independent

The National Federation of Federal Employees started out in 1917 as the AFL union of federal-government employees and has since gone through several significant changes in character. As noted previously, NFFE left the AFL in 1931 because of jurisdictional and policy differences with the craft unions; NFFE supported the adoption of the general-service schedule and a civil-service-type compensation plan, while the crafts adhered to the wage-board approach and the tying of individual craft rates to the prevailing private-sector union rate for that craft. At the time of the withdrawal, NFFE reportedly had almost 50,000 members, but membership declined over the next 30 years as a result of AFGE inroads.

When Executive Order 10988 was issued in 1962, NFFE condemned it and brought an unsuccessful court suit challenging the constitutionality of the President's action. Only after a two-year losing battle accompanied by a further decline in membership did the union reverse its position. The reversal was brought about by the newly elected president, Nathan T. Wolkomir, who defeated the incumbent who had opposed the executive order. Under Wolkomir's leadership, NFFE rebuilt its membership and increased the number of employees it represents from about 32,000 in 1967 to 150,000 in 1985. It should be kept in mind, however, that only about 34,000 of these employees pay dues to the organization....

The National Treasury Employees Union (NTEU), Independent

The National Treasury Employees Union is an unusual union. Originally organized by the professionals in the Internal Revenue Service, it has extended its occupational jurisdiction to cover clerical employees, and its agency jurisdiction to cover all of the Treasury Department and also employees of other agencies.

The predecessor organization to NTEU, the National Association of Collectors of Internal Revenue, was formed in 1938 by field employees in that agency who were seeking civil service status. In the 1950s, as the Internal Revenue Service was restructured, the organization expanded its jurisdiction to cover all IRS employees and changed its name to the National Association of Internal Revenue Employees (NAIRE). The organization changed its name again in

1973 to NTEU, in recognition of its further expansion within the Treasury Department. As of 1985 NTEU represented slightly more than 100,000 employees, of whom about 50 percent are dues-paying members.

Vincent Connery, the president of NTEU from 1966 to 1983, was a strong leader who formulated and developed the program carried on by his successor, Robert Tobias. Tobias, who had been the general counsel of the union, was elected to a four-year term as president in 1983 with Connery's blessing. Connery believed in central control of the union and reliance on a paid professional staff to service local unions, in contrast to the other federal unions that featured many elected officers, decentralized administration, and shared power. The union undertook important legal actions to preserve its rights and aggressive organizing efforts to gain representation rights outside the Treasury Department. Also, the centralized NTEU benefited from the system of labor relations that permitted unions which won unit consolidation elections to negotiate with the government agency on a national level, thereby expanding the scope of bargaining beyond that available to individual units....

Professional Air Traffic Controllers Organization (PATCO), AFL-CIO

It would be inappropriate to conclude this section about federal unions without reference to the demise of the Professional Air Traffic Controllers Organization (PATCO) in 1981. PATCO had represented a 17,000-person national unit of air traffic controllers from 1972 until 1981 when it engaged in an illegal and unsuccessful strike. Most of the strikers ignored a presidential back-to-work order and were fired, and the organization was decertified. Less than six years later, however, a replacement organization, the National Air Traffic Controllers Association (NATCA), an autonomous affiliate of the Marine Engineers Beneficial Association (MEBA), held its founding convention and subsequently won a new national unit of 12,800 employees.

Just prior to the 1981 PATCO strike the administration had engaged in bargaining with the union about matters excluded from the scope of the Civil Service Reform Act. In effect, the government had bowed to pressure from PATCO to bargain about wages and hours. Although the administration had rejected the demand for a 32-hour week, it had agreed to pay overtime after 36 hours, thereby giving controllers 42-hours pay for 40-hours work. Also, it had agreed to give controllers a 6 percent wage increase in addition to the 4.8 percent increase proposed for all federal employees later that year.

If this package had been ratified by PATCO and by congressional legislation, it would have represented the breakthrough that federal unions are still seeking in 1987. From the point of view of those who advocate broad-scope bargaining by federal employees on an agency basis, the decision of PATCO to reject the government offer and to engage in a losing strike was a significant setback. If there had not been a strike and Congress had ratified the administration's settlement with PATCO, a new bargaining procedure would have been established for at least one group of federal employees and might very well have spread to others.

Unions in Education

The dramatic shift in image from the milquetoast-like teacher to the militant unionist which has accompanied the adoption of collective bargaining procedures by teachers at all levels of instruction is one of the well-publicized developments in public-sector labor relations. The three major unions in the field and their estimated membership in 1985 are as follows: National Education Association (NEA), independent, membership about 1.7 million; American Federation of Teachers (AFT), AFL-CIO, membership about 610,000; and American Association of University Professors (AAUP), independent, membership about 55,000 active nonstudent members.

In contrast to union experience in the federal sector, union and association membership in the education field exceeds the extent of collective bargaining coverage. Some AAUP members belong to chapters that do not engage in collective bargaining. Many NEA members are in locals in southern states where there is no bargaining. And, because of the rivalry between the NEA and AFT, some teachers may be paying a service fee to one organization while maintaining membership in the other.

In education, as in other parts of local and state government, the national union usually is not involved in the collective bargaining process. The key decision-makers are either local union officers or officials of district councils, UniServ districts (discussed later in this chapter), or state councils. For this reason, national office-holders and national policy are less important in these organizations than in industrial unions in the private sector.

The National Educational Association (NEA), Independent

The predecessor organization to the present-day National Education Association was founded in Philadelphia in 1857 by educational administrators and college professors. For most of its long existence, it has functioned as a professional organization promoting the cause of public education and the improvement of teaching. In the 25 years since 1962 when the NEA was defeated by the American Federation of Teachers (AFT) in the battle to represent New York City school teachers, the organization has undergone a sharp metamorphosis. Today in many sections of the country it is indistinguishable from the AFT insofar as its bargaining stance is concerned. In several respects, however, it still differs from the AFT.

First, as a matter of ideology the NEA has maintained that affiliation with the AFL-CIO is not desirable. Second, in states where bargaining is not well rooted, school administrators have been influential in the affairs of the organization. Third, in part because of membership losses to the AFT in major cities in the Northeastern, Middle Atlantic, and North Central states, more conservative positions on policies have been adopted than otherwise would be the case....

Key officials of the NEA are appointed rather than elected directly by the rank and file or convention delegates. At the national level, the key position is that of executive director. It is filled by someone hired by the nine-person executive committee that consists of the three full-time national officers and six board members at large — all of whom are elected at the representative assembly and who serve also on the board of directors, a group of about 125 people elected by the state affiliates.

Similarly, at the state level, state executive directors are appointed by state officers and boards of directors, who, in turn, have been elected by delegates to state conventions. National staff members and state staff members in states without bargaining laws are concerned with the usual broad range of activities, other than bargaining, carried on by most unions — political and legislative activity, organizing, legal actions, education, research, affirmative action, and special-projects and crisis-related functions. In states where bargaining has statutory protection and is widespread, the state office may help local unions and UniServ districts, particularly in strike situations.

The UniServ district is a structural unit of the organization created to administer bargaining activities. Typically, there is a local union for each school district and each local union has a contract which it has negotiated with the school board. But most districts, except the largest ones with a thousand or more teachers, cannot pay the salaries of full-time negotiators — nor is there a need for a full-time staff representative for each small unit. By persuading independent local unions in the same general geographic area to combine forces in maintaining a UniServ office and staff, the NEA has created the mechanism for providing staff help in contract negotiation and administration....

The American Federation of Teachers (AFT), AFL-CIO

The American Federation of Teachers was formed in 1916 by about two dozen teachers' groups across the country with a total membership of approximately 3,000 members. The Chicago Federation of Teachers, which had existed since the turn of the century and which had joined the AFL in 1913, was the key group in early AFT activities. Its long-time leader, Carl Megel, was president of the AFT from 1952 to 1964. In the 1960s when the New York City local of the AFT, the United Federation of Teachers (UFT), gained bargaining rights for the New York City teachers after defeating the NEA affiliate in an election, the balance of power shifted from Chicago to New York, and Charles Cogen, past president of the New York group, was elected AFT president. In 1974, Albert Shanker, who was then the president of the UFT and an AFL-CIO vice president, became president of the AFT. His decision to retain the presidency of the New York City local until 1987 while serving as the national president reflects the fact that the important bargaining decisions vitally affecting the life of the union are made at the local level.

The 610,000-member AFT is primarily the union of teachers in major cities and holds bargaining rights in New York, Chicago, Philadelphia, Detroit, Boston, Pittsburgh, Cleveland, Minneapolis, Denver, and Baltimore. Leaders of these locals serve as unpaid national officers and guide AFT activities between conventions. The only full-time national officer paid by national funds is the secretary-treasurer who directs the daily activities of the AFT. The president, Albert Shanker, and the 34 vice presidents who comprise the AFT executive board receive expenses but no salaries from the national organization. As local officials, however, these national AFT officers receive salaries from their locals and devote most of their time to local union activities. The AFT structure, like the NEA structure, reflects the importance of bargaining decisions made at the local level.

The AFT has approximately 2,200 local unions. The national office supplies the same wide range of nonbargaining services to its units as does the NEA. The national office also supplies the organizers and conducts the campaigns to persuade teachers to join the AFT rather than the NEA. In states where there are local unions, the AFT maintains a state organization that handles legislative matters, participates in organizational drives, and helps the locals handle bargaining problems. In some areas, locals have banded together to form area councils. Since AFT strength is in its big-city locals, however, the elected officials and staff of these locals provide the essential services to most AFT members.

At its 1977 convention, the AFT, like the NEA, faced the question of organizing groups other than teachers. But unlike the NEA, which declined to give paraprofessionals full rights at that time, the AFT passed a constitutional amendment permitting it to organize workers outside of schools and educational institutions. In the 10-year period since that decision was made, the AFT has organized a substantial number of employees in the health-care field and in state civil-service positions as well as paraprofessionals and school-related personnel (referred to as PSRP units) and faculty and PSRPs at community colleges and other institutions.

At its 1986 convention, the AFT reported that it had increased its membership by nearly 154,000, to 624,000, in the past 10 years. This increase of approximately 33 percent during a period when most unions were shrinking is quite unusual. Some of these new members were formerly members of independent groups, such as state civil-service associations, but many are new members in units that have gained bargaining rights during this period. Although there are periodic discussions of the desirability of an NEA/AFT merger, the rivalry between the two organizations continues unabated. The AFT reported that between November 1984 and June 1986, the AFT was successful in fending off raids on units in Detroit, Baltimore, Washington, D.C., St. Louis, and Broward County, Florida, involving a total of almost 58,000 school employees. The NEA and AFT also continue their competition to gain representation rights of higher education units throughout the country....

The American Association of University Professors (AAUP), Independent

From the 1960s to the present (1987), the AAUP has struggled with the question of identifying its role in higher education when collective bargaining comes to the campus. Essentially, it has been forced by the organizing efforts of the NEA and AFT to establish arrangements under which it could become the bargaining agent, singly or jointly with the NEA or AFT, while at the same time attempting to continue its traditional role in the areas of academic freedom, protection of individual rights, and promotion of higher education. The effort to reconcile its function "as a broad based professional association concerned with protecting academic freedom and tenure" with its role as the "collective bargaining agent for university faculty" seems to be a perennial question engendering debate at almost every annual conference.

In 1966 the AAUP adopted a policy stating that it "should oppose the extension of the principle of exclusive representation to faculty members in institutions of higher education...." It reaffirmed its support of faculty governance in 1969, but "recognize[d] the significant role which collective bargaining may play in bringing agreement between faculty and administration on economic and academic issues." In 1972 the AAUP abandoned its opposition to exclusive representation and stated: "The AAUP will pursue collective bargaining, as a major additional way of realizing the Association's goals in higher education, and will allocate such resources and staff as are necessary for a vigorous selective development of this activity beyond present levels." It is clear that the AAUP changed its policy because of the pressure from local chapters on campuses where NEA or AFT affiliates were likely to become sole representatives of the faculty if the AAUP did not attempt to become the bargaining agent.

At its annual meeting in 1984, the AAUP approved without debate a revision of its collective-bargaining policy that expresses a more positive endorsement of collective bargaining than did the 1972 statement. The stronger endorsement of bargaining did not mean, however, that the conflict between the AAUP role as a professional association and as a bargaining agent had been resolved. What it did mean was that the two groups — the "traditionalists" and the leaders of the Collective Bargaining Congress of the AAUP — believed that neither group was strong enough to flourish separately and, therefore, that it was necessary to continue the search for the best structural arrangements for continuing both the traditional and the bargaining activities of the AAUP.

This conflict within the AAUP was reflected in the changes in both the number and types of members. At the beginning of the 1970s, the AAUP had approximately 90,000 members, most of whom were individual members not covered by bargaining. By 1984, the membership had dropped to 52,000 active members, two-thirds of whom were in chapters engaged in collective bargaining. The rise of collective bargaining also created financial problems for the organization by increasing the need of local chapters for funds to carry on bargaining and diminishing their willingness to contribute full dues to the national AAUP office to finance traditional activities....

Unionism in Municipal and State Governments

Although the American Federation of State, County and Municipal Employees (AFSCME), AFL-CIO, is the dominant union of local and state government employees outside of education, many other organizations represent sizable numbers of public employees. In many states there are heated organizational battles among various AFL-CIO unions, as well as between AFSCME and independent unions such as the Teamsters and the National Education Association....

The organizing conflict has been extensive within two groups: the state civil-service employees who have been represented by independent organizations and the clerical and other nonteacher units in school systems. AFSCME's victories in Ohio are in part attributable to the fact that the formerly independent Ohio State Classified Employees Association had affiliated with AFSCME prior to the representation elections. In the 1981-1983 period, 943,000 state employees were in bargaining units. AFSCME represented 44 percent of these employees and independent associations represented 8 percent of them. Also, state employees in various parts of the country are represented by the CWA, Teamsters, UFCW, and other unions.

Most of the contests for nonteacher units in school systems have been between AFSCME and the local NEA affiliate that represents the teachers. In some instances, however, it is reported that the Service Employees International Union (SEIU), Teamsters, Laborers' International Union of North America (LIUNA), and United Automobile Workers Union (UAW) have sought to represent these employees.

In the health-care field, the American Nurses Association (ANA), similar to professional associations in education, has been drawn into the collective-bargaining arena in order to maintain its representation function. The ANA bargains for private-sector nurses covered by the National Labor Relations Act as well as for nurses employed by city, county, and state governments. In recent years, some groups of salaried doctors in both the private and public sectors have sought to bargain with their employers. Competition to represent the non-professional employees of hospitals and nursing homes in both the private and public sectors reflects the continuing fight of [Local] 1199 [of the Retail, Wholesale and Department Store Union (RWDSU), AFL-CIO], AFSCME, SEIU, and LIUNA for bargaining rights.

In the protective-services field, the International Association of Fire Fighters (IAFF), AFL-CIO, has little competition for the right to represent firefighters, in contrast to the situation among police where several organizations are active. It is estimated that slightly over half of the 600,000 full-time police officers are members of unions, and about half are members of the Fraternal Order of Police. For the most part, police officers are organized into independent organizations at the local level which combine loosely at the state level. The SEIU has organized some police on the West Coast and also, by virtue of its absorption of the National Association of Government Employees (NAGE), acquired the New England-based police groups that had belonged to NAGE.

National membership figures can be misleading in specific situations because some unions tend to be strong in one region and weak in others. For example, SEIU has considerable strength in the California public sector and almost none in Wisconsin. The UAW is a factor in public-sector unionization in Michigan and the Teamsters have organized public employees in various locations. Another factor making it more difficult to analyze public-sector unions is the degree to which bargaining is local in character. Local unions and district councils are relatively autonomous groups where bargaining strategy is concerned. One unit may be militant, favoring the strike, while another may prefer arbitration....

This review of public-sector unions is made more complicated by the shift of the local transit industry in the past 35 years from the private sector to the public sector. Practically all major city transit systems have gone public during this period and, strictly speaking, the unions in this industry which traditionally have not been thought of as public-sector unions should be included in that category.

The three major unions representing bus drivers and other local transit employees are the Amalgamated Transit Union (ATU) and the Transport Workers Union (TWU), each with approximately 140,000 members, and the local transit division of the United Transportation Union (UTU), which represents a smaller number of local transit workers than the other two unions. Although the ATU is the dominant union in the field nationally, the TWU represents bus drivers in New York City, Philadelphia, San Francisco, and Miami, and the UTU represents drivers in several other cities including Los Angeles and surrounding communities. Bargaining procedures and union policies in the local transit industry frequently were quite different from those covering other public employees of the same city or county; however, as public-transit labor relations is integrated into the public-sector labor relations policies of the employer, bargaining policies and procedures in transit unions are becoming more like those of other public-sector unions....

The American Federation of State, County and Municipal Employees (AFSCME), AFL-CIO

The American Federation of State, County and Municipal Employees was founded in the early 1930s by scattered groups of public employees who had affiliated individually with the AFL. The pioneering organization to affiliate in 1932 was the Wisconsin State Employees Association under the leadership of Arnold Zander, who subsequently became the first president of AFSCME. Originally, the individual units of local-government employees were included within AFGE, but in 1936 AFSCME was chartered separately by the AFL. At the time it had about 10,000 members, and by 1950 its membership had increased to over 80,000. When the AFL and CIO merged in 1955, the 30,000-member, public-employee CIO affiliate, the Government and Civil Employees Organizing Committee, merged with AFSCME. By 1960, the union had about 180,000 members and was entering a period of internal strife.

Jerry Wurf, the executive director of the large New York City AFSCME District 37, defeated Arnold Zander for the AFSCME presidency in 1964. In his campaign, he argued that the union must devote more of its efforts to collective bargaining. Over the following 17 years, the union, under Wurf's leadership, increased its membership from a little more than 200,000 members to almost one million members, and became the third largest AFL-CIO union. After Wurf died of a heart attack late in 1981, Gerald W. McEntee, a long-time AFSCME vice president and executive director of the large Pennsylvania AFSCME council, was elected by AFSCME's executive board to fill out the presidential term expiring in 1984. Although McEntee was opposed by William Lucy, the black secretary-treasurer in 1981, and won only narrowly, he was not opposed when he ran for a full four-year term in 1984. Lucy was reelected secretary-treasurer.

In the 1984-1986 period, AFSCME became the largest union in the AFL-CIO, reporting more than one million members in a 1984 tally of its membership. It had 400,000 members in the health-care field, 190,000 clericals, 110,000 technicals and professionals, and 100,000 in law enforcement. It had members in 47 states under almost 3,500 contracts. More than 400,000 of its members are women and about 30 percent of its membership is black or Hispanic....

Despite the spotlight on the national leaders, it should be kept in mind that bargaining is essentially decentralized and that the most important bargaining decisions are being made at the municipal- and state-government bargaining-unit levels. The key decision maker in AFSCME bargaining in the smaller municipalities is the full-time district-council representative helping the local negotiate the contract. In the larger cities, key decisions are usually made by the full-time executive director of the AFSCME district council in the area, with the approval of the bargaining team. Victor Gotbaum, executive director of the New York City AFSCME council, and his counterparts throughout the nation have considerable power and autonomy. However, in contrast to major steel and auto bargaining, national AFSCME leadership usually does not participate in these contract negotiations....

NOTES

1. The continuing surge in the unionization of public employees is revealed by the rapid growth which many public sector unions and employee organizations have experienced. The membership of eight of the major public sector unions and associations as of 1989 is as follows:

American Federation of Government Employees (AFGE) 215,000
American Federation of State, County and Municipal
   Employees (AFSCME) 1,200,000
American Federation of Teachers (AFT) 770,000
American Postal Workers Union (APWU) 365,000
Fraternal Order of Police (FOP) 203,000
International Association of Fire Fighters (IAFF) 142,000
National Association of Letter Carriers (NALC) 314,214
National Education Association (NEA) 2,000,000

C. Gifford, Directory of U.S. Labor Organizations, 1990-91 Edition (BNA 1990).

2. For a particularly comprehensive study of public sector unions and associations, see J. Stieber, Public Employee Unionism: Structure, Growth, Policy (1973). See also L. Troy & N. Sheflin, U.S. Union Sourcebook: Membership, Finances, Structure, Directory (1st ed. 1985); C. Gifford, Directory of U.S. Labor Organizations, 1990-91 Edition (1990); Freeman, *Unionism Comes to the Public Sector,* 24 J. Econ. Lit. 41 (March 1986).

3. For an extensive account of the founding and growth of AFSCME, see L. Kramer, Labor's Paradox — The American Federation of State, County, and Municipal Employees, AFL-CIO (1962); R. Billings & J. Greenya, Power to the Public Worker (1974). The history of AFGE is traced in J. & L. Nevin, AFGE-Federal Union: The Story of the American Federation of Government Employees (1976).

4. Among the many studies of the AFT and the NEA are West, The National Education Association: The Power Base for Education (1980); M. Donley, Power to the Teacher (1976); M. Lieberman & M. Moskow, Collective Negotiations for Teachers (1966); C. Perry & W. Wildman, The Impact of Negotiations in Public Education: The Evidence from the Schools (1970); M. Moskow & R. Doherty, *United States,* in Teacher Unions and Associations 295 (A. Blum ed. 1969). For a critical examination of the AFT, see R. Braun, Teachers and Power (1972). For an excellent article on the development of collective bargaining between the New York City Board of Education and the United Federation of Teachers, see Klaus, *The Evolution of a Collective Bargaining Relationship in Public Education: New York City's Changing Seven-year History,* 67 Mich. L. Rev. 1033 (1969).

5. The development of collective bargaining among faculty members at colleges and universities is explored in Garbarino, *Faculty Collective Bargaining: A Status Report,* in Unions in Transition 265 (S. Lipset ed. 1986); F. Kemerer & J. Baldridge, Unions On Campus (1975); Academics at the Bargaining Table: Early Experience (J. Begin ed. 1973); E. Duryea, R. Fisk, & Associates, Faculty Unions and Collective Bargaining (1973); Faculty Bargaining in the Seventies (T. Tice & G. Holmes eds. 1973); Faculty Power: Collective Bargaining on Campus (T. Tice ed. 1972); *Collective Negotiations in Higher Education: A Symposium,* 1971 Wis. L. Rev. 1; Brown, *Professors and Unions: The Faculty Senate: An Effective Alternative to Collective Bargaining in Higher Education,* 12 Wm. & Mary L. Rev. 252 (1970).

2. THE RISE AND FALL OF THE SOVEREIGNTY DOCTRINE

K. HANSLOWE, THE EMERGING LAW OF LABOR RELATIONS IN PUBLIC EMPLOYMENT 11-20 (1967)*

[V]arying policies have grown up at the state and federal levels with respect to the organizing and bargaining rights of public employees and ... a discernible trend toward enhanced recognition and protection of these rights is now evident. At one time and place or another, however, virtually all aspects of collective bargaining have been deemed incompatible with government employment. Thus, courts have ruled that public employees can be prohibited from joining unions. To the assertion that this interferes with the constitutional right of freedom of association, government has responded that, there being no constitutional right to government employment, it may insist on non-membership as a condition of such employment because of the governmental right and need to maintain operations without interference and interruption. Consequently, it has been ruled that state governments may condition employment on relinquishment of the right to organize, and that no one has a constitutional right to work for the government on his own terms.

Even where public employees are allowed to join unions, this right has often been restricted to organizations not affiliated with the general labor movement. Where not so restricted, affiliation, in any event, must not be with an organization that asserts the right to strike against the government. The reason for the latter restriction is fairly obvious. Strikes of government employees are almost universally deemed to be unlawful. The reasons for the former restriction are thought to be as follows:

(1) Affiliation increases the possibility that conflicting loyalties will arise. For example, it is argued that policemen who are members of a labor federation such as AFL-CIO, or who are members of an international union also representing employees in private industry, cannot be expected to perform in disinterested fashion and with no reservations when called out to eliminate violence on a picket line maintained by their fellow union members.

(2) Affiliation increases the funds available to public employee organizations and thereby increases their capacity to strike.

---

*Reprinted by permission of the New York State School of Industrial and Labor Relations, Cornell University.

(3) Affiliation increases the likelihood of sympathetic strikes by private or public employees to help their fellow union members.

(4) Affiliation with the general labor movement may result in placing too much power in the hands of organized labor. Employees in both sectors might use their respective political and economic power each to enhance the position of the other group at the expense of the rest of society.

The government trend in recent years has been to relax previous restrictions on affiliation. Most jurisdictions which now allow their public employees to organize, also allow them to affiliate with the general labor movement, at least so long as the affiliations are not with organizations asserting the right to strike against the government. More stringent restrictions can still be found in some instances, however, especially with respect to bans on the affiliation of policemen's organizations with other unions.

Other facets of collective bargaining, familiar in the private sector, have been similarly deemed inappropriate in government employment. This is true not only of the strike, but of exclusive recognition of an organization representing a majority of the employees involved, the closed or union shop, the checkoff by the employer of union dues from the employees' wages, and the arbitration of disputes as well. Indeed, the very possibility of *bargaining* with the government has been questioned; and agreements reached between public officials and labor unions have been held invalid as constituting unauthorized abdications of governmental power with respect to conditions of public employment.

These views are reflected in legal opinion. For instance, the attorney general of Florida advised the city manager of Miami that:

... no organization, regardless of who it is affiliated with, union or non-union, can tell a political sub-division possessing the attributes of sovereignty, who it can employ, how much it shall pay them, or any other matter or thing relating to its employees. To even countenance such a proposition would be to surrender a portion of the sovereignty that is possessed by every municipal corporation and such a municipality would cease to exist as an organization controlled by its citizens, for after all, government is no more than the individuals that go to make up the same and no one can tell the people how to say, through their duly constituted and elected officials, how the government should be run under such authority and powers as the people themselves give to a public corporation such as a city.[10]

A judicial decision, in 1946, asserted:

There is an abundance of authority, too numerous for citation, which condemns labor union contracts in the public service. The theory of these decisions is that the giving of a preference [to unions and their members] is against public policy. It is declared that such preferences, in whatever form, involve an illegal delegation of disciplinary authority, or of legislative power, or of the discretion of public officers; that such a contract disables them from performing their duty; that it involves a divided allegiance; that it encourages monopoly; that it defeats competition; that it is detrimental to the public

---

[10] Florida Attorney General's Opinion, March 21, 1944, reproduced in Rhyne, Labor Unions and Municipal Employee Law (Washington: National Institute of Municipal Law Offices, 1946), pp. 252-54.

welfare; that it is subversive of the public service; and that it impairs the freedom of the individual to contract for his own services....[11]

At the core of this position is the concept of sovereignty.

... In our polity, sovereignty, of course, ultimately reposes in the people but is, out of the practical necessities of circumstance, exercised for them by the constituted state governments and the federal government. It is these governments and their delegates (such as local governments, municipalities, and executive and administrative agencies) which exercise, within constitutional and statutory limitations, the sovereign power to make and enforce law. To the extent that collective bargaining entails joint determination of conditions of employment, such bargaining with the government is seen as unavoidably creating an interference in the sovereign's affairs. Unionization is similarly thought to involve intolerable splitting of the civil servant's loyalty between the government of which he is a part and his union. Furthermore, such practices as exclusive recognition, the closed or union shop, and the checkoff of union dues are thought not only to invite organized interference with the conduct of public business but to involve improper preference for one group at the expense of others in society. The use of arbitrators to resolve disputes is seen to entail an improper abandonment by the sovereign of a portion of his authority. And the strike, needless to say, involving, as it does, concerted coercion of the employer, falls little short of insurrection when the employer is the government.

What this position comes down to is that governmental power includes the power, through law, to fix the terms and conditions of government employment, that this power reposes in the sovereign's hand, that this is a unique power which cannot be given or taken away or shared, and that any organized effort to interfere with this power through a process such as collective bargaining is irreconcilable with the idea of sovereignty and is hence unlawful.

The [police] commission ... not only had the power but it was the manifest duty to adopt and enforce the resolution [prohibiting policemen from joining a labor union].... The failure to do so in effect would have amounted to a surrender of power, a dereliction of duty, and a relinquishment of supervision and control over public servants it was their sworn duty to supervise and direct.[12]

This is the orthodox position. We shall see below that in practice it has been widely modified, although not wholly abandoned.

Still another line of analysis must be indicated. What has been said thus far flows from political or legal theory. It can also be argued that the theory is grounded in functional necessity. The sovereign, whether absolute or representative, acts for the entire political entity involved. The functions which the sovereign performs are governmental tasks which need to be discharged on behalf of the whole society. These tasks, whether they be national defense, local security, running an educational system, or whatever, are carried on to further the public weal. Any conduct which interferes with the performance of these tasks is inimical to that weal and is therefore intolerable. Strikes of civil servants

---

[11]*Mugford v. Mayor and City Council of Baltimore*, opinion Nov. 6, 1944, *aff'd*, 185 Md. 266, 44 A.2d 745 (1946).

[12]*Perez v. Board of Police Commissioners*, 78 Cal. App. 2d 638, 651, 178 P.2d 537, 545 (1947).

clearly constitute such interference. So, likewise, to the extent that unionization and collective bargaining may have a tendency to lead to strikes, they can and, indeed, must be outlawed as running counter to the public interest. Thus, the functional necessity of governmental tasks is asserted to combine with the theoretical nature of sovereign power to render collective bargaining on the part of public employees undesirable and unlawful.

Sovereignty Delimited

So goes the traditional argument. Its difficulty lies in the circumstance that life has a way of running ahead of logic and that history tends to be more complex than political theory. Implicit in the argument is the idea that the sovereign is absolute, all-powerful, and always right. The idea is open to question.

We derive our notions of sovereignty from the English common law which reposed sovereign authority in the king as the fountainhead of law, justice, and government. "The king can do no wrong," wrote Blackstone in his *Commentaries.* This maxim assumed concrete meaning in the context of lawsuits by citizens against the Crown. If the king can indeed do no wrong, the Crown is necessarily immune from suit. Applied to government employment, the Blackstone maxim means that, when the sovereign has fixed the terms of public employment, these are inescapably fair and just, and hence any employee effort to alter them is wrong and runs counter to law.

One difficulty with this is that, insofar as sovereign immunity from suit is concerned, the Blackstone maxim has been misunderstood, and the English kings did not enjoy the absolute immunity commonly thought to be conveyed by the notion that they could "do no wrong." Professor Louis Jaffe writes:

> It is the prevailing view among students of this period that the requirement of consent [to be sued] was not based on a view that the King was above the law. "[T]he king, as the fountain of justice and equity, could not refuse to redress wrongs when petitioned to do so by his subjects." Indeed, it is argued by scholars on what seems adequate evidence that the expression "the King can do no wrong" originally meant precisely the contrary to what it later came to mean. "[I]t meant that the king must not, was not allowed, not entitled to do wrong...." It was on this basis that the King, though not suable in his court ..., nevertheless endorsed on petitions "let justice be done," thus empowering his courts to proceed.[13]

The petitions referred to were "petitions of right." They were granted when other remedies against the government were unavailable. Thus, legal procedure combined with political theory to delimit sovereign immunity even at its source — the kings of England. By what Professor Jaffe calls a "magnificent irony," these limitations upon sovereign immunity were substantially destroyed in North America when the Colonies, by revoking their allegiance to the Crown, eliminated the king who could "let justice be done."

So it seems that the king was not always absolutely right, and he has, of course, for a long time not been absolute. Absence of absolute power has, in any

---

[13] Louis Leventhal Jaffe, Judicial Control of Administrative Action (Boston: Little, Brown & Company, 1965), p. 199. Professor Jaffe's footnotes have been omitted.

case, been a dominant characteristic of American government from the start. Yet the doctrine of sovereign immunity has had a sturdy history in American law which, perhaps, helps to explain the reluctance with which American governments have moved in the direction of accepting collective bargaining with their employees....

Mr. Justice Holmes spoke in favor of the immunity of the sovereign:

A sovereign is exempt from suit, not because of any formal conception or obsolete theory, but on the logical and practical ground that there can be no legal right as against the authority that makes the law on which the right depends.[14]

Nevertheless, the doctrine of sovereignty, in areas other than the labor relations context, as well as in the labor relations field itself, has come to be limited. Indeed, Professor Kenneth Culp Davis has recently written: "Sovereign immunity in state courts is on the run."

The traditional position, for one thing, has been substantially modified by legislative enactments, the effect of which is to "waive" sovereign immunity for certain purposes. A court of claims was established in 1855 to entertain citizens' claims that their private property has been unconstitutionally taken by the federal government for public use without just compensation. Tort claims against the federal government may be asserted under the Federal Tort Claims Act of 1946. Contract claims may be similarly asserted under the Tucker Act of 1948. Several states have legislated in similar vein....

More recently the courts, often without legislative aid, have, in Professor Davis' words, "abolish[ed] large chunks of immunity." According to Professor Davis, thirteen jurisdictions have so acted between 1957 and 1965. Some of the decisions collected by Professor Davis speak in such terms as:

"[S]overeign immunity" may be a proper subject for discussion by students of mythology but finds no haven or refuge in this Court.[15]

With respect to municipal tort liability, the Supreme Court of Florida made this observation:

The modern city is in substantial measure a large business institution.... To continue to endow this type of organization with sovereign divinity appears to us to predicate the law of the Twentieth Century upon an Eighteenth Century anachronism.[16] ...

One may well ask, therefore, whether conceptions of sovereignty should remain as a barrier to collective bargaining in governmental labor relations. If the "sovereign" government is increasingly assuming ordinary legal responsibility in its relations with its citizens, why should not the same hold true for governmental relations with civil servants?

One point emerges. Whatever immunities the sovereign may possess, there is no barrier to such immunities being delimited. The sovereign power does, indeed, include the power within constitutional limitations to make policy. But

---

[14] *Kawananakoa v. Polyblank*, 205 U.S. 349, 353 (1907).
[15] *Colorado Racing Commission v. Brush Racing Ass'n*, 136 Colo. 279, 284 (1957).
[16] *Hargrove v. Town of Cocoa Beach*, 96 So. 2d 130, 133 (Fla. 1957).

does this not include the power to establish, as a matter of public personnel policy, a system of collective bargaining with respect to civil servants. This is, in fact, the position which seems to be emerging. One leading writer has concluded that, while *"the* [sovereignty] *doctrine is a clear and effective bar to any action on the part of government employees to compel the government to enter involuntarily into any type of collective bargaining relationship, ... the doctrine does not preclude the enactment of legislation specifically authorizing the government to enter into collective bargaining relationships with its employees."* ...[17]

NOTES

1. While the judge in the *Mugford* case quoted by Hanslowe condemned an agreement that gave the union a preferential position which was specifically denied to any other organization, the judge nevertheless stated:

> With the pattern of collective dealing so firmly established in the industrial field, is it reasonable to expect to maintain the fiction of personal relationship between employer and employe in the municipal field among a large number of workers engaged in performing the same tasks as are performed in the industrial field? I think not. To maintain even a semblance of individual contact with a large force of workers would require an increase of supervisory workers, who would still fail to detect and deal with grievances and complaints as effectively as an organization of workers would do. The right to organize, and to deal collectively, can be exercised without interference with the exercise of the discretion committed to public officers, without preferment of organization members, without discrimination against others, and without detriment to the public service. *Mugford v. Mayor & City Council* (Cir. Ct. No. 2, Baltimore City, 1944), reproduced in C. Rhyne, Labor Unions and Municipal Employe Law 166, 168 (1946).

2. In denying public employees many of the rights which their counterparts in the private sector possessed, the courts also relied on the theory that public employees owed extra loyalty to their governmental employers. The following critique of this "extra-loyalty" theory is contained in Edwards, *The Developing Labor Relations Law in the Public Sector,* 10 Duquesne L. Rev. 357, 360-61 (1972):

> A close relative of the sovereignty doctrine is the theory that public employees have a commitment to further the programs of government even at a sacrifice of their own interests....
>
> It would seem the extra-loyalty theory is open to the same criticism as the sovereignty theory: it too is vague, conclusory, and not adequately founded in the realities of the modern situation. Based upon an assumed consensus as to the proper role of government in society, it offers no guidance as to what the employee must give up. Further, it puts forth no reason for this sacrifice, save the equation government equals sovereign equals absolute fealty. Such an equation is hardly a viable alternative in our modern society. Indeed, with so many "urgent" demands on the government's admittedly inadequate resources — coupled with the great gains of private sector unions (creating a considerable controversy as to just what the public employee's fair share really

---

[17] Wilson R. Hart, Collective Bargaining in the Federal Civil Service (New York: Harper & Row, 1961), p. 44.

is) — it outrages modern notions of industrial democracy to relegate a large segment of the work force to dependence upon the conscience of the government. A degree of self-determinism has become a way of life for the American worker, and nowhere is it more necessary than in the public sector.

NORWALK TEACHERS' ASSOCIATION v. BOARD OF EDUCATION

138 Conn. 269, 83 A.2d 482 (1951)

JENNINGS, J. This is a suit between the Norwalk Teachers' Association as plaintiff and the Norwalk board of education as defendant for a declaratory judgment, reserved on the admitted allegations of the complaint for the advice of this court.

The complaint may be summarized as follows: The plaintiff is a voluntary association and an independent labor union to which all but two of the teaching personnel of approximately 300 in the Norwalk school system belong. In April, 1946, there was a dispute between the parties over salary rates. The board of estimate and taxation was also involved. After long negotiations, 230 members of the association rejected the individual contracts of employment tendered them and refused to return to their teaching duties. After further negotiations, in which the governor and the state board of education took part, a contract was entered into between the plaintiff and the defendant, and the teachers returned to their duties. The contract, subject to conditions precedent therein set forth, recognized the plaintiff as the bargaining agent for all of its members, defined working conditions and set up a grievance procedure and salary schedule. Similar contracts were entered into for the succeeding school years, including 1950-51. From September, 1946, to the present, and particularly with reference to the contract for 1950-1951, much doubt and uncertainty have arisen concerning the rights and duties of the respective parties, the interpretation of the contract and the construction of the state statutes relating to schools, education and boards of education. "In addition," the complaint states, "there has been the possibility of strikes, work stoppage or collective refusals to return to work by the teachers through their organization and the possibility of discharges or suspensions by the defendant by reason of difficult personnel relations, all of which tends to disharmony in the operation of the school system and to the ever present possibility that either, or both, the parties may be unwittingly violating statutes by reason of mistaken or erroneous interpretation thereon." The parties agreed that the contract for the school year 1949-1950 would govern their relations for the school year 1950-1951, that they would join in the action, and "that whatever contractual obligations exist will be forthwith modified so soon as they shall have received from the Court judgments and orders declaring their respective rights, privileges, duties and immunities." The specific points of dispute are stated in the questions reserved, printed in the footnote.[1] ...

---

[1] The plaintiff claimed a declaratory judgment answering and adjudicating the following questions:

"(a) Is it permitted to the plaintiff under our laws to organize itself as a labor union for the purpose of demanding and receiving recognition and collective bargaining?

"(b) Is it permitted to the plaintiff organized as a labor union to demand recognition as such and collective bargaining?

... Question (e) will be considered first.

Under our system, the government is established by and run for all of the people, not for the benefit of any person or group. The profit motive, inherent in the principle of free enterprise, is absent. It should be the aim of every employee of the government to do his or her part to make it function as efficiently and economically as possible. The drastic remedy of the organized strike to enforce the demands of unions of government employees is in direct contravention of this principle. It has been so regarded by the heads of the executive departments of the states and the nation. Most of the text writers refer to one or more of the following statements by three of our recent presidents. They are quoted, for example, in 1 Labor Law Journal 612 (May, 1950): "There is no right to strike against public safety by anybody anywhere at any time" (Calvin Coolidge on the Boston police strike). This same strike was characterized by President Wilson as "an intolerable crime against civilization." President Franklin D. Roosevelt said in a letter to the president of the National Federation of Federal Employees on August 16, 1937: "Particularly, I want to emphasize my conviction that militant tactics have no place in the functions of any organization of Government employees.... [A] strike of public employees manifests nothing less than an intent on their part to prevent or obstruct the operations of Government until their demands are satisfied. Such action, looking toward the paralysis of Government by those who have sworn to support it, is unthinkable and intolerable." As the author of the article cited says, "The above statement by President Roosevelt, who certainly was no enemy of labor unions, epitomizes the answer to the problem. It seems to be axiomatic."

The commentators, generally, subscribe to this proposition. National Institute of Municipal Law Officers Reports No. 76, 116, 129; 1 Teller, Labor Disputes & Collective Bargaining (1947 Sup.) § 171; 18 N.Y.U. L.Q. Rev. 247; 94 U. of Pa. L. Rev. 427. Notwithstanding this fact, Ziskind was able to publish a well-documented book entitled "One Thousand Strikes of Government Employees," which contains an elaborate bibliography. See also Spero, Government as Employer. This would indicate that the law on the subject is still in the process of development.

Few cases involving the right of unions of government employees to strike to enforce their demands have reached courts of last resort. That right has usually

---

"(c) Is it permissible under Connecticut law for the defendant to recognize the plaintiff for the purpose of collective bargaining?

"(d) Is collective bargaining to establish salaries and working conditions permissible between the plaintiff and the defendant?

"(e) May the plaintiff engage in concerted action such as strike, work stoppage, or collective refusal to enter upon duties?

"(f) Is arbitration a permissible method under Connecticut law to settle or adjust disputes between the plaintiff and the defendant?

"(g) Is mediation a permissible method under Connecticut law to settle or adjust disputes between the plaintiff and the defendant?

"(h) If the answer to the previous questions is yes, are the State's established administrative facilities, such as the State Board of Mediation and Arbitration and the State Labor Relations Board, available, as they are available in industrial disputes, to the plaintiff and the defendant?

"(i) Does the continuing contract law, so-called, create a status of employment within which the plaintiff may claim employment subject to the right to bargain salaries and working conditions?

"(j) Has the plaintiff the right to establish rules, working conditions and grievance resolution procedures by collective bargaining?"

been tested by an application for an injunction forbidding the strike. The right of the governmental body to this relief has been uniformly upheld. It has been put on various grounds: public policy; interference with governmental function; illegal discrimination against the right of any citizen to apply for government employment (where the union sought a closed shop). The following cases do not necessarily turn on the specific right to strike, but the reasoning indicates that, if faced with that question, the court would be compelled to deny that right to public employees. For example, *Perez v. Board of Police Commissioners,* 78 Cal. App. 2d 638, 178 P.2d 537, held that the board could, by rule, prevent police officers from joining a labor union. If it could do this, it would certainly be upheld in an attempt to enjoin a strike called by the union.... [Citations omitted.] The court puts the matter succinctly in the *Miami* case [*Miami Water Works Local 654 v. Miami,* 157 Fla. 445, 26 So. 2d 194 (1946)]: "While strikes are recognized by the statute to be lawful under some circumstances, it would seem that a strike against the city would amount, in effect, to a strike against government itself — a situation difficult to reconcile with all notions of government."

The plaintiff, recognizing the unreasonableness of its claims in the case of such employees as the militia and the judiciary, seeks to place teachers in a class with employees employed by the municipality in its proprietary capacity. No authority is cited in support of this proposition. "A town board of education is an agency of the state in charge of education in the town...." *Board of Education of Stamford v. Board of Finance,* 127 Conn. 345, 349, 16 A.2d 601. In fulfilling its duties as such an agency, it is acting in a governmental, not a proprietary, capacity....

In the American system, sovereignty is inherent in the people. They can delegate it to a government which they create and operate by law. They can give to that government the power and authority to perform certain duties and furnish certain services. The government so created and empowered must employ people to carry on its task. Those people are agents of the government. They exercise some part of the sovereignty entrusted to it. They occupy a status entirely different from those who carry on a private enterprise. They serve the public welfare and not a private purpose. To say that they can strike is the equivalent of saying that they can deny the authority of government and contravene the public welfare. The answer to question (e) is "No."

Questions (a) and (b) relate to the right of the plaintiff to organize itself as a labor union and to demand recognition and collective bargaining. The right to organize is sometimes accorded by statute or ordinance. See, for example, the Bridgeport ordinance adopted June 17, 1946 (Bridgeport Munic. Reg. [1947] p. 15), discussed in National Institute of Municipal Law Officers Report No. 129, p. 51. The right to organize has also been forbidden by statute or regulation. *Perez v. Board of Police Commissioners,* 78 Cal. App. 2d 638, 178 P.2d 537. In Connecticut the statutes are silent on the subject. Union organization in industry is now the rule rather than the exception. In the absence of prohibitory statute or regulation, no good reason appears why public employees should not organize as a labor union. *Springfield v. Clouse,* 356 Mo. 1239, 1246, 206 S.W.2d 539. It is the second part of question (a) that causes difficulty. The question reads: "Is it permitted to the plaintiff under our laws to organize itself as a labor union for the purpose of demanding and receiving recognition and collective bargaining?" The question is phrased in a very peremptory form. The common method of enforcing recognition and collective bargaining is the strike. It appears that this method has already been used by the plaintiff and that the threat of its use again is one of the reasons for the present suit. As has been said, the strike is not a permissible method of enforcing the plaintiff's demands. The answer to questions (a) and (b) is a qualified "Yes." There is no objection to the organization of the plaintiff as a labor union, but if its organization is for the purpose of "demanding" recognition and collective bargaining the demands must be kept within legal bounds. What we have said does not mean that the plaintiff has the right to organize for all of the purposes for which employees in private enterprise may unite, as those are defined in § 7391 of the General Statutes. Nor does it mean that, having organized, it is necessarily protected against unfair labor practices as specified in § 7392 or that it shall be the exclusive bargaining agent for all employees of the unit, as provided in § 7393. It means nothing more than that the plaintiff may organize and bargain collectively for the pay and working conditions which it may be in the power of the board of education to grant.

Questions (c) and (d) in effect ask whether collective bargaining between the plaintiff and the defendant is permissible. The statutes and private acts give broad powers to the defendant with reference to educational matters and school management in Norwalk. If it chooses to negotiate with the plaintiff with regard to the employment, salaries, grievance procedure and working conditions of its members, there is no statute, public or private, which forbids such negotiations. It is a matter of common knowledge that this is the method pursued in most school systems large enough to support a teachers' association in some form. It would seem to make no difference theoretically whether the negotiations are with a committee of the whole association or with individuals or small related groups, so long as any agreement made with the committee is confined to members of the association. If the strike threat is absent and the defendant prefers to handle the matter through negotiation with the plaintiff, no reason exists why it should not do so. The claim of the defendant that this would be an illegal delegation of authority is without merit. The authority is and remains in the board. This statement is not to be construed as approval of the existing contracts attached to the complaint. Their validity is not in issue.

As in the case of questions (a) and (b), (c) and (d) are in too general a form to permit a categorical answer. The qualified "Yes" which we give to them should not be construed as authority to negotiate a contract which involves the surrender of the board's legal discretion, is contrary to law or is otherwise ultra vires. For example, an agreement by the board to hire only union members would clearly be an illegal discrimination. *Mugford v. Baltimore,* 185 Md. 266, 270, 44 A.2d 745; Rhyne, Labor Unions & Municipal Employe Law, pp. 34, 137, 157. Any salary schedule must be subject to the powers of the board of estimate and taxation. "The salaries of all persons appointed by the board of education ... shall be as fixed by said board, but the aggregate amount of such salaries ... shall not exceed the amount determined by the board of estimate and taxation...." 21 Spec. Laws 285, No. 315, § 3; *Board of Education of Stamford v. Board of Finance,* 127 Conn. 345, 349, 16 A.2d 601. One of the allegations of the complaint is that the solution of the parties' difficulties by the posing of specific issues is not satisfactory. Whether or not this is so, that course will be necessary if this discussion of general principles is an insufficient guide.

Question (f) reads, "Is arbitration a permissible method under Connecticut law to settle or adjust disputes between the plaintiff and the defendant?" The power of a town to enter into an agreement of arbitration was originally denied on the ground that it was an unlawful delegation of authority. *Griswold v. North Stonington,* 5 Conn. 367, 371. It was later held that not only the amount of damages but liability could be submitted to arbitration. *Hine v. Stephens,* 33 Conn. 497, 504; *Mallory v. Huntington,* 64 Conn. 88, 96, 29 A. 245. The principle applies to the parties to the case at bar. If it is borne in mind that arbitration is the result of mutual agreement, there is no reason to deny the power of the defendant to enter voluntarily into a contract to arbitrate a specific dispute. On a proposal for a submission, the defendant would have the opportunity of deciding whether it would arbitrate as to any question within its power. Its power to submit to arbitration would not extend to questions of policy but might extend to questions of liability. Arbitration as a method of setting disputes is growing in importance and, in a proper case, "deserves the enthusiatic support of the courts." *International Brotherhood of Teamsters v. Shapiro,* 138 Conn. 57, 69, 82 A.2d 345. Agreements to submit all disputes to arbitration, commonly found in ordinary union contracts, are in a different category. If the defendant entered into a general agreement of that kind, it might find itself committed to surrender the board discretion and responsibility reposed in it by law. For example, it could not commit to an arbitrator the decision of a proceeding to discharge a teacher for cause. So, the matter of certification of teachers is committed to the state board of education. General Statutes §§ 1432, 1433, 1435. The best answer we can give to question (f) is, "Yes, arbitration may be a permissible method as to certain specific, arbitrable disputes."

From what has been said, it is obvious that, within the same limitations, mediation to settle or adjust disputes is not only permissible but desirable. The answer to question (g) is "Yes." The state board of mediation and arbitration and the state labor relations board, however, are set up to handle disputes in private industry and are not available to the plaintiff and defendant for reasons given in the opinion of the attorney general dated July 6, 1948. 25 Conn. Atty. Gen. Rep. 270. This was confirmed as to Norwalk teachers by an opinion dated June 12, 1950, not yet published. See also *United States v. United Mine Workers,* 330 U.S. 258, 269. The answer to question (h) is "No."

General Statutes, Sup.1949, § 160a, provides in part: "The contract of employment of a teacher shall be renewed for the following school year unless such teacher has been notified in writing prior to March first of that year that such contract will not be renewed." Question (i) asks whether this law creates "a status of employment within which the plaintiff may claim employment subject to the right to bargain salaries and working conditions?" The meaning of this is not clear and the briefs do not clarify it. It is the type of question that should be related to a specific state of facts. It cannot be answered in vacuo.

As to question (j), the plaintiff has no right to establish rules. As stated above, the right is and remains in the board....

NOTES

1. For a good review of the case law prior to 1953, see Annot., 31 A.L.R.2d 1142 (1953).

2. The *Norwalk* case at the time of its issuance in 1951 was hailed by public sector unions since the court recognized that collective bargaining was permissible in the public sector. Although the sovereignty doctrine was not utilized to prevent collective bargaining, the court clearly felt that it was pertinent to the various issues presented for decision.

3. The issues which were raised in the *Norwalk* case mirror many of the issues which are explored in subsequent chapters, e.g., the right of public employees to join and form unions, the authority of a public employer to recognize and negotiate with a union, the right to strike, the legality of an agreement to arbitrate disputes, and so forth.

4. The changing judicial attitude concerning the applicability of the sovereignty theory is graphically illustrated by two New York court decisions issued thirteen years apart. In *Railway Mail Ass'n v. Murphy,* 180 Misc. 868, 44 N.Y.S.2d 601, 607-08 (1943), *rev'd on other grounds,* 326 U.S. 88 (1945), the court stated:

> To tolerate or recognize any combination of Civil Service employees of the Government as a labor organization or union is not only incompatible with the spirit of democracy, but inconsistent with every principle upon which our Government is founded. Nothing is more dangerous to public welfare than to admit that hired servants of the state can dictate to the Government the hours, the wages and conditions under which they will carry on essential services vital to the welfare, safety and security of the citizen. To admit as true that Government employees have power to halt or check the functions of Government, unless their demands are satisfied, is to transfer to them all legislative, executive and judicial power. Nothing would be more ridiculous....
>
> Collective bargaining has no place in government service. The employer is the whole people. It is impossible for administrative officials to bind the Government of the United States or the State of New York by any agreement made between them and representatives of any union. Government officials and employees are governed and guided by laws which must be obeyed and which cannot be abrogated or set aside by an agreement of employees and officials.

Thirteen years later the court in *Civil Serv. Forum v. New York City Transit Auth.,* 3 Misc. 2d 346, 151 N.Y.S.2d 402, 408 (Sup. Ct. 1956), *rev'd on other grounds,* 4 App. Div. 2d 117, 163 N.Y.S.2d 476 (1957), stated:

> The agreement ... executed with these unions was negotiated for the purpose of protecting the health, safety and vital interests of the people of the City and State of New York and to establish and maintain harmonious and stable labor relations with the unions. In the circumstances it seems clear that these compelling reasons were sufficient to warrant the defendant authority in fostering a peaceful settlement of its prospective labor disputes by entering into the challenged agreement.

5. The full text of President Roosevelt's frequently quoted letter to the President of the National Federation of Federal Employees is reproduced in C. Rhyne, Labor Unions and Municipal Employe Law 436-37 (1946). This book, by the General Counsel of the National Institute of Municipal Law Officers, contains an invaluable collection of decisions, attorney general's opinions, and other documentation concerning public sector labor relations prior to 1946. For the period from 1946 to 1949, see C. Rhyne, *Labor Unions and Municipal Employee Law — A Supplementary Report,* Nat'l Institute Mun. L. Officers Rep. No. 129 (1949).

B. THE SIMILARITIES AND DIFFERENCES BETWEEN THE PUBLIC AND PRIVATE SECTORS

1. GENERALLY

STATEMENT OF R. SCOTT FOSLER, DIRECTOR OF GOVERNMENT STUDIES, COMMITTEE FOR ECONOMIC DEVELOPMENT

Hearings Before the Subcomm. on the City of the House Comm. on Banking, Finance and Urban Affairs, 95th Cong., 2d Sess., 397-402 (July 26, 1978)

The Fuzzy Dichotomy: Public and Private Sectors

Definitions of and distinctions between "business" and "government," or "private sector" and "public sector," are increasingly vague. A business may be anything from a small candy store to a large multinational corporation, and may be involved in manufacturing, services, finance, retailing, transportation, or other diverse pursuits. The nature of a government agency can be equally variable. The Department of Defense is a quite different operation from the Social Security Administration. The sanitation department of New York City is an altogether different operation from the sanitation department of Inglewood, California.

Some private sector organizations that are called businesses may be so heavily regulated or bureaucratic that they tend to behave more like the stereotype of a government agency. Some government institutions, on the other hand, may have an entrepreneurial spirit, independent sources of revenue, and flexibility in administrative structure that tend to resemble what we traditionally think of as a business.

A publicly operated hospital has more in common with a privately operated profit-making hospital than with a publicly operated land fill. The characteristic of being a hospital in this instance is more critical than the characteristic of being a government operation. On the other hand, the public hospital will not necessarily benefit from the management techniques used by a neighborhood camera shop, even though it is a business.

Nor should it be assumed that all businesses are necessarily better managed than government agencies. There has been notable improvement in the quality of public management over the years. For all the criticism of government inefficiency, examples are abundant — at the Federal, state, and local levels — of public institutions that are unusually well run and staffed by highly trained and proficient managers. The city management profession clearly has raised the level of public management in city governments.

It should also be recognized that the scale of operations of state and local governments would rank them among the top corporations in the country in terms of total budget or number of employees. New York City is, of course, in a class by itself, in size if not in other ways. Fairfax County, Virginia, with an annual budget in excess of one-half billion dollars, would rank in the fourth quintile of the Fortune 500 largest industrial corporations. The Community Services Division of the Department of Social and Health Services of the State of Washington would rank about 175th with a budget in excess of $1 billion. Such government operations as these in recent years have attracted top quality personnel whose management ability would compare favorably and perhaps superiorly to that of the nation's top corporations.

Nonetheless, while progress has been made in improving public sector management, it is still safe to say that, in general, government can still learn from business. The question is what can they learn, and under what circumstances?

Characteristics Common to Business and Government

To suggest that business possesses expertise that may be applicable to government assumes that there are certain similarities between the two. The key similarities include the following:

First, both business and government are organizations, and hence are subject to principles that seem to be common to all organizations.

Second, both are organizations that presumably have the purpose of producing something of value to others outside of the organization. This distinguishes them, for example, from other organizations whose principal purpose is to produce something of value principally or exclusively to those within the organization, such as most political and social organizations whose essential purpose is to promote the interests of their members.

Third, many business and government organizations are large, both in terms of the numbers of people employed, the size of their budgets, and the amount of capital employed. Principles and techniques for managing large-scale operations are applicable to both in general.

Fourth, many business and government organizations are complex, partly due to their size alone, and partly because of the degree of specialization required for production, the nature of technology employed, the multiplicity and ambiguity of goals, and the corresponding complexity of the environment in which they must function.

Fifth, the nature of the work force employed by both is more or less the same in terms of cultural and social background, education and training, experience, skills, and values.

Distinctions Between Business and Government

While the characteristics held in common suggest that there would be substantial opportunity for the application of techniques of management from one to the other, there are also important distinctions between the two which limit that applicability or require a substantial degree of modification.

First, the principal goals of government are politically determined. They consequently tend to be multiple and often ambiguous or intangible goals — even more so than in business. The political goals of government include not only the stated intent of public programs, but also contracts, prestige, power and other such values which are not necessarily related to the presumed "output" of public service organizations.

A second distinction deriving from the first is that in government the measure of output or results is much more cumbersome and less precise than it tends to be in business. Even in those instances where business goals are intangible and in some cases tend to be quite similar to government, business performance is ultimately measurable in terms of the profit and loss statement, whereas government typically does not have so precise a "bottom-line."

A third distinction is in the source of funding. Business revenue derives from sales of the good or service produced, whereas the revenue of most government agencies derives from a budget allocation of taxes collected from the public at large. Businesses and government agencies both have an interest in increasing their revenues, but whereas to do so business must increase the quantity or price of its output (presumably requiring it to be sensitive to consumer tastes and pocketbooks), government agencies can increase the size of their budgets through more skillful competition in the budget process which may require little or no attention to the quantity or quality of its services.

Fourth, government tends to plan and manage on a shorter time perspective than does business. Public policy making is geared as much to the cycle of two or four year elections as to the solving of problems, whereas business decisions have relatively greater flexibility to plan activities according to the time required to meet long-term goals.

A fifth important distinction lies in the structure of employment. Employees in government participate actively in the selection of their employers, i.e., elected officials, in contrast to business where management is selected by means that do not directly involve employees. An elected official, consequently, is in the position of being both the employer of his workers, at the same time that he is their employee in that they are also citizens, taxpayers, and voters. Civil service regulations also limit government management in assigning responsibilities, rewarding performance, and penalizing non-performance.

Finally, government also has fundamental responsibilities for the protection of life and property, the maintenance of order, and the assurance of justice. The government manager works within a complex set of constraints imposed by legislatures and higher levels of governments which presumably are designed to meet a range of public purposes, and which complicate his immediate tasks.

REHMUS, LABOR RELATIONS IN THE PUBLIC SECTOR, Paper prepared for the 3d World Congress, International Industrial Relations Association, London, England (Sept. 3-7, 1973)*

... A basic underlying reason for the extension of collective bargaining rights to public sector employees in the United States is the argument that collective bargaining rights which have been mandated by law in the private sector should in equity be given to the government's own employees. This is not to suggest that there are not important differences between private and public employment, however, and that these differences have not created some difficult problems as the private sector bargaining model increasingly pervades the public sector.

---

*Reprinted by permission of the Institute of Labor and Industrial Relations.

Probably the most fundamental of these problems lies in the different purposes of public and private undertakings. The public employer is an artificial creature of the electorate established to minister to the needs and desires of the public and to provide the mechanical and administrative structure to carry on these functions. In a democratic system of government it is elected officials who are normally charged with the control and determination of budget and tax rates, which is the primary way of setting goals and priorities. While extraparliamentary influences are both inevitable and necessary elements of the democratic process, they should not be allowed to overcome the fact that elected legislative bodies are supposed to be essentially deliberative bodies. If democratic governments are to distinguish between public passions and public interests, legislatures have to be at least partially insulated from group pressures. In a number of major American cities the crisis pressures that result from actual or threatened withdrawal of public employment services has at times usurped the legislature's deliberative process in this most fundamental governmental function of setting goals and priorities.

A second problem lies in the existence of the merit system and civil service in the public sector in the United States. These systems, basically designed to ensure that the selection, retention, and promotion of public employees is based on qualifications and meritorious performance alone, are often considered to be the warp and woof of public employment. To employees, however, merit is sometimes considered a euphemism for favoritism. Public employee organizations therefore attempt to weave into this tight fabric somewhat coarser threads such as strict seniority, across-the-board wage adjustments, and the like. It is a yet-unsettled question whether civil service and the merit system can survive the assault of traditional collective bargaining practices. It is clear that the protection of public employees' right to continued employment, assuming meritorious service, is increasingly being enforced through bargained grievance procedures culminating in binding neutral arbitration rather than through statutory devices such as the tenure system.

A third general problem is that of supervisory unionism. In private industry in the United States the lines of authority and supervision are ordinarily clearly drawn, even in areas of white collar employment. In the public sector, however, the lines between supervisor and employee are far more indistinct. There are several reasons for this. The appellation of supervisor tends to be pushed further down in the organizational hierarchy in public than in private bureaucracies. Where all are dedicated to serving the public, there is a greater community of interest among all employees. In the public service both supervisors and nonsupervisors alike are often compensated within an identical and fairly rigid salary payment structure. As a reflection of these facts many existing state collective bargaining laws have not drawn traditional distinctions between supervisors and employees. Hence labor relations boards that implement the state laws have permitted supervisory unionism. In some cases they have required the recognition of supervisory units as components of the same union that organized those who are supervised. Whether conflict of interest is inevitable between the supervisory goals of the organization and the fraternal goals of the union is as yet uncertain. It is clearly a danger, however.

A fourth serious problem in public employee bargaining arises because of the diffusion of decision-making authority which frequently exists in the public sector. Parliamentary systems of government permit a greater unity of legislative and executive authority than is common in United States governmental systems which are more often characterized by division of authority with checks and balances operating between the executive and legislative powers. In federal, state and local governments an agency head may have authority to negotiate only on a portion of the issues which are normally subjects of collective bargaining — other bargainable subjects may be retained within the control of the legislative body or an independent civil service board. Often a chief executive may not have final authority on distribution of funds and can only submit recommendations to the appropriate legislature. May the legislative body repudiate his decisions? Does it have the responsibility to provide the funds to pay for the salary structure which the chief executive has negotiated? Finally, where voter approval of increased millage is necessary to pay for the negotiated increases, local taxpayer revolts and disapproval are increasingly common. What is to be done in these situations? Questions of this kind are extremely difficult within many, though not all, governments in the United States. But the inherent logic of public employee bargaining is leading to considerable centralization of power and to increased executive power vis-à-vis both legislatures and civil service boards.

Related to but distinguishable from the previous problem is one characterized as "end-run" or "double-deck" bargaining. Some public employee unions attempt by lobbying to secure from the state legislature those items which they had failed to obtain or which were traded away at the municipal bargaining table. In many states, civil service organizations have been one of the strongest lobbies in the state legislature. These powers can hardly be taken away from such organizations. But from the municipal government's point of view, freedom to trade cost reductions in one area for contractually bargained new expenditures in another is an essential element of bargaining flexibility and bargaining equality. Where state legislatures mandate wage and fringe bargaining at the municipal level and yet continue to legislate on municipal employee benefits they place local units of government in a Procrustean bed. Public employee bargaining may be desirable and inevitable, but public employees hardly seem entitled to the benefits both of collective bargaining and of traditional protective state laws.

SUMMERS, PUBLIC SECTOR BARGAINING: PROBLEMS OF GOVERNMENTAL DECISIONMAKING, 44 U. Cin. L. Rev. 669, 669-73 (1975)*

I. The Uniqueness of Public Sector Bargaining

It is a threadbare truism that bargaining in the public sector is different from bargaining in the private sector, but the differences are often described in unhelpful detail, too much like the four blind men describing an elephant. Such descriptions will not help us either to make it work or to keep it under control.

---

*Reprinted by permission.

We ought, therefore, to describe the differences in more general and fundamental terms. To do that, we must start with the basic question: What, exactly, is
unique about public sector bargaining?

There is nothing unique about public employees; they are no different from
employees in the private sector. They have the same capacities, the same needs,
and the same values; they seek the same advantages and the same gains. Many
public sector employees previously have been, and with present trends perhaps
even more will again become, private sector employees.

There is nothing unique about the work which public employees perform.
The private sector has school teachers, nurses and social workers, as well as
secretaries, bookkeepers, janitors, maintenance employees, construction
workers, and rubbish collectors. There are private police, private detectives,
private armed guards, and even private firefighters. Nor is the work necessarily
any more critical because it is performed by public employees. Strikes by parochial school teachers create substantially the same inconvenience as strikes by
public school teachers. A strike by janitors in public buildings may create fewer
problems than a strike by janitors in private apartment buildings. A disruption
in garbage collection may be less serious than a disruption in electric power or
telephone service.

The uniqueness of public employment is not in the employees nor in the
work performed; the uniqueness is in the special character of the employer.
The employer is government; the ones who act on behalf of the employer are
public officials; and the ones to whom those officials are answerable are citizens
and voters. We have developed a whole structure of constitutional and statutory
principles, and a whole culture of political practices and attitudes as to how
government is to be conducted, what powers public officials are to exercise, and
how they are to be made answerable for their actions. Collective bargaining by
public employers must fit within the governmental structure and must function
consistently with our governmental processes; the problems of the public employer accommodating its collective bargaining function to government structures and processes is what makes public sector bargaining unique.

To state the difference another way, in private sector bargaining we have
never been concerned with how the employer decided on the policy to be
brought to the bargaining table. We have been concerned with the union's
decisionmaking process, requiring the union to observe minimal democratic
standards, but we have not been concerned with the corporation's decisionmaking process. All that the law has required is that the employer send someone to
the bargaining table who has authority to speak for and to bind the employer.
Who instructs the negotiator, how his instructions are determined, and what his
instructions may be is for the corporation to decide. The corporation's decision-
making process is of no concern in collective bargaining; it is of little concern to
the law.

When the employer is government, however, the employer's decisionmaking
process becomes of central concern in both legal and political terms. The policies brought to the bargaining table are governmental policies. State constitutions and statutes, city charters and ordinances may prescribe procedures as to
how those policies are to be decided, specify what bodies or officials shall make
those decisions, and impose limitations on the decisions which can be made.

More specifically, in the private sector, the employer must send someone to the bargaining table with authority to make a binding agreement. In the public sector this may not be legally possible or politically sensible. Wages and other benefits directly affect the budget and the tax rates; but adopting budgets and levying taxes are considered, within our governmental system, fundamental legislative policies to be decided by the legislative body, not by a negotiator at the bargaining table. Dismissal procedures may be subject to constitutional requirements which limit the procedures which can be negotiated. Promotion policies may be governed by civil service principles which are written into the city charter and cannot be eliminated by bargaining. Modifications in state pension plans cannot, in most states, be made binding by negotiators, but must be ratified by the legislature. In the public sector, agreement at the bargaining table may be only an intermediate, not a final, step in the decisionmaking process.

Collective bargaining by a governmental employer is different because governmental decisionmaking is different. The unique problems, and the ones of central concern, focus on how government makes its decision. The unique and interesting legal problems are created by legal limitations on governmental decisionmaking. Beyond the legal problems, however, are the far more important ones of how the governmental decisions in collective bargaining ought to be made. The problems are more in the realm of political science than of labor relations. Our central concern is not, as in the private sector, with what will facilitate bargaining and reaching agreement, but with what are appropriate processes for governmental decisionmaking.

Two cases illustrate this crucial difference between the central questions in public sector and private sector bargaining. In *Madison School District v. Wisconsin Employment Relations Board,*[18] a school teacher at a public meeting of the school board presented a petition urging the board not to agree to a "fair shares" provision in the agreement then being negotiated with the union. The board was charged with a prohibited labor practice for allowing the teacher to speak and for accepting the petition. In the private sector such conduct is barred because it may weaken the union's position as exclusive representative and may interfere with the bargaining process. In the public sector, we must confront the question whether citizens, teachers or otherwise, shall be allowed to make their views known to public officials on public issues. Beyond the constitutional issues of free speech and the right to petition is the judgmental question whether those making governmental decisions should be barred from hearing all views and opinions of all citizens before making decisions. The central concern is not the collective bargaining process but the governmental process.

In *Detroit Police Officers v. City of Detroit,*[19] the voters of the city wrote into the city charter the benefits payable under the police and firemen's pension plan. As a result, those benefits could be changed only by referendum. This, of course, impeded the bargaining process; but that does not end the inquiry in the public sector. The legal question is whether the collective agreement can

---

[18] 231 N.W.2d 206 (Wis. 1975). [Editors' note: The Supreme Court's decision is set out *infra.*]
[19] 214 N.W.2d 803 (1972) 341 Mich. 44. [Editors' note: The text of this decision is set out *infra.*]

override the results of a referendum, but the crucial political question is who should have the final voice in determining the city's pension obligations. When we realize that the pension plan may create a larger long-term obligation than any bond issue, creating a lien of undefined size for an indeterminate period, there are strong arguments for requiring voter approval, even though that impedes bargaining. Again the question is not what will facilitate bargaining, but what is the appropriate way of making the governmental decision. If certain acts may, in some measures, impede bargaining as we have known it in the private sector, that cannot end our inquiry. Our ultimate concern is not to make collective bargaining work, but to make government work. My first and basic proposition, then, is that in public employee bargaining, the fundamental issue to which we should be addressing ourselves is how the decisions of government should be made.

II. The Political Nature of Public Sector Bargaining

My second and subordinate proposition is that the major decisions made in bargaining with public employees are inescapably political decisions. They are political decisions in at least three senses. First, they involve critical policy choices. The matters debated at the bargaining table and decided by the contract are not simply questions of wages, hours, vacations and pensions. Directly at issue are political questions of the size and allocation of the budget, the tax rates, the level of public services, and the long term obligations of the government. These decisions as to budgets, taxes, services, and debts are political in the second sense that, within our system of government, they are to be made by the political branches of government — by elected officials who are politically responsible to the voters. Indeed, these decisions generally are considered uniquely legislative and not subject to delegation. Finally, these decisions are political in the ultimate sense that those making the decisions will do in the political market what businessmen do in the economic market — maximize their gains and minimize their losses. Politically elected officials in bargaining seek to maximize votes rather than profits.

The major decisions made in public employee bargaining not only are political, but in my view must be, and ought to be, political. The size of the budget, the taxes to be levied, the purposes for which tax money is to be used, the kinds and levels of governmental services to be enjoyed, and the level of indebtedness are issues that should be decided by officials who are politically responsible to those who pay the taxes and seek the services. The notion that we can or should insulate public employee bargaining from the political process either by arbitration or with some magic formula is a delusion of reality and a denigration of democratic government.

2. PUBLIC EMPLOYERS — SOME DEFINITIONAL CONSIDERATIONS

In our complex society a seemingly endless variety of legal entities have been established for a wide variety of purposes. Entities such as states, cities and counties are clearly public employers; others such as corporations that are privately owned, financed, and operated are clearly private employers. While it is an easy task at the extremes to distinguish a public employer from a private employer, there is a gray area in which the entity has the attributes of both a public employer and a private employer. Courts and the various agencies administering labor relations legislation are not infrequently faced with the threshold question of determining whether an employer is public or private. This determination is important in order to ascertain which statutory provisions, if any, are applicable to a given employer and thus to determine the rights and obligations of both the employer and its employees. This is particularly significant in those states where public employees are prohibited from striking.

NLRB v. NATURAL GAS UTILITY DISTRICT

402 U.S. 600, 91 S. Ct. 1746, 29 L. Ed. 2d 206 (1971)

JUSTICE BRENNAN delivered the opinion of the Court.

Upon the petition of Plumbers and Steamfitters Local 102, the National Labor Relations Board ordered that a representation election be held among the pipefitters employed by respondent, Natural Gas Utility District of Hawkins County, Tennessee, 167 N.L.R.B. 691 (1967). In the representation proceeding, respondent objected to the Board's jurisdiction on the sole ground that as a "political subdivision" of Tennessee, it was not an "employer" subject to Board jurisdiction under § 2(2) of the National Labor Relations Act, as amended by the Labor Management Relations Act, 1947, 61 Stat. 137, 29 U.S.C. § 152 (2).[1] When the Union won the election and was certified by the Board as bargaining representative of the pipefitters, respondent refused to comply with the Board's certification and recognize and bargain with the Union. An unfair labor practice proceeding resulted and the Board entered a cease-and-desist order against respondent on findings that respondent was in violation of §§ 8(a)(1) and 8(a)(5) of the Act, 29 U.S.C. §§ 158 (a)(1) and 158(a)(5). 170 N.L.R.B. 1409 (1968). Respondent continued its noncompliance and the Board sought enforcement of the order in the Court of Appeals for the Sixth Circuit. Enforcement was refused, the court holding that respondent was a "political subdivision," as contended. 427 F.2d 312 (1970). We granted certiorari, 400 U.S. 990 (1971). We affirm.

The respondent was organized under Tennessee's Utility District Law of 1937, Tenn. Code Ann. §§ 6-2601 to 6-2627 (1955). In *First Suburban Water Utility District v. McCanless,* 177 Tenn. 128, 146 S.W.2d 948 (1941), the Tennessee Supreme Court held that a utility district organized under this Act was an operation for a state governmental or public purpose. The Court of Appeals held that this decision "was of controlling importance on the question whether the District was a political subdivision of the state" within § 2(2) and "was binding on the Board." 427 F.2d, at 315. The Board, on the other hand, had held that "while such State law declarations and interpretations are given careful

---

[1]Section 2 (2), 29 U.S.C. § 152(2), provides: "The term 'employer' includes any person acting as an agent of an employer, directly or indirectly, but shall not include the United States or any wholly owned Government corporation, or any Federal Reserve Bank, or any State or political subdivision thereof, or any corporation or association operating a hospital, if no part of the net earnings inures to the benefit of any private shareholder or individual, or any person subject to the Railway Labor Act, as amended from time to time, or any labor organization (other than when acting as an employer), or anyone acting in the capacity of officer or agent of such labor organization."

consideration ..., they are not necessarily controlling." 167 N.L.R.B., at 691. We disagree with the Court of Appeals and agree with the Board. Federal, rather than state, law governs the determination, under § 2(2), whether an entity created under state law is a "political subdivision" of the State and therefore not an "employer" subject to the Act.

The Court of Appeals for the Fourth Circuit dealt with this question in *NLRB v. Randolph Electric Membership Corp.,* 343 F.2d 60 (1965), where the Board had determined that Randolph Electric was not a "political subdivision" within § 2(2). We adopt as correct law what was said at 62-63 of the opinion in that case:

> "There are, of course, instances in which the application of certain federal statutes may depend on state law....
>
> "But this is controlled by the will of Congress. In the absence of a plain indication to the contrary, however, it is to be assumed when Congress enacts a statute that it does not intend to make its application dependent on state law. *Jerome v. United States,* 318 U.S. 101, 104 ... (1943).
>
> "The argument of the electric corporations fails to persuade us that Congress intended the result for which they contend. Furthermore, it ignores the teachings of the Supreme Court as to the congressional purpose in enacting the national labor laws. In *National Labor Relations Board v. Hearst Publications,* 322 U.S. 111, 123 ... (1944), the Court dealt with the meaning of the term 'employee' as used in the Wagner Act, saying:
>
> "'Both the terms and the purposes of the statute, as well as the legislative history, show that Congress had in mind no ... patchwork plan for securing freedom of employees' organization and of collective bargaining. The Wagner Act is federal legislation, administered by a national agency, intended to solve a national problem on a national scale.... Nothing in the statute's background, history, terms or purposes indicates its scope is to be limited by ... varying local conceptions, either statutory or judicial, or that it is to be administered in accordance with whatever different standards the respective states may see fit to adopt for the disposition of unrelated, local problems.'
>
> "Thus, it is clear that state law is not controlling and that it is to the actual operations and characteristics of [respondents] that we must look in deciding whether there is sufficient support for the Board's conclusion that they are not 'political subdivisions' within the meaning of the National Labor Relations Act."

We turn then to identification of the governing federal law. The term "political subdivision" is not defined in the Act and the Act's legislative history does not disclose that Congress explicitly considered its meaning. The legislative history does reveal, however, that Congress enacted the § 2(2) exemption to except from Board cognizance the labor relations of federal, state, and municipal governments, since governmental employees did not usually enjoy the right to strike.[3] In the light of that purpose, the Board, according to its Brief, p. 11, "has limited the exemption for political subdivisions to entities that are either (1) created directly by the state, so as to constitute departments or administrative

---

[3] See 78 Cong. Rec. 10351 et seq.: Hearings on Labor Disputes Act before the House Committee on Labor, 74th Cong., 1st Sess., 179; 93 Cong. Rec. 6441 (Sen. Taft). See also C. Rhyne, Labor Unions and Municipal Employee Law 436-437 (1946); Vogel, *What About the Rights of the Public Employee?,* 1 Lab. L.J. 604, 612-615 (1950).

arms of the government, or (2) administered by individuals who are responsible to public officials or to the general electorate."

The Board's construction of the broad statutory term is, of course, entitled to great respect. *Randolph Electric, supra,* at 62. This case does not however require that we decide whether "the actual operations and characteristics" of an entity must necessarily feature one or the other of the Board's limitations to qualify an entity for the exemption, for we think that it is plain on the face of the Tennessee statute that the Board erred in its reading of it in light of the Board's own test. The Board found that "the Employer in this case is neither created directly by the State, nor administered by State-appointed or elected officials." 167 N.L.R.B., at 691-692 (footnotes omitted). But the Board test is not whether the entity is administered by "State-appointed or elected officials." Rather, alternative (2) of the test is whether the entity is "administered *by individuals who are responsible to public officials* or to the general electorate" (emphasis added), and the Tennessee statute makes crystal clear that respondent is administered by a Board of Commissioners appointed by an elected county judge, and subject to removal proceedings at the instance of the Governor, the county prosecutor, or private citizens. Therefore, in the light of other "actual operations and characteristics" under that administration, the Board's holding that respondent "exists as an essentially private venture, with insufficient identity with or relationship to the State of Tennessee," 167 N.L.R.B., at 691, has no "warrant in the record" and no "reasonable basis in law." *NLRB v. Hearst Publications,* 322 U.S. 111, 131 (1944).

Respondent is one of nearly 270 utility districts established under the Utility District Law of 1937. Under that statute, Tennessee residents may create districts to provide a wide range of public services such as the furnishing of water, sewers, sewage disposal, police protection, fire protection, garbage collection, street lighting, parks, and recreational facilities as well as the distribution of natural gas. Tenn. Code Ann. § 6-2608 (Supp. 1970). Acting under the statute, 38 owners of real property submitted in 1957 a petition to the county court of Hawkins County requesting the incorporation of a utility district to distribute natural gas within a specified portion of the county. The county judge, after holding a required public hearing and making required findings that the "public convenience and necessity requires the creation of the district," and that "the creation of the district is economically sound and desirable," Tenn. Code Ann. § 6-2604 (Supp. 1970), entered an order establishing the District. The judge's order and findings were appealable to Tennessee's appellate courts by any party "having an interest in the subject-matter." Tenn. Code Ann. § 6-2606 (1955).

To carry out its functions, the District is granted not only all the powers of a private corporation, Tenn. Code Ann. § 6-2610 (1955), but also "all the powers necessary and requisite for the accomplishment of the purpose for which such district is created, capable of being delegated by the legislature." Tenn. Code Ann. § 6-2612 (1955). This delegation includes the power of eminent domain, which the District may exercise even against other governmental entities. Tenn. Code Ann. § 6-2611 (1955). The District is operated on a nonprofit basis, and is declared by the statute to be "a 'municipality' or public corporation in perpetuity under its corporate name and the same shall in that name be a body politic and corporate with power of perpetual succession, but without any power to levy or collect taxes." Tenn. Code Ann. § 6-2607 (Supp. 1970). The property and revenue of the District are exempted from all state, county, and municipal taxes, and the District bonds are similarly exempt from such taxation, except for inheritance, transfer, and estate taxes. Tenn. Code Ann. § 6-2626 (1955).

The District's records are "public records" and as such open for inspection. Tenn. Code Ann. § 6-2615 (Supp. 1970). The District is required to publish its annual statement in a newspaper of general circulation, showing its financial condition, its earnings, and its method of setting rates. Tenn. Code Ann. § 6-2617 (Supp. 1970). The statute requires the District's commissioners to hear any protest to its rates filed within 30 days of publication of the annual statement at a public hearing, and to make and to publish written findings as to the reasonableness of the rates. Tenn. Code Ann. § 6-2618 (1955). The commissioners' determination may be challenged in the county court, under procedures prescribed by the statute. *Ibid.*

The District's commissioners are initially appointed, from among persons nominated in the petition, by the county judge, who is an elected public official. Tenn. Code Ann. § 6-2604 (Supp. 1970). The commissioners serve four-year terms and, contrary to the Board's finding that the State reserves no "power to remove or otherwise discipline those responsible for the Employer's operations," 167 N.L.R.B., at 692, are subject to removal under Tennessee's General Ouster Law, which provides procedures for removing public officials from office for misfeasance or nonfeasance. Tenn. Code Ann. § 8-2701 et seq. (1955); *First Suburban Water Utility District v. McCanless,* 177 Tenn., at 138, 146 S.W.2d, at 952. Proceedings under the law may be initiated by the Governor, the state attorney general, the county prosecutor, or ten citizens. Tenn. Code Ann. §§ 8-2708, 8-2709, 8-2710 (1955). When a vacancy occurs, the county judge appoints a new commissioner if the remaining two commissioners cannot agree upon a replacement. Tenn. Code Ann. § 6-2614 (Supp. 1970). In large counties, all vacancies are filled by popular election. *Ibid.* The commissioners are generally empowered to conduct the District's business. They have the power to subpoena witnesses and to administer oaths in investigating District affairs, Tenn. Code Ann. § 6-2616(5) (1955), and they serve for only nominal compensation. Tenn. Code Ann. § 6-2615 (Supp. 1970). Plainly, commissioners who are beholden to an elected public official for their appointment, and are subject to removal procedures applicable to all public officials, qualify as "individuals who are responsible to public officials or to the general electorate" within the Board's test.

In such circumstances, the Board itself has recognized that authority to exercise the power of eminent domain weighs in favor of finding an entity to be a political subdivision. *New Jersey Turnpike Authority,* 33 L.R.R.M. 1528 (1954). We have noted that respondent's power of eminent domain may be exercised even against other governmental units. And the District is further given an extremely broad grant of "all the powers necessary and requisite for the accomplishment of the purpose for which such district is created, capable of being delegated by the legislature." Tenn. Code Ann. § 6-2612 (1955). The District's "public records" requirement and the automatic right to a public hearing and written "decision" by the commissioners accorded to all users betoken a state, rather than a private, instrumentality. The commissioners' power of subpoena and their nominal compensation further suggest the public character of the District.

Moreover, a conclusion that the District is a political subdivision finds support in the treatment of the District under other federal laws. Income from its bonds is exempt from federal income tax, as income from an obligation of a "political subdivision" under 26 U.S.C. § 103. Social Security benefits for the District's employees are provided through voluntary rather than mandatory coverage since the District is considered a political subdivision under the Social Security Act. 42 U.S.C. § 418.

Respondent is therefore an entity "administered by individuals [the commissioners] who are responsible to public officials [an elected county judge]" and this together with the other factors mentioned satisfies us that its relationship to the State is such that respondent is a "political subdivision" within the meaning of § 2(2) of the Act. Accordingly, the Court of Appeals' judgment denying enforcement of the Board's order is

Affirmed.

[The dissenting opinion of Justice Stewart is omitted.]

MILWAUKEE AUDITORIUM BOARD

Decision No. 6543 (Wis. Emp. Relations Comm'n 1963)

The Union petitioned the Board to conduct an election to determine what, if any, representation the operating engineers employed by the Employer desired, pursuant to Section 111.05 of the Wisconsin Employment Peace Act. At the hearing the Employer, by its Counsel, contended that the Employer was a political subdivision of the state within the meaning of Section 111.70 and that therefore any election by the one operating engineer in its employ should be held pursuant to that subsection.

The Employer operates an auditorium and arena for the purpose of providing facilities for public meetings, conventions, expositions, and other purposes of a public nature for which its buildings are suitable. The Employer is in the nature of a joint Employer having two distinct and separate parts. The first is a private corporation and the second is the City of Milwaukee. This form of organization permitted the Employer to acquire some of the necessary capital for the construction of the auditorium. However, the arena was constructed entirely from public funds. The city owns the land and buildings of the Employer and controls the operation of the Employer by virtue of the fact that a majority of the board of trustees of the Employer are city officials. In recent years, the city has acquired portions of the stock of the corporation. However, not all of the corporation stock of the Employer has been transferred to the city since in such event the corporation would be dissolved and the board of trustees would consist of the city officials exclusively.

The Board has held that the fact that a corporation is authorized to disburse public moneys in performing a public purpose and furthermore that it is, by virtue of its organization and statutory limitations, substantially controlled by the State, is not determinative of the question whether such corporation is a state agency or political subdivision of the state.[1] In this same case, the Board looked to the particular language used in the Statute creating the Employer in determining whether such Employer should be deemed a political subdivision of the state. Section 43.44 Wisconsin Statutes provides in part:

"(1) Any city of the first class may establish and maintain public auditoriums and music halls; and may establish, maintain and operate the same jointly, share and share alike, by agreement between the common council of such city and private corporation duly organized for that purpose.

"(2) Such private corporation shall execute to the city a bond, in a sum determined and with sureties approved by said common council, conditioned that the said corporation will furnish its share of money as the same shall be required for the purposes specified in subsection (1)....

"(5) Whenever the city shall have acquired all the stock of such corporation, the said corporation shall ipso facto be dissolved and the title to all its property of whatsoever nature, shall vest in said city; thereupon the auditorium board provided for in section 43.45 shall consist of only the ex officio members specified in said section....

"(7) Any such city may build additions to such auditoriums and for the purposes of any such addition, by action of the common council, issue revenue bonds under the provisions of section 66.51 payable exclusively from income and revenues of any such addition and of any auditorium to which it is added which said auditoriums and additions thereto for such purpose are declared a public utility. Said private corporation shall not be required to contribute to any such addition. Any such addition shall be subject in all other respects to the provisions of sections 43.44 to 43.48."

The statutory language recognizes that a portion of the Employer's operation will be carried on by a private corporation operating jointly with the city. Part of the funds necessary to build the auditorium were furnished by the corporation. The corporation elects five members to the eleven member board of trustees which is charged by statute with full and complete control of the Employer. The statute further recognizes that stock in the corporation may be transferred to the city and that the corporation may assume a secondary role in furnishing capital for new buildings for the Employer. Nevertheless, the corporation retains its corporate entity, elects the members of the board of trustees that it is entitled to elect, and shares in the operation of the Employer, share and share alike, until such time as all of the stock of the corporation is transferred to the city. Such being the case, the Employer must be deemed a joint operation between a private corporation and a municipality.

The Petitioner herein petitioned the Board to conduct a representation election in a bargaining unit consisting of one operating engineer employed by the Milwaukee Auditorium Board pursuant to 111.05 of the Wisconsin Statutes. The Employer contends that the election should be conducted pursuant to 111.70(4) (d) of the Wisconsin Statutes since it is a municipal employer and not a private employer subject to the provisions of the Wisconsin Employment Peace Act.

Employes of private employers have greater rights than employes of municipal employers. Section 111.04 grants employes in private industry the right to

---

[1] *Milwaukee County War Memorial, Inc.,* Decision No. 6325, 4/63.

"engage in collective bargaining through representatives of their own choosing, and to engage in lawful concerted activities, such as strikes, picketing, and bargaining, or other mutual aid or protection," which refers to lawful concerted activities, such as strikes, picketing and boycotts, labor unions traditionally use to induce employers to accede to their demands. Section 111.70(a), while granting the right to representation in collective bargaining, omits the right to engage in concerted activities. Section 111.70(1) prohibits strikes by municipal employes and, in its stead, in Section 111.70 (e) through (g) establishes fact finding procedures for the resolution of disputes. The question here before the Board is not merely an administration matter as to which section of the statutes shall be cited when the Board directs its election, but is determinative of the right of the employe involved to engage in certain concerted activity. The representative of the Petitioning Union indicated his awareness of the basic issue when he stated on the record he sought in this proceeding the right to strike. The Milwaukee Auditorium Board operates the Milwaukee Arena and Auditorium. The operation is controlled by a private corporation established by the Wisconsin Statutes and by representatives of the City of Milwaukee. The private corporation was formed to acquire some of the necessary capital, for the construction of the auditorium. However, the latter building, the Arena, is constructed entirely from municipal funds. The City of Milwaukee has title to the land and buildings and controls the operation by virtue of the fact that a majority of the board of trustees are city officials. Furthermore in recent years the City of Milwaukee has been acquiring portions of the stock of the corporation and eventually all the corporate stock will be transferred to the City of Milwaukee. It appears to the Board that the City of Milwaukee is the senior partner in this organization having the greater control and having made the greater financial contribution and therefore any employes employed by the Milwaukee Auditorium Board are to be deemed municipal employes. Therefore the election shall be conducted pursuant to 111.70(4)(d) of the Wisconsin Statutes.

NOTES

1. In *Roza Irrigation Dist. v. State,* 80 Wash. 2d 633, 497 P.2d 166 (1972), the Washington Supreme Court was faced with a question of whether an irrigation district was a "municipal corporation" and thus covered by the Washington public sector collective bargaining statute. In giving the term "municipal corporation" a broad construction, the court stated:

We find no such restrictive intent expressed in the statute. The service which irrigation district employees render is a vital one in the areas which they serve. It is in the public interest to avoid interruption of irrigation services, just as it is to avoid interruption of services rendered by a city's fire or police department. We are given no plausible reason why the legislature should have chosen to deny such employees the protection of the act or to regard them as private employees, having the right to strike.

2. In *Nassau Library Sys.,* 1 P.E.R.B. ¶ 399.47 (1968), the New York Public Employment Relations Board held that the library in question was not a "government" or a "public employer" within the meaning of the Taylor Law and that, therefore, it did not have jurisdiction over the employer. The PERB noted:

> It would clearly be improper to apply the term "instrumentality or unit of government" to *any* corporate entity solely on the basis of the state or county aid it receives, the fact that it was established pursuant to a charter by permission of the legislature, or the fact that it performs a public service which is performed by other organs in the public sector as well.

Subsequently the NLRB ruled that it likewise did not have jurisdiction. *Nassau Library Sys.*, 196 N.L.R.B. 864 (1972). In declining to assert jurisdiction over the Nassau Library System, the Board pointed to the "unique relationship" between the System and the state and county, stating:

> [V]irtually all of the System's operating income is derived either directly or indirectly from the State of New York and Nassau County. In addition, the System's board of trustees is appointed by, and the System itself services, various public libraries....
>
> Moreover, the State of New York has intervened in the past over the System's day-to-day operations. The State of New York also places stringent requirements on the System to see that its plan of service is adequate, that its funds are invested in preapproved securities, and that it complies with state regulations regarding the purchase of books.
>
> For these reasons, we conclude, without deciding the System's status under Section 2(2) of the Act, that it would not effectuate the policies of the Act to assert jurisdiction over the System. Accordingly, we shall dismiss the petition.

In view of these holdings by the New York PERB and the NLRB, where else could a union seeking to represent the System's employees turn? By virtue of these decisions, has a no-man's land been created?

3. For many years the NLRB declined to assert jurisdiction over a private entity where the operations of such a private entity were intimately connected with the statutorily mandated functions carried out by a governmental entity. In these cases the NLRB held that the private entity shared the public employer's exemption from coverage under the National Labor Relations Act. See, e.g., *Camptown Bus Lines*, 226 N.L.R.B. 4 (1976); *Roesch Lines*, 224 N.L.R.B. 203 (1976). In *National Transp. Inc.*, 240 N.L.R.B. 565 (1979), however, the NLRB abandoned its adherence to the "intimate connection" test and asserted jurisdiction over a bus company that provided school bus service to several public school systems. The Board held that the sole test in such cases should be whether the private entity "retains sufficient control over its employees to enable it to engage in meaningful bargaining over conditions of employment with a labor organization." Subsequently, in *Res-Care*, 280 N.L.R.B. 670 (1986), the NLRB held that when a private entity "lacks the ultimate authority to determine primary terms and conditions of employment, such as wage and benefit levels, it lacks the ability to engage in the necessary 'give and take' which is a central requirement of good-faith bargaining and which makes bargaining meaningful." See *Trailways Commuter Transit, Inc.*, 284 N.L.R.B. 935 (1987) (applying the principles set forth in *National Transportation Service,* as amplified in *Res-Care,* the Board asserted jurisdiction over private commuter transit company based on "the overall independence ... [which it] exercises over its labor relations"). *Accord NLRB v. Parents and Friends of the Specialized Living Center,* 879 F.2d 1442 (7th Cir. 1989).

4. In *Holodnak v. Avco Corp.,* 514 F.2d 285 (2d Cir. 1975), the court held that where nearly all the land, buildings, machinery and equipment of an employer's plant were owned by the federal government and where most of the work done at the plant was defense-related, the links between the employer and the federal government were sufficient to make the employer's action in discharging an employee "state action" and, therefore, actionable under the first and fourteenth amendments. The court held that there was such a symbiotic relationship between the employer and the federal government that the federal government in effect became a partner or joint venturer in the enterprise. Would the employees of such an entity be considered federal employees for the purposes of the statutory ban against strikes by federal employees? In *United States v. United Mine Workers,* 350 U.S. 258 (1947), the Supreme Court held that the employees in coal mines that were seized by the government pursuant to executive order were employees of the United States and that, as a result, the Norris-LaGuardia Anti-Injunction Act was not applicable to a strike by such employees.

C. THE ROLE OF THE FEDERAL GOVERNMENT

1. CONSTITUTIONAL CONSIDERATIONS

GARCIA v. SAN ANTONIO METROPOLITAN TRANSIT AUTHORITY

469 U.S. 528, 105 S. Ct. 1005, 83 L. Ed. 2d 1016 (1985)

JUSTICE BLACKMUN delivered the opinion of the Court.

We revisit in these cases an issue raised in *National League of Cities v. Usery,* 426 U.S. 833 (1976). In that litigation, this Court, by a sharply divided vote, ruled that the Commerce Clause does not empower Congress to enforce the minimum-wage and overtime provisions of the Fair Labor Standards Act (FLSA) against the States "in areas of traditional governmental functions." *Id.,* at 852. Although *National League of Cities* supplied some examples of "traditional governmental functions," it did not offer a general explanation of how a "traditional" function is to be distinguished from a "nontraditional" one. Since then, federal and state courts have struggled with the task, thus imposed, of identifying a traditional function for purposes of state immunity under the Commerce Clause.

In the present cases, a Federal District Court concluded that municipal ownership and operation of a mass-transit system is a traditional governmental function and thus, under *National League of Cities,* is exempt from the obligations imposed by the FLSA. Faced with the identical question, three Federal Courts of Appeals and one state appellate court have reached the opposite conclusion.

Our examination of this "function" standard applied in these and other cases over the last eight years now persuades us that the attempt to draw the boundaries of state regulatory immunity in terms of "traditional governmental function" is not only unworkable but is inconsistent with established principles of federalism and, indeed, with those very federalism principles on which *National League of Cities* purported to rest. That case, accordingly, is overruled.

I

The history of public transportation in San Antonio, Tex., is characteristic of the history of local mass transit in the United States generally. Passenger transportation for hire within San Antonio originally was provided on a private basis by a local transportation company. In 1913, the Texas Legislature authorized the State's municipalities to regulate vehicles providing carriage for hire. 1913 Tex. Gen. Laws, ch. 147, § 4, ¶ 12, now codified, as amended, as Tex. Rev. Civ. Stat. Ann., Art. 1175, §§ 20 and 21 (Vernon 1963). Two years later, San Antonio enacted an ordinance setting forth franchising, insurance, and safety requirements for passenger vehicles operated for hire. The city continued to rely on such publicly regulated private mass transit until 1959, when it purchased the privately owned San Antonio Transit Company and replaced it with a public authority known as the San Antonio Transit System (SATS). SATS operated until 1978, when the city transferred its facilities and equipment to appellee San Antonio Metropolitan Transit Authority (SAMTA), a public mass-transit authority organized on a countywide basis. See generally Tex. Rev. Civ. Stat. Ann., Art. 1118x (Vernon Supp. 1984). SAMTA currently is the major provider of transportation in the San Antonio metropolitan area; between 1978 and 1980 alone, its vehicles traveled over 26 million route miles and carried over 63 million passengers.

As did other localities, San Antonio reached the point where it came to look to the Federal Government for financial assistance in maintaining its public mass transit. SATS managed to meet its operating expenses and bond obligations for the first decade of its existence without federal or local financial aid. By 1970, however, its financial position had deteriorated to the point where federal subsidies were vital for its continued operation. SATS' general manager that year testified before Congress that "if we do not receive substantial help from the Federal Government, San Antonio may ... join the growing ranks of cities that have inferior [public] transportation or may end up with no [public] transportation at all."

The principal federal program to which SATS and other mass-transit systems looked for relief was the Urban Mass Transportation Act of 1964 (UMTA), Pub. L. 88-365, 78 Stat. 302, as amended, 49 U.S.C. App. §§ 1601 et seq., which provides substantial federal assistance to urban mass-transit programs. See generally *Jackson Transit Authority v. Transit Union,* 457 U.S. 15 (1982). UMTA now authorizes the Department of Transportation to fund 75 percent of the capital outlays and up to 50 percent of the operating expenses of qualifying mass-transit programs. §§ 4(a), 5(d) and (e), 49 U.S.C. App. §§ 1603(a), 1604(d) and (e). SATS received its first UMTA subsidy, a $4.1 million capital grant, in December 1970. From then until February 1980, SATS and SAMTA received over $51 million in UMTA grants — more than $31 million in capital grants, over $20 million in operating assistance, and a minor amount in technical assistance. During SAMTA's first two fiscal years, it received $12.5 million in UMTA operating grants, $26.8 million from sales taxes, and only $10.1 million from fares. Federal subsidies and local sales taxes currently account for about 75 percent of SAMTA's operating expenses.

The present controversy concerns the extent to which SAMTA may be subjected to the minimum-wage and overtime requirements of the FLSA. When the FLSA was enacted in 1938, its wage and overtime provisions did not apply to local mass-transit employees or, indeed, to employees of state and local governments. §§ 3(d), 13(a)(9), 52 Stat. 1060, 1067. In 1961, Congress extended minimum-wage coverage to employees of any private mass-transit carrier whose annual gross revenue was not less than $1 million. Fair Labor Standards Amendments of 1961, §§ 2(c), 9, 75 Stat. 65, 71. Five years later, Congress extended FLSA coverage to state and local-government employees for the first time by withdrawing the minimum-wage and overtime exemptions from public hospitals, schools, and mass-transit carriers whose rates and services were subject to state regulation. Fair Labor Standards Amendments of 1966, §§ 102(a) and (b), 80 Stat. 831. At the same time, Congress eliminated the overtime exemption for all mass-transit employees other than drivers, operators, and conductors. § 206(c), 80 Stat. 836. The application of the FLSA to public schools and hospitals was ruled to be within Congress' power under the Commerce Clause. *Maryland v. Wirtz*, 392 U.S. 183 (1968).

The FLSA obligations of public mass-transit systems like SATS were expanded in 1974 when Congress provided for the progressive repeal of the surviving overtime exemption for mass-transit employees. Fair Labor Standards Amendments of 1974, § 21(b), 88 Stat. 68. Congress simultaneously brought the States and their subdivisions further within the ambit of the FLSA by extending FLSA coverage to virtually all state and local-government employees. §§6(a)(1) and (6), 88 Stat. 58, 60, 29 U. S. C. §§ 203(d) and (x). SATS complied with the FLSA's overtime requirements until 1976, when this Court, in *National League of Cities, supra,* overruled *Maryland v. Wirtz,* and held that the FLSA could not be applied constitutionally to the "traditional governmental functions" of state and local governments. Four months after *National League of Cities* was handed down, SATS informed its employees that the decision relieved SATS of its overtime obligations under the FLSA.[3]

Matters rested there until September 17, 1979, when the Wage and Hour Administration of the Department of Labor issued an opinion that SAMTA's operations "are not constitutionally immune from the application of the Fair Labor Standards Act" under *National League of Cities.* Opinion WH-499, 6 LRR 91:1138. On November 21 of that year, SAMTA filed this action against the Secretary of Labor in the United States District Court for the Western District of Texas. It sought a declaratory judgment that, contrary to the Wage and Hour Administration's determination, *National League of Cities* precluded the application of the FLSA's overtime requirements to SAMTA's operations. The Secretary counterclaimed under 29 U. S. C. § 217 for enforcement of the overtime and record-keeping requirements of the FLSA. On the same day that SAMTA filed its action, appellant Garcia and several other SAMTA employees brought suit against SAMTA in the same District Court for overtime pay under the FLSA. *Garcia v. SAMTA,* Civil Action No. SA 79 CA 458. The District Court has stayed that action pending the outcome of these cases, but it allowed Garcia to intervene in the present litigation as a defendant in support of the

---

[3] Neither SATS nor SAMTA appears to have attempted to avoid the FLSA's minimum-wage provisions. We are informed that basic wage levels in the mass-transit industry traditionally have been well in excess of the minimum wages prescribed by the FLSA. See Brief for National League of Cities et al. as *Amici Curiae* 7-8.

Secretary. One month after SAMTA brought suit, the Department of Labor formally amended its FLSA interpretive regulations to provide that publicly owned local mass-transit systems are not entitled to immunity under *National League of Cities.* 44 Fed. Reg. 75,630 (1979), codified as 29 CFR § 775.3(b)(3) (1983).

On November 17, 1981, the District Court granted SAMTA's motion for summary judgment and denied the Secretary's and Garcia's cross-motion for partial summary judgment. Without further explanation, the District Court ruled that "local public mass transit systems (including [SAMTA]) constitute integral operations in areas of traditional governmental functions" under *National League of Cities.* Juris. Statement in No. 82-1913, p. 24a. The Secretary and Garcia both appealed directly to this Court pursuant to 28 U.S.C. § 1252. During the pendency of those appeals, *Transportation Union v. Long Island R. Co.,* 455 U.S. 678 (1982), was decided. In that case, the Court ruled that commuter rail service provided by the state-owned Long Island Rail Road did not constitute a "traditional governmental function" and hence did not enjoy constitutional immunity, under *National League of Cities,* from the requirements of the Railway Labor Act. Thereafter, it vacated the District Court's judgment in the present cases and remanded them for further consideration in the light of *Long Island.* 457 U.S. 1102 (1982).

On remand, the District Court adhered to its original view and again entered judgment for SAMTA. *San Antonio Metropolitan Transit Authority v. Donovan,* 557 F. Supp. 445 (1983). The court looked first to what it regarded as the "historical reality" of state involvement in mass transit. It recognized that States not always had owned and operated mass-transit systems, but concluded that they had engaged in a longstanding pattern of public regulation, and that this regulatory tradition gave rise to an "inference of sovereignty." *Id.,* at 447-448. The court next looked to the record of federal involvement in the field and concluded that constitutional immunity would not result in an erosion of federal authority with respect to state-owned mass-transit systems, because many federal statutes themselves contain exemptions for States and thus make the withdrawal of federal regulatory power over public mass-transit systems a supervening federal policy. *Id.,* at 448-450. Although the Federal Government's authority over employee wages under the FLSA obviously would be eroded, Congress had not asserted any interest in the wages of public mass-transit employees until 1966 and hence had not established a longstanding federal interest in the field, in contrast to the century-old federal regulatory presence in the railroad industry found significant for the decision in *Long Island.* Finally, the court compared mass transit to the list of functions identified as constitutionally immune in *National League of Cities* and concluded that it did not differ from those functions in any material respect. The court stated: "If transit is to be distinguished from the exempt [*National League of Cities*] functions it will have to be by identifying a traditional state function in the same way pornography is sometimes identified: someone knows it when they see it, but they can't describe it." 557 F. Supp., at 453.[4]

---

[4] The District Court also analyzed the status of mass transit under the four-part test devised by the Sixth Circuit in *Amersbach v. City of Cleveland,* 598 F.2d 1033 (1979). In that case, the Court of Appeals looked to (1) whether the function benefits the community as a whole and is made available

The Secretary and Garcia again took direct appeals from the District Court's judgment. We noted probable jurisdiction. 464 U.S. 812 (1983). After initial argument, the cases were restored to our calendar for reargument, and the parties were requested to brief and argue the following additional question:

"Whether or not the principles of the Tenth Amendment as set forth in *National League of Cities v. Usery,* 426 U.S. 833 (1976), should be reconsidered?"

468 U.S. 1213 (1984). Reargument followed in due course.

II

Appellees have not argued that SAMTA is immune from regulation under the FLSA on the ground that it is a local transit system engaged in intrastate commercial activity. In a practical sense, SAMTA's operations might well be characterized as "local." Nonetheless, it long has been settled that Congress' authority under the Commerce Clause extends to intrastate economic activities that affect interstate commerce. See, e. g., *Hodel v. Virginia Surface Mining & Recl. Assn.,* 452 U.S. 264, 276-277 (1981); *Heart of Atlanta Motel, Inc. v. United States,* 379 U.S. 241, 258 (1964); *Wickard v. Filburn,* 317 U.S. 111, 125 (1942); *United States v. Darby,* 312 U.S. 100 (1941). Were SAMTA a privately owned and operated enterprise, it could not credibly argue that Congress exceeded the bounds of its Commerce Clause powers in prescribing minimum wages and overtime rates for SAMTA's employees. Any constitutional exemption from the requirements of the FLSA therefore must rest on SAMTA's status as a governmental entity rather than on the "local" nature of its operations.

The prerequisites for governmental immunity under *National League of Cities* were summarized by this Court in *Hodel, supra.* Under that summary, four conditions must be satisfied before a state activity may be deemed immune from a particular federal regulation under the Commerce Clause. First, it is said that the federal statute at issue must regulate "the 'States as States.'" Second, the statute must "address matters that are indisputably 'attribute[s] of state sovereignty.'" Third, state compliance with the federal obligation must "directly impair [the States'] ability 'to structure integral operations in areas of traditional governmental functions.'" Finally, the relation of state and federal interests must not be such that "the nature of the federal interest ... justifies state submission." 452 U.S., at 287-288, and n. 29, quoting *National League of Cities,* 426 U.S., at 845, 852, 854.

The controversy in the present cases has focused on the third *Hodel* requirement — that the challenged federal statute trench on "traditional governmental functions." The District Court voiced a common concern: "Despite the abundance of adjectives, identifying which particular state functions are immune remains difficult." 557 F. Supp., at 447. Just how troublesome the task has been is revealed by the results reached in other federal cases. Thus, courts have held that regulating ambulance services, *Gold Cross Ambulance v. City of Kansas City,* 538 F. Supp. 956, 967-969 (WD Mo. 1982), aff'd on other grounds, 705

---

at little or no expense; (2) whether it is undertaken for public service or pecuniary gain; (3) whether government is its principal provider; and (4) whether government is particularly suited to perform it because of a community-wide need. *Id.,* at 1037.

F.2d 1005 (CA8 1983), cert. pending, No. 83-183; licensing automobile drivers, *United States v. Best,* 573 F.2d 1095, 1102-1103 (CA9 1978); operating a municipal airport, *Amersbach v. City of Cleveland,* 598 F.2d 1033, 1037-1038 (CA6 1979); performing solid waste disposal, *Hybud Equipment Corp. v. City of Akron,* 654 F.2d 1187, 1196 (CA6 1981); and operating a highway authority, *Molina-Estrada v. Puerto Rico Highway Authority,* 680 F.2d 841, 845-846 (CA1 1982), are functions *protected* under *National League of Cities.* At the same time, courts have held that issuance of industrial development bonds, *Woods v. Homes and Structures of Pittsburgh, Kansas, Inc.,* 489 F. Supp. 1270, 1296-1297 (Kan. 1980); regulation of intrastate natural gas sales, *Oklahoma ex rel. Derryberry v. FERC,* 494 F. Supp. 636, 657 (WD Okla. 1980), aff'd, 661 F.2d 832 (CA10 1981), *cert. denied sub nom. Texas v. FERC,* 457 U.S. 1105 (1982); regulation of traffic on public roads, *Friends of the Earth v. Carey,* 552 F.2d 25, 38 (CA2), *cert. denied,* 434 U.S. 902 (1977); regulation of air transportation, *Hughes Air Corp. v. Public Utilities Commission,* 644 F.2d 1334, 1340-1341 (CA9 1981); operation of a telephone system, *Puerto Rico Tel. Co. v. FCC,* 553 F.2d 694, 700-701 (CA1 1977); leasing and sale of natural gas, *Public Service Co. v. FERC,* 587 F.2d 716, 721 (CA5), *cert. denied sub nom. Louisiana v. FERC,* 444 U.S. 879 (1979); operation of a mental health facility, *Williams v. Eastside Mental Health Center, Inc.,* 669 F.2d 671, 680-681 (CA11), *cert. denied,* 459 U.S. 976 (1982); and provision of in-house domestic services for the aged and handicapped, *Bonnette v. California Health and Welfare Agency,* 704 F.2d 1465, 1472 (CA9 1983), are *not* entitled to immunity. We find it difficult, if not impossible, to identify an organizing principle that places each of the cases in the first group on one side of a line and each of the cases in the second group on the other side. The constitutional distinction between licensing drivers and regulating traffic, for example, or between operating a highway authority and operating a mental health facility, is elusive at best.

Thus far, this Court itself has made little headway in defining the scope of the governmental functions deemed protected under *National League of Cities.* In that case the Court set forth examples of protected and unprotected functions, see 426 U.S., at 851, 854, n. 18, but provided no explanation of how those examples were identified. The only other case in which the Court has had occasion to address the problem is *Long Island.* We there observed: "The determination of whether a federal law impairs a state's authority with respect to 'areas of traditional [state] functions' may at times be a difficult one." 455 U.S., at 684, quoting *National League of Cities,* 426 U.S., at 852. The accuracy of that statement is demonstrated by this Court's own difficulties in *Long Island* in developing a workable standard for "traditional governmental functions." We relied in large part there on "the *historical reality* that the operation of railroads is not among the functions *traditionally* performed by state and local governments," but we simultaneously disavowed "a static historical view of state functions generally immune from federal regulation." 455 U.S., at 686 (first emphasis added; second emphasis in original). We held that the inquiry into a particular function's "traditional" nature was merely a means of determining whether the federal statute at issue unduly handicaps "basic state prerogatives," *id.,* at 686-687, but we did not offer an explanation of what makes one state function a "basic prerogative" and another function not basic. Finally, having disclaimed a rigid reliance on the historical pedigree of state involvement in a particular area, we nonetheless found it appropriate to emphasize the extended historical record of *federal* involvement in the field of rail transportation. *Id.,* at 687-689.

Many constitutional standards involve "undoubte[d] ... gray areas," *Fry v. United States,* 421 U.S. 542, 558 (1975) (dissenting opinion), and, despite the difficulties that this Court and other courts have encountered so far, it normally might be fair to venture the assumption that case-by-case development would lead to a workable standard for determining whether a particular governmental function should be immune from federal regulation under the Commerce Clause. A further cautionary note is sounded, however, by the Court's experience in the related field of state immunity from federal taxation. In *South Carolina v. United States,* 199 U.S. 437 (1905), the Court held for the first time that the state tax immunity recognized in *Collector v. Day,* 11 Wall. 113 (1870), extended only to the "ordinary" and "strictly governmental" instrumentalities of state governments and not to instrumentalities "used by the State in the carrying on of an ordinary private business." 199 U.S., at 451, 461. While the Court applied the distinction outlined in *South Carolina* for the following 40 years, at no time during that period did the Court develop a consistent formulation of the kinds of governmental functions that were entitled to immunity. The Court identified the protected functions at various times as "essential," "usual," "traditional," or "strictly governmental." While "these differences in phraseology ... must not be too literally contradistinguished," *Brush v. Commissioner,* 300 U.S. 352, 362 (1937), they reflect an inability to specify precisely what aspects of a governmental function made it necessary to the "unimpaired existence" of the States. *Collector v. Day,* 11 Wall., at 127. Indeed, the Court ultimately chose "not, by an attempt to formulate any general test, [to] risk embarrassing the decision of cases [concerning] activities of a different kind which may arise in the future." *Brush v. Commissioner,* 300 U.S., at 365.

If these tax immunity cases had any common thread, it was in the attempt to distinguish between "governmental" and "proprietary" functions. To say that the distinction between "governmental" and "proprietary" proved to be stable, however, would be something of an overstatement. In 1911, for example, the Court declared that the provision of a municipal water supply "is no part of the essential governmental functions of a State." *Flint v. Stone Tracy Co.,* 220 U.S. 107, 172. Twenty-six years later, without any intervening change in the applicable legal standards, the Court simply rejected its earlier position and decided that the provision of a municipal water supply *was* immune from federal taxation as an essential governmental function, even though municipal water works long had been operated for profit by private industry. *Brush v. Commissioner,* 300 U.S., at 370-373. At the same time that the Court was holding a municipal water supply to be immune from federal taxes, it had held that a state-run commuter rail system was *not* immune. *Helvering v. Powers,* 293 U.S. 214 (1934). Justice Black, in *Helvering v. Gerhardt,* 304 U.S. 405, 427 (1938), was moved to observe: "An implied constitutional distinction which taxes income of an officer of a state-operated transportation system and exempts income of the manager of a municipal water works system manifests the uncertainty created by the 'essential' and 'non-essential' test" (concurring opinion). It was this uncertainty and instability that led the Court shortly thereafter, in *New York v.*

United States, 326 U.S. 572 (1946), unanimously to conclude that the distinction between "governmental" and "proprietary" functions was "untenable" and must be abandoned. See *id.,* at 583 (opinion of Frankfurter, J., joined by Rutledge, J.); *id.,* at 586 (Stone, C.J., concurring, joined by Reed, Murphy, and Burton, JJ.); *id.,* at 590-596 (Douglas, J., dissenting, joined by Black, J.). See also *Massa-chusetts v. United States,* 435 U.S. 444, 457, and n. 14 (1978) (plurality opinion); *Case v. Bowles,* 327 U.S. 92, 101 (1946).

Even during the heyday of the governmental/proprietary distinction in inter-governmental tax-immunity doctrine the Court never explained the constitutional basis for that distinction. In *South Carolina,* it expressed its concern that unlimited state immunity from federal taxation would allow the States to undermine the Federal Government's tax base by expanding into previously private sectors of the economy. See 199 U.S., at 454-455. Although the need to reconcile state and federal interests obviously demanded that state immunity have some limiting principle, the Court did not try to justify the particular result it reached; it simply concluded that a "line [must] be drawn," *id.,* at 456, and proceeded to draw that line. The Court's elaborations in later cases, such as the assertion in *Ohio v. Helvering,* 292 U.S. 360, 369 (1934), that "[w]hen a state enters the market place seeking customers it divests itself of its *quasi* sovereignty *pro tanto,*" sound more of *ipse dixit* than reasoned explanation. This inability to give principled content to the distinction between "governmental" and "proprietary," no less significantly than its unworkability, led the Court to abandon the distinction in *New York v. United States.*

The distinction the Court discarded as unworkable in the field of tax immunity has proved no more fruitful in the field of regulatory immunity under the Commerce Clause. Neither do any of the alternative standards that might be employed to distinguish between protected and unprotected governmental functions appear manageable. We rejected the possibility of making immunity turn on a purely historical standard of "tradition" in *Long Island,* and properly so. The most obvious defect of a historical approach to state immunity is that it prevents a court from accommodating changes in the historical functions of States, changes that have resulted in a number of once-private functions like education being assumed by the States and their subdivisions. At the same time, the only apparent virtue of a rigorous historical standard, namely, its promise of a reasonably objective measure for state immunity, is illusory. Reliance on history as an organizing principle results in linedrawing of the most arbitrary sort; the genesis of state governmental functions stretches over a historical continuum from before the Revolution to the present, and courts would have to decide by fiat precisely how longstanding a pattern of state involvement had to be for federal regulatory authority to be defeated.

A nonhistorical standard for selecting immune governmental functions is likely to be just as unworkable as is an historical standard. The goal of identifying "uniquely" governmental functions, for example, has been rejected by the Court in the field of government tort liability in part because the notion of a "uniquely" governmental function is unmanageable. See *Indian Towing Co. v. United States,* 350 U.S. 61, 64-68 (1955); see also *Lafayette v. Louisiana Power & Light Co.,* 435 U.S. 389, 433 (1978) (dissenting opinion). Another possibility would be to confine immunity to "necessary" governmental services, that is, services that would be provided inadequately or not at all unless the government provided them. Cf. *Flint v. Stone Tracy Co.,* 220 U.S., at 172. The set of services that fits into this category, however, may well be negligible. The fact that an unregulated market produces less of some service than a State deems desirable does not mean that the State itself must provide the service; in most if not all cases, the State can "contract out" by hiring private firms to provide the service or simply by providing subsidies to existing suppliers. It also is open to question how well equipped courts are to make this kind of determination about the workings of economic markets.

We believe, however, that there is a more fundamental problem at work here, a problem that explains why the Court was never able to provide a basis for the governmental/proprietary distinction in the intergovernmental tax immunity cases and why an attempt to draw similar distinctions with respect to federal regulatory authority under *National League of Cities* is unlikely to succeed regardless of how the distinctions are phrased. The problem is that neither the governmental/proprietary distinction nor any other that purports to separate out important governmental functions can be faithful to the role of federalism in a democratic society. The essence of our federal system is that within the realm of authority left open to them under the Constitution, the States must be equally free to engage in any activity that their citizens choose for the common weal, no matter how unorthodox or unnecessary anyone else — including the judiciary — deems state involvement to be. Any rule of state immunity that looks to the "traditional," "integral," or "necessary" nature of governmental functions inevitably invites an unelected federal judiciary to make decisions about which state policies it favors and which ones it dislikes. "The science of government ... is the science of experiment," *Anderson v. Dunn,* 6 Wheat. 204, 226 (1821), and the States cannot serve as laboratories for social and economic experiment, see *New State Ice Co. v. Liebmann,* 285 U.S. 262, 311 (1932) (Brandeis, J., dissenting), if they must pay an added price when they meet the changing needs of their citizenry by taking up functions that an earlier day and a different society left in private hands. In the words of Justice Black:

> "There is not, and there cannot be, any unchanging line of demarcation between essential and non-essential governmental functions. Many governmental functions of today have at some time in the past been non-governmental. The genius of our government provides that, within the sphere of constitutional action, the people — acting not through the courts but through their elected legislative representatives — have the power to determine as conditions demand, what services and functions the public welfare requires." *Helvering v. Gerhardt,* 304 U.S., at 427 (concurring opinion).

We therefore now reject, as unsound in principle and unworkable in practice, a rule of state immunity from federal regulation that turns on a judicial appraisal of whether a particular governmental function is "integral" or "traditional." Any such rule leads to inconsistent results at the same time that it disserves principles of democratic self-governance, and it breeds inconsistency precisely because it is divorced from those principles. If there are to be limits on the Federal Government's power to interfere with state functions — as undoubtedly there are — we must look elsewhere to find them. We accordingly return to the underlying issue that confronted this Court in *National League of*

Cities — the manner in which the Constitution insulates States from the reach of Congress' power under the Commerce Clause.

III

The central theme of *National League of Cities* was that the States occupy a special position in our constitutional system and that the scope of Congress' authority under the Commerce Clause must reflect that position. Of course, the Commerce Clause by its specific language does not provide any special limitation on Congress' actions with respect to the States. See *EEOC v. Wyoming,* 460 U.S. 226, 248 (1983) (concurring opinion). It is equally true, however, that the text of the Constitution provides the beginning rather than the final answer to every inquiry into questions of federalism, for "[b]ehind the words of the constitutional provisions are postulates which limit and control." *Monaco v. Mississippi,* 292 U.S. 313, 322 (1934). *National League of Cities* reflected the general conviction that the Constitution precludes "the National Government [from] devour[ing] the essentials of state sovereignty." *Maryland v. Wirtz,* 392 U.S., at 205 (dissenting opinion). In order to be faithful to the underlying federal premises of the Constitution, courts must look for the "postulates which limit and control."

What has proved problematic is not the perception that the Constitution's federal structure imposes limitations on the Commerce Clause, but rather the nature and content of those limitations. One approach to defining the limits on Congress' authority to regulate the States under the Commerce Clause is to identify certain underlying elements of political sovereignty that are deemed essential to the States' "separate and independent existence." *Lane County v. Oregon,* 7 Wall. 71, 76 (1869). This approach obviously underlay the Court's use of the "traditional governmental function" concept in *National League of Cities.* It also has led to the separate requirement that the challenged federal statute "address matters that are indisputably 'attribute[s] of state sovereignty.'" *Hodel,* 452 U.S., at 288, quoting *National League of Cities,* 426 U.S., at 845. In *National League of Cities* itself, for example, the Court concluded that decisions by a State concerning the wages and hours of its employees are an "undoubted attribute of state sovereignty." 426 U.S., at 845. The opinion did not explain what aspects of such decisions made them such an "undoubted attribute," and the Court since then has remarked on the uncertain scope of the concept. See *EEOC v. Wyoming,* 460 U.S., at 238, n. 11. The point of the inquiry, however, has remained to single out particular features of a State's internal governance that are deemed to be intrinsic parts of state sovereignty.

We doubt that courts ultimately can identify principled constitutional limitations on the scope of Congress' Commerce Clause powers over the States merely by relying on *a priori* definitions of state sovereignty. In part, this is because of the elusiveness of objective criteria for "fundamental" elements of state sovereignty, a problem we have witnessed in the search for "traditional governmental functions." There is, however, a more fundamental reason: the sovereignty of the States is limited by the Constitution itself. A variety of sovereign powers, for example, are withdrawn from the States by Article I, § 10. Section 8 of the same Article works an equally sharp contraction of state sovereignty by authorizing Congress to exercise a wide range of legislative powers and (in conjunction with the Supremacy Clause of Article VI) to displace contrary state legislation. See *Hodel,* 452 U.S., at 290-292. By providing for final review of questions of federal law in this Court, Article III curtails the sovereign power of the States' judiciaries to make authoritative determinations of law. See *Martin v. Hunter's Lessee,* 1 Wheat. 304 (1816). Finally, the developed application, through the Fourteenth Amendment, of the greater part of the Bill of Rights to the States limits the sovereign authority that States otherwise would possess to legislate with respect to their citizens and to conduct their own affairs.

The States unquestionably do "retai[n] a significant measure of sovereign authority." *EEOC v. Wyoming,* 460 U.S., at 269 (POWELL, J., dissenting). They do so, however, only to the extent that the Constitution has not divested them of their original powers and transferred those powers to the Federal Government. In the words of James Madison to the Members of the First Congress: "Interference with the power of the States was no constitutional criterion of the power of Congress. If the power was not given, Congress could not exercise it; if given, they might exercise it, although it should interfere with the laws, or even the Constitution of the States." 2 Annals of Cong. 1897 (1791). Justice Field made the same point in the course of his defense of state autonomy in his dissenting opinion in *Baltimore & Ohio R. Co. v. Baugh,* 149 U.S. 368, 401 (1893), a defense quoted with approval in *Erie R. Co. v. Tompkins,* 304 U.S. 64, 78-79 (1938):

> "[T]he Constitution of the United States ... recognizes and preserves the autonomy and independence of the States — independence in their legislative and independence in their judicial departments. [Federal] [s]upervision over either the legislative or the judicial action of the States is in no case permissible except as to matters by the Constitution specifically authorized or delegated to the United States. Any interference with either, except as thus permitted, is an invasion of the authority of the State and, to that extent, a denial of its independence."

As a result, to say that the Constitution assumes the continued role of the States is to say little about the nature of that role. Only recently, this Court recognized that the purpose of the constitutional immunity recognized in *National League of Cities* is not to preserve "a sacred province of state autonomy." *EEOC v. Wyoming,* 460 U.S., at 236. With rare exceptions, like the guarantee, in Article IV, § 3, of state territorial integrity, the Constitution does not carve out express elements of state sovereignty that Congress may not employ its delegated powers to displace. James Wilson reminded the Pennsylvania ratifying convention in 1787: "It is true, indeed, sir, although it presupposes the existence of state governments, yet this Constitution does not suppose them to be the sole power to be respected." 2 Debates in the Several State Conventions on the Adoption of the Federal Constitution 439 (J. Elliot 2d ed. 1876) (Elliot). The power of the Federal Government is a "power to be respected" as well, and the fact that the States remain sovereign as to all powers not vested in Congress or denied them by the Constitution offers no guidance about where the frontier between state and federal power lies. In short, we have no license to employ freestanding conceptions of state sovereignty when measuring congressional authority under the Commerce Clause.

When we look for the States' "residuary and inviolable sovereignty," The Federalist No. 39, p. 285 (B. Wright ed. 1961) (J. Madison), in the shape of the constitutional scheme rather than in predetermined notions of sovereign power, a different measure of state sovereignty emerges. Apart from the limitation on federal authority inherent in the delegated nature of Congress' Article I powers, the principal means chosen by the Framers to ensure the role of the States in the federal system lies in the structure of the Federal Government itself. It is no novelty to observe that the composition of the Federal Government was designed in large part to protect the States from overreaching by Congress. The Framers thus gave the States a role in the selection both of the Executive and the Legislative Branches of the Federal Government. The States were vested with indirect influence over the House of Representatives and the Presidency by their control of electoral qualifications and their role in presidential elections. U.S. Const., Art. I, § 2, and Art. II, § 1. They were given more direct influence in the Senate, where each State received equal representation and each Senator was to be selected by the legislature of his State. Art. I, § 3. The significance attached to the States' equal representation in the Senate is underscored by the prohibition of any constitutional amendment divesting a state of equal representation without the State's consent. Art. V.

The extent to which the structure of the Federal Government itself was relied on to insulate the interests of the States is evident in the views of the Framers. James Madison explained that the Federal Government "will partake sufficiently of the spirit [of the States], to be disinclined to invade the rights of the individual States, or the prerogatives of their governments." The Federalist No. 46, p. 332 (B. Wright ed. 1961). Similarly, James Wilson observed that "it was a favorite object in the Convention" to provide for the security of the States against federal encroachment and that the structure of the Federal Government itself served that end. 2 Elliot, at 438-439. Madison placed particular reliance on the equal representation of the States in the Senate, which he saw as "at once a constitutional recognition of the portion of sovereignty remaining in the individual States, and an instrument for preserving that residuary sovereignty." The Federalist No. 62, p. 408 (B. Wright ed. 1961). He further noted that "the residuary sovereignty of the States [is] implied *and secured* by that principle of representation in one branch of the [federal] legislature" (emphasis added). The Federalist No. 43, p. 315 (B. Wright ed. 1961). See also *M'Culloch v. Maryland,* 4 Wheat. 316, 435 (1819). In short, the Framers chose to rely on a federal system in which special restraints on federal power over the States inhered principally in the workings of the National Government itself, rather than in discrete limitations on the objects of federal authority. State sovereign interests, then, are more properly protected by procedural safeguards inherent in the structure of the federal system than by judicially created limitations on federal power.

The effectiveness of the federal political process in preserving the States' interests is apparent even today in the course of federal legislation. On the one hand, the States have been able to direct a substantial proportion of federal revenues into their own treasuries in the form of general and program-specific grants in aid. The federal role in assisting state and local governments is a longstanding one; Congress provided federal land grants to finance state governments from the beginning of the Republic, and direct cash grants were awarded as early as 1887 under the Hatch Act. In the past quarter-century alone, federal grants to States and localities have grown from $7 billion to $96 billion. As a result, federal grants now account for about one-fifth of state and local government expenditures. The States have obtained federal funding for such services as police and fire protection, education, public health and hospitals, parks and recreation, and sanitation. Moreover, at the same time that the States have exercised their influence to obtain federal support, they have been able to exempt themselves from a wide variety of obligations imposed by Congress under the Commerce Clause. For example, the Federal Power Act, the National Labor Relations Act, the Labor-Management Reporting and Disclosure Act, the Occupational Safety and Health Act, the Employee Retirement Insurance Security Act, and the Sherman Act all contain express or implied exemptions for States and their subdivisions. The fact that some federal statutes such as the FLSA extend general obligations to the States cannot obscure the extent to which the political position of the States in the federal system has served to minimize the burdens that the States bear under the Commerce Clause.[17]

We realize that changes in the structure of the Federal Government have taken place since 1789, not the least of which has been the substitution of popular election of Senators by the adoption of the Seventeenth Amendment in 1913, and that these changes may work to alter the influence of the States in the federal political process. Nonetheless, against this background, we are convinced that the fundamental limitation that the constitutional scheme imposes on the Commerce Clause to protect the "States as States" is one of process rather than one of result. Any substantive restraint on the exercise of Commerce Clause powers must find its justification in the procedural nature of this basic limitation, and it must be tailored to compensate for possible failings in the national political process rather than to dictate a "sacred province of state autonomy." *EEOC v. Wyoming,* 460 U.S., at 236.

Insofar as the present cases are concerned, then, we need go no further than to state that we perceive nothing in the overtime and minimum-wage requirements of the FLSA, as applied to SAMTA, that is destructive of state sovereignty or violative of any constitutional provision. SAMTA faces nothing more than the same minimum-wage and overtime obligations that hundreds of thousands of other employers, public as well as private, have to meet.

In these cases, the status of public mass transit simply underscores the extent to which the structural protections of the Constitution insulate the States from federally imposed burdens. When Congress first subjected state mass-transit systems to FLSA obligations in 1966, and when it expanded those obligations in 1974, it simultaneously provided extensive funding for state and local mass transit through UMTA. In the two decades since its enactment, UMTA has

---

[17]Even as regards the FLSA, Congress incorporated special provisions concerning overtime pay for law enforcement and firefighting personnel when it amended the FLSA in 1974 in order to take account of the special concerns of States and localities with respect to these positions. See 29 U.S.C. § 207(k). Congress also declined to impose any obligations on state and local governments with respect to policymaking personnel who are not subject to civil service laws. See 29 U.S.C. § 203(e)(2)(C)(i) and (ii).

provided over $22 billion in mass transit aid to States and localities. In 1983 alone, UMTA funding amounted to $3.7 billion. As noted above, SAMTA and its immediate predecessor have received a substantial amount of UMTA funding, including over $12 million during SAMTA's first two fiscal years alone. In short, Congress has not simply placed a financial burden on the shoulders of States and localities that operate mass-transit systems, but has provided substantial countervailing financial assistance as well, assistance that may leave individual mass transit systems better off than they would have been had Congress never intervened at all in the area. Congress' treatment of public mass transit reinforces our conviction that the national political process systematically protects States from the risk of having their functions in that area handicapped by Commerce Clause regulations.[21]

IV

This analysis makes clear that Congress' action in affording SAMTA employees the protections of the wage and hour provisions of the FLSA contravened no affirmative limit on Congress' power under the Commerce Clause. The judgment of the District Court therefore must be reversed.

Of course, we continue to recognize that the States occupy a special and specific position in our constitutional system and that the scope of Congress' authority under the Commerce Clause must reflect that position. But the principal and basic limit on the federal commerce power is that inherent in all congressional action — the built-in restraints that our system provides through state participation in federal governmental action. The political process ensures that laws that unduly burden the States will not be promulgated. In the factual setting of these cases the internal safeguards of the political process have performed as intended.

These cases do not require us to identify or define what affirmative limits the constitutional structure might impose on federal action affecting the States under the Commerce Clause. See *Coyle v. Oklahoma*, 221 U.S. 559 (1911). We note and accept Justice Frankfurter's observation in *New York v. United States*, 326 U.S. 572, 583 (1946):

"The process of Constitutional adjudication does not thrive on conjuring up horrible possibilities that never happen in the real world and devising doctrines sufficiently comprehensive in detail to cover the remotest contingency. Nor need we go beyond what is required for a reasoned disposition of the kind of controversy now before the Court."

Though the separate concurrence providing the fifth vote in *National League of Cities* was "not untroubled by certain possible implications" of the decision, 426 U.S., at 856, the Court in that case attempted to articulate affirmative limits on the Commerce Clause power in terms of core governmental functions and fundamental attributes of state sovereignty. But the model of democratic decisionmaking the Court there identified underestimated, in our view, the solici-

---

[21]Our references to UMTA are not meant to imply that regulation under the Commerce Clause must be accompanied by countervailing financial benefits under the Spending Clause. The application of the FLSA to SAMTA would be constitutional even had Congress not provided federal funding under UMTA.

tude of the national political process for the continued vitality of the States. Attempts by other courts since then to draw guidance from this model have proved it both impracticable and doctrinally barren. In sum, in *National League of Cities* the Court tried to repair what did not need repair.

We do not lightly overrule recent precedent. We have not hesitated, however, when it has become apparent that a prior decision has departed from a proper understanding of congressional power under the Commerce Clause. See *United States v. Darby*, 312 U.S. 100, 116-117 (1941). Due respect for the reach of congressional power within the federal system mandates that we do so now.

National League of Cities v. Usery, 426 U.S. 833 (1976), is overruled. The judgment of the District Court is reversed, and these cases are remanded to that court for further proceedings consistent with this opinion.

It is so ordered.

JUSTICE POWELL, with whom THE CHIEF JUSTICE, JUSTICE REHNQUIST, and JUSTICE O'CONNOR join, dissenting.

The Court today, in its 5-4 decision, overrules *National League of Cities v. Usery*, 426 U.S. 833 (1976), a case in which we held that Congress lacked authority to impose the requirements of the Fair Labor Standards Act on state and local governments. Because I believe this decision substantially alters the federal system embodied in the Constitution, I dissent.

I

There are, of course, numerous examples over the history of this Court in which prior decisions have been reconsidered and overruled. There have been few cases, however, in which the principle of *stare decisis* and the rationale of recent decisions were ignored as abruptly as we now witness. The reasoning of the Court in *National League of Cities,* and the principle applied there, have been reiterated consistently over the past eight years. Since its decision in 1976, *National League of Cities* has been cited and quoted in opinions joined by every member of the present Court. *Hodel v. Virginia Surface Mining & Recl. Assn.*, 452 U.S. 264, 287-293 (1981); *United Transportation Union v. Long Island R. Co.*, 455 U.S. 678, 684-686 (1982); *FERC v. Mississippi*, 456 U.S. 742, 764-767 (1982). Less than three years ago, in *Long Island R. Co., supra,* a unanimous Court reaffirmed the principles of *National League of Cities* but found them inapplicable to the regulation of a railroad heavily engaged in interstate commerce. The Court stated:

"The key prong of the *National League of Cities* test applicable to this case is the third one [repeated and reformulated in *Hodel*], which examines whether 'the states' compliance with the federal law would directly impair their ability to structure integral operations in areas of traditional governmental functions." 455 U.S., at 684.

The Court in that case recognized that the test "may at times be a difficult one," *ibid.,* but it was considered in that unanimous decision as settled constitutional doctrine.

As recently as June 1, 1982 the five Justices who constitute the majority in this case also were the majority in *FERC v. Mississippi.* In that case, the Court said:

"In *National League of Cities, supra,* for example, the Court made clear that the State's regulation of its relationship with its employees is an 'undoubted attribute of state sovereignty.' 426 U.S., at 845. Yet, by holding 'unimpaired' *California v. Taylor,* 353 U.S. 553 (1957), which upheld a federal labor regulation as applied to state railroad employees, 426 U.S., at 854, n. 18, *National League of Cities* acknowledged that not all aspects of a State's sovereign authority are immune from federal control." 426 U.S., at 764, n. 28.

The Court went on to say that even where the requirements of the *National League of Cities* standard are met, "'[t]here are situations in which the nature of the federal interest advanced may be such that it justifies state submission.'" *Ibid.,* quoting *Hodel, supra,* 452 U.S., at 288 n. 29. The joint federal/state system of regulation in *FERC* was such a "situation," but there was no hint in the Court's opinion that *National League of Cities* — or its basic standard — was subject to the infirmities discovered today.

Although the doctrine is not rigidly applied to constitutional questions, "any departure from the doctrine of *stare decisis* demands special justification." *Arizona v. Rumsey,* 467 U.S. 203, 212 (1984). See also *Oregon v. Kennedy,* 456 U.S. 667, 691-692 n. 34 (1982) (STEVENS, J., concurring). In the present case, the five Justices who compose the majority today participated in *National League of Cities* and the cases reaffirming it.[2] The stability of judicial decision, and with it respect for the authority of this Court, are not served by the precipitous overruling of multiple precedents that we witness in this case.

Whatever effect the Court's decision may have in weakening the application of *stare decisis,* it is likely to be less important than what the Court has done to the Constitution itself. A unique feature of the United States is the *federal* system of government guaranteed by the Constitution and implicit in the very name of our country. Despite some genuflecting in the Court's opinion to the concept of federalism, today's decision effectively reduces the Tenth Amendment to meaningless rhetoric when Congress acts pursuant to the Commerce Clause. The Court holds that the Fair Labor Standards Act ["FLSA"] "contravened no affirmative limit on Congress' power under the Commerce Clause" to determine the wage rates and hours of employment of all state and local employees. *Ante,* at 27. In rejecting the traditional view of our federal system, the Court states:

"Apart from the limitation on federal authority inherent in the delegated nature of Congress' Article I powers, the principal means chosen by the Framers to ensure the role of the states in the federal system lies in the *structure* of the Federal Government itself." *Ante,* at 21-22 (emphasis added).

To leave no doubt about its intention, the Court renounces its decision in *National League of Cities* because it "inevitably invites an unelected federal judiciary to make decisions about which state policies it favors and which ones it

---

[2] JUSTICE O'CONNOR, the only new member in the Court since our decision in *National League of Cities,* has joined the Court in reaffirming its principles. See *United Transportation Union v. Long Island R. Co.,* 455 U.S. 678 (1982), and *FERC v. Mississippi,* 456 U.S. 742, 775 (1982) (O'CONNOR, J., dissenting in part).

dislikes." *Ante,* at 17. In other words, the extent to which the States may exercise their authority, when Congress purports to act under the Commerce Clause, henceforth is to be determined from time to time by political decisions made by members of the federal government, decisions the Court says will not be subject to judicial review. I note that it does not seem to have occurred to the Court that *it* — an unelected majority of five Justices — today rejects almost 200 years of the understanding of the constitutional status of federalism. In doing so, there is only a single passing reference to the Tenth Amendment. Nor is so much as a dictum of any court cited in support of the view that the role of the States in the federal system may depend upon the grace of elected federal officials, rather than on the Constitution as interpreted by this Court.

In my opinion that follows, Part II addresses the Court's criticisms of *National League of Cities.* Part III reviews briefly the understanding of federalism that ensured the ratification of the Constitution and the extent to which this Court, until today, has recognized that the States retain a significant measure of sovereignty in our federal system. Part IV considers the applicability of the FLSA to the indisputably local service provided by an urban transit system.

II

The Court finds that the test of State immunity approved in *National League of Cities* and its progeny is unworkable and unsound in principle. In finding the test to be unworkable, the Court begins by mischaracterizing *National League of Cities* and subsequent cases. In concluding that efforts to define state immunity are unsound in principle, the Court radically departs from long settled constitutional values and ignores the role of judicial review in our system of government.

A

Much of the Court's opinion is devoted to arguing that it is difficult to define *a priori* "traditional governmental functions." *National League of Cities* neither engaged in, nor required, such a task. The Court discusses and condemns as standards "traditional governmental function[s]," "purely historical" functions, "'uniquely' governmental functions," and "'necessary' governmental services." *Ante,* at 10-11, 15, 16. But nowhere does it mention that *National League of Cities* adopted a familiar type of balancing test for determining whether Commerce Clause enactments transgress constitutional limitations imposed by the federal nature of our system of government. This omission is noteworthy, since the author of today's opinion joined *National League of Cities* and concurred separately to point out that the Court's opinion in that case "adopt[s] a balancing approach [that] does not outlaw federal power in areas … where the federal interest is demonstrably greater and where state … compliance with imposed federal standards would be essential." 426 U.S., at 856 (BLACKMUN, J., concurring).

In reading *National League of Cities* to embrace a balancing approach, JUSTICE BLACKMUN quite correctly cited the part of the opinion that reaffirmed *Fry v. United States,* 421 U.S. 542 (1975). The Court's analysis reaffirming *Fry* explicitly weighed the seriousness of the problem addressed by the federal

legislation at issue in that case, against the effects of compliance on State sovereignty. 426 U.S., at 852-853. Our subsequent decisions also adopted this approach of weighing the respective interests of the States and federal government. In *EEOC v. Wyoming,* 460 U.S. 226 (1983), for example, the Court stated
that "[t]he principle of immunity articulated in *National League of Cities* is a
functional doctrine ... whose ultimate purpose is not to create a sacred province
of state autonomy, but to ensure that the unique benefits of a federal system ...
not be lost through undue federal interference in certain core state functions."
Id., at 236. See also *Hodel v. Virginia Surface Mining & Reclamation Assn.,* 452
U.S. 264 (1981). In overruling *National League of Cities,* the Court incorrectly
characterizes the mode of analysis established therein and developed in subsequent cases.

Moreover, the statute at issue in this case, the FLSA, is the identical statute
that was at issue in *National League of Cities.* Although JUSTICE BLACKMUN'S
concurrence noted that he was "not untroubled by certain possible implications
of the Court's opinion" in *National League of Cities,* it also stated that "the
result with respect to the statute under challenge here [the FLSA] is *necessarily
correct.*" 426 U.S., at 856 (emphasis added). His opinion for the Court today
does not discuss the statute, nor identify any changed circumstances that warrant the conclusion today that *National League of Cities* is *necessarily wrong.*

B

Today's opinion does not explain how the States' role in the electoral process
guarantees that particular exercises of the Commerce Clause power will not
infringe on residual State sovereignty. Members of Congress are elected from
the various States, but once in office they are members of the federal government. Although the States participate in the Electoral College, this is hardly a
reason to view the President as a representative of the States' interest against
federal encroachment. We noted recently "the hydraulic pressure inherent
within each of the separate Branches to exceed the outer limits of its power ...."
Immigration and Naturalization Service v. Chadha, 462 U.S. 919, — (1983).
The Court offers no reason to think that this pressure will not operate when
Congress seeks to invoke its powers under the Commerce Clause, notwithstanding the electoral role of the States.

The Court apparently thinks that the States' success at obtaining federal
funds for various projects and exemptions from the obligations of some federal
statutes is indicative of the "effectiveness of the federal political process in
preserving the States' interests...." *Ante,* at 23-24. But such political success is
not relevant to the question whether the political *processes* are the proper
means of enforcing constitutional limitations. The fact that Congress generally
does not transgress constitutional limits on its power to reach State activities
does not make judicial review any less necessary to rectify the cases in which it
does do so. The States' role in our system of government is a matter of constitutional law, not of legislative grace. "The powers not delegated to the United
States by the Constitution, nor prohibited by it to the States, are reserved to the
States, respectively, or to the people." U.S. Const., Amend. 10.

More troubling than the logical infirmities in the Court's reasoning is the
result of its holding, i.e., that federal political officials, invoking the Commerce

Clause, are the sole judges of the limits of their own power. This result is inconsistent with the fundamental principles of our constitutional system. See, e.g., The Federalist No. 78 (Hamilton). At least since *Marbury v. Madison* it has been the settled province of the federal judidicary "to say what the law is" with respect to the constitutionality of acts of Congress. 1 Cranch 137, 177 (1803). In rejecting the role of the judiciary in protecting the States from federal over-reaching, the Court's opinion offers no explanation for ignoring the teaching of the most famous case in our history.

III

A

In our federal system, the States have a major role that cannot be preempted by the national government. As contemporaneous writings and the debates at the ratifying conventions make clear, the States' ratification of the Constitution was predicated on this understanding of federalism. Indeed, the Tenth Amendment was adopted specifically to ensure that the important role promised the States by the proponents of the Constitution was realized.

Much of the initial opposition to the Constitution was rooted in the fear that the national government would be too powerful and eventually would eliminate the States as viable political entities. This concern was voiced repeatedly until proponents of the Constitution made assurances that a bill of rights, including a provision explicitly reserving powers in the States, would be among the first business of the new Congress. Samuel Adams argued, for example, that if the several States were to be joined in "one entire Nation, under one Legislature, the Powers of which shall extend to every Subject of Legislation, and its Laws be supreme & controul the whole, the Idea of Sovereignty in these States must be lost." Letter from Samuel Adams to Richard Henry Lee (Dec. 3, 1787), reprinted in Anti-Federalists versus Federalists 159 (J. Lewis ed. 1967). Likewise, George Mason feared that "the general government being paramount to, and in every respect more powerful than the state governments, the latter must give way to the former." Address in the Ratifying Convention of Virginia (June 4-12, 1788), reprinted in Anti-Federalists versus Federalists, *supra,* at 208-209.

Antifederalists raised these concerns in almost every State ratifying convention. See generally 1-4, Debates in the Several State Conventions on the Adoption of the Federal Constitution (J. Elliot 2d ed. 1854). As a result, eight States voted for the Constitution only after proposing amendments to be adopted after ratification. All eight of these included among their recommendations some version of what later became the Tenth Amendment. *Ibid.* So strong was the concern that the proposed Constitution was seriously defective without a specific bill of rights, including a provision reserving powers to the States, that in order to secure the votes for ratification, the Federalists eventually conceded that such provisions were necessary. See Schwartz, The Bill of Rights: A Documentary History, 505 and *passim* (1971). It was thus generally agreed that consideration of a bill of rights would be among the first business of the new Congress. See generally 1 Annals of Congress 432-437 (June 8, 1789) (remarks of James Madison). Accordingly, the 10 amendments that we know as the Bill of

Rights were proposed and adopted early in the first session of the First Congress. Schwartz, The Bill of Rights, *supra*, 983-1167.

This history, which the Court simply ignores, documents the integral role of the Tenth Amendment in our constitutional theory. It exposes as well, I believe, the fundamental character of the Court's error today. Far from being "unsound in principle," *ante*, at 18, judicial enforcement of the Tenth Amendment is essential to maintaining the federal system so carefully designed by the Framers and adopted in the Constitution....

The Framers believed that the separate sphere of sovereignty reserved to the States would ensure that the States would serve as an effective "counterpoise" to the power of the federal government. The States would serve this essential role because they would attract and retain the loyalty of their citizens....

Thus, the harm to the States that results from federal overreaching under the Commerce Clause is not simply a matter of dollars and cents. *National League of Cities,* 426 U.S., at 846-851. Nor is it a matter of the wisdom or folly of certain policy choices. Cf. *ante,* at 17. Rather, by usurping functions traditionally performed by the States, federal overreaching under the Commerce Clause undermines the constitutionally mandated balance of power between the States and the federal government, a balance designed to protect our fundamental liberties.

C

The emasculation of the powers of the States that can result from the Court's decision is predicated on the Commerce Clause as a power "delegated to the United States" by the Constitution....

To be sure, this Court has construed the Commerce Clause to accommodate unanticipated changes over the past two centuries. As these changes have occurred, the Court has had to decide whether the federal government has exceeded its authority by regulating activities beyond the capability of a single state to regulate or beyond legitimate federal interests that outweighed the authority and interests of the States. In so doing, however, the Court properly has been mindful of the essential role of the States in our federal system.

The opinion for the Court in *National League of Cities* was faithful to history in its understanding of federalism. The Court observed that "our federal system of government imposes definite limits upon the authority of Congress to regulate the activities of States as States by means of the commerce power." 426 U.S., at 842. The Tenth Amendment was invoked to prevent Congress from exercising its "power in a fashion that impairs the States' integrity or their ability to function effectively in a federal system." *Id.,* at 842-843, quoting *Fry v. United States,* 421 U.S. 542, 547 n. 7 (1975)....

IV

The question presented in this case is whether the extension of the FLSA to the wages and hours of employees of a city-owned transit system unconstitutionally impinges on fundamental state sovereignty. The Court's sweeping holding does far more than simply answer this question in the negative. In overruling *National League of Cities,* today's opinion apparently authorizes federal control, under the auspices of the Commerce Clause, over the terms and conditions of employment of all state and local employees. Thus, for purposes of federal regulation, the Court rejects the distinction between public and private employers that had been drawn carefully in *National League of Cities*. The Court's action reflects a serious misunderstanding, if not an outright rejection, of the history of our country and the intention of the Framers of the Constitution.

I return now to the balancing test approved in *National League of Cities* and accepted in *Hodel, Long Island R. Co.,* and *FERC v. Mississippi*. See n. 5, *supra*. The Court does not find in this case that the "federal interest is demonstrably greater." 426 U.S., at 856 (BLACKMUN, J., concurring). No such finding could have been made, for the state interest is compelling. The financial impact on States and localities of displacing their control over wages, hours, overtime regulations, pensions, and labor relations with their employees could have serious, as well as unanticipated, effects on state and local planning, budgeting, and the levying of taxes. As we said in *National League of Cities,* federal control of the terms and conditions of employment of State employees also inevitably "displaces state policies regarding the manner in which [States] will structure delivery of those governmental services that citizens require." *Id.,* at 847.

The Court emphasizes that municipal operation of an intracity mass transit system is relatively new in the life of our country. It nevertheless is a classic example of the type of service traditionally provided by local government. It is *local* by definition. It is indistinguishable in principle from the traditional services of providing and maintaining streets, public lighting, traffic control, water, and sewerage systems. Services of this kind are precisely those "with which citizens are more 'familiarly and minutely conversant.'" The Federalist, No. 46, p. 316. State and local officials of course must be intimately familiar with these services and sensitive to their quality as well as cost. Such officials also know that their constituents and the press respond to the adequacy, fair distribution, and cost of these services. It is this kind of state and local control and accountability that the Framers understood would insure the vitality and preservation of the federal system that the Constitution explicitly requires. See *National League of Cities, supra,* at 847-852.

V

Although the Court's opinion purports to recognize that the States retain some sovereign power, it does not identify even a single aspect of state authority that would remain when the Commerce Clause is invoked to justify federal regulation. In *Maryland v. Wirtz,* 392 U.S. 183 (1968), overruled by *National League of Cities* and today reaffirmed, the Court sustained an extension of the FLSA to certain hospitals, institutions, and schools. Although the Court's opinion in *Wirtz* was comparatively narrow, Justice Douglas, in dissent, wrote presciently that the Court's reading of the Commerce Clause would enable "the National Government [to] devour the essentials of state sovereignty, though that sovereignty is attested by the Tenth Amendment." *Id.,* at 205. Today's decision makes Justice Douglas's fear once again a realistic one.

As I view the Court's decision today as rejecting the basic precepts of our federal system and limiting the constitutional role of judicial review, I dissent.

JUSTICE REHNQUIST, dissenting.

I join both JUSTICE POWELL's and JUSTICE O'CONNOR's thoughtful dissents. JUSTICE POWELL's reference to the "balancing test" approved in *National League of Cities* is not identical with the language in that case, which recognized that Congress could not act under its commerce power to infringe on certain fundamental aspects of state sovereignty that are essential to "the States' separate and independent existence." Nor is either test, or JUSTICE O'CONNOR's suggested approach, precisely congruent with JUSTICE BLACKMUN's views in 1976, when he spoke of a balancing approach which did not outlaw federal power in areas "where the federal interest is demonstrably greater." But under any one of these approaches the judgment in this case should be affirmed, and I do not think it incumbent on those of us in dissent to spell out further the fine points of a principle that will, I am confident, in time again command the support of a majority of this Court.

JUSTICE O'CONNOR, with whom JUSTICE POWELL and JUSTICE REHNQUIST join, dissenting.

The Court today surveys the battle scene of federalism and sounds a retreat. Like JUSTICE POWELL, I would prefer to hold the field and, at the very least, render a little aid to the wounded. I join JUSTICE POWELL's opinion. I also write separately to note my fundamental disagreement with the majority's views of federalism and the duty of this Court.

The Court overrules *National League of Cities v. Usery,* 426 U.S. 833 (1976), on the grounds that it is not "faithful to the role of federalism in a democratic society." *Ante,* at 17. "The essence of our federal system," the Court concludes, "is that within the realm of authority left open to them under the Constitution, the States must be equally free to engage in any activity that their citizens choose for the common weal...." *Ibid. National League of Cities* is held to be inconsistent with this narrow view of federalism because it attempts to protect only those fundamental aspects of state sovereignty that are essential to the States' separate and independent existence, rather than protecting all state activities "equally."

In my view, federalism cannot be reduced to the weak "essence" distilled by the majority today. There is more to federalism than the nature of the constraints that can be imposed on the States in "the realm of authority left open to them by the Constitution." The central issue of federalism, of course, is whether any realm *is* left open to the States by the Constitution — whether any area remains in which a State may act free of federal interference. "The issue ... is whether the federal system has any *legal* substance, any core of constitutional right that courts will enforce." C. Black, Perspectives in Constitutional Law 30 (1963). The true "essence" of federalism is that the States *as States* have legitimate interests which the National Government is bound to respect even though its laws are supreme. *Younger v. Harris,* 401 U.S. 37, 44 (1971). If federalism so conceived and so carefully cultivated by the Framers of our Constitution is to remain meaningful, this Court cannot abdicate its constitutional responsibility to oversee the Federal Government's compliance with its duty to respect the legitimate interests of the States.

Due to the emergence of an integrated and industrialized national economy, this Court has been required to examine and review a breathtaking expansion of the powers of Congress. In doing so the Court correctly perceived that the Framers of our Constitution intended Congress to have sufficient power to address national problems....

It would be erroneous, however, to conclude that the Supreme Court was blind to the threat to federalism when it expanded the commerce power. The Court based the expansion on the authority of Congress, through the Necessary and Proper Clause, "to resort to all means for the exercise of a granted power which are appropriate and plainly adapted to the permitted end." *United States v. Darby, supra,* at 124. It is through this reasoning that an intrastate activity "affecting" interstate commerce can be reached through the commerce power. Thus, in *United States v. Wrightwood Dairy Co.,* 315 U.S. 110, 119 (1942), the Court stated:

> "The commerce power is not confined in its exercise to the regulation of commerce among the states. It extends to those activities intrastate which so affect interstate commerce, or the exertion of the power of Congress over it, as to make regulation of them appropriate means to the attainment of a legitimate end, the effective execution of the granted power to regulate interstate commerce. See *McCulloch v. Maryland,* 4 Wheat. 316, 421 ...."

United States v. Wrightwood Dairy Co. was heavily relied upon by *Wickard v. Filburn,* 317 U.S. 111, 124 (1942), and the reasoning of these cases underlies every recent decision concerning the reach of Congress to activities affecting interstate commerce. See, e.g., *Fry v. United States, supra,* at 547; *Perez v. United States, supra,* at 151-152; *Heart of Atlanta Motel, Inc. v. United States, supra,* at 258-259.

It is worth recalling the cited passage in *McCulloch v. Maryland,* 4 Wheat. 316, 421 (1819), that lies at the source of the recent expansion of the commerce power. "Let the end be legitimate, let it be within the scope of the constitution," Chief Justice Marshall said, "and all means which are appropriate, which are plainly adapted to that end, which are not prohibited, but consist with the letter *and spirit* of the constitution, are constitutional." (emphasis added). The *spirit* of the Tenth Amendment, of course, is that the States will retain their integrity in a system in which the laws of the United States are nevertheless supreme. *Fry v. United States, supra,* at 547, n. 7.

It is not enough that the "end be legitimate"; the means to that end chosen by Congress must not contravene the spirit of the Constitution. Thus many of this Court's decisions acknowledge that the means by which national power is exercised must take into account concerns for state autonomy....

This principle requires the Court to enforce affirmative limits on federal regulation of the States to complement the judicially crafted expansion of the interstate commerce power. *National League of Cities v. Usery* represented an attempt to define such limits. The Court today rejects *National League of Cities* and washes its hands of all efforts to protect the States. In the process, the Court opines that unwarranted federal encroachments on state authority are and will remain "'horrible possibilities that never happen in the real world.'" *Ante,* at 27, quoting *New York v. United States, supra,* at 583 (opinion of Frankfurter, J.). There is ample reason to believe to the contrary.

The last two decades have seen an unprecedented growth of federal regulatory activity, as the majority itself acknowledges. *Ante,* at 15, n. 10. In 1954, one could still speak of a "burden of persuasion on those favoring national intervention" in asserting that "National action has ... always been regarded as exceptional in our polity, an intrusion to be justified by some necessity, the special rather than the ordinary case." Wechsler, *The Political Safeguards of Federalism: The Role of the States in the Composition and Selection of the National Government,* 54 Colum. L. Rev. 543, 544-545 (1954). Today, as federal legislation and coercive grant programs have expanded to embrace innumerable activities that were once viewed as local, the burden of persuasion has surely shifted, and the extraordinary has become ordinary. See Engdahl, *Sense and Nonsense About State Immunity,* 2 Constitutional Commentary 93 (1985). For example, recently the Federal Government has, with this Court's blessing, undertaken to tell the States the age at which they can retire their law enforcement officers, and the regulatory standards, procedures, and even the agenda which their utilities commissions must consider and follow. See *EEOC v. Wyoming,* 460 U.S. 226 (1983); *FERC v. Mississippi,* 456 U.S. 742 (1982). The political process has not protected against these encroachments on state activities, even though they directly impinge on a State's ability to make and enforce its laws. With the abandonment of *National League of Cities,* all that stands between the remaining essentials of state sovereignty and Congress is the latter's underdeveloped capacity for self-restraint.

The problems of federalism in an integrated national economy are capable of more responsible resolution than holding that the States as States retain no status apart from that which Congress chooses to let them retain. The proper resolution, I suggest, lies in weighing state autonomy as a factor in the balance when interpreting the means by which Congress can exercise its authority on the States as States. It is insufficient, in assessing the validity of congressional regulation of a State pursuant to the commerce power, to ask only whether the same regulation would be valid if enforced against a private party. That reasoning, embodied in the majority opinion, is inconsistent with the spirit of our Constitution. It remains relevant that a *State* is being regulated, as *National League of Cities* and every recent case have recognized. See *EEOC v. Wyoming, supra; Transportation Union v. Long Island R. Co.,* 455 U.S. 678, 684 (1982); *Hodel v. Virginia Surface Mining & Recl. Assn.,* 452 U.S. 264, 287-288 (1981); *National League of Cities,* 426 U.S., at 841-846. As far as the Constitution is concerned, a State should not be equated with any private litigant. Cf. *Nevada v. Hall,* 440 U.S. 410, 428 (1979) (BLACKMUN, J., dissenting) (criticising the ability of a state court to treat a sister State no differently than a private litigant). Instead, the autonomy of a State is an essential component of federalism. If state autonomy is ignored in assessing the means by which Congress regulates matters affecting commerce, then federalism becomes irrelevant simply because the set of activities remaining beyond the reach of such a commerce power "may well be negligible." *Ante,* at 16.

It has been difficult for this Court to craft bright lines defining the scope of the state autonomy protected by *National League of Cities.* Such difficulty is to be expected whenever constitutional concerns as important as federalism and the effectiveness of the commerce power come in to conflict. Regardless of the difficulty, it is and will remain the duty of this Court to reconcile these concerns in the final instance. That the Court shuns the task today by appealing to the "essence of federalism" can provide scant comfort to those who believe our federal system requires something more than a unitary, centralized government. I would not shirk the duty acknowledged by *National League of Cities* and its progeny, and I share JUSTICE REHNQUIST's belief that this Court will in time again assume its constitutional responsibility.

I respectfully dissent.

NOTES

1. In *Municipal Gov't, City of Newark & State, County & Mun. Workers of Am., Local 277, CIO,* Case Nos. 47 and 726 (December 23, 1942), reprinted in C. Rhyne, Labor Unions and Municipal Employe Law 226 (1946), the National War Labor Board unanimously held that it did not have jurisdiction over labor disputes between state governments, including political subdivisions thereof, and their public employees. In so ruling, the Board, in an opinion written by Wayne Morse, stated:

It has never been suggested that the Federal Government has the power to regulate with respect to the wages, working hours, or conditions of employment of those who are engaged in performing services for the states or their political subdivisions. Any action by the National War Labor Board in attempting to regulate such matter by directive order would be beyond its powers and jurisdiction. The employees involved in the instant cases are performing services for political subdivisions of state governments. Any directive order of the National War Labor Board which purported to regulate the wages, the working hours, or the conditions of employment of state or municipal employees would constitute a clear invasion of the sovereign rights of the political subdivisions of local state government.

Among the labor members who concurred in the foregoing opinion was George Meany, the long-time President of the AFL-CIO. George W. Taylor, the principal author of the New York public sector collective bargaining law, was a public member who likewise concurred in the opinion.

2. In response to concerns raised by public employers with respect to application of the Fair Labor Standards Act (FLSA) to public employers following the Supreme Court's decision in *Garcia,* Congress in November 1985 passed the Fair Labor Standards Amendments Act of 1985. Pub. L. 99-150, 99 Stat. 787 (1985). This Act delayed the effective date of enforcement of the FLSA until April 15, 1986. In addition, under the Act public employees may be offered compensatory time in lieu of cash overtime under the following specific circumstances:

(1) There must be an agreement or an existing practice between the employees or their union and the employer prior to the performance of the overtime work.

(2) Compensatory time must be allowed at the overtime premium; that is, three hours of compensatory time must be allowed for two hours of overtime.

(3) There are limits on the amount of compensatory time that can be accumulated or banked. Public safety, emergency response, and seasonal em-

ployees may bank up to 480 hours of compensatory time before the employer is forced to pay the premium cash rate. All other employers are limited to the accrual of 240 hours of compensatory time.

So as not to discourage volunteer activities, the 1985 amendments to the FLSA exempt from coverage individuals who volunteer their services to state and local governments and receive no compensation other than expenses, reasonable benefits, nominal fees, or some combination thereof. However, an individual will not be considered a volunteer if he or she is otherwise employed by the same public agency to perform the same type of services as those for which he or she proposes to volunteer.

In *Ackinclose v. Palm Beach Cty.,* 845 F.2d 931 (11th Cir. 1988), the court observed that the one-year grace period "was to provide lead-time to state and local governments so that they might complete the reordering of their budgetary priorities made necessary by *Garcia* while maintaining fiscal stability." The court held, however, that Section 2(c)(1) of the 1985 amendments "was not intended to limit the ability of state and local government employees working outside areas of traditional governmental function to bring suit to enforce the minimum wage/overtime compensation protections afforded to them by the FLSA." Accordingly, the court concluded "that Section 2(c)(1) of the Fair Labor Standards Amendments of 1985 does not bar appellants from pursuing this FLSA enforcement action, provided they can establish that the work performed during the period at issue did not fall within an area of traditional governmental function."

3. The Age Discrimination in Employment Act (ADEA), which is part of the Fair Labor Standards Act, was amended in 1986 to permit public employers to set mandatory retirement ages for police and firefighters. 29 U.S.C. § 623(i). In *Boylan v. State,* 116 N.J. 236, 561 A.2d 552 (1989), *cert. denied,* 110 S. Ct. 1539 (1990), the New Jersey Supreme Court ruled that a New Jersey law which required firefighters and police officers in supervisory or administrative positions to retire at age 65 did not violate the ADEA, reasoning that Congress intended the 1986 amendment "to apply to all law-enforcement officers and firefighters, whether or not they are 'line' employees or supervisors."

4. In *Gregory v. Ashcroft,* 898 F.2d 598 (8th Cir.), *petition for cert. granted,* 111 S. Ct. 507 (1990), the Eighth Circuit Court of Appeals held that a Missouri constitutional provision requiring appointed judges to retire at age 70 did not violate either the ADEA or the fourteenth amendment's equal protection clause. The court agreed with the First Circuit's decision in *EEOC v. Massachusetts,* 858 F.2d 52 (1st Cir. 1988), that judges are involved in policy-making and are therefore exempt from coverage under the ADEA. Contra *EEOC v. Vermont,* 904 F.2d 794 (2d Cir. 1990).

5. In *Jackson Transit Auth. v. Local Div. 1285, Amalgamated Transit Union,* 457 U.S. 15, 102 S. Ct. 2202, 72 L. Ed. 2d 639 (1982), the Supreme Court held that section 13(c) does not provide a union with a federal cause of action for alleged breaches of section 13(c) of the Urban Mass Transportation Act and related collective bargaining agreements. After noting that such agreements, "like ordinary contracts, [are] enforceable by private suit upon a breach," the Court noted that the issue was "not whether Congress intended the union to be able to bring contract actions for breaches of the two contracts, but whether Congress intended such contract actions to set forth federal, rather than state, claims." After reviewing in detail the legislative history of section 13(c), the Court concluded:

> Congress made it clear that it did not intend to create a body of federal laws applicable to labor relations between local government entities and transit workers. Section 13(c) would not supersede state law, it would leave intact the exclusion of local government employers from the National Labor Relations Act, and state courts would retain jurisdiction to determine the application of state policy to local government transit labor relations. Congress intended that § 13(c) would be an important tool to protect the collective bargaining rights of transit workers, by insuring that state law preserved their right before federal aid could be used to convert private companies into public entities ... but Congress designed § 13(c) as a means to accommodate state law to collective bargaining, not as a means to substitute a federal law of collective bargaining for state labor law.

2. FEDERAL REGULATION OF STATE AND LOCAL GOVERNMENT COLLECTIVE BARGAINING

Starting with the 91st Congress in 1970, bills have been submitted in every session which would make state and local government labor relations subject to federal regulation. Two distinct approaches have been advanced by the principal advocates of federal legislation. First, organizations such as AFSCME have advocated the enactment of comprehensive legislation which would apply to the entire state and local public sector under separate legislation administered by a five-member National Public Employment Relations Commission. Such legislation was introduced as H.R. 7684 in the 92d Congress and as H.R. 8677 and S. 3295 in the 93d Congress. As introduced in the 93d Congress, this legislation would:

1. Authorize supervisory bargaining units.

2. Describe the scope of bargaining broadly to cover "terms and conditions of employment and other matters of mutual concern relating thereto."

3. Provide for compulsory arbitration or strikes as the mechanism for resolving collective bargaining impasses, the choice to be made by the exclusive bargaining representative.

4. Guarantee public employees the right to strike and specifically supersede any inconsistent state laws that prohibit public employee strikes.

5. Override and supersede inconsistent state and local enactments in that the Act would "take precedence over all ordinances, rules and regulations, or other enactments of any State, territory, or other possession of the United States, or any political subdivision thereof."

6. Provide that the Act applies to all state and local jurisdictions unless the five-member National Public Employment Relations Commission determines that a state or local enactment "is substantially equivalent to the system established herein."

On the other hand, H.R. 12532 introduced in the 92d Congress and H.R. 8677 and S. 3294 introduced in the 93d Congress would have brought the entire state and local public sector under the National Labor Relations Act (NLRA). Thus, these latter bills would have removed the exclusion of "any state or political subdivision thereof" from the definition of employers covered by the NLRA.

Hearings on the proposed federal public sector collective bargaining legislation were held in the House of Representatives during the 92d Congress and in the Senate during the 93d Congress. See Hearings on H.R. 12532, H.R. 7684 & H.R. 9324 before the Special Subcomm. on Labor of the House Comm. on Education and Labor, 92d Cong., 2d Sess. (1972); Hearings on S. 3295 & S. 3294 before the Subcomm. on Labor of the Senate Comm. on Labor and Public Welfare, 93d Cong., 2d Sess. (1974). The varying views of some of the principal proponents and opponents of federal legislation governing state and local collective bargaining are set forth below. While the movement towards the enactment of federal legislation was slowed down by the Supreme Court's decision in *National League of Cities,* it is an issue which may well be the subject of renewed interest in light of *Garcia v. San Antonio Metropolitan Transit Authority.*

STATEMENT OF JERRY WURF, INTERNATIONAL PRESIDENT, AMERICAN FEDERATION OF STATE, COUNTY, AND MUNICIPAL EMPLOYEES, AFL-CIO

Hearings on H.R. 12532, H.R. 7684, & H.R. 9324
Before the Special Subcomm. on Labor of the House Comm. on Education
and Labor, 92d Cong., 2d Sess., 25, 28, 31-32 (1972)

... We appear before you this morning in behalf of the over 525,000 public employees who are members of our Union to urge the enactment of Federal legislation dealing with labor relations in state and local government. We are convinced that only through national legislation can public employees be guaranteed full rights to organize and bargain collectively and thereby end unnecessary labor strife in the public sector.

Our views also reflect the concerns and interests of the Coalition of Public Employee Organizations, representing more than two million public employees throughout the nation. This Coalition, formed last March, includes our union, the National Education Association and the International Association of Fire Fighters, AFL-CIO. The Coalition was established to bring the collective power of public employees to bear on matters of mutual concern.

Over the past several months, our organizations have been working toward a common position on Federal legislation to establish a uniform national labor relations policy in the public sector. We have reached agreement on the substantive provisions of such a bill and the specific legislative recommendations made in behalf of the American Federation of State, County, and Municipal Employees this morning are shared by the other oganizations associated with this Coalition....

In the absence of a national uniform labor-management relations policy, labor law in the public sector has developed on a piecemeal, state-by-state, city-by-city basis. State laws are a shameful hodgepodge designed largely to frustrate unionization and collective bargaining.

Inconsistency and confusion best describe the legal setting of labor relations for state and local government employees. Each of the 50 states and the 80,000 units of local government does its own thing. There is no set pattern. The labor programs are regulated by state laws, city ordinances, court decisions, attorneys general opinions, county charters, civil service rules, executive orders, school board policies, and other regulations....

There is clear need for change in public sector labor relations. The choice, in our view, is between continued chaos or Federal legislation.

New state laws are proliferating. Each is different. Most merely add to the confusion and chaos that already exists. Hawaii and Pennsylvania are outstanding exceptions. Although both have provisions with which we disagree, or lack provisions we believe necessary.

The frustrations deriving from the astonishing jungle of state laws, have led our Union to the call for a single, comprehensive Federal law addressing itself to labor relations in the public sector.

There have been enough confrontations. There have been enough studies and experiments. It is time for responsible change.

The problem is national in scope and it requires a national solution.

We need uniformity of law in the public sector, so that a body of law and tradition and practice can be developed. This will only occur under Federal legislation, much like that which governs labor relations in business and industry. We are convinced that the majority of the states are either unwilling or unable to move toward the establishment of rational and reasonable mechanisms.

The needs of public employees do not differ across state lines. They are one and the same throughout the nation. There should be no more difference between the job rights of a public employee in Wisconsin and Virginia than there is between an aerospace worker in California and New York. The labor relations situation of public employees today is different in every city, county, and state — not just between states, but between cities and counties within the same state. There is no more reason to justify fragmentation of labor relations between states and their cities and counties than there is to fragment any other system of dealing with problems on a national level.

We believe it is outrageous to conduct labor relations without a set of uniform rules. We are advocating uniformity of law of this matter for the same reason we advocate government by law rather than by force.

You can say what you want about labor relations in business and industry, but a free society could not get along without the mechanisms that exist there. The mechanisms are firmly established and clearly understood. They have a history of legal precedents applicable to almost every work place in America. Contrast that with the public sector where you can go from one city to the next and find a different mechanism and a different set of precedents and procedures.

Finally, we know what state legislatures have to offer us in the way of labor legislation. We know what the needs are. The two just don't fit and probably never will. We are not turning our backs on the new laws in Hawaii and Pennsylvania. They are good laws, although we have serious points of difference with them. If we continue to rely on state legislation, we will continue to face a crazy quilt-work pattern of law. A national approach is the only answer to meeting them uniformly and fairly....

STATEMENT OF ALBERT SHANKER, PRESIDENT, AMERICAN
FEDERATION OF TEACHERS, AFL-CIO

Hearings on S. 3295 & S. 3294 Before the Subcomm. on Labor of the Senate
Comm. on Labor and Public Welfare, 93d Cong., 2d Sess., 281-84 (1974)

This Committee is considering two bills — S. 3294 and S. 3295. These bills provide for Federal regulation of labor relations in the public sector at the state and local level. The AFT firmly believes that the time for such regulation has come.

There has been much activity in recent years toward giving state and local public employees basic recognition rights, and thereby eliminating the need for strikes conducted for the purpose of gaining recognition. In most areas where bargaining rights for public employees exist, they are very limited in comparison to those which exist for private sector workers, both with respect to the bargaining process and with respect to who is covered by the various state public employee bargaining laws.

At present, 13 states still have no provision for recognition of public employees for the purpose of collective bargaining or even "meeting and conferring." As the National Labor Relations Act currently excludes from coverage employees of "... any State or political subdivision thereof," there is no framework whatever for the exercise of what the AFT believes is a basic right in a democracy — the right of any worker, in the private or public sector, to have a say in determining the conditions under which he or she must work.

In the 37 remaining states, either by statute or by Executive Order, there is some mechanism by which public employees can be heard but the picture can only be described as imperfect at best and repressive at worst.

1. The coverage of the various state statutes and Executives Orders wanders all over the map. Some states have comprehensive public employee labor relations laws applying to all groups of public employees while others have separate statutes, often granting different degrees of recognition, representation and negotiation rights for different groups of public employees — many even differentiating by location.

2. In some states, groups of public employees can choose through majority vote an organizational spokesman to speak for them but in others, all organizations purporting to represent public employees in any particular unit must be represented at the discussion table.

3. In some states, public employees are only given the right to "meet and confer" with their public employers but there is no requirement on the employer to negotiate in good faith and participate in the kind of give and take which solves problems. In other states, there is a duty on both parties to engage in good faith negotiations with a host of impasse resolution services provided but if these fail, the public employer can still do whatever it chooses. Only in 7 states is there currently even a qualified right to strike for public employees.

4. In some states (California, Texas, Arizona, South Dakota and most of the Southern States), binding arbitration of grievances of public employees has been held to be illegal while in others the arbitration of grievances has increased stability and lessened strife in public employment.

The AFT believes there is a strong Federal interest in rationalizing this hodgepodge of state public employee labor relations legislation. State and local government is one of the fastest growing sectors in the American economy....

The underlying rationale for the original Wagner Act and the present NLRA is that breakdowns in labor-management relations impede commerce and are contrary to the general welfare of the nation. When these laws were enacted, disruptions of government services due to labor disputes in the public sector were minimal. Over the last 20 years, however, public employees have demanded the same collective bargaining rights as those in the private sector. Clearly, the same rationale applies now in the public sector as first applied 39 years ago in the private sector and for this reason, a Federal statute governing state and local public employee labor relations is a necessity.

Before commenting on the two proposals being considered by the Committee, I want to state in no uncertain terms that the AFT considers the right to strike to be an absolutely basic element in any system of labor relations which has as its aim the granting of employees that fundamental right of having a say in determining the conditions under which they must work through meaningful collective bargaining. When the right to withhold labor is limited then the bargaining loses its meaning because the power of employees is dissipated. With the strike tool, the employer is forced to consider alternatives — does the public value the service enough to indicate meeting the demands; how much of a tax increase is the public willing to assume; is the public willing to do without the service for a time? Without the strike, there is no meaningful pressure on the employer to reach agreement with its employees. At present, none of the state public employee labor relations statutes contains an unlimited right to strike, and as stated, there are only 7 states which grant public employees even a limited right to strike. But, strikes do take place, often in spite of heavy fines and jail sentences.

Any blanket qualifying provision on the right to strike for public employees appearing in any legislative proposal for the Federal regulation of state and local public employee labor relations will be vigorously opposed by the AFT just as we fight that battle on the state and local levels. Furthermore, if a ban against public employee strikes in general is the price of Federal legislation in this area, it is a price that the AFT would not be willing to pay, no matter how otherwise favorable that legislation might be.

Some opponents of public employee strikes suggest compulsory arbitration as a substitute for the right to strike. Let me point out that we have no objection to employers and employee representatives agreeing in advance to submit differences to binding arbitration. But this is arbitration jointly and voluntarily agreed to, not compulsory arbitration which destroys the bargaining process by removing all incentive for compromise. Furthermore, I want to make clear that this discussion is in reference to what is known as interest negotiation — negotiation of a contract. A negotiated grievance procedure with a top step of compulsory binding arbitration as part of a contractual agreement has long been recognized as a legitimate means of resolving disputes during the life of a collective bargaining agreement. But of course, that initial agreement should always be arrived at by a voluntary process or collective bargaining has no meaning.

The two bills before the Committee take two distinctly different approaches to Federal regulation of public sector labor relations at the state and local level. S. 3294, in extending the NLRA to state and local government workers, will bring about a situation in which private and public sector workers and their employers will be subject to the same labor relations laws. S. 3295 establishes a separate legal structure and enforcement apparatus for public employees.

The AFT strongly supports the former approach — S. 3294 — because it reflects a fundamental philosophy which we have been preaching for a long time. That philosophy is that the interests, concerns and problems that public employees have with respect to their jobs are in no basic way different than the interests, concerns and problems of private sector workers. This viewpoint is strengthened by what we believe to be the absolutely absurd situation of the professor of history at New York University having the right to strike, the professor of history at the City University of New York not having the right to strike and the professor of history at the University of Illinois not even allowed to engage in any form of collective negotiation through a recognized representative. This is true not only of professors but of employees of elementary and secondary schools, transit systems, utilities, nursing homes and hospitals to name a few. The fact is that under the present structure of labor relations in the United States, the extent of an employee's right to have a say in the conditions under which he or she must work depends not at all on what he or she does but whom the employer happens to be — public or private sector.

Certainly the co-existence of distinct legislative and administrative bodies in the public sector is a unique aspect of public employment but our experience in collective bargaining convinces us that any special accommodations that are necessary can easily be accomplished within the labor relations framework of the NLRA if public employees are covered. The AFT does not believe there is any justification for the exclusively public employment body of law and structure envisioned in S. 3295.

At its Tenth Constitutional Convention, in October 1973, the AFL-CIO was presented with a clear choice and strongly endorsed the approach embodied in S. 3294 — extending NLRA coverage to state and local public employees. Delegates representing the American Federation of State, County and Municipal Employees did introduce a resolution entitled "Collective Bargaining for Public Employees" which stated in part:

Resolved, This convention supports a federal collective bargaining law which gives negotiating equity to public employees, while at the same time taking into account the special problems of collective bargaining in state and local government: the problems of impasse resolution and strikes, the budgetary processes, the relationships between the administrative and the legislative arms of the government.

The AFL-CIO Convention Resolutions Committee rejected the AFSCME resolution and approved a substitute. The substitute resolution which was unanimously adopted by the full convention reads in part:

"Whereas, in many areas of federal and state legislation public employees are still excluded from the full benefits of such legislation, or are frequently discriminated against in separate public employee legislation; therefore be it

"*Resolved,* That the time has come to recognize that public employees are workers who should enjoy the rights and benefits equal to those guaranteed under law to workers in the private sector, and therefore be it further

"*Resolved,* That this convention supports the extension of these rights and benefits — such as the right to collective bargaining, and the right to economic and social insurance legislation — to all public employees through coverage under existing federal, state and local laws." ...

STATEMENT OF JOHN HANSON, PRESIDENT, NATIONAL PUBLIC EMPLOYER LABOR RELATIONS ASSOCIATION

Hearings on S. 3295 & S. 3294 Before the Subcomm. on Labor of the Senate
Comm. on Labor and Public Welfare, 93d Cong., 2d Sess., 360-62 (1974)

The National Public Employer Labor Relations Association is a relatively young professional association, with more than two hundred members who represent state, county and municipal governments in their labor relations. Its membership includes chief negotiators for many of the major cities in the country.

We fully support collective bargaining for the public sector. We believe that the several states should be encouraged to continue to meet their responsibilities in this area by enacting effective legislation that will meet local priorities and establish a firm framework for conducting labor relations at the state and local levels.

We are opposed to the enactment of federal legislation covering public sector collective bargaining at the state and local levels. Because of the vast differences between the several states and their political subdivisions with respect to the manner in which wages, hours and working conditions are established, collective bargaining legislation is not a matter that is susceptible to uniform federal regulation. NPELRA supports the following conclusion of Professors Harry Wellington and Ralph Winter, in a study prepared for the Brookings Institution:

"When an issue is a matter of low federal priority, considerations of federalism dictate that governmental action be left to state or local initiative. One can claim more, however, than that municipal public employee bargaining should have a low priority on any agenda for Congressional action. One can claim that intervention at the national level would be positively harmful. Federal legislation or regulation necessarily tends to a uniform rule. In the case of public employee unionism, uniformity is most undesirable and diversity in rules and structures virtually a necessity."[20]

In examining this question, any objective observer must recognize that there are substantial differences between public sector and private sector collective bargaining. Many of these differences have been identified by either proponents or opponents of the proposed legislation before this Committee. As pointed out by Arvid Anderson, Chairman, Office of Collective Bargaining, New York City, in his testimony of October 1, 1974, Congress, itself, in enacting labor relations legislation for the Postal Service, made a major change from private law by the substitution of interest arbitration for the right to strike.

---

[20]H. Wellington & R. Winter, The Unions and The Cities 52-53 (1971).

We should like to emphasize two other significant differences which we believe your Committee should keep in mind.

First of all, in the public sector a union has four different methods of influencing, or representing its interest with the public employer as follows:

1. Legislation
2. Pressure on elected officials
3. Campaigning for election of officials who will support the union position, and
4. Collective bargaining

In the private sector there are only two ways of influencing the bargaining process:

1. Legislation
2. Collective bargaining

The result constitutes a significant difference in the union bargaining power between the public and private sector. For example, the public sector bargaining representative is often frustrated by attempts of union representatives, in the midst of bargaining, to deal directly with his elected bosses in an effort to secure benefits not obtained in the process of negotiations. At the same time, this technique places heavy pressure on the elected official.

Secondly, the environment in which local government employees and employers function is different from that in which private sector labor relations is conducted. It is localized geographically. The attitude of the citizens toward public employees varies and thus the framework adopted will also vary.

Then the public official is elected by all the people and is accountable to the general public. The ultimate policy making positions are held by election, not by private appointment. State officials are limited and function under constitutional authority and the local laws and ordinances which vary from state to state.

The impact of Federal legislation is difficult to ascertain. Involved in the process are the state constitution, home rule charters, state civil service laws, tenure laws and the like. Necessarily, attention must be given to federal-state relationships and the impact of labor relations legislation on the separation of powers doctrine within the states (e.g., when a governor agrees to a contract, what is the obligation of the state legislature?). These kinds of issues do not exist in the private sector and their consideration and resolution must precede Federal legislation, if it is to contribute to effective government at all levels.

In light of these differences, we are convinced that Federal legislation covering public sector collective bargaining is inappropriate, improper and unnecessary.

Federal legislation is inappropriate because no ideal solution has been achieved. The States are acting to meet the problems as they are seen locally and intimately. The approaches vary but this is not unhealthy. As the Advisory Committee on Intergovernment Relations noted "... experimentation and flexibility are needed, not a standardized, Federal preemptive approach."[21]

The enactment of federal legislation would stifle the experimentation and search for alternative selections that are now going on. The uniformity that

---

[21] Advisory Commission on Intergovernmental Relations, Labor-Management Policies for State and Local Government, 113 (1969).

would be an inevitable product of federal legislation would achieve not a solution to the many complex problems faced by state and local governments, but an untoward and premature harnessing of the vital energies of both management and labor that might otherwise make substantial contributions to a new and better system of labor relations.

In reaching this position, we are not, as has been suggested by some advocates of federal legislation, suggesting that any of the states should be encouraged to withhold the basic rights that are necessary to protect employees' freedom of choice and the development of stable labor relations. We are suggesting that these goals can be better achieved by encouraging the states to meet their own local problems.

Federal legislation is improper, because it would contradict the current posture of Congress, which has been to encourage state and local governments to have and exercise greater authority over their own affairs. The development of the latent principle of federalism has been welcomed by the people of all the states, is reflected in the revenue-sharing programs developed by Congress and is supported by the statements of many Senators and Representatives who recommend the desirability of maintaining as much local autonomy as possible.

ANDERSON,* PROSPECTS FOR NATIONAL PUBLIC SECTOR BARGAINING LAWS, Address prepared for NLRB Tenth Region Labor Management Seminar, Atlanta, Georgia (June 2, 1977)

As for my personal view regarding a federal bargaining law, I remain committed to the position of the Association of Labor Mediation Agencies which favors a non-preemptive federal minimum standards law. Such standards would, as a minimum, contain the following:

—Public employees should be granted the right to organize, to join employee organizations, and to bargain with respect to their terms and conditions of employment.

—Standards should be provided for resolution of representation disputes, unit determinations and elections to determine bargaining agents.

—Broadly defined unfair labor practices should be included and should be applicable to both employers and employee organizations.

—At the state or local level a neutral and politically independent administrative agency shall be required to implement the foregoing standards.

—A framework for the resolution for impasses should be mandated, but wide latitude for experimentation should be permitted.

For example, impasse procedures could give the states the right to decide on whether to permit or prohibit strikes, authorize or require binding arbitration of new contracts or merely provide for non-binding fact finding with recommendations.

Under these proposals, if a state or local government chooses to administer and implement its own public employee labor relations statute providing for a system of collective bargaining under the federal minimum standards, it would be permitted to do so without a presumption of federal preemption. Any con-

---

*Arvid Anderson was the Chairman of the New York City Office of Collective Bargaining from 1967 to 1987.

troversy as to whether a specific provision in a state or local statute was not consistent with the minimum federal standards would be resolved in the federal courts and such proceedings could only be initiated by a federal agency. Thus, the burden of proof of non-compliance with federal minimum standards would fall on the federal agency rather than on the states.

I stress that federal law should not be preemptive because the experience of the administration of the Labor Management Relations Act by the National Labor Relations Board throughout its entire history demonstrates conclusively that a federal administrative agency will, if left to its own discretion, refuse to cede to any competent state authority administration over any phase of its statute. The administrators of the National Labor Relations Board have consistently held the position that those sections of the national act which provide the basis to cede certain administrative authority to states if such state laws or administration are not inconsistent with federal law, that the state statute must be identical with federal law, and, thus, in effect, have refused to cede any authority to the states.

I don't think the problem is the language of the statute; it is the lack of willingness of the federal authorities to cede any jurisdiction to state agencies. Thus, states with competent professional administrative agencies in the private sector, such as Wisconsin, New York, Connecticut and Michigan, although they repeatedly tried to obtain the consent of the federal government to assume some responsibility over the administration of private sector labor relations, were unable to complete such agreements.

In June 1975, Betty Southard Murphy, then Chairman of the NLRB, testifying before the House Labor Subcommittee on Labor-Management Relations with regard to proposals to include state and local public employees under the National Labor Relations Act, stated that:

> Our experience has convinced us that the Congressional policy of a national labor law favorably contributes to industrial peace by providing a uniform framework within which management and labor may function. Separate State labor policies would inevitably create jurisdictional problems between and among the States and subject multi-State employers and national labor organizations to a wide variety of inconsistent labor policies and regulations.

She further stated that the question of ceding NLRB jurisdiction "involves a basic policy decision as to whether a uniform national policy should remain paramount or whether there should be some sacrifice in uniformity to permit a degree of cession to state agencies."

A close look at the different union positions on a federal bargaining law makes clear that the "uniformity" they seem to favor does not include a federal preemption of existing tenure, civil service or pension rights which are presently codified in state and local statutes and state constitutions. The unions apparently favor federal preemption of bargaining structures but not of existing employee benefits.

I question the need for total uniformity in a federal bargaining law for state and local government employees. Certainly, the basic right to organize and bargain collectively, and the protection of those rights, should be uniform, but it does not follow that all states or all categories of employees should have the same bargaining structure or method of impasse resolution. Why should not the states decide whether the strike route or binding arbitration, or some combination thereof, is to be an appropriate means of impasse resolution? In other words, everyone need not wear a size 9 shoe.

I also believe that state agencies and local agencies are generally competent and, because of their thorough knowledge of the local scene, are as well or better equipped than a federal agency to administer a public sector labor relations statute. I firmly believe that the right of the states to do so should be protected and that, in the absence of federal judicial restraint, state and local procedures should continue. Total uniformity is not necessary provided there is substantial equivalence in the implementation of a state law to the federal statute. A limitation on federal preemption would permit the freedom of state experimentation which now exists to continue and would encourage additional states to enact bargaining procedures for their state and local employees.

A limitation similar to that which I propose here has worked effectively under the New York State Taylor Law with respect to its relationship to the New York City Collective Bargaining Law. The New York City Law is not identical to the Taylor Law; but it is our belief that its purposes and administration are substantially equivalent to the Taylor Law. Such procedures have worked for the past ten years even though both laws have been amended during that period....

AARON, THE FUTURE OF COLLECTIVE BARGAINING IN THE PUBLIC SECTOR, in Public-Sector Bargaining 324-26 (B. Aaron, J. Grodin & J. Stern eds. 1988)*

Whatever barriers *National League of Cities* may have erected against a federal preemptive law uniformly regulating labor relations between the states and their employees have thus been removed [by *Garcia*], but pursuit of that objective seems both unlikely and undesirable. There are at least four reasons for that conclusion.

First, at the level of practical politics, organized labor as a whole — its membership drastically reduced and declining — is in no position to lobby effectively for such a revolutionary change in the law. Although government employment bargaining organizations continue to grow, they still lack the power to accomplish such a formidable coup. In addition, any such change would prompt a firestorm of protest from the states.

Second, administrative agencies tend to reflect the ideology of the incumbent administration. The NLRB has thus become the target of official union outrage over the labor policies of the Reagan administration, and it is doubtful that there is any support in labor's ranks, at least at the present time, either for expanding the Board's jurisdiction over state and local government employees or for creating a similar federal agency to deal with their labor relations problems.

Third, most states now have collective bargaining laws for government employees, and many administer them (from the unions' point of view) at least as favorably, and probably more favorably, than the NLRB administers the NLRA.

---

*Reprinted by permission of the Industrial Relations Research Association.

Finally, allowing the states to develop their own policies for dealing with labor relations with their employees has worked well. The number of state laws on this subject has steadily increased during the last two decades. Three of the four major states that had not passed government employee collective bargaining laws in 1974 — California, Illinois, and Ohio — have now done so; only Texas remains outside the fold. Although there has been a certain amount of statutory inbreeding, the individual laws are for the most part tailored to meet the issues that are important to each state's citizens. Some statutory provisions, especially those dealing with the resolution of impasses, reveal considerable imagination. To be sure, there are a few states that have no statutes dealing with collective bargaining for any group of government employees, but that hardly warrants imposing a Procrustean federal model, even in the extremely unlikely event that it is politically possible to do so.

The experience to date with statutory and judicial regulation of collective bargaining by government employees, especially in the area of unfair labor practices and strikes, suggests that further reference to the NLRA or the LMRA as models is unnecessary and undesirable. From now on, the federal government and the states will develop and modify collective bargaining laws applicable to their own employees on the basis of conditions and public attitudes within their respective spheres. Little, if anything, in the decisions of the current NLRB seems likely to have much relevance to collective bargaining in the public sector. To the extent that NLRB decisions may be relevant, they are not precedents that should be followed. It is not so much that strikes in government employment give rise to problems radically different from those associated with strikes in the private sector, but labor-management relations in government employment in the various states have their own history, structure, and practices that should be taken into account by those who fashion the laws governing those relations. It may well be that certain labor relations practices in the private sector are relevant to collective bargaining in government employment, and that they will in time be adopted in the public sector. It is also possible that certain collective bargaining laws and practices in government employment will commend themselves to the private sector. Indeed, this latter possibility may be the more likely of the two. If such changes come to pass, however, they will result primarily from voluntary decisions by the collective bargaining parties themselves, rather than from statutory mandates or judicial edicts. That is, at least, an outcome devoutly to be wished.

NOTE

The legal and practical ramifications of the possible enactment of federal legislation governing state and local government collective bargaining have been examined in numerous articles and monographs, including Federal Legislation for Public Sector Collective Bargaining (T. Colosi & S. Rynecki eds. 1975); Baird, *National Legislation for Public Employees: "End Run" on the Wagner Act,* 61 Ill. B.J. 410 (1973).

D. THE IMPACT OF PUBLIC SECTOR UNIONS

REHMUS, LABOR RELATIONS IN THE PUBLIC SECTOR, Paper prepared for the 3d World Congress, International Industrial Relations Association, London, England (Sept. 3-7, 1973)*

The coming of collective bargaining to the public sector is the most significant development in the industrial relations field in the United States in the last thirty years. Its growth has been both rapid and extensive and appears to be continuing. Even now, however, bargaining does not occur in more than half of all governmental jurisdictions in the United States. In many areas where bargaining has begun it is less than ten years old. Hence one must be cautious in making generalizations about the future of public employee labor relations. A few may be put forward tentatively, however.

The coming of unionism to the public sector has provided enough new recruits to the labor movement to reverse the decline in trade union membership which took place during the latter 1950's and early 1960's. Moreover, it is at least possible that as government employees join unions, or convert their traditional professional associations to union-like behavior, that this will change the general blue-collar image of the labor movement in the United States. Private sector trade unionism has never exceeded 30 percent of the non-agricultural workforce and has never had any strong appeal to white collar workers. Organizing successes among white collar and professional employees in the public sector may make unionism acceptable and normal to private sector white collar workers who in the near future, if not already, will represent a majority of employment in private industry. In summary, public employee unionism has halted the decline in trade union size in the United States and may in fact contribute to substantial new growth in the private sector in the next decade or two.

Public employee unionism appears to have contributed to the centralization of governmental decision-making power in the United States, though it is by no means the sole cause of such developments. At the municipal level it is clear that the exigencies of collective bargaining have forced decision-making power toward the chief executive at the expense of municipal legislatures and civil service boards. In the educational field organized teacher pressures along with a number of constitutional decisions are forcing a shift away from the local property tax toward the state-imposed income tax as the primary means of financing public education. Almost inevitably this will mean that many financial decisions will be removed from local school boards and centralized to intermediate or statewide decision-making bodies. At the federal level the movement toward nation-wide bargaining units of federal civil servants may slow or halt efforts toward federal decentralization that were undertaken in the 1960's. In short, public employee unionism appears in many areas to be leading to more centralized decision-making in the United States, similar to the way it has in many other industrialized democracies.

The economic results of public employee bargaining are as yet unclear and controversial. Some authorities believe that public employees have driven their

---

*Reprinted by permission of the Institute of Labor and Industrial Relations.

salary and benefit levels far higher than would have been the case in the absence of collective bargaining, and higher than can be justified on the basis of economic equity. Others challenge this assumption. They state that recent increases in public employee compensation are largely reflective of inflationary pressures in the society and the temporary need for public employees to "catch up" with others to whom their wages and salaries should be compared. Quantitative data that would support either argument are still scanty. Public employees in some occupations clearly have fared more favorably in recent years than has the average employee in the private sector. The differences are not large, however, and during 1971 and 1972 increases in both sectors were held down by government wage policies.

As yet, at least, the impact of public employee unionism on governmental decision-making has not been as great as the numerical increase in public union membership and bargaining unit growth might suggest. In the federal sector it is estimated that employees as yet have the right to bargain on perhaps only 25 percent of the subjects that are bargainable in the private sector. Though the scope of bargaining is increasing at the federal level, and is already more extensive at the local and educational levels, it cannot be said with any certainty that the large majority of governmental and public policy decisions are fundamentally different than they would have been in the absence of collective bargaining.

Finally, and most speculatively, it is possible that public employee unionism will bring changes to the whole of the labor relations environment in the United States. As previously noted, white collar and professional organization in the public sector may bring a greater acceptability of white collar unionization in the private sector. If devices such as compulsory arbitration become common and effective for resolving collective bargaining impasses in the public sector, such devices may increasingly be urged for use in the private sector. In general, and with many obvious exceptions, public sector labor relations practices and laws in the United States have thus far been strongly modeled on the private sector structures which had evolved earlier. Over time, experience in the public sector may prove certain procedures and practices, now uncommon or unknown in the private sector, to be useful or effective. It is not at all unlikely that such practices might then become acceptable in the private sector. In sum, the future may well be one of simultaneous changes in both sectors, each tending generally to become more like the other.

FREEMAN & ICHNIOWSKI, INTRODUCTION: THE PUBLIC SECTOR LOOK OF AMERICAN UNIONISM, in When Public Sector Workers Unionize 1-13 (R. Freeman & C. Ichniowski eds. 1988)*

After decades in which collective bargaining with the government was considered virtually "impossible" in America,[1] unionization achieved in the 1970s and 1980s greater strength in the public sector than in the private sector. In 1986 over a third of public sector workers were organized into unions, and over 40

---

*Reprinted by permission of the author and The University of Chicago Press.

[1] In 1962 George Meany was quoted as declaring that it is "impossible to bargain collectively with the government." See Kramer, (1962, 41).

percent were covered by collective agreements compared to a union density in the private sector of 14 percent. Nearly one in three union members was a public employee. The National Education Association, the American Federation of Teachers, the American Federation of State, County, and Municipal Employees, and the Service Employees International Union (with nearly half its membership in the public sector) were among the largest unions in the country. Unions of fire fighters and police were well-established exemplars of the craft-type organizations that once dominated American labor. Public sector unionism had become *the* vibrant component of the American labor movement.

Why did union density and collective bargaining prosper in the public sector while declining elsewhere? What does the new public sector "look" of organized labor mean for the economy? Do labor-management relations in the public sector mirror private sector patterns or do they represent something novel on the labor scene? What can the private sector learn from the success of collective bargaining in the public sector?

... [N]ew data permit analyses of public sector unionism that go beyond estimating the impact of a 0-1 union variable on wages that has been the focus of much past work. The research highlights fundamental differences between public and private sector labor relations in the conditions that foster or undermine unionism; the pay and employment outcomes unions produce; and the procedures by which unions secure benefits for their members.

Studies of the growth of public sector collective bargaining attribute the 1970s and 1980s spurt largely to the enactment of comprehensive labor laws that impose a duty to bargain on managers, often with compulsory arbitration to resolve disputes. The greater effectiveness of these laws than that of the National Labor Relations Act, which governs private sector unionism, is explained by the political incentives that keep public sector managers from opposing unions and committing unfair labor practices to the extent done in the private sector.

The studies of union impacts find that public sector unions have different or more pronounced effects than private sector unions in several areas: reducing layoffs and unemployment and increasing employment of members; raising wages of nonunion workers through "spillover" or "threat" effects; and increasing expenditures in organized departments. In addition, teacher unionism has been found to be associated with higher student test scores. As a result of these impacts, the wage differential between union and nonunion workers, commonly used to measure what unions do, *understates* the impact of unionism on the public sector.

Finally, the research shows that public sector unionism affects outcomes in ways that go beyond standard collective bargaining: through lobbying and political campaigning that influence both the goals and behavior of management and citizens' views about desired public services, and through the use of final outcome arbitration to resolve impasses rather than the traditional strike weapon.

The Central Role of Labor Laws in Public Sector Labor Relations

Students of the U.S. Labor movement have long debated the role of labor law in unionization. Some argue that laws are a fundamental determinant of union strength, crediting (blaming) the National Labor Relations Act of 1936 [sic] and decisions of the War Labor Board for much of the rise of private sector unionism in the 1940s, and blaming (crediting) union decline in the 1970s and 1980s on the ensuing failure of labor law to control illegal management activities in representation elections. Others, noting union successes in periods of legal adversity and the ability of management and labor to circumvent legal restrictions, feel that laws have little effect on unionism.[3]

The variation in public sector labor laws among states and occupations at a point in time and over time — which ranges from outlawing collective bargaining to providing arbitration mechanisms to resolve contract disputes — provides a "natural experiment" to evaluate the role of legal enactment in the evolution of collective bargaining. Accordingly, NBER [National Bureau of Economic Research] researchers developed a data set measuring public sector labor law from 1955, when bargaining with the government seemed impossible, to 1984, when many states had enacted comprehensive public sector labor laws; they obtained data on collective contracts in Ohio and Illinois, industrial states whose public sector unionization prior to enactment of laws are oft-cited counter examples to the claim that laws are important; and they determined the dates when police departments first signed collective contracts in cities throughout the country. Analyses of these data yield five broad conclusions about the role of labor law in the rise of collective bargaining in the public sector.

1. The legal environment is critical in determining whether or not public sector employers bargain collectively with their workers.

The evidence is threefold. First, favorable state public sector labor laws increase the probability that a municipal department is governed by a collective contract, even when other diverse determinants of contract status, including extent of union membership and the city in which a department is located, are held fixed (Freeman and Valletta, this volume, chap. 3, tables 3.2 and 3.3) [omitted]. Second, passage of comprehensive public sector labor laws induced sharp increases in the percentage of departments bargaining within a state. Among police, research indicates that the impact of laws is so substantial that within eight years of enactment of laws mandating arbitration virtually all departments bargain contractually with their workers, while in the absence of laws it would take "forever" (252 years) for workers to achieve such coverage (Ichniowski, this volume, chap. 1, table 1.2, figure 1.2) [omitted]. Third, analysis of Ohio and Illinois shows that the 1983 comprehensive public sector laws enacted in these "exceptions" induced dramatic spurts in contract coverage: in Illinois the probability that school districts signed contracts increased by 32 percentage points within a year of enactment (Saltzman, this volume, chap. 2, table 2.4) [omitted]. Moreover, unionism prior to passage of the laws was abetted by favorable court decisions on the legality of collective bargaining. While not "necessary" for unionization, favorable public sector labor laws seem to be a sufficient condition for rapid growth.

---

[3] John Dunlop, in particular, has argued that union growths occurs in spurts not necessarily related to legal developments (pers. comm. 1987). For the public sector, Burton (1979) has advanced the argument that policy changes are no more important than several other factors.

2. Economic benefits and costs do not readily explain the timing of public sector labor laws.

The trend in public sector labor law has been, first, to legalize union activity and require managers to "meet and confer" with unions; second, to require managers to bargain with unions; and, third, to mandate arbitration or other final closure mechanisms to guarantee a contract (Valletta and Freeman, this volume, appendix B) [omitted]. To the extent that passage of the laws themselves depends on fundamental economic forces, the factors that determine enactment of laws should be part of the economic analysis of union growth. Can we identify such factors?

While cross-state comparisons show that state characteristics such as per capita income and public expenditures are associated with public sector laws favorable to unionism (Kochan 1973; Faber and Martin 1980; Hunt, White, and Moore 1985), analysis of changes over time fail to turn up systematic factors that cause states to enact laws earlier rather than later (Farber, this volume, chap. 5) [omitted]. Different states moved at different speeds toward comprehensive public sector labor laws, apparently for "idiosyncratic" political reasons involving patronage, personalities, and union rivalry rather than broad economic or social factors. That Ohio and Illinois did not enact comprehensive labor laws until 1983 is consistent with this pattern. Viewed negatively, the inability to explain the timing of state labor laws suggests limits to economic analysis of legal developments and the need for detailed legislative histories to understand changes. Viewed positively, the finding suggests that treating the timing of the laws as exogenous does not create significantly biases in analyzing the impact of laws on bargaining and thus strengthens the conclusion that laws can be treated as an independent cause of the growth of collective bargaining.

3. Public sector laws favorable to collective bargaining raise wages in nonunion as well as union departments but have substantial adverse employment consequences only for nonunion departments.

By spurring collective bargaining, public sector labor laws are indirectly responsible for union-induced charges in wages and employment. In addition, the laws affect economic outcomes by enhancing the bargaining power of unions and altering management decisions in nonunion departments as well.

Indicative of the impact of laws on union bargaining strength, unionized workers in municipal departments in states with laws favorable to collective bargaining receive about 6 percent higher pay than those in states with unfavorable laws and appear to experience a comparable increase in pay following passage of favorable laws. Indicative of the apparent impact of the laws on nonunion departments, the pay of nonunion municipal workers is about 3 percent higher in states with comprehensive public sector labor laws than in other states, seemingly as a result of the "threat" that those workers will also unionize. The employment consequences of strong collective bargaining laws, by contrast, differ between union and nonunion departments; unionized departments experience only marginally lower employment in favorable legal environments despite higher wages whereas nonunion departments suffer considerable job loss, suggesting that unions use some of the power they attain from favorable legislation to maintain employment (Freeman and Valletta, this volume, chap. 3, tables 3.5 and 3.7) [omitted].

4. Among states that obligate employers to bargain, wages are no higher with compulsory arbitration than with other dispute resolution mechanisms, whereas wages are noticeably higher with strike-permitted laws.

One of the hallmarks of public sector labor relations is the use of dispute resolution mechanisms, including compulsory interest arbitration of various forms, in place of strikes and lockouts. While at one time public sector unions opposed such alternatives to the strike, more recently management has alleged that arbitration favors unions. Dramatizing this complaint in 1977, one Massachusetts mayor stripped to his shorts before television cameras to show that arbitration was "stripping" the city of its money (New Bedford Standard-Times, 25 January 1977). Extant research, however, finds that arbitrated settlements are, if anything, lower than negotiated settlements (Ashenfelter and Bloom 1984). This leaves only one possible way for arbitration to raise wages: by creating an environment in which cities agree to high negotiated settlements for fear that arbitrators will impose even higher wages. If this were true, cities in states with compulsory arbitration would pay more for comparable labor (all else the same) than cities in states that simply require employers to bargain with unions; pay would rise especially rapidly when state laws changed from duty-to-bargain to compulsory arbitration. The evidence, however, shows that pay in states with compulsory arbitration laws does not differ noticeably from that in other duty-to-bargain states, whereas pay is on the order of 2-9 percent higher in states that permit strikes (Freeman and Valletta, this volume, chap. 3, table 3.8) [omitted]. That arbitration has little impact on wages in states that encourage bargaining is important in light of evidence that arbitration laws reduce strike rates (Ichniowski 1982), for it suggests that compulsory arbitration resolves impasses without strikes — the aim of these laws — without increasing wages and salaries.

5. Arbitrators do not favor one side or the other nor respond greatly to the facts of a case when labor and management make "reasonable" proposals; rather, they tend to "split the difference."

The question of the extent to which arbitrators split the difference between offers as opposed to making independent judgments based on the facts is a long-standing one. One way to evaluate arbitrator behavior is to devise "laboratory-type experiments" in which the researcher asks arbitrator to settle pseudocases that isolate the effect of given conditions on outcomes. In an NBER experiment, the researcher asked arbitrators to resolve cases patterned after actual contract disputes and varied the settlements proposed by labor and management. In a set of identical cases, arbitrators tended to split the differences between offers, giving higher (lower) awards when management or labor offers were high (low) even under identical factual situations (Bloom, this volume, chap. 4) [omitted]. At first blush this might suggest that the best strategy for unions and management is to make extreme proposals regardless of the facts. This would be an incorrect inference, however, as arbitrators do indeed place primary weight on facts when offers and facts are unrelated (Bazerman and

Farber 1985). Arbitrators split the difference when they feel the proposals of the two sites reflect the facts. As in actual cases both sides generally base offers on the facts, the result is that arbitrators often split the differences in actual practice.

The Effects of Public Sector Collective Bargaining on Wages

Following the private sector union literature, much research on public sector unionism has examined the impact of unions on wages. Reviewing this extensive body of research, Lewis (this volume, chap. 6) [omitted] concludes that:

6. Union/nonunion earnings differences tend to be smaller in the public sector than in the private sector but vary considerably among workers and are far from negligible.

On average the earnings of union workers exceed those of nonunion workers by 8-13 percent in the public sector, which is about 5 percentage points lower than union/nonunion earnings differences in the private sector. However, some groups of unionized public sector workers obtain as large (local government workers) or larger (public school teachers) earnings advantages over nonunion workers as does the average unionized private sector worker. Looking at demographic groups, union/nonunion earnings differences are higher for women than for men in the public sector but are about the same for black as for white workers. Among occupations outside of teaching, union earnings advantages are smaller for blue-collar workers in the public sector than in the private sector, at least among males, and are modest for police, fire fighters, and most hospital workers.

The new NBER research adds to and modifies the findings of earlier work, leading to three further findings:

7. Nonunion workers appear to benefit from the presence of unionism in the public sector, receiving higher pay in states with laws favorable to collective bargaining and in cities where other workers are unionized.

The first bit of evidence of wage spillovers in the public sector is the finding, noted under point 3 above, that the earnings of nonunion workers in states with laws that favor collective bargaining are higher than the earnings of nonunion workers in other states, all else held fixed. The second piece of evidence is that nonunion workers earnings increased especially rapidly in states that enacted comprehensive collective bargaining laws compared to nonunion worker earnings in other states (Freeman and Valletta, this volume, chap. 3, tables 3.5 and 3.7) [omitted]. The third piece of evidence is that workers in unorganized departments of a city receive higher pay when workers in other departments are organized (Zax and Ichniowski, this volume, chap. 12, tables 12.3 and 12.6) [omitted]. Wage "spillover" from organized police to fire fighters, where pay parity is an explicit issue in collective bargaining, is especially pronounced. The interpretation of these relations as resulting from the threat of union organization is supported by other research showing that, among police at least, low-wage departments have the highest chances of being organized (Ichniowski, Freeman, and Lauer 1987).

8. Public sector wages rise with size of department, partly because larger cities have a greater ability to pay, as reflected in property values and family incomes, while wage differences between union and nonunion public sector workers depend modestly on the city's ability to pay.

In the private sector, pay increases with the size of firm or establishment, particularly in the nonunion sector, implying that unions raise wages less at large workplaces. Do wages rise with size and union premiums fall with size in the public sector as well? What is the effect of controlling for measures of the size of department or city and the ability to pay on the union wage premium?

Increases in pay with size in the public sector are about as large as the increase in pay with size in the private sector, but they reveal a different pattern by union status, with union effects on wages independent or increasing with size. Data on individuals from the Current Population Survey (CPS) indicate that a 10 percent increase in the size of a government unit is associated with a 0.2 percent increase in wages and a rise in the union wage premium of about 0.4 percent, other factors held fixed. The rise in the union premium at larger workplaces may reflect greater union political power where employment is greater or possibly the ability of strong unions to raise employment as well as wages (see point 10 below). Data from the Survey of Governments (SOG) on municipal departments show a more pronounced relation between size and pay, with a 10 percent increase in size associated with a 0.4 percent increase in pay, but no change in the union premium with size (Brown and Medoff, this volume, chap. 7, table. 7.3) [omitted]. As far as can be told, moreover, only about a fifth of the increase in pay with city size results from factors such as property values that measure a city's "ability to pay." Similarly, while some of the public sector union/nonunion wage differential can be attributed to disproportionate unionization of larger departments and of workers in cities with greater ability to pay, the vast bulk of the effect must be attributed to unionism per se rather than to these correlates.

9. Despite the fact that federal employee unions do not negotiate pay, many federal workers earn more than they would in the private sector, producing queues for federal jobs.

The question of whether federal employees are paid more or less than otherwise comparable workers in the labor market has generated considerable controversy. Comparisons of wages based on the CPS, which contains information for individual characteristics, show federal employees to be relatively highly paid (Smith 1977), with the greatest differences being among minorities and women (Asher and Popkin 1984). Comparisons of wages in narrowly defined occupations gives, however, the opposite pattern, with significant pay disadvantage to federal workers in the late 1970s and 1980s (Freeman 1988). Which picture of federal pay is right?

Evidence from workers who move between federal and private employment supports the view that federal pay is relatively high for average workers, as those who move from private to federal employment obtain larger wage gains than those who move from on private employer to another. In addition, Civil Service Commission data show sizeable queues for federal employment

(Krueger, this volume, chap. 8) [omitted]. As federal worker unions do not negotiate pay, these wage advantages cannot be attributed to collective bargaining. One possible reason for high pay, consistent with the increase in pay by size in the public sector, is that the federal government is by far the nation's largest employer. Another possibility is that the federal government's national pay scale — chosen for reasons of administrative ease, internal labor market mobility, and politics — requires that average pay be high enough to attract labor in high-wage local markets.

The Effects of Public Sector Unionism on Employment, Labor Turnover, Output, and Budgets

Because union wage effects are smaller in the public than in the private sector, it is common to conclude that public sector unions are weaker than their private sector counterparts. NBER research rejects this notion because of the pronounced effects of public sector unionism on other labor market outcomes — employment, layoffs, output, and budgets.

10. Public sector unionism raises employment of organized workers.

It is generally held that public sector union wage gains come at the expense of employment, as enterprises economize on more expensive labor. The pattern in the public sector seems to be quite different. Consistent with earlier work (Zax 1985), comparisons of employment across cities show that with diverse factors held fixed, departments that bargain collectively hire more workers than otherwise similar departments that do not bargain collectively (Freeman and Valletta, this volume, chap. 3, tables 3.5 and 3.6; Zax and Ichniowski, this volume, chap. 12, tables 12.1-12.3) [omitted]. Coupled with the positive impact of collective bargaining on wages, this implies that payrolls are higher in union departments and also produce higher total expenditures in those departments (Zax and Ichniowski, this volume, chap. 12, tables 12.4 and 12.5) [omitted]. Only among teachers have NBER researchers failed to find a positive bargaining effect on employment (Kleiner and Petree, this volume, chap. 11, table 11.6) [omitted], though here other recent research has detached such effects (Eberts and Stone 1986).

There are two possible reasons why employment of unionized labor might be higher in the public sector despite higher wages. One is that public sector unions shift the demand for members' services through political activity — lobbying and campaigning for additional public expenditures that increase both wages and employment. An alternative explanation is that unions use their bargaining strength to force employers off demand curves in accord with union preferences for jobs (producing so-called efficient contracts), for instance, by demanding contract clauses that specify a minimum number of police per cruiser, or fire fighters per shift or piece of equipment, or pupils per classroom. Without denying union use of collective bargaining to alter employment, the fact that city councils and legislatures need not appropriate the money to finance negotiated settlements forces unions to complement contract provisions with political and lobbying activities that affect the level of demand. In the public sector unions cannot rely exclusively on collective bargaining behind closed doors to obtain desired agreements, efficient or not.

11. Public sector unionism reduces layoffs and unemployment but has only marginal effects on quits.

The impact of unionism on turnover [is] strikingly different in the public sector than in the private sector (Allen, this volume, chap. 10) [omitted]. Unions in the public sector reduce substantially temporary and indefinite layoffs, whereas they increase those layoffs in the private sector (Medoff 1979). The magnitudes of the public sector effects are, moreover, quite large: in the mid-to-late 1970s the likelihood that public sector employees would be on temporary or indefinite layoff was 40 percent less for unionized than nonunion employees, whereas in the private sector unionists were three times more likely to be on temporary or indefinite layoff than nonunion workers (Allen, this volume, chap. 10, table 10.3) [omitted]. On the other hand, quit rates, which unionism lowers markedly in the private sector (Freeman 1980), are barely affected by union status in the public sector (Allen, this volume, chap. 10, tables 10.5 and 10.6) [omitted]. The net of these two effects — reductions in layoffs and modest impacts on quits — is that unionism in the public sector appears to increase job stability and reduce the probability of unemployment for members. This is consistent with the finding that public sector unionism raises employment (see point 10) and is a major element in our conclusion that public sector unions have more substantial economic effects than shown in simple comparisons of union and nonunion wages.

12. Teacher unionism is associated with increased student test scores, but the reasons for this association are not well determined.

Extant research on the impact of unionism on productivity in the public sector presents a mixed picture: some studies show positive union effects, others find negative effects, while others report no effects leading to the generalization that on net unionism is neutral to productivity in the public sector (Freeman 1986; Methe and Perry 1980). Using special tabulations of student test scores and other indicators to measure outputs in education, NEBR researchers found educational productivity to be somewhat higher, other factors held fixed, in more highly unionized states. Longitudinal data that contrast scores in the same state over time show a comparable result, though whether the effects come from the presence of a labor organization per se or from collective bargaining is unclear (Kleiner and Petree, this volume, chap. 11, table 11.8) [omitted]. Working separately with data for individual students rather than states, Eberts and Stone (1986) report comparable results for students with average achievement levels, but more complex ones for more/less able students. Unfortunately neither study is able to identify the particular factors — better management due to union pressures? lower turnover? greater teacher effort? — by which unionism is associated with greater educational productivity.[8]

---

[8] The failure of these studies to identify the mechanism underlying the improved performance of schools in a union environment mirrors the general failure of economists to determine causes of

13. State aid to local school districts does not increase wages or employment in a unionized setting but, rather, reduces taxes.

When a state awards a school district unexpected grants-in-aid, how much of the funds show up in higher teacher pay or employment or other educational expenditures as opposed to reductions in local taxes? Surprisingly, in highly unionized states such as New York (Ehrenberg and Chaykowski, this volume, chap. 9) [omitted] and Michigan (Murnane, Singer, and Willett 1986), districts have used such money largely to reduce property taxes. Why? One possibility is that school districts were unwilling to make major salary or employment commitments based on state financing that they view as uncertain. Another possibility is that the failure to raise wages or employment is a "period effect" due to the 1970s and early 1980s "tax revolt" at the state and local levels. Finally, it is possible that in these states unions used their lobbying resources to increase educational spending from normal funding sources to such an extent that taxpayers were unwilling to finance additional resources for schooling. Whichever interpretation is correct, the fact that state relief does not augment school spending highlights the limitations on the ability of unions to raise spending through collective bargaining and thus helps explain union pressure for state laws that earmark increased state aid for higher minimum salaries, as in New Jersey, or for general teachers' salaries, as in New York, and the importance of activity outside normal collective bargaining.

14. Public sector collective bargaining raises expenditures on unionized functions but appears to have little impact on total municipal expenditures.

Further evidence on the limited ability of public sector unions to affect outcomes through bargaining is given by the surprising fact that while cities that bargain with unions is four municipal functions (police, fire, sanitation, and street and highway workers) spend more on these activities than other cities, they do not have higher *total* city budgets than cities that do not bargain with unions (Zax and Ichniowski, this volume, chap. 12, table 12.4) [omitted]. The implication is that the bulk of union-induced increases in expenditures on organized activities is funded by reallocating city moneys from nonorganized to organized activities rather than by increasing total spending and taxes. If this finding is correct, public sector unions would seem to have greater ability to alter line items in a given city budget than to increase taxes and budgets, perhaps because taxpayers pay more attention to total tax bills than to expenditures on specific services. By contrast, private sector unions are more likely to impact bottom-line profits than the allocation of moneys within a firm.

Interpreting Public Sector Labor Relations

Despite comprehensive labor laws that mimic the National Labor Relations Act and a tradition of drawing on the experience of the private sector, public sector unions and management have evolved of a new and different labor

---

productivity advance and the more specific problem in determining why productivity tends to be higher in unionized settings in the private sector.

relations system. Why? What explains the features of public sector labor relations found in this volume and in other research?

Our analysis stresses the distinct incentives and constraints that operate in political as opposed to economic markets, in particular the fact that public sector management and labor, unlike private employers and unions, must appeal to voters to support their actions. For unions, this creates an opportunity to affect the agenda of the employers who face them across the bargaining table. At the same time it makes them frame demands and set policies on the allocation of resources to public services broadly defined as well as on benefits to members, and thus go beyond the bargaining table to convince those who ultimately foot the bill of the virtue of their case. Since political influence depends in part on how large a group one can muster, moreover, public sector unions tend to place great weight on employment outcomes (see Courant, Gramlich, and Rubinfeld 1979). On the employer side, the fact that management is beholden to an electorate that includes public sector workers and politically active unions induces management to take a less adversarial approach to collective bargaining than do private sector managers beholden to shareholders. Further reducing the adversarial relation is the fact that unions can be an important ally in convincing the electorate, or the legislature, or other governmental bodies of the need to increase budgets. Finally, the belief that government employees should not have the right to strike has spurred public sector development of arbitration to resolve impasses, which itself alters the nature of the management-labor conflict.

Another important factor that differentiates the public sector from the private sector in the United States (though not in most countries) is the setting of public sector labor law on a decentralized state basis. Decentralization of the law allows areas of the country favorably inclined to unionism to encourage collective bargaining and areas with unfavorable attitudes to restrict it. It also has led to numerous "experiments" with different modes of regulating union and management conduct and conflicts, encouraging institutional innovation and diversity. In contrast to the private sector, where workers and employers have been limited to the traditional model of exclusive representation, bargaining-to-contract, and strikes to settle impasses, the public sector has offered a range of unions and union-type organizations from worker associations with whom employers need not bargain to full-fledged collective bargaining organizations with diverse alternative modes of impasse resolution.

Given the greater success of collective bargaining in the public sector than in the private sector in the 1970s and 1980s, the time would seem to have come for researchers and practitioners to begin to ask what the private sector might learn from the public sector experience rather than the converse.

NOTES

1. Collective bargaining in the public sector has been the subject of numerous books and symposia. The following are particularly useful in gaining a broad overview of the issues and problems: Public-Sector Bargaining (B. Aaron, J. Grodin & J. Stern eds. 1988); When Public Sector Workers Unionize (R. Freeman & C. Ichniowski eds. 1988); The Evolving Process—Negotiations in Public Employment (J. Lefkowitz ed. 1985); M. Lieberman, Public-Sector Bargaining: A Policy Appraisal (1980); H. Wellington & R. Winter, The Unions and the

Cities (1971); Public Workers and Public Unions (S. Zagoria ed. 1972); Labor Relations Law in the Public Sector (A. Knapp ed. 1977); Public Employee Unions: A Study of the Crisis in Public Sector Labor Relations (A. Chickering ed. 1976); S. Spero & J. Capozzola, The Urban Community and Its Unionized Bureaucracies (1973); P. Feuille & T. Kochan, Public Sector Labor Relations: Analysis and Readings (1977); M. Moskow, J. Loewenberg, E. Koziara, Collective Bargaining in Public Employment (1970). One of the most concise yet most perceptive discussions of the principal policy issues raised by public sector unionism is D. Bok & J. Dunlop, *Collective Bargaining and the Public Sector,* in Labor and the American Community 312 (1970).

2. The reports and recommendations of various advisory commissions are another invaluable source of information on public sector collective bargaining. See generally Committee on Economic Development, Improving Management of the Public Work Force: The Challenge to State and Local Government (1978); Advisory Commission on Intergovernmental Relations, Labor-Management Policies for State and Local Government (1969); 1967 Executive Committee, National Governors' Conference, Report of Task Force on State and Local Government Labor Relations (1967), and 1968, 1969 and 1970 Supplements to Report of Task Force on State and Local Government Labor Relations; The Council of State Governments, State-Local Employee Labor Relations (1970); Twentieth Century Fund Task Force on Labor Disputes in Public Employment, Pickets at City Hall (1970). Many of the reports issued by state and local advisory commissions are also useful. For one of the most comprehensive, see Final Report of the Assembly Advisory Council on Public Employee Relations, State of California (March 15, 1973). See also Public Employer-Employee Relations Study Comm'n, Report to the Governor and the Legislature (N.J. 1976); Governor's Advisory Comm'n on Labor-Management for Public Employees, Report and Recommendations (Ill. 1967). See generally Smith, *State and Local Advisory Reports on Public Employment Labor Legislation: A Comparative Analysis,* 67 Mich L. Rev. 891 (1969).

3. For an assessment of the impact of unions on education in elementary, secondary and higher education, see Faculty and Teacher Bargaining (G. Angell ed. 1981).

4. The development of collective bargaining among federal employees is comprehensively treated in M. Nesbitt, Labor Relations in the Federal Government Service (1976). See generally S. Levitan & A. Noden, Working for the Sovereign: Employee Relations in the Federal Government (1983).

5. In Fogel & Lewin, *Wage Determination in the Public Sector,* 27 Indus. & Lab. Rel. Rev. 410, 430 (1974), the authors concluded:

> The available data indicate that public-privacy pay relationships in the United States can be explained, at least in part, by a combination of two factors: a discretion that public employers must exercise in implementing the prevailing wage rule adopted by most cities and larger government units and the nature of the political forces that affect governmental wage decisions. The result is an occupational pay structure that is more "equalitarian" in the public sector than in private industry, in the sense that public employers tend to pay more than private employers for low-scale and craft jobs to pay less for top executive jobs.

Chapter 2

THE RIGHT TO JOIN AND FORM UNIONS

A. CONSTITUTIONAL PROTECTION

ATKINS v. CITY OF CHARLOTTE

296 F. Supp. 1068 (W.D.N.C. 1969)

CRAVEN, CIRCUIT JUDGE: This is a civil action brought to obtain a declaratory judgment and injunctive relief declaring unconstitutional and preventing enforcement of Sections 95-97, 95-98 and 95-99 of the General Statutes of North Carolina.* We hold G.S. 95-97 unconstitutional on its face. We hold G.S. § 95-98 a valid and constitutional exercise of the legislative authority of the General Assembly of North Carolina. As for G.S. § 95-99, we hold it to be so related to G.S. § 95-97 that it cannot survive the invalidation of that section.

... [T]he court finds the facts to be as follows:

Facts

The statutes sought to be invalidated are these:

N.C.G.S. § 95-97: ... [Prohibits any employee employed by any governmental unit engaged full-time in law enforcement or fire protection activity from being or becoming a member of any labor organization or aiding or assisting any labor organization] which is, or may become, a part of or affiliated in any way with any national or international labor union, federation, or organization, and which has as its purpose or one of its purposes, collective bargaining....

N.C.G.S. § 95-98: ... [Any agreement or contract between any unit or government and any labor organization] is hereby declared to be against the public policy of the State, illegal, unlawful, void and of no effect.

N.C.G.S. § 95-99: ... [Violations of §§ 95-97 and 95-98 are misdemeanors] punishable in the discretion of the court.

All of the plaintiffs are members of the Charlotte Fire Department, and the gist of the complaint is that the statutes are overbroad and prohibit constitutionally guaranteed rights of the plaintiffs in violation of the First Amendment and the Due Process and Equal Protection Clauses of the Fourteenth Amendment to the Constitution of the United States. Specifically, plaintiffs want to become dues paying members of a Local which would become affiliated with International Association of Fire Fighters, the intervenor. Affidavits of some 400 fire

---

*Editors' note: The suit was brought pursuant to, *inter alia,* 42 U.S.C. § 1983, which reads as follows: "Every person who, under color of any statute, ordinance, regulation, custom, or usage, of any State or Territory, subjects, or causes to be subjected, any citizen of the United States or other person within the jurisdiction thereof to the deprivation of any rights, privileges, or immunities secured by the Constitution and laws, shall be liable to the party injured in an action at law, suit in equity, or other proper proceeding for redress."

fighters of the Charlotte Fire Department have been put into evidence to the effect that, if allowed to do so by law, affiants would join the Union.

The City of Charlotte is a municipal corporation which operates and maintains the Charlotte Fire Department pursuant to the City Charter. The Chief of the Department is appointed by the City Council and is accountable to the Council for the faithful performance of his duties. He is responsible for the discipline and efficiency of the Department and for carrying out all orders, rules and regulations approved by the Council. He is also responsible for approving all promotions of members in the Department subject to the approval of the Civil Service Board.

The Department has approximately 438 employees, consisting of the Chief, two assistant chiefs, 14 deputy chiefs, 60 fire captains, and 56 fire lieutenants, with the remainder being fire fighters, inspectors, fire alarm personnel and office personnel. The plaintiffs consist of deputy chiefs, captains, lieutenants and fire fighters and range in service with the department from two to 40 years.

For many years prior to the enactment in 1959 of the North Carolina General Statutes complained of, the International Association of Fire Fighters operated or maintained a union made up of Charlotte Fire Department members and designated as Local 660, an affiliate of the International Association of Fire Fighters. A number of Fire Department members paid dues to that organization which was engaged in collective bargaining activity. Further, the City checked off dues for union membership.

During 1959, the North Carolina Legislature enacted General Statutes §§ 95-97 through 95-99. Following the enactment of these statutes, Local 660 terminated its affiliation with the International Association of Fire Fighters and became, or took the name, Charlotte Fire Fighters Association. This organization continued the activities and representations very much as had been the practice with Local 660. The Fire Fighters Association continued to negotiate with the City and to represent the Charlotte firemen with respect to wages, grievances, and other conditions of employment, and the City continued its recognition of the association and permitted dues check-off. This practice continued from 1959 until 1962. On January 29, 1962, the City Council received and approved a report compiled by the City Manager. One of the recommendations of this report as it was approved established as a condition of continued employment in the Fire Department non-membership in the Fire Fighters Association or in any successor thereto. The City Council approved this report after having been advised by the City Attorney that the Fire Fighters Association was not illegal per se under the statutes complained of, but that the association and its recognition by the City was in violation of public policies of the State. Sometime after this action on the part of the City Council, the Fire Fighters Association terminated its activities and the City discontinued its recognition and dues check-off. A grievance procedure was established to allow individual employees to process grievances, but no provisions were made for group grievance procedure or for collective bargaining with respect to grievances, wages, and conditions of employment.

During March of 1967, members of the Charlotte Fire Department, the plaintiffs herein, organized the Charlotte Firemen's Assembly. This organization has as its purpose collective bargaining with the City of Charlotte with respect to wages, grievances, hours of employment and other conditions of employment. It would like to become a local affiliate of intervenor but is prevented by the statutes. The Firemen's Assembly has not been recognized by the City as a representative of firemen....

The Constitutional Question and the Remedy

We think N.C.G.S. § 95-97 is void on its face as an abridgment of freedom of association protected by the First and Fourteenth Amendments of the Constitution of the United States. The flaw in it is an intolerable "overbreadth" unnecessary to the protection of valid state interests. Cf. *United States v. Robel,* 389 U.S. 258 (1967). The Supreme Court of the United States has accorded "freedom of association" full status as an aspect of liberty protected by the Due Process Clause of the Fourteenth Amendment and by the rights of free speech and peaceful assembly explicitly set out in the First Amendment. In *NAACP v. Alabama ex rel. Patterson,* the Court said:

> "It is beyond debate that freedom to engage in association for the advancement of beliefs and ideas is an inseparable aspect of the 'liberty' assured by the Due Process Clause of the Fourteenth Amendment, which embraces freedom of speech. [Citations omitted.] Of course, it is immaterial whether the beliefs sought to be advanced by association pertain to political, *economic,* religious or cultural matters, and state action which may have the effect of curtailing the freedom to associate is subject to the closest scrutiny." 357 U.S. 449, 460-461 (1958). (Emphasis ours.)

The Court had previously noted the close connection between the freedoms of speech and assembly. In *DeJonge v. Oregon,* 299 U.S. 353, 364 (1937), the Court held that the right of peaceable assembly is a right cognate to those of free speech and free press and equally fundamental. It was said that the right is one that cannot be denied without violating fundamental principles of liberty and justice which lie at the base of all civil and political institutions. The Court made a careful distinction between the proper exercise of legislative power to protect against abuse of the right of assembly and legislative infringement per se of that right, holding that the latter is not permissible. Especially pertinent to the problem confronting us is the following:

> "[C]onsistently with the Federal Constitution, peaceable assembly for lawful discussion cannot be made a crime. The holding of meetings for peaceable political action cannot be proscribed. Those who assist in the conduct of such meetings cannot be branded as criminals on that score. The question, if the rights of free speech and peaceable assembly are to be preserved, is not *as to the auspices under which the meeting is held* but as to its purpose...." *DeJonge v. Oregon,* 299 U.S. 353, 365 (1937). (Emphasis ours.)

We would make the same distinction here. It matters not, we think, whether the firemen of the City of Charlotte meet under the auspices of the intervenor, a national labor union, but whether their proposed concerted action, if any, endangers valid state interests. We think there is no valid state interest in denying firemen the right to organize a labor union — whether local or national in scope. It is beyond argument that a single individual cannot negotiate on an equal basis with an employer who hires hundreds of people. Recognition of this fact of life is the basis of labor-management relations in this country. Charlotte concedes in its brief that the right of public employees to join labor unions is becoming increasingly recognized (with the exception of firemen and policemen) and even admits that collective bargaining might be beneficial in many situations in the case of municipal firemen. But Charlotte insists that the State has a valid interest in forbidding membership in a labor union to firemen. It is said that fire departments are quasi-military in structure, and that such a structure is necessary because individual firemen must be ready to respond instantly and without question to orders of a superior, and that such military discipline may well mean the difference between saving human life and property, and failure. The extension of this argument is, of course, that affiliation with a national labor union might eventuate in a strike against the public interest which could not be tolerated, and the very existence of which would imperil lives and property in the City of Charlotte. This is the only state interest that can be validly asserted for N.C.G.S. § 95-97. The thought of fires raging out of control in Charlotte while firemen, out on strike, Neroicly watch the flames, is frightening. We do not question the power of the State to deal with such a contingency. We do question the overbreadth of G.S. § 95-97, which quite unnecessarily, in our opinion, goes far beyond the valid state interest that is suggested to us, and strikes down indiscriminately the right of association in a labor union — even one whose policy is opposed to strikes.

Since the only valid state interest suggested by defendants in support of the constitutionality of G.S. § 95-97 is the quite legitimate fear that fire protection for the people of Charlotte might be disrupted by violence or by strike, it seems quite clear that the statute must be invalidated for "overbreadth."

The Supreme Court "has repeatedly held that a governmental purpose to control or prevent activities constitutionally subject to state regulation may not be achieved by means which sweep unnecessarily broadly and thereby invade the area of protected freedoms." *NAACP v. Alabama ex rel. Flowers,* 377 U.S. 288, at 307 (1964).

Again, "even though the governmental purpose be legitimate and substantial, that purpose cannot be pursued by means that broadly stifle fundamental personal liberties when the end can be more narrowly achieved." *Shelton v. Tucker,* 364 U.S. 479, 488 (1960). As previously indicated, the plaintiffs and intervenor do not question the power of the State to prohibit strikes against the public interest.

What we have said thus far supports our ultimate conclusion: that the firemen of the City of Charlotte are granted the right of free association by the First and Fourteenth Amendments of the United States Constitution; that that right of association includes the right to form and join a labor union — whether local or national; that membership in such a labor organization will confer upon the firemen no immunity from proper state regulation to protect valid state interests which are, in this case, the protection of property and life from destruction by fire. We think such a conclusion flows inevitably from the enunciations of the United States Supreme Court set out above. Our decision is consistent with that of the Seventh Circuit according the same right to teachers. *McLaughlin v. Tilendis,* 398 F.2d 287 (7th Cir. 1968). We do not think the *McLaughlin* decision is distinguishable on the asserted ground that the State in that case had not undertaken to prohibit membership in a teachers' labor union. The court's recitation that there was no such state legislation went to the question of whether there was a valid state interest. It held that there was no such state interest, and that the right of a teacher to join a labor union rested upon the First Amendment to the United States Constitution. In our case, we hold that the valid state interest may be served by more narrowly drawn legislation so as not to infringe the First Amendment.

We find nothing unconstitutional in G.S. § 95-98. It simply voids contracts between units of government within North Carolina and labor unions and expresses the public policy of North Carolina to be against such collective bargaining contracts. There is nothing in the United States Constitution which entitles one to have a contract with another who does not want it. It is but a step further to hold that the state may lawfully forbid such contracts with its instrumentalities. The solution, if there be one, from the viewpoint of the firemen, is that labor unions may someday persuade state government of the asserted value of collective bargaining agreements, but this is a political matter and does not yield to judicial solution. The right to a collective bargaining agreement, so firmly entrenched in American labor-management relations, rests upon national legislation and not upon the federal Constitution. The State is within the powers reserved to it to refuse to enter into such agreements and so to declare by statute....

Finally, we are asked to enjoin the defendants from enforcing these statutes now adjudged to be unconstitutional, *viz.*, N.C.G.S. § 95-97 and § 95-99. We decline to do so. There has not been the slightest intimation that our decision adjudging these statutes invalid will be ignored by the City of Charlotte or by any of the other defendants. If our decision should be thought wrong, we may properly assume it will be appealed — not ignored. There is no evidence that the solicitor of the district has sought indictments against any firemen or that he intends doing so. We adhere to the philosophy of federalism and think it unseeming that a federal court should issue its injunctive process against state or local officers except in situations of the most compelling necessity. Entry of a declaratory judgment decreeing G.S. § 95-97 and § 95-99 invalid because in violation of the First and Fourteenth Amendments of the United States Constitution seems to us, on the facts of this case, a fully sufficient remedy.

Declaratory judgment granted. Injunction denied.

ADDENDUM: The Eighth Circuit has decided that public employees have a right, grounded in the Constitution, to join a labor union, in the absence of a "paramount public interest of the State of Nebraska or the City of North Platte [which] warranted limiting the plaintiffs' right to freedom of association." See *American Federation of State, County, and Municipal Employees v. Woodward*, 406 F.2d 137 (8th Cir. Jan. 17, 1969) (Jan. 28, 1969).

NOTES

1. Prior to the decision in *McLaughlin v. Tilendis*, 398 F.2d 298 (7th Cir. 1968), a case relied on by the court in *Atkins*, the courts had generally upheld regulations or ordinances which prohibited public employees from joining labor organizations. For example, in *Perez v. Board of Police Comm'rs*, 78 Cal. App. 638, 178 P.2d 537 (1947), the court upheld a regulation prohibiting police officers from becoming members of any organization identified with "any trade association, federation or labor union which admits to membership persons who are not members of the Los Angeles Police Department, or whose membership is not exclusively made up of employees of city of Los Angeles." Accord *AFSCME Local 201 v. City of Muskegon,* 369 Mich. 384, 120 N.W.2d 197, *cert. denied,* 375 U.S. 833 (1963); *King v. Priest,* 357 Mo. 68, 206 S.W.2d 547 (1947), *appeal dismissed,* 333 U.S. 852 (1948).

2. Must a public employee first exhaust whatever state *judicial* remedies may exist before maintaining a suit in federal court under the Civil Rights Act of 1871? The courts have held that "exhaustion of state *judicial* remedies is not a prerequisite to the invocation of federal relief under Section 1983 since the cause of action established by that statute is fully supplementary to any remedy, adequate or inadequate, that might exist under state law." *Hobbs v. Thompson,* 448 F.2d 456 (5th Cir. 1971).

3. Most of the comprehensive state public employee labor relations statutes specifically provide that it is an unfair labor practice for a public employer to discriminate against a public employee because of his union activities. Most of these statutes further establish a public employee relations agency to hear complaints of alleged unfair labor practices and authorize the agency to issue orders remedying any unfair labor practices that are found to exist. Where such a state *administrative* remedy exists, should the employee be required to exhaust this remedy before seeking relief in the federal courts under the Civil Rights Act of 1871?

In *Patsy v. Board of Regents,* 457 U.S. 496, 102 S. Ct. 2557, 73 L. Ed. 2d 172 (1982), the Supreme Court in a 7-2 decision held that in Section 1983 suits there is no requirement that state administrative remedies be exhausted. The Court observed that its prior decisions had "stated categorically that exhaustion is not a prerequisite to an action under § 1983." The Court held that these prior decisions were in accord with the tenor of the legislative debate over the predecessor to Section 1983 and that this legislative history supported its "conclusion that exhaustion of administrative remedies in § 1983 actions should not be judicially imposed." The Court observed that the question whether exhaustion of state administrative remedies should be required in some or all Section 1983 suits should be addressed to Congress.

Does the result in *Patsy* make sense in the labor relations context, where the public employee's right to join and form unions is affirmatively protected and where the state provides an administrative remedy to protect such right? Should exhaustion be required where such an administrative remedy exists and the inquiry is essentially factual in nature, involving, e.g., whether a public employer unlawfully discriminated against the public employee because of his or her union activities?

4. While most Section 1983 lawsuits are instituted in federal court, state courts have concurrent jurisdiction. Where a plaintiff files a Section 1983 lawsuit in state court, is there any requirement that the plaintiff exhaust any state administrative remedies that may be available? In *Givney v. Toledo Bd. of Educ.,* 40 Ohio St. 3d 152, 532 N.E.2d 1300 (1988), the Ohio Supreme Court held that plaintiffs were not required to exhaust the administrative remedies contained in the Ohio collective bargaining law as a prerequisite to filing suit under Section 1983 to challenge the constitutionality of fair share fees. Relying on the Supreme Court's decision in *Felder v. Casey,* 108 S. Ct. 2302 (1988), the court stated that it was its "view that the Supreme Court has rejected the use of exhaustion requirements in state-court Section 1983 actions unless Congress has provided otherwise." The Court noted that if it imposed "an exhaustion requirement on those filing Section 1983 actions in ... state courts,... [it] would be forcing such civil rights victims to comply with a requirement that is entirely absent from civil rights litigation of this sort in federal courts."

5. Although a plaintiff in a Section 1983 suit cannot be required to exhaust state administrative remedies, can a court in a Section 1983 case abstain from making a decision based on a determination that a state administrative proceeding might eliminate or significantly alter the constitutional issues that the federal court would otherwise have to address? In *Jordi v. Sauk Prairie Sch. Bd.,* 651 F. Supp. 1566 (W.D. Wis. 1987), the court held that abstention in such circumstances was appropriate, noting:

> The doctrines of exhaustion and abstention are distinct. Exhaustion is the requirement that a litigant avail himself of all available state remedies before filing in federal; it is a prerequisite to federal subject matter jurisdiction in certain kinds of cases. In contrast, abstention involves the question of whether a federal court that has subject matter jurisdiction should decline to exercise it. The lack of an exhaustion requirement in civil rights cases is not relevant to the question whether this court should exercise its jurisdiction or abstain from doing so. The fact that civil rights are involved does not mean that abstention is necessarily inappropriate.

Based on the foregoing, the court abstained from ruling on a Section 1983 suit challenging the constitutionality of fair share agreements in view of "the Wisconsin Employment Relations Commission's efforts to establish a coherent Wisconsin policy concerning fair share agreements in a public school context...."

6. If a public employee, whether required to or not, exhausts his or her state administrative remedy and a decision is issued finding that his or her right to engage in union activity was not unlawfully interfered with, may the employee subsequently relitigate the same matter in a suit in federal court? In *Migra v. Warren City Sch. Dist. Bd. of Educ.,* 465 U.S. 75, 104 S. Ct. 892, 79 L. Ed. 2d 56 (1984), the Supreme Court held that a state court judgment precluded a subsequent lawsuit under Section 1983 with respect to issues that were litigated or could have been litigated in the state court proceeding. The Court ruled "that petitioner's state-court judgment in this litigation has the same preclusive effect in federal court that the judgment would have in the Ohio state courts." Two years later, in *University of Tenn. v. Elliot,* 478 U.S. 788, 106 S. Ct. 3220, 92 L. Ed. 2d 635 (1986), the Supreme Court gave preclusive effect to factfinding by a state administrative tribunal in a subsequent Section 1983 lawsuit.

However, in *McDonald v. City of West Branch,* 466 U.S. 284, 104 S. Ct. 1799, 80 L. Ed. 2d 302 (1984), the Supreme Court held that an arbitration award rendered pursuant to the terms of a collective bargaining agreement which upheld the termination of a city police officer did not have a res judicata or collateral estoppel effect on the officer's right to institute a subsequent lawsuit under Section 1983. The Court observed that while "arbitration is well suited to resolving contractual disputes, ... it cannot provide an adequate substitute for a judicial proceeding in protecting the federal statutory and constitutional rights that § 1983 is designed to safeguard." The Court did note that "an arbitral decision may be admitted as evidence in a § 1983 action."

7. The Civil Rights Attorney's Fees Award Act of 1976, 42 U.S.C. § 1988 (1981), provides that, *inter alia,* in any action under 42 U.S.C. §§ 1981, 1982, 1983, 1985, and 1986, "the court, in its discretion, may allow the prevailing party, other than the United States, a reasonable attorney's fee as part of the costs." In *Bond v. Stanton*, 555 F.2d 172, 174 (7th Cir. 1977), *cert. denied*, 98 S. Ct. 3146 (1978), the court held that this act was intended by Congress "to apply to actions against state officials in their official capacity" and that the imposition of liability for attorneys' fees on state officials acting in their official capacity was constitutional, notwithstanding the eleventh amendment. See *Garrison v. Hickey*, 464 F. Supp. 276 (E.D. Ark. 1979) (reasonable attorney's fee awarded where court found that a firefighter had been improperly discharged due to his union activity).

In *Texas State Teachers Ass'n v. Garland Indep. Sch. Dist.*, 109 S. Ct. 1486 (1989), the Supreme Court held that a litigant need not prevail on the "central issue" in a Section 1983 case in order to be considered a "prevailing party" for the purpose of obtaining attorney's fees under 42 U.S.C. § 1988, but need only succeed on "any significant issue" that materially alters the legal relationship between the parties. The Court reasoned as follows:

> The touchstone of the prevailing party inquiry must be the material alteration of the legal relationship of the parties in a manner which Congress sought to promote in the fee statute. Where such a change has occurred, the degree of the plaintiff's overall success goes to the reasonableness of the award under *Hensley*, not the availability of a fee award *vel non*.

On the other hand, "[w]here the plaintiff's success on a legal claim can be characterized as purely technical or *de minimis*, a district court would be justified in concluding that even the 'generous formulation' we adopt today has not been satisfied."

8. In *Board of Regents v. Tomanio*, 446 U.S. 478, 100 S. Ct. 1790, 64 L. Ed. 2d 440 (1980), the Supreme Court held that the applicable state statute of limitations and the state tolling rules govern actions brought under 42 U.S.C. § 1983. Subsequently, in *Chardon v. Soto*, 462 U.S. 650, 103 S. Ct. 2610, 77 L. Ed. 2d 74 (1983), the Supreme Court held that state law governed with respect to whether a state statute of limitations was tolled during the period a class action was pending. The Court stated that "[u]ntil Congress enacts a federal statute of limitations to govern § 1983 litigation ... federal courts must continue the practice of 'limitations borrowing' outlined in *Tomanio*." And, in *Burnett v. Grattan*, 468 U.S. 42, 104 S. Ct. 2924, 82 L. Ed. 2d 36 (1984), the Court held that it was inappropriate to borrow the limitations period from an administrative employment discrimination statute in view of the practical differences between litigation and an administrative proceeding, and the divergence in the objectives of the federal cause of action and the state administrative procedure. The Court observed "that borrowing an administrative statute of limitations ignores the dominant characteristics of civil rights actions; they belong in court." The Court held that the appropriate state limitations period to be borrowed "must be responsive to [the] characteristics of litigation under the federal [civil rights] statutes."

In *Wilson v. Garcia*, 471 U.S. 261, 105 S. Ct. 1938, 85 L. Ed. 2d 254 (1985), the Supreme Court held that a state's personal injury statute of limitations should be applied to all Section 1983 claims, because Section 1983 claims "are best characterized as personal injury actions." But what is the appropriate state statute of limitations to borrow for lawsuits instituted under Section 1983 where the state in which the action arose has multiple statutes of limitations for personal injury actions? In *Owens v. Okure*, 109 S. Ct. 573 (1989), the Supreme Court said that its task was "to provide courts with a rule for determining the appropriate personal injury limitation statute that can be applied with ease and predictability in all 50 states." Accordingly, it held that the residual or general personal injury statute of limitations should be used, noting that "[i]n marked contrast to the multiplicity of state intentional tort statutes of limitation, every State has one general or residual statute of limitations governing personal injury actions."

9. If it is determined that a public employee has been unlawfully discharged because of his or her union activities and reinstatement with backpay is ordered, is the public employer liable for the backpay or is this the responsibility of the public official or officials who discharged the employee in question? In *Monell v. Department of Social Servs.*, 436 U.S. 658, 98 S. Ct. 2018, 56 L. Ed. 2d 611 (1978), the Supreme Court, reversing *Monroe v. Pape*, 365 U.S. 167, 81 S. Ct. 473, 5 L. Ed. 2d 492 (1961), held that municipalities, including school boards, were "persons" for the purposes of Section 1983. While the court held that "a local government may not be sued for an injury inflicted solely by its employees or agents," it held that such a government may be sued for monetary, declaratory, and injunctive relief under Section 1983 "when execution of a government's policy or custom, whether made by its lawmakers or by those whose edicts or acts may fairly be said to represent official policy, inflicts the injury."

In *Smith v. Wade*, 461 U.S. 30, 103 S. Ct. 1625, 75 L. Ed. 2d 632 (1983), the Supreme Court held that in an action under Section 1983 punitive damages may be assessed against public officials when their "conduct is shown to be motivated by evil motive or intent, or when it involves reckless or callous indifference to the federally protected rights of others."

10. Does a union have standing to bring an action under Section 1983 alleging that a public employer interfered with the constitutional right of public employees to join or become members of the union? In *Elk Grove Firefighters Local No. 2340 v. Willis*, 391 F. Supp. 487 (N.D. Ill. 1975), the court held that a union had standing to sue under Section 1983, in both its representative and individual capacity. Accord *SEIU v. County of Butler*, 306 F. Supp. 1080 (W.D. Pa. 1969). Contra *Lontine v. VanCleave*, 80 L.R.R.M. 3240 (D. Colo. 1972), *aff'd on other grounds*, 483 F.2d 966 (10th Cir. 1973).

VICKSBURG FIREFIGHTERS ASSOCIATION, LOCAL 1686 v. CITY OF VICKSBURG

761 F.2d 1036 (5th Cir. 1985)

Before RUBIN, RANDALL and HIGGINBOTHAM, CIRCUIT JUDGES.

RANDALL, CIRCUIT JUDGE:

In this civil rights case, plaintiffs seek, *inter alia*, to enjoin the City of Vicksburg, Mississippi, from giving force and effect to a municipal resolution prohibiting captains of the Vicksburg Fire Department from belonging to a union or labor organization having in its membership rank-and-file firefighters of that department. The district court refused to issue the injunction on the ground that captains in the Vicksburg Fire Department are supervisors with interests adverse to those of the lesser-ranked firefighters and that therefore, the prohibition against membership in a union representing the rank and file was a valid limitation on the exercise of the captains' first amendment rights. Finding ourselves in substantial agreement with the district court, we affirm.

I.

The Vicksburg Firefighters Association, Local 1686 is a voluntary unincorporated labor organization affiliated with the International Association of Firefighters, AFL-CIO, CLC. While the membership of Local 1686 is comprised mostly of firefighters holding the rank of private or lieutenant, since the organization's inception captains in the Vicksburg Fire Department have been allowed to join and become officers. The purpose of Local 1686 is to assist its members to work collectively for their mutual benefit and protection and to engage in legislative lobbying activities to promote the employment-related interests of its members. In addition, Local 1686 over the years has held fire safety programs for the citizens of Vicksburg, sponsored training programs for its members to enhance fire safety and performance, and raised funds for the Muscular Dystrophy Association and the Mississippi Burn Center. The City of Vicksburg is under no obligation to recognize Local 1686 as a collective bargaining representative[1] and has not done so. Nor has the City signed a collective bargaining agreement with any other organization of firefighters or even engaged in any collective bargaining with its firefighters.

It is undisputed that the Vicksburg Fire Department has generally functioned well and has enjoyed good relations between superior officers and their subordinates. Since the creation of Local 1686 in 1967, there have been no strikes or work stoppages. In September of 1978 and September of 1980, however, off-duty members of Local 1686 engaged in informational picketing in an effort to gain public support for a wage increase. Approximately ten captains were members of Local 1686 at the time of the picketing.

On April 19, 1982, the Mayor and Board of Aldermen of the City of Vicksburg adopted the following resolution:

> WHEREAS, it has come to the attention of the Mayor and Board of Aldermen that some of the captains in the City Fire Department are members of Local 1686, International Association of Firefighters, AFL-CIO and CIC; and
>
> WHEREAS, the captains in the Fire Department are in supervisory positions and exercise supervision over the other members of the Fire Department at various stations and on various shifts; and,
>
> WHEREAS, under the National Labor Relations Act, employers are not compelled to regard supervisiors as employees for purposes of collective bargaining, and under the Taft-Hartly Act, a policy is expressed that supervisory membership in rank and file unions is inimical to efficiency; and,
>
> WHEREAS, although the National Labor Relations Act and the Taft-Hartley Act do not apply to public employers, the Mayor and Board of Aldermen believe that the policies established by these Acts are the proper policies for the City to follow and believes [sic] that captains by virtue of their supervisory responsibilities, should have complete and undivided loyalty to the Fire Department and, therefore, should not be members of a union or labor organization having as members those fire fighters whom said captains are employed to supervise.

---

[1]See generally *Smith v. Arkansas State Highway Employees, Local 1315,* 441 U.S. 463, 99 S. Ct. 1826, 60 L. Ed. 2d 360 (1979) (government has no constitutional duty to bargain collectively with an exclusive bargaining agent).

NOW, THEREFORE, BE IT RESOLVED by the Mayor and Board of Aldermen of the City of Vicksburg, that it is hereby accepted as the policy of said City that individuals occupying the position of captain in the Vicksburg Fire Department will not be permitted to belong to a union or labor organization having as members rank and file fire fighters of the Vicksburg Fire Department.

Under the resolution, in order to retain their present rank, thirteen captains of the Vicksburg Fire Department who belonged to Local 1686 were required to resign from that organization. The resolution, however, did not prohibit membership in the union by lesser-grade firefighters or preclude captains from joining any labor organization whose membership did not consist of rank-and-file firefighters of the Vicksburg Fire Department.

Following adoption of the resolution, the plaintiffs—consisting of Local 1686, firefighters in the Vicksburg Fire Department holding the rank of captain, and lieutenants who have passed their captain examinations but have not yet been promoted—filed the instant action in the District Court for the Southern District of Mississippi pursuant to 42 U.S.C. §§ 1983 and 1985. Asserting that the resolution unconstitutionally infringed on first amendment and due process rights, the plaintiffs sought declaratory and injunctive relief as well as damages against the City of Vicksburg, its Mayor, and its Board of Aldermen. The district court ordered the resolution held in abeyance pending disposition of the case, and, after a two-day trial, upheld the resolution as a legitimate restriction on constitutional rights. Judgment was entered accordingly, and this appeal followed.

II.

There can be no doubt that the City of Vicksburg's resolution forbidding captains from belonging to labor organizations comprised of rank-and-file firefighters implicates important first amendment protections. The first amendment's freedom of association provides both public and private employees the right to organize, solicit members for, and belong to labor unions. See *Smith v. Arkansas State Highway Employees, Local 1315,* 441 U.S. 463, 464-66, 99 S. Ct. 1826, 1827-28, 60 L. Ed. 2d 360 (1979); *Thomas v. Collins,* 323 U.S. 516, 532, 65 S. Ct. 315, 319, 89 L. Ed. 430 (1945). These rights, however, are not absolute, especially with respect to public employees. While the government cannot condition public employment on the relinquishing of first amendment protection, *Perry v. Sindermann,* 408 U.S. 593, 596-98, 92 S. Ct. 2694, 2696-98, 33 L. Ed. 2d 570 (1972); *Keyishian v. Board of Regents,* 385 U.S. 589, 605, 87 S. Ct. 675, 685, 17 L. Ed. 2d 629 (1967), the government has legitimate interests as an employer in regulating the first amendment conduct of its employees that differ significantly from those it possesses in connection with the population in general. See *Connick v. Myers,* 461 U.S. 138, 140, 103 S. Ct. 1684, 1686, 75 L. Ed. 2d 708 (1983); *Pickering v. Board of Education,* 391 U.S. 563, 568, 88 S. Ct. 1731, 1734, 20 L. Ed. 2d 811 (1968). "The problem is to balance the rights of the employees as citizens against the interests of the state in promoting efficient public service." *Battle v. Mulholland,* 439 F.2d 321, 324 (5th Cir. 1971); see also *McBee v. Jim Hogg County,* 730 F.2d 1009 (5th Cir. 1984) (en banc); *Bickel v. Burkhart,* 632 F.2d 1251, 1256 (5th Cir. 1980). In order for an intrusion on associational rights to withstand judicial scrutiny, the government must show that the regulation serves a legitimate and substantial government interest and that the means employed are the least drastic restriction of constitutional rights. *Elrod v. Burns,* 427 U.S. 347, 363, 96 S. Ct. 2673, 2684, 49 L. Ed. 2d 547 (1976); *Shelton v. Tucker,* 364 U.S. 479, 488, 81 S. Ct. 247, 252, 5 L. Ed. 2d 231 (1960); see generally *Developments in the Law—Public Employment,* 97 Harv. L. Rev. 1611, 1678 (1984).

In holding that the City of Vicksburg's resolution was a legitimate limitation on the exercise of first amendment rights, the district court relied heavily on the case of *Local 2263, International Ass'n. of Fire Fighters v. City of Tupelo,* 439 F. Supp. 1224 (N.D. Miss. 1977). *Tupelo* as well as two other cases—*York County Fire Fighters Ass'n., Local 2498 v. County of York,* 589 F.2d 775 (4th Cir. 1978), and *Elk Grove Firefighters Local 2340 v. Willis,* 400 F. Supp. 1097 (N.D. Ill. 1975), aff'd mem., 539 F.2d 714 (7th Cir. 1976)—concerned the constitutionality of municipal resolutions that were substantially identical to the one at bar.[3] We think these cases were correctly decided and accordingly adopt their reasoning. We hold that prohibiting firefighters properly characterized as supervisors from belonging to labor organizations composed of the rank and file serves a legitimate and substantial government interest in maintaining efficient and dependable firefighting services. "Management, like labor, must have faithful agents." *Beasley v. Food Fair of North Carolina, Inc.,* 416 U.S. 653, 660, 94 S. Ct. 2023, 2027, 40 L. Ed. 2d 443 (1974) (quoting H.R. Rep. No. 245, 80th Cong., 1st Sess. 16 (1974)). An identity of interests on the part of supervisors with the rank and file poses a significant threat that the loyalties of the supervisors will be divided and that consequently the discipline and effectiveness of the fire department will be impaired. Indeed, it is not difficult to imagine numerous instances in which the interests of the supervisors and those of the union would come into direct conflict, such as when the department determines that overtime is necessary to ensure the provision of effective fire protection services or when the union orders a picket, a work slow down, or a strike. In these cases, the supervisor cannot fulfill his obligation to both the city and the union, and the city's determination to spare itself the uncertain and perhaps dire consequences to persons and property of such a conflict of interest cannot be said to be constitutionally infirm. Cf. *Connick v. Myers, supra,* at 152, 103 S. Ct. at 1692 ("[W]e do not see the necessity for an employer to allow events to unfold to the extent that the disruption of the office and the destruction of working relationships is manifest before taking action.").[4]

---

[3]See also *Key v. Rutherford,* 645 F.2d 880, 885 (105h Cir. 1981) (remand for determination whether police chief's membership in "fraternal" organization conflicts with city's interest in an efficient police department); *Norbeck v. Davenport Community School Dist.,* 545 F.2d 63, 68 (8th Cir. 1976) (holding that school district had legitimate interest in preventing school principal from being a bargaining agent for an association of teachers).

[4]Our conclusion that government has a legitimate and substantial interest in prohibiting supervisors from joining a union composed of rank-and-file firefighters is bolstered by § 14(a) of the Labor Management Relations Act (LMRA), 29 U.S.C. § 164(a), which excludes supervisors from the protection afforded rank-and-file employees under the National Labor Relations Act. The purpose of § 14(a) is "to assure management of the undivided loyalty of its supervisory personnel by making sure that no employer would have to retain as its agent one who is obligated to the union." *NLRB v. Southern Plasma Corp.,* 626 F.2d 1287, 1299 (5th Cir. 1980); see also *Florida Power & Light v. International Bhd. of Elec. Workers, Local 641,* 417 U.S. 790, 808, 94 S. Ct. 2737, 2746, 41 L. Ed.

The plaintiff's do not appear to disagree with the basic proposition that governement is entitled to the undivided allegiance of its supervisory personnel. Rather, they argue that for more specific reasons barring captains of the Vicksburg Fire Department from holding membership in a union representing rank-and-file firefighters does not significantly advance this government interest. First, the plaintiffs contend that, because the City of Vicksburg refuses to recognize Local 1686 or any other labor organization as the collective bargaining agent for the rank-and-file firefighters, the opportunity for conflict to arise between the needs of the City and the interests of the union is substantially reduced. Any remaining fear of conflict, the plaintiffs argue further, has been fully allayed by Local 1686's pledge that no captain will ever engage in a strike or work stoppage or hold union office if to do so would be inconsistent with the needs of the department. This argument is unpersuasive. Although Local 1686 is not the recognized agent for the employees, the union is still able to take an active role in promoting the employment-related interests of the rank and file, as the informational picketing conducted by union members in 1978 and 1980 demonstrates. Consequently, as the Fourth Circuit observed, "membership by supervisory personnel in a union to which the rank and file fire fighter also belongs has substantially the same potential disruptive effect, irrespective of whether the employer has statutory authority to bargain with the union or not." *York County Fire Fighters, supra,* at 778. Similarly, the pledge of the union, even if effective, would hardly be sufficient to dissipate the identity of interests union membership would foster between supervisors and the rank and file or guarantee to the City that discipline and efficiency in providing fire protection services will not be affected.

We also reject the plaintiff's second contention that the resolution cuts too broad a swath through constitutionally protected freedoms. As noted above, under the resolution, captains of the Vicksburg Fire Department are only prohibited from belonging to those unions that have rank-and-file firefighters in their membership. Captains therefore are not prevented from joining labor organizations whose membership does not consist of rank-and-file members of the Vicksburg Fire Department. In addition, while the resolution necessarily prevents captains from continuing to participate directly in the various charitable and professional activities conducted by the rank-and-file unions, captains are not precluded from engaging in such activities either on their own or through other unions. Moreover, nothing in the resolution would prevent a union comprised of captains and other persons not including rank-and-file firefighters from working on charitable or other projects, such as conducting safety programs for the public or raising funds for medical research, in conjunction with the unions representing rank-and-file firefighters. For these reasons, we find the proscription on union activities, limited as it is, to be narrowly tailored to achieve the City of Vicksburg's legitimate ends. See *Tupelo, supra,* at 1231-32; *Elk Grove, supra,* at 1103.

Finally, the plaintiffs argue at great length that captains of the Vicksburg Fire Department are not properly characterized as "supervisors," but are rather

---

2d 477 (1974). The LMRA reflects a congressional judgment that the unionizing of supervisors threatens the overlapping goals of increasing productivity and promoting labor peace. *Beasley, supra,* at 661, 94 S. Ct. at 2028.

"crew leaders" who possess no actual supervisory authority. Consequently, it is contended, irrespective of the City's ability to restrict the union affiliations of higher-ranking officers of the Vicksburg Fire Department, the resolution's intrusion on the associational rights of captains does not effectively serve any legitimate government interest and is violative of the first amendment.

In concluding that captains of the Vicksburg Fire Department were supervisors, the district court relied heavily on the definition of that term in section 2(11) of the National Labor Relations Act, as amended, which provides:

> The term "supervisor" means any individual having authority, in the interest of the employer, to hire, transfer, suspend, lay off, recall, promote, discharge, assign, reward, or discipline other employees, or responsibly to direct them, or to adjust their grievances, or effectively to recommend such action, if in connection with the foregoing the exercise of such authority is not of a merely routine or clerical nature, but requires the use of independent judgment.

29 U.S.C. § 152(11). The functions of a supervisor listed in the statute are disjunctive; it need not be shown that an employee performed all or several of the functions to support a finding of supervisory status. *NLRB v. Dadco Fashions, Inc.,* 632 F.2d 493, 496 (5th Cir. 1980); *Sweeney & Co. v. NLRB,* 437 F.2d 1127, 1131 (5th Cir. 1971).

While the foregoing provision of the Act is of course not directly applicable in the public employment context, we agree with the district court that its definition of the term "supervisor" is a helpful guide in determining whether captains engage in the type of activity that would render their interests sufficiently adverse to those of the rank and file to warrant the prohibition against joining a common union. Certainly, if an employee regularly performs one of the functions delineated in the statute and, in so doing, exercises independent judgment in the interests of management, membership in a union comprised of the rank and file would result in a real possibility of a conflict of interest that would be inimical to efficient fire protection. Because the district court's conclusion that captains in the Vicksburg Fire Department qualify as supervisiors under section 2(11) is a finding of fact, we review it under the clearly erroneous standard of Federal Rule of Civil Procedure 52(a). Under this standard, the district court's decision cannot be reversed unless a review of the entire evidence leaves us "'with the definite and firm conviction that a mistake has been committed.'"...

The record reveals the following. In the Vicksburg Fire Department's chain of command, thirteen captains are superior officers to fifty-nine subordinates of whom fourteen are lieutenants and forty-five are privates. Captains in turn are subordinate to five assistant chiefs, who themselves are under the command of a deputy chief and the fire chief. Captains work directly with lieutenants and privates at each of the firehouses and in actually fighting fires. On fire runs outside city limits, although radio contact with the central station is maintained, the captain is usually solely in charge of the fire situation from the time the report of a fire is called into the station until the fire is extinguished. Upon arrival at the fire, the captain makes all determinations and decisions regarding the type of fire, whether inflammables are involved, appropriate safety-and-rescue measures, methods of extinguishment, and whether additional firefighting equipment and personnel are needed to assist. With respect to fires within city limits, the captain is in charge of the fire until the assistant chief arrives. Even then, however, the authority of the captain is not diminished; he continues to make decisions, working and placing subordinate personnel in positions appropriate to combatting fires. While not on fire runs, the captain is generally responsible for the cleanliness of his station and for the apparatus, tools, and other equipment stored therein. The captain also delegates station maintenance duties. Although the captain has no authority to hire, transfer, promote, discharge, or reward employees directly responsible to him, the captain is authorized to evaluate and file reports on subordinate personnel performance and to reprimand subordinate personnel in the absence of superior officers. In addition, the captain can temporarily suspend a lieutenant or a private for such infractions of the rules as intoxication or fighting. Upon return of the suspended employee, the captain recommends to his superior whether further suspension is necessary. All recommendations by the captain are subject to independent review.

While the question is a close one, based on the foregoing, the district court's finding that captains in the Vicksburg Fire Department engage in supervisory activities and do so in the interests of management is not clearly erroneous. The authority of the captain to suspend subordinates, albeit temporarily, and issue reprimands indicates that they perform a distinct disciplinary function over the rank-and-file firefighters in the department. Moreover, especially on fire runs outside city limits, the responsibility of the captain often is equivalent to that of the assistant chief. The district court could have reasonably determined that at these times, rather than being a mere conduit for management directives, the captain possesses plenary control over the activities of the other firefighters and must exercise independent judgment in the direction of firefighting operations. We think that sufficient evidence exists to support the court's findings and therefore uphold the determination that captains in the Vicksburg Fire Department were properly characterized as supervisors. We conclude that the City of Vicksburg's resolution was constitutionally adopted in furtherance of its legitimate concern over maintaining an effective and efficient fire department.

III.

Because the City of Vicksburg's resolution does not impermissibly intrude upon first amendment freedoms, the judgment of the district court is affirmed.

Affirmed.

NOTES

1. In *Wilton v. Mayor & City Council of Baltimore,* 772 F.2d 88 (4th Cir. 1985), the Fourth Circuit held that an employer's interest in assuring the undivided loyalty of its supervisors justified its delay in promoting two union activists to supervisory positions. Referring to the Fourth Circuit's earlier decision in *York Cty. Firefighters Ass'n v. County of York,* the Fourth Circuit stated:

> *York County Firefighters* authorizes a government employer not only to ask of managerial candidates but also to answer for them the question that sparks such controversy at the Wilton and Sullivan interviews, "Can you effectively

wear two hats, that of a supervisor and a union representative?" The fact that this concern may have been bluntly or colloquially communicated to Wilton and Sullivan does not change the result. Nor can the bitterness of labor-management relations, though regrettable, logically diminish the legitimacy of concerns over supervisory loyalty.... In deciding that the applicants could not serve both masters [the employer] reached the same conclusion for Wilton and Sullivan that York County reached for its entire firefighting force. In both instances the government employer's attention to conflicting tugs of allegiance did not violate any constitutional rights that may be enjoyed by the employees.

2. In *State Mgt. Ass'n of Conn. v. O'Neill*, 204 Conn. 746, 529 A.2d 1276 (1987), the Connecticut Supreme Court upheld the constitutionality of a state law which denied managerial employees the right to union representation and the right to bargain collectively. In rejecting the plaintiff's contention that such a prohibition violated equal protection rights, the court held that the need for an employer to have loyal supervisors and managers who were independent from rank and file employees was rational, noting that "it is widely believed that this objective is equally applicable to and more important in the public sector."

3. The New Jersey Act states that unless "established practice, prior agreement, or special circumstances dictate the contrary, no policeman shall have the right to join an employee organization that admits employees other than policemen to membership." N.J. Stat. Ann. § 34:13A-5.3 (West Supp. 1968). Is this provision constitutional? Are there any legitimate reasons for restricting the kind of labor organization that police officers can join? In ABA Project on Standards for Criminal Justice, The Urban Police Function 171 (Tentative Draft, March 1972), the Advisory Committee on the Police Function made the following recommendations:

> The need to preserve local control over law enforcement and over the resolution of law enforcement policy issues requires that law enforcement policy not be influenced by a national police union.
> The maintenance of police in a position of objectivity in engaging in conflict resolution requires that police not belong to a union which also has non-police members who may become party to a labor dispute.

See also Illinois Governor's Advisory Commission on Labor-Management Policy for Public Employees 14 (March 1967).

Section 9(b)(3) of the NLRA provides that no unit shall be established if it includes any guard together with any other employees. Is this provision constitutional? In terms of a constitutional challenge, is there any difference between this provision and the provision contained in the New Jersey Act? *International Bhd. of Teamsters Local 344 v. NLRB*, 568 F.2d 12 (7th Cir. 1978) (NLRA prohibition against NLRB certifying unit of guards if the union seeking said representation admits to membership employees other than guards held constitutional).

In *Brennan v. Koch*, 564 F. Supp. 322 (S.D.N.Y. 1983), the court rejected a constitutional challenge to the following provision of the New York City collective bargaining law:

> No organization seeking or claiming to represent members of the police force of the police department shall be certified if such organization (i) admits to membership, or is affiliated directly or indirectly with an organization

which admits to membership, employees other than members of the police force of the department, or (ii) advocates the right to strike.

The court held that the city could properly "recognize and prevent the divided loyalties that could develop if police officers were called upon to police labor disputes involving labor groups with which they were affiliated." Moreover, the court noted that the city "must be allowed the freedom to legislate with respect to its own situation and cannot constitutionally be precluded from doing so merely because other legislators in other places may have made equally rational decisions to the contrary."

PERRY EDUCATION ASSOCIATION v. PERRY LOCAL EDUCATORS' ASSOCIATION

460 U.S. 37, 103 S. Ct. 948, 74 L. Ed. 2d 794 (1983)

JUSTICE WHITE delivered the opinion of the Court.

Perry Education Association is the duly elected exclusive bargaining representative for the teachers of the Metropolitan School District of Perry Township, Ind. A collective bargaining agreement with the Board of Education provided that Perry Education Association, but no other union, would have access to the interschool mail system and teacher mailboxes in the Perry Township schools. The issue in this case is whether the denial of similar access to the Perry Local Educators' Association, a rival teacher group, violates the First and Fourteenth Amendments.

I

The Metropolitan School District of Perry Township, Ind., operates a public school system of 13 separate schools. Each school building contains a set of mailboxes for the teachers. Interschool delivery by school employees permits messages to be delivered rapidly to teachers in the District.[1] The primary function of this internal mail system is to transmit official messages among the teachers and between the teachers and the school administration. In addition, teachers use the system to send personal messages and individual school building principals have allowed delivery of messages from various private organizations.[2]

Prior to 1977, both the Perry Education Association (PEA) and the Perry Local Educators' Association (PLEA) represented teachers in the school district and apparently had equal access to the interschool mail system. In 1977, PLEA challenged PEA's status as *de facto* bargaining representative for the Perry Township teachers by filing an election petition with the Indiana Education

---

[1] The United States Postal Service, in a submission as *amicus curiae,* suggests that the interschool delivery of material to teachers at various schools in the District violates the Private Express statutes, 18 U.S.C. §§ 1693-1699 and 39 U.S.C. §§ 601-606, which generally prohibit the carriage of letters over postal routes without payment of postage. We agree with the Postal Service that this question does not directly bear on the issues before the Court in this case. Accordingly, we express no opinion on whether the mail delivery practices involved here comply with the Private Express statutes or other Postal Service regulations.

[2] Local parochial schools, church groups, YMCA's, and Cub Scout units have used the system. The record does not indicate whether any requests for use have been denied, nor does it reveal whether permission must separately be sought for every message that a group wishes delivered to the teachers.

Employment Relations Board (Board). PEA won the election and was certified as the exclusive representative, as provided by Indiana law. Ind. Code § 20-7.5-1-2(l) (1982).

The Board permits a school district to provide access to communication facilities to the union selected for the discharge of the exclusive representative duties of representing the bargaining unit and its individual members without having to provide equal access to rival unions.[3] Following the election, PEA and the School District negotiated a labor contract in which the school board gave PEA "access to teachers' mailboxes in which to insert material" and the right to use the interschool mail delivery system to the extent that the School District incurred no extra expense by such use. The labor agreement noted that these access rights were being accorded to PEA "acting as the representative of the teachers" and went on to stipulate that these access rights shall not be granted to any other "school employee organization" — a term of art defined by Indiana law to mean "any organization which has school employees as members and one of whose primary purposes is representing school employees in dealing with their employer." The PEA contract with these provisions was renewed in 1980 and is presently in force.

The exclusive-access policy applies only to use of the mailboxes and school mail system. PLEA is not prevented from using other school facilities to communicate with teachers. PLEA may post notices on school bulletin boards; may hold meetings on school property after school hours; and may, with approval of the building principals, make announcements on the public address system. Of course, PLEA also may communicate with teachers by word of mouth, telephone, or the United States mail. Moreover, under Indiana law, the preferential access of the bargaining agent may continue only while its status as exclusive representative is insulated from challenge. Ind. Code § 20-7.5-1-10(c)(4) (1982). While a representation contest is in progress, unions must be afforded equal access to such communication facilities.

PLEA and two of its members filed this action under 42 U.S.C. § 1983 against PEA and individual members of the Perry Township School Board. Plaintiffs contended that PEA's preferential access to the internal mail system violates the First Amendment and the Equal Protection Clause of the Fourteenth Amendment. They sought injunctive and declaratory relief and damages. Upon cross-motions for summary judgment, the district court entered judgment for the defendants. *Perry Local Educators' Assn. v. Hohlt,* IP 79-189-C (SD Ind., Feb. 25, 1980).

The Court of Appeals for the Seventh Circuit reversed. *Perry Local Educators' Assn. v. Hohlt,* 652 F.2d 1286 (1981). The court held that once the School

---

[3] See *Perry Local Educators' Assn. v. Hohlt,* 652 F.2d 1286, 1291, and n. 13 (CA7 1981). It is an unfair labor practice under state law for a school employer to "dominate, interfere or assist in the formation or administration of any school employee organization or contribute financial or other support to it." Ind. Code § 20-7.5-1-7(a)(2) (1982). The Indiana Education Employment Relations Board has held that a school employer may exclude a minority union from organizational activities which take place on school property and may deny the rival union "nearly all organizational conveniences." *Pike Independent Professional Educators v. Metropolitan School Dist. of Pike Township,* No. U-76-16-5350 (Oct. 22, 1976) (holding that denying rival union use of a school building for meetings was not unfair labor practice, but that denying the union use of school bulletin boards was unfair labor practice).

District "opens its internal mail system to PEA but denies it to PLEA, it violates both the Equal Protection Clause and the First Amendment." *Id.*, at 1290. It acknowledged that PEA had "legal duties to the teachers that PLEA does not have" but reasoned that "[w]ithout an independent reason why equal access for other labor groups and individual teachers is undesirable, the special duties of the incumbent do not justify opening the system to the incumbent alone." *Id.*, at 1300....

... The constitutional issues presented are important and the decision below conflicts with the judgment of other federal and state courts. Therefore, regarding PEA's jurisdictional statement as a petition for a writ of certiorari, we grant certiorari.

III

The primary question presented is whether the First Amendment, applicable to the States by virtue of the Fourteenth Amendment, is violated when a union that has been elected by public school teachers as their exclusive bargaining representative is granted access to certain means of communication, while such access is denied to a rival union. There is no question that constitutional interests are implicated by denying PLEA use of the interschool mail system. "It can hardly be argued that either students or teachers shed their constitutional rights to freedom of speech or expression at the schoolhouse gate." *Tinker v. Des Moines School District,* 393 U.S. 503, 506 (1969); *Healy v. James,* 408 U.S. 169 (1972). The First Amendment's guarantee of free speech applies to teacher's mailboxes as surely as it does elsewhere within the school, *Tinker v. Des Moines School District, supra,* and on sidewalks outside, *Police Department of Chicago v. Mosley,* 408 U.S. 92 (1972). But this is not to say that the First Amendment requires equivalent access to all parts of a school building in which some form of communicative activity occurs. "[N]owhere [have we] suggested that students, teachers, or anyone else has an absolute constitutional right to use all parts of a school building or its immediate environs for ... unlimited expressive purposes." *Grayned v. City of Rockford,* 408 U.S. 104, 117-118 (1972). The existence of a right of access to public property and the standard by which limitations upon such a right must be evaluated differ depending on the character of the property at issue.

A

In places which by long tradition or by government fiat have been devoted to assembly and debate, the rights of the State to limit expressive activity are sharply circumscribed. At one end of the spectrum are streets and parks which "have immemorially been held in trust for the use of the public, and, time out of mind, have been used for purposes of assembly, communicating thoughts between citizens, and discussing public questions." *Hague v. C.I.O.,* 307 U.S. 496, 515 (1939). In these quintessential public forums, the government may not prohibit all communicative activity. For the State to enforce a content-based exclusion it must show that its regulation is necessary to serve a compelling state interest and that it is narrowly drawn to achieve that end. *Carey v. Brown,* 447 U.S. 455, 461 (1980). The State may also enforce regulations of the time, place, and manner of expression which are content-neutral, are narrowly tailored to serve a significant government interest, and leave open ample alternative channels of communication....

A second category consists of public property which the State has opened for use by the public as a place for expressive activity. The Constitution forbids a State to enforce certain exclusions from a forum generally open to the public even if it was not required to create the forum in the first place. Although a State is not required to indefinitely retain the open character of the facility, as long as it does so it is bound by the same standards as apply in a traditional public forum. Reasonable time, place, and manner regulations are permissible, and a content-based prohibition must be narrowly drawn to effectuate a compelling state interest. *Widmar v. Vincent, supra,* [454 U.S.,] at 269-270.

Public property which is not by tradition or designation a forum for public communication is governed by different standards. We have recognized that the "First Amendment does not guarantee access to property simply because it is owned or controlled by the government." *United States Postal Service v. Council of Greenburgh Civic Assns., supra,* [453 U.S.,] at 129. In addition to time, place, and manner regulations, the State may reserve the forum for its intended purposes, communicative or otherwise, as long as the regulation on speech is reasonable and not an effort to suppress expression merely because public officials oppose the speaker's view. 453 U.S., at 131, n. 7. As we have stated on several occasions, "[t]he State, no less than a private owner of property, has power to preserve the property under its control for the use to which it is lawfully dedicated." *Id.,* at 129-130; *Greer v. Spock,* 424 U.S. 828, 836 (1976); *Adderley v. Florida,* 385 U.S. 39, 48 (1966).

The school mail facilities at issue here fall within this third category. The Court of Appeals recognized that Perry School District's interschool mail system is not a traditional public forum: "We do not hold that a school's internal mail system is a public forum in the sense that a school board may not close it to all but official business if it chooses." 652 F.2d, at 1301. On this point the parties agree. Nor do the parties dispute that, as the District Court observed, the "normal and intended function [of the school mail facilities] is to facilitate internal communication of school related matters to teachers." *Perry Local Educators' Assn. v. Hohlt,* IP 79-189-C (SD Ind., Feb. 25, 1980), p. 4. The internal mail system, at least by policy, is not held open to the general public. It is instead PLEA's position that the school mail facilities have become a "limited public forum" from which it may not be excluded because of the periodic use of the system by private non-school-connected groups, and PLEA's own unrestricted access to the system prior to PEA's certification as exclusive representative.

Neither of these arguments is persuasive. The use of the internal school mail by groups not affiliated with the schools is no doubt a relevant consideration. If by policy or by practice the Perry School District has opened its mail system for indiscriminate use by the general public, then PLEA could justifiably argue a public forum has been created. This, however, is not the case. As the case comes before us, there is no indication in the record that the school mailboxes and interschool delivery system are open for use by the general public. Permission to use the system to communicate with teachers must be secured from the individual building principal. There is no court finding or evidence in the record which demonstrates that this permission has been granted as a matter of course to all who seek to distribute material. We can only conclude that the schools do allow some outside organizations such as the YMCA, Cub Scouts, and other civic and church organizations to use the facilities. This type of selective access does not transform government property into a public forum. In *Greer v. Spock, supra,* at 838, n. 10, the fact that other civilian speakers and entertainers had sometimes been invited to appear at Fort Dix did not convert the military base into a public forum. And in *Lehman v. Shaker Heights,* 418 U.S. 298 (1974) (opinion of BLACKMUN, J.), a plurality of the Court concluded that a city transit system's rental of space in its vehicles for commercial advertising did not require it to accept partisan political advertising.

Moreover, even if we assume that by granting access to the Cub Scouts, YMCA's, and parochial schools, the School District has created a "limited" public forum, the constitutional right of access would in any event extend only to other entities of similar character. While the school mail facilities thus might be a forum generally open for use by the Girl Scouts, the local boys' club and other organizations that engage in activities of interest and educational relevance to students, they would not as a consequence be open to an organization such as PLEA, which is concerned with the terms and conditions of teacher employment.

PLEA also points to its ability to use the school mailboxes and delivery system on an equal footing with PEA prior to the collective bargaining agreement signed in 1978. Its argument appears to be that the access policy in effect at that time converted the school mail facilities into a limited public forum generally open for use by employee organizations, and that once this occurred, exclusions of employee organizations thereafter must be judged by the constitutional standard applicable to public forums. The fallacy in the argument is that it is not the forum, but PLEA itself, which has changed. Prior to 1977, there was no exclusive representative for the Perry School District teachers. PEA and PLEA each represented its own members. Therefore the School District's policy of allowing both organizations to use the school mail facilities simply reflected the fact that both unions represented the teachers and had legitimate reasons for use of the system. PLEA's previous access was consistent with the School District's preservation of the facilities for school-related business, and did not constitute creation of a public forum in any broader sense.

Because the school mail system is not a public forum, the School District had no "constitutional obligation *per se* to let any organization use the school mail boxes." *Connecticut State Federation of Teachers v. Board of Ed. Members,* 538 F.2d 471, 481 (CA2 1976). In the Court of Appeals' view, however, the access policy adopted by the Perry schools favors a particular viewpoint, that of the PEA, on labor relations, and consequently must be strictly scrutinized regardless of whether a public forum is involved. There is, however, no indication that the School Board intended to discourage one viewpoint and advance another. We believe it is more accurate to characterize the access policy as based on the *status* of the respective unions rather than their views. Implicit in the concept of the nonpublic forum is the right to make distinctions in access on the basis of subject matter and speaker identity. These distinctions may be impermissible in a public forum but are inherent and inescapable in the process of limiting a nonpublic forum to activities compatible with the intended purpose of the property. The touchstone for evaluating these distinctions is whether they are reasonable in light of the purpose which the forum at issue serves.

B

The differential access provided PEA and PLEA is reasonable because it is wholly consistent with the district's legitimate interest in """"preserv[ing] the property ... for the use to which it is lawfully dedicated."""*United States Postal Service,* 453 U.S., at 129-130. Use of school mail facilities enables PEA to perform effectively its obligations as exclusive representative of *all* Perry Township teachers. Conversely, PLEA does not have any official responsibility in connection with the School District and need not be entitled to the same rights of access to school mailboxes. We observe that providing exclusive access to recognized bargaining representatives is a permissible labor practice in the public sector.[11] We have previously noted that the "designation of a union as exclusive representative carries with it great responsibilities. The tasks of negotiating and administering a collective-bargaining agreement and representing the interests of employees in settling disputes and processing grievances are continuing and difficult ones." *Abood v. Detroit Bd. of Ed.,* 431 U.S. 209, 221 (1977). Moreover, exclusion of the rival union may reasonably be considered a means of insuring labor peace within the schools. The policy "serves to prevent the District's schools from becoming a battlefield for inter-union squabbles."

The Court of Appeals accorded little or no weight to PEA's special responsibilities. In its view these responsibilities, while justifying PEA's access, did not justify denying equal access to PLEA. The Court of Appeals would have been correct if a public forum were involved here. But the internal mail system is not a public forum. As we have already stressed, when government property is not dedicated to open communication the government may — without further justification — restrict use to those who participate in the forum's official business.

Finally, the reasonableness of the limitations on PLEA's access to the school mail system is also supported by the substantial alternative channels that remain open for union-teacher communication to take place. These means range from bulletin boards to meeting facilities to the United States mail. During election periods, PLEA is assured of equal access to all modes of communication. There is no showing here that PLEA's ability to communicate with teachers is seriously impinged by the restricted access to the internal mail system. The variety and type of alternative modes of access present here compare favorably with those in other non-public forum cases where we have upheld restrictions on access.

---

[11]See, e.g., *Broward County School Board,* 6 FPER ¶ 11088 (Fla. PERC, 1980); *Union County Board of Education,* 2 NJPER 50 (N.J. PERC, 1976). Differentiation in access is also permitted in federal employment, and, indeed, it may be an unfair labor practice under 5 U.S.C. § 7116(a)(3) (1976) to grant access to internal communication facilities to unions other than the exclusive representative. That provision states that it shall be an unfair labor practice for an agency to "sponsor, control or otherwise assist any labor organization" aside from routine services provided other unions of "equivalent status." A number of administrative decisions construing this language as it earlier appeared in Executive Order 11491, § 19(a)(3), have taken this view. See, e.g., Dept. of the Army, Asst. Sec. Labor/Management Reports (A/SLMR) No. 654 (U.S. Dept. of Labor, 1976); Commissary, Fort Meade, Dept. of the Army, A/SLMR No. 793; (U.S. Dept. of Labor 1977); Dept. of the Air Force, Grissom Air Force Base, A/SLMR No. 852 (U.S. Dept. of Labor, 1977); Dept. of Transportation, Federal Aviation Administration, 2 FLRA No. 48 (1979)....

See, e.g., *Greer v. Spock*, 424 U.S., at 839 (servicemen free to attend political rallies off base); *Pell v. Procunier*, 417 U.S. 817, 827-828 (1974) (prison inmates may communicate with media by mail and through visitors).

IV

The Court of Appeals also held that the differential access provided the rival unions constituted impermissible content discrimination in violation of the Equal Protection Clause of the Fourteenth Amendment. We have rejected this contention when cast as a First Amendment argument, and it fares no better in equal protection garb. As we have explained above, PLEA did not have a First Amendment or other right of access to the interschool mail system. The grant of such access to PEA, therefore, does not burden a fundamental right of the PLEA. Thus, the decision to grant such privileges to the PEA need not be tested by the strict scrutiny applied when government action impinges upon a fundamental right protected by the Constitution. See *San Antonio Independent School District v. Rodriguez*, 411 U.S. 1, 17 (1973). The School District's policy need only rationally further a legitimate state purpose. That purpose is clearly found in the special responsibilities of an exclusive bargaining representative. See *supra*, at 51-52.

The Seventh Circuit and PLEA rely on *Police Department of Chicago v. Mosley*, 408 U.S. 92 (1972), and *Carey v. Brown*, 447 U.S. 455 (1980). In *Mosley* and *Carey*, we struck down prohibitions on peaceful picketing in a public forum. In *Mosley*, the City of Chicago permitted peaceful picketing on the subject of a school's labor-management dispute, but prohibited other picketing in the immediate vicinity of the school. In *Carey*, the challenged state statute barred all picketing of residences and dwellings except the peaceful picketing of a place of employment involved in a labor dispute. In both cases, we found the distinction between classes of speech violative of the Equal Protection Clause. The key to those decisions, however, was the presence of a public forum. In a public forum, by definition, all parties have a constitutional right of access and the state must demonstrate compelling reasons for restricting access to a single class of speakers, a single viewpoint, or a single subject.

When speakers and subjects are similarly situated, the State may not pick and choose. Conversely on government property that has not been made a public forum, not all speech is equally situated, and the State may draw distinctions which relate to the special purpose for which the property is used. As we have explained above, for a school mail facility, the difference in status between the exclusive bargaining representative and its rival is such a distinction.

V

The Court of Appeals invalidated the limited privileges PEA negotiated as the bargaining voice of the Perry Township teachers by misapplying our cases that have dealt with the rights of free expression on streets, parks, and other fora generally open for assembly and debate. Virtually every other court to consider this type of exclusive access policy has upheld it as constitutional and today, so do we. The judgment of the Court of Appeals is

Reversed.

JUSTICE BRENNAN, with whom JUSTICE MARSHALL, JUSTICE POWELL, and JUS-
TICE STEVENS join, dissenting.

The Court today holds that an incumbent teachers' union may negotiate a
collective-bargaining agreement with a school board that grants the incumbent
access to teachers' mailboxes and to the interschool mail system and denies such
access to a rival union. Because the exclusive access provision in the collective
bargaining agreement amounts to viewpoint discrimination that infringes the
respondents' First Amendment rights and fails to advance any substantial state
interest, I dissent.

I ....

The Court fundamentally misperceives the essence of the respondents' claims
and misunderstands the thrust of the Court of Appeals' well-reasoned opinion.
This case does not involve an "absolute access" claim. It involves an "equal
access" claim. As such it does not turn on whether the internal school mail
system is a "public forum." In focusing on the public forum issue, the Court
disregards the First Amendment's central proscription against censorship, in
the form of viewpoint discrimination, in any forum, public or nonpublic.

A ....

Once the government permits discussion of certain subject matter, it may not
impose restrictions that discriminate among viewpoints on those subjects
whether a nonpublic forum is involved or not. This prohibition is implicit in the
Mosley line of cases, in *Tinker v. Des Moines School District,* 393 U.S. 503
(1969), and in those cases in which we have approved content-based restrictions
on access to government property that is not a public forum. We have never
held that government may allow discussion of a subject and then discriminate
among viewpoints on that particular topic, even if the government for certain
reasons may entirely exclude discussion of the subject from the forum. In this
context, the greater power does not include the lesser because for First Amendment purposes exercise of the lesser power is more threatening to core values.
Viewpoint discrimination is censorship in its purest form and government regulation that discriminates among viewpoints threatens the continued vitality of
"free speech."

B

Against this background, it is clear that the Court's approach to this case is
flawed. By focusing on whether the interschool mail system is a public forum,
the Court disregards the independent First Amendment protection afforded by
the prohibition against viewpoint discrimination. This case does not involve a
claim of an absolute right of access to the forum to discuss any subject whatever.
If it did, public forum analysis might be relevant. This case involves a claim of
equal access to discuss a subject that the board has approved for discussion in
the forum. In essence, the respondents are not asserting a right of access at all;
they are asserting a right to be free from discrimination. The critical inquiry,
therefore, is whether the board's grant of exclusive access to the petitioner
amounts to prohibited viewpoint discrimination.

II ....

On a practical level, the only reason for the petitioner to seek an exclusive access policy is to deny its rivals access to an effective channel of communication. No other group is explicitly denied access to the mail system. In fact, as the Court points out, *ante,* at 47-48, many other groups have been granted access to the system. Apparently, access is denied to the respondents because of the likelihood of their expressing points of view different from the petitioner's on a range of subjects. The very argument the petitioner advances in support of the policy, the need to preserve labor peace, also indicates that the access policy is not viewpoint-neutral.

In short, the exclusive-access policy discriminates against the respondents based on their viewpoint. The Board has agreed to amplify the speech of the petitioner, while repressing the speech of the respondents based on the respondents' point of view. This sort of discrimination amounts to censorship and infringes the First Amendment rights of the respondents. In this light, the policy can survive only if the petitioner can justify it.

III .... A

The petitioner attempts to justify the exclusive-access provision based on its status as the exclusive bargaining representative for the teachers and on the State's interest in efficient communication between collective bargaining representatives and the members of the unit. The petitioner's status and the State's interest in efficient communication are important considerations. They are not sufficient, however, to sustain the exclusive-access policy....

B

The petitioner ... argues, and the Court agrees, *ante,* at 52, that the exclusive access policy is justified by the State's interest in preserving labor peace. As the Court of Appeals found, there is no evidence on this record that granting access to the respondents would result in labor instability. 652 F.2d, at 1301. In addition, there is no reason to assume that the respondents' messages would be any more likely to cause labor discord when received by members of the majority union than the petitioner's messages would when received by the respondents. Moreover, it is noteworthy that both the petitioner and the respondents had access to the mail system for some time prior to the representation election. See *ante,* at 39. There is no indication that this policy resulted in disruption of the school environment.

Although the State's interest in preserving labor peace in the schools in order to prevent disruption is unquestionably substantial, merely articulating the interest is not enough to sustain the exclusive access policy in this case. There must be some showing that the asserted interest is advanced by the policy. In the absence of such a showing, the exclusive access policy must fall....

NOTES

1. In *Reid v. Barrett,* 467 F. Supp. 124 (D.N.J. 1979), *aff'd,* 615 F.2d 1354 (3d Cir. 1980), the court held that a school superintendent did not violate the first amendment in prohibiting a union's attempt to distribute letters to parents

by giving them to students to take home. The court noted that since "the Super-intendent had no constitutional obligation to let any organization use the pupils to carry messages home, and the use of the students for that purpose may be denied altogether, his order barring distribution in the instant case does not work a constitutional deprivation."

2. In *Henrico Prof. Fire Fighters Ass'n, Local 1568 v. Board of Supvrs.,* 649 F.2d 237 (4th Cir. 1981), the question presented was "whether a government board that routinely permits individuals and representatives of organizations to present their views to it during regularly scheduled public meetings on any matters on which the board is empowered to act, may, through a single excep-tion to the otherwise general rule, constitutionally prevent a representative of an association of its employees from presenting to it the collective views of its members solely because the speaker appears in the guise of a representative of an association of employees." In holding that the limitation did not pass consti-tutional muster, the court stated:

[W]e hold that representatives of a public employee association may not be denied the equal protection of the First and Fourteenth Amendments when (1) a public meeting has been generally opened for discussion by individuals of the topic the association wishes to address, (2) nonemployee associations are welcomed and allowed to discuss topics of interest to them, and (3) any topic is deemed relevant if it concerns matters with which the body holding the meeting has power to deal. Government may not discriminate among those it will hear on the basis of the speaker's status as a labor organization, rather than an individual employee, or because the particular association is composed of public employees.

At the same time, allowing Captain McClure an opportunity to speak means only that. It does not call for "recognition" as that term is used in the labor relations context. It does not compel the Board to bargain with the Association. It does not even require that the Board pay attention. We only decide that it was incumbent on the Board to afford him, as a representative of the Association and its members, the right to speak.

3. In *Texas State Teachers Ass'n v. Garland Indep. Sch. Dist.,* 777 F.2d 1046 (5th Cir. 1985), *aff'd,* 479 U.S. 801, 107 S. Ct. 41, 93 L. Ed. 2d 4 (1986), the Fifth Circuit held that where teachers were permitted to use a school district's bulletin boards and internal mail system for any reason, including purely per-sonal matters, it was unconstitutional to prohibit teacher communications relat-ing to employee organizations. The court stated:

Teachers who have access to school media facilities for even purely personal matters cannot be prohibited from the exercise of that right simply because their internal speech may concern "employee organizations." We therefore hold that [school district] policies preventing teachers from using school mail facilities to mention "employee organizations" are unconstitutional. So are prohibitions against the use of whatever billboard facilities may be set aside for teachers' personal messages. No "material and substantial" disruption has been shown.

On the other hand, the Fifth Circuit held that a regulation prohibiting repre-sentatives of outside employee organizations from using school media facilities was not unconstitutional based on its finding that the school district had "not created a public forum in its communications facilities," even though certain civic and commercial groups had been allowed to distribute literature through such facilities. Citing *Perry,* the court "held that 'this [t]ype of selective access does not transform government property into a public forum.'"

4. In *Regents of Univ. of Cal. v. PERB,* 108 S. Ct. 1404 (1988), the Supreme Court held that a state university's refusal to permit a union seeking to organize its employees access to its internal mail system to distribute organizational literature was not unlawful, because granting such use would be in violation of the Private Express Statutes, which establish a postal monopoly for the United States Postal Service. The Court ruled that "neither of the statutory exceptions proffered by appellees — the letters-of-the-carrier exception and the private-hands exception — permits appellant [state university] to carry the Union's letters in its internal mail system."

B. STATUTORY PROTECTION

Virtually all of the public sector collective bargaining statutes set forth the rights of public employees. This statutory statement frequently parallels the statement of the rights of employees in § 7 of the National Labor Relations Act, as amended. For example, the Pennsylvania statute, 43 Pa. Cons. Stat. Ann. § 1101.401 (Purdon 1991), provides that:

It shall be lawful for public employes to organize, form, join or assist in employe organizations or to engage in lawful concerted activities for the purpose of collective bargaining or other mutual aid and protection or to bargain collectively through representatives of their own free choice and such employes shall also have the right to refrain from any or all such activities, except as may be required pursuant to a maintenance of membership provision in a collective bargaining agreement.

Most of the comprehensive statutes, again adopting the NLRA model, specify unfair labor practices by both public employers and employee organizations. Thus, these comprehensive statutes generally provide that it is an unfair labor practice (sometimes referred to as an "improper practice" or "prohibited practice") for a public employer to:

(1) interfere with, restrain, or coerce public employees in the exercise of their enumerated rights;

(2) dominate or interfere with the formation or administration of an employee organization;

(3) discriminate in regard to hire or tenure of employment or any term or condition of employment to encourage or discourage membership in any employee organization;

(4) discharge or otherwise discriminate against an employee because he has filed charges or given testimony under the act; and

(5) refuse to bargain in good faith with the duly designated bargaining agent.

Similarly, these statutes also provide, with some exceptions, that it is an unfair labor practice for an employee organization to:

(1) restrain or coerce employees in the exercise of their enumerated rights;

(2) cause or attempt to cause an employer to interfere with, restrain, or coerce employees in the exercise of their enumerated rights;

(3) restrain or coerce employers in the selection of their representatives for the purposes of collective bargaining or the adjustment of grievances; and

(4) refuse to bargain in good faith.

Some of the comprehensive statutes, however, contain broader proscriptions than those set forth in the NLRA. For example, some of the laws make it an unfair labor practice for *both* public employers and unions to:

(1) refuse or fail to participate in good faith in statutory impasse procedures: United States, California (teachers), Connecticut (teachers), Hawaii, Iowa, Kansas, Massachusetts, Oregon, Pennsylvania, and Tennessee (teachers);

(2) violate any rules and regulations issued to regulate the conduct of representation elections: Connecticut (municipal and state employees), Illinois, Minnesota, and Pennsylvania;

(3) refuse to comply with any provision in the act: United States, Hawaii, Indiana (teachers), New Hampshire, and Oregon;

(4) violate the terms of a collective bargaining agreement: Hawaii, New Hampshire, Oregon, and Wisconsin (municipal and state employees);

(5) refuse to comply with or accept an arbitration award: Connecticut (municipal employees), Illinois (educational employees), Minnesota, Oregon, Pennsylvania, and Wisconsin (municipal and state employees); and

(6) discriminate on the basis of race, color, religion, sex, handicap or national origin: District of Columbia, Nevada, and Vermont (state and municipal employees).

In addition, some of the laws provide that it is a *union* unfair labor practice to:

(1) instigate a strike or other concerted refusal to work: District of Columbia, Florida, Iowa, Kansas, Maine (state and municipal employees), Minnesota, Nebraska, New Hampshire, Vermont (state and municipal employees), and Wisconsin (state employees);

(2) engage in secondary boycotts: District of Columbia, Iowa, Minnesota, Ohio, Pennsylvania, Tennessee (teachers), and Vermont (state and municipal employees);

(3) engage in jurisdictional strikes: Iowa, Minnesota, Ohio, and Pennsylvania;

(4) engage in recognitional picketing: Illinois (non-educational employees), and Vermont (state and municipal employees);

(5) induce or encourage any individual to picket the residence or place of private employment of any public official or representative of a public employer: Ohio;

(6) cause or attempt to cause a public employer to pay for services not performed, or which are not needed or required by a public employer: Minnesota and Vermont (state and municipal employees);

(7) hinder or interfere with an employee's work performance or productivity: United States and New Mexico;

(8) coerce or intimidate a supervisor working at the same trade or profession as employees to induce him or her to become a member of or act in concert with the employee organization of which employees are members: Wisconsin (state and municipal employees);

(9) solicit or advocate support from students for an employee organization's activities: Connecticut (teachers) and Florida;

(10) distribute organizational literature or solicit public school employees during working hours in areas where such employees work in a manner which would hinder or interfere with school operations: Delaware (teachers);

(11) communicate during negotiations with officials other than those designated to represent the public employer concerning employment relations: Oregon;

(12) blacklist public employers for the purpose of preventing them from filling employee vacancies: Maine;

(13) endorse candidates, spend income for partisan or political purposes, or advocate or oppose elections of candidates for public office: Kansas;

(14) use agency shop fees for contributions to political candidates or parties at state or local levels: Montana; and

(15) discriminate against any employee with respect to membership in an employee organization on the basis of race, color, creed, national origin, sex, age, preferential or non-preferential civil service status, political affiliation, marital status, or handicapping conditions: United States.

Finally, the laws in some states make it an unfair labor practice for a *public employer* to:

(1) institute a lockout: Connecticut, Iowa, Kansas, Nebraska, New Hampshire, and Ohio;

(2) deny an employee organization the rights accompanying certification or recognition: Iowa and Kansas;

(3) blacklist employees: Maine (municipal and state employees) and Minnesota;

(4) communicate directly with bargaining unit employees during negotiations concerning employment matters, except where related to work performance: Oregon;

(5) refuse to appropriate sufficient funds to implement a written collective bargaining agreement: Vermont (municipal employees);

(6) refuse to provide an exclusive representative, upon request, all information pertaining to a public employer's budget: Minnesota;

(7) refuse to permit employee organization to have reasonable access to bulletin boards, mailboxes and other communication media: Tennessee (teachers);

(8) refuse to continue terms of an expired agreement until a new agreement is negotiated, unless the employee organization engages in a prohibited strike: New York; and

(9) Spend public funds for external assistance in attempting to influence the outcome of a representation election, provided that this prohibition does not limit a public employer's right to internally communicate with its employees or to seek or obtain advice from legal counsel: Illinois.

The determination of whether an unfair labor practice has occurred is generally left to a public employment relations agency. If the agency finds that the person named in the complaint has engaged in or is engaging in an unfair labor practice, the agency is generally empowered, as the Pennsylvania Act provides, to "cause to be served on such person an order requiring such person to cease and desist from such unfair practice, and to take such reasonable affirmative action, including reinstatement of employes, discharged in violation of Article XII of this act, with or without back pay, as will effectuate the policies of this act." 43 Pa. Cons. Stat. Ann. § 1101.1303 (Purdon 1991).

Statute of Limitations. The statute of limitations for filing an unfair labor practice charge is typically six months, the same as under the NLRA; however, several laws or ordinances specify a shorter period. The New Mexico State Personnel Board regulations and the District of Columbia Personnel Manual provide that unfair labor practice charges must be filed within 30 and 60 days, respectively, of the alleged offense. N.M. State Personnel Bd., § 17(a)(2); D.C. Personnel Manual, Ch. 25, § a, Item 18(c). Both the Iowa and Ohio statutes have a 90-day period for filing charges. Iowa Code Ann., § 20.11(1) (West 1989); Ohio Rev. Code § 4117.12(B) (Anderson 1991).

NOTES

1. Should the complaining party have the burden of prosecuting an unfair labor practice charge before a public employment relations agency? The contrasting approaches under the NLRA and under several of the comprehensive public sector statutes is discussed in 1967 Executive Committee, National Governor's Conference, Report of Task Force on State and Local Government Labor Relations 15 (1967):

> In the administration of the unfair labor practice provisions of their statutes, the states have tended *not* to follow the National Labor Management Relations Act. The federal act originally conferred responsibility for investigating, prosecuting, and determining the merits of charges of unfair practices to the National Labor Relations Board. This led to the accusation that the board was both prosecutor and judge. Later the judicial functions were administratively separated from the investigatory and prosecuting functions. This softened the accusation but did not totally eliminate it. To avoid this functional conflict, the state laws in Wisconsin and Michigan have restricted the board's function to hearing and deciding a charge, and leaving to the complaining party the responsibility of raising the issue at the outset and also of making a valid case in support of the charge. The Illinois Commission reviewed these procedural questions and concluded that it was basically sound to limit the board's function to deciding charges even though this practice might in some instances place a burden on an individual employee. At the same time, it also warned the board against holding formal hearings on trivial charges.

In *Crestwood Educ. Ass'n v. MERC*, 80 Mich. App. 409, 276 N.W.2d 592 (1979), the court rejected a contention that the Michigan Employment Relations Commission had a statutory duty to investigate and prosecute unfair labor practice charges. After noting that the Michigan Act, unlike the NLRA, did not specifically authorize the Commission to investigate and prosecute complaints, the court stated that it was "unable to conclude that the omission of investigatory and prosecutorial powers was accidental." Accordingly, the court held "that MERC properly limited its role ... to that of adjudicating the dispute before it."

2. Under Executive Order 11491, a charging party had the responsibility of prosecuting an unfair labor practice charge. However, under the Federal Service Labor Management and Employee Relations Law, which was enacted as part of the Civil Service Reform Act of 1978, the position of General Counsel has been created, and the General Counsel is given the authority to "investigate alleged unfair labor practices" and to "file and prosecute complaints." Civil Service Reform Act of 1978, Pub. L. No. 95-454, 92 Stat. 1111, codified at 5 U.S.C. § 7104(f)(3)(A)&(B).

3. The Illinois statute covering non-educational employees provides that the state and local labor relations boards are required to issue rules and regulations providing for the appointment of an attorney to represent a charging party where the charging party is able "to demonstrate an inability to pay for or inability to otherwise provide for adequate representation before a governing board." Ill. Rev. Stat., ch. 48, § 1605(k) (1986).

4. Although attorney's fees and costs are typically not recoverable, the Florida law provides that the Commission's order in an unfair labor practice case "may award to the prevailing party all or part of the costs of litigation and reasonable attorney's fees and expert witness fees whenever the commission determines that such an award is appropriate." Fla. Stat. Ann. § 447.503(6)(c) (West 1981). In *City of Venice,* 4 FPER ¶4107 (Fla. PERC 1978), the Florida PERC held that attorney's fees should only be awarded where there is "something special about the circumstances from which the case arose or something distinguishing about the manner in which the case is litigated."

After referring to decisions under the National Labor Relations Act, the Washington Supreme Court in *Washington Fed'n of State Emps. v. Central Wash. Univ.,* 93 Wash. 2d 60, 605 P.2d 1252 (1980), held that the Washington Higher Education Personnel Board was empowered under the state public sector collective bargaining act to award attorneys' fees. The court reasoned as follows:

> We believe "remedial" action encompasses the power to award attorneys' fees under appropriate circumstances. We hold that [the Washington Act] is broad enough to permit a remedial order containing an award of litigation expenses when that is necessary to make the order effective. Such an allowance is not automatic, but should be reserved for those cases in which a defense to the unfair labor practice charge can be characterized as frivolous or meritless. The term "meritless" has been defined as meaning groundless or without foundation. See *Christiansburg Garment Co. v. Equal Employment Opportunity Comm'n,* 434 U.S. 412, 421 (1978). Awards should not be permitted routinely, simply because the charging party prevails.

In *Washburn Teachers Ass'n v. Barnes,* Case No. 83-21 (Me. LRB 1983), the Maine Labor Relations Board held that where an employer had been subject to a previous remedial order and had thereafter committed flagrant violations of the act, it was appropriate to order the employer to reimburse the union for documented expenses relative to its investigation and preparation of the case, and any costs incurred by its witnesses for travel, meals, and lodging.

5. Does a PERB or PERC have authority to award punitive damages or damages of emotional or psychological injuries as remedies in an unfair labor practice proceeding? See *State of California,* 14 PERC ¶21115 (Cal. 1990) ("... PERB is without authority to award punitive damages or damages for emotional or psychological injuries in unfair practice cases").

6. As noted above, most of the comprehensive statutes protect the right of public employees to bargain collectively and specifically provide that it is an unfair labor practice for an employer to refuse to bargain collectively. This area is discussed in detail in Chapter 4.

7. In *Wines v. City of Huntington Woods,* 97 Mich. App. 86, 293 N.W.2d 730 (1980), the court reversed a MERC decision and held that an unfair labor practice complaint was timely, even though it was filed more than six months from the date of the act which allegedly constituted the unfair labor practice. The court held that the complaint was timely since the six-month statutory limitation period does not begin to run until the employee has actual knowledge, or reason to know that the act that allegedly constitutes an unfair labor practice has been committed. The court observed that a contrary ruling would allow "unscrupulous employers to conceal unfair labor practices until expiration of the six-month limitations period."

8. Does the filing of an unfair labor practice charge with the NLRB by an employee toll the statute of limitations for filing the charge with the appropriate state PERB or PERC? In *North Broward Med. Center,* 16 FPER ¶ 21054 (Fla. 1990), the Florida Commission held that a "timely appeal to the National Labor Relations Board will not toll the statute of limitations requirements" set forth in the Florida act.

9. Normally a labor relations agency conducts an investigation to determine whether an unfair labor practice charge has any merit. If the agency dismisses the charge, to what extent can the individual seek judicial review of such a determination? Under the National Labor Relations Act, the courts have uniformly held that the exercise of discretion by the NLRB General Counsel in dismissing an unfair labor practice charge is not subject to judicial review. See, e.g., *United Elec. Contrs. Ass'n v. Ordman,* 366 F.2d 766 (2d Cir. 1966) (per curiam), *cert. denied,* 385 U.S. 1026 (1967); *Hourihan v. NLRB,* 201 F.2d 187 (D.C. Cir. 1952), *cert. denied,* 345 U.S. 930 (1953).

Some state acts, however, specifically permit a party to seek judicial review when an unfair labor practice charge is dismissed. For example, Section 16(a) of the Illinois Public Labor Relations Act provides that "[a] charging party or any person aggrieved by a final order of the Board granting or denying in whole or in part the relief sought may apply for and obtain judicial review of an order of the Board entered under this Act...." Ill. Rev. Stat. ch. 48, ¶ 1716(a) (Supp. 1990).

10. Section 14(b) of the NLRA permits the states to enact right-to-work legislation, 29 U.S.C. § 164(b) (1970), and at present twenty-one states have enacted right-to-work laws: Alabama, Arizona, Arkansas, Florida, Georgia, Idaho, Iowa, Kansas, Louisiana, Mississippi, Nebraska, Nevada, North Carolina, North Dakota, South Carolina, South Dakota, Tennessee, Texas, Utah, Virginia, and Wyoming. The general purpose of most of these laws is to make it illegal to condition employment on membership *or* non-membership in a labor organization. Although right-to-work laws have been vehemently attacked by organized labor, public sector unions have occasionally relied on such laws to support their contention that public employees have the right to join labor organizations of their own choosing. For example, in *Levasseur v. Wheeldon,* 79 S.D. 442, 112 N.W.2d 894 (1964), a resolution adopted by a municipality which prohibited fire, police, and health department employees from becoming members of any labor organization whose membership was not exclusively confined to employees of the municipality was held to contravene the "right-to-work" provision in the state's constitution. The court held that the "constitutional amendment does not exclude public employment and that membership among city employees cannot be banned by municipal legislation or rule." Accord *Potts v. Hay,* 229 Ark. 830, 318 S.W.2d 826 (1958); *Beverly v. City of Dallas,* 292 S.W.2d 172 (Tex. Civ. App. 1956). Contra *Keeble v. City of Alcoa,* 204 Tenn. 286, 319 S.W.2d 249 (1958).

1. INTERFERENCE, RESTRAINT AND COERCION

MONTGOMERY COUNTY GERIATRIC & REHABILITATION CENTER

13 PPER ¶ 13242 (Penn. Labor Rel. Bd. 1982)

[The PLRB made the following relevant findings of fact: that an employee "was told by his supervisor that he was being terminated for 'soliciting, being in an unauthorized work place and lounging out'" and that this "solicitation involved the handing out of union cards"; that a supervisor, Mr. Arapolu, "told Ms. Beers and Ms. Deevy that any further impermissible solicitation would result in their termination"; and that although supervisors had observed "employees collecting money and selling raffles while on break, no warning or other comment had been made about their soliciting for those purposes."]

The Employer argues that the no solicitation rule which appears in the employe handbook had been promulgated several years earlier and was applied to all groups, union and nonunion, who were involved in any kind of solicitation on company property during working time. The Employer contends that this nondiscriminatory application of the rule was valid as it was applied so as to limit employes only on working time in working places. The rule as written in the employe handbook, however, states that "no employe ... shall be permitted to solicit ... on Montgomery County Center premises or during working time." Thus the blanket prohibition affects all solicitation on the premises of the Employer. In *Solo Cup Company*, 144 NLRB 1481 (1963), the NLRB addressed a similar rule promulgated by an employer.

> The rule prohibited all "unauthorized" solicitation on company property and the respondent claims that "unauthorized" referred to working time and did not mean that company approval was required before solicitations could be made.

144 NLRB at 1481. Citing a Court of Appeals decision, the Board went on to say that

> [T]he reasonably foreseeable effects of the wording of the rule on the conduct of the employes will determine its legality, and that where the language ... may ... cause [employes] to refrain from exercising their statutory rights, then the rule is invalid even if interpreted lawfully by the employer in practice. A number of Board cases have also followed the view that the conduct of the employes is deemed to be guided by the wording of the rule itself and not the unexpressed limitations or interpretations that are given to it by the employer. (list of citations omitted)

144 NLRB at 1481-82.

The National Board decisions on this issue have followed the dictates of the U.S. Supreme Court. In *Republic Aviation Corp. v. NLRB*, 324 U.S. 793 (1945), rehearing denied, the Supreme Court held invalid a broad no solicitation rule. The Court said:

> It is no less true that time outside working hours, whether before or after work or during luncheon or rest periods, is an employe's time to use as he wishes without unreasonable restraint, although the employe is on company property. It is therefore not within the province of an employer to promul-

gate and enforce a rule prohibiting union solicitation by an employe outside of working hours, although on company property. Such a rule must be presumed to be an unreasonable impediment to self organization and therefore discriminatory in the absence of evidence that special circumstances make the rule necessary in order to maintain production or discipline.

324 U.S. at 803 fn. 10. In the case before the Board the Employer has alleged no evidence of special circumstances making the rule necessary to maintain production or discipline.

The Supreme Court, in *Republic Aviation,* went on to explain:

> Petitioner urges that irrespective of the validity of the rule against solicitation, its application in this instance did not violate [the Act] because the rule was not discriminatorily applied against union solicitation but was impartially enforced against all solicitors.

324 U.S. at 805. If the rule is invalid, said the Court, then discharge or threat of discipline becomes discriminatory because it discourages membership in a labor organization. In this case the no solicitation rule as published in the handbook emphatically states:

> Violation of this policy shall be considered serious enough to be grounds for immediate dismissal. (Union Exhibit 1)

The Employer's argument that employes were told they could solicit in specified area at specified times is insufficient to save the broad wording of the no solicitation rule as presented in the employees handbook. Moreover, Ms. Beers and Ms. Deevy both testified that they were told by Mr. Arapolu that they were prohibited from soliciting signatures anywhere on the premises on pain of discharge; it appears, moreover, that no warning or comment accompanied solicitation for other purposes.

Affirming an NLRB decision that the possibility of disruption in patient care was remote, the U.S. Supreme Court has held that prohibiting solicitation throughout the premises of a hospital during non-working time was an unreasonable interference with employee rights. In *Beth Israel Hospital v. NLRB,* 437 U.S. 483 (1978), the Court said:

> We have long accepted the Board's view that the right of employees to self-organize and bargain collectively ... necessarily encompasses the right effectively to communicate with one another regarding self-organization at the job site.

437 U.S. at 491. That right, the Supreme Court recognized, must be weighed against the right of the public employer to manage the enterprise in the public interest. Self-organization is a "fundamental right" guaranteed by PERA and thus weighs heavily on the side of the employes. *PLRB v. Altoona Area School District,* 480 Pa. 148, 389 A.2d 553, 557, 9 PPER 9181 (1978).

OREGON PUBLIC EMPLOYES UNION, LOCAL 503
v. DEPARTMENT OF REVENUE

6 PECBR 4901 (Or. Emp. Relations Bd. 1981)

On April 8, 1981, the Oregon Public Employes Union, Local 503, SEIU, AFL-CIO, (Union) filed an unfair labor practice complaint against the Department of Revenue, Robyn L. Godwin, Director, Executive Department, State of Oregon (State). As amended April 30, 1981, the complaint charged that the State had violated ORS 243.672(1) (a) by refusing to permit employes to distribute the Union's literature in employe work areas. The State's answer, filed on June 2, 1981, admitted all the material facts alleged by the complaint but denied that it had violated the Act as alleged....

Findings of Fact ....

On or about February 10, 17 and March 11, 1981, the State informed a Union shop steward, an employe named Ronald D. Swanson, that he would not be allowed to distribute the Union's bargaining newsletter in the work area of the Assessment and Appraisal Division of the State's Department of Revenue in Salem, Oregon. There is no evidence tending to indicate that Swanson sought to distribute literature only during his lunch or coffee break periods. It also cannot reasonably be inferred from the record that the employes to whom he gave literature were on their lunch or coffee breaks.

The Assessment and Appraisal Division is a production-oriented work unit, in which employes working at desks in an open area draft cadastral maps for use in assessment work. Employes in the unit work "flextime" schedules, starting and ending their work days at assorted hours and taking their coffee and lunch breaks at various times during the work day. Coffee and lunch breaks may be taken at the employe's desk, in an adjacent conference room, in a smoking room on another floor, or in the building cafeteria.

The State has consistently permitted nonwork related materials, such as blood donor drive information, United Way information, cancer drive information, announcements of social events, birthday cards and the "Working Woman" magazine to be distributed in the work area during working hours. Such material is often circulated by "route" slip to employes at their desks, rather than by individual distribution, unlike the Union literature. This other nonwork related material has not been distributed as frequently as the Union literature. While distribution of Union literature was occurring on an average of two to three times per week, distribution of material for campaigns such as United Way occurred six or seven times a year, for party announcements once or twice a year and for get well cards, once or twice a month. No evidence was presented concerning frequency of distribution of other nonwork related material, such as the "Working Woman" magazine or birthday cards.

The State maintains that a prohibition on distribution of Union material was made necessary because of the controversy generated by this material. There is no sample of the Union material in the record, nor is it otherwise described than simply as the "OPEU Bargaining Newsletter." The work unit includes some employes who are vigorously opposed to the Union and who complained about distribution of this Union literature. Also, discussions between pro-Union and anti-Union employes generated by the Union literature were occurring, prior to the ban, during working time. The State has given Swanson permission to distribute the literature in a conference room adjacent to the work unit and to adjust his own lunch hour so that it overlaps most other employes' lunch periods. The State has given the Union the names and home addresses of employes in the bargaining unit. There is no evidence that the Union has requested, or that the State has permitted or would permit, distribution of the Union's literature by means of a route slip.

On or about April 27, 1981, an employe named Annie Clemens was refused permission by her supervisor to distribute Union bargaining information in the work area of the Administrative Services Division of the State's Department of Revenue, in Salem, Oregon. This Division is also a production-oriented work unit, responsible for the Division's word processing. Employes in this unit, like the employes in the Assessment and Appraisal Division, work flexible hours and may take coffee and lunch breaks at their desks in the common work area, at a conference table adjacent to the work area, or in the building's cafeteria. On May 26, 1981, Clemens was cautioned in writing about continued distribution of Union literature during her working hours and about her overuse of the telephone. While the distribution of Union literature is not a matter which generates controversy among employes in this work unit, the supervisor of this unit has a continuing problem involving too much "visiting" between employes during work time. When she was supposed to be working, Clemens was distributing Union material to employes who also were supposed to be working. The State believes the Union could appropriately distribute its literature at the large conference table near the work area, rather than distribute literature in the employe work area.

On April 27, 1981, the first day Clemens was cautioned about distribution of Union literature, the State permitted a party announcement to be circulated in this work area during work hours. There is no evidence tending to show that the Union has been granted an opportunity to circulate its literature by the route slip means used for circulation of the party announcement. It does appear that there is a greater disparity in this division between distribution frequency of Union literature and distribution frequency of other nonwork related literature than in the Assessment and Appraisal Division. Here, Union literature was distributed at least once a week and maybe more often, whereas there is unrebutted evidence that other nonwork related information was very seldom circulated.

The record does not include detailed descriptions of the Union literature which was distributed in this work unit. The State admitted refusing permission to Clemens to distribute "union bargaining information." On one occasion, this information consisted of "buttons" relating to an upcoming informational strike.

Conclusions of Law ....

This case presents an issue of first impression for this Board. However, in the private sector, the NLRB and the federal courts have developed a substantial body of case law concerning distribution of union literature in the work place. The guidelines which have been established by this case law flow from the basic principle that an employer must allow employes to distribute union literature in nonworking areas during nonworking time. See, *Eastex, Inc. v. NLRB,* 437 U.S. 556, 98 LRRM 2717 (1978); *Republic Aviation Corporation v. NLRB,* 324; U.S. 793, 16 LRRM 620 (1945); *Time-O-Matic, Inc. v. NLRB,* 264 F.2d 96, 43 LRRM 2661 (CA 7, 1959); and, *Stoddard-Quirk Mfg. Co.,* 138 NLRB 615, 51 LRRM 1110 (1962). Under those cases, an employer rule regulating distribution of material in nonwork areas or on nonwork time is presumptively invalid, although the presumption of invalidity may be rebutted where, for example, special circumstances make the rule necessary to maintain production or discipline and where the employer's interest by reason of the special circumstances in controlling such distribution outweighs the employes' interest in making the distribution. See, *McDonnell Douglas Corporation,* 472 F.2d 539, 82 LRRM 2393 (CA 8, 1973). On the other hand, a rule prohibiting distribution of material in working areas or during working time[3] is presumptively valid, a presumption which can be rebutted by a showing that the rule was discriminatorily promulgated or enforced. See, *Beth Israel Hospital v. NLRB,* 437 U.S. 483, 98 LRRM 2727 (1978); *American Cast Iron Pipe Co. v. NLRB,* 600 F.2d 132, 101 LRRM 2522 (CA 8, 1979); *NLRB v. Olympic Medical Corp.,* 608 F.2d 762, 102 LRRM 2904 (CA 9, 1979); *Midwest Stock Exchange v. NLRB,* 635 F.2d 1255, 105 LRRM 3172 (CA 7, 1980); and, *Clougherty Packing Company,* 240 NLRB 932, 100 LRRM 1442 (1979).

Both parties to this case have relied on private sector precedent in arguing their respective positions to this Board. We find the private sector precedent helpful by analogy and, for the most part, highly persuasive. Neither party has urged that any special circumstances peculiar to public sector employment ought to warrant selection by this Board of some different rules governing this no-distribution issue and we are not aware of any such special circumstances. Therefore, we adopt the principles enunciated in the private sector and outlined above as our own and will proceed to apply those principles to the facts before us.

At the outset, we find that the State's no-distribution rule is of a presumptively valid variety. As promulgated, this rule is a somewhat informal and largely oral ban on distribution of material in working areas during working time. It is undisputed that the banned distributions occurred in employe work areas, rather than at adjacent conference tables or in nearby conference rooms. It has been neither urged nor proven that Swanson, Clemens and the employes to whom material was distributed were all on lunch, coffee or other permissible work "breaks" when the distributions took place. The evidence is clear that the State does not ban distribution of union literature outside the work area during employe "break" times and has even facilitated such distribution by suggesting acceptable places for it.

We also conclude that the State has not applied its no-distribution rule in a discriminatory fashion. The unrebutted evidence is that distribution of union

---

[3] In *Essex International, Inc.,* 211 NLRB 749, 86 LRRM 1411 (1974), the NLRB held that while rules that prohibit solicitation or distribution during "working time" or "work time" are presumed valid, rules that prohibit solicitation or distribution during "working hours" are presumed invalid unless their impact on lunch and break time is clarified to reflect that the lunch and break times are not considered included in the "working hours."

literature in the employe work areas during work time was occurring, in the Assessment and Appraisal Division, on an average of two or three times per week, and in the Administrative Services Division, at least once a week. By contrast, unrebutted evidence of discrimination in favor of distribution of other nonwork related material consists of five or six circulations per year for charitable campaigns such as United Way in one Division, circulation of one or two party announcements per year in each Division, circulation of get well cards once or twice a month in one Division and an unknown frequency of distribution of birthday cards and a magazine called "Working Woman." Clearly, the nonunion "social" distributions are so outnumbered in frequency by the Union literature distributions that the social distributions must be regarded as isolated occurrences by comparison. By permitting an occasional distribution of social material, while prohibiting the distribution of Union literature, the State has not discriminated against the Union in interference with employe rights under ORS 243.672 (1) (a). See *NLRB v. Electro Plastic Fabrics, Inc.,* 381 F.2d 374, 65 LRRM 3127 (CA 4, 1967); *American Cast Iron Pipe Co., supra;* and *Midwest Stock Exchange v. NLRB, supra.*[6]

Having concluded that the State did not violate ORS 243.672(1) (a) as alleged, we have no occasion to consider possible defenses to the charge, such as waiver or special circumstances.[7]

NOTES

1. Can a public employer prohibit solicitation and distribution of union materials on its premises by *nonemployees* ? Under the NLRA, the courts and the NLRB have made a distinction between the rights of employees and the rights of nonemployees. The leading NLRB decision concerning the legality of an employer's no-solicitation and no-distribution rules is *Stoddard-Quirk Mfg. Co.,* 138 N.L.R.B. 615 (1962). In *NLRB v. Babcock & Wilcox Co.,* 351 U.S. 105 (1956), the Court stated:

an employer may validly post his property against nonemployee distribution of union literature if reasonable efforts by the union through other available channels of communication will enable it to reach the employees with its message and if the employer's notice or order does not discriminate against the union by allowing other distribution.

---

[6] In *NLRB v. Electro Plastic Fabrics, Inc., supra,* the employer's no-solicitation rule was found unlawfully discriminatory because the permitted nonunion kinds of solicitation were "widespread and variegated" and included active anti-union solicitation. In *American Cast Iron Pipe Co. v. NLRB, supra,* the Court determined that where a politician, the Girl Scouts and several charities had been allowed to distribute literature or make collections on company property in a six-months' time frame, these distributions were, among other things, not too isolated to constitute discrimination. In *Midwest Stock Exchange v. NLRB, supra,* it was noted that: "[S]uch drives as the Crusade of Mercy, collection of blood in a bloodmobile which was brought to the Exchange's premises, the selling of Avon products, Tupperware, boat cruise tickets, raffle tickets, Girl Scout cookies, and a number of other items...." (105 LRRM at 3184) regularly took place at the company. The Court there found discriminatory a "double standard" applied to ban distribution of union literature. The very few social distributions permitted here by the State cannot compare in quantity or frequency to the social distributions found discriminatory in the foregoing private sector cases.

[7] We also note that while the State presented evidence tending to show that distribution of union literature caused dissension among some employes, it appears that the Union has correctly argued that controversy which is or might be generated by union literature is not generally a successful defense to a charge of discriminatory enforcement of a no-distribution rule. See *NLRB v. Container Corp.,* 107 LRRM 2545 (CA 6, May 18, 1981).

Should the same distinction be made in the public sector where public property rather than private property is involved? In *Okaloosa-Walton Junior College v. PERC*, 372 So. 2d 1378 (Fla. Dist. Ct. App. 1979), the court upheld the Florida PERC's adoption of the no-solicitation and no-distribution rules set forth by the NLRB in *Stoddard-Quirk*.

2. Does an employer interfere with protected employee rights if it refuses to accept a paid advertisement from a union for publication in an employer newspaper? In *Department of Air Force, Scott Air Force Base, Ill.*, FLRA Case No. 5-CA-70175 (1990), the FLRA affirmed an Administrative Law Judge's decision that a union has no statutory right to advertise in an employer-controlled newspaper. The Administrative Law Judge had ruled that "denial of the right to communicate does not automatically constitute interference within the meaning of Section 7116(a)(1) of the statute because there must be a general right to communicate through the means sought to be used." In affirming the ALJ's decision, the FLRA stated:

> Because placing an advertisement in an agency-controlled newspaper is analogous to posting material on agency property and because a union does not have a statutory right to post material on an agency's property, we find that a union does not have a statutory right ... to advertise in an agency's newspaper.

3. Occasionally an employee organization's right of access, as well as the limitations on such right, are spelled out in considerable detail in the applicable law. For example, the Tennessee Education Professional Negotiations Act specifically provides that it is unlawful for a board of education to

> refuse to permit a professional employees' organization to have access at reasonable times to areas in which professional employees work, to use institutional bulletin boards, mail boxes, or other communication media, or to use institutional facilities at reasonable times for the purpose of meeting concerned with the exercise of the rights guaranteed by this act; provided, that if a representative has been selected or designated pursuant to the provisions of this part, a board of education may deny such access and/or usage to any professional employees' organization other than the representative until such time as a lawful challenge to the majority status of the representative is sustained pursuant to this part.

Tenn. Code Ann. § 49-5-609(a)(4) (1990).

4. Even though an employee's right to join and form a union is affirmatively protected by statute or executive order, are there any legitimate restrictions which an employer can place on such activity? In *Department of Transp., Fed. Aviation Admin.*, FLRC No. 72A-1 (1973), the Federal Labor Relations Council held that the teacher-student relationship between instructors and new employees justified greater restrictions on union activity than those which may be placed on other employees. The FLRC stated:

> It is a generally-felt belief that instructors have suasion over their students, even if they do not "supervise" the students. Students inherently feel pressure to "please" instructors and to be deferential to their desires. This is particularly significant in the circumstances of this case where students are often in attendance at the academy and away from their normal workplaces for extended periods of time. If the student is "solicited" by the instructor — for example, is asked to sign a union authorization card or membership application or to tender an initiation fee, this places undue pressure upon the stu-

dent to respond affirmatively, notwithstanding the sophisticated judgment that the instructor is neither a management official nor a supervisor. Further, such action on the part of an instructor places agency management in an equally untenable position. The agency must insure the efficiency of its employees and the administration of a total labor relations program. It is required to insure that undue pressures do not distort true employee choices or the viability of the representation process or impair the efficiency of agency operations.

The FLRC held, however, that it was an unfair labor practice for the agency to ban instructors from wearing union buttons:

There is a great difference between actively soliciting in behalf of a labor organization and merely wearing a union membership button, particularly in the facts of the instant case where the buttons at issue are described as "unobtrusive membership pins bearing no campaign propaganda." We see no reasonable potential for employee coercion or adverse impact on the operation of the facility resulting from instructors wearing union membership buttons. While a balancing of competing rights and obligations justifies permitting the agency to restrict the right of instructors to solicit students in behalf of a labor organization, the same kinds of considerations do not exist — certainly, at least, not to a comparable degree — when the restriction goes to the very personal act of wearing a union membership button.

5. The statutory proscription against interfering with, restraining, or coercing an employee in the exercise of his rights to join or form a union and to engage in collective bargaining has been held to cover numerous matters:

(a) *Surveillance.* An employer's surveillance of union activities constitutes illegal interference, restraint, and coercion. For example, in *Green Lake County,* Decision No. 6061 (Wis. ERC 1962), the Wisconsin Employment Relations Commission held that it was illegal for an employer to spy on a union meeting for the purpose of determining who attended. In *City of Midland,* 1971 MERC Lab. Op. 1129 Mich., the Michigan Commission held that "[t]he representation of a city government in the bargaining process does not include infiltration and subversion of the union's strategy meetings." See also *Pennsylvania Game Comm'n,* 657 GERR B-8 (Pa. PLRB 1976).

(b) *Interrogation.* An employer's action in interrogating or questioning employees about their union activities, about whether they have signed union cards, about how they intend to vote in a representation election, etc., constitutes illegal interference. See *Hardin Cty. Community Unit Sch. Dist. No. 1 v. IELRB,* 174 Ill. App. 3d 168, 528 N.E.2d 737 (1988); *Wisconsin Council of County & Mun. Employees,* Case No. 17768 MP-345 (Wis. ERC 1977); *Jess Parrish Mem. Hosp.,* 4 FPER ¶ 4007 (Fla. PERC 1977).

(c) *Promise of benefit or threat of reprisal.* The granting or withholding of benefits for the purpose of influencing employees with respect to union activity constitutes illegal interference, restraint, and coercion. As the Supreme Court stated in *NLRB v. Exchange Parts Co.,* 375 U.S. 405, 84 S. Ct. 457 (1964):

We think the Court of Appeals was mistaken in concluding that the conferral of employee benefits while a representation election is pending, for the purpose of inducing employees to vote against the union, does not "interfere with" the protected right to organize.

... The danger inherent in well-timed increases in benefits is the suggestion of a fist inside the velvet glove. Employees are not likely to miss the inference that the source of benefits now conferred is also the source from which future benefits must flow and which may dry up if it is not obliged. The danger may be diminished if, as in this case, the benefits are conferred permanently and unconditionally. But the absence of conditions or threats pertaining to the particular benefits conferred would be of controlling significance only if it could be presumed that no question of additional benefits or renegotiation of existing benefits would arise in the future; and, of course, no such presumption is tenable.

... Other unlawful conduct may often be an indication of the motive behind a grant of benefits while an election is pending, and to that extent it is relevant to the legality of the grant; but when as here the motive is otherwise established, an employer is not free to violate § 8(a)(1) by conferring benefits simply because it refrains from other, more obvious violations. We cannot agree with the Court of Appeals that enforcement of the Board's order will have the "ironic" result of "discouraging benefits for labor." 304 F.2d, at 376. The beneficence of an employer is likely to be ephemeral if prompted by a threat of unionization which is subsequently removed. Insulating the right of collective organization from calculated good will of this sort deprives employees of little that has lasting value.

In addition to the actual conferral or withdrawal of benefits, employer statements which contain promises of benefit or threats of reprisal constitute unlawful interference, restraint, and coercion. See, e.g., *City of Marysville*, 1970 MERC Lab. Op. 458 (Mich.).

6. A wide variety of activities has been held to constitute "protected concerted activity" and therefore covered by statutes making it an unfair labor practice for a public employer to interfere with or discriminate against employees because of their involvement in such activities. Examples include:

(a) peaceful picketing on employees' own time, *City of Fitchburg*, Case No. MUPL-72 (Mass. LRC 1975);

(b) communicating with newspaper reporter about matter of concern to fellow employees, *City of Venice*, 4 FPER ¶4059 (Fla. PERC 1978);

(c) publishing newspaper ad authorized by union questioning adequacy of fire protection following layoffs in fire department, *Town of Johnson*, Case No. ULP-3236 (R.I. SLRB 1975);

(d) union petition to fire chief and city officials expressing lack of confidence in fire captain and requesting his termination, *City of Dunedin*, 4 FPER ¶4258 (Fla. PERC 1978).

The various commissions and boards, however, have distinguished between activities which involve a single employee as opposed to activities which benefit or involve two or more employees. For example, the Florida PERC in *City of Hollywood*, 4 FPER ¶4131 (Fla. PERC 1978), noted that "[w]here an employee engages in activities for his benefit alone, his action is not *concerted* protected activity." (Emphasis in original.)

7. Does an employee engage in protected activity when he or she does work on behalf of a sister union? In rejecting a California PERB decision that such conduct was not protected activity, the California Court of Appeals in *McPherson v. PERB*, 189 Cal. App. 293, 234 Cal. Rptr. 428 (1987), held that "[s]ince the early days of the NLRA, it has been recognized that association with, and assistance to, employees outside the bargaining unit is an integral part of normal organizational activities and is therefore protected from employer reprisal. The court further ruled that "an employee is engaged in protected concerted activity by assisting other labor organizations, even if that employee is the only individual in his or her own bargaining unit who is taking such action."

8. Unlike the National Labor Relations Act and many other public sector statutes, the New York Taylor Law does not affirmatively protect the right of employees to "engage in other concerted activities for the purpose of collective bargaining or other mutual aid and protection." Rather, Section 202 of the Taylor Law provides that "[p]ublic employees shall have the right to form, join and participate in, or refrain from forming, joining, or participating in, any employee organization of their own choosing." In *Rosen v. PERB*, 72 N.Y.2d 42, 526 N.E.2d 25, 530 N.Y.S.2d 534 (1988), New York's highest court held that the different language in Section 202, together with the Taylor Law's more limited definition of what constitutes an employee organization, "... evinces a legislative desire that the Taylor Law protect the formal organization of employees, or efforts to form an actual organization, rather than activity, albeit concerted, that is an informal and infrequent airing of grievances without recognized representatives...." After observing that "the Legislature sought to exclude from a statutory scheme regulating public employment certain rights and advantages conferred upon those in the private sector," the court concluded:

> ... Not only is the scope of the protected right to organize drawn more restrictively in Section 202 of the Taylor Law than in section 7 of The NLRA, but a comparison of the corresponding definitions of the term employee organization reveals that the Taylor Law was not intended to protect unorganized — though concerted — activity. Having concluded that petitioner and the other teachers had not formed, or sought to form, an employee organization, and had not exercised any right guaranteed by Section 202, PERB correctly determined that the college therefore did not commit an improper practice within the meaning of Section 209-a(1).

TOWNSHIP OF SHALER

11 PPER ¶ 11347 (Penn. Labor Rel. Bd. 1980)

The instant case is a matter of first impression which requires the Board to determine whether we will apply the rule enunciated by the United States Supreme Court in *NLRB v. J. Weingarten, Inc.,* 420 U.S. 251 (1975) to disputes arising under the PLRA and Act 111. In *Weingarten,* the Supreme Court declared that an employer's denial of an employee's request that a union representative be present at an investigatory interview, which the employee reasonably believed might result in disciplinary action, interfered with, restrained and coerced the employee's right to engage in concerted activities for mutual aid and protection, thus constituting an unfair labor practice....

The Supreme Court's decision in *Weingarten* is premised upon the principle that:

> "Requiring a lone employee to attend an investigatory interview which he reasonably believes may result in the imposition of discipline perpetuates the inequality the Act was designed to eliminate, and bars recourse to the safeguards the Act provided 'to redress the perceived imbalance of economic power between labor and management. (citation omitted)....
>
> "The action of an employee in seeking to have the assistance of his union representative at a confrontation with his employer clearly falls within the

literal wording of § 7[1] that 'employees shall have the right ... to engage in ... concerted activities for the purpose of ... mutual aid or protection.' (citation omitted). This is true even though the employee alone may have an immediate stake in the outcome; he seeks 'aid or protection' against a perceived threat to his employment security. The union representative whose participation he seeks is, however, safeguarding not only the particular employee's interest, but also the interests of the entire bargaining unit by exercising vigilance to make certain that the employer does not initiate or continue a practice of imposing punishment unjustly. (footnote omitted). The representative's presence is an assurance to the other employees in the bargaining unit that they too, can obtain his mutual aid and protection if called upon to attend a like interview." 95 S. Ct. at 965-966.

Respondent argues that this federal private sector precedent has no application in the public sector insofar as statutory procedures already exist for allowing public employes to contest employer disciplinary actions. We cannot agree with this position.

The Pennsylvania Supreme Court has on numerous occasions declared that when private sector policy considerations are similar to and compatible with public sector labor relations, it is proper to apply federal precedent in a public sector setting. Cf. *PLRB v. Williamsport Areas School District,* 486 Pa. 375, 406 A.2d 329, 10 PPER 10265 (1979); *Appeal of Cumberland Valley School District,* 483 Pa. 134, 394 A.2d 946, 9 PPER 9291 (1978); *PLRB v. Mars Area School District,* 480 Pa. 295, 389 A.2d 1073, 9 PPER 9163 (1978). There is no evidence in the labor legislation of this Commonwealth, nor in any decision rendered by a court of this Commonwealth, that would suggest, as Respondent contends, that merely because police employes play a vital function in safeguarding the health and welfare of the citizenry-at-large and that they are part of a paramilitary organization, they are not to be afforded the full range of rights which flow from the establishment of a collective bargaining relationship. We believe that the United States Supreme Court's holding in *Weingarten* has the salutary effect of providing employes with meaningful representation at a critical period in the disciplinary process and that such a result is not incompatible with existing statutory provisions. Accordingly, we will look to the *Weingarten* decision for guidance in resolving the instant matter.

The facts of this case may be summarized as follows: On February 5, 1979, during an investigation of a possible homicide, Complainant was reprimanded by Lt. Duss on at least three occasions for improperly conducting his investigation. On one of these occasions, Complainant responded in a loud manner to Lt. Duss in the presence of other personnel and because of this he was ordered to leave the crime scene. Upon their return to the police station, Lt. Duss informed Complainant that he wished to speak to Complainant in the locker room. When Lt. Duss entered the locker room and asked Complainant to sit down so they could talk, Complainant immediately jumped up, forcing Lt. Duss against a wall, and began demanding that Officer Reiber, a grievance representative, be present on Complainant's behalf. Lt. Duss told Complainant that this was a matter between himself and Complainant and that Officer Reiber's pres-

---

[1] 29 U.S.C. § 157. The Board notes that the language of § 7 of the NLRA is virtually identical to that set forth at § 5 of the PLRA.

ence was not necessary. Complainant, in a loud voice, continued to demand that Officer Reiber be present. Sgt. Hieber, who was also present in the locker room, believing that things might get out of hand, put his hand on Complainant's shoulder in an effort to calm him down. Whereupon, Complainant, again in a very loud voice, told Sgt. Hieber to "get his f...... hands off (Complainant)." When Complainant continued to demand that Officer Reiber be present, Lt. Duss terminated the meeting telling Complainant that they would discuss the matter the next day in Chief Sobehart's office. The incident in the locker room caused a loud commotion which was overheard by other department personnel as well as county detectives who were present at the police station.

The day after the locker room incident, a meeting was held in Chief Sobehart's office to discuss the previous day's events which were summarized in a memo written by Lt. Duss to Chief Sobehart. Complainant was provided with a copy of the memo. Chief Sobehart, Lt. Duss, Sgt. Hieber and Complainant were present at this meeting. Chief Sobehart asked Complainant if Complainant wanted a representative to be present. Complainant did not request representation at the meeting nor did he respond to the Chief's offer of representation. Subsequent to this meeting, Chief Sobehart filed formal charges against Complainant with the Shaler Township Public Safety Committee. The charges were based upon Complainant's insubordination both at the crime scene and in the locker room. As a result of the Public Safety Committee hearing, Complainant was suspended for seven days. The Committee's decision to suspend Complainant was upheld by the Civil Service Commission.

Complainant contends that the locker room meeting held by Lt. Duss violated his right to representation established under *Weingarten*. The *Weingarten* decision sets forth three conditions which must be met in order to establish a violation of the employee's right to representation at an investigatory interview. First, the Complainant must demonstrate that he reasonably believed that the interview might result in disciplinary action. Second, the Complainant must request that a union representative be present and that such request must be denied. Finally, that subsequent to the employer's denial of representation, the employer must compel the employee to continue with the interview. In applying this three-part test to the facts of record, we must conclude that Complainant has failed to establish all of the three conditions necessary for finding a violation of his right to representation.

The record discloses that Lt. Duss had reprimanded Complainant for his conduct at the crime scene on at least three occasions prior to the locker room meeting and that Lt. Duss informed Complainant prior to the locker room meeting that he wished to speak to Complainant. Since Complainant had been reprimanded on several occasions and formally ordered to leave the crime scene, it was reasonable for him to assume that he was going to be disciplined and that the locker room meeting was for the purpose of discussing this matter. However, the record also reveals that while Lt. Duss may have denied Complainant's request for representation at the locker room meeting. Lt. Duss terminated the meeting and did not compel the Complainant to continue the interview without having a representative present. As the Supreme Court stated in *Weingarten, supra*:

"Exercise of the right (to have a representative present at an investigatory interview) may not interfere with legitimate employer prerogatives. The employer has no obligation to justify his refusal to allow union representation, and despite refusal, the employer is free to carry on his inquiry without interviewing the employee, and thus leave to the employee the choice between having an interview unaccompanied by his representative, or having no interview and foregoing any benefits that might be derived from one. As stated in *Mobil Oil*:

'The employer may, if it wishes, advise the employee that it will not proceed with the interview unless the employee is willing to enter the interview unaccompanied by his representative.The employee may then refrain from participating in the interview, thereby protecting his right to representation, but at the same time relinquishing any benefit which might be derived from the interview. The employer would then be free to act on the basis of information obtained from other source.' 196 NLRB, at 1052.

"The Board explained in *Quality* [*Mfg. Co.,* 195 N.L.R.B. 197 (1972)]:

'This seems to us to be the only course consistent with all of the provisions of our Act. It permits the employer to reject a collective course in situations such as investigative interviews where a collective course is not required but protects the employee's right to protection by his chosen agents. Participation in the interview is then voluntary, and, if the employee has reasonable ground to fear that the interview will adversely affect his continued employment, or even his working conditions, he may choose to forego it unless he is afforded the safeguard of his representative's presence. He would then also forego whatever benefit might come from the interview. And, in that event, the employer would, of course, be free to act on the basis of whatever information he had and without such additional facts as might have been gleaned through the interview.' 95 N.L.R.B., at 198-199." 95 S.Ct. at 964.

Based upon the foregoing discussion, it is clear that the evil sought to be remedied in *Weingarten* is a situation in which an employe is compelled to *involuntarily* participate in an investigatory or disciplinary-related interview without the benefit of a union representative being present. Once the employe has requested representation, there is nothing in the *Weingarten* decision which would preclude the employer from terminating the interview and thereafter proceeding with whatever further investigatory or disciplinary action it may deem appropriate.

In the instant case, Lt. Duss terminated the locker room meeting after Complainant requested Officer Reiber to be present and Complainant was never forced to participate in an involuntary investigatory interview. It should also be noted that during the subsequent interview in Chief Sobehart's office, Complainant was expressly asked if he desired a representative to be present and Complainant did not take advantage of this offer. Under these circumstances, we can find no attempt by the Respondent to deny Complainant of his right to representation.

Complainant also alleges that his request for representation played a significant part in the disciplinary charges which were ultimately brought against him.
This charge was expressly denied at hearing by the Respondent.

It is an axiom of employe relations that an employer has the right to discipline
an employe for any reason as long as it does not violate a statute or collective
bargaining agreement. *PLRB v. Elk Motor Sales Co.*, 388 Pa. 173 (1957); *PLRB
v. Sansom House Enterprises, Inc.*, 378 Pa. 385 (1954). An employe's insubordinate conduct toward a supervisor clearly provides a legitimate basis for an
employer's decision to take disciplinary action. Cf. *National Steel Corp., Great
Lakes Division*, 238 NLRB No. 38, 99 LRRM 1241, 1242 (1978); *Court Square
Press, Inc.*, 235 NLRB No. 22, 98 LRRM 1076 (1978); *General Dynamics Corp.,
Electrical Boat Div.*, 234 NLRB No. 22, 97 LRRM 1216 (1978). In the instant
case the charges filed by Respondent with the Public Safety Committee were
based upon Complainant's alleged insubordination both at the crime scene and
in the locker room. The record demonstrates that on both occasions in question,
Complainant responded in a loud manner toward a superior officer and on one
occasion spoke in a vulgar manner to a superior officer. The record further
discloses that all of these events took place in the presence of or in hearing
distance of county detectives and other department personnel.

The burden of proving an unfair practice rests upon the Complainant. The
finding of an unfair practice must be supported by substantial and legally credible evidence. Substantial evidence as indicated in a number of cases is more
than a mere scintilla. Substantial evidence must do more than create a suspicion
of the facts to be established. In this case, the employer gave a lawful comprehensible reason for the action taken against Complainant. The burden is upon
Complainant to prove that the real motive of the Respondent was an improper
one. We have carefully reviewed all the testimony and documentary evidence of
record and are compelled to conclude that the Complainant has not met his
burden of proof. The best that can be said for Complainant's evidence is that it
raises a suspicion, however, this suspicion was refuted and rebutted by Respondent's witnesses who explained their motivation amply on the record. Accordingly, the charge of unfair practices must be dismissed.

NOTES

1. Accord *Fremont Union High Sch. Dist.*, 6 PERC 13047 (Cal. 1982); *East
Brunswick Bd. of Educ.*, 5 NJPER ¶ 10,206 (N.J. PERC 1979); *Conneaut Sch.
Dist.*, 12 PPER ¶ 12,155 (Pa. PLRB 1981); *Regents of Univ. of Mich.*, 1977
MERC Lab. Op. 496 (Mich.).

2. In *Duval Cty. Sch. Bd.*, 4 FPER ¶ 4154 (Fla. PERC 1978), the Florida
Commission adopted *Weingarten,* but added an additional exception for emergency situations "in which (1) the employer must conduct a prompt investigation in order to resolve an existing or imminent problem, (2) a union representative is not readily available, and (3) delay in conducting the interview may
reasonably be expected to jeopardize some significant interest of the employer."
In *Commonwealth of Mass., Comm'r of Admin. & Fin.*, Case No. SUP-2665
(Mass. LRC 1983), the Massachusetts Labor Relations Commission held that a
union does not have a statutory right under the Massachusetts bargaining law to
participate in a management-initiated meeting with an employee to investigate
alleged misconduct on the employee's part in the absence of a request by the

affected employee. The Massachusetts Commission noted that "the union's interest in participating in investigations is derivative of the right of the individual employee, and dependent on the assertion of that right by the individual."

3. Does an employee have the right to select his or her representative? In *State of Conn., Dep't of Cors.,* Dec. No. 2582 (Conn. SBLR 1987), the Connecticut Board ruled that "where there are two or more equally available union stewards and the employee expresses a preference for one of them, ... the employee and not the employer has the right to select among them".

4. Does an employee's right to union representation extend to questions asked by a co-worker at the behest of management? In *NTEU v. FLRA,* 835 F.2d 1446 (D.C. Cir. 1987), the court held that it did not, since the employee could not have reasonably believed that her responses might result in disciplinary action against her. In his opinion on behalf of the court, Judge Edwards stated:

> Because Franken was totally unaware that a special investigator had formulated the questions she was asked and that he was tape recording her replies, she could not have had a reasonable apprehension of punishment. Franken therefore lacked a right to union representation.

After noting that its decision was consistent with the rationale of the Supreme Court's decision in *Weingarten,* the court noted that "[i]t remains for Congress to repair the Statute if it deems the results in this and similar cases to be untoward."

5. In *AFSCME Council 13 v. Pennsylvania Labor Rels. Bd.,* 1986-88 PBC ¶ 34,871 (Pa. Commw. Ct. 1986), the court upheld a PLRB decision holding that an employee did not have a *Weingarten* right to union representation at an employer-conducted "desk audit" designed to accurately determine an employee's job responsibilities as part of a classification review. In holding that such a "desk audit" did not fall within the purview of *Weingarten,* the court noted that a desk audit was not part of a disciplinary procedure.

6. Do an employee's *Weingarten* rights include the right to be represented by a private attorney? In *McLean Hosp.,* 264 N.L.R.B. 459 (1982), the NLRB held that "[r]epresentation by private counsel is not tantamount to union representation within the rule of *Weingarten,* nor does representation of an employee by private counsel constitute concerted activities within the purview of the Act...." Accord *TCC Center Cos.,* 275 N.L.R.B. 604 (1985).

7. What is the appropriate remedy if a labor relations agency finds that an employer has improperly denied an employee's request to have a union representative present during an investigatory interview that could lead to disciplinary action? In *Department of Justice, Bur. of Prisons and American Fed'n of Gov't Emps. Local 2313,* 35 FLRA No. 56 (1990), the FLRA held that a make whole remedy for an employee who was suspended for ten days without pay after his request for union representation at a disciplinary interview had been denied was not appropriate where the only violation was the improper denial of the employee's request to have a union representative at the investigatory interview. In ordering that the agency repeat the investigatory interview with the union representative being present and to reconsider the disciplinary action, the FLRA concluded that this remedy would "protect employee rights and promote the efficiency of government — matters that Congress has determined to be in the public interest." See also *State of Conn., Dep't of Cors.,* Dec. No. 2582 (Conn. SBLR 1987) (although back pay was denied, the Board ordered the reinstatement of two employees, noting that "more than a mere cease and desist order is required to effect the purposes of the Act, especially in light of the capriciousness and hostility which infected the behavior and attitude of the Respondent's agents at the time of the interviews in which the violations occurred").

8. Does an employer commit an unfair labor practice by disciplining an employee who is a union representative for giving another employee mistaken, albeit in good faith, advice about his *Weingarten* rights? In *City of Troy,* 1989 MERC Lab. Op. 291 (Mich.), the Michigan Commission answered this question affirmatively, holding that such conduct is protected activity. It reasoned "that exposing a union steward to discipline for providing good faith, but mistaken advice would have a chilling effect on union activities and would expose stewards to charges that they failed their duty of fair representation."

9. In *Materials Research Corp.,* 262 N.L.R.B. 1010 (1982), the NLRB in a 3-2 decision extended the *Weingarten* right to representation to unrepresented employees. However, in *Sears, Roebuck & Co.,* 274 N.L.R.B. 230 (1985), the NLRB overruled *Materials Research* and held that *Weingarten* rights are not applicable to unrepresented employees.

10. Can a public employee's right to representation as enunciated in the principal case be contractually waived? In *Prudential Life Ins. Co. of Am. v. NLRB,* 661 F.2d 398 (5th Cir. 1981), the court held that although the *Weingarten* right is an individual right under the NLRA, this did not "mean that it cannot be contractually waived by the union." Thus, the court held that a union can agree to "waive the employee's *Weingarten* right for other concessions during negotiations."

11. Although a union's failure to fairly represent all employees is not typically specified as an unfair labor practice, the various commissions have generally held that a union's failure to fairly represent all unit employees is an unfair labor practice. For example, in *AFSCME Local 1633,* 4 FPER ¶ 4168 (Fla. PERC 1978), the Florida Commission held that the privilege of exclusive representation granted by the Florida law "required the correlative duty of fair representation to all unit employees" and that "any default in the performance of [the duty of fair representation] constitutes infringement of [the rights granted to employees under the Act] and is therefore enforceable as an unfair labor practice." In *Auburn Adm'rs Ass'n,* 11 PERB ¶ 3086 (N.Y. 1978), the New York PERB held that it was an unfair labor practice for a union to tell a non-member that it would not represent him in negotiations because of his non-member status. The New York PERB ruled that "[a]n aspect of an employee organization's duty to represent all unit employees fairly without regard to membership is that it may not coerce employees into joining by implying that it will not honor that duty faithfully as to them."

12. Where a union's breach of its duty of fair representation is an unfair labor practice under a state act, can a duty of fair representation lawsuit be filed without exhausting the administrative remedy? Compare *Norton v. Adair Cty.,* 441 N.W.2d 347 (Iowa S. Ct. 1989) (courts and PERB have concurrent jurisdiction) with *Gray v. City of Toledo,* C.A. No. L-86-113 (Ohio Ct. App. 1987) (State Employment Relations Board has exclusive jurisdiction).

2. EMPLOYER DISCRIMINATION

MUSKEGO-NORWAY CONSOLIDATED SCHOOLS v. WERB

35 Wis. 2d 540, 151 N.W.2d 617 (1967)

... In 1960 the Muskego-Norway Education Association (MNEA), an organization composed of practically 100 percent of all teaching and administrative personnel in the employ of the school district, was organized. The MNEA is affiliated with the Wisconsin Education Association (WEA), which renders assistance to local affiliates in regard to their representation of teachers in conferences and negotiations concerning salaries and other conditions of employment.

This controversy concerns certain activities in the school district during the period from 1960 through early 1964. On the one hand is a group of teachers employed by the district who in May, 1964, complained of violations of sec. 111.70, Stats., on the part of the school board and certain of its supervisory personnel. These teachers alleged that the school district ... discouraged labor activity on the part of the teachers by its failure to renew the teaching contract of Carston C. Koeller because of his labor activities on behalf of the MNEA.

On the other hand are the school district; Robert J. Kreuser, superintendent of schools; Jack C. Refling, high school principal; Paul J. Ussel, assistant principal; and Charles A. Ladd, coordinator of instruction.

Certain facts in this involved dispute are uncontroverted and best be set forth here. Other pertinent facts, some controverted, are detailed in the opinion....

Carston Koeller, a first-year teacher in the district, was elected chairman of a reorganized and enlarged MNEA welfare committee for the 1963-1964 year. (He remained chairman at all times pertinent herein.) In September of 1963 the committee began operations by requesting salary information from Superintendent Kreuser. When this information was not forthcoming, the committee obtained it by circulating questionnaires to the teachers. The MNEA also began sending representatives to board meetings. Largely through Koeller's efforts, this information was tabulated prior to mid-January, 1964, and proposals for the year 1964-1965 were formulated. The committee worked hard and held as many as 26 meetings. Its proposals, which were very comprehensive and were approved by the MNEA membership, were presented to the personnel committee of the school board. The proposals dealt with matters of teacher salaries, insurance, personal and sabbatical leaves, class size and load, job security, teacher qualifications, and other matters supporting said proposals including various tables and graphs.

The personnel committee took these proposals under advisement. The personnel committee met again with MNEA representatives and questioned the accuracy of these proposals and whether they represented the wishes of a majority of the teachers. Further questionnaires were circulated and modified proposals were submitted (as approved by the MNEA membership). The report and proposals were submitted to the board meeting on March 2, 1964. What transpired at that meeting and subsequently will be described later in the statement of facts.

Paralleling in importance the development of the MNEA as an effective representative of the teachers are the activities of the chairman of its welfare committee, Carston Koeller, both educational and as a leader in the MNEA. Mr.

Koeller was hired by the school district in 1962 following three years of teaching experience in the air force and one year at Belleville, Wisconsin. Mr. Koeller taught five classes of general mathematics, a subject taken by students deficient in mathematics and incapable of comprehending algebra. These students were also slower learners in other subjects as well. In 1963, at the end of Koeller's first year of teaching, a report was filed by the then principal, Donald Helstad, listing him in the bottom quarter of the faculty in teaching ability, although this did not necessarily mean he was a poor teacher. Helstad advised that Koeller had shown as much progress as any other high school teacher at the time and Helstad unqualifiedly recommended that Koeller be rehired for the year 1963-1964. Koeller was retained. Subsequently, Koeller engaged in a number of activities related to his duties as a teacher rather than to his extracurricular duties with the MNEA.

1. On October 2, 1963, Koeller mailed to six parents a statement asking them to sign a request to give Mr. Koeller permission to use whatever physical means was necessary in order to enforce discipline. On October 7th the new principal, Refling, held a conference with Koeller informing him he was not to determine a course of discipline contrary to established school procedures. At this conference, Koeller's difficulty in handling students in study hall was also discussed. (Koeller had placed a female student in a large unlighted closet as a disciplinary procedure.)

2. On October 14th Koeller suggested in writing to a committee of teachers established to create procedures for disciplining study halls that enforcement of discipline could be implemented by "tweak or pull an ear, rap on head, pull hunk of hair or sit in front closet with door shut."

3. In the fall of 1963, football players were excused from their seventh-hour classes on the day of the game. On October 22d Koeller sent a note to Principal Refling, objecting to this practice. Koeller was then called into a conference with Ussel and Refling, in which conference Koeller's disagreement with school policies and his lack of judgment in handling student situations were discussed. Koeller then appealed by letter directly to Mr. Guhr (school board president) but was told to go through the normal grievance procedures. No further action was taken on this matter except that on October 28th Refling sent Koeller a letter warning him about insubordination.

4. On December 2, 1963, following a visit to Koeller's classroom, coordinator of instruction Ladd made the following comments and suggestions for improving inadequacies in Koeller's teaching techniques: (a) More student "involvement," (b) "less teacher talk," (c) the elicitation of "clear, confident responses" from students, (d) personal supervision of assignments, (e) various approaches to various students, and (f) permitting students to make their own evaluations. Koeller visited an experienced mathematics teacher from a Racine school and his class, and thereafter Ladd noticed that Koeller's teaching techniques improved.

5. On December 10, 1963, as a layman, Koeller wrote the state department of public instruction, concerning state aids formulas and the financial condition of the Muskego-Norway district. In this letter Koeller complained of inadequate facilities in the district.

6. On January 28, 1964, Koeller scheduled a meeting of the National Honor Society which conflicted with the meeting of the high school P. T. A. Koeller was given oral confirmation from Ussel but school policy required a written approval. A memo from the principal chastized Koeller for failing to obtain the approval of the principal, and Koeller circulated the memo.

7. On February 5, 1964, Koeller sent a student to the office with a note indicating he had suspended the student for three days. Koeller was told that the administration decided whether suspensions were in order. Koeller then publicly challenged the position of the administration in the MNEA newsletter, quoting from the private memo he had received from the administration. In the newsletter, Koeller maintained he had the right to suspend students for disciplinary reasons. Koeller was called into conference with the principal, where he was advised he was skating on "thin ice" in utilizing the MNEA newsletter to vent a private grievance.

8. On February 18th Koeller read the memo received in regard to the scheduling problem to the National Honor Society students and announced that this was the reason for resigning as adviser from the group. Koeller then sent Kreuser a note explaining his reasons for resigning and charging that Kreuser had exhibited vindictiveness toward him. Koeller subsequently withdrew this statement.

9. Koeller's record as a teacher includes having 43 disciplinary referrals to Principal Refling, while the 49 other teachers on the faculty had a total of 150 disciplinary referrals.

There is a dispute about what transpired at the March 2, 1964, meeting of the board. In addition to the salary-and-working-conditions proposals of the MNEA during executive session the board also considered whether to rehire Koeller. Kreuser denied that he made any recommendations at that session against renewing Koeller's contract. He denied that the subject was even discussed. Yet board member Vogel recalled that Kreuser had advised him on March 3d that Kreuser had made this recommendation at the meeting the previous night. Between March 2 and March 9, 1964, a summary of Koeller's activities was prepared and, upon the recommendation of Kreuser, at another executive session on March 9, 1964, the school board formally determined not to offer Koeller a teacher's contract for 1964-1965. On March 11, 1964, conditions of employment were again announced at a general teachers' meeting. No prior notice of action taken on its proposals was received by the MNEA.

On March 12, 1964, Koeller was called to Kreuser's office and given a notice that his contract would not be renewed. Kreuser read from a sheet of paper a number of reasons for the dismissal, but he did not give Koeller a copy of the list of the reasons even though Koeller requested one. Kreuser also advised Koeller that a successful contest of the discharge was unlikely, because all statutory requirements had been met. Further, Kreuser advised Koeller that such an appeal would be professional suicide because Koeller needed Kreuser's signature to obtain a life-time teaching certificate.

A dispute exists as to whether or not Kreuser first offered to give Koeller a recommendation for another job if Koeller would resign. Koeller's testimony indicates this is true while the testimony of Kreuser and Refling is that Koeller was only offered the opportunity to resign. Nonetheless, Koeller refused to resign and was then handed a prepared notice of termination, the letter stating that the action was "deemed advisable in view of actions and conduct on your part which have previously been discussed with you."

After a full hearing on the complaints, the WERB found:

"29. That the primary motivation of Kreuser's recommendation to the School Board not to renew Koeller's teaching contract for the 1964-1965 school year was not based on any shortcomings Koeller may have had as a teacher, nor upon his differences with certain policies with the School Board, but rather upon Koeller's activity and efforts on behalf of the MNEA Welfare Committee as the collective bargaining representative of the majority of the professional teaching personnel in the employ of the School District; that the discriminatory refusal of the School Board to renew Koeller's teaching contract and the recommendations with respect thereto made by Superintendent Kreuser and other supervisory employes of the School District, interfered, restrained and coerced not only Koeller, but also the remaining teachers in the employ of the School District in the exercise of their right to engage in lawful concerted activities."

And it reached the following conclusion of law:

"2. That Muskego-Norway Consolidated Schools Joint School District No. 9, Town of Muskego, Waukesha County, and Town of Norway, Racine County, by its School Board, by refusing and failing to renew Carston C. Koeller's teaching contract for the year 1964-1965 upon the recommendation of Kreuser, Refling, Ussel and Ladd, discriminated against him in regard to the conditions of his employment, for the purpose of discouraging membership in and activities on behalf of the Muskego-Norway Education Association and, thereby, has committed, and is committing, prohibited practices, within the meaning of Section 111.70 (3) (a)1 and 2 of the Wisconsin Statutes." ...

The WERB ordered the school district ... to offer Koeller his former position without prejudice, to pay Koeller any damages he may have suffered and to post a notice to all teachers notifying them of the actions taken and future policy to be followed by the district.

A petition for review of the WERB's order was filed under ch. 227, Stats. Thereafter, judgment was entered setting aside the order of the WERB. On the merits the trial court found that the finding of the WERB that the school board's primary motivation for firing Koeller was his labor activities was based on speculation and conjecture.... Further, the trial court ruled that there had been no proof of any relationship between the school board and the administrators. The WERB has appealed.

WILKIE, J. Four issues are raised on this appeal:

First, is the authority of school boards under secs. 40.40 and 40.41, Stats., subject to the limitations of sec. 111.70? ...

Third, is the WERB finding that the refusal of respondents to renew Koeller's contract was prompted by his labor activities supported by substantial evidence?

Fourth, must the WERB make an express finding that Kreuser, Refling, Ladd and Ussel were agents of the Muskego-Norway school board in order to impute their actions to the board in deciding whether unfair labor practices were committed?

Relation of Secs. 40.40, 40.41 and 40.45 and Sec. 111.70, Stats.

One of the principal premises for the trial court's decision was that secs. 40.40 and 40.41, Stats., require the school board to contract individually with each teacher each year....

The provisions of sec. 111.70, Stats., apply to the authority of school districts to the same extent as the authority of other municipal governing bodies. Sec. 111.70 was enacted after secs. 40.40 and 40.41 and is presumed to have been enacted with a full knowledge of preexisting statutes. Construction of statutes should be done in a way which harmonizes the whole system of law of which they are a part, and any conflict should be reconciled if possible....

Respondents ... contend that secs. 40.40 and 40.41, Stats., permit the school board to refuse to rehire on any ground or for no reason at all. Assuming this to be true, secs. 40.40 and 40.41 can be modified by subsequent statutes which forbid refusing to rehire a teacher for a particular reason. For example, a school board may not refuse to rehire a teacher because of his race, nationality or political or religious affiliations. Modification of statutes is a question of legislative policy. In 1959 the legislature enacted sec. 111.70 (3) (a), which prohibits municipal employers, including school districts, from:

"1. Interfering with, restraining or coercing any municipal employe in the exercise of the rights provided in sub. (2).

"2. Encouraging or discouraging membership in any labor organization, employe agency, committee, association or representation plan by discrimination in regard to hiring, tenure or other terms or conditions of employment."

This also restricts the reasons a teacher can be refused re-employment. A school board may not terminate a teacher's contract because the teacher has been engaging in labor activities.

Scope of Judicial Review

The second and third issues concern whether crucial findings of the WERB are supported by credible evidence. This makes it necessary to state the standard of judicial review of the findings of the WERB. It is well established that under sec. 227.20 (1) (d), Stats., judicial review of the WERB findings is to determine whether or not the questioned finding is supported "by substantial evidence in view of the entire record." This court has held that the key to the application of this standard is to determine what is meant by "substantial evidence."[10]

In *Copland* this court quoted from an article by E. Blythe Stason[11] as follows:

"'[T]he term "substantial evidence" should be construed to confer finality upon an administrative decision on the facts when, upon an examination of the entire record, the evidence, including the inferences therefrom, is found to be such that a reasonable man, acting reasonably, *might* have reached the decision; but, on the other hand, if a reasonable man, acting reasonably, *could not* have reached the decision from the evidence and its inferences then

---

[10] *Copland v. Department of Taxation* (1962), 16 Wis. (2d) 543, 554, 114 N.W. (2d) 858.
[11] *"Substantial Evidence" in Administrative Law,* 89 University of Pennsylvania Law Review (1941), 1026, 1038.

the decision is not supported by substantial evidence and it should be set aside.'"

Moreover, in *Copland* we reiterated that "'substantial evidence' is 'such relevant evidence as a *reasonable mind* might accept as adequate to support a conclusion.' (Emphasis supplied.)"[13] In *Copland* we declared that the test of reasonableness "is implicit in the statutory words 'substantial evidence,'" and that the "[u]se of the statutory words 'in view of the entire record as submitted' strongly suggests that the test of reasonableness is to be applied to the evidence as a whole, not merely to that part which tends to support the agency's findings." ...

Termination of Employment for Labor Activities

The WERB found that the primary motivation for the refusal of the school board to renew Koeller's contract was because of his activities and efforts on behalf of the MNEA welfare committee. The WERB concluded that the school board discriminated against Koeller in regard to the conditions of his employment for the purpose of discouraging membership in and activities on behalf of the MNEA and was thereby committing a prohibited practice under sec. 111.70 (3) (a), Stats.

A major premise in the trial court's argument for reversing the WERB's determination in this respect is that if a valid reason for discharging an employee exists, this is a sufficient basis for holding that the employee was not dismissed for union activities. The trial court quotes *Wisconsin Labor Relations Board v. Fred Rueping Leather Co.* as follows:

"... When a valid reason as heretofore defined is found to be present, it is relatively difficult and may be impossible to more than guess which reason motivated the discharge. The board could find discrimination here only by finding that the assigned reason for the discharge of Assaf was false because if it was not, the evidence is in such state that a finding of discrimination would be pure conjecture. Furthermore, we have some misgivings whether, if a valid and sufficient reason for discharge exists, the real or motivating reason has any materiality whatever, unless it can be shown that in other cases where similar grounds for discharge of nonunion men existed, no such action was taken." [228 Wis. 473, 499, 279 N.W. 673, 684 (1938).]

In other words, if there was good reason for terminating Koeller's employment because of teaching deficiencies and his differences of teaching philosophy with the school board and the supervisory personnel, it would not matter whether the contract was not renewed for his labor activities. But this is not the law. In *Rueping* there was no speculation as to what the real reason for the discharge was. Moreover, the law concerning discharge for labor activities has changed since 1938. In *N.L.R.B. v. Great Eastern Color Lithographic Corp.* [309 F.2d 352, 355 (2d Cir. 1962),] the federal courts [sic] stated:

"The issue before us is not, of course, whether or not there existed grounds for discharge of these employees apart from their union activities. *The fact that the employer had ample reason for discharging them is of no moment. It*

---

[13] *Copland v. Department of Taxation, supra,* footnote 10, at page 554, quoting from *Gateway City Transfer Co. v. Public Service Comm.* (1948), 253 Wis. 397, 405, 406, 34 N.W. (2d) 238; and *Consolidated Edison Co. v. National Labor Relations Board* (1938), 305 U.S. 197.

was free to discharge them for any reason good or bad, so long as it did not discharge them for their union activity. And even though the discharges may have been based upon other reasons as well, if the employer were partly motivated by union activity, the discharges were violative of the Act." (Emphasis added.)

Several other federal cases are in accord. Although these cases all involve a construction of unfair labor practices under the Wagner Act, the case of *St. Joseph's Hospital v. Wisconsin Employment Relations Board* adopts their legal conclusion that an employee may not be fired when one of the motivating factors is his union activities, no matter how many other valid reasons exist for firing him.

The trial court opined that the WERB reached finding of fact No. 29 "purely upon conjecture." It concluded that there was ample reason for the school board's actions for Koeller's deficiencies as a teacher and his philosophical differences with the individual respondents on school matters.

But in this court's judicial review we are not required to agree in every detail with the WERB as to its findings, conclusions and order. We must affirm its findings if they are supported by substantial evidence in view of the entire record. Sec. 227.20 (2), Stats., requires that upon such review due weight shall be accorded the experience, technical competence, and specialized knowledge of the agency involved. In short, this means the court must make some deference to the expertise of the agency.

In *St. Joseph's Hospital v. Wisconsin Employment Relations Board* the WERB found that the discharge of an employee was primarily because of her union activities. The court discussed the scope of review of this finding as follows:

"Finding 20 is a finding of ultimate fact and is of necessity based upon inferences from other testimony before the board. Such inferences may not be based upon conjecture but must be drawn from established facts which logically support them. The drawing of inferences from other facts in the record is a function of the board and the weight to be given to those facts is for the board to determine. International Union v. Wisconsin E.R. Board, 258 Wis. 481, 46 N.W.(2d) 185. Such findings, when made, cannot be disturbed by a court unless they are unsupported by substantial evidence in view of the entire record submitted."

The board is the judge of the credibility of the witnesses and the reviewing court is not to substitute its judgment for the judgment of the board.

In essence, in the instant case we must decide whether the WERB's crucial findings, conclusions and order are based on inferences reasonably drawn on the entire record or whether they are the result of conjecture on the part of the WERB.

On the whole record we conclude that WERB's finding No. 29 is supported by substantial evidence and reasonable inferences drawn therefrom in view of the entire record, that the failure to renew Koeller's teaching contract was motivated by his activities as chairman of the welfare committee of MNEA and not on any shortcomings Koeller may have had as a teacher nor upon his differences with certain policies of the school board and the respondent supervisory personnel.

The WERB's finding No. 29 is the logical final determination as to the motivation behind the failure to renew Koeller's contract following the stepped-up labor activities of the welfare committee in which Koeller had such a major part and the difficulties [he] had in assembling and presenting proposals on salaries and working conditions to Kreuser and the school board.

The WERB placed heavy emphasis on the timing and manner of the dismissal. Although there was dispute about it the WERB could reasonably find that the first recommendation of Koeller's nonrenewal was made at the executive session of the school board on March 2, 1964, immediately following the very meeting when the MNEA proposals for 1964-1965 were submitted to the school board for the first time and were discussed; that at that time no written reasons were given for the dismissal; that on March 9, 1964, a summary of reasons having been prepared since March 2d, the school board acted formally to terminate Koeller's services; that Koeller was not notified of this action until March 12, 1964, the day after the school teachers were called together and told of the school board's determinations about salaries and working conditions for the year 1964-1965 (there having been no negotiations about the MNEA proposals).

In a memorandum accompanying its findings of fact, conclusions of law and order the WERB discussed its reasons for concluding that the respondents were motivated by Koeller's labor activities in ending his employment. The WERB also thoroughly discussed and rejected the other reasons that were alleged to have motivated the respondents relating to the shortcomings of Koeller as a teacher and his disagreement with certain policies established by the school board.

The WERB carefully considered each one of the reasons compiled in the summary prepared by supervisory personnel prior to the school board's final action on March 9th as to why Koeller's contract should not be renewed. The WERB's analysis is summed up as follows:

> "It seems incredible to us that the Superintendent could be sincere in the gravity of complaints made against Koeller and at the same time offer to recommend him to another position. We believe this to be a gross act of intimidation."

The WERB concluded:

> "... in light of the entire record, we do not find that Koeller's competence as a teacher or disciplinarian motivated the determination not to extend his teaching contract.
> "We have therefore concluded that the Respondent School District refused Koeller a contract in order to discourage membership and collective bargaining activities on behalf of the Welfare Committee of the MNEA."

In any event, it may be assumed arguendo that the school board would have been warranted in terminating Koeller's services on these grounds if the motivation for the action were not connected with his labor activities. Yet the WERB could reasonably find, as it did, that the motivation for failing to renew Koeller's contract was his activities in the MNEA and on behalf of his fellow teachers' welfare.

Agency

The WERB specifically found that Kreuser, Refling, Ussel, and Ladd were supervisory personnel in the employ of the Muskego-Norway school district. The WERB considered the actions of these supervisory personnel in determining whether unfair labor practices had been committed by the school board and the school district. The trial court ruled that there was nothing in the findings of the WERB or in the evidence to establish that these supervisory personnel were agents of the Muskego-Norway school board. Therefore, ruled the trial court, actions of the supervisory personnel could not be attributed to the board in determining whether unfair labor practices had been committed, and only actions by school board members could be considered.

The trial court's ruling places form over substance. Where the WERB expressly found that Kreuser, Refling, Ussel, and Ladd were "supervisory personnel in the employ of said School District," such employment is sufficient to constitute an agency relationship. The employment policies of the school district are implemented through the actions of the supervisory personnel. Under the trial court's ruling, the school board could tacitly engage in unfair labor practices through actions by the supervisory personnel, and the employees discriminated against would have no effective recourse. Such a technical interpretation — as made by the trial court — of the findings of the WERB deprives sec. 111.70(3), Stats., of any real substance.

By the Court. — Judgment reversed.

WASHINGTON PUBLIC EMPLOYEES ASSOCIATION v. COMMUNITY COLLEGE DISTRICT 9

31 Wash. App. 203, 642 P.2d 1248 (1982)

PETRICH, JUDGE. This is an appeal by the Washington Public Employees Association (WPEA) and John P. Clayton, from an order of the Superior Court denying their petition for a writ of mandamus compelling enforcement of an order of the Higher Education Personnel Board (HEP Board) finding that Highline Community College committed an unfair labor practice. Because the HEP Board did not apply the appropriate standard in determining that an unfair labor practice existed, we remand the case to the HEP Board for further proceedings.

John P. Clayton was employed by Highline Community College as an Accountant III (chief accountant) from June 1968 until August 1977. On August 9, 1977, Clayton received notice that he was being suspended without pay effective August 9, 1977, and terminated effective August 23, 1977, because of continued neglect of duty, inefficiency, and incompetence. Clayton challenged the suspension and termination, filing both an appeal under RCW 28B.16.120 and chapter 251-12 WAC, and an unfair labor practice complaint pursuant to RCW 41.56.140. After being advised that the HEP Board would not hear the unfair labor practice charge while an appeal was pending, see WAC 251-14-090, Clayton withdrew his appeal. Clayton did not seek judicial review of the HEP Board's ruling prohibiting him from pursuing both his appeal and unfair labor practice complaint simultaneously.

Hearings were held on the unfair labor practice complaint. At the hearings evidence was introduced establishing:

1. Dr. Eade, Clayton's immediate supervisor, noted problems with Clayton's work as early as 1974.

2. The Highline Community College accounting department began using a new computer system in July, 1975; the change in systems caused some problems.

3. In December 1975, Dr. Eade learned that the general ledger had been out of balance for 3 months. A trainer was called in to assist Clayton in balancing the ledger.

4. On March 19, 1976, Don Slaughter, Highline Business Manager, published and distributed a memorandum entitled "The Union Shop — Have You Thought It Through" to all classified employees.

5. During the week of March 19, 1976, Clayton refused to sign an anti-union statement being circulated by Dr. Eade's secretary.

6. On March 22, 1976, Dr. Eade, a member of the bargaining unit, issued a memorandum entitled "Grumpy Editorial Comment."

7. Prior to the election Dr. Eade asked Clayton where he stood on the union shop issue. When Clayton told Dr. Eade that he favored the adoption of a union shop, Dr. Eade became visibly disturbed.

8. The election was held on March 25, 1976. On April 5, 1976, the WPEA was certified as the union shop representative.

9. Prior to May 10, 1976, Eade met with Clayton and discussed six concerns that Eade had about Clayton's work. Eade testified that Clayton acknowledged that he had problems but felt that he could solve them.

10. On May 10, 1976, Eade sent Clayton a memorandum requesting that Clayton give a 30-minute presentation on May 13, 1976, to Eade and Slaughter on the efforts that were necessary to balance the new accounting system. Clayton testified that there was no way he could collect the information requested within the time frame granted. Eade testified that such knowledge should have been within Clayton's immediate grasp and that Clayton had not indicated to him that he would not have enough time to prepare for such presentation. After the meeting, Eade told Clayton that his presentation had not been responsive.

11. During the summer of 1976, Clayton missed six weeks of work as a result of a cancer operation.

12. During 1976 and 1977, Clayton committed a number of significant accounting errors.

Based on the testimony and evidence taken at the hearings, the HEP Board found that Clayton's termination was "a contrived, anti-union action in violation of WAC 251-14-070(1)" and ordered Clayton's reinstatement. Highline Community College did not comply with the Board's order and the WPEA and Clayton applied to the Thurston County Superior Court for a writ of mandamus compelling enforcement of the Board's order. The trial court found that the HEP Board's order was "clearly erroneous" and denied the writ. Clayton now seeks review....

Although at some point it will be necessary for the legislature or the courts to determine the standard for judicial review of orders of the HEP Board, in unfair labor practice cases, we find it unnecessary to decide the issue at this time. In this case, we are not concerned with the degree of judicial deference accorded to an administrative agency in resolving factual issues or the application of the agency's special expertise in interpreting the factual or legal issue involved. The issue, rather, is whether the HEP Board applied the appropriate legal standard in determining that Highline Community College committed an unfair labor practice. This determination is peculiarly within the province of the court. For the reasons set forth below, this court finds that the Board did not apply the proper standard. Thus, applying either of the standards of review discussed above, the Superior Court, while stating the wrong reason, acted properly when it refused to grant an order enforcing the decision of the HEP Board.

Legal Standard to Be Applied in Unfair Labor Practice Cases Alleging Discriminatory Discharge

Complaints alleging that an employer's discharge of an employee constitutes an unfair labor practice fall into three categories: (1) cases in which the employer asserts no legitimate ground for discharge; (2) cases in which the employer's asserted justification for discharge is a sham and no legitimate business justification for discharge in fact exists (pretextual firings); and (3) cases in which there is both a legitimate and impermissible reason for the discharge (dual motive discharges). The first two types of discharge constitute unfair labor practices. The third type may or may not constitute an unfair labor practice.

The NLRB and United States Court of Appeals have applied several different tests in determining whether a particular discharge constitutes an unfair labor practice. Up until August, 1980, the NLRB applied an "in part" test in dual motive cases. *Wright Line, A Division of Wright Line, Inc.,* 251 NLRB Dec. (1980); *The Youngstown Osteopathic Hospital Ass'n,* 224 NLRB Dec. (1976). Under the "in part" test, if the discharge was motivated "in part" by protected activities of the employee, the discharge constitutes an unfair labor practice. This is true even if a legitimate business reason for the discharge also exists. A number of circuits have refused, however, to apply this test stating that the test ignores the legitimate business motives of the employer and places the union activist in an almost impregnable position once anti-union animus is established. *NLRB v. Billen Shoe Co.,* 397 F.2d 801 (1st Cir. 1968); *NLRB v. Patrick Plaza Dodge, Inc.,* 522 F.2d 804 (4th Cir. 1975); *Cain's Coffee Co. v. NLRB,* 404 F.2d 1172 (10th Cir. 1968).

Instead of the "in part" test, the First Circuit, at least until recently, applied a "dominant motive" test. Under the First Circuit test, if both a good and bad reason for the discharge exist, the Board, when it seeks an enforcement order, has to establish that the discharge would not have occurred but for the employee's union activity or the employer's anti-union animus. *NLRB v. Fibers International Corp.,* 439 F.2d 1311 (1st Cir. 1971); *NLRB v. Gotham Ind., Inc.,* 406 F.2d 1306 (1st Cir. 1969). The Third and Fifth Circuits have held that an employer commits an unfair labor practice if anti-union animus is the "real reason" or "real motive" for the discharge. *Gould, Inc. v. NLRB,* 612 F.2d 728 (3rd Cir. 1979); *Berry Schools v. NLRB,* 627 F.2d 692 (5th Cir. 1980). The Seventh Circuit has applied both the NLRB's "in part" test and an "any significant part" test. See *Nacker Packing Co. v. NLRB,* 615 F.2d 456 (7th Cir. 1980); *NLRB v. Pfizer, Inc.,* 629 F.2d 1272 (7th Cir. 1980). The Ninth Circuit has applied both a "dominant motive" and "but for" test. *NLRB v. Adams Delivery Service, Inc.,* 623 F.2d 96 (9th Cir. 1980); *NLRB v. Sacramento Clinical Laboratory, Inc.,* 623 F.2d 110 (9th Cir. 1980). The Tenth Circuit looks to see whether the "contributing motivation" in a discharge was an anti-union animus. *Coors Container Co. v. NLRB,* 628 F.2d 1283 (10th Cir. 1980).

In August, 1980, the NLRB adopted a new test. See *Wright Line, Inc., supra.* The new test, modeled after the test established by the United States Supreme Court in *Mount Healthy City School Dist. Bd. of Education v. Doyle,* 429 U.S. 274 (1977), to determine whether a teacher's contract was not renewed due to the teacher's constitutionally protected conduct, initially places the burden on the employee to show that his conduct was protected and that such conduct was a substantial or motivating factor in the employer's decision to discharge him. Once this is accomplished, the burden shifts to the employer to demonstrate that it would have discharged the employee even absent the protected conduct. The test effectively balances the interest of the employee in protected activity against the interest of the employer in operating his business in a particular manner. As the NLRB stated in *Wright Line,* 251 NLRB Dec. at 1089:

> Under the *Mt. Healthy* test, the aggrieved employee is afforded protection since he or she is only required initially to show that protected activities played a role in the employer's decision. Also, the employer is provided with a formal framework within which to establish its asserted legitimate justification. In this context, it is the employer which has "to make the proof." Under this analysis, should the employer be able to demonstrate that the discipline or other action would have occurred absent protected activities, the employee cannot justly complain if the employer's action is upheld. Similarly, if the employer cannot make the necessary showing, it should not be heard to object to the employee's being made whole because its action will have been found to have been motivated by an unlawful consideration in a manner consistent with congressional intent, Supreme Court precedent, and established Board processes.

In this case, neither the HEP Board nor the Superior Court specifically stated which standard was used in deciding complaints filed under sections 41.56.140 through 41.56.190 RCW. The HEP Board simply found "the *preponderance of the credible evidence* indicates that the *substantive reason* for Mr. Clayton's ultimate dismissal was his support of the Washington Public Employees Association and the union shop condition ..." (Emphasis added).

It is the opinion of this court that the appropriate legal standard is the *Mt. Healthy* standard adopted by the NLRB in *Wright Line.* The in-part test previously applied by the NLRB did not adequately protect the employer's rights; the dominant motive and other similar tests did not protect the legitimate interests of the employee. In contrast, the *Mt. Healthy* test, if properly applied, provides an effective mechanism for balancing the legitimate interests of both the employer and the employee. Accord, *NLRB v. Nevis Ind., Inc.,* 647 F.2d 905 (9th Cir. 1981); *Peavey Co. v. NLRB,* 648 F.2d 460 (7th Cir. 1981); *Statler Ind., Inc. v. NLRB,* 644 F.2d 902 (1st Cir. 1981).

Remand to the HEP Board for Consideration of Evidence and Testimony in Light of Appropriate Legal Standard

Because the HEP Board did not apply the appropriate legal standard, the trial court acted properly in refusing to enforce the Board's order. Clayton is, however, entitled to some relief. When an administrative agency applies an inappropriate legal standard, the weight of authority dictates that the reviewing court remand the case to the administrative agency with instructions to apply the appropriate legal standard. See *NLRB v. Gulf State Canners, Inc.,* 585 F.2d 757 (5th Cir. 1978); *Blackman-Uhler Chemical Div., Synalloy Corp. v. NLRB,* 561 F.2d 1118 (4th Cir. 1977); *NLRB v. Mosey Mfg. Co.,* 595 F.2d 375 (7th Cir. 1979). See also *NLRB v. Food Store Employees Union Local 347,* 417 U.S. 1 (1974). A new hearing will not be required. The HEP Board need only evaluate the testimony and evidence received at the previous hearings in light of the legal standard we have set forth in this opinion.

NOTES

1. In *Mt. Healthy City Sch. Dist. Bd. of Educ. v. Doyle,* 429 U.S. 274, 97 S. Ct. 274, 50 L. Ed. 2d 236 (1977), discussed in the principal case, a teacher was terminated because of (1) his statement to a radio station, and (2) his use of obscene gestures to students. In reversing the district court's holding that the teacher had to be reinstated since the teacher's exercise of his first amendment rights played a part in his termination (i.e., his statement to the radio station), the Court unanimously stated:

A rule of causation which focuses solely on whether protected conduct played a part, "substantial" or otherwise, in a decision not to rehire, could place an employee in a better position as a result of the exercise of constitutionally protected conduct than he would have occupied had he done nothing. The difficulty with the rule enunciated by the District Court is that it would require reinstatement in cases where a dramatic and perhaps abrasive incident is inevitably on the minds of those responsible for the decision to rehire, and does indeed play a part in that decision — even if the same decision would have been reached had the incident not occurred. The constitutional principle at stake is sufficiently vindicated if such an employee is placed in no worse a position than if he had not engaged in the conduct. A borderline or marginal candidate should not have the employment question resolved against him because of constitutionally protected conduct. But that same candidate ought not to be able, by engaging in such conduct, to prevent his employer from assessing his performance record and reaching a decision not to rehire on the basis of that record, simply because the protected conduct makes the employer more certain of the correctness of its decision....

Initially, in this case, the burden was properly placed upon respondent to show that his conduct was constitutionally protected, and that this conduct was a "substantial factor" — or to put it in other words, that it was a "motivating factor" in the Board's decision not to rehire him. Respondent having carried that burden, however, the District Court should have gone on to determine whether the Board had shown by a preponderance of the evidence that it would have reached the same decision as to respondent's reemployment even in the absence of the protected conduct.

429 U.S. at 285-87.

2. In *Board of Trustees of Billings Sch. Dist. No. 2 v. State,* 185 Mont. 89, 604 P.2d 770 (1979), the Montana Supreme Court adopted the *Mt. Healthy* "but for" test "for dual-motivation cases under Montana's Collective Bargaining Act." The Montana Supreme Court stated that "[l]abor law rights under Montana law should not be given a higher degree of protection than federal First Amendment rights are given." Similarly, the Federal Labor Relations Authority in *Internal Revenue Serv. & National Treas. Emps. Union,* 6 FLRA 23 (1981), adopted the *Mt. Healthy* test, stating:

> In the Authority's view, the application of such a test will serve to balance the legitimate interests and purposes of government with those rights assured to employees and their representatives under the Statute.... Such a test serves the purposes of the Statute by making it possible to more thoroughly analyze the relationship between the agency action and the protected conduct of an employee. Under this test, therefore, both the General Counsel and the agency will have an opportunity to adduce evidence as to the motivating factors involved in the action or decision of the agency which is the basis of the complaint. If it is established by a preponderance of the evidence that the same action or decision of the agency would have taken place even in the absence of the protected activity, a complaint of violation of Section 7116(a)(1) and (2) of the Statute will not be sustained. Conversely, if it is not established by a preponderance of the evidence that the action or decision would have taken place in any event, the Authority will find a violation under Section 7116(a)(1) and (2) of the Statute.

3. In *Wright Line,* 251 NLRB 1083 (1980), the NLRB adopted the *Mt. Healthy* test "of causation for cases alleging violations of Section 8(a)(3) of the Act." Subsequently, in *NLRB v. Transp. Mgt. Corp.,* 463 U.S. 393, 103 S. Ct. 2469, 76 L. Ed. 2d 667 (1983), the Supreme Court upheld the Board's *Wright Line* test, stating:

> In *Mt. Healthy City Board of Education v. Doyle,* 429 U.S. 274 (1977), we found it prudent, albeit in a case implicating the Constitution, to set up an allocation of the burden of proof on which the Board heavily relied on and borrowed from in its *Wright Line* decision. There, we held that the plaintiff had to show that the employer's disapproval of his First Amendment protected expression played a role in the employer's decision to discharge him. If that burden of persuasion were carried, the burden would be on the defendant to show by a preponderance of the evidence that he would have reached the same decision even if, hypothetically, he had not been motivated by a desire to punish plaintiff for exercising his First Amendment rights. The analogy to *Mt. Healthy* drawn by the Board was a fair one.

103 S. Ct. at 2475.

The NLRB's *Wright Line* test has been adopted in many jurisdictions. See, e.g., *Hardin Cty. Community Unit Sch. Dist. No. 1,* 174 Ill. App. 3d 168, 528 N.E.2d 737 (1988); *Maine State Emps. Ass'n v. State Dev. Office,* 499 A.2d 165 (Me. 1985); *Township of Bridgewater,* 95 N.J. 235, 471 A.2d 1 (1984); *McPherson v. PERB,* 189 Cal. App. 3d 293, 234 Cal. Rptr. 428 (1987).

4. Despite the Supreme Court's decision in *Mt. Healthy* and its subsequent adoption in many public sector "dual motive" cases, the Wisconsin Employment Relations Commission, with court approval, has continued to apply the "in part" test set forth in *Muskego-Norway.* In *State v. WERC,* 122 Wis. 2d 132, 361 N.W.2d 660 (1985), the court affirmed a WERC decision holding that an employer committed an unfair labor practice when it terminated an employee "when one of the employer's motivating factors is the employee's union activities even though many other valid reasons exist for firing the employee." In rejecting the employer's contention that the *Muskego-Norway* rule should be reversed, the Wisconsin Supreme Court stated:

> We recognize that the *Wright Line* test is obviously more advantageous to the employer than to the employee. Application of this standard permits an employer to voice his or her hostility toward union activists and even fire employees engaging in union activity, as long as he or she can provide a legitimate reason for terminating employment. Conduct of this nature will not be encouraged or tolerated by this court, and we therefore, refuse to join the NLRB in the use of the *Wright Line* test. In reaching this conclusion, we generally recognize the delicate balance that exists between management and labor. On one hand, the state of Wisconsin should be a paragon of fairness toward labor unions. Indeed, Wisconsin has had an admirable history of fostering a favorable climate for labor unions. However, the laws of this state must also be flexible enough to allow for efficiency and productivity in the marketplace. We believe that the *Wright Line* test would disrupt the relative balance between management and labor that this state strives for. For the reasons listed below, we reaffirm the validity of the "in part" test of *Muskego-Norway*.

5. The Illinois State Labor Relations Board in *State of Ill. (Dep'ts of Cent. Mgt. Servs. & Cors.),* 1 PERI ¶ 2020 (Ill. SLRB 1985), adopted the following analysis in determining whether remedial orders should be issued in "mixed motive" cases:

> When a Charging Party demonstrates that an adverse employment action was motivated, at least on part, by his having engaged in protected activities, we will find a violation of the Act, which will raise a presumption that the standard make whole remedy is appropriate. To rebut this presumption, the burden will be upon the employer to demonstrate that the same action would have been taken for legitimate reasons even in the absence of the protected activities. If the employer fully meets this burden in a discharge situation, it will not be required to grant the Charging Party reinstatement and back pay. Rather, the only remedy will be the posting of a notice. This approach safeguards the interests of both parties. Using this standard, an employer will not be free to use illegal motives in its disciplinary process; if it does so, it will be found guilty of an unfair labor practice and will, at a minimum, be required to post a notice so advising its employees. Therefore, the right of all employees to be free from discriminatory employment actions is protected. Conversely, an employer will not be required to provide a full remedy to an employee whose own misconduct would have resulted in discipline for the legitimate reasons, merely because his protected activities may also have been considered. This approach is a modification of both the NLRB's current *Wright Line* standard and its previous "in part" test and accomplishes, we believe, the Act's objectives more fully than either.

6. What obligations does an employee who has been discriminatorily terminated have to mitigate damages by seeking interim employment? In *Town of Pembroke Pines v. Florida State Lodge, FOP,* 501 So. 2d 1294 (Fla. Dist. Ct. App. 1986), the court upheld a Florida Commission decision holding that in future back pay proceedings a claimant would have the obligation of producing contemporaneous written documentation of efforts to seek employment as a prerequisite to obtaining an award of back pay. The court, however, upheld the Commission's decision to not apply the standard in the case before it since the public had not been sufficiently advised of the Commission's intention to adopt such a standard.

MIDDLESEX COUNTY ENGINEERING DEPARTMENT

Case No. MUP-472 (Mass. Labor Rel. Comm'n 1973)

[During an election campaign involving the seats of two of the three Middlesex County Commissioners, two "reform" candidates, Tsongos and Ralph, promised to reduce the size of the engineering department which had grown from 25-30 employees in 1962 to approximately 125 in 1972. After the reform candidates had pledged to reduce the size of the engineering department, a union organizing meeting was held and by September, 1972, approximately 90% of the engineering department employees had signed union authorization cards. In September a seven member union organizing committee was elected and the names of the members were announced in mid-November. Tsongos and Ralph were successful in defeating the two incumbent commissioners in the primary election and were elected in the general election in November 1972. On December 1, 1972, a petition was filed by the American Federation of State, County and Municipal Employees (AFSCME) for certification of a bargaining unit consisting of the employees in the engineering department. The petition was held in abeyance pending the outcome of the instant proceeding.

After Tsongos and Ralph took their positions as county commissioners on January 3, 1972, Commissioner Tsongos requested certain employees in the engineering department to draw up lists of 50 employees that they would recommend be retained. Data from the six lists that were received was compiled by the staff aides for the two new commissioners. Based on these compilations, 46 employees were terminated on January 26, 1973. Of the seven-member union organizing committee, three were terminated (including the Chairman, Gino Porreca) and four were retained.

A prohibited practice charge was filed on February 27, 1973, alleging that the county commissioners interfered with and restrained

employees from the formation, organization and creation of an employee organization by terminating the employment, summarily, of all employees having been designated as members of the Negotiating Committee to represent the Engineering Department and others active in the formation and organization of the employee organization.

Following an investigation, the Massachusetts Labor Relations Commission on March 29, 1973, issued a complaint alleging "that all forty-six (46) employees involved were active in the formation of an employee organization" and that their "dismissal was an interference and restraint on the formation of said employee organization."

At the hearing the chairman of the local union organizing committee, Gino Porreca, characterized four of the six individuals who submitted lists as "anti-union," and that the remaining two "were friendly." This same witness testified that he was in charge of patronage for the two defeated commissioners and knew that employees came into the department under the sponsorship of a commissioner. He further testified that he was aware of the pledge made by Tsongos and Ralph to reduce the size of the engineering department.]

The Petitioner [Gino Porreca] avers that he and others were discharged for joining, assisting, and participating in lawful union activity. The Municipal Employer denies this, and says all were discharged in accordance with procedures for reducing the overall size of the Middlesex County Engineering Department....

The question raised in the instant case is whether certain employees of the County Government of Middlesex County were discriminatorily terminated because of their activity on behalf of a labor organization. When a Municipal Employer violates individual rights guaranteed by *General Laws Chapter 149, Section 178* by terminating the employment of individuals for having engaged in protected activity, it is the responsibility of the Labor Relations Commission to remedy that violation and make whole the injured party by ordering his reinstatement, ... and, in appropriate cases, awarding back pay.... Where, however, such motive is not established, this Commission will not substitute its judgment for the legitimate authority of the Employer....

We begin, then, from the premise that, where an improper motive is not shown, the Commission cannot question the personnel policies and practices of a Municipal Employer. This rationale applies equally whether the employee is discharged, suspended or laid off. Cf. *McNeil v. Mayor and City Council of Peabody,* 297 Mass. 499 (1937), where the Court held that the purpose of the Civil Service legislation was to "protect public employees from partisan political control.... But it was not designed to prevent a city from undertaking in good faith a reorganization of a political department in order to promote effectiveness and economy."

The Seventh Circuit Court of Appeals stated the matter succinctly in interpreting sections 8 (a) (1) and (3), National Labor Relations Act, which General Laws Chapter 149, section 178 (L) closely parallels:

> "The mere coincidence of the layoffs with the union activity, without more, is not substantially indicative of a discriminatory motive." *Beaver Valley Canning Co. v. N.L.R.B.,* 332 F.2d 429 (7th Cir. 1964).

The burden is on the charging party to demonstrate by direct testimony or fair inference that the layoffs were improperly motivated. *N.L.R.B. v. Whitin Machine Works,* 264 F.2d 383 (1st Cir. 1953). The New York P.E.R.B. has similarly held "the charging party had to initially establish by a preponderance of the credible evidence that the respondent ... was unlawfully motivated. It had to establish respondent's anti-charging party animus." *General School District No. 3, Town of Huntington and Babylon, Suffolk County and Half Hills Teachers Ass'n, Inc.,* 5 PERB ¶4515 (1972).

We find the reasoning of these and similar cases persuasive. To find a violation of General Laws Chapter 149 section 178 (L) the record must reveal more evidence from which the implication of discriminatory intent may fairly be drawn.

We note in this regard that the so-called "reform" slate had announced its intention of reducing staff size prior to the commencement of any union activity and that reduction of staff size was a major plank in the "reformers'" campaign platform. We therefore find that the decision to layoff was not discriminatively motivated, and unless we are to conclude that the layoff was carried out in a discriminatory manner, there was no violation of the Act.

The record does not support such a conclusion. Although three members of the union steering committee were laid off, four were retained. In the total staff reduction, the percentage of pro-union employees laid off does not appear to be disproportionate. The record does not disclose any substantial anti-union animus on the part of either the selection committee or the Commissioners. Mr. Porreca testified to his "feelings" that several members of the rating panel were against the union. Others, however, were in favor. At least one member of the panel had signed an authorization card. There is no credible evidence that any member of the rating panel was selected because of his anti-union bias, or that anti-union motives influenced the evaluations. Rather, the testimony indicates that if the members of the rating panel were influenced by any factor other than the ability of employees to perform their jobs, that factor was political partisanship. Such a claim, while not free from legal complexity, is potentially within the jurisdiction of this Commission.

Non-tenured public employees do not forfeit First and Fourteenth Amendment rights by the mere act of accepting such employment. While it has been held that a non-tenured public employee has no constitutionally protected right to his continued employment, *Bailey v. Richardson,* 182 F.2d 46 (D.C. Cir. 1950), *aff'd per curiam,* 341 U.S. 918 (1950), recent federal decisions indicate that such employees may not be discharged solely because of the exercise of First Amendment rights to freedom of speech and association. *Wieman v. Updegraff,* 344 U.S. 183 (1952); *Pickering v. Board of Education,* 391 U.S. 563; *Perry v. Sindermann,* 400 U.S. 593 (1972), and cases cited therein. Recently courts have been faced with the issue of whether a political partisan may be discharged from a non-tenured public position solely on the basis of past or present political affiliations. The circuits have divided on the issue.... [Editors' Note: In *Elrod v. Burns, infra,* the Supreme Court held that public employees in non-policymaking positions could not be terminated solely because of their political affiliations.]

While the Labor Relations Commission is not, strictly speaking, empowered to decide constitutional questions, public employee labor relations is often inextricably intertwined with the political process. This Commission has recognized, for example, that the right of access to the press is a necessary and proper tool of both labor organizations and employers, in attempting to persuade and inform the public of their respective positions. See *Quincy School Committee and National Association of Government Employees,* MUPL-18 (4/25/72). We might, at some point, have to determine whether certain activity, such as petitioning a legislative body for passage or defeat of a measure, or even political activity on behalf of certain candidates constitutes protected activity within the meaning of the Statutes we are empowered to interpret and enforce. We refrain from further consideration of arguably constitutional questions, however, since we are satisfied that, on the record in this case, they are not properly raised.

Despite being given every opportunity to do so, neither party herein has argued that the discharges were in any way politically motivated. That the parties could mutually agree on this point strains our credulity, but the charging parties are bound by their testimony on the record specifically denying that the discharges were purely political in the pejorative sense....

Since it has been determined previously that the layoff of the employees involved was not related to their belated organizational efforts on behalf of a union, the complaint should be, and hereby is, *Dismissed.*

NOTES

1. Accord *City of Philadelphia & Register of Wills,* 8 PPER 78 (Pa. PLRB 1977) (termination of employees for political reasons did not violate act where not motivated by anti-union animus).

2. In *City of New Berlin,* WERC Decision No. 7293 (1966), the Wisconsin Employment Relations Commission, in holding that an employee's termination was not motivated because of union activities, stated:

The most that Complainant can assert under the circumstances is that his selection for termination was arbitrary; but if the reason for discharge is not for an unlawful purpose prescribed [sic] by Section 111.70(3)(a), this Board has no jurisdiction to remedy mere arbitrary action.

Accord *Westport Transport Dist.,* Case No. MPP-3447 (Conn. SBLR 1977) (board has no jurisdiction to decide whether discharge is too severe in absence of proof action was motivated by employee's union or protected activities).

TOWN OF DEDHAM v. LABOR RELATIONS COMMISSION

365 Mass. 392, 312 N.E.2d 548 (1974)

KAPLAN, JUSTICE. We face again the problem of meshing the new labor rights guaranteed to public employees with earlier provisions of law. On the present appeal we have to deal with an accommodation between the statute empowering the Labor Relations Commission to rectify alleged interference by municipal employers with the protected mutual-aid activities of their employees, and the older statute establishing the Civil Service Commission as a guard against arbitrary disciplining of classified employees by their public employers. The field is dynamic....

1. *Facts.* On September 9, 1970, Warren W. Vaughan, a Dedham firefighter, one of the interveners-appellants herein, engaged in a "heated conversation" with the deputy chief of the fire department, James Hall, at the Dedham fire station. On September 14 the chief of department, John L. O'Brien, one of the appellees, notified Vaughan that commencing that day he was suspended for five days with loss of pay for "insubordination" toward a superior officer arising out of the incident with Deputy Chief Hall.

On September 23 Vaughan requested a hearing before a member of the Civil Service Commission pursuant to G.L. c. 31, § 43(e), as to whether the suspension was for "just cause." A week later, on September 30, Vaughan filed a complaint with the Labor Relations Commission charging a prohibited labor practice on the part of the appellees town of Dedham and its fire chief within the meaning of c. 149, § 178L(1), in that they had violated his protected rights under § 178H(1) to engage in activities on behalf of the firefighters for mutual aid free from interference, restraint, or coercion.

A Civil Service Commissioner held a hearing on October 20 attended by Vaughan and counsel, and on January 13, 1971, the Civil Service Commission notified the fire chief that the suspension was justified but that the penalty should be reduced to a two-day suspension with loss of pay. The present record on appeal does not indicate what issues were considered, nor are any particular findings set out. Meanwhile the Labor Relations Commission, after investigation by its agents, issued its formal complaint on November 5, 1970, against the town and fire chief. At a hearing on January 5, 1971, before a Labor Relations Commissioner, the town and fire chief moved to dismiss the complaint on the ground that the commission lacked jurisdiction of the subject matter. The motion was not allowed. Testimony was taken and recorded, and the following facts as to the September 9 incident appeared, embodied in the "Findings of Fact and Decision" of the commission, made part of its "Decision and Order" contained in the record on appeal.

Vaughan was a member of the executive board and past president of Local 1735, Dedham Firefighters Association. He was off duty on September 9, when he got into the "heated conversation" with Deputy Chief Hall in the presence of another firefighter. The subject was the duties to be performed by firefighters on holidays (such as Labor Day just passed). Vaughan objected to the men's being assigned window washing and similar chores and said this was in violation of the practice of "holiday routine" by which the men were to be excused certain maintenance jobs. Deputy Chief Hall refused to discuss this issue on the ground that "Vaughan was not running the Department." Vaughan told the deputy chief that he was going to bring the matter up at the next union meeting. He advised the men not to do work on holidays in the future beyond the "holiday routine." He then left the fire station.

On evidence going beyond the immediate incident, the Labor Relations Commission also found that Vaughan had an excellent record as a firefighter. In processing grievances and negotiating on labor matters over the previous two years, he had had many heated discussions with the fire chief. Examining the circumstances surrounding the fire chief's decision to suspend Vaughan, the commission found that the chief had ordered the suspension for other than disciplinary reasons. It may be added that the commission found there had in fact been a right to a "holiday routine" which had become vested by practice over a period of years despite "rules and regulations" promulgated by the fire chief.

On the whole case, the commission concluded that the formal complaint it had issued was supported by the testimony. Accordingly, it issued its order in two parts: first, that the appellees, town of Dedham and its fire chief, cease and desist from interfering with their employees in the exercise of their protected rights under the statute; second, that they take affirmative action to "reinstate" Vaughan and make him whole by payment of the withheld salary, make available on request the records as to back pay, post a notice announcing their intention to comply with the directions to cease and desist and to reinstate, and notify the commission as to steps taken to comply with the order.

The appellees petitioned the Superior Court under the State Administrative Procedure Act, G.L. c. 30A, § 14, for review of the decision and order of the Labor Relations Commission. Although the pleader recited all plausible grounds of review listed in § 14(8), the two distinctive grounds that appear pertinent were lack of jurisdiction of the Labor Relations Commission, and lack of substantial evidence to support the decision. The judge of the Superior Court held for the appellees on the first ground, ruling that the matter was beyond the jurisdiction of the Labor Relations Commission and "fell exclusively within the jurisdiction of the Civil Service Commission" under c. 31, § 43; thus the appellees' motion to dismiss should have been allowed, and the commission's prohibited practice complaint was now to be dismissed. The judge rested essentially on c. 149, § 178N, which states that "[n]othing in sections one hundred and seventy-eight F to one hundred and seventy-eight M, inclusive [the sections of c. 149 setting forth the rights and duties of municipal employees, and the relevant responsibilities of the Labor Relations Commission], shall diminish the authority and power of the civil service commission, or any retirement board or personnel board established by law, nor shall anything in said sections constitute a grant of the right to strike to employees of any municipal employer." The judge did not reach the question of substantial evidence. Appeal from the final decree was claimed by the Labor Relations Commission and the interveners, Vaughan and Local 1735.

2. *Statutes.* Until 1958, public employees in the Commonwealth, as in most States, had virtually none of the rights that had been widely guaranteed since the nineteen thirties to employees in private business to organize and bargain collectively and to be protected in the associated activities of asserting and negotiating grievances. Classified public employees were indeed entitled to the benefits of a civil service system, designed, according to the "merit principle," to bring nonpartisanship and rationality into the processes of hiring, promotion, transfer, and discipline. These employees were protected against arbitrary punishment, the usual issues being whether the charges made by the public authority as grounds for dismissals or suspensions — neglect of duty, incompetency, insubordination, venality, or the like — could be supported in fact. The question whether the charges were being used by the employers as excuses or masks for interference with the employees' rights to organize, present grievances, and so forth, had no particular place in proceedings before the Civil Service Commission because the rights themselves had not received recognition by law.

The civil service statute to this day does not in terms reflect labor rights of this character. Dismissal or suspension may be exacted only for "just cause," see G.L. c. 31, § 43, a formula that is not less than seventy years old. The pattern of the procedure now is that the employee receives written notice from the "appointing authority" of the reason for its action, whereupon the employee may request a hearing by that authority; if the decision is unfavorable, he may request a hearing before a member of the Civil Service Commission, who reports his findings to the commission, which acts to affirm, reverse, or modify. From an adverse determination, the employee may petition for review by a District Court (or the Municipal Court of the City of Boston), with the appointing authority and the commission named as repondents. § 45.

Turning to the origin of the labor statute, the traditional hostility to organizational rights on the part of public employees gradually diminished in the postwar period, and in 1958 Massachusetts was among the first States to take steps — but they were quite ineffectual steps — to afford a measure of recognition to those rights. See St. 1958, c. 460, adding G.L. c. 149, § 178D. The Presidential Executive Order of 1962 (No. 10988, 5 U.S.C.A. § 7301 at 300 [1967], replaced by No. 11491 [1969], as amended, 3 C.F.R. 262 [1973]) granting rights of collective bargaining to Federal employees added to the respectability and impetus of the movement, and by 1965 there had been much growth of unionization among public employees. 1971 Ann.Surv. of Mass.Law, §§ 6.1, 6.2. Legislation of 1964 and 1965 provided a fairly comprehensive code of collective bargaining law, both substantive and procedural, for the benefit of State and municipal employees, and it is this code which applied at the time of the events in suit and with which we are here concerned. St. 1964, c. 637, adding c. 149, § 178F. St. 1965, c. 763, adding c. 149, §§ 178G-178N.

All municipal employees are embraced in the 1965 code, "whether or not in the classified service of the municipal employer," except elected officials and certain others. § 178G. Passing over the rather elaborate provisions directed to the process of collective bargaining itself (§§ 178I-178K), § 178H(1) states the basic rights of employees to self-organization and to engage in the various ancillary concerted activities. By § 178L, first paragraph, municipal employers are prohibited from interfering with those guaranteed rights (subdivision [1]), and from committing certain acts more particularly enumerated, such as "refusing to discuss grievances with the representatives of an employee organization recognized or designated as the exclusive representative in an appropriate unit" (subdivision [5]). Certain prohibitions are also laid on employee organizations (second paragraph). When complaint is made to the Labor Relations Commission that a prohibited practice has been committed, the commission may dismiss, or order a hearing, or an investigation to be followed by hearing, which may be conducted before the commission itself or by a member of the commission. The proceeding is then in the name of the commission against the allegedly offending municipal employer, employee, or other person, who may appear to defend; others, including the original complainant, may be admitted as interveners. A transcript of the testimony is taken. There is a right of review from the Commissioner to the commission, which may receive further testimony. If, on all the proof, the commission finds that a prohibited practice has occurred, it makes findings of fact and issues an order against the offender to cease and desist and to take such affirmative action as will comply with the provisions of § 178L, including an order for "reinstatement with or without back pay of an employee discharged or discriminated against" in violation of the first paragraph. Review of an order of the commission, available to any party aggrieved, may be had by petition to the Superior Court under the State Administrative Procedure Act, c. 30A, § 14. Section 178N contains the saving clause, quoted above, relating to the Civil Service Commission and other agencies. (As noted, material changes are brought into the scheme by legislation effective July 1, 1974.)

3. *Discussion.* The Legislature's attempt to solve the whole problem of the interrelation of the labor statute with the civil service law by the general saving

clause of § 178N "invites litigation," as we said of a similar facile effort in *Mathewson v. Contributory Retirement Appeal Bd.*, 335 Mass. 610, 614, 141 N.E.2d 522 (1957). As elsewhere in the field of labor law, "it ... [becomes] the task of the courts to accommodate, to reconcile the older statutes with the more recent ones." *Boys Mkts., Inc. v. Retail Clerks Union, Local 770*, 398 U.S. 235, 251 (1970).

The judge below read § 178N to mean that upon a complaint by a municipal civil service employee under c. 31, § 43, that there was not just cause for his suspension (or dismissal) on the ground of alleged "insubordination," the matter was to be handled exclusively by the Civil Service Commission and the Labor Relations Commission was wholly excluded and without jurisdiction to take any action; just as such a case would be handled solely by the Civil Service Commission before the creation of the Labor Relations Commission, so, according to the judge, it must be handled now.

This seems to us not a reasonable accommodation. Neither § 178N nor any other statutory provision purports to confer "exclusive" jurisdiction on either commission. Such routing of cases involving municipal employees under civil service solely through the Civil Service Commission, while cases of municipal employees not under civil service alleging prohibited practices could move only through the Labor Relations Commission, would result in distortions and disregard of enacted law that would call in question any supposed legislative purpose to create that kind of dual system.

If the Civil Service Commission were to administer in such cases only the substantive law which it has historically fashioned under the title of "just cause," and no recourse could be had there or before the Labor Relations Commission to the new labor statute in its material aspects, then a plain perversion of the legislative purpose would occur and a gulf would be created between the treatment of classified and nonclassified municipal employees that could not be justified in policy or logic. The opinion below does not disavow this result.

But if it be suggested that the Civil Service Commission should attempt in those cases to apply the labor law as well, with the Labor Relations Commission wholly excluded — a suggestion made by the appellees in their brief, although with little elaboration — then there would still be a plain defiance of the definitional clause of § 178G, already quoted, joining together classified and nonclassified employees for the purposes, procedural and substantive, of the labor statute.

Employees of both classes (and their employers as well) are entitled to the specialized services of the Labor Relations Commission in the administration of the labor rights, and to the related adjective arrangements. Considering the indissoluble linkage of the character of a tribunal, its procedure, and the substantive law that it enforces, it seems clear that the parties before the Civil Service Commission would not — and in the nature of things could not — secure from that body alone substantive rights equivalent to those assigned by the statute for enforcement to the other commission. So the idea of using the Civil Service Commission to act as a substitute for the Labor Relations Commission in cases involving employees in the civil service would turn out to be quite unsatisfactory. It must, after all, have been a prime legislative purpose in creating the Labor Relations Commission to promote uniformity rather than disuniformity of interpretation and application of the labor law. In this light we need hardly point out that "cease and desist" and "affirmative" remedies, not only available but required in certain cases under the labor statute, could in no event attach to determinations by the Civil Service Commission, and that the nature and course of judicial review of orders of the Civil Service Commission depart from those prescribed for review of orders of the Labor Relations Commission.

In our view, the statutes can be read "so as to constitute a harmonious whole" (*Mathewson v. Contributory Retirement Appeal Bd., supra,* 335 Mass. at 614, 141 N.E.2d at 525) by attributing to the Legislature certain commonsense general purposes. There was a legislative design to introduce new substantive law as to the rights of municipal employees which must in ultimate effect impinge on the traditional "just cause" formula. The Civil Service Commission was to remain concerned with the functions and with protection of the interests with which it had long been associated, while the Labor Relations Commission was to be engaged in the new tasks and protection of the new interests. But neither agency should be oblivious of the actions of the other. It could follow that some marginal litigious events — relatively few in comparison with the bulk — might have to be handled by both agencies. With mutual restraint, aided by cooperation of those representing employees and employers, the two agencies could reach a fair adjustment, and the precept of § 178N would be reasonably satisfied.[18]

Preliminarily we observe that it was open to the Legislature in writing the new law to prescribe, as a ground for examining, and in proper cases overturning disciplinary action by a municipal employer (as well as for securing independent relief against it), that it had engaged in a prohibited practice. This the Legislature did by means of §§ 178H and 178L. Though the new law can be thought of as amending or affecting the civil service law, with its traditional reading of "just cause," it did not exceed legislative power, or in itself qualify the policy of § 178N....

Nor is § 178N abused when functional lines are respected within reason in the conduct of particular dismissal or suspension cases. The present case was evidently conducted on all sides without forethought as to the optimum procedure to be used, but the functional idea may still be followed to a solution. Although the charge before the Civil Service Commission was "insubordination," it was not improbable that the question of anti-union bias might come up in the unfolding of the facts as possibly qualifying or negating the charge. The record, however, does not disclose that the question did come up; if it did, there is no indication of what attention it actually received. In this situation, it would be strange indeed to say that the Labor Relations Commission lacked "jurisdiction" to proceed with an inquiry into anti-union bias upon a complaint before it charging a prohibited practice. This consideration is enough to dispose of the present appeal.

We think we should go on to say that, had the Civil Service Commission examined into the motivation of the suspension as a phase of the question

---

[18] To make anything turn on whether one agency has some priority in time over the other would be without support in the statutes and might encourage regrettable competitive races between the agencies.

whether the employee was in fact insubordinate, and had it ruled against the employee, then the Labor Relations Commission, in comity, could properly take the ruling of the other agency into account as support for a determination to dismiss the employee's concurrent complaint charging a prohibited practice. But the Labor Relations Commission would not be deprived of "jurisdiction," and if not satisfied that the question of anti-union bias had been sufficiently explored, could decline to dismiss, issue its own complaint, and proceed to prosecute and later grant relief which might comprehend "reinstatement" and more.[20]

Whether the Labor Relations Commission, acting within its "jurisdiction" in the present case, reached the right decision in substance, can be tested when the cause is remanded to the Superior Court and the employers' petition for review under the State Administrative Procedure Act is proceeded with there. If the employers succeed, the suspension stands, and no offence is given to § 178N. It is very unlikely that there can be any such offence if the employers fail and the employee's suspension is wiped out by an order for "reinstatement." This follows from two added considerations. An employer's commission of a prohibited practice usually, if not always, so far pervades and dominates a case as to call for revoking the discipline ordered by the employer even if the employee could otherwise be properly called insubordinate (and other relief, negative and affirmative, would then also be in order). The "insubordination" that was found is not negated but may be taken to be outweighed. Second, the Labor Relations Commission operates on a basis different from that of the Civil Service Commission. The latter agency vindicates a private right of the complaining employee (although of course the right is given in part to serve a public purpose). The former agency, although stirred to action by a private complaint, acts when it chooses to do so in its own name as a public prosecutor to test a public right, with the possible remedy not limited to the grievance of the particular employee.[22]

In retrospect, considering the apparent seriousness with which the prohibited practice charge was here being pressed, one imagines that it would have been advantageous to hold the civil service proceeding in abeyance by consent or otherwise while the Labor Relations Commission acted. A finding of prohibited practice against the municipal employer would likely have ended the matter (subject to review in the Superior Court on the employer's petition); a finding by the commission for the employer on that charge (or reversal of a contrary finding on review) would leave the employee with his § 43 route to protest that he was not "insubordinate."

We have, of course, been speaking of the rare cases with potentialities of conflict between the agencies. The much larger number will fall to one or the

---

[20] Analogy can be found in the attitude of deference that may be taken by the National Labor Relations Board toward certain arbitral decisions, although it does not yield ultimate jurisdiction. See The Developing Labor Law, 488-495 (A.B.A., Section of Labor Relations Law, ed. Morris, 1971); *Yourga Trucking, Inc.,* 197 N.L.R.B. No. 130, 80 L.R.R.M. 1498 (1972). Cf. n. 23 below.

[22] This difference in the operations of the agencies is among the reasons why an employee's application to either agency should not be considered an "election" against or a "waiver" of resort to the other. So also it is immaterial that the employee here did not attempt judicial review of the determination of the Civil Service Commission (which, according to the judge below, the employee thought to be a futile course). See n. 23 below.

other as a matter of routine. In the present situation, indeed, the employee might well have applied only to the Labor Relations Commission. On a favorable decision there, he would be reinstated, and this would not interfere in any way with the Civil Service Commission, which would not have been applied to. Otherwise the suspension would stand.

While some awkwardness must be felt in those few cases where a single episode may be twice examined at the administrative level, there is in fact considerable precedent for giving the employee more than one string to his bow. Thus in the recent case of *Alexander v. Gardner-Denver Co.*, 415 U.S. 36, the Supreme Court held that the employee could maintain an action under Title VII of the Civil Rights Act of 1964, 42 U.S.C. § 2000e et seq. (1970), for a discharge based on alleged racial discrimination, although he had failed in a previous arbitration under the collective bargaining agreement with his employer where he (with his union) had charged the same wrongful discrimination. Justice Powell observed that "legislative enactments in this area have long evinced a general intent to accord parallel or overlapping remedies against discrimination." *Id.* at 47. Where our statutes allow alternative remedies or avenues of relief there is perhaps less anomaly, because as we have seen the interests protected are not the same, and in the one case it is the individual, in the other an agency of the Commonwealth, that seeks vindication of the interest.[23]

4. *Conclusion.* The decree appealed from, dismissing the proceeding before the Labor Relations Commission for lack of jurisdiction, is reversed, and the cause is remanded to the Superior Court for further proceedings consistent with this opinion.

NOTES

1. In *Hinfey v. Matawan Reg'l Bd. of Educ.*, 77 N.J. 514, 391 A.2d 899 (1978), the New Jersey Supreme Court held that where concurrent administrative jurisdiction exists, it is the responsibility of both agencies to make a comparative analysis of their respective statutes and determine which agency is best equipped to resolve a particular dispute.

2. The New Hampshire Public Employee Bargaining Law provides that "[t]he board shall have primary jurisdiction of all violations ..., but no complaints may be filed with the board for violation of [the equivalent of Section 8(a)(3) and (4) of the NLRA] until the complainant has exhausted the administrative remedies provided by statutes other than this chapter." N.H. Rev. Stat. Ann. § 273-A:6 (1976).

---

[23] Justice Powell's opinion in the *Alexander* case will be found rich in suggestion about the nonapplicability of "election" and "waiver" (415 U.S. at 49-54 (1974) [42 U.S.L. Week at 4218-4219] and about a court's possible deference to or acceptance of findings made by the arbitrator (415 U.S. at 55-60 (1974) [42 U.S.L. Week at 4220-4221]).

Chapter 3

ESTABLISHMENT OF THE COLLECTIVE BARGAINING RELATIONSHIP

A. QUALIFICATION OF THE PROPOSED BARGAINING REPRESENTATIVE

Most of the state labor relations acts provide that labor organizations can file representation petitions seeking to represent employees in an appropriate unit. A preliminary question is occasionally raised as to whether a given organization or group constitutes a "labor organization" or "employee organization" within the meaning of the act. Many of the acts contain the definition of labor organization that is set forth in Section 2(5) of the National Labor Relations Act:

The term "labor organization" means any organization of any kind, or any agency or employee representation committee or plan, in which employees participate and which exists for the purpose, *in whole or in part,* of dealing with employers concerning grievances, labor disputes, wages, rates of pay, hours of employment, or conditions of work. 29 U.S.C. § 152(5) (1973) (emphasis added).

This definition has been given an expansive interpretation. Thus, an organization that has as one of its purposes negotiations with an employer is a labor organization even though it has no written constitution or by-laws, its officers do not serve for a specified period of time, and it is funded by voluntary contributions. *Yale Univ.,* 184 N.L.R.B. 860 (1970). Moreover, the Supreme Court has held that an organization that deals with an employer concerning grievances is a labor organization within the meaning of the act, even though it does not negotiate collective agreements with the employer in the usual sense. *NLRB v. Cabot Carbon Co.,* 360 U.S. 203 (1959). Social clubs and "flower" committees have also been held to be labor organizations if they serve as the medium for the presentation of employee recommendations and grievances to the employer. *NLRB v. Precision Castings Co.,* 130 F.2d 639 (6th Cir. 1942).

Where the state act's definition of the term "labor organization" parallels the definition found in the National Labor Relations Act, the term has likewise been interpreted liberally. For example, in *Wayne Cty. Bd. of Supvrs.,* 1965-1966 MERC Lab. Op. 320 (Mich.), the Michigan Employment Relations Commission held that a bar association was a labor organization even though its by-laws did not list collective bargaining as one of the purposes of the organization. And in *Wayne State Univ.,* 1969 MERC Lab. Op. 670 (Mich.), the MERC held that an organization composed entirely of students was a "labor organization," rejecting the contention that such an organization "would not have the permanence, experience, or strength necessary to constitute" a labor organization within the meaning of the Michigan Act. See also *Kalama Sch. Dist. No. 402,* Decision No. 873 (Wash. PERC 1980) (informal organization with no by-laws or dues structure and which was generally dormant following contract ratification held to be an "employee organization").

In contrast to the NLRA-type definition, the New York Taylor Law, as well as several other state statutes, defines the term "labor organization" or "employee organization" to mean "an organization of any kind having as its primary purpose the improvement of terms and conditions of public employees." N.Y. Civ. Serv. Law § 201(5) (McKinney 1983). In view of this definition, it was contended that an organization whose membership included both public employees and private employees was not an "employee organization." The New York PERB refused to accept this interpretation. *City of Ogdensburg,* 1 PERB ¶ 414 (N.Y. 1968). Joseph Crowley, a member of the New York PERB, explained the Board's position as follows:

> In those situations where the employee organization does admit to membership both public and private employees, it has been held that if the public employee members of the organization select their own negotiating committee and, without participation by private sector members, ratify negotiation agreements, the organization is an employee organization within the meaning of section 201(5). The reasoning of the Board is that the public employees who are responsible for the conduct of the negotiations would, therefore, not be submerged in an organizational structure dominated by private sector employees. Hence, where the independence of action of public employee members involved is protected, such organizations have been found to be within the purview of section 201(5) of the Law.

Crowley, *The Resolution of Representation Status Disputes Under the Taylor Law,* 37 Fordham L. Rev. 517, 529-30 (1969).

In *State of N.Y. (State Univ. of N.Y.),* 2 PERB ¶ 3070 (N.Y. 1969), the New York PERB held that a faculty senate was an "employee organization" for purposes of the Taylor Law, agreeing with the following conclusion of its director of representation (2 PERB ¶ 2010):

> The record makes it clear that the senate, in its role as faculty governor, has represented the faculty position with regard to economic goals as well as a number of matters of educational concern, such as admissions policies, faculty hiring, promotion and tenure procedures, curriculum, and class size. It is equally clear that many of these matters would constitute, to some degree, negotiable terms and conditions of faculty employment. Moreover, the "purpose" clause of the senate's constitution was revised in late 1968 to specifically mandate the senate to work to improve the terms and conditions of employment of all members of the professional staff. Clearly then, there is no basis in fact for finding that the senate's "primary purpose" is other than the improvement of terms and conditions of employment. Therefore, I find that the senate satisfies the statutory definition of an "employee organization."

CONNECTICUT STATE BOARD OF LABOR RELATIONS, TWENTY-FIRST ANNUAL REPORT 8-9 (1967)

The Act defines this term ["employee organization"] as meaning "any lawful association, labor organization, federation or council having as a primary purpose the improvement of wages, hours and other conditions of employment among employees of municipal employers."...

In two cases where employee associations met this primary purpose requirement, they were challenged on the ground that supervisors, excluded from the unit by the Act, were active members and officers of the association. The Board, following decisions by the federal courts, the National Labor Relations Board, and the New York State Labor Relations Board, ruled that such membership rendered the organization ineligible to be a bargaining representative of municipal employees under the Act. Such membership "inevitably conflicts with the policy of the Act 'to insulate employees' jobs from their organizational rights." *Local 636, United Association of Journeymen, etc. v. NLRB,* 287 F.2d 354, 362 (D.C. Cir. 1961). Therefore the Board concluded:

"These decisions did not, of course, involve the Connecticut statute which we must construe and administer. They were, however, made under statutes which were similar to ours in forbidding domination or interference by the employer in the associations which are to represent the employees. And we find the federal and New York decisions persuasive that the policies underlying this prohibition are violated when supervisory personnel excluded from the bargaining unit are allowed to become active voting members of the association; and more clearly violated when such supervisors became officers of the association.

"The next question is whether an association which permits such supervisors to be active members or officers is a 'lawful association' within Section 1(3) of our Act. The giving of such permission is not made a prohibited practice on the part of an employee organization under Section 4(b) of the Act, nor is it unlawful in the sense that it will subject the association to criminal penalties, but this is not, we feel, dispositive of the question. We believe that the legislature used the words 'lawful association' in this connection to mean broadly an association which is so constituted and organized that it is fully capable of serving the law's policy to have a disinterested and independent bargaining representative for employee units which want representation. And we find that an association which acquiesces in or permits voting membership or office-holding by supervisors excluded from the bargaining unit is thereby acquiescing in a practice which is prohibited because it tends to subvert the policies of the Act and render the association incapable of fulfilling the law's policies. This prevents it from being a 'lawful association' within the meaning and purposes of this provision." *City of Stamford (Public Works Department),* Dec. No. 682, April 1, 1966; *City of Hartford,* Dec. No. 681, April 6, 1966.

CITY OF MILWAUKEE

Decision No. 6960 (Wis. Emp. Relations Comm'n 1964)

Effect of Supervisory Employes as Members of Employe Organization

The Board is confronted herein with a problem as to whether it should permit an employe organization to be on a ballot in an election proceeding which organization has a substantial number of supervisors among its membership. In *Joint School District No. 1 of the City of West Allis, etc.,* [Decision No. 6544,] the Board stated:

"The fact that supervisory personnel are members of, or any hold office in, any labor organization subject to the provision of Section 111.70 may raise a suspicion, but does not in itself establish domination or interference with the organization by the Municipal Employer employing such supervisory personnel. The number of supervisors among the members of the organization and the ratio of supervisors to other members are factors to be evaluated in each case. Likewise, the office held by supervisors and the extent to which they formulate the bargaining policy and programs of their labor organizations will also be scrutinized in each case."

In said case the issue of participation by supervisors, as members, in a labor organization was raised in a prohibitive practice proceeding before the Board and not in a representation case. The function of the Board in a representation proceeding is to determine whether or not a question of representation exists, to take evidence with respect to the appropriate collective bargaining unit and with respect to the employes eligible to participate in the election if one is ordered by the Board. It is now our opinion that the Board should not, in a representation proceeding, question the internal affairs of an organization, which the Board is satisfied exists for the purpose of representing municipal employes in conferences and negotiations with municipal employers on matters pertaining to wages, hours and conditions of employment. Therefore, in a representation proceeding, we do not believe that we should impose conditions on any organization seeking to represent municipal employes, which conditions would limit the right of such organizations to establish rules for the acquisition, retention and rejection of membership. To do so in a representation proceeding would impinge on the voluntary nature of such organizations. If the rules of such an organization permit supervisors to membership and/or exclude classes of employes from membership, the employes involved have a right to refuse to become members thereof, and if said organization is seeking to represent the employes in an election proceeding before this Board, the employes can vote to reject such organization as their collective bargaining representative. If it can be established, in a prohibitive practice proceeding, that any labor organization which has been selected as the collective bargaining representative of municipal employes in an election conducted by the Board, that the rules and regulations of such an organization interfere with the rights of employes under Section 111.70 or that supervisory employes have dominated that organization and thus interfered with the rights granted to the employes, we will, among other remedies, set aside the certification.

We have held that supervisory employes should be barred from the collective bargaining unit since we do not consider them to be employes within the meaning of Section 111.70. Since supervisors are not employes within the meaning of the Statute then they should not participate in the activities of an employe organization concerned with wages, hours and conditions of employment.

As noted previously herein, the inclusion of supervisors in the same bargaining unit with employes would create a conflict of interest since supervisors are agents of the municipal employer. Where supervisory employes are members of the rank and file employe organization, the fact that they are not included in the appropriate collective bargaining unit would not eliminate the possible conflict of interest above noted. Supervisors who are members of an employe organization, with rights and privileges extended to employe members, could exercise a voice and vote in the administration and in the deliberations of the affairs of that employe organization. Their membership in the employe organization would permit them to run for office, to nominate candidates for office, to vote on candidates for office, to act on committees meeting in conferences and negotiations with the municipal employer on questions concerning hours, wages and conditions of employment and to vote and participate in such matters. By such membership they could actively exercise an interest in conflict with that of the employes and thereby dominate or interfere with the internal affairs of the employe organization. The active participation by supervisory employes in the affairs of an employe organization could result in impeding and defeating the primary purpose of the employe organization — that of representing municipal employes in conferences and negotiations concerning their wages, hours and conditions of employment. Since supervisors are the agents of the municipal employer, a municipal employer, by permitting supervisory employes to participate actively, in any manner similar to that described above, in the affairs of an organization representing employes for the purposes set forth in Section 111.70, could, in the proper proceedings, be found to have committed prohibitive practices by interfering, restraining and coercing its employes in the exercise of their rights granted to them under the law. As previously noted in this case, the president of the Association and two members of its Board of Directors have been found to be supervisors by the Board. Whether the activities of supervisors as members of a labor organization constitute prohibitive practices under Section 111.70 will be determined by the Board in formal complaint proceedings before the Board and by the facts established in each case.

Effect of Limiting Membership to Certain Employes

As noted above, during the hearings in the matter, a question arose as to whether or not the Board would consider the Association as a qualified labor organization under Section 111.70 since it admitted to membership only registered engineers and architects, or those who had obtained a degree in their respective fields. The Board has found the unit appropriate here not only to include certain classifications of engineers and architects, but also the Engineering Technician IV, V and VI classifications, the incumbents of which, although not degreed or registered, are performing duties identical to various degreed or registered employes employed in the engineering and architectural classifications.

Section 111.70(2) confers upon municipal employes the right to affiliate with employe organizations of their own choosing. In our view this provision does not limit employe organizations from adopting reasonable rules for the acquisition, retention or rejection of membership. As noted above, we have indicated that we will not, in a representation proceeding, prescribe or review the rules governing the internal affairs of labor organizations representing municipal employes and, therefore, the fact that the Association's constitution and by-laws do not provide membership for non-degreed or non-registered employes does not affect the right of the Association to appear on the ballot in this election proceeding. Any labor organization selected by a majority of employes in an appropriate collective bargaining unit has the duty and obligation to represent all of the employes in the bargaining unit with equal vigor, whether members of the organization or not. If any labor organization certified by the Board as the exclusive bargaining representative for employes in an appropriate unit fails in that duty and obligation, the Board can, in a proper proceeding, vacate its certification and eliminate the right of such organization to continue as the exclusive collective bargaining representative of said employes....

NOTES

1. The New York PERB in *State of N.Y. (State Univ. of N.Y.)*, 2 PERB ¶ 3070 (N.Y. 1969), held that questions of employer domination should be handled in a prohibited practice proceeding "separate and apart from a representation proceeding."

2. The NLRB considers the effect of supervisory membership on labor organization status in representation proceedings. See, e.g., *International Paper Co.*, 172 N.L.R.B. 933 (1968).

3. The constitutionality of the Taylor Law's requirement that an employee organization must affirm that it does not assert the right to strike before it can be certified as a collective bargaining representative was upheld by the New York Appellate Division in *Rogoff v. Anderson*, 34 App. Div. 2d 154, 310 N.Y.S.2d 174 (1970), *aff'd*, 28 N.Y.2d 880, 271 N.E.2d 553, 322 N.Y.S.2d 718, *appeal dismissed for want of a substantial federal question*, 404 U.S. 805 (1971). The union argued "that the requirement for an affirmation that Respondent does not assert the right to strike is a violation of Respondent's right of free speech under the Federal and State Constitutions," relying on the decision in *National Ass'n of Letter Carriers v. Blount*, 305 F. Supp. 546 (D.D.C. 1969), *appeal dismissed*, 400 U.S. 801 (1970), in which the court struck down as unconstitutional a statutory provision that made it illegal for federal employees to belong to employee organizations that asserted the right to strike. In distinguishing this case, the court held the problem "was not job acquisition for retention, but certification with its attendant benefits." As a result, the court held that "the condition imposed is reasonable for the benefits conferred, and is reasonably calculated to achieve the ultimate desired end." The court further observed that it did not construe the statutory requirement as an infringement "upon the exercise of rights protected by the First Amendment."

4. The Georgia Fire Fighters Bargaining Law provides that a municipal employer shall recognize the organization selected by a majority of the fire fighters in a given fire department if said "organization does not advocate striking and has a 'no-strike' clause in its constitution and bylaws." Ga. Code Ann., ch. 25-5-5 (Harrison 1990). The Nevada statute provides that a local government employer may only recognize an employee organization that has affirmatively pledged "in writing not to strike against the local government employer under any circumstances." Nev. Rev. Stat. § 288.160(1)(c) (1987). Are either or both of these requirements unconstitutional? In determining the constitutionality of prohibiting the granting of recognition to an employee organization that advocates striking, would it make any difference if the jobs of the employees in question are essential to the safety and health of the public?

B. EXISTENCE OF QUESTION CONCERNING REPRESENTATION

1. SHOWING OF INTEREST

A condition precedent to invoking the representation procedures under most of the public sector collective bargaining statutes is a showing by the union or employee organization that it has substantial support among the employees in the bargaining unit petitioned for. The purpose of such a requirement is "to avoid needless dissipation of P.E.R.B.'s resources on frivolous representation claims." *Civil Serv. Emps. Ass'n v. Helsby,* 63 Misc. 2d 403, 312 N.Y.2d 386 (Sup. Ct. 1970), *aff'd,* 35 App. Div. 2d 655, 314 N.Y.S.2d 159 (1971). Most of the statutes incorporate the long-standing NLRB rule that the union or employee organization must affirmatively demonstrate that it has the support of at least 30 percent of the employees in the unit claimed to be appropriate. Although there are some statutory variations, this showing of interest is usually made by submitting membership cards or dues checkoff authorizations to the labor relations agency. These cards or authorizations are then checked against a list of employees submitted by the employer. Following the private sector precedent, the determination of whether the employee organization has submitted the requisite showing of interest has been held to be an administrative matter that is within the discretion of the agency to determine and is not a matter that can be litigated. *Kane Cty. v. Illinois State Lab. Rel. Bd.,* 165 Ill. App. 3d 614, 518 N.E.2d 1339 (1988); *Civil Serv. Emps. Ass'n v. Helsby, supra; Union Free Sch. Dist. No. 21,* 1 PERB ¶ 405 (N.Y. PERB 1968); *Commonwealth of Mass.,* 10 MLC 1557 (Mass. LRC 1984). See also *Helper v. State of Mich., Dep't of Labor,* 64 Mich. App. 78, 235 N.W.2d 161 (1975) (MERC administrative determination that there was an insufficient showing of interest will not be set aside "[a]bsent a showing that MERC's discretionary decision is so perverse or palpably wrong as to effectively amount to a breach of its statutory duty"). Several PERBs have promulgated rules to this effect. For example, Section 95.17 of the Rules of the Pennsylvania Labor Relations Board provides that the administrative determination of the showing of interest "shall not be subject to collateral attack in any hearing."

Unlike other statutory schemes, the Florida law provides that "[a]ny employee, employers, or employee organization having sufficient reason to believe any of the employee signatures were obtained by collusion, coercion, intimidation or misrepresentation, or are otherwise invalid shall be given a reasonable opportunity to verify and challenge signatures appearing on the petition." Fla. Stat. § 447.307(2) (West 1981). In *School Bd. of Marion Cty. v. PERC,* 334 So. 2d 582 (Fla. 1976), the Florida Supreme Court interpreted this provision "to mean that a public employer's good faith allegation of one of the grounds enumerated in the statute is sufficient to require the Commission to give access to the authorization cards, and that the Commission is not authorized to review or test the employer's judgment or assertions at that stage of the proceedings."

NOTES

1. Many of the public sector statutes specifically provide that a decertification petition must be supported by a 30 percent showing of interest. If a decertification petition is filed within the applicable "window period," is it permissible for the petitioner to submit its showing of interest after the "window period"? In *California Dep't of Personnel Admin.*, 7 PERC ¶ 14200 (Cal. PERB 1983), the California PERB dismissed a petition since the showing of interest was submitted following the close of the window period.

2. Where a given statute specifically authorizes employees to file a decertification petition but makes no provision for an employer to do so, may an employer nevertheless file a petition challenging the continued majority status of the collective bargaining representative? May an employer test the union's majority status by refusing to bargain with the union and assert as its defense that the union no longer represents a majority of the employees in the appropriate bargaining unit? See *PLRB v. Houtzdale Mun. Auth.*, 6 PPER 283 (Pa. PLRB 1975) (unfair labor practice for employer to refuse to bargain based on doubt as to union's majority status; proper course of action is for employer to file a decertification petition).

3. The NLRB, like the WERC, has held that an employer may file a petition challenging a union's majority status if it can establish that it has a good faith doubt based on objective considerations that the union has lost its majority status. *United States Gypsum Co.*, 157 N.L.R.B. 652 (1966). The NLRB has further held that the determination as to whether the employer has presented sufficient objective considerations is an administrative matter and cannot be litigated. *United States Gypsum Co.*, 161 N.L.R.B. 601 (1966). See *Wauwatosa Bd. of Educ.*, Decision No. 8300-A (Wis. ERC), aff'd, 1 PBC ¶ 10,303 (Wis. Cir. Ct. 1968) ("An employer petitioning for an election in an existing unit must demonstrate to this agency at the hearing, by objective considerations, that it has reasonable cause to believe that the incumbent organization has lost its majority status since its certification or the date of voluntary recognition").

4. The Nevada statute is unique in that it expressly provides that a public employer may withdraw recognition if the employee organization "ceases to be supported by a majority of the local government employees in the negotiating unit for which it is recognized." Nev. Rev. Stat. § 288.160(3)(c) (1971). The employee organization may appeal, however, to the Local Government Employee-Management Relations Board. The Board is given the authority to direct an election if it "in good faith doubts whether any employee organization is supported by a majority of the local government employees in a particular negotiating unit." Nev. Rev. Stat. § 288.160(4) (1987). See *Nevada Classified Sch. Emps. Ass'n v. Carson City Sch. Dist.*, Item No. 99 (Nev. LGE-MRB 1980).

5. Can a public employer withdraw recognition from an employee organization because it has engaged in an illegal strike? In *IBEW Local 1225 v. City of Gridley*, 113 L.R.R.M. 3729 (Cal. 1983), the California Supreme Court held that under the Meyers-Milias-Brown Act, a public employer does not have the right to revoke a union's recognition as exclusive representative because of its instigation of an illegal strike. The court noted "that the guiding principle of the statute insofar as recognition of employee organizations goes is employee choice" and that "[t]he City's action, revoking recognition of the union, was inconsistent with that principle." In a footnote, the court noted that "although seven states explicitly authorize revocation of union recognition as a sanction for strike activity … , the few appellate courts that have considered the sanction have been reluctant to uphold it, expressing concern that it interferes with employees' rights to be represented by organizations of their own choosing."

In *PATCO v. FLRA*, 685 F.2d 547 (D.C. Cir. 1982), the court affirmed an order of the Federal Labor Relations Authority revoking PATCO's certification following the 1981 air traffic controllers' strike. The authority of the FLRA to revoke an exclusive representative's certification as majority representative is specifically authorized as a sanction for strike activity by the Federal Labor-Management Relations Act. 5 U.S.C. § 7120(f), 5 U.S.C. § 7103(a)(4)(D) (1980).

2. EFFECT OF AN EXISTING AGREEMENT (CONTRACT BAR DOCTRINE)

TOWN OF MANCHESTER

Decision No. 813 (Conn. State Bd. of Labor Rels. 1968)

The Municipal Employees' Group, Inc., on March 7, 1968, petitioned for an election in a unit consisting of salaried employees. The employees in this unit are presently represented by the Intervenor, Local 991, of Council #4, American Federation of State, County and Municipal Employees, AFL-CIO, and are covered by a collective agreement between the Intervenor and the Municipal Employer. That Agreement is due to expire January 1, 1969.

The Intervenor objects to the petition on the ground that an election is barred by the present contract and that a petition filed ten months prior to the termination of the contract is premature. We agree and order the petition dismissed. However, because our past decisions have raised some questions as to the operation of the contract bar principle in the field of municipal employment and when a petition will be considered to be timely filed, we feel it appropriate to provide as much clarification as our evolving experience presently permits.

We start with the basic statutory premise that employees have a right to bargain through representatives of their own choosing. That freedom of choice includes the freedom to change their mind as to which, if any, employee organization they want to represent them. At the same time, the purpose of choosing a representative is for collective bargaining, and that purpose cannot be realized unless there is some stability of representation. The employees must be permitted periodically to reconsider their choice, but this ought to be done at a time when it will not disrupt the bargaining process any more than necessary. To that end, the National Labor Relations Board developed the contract bar rule which this Board has generally followed. The least disruptive time for a change of representative is at the end of the contract term. Therefore, the appropriate time for a petition for an election is in that period prior to the end of the contract when a change in the bargaining representative can be most smoothly effectuated with the least disruption of the bargaining process.

The National Labor Relations Board evolved a set of subsidiary rules governing the timeliness of a petition prior to the end of the contract. See Leedom, *Industrial Stability and Freedom of Choice,* in Collective Bargaining and the Law (1959), p. 63; Reed Roller Bit Co., 72 N.L.R.B. 927 (1947). Petitions filed more than 150 days prior to the end of the contract would not be accepted because the holding of an election would leave the incumbent union as a lame duck in administering the old contract. Also, petitions filed less than 60 days prior to the end of the contract would not be accepted so that the parties would have the last 60 days of bargaining undisrupted by any doubts as to the union's status in election proceedings. To these rules governing the timeliness of a petition, the NLRB added a third rule that a petition would not be barred by the negotiation of a new contract prior to the end of the time for filing a petition. Deluxe Metal Furniture Co., 121 N.L.R.B. 995 (1958). For example, if the contract were to expire on December 31, a petition filed on October 30 would not be barred by a new contract made prior to that date. The challenging union could not be blocked by the incumbent union's premature renewal of the contract. Later the NLRB modified these time limits to require filing not more than 90 days or less than 60 days prior to the end of the contract. Leonard Wholesale Meats, Inc., 136 N.L.R.B. 1000 (1962).

These rules were developed by the National Labor Relations Board for collective bargaining in the private sector. Although we have never adopted the rigid time limits set down by the NLRB, we believe that the principles they are built upon are sound and that the time spans indicated are generally appropriate in the sphere for which they were designed. That is, for collective bargaining in the private sector.

Collective bargaining in the public sector raises different considerations. Experience during the last two years has suggested that the bargaining process in public employment is often more protracted than in private employment. This means that bargaining for a new contract may begin longer in advance of the end of the contract term. If there is to be a change of the bargaining representative, that change can be most smoothly made at the time when contract negotiations would normally begin. Therefore, a petition filed somewhat more than 90 days prior to the end of the contract would be at an appropriate time. Our experience is too limited to now fix limits with certainty, but we are presently persuaded that a petition filed as much as four months prior to the end of that contract should not be considered premature.

Collective bargaining in the public sector often requires quite different time limits for filing petitions for another reason. Collective agreements are often timed to expire at the end of the fiscal year. In that case, the parties usually contemplate that negotiations for a new contract will be held while the budget is being prepared so that when the budget is presented and adopted, it will reflect the costs of the new collective agreement.

Where the collective bargaining process is thus coordinated with the budget-making processes, the normal time for beginning negotiations may be as much as five or six months before the end of the contract term. This time is considered necessary to complete negotiations, get the results of the negotiations reflected in the budget and have the budget adopted before the end of the fiscal year. A petition filed for a change of representatives at the time when negotiations for a new contract normally begin cannot be considered to be premature. On the contrary, it might well be considered to be at the most appropriate time. It would avoid having negotiations disrupted in mid-course by a change of bargaining representatives. For this reason, we ordered an election in the Greenwich case (Case No. ME-1631, April 17, 1968), even though the collective agreement still had several months to run.

We are not prepared at this time to establish any rigid time limit in such cases, for our experience is yet too limited to say with any assurance how long a time may be required. Nor do we know in practical terms what difficulties the incumbent union may have in administering the remainder of the existing contract. For the present, we will follow the general guide that a petition filed within a month prior to the time when negotiations will normally begin will be considered timely. We consider it preferable that when negotiations normally begin, everyone will know who are the proper negotiators.

In this case, the contract is not scheduled to coordinate with the fiscal year, but is to expire on January 1, 1969. The parties have testified that, as in private employment, negotiations would normally begin about three months prior to the end of the contract. To hold an election in May could mean that the incumbent union could continue to administer the contract for seven or eight months in a lame duck status. Such problems should and can be avoided. The appropriate time for a petition to be filed in this case is after the first of September. This will permit the question of representation to be resolved in time for negotiations to take their regular course. A petition filed any earlier than the first of September will, in this case, be considered premature.

The petitioner here need have no fear that it will be barred by a new contract made before it files a new petition. If a petition is filed at any time between September 1, and November 1, then a new agreement made prior to the filing of the petition will not constitute a bar to an election.

The petition is hereby dismissed.

NOTES

1. Who administers an existing agreement if a rival union decertifies the incumbent union prior to the expiration date of the agreement? The Wisconsin Employment Relations Commission in *City of Milwaukee,* Decision No. 8622 (Wis. ERC 1968), held that if a rival union unseats an incumbent union prior to the expiration of the agreement, the rival union administers the agreement for the balance of its term. Accord *Old Orchard Beach Police Dep't,* CCH Lab. Law Rep., 3 State Laws ¶ 49,999C.44 (Me. PELRB 1974). In *State of N.Y.,* 5 PERB ¶ 3060 (N.Y. 1972), *aff'd sub nom. Police Benevolent Ass'n v. Osterman,* 73 Misc. 2d 184, 340 N.Y.S.2d 291 (Sup. Ct. 1973), the New York PERB held that the successor organization administers the agreement "until a new agreement can be negotiated effective upon the start of a new fiscal year of the employer or the expiration of the old agreement, whichever is sooner." On the other hand, the Connecticut State Board of Labor Relations in *City of Norwich,* Decision No. 804 (1968), held that:

> even though an election is held prior to the termination date of the contract, it is for determining the status of the bargaining agent after the termination of the contract. During the remainder of the contract term, the Union retains its right to recognition and its authority to represent the employees, regardless of the outcome of the election.

In *County of Delaware v. PLRB,* 89 Pa. Commw. 402, 492 A.2d 506 (1985), the court held that a successor union had the right to negotiate during the term of an existing contract that was the result of interest arbitration. The court held that interest arbitration was final and binding only on the parties that participated in the arbitration proceeding and was not final and binding on the successor union.

Under the NLRA if an incumbent union is decertified, it loses its status as the bargaining agent and it has no right to administer the agreement for the balance of its term. See *Modine Mfg. Co. v. Grand Lodge Int'l Ass'n of Machinists,* 216 F.2d 326 (6th Cir. 1954); *Farmbest, Inc.,* 154 N.L.R.B. 1421 (1965), *en-*

forced as modified, 370 F.2d 1015 (8th Cir. 1967). The Supreme Court in *NLRB v. Burns Int'l Sec. Serv.,* 406 U.S. 272, 284 n.8 (1972), held that "[w]hen the union that has signed a collective-bargaining contract is decertified, the succeeding union certified by the Board is not bound by the prior contract, need not administer it, and may demand negotiations for a new contract, even if the terms of the old contract have not yet expired." What are the advantages and disadvantages of each approach? Which approach is more likely to promote labor relations stability?

2. Not infrequently the period of time within which a representation petition may be filed where there is an existing collective bargaining agreement is specifically set forth in the applicable statute. For example, Section 967(2) of the Maine Municipal Public Employees Labor Relations Act provides that "[w]here there is a valid collective bargaining agreement in effect, no question concerning unit or representation may be raised except during the period not more than 90 nor less than 60 days prior to the expiration date of the agreement." Me. Rev. Stat. Ann. tit. 26, § 967(2) (1974 & Supp. 1983). The Hawaii statute contains a similar provision. Hawaii Rev. Stat. § 89-7 (1985). In other instances the contract bar rules are set forth in rules and regulations promulgated by the agency administering the act.

3. Normally, a representation petition is timely if it is filed after the expiration date of a collective bargaining agreement. Suppose, however, that prior to the expiration date the parties had reached agreement on all but one issue and had agreed to submit that issue to binding arbitration. Would a representation petition filed by a rival union be timely if it was filed after the termination date of the agreement but prior to the receipt of the arbitrator's award that would resolve the one remaining issue in negotiations between the employer and the incumbent union? In *City of Norwich,* Decision No. 804 (Conn. SLRB 1968), the Connecticut State Board of Labor Relations stated:

> [T]he agreement to submit the principal issue in dispute to binding arbitration creates a contractual relationship between the Union and the employer which bars an election, and if that arbitration leads directly to the concluding of a collective agreement, an election is barred until the termination of that collective agreement. The purpose of the contract bar is to promote stability in collective bargaining relations. The arbitration agreement substantially settles the parties' relation and removes the uncertainty and instability of unsettled negotiations. To open the question of representation during the time required for arbitration to crystalize into a completed contract would be to disrupt this peaceful method of resolving disputes. Uncertainty as to the union's status would undermine or distort the arbitration and open the award to a kind of collateral attack.

Accord *City of Prescott,* Decision No. 1874 (Conn. SBLB 1981). Would the same considerations be applicable if the parties had agreed to submit the unresolved issues to non-binding fact finding as opposed to binding arbitration? Would it make any difference if non-binding fact finding was legislatively mandated? See *City of Appleton,* Decision No. 7423 (Wis. ERC 1966).

4. Does a two-year collective bargaining agreement that contains a limited reopening clause permitting negotiations for wages and one or two fringe benefit items for the second year constitute a bar for the full two-year term? In *Douglas Cty.,* Decision No. 20608 (Wis. ERC 1983), the Wisconsin Commission held that such a contract constituted a contract bar and that the reopener did not trigger the window period within which a representation petition could be filed.

CITY OF GRAND RAPIDS (HEALTH DEPARTMENT)
1968 MERC Lab. Op. 194 (Mich. Emp. Relations Comm'n)

... On July 11, 1967, MNA [Michigan Nurses Association] petitioned the Board for a representation election in a unit defined as:

> "All registered nurses employed by the Health Department of the City of Grand Rapids."

AFSCME and the City oppose this petition on the grounds that ... there existed as of July 11, 1967, a collective bargaining agreement sufficient under section 14 of PERA to bar the Board from conducting any election....

The 1966 contract contained an expiration date of June 30, 1967. In March, 1967, AFSCME and the City commenced negotiations for a new agreement. Since no new agreement had yet been reached as of June 28, 1967, the parties extended the 1966 agreement to July 7, 1967. On July 5, 1967, the City Commission adopted Ordinance No. 67-43, a general salary ordinance which set pay ranges for the various classifications of work. On July 7, the City Manager completed negotiations with AFSCME and reached an oral agreement on salaries and all other working conditions. This oral agreement called for certain salary increases beyond those just provided in Ordinance No. 67-43 of July 5, 1967. The City Commission followed through by adopting Ordinance No. 67-44, on July 11, 1967, upping salaries to the level orally agreed to on July 7, 1967 by the City Manager and AFSCME. Also on July 11, a two page "letter of agreement" was signed by the City Manager and AFSCME officials, agreeing that the old 1966 Contract would remain in effect until May 31, 1968, with several specific modifications, including the substance of Salary Ordinance 67-43 as amended by 67-44. Other modifications affected the grievance procedure, compensatory time off, pay for work out of classification, vacation pay, number of holidays, hospitalizations, life insurance, safety committee, uniforms, tool allowance, and a parking facilities study committee. The MNA's election petition, as noted earlier, was filed with the Board on July 11, 1967, the same date as the "letter of agreement" and Ordinance No. 67-44. The election petition was not served upon the City and AFSCME until several days later. Section 14 of PERA provides in pertinent part:

> "*No election shall be directed* in any bargaining unit or subdivision thereof *where there is in force and effect a valid collective bargaining agreement* which was not prematurely extended and which is of fixed duration...." (emphasis added)

The ultimate issue is whether there was in force and effect as of July 11, 1967, a valid collective bargaining agreement between the City and AFSCME. What existed as of that date was a written agreement between the City Manager and AFSCME, covering all areas of wages and working conditions, coupled with City Commission ordinances confirming the salary portion of the City Manager's agreement. The ordinances were silent as to the several other contract modifications agreed to in the "letter of agreement," except for the following relevant provision of Ordinance No. 67-43:

> "Section 21. The City Manager shall make rules not in conflict with Civil Service provisions, *and subject to the approval of the City Commission,* on the subjects of sick leave, annual leave (vacation), military leave, leave without pay, holidays, working hours, and other personnel matters. *Until such rules are approved existing resolutions and rules on such subjects shall remain in full force and effect.*" (emphasis added)

It is clear from the above that the several non-salary modifications agreed to by the City Manager were to be of no effect until the City Commission approved them. There is no evidence that the City Commission ever formally approved these modifications to which the City Manager had agreed. Accordingly, it is concluded that the only collective bargaining agreement "in force and effect" (Section 14 of PERA) as of the date the election petition was filed was the agreement on a salary schedule.[1] The City Manager patently lacked power to bind the City or its City Commission to terms for a new contract. While he was authorized by a 1965 Commission action to "represent" the City in union matters, the Commission never pretended to delegate to him the power to legislate wages and working conditions without the Commission's ratification of any agreement reached by him at the bargaining table. Inasmuch as the "letter of agreement" was legally unenforceable without Commission approval taken at a Commission meeting, it is found that no "collective bargaining agreement" was "in force and effect" as of July 11, 1967, except for the salary agreement which was adopted by Commission Ordinances Nos. 67-43 and 67-44.

As a general rule the Board will follow a policy of treating as a section 14 bar only such agreements of public employers as have been rendered legally enforceable by virtue of having been duly enacted, adopted or approved by the competent governing body, e.g., city council or commission, board of education, or county board of supervisors. However, it is apparent that the unavoidable delay[3] between tentative agreement by negotiators at the bargaining table and the convening of an official meeting of the legislative body encourages disruptive rival union activity and consequent raids if the tentative agreement does not serve to bar an election. This is so because it encourages dissident groups of employees to make capital out of their asserted ability to negotiate an even better contract. Such a situation discourages reasonable settlements and responsible representation. Accordingly, in the interest of striking a balance between employee freedom of choice and stability of existing bargaining relationships,

---

[1] The Charter of the City of Grand Rapids, Title V, vests all City legislative and administrative powers in the City Commission (sec. 1(a)); provides that no monies shall be paid out except in pursuance of appropriations approved by the City Commission (sec. 20); and provides that the City Commission shall fix by ordinance the salary or rate of compensation of all officers and employees of the City (sec. 35).

[3] Administrative notice is taken of the fact that the majority of such local legislative bodies, are composed of citizens who have other occupations, serve on a voluntary basis, and are unable to meet on a continuous basis because of other commitments.

the Board announces the following policy which will be applied in implementing PERA section 14 for all petitions filed after the date of this order:

A complete written collective bargaining agreement made between and executed by, authorized representatives of a public employer and the exclusive bargaining agent of its employees will, for a period of up to thirty days thereafter, bar a rival union election petition or a decertification petition pending subsequent action on the agreement by the legislative body. A petition filed within the thirty day period will not be dismissed if the legislative body meets and votes to reject the proposed agreement or takes no action within the thirty day period. If the legislative body approves the collective bargaining agreement negotiated by its representative within the thirty day period, the petition will be dismissed.

The determinative issue in this case is whether the salary agreement (the only agreement approved by the governing City Commission *at any time*) was sufficient *in scope* to constitute the type of agreement contemplated by section 14 as barring an election.[4] This question must be answered in the negative, consistent with the holding in *School District No. 61, Berrien County-Buchanan Public Schools,* 1967 Labor Opinions, 518, 520 wherein we stated:

"The National Labor Relations Board consistently refuses to treat an agreement as a bar to an election petition unless it contains substantial terms and conditions of employment deemed sufficient to stabilize the bargaining relationship. A contract limited to wages only or to one or several insubstantial provisions is not recognized as a bar. *Appalachian Shale Products Co.,* 121 NLRB 1160. We have adopted the NLRB rule. *South Redford School District* MLMB R65 J-184, 1966 Labor Opinions 160; *Sterling Township,* MLMB R65 H-20, 1966 Labor Opinions 9. Accordingly, the agreement of June 20, 1966, being limited to a wage schedule, is not a bar, under section 14 of PERA, to the conduct of an election at this time."

Accordingly, it is concluded that no section 14 bar exists to the direction of an election....

NOTES

1. In *Lake Superior State College,* 1984 MERC Lab. Op. (Mich.), the Michigan Commission extended the *Grand Rapids* rule to a situation in which a tentative agreement was subject to ratification by *both* the public employer and the union. Thus, the Michigan Commission ruled that "a tentative agreement entered into by a public employer and a labor organization, if complete and properly signed and dated, bars a rival petition for 30 days from the date of the tentative agreement, during which time the ratification process by both parties is taking place."

2. The NLRB has held that "[w]here ratification is a condition precedent to contractual validity by express contractual provision, the contract will be ineffectual as a bar unless it is ratified prior to the filing of the petition." *Appalachian Shale Prods. Co.,* 121 N.L.R.B. 1160 (1958). The New Jersey Public Employ-

---

[4] It is unnecessary to apply the 30 day rule, announced above, in reaching a decision in the instant case, since the record contains no evidence that the City Commission *ever* met and approved a complete collective bargaining agreement.

ment Relations Commission adopted a similar policy in *Camden Cty. Welfare Bd.,* Decision No. 65 (N.J. PERC 1972).

3. The Michigan Employment Relations Commission, following the uniform practice of the NLRB, has ruled that "a contract to act as a bar to an election must embrace a unit that is appropriate to the extent that the unit is one neither prohibited by PERA nor contrary to Board policy." *Kent Cty. Rd. Comm'n,* 1969 MERC Lab. Op. 34 (Mich.).

4. Does a contract that does not include any wage or fringe benefit provisions constitute a bar to a representation proceeding? The New York City Office of Collective Bargaining has held that a contract that "contains substantial non-economic provisions" was sufficient to be a bar since the wages and fringe benefits were mandated by the state's "prevailing rate" law and bargaining was prohibited on subjects covered by the law. *Teamsters Local Union 237,* Decision No. 11-71, GERR No. 396, B-7 (N.Y.C. OCB 1971). On the other hand, in *Bridgeport Hous. Auth.,* Decision No. 1897 (Conn. SBLR 1980), the Connecticut Board held that a contract which did not cover money items did not bar the filing of a representation petition.

5. Does the inclusion of an illegal union security clause remove the contract as a bar to an election? In the private sector, the NLRB has uniformly held that a contract which contains a union-security clause or a checkoff clause which is illegal on its face or has been determined to be illegal in an unfair labor practice proceeding does not bar a representation election. *Paragon Prods. Corp.,* 134 N.L.R.B. 662 (1961); *Gary Steel Supply Co.,* 144 N.L.R.B. 470 (1963). What are the advantages and disadvantages of adopting this policy in the public sector?

6. Does an agreement that is conditioned upon the appropriation of funds by another public body operate as a bar prior to the time the condition is met? In *Camden Cty. Welfare Bd.,* Decision No. 65 (N.J. PERC 1972), the New Jersey PERC stated:

> The incorporation of two conditions regarding funds for salary increases in no way detracts from the substance of the agreement. It simply represents the most that a public employer could do under the circumstances at that time. A collective negotiations agreement in public employment frequently requires a later appropriation of funds after execution of the agreement in order to implement it. Even if that subsequent appropriation is not made an express condition in the contract, it is nevertheless a fundamental condition which is incorporated by necessary implication. Many, probably most, public employers are not self-appropriators; they are dependent for funds upon a political mechanism outside of their direct control. The conditions involved here are of that kind; the contract does not contain a condition, the fulfillment of which is reserved to one of the parties. The parties struck a bargain, the funding of which was necessarily conditioned by the Board's limitations. The expression of these conditions in their agreement merely recognizes a fact of political life. Under the circumstances, we conclude that the execution date of their written agreement, January 13, 1971, should control for purposes of applying the contract bar rule.

7. Where there is an incumbent union, can a public employer continue to bargain with the incumbent union after a representation petition has been filed by a rival union or after a decertification petition has been filed? Under the NLRB's *Midwest Piping* doctrine, an employer faced with a pending representation petition filed by a rival union committed an unfair labor practice if it did not cease bargaining with the incumbent union during the pendency of representation proceeding. *Midwest Piping & Supply Co.,* 63 N.L.R.B. 1060 (1945); *Shea Chem. Corp.,* 121 N.L.R.B. 1027 (1958). Subsequently, however, the NLRB in *RCA Del Caribe, Inc.,* 262 N.L.R.B. 963 (1982), modified its *Midwest Piping* doctrine and held that the mere filing of a representation petition by a rival union would no longer "require or permit" an employer to refrain from bargaining with the incumbent union. In *RCA Del Caribe,* the NLRB further held that an employer commits an unfair labor practice if it refuses to bargain with the incumbent union based solely on the fact that a petition has been filed by a rival union. Similarly, in *Dresser Indus.,* 264 N.L.R.B. 1088 (1982), the NLRB held that the mere filing of a decertification petition would no longer require or permit an employer to withdraw from bargaining or executing a contract with an incumbent union unless the employer had a good faith doubt, supported by objective considerations, of the incumbent union's continuing majority status.

Most of the public sector boards that have considered the issue, both before and after the NLRB's decision in *RCA Del Caribe,* have generally endorsed the *Midwest Piping* doctrine, i.e., that a public employer commits an unfair labor practice if it bargains with an incumbent union after a representation petition has been filed by a rival union. See *Williamsport-Lycoming Cty. Rec. Auth.,* 14 PPER ¶ 14128 (Penn. LRB 1983) (the Pennsylvania Board, however, has ruled that a question concerning representation arises for purposes of applying the *Midwest Piping* doctrine only after the Board orders a representation hearing or a pre-hearing conference, rather than upon the mere filing of a petition); *Middlesex Cty. (Roosevelt Hosp.),* 7 NJPER ¶ 12118 (N.J. PERC 1981); *Commonwealth of Mass. & NAGE,* Case No. SUP-2380 (Mass. LRC 1980); *Rockland Cty.,* 10 PERB ¶ 3098 (N.Y. PERB 1977). Contra *Galesburg Community Unit Sch. Dist. 205,* 1 PERI ¶ 1155 (Ill. ELRB 1985) (new NLRB policy adopted; an "incumbent representative's bargaining rights, including the right to negotiate a new contract, should remain fully intact until the completion of the selection of a new representative").

3. ELECTION, CERTIFICATION AND RECOGNITION BARS

Election Bars. In order to balance the right of employees freely to decide whether they wish to be represented with the desirability of providing some degree of finality to the results of an election, most public sector collective bargaining statutes provide for a one-year election bar. Section 23.40.100(c) of the Alaska statute, which parallels Section 9(c)(3) of the NLRA, is typical: "An election may not be held in a bargaining unit or in a subdivision of a bargaining unit if a valid election has been held within the preceding 12 months." Alaska Stat. § 23.40.100(c) (1983). There are some variations, however. The Los Angeles ordinance states that "At least six months shall lapse following an election without a majority representative being chosen before a petition for certification may be filed covering the same group of employees." Los Angeles, Cal., Admin. Code, div. 4, ch. 8, § 4.822(c)(6) (1971). On the other hand, Section 213.1 of the rules promulgated by the Indiana Education Employment Relations Board provides that "no election shall be conducted until at least 24 months after a previous election." An election bar, however, does not prohibit the holding of a runoff election or a second election if the first election has been set aside on the basis of objections filed by a party to the election or has otherwise been ruled invalid.

Under the NLRA the period of time within which another election is barred is computed from the date of the election, not the date on which the results of the election are certified. *Bendix Corp., Automation & Measurement Div.,* 179 N.L.R.B. 140 (1969). Accord *Holland Bd. of Pub. Works,* 1968 MERC Lab. Op. 853 (Mich.). While an election in a broad bargaining unit bars an election in a smaller bargaining unit for the specified period of time, an election in a smaller unit does not bar an election in a broader unit. For example, if a group of craft employees were included in a broad overall unit, a subsequent election limited to the craft employees would be barred for the specified period. See *Vickers, Inc.,* 124 N.L.R.B. 1051 (1959). On the other hand, if an election were held in a unit limited to craft employees, it would not bar an election in a larger bargaining unit that included the craft employees, even though the specified period of time had not elapsed. See *Thiokol Chem. Co.,* 123 N.L.R.B. 888 (1959). Would the same results be required under the Los Angeles ordinance quoted above?

Suppose a valid election is held on June 1 in which Union *A* fails to poll a majority of the votes cast. Suppose further that within three months thereafter Union *B* obtains authorization cards from a substantial majority of the same employees that voted in the June 1 election. Does the employer, knowing *B* represents a majority of its employees, commit an unfair labor practice if it refuses to recognize *B* where the act bars the holding of an election if a valid election has been held within the twelve preceding months? Would it be necessary to show that the employer has engaged in unfair labor practices aimed at dissipating the union's majority support? See *Conren, Inc. v. NLRB,* 368 F.2d 173 (7th Cir. 1966), *cert. denied,* 386 U.S. 974 (1967), *noted* 80 Harv. L. Rev. 1805 (1967).

Certification Bars. Several public sector collective bargaining statutes expressly provide that no question concerning representation can be raised during a designated period of time from the date of the employee organization's certification as the collective bargaining representative. A one-year period is typically specified. The Maryland and Tennessee teachers' statutes are exceptions; they provide that the designation or certification of an exclusive representative shall be for a minimum period of two years. Md. Educ. Code § 6-406(a) (1989); Tenn. Code Ann. § 49-5-605(c) (1983). Under the NLRA there is a conclusive presumption that a union, in the absence of unusual circumstances, continues to represent a majority of the employees during the year following certification and no question concerning representation can be raised during the certification year. *Brooks v. NLRB,* 348 U.S. 96 (1954). The Michigan Employment Relations Commission has adopted a similar policy. *Sunshine Hosp.,* 1968 MERC Lab. Op. 440 (Mich.); *City of Bay City,* 1967 MERC Lab. Op. 155. One of the underlying premises is that "a union should be given ample time for carrying out its mandate on behalf of its members, and should not be under exigent pressure to produce hothouse results or be turned out." *Brooks v. NLRB, supra.*

In *Kenosha Bd. of Educ.,* WERC Decision No. 8031 (Wis. ERC 1967), a local affiliate of the American Federation of Teachers filed a representation petition seeking to represent the District's teachers. In opposing the petition, the Kenosha Education Association, the incumbent bargaining representative, urged, inter alia, "that the Board adopt a rule to the effect that where the Board has previously certified an organization as the exclusive bargaining representative of employes in an appropriate unit, the second election should not be conducted within two years of the date of the certification of the results of the first election, and further, that said two-year certification bar rule be extended at two-year intervals." With respect to this contention, the WERC stated:

The Board has seriously considered whether it should adopt a two-year certification bar rule. That is to say, whether the Board should not conduct a second election in a period earlier than two years from the certification of the results of a previous election. In such consideration we must weigh the right of the employes to select or change their bargaining representative with the interest of preserving the stability of the established collective bargaining relationship. The problem is aggravated as a result of the fact that collective bargaining agreements in public employment, and especially those involving teachers, are not coextensive in time with budgetary considerations. Because of its statutory budgetary deadline and because of the nature of teacher employment, the School Board herein normally commences bargaining in May of each year for terms and conditions of employment for the following school year. It therefore becomes a necessity that if the employes are to select a new collective bargaining representative, said representative should be given a reasonable time to negotiate the collective bargaining agreement. If the ordinary contract bar rules were to apply, the election would not be held during the term of an existing agreement, and the selected collective bargaining representative, therefore, normally would not have a reasonable period of time to negotiate a collective bargaining agreement to succeed the existing agreement.

No rule with respect to certification bar is being established because the history of employment relations in municipal employment has not been such as to require such a rule at the present time, and because that history is not sufficiently developed to indicate a pattern of similar conditions. The conditions to be regulated are still too vaguely defined, and the Board prefers to wait until it is sufficiently certain that its rule, once adopted, will not be eroded by exceptions. Each case will be reviewed and determined on its own facts in order to balance the objective of employe choice with the objective of a stable bargaining relationship.

In determining how the two objectives will best be balanced and achieved, the Board will be influenced by various factors such as (1) the presence or absence of a current agreement; (2) the presence or absence of current and active negotiations for an agreement and how long such negotiations have been in progress; (3) the budgetary deadlines imposed upon the parties; (4) the special deadlines imposed by statute, such as the case with respect to teachers' personal contracts; (5) whether the current bargaining agent was certified or recognized; (6) the period of time since the current bargaining agent was certified or recognized; and (7) the employment relations history involved.

What effect would a finding that an employer had not bargained in good faith have on the computation of the certification year? In *City of Norwich,* Decision No. 804 (Conn. SBLR 1968), the Connecticut State Board of Labor Relations stated:

There remains the question whether the petition in this case should be barred by the Municipal Employer's past prohibited labor practices in refusing to fulfill its statutory obligation to bargain collectively. In a number of cases under the National Labor Relations Act, it has been held that where a union's majority was dissipated after an employer has engaged in unfair labor practices, particularly the refusal to bargain collectively, the Union is entitled to recognition for a reasonable period even though it has lost its majority support. For example, in *Franks Bros. v. NLRB*, 321 U.S. 702 (1944) the Supreme Court held that even though the union had lost its majority the employer should be compelled to continue bargaining with it for a reasonable period. The underlying principle expressed by the Court was that the union was entitled to a period of recognition and stability in order to demonstrate to the employees its capacity to represent them and to obtain benefits on their behalf. See also *NLRB v. Warren Co. Inc.*, 350 U.S. 107 (1955); *NLRB v. John S. Swift Co.*, 302 F.2d 342 (7th Cir. 1962); *Irving Air Chute Co. v. NLRB*, 350 F.2d 176 (2nd Cir. 1965).

We subscribe to this general principle. The employees can have no freedom of choice between whether they will engage in collective bargaining or not if the employer's refusal to bargain has prevented them from experiencing collective bargaining. We will not entertain a petition for an election where the employer's unfair labor practices have undermined the union's majority before it has had an opportunity to demonstrate its capabilities of representing the employees in collective bargaining.

Recognition Bars. Under many public sector bargaining statutes an employer may voluntarily grant recognition to an employee organization if it represents a majority of the employees in an appropriate unit. Should such a voluntary grant of recognition likewise constitute a bar to a representation petition filed by a rival organization? The NLRB has held that voluntary recognition bars a representation election "for a reasonable period." *Keller Plastics E., Inc.*, 157 N.L.R.B. 583 (1969). The so-called "reasonable period" is determined on a case-by-case basis and is frequently much less than one year from the date recognition was granted. Compare *Universal Gear Serv. Corp.*, 157 N.L.R.B. 1169 (1969) (two month period not reasonable), with *Brennan's Cadillac, Inc.*, 231 N.L.R.B. 225 (1977) (three month period reasonable). What reasons, if any, are there for establishing different periods of unchallenged representation depending on whether the union is certified or voluntarily recognized by the employer? Should the same policy be adopted in the public sector? See *Town of S. Winsor,* Decision No. 2076 (Conn. SBLR 1981) ("A reasonable time for a recognized representative to make substantial headway towards obtaining a contract is one year from the date of recognition and we interpret the Act as prescribing such a duration for the recognition and its exclusive quality").

4. EFFECT OF AFL-CIO INTERNAL DISPUTES PLAN

The purpose of the AFL-CIO Internal Disputes Plan as set forth in Article XX of the AFL-CIO Constitution is to prevent member unions from raiding the jurisdiction of other member unions. Article XX provides that if a member union feels that another member union is invading its jurisdiction, it can file a complaint and have the complaint heard by the Internal Disputes Tribunal. Article XX provides that the decision of the impartial tribunal is binding on member unions. The NLRB, however, has uniformly refused to dismiss a representation petition on the basis that an appeal to the AFL-CIO Internal Disputes Plan is being made or the petitioner has been found to be in violation of Article XX. In *S.G. Adams Co.*, 115 N.L.R.B. 1012, 1013 n.1 (1956), the Board stated:

> [T]he pendency of proceedings before an intra-union tribunal for adjudication of representation questions does not affect the duty of the Board to resolve such questions.... Nor is the fact that the filing of a representation petition violates a union constitutional provision sufficient ground under Board policy for dismissing the petition. The Board has frequently held that it will not concern itself with the internal regulations of a labor organization.

Accord *Weather Vane Outerware Corp.*, 233 N.L.R.B. 414 (1977).

That the same approach may be adopted in the public sector is indicated by the decision of the New York City Office of Collective Bargaining in *Local Union No. 3, IBEW and City of N.Y.*, Decision No. 36-69, GERR No. 305, B-4 (N.Y.C. OCB 1969), wherein the New York City OCB stated:

> Although Article XX may constitute a binding contract between affiliates of the AFL-CIO, it is not binding on third parties. In the State of New York, public employees have the statutory right to bargain collectively through representatives of their own choosing.... That statutory right manifestly is paramount to the contract between AFL-CIO affiliates, and must be recognized and effectuated by this Board.

The New York City OCB further noted that "the paramount right of the employees to select a bargaining representative cannot and should not be stultified by the fact that a rival union had represented employees in the past." Accord *SEIU, California State Emps. Ass'n*, 8 PERC ¶ 15123 (Cal. PERB 1984); *Elizabeth Bd. of Educ.*, Docket No. RO-792 (N.J. PERC 1974). But see *Sevey v. AFSCME*, 48 Cal. App. 3d 64, 89 L.R.R.M. 3049 (1975) (umpire's award in Article XX proceeding upheld despite potential conflict with employees' right to choose a bargaining representative).

C. DETERMINATION OF THE APPROPRIATE BARGAINING UNIT

1. INTRODUCTION

KURTZ, BARR & DENACO, BARGAINING UNITS IN THE PUBLIC SECTOR, in The Evolving Process — Collective Negotiations in Public Employment 108-12 (1985)*

Significance of the Appropriate Bargaining Unit

There is no more important problem existing in collective bargaining in the public sector than the appropriate unit question. The determination of the appropriate bargaining unit may control whether the parties ever get to the bargaining table, the extent and nature of the benefits sought and obtained at the bargaining table, and the way employees work on the job and are supervised. Determination of the size and composition of the bargaining unit can be decisive of the question of whether any employee organization will achieve

*Reprinted by permission of LRP Publications, 747 Dresher Road, P.O. Box 980, Horsham, PA 19044-0980, Tel. (215)784-0860.

majority support, and consequent recognition or certification, and if so, which of competing organizations. The scope and nature of the unit found to be appropriate will also affect the employee organization's basic economic strength, its ability to bargain over economic issues, the range of subjects that can be meaningfully negotiated, the likelihood of specific resolution of disputes, and the ultimate success and acceptance of the collective bargaining process in the public sector. The time should be past when the public employer and the union give little thought to the appropriateness of a requested bargaining unit.

The bargaining unit is composed of jobs or job categories, and not of the particular persons working at those jobs at any given time. It may be the jobs connected with a particular type of operation, the jobs in a department, residual groups of jobs not otherwise grouped together, all the jobs of the employer, or some other combination. The fundamental question, therefore, is the appropriate combination of jobs. What should be achieved is a well-balanced group of employees who have similar needs and demands that can be dealt with at the bargaining table. An effectively defined bargaining unit based on compatible job categories is intended to benefit both labor and management. Unfortunately, both public employers and employee organizations have not always recognized the long-term consequences of the appropriate bargaining unit. In developing their respective positions, they are likely to look ahead to the impact of alternative unit possibilities upon the forthcoming election, negotiations and contract administration.

Elections

Pragmatic and tactical considerations will often influence the position taken by both the employee organization and the employer to the unit question. Inasmuch as the unit determination controls election eligibility, and consequently whether a collective bargaining relationship between the parties will be established in the first place, the parties' unit considerations may be largely dictated by the election. The employee organization will tend to seek a unit which it thinks it can organize. If two unions both seek recognition for at least some of the same group of workers, they will be interested in a unit where their strength lies. Thus, one may seek a narrow unit, while the other will seek to overwhelm its opponent's strength in a wider grouping. Concern for the extent of organization will often mean that rival unions will take the opposite sides in two different unit questions, seeking a narrow unit in one dispute and a wider one in the other, and vice versa.

The employer's attitude toward the unit question may be influenced by similar considerations. If the employer wishes to avoid collective bargaining, it may seek a unit which it believes the employee organization will have difficulty winning. Usually, this is a wider unit than the employee organization wants. Management can "win" by persuading a majority of the people in a bargaining unit to vote for "no representation." In evaluating such a strategy, however, the employer should bear in mind that, historically, in both the public and private sectors, voter participation in bargaining unit elections has been relatively high, and certainly much higher than the rate of participation in national political elections. Specifically, in the public sector, union organizational efforts may be facilitated by three factors: 1) most public employer premises are, by law, regu-

lation or policy, subject to varying degrees of public access; 2) the newly emerging public sector can rely on nearly 50 years of experience under the National
Labor Relations Act, when a question arises as to the rights of union organizers
to reach public employees during an organizational and election campaign; and
3) public sector collective bargaining has won approval, in most jurisdictions, by
statutory mandate.

Obviously, there is an inherent risk in viewing the unit question solely in
terms of election strategy. If one argues for a certain unit structure solely in
order to influence the election result, the parties will be subsequently "stuck"
with that unit, if the union is successful in the election. The employer may then
find that the bargaining unit, as a continuing entity, does not meet its planning
and administrative needs and its concerns for stability and efficiency in its
relations with the work force. The union may face collateral problems of its
own, if there is not an adequate community of interest and commonality of
goals among the various job categories involved. In other words, what might be
a realistic position in attempting to fashion the bargaining unit to achieve a
certain voting result may not be appropriate when considering the types of
interest that the union must serve through the processing of grievances, interpretation of past practices, or the application of other precedents and policies
which do not fit conveniently for all members of the bargaining unit.

Negotiations

The size and nature of the bargaining unit will shape the kinds of issues that
will be addressed in collective bargaining and dealt with in the bargaining agreement. The employer will commonly favor a large unit. It is usually seen as
furthering the orderly and efficient administration of government. Certain cost
efficiencies may be anticipated by not having to negotiate too many separate
bargaining agreements and in standardizing a wage and benefit package in a
single agreement, rather than in several separate agreements. On the other
hand, fragmented units or a proliferation of units tend to bring administrative
headaches to the employer. Such units involve the greater cost and disruption
that comes with frequent bargaining cycles and expose the employer to "whip
saw" bargaining (and strikes) by employees in one unit who seek benefits which
inure cumulatively to the benefit of employees in other units.

The union will commonly favor a smaller unit. The employees may want a
unit which gives each individual the maximum amount of self-determination.
The smaller the unit, the greater the chance that the individual's vote will be
significant. The diversified constituency of a large unit, with employees of differing skills, attitudes and interests, may place strains upon the union's ability to
represent all unit employees fairly in negotiating and administering the collective bargaining contract. The larger and/or more vocal elements of the bargaining unit may have more success in putting forward their bargaining demands. A
large unit, which does not appropriately integrate common job categories, increases the possibility of fractionalization within the bargaining unit. If membership objectives have a certain amount of commonality, it can be reflected in
unified and consistent demands by both parties at the bargaining table. If
fractionalization is a consequence of a large unit, it may result in the ultimate
breaking apart of the bargaining unit (by further decertification proceedings,

mutual agreement of the parties, or otherwise). The employer may then be confronted with the smaller, fragmented units, which it initially sought to avoid, and faced with the dangers of multiple bargaining, which have been alluded to. Even if the bargaining unit does not break up, the fractionalization could make it difficult for a union to secure ratification of the agreements it reaches. This could result in unnecessary polarization of the parties.

Contract Administration

Beyond the election campaign and the negotiation of the collective bargaining agreement, the bargaining unit plays an important role in contract administration. The jobs contained in the bargaining unit may well determine the way the employees work and are supervised. The notions of "span of control," "supervisory effectiveness," and the more esoteric "management by objective" all function differently, depending upon the cohesiveness of the bargaining unit, the work locations of the members, the distinction between the hourly and salaried employees, and many other considerations relating to the various type of fringe benefits accorded to members of the bargaining unit.

....

It is quite obvious that the interests of both labor and management and the public will be served by a properly constituted bargaining unit. It should be neither too large nor too small and should reflect the interests which are common to the members of the unit and the interests of the public employer in an orderly and efficient administration of government.

SHAW & CLARK, DETERMINATION OF APPROPRIATE BARGAINING UNITS IN THE PUBLIC SECTOR: LEGAL AND PRACTICAL PROBLEMS, 51 Or. L. Rev. 152, 152-54, 157-58 (1971)*

Determination of the appropriate bargaining unit in the public sector is of fundamental importance. It is both a prerequisite to negotiations and a vital factor in their structure and outcome. The more bargaining units public management deals with, the greater the chance that competing unions will be able to whipsaw the employer. Moreover, a multiplicity of bargaining units makes it difficult, if not impossible, to maintain some semblance of uniformity in benefits and working conditions. Unfortunately, in many states and localities bargaining units have been established without consideration of the effect such units will have on negotiations or on the subsequent administration of an agreement. The resulting crazy-quilt pattern of representation has unduly complicated the collective bargaining process in the public sector....

The Legal Framework

State Legislation. In states which do not have applicable legislation, the determination of the appropriate bargaining unit is made by the parties. With increasing frequency, however, the determination of whether a unit is appropriate, in the absence of voluntary agreement by the parties, is made by a public employee relations board. Wisconsin, in 1959, was the first state to enact a

---

comprehensive statute concerning collective bargaining by public employees. Since then there has been a virtual onslaught of legislation. More than thirty states have enacted legislation covering some or all categories of public employees. Various criteria have been suggested for determining the appropriate bargaining unit;[1] the following considerations are most frequently mentioned: (1) whether the employees concerned have a clear and identifiable community of interest; (2) whether the proposed unit will result in effective dealings and efficiency of operations; and (3) whether the employees have a history of representation. Generally the extent of organization may not be a controlling consideration.

Recently, there has been a distinct trend toward prescribing criteria explicitly designed to avoid fragmented bargaining units. The Pennsylvania Act, for example, provides that the board, in determining the appropriate bargaining unit, must take into consideration the effects of over-fragmentation and the existence of an identifiable community of interest. It further requires the board to consider "that when the Commonwealth is the employer, it will be bargaining on a statewide basis unless the issues involve working conditions peculiar to a given governmental locale." Similarly, the Kansas Act directs the public employee relations board to consider "the effects of overfragmentation and the splintering of a work organization."

Hawaii has gone one step further; it has legislatively established statewide bargaining units. Thus, there are separate units for supervisory and nonsupervisory employees in blue-collar positions. The same is true for white-collar groups. There are separate units for teachers, for faculty of the University of Hawaii and the community college system, and for employees of the university and community college system other than faculty. Optional appropriate bargaining units are designated for registered nurses, nonprofessional hospital and institutional workers, firemen, policemen, and professional and scientific employees other than nurses.

On both the state and national level, statutory criteria necessarily determine the framework within which decisions of the various public employee relations boards can be made. The Wisconsin and New York statutes illustrate how the statutory framework affects bargaining unit determinations....

Occupational Group Statutes. The Wisconsin and New York statutes are comprehensive in that they (1) cover all categories of employees, (2) provide a method for resolving questions concerning representation, and (3) establish a public employee relations board to administer the act. It should be noted, however, that there are numerous statutes that apply to only one occupational group, such as firefighters, policemen, or teachers. In contrast to the general criteria for determining the appropriate unit set forth in the comprehensive statutes, the occupational group statutes prescribe the boundaries of the bargaining unit. Furthermore, these statutorily prescribed bargaining units usually include supervisory and managerial personnel.[2]

---

[1]Most of the statutes covering specific occupational groups such as firefighters, policemen or teachers specifically set forth the boundaries of the collective bargaining unit....

[2]The statutes covering firefighters are a prime example. Occasionally, individual units are prescribed within a comprehensive act. The Michigan Act, for example, provides that "... in any fire department, or any department in whole or part engaged in, or having the responsibilities of, fire

The ... Georgia, Idaho, Rhode Island, and Wyoming statutes [provide] that the organization selected by the majority of the firefighters shall be the sole and exclusive bargaining agent for *all* the classified members of the fire department.

NOTES

1. Section 23.40.090 of the Alaska Public Employment Act specifically provides that "bargaining units shall be as large as is reasonable and unnecessary fragmenting shall be avoided." Alaska Stat. § 20.40.090 (1983).

2. The Nevada statute provides that where a local government employer has recognized one or more employee organizations, the employer is to determine the appropriate bargaining unit, after consultation with the employee organization or organizations, pursuant to the criteria set forth in the statute. If an employee organization disagrees with the unit determination, it may appeal to the PERB which is directed to apply "the same criterion" as the government employer. Nev. Rev. Stat. § 288.170(1), (5) (1987).

3. In states where public employers have the authority to engage in collective bargaining in the absence of applicable legislation, the employer has wide discretion in establishing bargaining units, both in terms of their breadth and in terms of categories of employees who are to be included in or excluded from bargaining units. Thus, a public employer in this situation can normally condition its willingness to engage in collective bargaining upon the establishment of bargaining units that it deems appropriate. For example, in *Fraternal Order of Police v. City of Dayton,* 60 Ohio App. 2d 259, 396 N.E.2d 1045 (1978), the Ohio Court of Appeals upheld a city ordinance which excluded supervisory employees from inclusion in any bargaining units recognized by the city. The Fraternal Order of Police (FOP) and the International Association of Fire Fighters (IAFF) challenged the constitutionality and legality of this ordinance since it had the effect of excluding sergeants, lieutenants and captains from the police bargaining unit and lieutenants, captains and district chiefs from the fire fighters bargaining unit. In upholding the supervisory exclusion, the Ohio Court of Appeals stated:

> There is no provision in the Ohio Constitution or Statute that requires the City of Dayton to bargain collectively with its employees through their representatives FOP and IAFF. Since the city is not required to bargain collectively with its employees it may refrain from doing so or it may set conditions under which it elects to do so. If the employees' bargaining unit chooses not to comply with those conditions, the alternative is no agreement to bargain. The City of Dayton has not violated any constitutional provisions in barring supervisory employees from the bargaining units.

See also *Tobin v. Cook Cty. Hosp. Comm'n,* 66 Ill. App. 3d 564, 384 N.E.2d 77 (1978) (in absence of legislation, public employer is "empowered to determine the parameters of a bargaining unit of its employees"); *Chicago High Sch. Assistant Principals Ass'n v. Board of Educ.,* 5 Ill. App. 3d 672, 284 N.E.2d 14 (1972).

In some instances where the parties have been unable to reach agreement on the appropriate bargaining unit, they have submitted the question to a mutually selected arbitrator. See, e.g., *Rochester Bd. of Educ.,* 52 Lab. Arb. 1062 (Arb. Jean McKelvey, 1969). See generally Rehmus, *Arbitration of Representation*

---

fighting, no person subordinate to a fire commission, safety director, or other similar administrative agency shall be deemed to be a supervisor." Mich. Comp. Laws Ann. § 423.213 (1967).

and Bargaining Unit Questions in Public Employment Disputes, in National Academy of Arbitrators, The Arbitrator, The NLRB, and the Courts, Proceedings of the Twentieth Annual Meeting 251 (1967).

ROCK, THE APPROPRIATE UNIT QUESTION IN THE PUBLIC SERVICE: THE PROBLEM OF PROLIFERATION, 67 Mich. L. Rev. 1001, 1001-08 (1969)*

I. Introduction

It is becoming increasingly clear that of the numerous problems which complicate the practice of collective bargaining in the public sector, none is more important than the appropriate unit question. In the public sector as well as in private industry, determination of the size and composition of the bargaining unit at the initial stages of organization and recognition can be decisive of the question of which employee organization will achieve majority recognition, or whether any organization will win recognition. Save for the employee organization which limits its jurisdiction along narrow lines such as the craft practiced by its members, the normal tendency may be to request initially a unit whose boundaries coincide with the spread of the organization's membership or estimated strength. The public employer, on the other hand, may seek to recognize a unit in which the no-union votes will be in the majority, or a favored employee organization will have predominant strength; or the employer may simply seek to avoid undue proliferation of bargaining units.

The problem in the public sector, however, is of far greater depth than the initial victory-or-defeat aspect of recognition. In the private sector, it is clear that the scope and nature of the unit found to be appropriate for bargaining has acted as an important determinant of the union's basic economic strength — that is, its bargaining over bread-and-butter economic issues. In the public sector, it seems clear that the scope and nature of the unit found to be appropriate will also affect the range of subjects which can be negotiated meaningfully, the role played in the process by the separate branches of government, the likelihood of peaceful resolution of disputes, order versus chaos in bargaining, and ultimately, perhaps, the success of the whole idea of collective bargaining for public employees.

Although the appropriate unit question has received much attention in the private sector during the past thirty years, it has not received the same attention for public sector employees until recently. The purpose of this Article is to focus on certain distinguishing aspects of both the problem and the experience in the public sector, and to discuss a possible approach or philosophy for the future. The primary concern here is undue proliferation of units among the large pool of blue-collar and white-collar employees in the public service.

II. Past Tendencies and Patterns

Traditionally, the public employer and union have given little thought to the appropriateness of a unit that requested recognition. More often than not, in the years prior to the enactment of definitive rules for recognition of public

---

*Reprinted by permission of the Michigan Law Review Association.

employees, a union requesting and receiving some form of recognition was considered the spokesman for its members — in whatever job classifications, functional departments, or physical locations they happened to be. This lenient approach was facilitated by (and perhaps had its start in) the fact that "recognition" frequently carried no legal consequences beyond the ability to appear before legislative or executive bodies hearing budgetary requests or the power to lobby with key political figures. Even when recognition was followed by a procedure similar to bargaining — including in some instances an embodiment of the bargain in a written agreement or memorandum — little if any consideration was given to the appropriateness of the unit being dealt with. Apart from the obvious problems stemming from the failure to grant "exclusive bargaining rights" to these early public employee units and from the inattention to the matter of excluding supervisors from the units representing those whom they supervise, a groundwork was laid for the creation of illogical unit lines. All too frequently the result was a proliferation of bargaining units. The task of changing this ill-conceived basis has often proved troublesome in the current period of rule-oriented bargaining.

Nor has the enactment of rules in the past ten years invariably led to a different pattern. For example, under New York City's Executive Order 49, issued by Mayor Wagner in the late fifties, certificates of recognition were granted for over 200 separate units, some containing as few as two employees. The proportion of units to number of member-employees found in New York City is perhaps exceeded only in Detroit, where some seventy-eight separate units have come into existence. At the federal level, marked proliferation of units has also characterized the pattern of recognition under Executive Order No. 10,988; a similar tendency seems inherent in a number of recently enacted state legislative standards for unit determination.

Notwithstanding this rather pessimistic summary, the past ten years have clearly been the decisive decade for all aspects of public sector bargaining, and this is particularly true for the specific rules regarding unit determination. A major example of this development occurred in 1962 with President Kennedy's promulgation of Executive Order No. 10,988. In this document, which was originally regarded as the federal employee's Magna Carta of labor relations, the following general standards are specified for appropriate unit determination when "exclusive" recognition is sought by a majority organization:

> Units may be established on any plant or installation, craft, functional or other basis which will ensure a clear and identifiable community of interest among the employees concerned, but no unit shall be established solely on the basis of the extent to which employees in the proposed unit have organized.

Another section of the Order also provides for "formal" recognition in a "unit as defined by the agency" when an employee organization has ten percent of the employees as members, and no other organization holds exclusive representation rights. Finally, another section provides for "informal" recognition when the employee organization does not qualify for exclusive or formal recognition, without regard to whether other employee organizations hold one of the other forms of recognition in the same unit.

Regardless of whether this three-sided format was justified under the state of recognition and bargaining then prevalent in the federal service, there can be little question that the system was calculated to encourage representational footholds on a mass scale within small units. And, it did result in proliferation of units, albeit on a reduced scale, as informal or formal recognition often led to exclusive recognition. Emphasis on the "community of interest" standard in the administration of Executive Order No. 10,988, and the use in some instances of the National Labor Relations Board's technique of the "*Globe* election" — a procedure in which the members of a homogeneous occupational group are allowed to vote on separate recognition for their own unit, as opposed to a rival organization's request that they be included in a larger unit — have undoubtedly contributed further to widespread fragmentation of units in federal employment.

At the state and local levels, virtually all of the significant legislation passed since 1960 has spelled out standards of some type for unit determination. In many instances these state enactments made possible further proliferation by adding to the existing illogical patterns of recognition new units made possible through espousal of the federal "community of interest" standard and its converse, separate units for groups having "conflicting interests"; by providing for *Globe*-type elections or similar approaches designed to facilitate small unit separation; and, in the states of Delaware and Minnesota, by permitting the government agency to rely on the extent of employee organization. Notwithstanding the fact that some of the state laws embody specific standards used by the National Labor Relations Board for the private sector, observers familiar with bargaining conditions in both sectors have contended that the degree of fragmentation in some of the states exceeds that of the private sector.

Clearly, at both state and federal levels the standards place a high premium on the subjective judgment of the decision-making body or individual, and results are also shaped to a high degree by the happenstance of the petitioning organization's requested unit at the time of the petition. Particularly when there is no rival organizational claim for a larger unit — which is often the case — the over-all effect has been to encourage recognition of the smaller unit. Even if a union succeeds in winning recognition in a large unit, employees in that unit are generally not required to become members of the union. The relative lack of union security clauses in the collective bargaining agreements of the public service assures that, to a degree unparalleled in the private sector, dissident small-unit groups are able to maintain their separate identities and to prolong the battle for break-off from the larger group's exclusive bargaining agent.

III. The Case for and Against the Small Unit

It cannot be assumed automatically that the pattern of many small units is wrong. A single craft, classification, department, or installation which would otherwise constitute a small minority if included in a larger unit can argue with some justification that its specialized interests and needs may be subordinated to the wishes of the larger unit's majority. Moreover, the smaller unit which performs a particularly essential function may also be capable of striking a better bargain for itself when left to do its own negotiating.

"Community of interest" is more than a catch phrase. It not only points up that like-situated employees will better understand their own problems and press their unique needs, but it also recognizes the instinct of exclusiveness which causes employees to *want* to form their own organization rather than become a part of a larger organization in which they may feel themselves strangers. The desire to possess such "freedom of choice" or "self-determination" should, it can be argued, receive greater weight for public employees, because they are "public," than for those in the private sector.

There is nothing inherently wrong in permitting an employee organization to gain a foothold in a smaller unit, if the employees in that unit select it; and, if the union is effective in the small unit, it may grow and achieve recognition in other separate units or in a single large unit. This consideration may be particularly significant in the early period after the promulgation of legislation or executive orders encompassing a vast group of employees whose right to representation had not previously been formally legitimized. It is frequently easier for unions to secure employees' allegiance in smaller, distinctive groups than in larger, heterogeneous ones.

At the same time, there are important considerations which, it seems, point toward a unique long-range need for larger units in the public sector. The special problems of unit determination in the public sector were most clearly recognized legislatively in 1967 in New York's Taylor Law, which included, in addition to the common standards of community of interest and necessity to promote the public welfare, the further requirement that in defining an appropriate unit the following standard should be taken into consideration: "the officials of government at the level of the unit shall have the power to agree, or to make effective recommendations to other administrative authority or the legislative body with respect to, the terms and conditions of employment upon which the employees desire to negotiate...." The latter clause clearly reflects awareness of the fact that the employer-negotiator in the public service frequently has only limited authority, and that this condition will affect the scope of bargaining. As pointed out by the New York Governor's Committee on Public Employee Relations, the picture in the public sector is fundamentally different from that in the private sector. In private business, the authority to bargain on all of the normally bargainable matters is present or can be delegated, no matter what the size or make-up of the bargaining unit. By contrast, in the public service the necessary authority may not be delegable to lower-level functional units; legal requirements and tradition often call for uniformity of certain working conditions for like categories of employees throughout the governmental entity, regardless of bargaining unit categorization; and, even at the top of the particular level of government involved, authority is normally divided at least three ways — among the executive branch, the legislative branch, and a civil service commission.

Inherent in the previously quoted section of the Taylor Law, therefore, is the necessity that some consideration be given to the nature of the subject matter sought to be bargained upon in seeking to arrive at the appropriateness of a unit. This provision of the Taylor Law also recognizes that the subject matter of bargaining must normally be limited by the scope of the "employer's" authority to make agreements or effective recommendations, and a likely consequence is that the smaller the unit decided upon, the more restricted the scope of the bargaining by that unit will be.

Apart from this inhibiting effect on the bargaining experience, an approach which permits or favors small units makes it very difficult to resolve other institutional complications which arise in bargaining in the public service. The New York Governor's Committee, in both its 1966 Report and its 1968 Report, pointed out the unique importance of completing a negotiation with public employees in time to incorporate the agreement's financial essence in the budget of the governmental unit — which, by law, generally must be submitted to the legislature by a specified date. However, many of the annual bargaining sessions in the public sector today are extraordinarily prolonged, starting with direct negotiation, followed by resort to mediation and the frequently used machinery of fact-finding or impasse panels. After all of this there may be further extensive dealings with upper-echelon individuals or groups in the executive and legislative branches. Thus, the sheer weight of the process[3] may lead to its breakdown if the trend toward proliferation of bargaining units in numerous jurisdictions continues unabated. It is noteworthy that in the City of Philadelphia[4] — which is frequently cited as an example of well-established, peaceful, and effective bargaining at the municipal level — all employees except policemen and firemen have been represented by a single unit for most of the last two decades. Even with only a single unit and without use of impasse resolution machinery, however, the experience in Philadelphia has been marked by many instances of abnormally prolonged annual negotiations. The Philadelphia experience also demonstrates the need to establish detailed liaison between the executive branch, the legislative branch, and the civil service commission during the course of an annual bargaining program in order to minimize the chaotic effects of overlapping authority on the government side.

While it is possible that a city the size of Philadelphia might also have had a history of successful labor relations in the public sector under a pattern which broke down the public employee bargaining group into a small number of separate units, there is little question that the success could not have been achieved under the patterns of excessive fragmentation found elsewhere. In any event, the existence of the single large unit clearly contributed significantly to that city's ability to surmount effectively the institutional obstacles complicating public sector bargaining. Moreover, proliferation can and does breed excessive competition among rival organizations. One consequence of this may be a high incidence of breakdowns in peaceful bargaining. To be sure, competition in bargaining is to some extent unavoidable; this condition is not necessarily undesirable socially, and will continue to characterize the experience in private and public sector alike, regardless of the size of units involved. Nevertheless, there is hardly a permanent justification for permitting what appears to be a greater proliferation of bargaining units in the public sector than that now

---

[3] For example, a February 27, 1968, report by an impasse panel for the unit of Detroit police officers recommended a procedure for future bargaining. The essential steps which the panel proposed were to extend over a period of nine months in a particular year. *Excerpts from Detroit Police Panel Report,* Gov't Employee Rel. Rep. [*hereinafter* GERR] No. 235, at D-1, D-10 (March 11, 1968).

[4] The author was the labor relations adviser to the City of Philadelphia between 1952 and 1962.

prevailing in the private sector. The institutional factors discussed above add a unique dimension to the task of achieving peaceful and successful bargaining in the public sector. Because of this, and because of the likelihood that proliferation will result in an increased number of breakdowns in the bargaining process, larger units must become the accepted norm in the public sector....

NOTE

For other useful discussions, see Rubin, Hickman, Durkee & Hayford, *Public Sector Unit Determination, Administrative Procedures and Case Law,* Final Report submitted to the United States Department of Labor, Labor Management Services Administration (1978); Mack, *Public Sector Collective Bargaining: Diffusion of Managerial Structure and Fragmentation of Bargaining Units,* 2 Fla. St. L. Rev. 281 (1974); H. Wellington & R. Winter, The Unions and the Cities 97-114 (1971). The NLRB's unit policies in the private sector are thoroughly explored in J. Abodeely, R. Hammer & A. Sandler, The NLRB and the Appropriate Bargaining Unit (1981).

2. CRITERIA CONSIDERED

CONNECTICUT STATE BOARD OF LABOR RELATIONS, TWENTY-FIRST ANNUAL REPORT 1-3 (1967)

Questions concerning the unit and the related questions concerning the supervisory level at which membership in a unit is to be cut off obviously involve competing legitimate interests. The municipal employer, for example, often wants the broadest possible unit for reasons of administrative simplicity and convenience. Some employee organizations also want wide units because of their own traditions and institutional patterns. Other employee organizations have different and narrower traditions and practices, sometimes stemming from those of the old-line trade or craft unions. And some groups, heretofore unorganized or loosely organized, have their own traditions and special communities of interest. The Legislature itself has resolved these conflicts by providing specific guides in the case of uniformed and investigatory members of the police and fire departments, and in the case of professional employees. Even these guides have presented some problems of interpretation. Beyond them the Legislature has charged the Board with the difficult and often delicate task of balancing these competing interests under the broad injunction to insure to employees "the fullest freedom in exercising their rights" under the Act, and "to insure a clear and identifiable community of interest among employees" included in a unit. The Commission which drafted the Act stated that it did "subscribe to the view that the units should be the broadest possible which will reflect a community of interest and at the same time will respect the special interests of certain groups of employees." Report of the Interim Commission to Study Collective Bargaining by Municipalities (1965), p. 15 (hereinafter Report).

In attempting to implement this broad legislative mandate, the Board has given attention to the following factors in cases where one or more of them were made to appear:

1. *Agreements by the parties.* The Commission's Report indicates that the framers of the Act believed that questions of this nature should be governed by

agreement of the parties where agreement can be had. Report, page 15. There has been such agreement in a majority of cases processed by the Agent during the reporting period, upon at least some aspects of the case. The Board has adopted the policy of approving such agreements unless the resulting unit clearly contravenes the policy of the Act, and this has not occurred in practice.

2. *The similarity (or dissimilarity) of work and working conditions.* This includes any aspects of the work which would tend to create a community of interest, or the reverse, and covers a great variety of matters. Whether the work is clerical or manual (white collar or blue collar); whether there is common supervision; whether the work is performed in a single location, are examples of the sort of things the Board will look for and try to weigh. Obviously these considerations may sometimes pull in opposite directions. Employees in the same department may, for instance, perform different kinds of work, and work classifications often cut across department lines. This was the case in *Greenwich,* Dec. No. 692, June 7, 1966.

3. *The convenience of the municipal employer* in the light of its personnel and other relevant policies and practices. Thus in *Town of Greenwich* the Board declined to carve a unit out of blue collar workers in the Public Works Department alone, when the Town showed that this would disrupt its policy of uniform treatment for all employees in the work classifications involved, many of whom were in other departments, and where there appeared to be no countervailing consideration. See also *City of Bridgeport,* Dec. No. 677, February 21, 1966.

4. *Past bargaining history, if any.* The Board has given weight to the municipal employer's past practices and patterns of negotiation and recognition where there have been any. It is true that these would have antedated the Act, and are not legally binding on the parties. Nevertheless they have some tendency to show what the parties themselves have considered appropriate and feasible and what they are used to. And the patterns are likely to reflect any traditions that have evolved in the municipal service. Patterns worked out in other cities and towns, where they have attained a measure of consistency, seem entitled to some consideration in determining what is appropriate (though less than the municipal employer's own practices). They may be compared roughly to the customs of an industry which have often been given similar consideration. Even the employee organization's overall pattern (in this country), where there is one, seems entitled to some weight, since it has at least a slight tendency on pragmatic grounds to show something about feasibility and about the kind of unit which the organization can effectively represent.

5. *The desires of the members of a group* to be associated together for bargaining purposes....

6. *The Commission's admonition to keep the unit as broad as possible,* where that is consistent with the need for community of interest, and respect for legitimate special interests....

The above discussion should indicate something of the complexity and difficulty of the Board's task. It should be quite apparent that many of the above considerations overlap, and many work at cross-purposes with each other. The problems and practices of the 169 cities and towns of the State vary infinitely, and the extent to which each of the factors listed above appears is not the same in any two of them.... For this reason there is great variety among the size and the kinds of units found appropriate in the cases decided by the Board during the reporting period. Just as the Commission "concluded that it would be impossible to lay down any hard and fast rules for the determination by the Board of appropriate units," ... so the Board has refrained from applying rules which would put a strait-jacket on the types of units it would find appropriate. Rather it has sought to determine the problems in each municipality by applying to them the broad principles which the Act lays down, and by weighing the factors which the Board believes to be relevant to those principles in each individual case.

CITY OF APPLETON

Decision No. 7423 (Wis. Emp. Relations Comm'n 1966)

Local 73, AFSCME, hereinafter referred to as the Petitioner, petitioned the Board to conduct an election among employes of the City of Appleton, employed in the Sewerage Division of the Department of Public Works, to determine what representation, if any, the employes therein desired for the purposes of collective bargaining, pursuant to Section 111.70 of the Wisconsin Statutes. At the hearing, Teamsters Local 563, hereinafter referred to as the Intervenor, was permitted to intervene on the basis of its claim to be the recognized representative for all hourly-paid employes employed in the Department of Public Works.

The Intervenor would have the Board dismiss the petition on two grounds, (1) that the unit sought by the Petitioner is inappropriate, and (2) that the petition was untimely filed.

Appropriateness of Unit

The Department of Public Works consists of five separate divisions, Street, Sanitation, Sewerage, Maintenance and Engineering. There are approximately 120 employes in the Department of Public Works, and 18 are employed in the Sewerage Division. The Intervenor, up until at least the date of the filing of the petition, September 27, 1965, has been recognized as the collective bargaining representative of all hourly-paid employes in the first four divisions. The Engineering Division consists of professional engineers and clericals.

While the Intervenor claims that it has been recognized as the representative of the employes in the Department of Public Works and that such a Department is an appropriate unit, it should be noted that the clerical employes in the Engineering Department have not been included as part of that departmental-wide unit.

The Sewerage Division is physically and functionally located separate and distinct from the remainder of the functions and divisions of the Municipal Employer. Its employes primarily carry out their functions at the Sewage Disposal Plant. It has its own Superintendent, who is in charge of the entire Division, and the employes in said Division are not subject to the supervision of any other agent or officer of the Municipal Employer. The employes perform duties which, except for the Laborer I and II classifications, of which there are four positions, are distinct from the duties performed by employes of the Municipal Employer employed in other divisions or departments. There are very few temporary transfers either to or from the Sewerage Division.

The Board's function with respect to the establishment of an appropriate collective bargaining unit of municipal employes is governed by the following statutory provisions:

"Section 111.70(4)(d). *Collective Bargaining Units.* Whenever a question arises between a municipal employer and a labor union as to whether the union represents the employes of the employer, either the union or the municipality may petition the board to conduct an election among said employes to determine whether they desire to be represented by a labor organization. Proceedings in representation cases shall be in accordance with ss. 111.02(6) and 111.05 insofar as applicable, except that where the board finds that a proposed unit includes a craft the board shall exclude such craft from the unit. The board shall not order an election among employes in a craft unit except on separate petition initiating representation proceedings in such craft unit."

"Section 111.02(6). The term 'collective bargaining unit' shall mean all of the employes of one employer ..., except that where a majority of such employes engaged in a single craft, division, department or plant shall have voted by secret ballot as provided in Section 111.05(2) to constitute such group a separate bargaining unit they shall be so considered, ..."

"Section 111.05(2). Whenever a question arises concerning the determination of a collective bargaining unit as defined in Section 111.02(6), it shall be determined by secret ballot, and the board, upon request, shall cause the ballot to be taken in such manner as to show separately the wishes of the employes in any craft, division, department or plant as to the determination of the collective bargaining unit."

Whenever a petition for an election is filed with the Board, and wherein the petitioner requests an election among certain employes not constituting all of the employes of the employer, the Board has no power, except if the employes constitute a single craft, to determine what constitutes an appropriate collective bargaining unit. It does determine whether the group of employes set out as being an appropriate bargaining unit does in fact constitute a separate craft, division, department or plant. The employes involved, if they do constitute a separate division, department, or plant, are given the opportunity to determine for themselves whether they desire to constitute a separate collective bargaining unit.

The Intervenor contends that the statutes should be interpreted to give weight to past bargaining history to determine whether a non-craft group should be permitted to establish itself as a separate unit, whether for the purpose of decertification or for substituting another union for its current bargaining agent. It emphasizes the bargaining history between the Intervenor and the Municipal Employer, and argues that the unit established through bargaining history should not be disturbed.

The bargaining and negotiations in the past have been conducted by the City's Personnel Committee for all of the employes in the Department of Public Works, with the City Personnel Committee consulting with and receiving the advice of the Director of Public Works. The wage increases, fringe benefits and work rules negotiated for the Department of Public Works have been applied to all the employes in the Department and, in some instances, on a City-wide basis. The recommendations made by the Sewerage Division Superintendent with respect to promotions, transfers, discipline and individual wage adjustments, are subject to the approval of the Director of Public Works, and are not made independently by the Superintendent of the Sewage Disposal Plant.

The Intervenor would have the Board establish an appropriate collective bargaining unit on criteria considered by the National Labor Relations Board in establishing appropriate units under the federal labor law. The National Labor Relations Board considers the following factors:

(1) Duties, skills and working conditions of the employes.

(2) History of collective bargaining.

(3) Extent of union organization among the employes.

(4) Desires of the employes where one or two units may be equally appropriate.

Similarly, in recently adopted labor laws applying to public employes, the Connecticut State Board of Labor Relations and the Michigan Labor Mediation Board determine appropriate collective bargaining units with due consideration to "... a clear and identifiable community of interest to employes concerned...."

However, the criteria established in the Wisconsin Employment Peace Act, as quoted above, do not permit the Board to rely on the bargaining history as grounds for denying elections among employes in a separate division to determine for themselves whether they desire to constitute a unit separate and apart from the other employes of the municipal employer.

The Board has also today issued a Direction of Elections in a case involving the City of Kenosha. Another local of the Teamsters filed a petition with the Board requesting the Board to conduct an election among employes in the Waste Division of the Department of Public Works. In that proceeding, another local of the AFSCME has been historically recognized as the representative of all civil service employes of that community, with the exception of uniformed employes. In the instant proceeding, the intervening Teamster's local objects to the fragmentation of an existing unit. In the City of Kenosha case, the petitioning Teamster's local would fragmentize the existing unit. The Intervenor AFSCME Local in the City of Kenosha case would retain the overall unit and opposes fragmentation of an existing unit, while in the instant proceeding, the petitioning AFSCME Local would fragmentize the existing unit. The position of the parties in said two proceedings are inconsistent and demonstrate the problems faced by the Board in establishing units as required by the Statute. Fragmentizing of larger units of employes may result in requiring a municipal employer to engage in conferences and negotiations with more than one labor organization representing the same general category of employes on wages, hours and working conditions of its employes, may encourage needless rivalry among labor organizations, and may disturb an existing legitimate relationship and tend to delay the collective bargaining process. However, these factors must be weighed against the rights of the employes, where they constitute a separate department or division, to determine for themselves whether they desire to constitute a separate appropriate collective bargaining unit and, further, what representation, if any, they desire for the purposes of conferences and negotiations with their municipal employer. It is interesting to note that there has been an insignificant number of cases where the Board has observed fragmentation of bargaining units, in accordance with the statutory requirements, among employes of private employers. Apparently, the employes, labor organizations and employers alike, at least in private employment, have recognized that an effective collective bargaining relationship is best maintained in the absence of fragmentizing an over-all collective bargaining unit. This observation is not intended to apply to those smaller units consisting of craft employes or employes with specialized skills....

The Board, therefore, is today issuing a Direction of Elections wherein the employes in the Sewerage Division will be given an opportunity to determine for themselves whether they desire to constitute a collective bargaining unit separate and apart from other employes of the Municipal Employer, and what, if any, representation they desire for the purposes of conferences and negotiations with the Municipal Employer on questions of wages, hours and conditions of employment.

The results of the unit vote will be tabulated first, and if there is no question that the required number of employes vote in favor of the separate unit, then the ballots with respect to the selection of the bargaining representative will be tallied. However, if the result of the vote on the unit determination does not establish a separate unit, the Board agent conducting the elections will immediately impound the ballots on the question of representation and the results thereof will not be determined....

NOTE

Chairman Morris Slavney of the Wisconsin Employment Relations Commission made the following comments with respect to the statutory provisions referred to in the principal case:

> [S]uch requirements with regard to the establishment of bargaining units have resulted in an overfragmentation of bargaining units in municipal employment in Wisconsin. For example, the City of Milwaukee has over 20 separate bargaining units. In the City of Appleton, somewhere in the neighborhood of 60,000 population, both AFSCME and Teamsters were engaged in organizational efforts among clerical employees in some six departments of the city hall. As a result of the statutory provision granting employees in each department an opportunity to establish separate units, the City of Appleton ended up with six units of stenographers and clericals in six departments. The Teamsters represented three of the departmental units while AFSCME was certified as the representative in the remaining three departments. You can imagine the frustration of management in having to bargain with two unions, who are forever competing with each other, for the same classification of employees under the same civil service system. Slavney, *Representation and Bargaining Unit Issues,* in Dispute Settlement in the Public Sector 35, 49-50 (T. Gilroy ed. 1972).

The Wisconsin Municipal Employment Law was subsequently revised to broaden the discretion of the WERC in determining appropriate bargaining units, while at the same time mandating it to avoid excessive fragmentation. Wis. Stat. Ann. § 111.70(4)(d) (West 1988) now provides, in relevant part, that:

The commission shall determine the appropriate bargaining unit for the purpose of collective bargaining and shall whenever possible avoid fragmentation by maintaining as few units as practicable in keeping with the size of the total municipal work force. In making such a determination, the commission may decide whether, in a particular case, the employees in the same or several departments, divisions, institutions, crafts, professions or other occupational groupings constitute a unit. Before making its determination, the commission may provide an opportunity for the employees concerned to determine, by secret ballot, whether or not they desire to be established as a separate collective bargaining unit.

STATE OF NEW YORK

1 PERB ¶ 399.85 (N.Y. Pub. Emp. Relations Bd. 1968), *aff'd per curiam sub nom.*
Civil Service Employees Ass'n v. Helsby, 32 App. Div. 2d 131, 300
N.Y.S.2d 424, *aff'd per curiam,* 25 N.Y.2d 842, 250 N.E.2d 731,
303 N.Y.S.2d 690 (1969)

On November 15, 1967, the State of New York, herein referred to as the employer, recognized the Civil Service Employees Association, Inc., herein referred to as CSEA, as negotiating representative of employees in a general unit made up of all State employees other than professional members of the State University of New York and members of the State Police. Timely petitions contesting the designation of the general unit and the recognition of CSEA were filed by many organizations, all of which proposed one or more negotiating units alternative to the unit designated by the employer.

The Petitioners and the Units They Claim

New York State Employees Council 50, American Federation of State, County and Municipal Employees, AFL-CIO, herein referred to as Council 50, directly and through several of its affiliated locals, seeks the following units:

1. All correction officers, correction youth camp officers and correction hospital officers in the Department of Correction, excluding all supervisors and all other persons.

This identical unit is claimed by another of the petitioners, Local 456 of the International Brotherhood of Teamsters, Chauffeurs, Warehousemen and Helpers of America, herein referred to as IBT.

2. All employees in the Psychiatric Attendant Series, including psychiatric attendant, psychiatric senior attendant, psychiatric staff attendant, psychiatric supervising attendant, psychiatric head attendant, psychiatric chief supervising attendant and all (T.B.) titles in this series.

3. All nonsupervisory employees in the Rehabilitation Counselor Series in the Department of Education, including counselors and senior counselors. There are a few rehabilitation counselors in the Department of Social Services and Mental Hygiene and in the State University. Council 50 takes no position on whether these rehabilitation counselors should also be included in the proposed unit.

4. All clerical employees of the Department of Labor proper.

5. All professional and technical employees of the Department of Labor proper, excluding managerial and confidential employees, nurses, attorneys and safety inspectors.

6. All professional and technical employees of the Division of Employment, excluding managerial and confidential employees, nurses and attorneys.

7. All clerical employees of the Division of Employment.

8. All nonsupervisory office and clerical employees of the State Insurance Fund.

9. All nonsupervisory professional and technical employees of the State Insurance Fund, excluding field service, confidential and managerial employees, nurses and attorneys.

10. All supervising professional and technical employees of the State Insurance Fund, excluding field service, confidential and managerial employees, nurses and attorneys.

11. All investigators of the Workmen's Compensation Board, Grade 12 through Grade 20.

12. All hearing officers of the Workmen's Compensation Board, Grade 14, and all those calendar clerks who are assigned to the Workmen's Compensation Board Referees' Bureau.

13. All assistant workmen's compensation examiners, Grade 8.

Local 30D, International Union of Operating Engineers, AFL-CIO, herein referred to as Operating Engineers, seeks a unit of:

14. Nonsupervisory employees in the power plants and related skilled trade shops.

The Safety Officers Benevolent Association, herein referred to as SOBA, seeks to represent:

15. All nonsupervisory safety officers. SOBA leaves to the discretion of this Board whether all nonsupervisory safety officers should be included in a single unit or whether there should be separate units for those employees in the Department of Mental Hygiene, Department of Correction, and the State University, respectively. It takes no position with respect to the inclusion or exclusion from the proposed unit or units of safety officers, if any, in the Department of Health.

Local 381 of the Building Service Employees International Union, AFL-CIO, herein referred to as BSEIU, seeks two units consisting, respectively, of:

16. Lifeguards employed by Long Island State Park Commission.

17. Seasonal patrolmen employed by Long Island State Park Commission.

District 15, International Association of Machinists and Aerospace Workers, AFL-CIO, herein referred to as IAM, seeks a unit of:

18. Long Island State Park Police, Grade 14 and Grade 16.

The Police Conference of New York, Inc., through two of its affiliates, seeks units of:

19. Niagara State Park Police, excluding the captain and lieutenants.

20. All Capital Buildings Police.

The Correction Officers Association claims a unit of:

21. All correction officers and their supervisors, excluding the deputy warden and correction deputy superintendent.

Local 223 of the Building Service Employees International Union, AFL-CIO, seeks a unit of:

22. Inspectors in the Division of Industrial Safety Service of the Department of Labor, excluding chief inspectors.

The Association of New York State Civil Service Attorneys, Inc., seeks a unit of:

23. Lawyers holding competitive class positions in the attorney series of titles for which permission to practice law in the State of New York is a mandatory requirement, and persons holding training-level positions whether or not admitted to practice law in New York State. It would exclude lawyers who hold competitive class positions as counsel to a department or agency.

The New York State Nurses Association seeks a unit consisting of:

24. All registered professional nurses and every person lawfully authorized by permit to practice as a registered professional nurse in nursing service or in nursing education. The proposed unit would include persons on the faculty of the State University and, therefore, not within the general unit designated by the employer.

The American Physical Therapy Association claims a unit of:

25. All physical therapists. This unit would include physical therapists employed on the faculty of the State University and, therefore, not within the general unit designated by the employer.

Petitions were also filed by SOBA for a unit of nonsupervisory narcotics security assistants in the Department of Mental Hygiene, by the New York State Council of Carpenters, AFL-CIO, for a unit comprising all carpenters; and by Local 200 of the Building Service Employees International Union, AFL-CIO, for a unit consisting of all nonsupervisory employees of the Syracuse State School. Each of these petitions was withdrawn, as was a petition of the Police Conference, Inc., on behalf of a unit of police officers of the Palisades Interstate Park Commission.

Council 50 and BSEIU both filed timely petitions to decertify CSEA as the negotiating representative of employees in the general unit, on the ground that the general unit is inappropriate for the purpose of collective negotiations....

[The Board denied a motion to disqualify the CSEA on the ground that it was not a labor organization within the meaning of the act. The Board granted motions disqualifying the American Physical Therapy Association and the Association of New York State Civil Service Attorneys, Inc., on this basis.]

Unit Determination of Director of Representation

With respect to the unit claims of the petitioners, the Director of Representation gave full consideration to the evidence produced and to the arguments made. He found that the employees within the general unit did not share a community of interest in that the range of their work assignments and of the training required for the performance of such assignments was inordinately broad. On the other hand, he found that, in the language of the employer:

none [of the petitioners] has related its unit to a meaningful pattern of collective negotiation. Each would leave the State with a jumble of mixed vertical and horizontal units. They would leave it to the State to bring order out of the chaos they had created.

We agree with this analysis of the Director of Representation.

The employees concerned in this representation dispute are employed in over 3,700 job classifications, categorized in some 90 occupational groupings. These job classifications far surpass in diversity and number those usually found in public or private employment. These classifications run the gamut from Aircraft Pilot to Wild Life Trapper.

The enormity of this diversity of occupations and the great range in the qualifications requisite for employment in these occupations would preclude effective and meaningful representation in collective negotiations if all such employees were included in a single unit. The occupational differences found here give rise to different interests and concerns in terms and conditions of employment. This, in turn, would give rise to such conflicts of interest as to outweigh those factors indicating a community of interest.

Thus, the implementation of the rights granted by the Act to all public employees mandates a finding that a single unit would be inappropriate.

On the other hand, to grant the type of narrow occupational fragmentation requested by the petitioners would lead to unwarranted and unnecessary administrative difficulties. Indeed, as the State contends, it might well lead to the disintegration of the State's current labor relations structure.

Having rejected the unit designated by the employer and those proposed by petitioners, the Director of Representation decided that there should be six negotiating units, as follows:

Operational Services Unit, Inspection and Security Services Unit, Health Services and Support Unit, Administrative Services Unit, Professional, Scientific and Technical Services Unit, and a unit of seasonal employees of the Long Island State Park Commission.

Excluded from all units are all other seasonal and part-time employees inasmuch as there is not sufficient evidence in the record to determine their proper unit placement, and persons claimed to be managerial or confidential employees by the employer. With respect to the latter group, the Director stated that further proceedings would be necessary to develop criteria to be utilized in categorizing an employee as managerial or confidential and to determine the desirability and practicality of their inclusion in the negotiating structure of State employees.

Both the employer and CSEA have contended on this appeal that the decision of the Director constitutes error, in that the units found in his decision do not coincide with any of the units petitioned for in this proceeding. Thus, a most basic question presented on this appeal is whether this Board, in a representation proceeding, may devise a unit that it deems to be most appropriate although such a unit is not sought by any of the parties.

We are convinced that this question must be answered in the affirmative. The statutory grant of authority to this Board to resolve disputes concerning representation status mandates this Board to define appropriate units and does not restrict its power simply to the approval or disapproval of units sought by a party or parties to the proceeding. Even apart from such clear statutory intent, the logic of the situation compels the same conclusion. If the Board's power herein were so restricted, a representation dispute might be interminable, in that it would continue until a party to the proceeding petitioned for a unit which the Board found to be appropriate in the light of statutory criteria. Such a restrictive interpretation of the Act would delay unduly participation by public employees in the determination of their terms and conditions of employment. It is for this reason that the Director of Representation has, in many proceedings, devised negotiating units which were not sought by any of the parties.

We believe that the statutory criteria that "the unit shall be compatible with the joint responsibilities of the public employer and public employees to serve the public" (Civil Service Law, § 207(c)) requires us to designate negotiating units which provide the employer with a comprehensive and coherent pattern for collective negotiations. Moreover, we believe that this statutory standard requires the designation of as small a number of units as possible consistent with the overriding requirement that the employees be permitted to form organizations of their own choosing to represent them in a meaningful and effective manner. It is our conviction that the approach of the Director of Representation in designating a limited number of negotiating units, each consisting of families of occupations, is reasonably designed to achieve this goal.

In evaluating the specific units determined to be appropriate by the Director of Representation, we defer consideration of the unit for the seasonal employees of the Long Island State Park Commission. The unit itself and the questions it raises regarding seasonal employees in parks and elsewhere throughout the State are separable from problems involving the other State employees. Further, these problems are not ripe for resolution as the seasonal employees of the Long Island State Park Commission are not presently on the State payroll and will not be until the advent of summer.

We find the following five units to be appropriate:

1. Operational Services Unit:

This unit is similar to that determined to be appropriate by the Director of Representation except that we delete those occupations associated with institutions and related to the preparation and distribution of food, and to personal and domestic services. For the reasons discussed below, these occupations are placed in Unit 3.

2. Security Services Unit:

This unit is a contraction of the Inspection and Security Services Unit determined to be appropriate by the Director of Representation in that we delete all inspectors, investigators and examiners from that unit. The unit now comprises all occupations involving the protection of persons and property; the enforcement of laws, codes, rules and regulations concerned with vehicle and highway safety; and the security aspects of correctional institutions. Inspectional services cover a broad range of occupations which are distinct from security services and cannot be properly allocated to the same unit. The inspectors, investigators and examiners who have been deleted from this unit have been placed in Units 4 and 5.

3. Institutional Services Unit:

This unit is an expansion of the Health Services and Support Unit determined to be appropriate by the Director of Representation in that the unit now includes those occupations associated with institutions and related to the preparation and distribution of food and to personal and domestic services. We find that working conditions in institutions are significantly different from working conditions elsewhere. Accordingly, we conclude that employees engaged in these occupations — which are unique to institutions — have a greater community of interest with their fellow institutional employees than with operational services employees.

4. Administrative Services Unit:

This unit is similar to the unit determined to be appropriate by the Director of Representation except that it also includes certain inspectors, investigators and examiners who were deleted from Unit 2. All inspectors, investigators and examiners are placed in this unit unless their responsibilities are of a professional, scientific or technical nature.

5. Professional, Scientific and Technical Services Unit:

This unit is similar to that determined to be appropriate by the Director of Representation except that it includes inspectors, investigators and examiners, the nature of whose responsibilities are of a technical, professional or scientific nature.

The implementation of these units in this representation proceeding requires a determination as to those eligible for inclusion in each unit. In making this determination, we must consider these as yet unanswered questions —

First — A determination as to which job titles shall be included in each unit. We feel that the delineation of the units heretofore made provides sufficient specificity to allocate the majority of job titles to their respective units. However, there may be a question with respect to some job titles as to which unit they belong.

Second — In his decision, the Director included in each unit those responsible for the supervision of the activities of that unit. It is our policy not to exclude all supervisors arbitrarily from a rank-and-file unit. Rather, supervisors have been excluded when there was a showing that their supervisory duties and obligations were of such a nature to give rise to such a conflict of interest as to preclude their inclusion in the same unit with rank-and-file. Thus, a determination must be made as to what supervisors will be excluded from any unit and the disposition of those excluded.

Third — The dimensions of the exclusion of managerial and confidential employees.

We believe that these specific questions of eligibility and exclusion can be resolved most expeditiously in the following manner: This Board shall prepare a list of job titles to be placed in each unit. This list shall include the Board's disposition of the supervision question. A second list prepared by the Board will indicate those excluded as managerial or confidential. Within seven days after these lists have been submitted to the parties, a conference will be scheduled by the Board, at which time the Board will consider and rule on any objections of the parties to such lists....

NOTES

1. Following the trend toward broad statewide units, the Maine Labor Relations Board in *Council 74, AFSCME,* GERR No. 682, E-1 (Me. LRB 1976), established seven statewide bargaining units: (1) administrative services, (2) professional and technical services, (3) institutional services, (4) law enforcement, public safety and regulatory services (non-police), (5) state police services, (6) operations maintenance and support services, and (7) supervisory personnel services. The Board in its decision made a special reference to the expert testimony that was presented concerning the experience in New York and Massachusetts with broad bargaining units at the state level.

2. In *State of Iowa & Iowa AFSCME Council 61,* 734 GERR 10 (Iowa PERB 1977), the Iowa PERB held that a unit of approximately 7000 technical employees constituted an appropriate unit. In holding that the broad unit that included classifications ranging from airplane pilots to seed analysts was appropriate, the Iowa PERB held that the statutory phrase "principles of efficient administration of government" required it to establish "the smallest number of bargaining units consistent with meaningful and effective representation of the employees so involved." In so ruling, the Iowa PERB held that a separate unit of licensed practical nurses (LPNs) was not appropriate in view of their community of interest with other health care classifications also included in the technical unit, as well as the need to avoid unnecessary fragmentation.

3. The Ohio Public Employment Relations Board in *In re State of Ohio,* 2 OPER ¶ 2423 (Ohio PERB 1985), in establishing fourteen bargaining units for state employees, stated that the units were established for the purpose of avoiding the splitting of a given job classification among different bargaining units and in order to maintain a commonality of promotions and transfers within a unit. The Ohio PERB also stated that special emphasis was placed on avoiding unit proliferation as well as in reducing the potential for fragmentation in the future.

4. In establishing appropriate bargaining units, is it necessary that the agency establish the *most* appropriate unit as distinguished from *an* appropriate unit? In the private sector the NLRB has uniformly held that the unit petitioned for does not have to be the most appropriate unit. In *Morand Bros. Beverage Co.,* 91 N.L.R.B. 409, 418 (1950), the Board stated that "there is nothing in the statute which requires that the unit of bargaining be the *only* appropriate unit, or the *ultimate* unit or the *most* appropriate unit; the Act requires only that the unit be appropriate. It must be appropriate to insure to employees, *in every case,* 'the fullest freedom in exercising the rights guaranteed by this Act.'" Although similar rulings have been made by several state labor relations boards, there are at least two noteworthy exceptions. In the principal case, the New York PERB held that the statutory criteria mandated the establishment of the most appropriate bargaining unit. The Michigan Employment Relations Commission (MERC) has adopted a position somewhere between the NLRB approach and the New York PERB approach. Thus, the MERC has stated that in making unit determinations it is guided by the following standard set forth by the Michigan Supreme Court in *Hotel Olds v. State Labor Mediation Bd.,* 333 Mich. 382, 387, 53 N.W.2d 302, 304 (1952): "In designating bargaining units as appropriate, a primary objective of the Commission is to constitute the largest unit which in the circumstances of the particular case is most compatible with the effectuation of the purposes of the law and to include in a single unit all common interests." Relying on the *Hotel Olds* decision, the MERC held in *City of Charlevoix,* 1970 MERC Lab. Op. 404 (Mich.), that a city-wide bargaining unit that included fire and police personnel was appropriate since "the larger overall unit is more in keeping with the policy of the State than separate departmental units, especially in a municipality where only a small number of employees are employed." On the other hand, in *Regents of the Univ. of Mich.,* 1971 MERC Lab. Op. 337 (Mich.), the MERC stated that "[t]he statute does not require that only the 'ultimate unit' can be certified. There may be smaller groupings within the employment of a single employer which are appropriate for collective bargaining." The California Educational Employment Relations Board has likewise eschewed adopting either the "most" or "an" appropriate unit standard. *Antioch Unified Sch. Dist.,* 1 PERC ¶ 517B (Cal. EERB 1977).

5. The Kansas Public Employee Relations Board in *Ft. Hays Kan. State College, Case No. 1 (1972),* GERR No. 487, B-3 (1973), stated that it "would allow public employees at each unit of higher education to organize on individual institutional units." The Kansas Board stated:

> Each institution, the Board feels, is a separate distinct operating entity with a complex relationship already existing between the public employees and the administration therein. The principles of efficient administration will be maintained inasmuch as the evidence before this Board indicates that most problems concerning conditions of employment with university employees have been handled on a local basis; *i.e.,* between the local university administration and the employee. Evidence before this Board also indicates that a distinct "community of interest" is enjoyed by employees at the individual institutions. Particularly, it was expressed that the workers with similar occupations at KU Medical Center and at Kansas University were working under different environments with different benefits in some cases. Contrasted with this, the employees at each institution had a common base in their working conditions and the evidence indicated a similarity of problems at each institution that is not evident between employees of separate institutions.
>
> ... The difficulties of employees organizing over a great distance (*i.e.,* the distance between Wichita and Ft. Hays) when considered in light of the fact that each institution has operated as a separate identity, made the unit determinations on an individual institutional basis seem most logical. The Board did not view the problems of overfragmentation and splintering of a work force as automatically requiring a statewide unit in every case, but that each case must be reviewed on its own merit, thus our decision of the individual institutional units.

STATE OF FLORIDA

Case No. 8H-R3 (Fla. Pub. Employees Relations Comm'n, June 17, 1976)

MACK, CHAIRMAN, and FILIPOWICZ and GITOMER, COMMISSIONERS: The State of Florida, filed a Petition on March 4, 1976 pursuant to §§ 120.54(b)(4) and 447.201(1), Fla. Stat. (1975) requesting the Commission to establish bargaining units for state employees by rule. In its petition, the State, through the Department of Administration, proposed that four statewide occupational units be established by rule in addition to the two units that have already been approved through the consent election process.

The Commission held a hearing on April 8, 1976 to consider the wisdom and propriety of adopting unit configurations for state employees through rulemaking....

The only questions which the Commission addressed at the April 8 hearing were the feasibility and legality of unit determination by rule. These issues were considered by the Massachusetts Labor Relations Commission at length in their decision of March 3, 1975, wherein a minimum of ten statewide occupationally based units were established for employees of the Commonwealth of Massachusetts. The Massachusetts Commission was faced with a crazy quilt of units that had been established under a statute granting to state employees limited collective bargaining rights in geographically determined single agency units. Under a comprehensive collective bargaining act, the Massachusetts Commissioner of Administration was delegated the duty of representing the Commonwealth of Massachusetts as the employer for collective bargaining purposes of all commonwealth employees. The Massachusetts Labor Relations Commission, following a petition by the Commonwealth to consolidate large numbers of pre-existing units, determined that establishing the configuration of a small number of units for these employees by rule was both wise and economical. Thereafter, following extensive public hearings, that Commission's Rules and Regulations were amended to provide minimum standards against which any petition for Commonwealth employees would be measured.

Florida, of course, had no formal collective bargaining structure for state employees prior to the passage of Chapter 74-100, Laws of Florida (§§ 447.201-.609, Fla. Stat. (1975)), hereinafter the Act. During the year and a half of experience under the Act, numerous petitions have been filed by organizations seeking to represent state employees. Of these petitions a significant number have been dismissed for proposing units which, we have found, do not comport with the standards established in § 447.307(4) of the Act and § 8H-3.31 of the Commission's Rules and Regulations. In the process of petition and dismissal, bargaining elections have been delayed by the absence of precedent in Florida public employee relations law and by the multifarious units that can legitimately be proposed for employees of the state. Thus, when the State of Florida proposed rulemaking as a means to expedite the weighty policy questions involving unit determinations for state employees, we were ready to listen to all those who wished to appear and argue the pros and cons of the State's petition.

The Administrative Procedure Act, Chapter 120, Florida Statutes, and other statutes under which this Commission operates provide us with two methods of devising rules and orders: quasi-legislative rulemaking and case by case adjudication. Rule-making is required for the promulgation of "… agency statement[s] of general applicability that [implement], interpret, or prescribe law policy…." Fla. Stat. § 120.52(13) (1975). Ad hoc adjudication, on the other hand, determines the statutory rights of particular parties to a particular controversy or legal question.

Before any administrative agency may adopt rules and regulations, it is required by statute to give notice of its proposed action, with a statement of the purpose and effect of the proposed rule, a summary of the rule, and a reference to the statutory authority for the particular proposed rule.[1] Fla. Stat. § 120.54(1) (1975). By law, we are required to "give affected persons an opportunity to present evidence and argument on all issues under consideration ap-

---

[1]Section 447.207(1) of the Act provides: "After public hearing, the commission shall adopt, promulgate, amend or rescind such rules and regulations as it deems necessary and administratively feasible to carry out the provisions of this part." In addition, § 447.307(4)(h) of the Act establishes for the determination of appropriate collective bargaining units "[s]uch other factors and policies as the commission may prescribe by regulations or by its decisions."

propriate to inform [us] of their contention," Fla. Stat. § 120.54(2) (1975), if an affected person timely requests such opportunity.[2]

In short, rulemaking provides the opportunity for an agency to receive and consider the arguments, positions and evidence presented by all parties affected by a policy decision before it decides questions that affect broad classes of persons. Since the Commission must give notice that rulemaking is under consideration and must further summarize its proposed action, those who would be affected by our decision are given the opportunity to:

"effectively advance their own policy by mobilizing their sources of information and experience and making them available to the Commission." Memorandum, "Why Establish Units By Rule Making Rather Than The Case-By-Case Method?"[3]

In rulemaking we may be provided the opinions of many interested and concerned parties; in adjudication our field of inquiry is limited to only those parties and those questions directly at issue in a particular case. Thus, the advantages of rulemaking hearings flow to the organizations and employees involved as well as to the state and to this Commission.

Many commentators on the administrative process have expressed doubts on the desirability of case by case adjudication of issues that result in broad policy decisions.[4] They would suggest, as an alternative to ad hoc decision making on policy matters by an administrative agency, the quasi-legislative rule-making procedure wherein the data and theories upon which policies may rest are subject to public scrutiny and review before the interests of individual parties are affected.

As the Massachusetts Commission recognized, certainly rulemaking provides an expeditious alternative to case by case adjudication.[5] "Clearly enunciated and properly drawn rules should reduce litigation by authoritatively advising affected parties what general types of units will or will not be deemed appropriate."[6]

While the National Labor Relations Board (NLRB) has chosen the adjudicatory method for the promulgation and amendment of substantive rules of law,

---

[2] See Note, "The Use of Agency Rule Making," 54 Iowa L. Rev. 1086, 1097, 1098 (1969): "An agency may consider and decide many broad policy issues in adjudicatory proceedings ... (but) formulating these broad policies in an adjudication eliminates or defers the participation of many parties who ultimately are affected by the decision. Making these same decisions in a rulemaking proceeding gives all interested parties notice and a chance to participate in the agency decisions."

[3] Memorandum, "Why Establish Units By Rule Making Rather Than The Case-By-Case Method?" (Mass. Lab. Rel. Comm'n, Nov. 13, 1974).

[4] H. Friendly, "The Federal Administrative Agencies," 146-147 (1962); I. K. Davis, "Administrative Law Treatise," § 6.13 (1965); Recommendations of Section of Labor Relations Law, American Bar Association, 42 LRRM 513 (1958); Peck, "The Atrophied Rule Making Powers of the National Labor Relations Board," 70 Yale L.J. 729 (1961); Shapiro, "The Choice of Rule Making or Adjudication in the Development of Administrative Policy," 76 Harv. L. Rev. 921, 942 (1965); Bernstein, "The NLRB's Adjudication-Rule Making Dilemma Under the Administrative Procedures Act," 79 Yale L.J. 571 (1970); Kahn, "The NLRB and Higher Education: The Failure of Policy Making Through Adjudication," 22 UCLA L. Rev. 63 (1973); Silverman, "The Case for the National Labor Relations Board's Use of Rule Making in Asserting Jurisdiction," Labor L.J. at 607 (October 1974); NLRB v. Wyman Gordon Co., 394 U.S. 759 (1969); NLRB v. Textron, Inc., 416 U.S. 267 (1974).

[5] Memorandum, "Why Establish Units by Rule Making Rather Than by the Case-by-Case Method?" (Mass. Lab. Rel. Comm'n November 13, 1974).

[6] Id. at 7.

it does so through the exercise of its own "informed discretion."[7] And indeed, when compared to the short time required for unit determinations under the NLRB's jurisdiction and the publication system available for dissemination of decisions, the rulemaking process is indeed cumbersome. However, the time heretofore required for unit determinations under our statute, the part-time nature of this Commission, and the difficulties encountered in providing our decisions to all potentially affected parties make rulemaking in the context of unit determinations for state employees expeditious, economical, and administratively feasible.

While certain questions have been raised as to our authority to promulgate specific standards for units for state employees, we conclude that both the Act and Florida administrative law grant the power which we have chosen to exercise. Adopting general unit configurations for state employees as standards against which petitions are measured is a policy decision which § 447.307(4)(h) of the Act specifically states may be promulgated by rule *or* decision. In addition, we have set forth above the factors which lead us to the conclusion that these standards are "necessary and administratively feasible to carry out the provisions of this part." Thus, we conclude that the Legislature has delegated to us the authority under which we propose to act.

Accordingly the Commission has determined to grant the petition of the State of Florida to institute rulemaking proceedings to determine the general type and kind of units which are appropriate for state employees under the Act.

Commissioner Stouffer dissents on the grounds that, in his opinion, the Commission has only the authority to determine the appropriateness or inappropriateness of particular bargaining units as they are proposed by petition. Commissioner Rose dissents only as to the wisdom of proceeding by rulemaking at this time.

NOTES

1. Following a hearing on the State's petition for adoption of a rule establishing six statewide bargaining units, the Florida Commission in *State of Fla.,* 2 FPER 166 (Fla. PERC 1976), adopted a rule establishing the following seven statewide bargaining units: (1) administrative and clerical services, (2) operational services, (3) human or institutional services, (4) health care professionals, (5) all other professionals, (6) law enforcement employees, and (7) supervisory employees. Rather than including all professional employees in one unit, the Commission included all health care professional employees in one unit and all other professional employees in a separate unit. For a review of the establishment of bargaining units at the state level in Florida, see McHugh, *The Florida Experience in Public Employee Collective Bargaining, 1974-1978: Bellwether for the South,* 6 Fla. St. U.L. Rev. 263, 302-06 (1978).

2. Using its rule making authority under the Illinois Educational Labor Relations Act, the Illinois Educational Labor Relations Board has established by rule

---

[7]*NLRB v. Textron, Inc.,* 416 U.S. 267, 294 (1974); *NLRB v. Wyman Gordon Co.,* 394 U.S. 759 (1969). Indeed, the United States Supreme Court recognized "that rulemaking would provide the Board with a forum for soliciting the informed views of those affected in industry and labor before embarking on a new course. But surely the Board has the discretion to decide that the adjudicative procedures in this case may also produce the relevant information necessary to mature and fair consideration of the issues." *NLRB v. Textron, Inc., supra* at 295.

presumptively appropriate bargaining units at both the Urbana and Chicago campuses of the University of Illinois. 80 Ill. Admin. Code 1135.20(a). A bargaining unit of University employees which is not one of the presumptively appropriate units may be established only if the petitioner can demonstrate the following by the clear and convincing evidence:

1) that the unit is otherwise appropriate under Section 7 of the Illinois Educational Labor Relations Act;

2) that special circumstances and compelling justifications make it appropriate for the Illinois Educational Labor Relations Board to establish a unit different from those set forth ... [in the rule];

3) that establishment of a different unit will not cause undue fragmentation of bargaining units or proliferation of bargaining units....

80 Ill. Admin. Code 1135.30 (a)(1), (2) and (3).

3. In *American Hosp. Ass'n v. NLRB,* 111 S. Ct. 1539 (1991), the Supreme Court unanimously upheld the NLRB's authority to promulgate by Rule eight defined employee bargaining units for acute care hospitals. After noting that a "decisionmaker has the authority to rely on rulemaking to resolve certain issues of general applicability unless Congress clearly expresses an intent to withhold that authority," the Court stated that the NLRA's "role of facilitating the organization and recognition of unions is certainly served by rules that define in advance the portions of the work force to which organizing efforts may properly be conducted." In responding to petitioner's contention that the NLRB's rule could result in an arbitrary result, the Court stated:

We consider it likely that presented with the case of an acute care hospital to which its application would be arbitrary, the Board would conclude that "extraordinary circumstances" justify a departure from the rule. See 29 C.F.R. § 103.30(a), (b) (1990). Even assuming, however, that the Board might decline to do so, we cannot conclude that the entire rule is invalid on its face.

4. Are there any limits on how broad bargaining units should be in the public sector? That the law of diminishing returns may be applicable is indicated in the following remarks of Clyde Summers:

City employment spans an exceedingly wide range of skills, from the professionally trained engineer and health officer to the unskilled janitor and park attendant. The work and working conditions of city employees vary so greatly that their interests may be better represented by separately chosen unions and their different problems may be better worked out in separate negotiations. A single union can, and commonly does, represent employees with varied and even competing interests. In fact, one function a union serves is to reconcile and compromise those interests by its internal processes. However, diverse interests within the union create internal tensions. If the diversity is too great the resulting tensions may be more than the union can manage. These tensions are then manifested at the bargaining table by the union making an array of demands designed to placate every group in the union. Bargaining becomes protracted and if the union is unable to resolve differences by its internal processes, it may be unable to work out compromises at the bargaining table or accept what might otherwise be considered a reasonable package. Thus, while multiple bargaining units add to the employer's negotiating burden, that cost may be less than negotiating with a conglomerate union which is trying to represent greater diversity than its internal pro-

cesses can reconcile. Moreover, if bargaining reaches an impasse, the consequences will be less disruptive if only one group of employees is involved than
if all employees are involved.

Summers, *Public Employee Bargaining: A Political Perspective*, 83 Yale L.J.
1156, 1190 (1974).

STATE OF NEW JERSEY

Decision No. 68, GERR No. 457, E-1 (N.J. Pub. Emp. Relations Comm'n 1972)

The above-captioned cases raise questions concerning the representation of
various groups of professional employees[2] employed by the State of New Jersey. Hearings were conducted on each of the petitions and thereafter Hearing
Officers made the following recommendations. In Case No. R-111 *ad hoc* Hearing Officer Joseph McCabe recommended that separate state-wide units of
supervisory and non-supervisory Registered Nurses be found appropriate. No
exceptions were timely filed to that recommendation. In Case No. RO-196,
wherein Petitioner sought certification in a unit of all Social Workers and Social
Worker trainees employed by the Bureau of Childrens Services, Hearing Officer Martin Pachman recommended dismissal of that petition on two grounds.
First, since not all social workers in state classified service were included, the
unit sought, being less than state-wide in scope, failed to meet the minimum
standards set forth by the Commission in its earlier disposition of other state
cases.[3] Second, even if that state-wide standard were not a requirement, the
exclusion of other social workers located in hospitals, training schools, etc., who
share the same characteristics of employment is not consistent with any reasonable definition of community of interest. In Case No. RO-230, wherein Petitioner sought certification in a unit of all Rehabilitation Counselors, their supervisors, aides and trainees employed by the Department of Labor and Industry,
the same Hearing Officer recommended dismissal of that petition essentially
because the unit, even though state-wide as to the titles sought, would exclude
employees with similar duties, skills, functions, goals and job qualifications and
thus there was a community of interest which extended beyond those titles
which that Petitioner sought to represent. Neither of the two Petitioners involved in these recommendations filed exceptions to the proposed dismissals of
their petitions. The Employer took exception to certain observations made by
the Hearing Officer which were not material to his recommendations above, but
which were relied on to support his suggested resolution of the larger question
of appropriate unit or units for professional employees of the State. Finally, in
Cases Nos. RO-164 and RO-208, which, by virtue of certain amendments,
amount to a single petition for a unit of all professional, non-supervisory, educational employees in the Departments of Education and Institutions and Agencies, Hearing Officer Jeffrey B. Tener recommended that a unit of all professional, educational employees be found appropriate. This is a modification of
Petitioner's unit, principally in that it also includes a small number of employees

---

[2] In most instances the parties do not contest the use of the term "professional" in describing the
employees involved. For purposes of this decision, there is an assumption, but no determination,
that such description is appropriate.

[3] *State of New Jersey (Neuro-Psychiatric Institute, et al.)*, P.E.R.C. No. 50.

in the Department of Higher Education.[4] The Employer filed exceptions to a variety of the Hearing Officer's findings and conclusions as well as to his ultimate recommendation on unit.

Following submission of all Hearing Officers' Reports and exceptions thereto, a three member panel of the Commission heard oral argument on the positions of the parties in these consolidated cases. The Commission has considered the record, briefs, Hearing Officer's Report and Recommendations, exceptions and oral argument in each of these cases and makes the following dispositions.

The cases will be discussed as one since the bases for disposition are the same in each. The Commission is not persuaded that the above units where recommended as appropriate for collective negotiations can be found so. There are two interrelated reasons for this conclusion, the statute's policy and the community of interest of the employees concerned.

It was the Legislature's express determination that Ch. 303 be enacted to promote permanent employer-employee peace and the health, welfare, comfort and safety of the people of the State. N.J.S.A. 34:13A-2. As the Supreme Court later observed, "The nature of the appropriate negotiating unit is a most significant factor in the production and maintenance of harmony and peace in public employment relations."[5]

Against this background the statute provides that the negotiating unit "... shall be defined with due regard for the community of interest among the employees concerned ..." N.J.S.A. 34:13A-5.3. Community of interest is an accepted term of art and the statute does not attempt to define it. There are several guidelines, however, only one of which is relevant here, namely, that in deciding which unit is appropriate for collective negotiations, the Commission may not include professional employees in the same unit with non-professional employees unless a majority of the former vote for inclusion. N.J.S.A. 34:13A-6(d).

When the Commission last examined the question of unit involving State employees, it concluded, with respect to the employees in question there, that to be appropriate the scope of the unit must be state-wide. Expressed and implied in that conclusion was an assessment that the strength and significance of the factors cited — in brief, a high degree of centralization of authority in the top echelon of State government and a general uniformity of major terms and conditions of employment for State employees — required a finding that the first distinctive level of common interest among employees extended state-wide and that this was the minimum level for meaningful negotiation of terms and conditions of employment. The Commission recognized but refused to give controlling weight to the variety of lesser but more particularized points of common employee interest known to exist in a specific institution or department. Admittedly, a reasonably persuasive case was made for establishing units at the institution or department level by highlighting local differences in conditions and duties, but on balance the factors demonstrating a broader community of interest were considered more compelling. Conceivably, the Commission could have stopped at that point and relied on the factors cited to conclude, as

---

[4] The unit does not contemplate inclusion of the teaching faculties found within the Department of Higher Education, most of whom are already represented.

[5] *Board of Education of the Town of West Orange v. Wilton*, 57 N.J. 404, 424 (1971).

one organization urged, that not only was this the first level of common interest, but that this was the only set of interests to be recognized in determining the unit question, meaning that there would be only one unit for all State employees. Instead, the Commission relied on that set of facts only to establish the base or scope of the unit. It then found, in agreement with the principal parties, that it was appropriate to fashion a unit, statewide in scope, to encompass all employees sharing a broad occupational objective or description. That is, it found an additional mutuality of employee interest arising from the kind of work performed, not expressed in terms of specific job titles or functions, but in terms of the nature of the service provided. As a result of that proceeding, the following three units of nonprofessional, nonsupervisory employees were established: Health, Care and Rehabilitation Services; Operations, Maintenance and Services; and Craft.

The Commission is now asked to find appropriate several units whose composition would conform to certain individual professions. To do so would require the Commission to recognize as controlling the common attributes and bonds which distinguish a particular profession, be it teaching, nursing, counseling, etc., and find therein the necessary regard for community of interest. The Commission views that concept in much broader perspective in these cases. Community of interest is, as the writers have said, an elusive concept. While it is purposely vague and undefined, a considerable number of factors has been identified as useful indicators. But in given cases some factors are emphasized over others, with still others regarded as insignificant; in other fact settings the weight given the same indicators may be substantially altered. It is essentially a question of weighing the facts in each case and deciding what will best serve the statutory policy.

For example, no one would dispute that registered nurses share an identity simply by virtue of their common background and qualifications required for licensure and by virtue of their common goal to provide care of various kinds to those in medical need. Yet, it is obvious that these professional characteristics do not necessarily create an exclusive community of interest. The statute, which generally provides little insight, does contemplate that there may, in fact, be an identity of interest between professionals and nonprofessionals. In that event it requires a majority vote by professionals for inclusion with nonprofessionals, thereby recognizing the professional interest. But material to this discussion is the recognition that such interest is not so unique that it must be insulated.[6] A fortiori, the lines between professional disciplines are not necessarily natural barriers. The goal of providing medical care is common to nurses but it is equally common to medical doctors, clinical psychiatrists and psychologists. True, the particular skills, functions and qualifications of these groups differ, but the same observation may be made of the shop teacher at Bordentown Youth Correction Institution, the teacher of the deaf at Marie Katzenbach and the curriculum consultant for elementary education, all of whom are sought to be included in the educational unit. Given the policy considerations of this

---

[6] A graphic example from recent private sector experience is found in *Barnes-Hind Pharmaceuticals*, 183 N.L.R.B. No. 38 where the Board found it would be appropriate to group professional scientists in the same unit with non-professional technicians and employees such as glassware washer and animal caretaker.

statute, the Commission believes that the characteristics of a particular profession should not be the determinant in establishing units for negotiations. If community of interest is equated with and limited to such characteristics, the stability and harmony which this Act was designed to promote are in jeopardy. Potentially, every recognized professional group would be segregated, presenting the Employer with multiplicity of units and the likelihood of attendant problems of competing demands, whipsawing, and continuous negotiations which, disregarding the Employer's inconvenience, are not judged to be in the public interest. Fragmentation to that degree cannot be justified on the ground that individual professional interests are so unique that they cannot be adequately represented in concert with others, especially in the absence of a determination that matters of a professional concern are in every instance negotiable as terms and conditions of employment. At this point in the statute's development the Commission is inclined to believe that the purposes of the Act will be better served if, when dealing with professional employees, the individual distinctions among the professions not be regarded as controlling, but rather the more elementary fact that they are simply professionals and on that basis alone to be distinguished from other groups of employees. This approach would parallel that taken in the case of craft employees where individual craft lines were not observed and the unit was established simply on the basis of a general craft distinction.

The Commission is not unmindful of the fact that several organizations were interested in representing all craft employees in one unit, whereas here the organizations concerned seek representation along the lines of separate professions. We consider the right to organize and be represented, not as an absolute right, but as one that is qualified by the statute's policy and purpose and by the requirement that the exercise of the right be channeled through units appropriate for negotiations. Moreover the Commission takes note of the fact that units already exist at state level containing substantial diversity of function and ranging in size up to 7,500 employees.

The Commission concludes for the reasons above that each of the petitions be and are hereby dismissed.

NOTES

1. The New Jersey Commission's decision that a statewide unit of professional employees is appropriate was affirmed by the New Jersey Supreme Court in *State v. Professional Ass'n of N.J. Dep't of Educ.*, 64 N.J. 231, 315 A.2d 1 (1974). The court, in relevant part, stated:

The contention of the petitioning organizations that designation of a statewide unit of professional employees ignores the statutory criterion of "due regard" for the "community of interest" of the employees concerned cannot be sustained. What is called for on the part of the Commission is "due regard for," not exclusive reliance upon such community of interest. We have shown above that the interests of the employer and of the public at large are also relevant factors. In any event, we conceive the State is not unreasonable in arguing that there is a common interest and character in relation to professional employees, as such, with respect to their status, training and functions, as well as with respect to their fairly common expectations concerning the range of compensation and working conditions negotiable on their behalf, in contradistinction to other groupings of employees....

As to the suggestion that in a general professional employees unit, the special problems and interests of the registered nurses will be submerged and inadequately dealt with by the common representative, this is always a problem where discrete categories are placed in a common negotiating unit. It must be assumed, however, except where shown to the contrary in a particular case, that the common representative will perform its duty fairly in respect of all within the unit and exercise its good faith judgment as to when or whether different characteristics within the group warrant different demands. See *Steele v. Louisville & Nashville R.R. Co.,* 323 U.S. 192, 203, 204, 89 L.Ed. 173, 183, 184, 15 LRRM 708 (1944).

2. Although the New York Taylor Law does not specifically provide that professional employees are entitled to separate units, the New York PERB has allowed professional employees to form their own units, primarily on the basis of their substantially different community of interest from that of nonprofessional employees. *Chemung Cty.,* 1 PERB ¶415 (1968); *New York State Thruway,* 1 PERB ¶423 (1968). In *New York State,* 1 PERB ¶424 (1968), the New York PERB placed all of the state's professional employees, e.g., doctors, lawyers, accountants, and economists, in one unit. A member of the New York PERB, Joseph Crowley, commented as follows concerning this decision:

Though the disciplines differed, the interest in the maintenance of professional standards and status would provide a common bond. Further experience is necessary to determine whether this grouping of professions may preclude effective and meaningful negotiations. The desire to avoid unwarranted fragmentation appears to dictate this approach. Fragmentation should be granted only where the evidence to support it is clear and convincing. Crowley, *The Resolution of Representation Status Disputes Under the Taylor Law,* 37 Fordham L. Rev. 517, 526 (1969).

3. Section 9(b) of the NLRA provides that

the Board shall not (1) decide that any unit is appropriate [for the purposes of collective bargaining] if such unit includes both professional employees and employees who are not professional employees unless a majority of such professional employees vote for inclusion in such unit.... 29 U.S.C. § 159(b)(1) (1973).

A premise underlying this provision is that professional employees should not be automatically included in bargaining units with nonprofessional employees against their wishes since they usually have distinct professional standards, different working conditions, and are frequently paid on a different basis than nonprofessional employees. In order to differentiate professional employees from nonprofessional employees, Congress defined the term "professional employee" as follows:

(a) any employee engaged in work (i) predominantly intellectual and varied in character as opposed to routine mental, manual, mechanical, or physical work; (ii) involving the consistent exercise of discretion and judgment in its performance; (iii) of such a character that the output produced or the result accomplished cannot be standardized in relation to a given period of time; and (iv) requiring knowledge of an advanced type in a field of science or learning customarily acquired by a prolonged course of specialized intellectual instruction and study in an institution of higher learning or a hospital, as distinguished from a general academic education or from an apprenticeship or from training in the performance of routine mental, manual or physical processes; or

(b) any employee, who (i) has completed the courses of specialized intellectual instruction and study described in clause (iv) of paragraph (a), and (ii) is performing related work under the supervision of a professional person to qualify himself to become a professional employee as defined in paragraph (a). 29 U.S.C. § 152(12) (1970).

4. One of the reasons advanced for allowing professional employees to establish separate bargaining units in the private sector is that they would constitute in many instances only a small minority of the bargaining unit if they were included with nonprofessionals. This consideration may not be as valid in the public sector. The Illinois Study Commission, for example, noted that "there are public agencies in which the nonprofessionals are a small portion of the total, and they should not automatically be blanketed in with a larger professional group that did not reflect their interests." Based on this finding, the Illinois Study Commission recommended that *both* "[p]rofessional and nonprofessional employees should be given the opportunity to decide whether they want to be included in the same unit if that issue is raised by either group." Illinois Governor's Advisory Commission on Labor-Management for Public Employees, Report and Recommendations 20 (Mar. 1967). Incorporating this approach, the Florida law provides that "no unit shall be established or approved for purposes of collective bargaining which includes both professional and nonprofessional employees unless a majority of each group votes for inclusion in such unit." Fla. Stat. Ann. § 447.307(3)(h) (West 1981). The Connecticut Board accomplished the same result by decision in *Clifford W. Beers Guidance Clinic,* Decision No. 1104 (Conn. SBLR 1973).

5. One of the current policies of government employers is to encourage job advancement of racial minorities. The Report of the Fortieth American Assembly on Collective Bargaining in American Government included the following recommendation:

As an increasing number of Americans obtain access to the rights inherent in a free society, there is a particular responsibility placed on public employers and public unions. Both unions and public employers have an afffirmative obligation to effectuate a change in the racial composition of government's work forces so that the number of minority employees on all levels more adequately reflects the racial balance of residents in the governmental unit. Unions have an affirmative obligation to the full extent of their bargaining capabilities to press employers to hire or promote minorities and to eliminate artificial, non-job related barriers which impede minority employment. Employers have the same obligation to remove such barriers and to withdraw or deny recognition from a union which impedes affirmative action....

None of this will be easy, but public employers and public unions as the beneficiaries of tax revenues derived from the population have a particular responsibility to act on these matters. They may have to revise or overcome collective bargaining agreements if exclusive rights for unions block necessary changes in the work force.

Report of the Fortieth American Assembly, Collective Bargaining in American Government 7 (1971). What effect does the establishment of separate bargaining units for professional and nonprofessional employees have on job mobility? Consider, for example, the various categories of jobs related to nursing, i.e., registered nurses, licensed practical nurses, and nurses' aides. If each of these three groups is allowed to form its own separate bargaining unit, it is quite possible that artificial barriers would be created in terms of advancement from a nurses' aide to a licensed practical nurse and finally to a registered nurse. This suggests that it might be necessary to reconsider the applicability of the usual statutory provision, borrowed from the private sector, which provides that professional employees may not be included in the same bargaining unit with nonprofessional employees unless they affirmatively vote to be included in such a unit. Perhaps some discretion should be given to the agency on a case-by-case basis to determine whether the appropriate unit should include both professional and nonprofessional employees. See *Anthon-OTO Community Sch. Dist. v. PERB,* 1986-88 PBC ¶ 34,820 (Iowa S. Ct. 1987) (PERB decision including both professional and non-professional employees in one bargaining unit upheld based on the unique "one-room school house" character of the school district); *State of Alaska,* Alaska State Labor Relations Agency Decision No. 1, GERR No. 492, G-1 (1973) (combined unit of technical, professional and clerical employees held appropriate since "the interests of these groups are intertwined and the distinctions between them are often blurred"); *Detroit Bd. of Educ. & Michigan Nurses Ass'n,* 1969 MERC Lab. Op. 229 (Mich.) (professional employees have no statutory right to separation from nonprofessional employees and may be included in same bargaining unit).

MICHIGAN STATE UNIVERSITY

1971 MERC Lab. Op. 82 (Mich. Emp. Relations Comm'n)

[The University College Chapter — MSU District of the Michigan Association for Higher Education filed a petition seeking an election among certain employees of Michigan State University. The American Association of University Professors — MSU Chapter was allowed to intervene on the basis of a sufficient showing of interest.]

Michigan State University, an institution of higher learning established under Article VIII, Section 5, of the Michigan Constitution of 1963, is composed of approximately fifteen colleges. The ... University employs approximately two thousand persons in its teaching faculty from the rank of instructor and up. The unit sought in the petition is composed of approximately two hundred and twenty teaching personnel including all academic rankings from instructor, associate professor, through full professor. While the Petitioner contends that this unit is appropriate, the Employer and the Intervenor take the position that only a university-wide unit of teaching personnel would be appropriate for collective bargaining.

The nature of this case is such that there is minimal dispute over the factual situation. The relationship of University College to the University in terms of administrative structure is comparable to that of the other colleges or schools making up the University. The petitioned for unit includes teaching personnel in all of the academic ranks as does every other college. The range of teaching duties and other obligations, counseling, research and related activities, required and expected of the faculty of University College is comparable, if not identical, with those of faculty members of all the other colleges and schools.

The employment relationships of the individual faculty member with the University is uniform throughout all the colleges. The general salary scale and the enjoyment of various employment benefits are uniform throughout the University.

The Petitioner introduced evidence by which it proposed to delineate University College and its faculty as a separate entity within the University with sufficient separate identity to warrant the finding of a unit limited to its faculty. The University catalog and other publications identify the College within the structure of Michigan State University as a separate college. As is the case with each of the other fifteen colleges, it has its own dean. It has two major responsibilities. It offers four courses which are required as a condition of graduation of substantially all students. It also enrolls and is responsible for the academic progress of substantially all freshmen and sophomores in the University. In addition to the four basic courses, which are embodied in four departments, the College maintains a noninstructional department which provides testing services within the college and for other colleges of the University. Virtually all of the students in the University College courses, therefore, are freshmen or sophomores and, it is not unfair to say, that their unique problems and needs form the primary concern of the college. It is one of the few colleges in the University which does not grant a degree.

The Petitioner presented evidence of the separate activities of the University College faculty. The University College faculty has promulgated a set of bylaws which govern its internal procedures. However, it should be noted that these bylaws refer primarily to intra-college matters and are authorized and controlled by the bylaws of the University. Its faculty periodically conducts meetings. It publishes a newsletter written by and distributed to its own faculty. It also publishes the "University College Quarterly," a journal related to the scholarly concerns of the faculty.

The University College faculty participate in a variety of university-wide committees and councils made up of elected or appointed representatives of the various colleges and schools. These committees and councils govern the broad spectrum of academic and internal activities of the University. The broadest based of these is the Academic Senate. All members of the University faculty are members of the Academic Senate of Michigan State University which is made up of all tenured faculty. University College elects representatives to the Academic Council of the University and its faculty are among the appointed Council members. Its faculty participates fully in all faculty standing committees. These standing committees relate in their activities to aspects of the University's functioning in which University College stands on equal footing with the other colleges and schools. Among these committees are the University Curriculum Committee, University Educational Policies Committee, University Faculty Affairs Committee, University Faculty Tenure Committee, and other committees reflecting the multiple concerns and activities of a large university.

With reference to faculty appointments, University College personnel are employed primarily within the College. Dual appointments, that is, an appointment of an individual to different colleges simultaneously, constitute a small percentage of the total appointments within the entire University and a slightly larger percentage of the faculty of this College. More common, although not involving University College, is the joint administration of a department by two or more colleges. This also involves a relatively small percentage of the total faculty.

Testimony of an administrative officer of the University emphasized the centralized control of vital aspects of University academic and personnel activities. As is implicit in the titles of several of the standing committees listed above, significant areas are within the purview of university-wide committees. The University Tenure Committee has jurisdiction over all faculty. Major curriculum decisions must be approved by a university-wide committee. Non-academic administrative control is uniform throughout the University. In matters such as appointments, promotions or tenure, recommendations originate with the department head or dean of the college involved but are then channeled through the office of the Provost and ultimately to the President and Board of Trustees. Recruiting is conducted by the individual department although ultimate approval must come from the central office of the University. Higher ranking appointments involve a personal interview by the office of the Provost, the highest academic officer of the University.

The budget of the University is prepared centrally and allocated by the Legislature to the University rather than to individual schools. The dean prepares the budget request for his school. After the final budget is returned to him, he has certain freedom, with approval of the Provost, to make adjustments. Some members of the University College faculty are involved in the Office of Evaluation Services of the College. These sixteen persons provide technical advice and assistance to other professors and departments in a variety of testing and evaluation procedures. They teach part-time either in University College or in other colleges in the University.

Analysis and Conclusions of Law

The picture painted by this record is one of dual levels of administrative authority within a large university. It reflects significant departmental freedom in many areas, although centralized authority and control is retained. Thus, there is substantial recognition of the competence of each department to find and recommend persons for hire based on their status as scholars and competence as teachers. Generally, recommendations of departmental faculty, approved by the individual dean, are followed by the University. Similarly, in granting tenure, the collegial decisions of each department are generally respected by the central administration. Within each school and within individual departments the chairman or dean is the direct and effective supervisor in terms of immediate day-to-day employment relations. However, policy decisions and administrative control are allocated, as appropriate, between various committees and the central administration.

The petitioner would now have us find a separate bargaining unit made up of one school composed of five departments. Our prior decisions have expressed the essential elements of evidence of an appropriate bargaining unit. The record must show that the sought-for unit has inherent cohesiveness, that is, an internal community of interest among the employees in the proposed unit, and a cleavage between the community of interest of those employees and all other employees of the employer. *City of Warren,* 1966 MERC Lab. Op. 225; 61

LRRM 1206; *Wayne State University Board of Governors,* 1969 MERC Lab. Op. 670. It is clear from this record that the employees in the proposed unit share a community of interest among themselves. They perform basically the same duties under the same conditions and under separate supervision. They are employed in a subdivision of the Employer which is nominally distinguished and, to a limited extent, administratively separate, from the balance of the employing institution.

We must search the record with substantial diligence, however, to discover factors that will create a cognizable line of demarcation between the employees in the proposed unit and the balance of the faculty. They perform the same function. The separate supervision of the College, to the extent that is shown by the record, is not sufficient to support a separate unit finding. *City of Warren, supra.* The intra-college activities, such as the journal and bylaws, do not significantly affect the community of interest question. No geographical or physical separation of this faculty school is reflected in the record. It is not contended that the professional or academic character of the petitioned for group is sufficiently distinguishable from the overall faculty as to constitute a basis for a separate finding. Although the College is primarily concerned with teaching freshmen and sophomores, there are at least three other colleges in the University which admit and conduct courses for lower classmen.

Accordingly, on the facts on this record, we find that the unit sought does not constitute an appropriate unit for collective bargaining and we will order the petition dismissed. *Wayne State University, Board of Governors,* 1969 MERC Lab. Op. 670; *Grand Rapids Board of Education,* 1966 MERC Lab. Op. 241.

NOTES

1. At the university level, the various labor relations agencies have differed on whether a graduate school within a university constitutes an appropriate unit. In the private sector, the NLRB has ruled that a graduate school within a university may, in appropriate circumstances, constitute a separate appropriate bargaining unit. For example, in *Fordham Univ.,* 193 NLRB 134 (1971), the Board held that the faculty of the Fordham Law School constituted a separate appropriate unit, based on a finding that they possessed a community of interest separate and apart from the balance of the university. In *University of Pittsburgh,* 7 PPER 21 (Pa. PLRB 1976), the Pennsylvania Board held that the medical, dental, and law school faculties constituted separate appropriate bargaining units in that "all Doctors, Dentists, and Lawyers are Doctors, Dentists, and Lawyers before they are teachers and their communities of interest are separate and apart from all other areas of the university if only by virtue of their much higher income." Accord *Temple Univ.,* 3 PPER 209 (Pa. PLRB 1973). But see *Coggins v. PERB,* 1977-78 PBC ¶ 36,416 (Kan. Ct. App. 1978) (not arbitrary for Kansas Board to include law faculty in campus-wide bargaining unit).

2. The state boards have also had to determine whether a faculty unit may be limited to one campus of a multi-campus university. In *State of N.Y. (State Univ. of N.Y.),* 2 PERB ¶ 3070 (1969), aff'd sub nom. *Wakshull v. Helsby,* 35 App. Div. 2d 183, 315 N.Y.S.2d 371 (1970), the New York PERB held that a university-wide faculty bargaining unit was appropriate. In so ruling, the PERB affirmed its Director of Representation who held that "the concomitant differences among the campuses do not establish such conflicts of interest between their respective professions as to warrant geographic fragmentation." Accord *Minnesota State College Bd. v. PERB,* 303 Minn. 453, 228 N.W.2d 551 (1974) (PERB erred in not finding appropriate a statewide unit of faculty employed at seven state colleges); *State of N.J.,* Docket Nos. RO-210 and RO-221 (N.J. PERC 1972), GERR No. 484, F-1 (1973) (statewide unit of faculties at six state colleges held appropriate). On the other hand, in *AAUP v. University of Neb.,* 198 Neb. 243, 253 N.W.2d 1 (1977), the Nebraska Supreme Court affirmed a decision of the Nebraska Court of Industrial Relations establishing separate bargaining units for the faculty of the University of Nebraska at Lincoln (UN-L) and the faculty of the University of Nebraska at Omaha (UN-O). The court observed that "the UN-L faculty has a separate community of interest, separate from the faculty of UN-O, which warrants a separate unit." Accord *Southern Ill. Univ. Bd. of Trustees,* 5 PERI ¶ 1197 (Ill. ELRB 1988) (separate bargaining units for both faculty and administrative professionals established at the Carbondale and Edwardsville campuses of SIU rather than systemwide units). See generally McHugh, *Collective Bargaining with Professionals in Higher Education: Problems in Unit Determinations,* 1971 Wis. L. Rev. 55.

3. The various state agencies have split on whether part-time faculty members should be included in faculty units. In *University of Mass.,* Case Nos. SCR 2079, 2082 (Mass. LRB 1976), part-time faculty were included in a faculty unit if "they ... taught one course for three consecutive semesters." In *Los Rios Community College Dist.,* Decision No. 18 (Cal. EERB 1977), part-time faculty were included if they "taught the equivalent of three or more semesters during the last six semesters inclusive." On the other hand, the NLRB in *New York Univ.,* 205 N.L.R.B. 4 (1973) held "that part-time faculty do not share a community of interest with full-time faculty and, therefore, should not be included in the same bargaining unit." See also *Eastern Mich. Univ. v. AAUP,* 84 L.R.R.M. 2079 (Mich. Ct. App. 1973), where the court reversed a MERC decision which included lecturers in a faculty bargaining unit.

4. With respect to elementary and/or secondary school districts, the state boards have uniformly denied requests for bargaining units on less than a system-wide basis. See, e.g., *Joint Sch. Dist. No. 8 (City of Madison),* Decision No. 6746 (Wis. WERC 1964); *Grand Rapids Bd. of Educ.,* 1966 MERC Lab. Op. 241 (Mich.).

5. In establishing teacher bargaining units, the question of whether "fringe" personnel such as counselors, nurses, psychologists, social workers, and the like, should be included in or excluded from the bargaining unit is frequently raised. In *Janesville Bd. of Educ.,* Decision No. 6678 (Wis. WERC 1964), the WERC set forth the following standard:

> Where there are issues with respect to the eligibles in an appropriate collective bargaining unit, the Board will usually include as eligible in a unit consisting of regular full-time certificated teaching personnel those certificated teachers who are regularly employed on a part-time basis and those who, although not directly engaged in normal classroom teaching, work directly with students or with teachers, other than in a supervisory capacity, in support of the education program.

Applying this standard, the WERC has included the following categories of personnel in teacher bargaining units: social workers and psychometrists, *La Crosse City Pub. Sch. Dist. Joint No. 5,* Decision No. 7347 (Wis. WERC 1965); psychologists, counselors and guidance personnel, reading teachers, and physical and occupational therapists, *Joint City Sch. Dist. No. 1,* Decision No. 6677 (Wis. WERC 1964).

3. SEVERANCE PETITIONS

CITY OF WENATCHEE

Decision No. 911 (Wash. Pub. Emp. Relations Comm'n 1980)

On October 8, 1979 the Wenatchee Police Guild filed with the Public Employment Relations Commission a petition for investigation of a question concerning representation of employees in the Police Department of the City of Wenatchee, other than uniformed personnel, and for certain court employees. The petition specifically seeks to represent "Dispatchers, Jailers, Jail Cook, Records and Identification, Parking Control, Parking Clerk-Matron, Court Clerks."

The incumbent bargaining representative, Washington State Council of County and City Employees (WSCCCE), made a timely motion for intervention, which was granted....

Background

WSCCCE Local No. 846W has represented a unit of non-uniformed employees of the City of Wenatchee since 1969. The petitioned-for employees were added to the unit by certification on January 30, 1975.... These bargaining units along with the Fire Fighter unit comprise the three groups of represented employees of the City.

There are a total of fourteen (14) employees in the unit which Petitioner seeks to sever from the city-wide bargaining unit represented by WSCCCE.

According to the City's Authorized Job Title and Classification Plan, the correct job titles of the petitioned-for employees are as follows: the Deputy Court Clerk, Matron, Dispatchers, Records and Identification employees are all Department Assistant II. The Department Assistant II classification is a broad, city-wide job title which covers employees doing general clerical work such as typing, filing and scheduling, as well as dispatching. Employees can and do transfer from one department to another and have seniority rights in applying for promotional positions.

The employees in the proposed bargaining unit work in, or out of, a building which is adjacent to the City Hall. They use the copy machine in the City Hall, and also do their mailing there. The non-commissioned personnel of the Police Department are supervised by various Police Officers who happen to be on duty during their shift. The Municipal Court employees are supervised by the Municipal Court Judge.

Positions of the Parties

The Petitioner states that the non-commissioned employees of the Police Department and the Municipal Court employees represent an appropriate bargaining unit and should be severed from the over-all city-wide unit. All of the employees in the petitioned-for unit fall within the Criminal Justice System and the training of these employees is coordinated through the Washington State Criminal Justice Training Commission. Petitioner points out that these employees all work in the same building separate from other city employees and have little contact with them. Further, these employees are alleged to have a high degree of commonality, working relationships and mutual interest with the Police Officers in the Police Department.

The employer opposed the severance petition, stating that it would be disruptive of the City's labor relations process. The City claims that an additional bargaining unit would be an additional burden in both time and expense. Since the same job classifications are found throughout the City, the ability to transfer employees would be sharply curtailed. The employer states the existing, historical unit has provided a very good bargaining relationship.

The Intervenor contends that the petitioned-for unit is inappropriate for severance from the existing unit. The duties, skills, and working conditions vary substantially within the proposed unit while there are similar work functions elsewhere in the City. Intervenor argues that the Criminal Justice System is no more distinct than the Sewage Treatment Plant which is included in the city-wide unit. Further, WSCCCE points out that there is no history of separate representation of the petitioned-for employees.

Discussion

In making a determination as to whether or not a petitioned-for unit is appropriate for purposes of collective bargaining the Commission is required to follow the criteria set forth in RCW 41.56.060 and base its decision on:

> "the duties, skills, and working conditions of the public employees, the history of collective bargaining by the public employees and their bargaining representatives; the extent of organization among the public employees; and the desires of the public employees." RCW 41.56.060.

In this case there is no history of separate representation of the petitioned-for employees and there is a long history of bargaining under which the petitioned-for employees have been included in the city-wide unit. Severance principles are applicable, *Mallinckrodt Chemical Works,* 162 NLRB 387 (1966); *Bremerton School District,* Decision 527 (PECB, 1978). It is necessary that the Petitioner demonstrate the viability of its proposed severance in order to justify disruption of the long-established bargaining relationship. It is concluded that it has failed to sustain that burden.

While the unified departmental effort certainly exists among both commissioned and non-commissioned employees of the Police Department and the Municipal Court employees, the record does not demonstrate a community of interest sufficient to justify fragmentation of the existing city-wide bargaining unit. Each department within the city faces the same basic situation. While not identical, the varied duties of the positions in separate departments are nevertheless somewhat similar when seen from an overview.

Persons hired through a central personnel office, having opportunity to routinely transfer to and from various departments, possessing similar job descriptions, and receiving similar pay and benefits have been found to be appropriately placed in a singular unit. *City of Tacoma,* Decision 204 (PECB, 1977). Employees sharing comparable wages, fringe benefits and general working conditions with other employees have been found to lack the unique community of interest and separate identity of a functionally distinct group. *Kent School District,* Decision 127 (PECB, 1976).

Although the non-commissioned police employees and the Municipal Court employees may work in a separate location on a different schedule and with limited interchange between other city employees, they share a community of interest, wages, hours and working conditions with other city employees. No changes of circumstance warranting a change of unit status [have] occurred. Establishment of a separate bargaining unit would merely have the effect of fragmenting the established unit.

NOTES

1. The Federal Labor Relations Council has upheld the Assistant Secretary's so-called *Davisville* rule in which he held that "where the evidence showed that an established, effective and fair collective bargaining relationship is in existence, a separate unit carved out of the existing unit will not be found to be appropriate except in unusual circumstances." *Department of Navy, Naval Air Station, Corpus Christi, Texas,* FLRC No. 72A-24 (1973).

2. In *Teamsters Local 14 v. City of Las Vegas,* Item #76 (Nev. Local Gov't Employee-Mgt. Relations Bd. 1978), aff'd, 641 P.2d 478 (Nev. 1982), the Nevada Board denied a union's petition to sever a group of blue collar employees from an overall unit of white collar and blue collar employees, reasoning as follows:

> The appellant has failed to present clear and convincing evidence that would persuade us that the best interests of the Local Government employees here involved would be served by carving out a blue collar unit from the current bargaining unit composed of the non-uniformed employees of the City. Although there may or may not be a community of interest among the blue collar workers, there is a greater and overriding community of interest among all of the non-uniformed employees of the City.

D. UNIT STATUS OF CERTAIN CATEGORIES OF EMPLOYEES

1. SUPERVISORS

HAYFORD & SINICROPI, BARGAINING RIGHTS STATUS OF PUBLIC SECTOR SUPERVISORS, 15 Indus. Rel. 44, 59-61 (1976)*

The bargaining rights status of public sector supervisors is far from being settled. While it is clear that a federal employment experience has paralleled that of the private sector, several state legislatures and/or administrative agencies have chosen a more expansive approach, which has taken two principal forms.

The first approach is reflected by Wisconsin, Oregon, and Connecticut which have chosen to exclude only bona fide supervisors from the coverage of their public employee collective bargaining laws. This has been accomplished by the application of a rigorous test of the statutory definition of "supervisor." Thus, many individuals with supervisory titles are not held to be supervisors for statu-

---

*Reprinted by permission of the Institute of Industrial Relations.

tory purposes. This policy is founded upon the often cited contention that many public employees in supervisory positions are not really managers. As a rule these "less than bona fide supervisors" are placed in the same bargaining units with rank-and-file employees.

The second view is exemplified by the actions of five states: Hawaii, Minnesota, New York, Massachusetts, and Michigan. They have elected to grant full bargaining rights protection to all supervisory employees. The policy makers in these states apparently do not see any conflict of interest (between the supervisors' role as a member of management and their participation in collective bargaining with management) when bona fide supervisors are allowed to bargain collectively. In these jurisdictions bona fide supervisors are placed in autonomous bargaining units, while less than bona fide supervisors are included in rank-and-file units. This approach is analogous to the final position adopted by the National Labor Relations Board prior to enactment of the Taft-Hartley amendments.

Several factors have contributed to the divergent direction taken by the states vis-à-vis the private sector and the federal government. Perhaps foremost among them is the desires of the supervisors themselves. In several jurisdictions public sector supervisors have demonstrated a strong desire to be included in the bargaining process. This desire is manifested in elections and unit determination petitions and also was no doubt felt through lobbying activities when much of the legislation was developed. This activity, coupled with the questionable managerial status of many supervisors in public employment, has undoubtedly weighed heavily upon the decisions of the various state legislatures and administrative agencies.

The early stage of development of public sector collective bargaining must also be considered a critical factor. In many public sector bargaining relationships the major emphasis has yet to shift from contract negotiation to contract administration. In the private sector, the grievance procedure is well institutionalized, and the supervisor's key role in contract administration is widely recognized. Since successful contract administration has not yet become the focus of the labor relations programs in the majority of public sector jurisdictions, the role of the supervisor in those labor relations structures has not been clearly delineated. Therefore, the role ambivalence felt by public sector supervisors has not yet emerged as a major concern which their superiors have considered in depth.

The diversity that presently exists in the statutory treatment of supervisors is not likely to persist. The major reason for this observation is the strong possibility that some form of national public employee collective bargaining legislation will be enacted in the immediate future. It appears likely that such national legislation will incorporate the private sector approach to supervisory bargaining rights. This conclusion is based upon three primary factors: the well established policy position of the federal government which essentially excludes all supervisors from any form of bargaining rights protection, the pervasive effect of the private sector treatment of supervisors, and the disruptive effect that a continuing expansion of supervisory bargaining rights in public employment will have upon private sector labor relations.

If national public employee legislation is enacted, it is reasonable to assume that the influence of the executive branch of the federal government would be considerable. The position of the executive branch on the supervisory bargaining rights issue is clear from the discussion here. The language of Executive Order 11838 gives no indication of a change in that policy.

A national public employee collective bargaining statute granting bargaining rights protection to supervisors would inevitably result in a demand by private sector supervisors for similar treatment. There is no evidence to suggest that Congress would be willing to amend the Taft-Hartley Act in such a manner. The disruptive effect of such an act upon the relatively stable collective bargaining structure in the private sector would be of such a magnitude as to make it politically infeasible. The convergence of private and public sector collective bargaining is clear. Because of the factors discussed here, it seems highly probable that, if national public employee collective bargaining legislation is enacted, supervisory bargaining rights is one area in which the private sector treatment will prevail.

Notwithstanding the persuasive arguments that all but the top echelon of public employees should be allowed to bargain collectively and the lack of negative reports from those jurisdictions pursuing such a policy, it is our feeling that an effective statutory structure must provide that true bona fide supervisors be excluded from statutory bargaining rights protection. The heart of a viable labor relations structure lies in effective contract administration. It is a widely accepted fact that in mature bargaining relationships, the key person in day-to-day contract administration is the front line supervisor. The formidable problems inherent in weakening that first line of management-labor communication and cooperation by allowing such individuals to bargain collectively are apparent.

Because there are many individuals in public employment with supervisory titles who do not have consequential management responsibilities or authority, the authors advocate a statutory and interpretative policy that requires substantial proof of "bona fide" supervisory status before an individual is excluded from bargaining rights protection. The policy and practice of the Wisconsin Employment Relations Commission best exemplify this approach.

The authors have advanced the view that only supervisors who possess consequential managerial responsibilities and authority should be excluded from bargaining rights protection. If such a policy is adopted by public employers, many factors which have prompted public sector supervisors to seek statutory bargaining rights protection will diminish in importance. The emergence of this type of labor relations structure should contribute greatly to the achievement of stability and maturity in public sector labor management relations.

NOTES

1. In recommending that bona fide supervisory employees be excluded from public sector collective bargaining units, the Committee on Economic Development (CED) stated:

> The structure of bargaining units can also have an impact on the effectiveness of middle management and supervisory personnel. In order to assure strong management direction and to have the ability to administer negotiated con-

tracts, bona fide supervisory personnel should be considered part of management, dealt with as management and encouraged to think of themselves as management. In the event of a strike or other job action, it is especially important that supervisory personnel be clearly allied with management so that they can be counted on to help provide a minimum level of essential services. We believe that supervisory personnel should be considered part of management and consequently should not be included in bargaining units. In those instances in which supervisory personnel do have bargaining rights, they should not be included in the same bargaining unit or belong to the same organization as nonsupervisory personnel. Committee on Economic Development, Improving Management of the Public Work Force: The Challenge to State and Local Government 68-69 (1978).

For a similar recommendation, as well as a good discussion of the policy issues involved, see Advisory Commission on Intergovernmental Relations, Labor-Management Policies for State and Local Government 95-96 (1970).

2. Among the many articles examining the status of supervisory personnel in the public sector are Rains, *Collective Bargaining in the Public Sector and the Need for Exclusion of Supervisory Personnel,* 23 Lab. L.J. 275 (1972); Bers, *The Status of Managerial, Supervisory and Confidential Employees in Government Employment Relations,* a report sponsored by the New York State Public Employment Relations Board (Jan. 1970).

CITY OF WAUSAU

Decision No. 6276 (Wis. Emp. Relations Comm'n 1963)

At the hearing the parties stipulated to the description of the collective bargaining unit as being all the employes of the Municipal Employer employed in the Board of Public Works, which consists of the Engineering, Sanitation, Electrical, Public Works and Inspection departments. However an issue exists with respect to whether individuals employed as supervisors should be included as eligibles in the unit.

The Municipal Employer contends that only those employes excluded from the term "municipal employe" as defined in Section 111.70 can be excluded from the unit. It argues that supervisory employes have a right to engage in concerted activity and to be represented for the purposes of collective bargaining since that right is given to "employes," and that therefore no basis exists for their exclusion from the eligibles in the bargaining unit.

The Union, on the other hand, takes the position that the Board should apply the same principles and rules that it applies in determining eligibles in elections conducted by the Board among employes of non-public employers pursuant to Section 111.05 of the Wisconsin Employment Peace Act.

Section 111.70(1)(b) defines the term "municipal employe" as follows:

"... any employe of a municipal employer except city and village policemen, sheriff's deputies and county traffic officers."

A municipal employer performs its functions and services through elected and appointed officials and by employes hired by the municipal employer through its administrative and managerial officials and employes. Broadly, any individual receiving compensation for services performed by him on behalf of the municipal employer, with the exception of those services performed under contract, can be said to be an employe of the municipal employer. Such application could encompass the mayor, city manager, alderman and department heads. A municipal employer as such is a corporate being. Governmental units, including municipal employers, are managed by persons who, among their duties, may represent the municipal employer in its relationship to employes thereof who are performing services and who have no connection with any managerial function. As in private industry, the managerial function of the municipal employer is not normally performed by any single individual. The usual chain of command originates with the mayor or city manager, and is channeled to various committees, boards, department heads, and through various supervisory personnel in the various departments. Managerial and supervisory functions are performed in the interest of the municipality as an employer. The representative of the municipal employer has the responsibility and authority connected with the municipal employer's operation and presumably perform their duties in what is the best interest of the municipality as the employer. Their inclusion in a collective bargaining unit consisting of employes whom they supervise is inconsistent with their obligation to the performance of their supervisory function on behalf of the municipal employer. Should supervisors be included in the same bargaining unit with employes they supervise said individuals would be in a position either to prefer the interest of employes over that of the municipal employer or to prefer the interest of the municipal employer as the agents thereof over that of the employes.

Supervisors are generally responsible for the direction of the work force, the maintenance of discipline and the processing of routine grievances. We do not believe that supervisors can properly carry out such responsibilities if they were included in the bargaining unit.

The rights conferred upon municipal employes under Section 111.70(2) to form and join labor organizations of their own choosing and the right to engage in conferences and negotiations with their municipal employer on the questions of wages, hours, and conditions of employment could be seriously impaired, if not nullified, if the agents of the municipal employer, with whom the representatives of the employes could be expected to negotiate, were included in the employes bargaining unit. To permit supervisory personnel to participate in the election of the representative of the employes he supervises would constitute an interference with their rights as provided in Section 111.70, for it may very well be possible that the ballots of supervisors, if permitted to vote, would affect the results of the representation election. If supervisors were not excluded from bargaining units, then presumably chief executive officers of a municipal employer could be included in the same bargaining unit as other employes. We believe such an interpretation would be clearly at variance with the statutory intent, for who would then be the statutory representative of the municipal employer with whom the municipal employes have a right to confer and negotiate?

Section 111.70(4)(d) provides:

"(d) *Collective bargaining units.* Whenever a question arises between a municipal employer and a labor union as to whether the union represents the employes of the employer, either the union or the municipality may petition the board to conduct an election among said employes to determine whether they desire to be represented by a labor organization. Proceedings in representation cases shall be in accordance with ss. 111.02(6) and 111.05 insofar as applicable, except that where the board finds that a proposed unit includes a craft the board shall exclude such craft from the unit. The board shall not order an election among employes in a craft unit except on separate petition initiating representation proceedings in such craft unit."

The legislature by making reference to the election provision in the Wisconsin Employment Peace Act has granted the Board the power to utilize procedures there provided which are not inconsistent with the substantive provisions of Section 111.70. The Board's determination to exclude supervisory personnel from collective bargaining units of public employes is consistent with the policy applied by the Board in elections conducted under Section 111.05 of the Wisconsin Employment Peace Act.

The Board therefore has and will continue to exclude managerial and supervisory personnel from collective bargaining units on the basis that they are agents of the municipal employer in the performance of the "employer" function....

NOTES

1. Unlike the employer in the principal case, employers generally argue for the exclusion of individuals whom they consider to be supervisors. Why do you think the city in the instant case sought to include supervisors in the bargaining unit? Sometimes the reason is the employer's belief that the individuals in question are likely to vote against union representation and therefore tip the vote in the employer's favor. Is such a short-range consideration valid from an employer's standpoint? Consider the following comments of Wellington and Winter:

Municipalities are frequently not well organized for collective bargaining and never will be if they cannot create positions with effective responsibility for the administration of collective agreements. Such positions must necessarily be filled by persons who identify with, and are part of, management, not by those who are unionized, whether or not the union is exclusively supervisory. Nor can such responsibilities be carried out by persons who are members, much less officers, of the other party to the contract, as might occur when supervisors are in a unit with regular employees. Indeed, the creation of such positions and the delegation of supervisory power are likely to constitute a principal change in municipal structure as a consequence of collective bargaining. The law should not discourage this trend by permitting the holders of these positions to organize or be in units with nonsupervisory employees. H. Wellington & R. Winter, The Unions and the Cities 114 (1971).

2. Under the National Labor Relations Act as initially enacted in 1935, there was no specific exclusion of supervisors from the definition of the term "employee." In interpreting the Act the National Labor Relations Board vacillated with respect to whether supervisory employees were entitled to organize and have representation petitions processed. Compare *Godchaux Sugars, Inc.,* 44 N.L.R.B. 874 (1942) (supervisory employees may organize in an affiliated union), with *Maryland Drydock Co.,* 49 N.L.R.B. 733 (1943) (unit of supervisory employees was not appropriate). In *Packard Motor Car Co. v. NLRB,* 330 U.S. 485 (1947), the Supreme Court upheld the authority of the Board to establish bargaining units for supervisory employees. In rejecting the various policy arguments that were proffered as to why supervisory employees should not be allowed to organize, the Court noted that "[t]hey concern the wisdom of the legislation; they cannot alter the meaning of otherwise plain provisions."

When Congress amended the National Labor Relations Act in 1947, it specifically excluded supervisors from the definition of the term "employee" and defined the term "supervisor" to mean

> any individual having authority, in the interest of the employer, to hire, transfer, suspend, lay off, recall, promote, discharge, assign, reward, or discipline other employees, or responsibly to direct them, or to adjust their grievances, or effectively to recommend such action, if in connection with the foregoing the exercise of such authority is not of a merely routine or clerical nature, but requires the use of independent judgment. 29 U.S.C. § 152(11) (1973).

The reasons why Congress excluded supervisors from coverage under the NLRA are indicated in the following excerpt from the relevant House Report:

> *Management, like labor, must have faithful agents.* — If we are to produce goods competitively and in such large quantities that many can buy them at low cost, then, just as there are people on labor's side to say what workers want and have a right to expect, there must be in management and loyal to it persons not subject to influence or control of unions....
>
> ... What the bill does is to say what the law always has said until the Labor Board, in the exercise of what it modestly calls its "expertness," changed the law: That no one, whether employer or employee, need have as his agent one who is obligated to those on the other side, or one whom, for *any* reason, he does not trust. 1 Legislative History of the Labor-Management Relations Act 307, 308 (1948).

See generally Daykin, *Legal Meaning of "Supervisor" Under the Taft-Hartley Act,* 13 Lab. L.J. 130 (1963).

3. In *Fraternal Order of Police, Lodge 44 v. State Emp. Rels. Bd.,* 22 Ohio St. 3d 1, 488 N.E.2d 181 (1986), the Ohio Supreme Court held that a provision in the Ohio collective bargaining law which excluded sergeants, lieutenants and captains employed by the City of Dayton from inclusion in any bargaining unit regardless of whether they fell within the act's definition of "supervisor" was unconstitutional, because it neither had uniform application throughout the state nor bore any reasonable relationship to the purposes of the statewide collective bargaining law.

4. The various labor relations agencies have had considerable difficulty in deciding whether department chairpersons should be considered "supervisors" and therefore excluded from faculty or teacher bargaining units, or considered "employees" and included in such units. Compare *University of Pittsburgh,* 7 PPER 21 (Pa. PLRB 1976) (department chairpersons held supervisors), with *Tamaqua Area Sch. Dist.,* 7 PPER 253 (Pa. PLRB 1976) (department heads held not supervisors), and *Southern Ill. Univ. Bd. of Trustees,* 5 PERI ¶ 1197 (Ill. ELRB 1988) (department chairs held not supervisors since they did not devote a "preponderance" of their time to supervisory duties as required by the Illinois Educational Labor Relations Act). The NLRB has likewise struggled with the question of whether department chairpersons are "supervisors." Compare *Fordham Univ.,* 193 NLRB 134 (1971) (held not supervisors), with *Syracuse Univ.,* 204 NLRB 641 (1973) (held supervisors). See generally Comment, *The*

Bargaining Unit Status of Academic Department Chairmen, 40 U. Chi. L. Rev. 442 (1973).

5. The unit status of supervisory officers in fire fighter bargaining units has generated considerable litigation over the years. Public employers typically seek to exclude lieutenants, captains, battalion chiefs, etc., from fire fighter bargaining units, while the International Association of Fire Fighters or the employee organization representing fire fighters seeks their inclusion. Compare *United States Naval Weapons Center, China Lake, Cal.,* A/SLMR No. 297 (1973), *on remand from* FLRC No. 72 A-11 (1973) (fire captains excluded as supervisors), and *St. Louis Cty. Fire Fighters Ass'n v. City of Univ. City,* Case No. 76-018 (Mo. SBM 1977) (fire captains excluded as supervisors), with *City of Davenport v. PERB,* 264 N.W.2d 307, 98 L.R.R.M. 2582 (Iowa 1978) (captains and lieutenants included in bargaining unit), and *Village of Wheeling v. Illinois State Lab. Rel. Bd.,* 135 Ill. 2d 499, 554 N.E.2d 155 (1990) (fire lieutenants held not supervisors since they did not spend a "preponderance" of their time engaged in supervisory duties as required by the Illinois act). See generally Wheeler, *Officers in Municipal Fire Departments,* 28 Lab. L.J. 721 (1977).

6. Where a civil service commission has the authority to hire and fire employees and to determine which employee is to be promoted, what effect, if any, does this have on the determination of supervisory status? In *Wauwatosa Bd. of Educ.,* Decision No. 6219-D (Wis. ERC 1967), the Wisconsin Employment Relations Commission made the following observation:

> Because certain conditions of employment are governed by civil service rules and regulations, the employees in the positions in question have limited authority with respect to hiring and promotion and discharge of employees. However, they can make recommendations with respect thereto. The lack of such authority, however, will not preclude the Commission from making a supervisory determination.

HILLSDALE COMMUNITY SCHOOLS

1968 MERC Lab. Op. 859 (Mich. Emp. Relations Comm'n),
aff'd, 24 Mich. App. 36, 179 N.W.2d 661 (1970)

The instant case arose when the Hillsdale Community Schools Principals and Supervisory Association (PSA), a labor organization under the Act, sought an election in a proposed bargaining unit:

> "High School, junior high, and elementary school principals, curriculum coordinator, reading coordinator, ESEA coordinator, cooperative education coordinator, head librarian, and physical education director; excluding: teachers, superintendent, assistant superintendent, business manager and all non-certificated employees."

The Hillsdale Education Association (HEA) is a labor organization which is recognized by the School District as exclusive bargaining agent for the District's non-supervisory certificated teachers.

The School District opposes the petition on the grounds that: (1) supervisors and executives have no rights to collective bargaining under PERA; (2) assuming, arguendo, that PERA allows such rights to principals and other supervisors, this Board should deny such rights as a matter of public policy; (3) the proposed unit is inappropriate because it contains six staff specialists who are supervised by seven principals, also included in the unit; and (4) PSA may not be certified as exclusive representative of principals and teachers' supervisors, since it is affiliated with the state organization (MEA) which is the parent organization of many teacher organizations, including the organization of teachers in the petitioner's District.

We now turn to the discussion of the issues individually.

1. The Unit of Supervisors.

The Trial Examiner, in his Report, rejected the School District's position on this issue, consistent with our decision in *Saginaw County Road Commission*, 1967 Labor Opinions 196. During oral argument, the School District and certain amici curiae prayed that we reverse *Saginaw* and hold that supervisory employees are excluded from statutory coverage.

We have studied the briefs and arguments urging reversal of our position, but we are not persuaded that the *Saginaw* decision is contrary to proper construction of PERA.

Our duty as described in Section 13 of PERA is to:

"... decide in each case, in order to insure *public employees* the full benefit of their right to self organization, to collective bargaining and otherwise to effectuate the policies of this act, *the unit appropriate for the purposes of collective bargaining as provided in Section 9e of Act No. 176* (Labor Mediation Act) ...." (Emphasis supplied)

From this section, the argument is made that "employees," as used in 9e, specifically excludes executives and supervisors; that is, "employees" as used in Section 9e is defined in Section 2(e) of LMA.[3] However, this argument ignores the use of "public employee" in Section 13 of PERA. "Public employee" is defined in Section 2 of PERA and not in Section 2(e) of LMA. PERA, Section 2, does not exclude supervisors or executives from the provisions of PERA as does its counterpart in LMA.

Section 9e is incorporated into PERA only for standards of unit determination and to provide a prohibition against supervisors and executives being included in the same unit with employees they supervise. There is no prohibition against supervisory units except by virtue of LMA's Section 2(e), which is not included by specific mention in PERA.

The School District maintains that our interpretation of the statutes ignores the canon of construction that statutes which have the same general purpose should be read *in pari materia* as constituting one law, especially where there is specific reference from one statute to the other. The purpose of this canon of statutory construction is to avoid a strict construction of one statute which defeats the main purpose of another statute or statutes relating to the same subject.

However, this construction of two statutes dealing with the general subject of labor relations is subject to being made more specific by other canons of construction. *Expressio unius est exclusio alterius* restricts the effect of a statute to

---

[3] The customary basis for prohibition of supervisory units is found in the definition of employee, which excludes supervisors. If supervisors are not employees, they cannot avail themselves of the provisions of the Act.

the area specifically mentioned, *i.e.,* public employment relations. *Expressum facit cessare tacitum* means that "when the law designates the actors none others can come upon the stage." PERA is restricted to public employees, which term is defined in the Act.

We affirm our *Saginaw* decision and adopt the Trial Examiner's Findings of Fact and Conclusions of Law on this issue.[7]

2. Public Policy.

The School District devotes a substantial portion of its brief to urging the adoption of a policy that supervisors should not be allowed rights under PERA. Our *Saginaw* decision was based on statutory construction, not policy. The School District's argument is that "(t)he policy as well as the letter of the law is a guide to decision."

We recognize this Board's responsibility as guardian of public policy discussed in *National Labor Relations Board v. Atkins & Company,* 331 U.S. 398 (1947). While there are certain areas of policy to be considered in every matter, this policy should not be used to frustrate the intent of the Legislature as we interpret it. Thus, it would be inconsistent for us to find supervisory status encompassed within the definition of "public employees," and then deny that status because we believed that the policy should be to the contrary.

We do note that competent authorities have expressed the opinion that supervisory personnel in the public sector have characteristics which differ from supervisors in private employment.[9] These differences, far from disqualifying public employment supervisors from representation, make a stronger case for allowing supervisors separate bargaining units, particularly when they are not excluded from the definition of "employee."[10]

---

[7] We find no merit to the contention that the principals in the instant case are distinguishable from the traffic director supervisor in *Saginaw* because principals have a policy function. This argument is a *non sequitur* if supervisors are not excluded from the definition of employee. We note that the New York State Public Employment Relations Board has included principals and assistant principals in bargaining units, stating that: "Principals act merely as conduits rather than as decision makers." *Board of Education, Union Free School District and Depew Teachers Organization, Inc.,* 255 GERR C-2 (1968). Similarly, see *Metropolitan Transit Authority,* 48 L.R.R.M. 1296 (Mass. Labor Relations Board, 1961). We also dismiss the argument concerning Governor Romney's veto of HB 3388, which bill would have amended PERA to allow the inclusion of police supervisors in the bargaining unit with patrolmen. The issue raised by the bill was solely the inclusion, or exclusion, of police supervisors in the same unit with the rank and file. Police supervisors had, on the enactment of PERA, the privilege to engage in concerted activities, including the choice of an exclusive bargaining representative in a designated unit.

[9] See, for example, Slavney, "The Public Employee — How Shall He Be Represented in Collective Negotiations?" Governor Rockefeller's Conference on Public Employment Relations, 269 GERR E-1 (1968). Mr. Slavney observes at p. E-4: "I think most of us here would admit that supervisors in public employment are for the most part different than supervisors in the private sector, not only in the concept of employer loyalty but also in the performance of identifiable supervisory functions. Under a civil service system, the authority supervisors might have with regard to the hire, transfer, suspension, layoff, recall and promotion is subject to more stringent review than in private employment. Further, in civil service, employees performing normal supervisory duties have the same rights and protections as do rank and file employees with respect to tenure, job security and civil service grievance procedures, and normally their salary increments and increases have a distinct relationship to increments and increases granted to non-supervisory personnel. These factors tend to create a community of interest with employees supervised rather than with management." See also, New York Public Library, 69-1 ARB ¶ 8067 (Yagoda, 1968).

[10] *Metropolitan New York Nursing Home Association,* 60 L.R.R.M. 1281 (N.Y. State Labor Relations Board, 1965).

There is a common interest among school boards, superintendents, principals and teachers to provide "a superior education for the nation's youth." All of those parties work professionally toward the same goal....

3. Appropriate Unit.

The Trial Examiner found that the petitioned for unit was appropriate although it contained purported principal supervision of the staff specialists. We affirm the Trial Examiner's Findings that the nature of the supervision was not sufficient to invoke the prohibition against supervisors being included in units with those employees they supervise.

The evidence reveals that the supervision is mere routine direction not requiring the exercise of independent judgment....

Regarding the unit in question, we find a community of interest between the staff specialists and the principals. There are similarities in administrative duties, professional skills and working conditions. Additionally, we agree with the Trial Examiner's conclusion that the staff specialists' distinct community of interest is insufficient to separate them from the principals.

Thus, we find the petitioned for unit appropriate for collective bargaining purposes under PERA.

4. MEA Domination of PSA.

The School District argues here that the parent organization (MEA), exercises an overwhelming degree of control over its affiliates, particularly respecting collective bargaining policy. Also, it is alleged that it is impossible for PSA to be truly independent within the MEA organizational framework. Where both the principals' and teachers' organizations are MEA affiliates, the School District maintains that there is a conflict of interest where principals are the first step in the grievance procedure. Hence, if the MEA exercises such a degree of control over its affiliates, it will control the initial stage of the grievance procedure. The Trial Examiner agreed with the School District's contentions.

Perhaps this situation may arise, but it is speculative. We are charged with the duty to protect the organizational rights of *all* public employees. Where, as here, principals are public employees, we should not restrict their free exercise of Sec. 9 rights, which includes the selection of a collective bargaining representative. *City of Escanaba,* 1966 Labor Opinions 451. The petitioning organization must, however, proceed with the normal proof establishing itself as a labor organization within the terms of the Act.

Similarly, there is no more basis for restricting the choice of bargaining agent to one not representing the rank and file employees here, than there is in restricting that choice respecting craft, technical, or professional employee units. Just as professional, craft, and technical employees are not restricted in their choice of bargaining representative, supervisory employees should also not be so restricted.

We agree with the principals [sic] enunciated by the New York State Labor Relations Board:[14]

---

[14] *Yonkers Raceway, Inc.,* 63 L.R.R.M. 1098, 1100 (N.Y. State Labor Relations Bd., 1966).

Before this position is interpreted as allowing the organization of "vice presidents" mentioned in the *Packard*[15] case, we note that there is a level at which organization must end. That level consists of "executive" employees, and is limited to those employees who formulate, determine and effectuate management policies.

The application of this exclusion is not necessary in this case because there is no evidence that the employees in the proposed unit act in any other manner than as resource people in collective bargaining or as conduits for labor relations policy established without their participation. We do not consider that employees who serve the employer at the first step of the grievance procedure are within the executive category by reason of that responsibility. Thus, we do not feel that our determination impinges upon management's right to have trusted personnel act in its behalf in formulating, determining and effectuating policies and in collective bargaining....

NOTES

1. Accord *Town of Needham,* 10 MLC 1312 (Mass. LRC 1983).

2. While the Michigan Employment Relations Commission (MERC) in *Hillsdale Community Schs.* held that the same employee organization can represent both rank-and-file and supervisory bargaining units, the Michigan Commission in *St. Clair County Rd. Comm'n,* 1982 MERC Lab. Op. 685 (Mich. ERC), held that the parent organization must provide separate internal governance of supervisory and rank-and-file bargaining units, as well as complete separation in bargaining. Accordingly, the Michigan Commission held that a public employer did not commit an unfair labor practice when it refused to negotiate with a rank-and-file employee in negotiations with respect to a supervisory unit.

3. A number of commentators have supported the view that supervisory employees should have the right to be represented for the purposes of collective bargaining. See, e.g., Schmidt, *The Question of the Recognition of Principal and Other Supervisory Units in Public Education Collective Bargaining,* 19 Lab. L.J. 283 (1968); Wheeler & Kochan, *Unions and Public Sector Supervisors: The Case of Fire Fighters,* Monthly Lab. Rev., vol. 100, no. 12, at 44-48 (1977).

4. In contrast to the principal case, the Nebraska Supreme Court in *Nebraska Ass'n of Pub. Emps. v. Nebraska Game & Parks Comm'n,* 247 N.W.2d 449, 94 L.R.R.M. 2428 (Neb. 1976), held that supervisory and managerial employees could not be represented by the same union that represented rank and file employees, reasoning as follows:

> To permit supervisory personnel to retain the same bargaining agent as the employees' union would be tantamount to permitting them to enter the same bargaining unit and such agent could, and doubtless would, manipulate its efforts jointly in behalf of each. We hold that supervisory or managerial

---

"We also have noted that the 'conflict of loyalties,' allegedly resulting from the selection of the same representative by supervisory or protection employees and by rank and file employees, is a misnomer; that it arises, if at all, from the employees' fundamental right of association which exists independent of statute; that the denial of all rights under the Act to one of the two groups of employees provides no solution; and that any problems which arise can and should be adjusted and resolved in the collective bargaining process, when, and if, that eventuality occurs." ...

[15] *Packard Motor Car Company v. NLRB,* 330 U.S. 485 (1947). The briefs of some amici curiae noted the comment by Mr. Justice Jackson.

personnel may not enter into a bargaining unit with rank and file employees and may not retain the same bargaining agent.

Accord *City of Richland,* Decision No. 1519-A (Wash. ERC 1983).

5. In *Appeal of Manchester Bd. of Sch. Comm.,* 523 A.2d 114, 1986-88 PBC ¶ 34,815 (N.H. 1987), the court held that a bargaining unit of school principals could not be represented by the same union that represented the teachers whom they supervised. The court reasoned that since the New Hampshire Act specifically prohibited supervisors from belonging to the same bargaining unit as the employees they supervised, to permit supervisors to be represented by the same bargaining agent as the employees they supervised would be tantamount to permitting them to belong to the same bargaining unit.

6. The California Educational Employment Relations Act permits employees in management or confidential positions to be represented for meet and confer purposes individually or by an employee organization "whose membership is composed entirely of employees designated as holding such positions, in his employment relationship with the public school employer." Cal. Educ. Code § 3543.4. In *Los Angeles Unified Sch. Dist. v. PERB,* 191 Cal. App. 3d 551 (1987), the court upheld a PERB determination that unions which represented a school district's supervisory employees and non-supervisory employees were the "same employee organization" for purposes of bargaining unit determination where they were both affiliated with the same international union. The court held that the California Educational Employment Relations Act was intended to prevent situations in which the loyalty of supervisors might be placed in jeopardy and that, therefore, representation of a unit of supervisory employees by a union affiliated with the same international union that represented the district's teachers was not appropriate.

7. In *Department of Energy v. FLRA,* 880 F.2d 1163 (10th Cir. 1989), the Tenth Circuit, in reversing an FLRA decision, held that a bargaining unit which includes both supervisors and non-supervisors is not an appropriate bargaining unit. Although Section 7135(a)(2) of the Civil Service Reform Act provides for recognition of units that historically or traditionally represented supervisors, the court concluded that the language of this section only required the recognition of units composed solely of supervisors and not units that mixed supervisors and non-supervisors. The court noted that its "conclusion is supported by the general reluctance in labor law of establishing mixed units of supervisors and non-supervisory employees, ... [a reluctance that] is a result of the inherent problems of conflict of interest and divided loyalties associated with mixed units."

8. In *East Greenbush Cent. Sch. Dist.,* 17 PERB ¶ 3083 (N.Y. PERB 1984), the Board excluded supervisors from a unit of teachers in which they had previously been included where the union president had placed pressure on a supervisor to change the manner in which he exercised his supervisory duties. The New York PERB held that the union's attempt to subvert supervisory authority warranted the removal of the supervisors from the teachers' bargaining unit and the establishment of a separate supervisory unit. Where a mixed supervisory/rank-and-file unit exists, the New York PERB commented that the union "must be exceedingly prudent in refraining from conduct that casts doubt upon the appropriateness of its unit."

2. MANAGERIAL EMPLOYEES

Many of the public sector statutes exclude managerial employees from the definition of the term "employee." The definition of the term "managerial employee" varies, but it usually refers to persons who are involved in formulating, determining or effectuating policies on behalf of the public employer. A number of labor relations agencies have excluded managerial employees, even though the applicable statute in question does not contain such a specific exclusion. The Michigan Employment Relations Commission, for example, in *City of Detroit & Govtl. Accountants & Analysts Ass'n,* 1969 MERC Lab. Op. 187 (Mich.), excluded them on the ground that they are creators of policy and thus should not be included in bargaining units. The NLRB has likewise determined, as a matter of policy, that managerial employees should be excluded. See J. Abodeely, R. Hammer & A. Sandler, The NLRB and the Appropriate Bargaining Unit 209-10 (1981).

STATE OF NEW YORK

5 PERB ¶ 3001 (N.Y. Pub. Emp. Relations Bd. 1972)

On September 21, 1971 the State of New York filed a timely application pursuant to CSL § 201.7, as amended,[1] seeking to have this Board designate as managerial or confidential certain employees of the State of New York in specified job titles....

Discussion

I. Authority of PERB

One of the points made by the State is that,

"The initial and primary fact in the determination of whether a position or person should be designated as managerial or confidential is the opinion of the public employer. Only the employer can accurately judge its needs. Accordingly, when the over-all position of the employer appears to be reasonable, the employer's judgment should be supported by this Board unless for particular positions the employer's judgment is not supported by substantial evidence."

In support of this proposition, the State argues that a managerial employee is defined as one who formulates policy or "may reasonably be required on behalf of the public employer" to exercise certain specified labor relations functions.

---

[1]CSL § 201.7 provides: "The term 'public employee' ... shall not include ... persons who may reasonably be designated from time to time as managerial or confidential upon application of the public employer to the appropriate board in accordance with procedures established pursuant to section two hundred five or two hundred twelve of this article, which procedures shall provide that any such designations made during a period of unchallenged representation pursuant to subdivision two of section two hundred eight of this chapter shall only become effective upon the termination of such period of unchallenged representation. Employees may be designated as managerial only if they are persons (a) who formulate policy or (b) who may reasonably be required on behalf of the public employer to assist directly in the preparation for and conduct of collective negotiations or to have a major role in the administration of agreements or in personnel administration provided that such role is not of a routine or clerical nature and requires the exercise of independent judgment. Employees may be designated as confidential only if they are persons who assist and act in a confidential capacity to managerial employees described in clause (b)."

According to the State, the words, "may reasonably be required on behalf of the public employer," express a legislative intent that this Board should adopt the employer's analysis of what it may reasonably require unless the employer has been arbitrary.

We do not read the quoted language of the statute as creating a presumption in favor of an employer's judgment concerning the employees whom it may reasonably require to conduct its labor relations responsibilities; we understand it as providing a criterion which PERB must observe in making its determination. While an employer's opinion as to the designation of employees as management or confidential is entitled to serious consideration, nevertheless, this Board's determination is not limited simply to a review of the opinion of the employer and of the reasons supporting such opinion. Rather, the determination is based upon the application of the statutory criteria to all the evidence offered by the parties.

The respective responsibilities of PERB and the public employer are set forth in the Taylor Law (CSL § 201.7), which provides for the exclusion of "persons who may reasonably be designated from time to time as managerial or confidential upon application of the public employer to the appropriate board...." It is the function of the public employer to apply; it is the responsibility of the Board to determine....

II. Managerial and Confidential Employees Before the 1971 Amendment of the Taylor Law

Even before the enactment of Chapters 503 and 504 of the Laws of 1971, there was a concept of managerial and confidential employment under the Taylor Law. This concept derived from the Report of the Taylor Committee. Although the Taylor Law did not expressly exclude persons who were managerial or confidential, the Office of Collective Bargaining of the City of New York interpreted the Taylor Law to require such an exclusion. This Board did not have occasion to rule on whether managerial and confidential employees were covered by the Taylor Law, but it did find that they could not be in the same units as rank-and-file employees because of the conflict of interest between them, and no separate unit of managerial and confidential employees had ever been designated by PERB.

IV. Comparison of Statutory Definition with Prior PERB Definition

The definition used by this Board to exclude persons from the five units established in 1968 was that a person is managerial or confidential if he:

"Formulates or determines State or agency policy (e.g., department and agency heads and their deputies); or

"Directs the work of an agency or a major subdivision thereof with considerable discretion in determining the methods, means and personnel by which State or agency policy is to be carried out (e.g., institution heads, administrative directors); or

"Is so closely related to or involved with the activities noted above as to present a potential conflict of interest or clash of loyalties in matters concerning employer-employee relationships (e.g., staff agents, confidential assistants), or in a geographically separated location is responsible for representing the State's position in dealing with a significant number of employees."

The first two paragraphs of the above-quoted PERB definition were intended by this Board to delineate persons who might be deemed "managerial." The two criteria set forth in those paragraphs were clearly not limited to labor relations functions or responsibilities, but were intended to cover all activities that might be deemed "managerial," such as the formulation and determination of State, agency or institutional policy. The Legislature, however, in defining "managerial" in the same broad sense simply said "persons ... who formulate policy."

A. Criterion One — Formulation of policy.

This criterion is but one of four criteria established by the Legislature for designating persons as managerial. The other three criteria are limited to labor relations functions or responsibilities of the public employer. Thus, it would appear to have been the intent of the Legislature that persons who formulate policy may be designated managerial even though they do not exercise a labor relations function.

We will first discuss the "policy" criterion and later the other three criteria. It would appear desirable to first consider the term "policy." Policy is defined in a general sense as "a definite course or method of action selected from among alternatives and in the light of given conditions to guide and determine present and future decisions."[10] In government, policy would thus be the development of the particular objectives of a government or agency thereof in the fulfillment of its mission and the methods, means and extent of achieving such objectives.

The term "formulate" as used in the frame of reference of "managerial" would appear to include not only a person who has the authority or responsibility to select among options and to put a proposed policy into effect, but also a person who participates with regularity in the essential process which results in a policy proposal and the decision to put such a proposal into effect. It would not appear to include a person who simply drafts language for the statement of policy without meaningful participation in the decisional process, nor would it include one who simply engaged in research or the collection of data necessary for the development of a policy proposal.

We conclude that this legislative criterion is similar in scope and meaning to the earlier one stated by this Board, namely, one who "formulates or determines State or agency policy."

B. Criterion Two — Involvement in collective negotiations.

The remaining three criteria for designating an employee as managerial all specifically relate to the labor relations functions of the employee. The first of these is that the employee "may reasonably be required on behalf of the public employer to assist directly in the preparation for and conduct of collective negotiations." This part of the definition is an addition to the criteria set forth in our decision In the Matter of the State of New York, 1 PERB ¶ 399.85 (1968), although many of the persons to whom it is applicable were designated as

---

[10] Webster's Seventh New Collegiate Dictionary.

managerial under other criteria then used and now restated. We interpret this criterion to include those who may reasonably be required to be directly involved in the preparation and formulation of the employer's proposals or positions in collective negotiations. We do not think that the Legislature intended, however, that if an employer consulted with supervisory personnel on the implication or feasibility of negotiation proposals that such supervisory personnel should be deemed managerial. Admittedly, such supervisory personnel would be assisting in the preparation for collective negotiations, but such assistance without participation in the actual conduct of negotiations would not satisfy the statutory criterion. Moreover, we take the phrase "to assist directly" to mean direct involvement or participation in the preparation for collective negotiations so as to be part of the decision-making process therein. Similarly, with respect to "conduct of collective negotiations," there must be direct involvement or participation in the negotiating process, and simply being present at the negotiations as an observer or other non-participatory role would not suffice. The largest group of persons not previously designated as managerial, but encompassed by this part of the definition, are persons holding positions in newly created titles specifically related to the preparation for and conduct of collective negotiations. Examples of these are Labor-Management Relations Officers and Employee Relations Representatives.

C. Criterion Three — Administration of agreements.

The third criterion is that a person is managerial if he has "a major role in the administration of agreements ... provided that such role is not of a routine or clerical nature and requires the exercise of independent judgment." The administration of an agreement involves basically two functions: (1) observance of the terms of the agreement and (2) interpretation of the agreement both within and without the grievance procedures of the contract. The observance of the terms of the agreement is largely a routine and ministerial function. Undoubtedly many supervisory employees have a responsibility to insure that terms and conditions of an agreement are adhered to, but this responsibility does not usually require "the exercise of independent judgment." There will be occasions where the implementation of an agreement will necessitate a change in a government's procedures or methods of operation. The person or persons who effect such implementation and change do exercise independent judgment and would have a "major role" in the administration of an agreement. Such a person is one the Legislature sought to exclude by this criterion.

Many supervisors are involved in grievance procedures. It does not appear, however, that supervisors who participate in first step grievances exercise independent judgment. Rather, such participation generally conforms to policy established at a higher level.

The interpretation of an agreement involving State agency or institution policy involving employee relations would constitute a "major role" in the administration of an agreement, and would require the exercise of independent judgment.

D. Criterion Four — Personnel administration.

The final criterion for defining managerial employees is that they "have a major role ... in personnel administration, provided that such role is not of a routine or clerical nature and requires the exercise of independent judgment." Many of the persons so defined were previously excluded under the old definition because they were "so closely related to or involved with the activities [of those who formulate policy or direct the work of major subdivisions] as to present a potential conflict of interest or clash of loyalties in matters concerning employer-employee relationships." To some extent, this final criterion is a compression of our prior definition. Some persons were previously excluded from the five units because their relationship to personnel administration was very close, even though it was of a routine or clerical nature. In any event, they are not managerial employees under the new statutory definition. Examples of these are the staff of the health services unit of the Department of Civil Service....

NOTE

Can prospective duties be considered in determining managerial and/or supervisory status? In *Jamestown Prof. Fire Fighters Ass'n, Local 1772 v. Newman,* 1986-88 PBC ¶ 35,059 (N.Y.S. Ct., App. Div. 1987), the court held that the New York PERB properly considered the future duties of four assistant fire chiefs pursuant to a proposed reorganization plan in determining that they were managerial employees. The court rejected the union's contention that the New York Act "requires employees to actually be performing managerial duties before the managerial designation may be made," holding that "[a]ll that is required is the reasonable expectation that such responsibilities will be given...."

UNIVERSITY OF PITTSBURGH

21 PPER ¶ 21203 (Pa. Lab. Rel. Bd. 1990)

On May 2, 1989, a Nisi Order of Certification was issued by the Board Representative certifying the results of an election conducted among certain part-time faculty of the University of Pittsburgh (University or Pitt).

The United Faculty of the University of Pittsburgh, AAUP, PaAAUP, AFT, PaFT (Union) excepts to the conclusion that the full-time and regular part-time tenure stream faculty and full-time non-tenure stream faculty are management level employes under Section 301(16) of the Public Employe Relations Act (Act). The hearing examiner concluded that these employes were management level due to their participation, as a faculty unit, in duties identified as managerial in Section 301(16) of the Act.

....

The Faculty as Managers

The parties have agreed to a stipulation of facts which outlines the duties of the faculty.[1] That stipulation was included in the hearing examiner's order of March 11, 1987, and also serves as the factual basis of our review of the exceptions. We begin our review by a brief summary of the role of the faculty, as a whole in the organizational and managerial structure of the University.

In the Stipulation and other evidence submitted in this proceeding the University's organizational structure demonstrates approximately 300 or more managers who serve in professional administrative positions and who are agreed by the parties not to be in the petitioned-for unit. They include the president and his support staff, the office of provost and support staff. The University employs vice-presidents for administration, public affairs, health sciences, and necessary support staff. The University also employs a vice-president for management and budget and, including its subdivision, has 119 full-time personnel including 71 professional administrative personnel. The office of vice-president for business and finance include 646 full-time personnel including 128 professional and administrative personnel. Additionally, the University employs 21 deans with appropriate assistants and associate deans, four campus presidents along with necessary professional administrative staff, and four senior directors also supported by professional administrative staff. The record does not accurately state the total number of these agreed upon employes but it would appear that there are 300 or more agreed upon professional and administrative management level employes employed by the University.

The University argues that the faculty, separate and apart from the above noted administration, is managerial due to their collective role in collegial decision-making. The faculty Senate is the only university-wide body which includes all faculty members. In arguing for the alleged managerial status of *all* faculty members, the role of the faculty in the Senate is therefore critical. The faculty Senate includes all full-time faculty having the title of instructor, assistant professor, associate professor, professor, part-time tenure stream faculty and full-time faculty librarian. Also included in the Senate are the president, 12 administrators appointed by the president, 21 deans, four regional campus presidents and 65 student members. The University Senate normally meets twice a year (stipulation, ¶5). The parties stipulated (stipulation, ¶5) that the Senate almost never takes action in general meetings of the Senate and that it is the fourteen standing committees, Faculty Assembly (approximately 70 faculty members), and Council of the Senate (approximately 35 faculty members) which do the work which the University argues makes the entire faculty managerial.

The parties' stipulation (Order Directing Submission of Eligibility List, pp. 8-14) disclosed that there is a distinction between the Senate, as a functioning body, and the 14 standing committees and two deliberative bodies (Faculty

---

[1] The facts stipulated to by the parties are set forth in Finding of Fact 147 of the hearing examiner's March 11, 1987 order. In an introduction to the agreed upon facts, the parties set forth a legal conclusion, that they agree that the facts show managerial status under *NLRB v. Yeshiva University,* 444 U.S. 672 (1980). While we accept the stipulation as the operative facts upon which our decision is based, we obviously are not bound by the legal conclusions drawn by either or both parties. Although the parties separately stipulated to the underlying facts, the conclusion to be drawn from those facts as to the appropriate unit is for the Board.

Assembly and Council of the Senate) which formulate the recommendations to the administration. For example, the Provost's Advisory Committee (19 faculty members, 5 academic administrators, 4 students) advises and makes recommendations regarding academic matters relating to undergraduate education and student admissions. The University Council of Graduate Study has primary responsibility for and authority over graduate programs. Under the Planning and Resource Management System, faculty bodies recommend to the administration actions regarding the initiation, review and approval of programmatic and related budgetary proposals for the University's academic and support programs. The stipulation shows that like processes exist within the University whereby various faculty committees make recommendations to the University which are often followed regarding matters of policy and programs. It is important that, as is above noted, approximately 175-200 faculty members so participate out of a total of 1678 faculty employees in the unit as originally petitioned for.

The parties' stipulation discloses a limited role of the Senate itself in the workings of the faculty committees. The purpose of the Senate is to create and maintain adequate communication channels between the administration and the faculty and students (stipulation, ¶ 6). On this record we find a clear distinction between the working role of the Senate and the working role of the standing committees and other deliberative faculty bodies as alleged managerial employes under the Act. The record shows that the 175-200 faculty members who participate in the Faculty Assembly, Council of the Senate and 14 standing committees perform managerial functions within the meaning of Section 301(16) of the Act. The question then becomes, for purposes of the Act, whether the remaining vast majority of faculty members who, the record shows, are not directly involved in managerial decisions, are managerial employes simply because they are "faculty" and by virtue thereof members of the University Senate.

The existence and role of university-wide faculty governance bodies is a crucial factor under federal law. Where a university has a faculty-wide governance body which formulates collective faculty input in establishment of university policy, the employes are generally regarded as managerial. *Yeshiva, supra; NLRB v. Lewis,* 765 F.2d 616 (7th Cir. 1985); *Ithaca College,* 261 NLRB 577 (1982); *Thiel College,* 261 NLRB 580 (1982); *Boston University,* 281 NLRB No. 115 (1986); *University of New Haven,* 267 NLRB 939 (1983); *Duquesne University of the Holy Ghost,* 261 NLRB 587 (1981); *Livingston College,* 286 NLRB No. 124 (1987). However, [where] a faculty-wide governance body does not directly participate in policy formulation, where it meets once or twice a year and policy is recommended rather by the standing committees, where the institution has a larger administrative staff, where the faculty's input is generally limited to academic matters, the faculty as a whole has not been found to be managerial. *NLRB v. Florida Memorial College,* 820 F.2d 1182 (11th Cir. 1987); *Cooper Union for the Advancement of Science,* 273 NLRB 1768 (1985); *Loretto Heights College,* 263 NLRB 1248 (1982); *St. Thomas University,* 298

NLRB No. 32 (1990). In *Florida Memorial College,* the Circuit Court stated as follows:

"In contrast to *Yeshiva,* the faculty at Florida Memorial lack a faculty-wide governing organization through which to formulate collective faculty input as to matters at the College. While there is a faculty council, this body apparently meets only once or twice yearly and then for the sole purpose of electing two faculty members to serve as non-voting delegates on the Board of Trustees. The absence of an effective faculty-wide governing organization is in distinct contrast to *Yeshiva* where the faculty within the substantially autonomous undergraduate and graduate schools met formally, and in some instances pursuant to written bylaws, to decide matters of institutional and professional concern."

820 F.2d at 1184.

This Board has previously addressed the question of the alleged managerial status of an entire bargaining unit where the record shows that the majority bargaining unit members do not perform duties which would exclude them while others in the unit perform duties which would exclude them from the Act's coverage. In this case, the record shows that for every faculty member who participates in the managerial activities as outlined in the stipulation there are ten or more faculty members who do not so participate.

This case is akin to others which have arisen before the Board wherein a majority of employes at issue do not perform duties which would suggest exclusion and a minority perform duties which suggest their exclusion from the petitioned-for unit. It has been the Board's obligation since the inception of the Act to assess the extent to which the bargaining unit as a whole participates in the processes which it is argued require exclusion of an entire classification of employes. *AFSCME v. PLRB,* 17 Pa. Commonwealth Ct. 83, 330 A.2d 300 (1975); *PLRB v. AFSCME,* 20 Pa. Commonwealth Ct. 572, 342 A.2d 155 (1975).

In those cases petitions for representation were filed to establish rank and file and first level supervisory units under the Act. The employer responded in those cases by arguing that on balance many employes in the alleged rank and file unit were supervisory employes and that many employes in the petitioned-for first level supervisory unit were managers. Hearings in those cases disclosed that while certain individual employes performed duties which could support their exclusion from the unit, the majority of the employes did not perform such duties and the Board certified the units to include classifications as a whole. In these decisions it was dispositive that minority participation in managerial or supervisory activities did not warrant denial of collective bargaining or meet and discuss rights to the majority of employes who were not involved in such activities. Comparison of this record and the records of the above cited cases discloses that relatively fewer faculty members at the University participate in activities which would support exclusion than the employes involved in the Commonwealth cases. In its best light the University's argument is that the vast majority of employes, who the parties have agreed are not involved in the managerial process as is outlined in the stipulation of facts, should be denied collective bargaining rights because a small minority of these employes, through faculty governance committees, have some participatory role in managerial decisions. The law of this Commonwealth however is that the participation by a limited number of the employes in those functions should not and does not artificially disenfranchise the remaining vast majority of faculty members who have no such direct participation.

This case is unlike *Employes of Carlynton School District v. Carlynton School District,* 31 Pa. Commonwealth Ct. 631, 377 A.2d 1033 (1977) and others where the record demonstrated that the majority or all of the unit at issue performed managerial functions at least part of the time. Our review of the case law under the Act discloses no decided authority where a distinct minority of the proposed bargaining unit actually participated in policy formulation or implementation which resulted in exclusion of all members of the unit. On the contrary, as the case authority (*Carlynton, AFSCME v. PLRB, PLRB v. AFSCME*) demonstrates, where the record shows that the unit as a whole does not actually participate in functions described in Section 301(16) of the Act, it is the Board's duty not to deny employes their right to organize.

The situation at the University where employes are selected from bargaining units for administrative/managerial functions on a temporary or fixed term basis also occurs elsewhere under the Act. There are instances where rank and file or supervisory employes are selected to temporarily assume positions which arguably support their exclusion from a unit. In many of these instances employes work "out of class" for the period of their assumption of duties which are in the normal course regarded as supervisory, managerial or confidential. *Monroe County,* 18 PPER ¶ 18002 (Final Order, 1986); *Center County Child Development Council,* 10 PPER ¶ 10276 (Order and Notice of Election, 1979); *Neville Township,* 12 PPER ¶ 12365 (Proposed Order of Unit Clarification, 1981). In this case the record discloses that faculty members are primarily engaged in classroom instruction, research and other scholarly activities which are not managerial in nature. Periodically, faculty employes are selected for a fixed period to serve on University governance committees and during these periods, in addition to their regular duties, participate in the activities set forth in the stipulation of the parties. After conclusion of their selection to and participation on these committees, they presumably return to their normal classroom instructional, research and scholarship activities. Assumedly there are some employes who may be selected or volunteer for such activity more frequently than others and there may well be instances where selected faculty members spend substantial periods of their careers at the University involved in service to University governance committees. However, the method by which employes participate and the usual structure of the University is that these assignments are fixed and employe participation is of a fixed duration subject to termination, reconsideration or reappointment at an appropriate time.

The Board, however, must in light of this situation make a decision which is fair and equitable to all parties. As the University would have it, even those employes who served their entire careers at the University of Pittsburgh, having never participated in any governance committees, should be denied bargaining rights under the Act due to the participation in managerial activities by relatively few members of the petitioned-for unit or the twice a year occasion to participate in the activity of the Senate. We find this suggested result unparalleled in any unit determination heretofore made by this Board under the PERA or Act 111. The hallmark of Board unit determination policy is a factual consideration of employes' work with due regard for the Act's policy of granting collective bargaining rights to employes, reasonably excluding employes who would otherwise enjoy bargaining rights but for their participation in excludable activities. *PLRB v. Altoona Area School District,* 480 Pa. 148, 389 A.2d 553 (1978); *School District of the Township of Millcreek v. Millcreek Education Association,* 64 Pa. Commonwealth Ct. 389, 440 A.2d 673 (1982); *Washington Township Municipal Authority v. PLRB,* __ Pa. Commonwealth Ct. __, 569 A.2d 402 (1990), *pet. for allowance of appeal den.,* August 1, 1990 at No. 57 M.D. Allocatur Dkt. 1990. As the University would have it, ten or more otherwise includable faculty members should be denied bargaining rights because of the participation of one employe in these various faculty committees. We do not find this result to have support in the Act or the decided case authority in the 20 years since the Act's adoption in 1970.

This result is supported by the difference between faculty participation in managerial decisions at Pitt as opposed to that of the faculty involved in *Yeshiva.* The University argues in this proceeding that the PLRB should adopt *Yeshiva.* Yeshiva is a private university and Pitt is a quasi-public university which is statutorily a part of the Commonwealth System of Higher Education. See 24 P.S. § 2510.201-2510.210.

Our review of the record in this case and our reading of *Yeshiva* discloses greater reliance on the faculty at Yeshiva with regard to matters beyond the academic expertise of the faculty. For example, in the area of budget, the record in *Yeshiva* shows substantially greater reliance on the recommendations of the faculty than is shown in the record of this case. Pitt, like other public and quasi-public universities, has a substantial administrative arm, separate and apart from the faculty members at issue here, whose responsibility includes budget and finance. The stipulation of the parties reveals that in the Offices of Vice-President for Management and Budget and Vice-President for Business and Finance, the University employs approximately 765 employes including approximately 200 professional and administrative personnel whose duty it is to address management's interest with regard to matters of budget and finance (stipulation, ¶ 3). Yeshiva, like many other private universities, does not have the administrative superstructure as exists at the University. The authority of this Board and the appellate courts discloses that matters of budget are key indicators of managerial authority. See, e.g., *AFSCME v. PLRB, supra; Fraternal Order of Police, Star Lodge No. 20 v. PLRB,* 104 Pa. Commonwealth Ct. 561, 522 A.2d 697 (1987), *aff'd,* 522 Pa. 149, 560 A.2d 145 (1989). The parties' stipulation indicates that although faculty committee recommendations are generally followed with regard to a wide range of academic matters, faculty recommendations regarding budgetary matters such as distribution of faculty salary increments and university investment policy are generally not followed (stipulation, ¶ ¶ 19, 27). The stipulation in our view reflects the University's deference to its faculty committees regarding matters within their academic expertise but not with regard to matters concerning the managerial and budgetary interests of the employer as a whole.

The Act in this regard distinguishes between professional and managerial employes.[2] Recently, the Commonwealth Court has addressed this difference in *Pennsylvania Association of State Mental Hospital Physicians v. PLRB,* 124 Pa. Commonwealth Ct. 28, 554 A.2d 1021 (1989). In that case, the PLRB found certain professional psychiatric physicians to be management level because their effective participation in managerial decisions included matters not limited to their medical professional expertise but pertaining to the employer's overall budget and administration of the mental institutions. For example, the record in *State Mental Hospital Physicians* shows that the budgetary recommendation of the physicians is followed by the superintendent of the institution approximately ninety to ninety-five percent of the time. Our review of this record however shows that the University relies on the professional expertise of its faculty regarding matters generally limited to the educational mission of the University.

The record in this case does not support the claim that the faculty members have an effective and meaningful role in the establishment of the employer's policies beyond the academic responsibilities normally associated with those of a teacher in an institution of higher education. In this regard, the faculty members' participation in matters beyond their educational expertise is merely that of an advisory body whose recommendations are considered and often not followed.

We must consider this case in light of the increased trend toward employe involvement in matters which have been historically regarded exclusively within the control of management. Increasingly, private and public employers are involving their employes in matters which have historically been regarded as beyond the participation of employes in the normal course of performance of their duties. Instances where employes are involved in providing suggestions to management concerning matters normally regarded as managerial, and where management does not generally follow the recommendations, pose grave danger for an overly broad exclusion of employes as managerial. We do not believe the Supreme Court in *Yeshiva* intended in 1980 to require, under the National Labor Relations Act, the disenfranchisement of employes who participate in advising an employer which retains all managerial authority to accept or reject such advice. Our reading of *Yeshiva* indicates that, unlike the faculty at Pitt, which has substantially more administrative superstructure, the faculty at Yeshiva participated in a broader range of managerial decisions, including non-academic decisions.

We have reviewed the decisions of other state level jurisdictions which have considered the question of adoption of *Yeshiva* in regard to state level institutions of higher education. See, e.g., *Wichita State University,* No. 75-00-1980 (PERB, 1981); *University of Alaska,* No. U.A. 80-2 (LRB, 1981); *Southern Oregon State College,* No. C-176-82 (ERB, 1985). It is significant that in the latter of these jurisdictions, as the University points out, the legislation at issue, unlike the Act, expresses an intention to include faculty employes. However, the Kansas and Alaska statutes are similar to the law in Pennsylvania in that the legislatures did not specifically address the status of higher education faculty. In

---

[2]See also *Montefiore Hospital,* 26 NLRB 569, 110 LLRM 1048 (1982).

the latter instances the *Yeshiva* approach has been expressly rejected and the wisdom of *Yeshiva* was openly questioned. We join with these other state jurisdictions and find that the faculty at the University of Pittsburgh should not be excluded from PERA's coverage for alleged managerial status.

The Supreme Court in reviewing *Yeshiva* focused on the problem of "divided loyalty" which it perceived to be presented by a petition for representation for faculty members who are involved in collegial decision-making. In this regard, the National Labor Relations Act denies organizational rights to supervisors and managers because they are considered an arm of management and share management's rights. As noted in a law review article addressing the question of organizational rights for higher education faculty:

> "This statutory exclusion is based upon the rationale that supervisors are an arm of management and thus cannot act in the employer's interest if they are also members of the same union as the employes they supervise."

Ripps, *The Professor as Manager in the Academic Enterprise,* 29 Cleve. St. L. Rev. 17, 26 (1980). Review of the Act, on the other hand, discloses two significant departures from the federal statutory scheme. The legislature in its enactment of the Act did not find as legislative policy the "divided loyalty" problem which should prevent first level supervisory employes from the right to organize for purposes of meet and discuss. In this regard, the Act represents a significant departure from the federal labor relations model. Section 604(5) of the Act expressly grants first level supervisory employes the statutory right to organize and form separate homogeneous units. Thereafter, Section 704 of the Act allows first level supervisory employes the right to meet and discuss with their public employer over wages, hours and working conditions. Thereafter, Section 1201(a)(9) makes it an unfair practice for a public employer to refuse to comply with requirements of meet and discuss. Further, the Board and the courts have held that first level supervisory employes may be represented by the same organization which represents the rank and file employes. *PLRB v. Commonwealth of Pennsylvania,* 46 Pa. Commonwealth Ct. 468, 397 A.2d 858 (1979). The Act contains no prohibition on the right of first level supervisory employes to join the same union which represents rank and file employes. It is the Pennsylvania legislative policy and the experience in the 20 years since the passage of the Act to depart from the traditional private sector labor relations model regarding the divided loyalty approach. In deciding whether to adopt *Yeshiva* under the Act we are guided in part by the fact that under federal law, the divided loyalty concept remains a cornerstone of the NLRA since the 1940's, while Pennsylvania's public sector labor laws have not rejected the notion that an employe may responsibly serve above the rank and file and also be a member of a unit for collective bargaining or meet and discuss purposes. While this Board has recognized and relied on the divided loyalty concept regarding management level employes (*Philadelphia School District,* 4 PPER 128 (Order and Notice of Pre-Election Hearing, 1974)) for the reasons above stated, we do not find that the faculty as a whole exercises managerial authority.

As further evidence of Pennsylvania legislative policy, following the *Yeshiva* decision in 1980, there is [the] pronouncement of the Pennsylvania legislature regarding organizational rights of teaching employes in higher education. The and full-time non-tenure stream faculty are not managerial level employes under Section 301(16) of the Act.

....

NOTE

Citing the Supreme Court's *Yeshiva* decision, the Illinois Appellate Court in *Salaried Emps. of N. Am. v. Illinois Local Lab. Rel. Bd.,* 202 Ill. App. 3d 1013, 560 N.E.2d 926 (1990), affirmed a decision of the Illinois Local Labor Relations Board holding that attorneys employed by the City of Chicago's Law Department were managerial employees. The court noted:

> ... the Law Department attorneys exercise a tremendous amount of discretion on behalf of the city and we do not believe the city should be forced to bear the divided loyalty that often follows unionization.... This is especially so where, as here, the interests of the employees are identical to, and cannot be separated from, those of the employer.

3. CONFIDENTIAL EMPLOYEES

SHAW & CLARK, DETERMINATION OF APPROPRIATE BARGAINING UNITS IN THE PUBLIC SECTOR: LEGAL AND PRACTICAL PROBLEMS, 51 Or. L. Rev. 152, 171 (1971)*

Another common exclusion from bargaining units is confidential employees. Although the breadth of this exclusion varies from state to state, the term "confidential employees" usually refers to "employees who assist and act in a confidential capacity to persons who formulate, determine, and evaluate management policies in the field of labor relations." The rationale for excluding confidential employees from larger bargaining units in the private sector was to separate those employees "who, in the normal performance of their duties may obtain advance information of the Company's position with regard to contract negotiations, the disposition of grievances, or other labor relations matters."

In some states, including Oregon, confidential employees are specifically excluded from bargaining units. In other states, such as Connecticut and Michigan, confidential employees have been excluded from bargaining units on a case-by-case basis by the public employee labor relations board. For example, the Michigan Employment Relations Commission has adopted the following rule:

> [W]e are of the opinion that the "confidential" employees rule should be applied cautiously. Only those employees whose work is closely related to that of supervisory employees and involves matters which should be held in confidence should be excluded from a bargaining unit with nonsupervisory employees.... [*Benton Harbor Bd. of Educ.,* 1967 MERC Lab. Op. 743, 746.]

Applying this rule, the MERC has held that the secretary to a public employer's negotiator, and the secretary to a director of budget, finance, and accounting were confidential employees. On the other hand, persons who from time to time may have access to confidential information are not necessarily confiden-

---

*Reprinted by permission. Copyright © 1971 by University of Oregon.

gan, confidential employees have been excluded from bargaining units on a case-by-case basis by the public employee labor relations board. For example, the Michigan Employment Relations Commission has adopted the following rule:

> [W]e are of the opinion that the "confidential" employees rule should be applied cautiously. Only those employees whose work is closely related to that of supervisory employees and involves matters which should be held in confidence should be excluded from a bargaining unit with nonsupervisory employees.... [*Benton Harbor Bd. of Educ.,* 1967 MERC Lab. Op. 743, 746.]

Applying this rule, the MERC has held that the secretary to a public employer's negotiator, and the secretary to a director of budget, finance, and accounting were confidential employees. On the other hand, persons who from time to time may have access to confidential information are not necessarily confidential employees. Similar decisions have been issued by other public employee relations boards.

NOTES

1. In *PLRB v. Altoona Area Sch. Dist.,* 389 A.2d 553 (Pa. 1978), the Pennsylvania Supreme Court upheld the test utilized by the PLRB to determine confidential employee status, i.e., "whether or not the employe acts in a confidential capacity to a person who formulates, determines or effectuates management policies in the field of labor relations." After finding that the considerations underlying the exclusion of confidential employees under the NLRA were identical to the Pennsylvania statutory exclusion of confidential employees, the court held that the PLRB properly considered NLRB precedent in "formulat[ing] a workable definition of that term as it appears in the Pennsylvania statute."

2. In *New Hampshire Univ. Sys. v. State,* 369 A.2d 1139 (N.H. 1977), the court, after essentially adopting the NLRB standards for determining confidential status, held that department chairpersons were not confidential employees since the recommendations they made concerning tenure and promotions did "not constitute confidential interaction between department chairmen and the administration on labor relations matters."

3. The NLRB's exclusion of confidential employees from bargaining units is thoroughly explored in Note, *Confidential Employees and the National Labor Relations Act,* 29 Wash. & Lee L. Rev. 350 (1972).

4. The Florida statute defines confidential employees as "persons who act in a confidential capacity to assist or aid managerial employees as defined in [the Act]." Fla. Stat. § 447.203(5) (1977). In *Palm Beach Cty. Sch. Bd. v. PERC,* 99 LRRM 3035 (Fla. Dist. Ct. App. 1978), the court held "that the personal secretary of a managerial employee such as a school principal is, by definition, 'one who aids or assists a managerial employee in confidential matters.'" In setting aside a PERC order, the court held that the statute "does not require a 'nexus' between the confidential matters and the particular managerial duties of the principal listed in [the statutory definition of a managerial employee]," i.e., the confidential aid or assistance does not have to necessarily relate to those duties and responsibilities deemed managerial in nature under the Florida act. In *School Bd. of Polk Cty. v. Polk Educ. Ass'n,* 480 So. 2d 1360 (Fla. Dist. Ct. App. 1985), a different district of the Florida District Court of Appeals upheld the Florida Commission's use of a "labor nexus" test in determining whether individuals were confidential employees under the Florida Act.

5. The Federal Labor-Management and Employees Relations Law provides that no unit shall be determined to be appropriate if it includes confidential employees or employees "engaged in personnel work in other than a purely clerical capacity." 5 U.S.C. § 7112(b)(2), (3) (1978). The term "confidential employee" is defined to mean "an employee who acts in a confidential capacity with respect to an individual who formulates or effectuates management policies in the field of labor-management relations." 5 U.S.C. § 7103(13) (1978). How does this definition differ from the definition construed by the Florida court in the *Palm Beach Cty. Sch. Bd.* case discussed in the note immediately above?

6. Are city attorneys who furnish legal opinions to various municipal agencies and in such capacity participate in negotiations between such agencies and the unions that represent their employees confidential employees? In *City of Milwaukee,* Decision No. 8100 (Wis. ERC 1967), *aff'd,* 43 Wis. 2d 596, 168 N.W.2d 809 (1969), the WERC stated:

> Although the Assistant City Attorneys do act in a confidential capacity with respect to the determination and implementation of management policies in the field of labor relations, the information available to these attorneys is not directly related to the relationship between the City and their representative. Employees who have access to confidential labor relations information of other employers, unrelated to the relationship between the employer and the employees included in the unit in question, does not mean that such employees should be excluded from one unit because they are "confidential employees."

The WERC did find, however, that the assistant city attorney who represented the city in negotiations and was regularly assigned to furnish legal assistance to the office of the city's labor negotiator should be excluded from the unit. The WERC noted that the individual in question "cannot possibly serve both parties" and that "his relationship with the office of the Labor Negotiator is too intimate to permit him to be included in the unit."

7. In *City of Burbank,* 1 PERI ¶ 2008 (Ill. SLRB 1985), the Illinois State Labor Relations Board stated that:

> ... considering the question of confidential status in a work place new to collective bargaining, this Board will look to the employee's (and his/her superior's) future role in collective bargaining based upon the employee's current job duties and a reasonable expectation that the employee alleged to be confidential will in fact be performing confidential duties which meet the statutory definition with the onset of collective bargaining in the work place. If such reasonable expectation test is met, the employee will be declared confidential and placed outside the unit. If it is not met, he/she will be placed in the unit.

4. MISCELLANEOUS CATEGORIES

REGENTS OF THE UNIVERSITY OF CALIFORNIA v. PERB

41 Cal. 3d 601, 715 P.2d 590, 224 Cal. Rptr. 631 (1986)

BIRD, CHIEF JUSTICE.

The Regents of the University of California (University) petitions for review of a decision by the Public Employment Relations Board (PERB or the Board).

The Board found that housestaff,[1] who are paid by the University while participating in residency programs at clinics, institutes or hospitals owned or operated by the University, are "employees" within the meaning of Government
Code section 3562, subdivision (f)[2] of the Higher Education Employer-Employee Relations Act (HEERA or the Act) (§ 3560 et seq.). Therefore, they are
entitled to collective bargaining rights. This court must review the propriety of
that ruling.

I

Prior to July 1, 1979, Physicians National Housestaff Association (PNHA)
chapters representing housestaff at the Irvine, San Francisco and Davis
campuses participated in meet-and-confer sessions with representatives of different hospital administrations. During this period, PNHA also received payroll
dues deductions from its members' paychecks.

In 1978, the California Legislature enacted HEERA, which extended collective bargaining rights to employees of the University of California, Hastings
College of the Law and the California State University[3] (§ 3560, subd. (b).)
Shortly after HEERA became effective (July 1, 1979), the University notified
PNHA that it did not consider housestaff to be "employees" within the meaning
of the Act. It then ceased making payroll deductions from housestaff salaries to
pay PNHA dues. On July 20, 1979, PNHA responded by filing an unfair labor
practice charge against the University, alleging that the University had violated
section 3571, subdivisions (a) and (b) and section 3585, by refusing to make such
deductions.

A hearing before a PERB hearing officer ensued. The evidence consisted of
the following:

The University operates medical schools at five of its campuses: Los Angeles
(UCLA), San Diego (UCSD), San Francisco (UCSF), Irvine (UCI) and Davis
(UCD). Through its medical schools, the University provides residency training
programs in most medical specialty and subspecialty areas and operates hospitals at which housestaff gain clinical experience. Other hospitals, both public
and private, are also affiliated with these medical schools. Many housestaff
rotate through these hospitals during the course of their training.

---

[1]"Housestaff" is a shorthand term used to describe medical interns, residents and clinical fellows. In the past, an individual in the first year of a residency program was called an "intern." That
term is no longer used. Such an individual is now referred to as a "Resident I" or a first-year
resident. The term "clinical fellow" describes those persons who have completed their residencies in
recognized areas of medical specialization and are continuing to train in a medical subspecialty.

[2]Section 3562, subdivision (f) provides: "'Employee' or 'higher education employee' means any
employee of the Regents of the University of California, the Directors of Hastings College of the
Law, or the Board of Trustees of the California State University, whose employment is principally
within the State of California. However, managerial, and confidential employees shall be excluded
from coverage under this chapter. The board may find student employees whose employment is
contingent on their status as students are employees only if the services they provide are unrelated
to their educational objectives, or, that those educational objectives are subordinate to the services
they perform and that coverage under this chapter would further the purposes of this chapter."
Hereafter, this provision will be referred to as subdivision (f)....

[3]Employees of these institutions were among the last California public employees to be accorded
collective bargaining rights. (Brownstein, *Medical Housestaff: Scholars or Working Stiffs? The
Pending PERB Decision* (1981) 12 Pacific L.J. 1127 [hereafter *Scholars or Working Stiffs*].)

In the spring of 1979, approximately 4,500 housestaff were participating in University residency programs. Approximately 2,000 of them were on the University payroll. The others were paid by the affiliated institutions at which they served.

In order to participate in a University residency program, an individual must have graduated from medical school with a doctor of medicine (M.D.) degree. To qualify to practice medicine in California and in most other states, such an individual must complete at least one year in an approved residency program. In California, he or she must also obtain a "physician's and surgeon's certificate" from the Board of Medical Quality Assurance. Until receipt of such a certificate, housestaff may practice medicine only under an approved residency program. (Bus. & Prof. Code, § 2065.)

Most residency programs take between two and six years to complete, depending upon the specialty. The programs are structured so that housestaff rotate through different hospital services relevant to their specialty. Upon successful completion of a residency, an individual receives a certificate entitling him or her to take a specialty board examination leading to board certification in a particular specialty. Board certification is not a requirement for specialty practice, but attests to the physician's competence in that field.

Board certification requires participation in a training program approved by the Liaison Committee on Graduate Medical Education (LCGME). LCGME sets standards for residency programs, reviews programs for compliance and grants accreditation to programs which meet those standards. In order for University residency programs to acquire LCGME approval, they must comply with the general requirements contained in an LCGME document entitled "Essentials of Accredited Residencies."

On April 9, 1980, the PERB hearing officer concluded that housestaff are not employees under HEERA and recommended that PNHA's unfair labor practice charge be dismissed.

PNHA filed exceptions to the proposed decision. On February 14, 1983, PERB rendered a written decision adopting the hearing officer's findings of facts and making additional factual findings. The Board found that the educational objectives were subordinate to the services housestaff perform and coverage of housestaff under HEERA would further the purposes of the Act. Based on these findings, the Board concluded that housestaff are "employees." It further held that the University had violated HEERA by refusing to make payroll deductions. The Board issued a cease and desist order and directed the University to reimburse PNHA for the dues lost during the period for which the University made no payroll deductions.

This matter is before the court on the University's petition for a writ of review.

II

The first question to be resolved is whether HEERA precludes housestaff from being considered employees under the Act.

....

The statute provides in relevant part that "[t]he board may find student employees whose employment is contingent on their status as students are employees only if the services they provide are unrelated to their educational objectives, or, that those educational objectives are subordinate to the services they perform and that coverage under this chapter would further the purposes of this chapter." (§ 3562, subd. (f).)

Although the statute is silent on the subject of housestaff, it clearly leaves open the possibility that such persons may come within it. As the words of the statute make clear, the Legislature intended that PERB determine whether a particular student qualifies as an employee under the Act.

The legislative history which accompanied the passage of HEERA supports this conclusion. HEERA was enacted by Assembly Bill No. 1091 during the 1977-1978 session. When that bill was first introduced, subdivision (f) contained no reference to students. That provision simply defined "employees" as "any employee" except managerial and confidential employees.... This section was subsequently amended to exclude "managerial, and confidential employees, and employees who are students on the same campus where they are employed and who work less than 10 hours per week."...

However, the bill was not passed in this form. On the Senate side, an amendment was passed which eliminated the distinction between student employees based on the number of hours worked. That amendment, which was enacted into law, prescribed a case-by-case assessment of the degree to which a student's employment is related to his or her educational objectives. The determination of student employee status was expressly left to PERB.... Although this amendment arguably made the status of housestaff more uncertain, it is clear that they were not eliminated from coverage under the Act.

When this statutory history is considered in conjunction with a Legislative Counsel's opinion prepared while the bill was pending, the conclusion is inescapable that the Legislature did not intend to exclude housestaff from coverage under the Act. The Legislative Counsel's opinion was prepared at a time when subdivision (f) contained the exclusion for students employed less than 10 hours per week. The opinion concluded that "[w]hile this [exclusion] indicates an intention to cover students who are employees under some circumstances, it does not resolve the essential issue imposed by the [NLRB] as determining the coverage of student employees."... The opinion also noted that "[g]enerally speaking, the provisions of A.B. 1091 parallel those of the National Labor Relations Act [NLRA], as amended (Sec. 151 et seq., Title 29, U.S.C.). The [NLRB] ... has concluded that interns and residents are 'primarily students' rather than 'employees' and thus are not covered by the National Labor Relations Act (*St. Clare's Hospital* [(1977) 229 NLRB 1000 [95 LRRM 1180]]; and *Cedars-Sinai Medical Center* [(1976) 223 NLRB 251 [91 LRRM 1398]]).... *We think that in the absence of any more definitive statements in A.B. 1091, the courts would conclude that a similar construction is intended under A.B. 1091* to that given the provisions of the National Labor Relations Act...."
....

The Legislature responded to this opinion by amending subdivision (f) to *include* a "more definitive statement" as to the status of student employees. That action strongly suggests that the Legislature intended to promulgate a new standard for determining this issue rather than to follow NLRB precedent and deny housestaff employee status. That action also indicates that the Legislature did not intend to foreclose the issue of housestaff organizational rights. Instead, its creation of a statutory standard distinct from NLRB precedent was intended to permit PERB to make an independent determination of the status of housestaff.

The dissent contends that the Legislature's amendment was intended to incorporate NLRB precedent into the Act and deny housestaff employee status. This argument requires a comparison of the NLRB precedent with the statutory language ultimately adopted.

The NLRB first addressed the issue of housestaff status in *Cedars-Sinai, supra,* 91 LRRM 1398. Over a strong dissent, the NLRB held that housestaff were not employees under the NLRA, since they "are primarily engaged in graduate educational training" and thus are in "an educational rather than an employment relationship [with the hospital]." (*Id.,* at p. 1400.)

In arriving at that determination, the NLRB focused primarily on the purpose of housestaff participation in such programs. The Board paid little attention to the actual services performed by them. It found that housestaff participate in such programs to gain an education, not to earn a living, and that their selection of programs is primarily motivated by the quality of the training they will receive, rather than the amount of compensation. Further, it noted that while housestaff do perform much unsupervised patient care, this is merely a part of the training they must receive to develop practical skills. (*Id.,* at p. 1400.)

Member Fanning vigorously dissented from the majority's approach. He argued that the fact that "hospitals are instructed to view the primary purpose of housestaff programs as educational has no bearing on whether the housestaff ultimately *performs a service for compensation....*" (*Cedars-Sinai, supra,* 91 LRRM at p. 1403.) Nor did Fanning find any relevance in "the fact that an individual desirous of becoming an orthopedic surgeon chooses a residency program based on its quality and the opportunity for extensive training." (*Id.,* at p. 1404.) "That is," Fanning observed, "not a unique approach in any field of endeavor, particularly professional ones." (*Ibid.*) Instead, Fanning thought the Board's inquiry should focus on the services *actually performed* by housestaff.

Member Fanning was not alone in his criticism of his colleagues' ruling. (See, e.g., Drake, *Labor Problems of Interns and Residents: The Aftermath of Cedars-Sinai* (1977) 11 U.S.F. L. Rev. 694; Maute, *Student-Workers or Working Students? A Fatal Question for Collective Bargaining of Hospital House Staff* (1977) 38 U. Pitt. L. Rev. 762, 767, 772, 786 [hereafter *Student-Workers or Working Students*]; see generally *Scholars or Working Stiffs, supra,* 12 Pacific L.J. 1127.) Other jurisdictions chose not to follow the *Cedars-Sinai* majority. (See, e.g., *House Officers, Etc. v. U. of Neb. Med. Ctr.* (1977) 198 Neb. 697, 255 N.W.2d 258, 261-262; *City of Cambridge and Cambridge Hospital House Officers Association* (1976) 2 MLC 1450, 1458-1459 (Mass. Labor Cases).)

One year after *Cedars-Sinai* was decided, the NLRB addressed the issue again in *St. Clare's, supra,* 95 LRRM 1180, noting that it "may not have been as precise as [it] might have been in articulating [its] views" in *Cedars-Sinai.* (95 LRRM at p. 1181, fn. omitted.)

In these decisions the Board basically adopted a "primary purpose" test, which gave paramount consideration to the students' subjective intent in participating in housestaff programs. "*Our conclusion that housestaff are 'primarily students' rather than employees connotes nothing more than the simple fact that* when an individual is providing services at the educational institution itself as part and parcel of his or her educational development *the individual's interest in rendering such services is more academic than economic.*" (*St. Clare's, supra,* 95 LRRM, at p. 1184, emphasis added.)

In *St. Clare's,* the NLRB also observed that *Cedars-Sinai* fit within its prior decisions which had classified students into four general categories. (95 LRRM at p. 1181.) Two of these categories concern commercial employers and are inapplicable here. The other two categories involved students employed by their own educational institutions either (1) in a capacity *unrelated* to their course of study (*id.,* at p. 1182), or (2) in a capacity *directly related* to their educational program (*id.,* at p. 1183). Both of these categories of students are denied collective bargaining rights. (*Id.,* at pp. 1182-1183.)

After reviewing the various categories of students and noting that housestaff fall within the latter category, the NLRB reaffirmed its conclusion that housestaff are not entitled to collective bargaining rights under the NLRA. "Since the individuals are rendering services which are directly related to — and indeed constitute an integral part of — their educational program, they are serving primarily as students and not primarily as employees." (*St. Clare's, supra,* 95 LRRM at p. 1183, fn. omitted.)[12]

It is true, as the University notes, that subdivision (f) uses the "related/unrelated" classification scheme that *St. Clare's* created. However, that is where any similarity between *St. Clare's* and the present statute ends. While *St. Clare's* held that both categories of students were per se, *not entitled* to collective bargaining rights under the NLRA, HEERA *expressly* permits PERB to find students in both categories *entitled* to collective bargaining rights in appropriate circumstances.

Under HEERA, the Board may find students who are employed in a capacity *unrelated* to their course of study to be "employees" within the meaning of the Act and therefore entitled to collective bargaining rights. Further, PERB may find students who are employed in a capacity *related* to their educational program entitled to such rights depending on a case-by-case evaluation of (1) whether their educational objectives are subordinate to the services they perform, and (2) whether coverage under HEERA would further the purposes of the Act.

Thus, in defining "employees" under HEERA, the Legislature specifically rejected the NLRB rulings. Under the NLRB precedent, the relevant inquiry is whether the student's objectives are primarily academic. Under HEERA, even if PERB finds that housestaff are motivated by "educational objectives," it may

---

[12] As the NLRB explained, "The rationale for dismissing such petitions [as this] is a relatively simple and straightforward one. Since the individuals are rendering services which are directly related to — and indeed constitute an integral part of — their educational program, they are serving primarily as students and not primarily as employees. In our view this is a very fundamental distinction for it means that the mutual interests of the students and the educational institution in the services being rendered are predominantly academic rather than economic in nature. Such interests are completely foreign to the normal employment relationship and, in our judgment, are not readily adaptable to the collective-bargaining process. It is for this reason that the Board has determined that the national labor policy does not require — and in fact precludes — the extension of collective-bargaining rights and obligations to situations such as the one now before us." (*St. Clare's, supra,* LRRM at p. 1183, fn. omitted.)

nevertheless classify them as "employees" if their objectives are "subordinate to the services they perform" and if granting collective bargaining rights would further the purposes of the Act. It is, therefore, clear that instead of denying collective bargaining rights to student employees of public educational institutions, the Legislature intended to permit PERB to grant such rights in situations not permitted under NLRB precedent. If, as the dissent suggests, the Legislature had intended to retain NLRB precedent, it could have easily done so by adopting the language of the NLRA verbatim.

....

The Legislature has instructed PERB to look not only at the students' goals, but also at the services they actually perform, to see if the students' educational objectives, however personally important, are nonetheless subordinate to the services they are required to perform. Thus, even if PERB finds that the students' motivation for accepting employment was primarily educational, the inquiry does not end here. PERB must look further — to the services actually performed — to determine whether the students' educational objectives take a back seat to their service obligations.

This interpretation is the only one which remains true to the statutory language. Moreover, it makes sense in light of the events surrounding the passage of HEERA. As noted above, the housestaff issue was clearly on the mind of the Legislature when it enacted this provision. The NLRB had just rendered two controversial decisions on the issue. In those decisions a majority of the Board concentrated primarily on the students' motivation for entering into housestaff programs. The NLRB dissenter thought the focus should be confined to the services they actually perform, disregarding as irrelevant their motive for taking such jobs.... Subdivision (f), as enacted, represents a compromise between the majority and dissenting opinions expressed in the NLRB decisions. HEERA took a middle road, requiring both factors to be considered. It is not the prerogative of this court to act as a super-legislature and alter that Legislative choice merely because it may be unwise....

Another provision of HEERA corroborates the conclusion that housestaff were not excluded, per se, from the benefits of collective bargaining. Section 3562, subdivision (o)(1) defines a "professional employee" as a person engaged in work (i) predominantly intellectual and varied in character, (ii) involving the consistent exercise of discretion, (iii) impossible to standardize with respect to output, and (iv) requiring knowledge of an advanced type acquired through a course of specialized intellectual instruction and study in an institution of higher learning or a hospital. A professional employee is also defined as an individual who has completed the courses of specialized intellectual instruction and study described in clause (iv) above and is performing related work under the supervision of a professional person to qualify to become a professional employee. (§ 3562, subd. (o)(2).) Housestaff fit precisely within this definition. The fact that housestaff so clearly fall within the definition of professional employee reinforces the view that the Legislature did not intend housestaff to be excluded under the Act.

It is noteworthy that at the time HEERA was enacted the vast majority of decisions from other jurisdictions had concluded that housestaff are employees within the meaning of their respective collective bargaining statutes. (See, e.g.,

House Officers, Etc. v. U. of Neb. Med. Ctr., supra, 255 N.W.2d 258; *Regents of Univ. of Mich. v. Michigan Emp. Rel. Com'n* (1973) 389 Mich. 96, 204 N.W.2d 218, 224 (hereafter *Regents-Michigan*); *City of Cambridge and Cambridge Hospital House Officers Association, supra,* 2 MLC 1450, 1463; *Wyckoff Heights Hospital* (1971) 34 SLRB 625, 631 (New York State Labor Relations Board); *Bronx Eye Infirmary, Inc.* (1970) 33 SLRB 245, 250; *The Long Island College Hospital* (1970) 33 SLRB 161, 172-173; *Brooklyn Eye and Ear Hospital* (1969) 32 SLRB 65, 74; see also *Albert Einstein College, Etc.* (1970) 33 SLRB 465, 467; but see *Pa. Ass'n of Int. & Res. v. Albert Einstein Med. Ctr.* (1977) 470 Pa. 562, 369 A.2d 711, 714.) Although these collective bargaining statutes did not contain a provision like subdivision (f), many of the factors which led to the conclusion that housestaff are employees are similar to those which are appropriately considered under a subdivision (f) analysis.

In view of the foregoing, it is clear that the Legislature did not intend to preclude housestaff from coverage under the Act. Rather, it left that determination to PERB. Under subdivision (f), the Board determines whether students are employees under the Act by assessing whether the educational objectives are subordinate to the services students perform and whether according them collective bargaining rights would further the purposes of the Act. Since PERB made such a finding here, the only remaining issue is whether there is substantial evidence to support it.

III

"[T]he relationship of a reviewing court to an agency such as PERB ... is generally one of deference."... Such deference is mandated by HEERA itself. "The findings of the board with respect to questions of fact, including ultimate facts, if supported by substantial evidence on the record considered as a whole, are conclusive." (§ 3564, subd. (c).)

This court recently reaffirmed the limited nature of judicial review of a labor board's determinations under the substantial evidence standard. "Of course, we do not reweigh the evidence. If there is a plausible basis for the Board's factual decisions, we are not concerned that contrary findings may seem to us equally reasonable, or even more so. [Citations.] We will uphold the Board's decision if it is supported by substantial evidence on the whole record. [Citations.]" ...

Under the substantial evidence standard, when a labor board chooses between two conflicting views, a reviewing court may not substitute its judgment for that of the Board. As the United States Supreme Court has observed, "To be sure, the requirement for canvassing 'the whole record' in order to ascertain substantiality does not furnish a calculus of value by which a reviewing court can assess the evidence. Nor was it intended to negative the function of the Labor Board as one of those agencies presumably equipped or informed by experience to deal with a specialized field of knowledge, whose findings within that field carry the authority of an expertness which courts do not possess and therefore must respect. Nor does it mean that even as to matters not requiring expertise a court may displace the Board's choice between two fairly conflicting views, even though the court would justifiably have made a different choice had the matter been before it *de novo.*" (*Universal Camera Corp. v. Labor Bd.* (1951) 340 U.S. 474, 488, 71 S. Ct. 456, 465, 95 L. Ed. 456.)

PERB's review of the evidence revealed that the patient care services performed by housestaff were an important part of the hospital's overall service delivery. The Board also found that although housestaff did receive educational benefits in the course of their programs, this aspect was subordinate to the services they performed. The Board made this determination based on (1) the substantial quantity of time housestaff spend on clinical activities and direct patient care, (2) the nature of the procedures housestaff perform with little or no supervision, (3) the professional guidance they provide for interns, medical students and other hospital employees such as nurses and technicians, (4) the extensive indicia of employment that characterize housestaff as employees rather than students, and (5) the extent of the educational benefit and training received by housestaff. A review of the record demonstrates that the Board's finding was supported by substantial evidence.

There was abundant testimony that housestaff provide valuable patient-care services. From their first year of residency, housestaff are immersed in all aspects of direct patient care. They perform physical examinations, obtain patients' medical histories, develop treatment plans, prescribe drugs, administer dangerous drugs which nurses are not permitted to administer, and perform various operations and procedures. First-year residents normally write all orders for patient treatment and prescriptions. Housestaff are also required to supervise other hospital personnel such as nurses and technicians.

. . . .

Housestaff also work very long hours. An 80- or 100-hour week is not uncommon. More than 75 percent of that time is usually spent in direct patient care.

The remaining time is spent in didactic, or instructional, activities. These activities consist of lectures, weekly "grand rounds" during which cases are discussed with faculty, and "attending rounds" during which housestaff visit patients with an attending physician or the chief resident. In some specialties, a portion of the resident's time is set aside for intensive classroom, instructional or research activity. Since patient care is their primary responsibility, it is not uncommon for housestaff to be absent from didactic activities.

The extensive indicia of employment status also weigh in favor of the Board's findings. Housestaff are paid with monthly payroll checks from which federal and state income taxes are withheld. In 1979, annual salaries ranged from $15,100 to $21,800. Housestaff receive annual step and cost of living increases. They complete personnel forms, signing as "employees."

Housestaff receive several fringe benefits including paid vacations and medical coverage. Their medical malpractice and workers' compensation insurance is paid for by the University. On the other hand, housestaff are not included in the University's retirement system and do not receive life insurance or state unemployment insurance benefits. However, these facts do not detract from other evidence which strongly indicates employee status.

In addition, most indicia of student status are lacking, an omission which provides further support for PERB's conclusion. Although housestaff are eligible for financial aid, they pay no tuition or student fees. They do not take University examinations. They receive no grades. They do not complete registration forms processed by the registrar's office. They receive no degrees after they have completed their residencies.

....

The University argues that residency programs are primarily of an educational nature. It contends that (1) housestaff participate in the residency programs in order to further their educational development, (2) residency programs are developed by the various departments of the different medical schools to ensure that educational objectives predominate, (3) clinical service and the various tasks and duties required of housestaff are of an educational value, (4) the programs include participation in various didactics such as grand rounds, lectures and efforts to keep informed of the latest medical literature, and (5) clinic service is required by the Essentials.

The fact that housestaff obtain an educational benefit from providing direct patient-care services does not mean services are subordinate to educational objectives. Such services are undertaken for a patient's welfare. Obviously, patient demands are such that services must be performed without regard to whether they will provide any educational benefit.

Many services housestaff perform become routine and do not have a continuing educational value. That housestaff must continue to perform them supports PERB's conclusion that the "educational" side of the scale is subordinate to the "services" side.

Also, housestaff do not administer procedures on patients simply to "polish their skills." Rather, their day-to-day routine, like that of regular physicians, is dictated almost entirely by the exigencies of injury and disease. In short, although housestaff obviously receive intensive professional training through their work, there is substantial evidence to support the Board's finding that educational objectives are subordinate to the services they perform. In light of that substantial evidence, this court must defer to PERB.

The next step in determining whether housestaff are employees under subdivision (f) is to assess the Board's finding that granting collective bargaining rights to housestaff would further the purposes of HEERA. This determination necessarily involves questions of fact and policy. It is also necessary to bear in mind PERB's expertise in this area.

In enacting HEERA, the Legislature found that the people of this state "have a fundamental interest in the development of harmonious and cooperative labor relations between the public institutions of higher education and their employees." (§ 3560, subd. (a).) The Legislature also found that it would be "advantageous and desirable" to grant collective bargaining rights to higher education employees. (See *id.*, subd. (b).) As the Legislature declared, "[i]t is the purpose of this chapter to provide the means by which relations between each higher education employer and its employees may assure that the responsibilities and authorities granted to the separate institutions ... are carried out in an atmosphere which permits the fullest participation by employees in the determination of conditions of employment which affect them." (*Id.*, subd. (e).) "It is the further purpose of this chapter to provide orderly and clearly defined procedures for meeting and conferring and the resolution of impasses, and to define and prohibit certain practices which are inimical to the public interest." (§ 3561, subd. (a).)

The Board found and the record demonstrates that there are substantial employment concerns which affect housestaff, particularly in the area of wages, hours and working conditions. Salaries, vacation time, fringe benefits and hours are manifestly amenable to collective negotiations and have a direct and primary impact on the employment relationship of housestaff with the University. The Board concluded that according housestaff collective bargaining rights would further the purposes of the Act because it would enable them to participate fully in the determination of employment conditions which affect them. Further, the interest of developing "harmonious and cooperative labor relations" would be advanced since a viable mechanism for resolving their differences would be available.

PERB also suggested that denying housestaff collective bargaining rights would have serious ramifications in the public health care field. In addition, PERB found that according collective bargaining rights to housestaff would provide a viable mechanism for resolving disputes and minimize the potential for strikes. Lastly, PERB recognized that the quality of patient care is no doubt affected by the conditions under which housestaff are required to render services, and that bargaining over such matters as hours and working conditions may result in higher quality health care.

Given PERB's expertise in this area and the reasonableness of its conclusions, deference to PERB's finding is warranted.

The University asserts that if collective bargaining rights were given to housestaff the University's educational mission would be undermined by requiring bargaining on subjects which are intrinsically tied to the educational aspects of the residency programs. This "doomsday cry" seems somewhat exaggerated in light of the fact that the University engaged in meet-and-confer sessions with employee organizations representing housestaff *prior* to the effective date of HEERA.

Moreover, the University's argument is premature. The argument basically concerns the appropriate scope of representation under the Act. (See § 3562, subd. (q).) Such issues will undoubtedly arise in specific factual contexts in which one side wishes to bargain over a certain subject and the other side does not. These scope-of-representation issues may be resolved by the Board when they arise, since it alone has the responsibility "[t]o determine in disputed cases whether a disputed item is within or without the scope of representation." (§ 3563, subd. (b).)

The University also argues that permitting collective bargaining for housestaff may lead to strikes. However, it is widely recognized that collective bargaining is an alternative dispute resolution mechanism which diminishes the probability that vital services will be interrupted. (See *San Diego Teachers Assn. v. Superior Court, supra,* 24 Cal. 3d at pp. 8-9, 13, 154 Cal. Rptr. 893, 593 P.2d 838.)

Finally, the University argues that the brief tenure of housestaff's relationship with the University undermines the conclusion that coverage would further the purposes of the Act. The University acknowledges that many other individuals whose relationship with the University is of short duration have been accorded employee status with full bargaining rights. Housestaff should not be treated differently. As the record demonstrates, housestaff in certain residency programs may be employed by the University for up to six years.

Since there is substantial evidence to support the Board's finding that educational objectives are subordinate to the services performed by housestaff and granting collective bargaining rights to them will further the purposes of the Act, the Board's conclusion that housestaff are employees must be affirmed.

IV

The HEERA does not preclude housestaff from being considered employees. The Legislature specifically intended that PERB determine whether students are employees under the Act by assessing whether the educational objectives are subordinate to the services students perform and whether according them collective bargaining rights would further the purposes of the Act. Here, the Board's determination to that effect is supported by substantial evidence. Therefore, the Board properly concluded that housestaff are employees under HEERA.

The Board's decision is affirmed. The matter is remanded to the Board for reconsideration of its remedy in light of the defunct status of PNHA....

MOSK, BROUSSARD and REYNOSO, JJ., concur.

[The dissenting opinion of Justice Lucas is omitted.]

NOTES

1. The Pennsylvania Supreme Court in *Philadelphia Ass'n of Interns & Residents v. Albert Einstein Med. Center,* 470 Pa. 565, 369 A.2d 711 (1976), held, that hospital interns, residents, and clinical fellows were not public employees covered by the Pennsylvania PERA since the primary thrust of their hospital affiliation was to continue their medical education rather than to provide services as normal wage earners. The court observed that the purpose of the Act was to provide "for stability accounted for by a continuous employer-employee relationship" and that "[t]he interns, residents, and fellows had no such interest."

2. Are prisoners in state correctional institutions entitled to representations for the purposes of collective bargaining? In *Prisoners' Labor Union v. Helsby,* 44 A.D.2d 708, 354 N.Y.S.2d 694 (1974), the court sustained PERB's dismissal of representation petitions filed by prisoners' labor unions seeking to represent inmates, noting that "[i]f there be merit in petitioners' claims of a right to organize and bargain collectively, it is for the Legislature so to determine." The Massachusetts Labor Relations Commission ruled in *Commonwealth of Mass. Dep't of Cors. & Walpole Chapter of the Nat'l Prisoners' Reform Ass'n,* GERR No. 532, B-1 (1973), that prisoners were not state employees for the purposes of the state collective bargaining law. Accord *Salah v. PLRB,* 95 L.R.R.M. 2731 (Pa. Ct. C.P. 1977). But see *Michigan Dep't of Cors.,* GERR No. 552, B-13 (1974), where the MERC dismissed a representation petition filed by a group of prisoners on the ground that it had no jurisdiction over state agencies, but nevertheless observed that there was a sufficient employer-employee relationship to warrant collective bargaining for prisoners.

In two states — Delaware and Hawaii — prison inmates are specifically excluded from coverage under the public sector bargaining law. Del. Code Ann. tit. 13, § 1301(b) (1977); Haw. Rev. Stat. § 89-6(c) (1985).

3. Does the separation of powers doctrine preclude applying a public sector collective bargaining statute to employees of the judiciary? In *County of Kane v.*

Carlson, 116 Ill. 2d 186, 507 N.E.2d 482 (1987), the Illinois Supreme Court held "that the inclusion of judicial employees within the [Public Labor Relations] Act does not by itself trench on the separation of powers principle or on the general administrative and supervisory authority granted by the Constitution to the judicial branch." While the court thus upheld the constitutionality of the Illinois Act to employees of the judicial branch, the court noted that the instant litigation involved "preliminary attempts to gauge the scope of the Act" and that "[p]articular problems, including some on a constitutional level, are sure to arise as the broad provisions of the Act are applied to the unique workings of the judicial branch ...." Contra *Matter of Mich. Emp. Rels. Comm'n's Order,* 406 Mich. 647, 281 N.W.2d 299 (1979) (principles of separation of power preclude MERC from assuming jurisdiction over the Michigan Supreme Court and its employees).

4. Where a state constitution grants public employees the right to bargain collectively, is it unconstitutional for the legislature to exclude a category of individuals such as graduate assistants from coverage under the state's public sector collective bargaining law? In *United Faculty of Fla., Local 1847 v. Board of Regents, State Univ. Sys.,* 417 So. 2d 1055 (Fla. Dist. Ct. App. 1982), the court held that the statutory exclusion of graduate assistants from the definition of public employees covered by the Florida Public Employment Relations Act was unconstitutional. The court ruled that there was no compelling state interest advanced which would permit denying graduate assistants the right to engage in collective bargaining.

E. SELECTION OF THE COLLECTIVE BARGAINING REPRESENTATIVE

1. SECRET BALLOT ELECTION

Most of the comprehensive public sector collective bargaining statutes provide, as the Alaska statute does, that "[i]f the labor relations agency finds that there is a question of representation, it shall direct an election by secret ballot to determine whether or by which organization the employees desire to be represented and shall certify the results of the election." Alaska Stat. § 23.40.100(b) (1972). Adopting the practice under the NLRA, most of the state acts further provide that an employee organization is to be certified if it receives a majority of the votes *cast* in the election. In other words, if there are 100 employees in the unit and 80 employees vote in the election, only 41 votes favoring representation would be needed for certification, even though this would not constitute a majority of the employees in the unit. There are some exceptions, however. For example, the Indiana law covering certificated school employees provides that "[c]ertification as the exclusive representative shall ... be granted only to a school employee organization that has been selected, in a secret ballot election, by a majority of all of the employees in an appropriate unit as their representative." Ind. Code Ann. § 20-7.5-1-10(c)(4) (Burns Supp. 1990).

In addition to conducting secret ballot elections, the various labor relations agencies are frequently called upon to decide who is eligible to vote in such elections. Employees who are not on the active payroll because of illness, vacation, leave of absence and those who are on layoff but have a reasonable expectation of being recalled are generally considered eligible to vote in representation elections. Occasionally, this is specifically spelled out in the applicable statute or ordinance. For instance, the Los Angeles ordinance provides that employees who did not work in the period immediately prior to the election "because of illness, vacation or authorized leaves of absence" are entitled to vote. Probationary employees are considered eligible voters since they share a community of interest with other employees in the unit and have a reasonable expectation of becoming permanent employees. See *Taylor Cty., Highway Dep't,* Decision No. 8178 (Wis. ERC 1967); *Department of Navy, Navy Exch., Mayport, Fla.,* A/SLMR No. 24 (1971).

2. CARD CHECK OR OTHER MEANS

Several of the comprehensive public sector collective bargaining statutes provide that the labor relations agency has the authority to ascertain whether the employees desire to be represented by methods other than conducting a secret ballot election. For example, section 207 of the New York Taylor Law gives the PERB the authority to resolve questions concerning representation "on the basis of dues deduction authorization and other evidences or, if necessary, by conducting an election." N.Y. Civ. Serv. Law § 207 (McKinney 1983). The Connecticut statute provides that the State Board of Labor Relations has the authority to either direct a secret ballot election, or "use any other suitable method to determine whether and by which employee organization the employees desire to be represented." Conn. Gen. Stat. Ann. § 7-471(1)(B) (West 1989). This latter provision is very similar to the language in the National Labor Relations Act as originally enacted in 1935. When Congress amended the NLRA in 1947, the phrase "any other suitable method" was deleted.

NOTES

1. The Idaho Fire Fighters Bargaining Law provides that

The organization selected by the majority of the firefighters in any city, county, fire district or political subdivision shall be recognized as the sole and exclusive bargaining agent for all of the firefighters in the Fire Department, unless and until recognition of said bargaining agent is withdrawn by a vote of the majority of the firefighters of such department. Idaho Code § 44-1803 (Supp. 1990.)

The Georgia and Wyoming Fire Fighter Bargaining Laws contain substantially similar provisions. Under such a provision, may an employer require that the petitioning organization demonstrate that it, in fact, has been selected by a majority of the members of a given fire department? May an employer, for example, condition the grant of recognition upon the holding of a secret ballot election? Under a similar provision in the Oklahoma law prior to its amendment, the Oklahoma Attorney General ruled that a city had no right to establish the standards and procedures for the selection of a bargaining agent. Okla. Op. Att'y Gen. No. 71-420 (Dec. 29, 1971).

2. In *Bowman v. Hackensack Hosp. Ass'n,* 116 N.J. Super. 260, 282 A.2d 48 (1971), the New Jersey Superior Court rejected an employer's contention that a bargaining order should not be entered until an election was held to determine the union's majority status. The court noted that there were relatively few employees in the bargaining unit and that the union's majority status had been established by the pro-union trial testimony of a substantial majority of the unit members.

3. Can previously unrepresented employees be added to an existing bargaining unit without an election? In *Polk Cty. Sch. Bd. v. PERC,* 399 So. 2d 520 (Fla. App. 1981), the court held that the Florida PERC had to conduct a self-determination election to determine whether unrepresented employees wanted to become part of an existing bargaining unit or whether they wanted to remain outside the unit and unrepresented. The court observed that there is no "public policy reason to deny public employees the same opportunity as private employees to vote on the matter before adding [previously unrepresented] employees to an existing collective bargaining unit."

3. POST-ELECTION OBJECTIONS TO REPRESENTATION ELECTION

BRANCH COUNTY ROAD COMMISSION

1969 MERC Lab. Op. 247 (Mich. Emp. Relations Comm'n)

[At an employee meeting three days before a scheduled representation election employees were informed that the Branch County Road Commission had previously decided to give the employees a 25 cents per hour wage increase but that it could not do so because the Teamsters had filed a petition for an election. The employees were also told that if the Teamsters did not win the election the Commission would bargain with the Employees Association (which did not participate in the election) and agree to a three-year contract with a cost-of-living provision, a benefit which the employees had not previously enjoyed. When the Teamsters lost the election, it filed objections to the election based on the foregoing conduct.]

These circumstances establish that the intent and purpose of the Road Commission and its agents in holding the meeting, was to discourage the employees from voting for representation by the Teamsters union, and in addition was showing favoritism towards another organization that was not participating in the election.

We agree with the statement of the National Labor Relations Board, in *Baltimore Catering Company,* 148 N.L.R.B. 970, wherein that Board stated:

"Although the granting of benefits during the relevant period preceding an election is not necessarily cause for setting aside an election, the Board has set aside elections where it appears that the granting of the benefits at that particular time was calculated to influence the employees in their choice of a bargaining representative. In the absence of evidence demonstrating that the timing of the announcement of changes and benefits was governed by factors other than the pendency of the election, the Board will regard interference with employee freedom of choice as the motivating factor. The burden of establishing a justifiable motive remains with the employer. The fact that the employees may have known about or otherwise anticipated the increase in wages is not necessarily controlling. The crucial determination is whether the benefits were conferred for the purpose of influencing the employees in their choice of bargaining representatives and were of a type reasonably calculated to have that effect."

Accordingly, we hereby sustain the Objections to Elections discussed above, and direct an Election Officer of the Board to conduct a new election according to the attached Direction of Second Election, to determine whether the employees in the unit desire to be represented by Teamsters, State, County and Municipal Workers, Local 214, or no labor organization.

NOTE

As in the principal case, where it is determined that objectionable conduct has taken place which affected the outcome of the election, the usual remedy is to direct that a new election be conducted. Suppose, however, an employer engages in serious misconduct which would make it difficult, if not impossible, to assure that a new election would be an adequate remedy for the proven misconduct. In such circumstances, does a PERB or PERC have the authority to order the public employer to recognize and bargain with the union based on authorization cards showing that the union once had majority support? In *NLRB v. Gissel Packing Co.,* 395 U.S. 575, 89 S. Ct. 1918, 23 L.Ed.2d 547 (1969), the Supreme Court held that the NLRB had the authority to issue a bargaining order in such a case, noting:

If the Board could enter only a cease-and-desist order and direct an election or a rerun, it would in effect be rewarding the employer and allowing him "to profit from [his] own wrongful refusal to bargain," *Franks Bros. supra,* at 704, while at the same time severely curtailing the employees' right freely to determine whether they desire a representative. The employer could continue to delay or disrupt the election processes and put off indefinitely his obligation to bargain; and any election held under these circumstances would not be likely to demonstrate the employees' true desires. [Brackets in *Gissel*]

Relying on *Gissel,* the Wisconsin Supreme Court in *WERC v. City of Evansville,* 69 Wis. 2d 140, 230 N.W.2d 688 (1975), held that the Wisconsin Commission had the remedial authority to issue a bargaining order, reasoning that "[i]f the Wisconsin Employment Relations Commission did not have the power to order union recognition under circumstances such as those in the instant case, employees of municipalities, who under ... [Wisconsin law] do not have the right to strike, would be defenseless and without any meaningful remedy against an employer who followed a course of threats and coercion." Cf. *Galloway Twp. Bd. of Educ. v. Galloway Twp. Ass'n of Educ. Secretaries,* 78 N.J. 1, 393 A.2d 207 (1978).

ILLINOIS STATE SCHOLARSHIP COMMISSION
2 PERI ¶ 1125 (Ill. Ed. Lab. Rel. Bd. 1986)

On March 25, 1986, Petitioner, American Federation of State, County and Municipal Employees, AFL-CIO ("AFSCME") filed Exceptions with the Illinois Educational Labor Relations Board ("Board") to the Hearing Officer's Recommended Decision and Order in this matter. The Respondent, Illinois State Scholarship Commission ("ISSC"), also filed Exceptions to the decision on that date and on April 23, 1986, filed a Brief in Response to AFSCME's Exceptions. On May 27, 1986, the Illinois Education Association-NEA ("IEA") filed a Brief Amicus Curiae challenging several of the Hearing Officer's conclusions and on August 13, 1986, ISSC filed a response to the amicus curiae brief. After reviewing the Hearing Officer's Recommended Decision and Order, all briefs submitted in this matter, and the hearing record, we hereby affirm the Hearing Officer's decision for the reasons stated herein.

I

ISSC is a state agency that administers various financial aid programs for post-secondary students. It operates out of offices located in Chicago, Deerfield and Springfield. On January 24, 1985, AFSCME filed a petition with the Board seeking representation of a unit of approximately 200 clerical and technical employees of ISSC. Of these employees, 190 work at ISSC's Deerfield facility. On February 20, 1985, AFSCME and ISSC executed an Agreement for Consent Election authorizing an election among the employees at the three facilities to determine whether they wanted to be represented by AFSCME. An election was held among the employees at ISSC's Chicago and Springfield offices on March 14, 1985, and at its Deerfield facility the following day. With 198 votes counted, the results of the election yielded 123 votes for "no representation" and 75 votes for representation by AFSCME.

On March 22, 1985, AFSCME filed timely objections to the conduct of the election at ISSC's Deerfield facility alleging that:

(1) Through statements and a course of conduct, the Employer threatened to contract out bargaining unit work should AFSCME become the bargaining representative.

(2) Through a course of conduct and statements to the employees, the Employer threatened loss of "flex" time should AFSCME become the bargaining representative.

(3) Through a course of conduct and statements, the Employer threatened harsher standards of determining employee misconduct leading to disciplinary action.

(4) Through statements, the Employer threatened to engage in protracted bargaining should AFSCME become the bargaining representative, culminating in the likelihood of a strike. Furthermore, the Employer threatened that should the strike occur, the striking employees would likely be permanently replaced with no right of reinstatement to active employment.

(5) Through statements, the Employer threatened to delay the bargaining process, should AFSCME become the bargaining representative, resulting in further delay in economic improvements for members of the bargaining unit.

(6) The Employer engaged in unlawful acts of surveillance and intimidation by requiring employees to submit to individual interrogation and meetings with respect to the Union election with supervisors.

....

(8) The Employer inequitably applied a rule prohibiting campaigning with respect to the representation election during working time by allowing an (sic) encouraging employees to solicit antiunion support during working time and by assigning supervisors to such activity.

....

After investigating the objections, the Executive Director found probable cause that improper conduct occurred which could have affected the outcome of the election and set the matter for hearing pursuant to Section 8 of the Illinois Educational Labor Relations Act, Ill. Rev. Stat., ch. 48, par. 1701 et seq. ("Act") and the Board's Rules at 80 Ill. Adm. Code 1110.150(d).

A hearing on the matter was held on April 10, 11, 12, 15, 29, on May 5, and on June 4, 5, 1985. The Hearing Officer issued a Recommended Decision and Order on February 5, 1986, overruling all the objections filed against ISSC.
....

In consideration of the merits of this case, we initially take cognizance of the source of our authority to review objections to an election and the purpose of such authority. The purpose of the Act as set forth in Section 1 is to promote orderly and constructive relationships between educational employees and their employers. In an attempt to achieve harmonious relationships between the two groups, the General Assembly granted employees the right to organize and bargain collectively through representatives of their own free choice, as well as the right to refrain from such activities. It also established procedures to provide for the exercise and protection of these rights, one of which is the representation election whereby educational employees vote on whether or not they wish to be represented by an exclusive representative for the purpose of collective bargaining.

Recognizing the potential for election impropriety, the General Assembly established a procedure by which objections to an election may be filed with the Board on the grounds that "improper conduct occurred which affected the outcome of the election." Where objections to an election are filed, the Board must fully inquire into the circumstances of the election to determine whether there is "probable cause that improper conduct occurred (which) could have affected the outcome of the election." If so, a hearing must be held and a new election ordered if "the outcome of the election was affected by improper conduct."[7]

In conducting that hearing, we will presume that ballots cast in an election conducted under the auspices of this agency, and under the safeguards of our election procedures, accurately reflect the desires of the employees. For that reason, the burden is on the objecting party to show that objectionable conduct occurred, and that such conduct affected the outcome of the election.

In determining whether election conduct "affected the outcome of the election," we will use our authority as a quasi-judicial body to draw reasonable inferences from the facts presented. No testimony regarding actual interference is necessary. Rather, we will draw on our experience to determine if the alleged misconduct reasonably could be expected to interfere with employees['] free choice, and thus affect the outcome of the election.

It is our judgment that employee free choice in representation matters is crucial. Therefore, it is our duty in regulating the election process to provide an election atmosphere not unlike a "laboratory" in which the true desires of the employees may be determined.[10] However, although we adopt a "laboratory"

---

[7]...

It is important to note that a finding of improper election conduct does not necessarily imply that the party charged with having engaged in the conduct may also be found to have committed an unfair labor practice under Section 14 of the Act which sets forth those practices that both employers and employee organizations are prohibited from engaging in. That the General Assembly established procedures to review election objections separate and apart from unfair labor practice charges is a recognition that there may exist conduct which impairs the integrity of the election process, though that same conduct does not constitute an unfair labor practice.

[10]See, *General Shoe Corp.*, 77 NLRB 124, 127, 21 LRRM 1337 (1948).

conditions standard, it is not at the expense of chilling a free and vigorous exchange of ideas. Accordingly, we will look at all of the facts realistically and practically, and will not insist upon a totally pristine preelection environment. Only where election misconduct, whether it be an unfair labor practice or otherwise, could reasonably be found to interfere with employee free choice will we set aside an election.[12] For only then would it "affect the outcome of the election" as required by the Act.

We acknowledge that not all of the cases brought before us may be amenable to easy application of the standard set forth above. Nevertheless, we will utilize our experience in the labor relations field to decide election objection issues brought before us on a case-by-case basis.

In the instant matter, AFSCME filed objections to the election based upon ten (10) separate allegations. As to those allegations, we affirm those factual findings of the Hearing Officer that were not challenged by the parties. After reviewing the record and ISSC's exceptions to specific findings of the Hearing Officer, we also affirm those findings that were challenged, and we have discussed them where relevant to our conclusions below.

Objection No. 1[13]

AFSCME first alleges that:

Through statements and a course of conduct, the Employer threatened to contract out bargaining unit work should AFSCME become the bargaining representative.

According to the Hearing Officer, AFSCME claimed that statements made by ISSC Deputy Executive Director Keith Jepsen on March 14, 1985, indicated that "an AFSCME victory would result in the loss of benefits, protracted and futile negotiations, and a great likelihood that work functions would be contracted out" (Decision at p. 22). The Hearing Officer found that Jepsen's comments regarding subcontracting and strike contingency planning were statements of "factual probabilities and circumstances related to union representation" within an employer's right to discuss, and that AFSCME failed to establish that a threat to subcontract had been made or that if a threat was made, it substantially interfered with the employee's free choice (Decision at p. 23). We affirm that determination for the reasons set forth below.

We initially rule that during an election campaign, employer threats to change terms and conditions of employees' employment if the employees vote to unionize, are objectionable conduct, which if objectively determined to have affected the election results, will sustain a challenge to the election because such

---

[12] In this regard, we specifically reject the NLRB's holding in *Dal-Tex Optical Co., Inc.*, 137 NLRB 1782, 50 LRRM 1489 (1962) in which it held that conduct violative of Section 8(a)(1) of the National Labor Relations Act is *a fortiori*, conduct which interferes with the exercise of a free and untrammeled choice in an election. Rather, we will look at all of the circumstances to determine if the alleged misconduct could reasonably be expected to interfere with the employees' free choice.

[13] Although AFSCME did not separately file exceptions to each objection, it has specifically challenged what it considers to be an implied standard established by the Hearing Officer for evaluating employer election conduct, that is that threats of reprisal for unionizing must be clear and unambiguous before they are deemed objectionable. In consideration of this exception, we will review, seriatim, the Hearing Officer's rulings as to alleged threats to employees' working conditions as set forth in AFSCME's Objections 1 through 5.

conduct renders employee free choice improbable.[14] However, as noted above, it is the burden of the objecting party to show that a particular statement or action constituted a threat and that the statement or action might reasonably be expected to have affected the outcome of the election.

In the instant matter, the Hearing Officer found that Deputy Executive Director Jepsen addressed a large group of ISSC employees on March 14, 1985 and read from a speech which included the following comments regarding subcontracting:

> Another thing you should remember about collective bargaining and adversarial relationships is that sometimes people get backed into a corner and do things that later seem like they could have been avoided. I ask you to read again, carefully, what I've written about strikes in Reason #9 to Vote NO. There are a lot of companies just 'chomping at the bit' to sell us contractual services. Some of them say they only need a matter of days to come in and 'hel[p] us out of a jam.' Of course, I hope such a 'jam,' as they call it, never occurs here.

> Incidentally, I'd like to correct a misunderstanding about our current outside contract and me. Even though my belief is that free enterprise can usually "do more with less" than government, in 1981 when I reduced the Scholarships and Grants staff by 50% and contracted out our *MAP* processing, *not one sole was put out of ISSC.* Every person who left Scholarships and Grants, and wanted to work for ISSC, was transferred to a position which most later said they enjoyed — some even saying enjoyed more. By the way, *if* Larry and I both wanted *to contract out* the rest of our work, don't you think we would have done it by now? Again, I ask you, please don't allow some union to paint ISSC into a corner, because the mission of ISSC supersedes *all of us* (emphasis in original text) (Dec. at p. 17).

Also, on March 6, 1985, in the "Staff Courier," an ISSC in-house publication, Jepsen responded to a series of written questions which had been proposed

---

[14] In this regard, we find instructive the Supreme Court's analysis of employer speech in *NLRB v. Gissel Packing Co.,* 395 U.S. 575, 71 LRRM 2481 (1969). In *Gissel,* the Court was faced with the employer's contention that its campaign rhetoric to employees is protected by the first amendment to the United State Constitution and by Section 8(c) of the Labor Management Relations Act of 1947 ("LMRA") which states that:

The expressing of any views, arguments, or opinion, or the dissemination thereof, whether in written, printed, graphic, or visual form, shall not constitute or be evidence of an unfair labor practice under any of the provisions of this Act, if such expression contains no threat of reprisal or force or promise of benefit.

The Court determined that the employer's right to freedom of speech guaranteed and incorporated in Section 8(c) should be balanced with the employees' right to organize and freely choose a bargaining representative in an untrammeled, noncoercive environment. Affirming the lower court's determination that the employer's statements were unlawful, the Court decided that in balancing the rights of the employer and the employees "an employer's free speech right to communicate his views to his employees is firmly established and cannot be infringed by a union or the (NLRB)...." The Court further stated, however, that an employer's right cannot outweigh the equal rights of the employees to associate freely, as those rights are embodied in (the LMRA) (p. 617).

Thus, [said] the Court, "an employer is free only to tell 'what he reasonably believes will be the likely economic consequences of unionization that are outside his own control' and not 'threats of economic reprisal to be taken solely on his own volition'" (p. 619).

In accordance with *Gissel,* we deem threats to change employees' working conditions to be statements of economic reprisal within the employer's control and beyond a mere predication of the likely economic consequences of unionization.

earlier by AFSCME. Specifically, he made the following response in ISSC's "Reason #9 to Vote No" discussed above in the first excerpt:

"Strikes are very rare," says the union organizer.

ANS: Consider the nightly news. It only takes one strike. When employees are out on an economic strike, they are not paid. It is our understanding of the new law that ISSC could, if needed, legally *hire permanent replacement* for economic strikers, as well as employ contractors to do the work. Permanent replacements are *entitled to the job even after the strike is over,* and the economic striker has no right to bump the replacement. ISSC would definitely bargain in good faith and would do everything reasonable to avoid a strike, but these are the facts (emphasis in original text).

In our view, these statements do not constitute a threat to contract out bargaining unit work simply because AFSCME might become the exclusive representative, and therefore are not objectionable. First, the aim of the first excerpt, especially when read in conjunction with the third excerpt above, is that there are companies willing to sell ISSC services on a contractual basis in the event of a strike by ISSC employees. Deputy Executive Director Jepsen then qualified the statement by saying that he hoped such a situation "never occurs here." Thus, Jepsen avoided giving the impression that ISSC would cause this to happen. Second, reading all three excerpts in context, we find that the thrust of the statements is that ISSC could subcontract services performed by its employees *in the event of a strike* and would conceivably do so *only* because of a strike. Again, however, Jepsen avoided giving the impression that ISSC would cause the strike. Notably, ISSC indicated in the third excerpt that based on its understanding of the new law, it could, if necessary, "legally *hire permanent replacements* for economic strikers, as well as employ contractors to do the work. Permanent replacements are *entitled to the job even after the strike is over,* and the economic striker has no right to bump the replacement...." (emphasis in original text).[15] Based on our reading of ISSC's statements, there is no suggestion that subcontracting would occur if the employees voted to unionize, but only possibly in the event of a subsequent strike. In fact, in the second excerpt, Jepsen reassured ISSC employees that even where ISSC had contracted out services in the past, it nonetheless retained all those employees that were affected. Therefore, we do not find that ISSC's statements constituted a threat to subcontract simply on the grounds of AFSCME's becoming the exclusive representative. Accordingly, we affirm the Hearing Officer's ruling.

---

[15]While neither the Act, the Board's Rules, nor case precedent under the act, expressly or impliedly indicates that an employer may lawfully hire permanent strike replacements or subcontract for services in the event of a strike, there is private sector precedent holding that permanent strike replacements may be hired where necessary to carry on the employer's business and where it is determined that the employer did not commit an unfair labor practice. See e.g., *NLRB v. McKay Radio and Telegraph Co.,* 304 U.S. 333, 2 LRRM 610 (1938). Based upon a reasonable interpretation of private sector precedent, we do not find it objectionable for ISSC to advise its employees of what it reasonably believes it may legally do with respect to subcontracting and striker replacement if presented with a strike.

Objection No. 2

In its second objection to the election, AFSCME alleges that:

Through a course of conduct and statements to the employees, the Employer threatened loss of "flex" time should AFSCME become the bargaining representative.

According to the Hearing Officer's findings, "flex" time is a policy that allows ISSC employees to choose starting times between 7:30 a.m. and 9:00 a.m. in half-hour increments as opposed to restricting employees to a fixed starting time. While the Hearing Officer did find that a major theme of ISSC's campaign was that electing AFSCME would mean a loss of flexibility in the workplace, she did not find that ISSC threatened employees that they would lose the ability to work on a "flex" time schedule. Rather, according to the Hearing Officer, ISSC stressed that "flex" time was a negotiable item like all other benefits and that it would probably be subject to negotiation in the collective bargaining process.

Our review of the record reveals that the Hearing Officer's findings are accurate, and therefore should not be disturbed. Based on these findings, we conclude that AFSCME has failed to establish that ISSC threatened employees with a loss of "flex" time or that it has engaged in other objectionable conduct in addressing the issue of "flex" time. Accordingly, we affirm the Hearing Officer and overrule AFSCME's objection.[18]

Objection No. 3

AFSCME's third objection to the election states that:

Through a course of conduct and statement, the Employer threatened harsher standards of determining employee misconduct leading to disciplinary action.

In its Exceptions, AFSCME presented no evidence to support this allegation. Therefore, we affirm the ruling of the Hearing Officer.

We note, however, that in analyzing this objection, the Hearing Officer considered the fact that ISSC informed employees that their complaints would have to be treated as formalized grievances under a union contract, which process would be controlled by AFSCME rather than the individual. The Hearing Officer determined that these statements did not constitute a threat to employees. She determined that ISSC's failure when discussing the grievance process to inform employees of their right under Section 3 of the Act to present their grievances to the employer without the intervention of the union, was an insufficient reason to set aside the election where there was no showing that the omission was done in a deceptive manner.

By focusing on the manner in which ISSC represented the grievance process, the Hearing Officer applied the private sector standard initially established by the NLRB in *Shopping Kart Food Market*, 228 NLRB 1311, 94 LRRM 1705 (1977) and recently reaffirmed in *Midland National Life Ins. Co.*, 263 NLRB

---

[18]See, *City of North Miami*, 4 FPER 4255 (Fla. PERC, July 11, 1978) (statements by employer that everything is negotiable held lawful); *AFSCME*, also *Wisconsin Council 40*, Case No. 16096-B (Wis. Empl. Rel. Comm., September 26, 1978), CCH Admin. Rulings, para. 40,780 (employer statements that informality of personnel relations could be lost if union won held lawful).

127, 110 LRRM 1489 (1982), holding that the NLRB "will set an election aside not because of the substance of the representation, but because of the deceptive manner in which it was made, a manner which renders employees unable to evaluate the forgery for what it is" (at p. 133). In *Midland,* the NLRB rejected its earlier holding in *Hollywood Ceramics,* 140 NLRB 221, 51 LRRM 1600 (1962) (later readopted in *General Knit of California,* 239 NLRB 619, 99 LRRM 1687 (1978)), that the NLRB would set aside elections:

> where there has been a misrepresentation or other similar campaign trickery, which involves a substantial departure from the truth, at a time which prevents the other party or parties from making an effective reply, so that the misrepresentation, whether deliberate or not, may reasonably be expected to have a significant impact on the election (at p. 224).

Reconsidering the *Hollywood Ceramics* standard, the NLRB in *Midland* stated that it would "no longer probe into the truth or falsity of the parties' campaign statements" or "set aside elections on the basis of misleading campaign statements" (*ibid.,* p. 133). Rather, the NLRB ruled that it would "intervene in cases where a party has used forged documents which render the voters unable to recognize propaganda for what it is" (*id.*).

Applying the *Midland* standard to the instant matter, the Hearing Officer found that ISSC's statements regarding grievance processing were not misrepresentations. We find the Hearing Officer's reliance on *Midland* appropriate and we hereby adopt that standard for application to election objections alleging that misrepresentations were made in a party's campaign statements.[20] We agree with the Hearing Officer's conclusion that ISSC's statements were not improper and we affirm her ruling overruling AFSCME's third objection.

Objection No. 4

AFSCME states as its fourth objection to the election that:

> Through statements, the Employer threatened to engage in protracted bargaining, should AFSCME become the bargaining representative, culminating in the likelihood of a strike. Furthermore, the Employer threatened that should the strike occur, the striking employees would likely be permanently replaced with no right of reinstatement to active employment.

In her decision, the Hearing Officer cited the following address delivered to ISSC employees by Deputy Executive Director Jepsen on March 14, 1985:

> Collective bargaining would be, in my opinion, a pain for all of us. And there's no guarantee anyone would be better off. Let me tell you some of what I've learned about the process. In talking with Pat Winn, the Assistant State's Attorney for Winnebago County, I learned that AFSCME won the right to

---

[20] By adopting the *Midland* standard for review of alleged misrepresentations, we acknowledge that our analysis in these instances will emphasize the parties' right of free speech, even if the exercise of that speech includes misstatements. We view employees subject of the Act as mature and intelligent voters who possess the ability to discriminate between campaign propaganda and hard facts. Moreover, we do not want to chill the parties' ability to wage a rigorous campaign by sitting in judgment of the propriety of their every word. This view is in conformity with our position taken earlier in this decision that robust debate and exposure to different viewpoints leads to more informed voters. In this case there was a great deal of discussion from both sides regarding the issues as well as wide dissemination of campaign literature.

represent county employees on February 2, 1984 — "Ground Hog Day"—
over a year ago. Negotiations *started* on about May 17, — *three and one-half
months* after AFSCME won. So far, they have had over 40 negotiation sessions of many hours duration and still no contract. Says Pat, (and I quote)
"There is considerable frustration among the approximately 400 employees
in the bargaining unit. Employees feel tremendous dissatisfaction as they
have had *no pay increase* since February 2, 1984. The union is not delivering
on their promises" (Emphasis in original text).

This statement continued:

I've also learned that in collective bargaining sometimes employees gain,
sometimes they stay the same, and sometimes they lost. It depends on the
situation and sometimes the negotiators (Jt. Exh. 160A).

Jepsen further asked the employees to consider whether they "really need(ed)
the anxiety of the protracted negotiations" like the situation in Winnebago
County (Rockford) (Jt. Exh. 160C).

The Hearing Officer also considered the following statement contained in
"Reason No. 9 to Vote No":

"Strikes are very rare," says the union organizer.

Consider the nightly news. It only takes one strike. When employees are out
on an economic strike, they are not paid. It is our understanding of the new
law that ISSC could, if needed, legally *hire permanent replacements* for economic strikers, as well as employ contractors to do the work. Permanent
replacements are *entitled to the job even after the strike is over,* and the
economic striker has no right to bump the replacement. ISSC would definitely bargain in good faith and would do everything reasonable to avoid a
strike, but these are the facts.

In the first excerpt, ISSC suggests that the process of collective bargaining may
be a lengthy one as evidenced by AFSCME's record in its representation of
employees in Winnebago County. ISSC's statement does not indicate that *it*
would protract negotiations, but rather, that either the collective bargaining
process itself or AFSCME *could* be the source of delays in bargaining. Moreover, according to the Hearing Officer's undisputed findings, ISSC recognized
and repeatedly acknowledged that it had a duty to bargain in good faith and
that it would fulfill that obligation. In this context, ISSC's references to the
protracted bargaining in Winnebago County would not be interpreted as a
threat by ISSC's employees.

We reach a similar conclusion as to the alleged threat to hire strike replacements or to subcontract bargaining unit work. As we stated in our analysis of
AFSCME's first objection, an employer's predictions of what may occur as a
result of unionization or what it may legally do in case of a strike, are not
improper so long as they are not based on conditions solely within the employer's control. The thrust of ISSC's statements regarding the impact of a
strike concerns the action ISSC reasonably believed it might legally take if a
strike occurred. See discussion at p. 19. Accordingly, we find that AFSCME has
failed to demonstrate that ISSC threatened employees with statements regarding delays in negotiations and its legal recourse in the event of a strike. We
therefore affirm the Hearing Officer's ruling overruling the objection.

Objection No. 5

AFSCME's fifth objection states that:

> Through statements, the Employer threatened to delay the bargaining pro-
> cess, should AFSCME become the bargaining representative, resulting in fur-
> ther delay in economic improvements for members of the bargaining unit.

The Hearing Officer found that this objection was based upon the same evidence AFSCME presented in its fourth objection, *supra,* and she overruled the
objection. However, she credited testimony by Supervisor McGarragher that he
warned employees that "if management was rotten enough they could start
everyone at base pay in negotiations and that if (AFSCME representatives)
Greenberg and Blocker did not like what was negotiated employees could wind
up on strike waiting for them to settle the agreement" (Dec. at p. 27). The
Hearing Officer ruled that even if that comment could be deemed threatening
to the employees, AFSCME failed to show that it affected the outcome of the
election since AFSCME supporters freely rebutted and ignored McGarragher's
comments.

We agree with the Hearing Officer's conclusion and affirm her ruling. In
reaching this result, we consider the fact that McGarragher is a relatively low-
level supervisor, with at least three levels of supervision above him (Tr. 4/29, p.
552), there was no evidence that his statement was widely disseminated and his
comment was offset by ISSC's repeated assurances that it would fulfill its duty to
bargain in good faith. Furthermore, we are not persuaded that a single, isolated
comment by one agent of ISSC, though arguably improper, threatened the
employees' free choice or affected the election results, especially where, as here,
the comment was freely rebutted by AFSCME supporters. See, e.g.,
Morgantown Full Fashioned Hosiery Company, 107 NLRB 1534 (1954) (employee mandate will not be set aside because of "a few isolated threats by over-
zealous minor supervisory personnel."); *Goodyear Clearwater Mill No. 2,* 109
NLRB 1017, 34 LRRM 1481 (1954) (several threats by supervisors insufficient
to set aside election); *The Swingline Company,* 256 NLRB 704, 717 (1981) ("not
every item of objectionable conduct, including acts of interference with employee exercise of rights guaranteed them by Section 7 of the Act, will merit
invalidating the election."); *Caron International, Inc.,* 246 NLRB 1120, 103
LRRM 1066 (1979) (election not set aside despite unlawful supervisor threat to
discharge union adherent).

Objection No. 6

In its sixth objection to the election, AFSCME alleges that:

> The Employer engaged in unlawful acts of surveillance and intimidation by
> requiring employees to submit to individual interrogation and meetings with
> respect to the Union election with supervisors.

The Hearing Officer found that on October 1, 1984, ISSC circulated a memo
to its managerial and supervisory staff giving them the imprimatur to talk to
small groups of employees about the union on agency time but not later than 24
hours before the election. She found that managers and supervisors did, in fact,
conduct small group meetings with employees and, in addition, initiated one-
on-one discussions with employees at their desks and in the employee lounge

area. Specifically, she found that there were several group meetings conducted by ISSC supervisors in which union issues were discussed.

The first of these two meetings was a staff meeting conducted by Client Support Services Supervisor Christine Peterson and was held in a conference room. This meeting was attended by three or four individuals representing approximately half of the employees in that department. The Hearing Officer found that approximately ten minutes into the meeting, Deputy Executive Director intervened and began discussing campaign issues. He initially stated ISSC's positions, but he also elicited comments from AFSCME supporters present as to AFSCME's position on the issues. According to the Hearing Officer, AFSCME supporters were also allowed to respond to questions from employees.

The second of the two small group meetings was convened by Supervisor of Collections McGarragher on March 11, 1985, with four employees in attendance, one of whom was not supervised by him. The meeting was held in the office of Manager of Systems and Procedures Craig Swift, an office that was used for employee meetings in Swift's absence (Tr. 175). McGarragher testified that he selected these employees because they appeared to be undecided and had questions regarding unionization. However, he testified, at the hearing that he could not recall any questions that these employees asked, and the Hearing Officer found that the employees vigorously rebutted McGarragher's statements.

The Hearing Officer further found that Manager of Claims and Collections Shirley Daniel had one-on-one discussions with employees concerning campaign issues while the employees were at their desk or in the employee lounge area. The Hearing Officer applied a totality-of-circumstances approach in analyzing ISSC's conduct described above. Under that analysis, she concluded that AFSCME failed to establish that the small group meetings were inherently coercive or that the one-on-one discussions threatened employees.

No exceptions were taken to the Hearing Officer's finding of fact, and we hereby affirm those findings. In addition, we find that the Hearing Officer applied the proper legal standard, and we agree with her conclusions. As noted by the Hearing Officer, the NLRB in analyzing the propriety of employer meetings with employees to discuss election issues, has alternately taken both a restrictive and a liberal approach. In 1957, in *Peoples Drug Stores,* 119 NLRB 643, 41 LRRM 1141, the NLRB sharply restricted the employer's ability to confer with employees and discuss union issues, holding that "the technique of calling employees individually or in small groups, into a private area removed from the employees' normal workplaces and urging them to reject the union is itself conduct which interferes with the conditions necessary to a free choice by the employees in the selection of a bargaining representative and warrants setting aside the election" (p. 636). However, nineteen years later in *NVF Co.,* 210 NLRB 663, 86 LRRM 1200 (1974), the NLRB overruled *Peoples Drug Stores* to the extent that it embodied a *per se* approach to employer interviews and ruled that it would instead carefully weight all the facts to determine whether such factors as the small size of the groups interviewed, the locus of the interview, the position of the interviewer in the employer's hierarchy, and the tenor of the speaker's remarks, interfered with the employees' free choice in the election. Under the NLRB's sound approach in *NVF Co., supra,* which we adopt, we find that the small group meetings conducted by ISSC supervisory and managerial personnel and the one-on-one discussions did not exceed the bounds of permissible employer speech nor obstruct the employees' right to freely choose a representative.

With regard to the meeting at which Deputy Executive Director Jepsen addressed election issues, we find that Jepsen did not single out employees to influence their vote, but rather opted to speak to all staff present. The findings show that employees were free to discuss the issues and that AFSCME supporters present at the meeting rebutted antiunion statements made by Jepsen. In addition, we do not find that this conference room was threatening to employees; it was a usual meeting place and, as such, would not reasonably be viewed as the locus of final authority.

Similarly, we are not persuaded that Supervisor McGarragher's meeting with employees in Manager Swift's office was improper conduct. We find that, as a low-level supervisor, the potential for McGarragher to interfere with employees' free choice in the election was substantially diminished. Moreover, the office in which the meeting was held — Manager Swift's office — was a regular meeting place and therefore lacked the aura of final authority.

Finally, we hold that the one-on-one meetings that took place between Manager Daniel and ISSC employees were not unlawful. Where, as here, the discussions took place amid a vigorously waged campaign in which AFSCME supporters consistently rebutted antiunion statements, we do not find that the discussions could have affected the outcome of the election.

....

Objection No. 8

The eighth objection AFSCME urges against the election is that:

> The Employer inequitably applied a rule prohibiting campaigning with respect to the representation election during working time by allowing an (sic) encouraging employees to solicit antiunion support during working time and by assigning supervisors to such activity.

The Hearing Officer found that AFSCME failed to prove that ISSC encouraged or supported antiunion campaigning by employees or that antiunion supporters were treated differently than prounion supporters, and, on review of the record, we sustain her finding.

More broadly, AFSCME urges in its exceptions that the Board prohibit public employers under its jursidiction from using their public office to campaign for or against union representation. We find no support in either the language of our statute or its legislative history for the proposition that this Board has the authority to prohibit employers from speaking freely during organizing campaigns. Absent evidence to the contrary, we must assume that the legislature intended to adopt for Illinois the policy on this issue which has long prevailed in the private sector and in most public sector jurisdictions, i.e., that the expression of noncoercive opinion, attitudes and facts by employers may be desirable and necessary to foster debate concerning relevant representation issues and produce informed voters. We also note that on March 25, 1986, House Bill 2939, which proposed to amend the Act to make it an unfair labor practice for a public employer to expend or cause the expenditure of public funds to influence the outcome of a representation election, was introduced to the Illinois House of Representatives. This bill was defeated on May 20, 1986. Accordingly, we cannot read into the act a prohibition that members of the General Assembly chose not to enact.[23]

In the alternative, AFSCME urges that we at least require equal application of workplace solicitation and nonsolicitation rules to employees and managerial or supervisory personnel alike. We decline to so hold.[24] Here again, we have no basis for finding that the legislature intended to modify long-established labor relations precedent in the public and private sectors as expressed in the United States Supreme Court's decision in *NLRB v. Steelworkers, CIO (Nutone, Inc.)*, 357 U.S. 357, 42 LRRM 2324 (1958). In that case, the Court held that enforcement of a valid no-solicitation rule by an employer, who at the same time engaged in antiunion solicitation is not a per se violation of the LMRA. The Court determined that finding a violation depends upon the circumstances of the individual case but expressly states that "it is highly relevant in determining wether a valid rule has been fairly applied" to establish that the rule "truly diminished the ability of the labor organizations involved to carry their message to the employees." The Court placed heavy emphasis on the availability of "alternative channels" of communication which rendered the union's ability to promote its views at least as great as that of the employer to campaign against the union.[25] Here, AFSCME makes no claim that it lacked the opportunity to communicate effectively with employees or that its opportunities were outweighed by those of ISSC. In fact, the evidence strongly indicates that AFSCME waged a very extensive campaign in which it widely communicated its position and vigorously rebutted antiunion statements.

....

VI

On the basis of the foregoing, the Hearing Officer's Recommended Decision and Order overruling AFSCME's objections to the election is affirmed. Accordingly, we hereby certify the results of the March 15, 1985 representation election.

---

[23] It is also noteworthy that the Michigan Employment Relation Commission concurs on this issue. See *Lapeer County General Hospital*, 1980 MERC Vol. XV, p. 534, in which the Commission adopted an administrative law judge's finding that the employer did not violate the Michigan Public Employment Relations Act by using public time and funds to campaign against the union. Accord, *School Board of Leon County*, 5 FPER 10144 (Fla. PERC, May 7, 1979); *Oregon State Employees Association*, Case No. C-19-75 (Oregon Empl. Rel. Bd., December 1, 1977), CCH Admin. Rulings, para. 40,662.

[24] Our holding here on permissible solicitation by either a union or employer is limited to the "office setting" facts of this case and could conceivably be subject to modification in an instructional environment.

[25] See also *Raley's Inc. v. NLRB*, 703 F.2d 410, 112 LRRM 3376 (9th Cir. 1983) and *Okaloosa-Walton Junior College Board of Trustees*, 3 FPER 153 (Fla. Pub. Emp. Rel. Comm., July 29, 1977). It is also noteworthy that this factor was dispositive in several public sector cases where it was held that employees' right to choose a representative had been interfered with because one union had access to the employer's facilities for communication with employees while the same access was denied to a competing union. See e.g., *University Federation of Teachers v. University of Minnesota*, 83 LRRM 2677 (1973); *Illinois State Employees Association*, 4 NPER 14-12018 (Illinois Office of Collective Bargaining, July 22, 1981).

NOTES

1. There is a continuing debate concerning the extent to which a public employer should be allowed to state its views on unionization to employees prior to a representation election. The Illinois Board in the principal case has adopted the NLRA private sector standard, i.e., an employer is permitted to state its views as long as such expressions of opinion do not contain any threat of reprisal or promise of benefit. The Report of the Fortieth American Assembly on Collective Bargaining in American Government recommended a similar approach, stating:

> Public employers at all levels of government should have the right to be active or passive in the face of a union organizing campaign. This right to free speech should not permit coercive conduct or dismissals of union adherents.

Report of the Fortieth American Assembly, Collective Bargaining in American Government 5 (1971). At the other extreme is the approach adopted by the federal government under Executive Order 11491, whereby the federal government, as an employer, maintains "a position of neutrality as far as union representation of its employees is concerned, and Government officials do not mount 'vote no' campaigns." Hampton, *Federal Labor-Management Relations: A Program in Evolution,* 21 Cath. U.L. Rev. 493, 502 (1972). See *Vandenberg Air Force Base,* A/SLMR No. 349 (1974) (election set aside where management did not maintain neutral posture). A position somewhere between these two approaches was recommended by the Federal Reserve System Labor Relations Panel. Thus in *Federal Reserve Bank of San Francisco,* Panel Report and Decision (July 19, 1971), GERR No. 413, A-6 (1971), the Panel, chaired by William E. Simkin, recommended that there be "greater restraint" by the various federal reserve banks in asserting their views on unionization than the NLRB would require of employers in the private sector.

2. In *Oregon Employee Ass'n. v. Department of Commerce,* 98 L.R.R.M. 3076 (Or. Ct. App. 1978), the court affirmed an order of the Oregon Employment Relations Board holding that a state agency was not prohibited "from using state time and funds to campaign against a labor organization in a representation election." The court quoted with approval the ERB's statement that "'[w]ithin the bounds of fair comment, and reasonable and timely opportunity to answer charges leveled, both sides may be heard.'"

3. In *City of New Haven,* Decision No. 1760 (Conn. SBLR 1979), the Connecticut Commission embraced the NLRB's decision in *Shopping Kart,* stating:

> We have always been uncomfortable with the paternalistic assumptions that underlie *Hollywood Ceramics.* Americans are steeped in democratic traditions, and one of the aspects of those traditions is campaign rhetoric or propaganda. Notoriously this does not always stick to the exact truth and American voters have become fairly sophisticated in recognizing such propaganda for what it is and discounting factual claims contained in it. It is only where the statement is made to appear as something other than campaign propaganda — where it is, for example, falsely attributed to a disinterested source that did not issue it (so as to be in effect a forgery) that the voters need this Board's protection.

Accord *Town of Springfield,* Docket Nos. 80-11 *et al.* (Vt. LRB 1980); *City of Ft. Lauderdale,* 4 FPER ¶ 4167 (Fla. PERC 1978).

4. The District of Columbia Board of Labor Relations in *Metropolitan Police Dep't of D.C.,* Decision No. 20 (D.C. BLR 1978), used the *Hollywood Ceramics* standard in setting aside an election based on a union's "serious and material misrepresentation." In this case, the District of Columbia Board specifically refused to adopt the *Shopping Kart* standard. Accord *State of Ill., Dep't of Commerce & Community Affairs,* ULP-133-OCB (Ill. OCB 1980).

5. In *Nebraska Ass'n of Pub. Emps. v. State,* 281 N.W.2d 544, 102 L.R.R.M. 3063 (Neb. 1979), the court, after reviewing the NLRB's decisions in *Hollywood Ceramics, Shopping Kart,* and *General Knit,* stated:

> Because of the unsettled state of the law in this very important area, as indicated by the foregoing authorities, we do not deem it advisable *at this time* to adopt either of the foregoing standards discussed above, nor are we required to follow them. It would appear, as pointed out by plaintiff-appellee NAPE in its brief, that it is fairly inferable from the opinion issued by the Court of Industrial Relations in this case that it has developed a standard which is somewhere between the Hollywood Ceramics philosophy and the new Shopping Kart philosophy, which standard appears to be that where there are material misrepresentations of relevant facts and where there is evidence that those misrepresentations influenced the voters or had a substantial impact on the outcome of the election, the Court of Industrial Relations would set aside the election. (Emphasis in original.)

The court then affirmed the decision of the Nebraska Court of Industrial Relations, holding that "it acted within the scope of its statutory authority, and that its action was not arbitrary, capricious, or unreasonable."

6. In a few jurisdictions rules have been promulgated setting forth the type and kind of conduct that would be sufficient to set aside an election. For example, Rule 5.4(3) of the Rules and Regulations of the Iowa PERB reads as follows:

> The following types of activity, if conducted during the period beginning with the filing of an election petition with the board and ending at the conclusion of the election, and if determined by the board that such activity could have affected the results of the election, shall be considered to be objectionable conduct sufficient to invalidate the results of an election:
>
> a. Electioneering within three hundred feet or within sound of the polling place established by the board during the conduct of the election;
>
> b. Misstatements of material facts by any party to the election or their representative without sufficient time for the adversely affected party to adequately respond;
>
> c. Any misuse of board documents, including an indication that the board endorses any particular choice appearing on the ballot;
>
> d. Campaign speeches to assembled groups of employees during working hours within the twenty-four-hour period before the election;
>
> e. Any polling of employees by a public employer which relates to the employees' preference for or against a bargaining representative;
>
> f. Commission of a prohibited practice;
>
> g. Any other misconduct or other circumstance which prevents employees from freely expressing their preferences in the election.

7. The NLRB in *Excelsior Underwear, Inc.,* 156 N.L.R.B. 1236 (1966), held that an employer is required to furnish a petitioning union, as well as any other employee organizations on the ballot, with the names and addresses of all eligible voters within a specified time period prior to the election and that an employer's failure to provide the names and addresses of its employees constitutes a valid ground for setting aside an election. The so-called *Excelsior* rule was upheld by the Supreme Court in *NLRB v. Wyman-Gordon Co.*, 394 U.S. 759 (1969). Accord *City of Quincy*, Case No. MCR-1311 (Mass. LRC 1974).

The Illinois Public Labor Relations Act provides that within seven days after a consent election agreement is approved or an election is directed "the public employer shall submit to the labor organization the complete names and addresses of those employees who are determined by the Board to be eligible to participate in the election." Ill. Rev. Stat. ch. 48, ¶ 1609(d) (1986). Although not mandated by statute, the state boards or commissions in Connecticut, Iowa, Maine, Michigan, South Dakota, and Washington have incorporated similar policies in their rules and regulations. In *PLRB v. Upper Darby Twp.*, Case No. C-3935-E (Pa. PLRB 1974), the Pennsylvania Board held it was an unfair labor practice for an employer to refuse to provide the names and addresses of all eligible voters.

8. The Florida PERC in *Laborers Int'l Union v. School Bd. of Alachua Cty.*, 10 FPER ¶ 15216 (Fla. PERC 1984), refused to reconsider its prior determination, contrary to long-established precedent under the National Labor Relations Act, that an employer's captive-audience speech within twenty-four hours of the time when a representation election is held does not constitute *per se* grounds for setting aside a representation election.

F. JUDICIAL REVIEW OF REPRESENTATION PROCEEDINGS

LINCOLN COUNTY MEMORIAL HOSPITAL v. MISSOURI STATE BOARD OF MEDIATION

549 S.W.2d 665, 95 L.R.R.M. 3110 (Mo. Ct. App. 1977)

WASSERSTROM, JUDGE. Lincoln County Memorial Hospital appealed under Section 105.525 (all statutory references herein being referred to RSMo 1969 unless otherwise noted) from a determination by the Missouri State Board of Mediation that all registered nurses of the Hospital, with one exception, constituted an appropriate unit for collective bargaining. From an affirmance by the circuit court of the Board's determination, the Hospital again appeals to this court....

On the present appeal, the Hospital assigns six points of error, the most serious of which complains of the inclusion in the bargaining unit of the nine registered nurses whom the Hospital insists are supervisors or managerial personnel. However, none of the errors assigned by the Hospital can be reached on this appeal unless this court has proper jurisdiction. That in turn depends on whether the Board's determination of the appropriate bargaining unit constitutes an appealable order. If it does not, then the circuit court lacks jurisdiction of the subject matter. *National Ass'n of Women's and Children's Apparel Salesmen, Inc. v. F.T.C.*, 479 F.2d 139, 144, footnote 9 (5th Cir. 1973); *Bd. of Tr. of Mem. Hosp. of Fremont County v. N.L.R.B.*, 523 F.2d 845 (10th Cir. 1975); *State Board of Registration for Healing Arts v. Masters*, 512 S.W.2d 150, 1. c. 159 (Mo. App. 1974).

And the want of jurisdiction by the circuit court would in turn deprive this court of the power to make any decision on the merits. *Shepler v. Shepler*, 348 S.W.2d 607, 609 (Mo. App. 1961); *Allen v. State Department of Public Health and Welfare*, 479 S.W.2d 183, 186 (Mo. App. 1972); *Swetnam v. U.S. By-Prod-*

ucts Corp., 510 S.W.2d 829, 831 (Mo. App. 1974). Even though this jurisdictional issue has not been raised by the parties, it is the duty of this court to consider the problem sua sponte....

The question of whether an appeal lies from an administrative determination of the appropriate bargaining unit, prior to determination of majority representative status, is not answered by the wording of § 105.525, which is ambiguous in this regard.[1] The same question has given rise to much litigation in other jurisdictions, with conflicting results. The rule followed uniformly in the federal courts under the National Labor Relations Act is that such an administrative determination is only interlocutory and is not separately appealable. Except in extraordinary situations, the aggrieved party must await the completion of the administrative process by an election certification and an order compelling the employer to enter into collective bargaining. This result is reached partially on the basis of the statutory language granting the right of appeal, contained in 29 U.S.C.A. § 160. However, these decisions, more importantly for our purposes, rest also in part upon grounds of public policy. Thus in a leading case, *American Federation of Labor v. N.L.R.B.,* 308 U.S. 401, 1. c. 409 (1940) the Supreme Court discussed and relied upon Congressional history to show a legislative purpose to eliminate delay which had occurred under the previous federal law (Public Resolution 44) and which had permitted judicial review at the stage of the determination of the appropriate bargaining unit. In this connection, the Supreme Court quoted the committee report as follows:

"'Weaknesses in Existing Law.... (6) *Obstacles to elections.* — Under Public Resolution 44, any attempt by the Government to conduct an election of representatives may be contested ab initio in the courts, although such election is in reality merely a preliminary determination of fact. This means that the Government can be delayed indefinitely before it takes the first step toward industrial peace. After almost a year not a single case, in which a company has chosen to contest an election order of the Board, has reached decision in any circuit court of appeals.' Sen. Rep. No. 573, Committee on Education and Labor, 74th Cong., 1st Sess., pp. 5, 6.

"After referring to the procedure for review under Public Resolution 44, the House Committee declared: 'The weakness of this procedure is that under the provision for review of election orders employers have a means of holding up the election for months by an application to the circuit court of appeals.... At the present time 10 cases for review of the Board's election orders are pending in circuit court of appeals. Only three have been argued and none have been decided.' House Rep. No. 1147, Committee on Labor, 74th Cong., 1st Sess., p. 6."

---

[1]Section 105.525 grants right of appeal as follows: "Issues with respect to appropriateness of bargaining units and majority representative status shall be resolved by the state board of mediation. In the event that the appropriate administrative body or any of the bargaining units shall be aggrieved by the decision of the state board of mediation, an appeal may be had to the circuit court of the county where the administrative body is located or in the circuit court of Cole County...." § 536.100 and Rule 100.03, governing judicial review of administrative rulings in contested cases generally, provide that the review be of "a final decision." The decisions from other jurisdictions hereinafter referred to generally address the question of whether determination of the appropriate bargaining unit, taken alone, constitutes "a final decision" of the administrative agency.

So also, in another leading case, *Boire v. Greyhound Corporation*, 376 U.S. 473, 1. c. 477-478 (1964), the Supreme Court made the following observations concerning the public policy involved:

"That this indirect method of obtaining judicial review imposes significant delays upon attempts to challenge the validity of Board orders in certification proceedings is obvious. But it is equally obvious that Congress explicitly intended to impose precisely such delays. At the time of the original passage of the National Labor Relations Act in 1935, the House Report clearly delineated the congressional policy judgment which underlay the restriction of judicial review to that provided for in § 9(d):
'When an employee organization has built up its membership to a point where it is entitled to be recognized as the representative of the employees for collective bargaining, and the employer refuses to accord such recognition, the union, unless an election can promptly be held to determine the choice of representation, runs the risk of impairment of strength by attrition and delay while the case is dragging on through the courts, or else is forced to call a strike to achieve recognition by its own economic power. Such strikes have been called when election orders of the National Labor Relations Board have been held up by court review.'"

The same policy of furthering labor peace by not permitting delays in elections is reiterated in *Bd. of Tr. of Mem. Hosp. of Fremont County v. N.L.R.B.*, supra, and in *Bishop v. N.L.R.B.*, 502 F.2d 1024, 1027 (5th Cir. 1974).

A number of state courts in the application of state labor relations statutes have followed the above federal rule. *City Manager of Medford v. State Labor Relations Commission*, 353 Mass. 519, 233 N.E.2d 310 (1968); *Worcester I.T.I. Instructors Ass'n v. Labor Relations Commission*, 357 Mass. 118, 256 N.E.2d 287 (1970); *Harrison v. Labor Relations Commission*, 363 Mass. 548, 296 N.E.2d 196 (1973); *Jordan Marsh Co. v. Labor Relations Commission*, 312 Mass. 597, 45 N.E.2d 925 (1942); *Town of Windsor v. Windsor Police Department Employees Ass'n*, 154 Conn. 530, 227 A.2d 65 (1967); *Southeast Furniture Co. v. Industrial Commission*, 100 Utah 154, 111 P.2d 153 (1941); *McGee v. Local No. 682*, 70 R.I. 200, 38 A.2d 303 (1944); *Klamath County v. Laborers Int'l Union of N.A., Local No. 915*, 534 P.2d 1169 (Or. App. 1975). The opinion last cited typically holds:

"Since (1) the designation of an appropriate bargaining unit is but one step in the process of certifying a bargaining agent with whom the employer is obligated to bargain, (2) several other actions by PERB are necessary to complete the process, and (3) the designation could be of no effect if the employes [sic] vote for no representation, we hold that the designation of an appropriate bargaining unit is not a 'final order' as the term is used in ORS 183.480."

On the other hand, New York, Minnesota and New Jersey have declined to follow the above approach and instead hold that the administrative determination of the appropriate bargaining unit does constitute a final order which is subject to immediate and separate judicial review. The leading case so holding is *Civil Service Employees Association v. Helsby*, 31 A.D.2d 325, 297 N.Y.S.2d 813 (1969), aff'd by a sharply divided vote of the New York Court of Appeals, 24 N.Y.2d 993, 302 N.Y.S.2d 822, 250 N.E.2d 230 (1969). Other cases following the lead of that case are: *Wakshull v. Helsby*, 35 A.D.2d 183, 315 N.Y.S.2d 371

(1970); *Minnesota State College Board v. Public Employment Relations Board,* 228 N.W.2d 551 (Minn. 1975); *County of Gloucester v. Public Employment Relations Commission,* 107 N.J. Super. 150, 257 A.2d 712, 714 (1969). See also the *Pennsylvania Labor Relations Act,* 43 P.S. § 211.9, applied in *Pennsylvania Labor Relations Board v. Butz,* 411 Pa. 360, 192 A.2d 707 (1963).

In determining which of these opposing views should be adopted in Missouri, the most persuasive factor is the public policy reflected in the United States Congressional debates. The potential for calculated stalling of collective bargaining by dilatory tactics, which led Congress to eliminate separate judicial review of the determination of an appropriate bargaining unit, is well illustrated in this very case. By the time this opinion is handed down, it will be more than two years since the Association filed its petition before the Board and there still has not been any certification of a bargaining representative, much less the commencement of any negotiations between the parties. Such a long frustration of the employees' right of collective bargaining is simply unfair. Moreover, the Missouri General Assembly, like the Federal Congress and the legislatures of many other states, has concluded that collective bargaining by public employees serves the public interest by being conducive to peaceful employment relationships in the public sector. Achievement of this public policy requires expeditious completion of the administrative process, and this can best be done by adoption of the federal rule requiring that the entire administrative process be terminated before judicial review can become operative.

The adoption of this rule will also harmonize with the general principle prevailing in this state as to what constitutes an appealable order. Only one which disposes of all the issues qualifies. *Spires v. Edgar,* 513 S.W.2d 372 (Mo. banc 1974); *P.I.C. Leasing, Inc. v. Roy A. Scheperle Construction Co., Inc., supra; Laclede Gas Co. v. Solon Gershman, Inc.,* 539 S.W.2d 574 (Mo. App. 1976). The reason for this principle is expedition of judicial business so that one appeal will cover all aspects of a case, rather than to permit successive piecemeal appeals. The same principle should apply, and with even more reason, in this labor relation situation.

Indeed, the adoption of this rule causes even less difficulty in Missouri than in the federal arena and in states having statutes closely patterned after the federal labor relations statute. The federal statute contains prohibition against unfair labor practices and judicial review of all representation questions is postponed until such time as the administrative board issues an unfair labor practice order. Then all questions between the parties, including the determination of the appropriate bargaining unit, are reviewed as part of the unfair labor practice case. The Missouri statute, § 105.500 et seq., contains no provision dealing with unfair labor practices and the entire administrative procedures are completed just as soon as the Board of Mediation has held an election and certifies the collective bargaining representative. Judicial review can therefore appropriately begin in Missouri at that time, a point which is much earlier than is permissible under the federal and similar state legislation.

Adoption of the federal rule does not foreclose the possibility that in a very unusual case, judicial review might be appropriate even before the holding of an election. The federal courts and the courts of the states following the federal rule do permit such exceptions in extraordinary circumstances. *Boire v. Grey-*

hound Corporation, supra; Jordan Marsh Co. v. Labor Relations Commission, supra; Bays v. Miller, 524 F.2d 631 (9th Cir. 1975). The adoption of the federal rule will therefore leave ample flexibility for special situations....

NOTES

1. Assume that Union *A* and Union *B* are vying for the right to represent the employees of a public employer and that Union *A* loses the election and subsequently files timely objections to the election alleging that Union *B* engaged in illegal pre-election conduct that affected the outcome of the election. Assume further that the PERB overrules the objections and certifies *B* as the exclusive bargaining representative of the employees. On the basis of the federal rule referred to in the principal case, could *A* obtain judicial review of the PERB decision overruling its objections?

2. In *Indiana Educ. Emp. Relations Bd. v. Benton Community Sch. Corp.,* 365 N.E.2d 752, 95 L.R.R.M. 3084 (Ind. 1977), the Indiana Supreme Court held that the Indiana Public Employees Collective Bargaining Act was unconstitutional because it precluded "judicial review of unit determinations and certification of exclusive bargaining representatives."

CIVIL SERVICE EMPLOYEES ASSOCIATION v. HELSBY

31 App. Div. 2d 325, 297 N.Y.S.2d 813, *aff'd per curiam,*
24 N.Y.2d 993, 250 N.E.2d 230, 302 N.Y.S.2d 822 (1969)

STALEY, JR., J. This is an appeal from a judgment of the Supreme Court at Special Term, entered in Albany County on January 9, 1969, which dismissed a petition in a proceeding under article 78 of the CPLR to review a determination of the Public Employment Relations Board in a representation status dispute, and denied an application to vacate an order issued by such board temporarily restraining the State Negotiating Committee from continuing negotiations with the Civil Service Employees Association pending final certification of representation status.

Following the enactment of the Public Employees' Fair Employment Act (Civil Service Law, art. 14; L. 1967, ch. 392, also known as the Taylor Law), the State Negotiating Committee determined that it would negotiate collectively with three units of State employees and recognized the Civil Service Employees Association to negotiate on behalf of employees of one such unit commonly called the general unit. Employee organizations opposed to the association filed petitions with the Public Employment Relations Board contesting both the establishment of the general unit and the recognition of the association. The board issued an order on November 30, 1967 restraining exclusive negotiations between the State Negotiating Committee and the association until the representation status dispute initiated by the filing of such petitions was resolved, which order was vacated in a prior proceeding in which the statute was construed as "conferring of power on the public employer to recognize and negotiate with employee organizations, untrammeled by representation dispute proceedings until they have been resolved by the Board through certifications of appropriate bargaining units and employee organizations." (*Matter of Civil Serv. Employees Assn. v. Helsby,* 21 N.Y.2d 541, 548.)

Following extensive hearings upon the petitions filed by the employee organizations opposed to the association, the board, on November 27, 1968, handed

down its decision which rejected the general unit designated by the State Negotiating Committee and found five separate units to be appropriate. The question of which job titles should be included in each unit and the ascertainment of
the employers' choice of employee organizations as their representatives were
reserved pending further proceedings before the board. The association
promptly commenced the present proceeding to review such determination by
petition and order to show cause issued November 27, 1968. Before service of
the petition and order to show cause was effected, the board issued an order,
also dated November 27, 1968, in which it ordered the State Negotiating Committee and the association to refrain from conducting further negotiations until
the representation status dispute was resolved through certifications of employee organizations for employees in each of the five units.

Respondents moved to dismiss the petition upon the ground that the determination sought to be reviewed is not final within the meaning of subdivision 1
of CPLR 7801, which motion was granted. Special Term also denied the association's application, apparently made upon the argument of the motion to dismiss
its petition, for judgment vacating the order restraining negotiations between
the State Negotiating Committee and the association.

The first issue raised on this appeal is whether the board's determination is
subject to judicial review under article 78 of the CPLR. CPLR 7801 provides
that article 78 "shall not be used to challenge a determination which is not final
or can be adequately reviewed by appeal to a court or some other body or
officer." It is this exception upon which the board relies to defer judicial review.

The board in its decision concluded that in a representative proceeding it was
empowered to devise a unit that it deemed most appropriate, although such a
unit was not specifically sought by any of the parties. It further held that the
general unit designated by the employer was not appropriate and approved five
separate units as appropriate. The board contends that its determination is not
final and, therefore, the association is not, at this time, free to question the
appropriateness of the units it has devised.

The pertinent provisions of the Taylor Law to the issues involved on this
appeal read as follows:

"§ 205. Public employment relations board.... 5. In addition to the powers
and functions provided in other sections of this article, the board shall have
the following powers and functions ... (f) To conduct studies of problems
involved in representation and negotiation, including, but not limited to ...
(ii) the problems of unit determination....

"§ 207. Determination of representation status. For purposes of resolving
disputes concerning representation status, pursuant to section two hundred
five or two hundred six of this article, the board or government, as the case
may be, shall

"1. define the appropriate employer-employee negotiating units taking
into account the following standards:

"(a) the definition of the unit shall correspond to a community of interest
among the employees to be included in the unit;

"(b) the officials of government at the level of the unit shall have the power
to agree, or to make effective recommendations to other administrative authority or the legislative body with respect to, the terms and conditions of
employment upon which the employees desire to negotiate; and

"(c) the unit shall be compatible with the joint responsibilities of the public employer and public employees to serve the public."

It should be noted that subdivision 1 of section 207 of the Civil Service Law provides for the determination of the negotiating unit, while subdivisions 2 and 3 provide for the implementation of the unit for the purpose of certification.

Nothing in the Taylor Law or the CPLR makes the certification of an employee organization a prerequisite to judicial review of the determination establishing separate negotiating units. If that determination is final as to the rights of the parties, with respect to the matter involved, it should be reviewable. The units deemed to be appropriate by the board are as final now as they will be upon certification. The matter involved in this proceeding is the propriety of the recognition of the association as a negotiating representative for the employees of the general unit, as contrasted with the board's determination that the general unit should be divided into five separate negotiating units. The determination mandated by subdivision 1 of section 207 of the Civil Service Law having been accomplished, the procedure provided by statute to implement that determination cannot alter the original determination. Whatever organization may ultimately be certified to represent the employees involved cannot affect the determination with respect to the structure of the five units.

The argument that the determination of the board establishing the five negotiating units should be reviewed only after certification as provided by subdivision 3 of section 207 of the Civil Service Law is contrary to prompt disposition of a dispute where a party is aggrieved as of the moment of the determination.

Judicial review at this time may avoid costly and time-consuming intermediate procedures. There would be no economy in deferring the question of the correctness of the board's determination until after all the proceedings required to ascertain and establish the employee representative for the five proposed units, should the courts ultimately decide that the five units established were not appropriate. Resolution of the issues in this proceeding at the earliest possible moment is in the best interest of the State and its employees. Unless there is some statutory prohibition, there is no reason to defer judicial review. As the Court of Appeals said of a comparable situation in *Long Is. Coll. Hosp. v. Catherwood* (23 N.Y.2d 20, 36): "A decision that the validity of the board's certification cannot be tested in the court until time-consuming mediation, factfinding and compulsory arbitration proceedings have been exhausted can only serve to delay a prompt determination of the representation issue — a delay which is not in the interest of the public, the nonprofitmaking hospitals or the unions, since unresolved representation issues may cause the very strife which the 1963 amendments were enacted to prevent."

We are here required to construe a unique statutory scheme, one that has as its main purpose the promotion of harmonious and cooperative relationships between government and its employees to protect the public by assuring at all times the orderly and uninterrupted operations and functions of government. Certainly such a statute should be construed with the liberality needed to carry out its public benefit purposes and, therefore, the determination involved should be afforded prompt and effective judicial review.

The board's decision finally and irrevocably rejected the bargaining unit designated by the State Negotiating Committee and determined appropriate alternate units. Such determination is in no sense interlocutory or merely an inter-mediate procedural ruling incident to the administrative process (cf. *Matter of Carville v. Allen,* 13 A.D.2d 866), but instead as to such matters it is final and thus reviewable under article 78....

NOTES

1. Accord *AAUP v. University of Neb.,* 198 Neb. 243, 253 N.W.2d 1 (1977) ("an order establishing bargaining units is a final order ..., and a party may appeal therefrom prior to the holding of elections"). See also *Laborer's Int'l Union of N. Am., Local 1280 v. SLRB,* 154 Ill. App. 3d 1045, 507 N.E.2d 1200 (1987) (order dismissing representation petition is an appealable final order; federal rule rejected because of difference in wording of NLRA and Illinois act).

2. In *New Hampshire Dep't of Revenue Admin. v. PELRB,* 380 A.2d 1085 (N.H. 1977), the court held that a bargaining unit determination was not an appealable final order. In holding "that final certification of representative capacity is the proper order to appeal," the court reasoned that until that time "no one's legal rights have been affected." Accord *Panama City v. PERC,* 333 So. 2d 470 (Fla. Dist. Ct. App. 1976) (certification following election constitutes final agency action from which petition for review of bargaining unit determi-nation can be filed); *Renton Educ. Ass'n v. PERC,* 24 Wash. App. 476, 103 L.R.R.M. 2453 (1979).

3. The California Educational Employment Relations Act provides that "[n]o employer or employee organization shall have the right to judicial review of a unit determination, except: (1) when the board in response to a petition from the employer or employee organization, agrees that the case is one of special importance, and joins in the request for such review; or (2) when the issue is raised as a defense to an unfair labor practice complaint." Cal. Educ. Code § 3542(a).

Chapter 4

THE OBLIGATION AND DUTY TO BARGAIN

A. THE OBLIGATION TO BARGAIN COLLECTIVELY

1. CONSTITUTIONAL CONSIDERATIONS

SMITH v. ARKANSAS STATE HIGHWAY EMPLOYEES, LOCAL 1315

441 U.S. 463, 99 S. Ct. 1826, 60 L. Ed. 2d 360 (1979)

PER CURIAM: — In grievance proceedings initiated by employees of the Arkansas State Highway Department, the State Highway Commission will not consider a grievance unless the employee submits his written complaint directly to the designated employer representative. The District Court for the Eastern District of Arkansas found that this procedure denied the union representing the employees the ability to submit effective grievances on their behalf and therefore violated the First Amendment. The United States Court of Appeals for the Eighth Circuit affirmed.[1] We disagree with these holdings; finding no constitutional violation in the actions of the Commission or its individual members, we grant certiorari and reverse the judgment of the Court of Appeals.

The First Amendment protects the right of an individual to speak freely, to advocate ideas, to associate with others, and to petition his government for redress of grievances. And it protects the right of associations to engage in advocacy on behalf of their members. *NAACP v. Button,* 371 U.S. 415; *Eastern Railroad Presidents Conf. v. Noerr Motor Freight Inc.,* 365 U.S. 127. The Government is prohibited from infringing upon these guarantees either by a general prohibition against certain forms of advocacy, *NAACP v. Button, supra,* or by imposing sanctions for the expression of particular views it opposes, e.g., *Brandenburg v. Ohio,* 395 U.S. 444, *Garrison v. Louisiana,* 379 U.S. 64.

But the First Amendment is not a substitute for the national labor relations laws. As the Court of Appeals for the Seventh Circuit recognized in *Hanover Township Federation of Teachers, Local 1954 v. Hanover Community School Corporation,* 457 F.2d 456 (1972), the fact that procedures followed by a public employer in bypassing the union and dealing directly with its members might well be unfair labor practices were federal statutory law applicable hardly estab-

---

[1]This suit was brought by the Arkansas State Highway Employees, Local 1315 and eight of its individual members, after the Commission refused to consider grievances submitted by the union on behalf of two of its members. The facts in these two cases are not in dispute: "[E]ach employee sent a letter to Local 1315, explaining the nature of their grievance and requesting the union to process the grievance on their behalf. In each case the union forwarded the employee's letter stating that it represented the employees and decided to set up a meeting. The employer's representative did not respond to the union's letter. Thereafter each employee filed a written complaint directly with the employer representative. Local 1315 represented each employee at subsequent meetings with the employer representative." *Arkansas State Highway Employees, Local 1315 v. Smith,* 99 LRRM 3168 (CA8 1978), Pet. App., at 2. The individual Commissioners of the Arkansas State Highway Commission and the Director of the State Highway Department were named as defendants, and are the petitioners in this Court.

lishes that such procedures violate the Constitution. The First Amendment right to associate and to advocate "provides no guarantee that a speech will persuade or that advocacy will be effective." *Id.,* at 461. The public employee surely can associate and speak freely and petition openly, and he is protected by the First Amendment from retaliation for doing so. See *Pickering v. Board of Education,* 391 U.S. 563, 574-575; *Shelton v. Tucker,* 364 U.S. 479. But the First Amendment does not impose any affirmative obligation on the government to listen, to respond or, in this context, to recognize the association and bargain with it.

In the case before us, there is no claim that the Highway Commission has prohibited its employees from joining together in a union, or from persuading others to do so, or from advocating any particular ideas. There is, in short, no claim of retaliation or discrimination proscribed by the First Amendment. Rather, the complaint of the union and its members is simply that the Commission refuses to consider or act upon grievances when filed by the union rather than by the employee directly.

Were public employers such as the Commission subject to the same labor laws applicable to private employers, this refusal might well constitute an unfair labor practice. We may assume that it would, and further, that it tends to impair or undermine — if only slightly — the effectiveness of the union in representing the economic interests of its members. Cf. *Hanover Township, supra.*

But this type of "impairment" is not one that the Constitution prohibits. Far from taking steps to prohibit or discourage union membership or association, all that the Commission has done in its challenged conduct is simply to ignore the union. That it is free to do.

The judgment of the Court of Appeals is therefore reversed.

JUSTICE POWELL took no part in the consideration or decision of this case.

[The dissenting opinion of Justice Marshall is omitted.]

NOTES

1. The courts have uniformly held that it is not a violation of the first amendment for a public employer to refuse to engage in collective bargaining with a bargaining representative chosen by the employees of the public employer. In *Alaniz v. City of San Antonio,* 80 L.R.R.M. 2983 (W.D. Tex. 1971), a three-judge federal court rejected the contention that the right to engage in collective bargaining is protected by the first amendment, reasoning as follows:

> While it is now clear that public employees have a constitutionally protected right to self-organization, this right has never been extended to include collective bargaining through a recognized group representative. The private employee's right to such concerted activity, now "fundamental" under national legislative policy in the private arena, is not guaranteed to public employees such as plaintiffs, either by national legislation or the constitution. The State [of Texas], in declaring its policy against bargaining-agent recognition and collective bargaining contracts in its dealing with public employees, is not interfering with any constitutionally protective [sic] rights of plaintiffs.

Accord *Hanover Twp. Fed'n of Teachers v. Hanover Community Sch. Corp.,* 457 F.2d 456 (7th Cir. 1972); *Winston-Salem/Forsyth Cty. Unit, N.C. Ass'n of Educ. v. Phillips,* 381 F. Supp. 644 (M.D.N.C. 1974); *Newport News Fire*

Fighters Ass'n, Local 794 v. City of Newport News, 339 F. Supp. 13 (E.D. Va. 1972); *Adkins v. City of Charlotte,* 296 F. Supp. 1068 (W.D.N.C. 1969); *Gary Teachers Union, Local 4 v. School City of Gary,* 427 Ind. App. 211, 284 N.E.2d 108 (1972). But see *School Comm. v. Westerly Teachers Ass'n,* 111 R.I. 96, 299 A.2d 441 (1973) (dissenting opinion).

2. Is it a violation of the equal protection clause for a public employer to refuse to bargain collectively with one group of employees while at the same time engaging in collective bargaining with a different group of employees? In *Charles Cty. Supporting Servs. Emps. Local Union 301 v. Board of Educ.,* 48 Md. App. 339, 427 A.2d 1025 (Md. Ct. Spec. App. 1981), the court held that there was no violation of the equal protection clause of the fourteenth amendment because non-certificated school employees were not afforded the same right to engage in collective bargaining that was extended to certificated employees. After holding that the union had the burden of establishing that there was no rational basis for the legislative classification, the court held that "the union did not show that there is no ground of difference between certificated and non-certificated employees, nor did it show that, given a ground of difference, there is no substantial relationship between that ground and the object of the legislation." Accord *Confederation of Police v. City of Chicago,* 529 F.2d 89 (7th Cir.), *vacated on other grounds,* 427 U.S. 902 (1976) (denial of collective bargaining rights to police officers not denial of equal protection even though non-academic employees of city board of education possessed such rights since board of education not comparable to police department for equal protection purposes). *AFSCME v. Jefferson Cty.,* 110 L.R.R.M. 2372 (W.D. Ky. 1982) (although a county engaged in a form of bargaining with its police officers, the county's refusal to bargain with its other employees did not violate the equal protection clause, since there were differences between the police officers and the county's other employees which established a rational basis for the county's refusal to bargain with its other employees).

CITY OF MADISON, JOINT SCHOOL DIST. NO. 8 v. WERC

429 U.S. 167, 97 S. Ct. 421, 50 L. Ed. 2d 376 (1976)

CHIEF JUSTICE BURGER delivered the opinion of the Court.

The question presented on this appeal from the Supreme Court of Wisconsin is whether a State may constitutionally require that an elected Board of Education prohibit teachers, other than union representatives, to speak at open meetings, at which public participation is permitted, if such speech is addressed to the subject of pending collective-bargaining negotiations.

The Madison Board of Education and Madison Teachers, Inc. (MTI), a labor union, were parties to a collective-bargaining agreement during the calendar year of 1971. In January 1971 negotiations commenced for renewal of the agreement and MTI submitted a number of proposals. One among them called for the inclusion of a so-called "fair-share" clause, which would require all teachers, whether members of MTI or not, to pay union dues to defray the costs of collective-bargaining. Wisconsin law expressly permits inclusion of "fair share" provisions in municipal employee collective-bargaining agreements. Wis. Stat. § 111.70(2) (1973). Another proposal presented by the union was a provision for binding arbitration of teacher dismissals. Both of these provisions were resisted by the school board. The negotiations dead-locked in November 1971 with a number of issues still unresolved, among them "fair share" and arbitration.

During the same month, two teachers, Holmquist and Reed, who were members of the bargaining unit, but not members of the union, mailed a letter to all teachers in the district expressing opposition to the "fair share" proposal.[2] Two hundred teachers replied, most commenting favorably on Holmquist and Reed's position. Thereupon a petition was drafted calling for a one year delay in the implementation of "fair share" while the proposal was more closely analyzed by an impartial committee.[3] The petition was circulated to all teachers in the district on December 6, 1971. Holmquist and Reed intended to present the results of their petition effort to the school board and to MTI at the school board's public meeting that same evening.

Because of the stalemate in the negotiations, MTI arranged to have pickets present at the school board meeting. In addition, 300 to 400 teachers attended in support of the union's position. During a portion of the meeting devoted to expression of opinion by the public, the president of MTI took the floor and spoke on the subject of the ongoing negotiations. He concluded his remarks by

---

[2]The text of the letter was as follows:

"Dear Fellow Madisonian Educator,

"E. C.—O. L. O. G. Y.

"*Educator's Choice—Obligatory Leadership Or Grievance by You*

"SAVE FREEDOM OF CHOICE

"A Closed Shop (agency shop) Removes This Freedom

"1. Does an organization which represents the best interests of teachers and pupils NEED mandatory membership deductions?

"2. Need relationships between administrators and teachers be further strained by LEGALLY providing for mandatory adversary camps?

"3. Should minority voices be mandatorily SILENCED?

"4. Could elimination of outside dissent produce NONRESPONSIVENESS to change?

"5. And ...
   isn't this lack of FREEDOM OF CHOICE undemocratic?

"*SUPPORT FREEDOM OF CHOICE—OPPOSE AGENCY SHOP*

"I wish to maintain freedom of choice:

"I oppose agency shop on principle

"I oppose agency shop and would sign a petition stating so

"I oppose agency shop and would work actively to maintain freedom of choice

"Let us hear from YOU.

"Al Holmquist /s/   E. C.—O. L. O. G. Y.
Al Holmquist   P.O. Box 5184
Ralph Reed /s/   Madison, WI 53705
Ralph Reed
   Teacher co-chairmen"

[3]The text of the petition was as follows:

"To: Madison Board of Education
Madison Teachers, Incorporated

"We the undersigned ask that the fair-share proposal (agency shop) being negotiated by Madison Teachers, Incorporated and the Madison Board of Education be deferred this year. We propose the following:

"1) The fair-share concept being negotiated be thoroughly studied by an impartial committee composed of representatives from all concerned groups.

"2) The findings of this study be made public.

"3) This impartial committee will ballot (written) all persons affected by the contract agreement for their opinion on the fair-share proposal.

"4) The results of this written ballot be made public."

presenting to the board a petition signed by 1,300-1,400 teachers calling for the expeditious resolution of the negotiations. Holmquist was next given the floor, after John Matthews, the business representative of MTI, unsuccessfully attempted to dissuade him from speaking. Matthews had also spoken to a member of the school board before the meeting and requested that the board refuse to permit Holmquist to speak. Holmquist stated that he represented "an informal committee of 72 teachers in 49 schools" and that he desired to inform the Board of Education, as he had already informed the union, of the results of an informal survey concerning the "fair share" clause. He then read the petition which had been circulated to the teachers in the district that morning and stated that in the 31 schools from which reports had been received, 53% of the teachers had already signed the petition.

Holmquist stated that neither side had adequately addressed the issue of "fair share" and that teachers were confused about the meaning of the proposal. He concluded by saying: "Due to this confusion, we wish to take no stand on the proposal itself, but ask only that all alternatives be presented clearly to all teachers and more importantly to the general public to whom we are all responsible. We ask simply for communication, not confrontation." The sole response from the school board was a question by the president inquiring whether Holmquist intended to present the board with the petition. Holmquist answered that he would. Holmquist's presentation had lasted approximately two and one-half minutes.

Later that evening, the board met in executive session and voted a proposal acceding to all of the union's demands with the exception of "fair share." During a negotiating session the following morning, MTI accepted the proposal and a contract was signed on December 14, 1976.

(1)

In January 1972 MTI filed a complaint with the Wisconsin Employment Relations Commission (WERC) claiming that the board had committed a prohibited labor practice by permitting Holmquist to speak at the December 6 meeting. MTI claimed that in so doing the board had engaged in negotiations with a member of the bargaining unit other than the exclusive collective bargaining representative, in violation of Wis. Stat. § 111.70(3)(a)1, 4. Following a hearing the Commission concluded that the board was guilty of the prohibited labor practice and ordered that it "immediately cease and desist from permitting employees, other than representatives of Madison Teachers, Inc., to appear and speak at meetings of the Board of Education, on matters subject to collective bargaining between it and Madison Teachers, Inc." The Commission's action was affirmed by the Circuit Court of Dane County.

The Supreme Court of Wisconsin affirmed. The court recognized that both the Federal and State Constitutions protect freedom of speech and the right to petition the government, but noted that these rights may be abridged in the face of "a clear and present danger that [the speech] will bring about the substantive evils that [the legislature] has a right to prevent." 69 Wis. 2d, at 211, 231 N.W.2d at 212, citing *Schneck v. United States,* 249 U.S. 47 (1919). The court held that abridgment of the speech in this case was justified in order "to avoid the dangers attendant upon relative chaos in labor-management relations." 69 Wis. 2d, at 212, 231 N.W.2d at 213.

(2)

The Wisconsin court perceived "clear and present danger" based upon its conclusion that Holmquist's speech before the school board constitued "negotiation" with the board. Permitting such "negotiation," the court reasoned, would undermine the bargaining exclusivity guaranteed the majority union under Wis. Stat. § 111.70(3)(a)4. From that premise it concluded that teachers' First Amendment rights could be limited. Assuming, *arguendo,* that such a "danger" might in some circumstances justify some limitation of First Amendment rights, we are unable to read this record as presenting such danger as would justify curtailing speech.

The Wisconsin Supreme Court's conclusion that Holmquist's terse statement during the public meeting constituted negotiation with the board was based upon its adoption of the lower court's determination that, "[e]ven though Holmquist's statement superficially appears to be merely a 'position statement,' the court deems from the total circumstances that it constituted 'negotiating.'" This cryptic conclusion seems to ignore the ancient wisdom that calling a thing by a name does not make it so. Holmquist did not seek to bargain or offer to enter into any bargain with the board, nor does it appear that he was authorized by any other teachers to enter into any agreement on their behalf. Although his views were not consistent with those of MTI, communicating such views to the employer could not change the fact that MTI alone was authorized to negotiate and to enter into a contract with the board.

Moreover, the school board meeting at which Holmquist was permitted to speak was open to the public. He addressed the school board not merely as one of its employees but also as a concerned citizen, seeking to express his views on an important decision of his government. We have held that teachers may not be "compelled to relinquish the First Amendment rights they would otherwise enjoy as citizens to comment on matters of public interest in connection with the operation of the public school in which they work." *Pickering v. Board of Education,* 391 U.S. 563, 568 (1968).... Where the State has opened a forum for direct citizen involvement, it is difficult to find justification for excluding teachers who make up the overwhelming proportion of school employees and are most vitally concerned with the proceedings. It is conceded that any citizen could have presented precisely the same points and provided the board with the same information as did Holmquist.

Regardless of the extent to which true contract negotiations between a public body and its employees may be regulated — an issue we need not consider at this time — the participation in public discussion of public business cannot be confined to one category of interested individuals. To permit one side of a debatable public question to have a monopoly in expressing its views to the government is the anthithesis of constitutional guarantees. Whatever its duties as an employer, when the board sits in public meetings to conduct public business and hear the views of citizens, it may not be required to discriminate between speakers on the basis of their employment, or the content of their speech. *See Police Department v. Mosley,* 408 U.S. 92, 96 (1972).

(3)

The Employment Relations Commission's order was not limited to a determination that a prohibited labor practice had taken place in the past; it also restrains future conduct. By prohibiting the school board from "permitting employees to appear and speak at meetings of the Board of Education" the order constitutes an indirect, but effective, prohibition on persons such as Holmquist from communicating with their government. The order would have a substantial impact upon virtually all communication between teachers and the school board. The order prohibits speech by teachers "on matters subject to collective bargaining." As the dissenting opinion below [omitted] noted, however, there is virtually no subject concerning the operation of the school system that could not also be characterized as a potential subject of collective bargaining. Teachers not only constitute the overwhelming bulk of employees of the school system, but they are the very core of that system; restraining teachers' expressions to the board on matters involving the operation of the schools would seriously impair the board's ability to govern the district....

JUSTICE BRENNAN with whom JUSTICE MARSHALL joins, concurring in the judgment.

By stating that "the extent to which true contract negotiations may be regulated [is] an issue we need not consider at this time," *ante*, at 426, the Court's opinion treats as open a question the answer to which I think is abundantly clear. Wisconsin has adopted, as unquestionably the State constitutionally may adopt, a statutory policy that authorizes public bodies to accord exclusive recognition to representatives for collective bargaining chosen by the majority of an appropriate unit of employees. In that circumstance the First Amendment plainly does not forbid Wisconsin from limiting attendance at a collective-bargaining session to school board and union bargaining representatives and denying Holmquist the right to attend and speak at the session. That proposition is implicit in the words of Mr. Justice Holmes, that the "Constitution does not require all public acts to be done in town meeting or an assembly of the whole." *Bi-Metallic Investment Co. v. State Board of Equalization*, 239 U.S. 441, 445 (1915). Certainly in the context of Wisconsin's adoption of the exclusivity principle as a matter of state policy governing relations between state bodies and unions of their employees, "There must be a limit to individual argument in such matters if government is to go on." *Ibid.* For the First Amendment does not command "that people who want to [voice] their views have a constitutional right to do so whenever and however and wherever they please." *Adderley v. Florida*, 385 U.S. 39, 48 (1966). For example, this Court's "own conferences [and] the meetings of other official bodies gathered in executive session" may be closed to the public without implicating any constitutional rights whatever. *Branzburg v. Hayes*, 408 U.S. 665, 684 (1972). Thus, the Wisconsin Supreme Court was correct in stating that there is nothing unconstitutional about legislation commanding that in closed-bargaining sessions a government body may admit, hear the views of, and respond to only the designated representatives of a union selected by the majority of its employees.

But the First Amendment plays a crucially different role when, as here, a government body has either by its own decision or under statutory command, determined to open its decisionmaking processes to public view and participation. In such case, the state body has created a public forum dedicated to the expression of views by the general public. "Once a forum is opened up to assembly or speaking by some groups, government may not prohibit others from assemblying or speaking on the basis of what they intend to say. Selective exclusions from a public forum may not be based on content alone, and may not be justified by reference to content alone." *Police Department of Chicago v. Mosley,* 408 U.S. 92, 96 (1972). The order sustained by the Wisconsin Supreme Court obviously contravenes that principle. Although there was a complete absence of any evidence that Holmquist's speech was part of a course of conduct in aid of an unfair labor practice by the Board, the order commands that the Board "shall immediately cease and desist from permitting employees other than [union] representatives ... to appear and speak at [Board] meetings, on matters subject to collective bargaining...." Obedience to that order requires that the Board, regardless of any other circumstances, not allow Holmquist or other citizens to speak at a meeting required by Wis. Stat. § 66.77 to be open and dedicated to expressions of views by citizens generally on such subjects, even though they conform with all procedural rules, even though the subject upon which they wish to speak may be addressed by union representatives, and even though they are part of the "public" to which the forum is otherwise open. The order is therefore wholly void. The State could no more prevent Holmquist from speaking at this public forum than it could prevent him from publishing the same views in a newspaper or proclaiming them from a soapbox.

I therefore agree that the judgment of the Wisconsin Supreme Court be reversed.

[The concurring opinion of Justice Stewart is omitted.]

NOTE

In *Hunterdon Cent. High Sch. Bd. of Educ. v. Hunterdon Cent. High Sch. Teachers Ass'n,* 174 N.J. Super. 568, 1979-80 PBC ¶ 37,003 (N.J. Super. Ct. App. Div. 1980), *aff'd,* 86 N.J. 43, 429 A.2d 354 (1981), the court held that a proposal to provide paid leaves of absence for religious purposes would violate the establishment clause of the first amendment and was therefore not a mandatory subject of negotiations. The New Jersey Supreme Court affirmed the Appellate Division's decision and in a concurring opinion Judge Handler stressed the "narrowness of the constitutional issue" presented for decision. While observing that the Appellate Court "correctly concluded that providing public employees with days off from work with pay for the exclusive purpose of religious observance without a deduction of either a personal day, vacation day, a day's wage, or the like, violated the Establishment Clause," Judge Handler stated that the court's decision "should not be construed to suggest that it is not constitutionally possible for public employers otherwise to accommodate the religious beliefs and practices of employees within the framework of subjects constituting terms and conditions of employment."

On the other hand, in *Americans United for Separation of Ch. & State v. County of Kent,* 97 Mich. App. 72, 107 L.R.R.M. 2050 (1980), the court held that clauses in a public employer's collective bargaining agreements which provided that employees were entitled to four hours of holiday pay on Good Friday did not violate the establishment clause of the first amendment. The court noted that "the decision to make Good Friday a partial holiday was the result of privately conducted negotiations authorized under a statute encouraging collective bargaining" and that it was undisputed that the parties had first agreed to the number of holidays and that if Good Friday had not been selected as a half holiday, "another half day would have been selected in its place." The court then observed that "the selection of Good Friday in the collective bargaining agreement did not increase the cost to the taxpayers or the number of hours County facilities would not be open for business." Finally, the court commented that "because nothing in the agreement encouraged employee attendance at Good Friday church services,... the agreements served a secular purpose of time off over the Easter holiday season." Accord *California Sch. Emps. Ass'n v. Sequoia Union High Sch. Dist.,* 67 Cal. App. 3d 157, 136 Cal. Rptr. 597 (1977). But see *Mandel v. Hodges,* 54 Cal. App. 3d 596, 127 Cal. Rptr. 247 (1976) (governor's directive closing state offices on Good Friday for three hours and granting state employees time off with pay violated the establishment clause of the first amendment).

MINNESOTA STATE BOARD FOR COMMUNITY COLLEGES v. KNIGHT

465 U.S. 271, 104 S. Ct. 1058, 79 L. Ed. 2d 299 (1984)

JUSTICE O'CONNOR delivered the opinion of the Court.

The State of Minnesota authorizes its public employees to bargain collectively over terms and conditions of employment. It also requires public employers to engage in official exchanges of views with their professional employees on policy questions relating to employment but outside the scope of mandatory bargaining. If professional employees forming an appropriate bargaining unit have selected an exclusive representative for mandatory bargaining, their employer may exchange views on nonmandatory subjects only with the exclusive representative. The question presented in this case is whether this restriction on participation in the nonmandatory-subject exchange process violates the constitutional rights of professional employees within the bargaining unit who are not members of the exclusive representative and who may disagree with its views. We hold that it does not.

I

A

In 1971, the Minnesota legislature adopted the Public Employment Labor Relations Act (PELRA), Minn.Stat. §§ 179.61 et seq. (1982), to establish "orderly and constructive relationships between all public employers and their employees...." *Id.,* § 179.61. The public employers covered by the law are, broadly speaking, the state and its political subdivisions, agencies, and instrumentalities. *Id.,* § 179.63. In its amended form, as in its original form, PELRA provides for the division of public employees into appropriate bargaining units and establishes a procedure, based on majority support within a unit, for the designation of an exclusive bargaining agent for that unit. *Id.,* §§ 179.67, 179.71, 179.741. The statute requires public employers to "meet and negotiate" with exclusive representatives concerning the "terms and conditions of employment," which the statute defines to mean "the hours of employment, the compensation therefor ... , and the employer's personnel policies affecting the working conditions of the employees." *Id.,* §§ 179.63, 179.67, 179.71. The employer's and employees' representatives must seek an agreement in good faith. *Id.,* § 179.63, subd. 16.

PELRA also grants professional employees, such as college faculty, the right to "meet and confer" with their employers on matters related to employment that are outside the scope of mandatory negotiations. *Id.,* §§ 179.63, 179.65. This provision rests on the recognition "that professional employees possess knowledge, expertise, and dedication which is helpful and necessary to the operation and quality of public services and which may assist public employers in developing their policies." *Id.,* § 179.73. The statute declares it to be the state's policy to "encourage close cooperation between public employees and professional employees" by providing for "meet and confer" sessions on all employment-related questions not subject to mandatory bargaining. *Ibid.* There is no statutory provision concerning the "meet and confer" process, however, that requires good faith efforts to reach agreement. See *Minneapolis Federation of Teachers Local 59 v. Minneapolis Special School Dist. No. 1,* Minn. 258 N.W.2d 802, 804, n. 2 (1977).

PELRA requires professional employees to select a representative to "meet and confer" with their public employer. Minn. Stat. § 179.73. If professional employees in an appropriate bargaining unit have an exclusive representative to "meet and negotiate" with their employer, that representative serves as the "meet and confer" representative as well. Indeed, the employer may neither "meet and negotiate" nor "meet and confer" with any members of that bargaining unit except through their exclusive representative. *Id.,* § 179.66, subd. 7. This restriction, however, does not prevent professional employees from submitting advice or recommendations to their employer as part of their work assignment. *Ibid.* Moreover, nothing in PELRA restricts the right of any public employee to speak on any "matter related to the conditions or compensation of public employment or their betterment" as long as doing so "is not designed to and does not interfere with the full, faithful and proper performance of the duties of employment or circumvent the rights of the exclusive representative if there be one." *Id.,* § 179.65, subd. 1.

B

Appellant Minnesota State Board for Community Colleges (State Board) operates the Minnesota community college system. At the time of trial, the system comprised eighteen institutions located throughout the state. Each community college is administered by a president, who reports, through the chancellor of the system, to the State Board.

Prior to 1971, Minnesota's community colleges were governed in a variety of ways. On some campuses, faculty had a strong voice in administrative policy-making, expressed through organizations such as faculty senates. On other campuses, the administration consulted very little with the faculty. Irrespective of the level of faculty involvement in governance, however, the administrations of the colleges retained final authority to make policy.

Following enactment of PELRA, appellant Minnesota Community College Faculty Association (MCCFA) was designated the exclusive representative of the faculty of the state's community colleges, which had been deemed a single bargaining unit. MCCFA has "met and negotiated" and "met and conferred" with the State Board since 1971. The result has been the negotiation of successive collective bargaining agreements in the intervening years and, in order to implement the "meet and confer" provision, a restructuring of governance practices in the community college system.

On the state level, MCCFA and the Board established "meet and confer" committees to discuss questions of policy applicable to the entire system. On the campus level, the MCCFA chapters and the college administrations created local "meet and confer" committees — also referred to as "exchange of views" committees — to discuss questions of policy applicable only to the campus. The committees on both levels have discussed such topics as the selection and evaluation of administrators, academic accreditation, student affairs, curriculum, and fiscal planning — all policy matters within the control of the college administrations and the State Board. App. to Juris. Statement A-49.

The State Board considers the views expressed by the state-wide faculty "meet and confer" committees to be the faculty's official collective position. It recognizes, however, that not every instructor agrees with the official faculty view on every policy question. Not every instructor in the bargaining unit is a member of MCCFA, and MCCFA has selected only its own members to represent it on "meet and confer" committees. Accordingly, all faculty have been free to communicate to the State Board and to local administrations their views on questions within the coverage of the statutory "meet and confer" provision. *Id.,* at A-50, A-52. They have frequently done so. With the possible exception of a brief period of adjustment to the new governance structure, during which some administrators were reluctant to communicate informally with faculty, individual faculty members have not been impeded by either MCCFA or college administrators in the communication of their views on policy questions. App. to Juris. Statement A-50. Nor has PELRA ever been construed to impede such communication.[4]

C

Appellees are twenty Minnesota community college faculty instructors who are not members of MCCFA. In December 1974, they filed suit in the United States District Court for the District of Minnesota, challenging the constitutionality of MCCFA's exclusive representation of community college faculty in both the "meet and negotiate" and "meet and confer" processes. A three-judge District Court was convened to hear the case. A Special Master appointed by the court conducted the trial in 1980 and submitted recommended findings of fact in early 1981. *Id.,* at A-54 to A-81. The three-judge District Court issued its

---

[4] The repeated suggestions in Justice Steven's dissent that the state employer and state employees have been prohibited or deterred by the statute from talking with each other on policy questions, e.g., post, at 1075-1078, 1080, 1081, 1086, misunderstand the statute and are flatly contradicted by the District Court's findings. All that the statute prohibits is the formal exchange of views called a "meet and confer" session. It in no way impairs the ability of individual employees or groups of employees to express their views to their employer outside that formal context, and there has been no suggestion in this case that, after an initial period of adjustment to PELRA, any such communication of views has ever been restrained because it was challenged as constituting a formal "meet and confer" session....

findings of fact in late 1981, *id.,* at A-32 to A-54, and its decision on the legal claims in early 1982, *id.,* at A-7 to A-32, 571 F. Supp. 1.

The court rejected appellees' attack on the constitutionality of exclusive representation in bargaining over terms and conditions of employment, relying chiefly on *Abood v. Board of Education,* 431 U.S. 209 (1977). The court agreed with appellees, however, that PELRA, as applied in the community college system, infringes First and Fourteenth Amendment speech and associational rights of faculty who do not wish to join MCCFA. By granting MCCFA the right to select the faculty representatives for the "meet and confer" committees and by permitting MCCFA to select only its own members, the court held, PELRA unconstitutionally deprives non-MCCFA instructors of "a fair opportunity to participate in the selection of governance representatives." App. to Juris. Statement A-23. The court granted declaratory relief in accordance with its holdings and enjoined MCCFA from selecting "meet and confer" representatives without providing all faculty the fair opportunity that its selection practice had unconstitutionally denied.

Appellees, the State Board, and MCCFA all filed appeals with this Court, invoking jurisdiction under 28 U.S.C. § 1253. The Court summarily affirmed the judgment insofar as the District Court held the "meet and negotiate" provisions of PELRA to be valid. 103 S. Ct. 1493 (1983). The Court thus rejected appellees' argument, based on *A.L.A. Schechter Poultry Corp. v. United States,* 295 U.S. 495 (1935), and on *Carter v. Carter Coal Co.,* 298 U.S. 238 (1936), that PELRA unconstitutionally delegated legislative authority to private parties. The Court's summary affirmance also rejected the constitutional attack on PELRA's restriction to the exclusive representative of participation in the "meet and negotiate" process.

On March 28, 1983, the Court noted probable jurisdiction in the appeals by the Board and MCCFA. 103 S. Ct. 1496. Several weeks later, following an election held pursuant to a newly established scheme for selecting "meet and confer" representatives, the three-judge District Court modified its injunction to require a specific voting system for the selection of faculty "meet and confer" representatives. This Court permitted appellants to add to their appeal a challenge to this new relief. 103 S. Ct. 2450 (1983). We now reverse the District Court's holding that the "meet and confer" provisons of PELRA deprive appellees of their constitutional rights.

II

A

Appellees do not and could not claim that they have been unconstitutionally denied access to a public forum. A "meet and confer" session is obviously not a public forum. It is a fundamental principle of First Amendment doctrine, articulated most recently in *Perry Education Assn. v. Perry Local Educators' Assn.,* 103 S. Ct. 948, 954 (1983), that for government property to be a public forum, it must by long tradition or by government designation be open to the public at large for assembly and speech. Minnesota college administration meetings convened to obtain faculty advice on policy questions have neither by long tradition nor by government designation been open for general public participation. The

District Court did not find, App. to Juris. Statement A-22, and appellees do not contend otherwise.

The rights at issue in this case are accordingly wholly unlike those at stake in *City of Madison Joint School District v. Wisconsin Public Employment Relations Comm'n*, 429 U.S. 167 (1976). The Court in that case upheld a claim of access to a public forum, applying standard public-forum First Amendment analysis. See *Perry Education Assn. v. Perry Local Educators' Assn.*, 103 S. Ct., at 955 (citing *City of Madison* as an example of a case involving a "forum generally open to the public" for expressive activity). The school board meetings at issue there were "opened [as] a forum for direct citizen involvement," 429 U.S., at 175, and "public participation [was] permitted," *id.*, at 169. The First Amendment was violated when the meetings were suddenly closed to one segment of the public even though they otherwise remained open for participation by the public at large. This case, by contrast, involves no selective closure of a generally open forum, and hence any reliance on the *City of Madison* case would be misplaced.

Indeed, the claim in this case is not even a claim of access to a *nonpublic* forum, such as the school mail system at issue in *Perry Education Assn.* A private organization there claimed a right of access to government property for use in speaking to potentially willing listeners among a group of private individuals and public officials not acting in an official capacity. The organization claimed no right to have anyone, public or private, attend to its message.... Appellees here make a claim quite different from those made in the nonpublic forum cases. They do not contend that certain government property has been closed to them for use in communicating with private individuals or public officials not acting as such who might be willing to listen to them. Rather, they claim an entitlement to a government audience for their views.

"Meet and confer" sessions are occasions for public employers, acting solely as instrumentalities of the state, to receive policy advice from their professional employees. Minnesota has simply restricted the class of persons to whom it will listen in its making of policy. Thus, appellees' principal claim is that they have a right to force officers of the state acting in an official policymaking capacity to listen to them in a particular formal setting. The nonpublic forum cases concern government's authority to provide assistance to certain persons in communicating with other persons who would not, as listeners, be acting for the government. As the discussion below makes clear, the claim that government is constitutionally obliged to listen to appellees involves entirely different considerations from those on which resolution of nonpublic forum cases turn. Hence, the nonpublic forum cases are largely irrelevant to assessing appellees' novel constitutional claim.

The District Court agreed with appellees' claim to the extent that it was limited to faculty participation in governance of institutions of higher education. The court reasoned that "issues of higher education have a special character." App. to Juris. Statement A-20. Tradition and public policy support the right of faculty to participate in policymaking in higher education, the court stated, and the "right of expression by faculty members also holds a special place under our Constitution." *Id.*, at A-20 to A-21. Because of the "vital concern for academic freedom," the District Court concluded, "when the state compels creation of a representative governance system in higher education and utilizes that forum for ongoing debate and resolution of virtually all issues outside the scope of collective bargaining, it must afford every faculty member a fair opportunity to participate in the selection of governance representatives." *Id.,* at A-22, A-23.

This conclusion is erroneous. Appellees have no constitutional right to force the government to listen to their views. They have no such right as members of the public, as government employees, or as instructors in an institution of higher education.

1

The Constitution does not grant to members of the public generally a right to be heard by public bodies making decisions of policy. In *Bi-Metallic Investment Co. v. State Board of Equalization,* 239 U.S. 441 (1915), this Court rejected a claim to such a right founded on the Due Process Clause of the Fourteenth Amendment. Speaking for the Court, Justice Holmes explained:

"Where a rule of conduct applies to more than a few people it is impracticable that every one should have a direct voice in its adoption. The Constitution does not require all public acts to be done in town meeting or an assembly of the whole. General statutes within the state power are passed that affect the person or property of individuals, sometimes to the point of ruin, without giving them a chance to be heard. Their rights are protected in the only way that they can be in a complex society, by their power, immediate or remote, over those who make the rule." *Id.,* at 445.

In *City of Madison Joint School District v. Wisconsin Employment Relations Commission, supra,* which sustained a First Amendment challenge to a restriction on access to a public forum, the Court recognized the soundness of Justice Holmes's reasoning outside the due process context. The Court stated: "Plainly, public bodies may confine their meetings to specified subject matter and may hold non-public sessions to transact business." 429 U.S., at 175 n. 8.

Policymaking organs in our system of government have never operated under a constitutional constraint requiring them to afford every interested member of the public an opportunity to present testimony before any policy is adopted. Legislatures throughout the nation, including Congress, frequently enact bills on which no hearings have been held or on which testimony has been received from only a select group. Executive agencies likewise make policy decisions of widespread application without permitting unrestricted public testimony. Public officials at all levels of government daily make policy decisions based only on the advice they decide they need and choose to hear. To recognize a constitutional right to participate directly in government policymaking would work a revolution in existing government practices.

Not least among the reasons for refusing to recognize such a right is the impossibility of its judicial definition and enforcement. Both federalism and separation-of-powers concerns would be implicated in the massive intrusion into state and federal policymaking that recognition of the claimed right would entail. Moreover, the pragmatic considerations identified by Justice Holmes in *Bi-Metallic Investment Co. v. State Board of Equalization, supra,* are as weighty today as they were in 1915. Government makes so many policy decisions affecting so many people that it would likely grind to a halt were policymaking constrained by constitutional requirements on whose voices must be heard. "There must be a limit to individual argument in such matters if government is to go on." 239 U.S., at 445. Absent statutory restrictions, the state must be free to consult or not to consult whomever it pleases.

However wise or practicable various levels of public participation in various kinds of policy decisions may be, this Court has never held, and nothing in the Constitution suggests it should hold, that government must provide for such participation. In *Bi-Metallic* the Court rejected due process as a source of an obligation to listen. Nothing in the First Amendment or in this Court's case law interpreting it suggests that the rights to speak, associate, and petition require government policymakers to listen or respond to individuals' communications on public issues. Indeed, in *Smith v. Arkansas State Highway Employees, Local 1315,* 441 U.S. 463, 464-466 (1979), the Court rejected the suggestion. No other constitutional provision has been advanced as a source of such a requirement. Nor, finally, can the structure of government established and approved by the Constitution provide the source. It is inherent in a republican form of government that direct public participation in government policymaking is limited. See The Federalist No. 10 (Madison). Disagreement with public policy and disapproval of officials' responsiveness, as Justice Holmes suggested in *Bi-Metallic, supra,* is to be registered principally at the polls.

2

Appellees thus have no constitutional right as members of the public to a government audience for their policy views. As public employees, of course, they have a special interest in public policies relating to their employment. Minnesota's statutory scheme for public-employment labor relations recognizes as much. Appellee's status as public employees, however, gives them no special constitutional right to a voice in the making of policy by their government employer.

In *Smith v. Arkansas State Highway Employees, Local 1315, supra,* a public employees' union argued that its First Amendment rights were abridged because the public employer required employees' grievances to be filed directly with the employer and refused to recognize the union's communications concerning its members' grievances. The Court rejected the argument.

"The public employee surely can associate, and speak freely and petition openly, and he is protected by the First Amendment from retaliation for doing so. See *Pickering v. State Board of Education,* 391 U.S. 563, 574-575 (1968); *Shelton v. Tucker,* 364 U.S. 479 (1960). But the First Amendment does not impose any affirmative obligation on the government to listen, to respond or, in this context, to recognize the association and bargain with it." 441 U.S., at 465 (footnote omitted).

The Court acknowledged that "[t]he First Amendment protects the right of an individual to speak freely, to advocate ideas, to associate with others, and to petition his government for redress of grievances." *Id.,* at 464. The government had not infringed any of those rights, the Court concluded. "[A]ll that the [government] has done in its challenged conduct is simply to ignore the union. That it is free to do." *Id.*, at 466.

The conduct challenged here is the converse of that challenged in *Smith*. There the government listened only to individual employees and not to the union. Here the government "meets and confers" with the union and not with individual employees. The applicable constitutional principles are identical to those that controlled in *Smith*. When government makes general policy, it is under no greater constitutional obligation to listen to any specially affected class than it is to listen to the public at large.

3

The academic setting of the policymaking at issue in this case does not alter this conclusion. To be sure, there is a strong, if not universal or uniform, tradition of faculty participation in school governance, and there are numerous policy arguments to support such participation. See American Association for Higher Education — National Education Association, Faculty Participation in Academic Governance (1967); Brief Amicus Curiae of American Association of University Professors 3-10. But this Court has never recognized a constitutional right of faculty to participate in policymaking in academic institutions.

In several cases the Court has recognized that infringement of the rights of speech and association guaranteed by the First and Fourteenth Amendment "'in the case of teachers brings the safeguards of those amendments vividly into operation.'" ... Those cases, however, involved individuals' rights to express their views and to associate with others for communicative purposes.... *Shelton v. Tucker, supra; Sweezy v. State of New Hampshire,* 354 U.S. 234 (1957). These rights do not entail any government obligation to listen. *Smith v. Arkansas State Highway Employees, Local 1315, supra.* Even assuming that speech rights guaranteed by the First Amendment take on a special meaning in an academic setting, they do not require government to allow teachers employed by it to participate in institutional policymaking. Faculty involvement in academic governance has much to recommend it as a matter of academic policy, but it finds no basis in the Constitution.

B

Although there is no constitutional right to participate in academic governance, the First Amendment guarantees the right both to speak and to associate. Appellees' speech and associational rights, however, have not been infringed by Minnesota's restriction of participation in "meet and confer" sessions to the faculty's exclusive representative. The state has in no way restrained appellees' freedom to speak on any education-related issue or their freedom to associate or not to associate with whom they please, including the exclusive representative. Nor has the state attempted to suppress any ideas.

It is doubtless true that the unique status of the exclusive representative in the "meet and confer" process amplifies its voice in the policymaking process. But that amplification no more impairs individual instructors' constitutional freedom to speak than the amplification of individual voices impaired the union's freedom to speak in *Smith v. Arkansas State Highway Employees, Local 1315, supra.* Moreover, the exclusive representative's unique role in "meet and negotiate" sessions amplifies its voice as much as its unique role in "meet and confer" sessions, yet the Court summarily affirmed the District Court's approval of that role in this case. Amplification of the sort claimed is inherent in government's freedom to choose its advisers. A person's right to speak is not infringed when government simply ignores that person while listening to others.

Nor is appellees' right to speak infringed by the ability of MCCFA to "retaliate" for protected speech, as the District Court put it, by refusing to appoint them to the "meet and confer" committees. The state of Minnesota seeks to obtain MCCFA's views on policy questions, and MCCFA has simply chosen representatives who share its views on the issues to be discussed with the state. MCCFA's ability to "retaliate" by not selecting those who dissent from its views no more unconstitutionally inhibits appellees' speech than voters' power to reject a candidate for office inhibits the candidate's speech. See *Branti v. Finkel,* 445 U.S. 507, 533 (1980) (JUSTICE POWELL, dissenting).

Similarly, appellees' associational freedom has not been impaired. Appellees are free to form whatever advocacy groups they like. They are not required to become members of MCCFA, and they do not challenge the monetary contribution they are required to make to support MCCFA's representation activities. Appellees may well feel some pressure to join the exclusive representative in order to give them the opportunity to serve on the "meet and confer" committees or to give them a voice in the representative's adoption of positions on particular issues. That pressure, however, is no different from the pressure they may feel to join MCCFA because of its unique status in the "meet and negotiate" process, a status the Court has summarily approved. Moreover, the pressure is no different from the pressure to join a majority party that persons in the minority always feel. Such pressure is inherent in our system of government; it does not create an unconstitutional inhibition on associational freedom.

C

Unable to demonstrate an infringement of any First Amendment right, appellees contend that their exclusion from "meet and confer" sessions denies them equal protection of the laws in violation of the Fourteenth Amendment. This final argument is meritless. The interest of appellees that is effected — the interest in a government audience for their policy views — finds no special protection in the Constitution. There being no other reason to invoke heightened scrutiny, the challenged state action "need only rationally further a legitimate state purpose" to be valid under the Equal Protection Clause. *Perry Education Assn. v. Perry Local Educators' Assn., supra,* 103 S. Ct., at 960. PELRA certainly meets that standard. The state has a legitimate interest in ensuring that its public employers hear one, and only one, voice presenting the majority view of its professional employees on employment-related policy questions, whatever other advice they may receive on those questions. Permitting selection of the "meet and confer" representatives to be made by the exclusive representative, which has its unique status by virtue of majority support within the bargaining unit, is a rational means of serving that interest.

If it is rational for the state to give the exclusive representative a unique role in the "meet and negotiate" process, as the summary affirmance in appellees' appeal in this case presupposes, it is rational for the state to do the same in the "meet and confer" process. The goal of reaching agreement makes it imperative for an employer to have before it only one collective view of its employees when "negotiating." See *Abood v. Detroit Board of Education, supra,* 431 U.S., at 224. Similarly, the goal of basing policy decisions on consideration of the majority view of its employees makes it reasonable for an employer to give only the exclusive representative a particular formal setting in which to offer advice on policy. Appellees' equal protection challenge accordingly fails.

III

The District Court erred in holding that appellees had been unconstitutionally denied an opportunity to participate in their public employer's making of policy. Whatever the wisdom of Minnesota's statutory scheme for professional employee consultation on employment-related policy, in academic or other settings, the scheme violates no provision of the Constitution. The judgment of the District Court is therefore

Reversed.

[The concurring opinion of Justice Marshall is omitted.]

Justice Brennan, dissenting.

Although I agree with much of Justice Stevens' dissent, I write separately to explain why, irrespective of other grounds, principles of academic freedom require affirmance of the District Court's holding that the "meet and confer" provisions deprive appellees of their constitutional rights.

It is crucial at the outset to recognize that two related First Amendment interests are at stake here. On the one hand, those faculty members who are barred from participation in "meet and confer" sessions by virtue of their refusal to join MCCFA have a First Amendment right to express their views on important matters of academic governance to college administrators. At the same time, they enjoy a First Amendment right to be free from compelled associations with positions or views that they do not espouse. In my view, the real vice of the Minnesota Public Employment Labor Relations Act (PELRA) is that it impermissibly forces non-union faculty members to choose between these two rights....

As we have often recognized, the use of an exclusive union representative is permissible in the collective-bargaining context because of the state's compelling interest in reaching an enforceable agreement, an interest that is best served when the state is free to reserve closed bargaining sessions to the designated representative of a union selected by public employees. See *Abood, supra,* 431 U.S., at 223-226. See also *Madison Joint School Dist. v. Wisconsin Employment Relations Commn.,* 429 U.S. 167, 178 (1976) (Brennan, J., concurring in the judgment). But in the distinctive context of "meet and confer" sessions — which embrace a broad array of sensitive policy matters and which serve only to provide information, not to establish any element of a collective-bargaining agreement — the state's interest in admitting no one other than an exclusive union representative to such sessions is substantially diminished. The views expressed by a union representative will only furnish college administrators with an incomplete and imperfect account of the wide-ranging views of the entire faculty.

The *Abood* rationale, therefore, does not justify this statutory restriction on the ability of non-union faculty members to convey to college administrators their views on matters of importance to the academic community.

Accordingly, I would affirm the judgment of the District Court.

JUSTICE STEVENS, with whom JUSTICE BRENNAN joins in all but Part III, and with whom JUSTICE POWELL joins in all but Part II, dissenting.

The First Amendment provides: "Congress shall make no law ... abridging the freedom of speech, or of the press ...." Laws enacted by state legislatures are subject to this prohibition. *Gitlow v. New York,* 268 U.S. 652 (1925). The question in this case is whether Minnesota's statute granting unions preferential access to the policymaking deliberations of public agencies, while prohibiting comparable access for others, is such a law.

We need not consider whether executives or legislators have any constitutional obligation to listen to unsolicited advice to decide this case. It is inherent in the republican form of government that high officials may choose — in their own wisdom and at their own peril — to listen to some of their constituents and not to others. But the First Amendment does guarantee an open marketplace for ideas — where divergent points of view can freely compete for the attention of those in power and of those to whom the powerful must account. The Minnesota statute places a significant restraint on that free competition, by regulating the communication that may take place between the government and those governed. As the District Court found, the statute gives only one speaker a realistic opportunity to present its views to state officials. All other communication is effectively prohibited, not by reference to the time, place or manner of communication, or even by reference to the officials' willingness to listen, but rather by reference to the identity of the speaker. The statute is therefore invalid because the First Amendment does not permit any state legislature to grant a single favored speaker an effective monopoly on the opportunity to petition the government.

I

The Minnesota Public Employment Labor Relations Act (PELRA), Minn. Stat. §§ 179.61-179.76 (1980), applies to the State itself, to its political subdivisions, and to its administrative agencies. While this case involves the state community colleges system, the statutory scheme applies to any public employer that engages in collective bargaining and has policymaking responsibilities in areas beyond its contractual relationships with its employees. It is its unique regulation of the public agencies' process of formulating policy concerning other subjects that makes the statute vulnerable to constitutional attack.

In this appeal, there is no dispute that Minnesota may limit the process of negotiation on the terms and conditions of public employment to the union that represents the employees in a given collective bargaining unit. This is accomplished by § 179.66(7) of the statute, which forbids an employer to "meet and negotiate" with anyone except the union's representatives. "Meet and negotiate" is defined as the process of collective bargaining on "terms and conditions of employment," § 179.63(16), which

> "means the hours of employment, the compensation therefor including fringe benefits except retirement contributions or benefits, and the employer's personnel policies affecting the working conditions of the employees. In the case of professional employees the term does not mean educational policies of a school district. The terms in both cases are subject to the provisions of section 179.66 regarding the rights of public employers and the scope of negotiations." § 179.63(18).

The portion of the statute under challenge here has nothing to do with the process of negotiating labor contracts. The challenged provisions prohibit the exchange of any "view" concerning the policies of the public employer between the employer and any employee except the majority union's representatives. The same portion of the PELRA that limits labor negotiations to the union's representative, also forbids public agencies to "meet and confer" with any employee or group of employees except a representative of the employees' union:

> "*The employer shall not* meet and negotiate or *meet and confer with any employee or group of employees* who are at the time designated as a member or part of an appropriate employee unit *except through the exclusive representative* ... provided that this subdivision shall not be deemed to prevent the communication to the employer, other than through the exclusive representative, of advice or recommendations by professional employees, when such communication is a part of the employee's work assignment." § 179.66(7) (emphasis supplied).

The provisions exempting individual communications from the otherwise all-encompassing abridgment of speech is limited to communication that "is a part of the employee's work assignment." Thus, a French professor could confer with his employer about Voltaire or Daudet but could not suggest that the football team needs a new coach, that the endowment fund should divest itself of South African investments, that the admissions committee should modify its affirmative action program, or that the faculty should organize a drive for the March of Dimes.

The breadth of the communication prohibited by this statute is remarkable. The "meet and confer" process in which only the majority union can participate is defined broadly to encompass: "the exchange of views and concerns between employers and their respective employees." § 179.63(15). The statute itself imposes no limit on the subjects that might be covered by the "meet and confer" system; in its application to other agencies, that system could encompass the entire range of public policy questions. Thus, in terms the statute says that a public employee may not exchange any views on virtually any public policy question with his or her employer. Appellants suggest no narrowing construction of these statutory terms, nor would it be appropriate for this Court to attempt in the first instance to construe the statute to mean something other than what it plainly says. The District Court found that the statute has been applied to mean what it says. In the community college program, the District Court found that the "subjects covered by the meet and confer system include new course proposals and other curriculum matters, budgetary planning, development of facilities, student rights and student affairs generally, evaluation of administrators, selection of college presidents, academic accreditation of the community college, and other matters." Jurisdictional Statement A-49.

Not only are employees who are not selected to represent the majority union's views disabled from expressing their own opinions to their employers, but the union is guaranteed ample opportunities to do what no one else can. The statute places public employers under an obligation to meet and confer with the majority union's representative at least once every four months. §§ 179.66(3), 179.73. Moreover, the statute acknowledges that the meet and confer process is critical to the process of formulating public policy.

As might be expected, the statutory prohibition has had an adverse impact on conversation and communication between teachers and administrators in the State's community college system. Although the meet and confer sessions with the majority union are open to all faculty members, no one can speak without the union's permission. In practice, observers have not been permitted to speak. The statute thus gives the majority union in the system an effective veto over the right of dissident faculty members to communicate their views to the administration. College administrators understand the PELRA to prohibit them from listening to the views except those of the majority union, and they have acted in accord with that understanding. As a result, much less communication between faculty members and college administrators occurs under the statute because both administrators and teachers fear that if they exchange views, especially when the exchange involves nonunion faculty members, they will be violating the PELRA. Those conversations that do still occur often are useless as a practical matter, since the administrator often responds only by saying that the subject must be discussed in a different forum. Thus the PELRA has substituted a union-controlled process for the formerly free exchange of views that took place between faculty and the administration. In practice, the union has a monopoly on the effective opportunity to present views to the administration on the wide range of subjects covered by the "meet and confer" process.

The District Court found that under the statute "the weight and significance of individual speech interests have been consciously derogated in favor of systematic, official expression." Jurisdictional Statement A-20. "The PELRA has made the formal meet and confer process the primary mechanism for *any significant faculty-administration communication* on such policy questions." *Id.,* at A-49 (emphasis supplied). It concluded that the meet and confer process "is the only significant forum for the faculty to resolve virtually every issue outside the scope of mandatory bargaining. *This structure effectively blocks any meaningful expression by faculty members who are excluded from the formal process." Id.,* at A-22 (emphasis supplied). These findings may not be set aside unless clearly erroneous, see *Inwood Laboratories v. Ives Laboratories,* 456 U.S. 844 (1982); *Pullman-Standard v. Swint,* 456 U.S. 273 (1982), and in any event are not challenged by appellants or the Court.

II

Both the plain language of the statute and the District Court's findings concerning its actual operation demonstrate that it is a law abridging the freedom of speech. This is true both because it grants unions especially favored positions in communicating with public policymaking bodies and because it curtails the ability of all other members of the public to communicate effectively with those public bodies.

There can be no question but that the First Amendment secures the right of individuals to communicate with their government. And the First Amendment was intended to secure something more than an exercise in futility — it guarantees a *meaningful* opportunity to express one's views. For example, this Court has recognized that the right to forward views might become a practical nullity if Government prohibited persons from banding together to make their voices heard. Thus, the First Amendment protects freedom of association because it makes the right to express one's views meaningful....

The First Amendment also protects the public employee's right *not* to associate. Just as "the Legislature could not require allegiance to a particular political faith as a condition of public employment," *Illinois State Employees Union, Council 34 v. Lewis,* 473 F.2d 561, 570 (7th Cir.1972), so is it equally clear that the Legislature could not require an employee to subscribe to the political tenets of a particular labor union....

IV

No one suggests that the Minnesota statute has been narrowly tailored to serve a compelling state interest. The only interest appellants claim the statute serves is in protecting the status of the public employees' exclusive representative. It is now settled law that a public employer may negotiate only with the elected representative of its employees, because it would be impracticable to negotiate simultaneously with rival labor unions. See *Abood v. Detroit Board of Education,* 431 U.S. 209, 224-226 (1977). But in *Abood* we explicitly held that exclusivity could not be extended to areas beyond the statutorily mandated subjects of collective bargaining, since such an extension would impair the associational rights of those who do not wish to join the union. See *id.,* at 232-237. Here, the area subject to the meet and confer process are by definition not subjects of collective bargaining. While a public employer cannot contract with more than one union at a time, as the Court points out, it can confer with as many groups as it desires. *Ante,* at 1065-1066. The need to conduct collective bargaining with only one employee representative does not justify prohibiting college administrators from conferring with other employees on topics not the subject of collective bargaining. That is the teaching of *Abood.*

There is a simple, but fundamental, reason why the state interest in exclusivity cannot sustain this statute. That interest creates a preference for the views of majority unions which itself infringes the principles of the First Amendment....

The majority claims that this principle does not apply to closed proceedings not open to any form of public access. *Ante,* at 1064-1065. In fact, however, the meet and confer sessions are open to the public and are held in public places. Moreover, the State permits participation by the union's representatives but no others. When a State permits some speakers but not others access to a forum for communication, it must justify its exclusions as viewpoint-neutral. See *Widmar v. Vincent,* 454 U.S. 263, 267-268 (1981); *Madison Joint School District v. Wisconsin Employment Relations Comm'n,* 429 U.S. 167, 175 and n. 8 (1976); *Southeastern Promotions, Ltd. v. Conrad,* 420 U.S. 546, 555-559 (1975). Surely that principle cannot be avoided by the simple expedient of using the speaker's point of view as the criterion for defining the scope of access to a publicly sponsored forum. Indeed, the case on which the majority principally relies, *Perry Education Assn. v. Perry Local Educators' Assn.*, 103 S. Ct. 948 (1983), states that government may not restrict access to channels of communication as an attempt "to discourage one viewpoint and advance another." 103 S. Ct. at 957....

The First Amendment favors unabridged communication among members of a free society — including communication between employer and employee. The process of collective bargaining requires that a limited exception to that general principle be recognized, but until today we have not tolerated any broadening of that exception beyond the collective bargaining process. The effect of the Minnesota statute is to make the union the only authorized spokesman for all employees on political matters as well as contractual matters. In my opinion, such state sponsored orthodoxy is plainly impermissible. The Court, however, relies on a newly found state interest in promoting conformity — the "interest in ensuring that its public employers hear one, and only one, voice presenting the majority view of its professional employees on employment-related policy questions, whatever other advice they may receive on those questions." *Ante*, at 1069. The notion that there is a state interest in fostering a private monopoly on any form of communication is at war with the principle that "the desire to favor one form of speech over all others" is not merely trivial; it "is illegitimate." *Carey v. Brown*, 447 U.S. 455, 468 (1980).

As I noted at the outset, we are concerned with the constitutionality of a law enacted by the legislature. That law requires all executives administering the community college system — as well as all other public employers — to adhere to the specific "meet and confer" process when formulating public policy. The invalidity of such a law need not impair the discretion exercised by individual public administrators with regard to the identity of the persons from whom, or the time, place, and manner in which, they will accept advice concerning their official conduct. But for the State to preclude the exercise of that discretion — to say that the ideas of all save the majority union may not compete on their merits — is to impose the kind of restraint on the free exchange of ideas that the First Amendment does not tolerate.

Because I am convinced that the statutorily mandated exclusive "meet and confer" process is constitutionally intolerable, I respectfully dissent.

2. AUTHORITY OF PUBLIC EMPLOYERS TO BARGAIN IN THE ABSENCE OF LEGISLATION

LITTLETON EDUCATION ASSOCIATION v. ARAPAHOE COUNTY SCHOOL DISTRICT NO. 6

191 Colo. 411, 553 P.2d 793 (1976)

DAY, JUSTICE. This appeal involves a determination of the validity of a collective bargaining agreement between defendant-appellee school board of Arapahoe County school district No. 6 (the board) and plaintiff-appellant Littleton Education Association (LEA)....

We do not adopt the court's ruling that, absent legislative authority, the board has no power to enter into collective bargaining agreements....

Collective bargaining negotiations entered into on a voluntary basis have resulted in agreements in 38 of the state's 181 school districts. In 1975 these contracts affected approximately 21,896 teachers in the state public school system.

In arguing for affirmance of the trial court's determination of the *per se* invalidity of such agreements, the board argues that this court's ruling in *Fellows v. LaTronica,* 151 Colo. 300, 377 P.2d 547 (1962), is controlling. In *Fellows* a municipal fireman claimed the city of Pueblo was required by a collective bargaining agreement to submit his dispute concerning vacation and sick leave to binding arbitration. The court held that the contract between the city and the labor union representing the firemen constituted an unlawful delegation of legislative responsibility by the municipality.

Upon reconsideration of the collective bargaining issue in light of subsequent case law, we now make it clear that *Fellows* should not be considered as per se invalidation of collective bargaining agreements in the public sector even though there is no express statutory authorization for the practice. See *Rockey v. School District #11,* 32 Colo. App. 203, 508 P.2d 796 (1973). Rather, *Fellows* should be limited to the holding on its facts: a public employer cannot be compelled to arbitrate *disputes* arising from collective bargaining agreements. This view is reflected in some of the dictum in the decision:

> "... A proper exercise of the legislative function might well involve consultation and negotiation with spokesmen for public employees, but the ultimate responsibility rests with the legislative body and, under the record here presented, that responsibility cannot be contracted away. For a complete annotation on the question see 31 A.L.R.(2d) 1142."

Also this view was elaborated upon in the specially concurring opinion of the present Chief Justice:

> "That public employees may organize in unions and may designate a representative to present their views as to terms and conditions of employment to the body charged with the duty of setting such terms and conditions if the body chooses to hear them seems now to be generally accepted. Agreements reached between the negotiating parties may be translated into effect by proper legislative action, providing such agreements do not conflict with constitutional, charter or statutory provisions."

It is to be noted that *Fellows* did not address the question of the bargained-for agreement itself. And we also point out that the subject agreement did not provide for binding arbitration on the points of disagreement when the negotiations broke down as involved in *Greeley Police Union v. City Council of Greeley,* Colo., 553 P.2d 790. On the contrary, only the services of an impartial fact finder are provided for. The agreement specifically states that the fact finder's report "... shall be advisory only ...." If the parties are still at an impasse after the advisory report of a fact finder, the agreement provides that "... the Board has the authority *to make the final decision and determination on all unresolved issues,* without further negotiation." (Emphasis added.)

The defect in the board's position that the subject agreement constitutes an unlawful delegation of authority and places control of a school system in the hands of an employee organization reflects a basic misperception of the negotiations process. Negotiations between an employer and an employee organization entered into voluntarily, as in this case, do not require the employer to agree with the proposals submitted by employees. Rather, the *ultimate* decisions regarding employment terms and conditions remain exclusively with the board. While the employees' influence is permitted and felt, the control of decision-making has not been abrogated or delegated.

Furthermore, school boards in this state are empowered with the general authority to contract. Section 22-32-101, C.R.S. 1973. Section 22-32-109(1)(f), C.R.S. 1973, indicates that school boards may contract for the purpose of performing their specific duty:

"To employ all personnel required to maintain the operations and carry out the educational program of the district, and to fix and order paid their compensation;"

Also, the district boards may, under section 22-32-110(1)(k), C.R.S. 1973, enter into a contract for the purpose of exercising their specific power:

"To adopt written policies, rules, and regulations, not inconsistent with law, which may relate to the efficiency, in-service training, professional growth, safety, official conduct, and welfare of the employees, or any classification thereof, of the district...."

In *Chicago Division v. Board of Education,* 76 Ill. App. 2d 456, 222 N.E.2d 243 (1966), the court held that a school board does not require legislative authority to enter into a collective bargaining agreement and that such an agreement is not against public policy.

In *Louisiana Teachers' Association v. New Orleans Parish School Board,* 303 So. 2d 564 (La.App.1974), *cert. denied,* 305 So. 2d 541 (La. S. Ct. 1975), a school board was held empowered to engage in collective bargaining in the absence of express legislative authority to do so. The court stated:

"The Board has the statutory authority to determine the number of teachers to be employed, to select such teachers, to hire them and to fix their salaries, as well as to determine the number and location of schools. [Citation omitted] The Board is further authorized to make rules and regulations for its own government, not inconsistent with law or with the regulations of the Louisiana State Board of Education.

"We hold that a school board, incidental to its statutory duties above enumerated, has the power and authority to collectively bargain with an agent selected by the employees, if the Board determines in its discretion that implementation of collective bargaining will more effectively and efficiently accomplish its objectives and purposes. In our opinion the Board can select reasonable means to carry out its duties and responsibilities incidental to the sound development of employer-employee relations, as long as the means selected are not prohibited by law or against public policy."

See also *Gary Teachers Union Local No. 4 v. School City of Gary,* 152 Ind. App. 591, 284 N.E.2d 108 (1972); and *Dayton Classroom Teachers v. Dayton Board of Education,* 41 Ohio St. 2d 127, 323 N.E.2d 714 (1975).

As one commentator has noted:

"If a public employer has the authority to execute individual employment contracts and is interested in efficiency and administrative simplicity, those individual contracts will contain standardized terms. Once one realizes that contracts negotiated for the same kind of work — office clerical, for example — are subject to standardization, it becomes apparent that a general power to contract can fairly encompass powers to confer exclusive recognition and execute collective bargaining contracts. A collective bargaining contract is essentially a master contract which sets the terms and conditions of employment for individual employees without requiring formal negotiation of these matters with each employee. If a public employer can standardize individual contracts of employment, it should also be able to utilize the more efficient master contract negotiated with an employee representative to achieve the same result. To say that standardized individual contracts are permissible, but a master contract is not, is to exalt form over substance." Dole, *State & Local Public Employee Collective Bargaining in the Absence of Specific Legislative Authority,* 54 Iowa L. Rev. 539 (1969).

In determining that a school board's participation in collective bargaining is not *per se* an unlawful delegation of its authority, we are cognizant of the fact that agreements reached pursuant to such procedures, in the absence of specific statutes to the contrary, must not conflict with existing statutes concerning the governance of the state school system.

We do not say, absent a statute so requiring, a school board can be compelled to enter into collective bargaining....

NOTES

1. In *AFSCME Local 2238 v. Stratton,* 131 L.R.R.M. 2424 (N.M. 1989), the New Mexico Supreme Court held that "in New Mexico, there is an implied authority to bargain collectively in the public sector as an incident to the express grant of authority under the Personnel Act." The court noted, however, that "collective bargaining contracts with governmental employees cannot in any way conflict with, contradict, expand or enlarge the Rules for Labor-Management Relations adopted by the State Personnel Board or any other governmental entity acting in this regard."

2. In a state without a collective bargaining law but in which the courts have held that public employers may voluntarily grant recognition and engage in collective bargaining, can a public employer which grants recognition subsequently withdraw such recognition and refuse thereafter to engage in bargaining? In *Naperville Police Union, Local 2233 v. City of Naperville,* 97 Ill. App. 3d 153, 422 N.E.2d 869 (1981), the court held that "the City's duty to bargain with the Union ended after the last agreement between the parties expired following unsuccessful dispute settlement procedures." The court further observed that "[h]aving chosen not to recognize the Union as the exclusive bargaining agent of the patrolmen on a voluntary basis, the City is under no enforceable legal duty to do so."

3. In *Peters v. Health & Hosps. Governing Comm'n,* 88 Ill. 2d 316, 430 N.E.2d 1128 (1981), two unions sought specific performance of their election agreements whereby the employer agreed to recognize and bargain in good faith with the unions in question unless the unions lost their majority status in accordance with the provisions of said election agreements. The Illinois Supreme Court held that the agreements were unenforceable, stating:

> This court has held that a public body may not delegate a discretionary public responsibility with which it is charged.... Although the courts have enforced collective bargaining agreements within the scope of those limitations, we find no authority in statutory or case law which supports the position that a public body can be ordered to negotiate such an agreement.

4. If a municipality, in the absence of applicable state legislation, enacts an ordinance establishing bargaining rights for its employees, can the ordinance be challenged on preemption grounds, i.e., that collective bargaining legislation is a matter of statewide concern and can only be enacted by the state legislature? Would it make any difference if the municipality had home rule powers? In *Louisville Fire Fighters v. Burke*, 75 L.R.R.M. 2001 (Ky. Cir. Ct., Jefferson County, 1970), the court upheld the power of the City of Louisville to enact a collective bargaining ordinance. The court noted, inter alia, "that the Legislature meant to and did confer home rule upon the City of Louisville except where specifically denied by statue." But see *Midwest Employers Council v. City of Omaha*, 177 Neb. 877, 131 N.W.2d 609 (1964), where the court held that the City of Omaha did not have authority to enact a fair employment practices ordinance since "the power relating to labor relations and practices, and civil rights lies in the state, and such matters are of statewide concern and not of local concern nor municipal government concern."

5. Although the decision in the principal case represents the clear majority view, there is precedent in several states supporting the proposition that a public employer has no authority to engage in collective bargaining in the absence of specific statutory authorization. For example, in *Virginia v. Arlington Cty. Bd.*, 232 S.E.2d 30 (Va. 1977), the Virginia Supreme Court held that a local governing body, in the absence of express statutory authority, could not recognize a union as the exclusive representative of a group of public employees and negotiate and enter into a binding collective bargaining agreement. The court reasoned as follows:

> For this court to imply the power here sought, we would be required to find that because local governmental boards possess the power to enter into contracts and to hire employees and fix the terms and conditions of their employment, the boards also possess the authority to bargain collectively with labor organizations. But if the power cannot be found in this source, the boards in the present case then would have us find that, nonetheless, they possess the power to bargain collectively because they have discretionary authority to select any reasonable method of exercising a power expressly granted but silent upon its mode or manner of execution.
>
> We cannot make either finding. To imply the contended for authority would constitute the creation of a power that does not exist or; at least, the expansion of an existing power beyond rational limits. To sanction the method of exercising authority which the boards have selected in this case, even giving the selection the benefit of any doubt, would result in an unreasonable and strained application of the doctrine of implied powers. To approve the actions taken in this case would ignore the lack of any support for the proposition that collective bargaining by the boards is necessary to pro-

mote the public interest. And, finally but not least important, to imply the power asserted by the boards would be contrary to legislative intent....

We are faced in this case with overwhelming indications of legislative intent concerning the concept of collective bargaining in the public sector. For this court to declare that the boards have the power to bargain collectively, when even the wisdom of incorporating the concept into the general law of the Commonwealth is the subject of controversial public and political debate, would constitute judicial legislation, with all the adverse connotations that term generates. Conscious of the respective roles of the General Assembly and the judiciary, we decline to intrude upon what the Attorney General succinctly describes as a "singularly political question."

Accord *Fayette Cty. Educ. Ass'n v. Hardy,* 626 S.W.2d 217 (Ky. Ct. App. 1980); *Int'l Union of Operating Eng'rs, Local 321 v. Water Works Bd.,* 276 Ala. 462, 163 So. 2d 619 (1964).

3. LEGAL AUTHORIZATION

Increasingly, the right of public employees to bargain collectively is established and protected by legislation, executive orders, or municipal ordinances. The right of federal employees to bargain collectively was initially authorized in 1962 by Executive Order 10988. In 1969, Executive Order 10988 was reissued and modified by Executive Order 11491. In 1978, the provisions of Executive Order 11491 were, to a very significant extent, codified as Title VII of the Civil Service Reform Act of 1978. 5 U.S.C. § 7101 et seq. (1980). The approximately 750,000 postal employees who were formerly covered by Executive Orders 10988 and 11491 are now covered by the labor relations provisions of the Postal Reorganization Act which incorporates most of the provisions of the National Labor Relations Act, as amended.*

Wisconsin in 1959 was the first state to enact legislation authorizing collective bargaining for public employees. Since then, well over half the states have enacted legislation permitting collective bargaining by some or all categories of public employees. The following is a summary of the legislation enacted to date:

Twenty-nine states have enacted reasonably comprehensive statutes of general applicability: Alaska (all public employees), California (substantially all public employees; three statutes),* Connecticut (all municipal employees, teachers, and state employees, three statutes), Delaware (all public employees; two statutes), Florida (all public employees), Hawaii (all public employees),* Illinois (all public employees; two statutes),* Iowa (all public employees), Kansas (all public employees; local option as to coverage), Maine (all municipal and state employees; several statutes), Massachusetts (all public employees; two statutes), Michigan (all public employees except classified state employees), Minnesota (all public employees), Missouri (all public employees except policemen and teachers),* Montana (all public employees), Nebraska (all municipal and state employees), Nevada (all local government employees including teachers), New Hampshire (classified state employees and non-academic university employees), New Jersey (all public employees), New York (all public employees),* North Dakota (all public employees), Ohio (all public employees), Oregon (all public

---

*Included in Statutory Appendix.

employees), Pennsylvania (all public employees, including fire fighters and police officers; two statutes),* Rhode Island (all public employees; five statutes), South Dakota (all public employees), Vermont (all public employees; three statutes), Washington (all state and local government employees; several statutes), Wisconsin (all state and municipal employees including teachers; two statutes).*

Fifteen states have enacted separate statutes granting teachers the right to bargain collectively: Alaska, California,* Connecticut, Delaware, Idaho, Indiana, Kansas, Maryland, Nebraska, North Dakota, Oklahoma, Rhode Island, Tennessee, Vermont, Washington.

Eleven states have enacted collective bargaining laws covering fire fighters and/or police officers: Alabama (fire fighters), Georgia (fire fighters), Idaho (fire fighters), Kentucky (both, but only covers Louisville and Jefferson County), New Hampshire (police officers), Oklahoma (both), Pennsylvania (both), Rhode Island (both; two statutes), South Dakota (both), Texas (both), Wyoming (fire fighters).

Several states have also enacted collective bargaining legislation that is limited to transit authorities, port authorities, or other special districts.

In addition to the numerous states laws referred to above, a number of municipalities in states that do not have collective bargaining legislation have passed charter provisions or enacted ordinances granting their employees the right to bargain collectively. Phoenix, Arizona, Baltimore, Maryland, and Washington, D.C., are three prominent examples.

NOTES

1. Whereas some states, such as New York and Hawaii, have one law which covers all public employees, other states, such as California and Rhode Island, have numerous statutory enactments covering various categories of public employees.

Most advisory commissions have recommended the enactment of one comprehensive statute rather than separate statutes for different categories of public employees. The Advisory Commission on Intergovernmental Relations in its Report "endorse[d] the single law approach," noting that "the State statute should deal with all occupational categories of public employees" since "separate statutory treatment of certain types of public employees is incompatible with the need for a smoothly-functioning labor-management relations process in the public sector." Advisory Comm'n on Intergovernmental Relations, Labor-Management Policies for State and Local Government 103-04 (1969). The Rhode Island Study Commission recommended that the state's five public sector collective bargaining laws be encompassed in one comprehensive law. In Discussion and Recommendations for Changing Public Employee Legislation in Rhode Island, GERR No. 498, E-1, E-2 (1973), the following critique was made of the state's existing patchwork of laws:

There is little question that the evolution of public sector legislation within the state was accomplished without any real consideration as to the totality of the impact of all of the legislation. We have in the state five collective bargaining laws each relating to a specific type of public employee, i.e., teachers, police, firefighters, municipal employees and state employees. Each of these

---

*Included in Statutory Appendix.

laws was framed only with reference to that particular class of employee. The major deficiency in this individual approach is that the impact of the bargains ultimately made draws upon common tax revenues and crosses administrative lines and if the laws are not considered together the administration of the acts as well as the requirements for dispute resolution are also inevitably handled independently. It is only incidental that the total economic and organizational impact is ever effectively understood. *In a word, we have over-legislated* and this "over legislation" in itself (since it has not taken into consideration the total system of impacts) has and will continue to have a serious, detrimental effect upon the collective bargaining process and the decisions made thereby.

2. Several of the state public sector bargaining laws permit local governmental jurisdictions to adopt their own procedures. The New York Law, for example, provides that provisions and procedures enacted by a local government, with certain exceptions, are applicable if the New York PERB has determined "that such provisions and procedures and the continuing implementation thereof are substantially equivalent to the provisions and procedures set forth ... with respect to the state." N.Y. Civil Serv. Law § 212 (McKinney 1983). With respect to New York City, however, the Act provides that the PERB is not required to make such a determination, but rather may file suit for declaratory judgment alleging that the provisions and procedures are not substantially equivalent. The Kansas Act requires that local provisions and procedures be "reasonably equivalent" rather than "substantially equivalent." Kan. Stat. Ann. § 75-4335 (Supp. 1983). What is the difference between "reasonably equivalent" and "substantially equivalent"? See Statement of Arvid Anderson, *supra.*

3. In a number of cases employee organizations and unions have contended that labor relations statutes that do not specifically cover public employers are nevertheless applicable to the public sector. The courts, however, have uniformly rejected this contention. For example, in *Westly v. Board of City Comm'rs,* 573 P.2d 1279, 97 L.R.R.M. 2580 (Utah 1978), the court stated that "[i]n the absence of explicit legislative language, statutes governing labor relations between employers and employees apply only to private industry and not to the sovereign or its political subdivisions." Accord *Retail Clerks Local 187 v. University of Wyo.,* 531 P.2d 884 (Wyo. 1975); *Local 283, IBEW v. Robison,* 91 Idaho 445, 423 P.2d 999 (1967).

B. SCOPE OF BARGAINING

1. PUBLIC POLICY CONSIDERATIONS

H. WELLINGTON & R. WINTER, THE UNIONS AND THE CITIES 21-30 (1971)*

The Public Sector Model: Nonmonetary Issues

In the private sector, unions have pushed to expand the scope of bargaining in response to the desires of their members for a variety of new benefits (pension rights, supplementary unemployment payments, merit increases). These benefits generally impose a monetary cost on the employer. And because employers are restrained by the market, an expanded bargaining agenda means that, if a union negotiates an agreement over more subjects, it generally trades off more of less for less of more.

---

*Reprinted by permission. Copyright 1971 by the Brookings Institution, Washington, D.C.

From the consumer's point of view this in turn means that the price of the product he purchases is not significantly related to the scope of bargaining. And since unions rarely bargain about the nature of the product produced, the consumer can be relatively indifferent as to how many or how few subjects are covered in any collective agreement. Nor need the consumer be concerned about union demands that would not impose a financial cost on the employer, for example, the design of a grievance procedure. While such demands are not subject to the same kind of trade-off as are financial demands, they are unlikely, if granted, to have any impact on the consumer. Their effect is on the quality of life of the parties to the agreement.

In the public sector the cluster of problems that surround the scope of bargaining are much more troublesome than they are in the private sector. The problems have several dimensions.

First, the trade-off between subjects of bargaining in the public sector is less of a protection to the consumer (public) than it is in the private. Where political leaders view the costs of union demands as essentially budgetary, a trade-off can occur. Thus, a demand for higher teacher salaries and a demand for reduced class size may be treated as part of one package. But where a demand, although it has a budgetary effect, is viewed as involving essentially political costs, trade-offs are more difficult. Our paradigmatic mayor, for example, may be under great pressure to make a large monetary settlement with a teachers' union whether or not it is joined to demands for special training programs for disadvantaged children. Interest groups tend to exert pressure against union demands only when they are directly affected. Otherwise, they are apt to join that large constituency (the general public) that wants to avoid labor trouble. Trade-offs can occur only when several demands are resisted by roughly the same groups. Thus, pure budgetary demands can be traded off when they are opposed by taxpayers. But when the identity of the resisting group changes with each demand, political leaders may find it expedient to strike a balance on each issue individually, rather than as part of a total package, by measuring the political power of each interest group involved against the political power of the constituency pressing for labor peace. To put it another way, as important as financial factors are to a mayor, political factors may be even more important. The market allows the businessman no such discretionary choice.

Where a union demand — such as increasing the disciplinary power of teachers — does not have budgetary consequences, some trade-offs may occur. Granting the demand will impose a political cost on the mayor because it may anger another interest group. But because the resisting group may change with each issue, each issue is apt to be treated individually and not as a part of a total package. And this may not protect the public. Differing from the private sector, nonmonetary demands of public sector unions do have effects that go beyond the parties to the agreement. All of us have a stake in how school children are disciplined. Expansion of the subjects of bargaining in the public sector, therefore, may increase the total quantum of union power in the political process.

Second, public employees do not generally produce a product. They perform a service. The way in which a service is performed may become a subject of bargaining. As a result, the nature of that service may be changed. Some of these services — police protection, teaching, health care — involve questions that are politically, socially, or ideologically sensitive. In part this is because government is involved and alternatives to governmentally provided services are relatively dear. In part, government is involved because of society's perception about the nature of the service and society's need for it. This suggests that decisions affecting the nature of a governmentally provided service are much more likely to be challenged and are more urgent than generally is the case with services that are offered privately.

Third, some of the services government provides are performed by professionals — teachers, social workers, and so forth — who are keenly interested in the underlying philosophy that informs their work. To them, theirs is not merely a job to be done for a salary. They may be educators or other "change agents" of society. And this may mean that these employees are concerned with more than incrementally altering a governmental service or its method of delivery. They may be advocates of bold departures that will radically transform the service itself.

The issue is not a threshold one of whether professional public employees should participate in decisions about the nature of the services they provide. Any properly run governmental agency should be interested in, and heavily reliant upon, the judgment of its professional staff. The issue rather is the method of that participation.

Conclusions about this issue as well as the larger issue of a full transplant of collective bargaining to the public sector may be facilitated by addressing some aspects of the governmental decision-making process — particularly at the municipal level — and the impact of collective bargaining on that process.

Public Employee Unions and the Political Process

Although the market does not discipline the union in the public sector to the extent that it does in the private, the municipal employment paradigm, nevertheless, would seem to be consistent with what Robert A. Dahl has called the "'normal' American political process," which is "one in which there is a high probability that an active and legitimate group in the population can make itself heard effectively at some crucial stage in the process of decision," for the union may be seen as little more than an "active and legitimate group in the population." With elections in the background to perform, as Mr. Dahl notes, "the critical role ... in maximizing political equality and popular sovereignty," all seems well, at least theoretically, with collective bargaining and public employment.

But there is trouble even in the house of theory if collective bargaining in the public sector means what it does in the private. The trouble is that if unions are able to withhold labor — to strike — as well as to employ the usual methods of political pressure, they may possess a disproportionate share of effective power in the process of decision. Collective bargaining would then be so effective a pressure as to skew the results of the "'normal' American political process."

One should straightway make plain that the strike issue is not simply the importance of public services as contrasted with services or products produced in the private sector. This is only part of the issue, and in the past the partial truth has beclouded analysis. The services performed by a private transit authority are neither less nor more important to the public than those that would be performed if the transit authority were owned by a municipality. A railroad or a dock strike may be more damaging to a community than a "job action" by police. This is not to say that governmental services are not important. They are, both because the demand for them is inelastic and because their disruption may seriously injure a city's economy and occasionally impair the physical welfare of its citizens. Nevertheless, the importance of governmental services is only a necessary part of, rather than a complete answer to, the question: Why be more concerned about strikes in public employment than in private?

The answer to the question is simply that, because strikes in public employment disrupt important services, a large part of a mayor's political constituency will, in many cases, press for a quick end to the strike with little concern for the cost of settlement. This is particularly so where the cost of settlement is borne by a different and larger political constituency, the citizens of the state or nation. Since interest groups other than public employees, with conflicting claims on municipal government, do not, as a general proposition, have anything approaching the effectiveness of the strike — or at least cannot maintain that relative degree of power over the long run — they may be put at a significant competitive disadvantage in the political process.

The private sector strike is designed to exert economic pressure on the employer by depriving him of revenues. The public employee strike is fundamentally different: its sole purpose is to exert political pressure on municipal officials. They are deprived, not of revenues but of the political support of those who are inconvenienced by a disruption of municipal services. But precisely because the private strike is an economic weapon, it is disciplined by the market and the benefit/unemployment trade-off that imposes. And because the public employee strike is a political weapon, it is subject only to the restraints imposed by the political process and they are on the whole less limiting and less disciplinary than those of the market. If this is the case, it must be said that the political process will be radically altered by wholesale importation of the strike weapon. And because of the deceptive simplicity of the analogy to collective bargaining in the private sector, the alteration may take place without anyone realizing what has happened.

Nor is it an answer that, in some municipalities, interest groups other than unions now have a disproportionate share of political power. This is inescapably true, and we do not condone that situation. Indeed, we would be among the first to advocate reform. However, reform cannot be accomplished by giving another interest group disproportionate power, for the losers would be the weakest groups in the community. In most municipalities, the weakest groups are composed of citizens who many believe are most in need of more power.

Therefore, while the purpose and effect of strikes by public employees may seem in the beginning designed merely to establish collective bargaining or to "catch up" with wages and fringe benefits in the private sector, in the long run strikes may become too effective a means for redistributing income; so effective, indeed, that one might see them as an institutionalized means of obtaining and maintaining a subsidy for union members.

As is often the case when one generalizes, this picture may be considered overdrawn. In order to refine analysis, it will be helpful to distinguish between strikes that occur over monetary issues and strikes involving nonmonetary issues. The generalized picture sketched above is mainly concerned with the former. Because there is usually no substitute for governmental services, the citizen-consumer faced with a strike of teachers, or garbage men, or social workers is likely to be seriously inconvenienced. This in turn places enormous pressure on the mayor, who is apt to find it difficult to look to the long-run balance sheet of the municipality. Most citizens are directly affected by a strike of sanitation workers. Few, however, can decipher a municipal budget or trace the relationship between today's labor settlement and next year's increase in the mill rate. Thus, in the typical case the impact of a settlement is less visible — or can more often be concealed — than the impact of a disruption of services. Moreover, the cost of settlement may fall upon a constituency much larger — the whole state or nation — than that represented by the mayor. And revenue sharing schemes that involve unrestricted funds may further lessen public resistance to generous settlements. It follows that the mayor usually will look to the electorate that is clamoring for a settlement, and in these circumstances the union's fear of a long strike, a major check on its power in the private sector, is not a consideration.[1] In the face of all of these factors other interest groups with priorities different from the union's are apt to be much less successful in their pursuit of scarce tax dollars than is the union with power to withhold services.[2]

With respect to strikes over some nonmonetary issues — decentralization of the governance of schools might be an example — the intensity of concern on the part of well-organized interest groups opposed to the union's position would support the mayor in his resistance to union demands. But even here, if the union rank and file back their leadership, pressures for settlement from the general public, which may be largely indifferent as to the underlying issue, might in time become irresistible.[3]

The strike and its threat, moreover, exacerbate the problems associated with the scope of bargaining in public employment. This seems clear if one attends in slightly more detail to techniques of municipal decision making.

Few students of our cities would object to Herbert Kaufman's observation that:

> Decisions of the municipal government emanate from no single source, but from many centers; conflicts and clashes are referred to no single authority, but are settled at many levels and at many points in the system: no single

---

[1]Contrast the situation in the private sector: "... management cannot normally win the short strike. Management can only win the long strike. Also management frequently tends, in fact, to win the long strike. As a strike lengthens, it commonly bears more heavily on the union and the employees than on management. Strike relief is no substitute for a job. Even regular strike benefits, which few unions can afford, and which usually exhaust the union treasury quite rapidly (with some exceptions), are no substitute for a job." E. Livernash, "The Relation of Power to the Structure and Process of Collective Bargaining," 6 Journal of Law & Economics 10, 15 (October 1963).

[2]A vivid example was provided by an experience in New Jersey. After a twelve-hour strike by Newark firefighters on July 11, 1969, state urban aid funds, originally authorized for helping the poor, were diverted to salary increases for firemen and police. See New York Times, Aug. 7, 1969, p. 25. Moreover, government decision makers other than the mayor (for example, the governor) may have interests different from those of the mayor, interests that manifest themselves in pressures for settlement.

[3]Consider also the effect of such strikes on the fabric of society. See, for example, M. Mayer, The Teacher Strike: New York, 1968 (Harper and Row, 1969).

group can guarantee the success of any proposal it supports, the defeat of every idea it objects to. Not even the central governmental organs of the city — the Mayor, the Board of Estimate, the Council — individually or in combination, even approach mastery in this sense.

Each separate decision center consists of a cluster of interested contestants, with a "core group" in the middle, invested by the rules with the formal authority to legitimize decisions (that is to promulgate them in binding form) and a constellation of related "satellite groups" seeking to influence the authoritative issuances of the core group.

Nor would many disagree with Nelson W. Polsby when, in discussing community decision making that is concerned with an alternative to a "current state of affairs," he argues that the alternative "must be politically palatable and relatively easy to accomplish; otherwise great amounts of influence have to be brought to bear with great skill and efficiency in order to secure its adoption."

It seems probable that such potential subjects of bargaining as school decentralization and a civilian police review board are, where they do not exist, alternatives to the "current state of affairs," which are not "politically palatable and relatively easy to accomplish." If a teachers' union or a police union were to bargain with the municipal employer over these questions, and were able to use the strike to insist that the proposals not be adopted, how much "skill and efficiency" on the part of the proposals' advocates would be necessary to effect a change? And, to put the shoe on the other foot, if a teachers' union were to insist through collective bargaining (with the strike or its threat) upon major changes in school curriculum, would not that union have to be considerably less skillful and efficient in the normal political process than other advocates of community change? The point is that with respect to some subjects, collective bargaining may be too powerful a lever on municipal decision making, too effective a technique for changing or preventing the change of one small but important part of the "current state of affairs."

Unfortunately, in this area the problem is not merely the strike threat and the strike. In a system where impasse procedures involving third parties are established in order to reduce work stoppages — and this is common in those states that have passed public employment bargaining statutes — third party intervention must be partly responsive to union demands. If the scope of bargaining is open-ended, the neutral party, to be effective, will have to work out accommodations that inevitably advance some of the union's claims some of the time. And the neutral, with his eyes fixed on achieving a settlement, can hardly be concerned with balancing all the items on the community agenda or reflecting the interests of all relevant groups.

The Theory Summarized

Collective bargaining in public employment, then, seems distinguishable from that in the private sector. To begin with, it imposes on society more than a potential misallocation of resources through restrictions on economic output, the principal cost imposed by private sector unions. Collective bargaining by public employees and the political process cannot be separated. The costs of such bargaining, therefore, cannot be fully measured without taking into account the impact on the allocation of political power in the typical municipality.

If one assumes, as here, that municipal political processes should be structured to ensure "a high probability that an active and legitimate group in the population can make itself heard effectively at some crucial stage in the process of decision," then the issue is how powerful unions will be in the typical municipal political process if a full transplant of collective bargaining is carried out.

The conclusion is that such a transplant would, in many cases, institutionalize the power of public employee unions in a way that would leave competing groups in the political process at a permanent and substantial disadvantage.

NOTES

1. The Advisory Commission on Intergovernmental Relations recommended that certain "management rights" be removed from the scope of bargaining. The Commission stated:

[The] Commission believes statutory description of management rights is necessary if well defined parameters to discussions are to be established. In a democratic political system, dealings between public employers and public employee organizations — whether they are called negotiations or discussions — must necessarily be limited by legislatively determined policies and goals. This may involve merely a restatement of basic management prerogatives and civil service precepts. Listing such rights in law eliminates many of the headaches of administrative elaboration and some of the cross pressures generated by ambiguities. Wages, hours, and other terms and conditions of employment, however, are left for the conference table. Hence, the framework for a meaningful dialogue remains intact. Advisory Commission on Intergovernmental Relations, Labor-Management Policies for State and Local Government 102-03 (1969).

The Committee on Economic Development similarly recommended that "[i]n enacting or revising public-sector collective bargaining legislation, states should identify the topics subject to bargaining and should also stipulate those management prerogatives not subject to bargaining." Committee on Economic Development, Improving Management of the Public Work Force 76-77 (1978).

On the other hand, the California Assembly Advisory Council chaired by Benjamin Aaron stated that it did "not see any compelling distinction between the public and private sector that would justify the inclusion of management-rights clauses in public employee relations statutes." Final Report of the Assembly Advisory Council on Public Employee Relations 139 (Cal. 1973).

2. Should the determination of whether public employees are allowed to strike have any bearing on the scope of bargaining? Bok and Dunlop answered affirmatively:

[T]he scope of bargaining will be influenced by the procedures adopted to resolve impasses in negotiations. If public employees are permitted to strike, the range of bargainable topics presumably should be closely confined. The exercise of economic pressure through disruption of public services is too haphazard a way of deciding significant issues affecting the public, such as institution of a police review board, decentralization of administrative services, and initiation or discontinuation of a specific government facility. This is especially true in the public sector, where decisions are much less restricted by competition and related market pressures. If disputes are settled by the more reasoned process of fact finding or arbitration, on the other hand, the scope of negotiation may be somewhat broader, although there will still be many important matters excluded from bargaining on the ground either that they should be within the province of management or that they seem more suited to resolution through the political process. Finally, a system that does not provide for strikes or arbitration, but reserves final power in a legislative body to settle bargaining disputes, can appropriately entrust a broad range of subjects to the bargaining process. D. Bok & J. Dunlop, Labor and the American Community 327 (1970).

WOLLETT, THE BARGAINING PROCESS IN THE PUBLIC SECTOR: WHAT IS BARGAINABLE?, 51 Or. L. Rev. 177, 177-82 (1971)*

Bargainability is a subject which seems to have a peculiar fascination for the National Labor Relations Board, and for lawyers, law professors, law students, directors of industrial relations, union representatives, and other persons in the labor relations business. A vast body of jurisprudence dealing with what the parties *must* bargain about, what they *may* bargain about, and what they *cannot* bargain about has developed in the last 30 years.

Predictably, as collective bargaining has come to public employment, the same concern has been demonstrated. For example, Professors Wellington and Winter have recently argued that collective bargaining is too powerful a lever on governmental decision-making and too effective a technique for changing or maintaining public policies to allow it to run unchecked. Therefore, the subject matter which is negotiable should be more sharply circumscribed in the public sector than in the private sector.

My thesis is that the vast literature concerning the scope of bargaining is much ado about nothing and that the preoccupation with this subject is mischievous as well as mistaken. Many practitioners will regard this as a glossing over of a fundamental issue, as an oversimplification, and as a blithe ignoring of vital matters.

The case for my thesis lies in the attitude which one brings to the bargaining table. If the negotiator conceives his function to be one of establishing immutable principles, winning points and outscoring the adversary, massaging his client's ego, or building a reputation as a protagonist of ordered government and managerial sovereignty, the issue of what is bargainable is fertile ground. If, on the other hand, he approaches the table in a spirit of meeting problems rather than avoiding them, and of trying to find ways to reach agreement rather than identifying obstacles which make a negotiated settlement impossible, I submit that the question of scope of bargaining becomes of little significance.

During my eight years of law practice in New York City, exclusively on the management side in the private sector, I cannot recall a single instance when my colleagues and I refused, on behalf of our client, to bargain about *anything* in the sense of refusing to discuss it on its merits. If we perceived that the proposal reflected a problem of genuine concern to the employees, we were willing to talk about it. In focusing on the facts, it often turned out that the problem was more fanciful than real, or that it could be more appropriately handled outside the context of periodic crisis bargaining, that it made no sense from either

---

*Reprinted by permission. Copyright © 1971 by University of Oregon.

party's point of view to deal with it as a fixed provision of a collective agreement, that it could be dealt with without invading interests in respect to which management felt it must retain the power to act unilaterally, or that it could be traded off. In my experience, this approach to scope of bargaining questions is both realistic and constructive. If one is willing to be imaginative in dealing with a proposal and is motivated by a desire to reach a negotiated settlement, an acceptable accommodation can generally be reached. If one is unwilling to consider new proposals, conflict is a certainty and exacerbation of the dispute a likelihood.

Although some union proposals represent institutional imperatives, most of them (in the public sector as well as in the private sector) are manifestations of the ambitions, fears, and frustrations of the employees represented. For purposes of this discussion, union proposals may be categorized into three groups. The first group contains those proposals which are psychological and political. These wash out in the bargaining process not because they are nonnegotiable but because they are frivolous, and for management to react to them by asserting that they invade prerogatives or sovereignty would be gratuitous and counter-productive. The second group includes those proposals which arguably intrude into policy matters usually thought to be within the sole control of management, which, while seriously made, are subject to trade-offs for improvements in wages, hours, and working conditions.[*] The third group consists of proposals which arguably intrude into managerial prerogatives or governmental sovereignty, which are seriously made and which are not readily tradable. The proposals in the last category do present problems, but they are not usually insoluble if they are dealt with on their merits rather than avoided on conceptualistic grounds.

The fourth set of negotiations between the New York City School Board and the United Federation of Teachers provides an excellent example of how problems encompassed in the third category above can be resolved. The fourth set of negotiations involved in part a proposal by the union that the collective bargaining agreement provide for the removal of disruptive children from regular classrooms. The parties had great difficulty with this issue because it involved educational policy as well as conditions of work, but the result of their negotiations was an acceptable compromise which preserved management's basic concern by agreeing that the procedures would be embodied in a "Special Circular" of the School Board which would be *appended to,* but would not be *a part of,* the collective bargaining agreement.

The Wellington-Winter thesis is based on two assumptions: (1) that public employee unions aspire to take over the responsibility for the management of governmental enterprises, and (2) that they have the power to do so. Both assumptions are, in my judgment, unsound. The scope of bargaining is partly a function of relative bargaining power, and most employee organizations in the public sector lack the power to force bargaining (or to force agreement) over such matters as operational efficiency, educational policy, and other matters which relate to the so-called "mission" of the enterprise.

---

[*]This subject is, of course, academic unless the aggressive party, usually the union, has enough bargaining power to compel trade-offs.

Most public employee unions, even those which are professional in nature, do not think of collective bargaining primarily as a vehicle for social change. They do not have ambitions to take over the responsibility for running the agency. Specific aspirations will vary, of course, according to the skills and traditions of the occupational group involved. For example, teachers as a group tend to be interested in social change; and some agreements resulting from teacher-school board bargaining have worked changes in educational programming. But it is not true, at least in my experience, that teachers use collective bargaining primarily as an instrumentality for promoting social change. Public employees, including those whose responsibilities and skills are professional or quasi-professional, think of collective bargaining primarily as a vehicle for protecting and advancing their interests as an employed occupational group.

The key word is "interests." If classes are large, teachers will express their concern at the bargaining table because the size of the class creates problems affecting their working conditions. The same is true of disruptive children and student disciplinary problems. If school facilities are inadequate or poorly designed, teachers will manifest their concerns at the bargaining table, not because they want to take over the schools, but because they are frustrated by their working milieu.

It is fashionable to argue that teachers must be held "accountable" for what students can or cannot do, what they learn or do not learn. The criteria for accountability and how these criteria apply are not clear, but student performance on achievement tests appears to be a major factor. Presumably, the teacher will be rewarded with merit salary increases or penalized with decreases or perhaps dismissal once the system of academic due process (i.e., tenure) has been "decimated." Given this threatening circumstance, one can expect teachers to have an expansive view of their occupational interests. At the bargaining table, they can be expected to demand authority over those areas for which they are held accountable. If they are to be held accountable for the behavior of their colleagues, they will want a voice in recruiting; if their accountability is to be determined by tests, they will want a voice in determining what those tests are and who applies them. Clearly they will want a voice over what is taught and how it is taught. Class size and procedures for handling the disruptive child will be more important than ever.

An argument frequently made in support of a limited scope of bargaining is that third-party intervenors (i.e., mediators, fact-finders, arbitrators) will, absent such constraints, invade the business of government itself. The contention is that even though an organization lacks the power to make a credible strike threat, it may be able to gain its ends by enlisting the support of an outsider.

This argument is unpersuasive. First, mediators or fact-finders who make recommendations in respect to matters regarded by management as being in the area of prerogatives or sovereignty will not be taken very seriously by the public employer unless the employee organization has sufficient bargaining power to enforce those recommendations. Thus a mediator or a fact-finder will not be able to force incursions into the prerogatives of management or government which the organization could not achieve on its own.

The situation is different when the arbitrator has the authority to bind the parties. However, the concern still seems more fanciful than real. To illustrate, what is an arbitrator likely to do in a typical situation where the parties have bargained on a package basis and a multiplicity of issues remain unresolved (for example, wages, holidays, shift premiums, overtime, transfer procedures, work rules, or seniority in general employee units; class size, student discipline, or curricular reform in education; or civilian review boards for police)? He will be inclined to deal solely with those issues with which he feels comfortable because these are acceptable criteria, ducking other issues in respect to which he feels uncomfortable, if not incompetent. It would be a rare arbitrator presumptuous enough to make a binding determination on class size, student discipline, curriculum reform, or the existence of a civilian police review board.

Law professors and management negotiators are not the only persons who are "uptight" about the scope of collective bargaining in public employment. Many legislative bodies suffer from the same syndrome.

The Nevada statute governing public employee bargaining specifies that a local government employer need not negotiate over its right to direct its employees, to hire, to promote, to classify, transfer, assign, retain, suspend, demote, discharge, or take disciplinary action against an employee, to relieve any employee from duty because of lack of work or for any other legitimate reason, to maintain the efficiency of its governmental operations, to determine the methods, means, and personnel by which its operations are to be conducted, and to take whatever actions may be necessary to carry out its responsibilities in emergency situations....

The Hawaiian statute goes even further. It makes it *illegal* for an employer and a labor organization to agree to any proposal which interferes with the right of a public employer to direct its employees, to determine qualifications, standards for work, the nature and content of examinations, to hire, to promote, transfer, assign, and retain employees in positions; to suspend, demote, discharge, or take other disciplinary action against its employees for proper cause; to relieve an employee from duty because of lack of work or other legitimate reasons; to maintain the efficiency of government operations; and to determine methods, means and personnel by which the employer's operations are to be conducted.

Even the most imaginative negotiators will have their work cut out for them under this language. Can they agree to a standard job security clause, to a provision requiring posting and bidding on promotions, to an article which makes seniority a controlling factor in lay-off and recall?

Such laws, which encourage or require public employers to avoid problems rather than deal with them, are mischievous because they produce strife and frustration rather than understanding and peaceful accommodation of conflicts between government and its employees. In the public sector, as well as the private, what is bargained about, as well as what the terms of the bargain are, should be a function of the bargaining process, not of abstract concerns over sovereignty or responsiveness to misconceived legislative constraints.

SUMMERS, PUBLIC EMPLOYEE BARGAINING: A POLITICAL
PERSPECTIVE, 83 Yale L.J. 1156, 1192-97 (1969)*

C. Subjects for Bargaining

Collective bargaining in the public sector, from the perspective of this inquiry, is a specially structured political process for making certain governmental decisions. The primary justification for this special process is that it gives the employees increased political effectiveness to help balance the massed political resistance of taxpayers and users of public services. One consequence of public employee bargaining is at least partial preclusion of public discussion of those subjects being bargained. And the effect of an agreement is to foreclose any change in matters agreed upon during the term of the agreement. Because it constitutes something of a derogation from traditional democratic principles, collective bargaining should be limited to those areas in which public employees do indeed encounter massed resistance. In other areas, disputes by public employees should be resolved through the customary channels of political decision-making.

Borrowing concepts of bargainable subjects from the private sector can be misleading for two reasons. First, in the private sector collective bargaining is the only instrument through which employees can have any effective voice in determining the terms and conditions of employment. One purpose of the duty to bargain is to provide employees a measure of industrial democracy; that duty, therefore, appropriately extends to all subjects which directly relate to their employment. In the public sector employees already have, as citizens, a voice in decisionmaking through customary political channels. The purpose of collective bargaining is to give them, as employees, a larger voice than the ordinary citizen. Therefore, the duty to bargain should extend only to those decisions where that larger voice is appropriate.

Second, in defining bargainable subjects in the private sector, the government is establishing boundaries for the dealings between private parties. In the public sector, however, government is establishing structures and procedures for making its own decisions. In the private sector the parties may agree at the bargaining table to expand the subjects of bargaining, but a public employee union and a public official do not have the same freedom to agree that certain decisions should be removed from the ordinary political processes and be decided by them in a special forum. The private employer's prerogatives are his to share as he sees fit, but the citizen's right to participate in governmental decisions cannot be bargained away by any public official.

In legal terms the principal question in the private sector is what the *mandatory* subjects of bargaining are, i.e., what decisions the employer *must* share with his employees. The principal question in the public sector is what the *permissible* subjects of bargaining are, i.e., what decisions *may* be made through the specially structured political process.

The special political structure and procedure of collective bargaining is particularly appropriate for decisions where the employees' interests in increased wages and reduced work load run counter to the combined interests of tax-

---

*Reprinted by permission of the Yale Law Journal Company and Fred B. Rothman & Co.

payers and users of public services. Therefore, decisions as to wages, insurance, pensions, sick leave, length of work week, overtime pay, vacations, and holidays should be considered proper subjects for bargaining. Collective bargaining, however, lacks the same claim of appropriateness for decisions where budgetary or level of service considerations are not dominant and where the political alignment of taxpayers and users against employees does not occur.

For example, a decision concerning the content of the school curriculum does not centrally involve salary levels or work loads of teachers on the one hand, or the size of the budget or the level of service on the other. Rather, the decision requires a choice of the kinds of services to be provided within the limitations of the funds available.[5] On such an issue there is no reason to assume that the teachers' views can be summarized by a single voice, nor is there reason to believe that taxpayers, parents, or users of other services have any unified position. Two-sided bargaining on such issues misrepresents both the range of views and the alignment of interests which should be considered in making the decision.

Furthermore, channeling discussion into closed bargaining sessions inhibits a full airing of viewpoints, for it precludes equal consideration of differing professional judgments of teachers and of differing judgments and concerns of parents, students, and other interested citizens. Even if all of these views are presented at the bargaining table, the decision is made by public representatives whose primary charge is to protect the public purse. Thus the decision is not made solely on the merits of the issue, but as part of a package which results from trading off unrelated items. Because of its structure and function, collective bargaining does not provide an appropriate political process for making such decisions.

To say that curriculum content is not a proper subject of bargaining does not mean that teachers have no legitimate interest in that subject or that they should not participate in curriculum decisions. It means only that the bargaining table is the wrong forum and the collective agreement is the wrong instrument. Because of the teachers' special interests and competence, the school board can properly be authorized, or even required, to consult with them before making a decision. But no organization should purport to act as an exclusive representative; the discussions should not be closed; and the decision should not be bargained for or solidified as an agreement. In addition, all of the ordinary political processes should remain open for individuals or groups of teachers to make their views known to the politically responsible officials and thus to influence the decision.[6]

---

[5]Collective bargaining on such matters as the content of the curriculum, the number of speech therapists, the choice of textbooks, and grading standards has been justified on the ground that teachers, as professionals, should have a greater voice in these decisions than politically sensitive lay boards of education and bureaucratic minded administrators, and that bargaining insulates decisionmaking from the pressures of the unenlightened populace. See Wollett, *The Coming Revolution in Public School Management,* 67 Mich. L. Rev. 1017 (1969). The assumption is that on all of these matters professional judgments should prevail over public choice. This assumption may be subject to question on several levels.... Undoubtedly, there are decisions which should be left to professional judgment, but submitting them to collective bargaining is a clumsy, inadequate, and even dangerous way of achieving that. Bargaining is a political process responding to political forces and leaves teachers vulnerable on some matters which should be beyond reach of local majorities.

[6]A wide variety of procedures can be developed to ensure that teachers participate in these decisions without depriving any interested group of an opportunity to be heard. Representatives of

This analysis, which restricts collective bargaining to subjects that substantially implicate budgetary issues, provides some guide for separating bargainable and nonbargainable subjects in the public sector. Yet it cannot provide a clear boundary line.

If teachers demand reduction in class size or policemen demand minimum manning of patrols, the interests of the employees may coincide with the interests of users of the particular service; the clear confrontation created by wage demands does not then exist. However, there remains the opposition of taxpayers and users of other services. Granting the union demands would almost certainly require increased appropriations for the schools or the police department. Even some parents may prefer that any increase in the school budget be spent to improve other aspects of the educational program. The configuration of political interest groups remains sufficiently similar to make the collective bargaining structure appropriate for resolving such issues.

Collective bargaining might initially seem inappropriate for subjects such as seniority, promotions, work assignments, and discipline, which do not directly affect budget allocation. But union demands on these subjects are commonly resisted on the grounds that they reduce efficiency and efficiency is an interest shared by both taxpayers and users of public services.

If the union's demands do not in fact affect efficiency, then the dispute is simply one between the employees in the bargaining unit and their supervisors, department heads, or personnel department. Such disputes do not involve the public's interest but rather concern the relative roles of opposing interest groups within the government in determining the terms and conditions of employment. These competing interests are represented at the two-sided bargaining table; the proper parties are on each side of the table. The structure and procedure seem quite appropriate for reconciling their interests and working out the rules to govern their relationships.

Demands by policemen for disciplinary procedures which effectively foreclose use of a public review board further illustrate the need to examine each subject to determine whether it should be decided within the special political process of collective bargaining. In making such a demand the union probably represents the consensus of the employees and can thus properly speak with a single voice. However, such a demand has no identifiable budget cost; those interested in more police protection are more likely to support than oppose the demand. Hence there is not the combined opposition which typified resolution of budgetary and level of service issues. Nor is there the opposition of supervisors which characterizes internal management and personnel issues, for the chief of police and the police commissioners who sit on the employer's side of the bargaining table find the prospect of a public review board equally frightening. Those who favor a public review board are those who fear that policemen will act abusively or unlawfully and that their superiors will not take appropriate disciplinary action. The interests of this group are not represented at the bar-

the union and other teacher groups can meet with the school board for full discussion of the problem. Committees can be elected by the affected teachers wholly outside the union framework. School faculties may discuss and make recommendations. And school boards can hold open public meetings at which teachers and their various spokesmen may present their views just as spokesmen for parents, students, and other groups do.

gaining table. Collective bargaining thus does not provide an appropriate political process for full discussion of the issue or for weighing and reconciling the competing interests.

Again, the conclusion that this subject should be nonbargainable does not mean that policemen have no legitimate interest in whether their conduct should be subject to public review. They certainly have a right to participate in that decision, but only through the ordinary avenues of the political process which are equally open to all competing views and interest groups.

NOTE

Among the many useful articles examining the scope of bargaining in the public sector are Scope of Public-Sector Bargaining (W. Gershenfeld, J. Loewenberg & B. Ingster eds. 1977); Clark, *The Scope of the Duty to Bargain in Public Employment,* in Labor Relations Law in the Public Sector 81 (A. Knapp ed. 1977); Sackman, *Redefining the Scope of Bargaining in Public Employment,* 19 B.C.L. Rev. 155 (1977); Sabghir, *The Scope of Bargaining in Public Sector Collective Bargaining,* A report sponsored by the New York State Employment Relations Board (Oct. 1970); U.S. Dep't of Labor, Scope of Bargaining in the Public Sector — Concepts and Problems (1972); Edwards, *The Emerging Duty to Bargain in the Public Sector,* 71 Mich. L. Rev. 885 (1973); Kilberg, *Appropriate Subjects for Bargaining in Local Government Labor Relations,* 30 Md. L. Rev. 179 (1970); Gerhart, *The Scope of Bargaining in Local Government Negotiations,* 20 Lab. L.J. 545 (1969); Blair, *State Legislative Control Over the Conditions of Public Employment: Defining the Scope of Collective Bargaining for State and Municipal Employees,* 26 Vand. L. Rev. 1 (1973); Vial, *The Scope of Bargaining Controversy: Substantive Issues vs. Procedural Hangups,* Cal. Pub. Employee Rel. no. 15, at 4 (Nov. 1972).

2. WAGES, HOURS AND WORKING CONDITIONS — WHAT IS NEGOTIABLE?

The determination of whether a given subject is mandatory or permissive has legal significance in at least five respects. *First,* while a party can propose a permissive subject of bargaining, it is generally an unfair labor practice for that party to insist on negotiations over a permissive subject to the point of impasse. Conversely, it is perfectly legal for the other party to refuse to negotiate over a permissive subject. In a few states like Pennsylvania an employer is required, upon request, to meet and confer but not negotiate on policy matters affecting wages, hours, and terms and conditions of employment.

Second, if a permissive subject is incorporated in a collective bargaining agreement, there is normally no obligation to negotiate over its deletion in a succeeding agreement. Thus, several PERBs have held that a permissive subject may be removed from a succeeding agreement upon the request of either party without any further obligation to negotiate over the subject. See, e.g., *Patterson Police Local v. City of Patterson,* 432 A.2d 847, (N.J. 1981) (permissive item is effective only for term of agreement and the "public employer is free to delete any permissive item from a successor agreement by refusing to negotiate with respect to that item"); *City of Troy,* 10 PERB ¶ 3015 (N.Y. 1977); *Town of Maplewood,* 4 NJPER 258 (N.J. PERC 1978).

Third, a public employer may not take unilateral action without first giving the union notice and an opportunity to negotiate to impasse over a mandatory subject of bargaining. This limitation on a public employer's right to take unilateral action does not, however, normally exist during the term of a collective bargaining agreement where the employer has specifically or implicitly retained the right to take the action in question.

Fourth, a public employer may take unilateral action on a permissive subject without any prior notice or bargaining with the union. Nevertheless, the employer may be required to negotiate over the *impact* of the action. See *City of New York & MEBA, Dist. No. 1, infra.*

Fifth, the determination of whether a given topic is mandatory or permissive affects what items can be submitted for resolution pursuant to a statutory impasse procedure. Under most impasse procedures, the fact finder or arbitrator, in the absence of mutual agreement, does not have the authority to make a recommendation or decision on permissive subjects of bargaining. In other words, if a party seeks to submit a permissive subject to an arbitrator, the other party can normally oppose consideration of this issue by the arbitrator on the ground that it is not a mandatory subject of bargaining.

WESTWOOD COMMUNITY SCHOOLS

1972 MERC Lab. Op. 313 (Mich. Emp. Relations Comm'n)

[The Westwood Education Association (Association) filed an unfair labor practice charge against the Westwood Community Schools (Employer) alleging, *inter alia* that the Employer violated Section 10(a) and (e) of the Michigan Public Employment Relations Act (PERA) by refusing to negotiate with the Association over the beginning and ending dates of the school term and by unilaterally establishing said dates. The Trial Examiner ruled "that there is no obligation on the Employer to bargain in regard to the opening of school and that subject is a voluntary subject of bargaining." The Association filed a timely exception to the Trial Examiner's recommendation that this portion of the Association's unfair labor practice charge be dismissed.]

The issue of whether the opening date of the school term is a mandatory subject of bargaining is one of first impression for this Commission. We have never definitively established a list of subjects which lie within the scope of bargaining, nor does PERA define such subjects. Section 15 of the statute provides that the collective bargaining duty of the Employer is "... to meet at reasonable times and confer in good faith with respect to wages, hours and other terms and conditions of employment...." Disputes involving bargainable subjects have been resolved on a case by case basis. *City of Detroit, Police Department,* 1971 MERC Lab. Op. 237, 241.

This ad hoc method of determination has, however, embraced the traditional private sector distinctions between mandatory, non-mandatory and illegal subjects of bargaining. *Bullock Creek School District,* 1969 MERC Lab. Op. 497, 504; *City of Detroit, Police Department, supra; Coleman Community Schools,* 1970 MERC Lab. Op. 813. While we have made no extensive analysis of these categories of bargaining proposals, we have held that the words "... other terms and conditions of employment ..." from Section 15 of PERA mean "those items which *affect* employees after they have become employees." *City of Detroit, Police Department, supra* at 249 (emphasis added).

The traditional classification of bargaining proposals was enunciated in the leading United States Supreme Court case, *National Labor Relations Board v. Wooster Division of Borg-Warner*, 356 U.S. 342, 42 L.R.R.M. 2034 (1958). Here, the employer insisted that its collective bargaining contract with some of its employees contain a ballot clause calling for a pre-strike secret vote of the employees as to the employer's last offer, and a recognition clause which excluded as a party to the contract the International Union which had been certified by the NLRB as the employees' exclusive bargaining agent and substituted for it the agent's uncertified local affiliate. The NLRB found that the employer's insistence upon either of such clauses amounted to an unlawful refusal to bargain. *Borg-Warner Corporation*, 113 N.L.R.B. 1288, 36 L.R.R.M. 1439 (1955). The Sixth Circuit of the United States Court of Appeals upheld the Labor Board's finding as to the recognition clause, but reversed on the ballot clause issue. *NLRB v. Wooster Division of Borg-Warner*, 236 F.2d 898, 38 L.R.R.M. 2660 (6th Cir., 1956). In reversing the Court of Appeals' decision as to the latter issue, the Supreme Court sustained the Labor Board's opinion.

The Court held that both the ballot clause and the recognition clause are not mandatory subjects of bargaining; thus, the employer could not insist upon contractual inclusion of these subjects. It reached this result by reading together Sections 8(a)(5) and 8(d) of the National Labor Relations Act. The former makes it an unfair labor practice for an employer to "refuse to bargain collectively with the representatives of his employees." National Labor Relations Act, 29 U.S.C. § 158(a)(5). The latter defines collective bargaining as the

"... performance of the mutual obligation of the employer and the representative of the employees to meet at reasonable times and confer in good faith with respect to wages, hours and other terms and conditions of employment ... but such obligation does not compel either party to agree to a proposal or require the making of a concession." *Id.*, 29 U.S.C. § 158(d).[3]

The court found that the duty to bargain is limited to the subjects (mandatory) "wages, hours and other terms and conditions of employment," and that neither party is legally obligated to yield. "As to other matters (non-mandatory), however, each party is free to bargain or not to bargain, and to agree or not to agree." 356 U.S. at 349, 42 L.R.R.M. at 2036. The Court explicitly held that "... (I)t is lawful to insist upon matters within the scope of mandatory bargaining and unlawful to insist upon matters without...." *Id.*, 42 L.R.R.M. at 2037.

Thus, the teaching of *Borg-Warner*, is that the employer cannot take unilateral action with regard to a mandatory subject of bargaining where there has been no bargaining. But the parties do not have to agree. In the absence of agreement, the employer may act unilaterally. *NLRB v. American National Insurance Co.*, 343 U.S. 395, 30 L.R.R.M. 2147 (1952). Under *Borg-Warner*, the employer may act without bargaining as to non-mandatory subjects of bargaining.

The elusive question that continually plagues courts, administrative tribunals and practitioners focuses on the phrase "other terms and conditions of employ-

---

[3] The PERA analogues to these provisions can be found at Sections 10(e) and 15 of the Act.

ment." No satisfactory answer has been formulated to resolve this problem; *Borg-Warner* provides little help.

The Supreme Court again dealt with this issue in *Fibreboard Paper Products Corp. v. NLRB,* 379 U.S. 203, 57 L.R.R.M. 2609 (1964). The Court held that an employer is required to bargain over the contracting out of bargaining unit work, within the limits of the evidence in that case. This decision has not been universally acclaimed; indeed, it has generated substantial criticism. M. Bernstein, "The NLRB's Adjudication-Rule Making Dilemma under the Administrative Procedure Act," 79 Yale L.J. 571, 580 (1970). However, the tests established in *Fibreboard* for the determination of a mandatory subject of bargaining are helpful. Summers, "Labor Law in the Supreme Court," 1964 Term, 75 Yale L.J. 59, 60 (1965). The Court noted that industrial practices in this country are a factor in determining a statutory subject of bargaining. The majority in *Fibreboard* held that bargaining is compelled to promote one of the primary purposes of the National Labor Relations Act, viz., "... the peaceful settlement of industrial disputes by subjecting labor-management controversies to the mediatory influence of negotiation...." 379 U.S. at 211, 57 L.R.R.M. at 2612. From this premise flow two tests: (1) Is the subject of such vital concern to both labor and management that it is likely to lead to controversy and industrial conflict? And (2) is collective bargaining appropriate for resolving such issues?

The most recent decision by the Court dealing with this issue reaffirmed the *Fibreboard* test. *Chemical Workers v. Pittsburgh Plate Glass Co.,* 40 U.S.L.W. 4043, 78 L.R.R.M. 2974 (U.S., Dec. 7, 1971). In holding that benefits of retired employees are not within the mandatory rule the Court said, "... in each case the question is ... whether it (the subject) vitally affects the terms and conditions of their (bargaining unit employees) employment." *Id.,* at 4050, 78 L.R.R.M. at 2982. However, the Court carefully pointed out in footnote No. 19 that the effect on the employer's freedom to conduct business must also be considered. *Id.*

This caveat specifically refers to Mr. Justice Stewart's concurring opinion in *Fibreboard,* wherein he argued that the majority's interpretation of the equivocal phrase "conditions of employment" "... seems to imply that any issue which may reasonably divide an employer and his employees must be the subject of compulsory collective bargaining." 379 U.S. at 221, 57 L.R.R.M. at 2616. After concluding that the term "conditions of employment" offers no workable guide, the opinion intuitively distinguished between "... managerial decisions which lie at the core of entrepreneurial control ... and (those) not in themselves primarily about conditions of employment." *Id.* at 223, 57 L.R.R.M. at 2617. Those decisions which are fundamental to the basic direction of a corporate enterprise should not be subject to compulsory bargaining. *Id.*

The instant case presents the challenge the Court faced in *Fibreboard.* The Employer argues that establishment of the opening day of school is a management function not subject to mandatory bargaining. The Education Association responds that the Employer's unilateral act affected a vital employee interest. We agree with the Association that the careful planning of summer interlude activities, e.g., advanced study, supplementary employment, travel and vacation, causes the teachers to have a substantial interest in the opening date of school. Thus, the classic confrontation between management rights and employee interests is created. This conflict can be appropriately reconciled by balancing the interests involved.

In this process, we are confined by the doctrine of illegal delegation of power which commands that certain discretionary decisions be made solely by a designated official rather than through the collective bargaining process. Wellington and Winter, "The Limits of Collective Bargaining in Public Employment," 78 Yale L.J. 1107, 1109 (1969). In the instant case, neither the Michigan Statutes nor the regulations of the State Department of Education interfere with a holding that the school calendar is a subject which must be bargained. With respect to the opening of school, the Michigan law provides only that the school year of all school districts shall commence on the first day of July. MCLA 340.353. State law also requires that every school district shall determine the length of the school term, but that the length of the term shall be a minimum of 180 days. MCLA 340.575, as amended. Since these rules are silent as to establishing the opening day of school, we find that there are no delegation problems created by submitting the school calendar to bargaining.

The rather substantial interest which the school teachers have in planning their summer activities outweigh any claim of interference with the right to manage the school district.

We agree with the holding of the Wisconsin Supreme Court, which has said, in affirming a Wisconsin Employment Relations Commission decision, that the school calendar (including the opening day of school) has a direct and intimate relationship to the salaries and working conditions of the teachers. *City of Madison v. Wisconsin Employment Relations Board,* 37 Wis. 2d 43, 155 N.W.2d 78, 65 L.R.R.M. 2488 (1967). In accord with that decision is *Norfolk Education Association v. South District of Norfolk,* Nebraska Court of Industrial Relations, Case No. 40, October 6, 1971, 430 GERR B-7 (December 6, 1971).

Since a Michigan school district has already been required to bargain collectively with respect to certain aspects of the school calendar, e.g., holiday and vacation dates (*Reese Public School District,* 1967 MERC Lab. Op. 489), requiring the employer to bargain about the beginning and terminating dates of the school term does not impair significantly its right to manage. Nor are we impressed by the argument that bargaining with the teachers over the school calendar would foreclose bargaining on this subject with other school district employees. Other subjects of bargaining affect more than one bargaining unit. Bargaining over such subjects as fringe benefits, holidays, hours and the work day, vacations and wages, as well as the school calendar, would be facilitated by joint or coalition bargaining. Furthermore, the order to bargain does not command that there be agreement; we only order that the parties bargain in good faith about this subject.

A balancing approach to bargaining may be more suited to the realities of the public sector than the dichotomized scheme — mandatory and non-mandatory — used in the private sector. The Supreme Court in *Fibreboard* argued that this private sector concept was necessary to preserve a primary purpose of the National Labor Relations Act — industrial peace. The Court argued that labor disputes should be peacefully settled by subjecting the controversies to the "mediatory influence of negotiation." This scheme prohibits the use of economic weapons to compel agreement to discuss non-mandatory subjects of bargaining but strikes are permissible once the point of impasse concerning mandatory subjects of bargaining is reached. Economic force is illegal in the public sector in Michigan as PERA prohibits strikes by public employees. In Michigan, in the public sector, economic battle is to be replaced by invocation of the impasse resolution procedures of mediation and fact finding.

An expansion of the subjects about which the public employer ought to bargain, unlike the private sector, should not result in a corresponding increase in the use of economic force to resolve impasses. In the absence of legal public sector strikes, our only proper concern in the area of subjects of bargaining is whether the employer's management functions are being unduly restrained. All bargaining has some limiting effect on an employer.

Therefore, we will not order bargaining in those cases where the subjects are demonstrably within the core of entrepreneurial control. Although such subjects may affect interests of employees, we do not believe that such interests outweigh the right to manage.

In reversing the Trial Examiner on this issue, we hold that the opening and terminating days of the school term are subjects about which the employer must bargain. However, we apply this decision prospectively, and we hold that the Employer did not commit an unfair labor practice in its unilateral setting of the opening day of school....

CHAIRMAN HOWLETT, dissenting: ...
The opening (and, indeed, the closing) date for the school year is a function which should be within the province of the school board. It is a power which should not be delegated, even to the extent of bargaining.

While Michigan statutes do not specifically vest this power in boards of education, it flows logically from MCLA 340.353 (Mich. Stat. Ann. 15.3353) which specifies that the school year of all school districts commences on the 1st day of July, and the requirement of MCLA 340.575 (Mich. Stat. Ann. 15.3375) that the length of the term shall be a minimum of 180 days. Within these two specifications, the school board should determine when the schools open and the period within which the 180 days (or more, at the option of the school board) shall be held.

It is urged that the opening day of school (as well as the calendar) has a direct and intimate relationship to the salaries and working conditions of the teachers. The majority opinion notes the contention of the Association "that the careful planning of summer activities, e.g., advance study, supplementary employment, travel and vacation causes the teachers to have a substantial interest in the opening date of school." And, the parents of children have summer interlude activities which cause them to have a substantial interest in the opening day of school. The parents are not — and should not be — part of the bargaining process. Under the school law, the members of the school board are elected to represent the citizens of the district, including the parents. The parents' interest in the opening date of school is equal, if not paramount, to that of the teachers. The interest of the citizens of the district, including the parents, is not, however, within the sphere of collective bargaining. Their rights are in the political (using the word in its broad sense) arena. The legislative body — the school board —

should make the decision of the period that school will be in session for all citizens of the district.

The majority notes that the United States Supreme Court, in *Allied Chemical and Alkali Workers v. Pittsburgh Plate Glass Co.,* — U.S. —, 92 S. Ct. 383, 78 L.R.R.M. 2974 (1971), said that "... in each case the question is ... whether it (the subject) vitally affects the terms and conditions of their (bargaining unit employees) *employment.*" (Emphasis supplied.)

Here I depart from the rationale of the majority. Is the opening date of school a term or condition of *employment?* While teachers may be considered employees for some purposes from the date they are required by law to notify the school board that they will return for the next school year (MCLA 38.83, Mich. Stat. Ann. 15.1983), or, in the case of non-tenured teachers, have signed a contract, teachers' active employment does not start until the day they are required to report at the beginning of the school year.

We have held, as the majority opinion notes, that bargaining is required with respect to holiday and vacation dates (*Reese Public School District,* 1967 MERC Lab. Op. 489). These are working conditions within the period of employment. Actual employment does not start until teachers report to work. There is no term or condition of employment prior to the *start* of employment. This is consistent with our decision in *City of Detroit, Police Department,* 1971 MERC Lab. Op. 237, that recruitment standards (before employment begins) are not included with "other terms and conditions of employment," as that phrase is used in Section 15 of PERA.[1]

Perhaps the nearest parallel in the private sector is the right of management to determine when an establishment shall be opened for the manufacture of the product produced or performing of the service offered, by the employer.

NOTES

1. Accord *Washington Teachers; Union Local 6, AFT v. District of Columbia,* 1986-88 PBC ¶ 35,035 (D.C. Sup. Ct. 1987); *Edmonds School Dist. No. 15,* Dec. No. 207-EDUC (Wash. PERC 1977).
2. The Maine Municipal Employees Labor Relations Act provides for negotiations over wages, hours, and working conditions, but specifically excludes "educational policies" from the scope of mandatory negotiations. Me. Rev. Stat. Ann. tit. 26, § 965(1)(C) (West 1988). In *City of Biddeford v. Biddeford Teachers Ass'n,* 304 A.2d 387 (Me. 1973), the court held that the scheduling and length of school vacations and the setting of the beginning and ending dates for the school year were "matters of 'educational policies' and, as such, non-negotiable and beyond the scope of binding arbitration." After noting that this issue involved "a substantial intermixing of judgments transcending teacher interests and embracing important interests of the general citizenry," the court observed that in establishing a calendar it is necessary to take into account "the plans and interests of families, the need to arrange for the presence of all non-teaching personnel who function while students are in attendance at school and the interests and concerns of all other parts of the community related to, or affected by, the times when students will be in attendance at school or on

---

[1]Teachers are often paid over the 12 months of the year. This is, in most instances, at the choice of the teacher. However, the teacher is paid for services *performed* from the day school opens until the day school closes.

vacation." Accord *Eugene Educ. Ass'n v. Eugene Sch. Dist. 4J*, Case No. C-65-78 (Or. ERB 1981); *Burlington Cty. Faculty Ass'n v. Burlington Cty. College*, 64 N.J. 10, 311 A.2d 733 (1973) (although "calendar undoubtedly has some practical effect on the faculty's employment arrangements ..., it is not a subject of mandatory negotiation"). See also *West Hartford Educ. Ass'n v. DeCourcy*, 162 Conn. 566, 295 A.2d 526 (1972), in which the court held that since the scope of bargaining under the Connecticut Teachers Act was limited to "salaries and other conditions of employment" and did not include "hours," the legislature intended to exclude such matters as length of the school day and school calendar from the scope of mandatory negotiations.

3. The scope of bargaining in the private sector and role of the NLRB has been the subject of extended discussion. Among the many excellent articles are Cox & Dunlop, *Regulation of Collective Bargaining by the National Labor Relations Board*, 63 Harv. L. Rev. 389 (1950); Cox, *The Duty to Bargain in Good Faith*, 71 Harv. L. Rev. 1401 (1958).

4. In *IFPTE Local 17 and Seattle*, Decisions 3051-A, *et al.* (Wash. PEBC 1989), the Washington PEBC held that a city committed an unfair labor practice when it implemented a tobacco use policy without first bargaining with the unions representing city employees. In rejecting the city's argument that a requirement that it bargain over this issue would seriously frustrate the city's desire to adopt a city-wide policy, the Washington Commission concluded that it was not persuaded "that a smoking policy must be city-wide, without exception, for every employee or every class of employees in every facility or segment of the workforce."

5. In *Department of Health & Human Servs., Indian Health Serv. v. FLRA*, 885 F.2d 911 (D.C. Cir. 1989), the D.C. Circuit affirmed an FLRA decision that the adoption and implementation of a smoking policy is a mandatory subject of bargaining.

6. In *Law Enforcement Labor Servs., Inc. v. Hennepin Cty.*, 449 N.W.2d 725 (Minn. 1990), the Minnesota Supreme Court unanimously held that a law enforcement agency's policy restricting employee hair, mustache, and fingernail length is not subject to mandatory bargaining.

7. While most public sector statutes define the scope of bargaining in general terms (e.g., wages, hours and other terms and conditions of employment), there are a few noteworthy exceptions. For example, the California Rodda Act covering certificated and classified educational personnel specifically sets forth what is negotiable and provides that all matters not specifically enumerated as mandatory subjects of bargaining "are reserved to the public school employer and may not be a subject of meeting and negotiating." Cal. Gov't Code, § 3543.2 (West Supp. 1991). In this situation, the legal subjects of bargaining are coterminous with the mandatory subjects set forth in the Act; there are not any permissive subjects. Unless specifically enumerated, a subject that might be considered as a permissive subject in other jurisdictions is an illegal subject under the Rodda Act in that a school board is legally prohibited from meeting and negotiating over such non-mandatory subjects.

8. In *Detroit Fire Fighters Ass'n, Local 344 v. City of Detroit*, 96 Mich. App. 543, 1979-80 PBC ¶37,038 (1980), the court held that an employer's proposal to exclude the positions of fire chief, assistant fire chief and fire marshal from the bargaining unit was a non-mandatory subject of bargaining and that the employer's insistence on this proposal to impasse constituted an unfair labor practice. See also *West Hartford Mun. Emps. v. Town of W. Hartford*, PEB

¶ 42,346 (Conn. SBLR 1981) (definition of bargaining unit a permissive subject of bargaining).

9. The Supreme Court has held that the public employer, in the absence of a statutory bar, can require public employees, as a condition of employment, to establish and maintain residency within the employer's boundaries. *McCarthy v. Philadelphia Civil Serv. Comm'n,* 424 U.S. 645 (1976). Most of the state courts and boards have held, however, that the establishment of residency requirements is a mandatory subject of bargaining. See, e.g., *Detroit Police Officers Ass'n v. City of Detroit,* 391 Mich. 44, 214 N.W.2d 803 (1974); *Boston Sch. Comm.,* 3 MLC 1603 (Mass. LRC 1977); *PLRB v. School Dist. of Erie,* PPER ¶ 9123 (Pa. LRB 1978); *City of Buffalo,* 9 PERB ¶ 3015 (N.Y. 1976); *City of Brookfield v. WERC,* 1 PBC ¶ 10,279 (Wis. Cir. Ct. 1974). See generally Hayford & Gurkee, *Residency Requirements in Local Government Employment: The Impact of the Public Employer's Duty to Bargain,* 29 Lab. L.J. 343 (1978). Would it make any difference if the residency requirement is only a condition of initial employment and is not a continuing condition of employment after being hired? In *Detroit Fed'n of Teachers, Local 231 v. Board of Educ.,* 237 N.W.2d 238, 92 L.R.R.M. 2121 (Mich. Ct. App. 1975), the court held that a residency requirement which is only a condition of initial hire is not a mandatory subject of bargaining. Accord *City of Buffalo, supra.*

10. Should evidence that other parties have included the disputed subject in agreements or that the parties' prior agreement contains the disputed item be a relevant factor in determining whether a given subject falls within the mandatory scope of negotiations? The Connecticut Supreme Court in *West Hartford Educ. Ass'n v. DeCourcy,* 162 Conn. 566, 295 A.2d 526 (1972), held that "the history and custom of the industry in collective bargaining" is a factor which "must [be] consider[ed] in order to determine if an item falls within the scope of negotiability." On the other hand, in *Town of Maplewood,* Decision No. 78-89 (N.J. PERC 1978), the New Jersey Commission stated, "The fact that a permissive subject of negotiations is included in a contract does not elevate that subject to mandatory status in negotiations for a successor agreement." Accord *Town of Ipswich v. IAFF, Local 1913,* Docket No. 4296 (Mass. 1977) ("Bargaining and agreeing on a permissive subject do not make the subject a mandatory subject of future bargaining"). See also *Allied Chem. & Alkali Workers v. Pittsburgh Plate Glass Co.,* 404 U.S. 157 (1971) (industry practices are not "determinative" and they "cannot change the law"); *U.S. Kirk Army Hosp.,* FLRC No. 70A-11 (1971) ("although other contracts may have included such provisions, as claimed by the union, this circumstance cannot alter the express language and intent of the Order [concerning negotiability] and is without controlling significance in this case"); *City of Troy,* 10 PERB ¶ 3105 (N.Y. 1977) ("agreement on a non-mandatory subject of negotiations does not obligate either party to negotiate over a demand to extend the agreement to a successor contract").

RIDGEFIELD PARK EDUCATION ASSOCIATION v. RIDGEFIELD PARK BOARD OF EDUCATION

78 N.J. 144, 393 A.2d 278 (1978)

PASHMAN, J. At issue herein is whether the 1974 amendments to the New Jersey Employer-Employee Relations Act, L. 1968, c. 303, as amended by L. 1974, c. 123, N.J.S.A. 34:13A-1 et seq. (the Act), created a class of permissively negotiable matters which, while not qualifying as mandatorily negotiable terms and conditions of employment, are nevertheless negotiable on a voluntary basis. The Public Employment Relations Commission (PERC) has concluded that such permissive category indeed exists.... PERC has also determined that disputes involving provisions of collectively negotiated agreements covering permissive matters may be resolved by binding arbitration if the matter is otherwise arbitrable, as is the case with those covering mandatorily negotiable matters.... The public employer herein contends that with respect to the issue of negotiability there are but two types of subjects — those as to which collective negotiation is mandatory and those as to which it is unlawful. The former category is comprised of those subjects which pertain to the terms and conditions of public employment while the latter includes all other subjects. It claims that any provision of a negotiated agreement which concerns subjects in the latter category is *ultra vires* and thus unenforceable.

The facts of this case are not in dispute. The collective agreement between plaintiff Association, the majority representative of the Board's teaching employees, and the defendant Board, which ran until July 1, 1977, defined a grievance as follows:

The term "grievance," means a complaint by an employee, group of employees, or the Association, that, as to him, there has been an inequitable, improper, or unjust application, interpretation, or violation of a policy, agreement, or administrative decision.

The contract provided for binding arbitration as the terminal step in the grievance process:

In the event the aggrieved party is dissatisfied with the determination of the Board he shall have the right to request arbitration pursuant to rules and regulations established by the Public Employment Relations Commission under the provisions of Chapter 303, Public Laws of 1968. The findings of the arbitrator shall be binding on all parties.

The collective agreement included a provision governing the subject of teacher transfers and reassignments.

Article XIV—Voluntary and Involuntary Transfers and Reassignments

A. Employees who desire a change in grade and/or subject assignment or who desire to transfer to another building may file a written statement(s) of such desire with the superintendent. Such statement(s) shall include the grade and/or subject to which the employee desires to be assigned and the school or schools to which he desires to be transferred, in order of preference.

As soon as practicable, and in no case later than June 1, the superintendent shall post in each school and deliver to the Association a system-wide schedule showing the names of all employees who have been reassigned or transferred and the nature of such reassignment or transfer.

B. In the determination of requests for voluntary reassignments and/or transfers, the wishes of the individual employee shall be honored, upon the recommendation of the superintendent and approval of the Board, to the extent that the transfer or reassignment does not conflict with the instructional requirements and best interests of the school system.

C. Notice of an involuntary transfer or reassignment shall be given to the employee as far in advance as practicable. In the case of teachers, except in an emergency situation, notice shall be given not later than April 30.

During the 1975-1976 and 1976-1977 school years certain teachers were involuntarily reassigned to teach courses or grades which they did not wish to teach, were refused a desired transfer to a different school, or were involuntarily transferred to another school. The Association filed grievances on behalf of these teachers. The Board denied all of them. The Association then sought to have these grievances resolved by binding arbitration, pursuant to the contractual arbitration clause. See *ante* at 280. The Board contended that the grievances pertained to matters outside the legal scope of negotiations, and hence were not arbitrable.

The Association instituted this action under N.J.S.A. 2A:24-1 and 3 seeking an order from the Chancery Division compelling the Board to submit the grievances involving transfers and reassignments to binding arbitration. The Board made a cross-application for an order enjoining the arbitrations. In the proceedings before the Chancery Judge, the Board admitted that it had a contractual duty to arbitrate the disputes herein, but submitted that the real issue was the legality of arbitrating these matters. The Board's request that the case be transferred to PERC for a decision on the negotiability of the issues involved in the grievances was denied. On March 4, 1977 the Chancery Division rendered an oral opinion adverse to the Board. On March 22, 1977 the Chancery Judge issued a judgment and order that the parties proceed to arbitration.

On March 2, 1977 the board had filed a Petition for Scope-of-Negotiations Determination with PERC pursuant to N.J.S.A. 34:13A-5.4(d). It sought an order from PERC enjoining arbitration on both an interim basis and on a permanent basis. The interim request was denied in an interlocutory decision on April 5, 1977. PERC No. 77-45, 3 NJPER 150. This denial was based on PERC's determination that its decisions in *In re Bridgewater-Raritan Regional Bd. of Ed., supra,* and *In re Bd. of Ed. of City of Trenton, supra,* mandated a conclusion that the matters in issue, though permissive and not mandatorily negotiable, would be arbitrable if otherwise within the contractual arbitration clause.

Meanwhile, the Board obtained a temporary stay of the enforcement of the Chancery judgment in order to enable it to apply for a stay from the Appellate Division. On April 20, 1977 a single judge of the Appellate Division denied the motion for a stay. However, arbitration had not commenced as of July 7, 1977, when a full panel of the Appellate Division granted the Board's motion for a stay.

PERC gave the matter a full hearing and issued its scope determination on August 17, 1977. PERC No. 78-9, 3 NJPER 319 (1977). PERC reaffirmed its earlier holding in *In re Bridgewater-Raritan Bd. of Ed., supra,* 3 NJPER at 25, that in enacting L. 1974, c. 123, the Legislature reacted to the restrictiveness of the standards enunciated by this Court in *Dunellen Bd. of Ed. v. Dunellen Ed. Ass'n,* 64 N.J. 17, 311 A.2d 737 (1973), concerning negotiability and arbitrability in the public sector. PERC observed that the critical factor in the Court's *Dunellen* holding was the L. 1968, c. 303 version of N.J.S.A. 34:13A-8.1, which provided, in effect, that negotiated agreements could not "annul or modify any statute or statutes of this State." Thus, great significance was ascribed to L. 1974, c. 123, § 6, which amended that statute effectively to provide that no negotiated agreement could "annul or modify any *pension* statute or statutes of this State." PERC also cited pertinent language from the 1974 amendments to N.J.S.A. 34:13A-5.3, which establishes the primacy of the negotiated grievance procedures in dispute resolution:

Notwithstanding any procedures for the resolution of disputes, controversies or grievances established by any other statute, grievance procedures established by agreement between the public employer and the representative organization *shall be utilized* for any dispute covered by the terms of such agreement. (emphasis added)

PERC concluded that one of the purposes of L. 1974, c. 123 was to expand the scope of arbitrable issues. So long as no specific statutes are violated and no overriding public policy contravened, PERC was of the opinion that both negotiation and arbitration of permissive matters are acceptable. In support of this view, PERC cited *In re Bd. of Ed. of City of Trenton, supra,* 2 NJPER at 352, where it had found that involuntary employee transfers were not precluded from negotiation by statute and were thus a permissible subject of negotiation, and *In re Bd. of Ed. of the Borough of Verona,* PERC No. 77-42, 3 NJPER 80 (1977), where it had found that a Board's decision to replace a teacher's non-teaching duty period with a classroom teaching period was also a permissibly negotiable subject. PERC held that the disputes herein were permissively negotiable and thus arbitrable if otherwise arbitrable under the agreement. 3 NJPER at 320-321.

The Board filed a motion for direct certification on July 18, 1977. On July 27, 1977 the Association appealed to this Court to vacate the interlocutory stay issued by the Appellate Division. In the alternative the Association requested direct certification. We directly certified this case while it was pending unheard in the Appellate Division, 75 N.J. 584, 384 A.2d 815 (1977).

I

Before we address the merits, some guidelines regarding proper procedure in these cases should be set. Under our existing legislative scheme it may be necessary to go to both PERC and the Superior Court in order to completely resolve a disagreement concerning the arbitrability of a particular dispute. When one party claims that a given dispute is arbitrable under the contract and the other party resists arbitration, the party desiring arbitration should seek an order from the Superior Court compelling arbitration. See N.J.S.A. 2A:24-1 et seq. Where the trial judge determines that the real controversy is not one of contractual arbitrability, but rather concerns the propriety of the parties negotiating and agreeing on the item in dispute, he should refrain from passing on the merits of that issue.

PERC has primary jurisdiction to make a determination on the merits of the question of whether the subject matter of a particular dispute is within the scope of collective negotiations. N.J.S.A. 34:13A-5.4(d).... However, the reach of this decision is limited. PERC discussed this point in *In re Hillside Bd. of Ed.,* PERC No. 76-11, 1 NJPER 55, 57 (1975):

The Commission is addressing the abstract issue: is the subject matter in dispute within the scope of collective negotiations. Whether that subject is within the arbitration clause of the agreement, whether the facts are as alleged by the grievant, whether the contract provides a defense for the employer's alleged action, or even whether there is a valid arbitration clause in the agreement, or any other question which might be raised is not to be determined by the Commission in a scope proceeding. Those are questions appropriate for determination by an arbitrator and/or the courts.

Of course, where the existence of a contractual obligation to arbitrate is not contested, the parties need only go to PERC for a ruling on whether the subject matter of the dispute whose grievability is contested is within the scope of collective negotiations. PERC can then afford complete relief. If PERC concludes that the dispute is within the legal scope of negotiability and agreement between the employer and employees, the matter may proceed to arbitration. Where PERC concludes that a particular dispute is not within the scope of collective negotiations, and thus not arbitrable, it must issue an injunction permanently restraining arbitration. *See Bd. of Ed. of Englewood v. Englewood Teachers,* 135 N.J. Super. 120, 124, 342 *A.2d* 866 (App.Div. 1975). Moreover, we agree with the decision in *Bd. of Ed. of Englewood v. Englewood Teachers, supra,* that PERC is empowered to order that arbitration proceedings be suspended during the pendency of a scope-of-negotiations proceeding. Where necessary, PERC may go to the Appellate Division to seek an appropriate order to compel compliance with its orders in scope proceedings. N.J.S.A. 34:13A-5.4(f). Where a party disagrees with PERC's determination on the scope question, an appeal to the Appellate Division is expressly authorized. N.J.S.A. 34:13A-5.4(d).

We agree with PERC that contract interpretation is a question for judicial resolution. Thus, where a party resists an attempt to have a dispute arbitrated, it may go to the Superior Court for a ruling on the issue of its contractual obligation to arbitrate. However, the issue of contractual arbitrability may not be reached if the threshold issue of whether the subject matter of the grievance is within the scope of collective negotiations is contested. In that event, a ruling on that issue must be obtained from PERC. Thus, the preferable procedure in the instant case would have been for PERC to have rendered its scope determination before the issue of contractual arbitrability was addressed. Where an item is within the scope of collective negotiations, and a court determines that the agreement contains a valid arbitration clause, the matter must proceed to arbitration.

The arbitrator's function is to comply with the authority the parties have given him in the agreement. Assuming that the item is a proper subject of arbitration under the agreement, the arbitrator will reach the merits and render an award. If the losing party is unwilling to abide by the award, the prevailing party may seek to have the award confirmed by the Superior Court. See N.J.S.A. 2A:24-7; *Amal. Transit Wkrs. Local 540 v. Mercer Cty. Impr. Authority,* 76 N.J. 245, 386 A.2d 1290 (1978).

Thus, PERC, the Superior Court and the arbitrator have distinct functions under our present scheme. To avoid needless procedural delays, we commend these guidelines to the bar.

II

By way of preliminary observation, we note that PERC was correct in concluding that under the test set forth in *Dunellen Ed. Assn. v. Dunellen Bd. of Ed.*, 64 N.J. 17, 25, 311 A.2d 737 (1973) and *Englewood Bd. of Ed. v. Englewood Teachers Ass'n*, 64 N.J. 1, 7, 311 A.2d 729 (1973), and today reaffirmed in *State v. State Supervisory Employees Ass'n, supra*, 78 N.J. at 67, 393 A.2d at 233, teacher transfers and reassignments are not mandatorily negotiable terms and conditions of employment. That test defined negotiable terms and conditions of employment as those matters which intimately and directly affect the work and welfare of public employees and on which negotiated agreement would not significantly interfere with the exercise of inherent management prerogatives pertaining to the determination of governmental policy. *State v. State Supervisory Employees Ass'n, supra*, 78 N.J. at 67, 393 A.2d at 233. The selection of the school in which a teacher works or the grade and subjects which he teaches undoubtedly have an appreciable effect on his welfare. However, even assuming that this effect could be considered direct and intimate, we find that this aspect of the transfer decision is insignificant in comparison to its relationship to the Board's managerial duty to deploy personnel in the manner which it considers most likely to promote the overall goal of providing all students with a thorough and efficient education. Thus, we find that the issue of teacher transfers is one on which negotiated agreement would significantly interfere with a public employer's discharge of inherent managerial responsibilities. Accordingly, it is not a matter as to which collective negotiation is mandatory.

III

To bolster its conclusion that L. 1974, c. 123 contemplated an expansion of negotiation into a permissive category of items, PERC makes several arguments. First, it points out that in passing L. 1974, c. 124, enacted on the same day as Chapter 123, which created a Public Employer-Employee Relations Study Commission, the Legislature implicitly assumed that there were already three categories of negotiating subjects. That statute directs the Commission, *inter alia*, to study

> Whether or not it is necessary and desirable either to define the phrase "terms and conditions of employment" as used in section 7 of the 1968 act [N.J.S.A. 34:13A-5.3] *and, in so doing, specify what subjects are mandatory, voluntary or illegal within the scope of bargaining or of grievance arbitration,* or to require that procedural guidelines be established for determining the same. [L. 1974, c. 124, § 3(c) (emphasis added)]

We do not accord the great degree of significance to this legislative action that PERC does. The mandate of the Study Commission was not necessarily limited to examining the law as it existed. Moreover, it is abundantly clear that a proposal to study and suggest changes is not given the same close scrutiny by legislators as is one which has the force of law. Thus, even legislators vehemently opposed to permissive negotiation may have voted in favor of setting up the Study Commission. Finally, the Legislature was well aware of the fact that we had held in *Burlington Cty. Fac. Assoc. v. Bd. of Trustees, supra*, that no expansive view of negotiations would be implied from ambiguous legislation.

We specifically required "clear and distinct phraseology" for a change of such magnitude.

PERC also alludes to L. 1977, c. 85, N.J.S.A. 34:13A-14 to 21, which provides for compulsory and binding "interest" arbitration of impasses in contract negotiations between local, county and state governments and policemen and firemen. That statute expressly contemplates a permissive category of negotiation:

> Factfinding shall be limited to those issues that are within the required scope of negotiations unless the parties to the factfinding agree to factfinding on permissive subjects of negotiation. [N.J.S.A. 34:13A-16b]

> Arbitration shall be limited to those subjects that are within the required scope of collective negotiations, except that the parties may agree to submit to arbitration one or more permissive subjects of negotiation. [N.J.S.A. 34:13A-16f(4)]

Of course, this enactment is not now before us. Neither is it of great importance to our interpretation of L. 1974, c. 123. It represents a specific decision on the part of the Legislature to authorize permissive negotiations with respect to police and firemen. Moreover, if it were so clear that L. 1974, c. 123 had created such a permissive area, we doubt that the Legislature would have had to provide carefully for a permissive category in L. 1977, c. 85. This recent statute covering a small percentage of all public employees may not be accorded dispositive effect in interpreting a more general statute passed three years earlier. We intimate no view as to the validity of the authorization for binding arbitration of "permissive subjects of negotiation" in N.J.S.A. 34:13A-16f(4).

PERC also cites federal precedents under the Labor Management Relations Act, 29 U.S.C. § 141 et seq. Illustrative of these cases is *NLRB v. Wooster Div. of Borg-Warner Corp.,* 356 U.S. 342, 349 (1958), where the United States Supreme Court held that under 29 U.S.C. § 158(a)(5) and § 158(d), collective bargaining was mandatory only as to terms and conditions of employment. As to other matters, each party was "free to bargain or not to bargain, and to agree to or not to agree." Of course, *Borg-Warner* dealt with the private sphere, and is therefore inapposite here.[2] In *Lullo v. Intern. Assoc. of Fire Fighters,* 55 N.J. 409, 436-441, 262 A.2d 681 (1970), we pointed out the significant differences between N.J.S.A. 34:13A-5.3 which grants a right to "collective negotiations" and 29 U.S.C. § 157 which grants a right to "collective bargaining."

> It is crystal clear that in using the term "collective negotiations" the Legislature intended to recognize inherent limitations on the bargaining power of public employer and employee.... And undoubtedly they were conscious also that public agencies, departments, etc., cannot abdicate or bargain away their continuing legislative or executive obligations or discretion. Consequently, absent some further changes in pertinent statutes public employers may not be able to make binding contractual commitments relating to certain subjects.... Finally, it signified an effort to make public employers and employees

---

[2] In *Galloway Tp. Bd. of Ed. v. Galloway Tp. Ass'n of Ed. Secretaries,* 78 N.J. 1, 393 A.2d 218 (1978), we held that since the unfair practice provisions of *N.J.S.A.* 34:13A-5.4 closely parallel those of the Labor Management Relations Act, 29 U.S.C § 158 and § 160, the federal precedents should guide our interpretation of this State act. However, this is not true with respect to scope of negotiability. We wish to specifically caution PERC and the Appellate Division of the limited relevance of private sector precedents with respect to scope-of-negotiations determinations.

realize that the process of collective bargaining as understood in the private employment sector cannot be transplanted into the public service. [55 N.J. at 440, 262 A.2d at 697]

Thus, federal precedents concerning the scope of collective bargaining in the private sector are of little value in determining the permissible scope of negotiability in public employment labor relations in New Jersey.

It is also contended that N.J.S.A. 34:13A-5.3, as amended by L. 1974, c. 123, § 4, see *ante* at 282, which mandates that grievance procedures negotiated by the parties supersede any mechanisms for the resolution of disputes provided by any statute, indicates that a category of permissively negotiable matters is now contemplated by the Act. PERC placed particular emphasis on the fact that the Legislature used the words "disputes and controversies" in the amended version of N.J.S.A. 34:13A-5.3, since they are the very words found in N.J.S.A. 18A:6-9 which gives the Commissioner of Education jurisdiction to resolve disagreements arising under the education laws. PERC contends that *Dunellen, supra,* 64 N.J. at 30-31, 311 A.2d 737, relied upon these words in N.J.S.A. 18A:6-9 to distinguish those matters which could be arbitrated from those matters which could not. Thus, the 1974 amendment is viewed by PERC as modifying the narrow scope of arbitration permitted by the Act which we found in *Dunellen.*

PERC errs in two respects. First, standing alone, N.J.S.A. 34:13A-5.3 is ineffective as a vehicle for expanding the permissible scope of arbitration. To be arbitrable, a matter must qualify as one on which the parties may negotiate. A matter which is not legally negotiable in the first place cannot be arbitrable. We have today held that the scope of grievability mandated by N.J.S.A. 34:13A-5.3 is limited to matters which affect the terms and conditions of public employment as that concept has been defined in our cases. *Tp. of West Windsor v. PERC,* 78 N.J. 98, 393 A.2d 255 (1978). Thus, only insofar as N.J.S.A. 34:13A-8.1 is viewed as increasing the legal scope of collective negotiation may N.J.S.A. 34:13A-5.3 be viewed as expanding the permissible coverage of contractual procedures for the resolution of grievances. Second, PERC and the Association both err in concluding that the *Dunellen* Trilogy was wholly based on statutory considerations. While our decisions in *Dunellen* and its companion cases were primarily based on the statutory language of L. 1968, c. 303 and the legislative intent underlying that enactment, we were not oblivious to more fundamental, constitutionally-rooted considerations of policy. As we observed in *Dunellen:*

> [*T]he Legislature,* in adopting the very general terms of L. 1968, c. 303, *did not contemplate that the local boards of education would or could* abdicate their management responsibilities for the local educational policies or that the State educational authorities would or could abdicate their management responsibilities for the State educational policies....

[64 N.J. at 25, 311 A.2d at 741 (emphasis added)]

Moreover, full application of PERC's view that everything which in any way affects the terms and conditions of public employment is negotiable at the option of the parties, unless such negotiation on a given topic is precluded by a specific statute, would be inconsistent with a successor statute in the education area. The Legislature has determined that community involvement in educational decisions, insuring some democratic control over such matters, is a significant part of a thorough and efficient system of education in this state. In passing the Public School Education Act of 1975, L. 1975, c. 212, now codified as N.J.S.A. 18A:7A-1 et seq., it gave that assumption the force of law:

(a) The Legislature finds and declares that: ...

(5) In order to encourage citizen involvement in educational matters, New Jersey should provide for free public schools in a manner which guarantees and encourages local participation consistent with the goal of a thorough and efficient system serving all of the children of the State:

(6) A thorough and efficient system of education includes local school districts in which decisions pertaining to the hiring and dismissal of personnel, the curriculum of the schools, the establishment of district budgets, and other essentially local questions are made democratically with a maximum of citizen involvement and self-determination and are consistent with Statewide goals, guidelines and standards; ....

[N.J.S.A. 18A:7A-2]

Literal application of PERC's interpretation of L. 1974, c. 123 would result in the emasculation of the intent of this later act. There would be little room for community involvement if agreements concerning educational policy matters could be negotiated behind closed doors and disputes concerning that agreement settled by an arbitrator who lacks public accountability. We simply find insufficient evidence of a legislative intent to permit this result to justify interpreting N.J.S.A. 34:13A-5.3 and 8.1 in the manner suggested by PERC.

Our holding herein is that L. 1974, c. 123 did not clearly indicate a legislative intent to create a permissive category of negotiations. Thus, we reaffirm our holding in *Dunellen* that there are but two categories of subjects in public employment negotiation — mandatorily negotiable terms and conditions of employment and non-negotiable matters of governmental policy. Since the subject of teacher transfers is not within the scope of mandatory negotiability, the Board acted in excess of its authority in agreeing to a provision of its collective agreement with the Association which would limit its managerial prerogatives on the subject. Accordingly, the contractual provision purporting to do so is invalid and may not be enforced against the Board in any arbitration proceeding. While a policy such as that expressed in the relevant contractual provision may be a salutary one, adherence to that policy is not something to which the Board could obligate itself in a collective agreement providing for binding arbitration.

IV

We are hesitant to find the existence of a permissive category of negotiable matters in public employment labor relations to be implicit in the amended act because such a classification might create serious problems in our democratic system. These potential difficulties should be carefully considered by the Legislature before taking any action expressly to authorize permissive negotiability with respect to all public employees. It is quite clear from our reading of the legislative history of L. 1974, c. 123 that the lawmakers did not purport to sanction the delegation of governmental policy decisions on every matter in any way touching upon the terms and conditions of public employment to the sphere of collective negotiation. We deem it appropriate for this Court to comment on these difficult questions concerning the permissibility of delegating governmental powers to private groups or of entrusting the formulation of governmental policy to an arena where the democratic voice of the electorate cannot be heard.

In *Tp. of West Windsor v. PERC,* 78 N.J. 98, 393 A.2d 255 (1978), we indicated that public employees' special access to government applies only where the government is acting in the capacity of an employer, and not where it is acting in its capacity as public policymaker. A private employer may bargain away as much or as little of its managerial control as it likes. *Tp. of West Windsor, supra.* However, the very foundation of representative democracy would be endangered if decisions on significant matters of governmental policy were left to the process of collective negotiation, where citizen participation is precluded. This Court would be most reluctant to sanction collective agreement on matters which are essentially managerial in nature, because the true managers are the people. Our democratic system demands that governmental bodies retain their accountability to the citizenry.

Our concern is with the very function of government. Both state and federal doctrines of substantive due process prohibit delegations of governmental policymaking power to private groups where a serious potential for self-serving action is created thereby.... To be constitutionally sustainable, a delegation must be narrowly limited, reasonable, and surrounded with stringent safeguards to protect against the possibility of arbitrary or self-serving action detrimental to third parties or the public good generally....

Since teachers possess substantial expertise in the education area, negotiations between teachers' associations and boards of education present a situation where an agreement which effectively determines governmental policy on various issues is especially likely. The impropriety of permitting such educational policy matters to be determined in the forum of collective negotiation — just as if they pertained to the terms and conditions of employment — is every bit as strong as it is in other areas of public employment. The interests of teachers do not always coincide with the interests of the students on many important matters of educational policy. Teachers' associations, like any employee organizations, have as their primary responsibility the advancement of the interests of their members. Arbitrators, to whom the resolution of grievances under collective agreements is generally entrusted, are concerned primarily with contractual rights and remedies. Of the relevant actors at the local level, only school boards have a primary responsibility to the public at large, as they have been delegated the responsibility of ensuring that all children receive a thorough and efficient education. These boards are responsible to the local electorate, as well as to the State, and may not make difficult educational policy decisions in a forum from which the public is excluded. Moreover, a multi-year contract covering policy matters would freeze the *status quo* and prevent a school board from making a flexible, creative response to changed circumstances, which might well preclude its acting in the best interests of the students.

The Legislature is of course free to exercise its judgment in determining whether or not a permissive category of negotiation is sound policy. We wish merely to point out that careful consideration of the limits which our demo-cratic system places on delegation of government powers is called for before any such action is taken. On the other hand, we are in no way prejudging the constitutionality of the concept of permissive negotiation *per se.*

We hold that the enactment of L. 1974, c. 123, §§ 4 and 6, N.J.S.A. 34:13A-5.3 and 8.1, did not have the effect of creating a new category of negotiating subjects in public employment labor relations comprised of matters negotiable at the option of the parties even though primarily concerned with governmental policy. PERC's scope-of-negotiations determination requiring that the Ridgefield Park Board of Education submit the propriety of teacher transfers and reassignments to binding arbitration is disapproved. In view of the foregoing, the Chancery Division order that the parties proceed to arbitra-tion is reversed and arbitration is permanently enjoined.

CONFORD. P.J.A.D. (temporarily assigned), concurring and dissenting.

I concur in the Court's judgment in this case that arbitration be permanently enjoined. But I do not reach that conclusion by the Court's rationale — i.e., that there is no legal category of permissively negotiable items in public employment relations but only the mandatorily negotiable category of "terms and condi-tions" of employment. I agree with the Public Employment Relations Commis-sion (PERC) that the Legislature has by L. 1974, c. 123 and L. 1977, c. 85 manifested its recognition of a class of permissive as well as of mandatory items for labor negotiation and with PERC's implementation by regulations of that understanding in the exercise of its scope-of-negotiations jurisdiction under L. 1974, c. 123 (N.J.S.A. 34:13A-5.4d.).

Practical recognition of negotiations in the permissive area has become a fact of life in the course of actual negotiations of collective agreements throughout the State in recent years and the validity thereof has been adjudicated in several leading jurisdictions beyond our borders. Today's holding by the Court is there-fore a backward step in the heretofore progressive development of public sector labor law in this State which will not conduce toward the legislative policy of promoting peace and stability in public employment relations.

However, I enter one qualification to my agreement with PERC's view as to this matter, and this will explain my concurrence in the Court's injunction against arbitration of the dispute in this case. Although, for reasons I shall presently set forth, a public employer may at its option choose to negotiate a permissive item, i.e., one which involves inherent managerial policy but also impacts appreciably upon the welfare of employees, it may not agree to binding arbitration of a dispute with respect to a negotiated item if so doing would transfer the making of an inherent managerial decision from a governmental official to an arbitrator....

NOTES

1. In *Board of Educ. v. Bernards Twp. Educ. Ass'n,* 79 N.J. 311, 399 A.2d 620 (1979), the court noted that while in *Ridgefield Park* it had held that "the parties could not encroach upon managerial prerogatives by contracting for binding arbitration," the court stated that it "did not ... express an opinion as to the validity of advisory arbitration as an intermediate procedural step in the resolution of disputes concerning the applicability of those managerial decisions

to a particular employee." In holding that such an agreement would be permissible, the court stated:

Advisory arbitration does not give rise to the adverse consequences that might ensue were binding arbitration deemed permissible....

Thus, an advisory arbitration clause does not interfere with the exercise of managerial prerogative. Moreover, its inclusion in a collective bargaining agreement will directly and intimately affect the work and welfare of the public employee. Consequently, a provision in a negotiated grievance procedure calling for advisory arbitration — even if it encompasses disputes concerning the applicability of managerial prerogatives — is itself a term and condition of employment, as that phrase is defined in our case law....

2. In *Maywood Bd. of Educ. v. Maywood Educ. Ass'n,* 168 N.J. Super. 45, 401 A.2d 711 (N.J. Super. Ct. App. Div. 1979), the court held that an employer could not be required to negotiate over the "impact" of the exercise of a managerial prerogative. The court stated:

unless the Legislature recognizes "permissive" negotiation the impact of a managerial decision on terms and conditions is not negotiable. To allow such impact to be negotiated would indirectly contravene the *Dunellen* analysis which was so strongly reaffirmed in *Ridgefield Park.*

Applying that conclusion to this case, there is no doubt but that the decision to reduce teacher personnel was based on a managerial prerogative. Therefore, the impact on the remaining teachers is not negotiable. Hence, the order directing the board to negotiate the impact of the reduced manning on the remaining librarian and teachers is reversed.

This decision should be contrasted with the decision of the New York City Office of Collective Bargaining in *City of N.Y. & MEBA, District No. 1, infra.*

3. In *Montgomery Cty. Educ. Ass'n v. Board of Educ.,* 311 Md. 303, 534 A.2d 980 (1987), the Maryland Court of Appeals held that under the Maryland statute covering teachers there was no "permissive" category of bargaining subjects. Accordingly, the court ruled that a local school board was either required to negotiate over a particular topic since it fell within the statutory scope of bargaining or it was not permitted to agree to negotiate over a subject since it fell outside the statutory scope of bargaining. In determining whether or not a particular subject is negotiable, the court endorsed the use of a balancing test. Utilizing these standards, the court upheld a State Board of Education determination that the issues of a school calendar and job reclassification were not negotiable.

4. Several states, including Alaska, Florida, Illinois, and Minnesota, specifically require that the parties include a grievance procedure ending in binding arbitration as part of their negotiated agreement. Other states, including Delaware (for teachers only), New Hampshire, and Ohio, provide that the agreement must contain a grievance procedure but do not necessarily mandate that the terminal step be binding arbitration.

5. Would a proposal by one party that any unresolved issues in the negotiations for a successor agreement be submitted to binding arbitration be a mandatory subject of bargaining? A permissive subject of bargaining? An illegal subject of bargaining? See *State Emps. Ass'n v. Mills,* 344 A.2d 6, 90 L.R.R.M. 2571 (N.H. 1975) (impasse arbitration held non-negotiable). Would it make any difference if the applicable statute provides, as the Pennsylvania act does, that nothing in the act "shall prevent the parties from submitting impasses to voluntary interest arbitration." 43 Pa. Cons. Stat. Ann. § 1101.804 (Purdon 1991). See *PLRB v. Richland Educ. Ass'n,* Case Nos. PERA-C-3477-C et al., 542 GERR B-7 (Pa. LRB 1974) (proposal for voluntary interest arbitration permissive subject of negotiations; neither party is required to negotiate over such a proposal). Under the National Labor Relations Act, the NLRB and the courts have uniformly held that interest arbitration is a non-mandatory subject of bargaining. See, e.g., *Massachusetts Nurses Ass'n,* 225 N.L.R.B. 678 (1976), aff'd, 557 F.2d 894 (1st Cir. 1977); *NLRB v. Sheet Metal Workers, Local 38,* 575 F.2d 394 (2d Cir. 1978).

In *Klauder v. San Juan Cty. Deputy Sherriff's Guild,* 107 Wash. 2d 338, 728 P.2d 1044 (1986), the Washington Supreme Court followed precedent under the NLRA and held that continuation of an interest arbitration provision in a collective bargaining agreement was not a mandatory subject of bargaining and that an interest arbitrator had no authority to order that such provision be incorporated as part of the parties' new collective bargaining agreement. The court ruled that "[t]he authority of the interest arbitrator is limited and cannot be extended to the establishment of future contracts over the objection of the party," noting that "[t]o lock either labor or management to unfriendly arbitrators for negotiation after negotiation would be intolerable." The court concluded that "[i]nterest arbitration provisions must terminate unless both parties agree to the continuation."

6. In *Keene State College Educ. Ass'n v. State,* 120 N.H. 25, 411 A.2d 156 (1980), the New Hampshire Supreme Court held "that faculty committees, observers and department chairmen are part of the management structure of the university" and that, as a result, the university under the New Hampshire statute had the "managerial prerogative ... to eliminate them" unilaterally. In dictum, the court stated:

> Because the purposes of the doctrine of exclusive representation are sometimes inapplicable in a university faculty setting, we hold that the doctrine need not bar the existence of advisory faculty committees or observers. Of course, we agree with the board that conditions of employment such as pay and hours remain proper subjects of union bargaining, while committees dealing with curriculum, honorary degrees or research topics would not impinge on exclusive union representation. We can offer no bright line distinction for the PELRB or administrators in this area. We prefer to leave some play in the joints rather than to constrict or destroy campus life in the name of [the New Hampshire statute].

7. In *Metropolitan Tech. Community College Educ. Ass'n v. Metropolitan Tech. Community College,* 203 Neb. 832, 281 N.W.2d 201 (1979), the court held that the number of instructor contact hours at a technical-vocational college involved "a foundational value judgment which is essential to [the College's] basic educational and learning philosophy and is therefore a prerogative of management and is not bargainable." The court set forth the following test to be utilized in determining whether or not a given item is a mandatory subject of bargaining:

> A matter which is of fundamental, basic or essential concern to an employee's financial and personal concern may be considered as involving working conditions and is mandatorily bargainable even though there may be some minor influence on educational policy or management prerogative. However, those matters which involve foundational value judgments, which strike at the very heart of the educational philosophy of the particular institu-

tion, are management prerogatives and are not a proper subject for negotiation even though such decisions may have some impact on working conditions. However, the impact of whatever decision management may make in this or any other case on the economic welfare of employees is a proper subject of mandatory bargaining.

Following the lead of the federal government, several states have also limited the scope of bargaining by enumerating certain management rights or prerogatives. Ohio, for example, provides that

Unless a public employer agrees otherwise in a collective bargaining agreement, nothing in Chapter 4117 of the Revised Code impairs the right and responsibility of each public employer to:
(1) Determine matters of inherent managerial policy which include, but are not limited to areas of discretion or policy such as the functions and programs of the public employer, standards of services, its overall budget, utilization of technology, and organizational structure;
(2) Direct, supervise, evaluate, or hire employees;
(3) Maintain and improve the efficiency and effectiveness of governmental operations;
(4) Determine the overall methods, process, means, or personnel by which governmental operations are to be conducted;
(5) Suspend, discipline, demote, or discharge for just cause, or lay off, transfer, assign, schedule, promote, or retain employees;
(6) Determine the adequacy of the work force;
(7) Determine the overall mission of the employer as a unit of government;
(8) Effectively manage the work force;
(9) Take actions to carry out the missions of the public employer as a govermental unit.
The employer is not required to bargain on subjects reserved to the management and direction of the governmental unit except as affect wages, hours, terms and conditions of employment, and the continuation, modification, or deletion of an existing provision of a collective bargaining agreement. A public employee or exclusive representative may raise a legitimate complaint or file a grievance based on the collective bargaining agreement.

Ohio Rev. Code Ann. § 4117.08(c) (Anderson 1991).
Hawaii, Kansas, New Hamsphire and Nevada have somewhat similar provisions.
The Minnesota act provides that

A public employer is not required to meet and negotiate on matters of inherent managerial policy, which include, but are not limited to, such areas of discretion or policy as the functions and programs of the employer, its overall budget, utilization of technology, the organizational structure and selection and direction and number of personnel. Minn. Stat. Ann. § 179A.06 (West Supp. 1991).

The Illinois and Pennsylvania acts contain nearly identical provisions, although the Illinois Act provides that employers are, nevertheless, "required to bargain collectively with regard to policy matters directly affecting wages, hours and terms and conditions of employment as well as the impact thereon upon request by employee representatives." In addition, the Illinois Act has a grandfather clause which provides that "employers shall be required to bargain collectively with regard to any matter concerning wages, hours or conditions of employment about which they have bargained for and agreed to in a collective bargaining agreement prior to the effective date of [the act]." Ill. Rev. Stat. ch. 48, ¶ 1604 (1989).

Vermont (for state employees) and California (for local government employees) have also exempted to a lesser extent certain management prerogatives from the scope of negotiations. Thus the California Act provides "that the scope of representation shall not include consideration of the merits, necessities, or organization of any service or activity provided by law or executive order." Cal. Gov't Code § 3504 (West 1980).

Numerous questions have arisen concerning the scope of bargaining under state statutes that include a statement of management prerogatives since most of these statutes also provide that the parties are required to negotiate in good faith over wages, hours and other terms and conditions of employment. The basic problem is to what extent are items which would otherwise be considered "wages, hours and other terms and conditions of employment" removed from the mandatory area of bargaining by a statutory statement of management rights. This problem is addressed in both the *Washoe* and *Illinois Departments* cases which follow.

WASHOE COUNTY SCHOOL DISTRICT & WASHOE COUNTY TEACHERS ASSOCIATION

Item #3 (Nev. Local Gov't Employee Mgt. Relations Bd. 1971), *aff'd*, 90 Nev. 442, 530 P.2d 114 (1974)

When Chapter 288, the Local Government Employee Relations Act, was enacted in 1969, valuable rights both on the part of the local government employees and the local government employer were relinquished in order to provide a more harmonious labor-management relationship on the local government level. NRS 288.180 declared strikes on the part of public employees to be illegal. NRS 288.150, Subsection 1, imposed upon the local government employer the duty of good faith negotiation with employee organizations on matters concerning wages, hours, and conditions of employment. However, NRS 288.150, Subsection 2, recognizes that the local government employer still maintains what is referred to as management prerogatives, i.e. the responsibility under appropriate situations to direct its employees; hire, promote, suspend, or terminate employees; maintain efficiency of its governmental operations; and to otherwise proceed to do such things, without reference to negotiation or any negotiated agreement which, if not done, would seriously infringe upon the local government employer's duty to the taxpayers and to the public.

Although it has been urged upon this Board by the counsel for the Washoe County School District that the provisions of Subsection 2 limit the areas of negotiability on matters relating to wages, hours, and conditions of employment if said matters also involve any items in Subsection 2, the Board rejects this view as untenable.

It is presumed the Legislature in enacting Chapter 288 did not enact a nullity. Under the school district's interpretation of the relationship between NRS 288.150, Subsection 1, and NRS 288.150, Subsection 2, any matter, including the very question of wage scale, involves management prerogative; and consequently, under said view would not be negotiable.

The Board does not believe that the Legislature so intended such an interpretation. Public employees by this Act have been denied perhaps their most valuable right — the right to strike. On the other hand, the local government employer has retained the right to define and recognize particular bargaining units, the right to exercise its management prerogatives without reference to negotiation or any prior negotiated agreement.

It is the opinion of the Board, therefore, that any matter significantly related to wages, hours, and working conditions is negotiable, whether or not said matters also relate to questions of management prerogative; and it is the duty of the local government employer to proceed and negotiate said items.

Findings of Fact

Based upon the evidence introduced, the Board makes the following findings of fact:

Class Size: Class size is significantly related to wages, hours, and working conditions inasmuch as student density directly affects a teacher's workload including the required hours of preparation and post-class evaluation; affects the teacher's control and discipline problems; affects the teacher's teaching and communication techniques; and affects the total amount of work required for a fixed compensation.

Article F. Professional Improvement: The professional improvement of a teacher is significantly related to working conditions since it directly affects his career opportunities within his profession as well as his ability to more effectively produce meritorious results in the classroom. However, no evidence has been presented to show that the determination of standards of the quality of education for a school district is so significantly related to wages, hours, and working conditions as to abrogate management prerogatives of the local government employer.

Article J. Student Discipline: The matter of student discipline is signficiantly related to a teacher's working conditions since the requirements for discipline at any given time usually demand a priority of the teacher's attention. The degree of control and discipline required in a classroom affects the demands on a teacher's ability to effectively teach the class.

Article K. School Calendar: The selection of those days that a teacher must work in a given school year is significantly related to the teacher's working conditions and the amount of work the teacher is expected to perform for a fixed compensation.

Article N. Teacher Performance: The evaluation of a teacher's performance is significantly related to wages and working conditions inasmuch as the evaluation affects transfer, retention, promotion and the compensation scale.

Article P. Special Student Program: The evidence produced in this hearing showed that management prerogatives predominate the entire subject matter as existing in Washoe County in that the Washoe County School District has provided a method and specialized staff to fulfill the sensitive responsibility of the school district to individual families in making determinations of which children are to be labeled special education cases. The evidence showed that the School District had relieved the teachers of this responsibility and there was insufficient evidence produced by the Teachers Association to demonstrate that the Association's proposal would signficantly affect or alter the teacher's working conditions.

Article S. Differentiated Staffing: Any plan of differentiated staffing which categorizes teachers on the basis of competency, experience, responsibilities and other factors, affects wages, hours, and working conditions of individual teachers relative to their peers.

Article W. Teacher Load: Where a teacher works, the amount of work done, and the kind of work done is a part of a teacher's working conditions. The remuneration for overtime for extra work assignments is a matter of wages and hours.

Article X. Instructional Supplies: The amount, type, quality, and availability of instructional supplies affects the ability of a teacher to discharge his job properly and is signficantly related to the teacher's working conditions and, in some cases, hours.

Conclusions of Law ....

[The Board held that all of the foregoing subjects were negotiable except for Article F on Professional Improvement which the Board held was "non-negotiable only in relation to the determination of the quality of education...."]

NOTES

1. In affirming the Commission's decision in the principal case, the Nevada Supreme Court stated:

> It is not conceivable that the legislature would give its extensive time and attention to study, draft, meet, hear, discuss and pass this important piece of legislation were it not to serve a useful purpose. For this court to hold that any item even though remotely relevant to management policy is beyond the pale of negotiation defeats the purpose of the legislation. Many matters involved in a teacher's work day bear somewhat on management policy and at the same time are inextricably linked to wages, hours and conditions of employment. What the legislature gave was not intended to immediately be taken away.

Washoe Cty. Teachers Ass'n v. Washoe Cty. Sch. Dist., 90 Nev. 442, 530 P.2d 114 (1974).

Subsequent to this decision, the Nevada statute was amended to limit the scope of negotiations to 20 enumerated items and to specifically provide that the management prerogatives reserved to a local government employer without negotiation "are not within the scope of mandatory bargaining." Nev. Rev. Stat. § 288.150 (1980). Class size, student discipline, and school calendar are not among the enumerated mandatory subjects of bargaining.

2. Utilizing an approach similar to that of the Nevada Commission in *Washoe,* the Rhode Island Supreme Court in *Barrington Sch. Comm. v. Rhode Island SLRB,* 120 R.I. 470, 388 A.2d 1369 (1978), held that the elimination of certain departmental chairmanships was a mandatory subject of bargaining. The court reasoned as follows:

> While we postulate no general rule, in the circumstances here, we conclude that the abolition of the 12 department chairmanships is not completely a matter of educational policy but is an appropriate matter for negotiating or bargaining concerning the effect on the individual teachers involved. In addition, to require the committee to bargain about the matter at issue would not in our opinion significantly abridge its freedom to manage and control the school system. We do not mean that the union should be able to dictate to the committee on matters strictly within the province of management. What we do say is that when, as here, the problem involved concerns both a question of management and a term or condition of employment, it is the duty of the committee to negotiate with the teachers involved.

ILLINOIS DEPARTMENTS OF CENTRAL MANAGEMENT SERVICES & CORRECTIONS

5 PERI ¶ 2001 (Ill. State Lab. Rel. Bd. 1988), aff'd sub nom.
AFSCME v. ISLRB, 190 Ill. App. 3d 259, 546 N.E.2d 687 (1989)

The issues in this matter arise from AFSCME's allegations that Respondent has violated Sections 10(a)(4) and 10(a)(1) of the Illinois Public Labor Relations Act (Act), Ill. Rev. Stat. 1987, ch. 48 pars. 1601 through 1627, by unilaterally implementing a drug testing policy during the term of a collective bargaining agreement.... The facts of the case are well stated in the Hearing Officer's Recommended Decision, and need not be discussed in detail here. Briefly, this dispute is the result of the Department of Corrections' (Corrections) decision to institute a drug testing plan to detect whether its employees are trafficking illegal drugs into State of Illinois correctional facilities.

AFSCME is the exclusive representative of over 8,000 employees of the Department of Corrections. The terms and conditions of employment for these employees are set forth in a master collective bargaining agreement, negotiated by AFSCME and the State of Illinois, with an effective term of July 1, 1986 through June 30, 1989. This agreement covers nearly 37,000 State employees represented by AFSCME in eight different collective bargaining units.

In early January, 1988, Respondent contacted AFSCME to inform it that Corrections wished to implement a policy to test its employees for the use of illegal drugs and that it was eager to meet and discuss the "impact" of the policy with AFSCME. The parties first met on January 22, 1988, at which time each made clear its respective position. Respondent stated that, through objective information gathered from its undercover investigations and subsequent arrests of those Corrections' employees trafficking illegal drugs into Illinois prisons, the overwhelming evidence demonstrated that these employees were drug users. As a result, Corrections wished to test those of its employees which it had "reasonable suspicion" of being under the influence of or using illegal drugs. Respondent contended that its decision to institute a drug testing policy was a management right; therefore, it asserted that, pursuant to Section 4 of the Act, it had no duty to bargain with AFSCME over the *decision* to test. Respondent asserted that it was obligated only to bargain over the "impact" of the policy, which, in this case, was limited to the disciplinary effects of being requested to take, or subsequently failing, a drug test.

AFSCME stated, however, that it was under no obligation to negotiate the proposal at all since the Respondent had no right to unilaterally implement the policy during the term of the existing collective bargaining agreement. AFSCME asserted that the Respondent's withdrawal of a drug testing proposal during the negotiations for the existing master collective bargaining agreement, and the subsequent inclusion of a "zipper clause" in the agreement, precluded Respondent from unilaterally implementing any policy involving drug testing during the term of the agreement. AFSCME contended that it was willing to listen to Respondent's proposal, but it insisted that, absent mutual agreement, Respondent could not implement any such policy.[2]

The parties' negotiators met on four occasions to discuss the policy and, as found by the Hearing Officer, agreed upon many of the items subsumed within the policy, including, but not limited to, testing and specimen collection procedures, laboratory qualifications, responsibility for bearing the time and cost of testing, and notification to AFSCME that Respondent was requesting an employee to take a test. Despite their agreement on various portions of the policy, the parties did not agree on the specific disciplinary penalties which would be imposed for refusing or failing a drug test. The parties also remained totally entrenched with regard to their bargaining obligations over the implementation of a drug testing policy. At the end of the fourth meeting, on February 23, 1988, Respondent declared that an impasse had been reached and that it would implement the policy.

As noted by the Hearing Officer in his well-reasoned recommendation in this matter:

> Drug testing at the work place has noticeably become a critical and controversial issue of national importance.... The horrible problem of the abuse of illegal drugs is indeed a serious social concern with which [sic] our nation must endeavor to solve. However, as we are a nation of laws, the methods employed to obliterate this evil must be instituted within constitutional and statutory limitations.

The concept of testing employees at the workplace for illegal drug use has recently become an active source of litigation and a widespread topic of publication. A large number of the public sector cases concerning drug testing involve the constitutionality of drug testing, that is[,] whether such testing may be considered an unreasonable search under the Fourth Amendment to the United States Constitution. The instant dispute involves no such constitutional ramifications; rather, the Charging Party's allegations are limited to Respondent's obligations under the Act as to the nature and scope of the duty to bargain over

---

[2]We reject AFSCME's argument that Corrections waived its right to institute a drug testing policy during the term of the contract. The facts, as found by the Hearing Officer, demonstrate that the proposal which Respondent withdrew at the bargaining table covered all State employees, not just those in Corrections. Moreover, the negotiation proposal provided for urine *and blood* testing under completely different circumstances than Corrections' policy based upon "reasonable suspicion" of drug use. After examination of these facts and the language of the "zipper-clause" in the agreement, we find that a "clear and unmistakable" waiver is not present. See *Rockwell International Corp.,* 260 NLRB 1346 (1982). As a result, we find that AFSCME's argument that the agreement's "zipper clause" constitutes a valid waiver in these circumstances is unpersuasive.

the matters at issue. Specifically, the threshold issue in this matter is whether the Respondent's decision to institute a drug testing policy is a "mandatory subject of bargaining."

Although we recognize that the nature of the subject matter in this case is emotional and sensitive, we find no reason to depart from the analysis that we have consistently applied to determine whether a particular topic is a "mandatory subject of bargaining" or a "management right." The Hearing Officer, after utilizing a balancing approach, determined that Corrections' interest in instituting a drug testing policy to further its statutory mission of protecting the health and safety of its employees and inmates outweighed the effect of the policy on the employees' conditions of employment. We agree.

Section 7 of the Act, which defines the duty to bargain, requires a public employer to bargain in good faith with the exclusive representative of its employees over wages, hours, and other conditions of employment, not excluded from the bargaining obligation by Section 4 of the Act. Section 4 of the Act provides, in pertinent part:

> Employers shall not be required to bargain over matters of inherent managerial policy, which shall include such areas of discretion or policy as the functions of the employer, standards of services, its overall budget, the organizational structure and selection of new employees, examination techniques and direction of employees. Employers, however, shall be required to bargain collectively with regard to policy matters directly affecting wages, hours and terms and conditions of employment as well as the impact thereon upon request by employee representatives.

Section 4 of the Act, therefore, is a specific limitation on a public employer's duty to bargain. Public employers, although required to bargain in good faith with respect to wages, hours and conditions of employment are not required to bargain over "matters of inherent managerial policy." See *State of Illinois, Department of Central Management Services* 1 PERI ¶ 2016 (Ill. SLRB 1985). Nevertheless, if the "inherent managerial policy" affects wages, hours and conditions of employment, the employer still must bargain over the "impact" (effects) of the policy.

The concepts of "terms and conditions of employment" and "inherent managerial policy," however, often overlap. Managerial policies frequently have an impact on an employee's conditions of employment and the converse is equally true. The problem of resolving this tension between an employer's managerial prerogatives and its employees' conditions of employment is one which has been addressed by various labor relations boards and courts. See, e.g., *Decatur School District No. 61*, 4 PERI ¶ 1076 (Ill. ELRB 1988); *Jacksonville School District No. 117*, 4 PERI ¶ 1075 (Ill. ELRB 1988); *Pennsylvania Labor Relations Board v. State College Area School District*, 337 A.2d 262 (Pa. 1975); *State v. State Supervisory Employees Associations*, 78 N.J. 54, 393 A.2d 233 (1978); *City of Beloit v. Wisconsin Employment Relations Commission*, 73 Wis. 2d 43, 242 N.W.2d 231 (1976); *City of New Rochelle*, 10 PERB ¶ 3078 (N.Y. PERB 1977); *Fibreboard Paper Products Corp. v. NLRB*, 379 U.S. 203 (1964).

Under the Act's statutory scheme, the overlap between management rights and employees' conditions of employment is manifested in the language found in Section 7 and in Section 4. In *City of Crest Hill*, 4 PERI ¶ 2030 (Ill. SLRB

1988), we stated that a balancing approach is the desirable method by which to resolve the tension between the duty to bargain over terms and conditions of employment and an employer's freedom to manage its own operations. See also *State of Illinois, Department of Central Management Services, supra*. Thus, to determine whether a subject is one over which the Act requires that the parties engage in collective bargaining, we must balance the competing interests and consider the extent to which collective negotiations will impair the employer's statutory right to determine government policy. See *In re IFPTE v. State*, 443 A.2d 187 (N.J. 1982). We conclude that when the employer demonstrates that the policy involved is a carefully tailored response to a need related to its mission, the employer may act unilaterally in the implementation of that policy, but only to the extent that its action does not significantly intrude on the protected interests of its employees. See *County of Niagara*, 21 PERB 3014, Case No. U-8615 (NY PERB March 11, 1988).

At the outset, we note that the special and unique statutory mission of Corrections includes maintaining order in the penal institutions of the State. In furtherance of this mission, Corrections has unilaterally implemented such policies as dog-sniffs, pat-downs and strip searches of employees to prevent the influx of contraband into prisons. The drug testing policy implemented here by Respondent is specifically and carefully developed to further the mission of Corrections. Corrections presented objective proof that some of its employees have been involved in the trafficking of illegal drugs within prison facilities, and nearly all of those employees caught trafficking drugs within prison facilities have been drug users. In response, Corrections has sought to implement a policy to drug test those of its employees whom it reasonably suspects are using narcotics. Thus, the policy is an investigatory tool to uncover criminal activity and to maintain institutional safety and security.

Moreover, it is clear that if the policy is to be an effective tool for Corrections to ferret out those of its employees who are trafficking illegal drugs to inmates, Respondent must be permitted to act unilaterally. If we did not permit Corrections to act unilaterally in an area so closely related to its statutory mission, we would be remiss in recognizing that, through Section 4 of the Act, the Legislature specifically provided that a public employer needs such freedom to effectively perform the services it is obligated to provide.[8]

AFSCME argues that the policy is a mandatory subject of bargaining because the Respondent's program intrudes upon its employees' privacy and directly

---

[8] The importance of a public employer's "mission" in the balance struck between the employer's right to establish governmental policy and the protected interest of its employees in their wages, hours and conditions of employment is most clearly portrayed in *County of Niagara*, 21 PERB 3014, Case No. U-8615 (NY PERB March 11, 1988). In this case, the County of Niagara maintained a skilled in-house nursing facility for the elderly. The employer, prompted by its concern over second-hand smoke hazards, instituted restrictions regarding employee smoking within certain areas of the facility, such as the main lobby, library and cafeteria. Although the New York State Public Employment Relations Board (PERB) found that the smoking ban affected the terms and conditions of employment of the employees, it concluded that the smoking restriction was directly related to the employer's statutory mission of treating the elderly ill. As a result, the PERB ruled that the employer could unilaterally ban smoking in those areas customarily used by patients; however, the PERB ordered the employer to rescind the ban in the library and cafeteria since those areas were not customarily used by patients and, therefore, the reason for the restriction in those areas was not directly related to the employer's mission.

affects the employees' conditions of employment. In support of its argument, AFSCME cites *Memorandum of Drug and Alcohol Testing*, Memorandum GC-87-5, dated September 8, 1987, issued by the General Counsel of the National Labor Relations Board (NLRB), in which the General Counsel advises that drug testing policies in the private sector are mandatory subjects of bargaining. We reject AFSCME's arguments. First, the policy proposed by the Respondent requires testing based upon "reasonable suspicion"; therefore, despite the awkward, but necessary, procedures that must be followed to obtain an unadulterated urine sample from an employee, the test is quite narrow and limited in its application to only those individuals with regard to whom Corrections possesses objective proof of drug use. Second, we find that the unique nature and environment involved in the employment relationship with Corrections requires that its employees be subject to reasonable regulations in the area of safety and security.

Further, we find the reasons and rationale of the NLRB's General Counsel, as set forth in her Memorandum GC 87-5, inapplicable. The Memorandum provides that drug testing is not a managerial prerogative because it is not fundamental to the basic function of the enterprise. In the private sector, however, "profit" is the function of the enterprise and the scope of bargaining is determined with regard to the employer's need to exercise discretion in the direction of the company's operations so as to ensure a profitable business. In the public sector, although budgetary concerns are present, the function of the employer is the delivery of public services, as determined by public officials and legislators who are held accountable to the voters and citizens; therefore, the scope of bargaining in the public sector must be determined with regard to the employer's statutory mission. As a result, the NLRB's General Counsel's Memorandum does not reflect the same employer interests and purposes that exist in the public sector and we therefore distinguish its applicability. Thus, the particular circumstances of this case demonstrate that the Respondent's interests in implementing the drug testing policy outweigh the Charging Party's interests. Consequently, the decision to test Corrections' employees for drug use, based upon a "reasonable suspicion," is a management prerogative and is not subject to the duty to bargain in good faith.[9]

Nonetheless, the Respondent is not completely free from the duty to bargain in good faith. Although an employer is not required to bargain collectively with an exclusive representative concerning matters of inherent managerial policy, the employer is required to bargain with the exclusive representative concerning the impact that such managerial decisions have upon employees' wages, hours and terms and conditions of employment. *State of Illinois, Department of Central Management Services, supra.* The Respondent contends that the only

---

[9] In making our decision today, we are mindful of the Florida Public Employees Relations Committee's decision in *City of Miami*, 12 FPER ¶ 17029 (FPERC 1985) in which, in a split decision, a majority held that mandatory drug testing of police officers is a mandatory subject of bargaining. Clearly, however, the facts in this case are extremely different. In our analysis, the unique and special interests of Corrections, the severity of the drug problem in Illinois prisons, and the "reasonable suspicion" aspect of the policy all have played a major role in our effort to strike a balance in this case. Therefore, Illinois public employers would be ill-advised in relying on our decision in this case as useful or broad authority for the unilateral implementation of drug testing programs for Illinois public employees.

"effect" of the decision upon employees' wages, hours and conditions of employment is the disciplinary portion of the policy. The Hearing Officer examined all of the subjects discussed at the bargaining table and found the range of "effects" much broader. The Hearing Officer concluded that all consequences of submitting to a drug test, including the ramifications of receiving test results indicating that no drugs were found in the employees' urine, discipline (including mandatory attendance at an employees' assistance program), specimen collection procedures, laboratory analysis procedures, the right to union representation, the time and cost involved in testing, the confidentiality of test results, and the criteria that determine when a test may be properly requested, are all subjects of bargaining because each has an impact on Corrections' employees as a result of Respondent's decision to institute drug testing.

Our review of the record, however, indicates that the parties were in agreement with respect to *all* of these topics, except for discipline and the effects of a negative test result.[10] Thus, regardless of their legal obligations concerning bargaining, the record is clear that the parties' negotiation sessions produced an accord on many of the policy's terms. As a result, we find it unnecessary to determine whether these areas constitute bargainable "effects" since the parties' obligation to bargain over these topics is no longer at issue. In this regard, we need not address the Hearing Officer's recommendations as to whether these subjects are within the area of "effects" bargaining.

By contrast, the parties did not agree on the subject of discipline. The Respondent, however, admitted that it was obligated to bargain over the disciplinary aspects that are attendant to the policy and did begin bargaining over them. Respondent claims that it ceased negotiations with AFSCME on the subject of discipline because an impasse was reached. Generally, where the parties have reached legitimate impasse, an employer may unilaterally implement changes in terms and conditions of employment consistent with its pre-impasse proposals. See *Kewanee Education Association, IEA-NEA, and Kewanee Community Unit School District No. 229,* 4 PERI 1136, Ill. ELRB Case No. 86-CA-0081-C (September 15, 1988) and cases cited therein. Therefore, the focus of our analysis now becomes whether the parties reached an impasse over negotiations solely on the subject of discipline.

Section 7 of the Act recognizes that parties engaged in collective bargaining are *not* required to reach a mutual agreement. In this context, the duty to bargain does not require a party "to engage in fruitless marathon discussions," see *NLRB v. American National Insurance Company,* 343 U.S. 395 (1952), as in instances where there are irreconcilable differences in the parties' positions after good-faith negotiations have exhausted the prospects of concluding an agreement. *Taft Broadcasting Co.,* 163 NLRB 475 (1967), *aff'd* 395 F.2d 622 (D.C. Cir. 1968). In *Taft Broadcasting Co., supra,* the NLRB discussed some of

---

[10] The parties did not agree on the subject referred to by the Hearing Officer as "negative test results." Apparently, AFSCME desired to bargain over the "effect" on an employee whose test results showed that he was drug-free. Failing to see how an employee's "condition of employment" is affected if he tests *negative* for drug use, we reject the Hearing Officer's conclusions regarding the bargaining obligations related to this type of proposal.

the factors to be considered in determining whether an impasse has been reached:

[t]he bargaining history, the good faith of the parties in negotiations, the length of the negotiations, the importance of the issue or issues as to which there is disagreement, the contemporaneous understanding of the parties as to the state of negotiations are all relevant factors....

163 NLRB at 478.

Upon review of the record, we find that although some give-and-take occurred on the subject of discipline, the discussions progressed very slowly. The reason for the parties' hesitancy seems clear: each had taken very strong and polarized positions on its bargaining obligations concerning the policy. Thus, despite agreement upon a number of subjects, such as testing procedures and specimen collection, the parties' ideological differences came to blows over the subject of discipline. Due to each of the parties' respective viewpoints of their legal duties, the negotiations were necessarily constrained.

The small number of meetings, and the complexity and novelty of the issues, while not alone conclusive proof of an absence of impasse, also added to the parties' problems engaging in thorough discussions. Indeed, now that the parties have been advised of their legal obligations, we expect that they can proceed with negotiations without the burdensome cloak of rhetoric and speculation. Clearly, the parties have not negotiated to the point where further bargaining over the subject of discipline would be futile; therefore, we find that an impasse has not been reached. Consequently, we will order the parties to return to the table and bargain in good faith over the disciplinary measures of the Respondent's policy until they reach an agreement or an impasse. Furthermore, when the parties reach agreement on disciplinary sanctions resulting from a request to take a drug test, we expect that they will reduce their agreement to writing to be fully incorporated into the existing collective bargaining agreement.

Finally, the Hearing Officer concluded that until the parties fulfilled their obligation to bargain over the disciplinary measures accompanying the policy, the Respondent was required to rescind the policy. The Hearing Officer reasoned that permitting the Respondent to institute drug testing without agreed-upon provisions for discipline would be unfair to the employees. We disagree. The parties, by providing in their collective bargaining agreement that employees will be subject to discipline only upon "just cause," have already agreed to the resolution of *all* disciplinary measures imposed upon bargaining unit employees. Consequently, the "just cause" provision will provide sufficient protections for the unit employees while the parties bargain over more specific disciplinary provisions.[14] See *Pennsylvania Bureau of Labor Relations,* 17 PPER ¶ 17134 (PA LRB 1985). In the meantime, AFSCME has the right to grieve any discipline arising from the Respondent's imposition of the drug

---

[14] Nonetheless, it is clear from the record that the parties desired and intended to bargain to agreement over the specific disciplinary actions to which Corrections' employees will [be] subjected should they be requested to take a drug test. Indeed, such bargaining is appropriate since the record lacks any evidence that the disciplinary and grievance provisions in the master agreement were ... bargained for with the drug testing program in mind. It is for these reasons that we have found that the parties must return to the table and be given the opportunity to conclude their negotiations.

testing policy. As a result, we conclude that the Respondent may implement its drug testing policy while the parties return to the bargaining table.

Finally, we request that the Board's Compliance Officer be in contact with the parties to ensure that bargaining over the subject of discipline ... commences immediately pursuant to this order. Should we find that either party is not complying with this order, we shall thereafter consider alternative methods to see that the parties' statutory bargaining obligations are met.

NOTES

1. There is no unanimity of authority on whether drug testing is a mandatory subject of bargaining. In line with the NLRB's decision in *Johnson-Bateman, Inc.,* 295 NLRB No. 26, 131 L.R.R.M. 1393 (1989), several jurisdictions have held that drug testing of current employees is a mandatory subject of bargaining. See *City of Detroit,* 1990 Lab. Op. 67 (Mich.) (random drug testing of police officers is a mandatory subject of bargaining since it "implicates discipline and employment security, and impacts upon safety in the workplace"); *Findlay City Sch. Dist. Bd. of Educ.,* 5 OPER ¶ 5049 (Ohio SERB 1987) ("The threat of disciplinary action ... brings the [drug and alcohol use] policy statement clearly within the scope of bargaining"); *City of New Haven,* Dec. No. 2554-A (Conn. SBLR 1987) (reasonable suspicion drug testing is a mandatory subject of bargaining). In other jurisdictions, however, drug testing has been held to be a nonmandatory subject of bargaining. See *City of Miami v. FOP Lodge 20,* 1990 Fla. App. LEXIS 2653 (1990) (en banc). The various labor relations boards, however, have uniformly held that drug testing of applicants for employment is not a mandatory subject of bargaining. See, e.g., *City of Detroit,* 1989 MERC Lab. Op. 788 (Mich.); *Star Tribune, Div. of Cowles Media Co.,* 295 NLRB No. 63, 131 L.R.R.M. 1404 (1989).

2. In *City of Buffalo (Police Department),* 20 PERB ¶ 3048 (N.Y. 1987), the New York PERB held that an employer could not compel a union to negotiate over random drug testing in view of a prior New York Court of Appeals decision which held that random drug testing was unconstitutional. In holding that random drug testing was a permissive subject of bargaining, the New York PERB noted that a union, although it could not be required to do so, could negotiate over and agree to random drug testing, observing that a "waiver of such constitutional rights can only occur upon consent" and that "the bargaining agent may act in the place of individual employees to grant or withhold consent."

3. In accord with the decision in the principal case, an increasing number of boards and courts are utilizing a balancing test to determine whether a given subject is mandatory or permissive. For example, in *Sutherlin Educ. Ass'n v. Sutherlin Sch. Dist. No.* 130, 25 Or. App. 85, 548 P.2d 208 (1976), the Oregon Court of Appeals stated that "the appropriate test to be applied in determining whether a proposed subject is a 'condition of employment' and therefore a mandatory subject of bargaining is to balance the element of educational policy involved against the effect that the subject has on a teacher's employment." Other decisions in which courts have adopted a balancing standard to resolve negotiability disputes include *Beloit Educ. Ass'n v. WERC,* 73 Wis. 2d 43, 242 N.W.2d 231 (1976), and *City of Biddeford v. Biddeford Teachers' Ass'n,* 304 A.2d 387, 83 L.R.R.M. 2098 (Me. 1973). See generally Clark, *The Scope of the Duty to Bargain in Public Employment,* in Labor Relations Law in the Public Sector 81 (A. Knapp ed. 1977).

In adopting the balancing test to resolve negotiability disputes, the New Jersey PERC in *Ridgefield Park Bd. of Educ.*, 3 NJPER 303 (1977), rejected the union's contention "that a 'significant relation' standard should be applied by the commission in rendering scope of negotiations determinations." After noting that "[t]his standard categorizes a specific issue as a required subject of collective negotiations if it is significantly related to wages, hours, and other terms and conditions of employment," the New Jersey PERC stated:

> The Commission in its scope determinations has not adopted the approach that a given subject is mandatorily negotiable if it is significantly related to wages, hours and other terms and conditions of employment. We have decided that this "significant relation" standard is inadequate because it does not properly recognize the competing interests at stake where there is an overlap between conditions of employment on the one hand and management prerogatives on the other. By focusing on only one half of this overlap situation, this standard would give undue, if not exclusive, weight to terms and conditions of employment.
>
> Instead, the Commission has applied a balancing test in determining whether a particular subject is a mandatory or permissive subject for collective negotiations. This pragmatic test openly acknowledges that there may be an overlap between terms and conditions of employment and certain management prerogatives which requires a careful consideration of the competing interests at issue.

Citing the New Jersey Commission's decision in *Ridgefield Park*, the New York PERB in *City of New Rochelle*, 10 PERB ¶ 3078 (1977), stated that "[b]alancing tests are appropriate in deciding whether or not a matter is a mandatory subject of negotiations."

4. Assuming a balancing test is utilized to determine whether a given item is a mandatory subject of bargaining, how should the following items be classified:

a. Institution of a civilian review board for police officers. Compare *Berkeley Police Ass'n v. City of Berkeley*, 76 Cal. App. 3d 931, 143 Cal. Rptr. 255, (1977) (managerial decision outside scope of negotiation), with *Pontiac Police Officers Ass'n v. City of Pontiac*, 397 Mich. 674, 246 N.W.2d 831 (1976) (mandatory subject of negotiations).

b. Decentralization of a school system.

c. Type of weapons and/or bullets issued to police officers.

d. Assignment of police officers to shifts on basis of seniority.

e. Student discipline.

f. Quality of patient care and the type and kind of medical equipment provided.

g. Promotions based on seniority.

h. Number of police officers assigned to a squad car.

i. Determination of a school or college curriculum.

j. Conditions under which police officer may use deadly force. See *San Jose Peace Officers Ass'n v. City of San Jose*, 78 Cal. App. 3d 935, 144 Cal. Rptr. 638 (1978).

What arguments could be made for and against mandatory negotiations of each of the foregoing items? Would it make any difference if compulsory interest arbitration is the terminal step of the statutory impasse procedure? See *Pontiac Police Officers Ass'n v. City of Pontiac*, 397 Mich. 674, 246 N.W.2d 831 (1976) (compulsory arbitration statute does "not affect the analysis of what constitutes mandatory subjects for collective bargaining under the 'other terms and conditions' language").

5. Contrast the Hawaii Act, which specifically provides that "[t]he employer and the exclusive representative shall not agree to any proposal which would be inconsistent with merit principles ... or which would interfere with the rights of a public employer to ...," Haw. Rev. Stat. § 89-9(d) (Supp. 1987), with the Pennsylvania Act, which provides that "[p]ublic employers shall not be required to bargain over matters of inherent managerial policy, which shall include but shall not be limited to such areas of discretion or policy as ..." 43 Pa. Cons. Stat. Ann. § 1101.702 (Purdon 1991). Whereas the parties are prohibited from bargaining over certain subjects by virtue of the Hawaii Act, the Pennsylvania Act only provides that the employer is not required to negotiate over certain matters. In other words, while the Pennsylvania Act specifically provides that certain matters are not *mandatory* subjects of bargaining, such matters may nevertheless be *permissible* subjects of negotiations, i.e., the employer could voluntarily negotiate over such matters and include any agreements reached in a written labor contract.

6. Would a public employer's proposal that supervisory employees who are excluded from an appropriate bargaining unit should be permitted to retain and accumulate seniority in the event they were assigned bargaining unit positions as a result of a layoff or reduction in force be a mandatory subject of bargaining? In *Marshalltown Educ. Ass'n v. PERB*, 299 N.W.2d 469, 1979-80 PBC ¶ 36, 135 (Iowa 1980), the court reversed the Iowa PERB's decision that such a proposal was a mandatory subject of bargaining. The court ruled that the proposal illegally sought "to impose mandatory bargaining for the benefit of persons who are excluded both from the act and from the bargaining unit." In this regard, the court noted that the exclusion of supervisory personnel from coverage under the act was "to protect the public and avoid the conflicts of interest inherent in the situation before us." But see *Hamden Bd. of Educ.*, Decision No. 2087 (Conn. SBLR 1981), in which the Connecticut Board held that a proposal which would permit administrators to bump into the teachers' bargaining unit if they had more teacher seniority was a mandatory subject of bargaining in negotiations between the school board and a unit of administrators. See also *Connecticut State Council of AFSA Locals*, Decision No. 2225 (Conn. SBLR 1983).

WEST IRONDEQUOIT BOARD OF EDUCATION

4 PERB ¶ 3070, *aff'd on rehearing*, 4 PERB ¶ 3089 (N.Y. Pub. Emp. Relations Bd. 1971), *aff'd*, 35 N.Y.2d 46, 315 N.E.2d 775, 358 N.Y.S.2d 720 (1974)

The West Irondequoit Teachers Association (charging party) filed an improper practice charge against the West Irondequoit Board of Education (employer) alleging that the employer violated Section 209-a.1(d) of the Public Employees' Fair Employment Act by refusing to negotiate on two issues.

The parties submitted the case to the hearing officer on stipulated facts. In summary, the charging party is the recognized negotiating representative for all of the full-time and part-time certificated personnel excluding some job titles which are immaterial herein.

During negotiations for the 1970-71 academic year, the charging party submitted a proposal entitled "Class Size and Teaching Load."[1]

In response to the charging party's proposal, the employer submitted it[s] own proposal.[2]

The charging party also submitted to the employer a proposal entitled "Promotional Policy."

The respondent in May 1970 informed the charging party that it would not negotiate with respect to numerical limitations of class size (hereinafter referred to as class size) or on promotional policy in that both subject matters involved nondelegable duties and responsibilities of the employer.

The charging party has contended that class size is a term and condition of employment and inasmuch as the negotiations on class size do not contravene any law, it is a mandatory subject of negotiations. Further, the charging party argued that since the employer in its counter-proposal stated that excessive class size may affect the emotional or mental well-being of a teacher, the employer had conceded that class size is a term and condition of employment.

The hearing officer stated that, in resolving this matter, we must weigh the duty of government officials to make decisions affecting the entire electorate against the statutory obligation of public employers to negotiate on subjects directly affecting the terms and conditions of employment.

The hearing officer further found that class size does have a major impact on a teacher's working conditions and that class size is not an expression of a primary policy goal of the basic direction of government. The hearing officer

---

[1]"Class Size and Teaching Load."
The pertinent provisions are: "B. Maximum Class Size:
(Definition: The number of pupils for whom a teacher is responsible during a single period in a single day.)
1. The class size of the kindergarten shall be 20 pupils.
2. The class size of the first grade in the elementary schools shall be 20 pupils.
3. The class size of the second-fourth grades in the elementary schools shall be 25 pupils.
4. The class size of the fifth-sixth grades and vocal music classes in the middle schools shall be 25 pupils.... [The proposal also specified class sizes for other grades.]
Classes that increase beyond the *maximum* must be agreed upon by the teacher and the building principal involved. Any disagreement over such an exception shall be subject to the procedure set forth in the Grievance Procedure." (emphasis in original)
[2]The pertinent provisions of respondent's proposal on "Class Size" are as follows:
D.1. Basic Understandings.
a. One key to effective learning is the quantity and quality of interrelations between and among pupils and teachers.
b. Excessive class size or teacher load may affect the emotional or mental well-being of the teachers.
c. A number of factors, such as available space, degrees of difficulty of the subject or grade level, the methodology utilized, the particular strengths of the teachers, and the individual characteristics of pupils must be considered by administrators when arranging classes and teacher assignments.
2. Agreements.
The Board and the Association agree that:
a. The relationships between effective learning and class size and teacher load shall be subject to continued examination by the parties, in order to determine optimal classroom conditions for pupils.
b. Administrative flexibility in arranging class sizes and teacher loads shall be maintained in order to allow for program diversity and innovation, and to allow for arrangements among teachers which are equitable. The district's administrators shall consider the guidelines established by the NYSTA Special Committee on the Duties of Teachers as optimal conditions in their planning for the 1971-72 school year.

concluded that class size is a term and condition of employment and, as such, is a mandatory subject of negotiation.[4]

The issue before this Board raised in this proceeding is a most serious one because of the effect such decisions will have upon school negotiations throughout the State.

In the *New Rochelle* case this Board stated that the determination as to the manner and means by which education service is rendered and the extent of such service is the duty and obligation of the public employer. A public employer should not be required to delegate this responsibility. The decisions of a public employer as to the carrying out of its mission — a decision to eliminate or curtail a service — are not decisions that a public employer should be compelled to negotiate with its employees.

Specifically in the *New Rochelle* case we held that budgetary cuts with concomitant job eliminations were not mandatory subjects of negotiations. Underlying this determination was the concept that basic decisions as to public policy should not be made in the isolation of a negotiation table, but rather should be made by those having the direct and sole responsibility therefor, and whose actions in this regard are subject to review in the electoral process. It would appear that class size is also a basic element of education policy. This follows our decision in the *New Rochelle* case. In that case, the budgetary decisions involved the elimination of a substantial number of teacher positions. These eliminations affected class size.

While we state that such decisions may be determined unilaterally by a public employer, nevertheless the employer is obligated to negotiate with the representative of its public employees on the impact of such decisions on terms and conditions of employment. Clearly such negotiations on the impact of decisions will have an effect on the allocation of resources. Nevertheless, impact is a matter for negotiations. Thus, it is not the thrust of this decision that an employer is not required to negotiate on subjects which affect the allocation of resources because salaries clearly have such an effect; rather, the thrust of this decision and the decision in the *New Rochelle* case is that basic policy decisions as to the implementation of a mission of an agency of government are not mandatory subjects of negotiations.[6]

It should be noted that the line of demarcation between a basic policy decision and the impact on terms and conditions of employment may not always be clear. For example, a policy decision as to class size may have an impact on teaching load. At first look, class size and teaching load may seem the same, but as we see them, they are not. The first represents a determination by the public employer as to an educational policy made in the light of its resources and other needs of its constituency. This decision may have an impact on hours of work and the number of teaching periods which are clearly mandatory subjects of negotiations.

---

[4]This conclusion of the hearing officer was reached prior to this Board's decision in *City School District of the City of New Rochelle v. New Rochelle Federation of Teachers*, 4 PERB ¶ 4-3060, 3704.

[6]However, the impact which such decisions have on the terms and conditions of employment is a mandatory subject of negotiation.

Further, we would make clear that this decision does not prohibit negotiations on class size. *A fortiori*, neither does it preclude a public employer, such as a school board, from consulting with teacher organizations in making basic decisions as to educational policies; rather this should be encouraged so as to take advantage of the teachers' professional expertise.

We, Therefore, modify the decision of the hearing officer and hold that class size is a policy decision of government and thus is not a mandatory subject of negotiations. As to that portion of the charge dealing with negotiation on promotional policy, we agree with the distinction and decision of the hearing officer and affirm and adopt the recommendations of the hearing officer.

Thus, we find that promotional policy for job titles outside the negotiating units, as well as the determination of qualifications for promotion into positions within the negotiating unit, are not terms and conditions of employment and, therefore, are not mandatory subjects of negotiations.

The employer is therefore

Ordered to negotiate upon the request of the charging party with respect to promotional policy relating to job titles within the negotiating unit; in all other respects, the charge herein is dismissed.

NOTES

1. Contrast the decision in the principal case with the decision of the Nevada Commission in *Washoe, supra.* Does the inclusion of a statutory management prerogatives clause make any difference in scope of bargaining determinations? What effect, if any, should the absence of a statutory reservation of management prerogatives have?

In *Fire Fighters Union, Local 1186 v. City of Vallejo,* 12 Cal. 3d 608, 526 P.2d 971, 116 Cal. Rptr. 507 (1973), the California Supreme Court was faced with the question of determining the scope of negotiations under a city charter which provided for negotiations on "wages, hours, and working conditions," but excluded from negotiations "matters involving the merits, necessity, or organization of any service or activity provided by law." Concerning the effect of this latter exclusion on the mandatory scope of negotiations, the California Supreme Court stated:

> Although the NLRA does not contain specific wording comparable to the "merits, necessity or organization" terminology in the city charter and the state act, the underlying fear that generated this language — that is, that wages, hours and working conditions could be expanded beyond reasonable boundaries to deprive an employer of his legitimate management prerogatives — lies imbedded in the federal precedents under the NLRA. As a review of federal case law in this field demonstrates, the trepidation that the union would extend its province into matters that should properly remain in the hands of employers has been incorporated into the interpretation of the scope of "wages, hours and terms and conditions of employment." Thus, because the federal decisions effectively reflect the same interests as those that prompted the inclusion of the "merits, necessity or organization" bargaining limitation in the charter provision and state act, the federal precedents provide reliable if analogous authority on the issue.

2. Did the New York PERB hold that the decisions with respect to class size or promotional policy are not conditions of employment? In *New Rochelle,* a decision referred to in the principal case, the New York Board noted that a proposed budgetary cut that would have resulted in the termination of 140 positions "[o]bviously ... does effect 'conditions of employment'.... However, it does not follow that every decision of a public employer which may affect job security is a mandatory subject of negotiations." *City Sch. Dist. of New Rochelle*, 4 PERB ¶ 3060 (N.Y. 1971).

3. Other decisions holding that class size is not a mandatory subject of bargaining include *Rapid City Educ. Ass'n v. Rapid City Area Sch. Dist. 51-4*, 376 N.W.2d 562 (S.D. 1985); *Beloit Educ. Ass'n v. WERC*, 73 Wis. 2d 43, 242 N.W.2d 231 (1976); *City of Biddeford v. Biddeford Teachers Ass'n*, 304 A.2d 387 (Me. 1973); *Seward Educ. Ass'n v. Sch. Dist.*, 188 Neb. 772, 199 N.W.2d 752 (1972); *Kenai Peninsula Dist. v. Kenai Peninsula Educ. Ass'n*, 557 P.2d 416, 97 L.R.R.M. 2153 (Alaska 1977); *Aberdeen Educ. Ass'n v. Aberdeen Bd. of Educ.*, 215 N.W.2d 837 (S.D. 1974); *Rutgers, The State University*, 2 NJPER 13 (N.J. PERC 1977). Contra *Decatur Bd. of Educ., Dist. No. 61 V. IELRB*, 180 Ill. App. 3d 770, 536 N.E.2d 743 (1989); *West Hartford Educ. Ass'n v. DeCourcy*, 162 Conn. 566, 295 A.2d 526 (1972); *Tigard Sch. Dist. 23J*, 11 PECBR 590 (Or. ERB 1989).

4. What has been the impact of negotiations, either de jure or de facto, over class size? In Hall & Carroll, *The Effect of Teachers' Organizations on Salaries and Class Size*, 26 Indus. & Lab. Rel. Rev. 834, 840 (1973), the authors concluded:

> [I]t appears that teachers' organizations are associated with a larger student-teacher ratio. This lends support to the common allegation that school boards are offering teachers higher salaries in exchange for larger classes and that these offers are being accepted. Certainly, there is nothing to suggest that teachers' organizations have had any success in reducing the number of pupils per classroom.

See generally C. Perry & W. Wildman, The Impact of Negotiations in Public Education: The Evidence from the Schools (1970).

5. In *Board of Higher Educ. of N.Y. City*, 7 PERB ¶ 3028 (1974), the New York PERB held that student membership on a faculty evaluation committee is not a mandatory subject of bargaining. The New York PERB stated "that the composition of committees that evaluate employees is not a term or condition of the employees being evaluated." In hesitating to allow college teachers to shut out non-faculty members, the Board noted that policy questions about a university's responsibilities

> Often involved issues of social concern to many groups within the community other than the public employer's administrative apparatus and its employees. It would be a perversion of collective negotiations to impose it as a technique for resolving such dispute and thus disenfranchising other interested groups.

Member Joseph Crowley dissented, rejecting what he regarded as the majority's overreliance on transposing an industrial model of collective bargaining into an academic setting. He noted that appointment and promotion matters have traditionally been matters for mandatory negotiation.

On the other hand, in *Compton Community College Dist.*, PERC ¶ 21078 (Cal. 1990), a student grievance policy which provided that students could evaluate a teacher's performance and that the resulting evaluation would be placed in the teacher's personnel file was held to be a mandatory subject of bargaining.

The California Board noted that evaluation of certificated personnel was one of the enumerated subjects of bargaining set forth in the California act.

CUYAHOGA COUNTY COMMISSIONERS

6 OPER ¶ 6279 (Ohio State Emp. Rel. Bd. 1989)

On June 17, 1987, the Cleveland Building and Construction Trades Council (Charging Party) filed an unfair labor practice charge against the Board of Cuyahoga County Commissioners (Respondent).

Pursuant to Ohio Revised Code (O.R.C.) § 4117.12, the Board conducted an investigation and found probable cause to believe that an unfair labor practice had been committed. Subsequently, a complaint was issued alleging that the Respondent had violated O.R.C. § 4117.11(A)(1) and (A)(5) by unilaterally implementing its decision to lay off employees and by refusing to bargain in good faith on this decision. The case was heard by a Board hearing officer.

The Board has reviewed the record, the hearing officer's proposed order, exceptions and responses. For the reasons stated in the attached opinion, incorporated by reference, the Board adopts ... the Findings of Fact as amended, Conclusions of Law and Recommendations.

O.R.C. § 4117.08 provides:

(A) All matters pertaining to wages, hours, or terms and other conditions of employment and the continuation, modification, or deletion of an existing provision of a collective bargaining agreement are subject to collective bargaining between the public employer and the exclusive representative, except as otherwise specified in this section....

(C) Unless a public employer agrees otherwise in a collective bargaining agreement, nothing in Chapter 4117 of the Revised Code impairs the right and responsibility of each public employer to:

(1) Determine matters of inherent managerial policy which include, but are not limited to areas of discretion or policy such as the functions and programs of the public employer, standards of services, its overall budget, utilization of technology, and organizational structure;

(2) Direct, supervise, evaluate, or hire employees;

(3) Maintain and improve the efficiency and effectiveness of governmental operations;

(4) Determine the overall methods, process, means or personnel by which governmental operations are to be conducted;

(5) Suspend, discipline, demote, or discharge for just cause, or lay off, transfer, assign, schedule, promote, or retain employees;

(6) Determine the adequacy of the work force;

(7) Determine the overall mission of the employer as a unit of government;

(8) Effectively manage the work force;

(9) Take actions to carry out the mission of the public employer as a governmental unit.

The employer is not required to bargain on subjects reserved to the management and direction of the governmental unit *except as affect wages, hours, terms and conditions of employment, and the continuation, modification, or deletion of an existing provision of a collective bargaining agreement.* A public employee or exclusive representative may raise a legitimate complaint or file a grievance based on the collective bargaining agreement. (Emphasis added.)

The obligation of an employer to bargain "as affect wages, hours, terms and conditions of employment" was well settled [in] *In re City of Lakewood,* 5 OPER 5513, SERB 88-009 (7-11-88), where the Board held:

The "as affects" proviso is an acknowledgment and a resolution of the following dilemma: while there are some matters upon which a public employer must be able to take independent action if it is to properly run its operation, such independent management authority may be essential only as to certain aspects of those actions; in other aspects and at other levels, those very actions can be inextricably related to the determination of "wages, hours, terms and other conditions of employment," and negotiation on those issues is essential to preserve meaningful collective bargaining rights. The "as affects" provision of O.R.C. § 4117.08(C) sets forth a clear standard for resolving this tension between the enumerated management rights and the subjects-of-bargaining provisions: when a matter "affects" wages, hours, terms and other conditions of employment, that matter is subject to bargaining.

Support for this position can be found in *Loraine City Bd. of Edn. v. State Emp. Relations Bd.* (1988), 40 Ohio St. 3d 257, 6 OPER 6187, 1989 SERB 4-2, at 4-4 (1988), where the Supreme Court stated:

Thus a reasonable interpretation of O.R.C. 4117.08(C) is that where the exercise of a management right causes a change in or "affects" working conditions or terms of a contract, then the decision to exercise that right is a mandatory subject of bargaining.

This standard, as adopted in *Lakewood, supra,* and applied to the instant case with regard to layoff decisions, has found application in the private sector as well. In *Lapeer Foundry and Machine, Inc.,* 289 NLRB No. 126, 129 LRRM 1603 (7/20/88), the National Labor Relations Board held:

We conclude that an employer's decision to lay off employees for economic reasons is a mandatory subject of bargaining and that the Respondent violated this Act by failing to bargain over its layoff decision and the effect of that decision.

Consequently, if a matter affects wages, hours, terms and other conditions of employment, it is fully bargainable. There is no doubt that in the case at issue the decision to lay off certain employees directly altered the employees' terms of employment and imposed a dramatic change in their working conditions. Since the decision to lay off clearly "affected" terms and conditions of employment, the decision to lay off had to be bargained in good faith.

. . . .

NOTES

1. In *Central City Educ. Ass'n v. IELRB,* 199 Ill. App. 3d 559, 557 N.E.2d 418 (1990), *leave to appeal granted,* the Illinois Appellate Court reversed a decision of the Illinois Educational Labor Relations Board and held that an economically motivated decision to reduce staff was a mandatory subject of

bargaining. After pointing to "the need for bargaining in those situations which are in fact 'amenable' to bargaining," the court stated:

> The Illinois Educational Labor Relations Board has expressed doubt that a labor cost analysis is of particular relevance in the public service sector, noting that while labor costs might be one of the factors to balance "it does not serve as a pivot point for the mandatory/permissive distinction as it does in the private sector." ... We agree that educational employers' concerns are different from private employers' aims to increase profits. Nevertheless, if the main reason for the layoff is to save money by eliminating teacher salaries ..., we believe that mandatory bargaining over that decision may well advance the policies of the Act by allowing the employees' representative to suggest cost-saving alternatives to the layoff....

2. In sharp contrast to the holdings in the principal case and *Central City Educ. Ass'n,* mentioned immediately above, a number of other jurisdictions have held that an economically motivated decision to lay off employees is not a mandatory subject of bargaining. See, e.g., *School Craft College Ass'n of Office Personnel/MESVA v. School Craft Comm. College,* 156 Mich. App. 754, 401 N.W.2d 915 (1986); *Stone v. Camden Cty. Bd. of Chosen Freeholders,* 280 N.J. Super. 430, 435 A.2d 143 (1981); *Harrisburg Sch. Dist.,* 13 PPER ¶ 13,077 (Pa. LRB 1982); *Oakland Unified Sch. Dist.,* 5 PERC ¶ 12149 (Cal. 1981); *City of New Rochelle,* 4 PERB ¶ 3060 (N.Y. 1971). See also *City of Brookfield v. WERC, infra.*

3. Following the lead of the United States Supreme Court in *Fibreboard Paper Prods. Corp. v. NLRB,* 379 U.S. 203 (1964), most state courts and boards have held that contracting out is a mandatory subject of bargaining if it affects bargaining unit employees. See, e.g., *Norwalk Bd. of Educ.,* Decision No. 2177 (Conn. SBLR 1983); *Heraldsburg Union High Sch. Dist.,* Decision No. 132 (Cal. PERB 1980); *Town of Burlington,* Case No. MUP-3519 (Mass. LRC 1980); *Van Buren Pub. Schs.,* 1973 MERC Lab. Op. 714 (Mich.), *aff'd,* 61 Mich. App. 6, 232 N.W.2d 278 (1975); *PLRB v. Sto-Rox Sch. Bd.,* 9 PPER ¶ 9065 (Pa. LRB 1978); *Saratoga Springs Sch. Dist.,* 11 PERB ¶ 3037 (N.Y. 1978); *State of R.I. (Univ. of R.I.),* Case No. EE-1899 (R.I. SLRB 1973); *Metropolitan Utilities Dist. Emp. Ass'n v. Metropolitan Utilities Dist.,* Case No. 59 (Neb. CIR 1972); *Teamsters Local 2 v. Board of Cty. Comm'rs,* ULP Case No. 4-76 (Mont. PBA 1976); *Unified Sch. Dist. v. WERC,* 81 Wis. 2d 89, 259 N.W.2d 724 (1977).

In *CWA Local 4501 v. Ohio State Univ.,* 24 Ohio St.3d 191, 494 N.E.2d 1082 (1986), the Ohio Supreme Court held that "[a] public employer's practice of letting out independent service contracts, rather than filling vacant civil service positions with employees who would perform the same work as the independent contractors, is a matter that pertains to 'wages, hours, or terms and other conditions of employment' and, as such, is a proper subject of collective bargaining between the public employer and the exclusive representative of an affected bargaining unit." As a general proposition, the court further noted "that in the absence of proof that a public employer was motivated by political considerations or a desire to set up a spoil system, the public employer 'may lawfully contract to have an independent contractor perform services which might also be performed by civil service employees,' ... so long as such practice is not violative of either the affected employees' collective bargaining agreement" or the Ohio collective bargaining law.

On the other hand, in *Local 195, IFPTE v. State,* 176 N.J. Super. 85 (1980), *aff'd in relevant part,* 443 A.2d 187 (N.J. 1982), the court was asked to review a

PERC decision holding that the following proposal was a mandatory subject of bargaining: "The State agrees to meet with the Union to discuss all incidences of contracting or subcontracting whenever it becomes apparent that a layoff or job displacement will result." In reversing the decision of the New Jersey PERC, the court held that it was "perfectly plain that a determination to subcontract out work is a matter of managerial prerogative." The court stated that PERC was "clearly wrong" in holding the clause negotiable because the subcontracting out of work could result in employees being terminated, reasoning as follows:

> The mere fact that the impact of a decision which is otherwise a matter of managerial prerogative is substantial on some employees makes the decision no less a matter of managerial prerogative.... The initial inquiry is thus a determination of the nature of the decision of the employer which is sought to be subjected to negotiation rather than its impact on the employee.

Accord *AFSCME Local 1116 v. Adams Cty.,* Case No. 494 (Neb. Comm. Indus. Rel. 1982); *AFSCME Dist. Council 37 & City of N.Y.,* Decision No. B-1-74 (N.Y.C. OCB 1974) (right to subcontract "would clearly be within the city's reserved management rights," but "it is equally clear that the practical impact of the decision to subcontract on the terms and conditions of employment of the affected employees must be bargained over").

4. Is a school board required to negotiate over a proposal to "tuition out" students to a neighboring school district? In *Midland Borough Sch. Dist. v. PLRB,* 126 Pa. Commw. 537, 560 A.2d 303 (1989), the court affirmed a PLRB decision that it was a mandatory subject of bargaining. As a result, the district was ordered to rescind the tuitioning-out agreement, to reinstate with back pay the teachers who had been laid off, and to otherwise return to the previous status quo.

5. In *In re Patrolmen's Benevolent Ass'n,* 1980-81 PBC ¶ 37,197 (N.Y. 1981), the court held that the City of New York was acting within its statutory management rights when it replaced uniformed police offices with civilian employees (civilianization) where it resulted in no layoffs, wage reductions, transfers out of the department, or adverse working conditions. Accord *City of New York & Uniformed Fire Fighters Ass'n, Local 94,* 87 App. Div. 235 (N.Y. 1982).

6. In *Chippewa Cty.,* Decision No. 25003 (Wis. ERC 1987), *aff'd,* 461 N.W.2d 286 (Wis. App. Ct. 1990), the Wisconsin Commission held that a union proposal which provided that the employer would not "contract, lease or sell [its health care center] or any of its property or physical plant to be used for the same purpose or for a similar purpose to that for which it is being used presently" was not a mandatory subject of bargaining. After noting that "the issue is one of determining the level of services provided by or through the municipal employer rather than whether services will be provided to citizens by any entity," the Wisconsin Commission held that "[w]here a municipal employer decides to get out of the health care service business, it need not bargain that choice with the union even though another entity may continue to provide such services to the citizens."

7. In *Southfield Police Officers Ass'n v. Southfield,* 433 Mich. 168, 445 N.W.2d 98 (1989), the Michigan Supreme Court upheld the MERC's "exclusivity" rule, under which an employer is not required to bargain over the transfer of bargaining unit work unless it is work exclusively done by bargaining unit employees. In *City of Lansing,* 1989 MERC Lab. Op. 1055 (Mich.), the Michigan Commission noted that the "exclusivity" rule provides a relatively clear test for parties attempting to determine the scope of the employer's duty to bargain over a decision to reassign work among its employees. The California Board in *Eureka City Sch. Dist.,* 9 PERC ¶ 16060 (Cal. 1985), adopted a similar "exclusivity" test to determine whether an employer committed an unfair labor practice by transferring bargaining unit work.

8. In *Whisman Elementary Sch. Dist.,* 14 PERC ¶ 21091 (Cal. 1990), the California Board held that an employer's unilateral transfer of work previously done by bargaining unit employees (i.e., providing after-school academic assistance to students) to volunteers was illegal, even though there had been a lapse of six years since the work had been done by bargaining unit employees. The Board noted that "by utilizing volunteers to staff the Homework Club, the District is depriving instructional aides of the opportunity to regain the additional hours and wages they lost when the Tutorial Center was closed and they were laid off."

CITY OF YAKIMA

Decision No. 1130-PECB (Wash. Pub. Emp. Rel. Comm'n 1981)

Background

On October 31, 1979, the City of Yakima filed an unfair labor practice complaint with the Public Employment Relations Commission against the Yakima Police Patrolman's Association. The city alleged that the association violated RCW 41.56.150(4) by insisting to impasse, and before an interest arbitration panel, that a nonmandatory bargaining subject, i.e., a manning clause, be included in their collective bargaining agreement. On November 12, 1980, a hearing was conducted in Yakima, Washington.

Facts

The City of Yakima is headed by a city council. The council elects one of its seven members to serve as mayor, and hires a city manager. The council sets city policy, including the determination of levels of service to be provided to the citizenry. Before it sets city policy on levels of service, it conducts public hearings and receives citizen input and staff advice. Its budgetary decisions are influenced by taxing power restrictions in the State constitution and by fluctuating receipts from federal revenue sharing. The city's population is 50,000 and has been rising, as have its crime statistics.

The city's police department has 87 police officers, about an average number for a city of its size. However, its ratio of criminal offenses committed within its borders to police officers is greater than that of the average city. The size of the police force has been decreasing since 1976, when it consisted of 106 police officers. The police force operates on three shifts. The A shift is scheduled from 6:30 a.m. until 2:30 p.m., the B shift from 2:30 p.m. until 10:30 p.m., and the C shift from 10:30 p.m. until 6:30 a.m. At the time of hearing, the department followed a flexible policy of maintaining seven officers on A shift, seven on B shift, and eight on C shift. The number of officers assigned to a particular shift may vary with the chief's perception of field requirements. Sometimes when there are absences, off duty personnel are called to duty to maintain the department's minimum manning policy. Sometimes shifts operate below the normal policy level.

The city and the association commenced bargaining for their 1980 collective bargaining agreement on July 2, 1979. By October, 1979, the parties were unable to reach agreement and resorted to interest arbitration.

One of the unresolved issues which the association submitted to the arbitrator was [its] proposal to have a minimum shift of seven officers each on A and B squads and eight officers on C squad. The city viewed shift strength as a nonmandatory subject of bargaining, refused to discuss it during negotiations, and objected to its consideration by the interest arbitrator. The city then filed the instant unfair labor practice complaint. The Executive Director of the Public Employment Relations Commission instructed the parties and the arbitrator that the issue of minimum shift strength should be held in abeyance pending the outcome of the unfair labor practice proceeding. With that understanding, a collective bargaining agreement was eventually executed. The parties stipulated that the association insisted to impasse on their minimum shift strength proposal.

The following statistics indicated the number of assaults on police officers in the city, and the number of resulting officer injuries for the years 1975 through 1979:

Year	Assaults on Officers	Injuries
1975	70	7
1976	53	7
1977	46	7
1978	44	2
1979	44	5

The department now has one officer in each patrol car, whereas they used to have two. The number of patrol cars in the field has fallen. The officer who is first on the scene of an emergency may have to act alone, since it may take up to five minutes before a backup patrol car arrives. An officer testified that some days he may respond to no emergency calls, on others he may respond to several. The police chief testified that in his 27 years as a police officer, he cannot recall a situation where a higher number of officers on duty would have prevented injury to an officer.

Shift staffing level decisions are made by the chief. The chief testified that these decisions are reevaluated based on community needs and crime statistics and that he requires flexibility to deal with unusual situations.

Positions of the Parties

The city contends that the association engaged in an unlawful refusal to bargain when it insisted to impasse on its minimum manning proposal. It reasons that the proposal is a nonmandatory subject for bargaining since establishing the level of police officer staffing is a fundamental management prerogative, and does not directly affect officer safety or workload.

The association asserts that the subject of minimum shift manning is a mandatory subject of bargaining because of its relationship to officer safety and workload.

Discussion

The Public Employees' Collective Bargaining Act provides in RCW 41.56.150(4) that "[i]t shall be an unfair labor practice for a public employer ... [t]o refuse to engage in collective bargaining."

"Collective bargaining" is defined in RCW 41.56.030(4) as:

... the performance of the mutual obligations of the public employer and the exclusive bargaining representative to meet at reasonable times, to confer and negotiate in good faith, and to execute a written agreement with respect to *grievance procedures and collective negotiations on personnel matters, including wages, hours and working conditions,* which may be peculiar to an appropriate bargaining unit of such public employer, except that by such obligation neither party shall be compelled to agree to a proposal or be required to make a concession unless otherwise provided in this chapter. (Emphasis supplied).

"[P]ersonnel matters, including wages, hours and working conditions" are mandatory subjects for bargaining. Subjects which are remote from such matters or are regarded as a prerogative of management are nonmandatory subjects for bargaining. *Federal Way School District,* PERC Decision No. 232-A (EDUC, 1977). The duty to bargain applies only to mandatory subjects. *Id.*; NLRB v. Wooster Division of Borg-Warner, 356 U.S. 342 (1958). In *Borg-Warner,* the court held that it is an unlawful refusal to bargain for a union or employer to insist as a condition to an agreement upon a matter which is a nonmandatory bargaining subject. Similarly, this Commission held:

A refusal by a bargaining representative to bargain collectively in good faith, including insistence on bargaining of non-mandatory subjects while at impasse and attempting to submit non-mandatory subjects of bargaining for interest arbitration under RCW 41.56.450, is an unfair labor practice in violation of RCW 41.56.150(4).

City of Wenatchee, Decision 780 (PECB, 1980); see also *Port of Ilwaco,* Decision No. 970 (PECB, 1980).

The Washington Supreme Court has said: "... that such managerial decisions which lie at the core of entrepreneurial control, are not subject to the duty to bargain collectively." *Spokane Education Association v. Barnes,* 83 Wn.2d 366 (1974), quoted in *Federal Way School District, supra.* See also Justice Stewart's concurring opinion in *Fibreboard Paper Products Corp. v. NLRB,* 379 U.S. 203 (1964).

In the private sector, strategic product decisions such as what product to manufacture or how many to produce, are not required to be bargained with the employees' collective bargaining representative. Such decisions are generally accepted as within management's prerogative. Similarly, in the public sector, the public officials are vested with the authority to make basic decisions to allocate resources and to determine the levels of service to be provided to the public. Whether a community will have a large police force, a small one, or none at all, is a very basic managerial decision which ultimately must be determined by the voting public through its elected representatives.

Other states have held police manning levels to be a nonmandatory subject of bargaining. *City of Cape May and Cape May P.B.A.,* 835 GERR 21 (N.J. PERC,

1979); *Matter of Newton Police Union Local 76 and City of Newton,* 3 CCH Public Employee Collective Bargaining Reporter, ¶ 40,621 (Iowa PERB,1978); *Police Association of Mount Vernon and City of Mount Vernon,* 3 CCH Public Employee Collective Bargaining Reporter, ¶ 42,096 (N.Y. PERB, 1980).

The union's contention that the staffing level directly affects the workload and safety[2] of police officers is unsupported by the record.

While there has been almost a twenty percent reduction in the number of the city's police officers since 1976, there was no showing that either the officers' workload or safety has been effected. In fact, the number of officer injuries has decreased considerably, and officers still respond to emergencies on an infrequent basis. The union points to the fact that the city has only one officer in a patrol car, rather than two as in the past, and that fewer remaining back-up officers may have to travel greater distances to lend assistance to an officer in danger. Yet an increase in the number of police officers on a shift does not directly address these perceived problems, and may not alleviate them. Whether the number of police officers in a patrol car or the emergency response procedures of the department are mandatory subjects of bargaining is not at issue here. That the number of police officers assigned to a shift may in some indirect manner relate to matters which arguably are mandatory bargaining subjects does not necessarily mean that the subject of manning levels is mandatory. See: *Federal Way School District, supra.*

The strategic service level decision on the number of police officers assigned to a shift must be considered a fundamental management prerogative. Further, it is too remote from "personnel matters, including wages, hours, and working conditions" to be considered a mandatory subject for bargaining. By insisting to impasse on a permissive subject of bargaining, the union violated RCW 41.56.150(4).

NOTE

In the absence of a specific statutory reservation of the employer's right to establish minimum manning, the courts and boards are divided over whether minimum manning proposals, especially with respect to fire and police departments, are mandatory or permissive subjects of bargaining. In addition to the principal case, other cases holding that minimum maning is not a mandatory subject of bargaining include *Hawaii Firefighters Ass'n,* Dec. No. 102 (Haw. PERB 1979); *Hillsborough Cty. Sch. Bd.,* 8 FPER ¶ 13074 (Fla. PERC 1982); *City of Manitowoc,* Dec. No. 18333 (Wis. ERC 1980); *City of Portland,* Case No. 83-01 (Me. LRB 1983); *City of Berlin,* Decision No. 81-42 (N.H. PELRB 1981); *International Ass'n of Fire Fighters v. Helsby,* 399 N.Y.S.2d 334, 97 L.R.R.M. 2297 (N.Y. App. Div. 1977); *City of W. St. Paul v. IAFF Local 1059,* 93 L.R.R.M. 2797 (Minn. Dist. Ct. 1976); *Cinnaminson Twp.,* 4 NJPER 310 (N.J. PERC 1978) ("the size of the police force, either in total or a particular crew size, relates to questions of manning requirements which is a permissive subject for negotiations"). Cases holding that minimum manning is a mandatory subject of bargaining include *City of Salem,* 7 PECBR 5819 (Or. ERB 1983); *Town of Narragansett v. IAFF Local 1589,* 119 R.I. 506, 380 A.2d 521 (1977); *City of*

---

[2]Concurring in *Fibreboard Paper Products Corp. v. NLRB, supra,* Justice Stewart said: "What one's hours are to be, what amount of work is expected during those hours, what periods of relief are available, what safety practices are observed, would all seem conditions of one's employment."

Alpena v. Alpena Fire Fighters Ass'n Local 623, 56 Mich. App. 568, 224 N.W.2d 672 (1974); *Fire Fighters Union, Local 1186 v. City of Vallejo,* 12 Cal. 3d 608, 526 P.2d 971, 116 Cal. Rptr. 507 (1974).

In *IAFF Local 699 v. City of Scranton,* 59 Pa. Commw. 235, 429 A.2d 779 (1981), the court held that the size of a municipal fire department was a managerial prerogative which could not be submitted to interest arbitration. The court noted that to hold otherwise would "give the public employees' union the right to have a major decision-making impact on governmental spending, budgeting, the level of police and fire protection that the municipality must provide, and even taxation, because salaries for the additional employees must come from public funds." The court, however, distinguished between the total number of employees on the force and the number of employees on duty at one station or assigned to a piece of equipment. The court held that the latter issue was negotiable and could be submitted to interest arbitration, noting: "The safety of a fire fighter is far more rationally related to the number of individuals fighting a fire with him, or operating an important piece of equipment at a fire, than it is to the total number of members of the entire force."

DEPARTMENT OF DEFENSE v. FLRA

659 F.2d 1140 (D.C. Cir. 1981), *cert. denied,*
455 U.S. 945 (1982)

J. SKELLY WRIGHT, CIRCUIT JUDGE: The Civil Service Reform Act of 1978 requires management officials of the federal agencies to bargain with employee representatives over conditions of employment. But the duty to engage in collective bargaining is not absolute. Section 7106 of the Reform Act enumerates certain reserved rights of management that cannot be lawful subjects of negotiation. It is permissible to bargain over the "procedures" by which those rights are exercised, but not over the substance of the rights themselves.

The consolidated cases raise important questions about the scope of management's duty to bargain under Section 7106. The issue arose when agency management refused to bargain over various union proposals for the terms of collective bargaining agreements. The negotiability of each of the proposals was considered in the first instance by the Federal Labor Relations Authority (FLRA or Authority). The Authority held three of the contested proposals to be mandatory subjects of collective bargaining; it found five to be excluded from the statutory obligation to bargain under the terms of Section 7106. We affirm the Authority in each of its holdings.

I

Labor relations within the federal civil service are governed by Title VII of the Civil Service Reform Act of 1978. Because these cases are among the first under that statute, see *Nat'l Federation of Federal Employees v. FLRA,* 652 F.2d 191 (D.C.Cir. 1981); *American Federation of Gov't Employees v. FLRA,* 653 F.2d 669 (D.C.Cir. 1981), it might be useful to sketch the background against which we consider the issues presented.

A

The questions before us arise on appeal from two decisions by the Federal Labor Relations Authority. An independent agency within the Executive

Branch, the FLRA was established under Reorganization Plan No. 2 of 1978. It was continued under and administers the labor relations section of the Civil Service Reform Act, Title VII. Its role is analogous to that of the National Labor Relations Board under the National Labor Relations Act. The Civil Service Reform Act invests the Authority with both rulemaking and adjudicatory powers. Among its specific mandates, the FLRA possesses authority to determine appropriate units for labor organization and bargaining, to conduct representation elections, to adjudicate unfair labor practice complaints, and to resolve exceptions to arbitrators' awards. With only minor exceptions, final orders of the Authority are subject to review in the Courts of Appeals. The Authority may petition any appropriate Court of Appeals for enforcement of its orders.

The FLRA has assumed its role as a successor agency to the Federal Labor Relations Council. Functioning pursuant to Executive Order 11491, issued by President Nixon in 1969, the Council was composed of three federal management officials: the Chairman of the Civil Service Commission, the Secretary of Labor, and the Director of the Office of Management and Budget. Its decisions were not subject to judicial review. The general framework for collective bargaining administered by the Council dated from 1962, the year in which Executive Order 10988, issued by President Kennedy, initially established a program of labor-management negotiations for federal employees.

B

The legislative history indicates that Title VII of the Civil Service Reform Act was intended to serve a variety of purposes. Congress sought at least in part to strengthen the authority of federal management to hire and to discipline employees. Representative Udall, who drafted the amendment that essentially became the labor relations chapter of the Reform Act, said explicitly that "one of the fundamental purposes of this bill is to make it easier and not harder to discharge incompetent employees...." But the Reform Act also aimed to strengthen the position of employee unions in the federal service. The statutory statement of congressional purpose asserts that "protection of the right of employees to organize [and] bargain collectively" "safeguards the public interest," "contributes to the effective conduct of public business," and "facilitates and encourages the amicable settlements of disputes...." Consistent with this view, the Reform Act replaced the Federal Labor Relations Council, which had been criticized as "defective" because its members "come exclusively from the ranks of management," with an independent and bipartisan FLRA. There was no suggestion that employee unions might not seek procedural protections against arbitrary or mistaken employee discharges. On the contrary, Representative Udall stressed that he intended his amendment "to meet some of the legitimate concerns of the Federal employee unions as an integral part of what is basically a bill to give management the power to manage and the flexibility that it needs." Other members articulated nearly identical sentiments during the floor debates. Endorsing the Udall amendment, Representative Ford agreed that "while considering the increased powers for management, we always had in mind that we would put together a totality here ... that we hoped would represent a fair package of balanced authority for management, balanced with a fair protection for at least the existing rights the employees have."

The balance of statutory purposes is evidenced, not only in the legislative history, but in the text of the Reform Act. On the one side, Section 7106(a) purports to define certain reserved rights of management:

§ 7106. Management rights

(a) Subject to subsection (b) of this section, nothing in this chapter shall affect the authority of any management official of any agency —

(1) to determine the mission, budget, organization, number of employees, and internal security practices of the agency; and

(2) in accordance with applicable laws —

(A) to hire, assign, direct, layoff, and retain employees in the agency, or to suspend, remove, reduce in grade or pay, or take other disciplinary action against such employees;

(B) to assign work, to make determinations with respect to contracting out, and to determine the personnel by which agency operations shall be conducted;

(C) with respect to filling positions, to make selections for appointments from —

(i) among properly ranked and certified candidates for promotion; or

(ii) any other appropriate source; and

(D) to take whatever actions may be necessary to carry out the agency mission during emergencies.

It is agreed that a union proposal intruding on protected management rights is not a proper subject of collective bargaining under the Act.

On the other side, the interest of employees in protecting their interests through collective bargaining is broadly recognized and protected. Federal management representatives are required to bargain in good faith over "conditions of employment" — a term that is expansively defined, subject only to express statutory exceptions, to include "personnel policies, and matters, whether established by rule, regulation, or otherwise, affecting working conditions ...." Even with regard to reserved management rights, the Act authorizes collective bargaining over the "procedures which management officials of the agency will observe in exercising [their] authority ...." Nor is the duty to bargain one that is lacking in practical effect. Although federal employees have no legal right to strike, management must make good faith efforts to reach agreement with employee representatives. Where bargaining fails to produce an accord, the Act provides for binding arbitration by the Federal Service Impasses Panel, or, if both parties agree and the procedure is approved by the Panel, by an outside arbitrator.

The possibility of binding arbitration and imposed settlement lends importance to the question whether a union contract proposal is a mandatory subject of collective bargaining under the Reform Act.[32] Procedures for resolving this question are provided by Section 7117 and by regulations issued by the FLRA.

---

[32] The Defense Department has stressed to this court that the Federal Service Impasses Panel frequently makes its arbitration decisions pursuant to a "final-offer selection" procedure. See reply brief for petitioners Department of Defense et al., No. 80-1119, at 2-3. Under this procedure the Panel will not itself attempt to structure a compromise of conflicting aims or positions, but will choose between the "final offers" submitted by the parties. Thus, the Department argues, any proposal held negotiable by the FLRA may in fact be imposed on the parties by the Impasses Panel,

Negotiability disputes characteristically arise when the union submits a proposal for inclusion in a collective bargaining agreement. If the agency believes that the proposal is contrary to law or applicable regulation, or is otherwise nonnegotiable under the statute, it may inform the union of its refusal to negotiate. Section 7117 thereupon provides a right to appeal the agency's determination of nonnegotiability to the FLRA.[35] The FLRA is required to decide the negotiability issue at the earliest possible date, issuing a written decision containing specific reasons for sustaining or setting aside the agency's allegation of nonnegotiability.[36] The FLRA's decision addresses only the negotiability of the union proposal under the Reform Act. It neither considers the merits of the proposal nor orders the agency to agree to it. If the proposal is found negotiable, the Authority holds only that the agency must bargain in good faith upon the union's request.

II

The issues before us in these cases stem from FLRA decisions concerning the negotiability of eight union proposals. They come to us in three separate appeals, involving two decisions issued by the Authority, which this court has consolidated for review.

A. *No. 80-1119,* Dix-McGuire

No. 80-1119 comes before us on a petition filed by the Department of Defense. In the course of its contract negotiations with the Army-Air Force Exchange Service, Dix-McGuire Exchange, Fort Dix, New Jersey (the agency), the American Federation of Government Employees, AFL-CIO, Local 1999 (the union) advanced the following proposal as a basis for collective bargaining:

> In the event of a disciplinary suspension or removal, the grievant will exhaust the review provisions contained in this Agreement before the suspension or removal is effectuated, and the employee will remain in a pay status until a final determination is rendered.

---

which, it contends, has no authority to undertake an independent review of the conformity of the proposals before it with applicable law and regulations. See *id.*

Section 7117(c) of the Civil Service Reform Act expressly imposes on the FLRA a duty to determine the negotiability of disputed proposals properly brought before it. We therefore agree with the Defense Department that the FLRA must determine whether union proposals, as they are actually drafted, satisfy the negotiability standards of the statute — standards that include consistency with applicable law and regulations. 5 U.S.C. § 7117(a)(1). The Authority may not approve a proposal not presently consistent with law by invoking the theory that the proposal will subsequently be rendered legally acceptable either by the parties or by the Impasses Panel. But we do not understand the FLRA to argue otherwise. Moreover, because the issue is not presented by the facts of the case before us, we express no opinion on the statutory authority of the Impasses Panel to determine for itself the legality of a union proposal under applicable law or regulations.

[35] See 5 U.S.C. § 7117. If the union wishes to appeal, it first obtains a written allegation from the agency explaining its reasons for holding the proposal nonnegotiable. 5 C.F.R. § 2424.3 (1980). The union then files a petition seeking FLRA determination of the negotiability issue. 5 C.F.R. § 2424.4 (1980). The agency is served with a copy of this petition, to which it may respond with a statement setting forth reasons supporting its position. 5 C.F.R. § 2424.6(a)(2) (1980). The union then has a final right of rebuttal. 5 C.F.R. § 2424.7 (1980).

[36] 5 U.S.C. § 7117(c)(6); see 5 C.F.R. § 2424.10 (1980). Although § 7117(b)(3) permits the Authority to hold a hearing before making a negotiability determination, none is ordinarily conducted. Brief for respondent FLRA, No. 80-1119, at 9 n.7.

The agency responded that the proposal was nonnegotiable. If adopted, if said, the proposed contract term would "so unreasonably delay and impede the exercise of the reserved right to suspend and separate employees as to negate that right and, hence, violates ... 5 U.S.C. 7106(a)(2)(A)." The union appealed this determination to the Authority.

Rejecting the management claim, the FLRA held the procedure to be negotiable. The FLRA based its decision on Section 7106(b)(2), which provides that the enumeration of reserved management rights contained in Section 7106(a) "does not preclude the negotiation of procedures which management will observe in exercising those rights." The Authority construed this section to license collective bargaining over proposed "procedures" for the exercise of management rights "except to the extent that ... negotiations would prevent agency management from acting at all." Although the arbitration process provided in the union proposal did not contain an express time limit, the FLRA found that the agency had failed to establish that its adoption would make it impossible for the agency to implement disciplinary actions. The proposal was therefore negotiable under the "acting at all" standard adopted by the Authority.

B. *No. 80-1351,* Wright-Patterson

There are two proposals at issue in No. 80-1351, brought before us by the Department of Defense. Like those presented for review in No. 80-1358, these proposals were submitted by the American Federation of Government Employees, AFL-CIO (the union) during contract negotiations between the union and the Air Force Logistics Command, Wright-Patterson Air Force Base, Ohio (the agency). The agency contended that a substantial number of the proposals would infringe protected management rights and therefore lay beyond the scope of the duty to bargain. Pursuant to 5 U.S.C. § 7117(c), the union appealed this allegation of nonnegotiability to the FLRA. Of the 16 proposals contested before the Authority, the FLRA held that eight were negotiable, that seven were not, and that one was partly negotiable and partly nonnegotiable. The two proposals at issue in No. 80-1351 are union Proposals III and XIV, both of which were held negotiable by the FLRA.

Proposal III provides:

Section 2. Details to Higher or Same Graded Positions
B. Unless the employer decides to use competitive procedures as outlined in Article — (Promotions), temporary assignment to higher or same grade/different duty positions shall be offered to qualified and available employees with requisite skills on the basis of seniority within the lowest organizational segment. If senior employees decline and it is necessary to detail an employee, the least senior employee shall be assigned.

In contesting the negotiability of the proposal the Defense Department argued that its adoption would infringe reserved management rights. According to the agency's construction, Section 7106(a)(2)(A) reserves a management right to make personnel assignments that may not be limited; management, it says, must retain full discretion to assign employees on any basis that it chooses. The FLRA rejected this argument. The Authority recognized that the right to make assignments encompasses more than the narrow right to decide whether or not to assign that particular employee identified by some agreed set of procedures: "Under section 7106(a)(2)(A) of the Statute, the agency retains discretion as to the personnel requirements of the work of the position, i.e., the qualifications and skills needed to do the work, as well as such job-related individual characteristics as judgment and reliability. Therefore, the right to assign an employee to a position includes the discretion to determine which employee will be assigned." Nevertheless, the Authority found the union proposal to be negotiable. The reason lay in the proposal's authorization of competitive selection procedures. As defined in the *Federal Personnel Manual,* competitive procedures preserve "management's right to select or not select from among a group of best qualified candidates." According to the FLRA, this reservation of management discretion brought the union proposal within the statutory duty to bargain: "Only if the agency chooses not to use competitive procedures must it select [an] individual on the basis of seniority. Because Union Proposal III preserves in this manner the agency's discretion to select, the proposal does not directly interfere with the agency's basic right to assign employees under section 7106(a)(2)(A) of the Statute."

Union Proposal XIV dealt with temporary promotion to "encumbered" positions:

> When an employee is temporarily assigned to an encumbered, but temporarily vacant[,] bargaining unit position of a higher grade for 30 days, the employee will receive the rate of pay for the higher position to which assigned, commencing on the 31st day.

The agency challenged this proposal as incompatible with its right under Section 7106(b)(1) to determine "the numbers, types, and grades of employees or positions ...." The incompatibility arises, it argued, because an employee cannot be paid for a position unless he has actually been promoted to it. Because two persons cannot hold the same position, the agency could not temporarily pay an employee at a higher rate without either assigning him to an already vacant position or creating a new one; and requiring management to do this, the agency asserted, would violate its reserved right to determine the number and grades of positions.The FLRA agreed with the agency that the law requires promotion as a prerequisite to increased pay. But the Authority found no barrier to temporary promotions of employees to encumbered but temporarily vacant positions. It therefore concluded that the proposal could be implemented without the Air Force being required to create new positions. Having rejected the agency's main objections, the Authority held Proposal XIV to be negotiable.

C. *No. 80-1358,* Wright-Patterson

The five proposals underlying No. 80-1358 were presented by the American Federation of Government Employees, AFL-CIO (the union) during the same contract negotiations with the Air Force Logistics Command, Wright-Patterson Air Force Base, Ohio (the agency) as those involved in No. 80-1351. These, however, were held by the FLRA to be nonnegotiable, and it is the union that brings this appeal.

Union Proposals IV, V, VI, and VII would all require management to make certain employee assignments on the basis of seniority. Proposal IV would compel the agency to rotate "details" to lower grade positions among qualified and available employees in inverse order of seniority. Proposal V, dealing with "loans" of employees to meet temporary or emergency needs outside their usual areas of employment, would similarly dictate selection of the least senior employees with requisite skills. Proposal VI mandates seniority as a selection criterion for temporary assignments outside the bargaining unit "[w]here conditions are less at the receiving location than is provided for by this contract ...." And Proposal VII would force the agency, in the absence of a volunteer for permanent reassignment from one duty station to another, to select the person to be assigned on an inverse seniority basis.

The FLRA upheld the agency's claim of nonnegotiability with regard to each of these proposals. All, it concluded, infringed management rights to make personnel assignments protected under Section 7106(a). The crucial failure of Proposals IV, V, VI, and VII, in the Authority's view, lay in their elimination of agency "discretion" in making assignments. "Discretion," it found, was "an essential part" of the package of rights reserved to management under Section 7106(a). "In thus compelling the selection of a particular individual for ... assignment," the FLRA held, Union Proposals IV, V, VI, and VII "each directly interfere[d] with" a reserved right of management.

Union Proposal XIII specified procedures for determining certain personnel assignments following a reduction in force.[61] It would normally have required the agency to act on the basis of employee preferences. In rejecting the proposal as nonnegotiable the FLRA reiterated its view that "the right of the agency to assign employees includes discretion as to the selection of the particular employee to be assigned." Because Proposal XIII eliminated such discretion, the Authority held it incompatible with the management rights reserved under Section 7106(a)(2)(A) and therefore outside the scope of the duty to bargain.

III

The disputes at the core of these cases issue primarily from the contested relationship between Sections 7106(a) and 7106(b) of Title VII of the Civil Service Reform Act of 1978. In the case of each of the disputed union proposals, the management parties purport to identify some infringement of a management right protected under Section 7106(a). Again in each case, the union responds that Section 7106(a) states explicitly that its own terms are "subject to subsection (b) ...." And subsection (b), Section 7106(b), clearly states:

---

[61] Proposal XIII states:

Article 16 Reduction in Force
Section 6.
B. Prior to any placement actions, the employer will establish lists of positions by grade, title, series, career potential and location into which personnel may be entitled to bump or retreat. Lists will contain all vacant positions and will be updated weekly. These lists will be made available to all individuals determined to be affected by the RIF. All affected employees will be offered an opportunity to list the preferred positions desired in each grade, in order of preference. The employer will assign employees, in retention order, to positions of preference for which qualified, in the order of preference, unless there are persuasive mission related reasons for not doing so, in which case the employer will provide the reasons in writing to the union and to the employee....

"Nothing in this section shall preclude any agency and any labor organization from negotiating ... *procedures* which management officials of the agency will observe in exercising any authority under this section ...." Because its proposals are cast in procedural terms, the union finds them compulsory subjects of bargaining under the statute.

Analysis of the competing arguments must begin with the language of the statute itself. See, e.g., *Ernst & Ernst v. Hochfelder*, 425 U.S. 185, 197 (1976); *Zerilli v. Evening News Ass'n*, 628 F.2d 217 (D.C.Cir. 1980). Although that language possesses troubling ambiguities, it does, we think, make clear the intent of Congress, expressed in a distinction between negotiable procedures and management's nonnegotiable substantive authority. There are substantive rights reserved to management under Section 7106(a), subject to — but only to — *procedures* to be negotiated under Section 7106(b).

The difficulty arises, of course, because the distinction between procedure and substance is not always crisp. Union proposals establishing "procedures" for employee selection illustrate the uncertain boundary between the categories. Selection on the basis of seniority, for example, defines a procedure for the exercise of management's right to hire or promote. But it is equally true that a proposal requiring selection based on seniority both establishes the substantive criterion pursuant to which selection will occur and identifies the particular employee to be chosen. Unless procedure is to be permitted to swallow substance entirely, it therefore becomes necessary to inquire into the range of proposals to be deemed "procedural" within the contemplation of the statute.

The need for an interpretive standard of this kind accounts for the various formulae enunciated by the FLRA and for those urged by the parties on this court. In *Dix-McGuire*, No. 80-1119, the Authority held that proposals structured in procedural language would be negotiable unless the effect of their adoption would be to stop management from "acting at all." In so doing it rejected the argument of the agency, which proposed to draw a different line between procedure and substance. The agency suggested that a proposal ceased to be procedural within the intent of the law if it was of such a character as to "unreasonably delay" management action. In the *Wright-Patterson* cases the FLRA again undertook to draw a line between proposals that are properly procedural within the meaning of the statute and those that impinge on substantive agency authority. The Authority held in these cases that various proposals advanced by the union were not negotiable, despite their being expressed in procedural terms, because their adoption would "directly interfere" with reserved management rights to make decisions of substance. The union now contests this standard, insisting on the propriety of the "acting at all" test propounded by the Authority in *Dix-McGuire*. It also argues that the Authority erred in applying different standards in the two cases.

Despite the inherent ambiguities of the distinction between procedure and substance, and the attendant difficulties in its application, the intent of Congress cannot be ignored. It is the task of the FLRA, authorized by statute to "provide leadership" in implementing the labor-management chapter of the Civil Service Reform Act, to develop workable standards consistent with the Act's underlying policies and intent.

In this regard, we think it appropriate to note what we perceive as a difference in kind among the cases calling for application of the statutory distinction between negotiable procedures and reserved substantive rights. There are, on the one hand, cases in which proposals cast in procedural language impinge on substantive management decisions by specifying the criteria pursuant to which decisions must be made. There are, on the other, more nearly "pure" procedures, which have less direct substantive repercussions — for example, procedures for use in determining which employees possess characteristics identified by management as appropriate criteria for choice. In view of this difference, we proceed to our discussion and decision of these consolidated cases without assuming beforehand that a standard found appropriate for one of these classes must also be applied to the other.

IV

A. *No. 80-1119,* Dix-McGuire

The sole negotiability issue in *Dix-McGuire* involves a proposed union contract term under which no employee could be removed or suspended from his job until completion of the review procedures provided under a collective bargaining agreement. Management objected that the proposal invited procedural delays incompatible with its reserved authority under Section 7106(a). Overruling this objection, the FLRA upheld the negotiability of the proposal.

As the FLRA recognized, the plain language of the statute strongly supports the union's position. Although Section 7106(a) asserts that nothing in the Reform Act "shall affect the authority of any management official" to hire, and take disciplinary action, it *also* provides that the terms of subsection (a) are "[s]ubject to subsection (b) ...." And subsection (b) clearly states that "[n]othing in this *section"* — which *includes* subsection (a), on which management's argument is based — "shall preclude any agency and any labor organization from negotiating ... procedures which management officials of the agency will observe in exercising any authority under this section ...." The language of Section 7106 thus seems to establish a hierarchy, in which the terms of subsection (b) hold priority over those of subsection (a). And the union proposal in this case, involving procedures to be followed prior to the exercise of management's right to discharge and discipline employees, appears to fall plainly within the language of Section 7106(b).

Before affirming this conclusion, however, we — like the FLRA — must take account of the management claim that the proposal in this case was not properly "procedural" within the meaning of the statute, because the effect of its adoption would be to "eviscerate" management rights enumerated in Subsection 7106(a). The FLRA weighed this argument, but concluded that this threatened effect would not occur. "[T]he procedural requirement established by the proposal," the Authority held, "relates only to *when* the suspension or removal may be effectuated, not to whether the agency ultimately will be able to implement those actions." The mere possibility of delay would not take a proposal outside the statutory obligation to negotiate. The test of negotiability, the FLRA held, was whether a union proposal would, if adopted, prevent agency management from "acting at all."

In its brief in this court the agency rests its claim for reversal of the FLRA's decision largely on an attack on this asserted rule of decision: the holding that procedural proposals are negotiable under the statute unless their adoption would stop the agency from "acting at all." In the context of this case — one involving a procedural proposal that does not directly mandate substantive criteria pursuant to which management must act — we find the attack to be unconvincing.

We note at the outset that the "acting at all" standard is a reasonable and natural construction of the statutory language, rendered by the agency given responsibility for administering the statute. The management power to act that is protected by Section 7106(a) may be limited by procedures under Section 7106(b), but only so far as the procedures do not have the effect of eliminating management authority by preventing its "acting at all."

Moreover, the "acting at all" standard finds support in — even if it is not necessarily mandated by — the legislative history. In this regard it stands in marked contrast with the alternative standard advanced by the management parties, who contend that a proposal should be held nonnegotiable if its adoption might occasion "unreasonable delay" in the exercise of management rights.

In its opinion below the FLRA justified its adoption of the "acting at all" standard largely by citation to a single passage in the report of the House-Senate conference committee that reported Title VII of the Civil Service Reform Act in the form in which it became law. In their briefs in this court the parties again treat this passage as central. It bears quotation in full:

> 3. [Proposed] Senate section 7218(b) provides that negotiations on procedures governing the exercise of authority reserved to management shall not *unreasonably delay* the exercise by management of its authority to act on such matters. Any negotiations on procedures governing matters otherwise reserved to agency discretion by subsection (a) may not have the effect of actually negating the authority as reserved to the agency by subsection (a). There are no comparable House provisions.
>
> *The conference report deletes these provisions. However, the conferees wish to emphasize that negotiations on such procedures should not be conducted in a way that prevents the agency from acting at all,* or in a way that prevents the exclusive representative from negotiating fully on procedures....

In our view, analysis restricted to this text alone reveals an inescapable ambiguity. The agency contends that the conference intended the "acting at all" standard to be applied to bar *negotiations* so protracted as to prevent management action; the substantive negotiability of union proposals, it says, should be judged against a standard of whether their *adoption* might cause the exercise of management rights to be unreasonably delayed. The FLRA, on the other hand, argues that the conference intended the "acting at all" test to apply to proposed contract provisions as well, as the ultimate measure of their negotiability under the statute.

Although the quoted passage is ambiguous at best, we believe that the legislative history, taken as a whole, gives stronger support to the view of the FLRA than to that of the agency....

The agency advances other arguments why this court should reject the "acting at all" standard enunciated by the FLRA. For example, the agency argues that it is implausible to think that Congress would pass a law countenancing, not merely delay, but "unreasonable delay," in implementation of management decisions. In the context, however, its argument is unconvincing. As the FLRA has emphasized, a negotiability standard is used only to determine whether a proposal is a proper subject of bargaining, not whether it ought to be implemented on the merits. In collective bargaining, government managers are presumably competent to look out for government interests. Congress has clearly acted on this premise in the enactment of other legislation, such as the labor-management chapter of the Foreign Service Act of 1980. Indeed, in reporting Section 1005 of the Foreign Service Act, a management rights provision that was modeled after Section 7106 of the Civil Service Reform Act, the House-Senate conference not only urged adoption of an "acting at all" standard; it cited Section 7106 of the Civil Service Reform Act as precedent for its decision to do so:

> [W]ith respect to negotiated procedures the [House and Senate] bills are consistent and reflect the conference report to accompany the Civil Service Reform Act of 1978 (S.Rept. 95-1271, p. 158), which stated that *the standard for determining whether a proposal is nonnegotiable is whether it "prevent[s] the agency from acting at all."*...

The conference report was "agreed to" by both the full Senate and the full House.

The agency also offers arguments that the FLRA's "acting at all" standard must be rejected as inconsistent with other provisions of the Reform Act. These claims do not require prolonged discussion.

The agency contends that toleration of lengthy delays prior to management removal of employees would be inconsistent with the statutory authority of management to "take whatever actions may be necessary to carry out the agency mission during emergencies." This argument is misdirected. The proposal under review deals only with *disciplinary* suspensions and removals. It does not necessarily apply to emergency assignments, even for disciplinary reasons.

The agency similarly argues that toleration of delays is inconsistent with the statutory command that any "negotiated grievance procedure ... shall provide for expeditious processing...." This provision may, indeed, place some limit on the kind of grievance procedures to which the parties could agree. But management has not shown that arbitration is so slow as to run afoul of this standard, and the FLRA was not required to conclude otherwise. The characteristic speed of arbitral dispute resolution also refutes the argument that the union's proposal in this case tolerates indefinite delay and thus should be declared nonnegotiable as impairing management's reserved authority even under the FLRA's "acting at all" standard.

Finally, the agency lodges an objection that the FLRA failed to consider relevant factors before reaching its challenged decision. This claim rests principally upon 5 U.S.C. § 7135(b), which states in pertinent part that "decisions issued under Executive Order[ ] 11491 ... shall remain in full force and effect ... unless superseded by specific provisions of this chapter or by regulations or decisions issued pursuant to this chapter." As construed by the agency, Section 7135(b) establishes that the decisions of the Federal Labor Relations Council —

including those holding union proposals nonnegotiable under an "unreasonable delay" standard — were due substantial deference from the FLRA. At a minimum, the agency says, the FLRA was required to explain its departure from Council precedents.

Our review of the legislative history should make obvious the weakness of this argument. The language of Section 7106 differs in important and relevant aspects from that of the parallel Section 12(b) of Executive Order 11491. Moreover, in opting for the new language the House and then the Senate-House conference explicitly rejected alternative proposals that would have retained the interpretive standards of the existing case law. Under the circumstances, it is apparent that the Council decisions to which the agency appeals were "superseded by specific provisions of this chapter" within the meaning of Section 7135(b).

B. *Nos. 80-1351 and 80-1358,* Wright-Patterson

Five of the seven union proposals at issue in Nos. 80-1351 and 80-1358 involve procedures that would have conditioned certain job assignments at least partly on an employee's seniority. These proposals obviously implicate substantive concerns. They identify a substantive criterion — namely, length of employment — on the basis of which personnel assignments would be made.

In weighing the negotiability of these proposals under Section 7106 the FLRA applied what the parties have characterized in this court as a "direct interference" test. Under this standard, as explicated by the Authority, a proposal for employee selection procedures would be held nonnegotiable if its implementation would "directly interfere with the agency's basic right to assign employees [as reserved] under section 7106(a)(2)(A)...." This is of course a different test of negotiability from the "acting at all" standard articulated by the Authority in *Dix-McGuire,* and the union has suggested here that this alleged inconsistency must be corrected.

We find no necessary incompatibility between the two approaches. Proposals to establish seniority as a basis for personnel assignments stand close to the uncertain border between procedure and substance. Such proposals are therefore different in kind from that involved in *Dix-McGuire* — a proposal that did not specify the criteria on which disciplinary action should be based, but only designated procedures for determining whether management criteria had in fact been satisfied in a particular instance. In view of the difference between the kinds of proposals under review, we cannot agree that an identical standard must be applied to both. Rejecting the challenge based on this point, we find no need to address the FLRA's contention in this court that application of the "acting at all" standard would have yielded the same results as those obtained under the "direct interference" formula.

In developing and applying the "direct interference" test, the FLRA appears to have reasoned from the premise that "[t]he right to assign employees in the agency under section 7106(a)(2)(A) of the Statute is more than merely the right to decide [whether] to assign an employee" after that employee has been identified by negotiable standards as uniquely eligible for the assignment. Management, in other words, must retain more than a right to say yes or no to an employee who is identified for assignment under selection standards negotiated with a union.

The union vigorously disputes this premise. It argues that "the authority to assign in [Section] (a)(2)(A) means just what the plain language states, and nothing more: the authority to assign — the legal entitlement to take an official personnel action." Because decisions about selection criteria do not effect any legal change in an employee's status, the union argues, they do not constitute "personnel action" within management's reserved authority.

The union's constrictively literalist construction of Section 7106(a) would permit collective bargaining over literally all personnel qualifications, no matter how essential to successful job performance, and would allow contractual requirements of selection based on a scaled ranking. We find this interpretation to be unsupportable. It ignores repeated assertions in the legislative history that Congress aimed to create a "balanced" statute that would, in the words of Representative Udall, the leading framer of Title VII, "give management the power to manage and the flexibility that it needs." Indeed, the union view would so thoroughly subordinate Section 7106(a) to Section 7106(b) as to read the former effectively out of the statute. Familiar canons of interpretation thus counsel rejection of the union's position. We must attempt to read the statute in a "manner which effectuates rather than frustrates the major purpose of the legislative draftsmen." *Shultz v. Louisiana Trailer Sales, Inc.,* 428 F.2d 61, 65 (5th Cir. 1970); see *Equal Employment Opportunity Comm'n v. Louisville & Nashville R. Co.,* 505 F.2d 610, 616-617 (5th Cir. 1974). Further, where alternative interpretations are possible, we should attempt to give effect to every word that Congress used. See *Reiter v. Sonotone Corp.,* 442 U.S. 330 (1979).

The Authority's construction of the statutory language, and its application of that construction to the proposals before it, accord far better with the teaching of these canons. Lacking clear guidance in the statutory language, the FLRA reasoned, consistent with the statute's purpose and its legislative history, that the right to establish personnel standards and qualifications was implicit in the reserved management right to make assignments: "An agency chooses to assign an employee to a position so that the work of that position will be done. Under section 7106(a)(2)(A) of the Statute, the agency retains discretion as to the personnel requirements of the work of the position ...." And these requirements, the FLRA continued, must be determined not on a general but on an individual basis. The agency, it held, must be able to decide whether a particular employee being considered for assignment has such "job-related individual characteristics as judgment and reliability." "Therefore," the Authority concluded, "the right to assign an employee to a position includes the discretion to determine which employee will be assigned."

The FLRA's decisions on the seniority proposals before it followed logically from its determination that Section 7106(a) protected the agency's right to exercise discretion at the conclusion of procedures to test and quantify employee qualifications. Union Proposals IV, V, VI, and VII would each have compelled selection of a particular individual, based on seniority, at least in some instances. Once the agency had "determined the particular qualifications and skills needed to perform the work of the position to which the employee will be assigned, and identified the employees in the unit who meet those requirements and would be available for assignment, selection from among the employees so identified of the particular employee who will be assigned must be on the basis of seniority." The Authority held the proposals nonnegotiable on this basis. "In ... compelling the selection of a particular individual for temporary assignment to another position" — and thus removing the agency's discretion to make individual judgments based on the judgment and reliability of particular persons — the proposals "directly interfere[d] with the right of the agency to assign employees."

Union Proposal III was subjected to an identical analysis. It, however, was held negotiable because it reserved to the agency the option of using "competitive procedures" to make its selections. As defined in the *Federal Personnel Manual,* "competitive procedures" retain the agency's right to "select or not select from among a group of best qualified candidates." To the Authority, this reserved discretion made a crucial difference:

> [U]nder Union Proposal III, the agency retains the option of exercising its discretion to select a particular employee for assignment. Only if the agency chooses not to use competitive procedures must it select the individual on the basis of seniority. Because Union Proposal III preserves in this manner the agency's discretion to select, the proposal does not directly interfere with the agency's basic right to assign employees under section 7106(a)(2)(A) of the Statute.

Under the circumstances presented by this case, we believe that the FLRA's decisions concerning Proposals III, IV, V, VI, and VII must be upheld. We begin with the recognition that courts must yield great deference to an interpretation of a statute by the agency entrusted with its administration.... The surface ambiguity of the central statutory distinction provides a further reason for us to defer to the considered judgment of the Authority. As we explained above, the task of distinguishing negotiable procedures from management's reserved substantive authority involves questions of judgment and balance, about which reasonable people could easily differ. And Congress intended the needed judgments to be made, not by this court, but by the Authority....

We find no compelling indications of error in the cases before us. On the contrary, the Authority's interpretation of the statute — as reserving a limited management discretion in employee selection — is entirely consistent with the admonition that "[t]he provisions of [Title VII of the Civil Service Reform Act] should be interpreted in a manner consistent with the requirement of an effective and efficient Government." ...

Proposal XIII

The FLRA held Union Proposal XIII to be nonnegotiable for essentially the same reasons that it had rejected Proposals IV, V, VI, and VII. Proposal XIII detailed procedures that would have dictated certain personnel assignments in cases involving reductions in force "unless there are persuasive mission related reasons for not doing so, in which case the employer will provide the reasons in writing to the union and to the employee." Concluding that the proposal would "compel the agency to assign an employee to a position on the basis of [the] employee's preference," the Authority held that it would "interefere[ ] with the discretion which is an essential part of the right to assign under section 7106(a)(2)(A) of the Statute."

Having upheld the Authority's interpretation of the statute as reserving a nonnegotiable agency right to exercise discretion in making personnel assignments, we cannot say that the FLRA wrongly applied that interpretive standard to Proposal XIII. The proposal's exception to mandatory assignment in cases involving "persuasive mission related reasons" might have permitted the FLRA to draw a different conclusion about the scope of discretion that it reserved to management and thus about its negotiability. As we have already said, however, "To sustain the [Authority's] application of [a] statutory term, we need not find that its construction is the only reasonable one, or even that it is the result we would have reached had the question arisen in the first instance in judicial proceedings." *Unemployment Compensation Comm'n v. Aragon, supra,* 329 U.S. at 153. We need find only that it was not arbitrary, capricious, or contrary to law. Under this deferential standard we have no difficulty in affirming the finding of the FLRA that the proposal would eviscerate an element of discretion protected under Section 7106(a)....

V

For the reasons stated herein, we conclude that the challenged holdings of the FLRA in these three consolidated cases should be upheld and that its orders here before us should be enforced.

NOTES

1. In *Veterans Admin. Med. Center, Tampa, Fla. v. FLRA,* 675 F.2d 260 (11th Cir. 1982), the court, in agreeing with the decision in the principal case, upheld a FLRA finding that a federal agency was obligated to negotiate over procedures to be followed in personnel actions since the proposed procedures would not prevent the agency from "acting at all." Judge Fay dissented, stating:

> To suggest that appropriate officials could operate at all if any decision to hire, assign, direct, lay off, retain, suspend, remove, reduce in grade or pay, transfer, etc., could be automatically stayed by merely making it the subject of a grievance or arbitration is too much for me. Nor do I find solace in the argument of counsel that this proposal would never become the final product of negotiations and certainly would not be imposed by the federal services impasses panel. Today's impossibilities seem to be tomorrow's realities.

Judge Fay concluded that the "proposal is so clearly contrary to the express provisions of the statute as to be outside any area of negotiability under either standard."

2. The tests to determine negotiability set forth in the principal case were refined as follows in *Dep't of Treasury, BATF v. FLRA,* 857 F.2d 819 (D.C. Cir. 1988):

> The "acting-at-all"/"directly interfere" tests, however, do not exist in a theoretical vacuum. The guidance provided in *Department of Defense* must be assessed not only in terms of the specific requirements a particular proposal would impose on management in the exercise of its protected rights, but on the circumstances which in real life allow it to exercise them. When a proposal stipulates procedures that so affect the environment within which an agency

is allowed to act that it places the equivalent of a substantive restraint on its ability to act, that proposal has forfeited its claim to procedural purety.

Applying this refinement to a union proposal that would require an agency to rank and consider current employees for promotion before soliciting or considering outside applicants, the court reversed the FLRA and held that the proposal was nonnegotiable since it "would constitute a direct and substantive impediment to management's exercise of its statutory right to select employees from any appropriate source."

3. In *Fort Stewart Schs. v. FLRA*, 110 S. Ct. 2043 (1990), the Supreme Court affirmed a decision of the Federal Labor Relations Agency that a school operated by the military was required to bargain over the wages and fringe benefits paid to its teachers. In holding that wages and fringe benefits were "conditions of employment" over which bargaining was required, the Court rejected as "unheard-of" the school's contention that the term "conditions of employment" "includes *other* insisted-upon prerequisites for continued employment, but does not include the insisted-upon prerequisite *par excellence*, wages." As for the school's argument that wages were not a mandatory subject of bargaining since the Federal Service Labor-Management Relations Statute (FSLMRS) requires bargaining only over "conditions of employment" and does not specifically include "wages" like both the National Labor Relations Act and the Postal Reorganization Act do, the Court noted that "those other statutes deal with labor-management relations in entirely different fields of employment, and the FSLMRS contains no indication that it is to be read *in pari materia* with them." Finally, the Court noted that although "[t]he wages and fringe benefits of the overwhelming majority of Executive Branch employees are fixed by law" and are not therefore negotiable, the teachers whose salaries were in question were "among a minuscule minority of federal employees whose wages are exempted from operation of the General Schedules." Accordingly, the Court rejected the school's reliance on numerous comments by members and committees of Congress that the FSLMRS did not permit bargaining over wages, observing that "[t]here is no conceivable persuasive effect in legislative history that may reflect nothing more than the speakers' incomplete understanding of the world upon which the statute will operate."

4. In *Department of Treasury, IRS v. FLRA*, 110 S. Ct. 1623 (1990), the Supreme Court reversed a decision of FLRA holding that the IRS had to negotiate over a union's proposal to submit to the contractual grievance and arbitration procedure claims that the IRS had failed to comply with Office of Management and Budget (OMB) Circular A-76 relating to the contracting out of work. The Court stated that "[t]he FLRA's position is flatly contradicted by the language of § 7106(a)'s command that '*nothing in this chapter*'—i.e., nothing in this entire Act—shall affect the authority of agency officials to make contracting-out determinations in accordance with applicable laws."

5. In *American Fed'n of Gov't Emps. Local 32 & Office of Personnel Mgt.*, 6 FLRA No. 76 (Aug. 19, 1981), the FLRA held that a proposal for free day care centers was a mandatory subject of bargaining. The Authority held that the mere fact that a proposal had an impact on the budget process did not necessarily require that a proposal be declared nonnegotiable. The FLRA noted that "[c]onsideration must be given to all the factors involved" and that "rather than basing a determination as to the negotiability of the proposal on increased cost alone, that one factor must be weighed against such factors as the potential for improved employee performance, increased productivity, reduced turnover, fewer grievances, and the like." The FLRA also rejected the contention that the

proposal was nonnegotiable on the ground that the agency had no authority to spend funds for day care centers unless approved by the Office of Management Budget and then by Congress, commenting:

> The thrust of this argument is that no duty to bargain exists in the absence of total discretion to implement any agreement reached. However, an Agency has a duty to bargain over conditions of employment to the extent it has any discretion concerning them. Thus, if the Agency's discretion in this case, as it claims, is limited to requesting approval from OMB, the Agency would be obligated to bargain to that extent. Further, in this connection, section 7114(b)(5) of the Statute provides that the duty of an agency to negotiate in good faith includes the obligation "to take such steps as are necessary to implement" any agreement reached between the parties. Thus, the circumstance that an agency might be unable to directly or completely implement an agreement reached through negotiations because of a limitation on its discretion would not render an otherwise negotiable proposal outside the duty to bargain. Rather, the agency would in those circumstances be obligated to take such steps as are within its discretion, including appropriate requests to third parties, to implement the agreement. In the present case, should it be necessary to request approval from OMB regarding any agreement to establish day care facilities that might be negotiated, the Agency would, pursuant to section 7114(b)(5) of the Statute, be obligated to seek such approval. Accordingly, the Agency's contention that it lacks discretion to directly implement any agreement reached does not support its allegation that the proposal is outside the duty to bargain.

6. See generally Robinson, Negotiability in the Federal Sector (1981).

PLAINVIEW-OLD BETHPAGE CENTRAL SCHOOL DISTRICT
17 PERB ¶ 3077 (N.Y. Pub. Emp. Relations Bd. 1984)

This matter comes to us on the exceptions of the Plainview-Old Bethpage Central School District (District) to the decision of an Administrative Law Judge (ALJ) that it violated its duty to negotiate in good faith with the Plainview-Old Bethpage Congress of Teachers, NEA-NY NEA (Congress) in that it executed a "parity" agreement with the Plainview-Old Bethpage Chairpersons' Association (Association) which tied certain benefits to the chairpersons to future negotiations with the Congress. The record establishes that the District and the Association entered into a collective bargaining agreement on May 25, 1984 which, among other things, assured chairpersons of any benefits that the Congress might achieve in subsequent negotiations on behalf of teachers dealing with workers' compensation, health insurance and several other matters. The District and the Association, which was permitted to intervene in the proceeding, argued that their agreement upon this parity clause was not improper. Relying on our decisions in *City of New York,* 10 PERB ¶ 3003 (1977), and *Rockville Centre Principals Assn.,* 12 PERB ¶ 3021 (1979), [the] ALJ found that it was.

The District and the Association argue that the Court of Appeals in *Niagara-Wheatfield Administrators Association v. Niagara-Wheatfield CSD,* 44 NY2d 68, 11 PERB ¶ 512 (1978) and the Appellate Division, Third Dept. in *City of Schenectady,* 85 AD2d 116, 15 PERB ¶ 7510 (1982), have determined that an agreement providing a parity clause is not improper. They further argue that, to the extent that these court decisions do not overrule our own decisions, *City of New York* should be distinguished on the ground that the employer there not only executed a parity clause but also used the clause as a shield against negotiation demands made by the union which bore the parity burden. This, it alleges, has not happened here.

Two other defenses raised by the District and the Association relate to the timing of the charge. The record shows that there was a similar parity clause in two prior agreements between the District and the Association covering a period of six years. They argue that by not objecting to that clause in the past, the Congress is barred by laches from objecting now. They also contend that the charge is not timely because it was brought four months and one day after the District's agreement with the Association was executed.

We find that the Congress is not barred by laches from filing the charge herein. Laches is an equitable defense that applies when there has been an excessive delay in asserting a right which prejudices an adverse party. There is no showing that the District or the Association have been prejudiced by the Congress' failure to contest the parity clauses in the prior agreements. Further, the failure of a union to object to improper conduct by an employer in one year does not amount to a waiver such as to preclude it from objecting to similar improper conduct taken in subsequent years. We also find no basis for concluding that the charge is not timely. There is no showing in the record that the Congress was aware of the contract between the District and the Association on the date of its execution. Thus, we conclude, its charge was brought within four months of the time when it knew or should have known of the alleged violation.

The rejection of these defenses confronts us with the parity issue. In *City of Albany,* 7 PERB ¶ 3079 (1974), this Board held parity to be a nonmandatory subject of negotiation. Later, in *City of New York,* we held parity to be a prohibited subject of negotiation "by reason of its inhibiting effect upon related collective negotiation." In *Niagara-Wheatfield,* the Court of Appeals ruled that a contract clause calling for the continuation of a contractual benefit was valid; the contract benefit in question was an assurance of parity. We nevertheless indicated our adherence to *City of New York* when the issue of parity next came before us in *Rockville Centre.* We reasoned that the Court of Appeals had not focused on the fact that the contract benefit being continued was a parity clause and that its specific and limited holding concerned the legality of a proposal for a continuation of benefits.

The issue next surfaced in *City of Schenectady.* The underlying facts were that the police and firefighters employed by Schenectady had negotiated a series of contracts *jointly* which contained parity clauses. An arbitrator awarded a benefit to the firefighters after the City had granted it to the police. Relying upon this Board's decisions, the City, unsuccessfully, contested the arbitrator's award. The Appellate Division rejected "any *per se* invalidation of such [parity] clauses.

Upon reconsideration, we believe that the police and firefighters' joint negotiations in the *Schenectady* case require us to reconsider our analysis of parity in prior decisions to the extent that we held a parity clause to be prohibited in all circumstances. A parity agreement is improper only to the extent that it trespasses upon the negotiation rights of a union that is not a party to the agreement. It does so by making it more difficult for the nonparty union to negotiate some benefits for employees it represents while imposing upon it a burden of negotiating for employees it does not represent. As evidenced by the facts in *Schenectady,* however, it cannot be assumed that the nonparty union will always object to the intrusion upon its negotiation rights affected [sic] by the parity agreement. We therefore agree with the court in *Schenectady* that there is no policy reason for barring parity clauses agreed to by both unions in joint bargaining with the employer or otherwise consented to by the nonparty union.

Our prior decisions failed to give sufficient recognition to the fact that litigation of parity clauses may not involve the rights of a nonparty union, but only the rights of the parties to the parity agreement. The above-cited court decisions involved only the parties to the parity agreement. In sustaining arbitration awards growing out of disputes between those parties, the courts perceived the dispositive public policy to be that set forth by the Court of Appeals in *District No. 3 v. Associated Teachers of Huntington,* 30 NY2d 122, 5 PERB ¶ 7057 (1972): having reached an agreement with the union a public employer should not be able to disavow it because it finds that the agreement has become disadvantageous.

Nevertheless, with respect to a nonparty union — the unwilling bargaining representative — we continue to believe that the policies underlying the Taylor Law require a different result. In our view, the interference with the rights of a union that may be effected by a parity agreement between an employer and another union is an improper practice within the exclusive jurisdiction of this Board.

Not being party to the parity agreement, a union may seek to vindicate its rights by bringing an improper practice charge before this Board. The parties to a parity agreement, in the ensuing improper practice proceeding, may defend their conduct by showing that the charging party had consented to the intrusion upon its negotiation rights. Such would have been the case had the joint bargaining situation in *Schenectady* emerged as an improper practice proceeding.

This analysis leads us to the conclusion that a parity clause is subject to nullification but is not prohibited *per se.* The relevant circumstances supporting the voiding of a parity clause can be established only in a timely improper practice charge brought by a union alleging that the parity clause trespasses upon its negotiation rights.

We now have before us such an improper practice charge, and the evidence is clear that the Congress did not consent to the parity clause. The Association contends that the parity clause itself does not trespass upon the negotiation rights of the Congress; only the use of that clause by the District as a shield to resist negotiation demands by the other union would be objectionable. It asserts that no such use of the parity clause was alleged in the instant case.

We reject this attempted distinction between the parity clause and its effect. The parity clause may not become an explicit issue in the Congresses' [sic] subsequent negotiations, but its effect will inevitably be present in the minds of the negotiators and constrict negotiating rights. The Connecticut State Labor

Relations Board has dealt with this problem persuasively in *City of New London,* MPP-2268 (1973). It said:

> What we find to be forbidden is an agreement between *one* group (e.g. firemen) and the employer that will impose equality for the future *upon another group* (e.g. policemen) that has had no part in making the agreement. We find that the *inevitable* tendency of such an agreement is to interfere with, restrain and coerce the right of the later group to have untrammeled bargaining. And this affects *all* the later negotiations (within the scope of the parity clause) even though it may be hard or impossible to trace by proof the effect of the parity clause upon any specific terms of the later contract (just as in the case before us). The parity clause will seldom surface in the later negotiations but it will surely be present in the minds of the negotiators and have a restraining or coercive effect not always consciously realized. And while the evidence in the present case may not have shown a specific connection between the parity clause and the terms of the Police contract, it certainly did not indicate the lack of such connection. The economic terms offered to policemen and finally accepted by them were just the same as those previously given to the firemen. (emphasis in original)

For the foregoing reasons, we affirm the decision of the ALJ.

NOTES

1. In *City of Barberton,* 5 OPER ¶5510 (Ohio SERB 1988), aff'd, 7 OPER 7915 (Ohio Ct. C.P. 1990), the Ohio Board held that a "me too" agreement was not a per se violation of an employer's duty to bargain in good faith, observing:

> ... If one were to adopt this premise [i.e., that agreeing to a "me too" agreement is a violation of the duty to bargain in good faith], in all practicality, a like charge could be leveled against any multi-unit employer by any dominant union during any negotiations; and, often, even against a single unit employer. For it is the force of the dominant union, the one with the clout, that normally sets the standard of pay and working conditions for the employer's other employees, both union and non-union, even without the presence of a "me too" agreement. Not to accept the practical implication of such negotiations ignores the dynamics of the collective bargaining process. Every employer must carefully calculate the impact his bargaining table concessions will have when dealing with his other employees who are not part of the subject bargaining unit.

2. In reversing the California Court of Appeals, the California Supreme Court in *Banning Teachers Ass'n, v. PERB,* 44 Cal. 3d 799, 750 P.2d 313, 244 Cal. Rptr. 671 (1988), held that parity agreements do not constitute a per se violation of the statutory provision requiring that nonteaching and teaching employees be separately represented. The court reasoned as follows:

> The Court of Appeals' concern with the obstruction of bargaining is unfounded. Parity agreements no more restrict the District's bargaining position than do the confines of a limited budget which exist absent such agreement. Each employee bargaining unit necessarily has an impact on the negotiations of every other unit, regardless of the order in which contracts are negotiated or whether the District enters into parity agreements.
>
> ....

To hold parity agreements per se illegal would place a burdensome limitation on public school employers to negotiate effectively in an already cumbersome environment of multi-unit collective bargaining. It would obstruct employment relations, thus defeating the stated purpose of Section 3512 "to foster peaceful employer-employee relations ...." It would also adversely affect the bargaining efficiency and strategy of school districts and public sector unions in California and would prolong bargaining, making settlements more difficult and labor unrest more frequent.

3. The Pennsylvania Labor Relations Board in *PLRB v. Commonwealth*, 9 PPER ¶ 9084 (1978), held that the Commonwealth committed an unfair labor practice when it entered into a "parity agreement" which provided that the contracting union would receive the same benefits as another union with which the Commonwealth was currently negotiating. The Pennsylvania PLRB stated that "parity agreements necessarily affect subsequent negotiations, impermissibly bringing another party to the bargaining table, and thereby interfere with good faith negotiations between the employer and the union not protected by the parity agreement." Accord *Town of Methuen*, Case No. MUP-507, 545 GERR B-17 (Mass. LRC 1974); *City of Plainfield*, 4 NJPER 255 (N.J. PERC 1978).

4. In *West Allis Prof. Policemen's Ass'n v. City of West Allis*, Decision No. 12706 (1974), the Wisconsin Employment Relations Commission held that it was not an unfair labor practice for the city to agree to pay fire fighters the same as police and to grant them any additional increases that the police union might negotiate. In rejecting the police union's contention that the parity clause in the fire fighters' agreement restrained and interfered with its statutory right to bargain collectively, the WERC stated:

Such [parity] agreements are not rare or limited to police and fire settlements and do, as the [police union] urges, affect the calculations of a municipal employer in its subsequent negotiations with other labor organizations. However, even in the absence of such agreements, employers ... calculate the effects of proposed settlements upon their relations with other groups of employees.... This is a "fact of life" in collective bargaining. The [police union] recognizes this, but distinguishes the present case on the basis of the existence of a formal agreement.... We hold that this distinction is artificial and not to be adopted herein....

The parity agreement does not place an absolute "ceiling" on settlements with the [police union]. It adds to the cost of higher settlements. The normal, unformalized considerations of employers, on the other hand, are very compelling, not only because of cost considerations, but because of very significant tactical considerations that an employer dealing with a number of unions must make respecting the relative positions of such unions. We would indeed be unrealistic and excessively legalistic if we attempted to minimize or eliminate these considerations. We would be engaging in unwarranted conclusions if we held agreements reflecting such considerations to be contrary to the duty to bargain in good faith....

5. In *Lewiston Fire Fighters Ass'n, Local 785 v. City of Lewiston*, 354 A.2d 154, 92 L.R.R.M. 2029 (Me. 1976), the court held that a charter provision which required the city to pay fire fighters wages that were "no less" than those paid to police officers was impliedly repealed by the enactment of the Maine public sector collective bargaining law. The court held that the procedures established by the Maine act "for determining the configuration of the unit whose wages will be determined by collective bargaining between its elected representatives and the employer are evaded by the parity pay provision which at the bargaining table, necessarily interjects the interests of the Lewiston Firefighters into the unit created to represent the Lewiston Police."

6. Can a public employer legally agree to a contractual provision whereby the wages for the employees in the bargaining unit are tied to the wages of a comparable group of public employees employed by *another* public employer? Compare *Voigt v. Bowen,* 53 App. Div. 2d 277, 385 N.Y.S.2d 600 (N.Y. App. Div. 1976) (contract which granted city police officers parity with county police officers held invalid as violation of New York Taylor Law and public policy), with *Kugler v. Yocum,* 69 Cal. 2d 371, 445 P.2d 303, 71 Cal. Rptr. 687 (1968) (ordinance providing that salaries for city fire fighters would be no less than average wage for fire fighters employed by two other public bodies upheld).

7. Would a union's demand that a negotiated wage increase be made retroactive be a mandatory subject of negotiation? In *Wisconsin Dep't of Admin. v. WERC,* 280 N.W.2d 150, 90 Wis. 2d 426 (1979), the Wisconsin Supreme Court was faced with the question of whether a retroactive wage adjustment for state employees is a mandatory subject of bargaining in view of a state constitutional provision that provided that the "legislature shall never grant any extra compensation to any public officer, agent, servant or contractor, after the services shall have been rendered or the contract entered into." In upholding the WERC's decision that retroactivity is a mandatory subject of bargaining, the court noted that the intent of the Act was to maintain "the continuity of the employment relationship during the period of time when employees are working without a contract." The court observed that "[i]f effective date of newly negotiated wage rates is not negotiable, the state would, in effect, have the unilateral power to set the effective date of any agreement" and that such an interpretation would contravene the express purposes of the state act. As for the constitutional proscription against extra compensation, the court held that it only prohibited "extra compensation for pay for wages previously agreed upon" and that there was no such previous agreement in the instant case. Accord *San Joaquin Cty. Emps. Ass'n v. County of San Joaquin,* 39 Cal. App. 3d 83, 113 Cal. Rptr. 912, 86 L.R.R.M. 2942 (1974), the court held that a similar constitutional prohibition did not prohibit a public employer from providing in a salary ordinance or by appropriate agreement for retroactive pay increases. Accord *Christie v. Port of Olympia,* 27 Wash. 2d 534, 179 P.2d 294 (1947).

8. See generally LaFranchise & Leibig, *Collective Bargaining for Parity in the Public Sector,* 32 Lab. L.J. 598 (1981).

CITY OF NEW YORK & MEBA, DISTRICT NO. 1

Decision No. B-3-75 (1975 N.Y.C. Office of Coll. Bar.)

[After the expiration of a collective bargaining agreement between the City of New York and the Marine Engineers Beneficial Association, District No. 1 (MEBA or Union), the Union initiated impasse proceedings. Subsequently, the city filed a petition alleging, *inter alia,* that Article II concerning job security in the parties' prior agreement was not a mandatory subject of bargaining and that this topic could not be raised before the impasse panel over the city's objection. While the OCB denied the City's motion to stay the impasse panel proceedings pending a determination of the negotiability of the disputed items, the OCB issued an interim order providing that in the absence of "the consent of both parties, the panel may not hear arguments on or make any determination on matters the bargainability of which has been challenged by the City until such time as the Board rules." Article II, entitled "Job Security," reads as follows:

> During the term of this agreement, the Employer will attempt to retain all per annum employees who hold positions by permanent appointment. If curtailment because of a reduced number of runs becomes necessary, the Employer will make every effort to re-employ such Employees in vacancies or to replace persons who have provisional appointments to positions for which such Employees are eligible, at the rates and working conditions prevailing in the department in which such Employees are re-employed. However, no such curtailment shall become effective without prior discussion with the Union.

The City's claim of non-bargainability is based upon its position that the issue of job security is a management right covered specifically by Section 1173-4.3(b) of the NYCCBL. Under that section, the Employer has the right to "relieve its employees from duties because of lack of work or for other legitimate reasons" as well as the right to determine standards of services to be offered, to maintain efficiency of government operations and to maintain complete control and discretion over its organization and the technology of performing its work.

The City also argues that the Board has previously held (in B-4-71 and B-1-70) that layoffs are a managerial right. Thus, the City is not obligated to negotiate a contract provision committing itself to "attempt to retain employees." The City further contends that terms and conditions of laid off employees who replace provisional employees are either covered by the Civil Service system or a contract covering the position into which the re-employed employee is returning.

The Union asserts that the Job Security provision challenged by the City is identical with a provision in the Agreement between the City and Local 333, United Marine Division, National Maritime Union, covering unlicensed ferry crew members employed in the same department. The Union alleges that the City's attempt to have this article of the prior agreement declared non-mandatory is based on discriminatory motivation of the City designed to interfere with employee rights and to discredit the Union.

Section 1173-4.3b of the NYCCBL specifically gives the City the right "to relieve its employees from duty because of lack of work or for other legitimate reasons." Where the employer is authorized by law to lay off employees for lack of work, that authority is not diminished by requiring the employer to negotiate a pledge that he will attempt not to lay off per annum permanent employees.

A second element of the Union's Job Security demand provides that the employer attempt to re-employ permanent per annum employees if vacancies occur. As we noted in Decision No. B-4-71 (*Assoc. of Building Inspectors and HDA*), however, the rights of competitive civil service employees with respect to Job Security are governed and protected by Civil Service Law....

The Union urges that the Job Security clause it seeks is supported by the United States Supreme Court's decision in *Fibreboard Paper Products Corp. v. NLRB*, 379 U.S. 203 (1964). That decision, however, dealt only with the narrow issue of private sector subcontracting under certain circumstances, and Chief Justice Warren, writing for the Court, noted that the *Fibreboard* holding was limited to "the facts of this case."

Clearly, the *Fibreboard* decision was based on a factual situation quite different from that in the instant matter, and it promulgated a narrow rule requiring bargaining in those circumstances where an employer, through subcontracting, replaces his own employees with others who will perform the same work under the same conditions, but for less money. Moreover, *Fibreboard* applies to the private sector and does not establish a precedent applicable to the matter before this Board.

In *City School District of New Rochelle v. New Rochelle Federation of Teachers, Local 280, AFL-CIO,* 4 PERB 3060 (1971), the Public Employment Relations Board determined that a managerial decision to approve budgetary cuts resulting in reduction of work force is a non-mandatory bargaining subject....

PERB concluded that although a decision to lay off workers necessarily affects working conditions, the employer is obligated to negotiate only the impact of its managerial decision.

This brings us to the third element of the instant Job Security demand, which would require discussion with the Union prior to effectuation of any layoffs. Insofar as we interpret this language to mean a demand for information and notification prior to implementation of a managerial decision to lay off, this requirement would not abridge a public employer's right to curtail or eliminate a service and would be a mandatory subject of bargaining. Under Section 1173-4.3b, the employer may unilaterally decide to relieve employees, but a Union demand for notice and discussion of imminent layoffs prior to their implementation relates directly to the Union's statutory right to negotiate on questions of the impact of managerial decisions on employees' working conditions....

In the instant case and with particular regard to the management prerogative to effect layoffs for lack of work, we find and herein decide that practical impact on those laid off or to be laid off is implicit in any exercise of that prerogative; and that wherever the employer exercises this particular power, a practical impact will be deemed to have occurred and to have been established.

Because practical impact is held herein to be implicit in any exercise by management of its prerogative to lay off, we further hold and enunciate as a rule in this Decision, that the Union need not wait until employees are, in fact, laid off before it exercises its right to negotiate the impact of management's decision. With respect to those issues over which the employer has discretion to act, and which relate to the practical impact of a managerial decision to lay off employees, the City is obligated to bargain immediately.

That aspect of the Union's Job Security demand which seeks to achieve re-employment rights falls within the area governed by Sections 80 and 81 of the Civil Service Law; it, therefore, is not a mandatory subject of bargaining to the extent that it would conflict with the cited sections of the Civil Service Law. Those issues, however, which fall within the practical impact of a managerial decision to lay off employees and which do not infringe Civil Service Law or § 1173-4.3b of the NYCCBL are mandatory subjects of bargaining. Notice and prior discussion of an intent to lay off employees is such an issue.

We do not hold herein that a per se practical impact flows from every exercise of a managerial prerogative. In certain situations, the impact of a management decision on working conditions, specifically job security, may be only slight or indirect and may involve questions of fact requiring hearings or other procedures to establish the facts. In the latter circumstance and in other circumstances, such as that underlying our Decision B-9-68, management's action may be so directly related to the mission of the agency that even if practical impact is alleged and subsequently determined by this Board to exist, management should first have the opportunity to act unilaterally to alleviate the impact.

In the instant decision, we determine only that a management decision to lay off employees will result per se in a practical impact and that this impact is immediately bargainable. Therefore, a union demand in collective negotiations for a contract provision that provides for impact-related procedures, such as notice and discussion, in the event the employer decides to relieve employees, is a mandatory subject.

Having decided this case differently than Decision B-9-68 with respect to practical impact, the Board thereby makes known its intention to determine other scope of bargaining disputes involving alleged practical impact on a case-by-case basis....

NOTES

1. The Florida PERC, in *United Faculty of Palm Beach Junior College v. Palm Beach Junior College Bd. of Trustees,* 7 FPER 12,300 (Fla. PERC 1981), *aff'd,* 475 S.W.2d 1221 (Fla. 1985), held a public employer's waiver proposal which would relieve the employer of its bargaining obligations over the impact of management decisions during the term of the agreement was not a mandatory subject of bargaining. The Florida PERC reasoned as follows:

[D]enomination of such a waiver provision as a required subject of bargaining would permit an employer to condition the implementation of a collective bargaining agreement containing provisions governing a wide range of other mandatory subjects upon the union's agreement to waive its statutory right to bargain over the effects of management decisions during the term of the agreement. In the private sector this result has been viewed as being justified because the union is free to use its economic weapons, including the strike, to counter the employer's attempt to extract a waiver....

This proposition simply does not have the same validity in the public sector where one of the parties is not "backed" by the public legal use of meaningful economic weaponry. Thus, a public sector union faced with an employer's insistence upon the inclusion of a waiver clause such as that proposed in this case has no effective lawful means to counter that insistence within our statutory scheme. The most likely result of permitting such insistence would be enhancement of frustration in the bargaining process and encouragement of unions to resort to remedies not sanctioned by law.

The Florida PERC noted, however, that since such a waiver proposal is not illegal per se, it is a permissive subject of bargaining and that an employer may propose that a bargaining representative "waive its right to negotiate over certain subjects the parties are otherwise required to negotiate."

2. In *Maine v. Maine State Emps. Ass'n,* 499 A.2d 1228 (Me. 1985), the court ruled that the following negotiated zipper clause waived a union's right to negotiate over the impact of several agency reorganizations on bargaining unit employees:

> Each party agrees that it shall not attempt to compel negotiations during the term of this Agreement on matters that could have been raised during negotiations that preceded this Agreement, matters that were raised during the negotiations that preceded this Agreement or matters that are specifically addressed in the Agreement.

The Maine Supreme Judicial Court held that this contract language "serves as a waiver of impact bargaining over the organizational changes expressly permitted under the Management Rights Article." The court further noted that "[u]nquestionably the parties may contractually waive the right to any mid-term negotiations."

3. Although an employer is normally obligated to negotiate over the impact of a decision on employee terms and conditions of employment, such obligation may be met by contract language that waives the union's right to any further negotiations. For example, in *PLRB v. Commonwealth of Pa.,* 19 PPER ¶ 19138 (Pa. LRB 1988), the Pennsylvania Board held that contract language which "set forth procedures regarding furloughs, recall and reemployment rights, and bumping ... clearly establishes that the Commonwealth fulfilled its obligation to bargain over the impact of the furloughs." Accord *Bd. of Trustees of Community College Dist. No. 516,* 4 PERI ¶ 1137 (Ill. ELRB 1988) (since the parties "bargained impact and memorialized their agreement with respect to the impact of the College's decision to retrench," issues relating to "impact did not remain a mandatory subject for the purpose of mid-term bargaining"); *South San Francisco United Sch. Dist.,* 7 PERC ¶ 14243 (Cal. PERB 1983).

4. Where there is a mid-term obligation to negotiate over impact and the parties are at impasse, is the dispute subject to a statutory impasse procedure? In *City of Newburg v. Newman,* 69 N.Y.2d 166, 505 N.E.2d 590, 513 N.Y.S.2d 79 (1987), the court held that unresolved negotiations between a city and a fire fighters union over the impact of the city's decision to reduce the number of fire fighters working on each shift were subject to the interest arbitration statute. The court ruled that requiring interest arbitration in such a case would foster harmonious and cooperative labor relations in the public sector and avoid strikes. On the other hand, in *Hartford Principals' & Supvrs.' Ass'n v. Shedd,* 202 Conn. 492 (1987), the court held that the mediation and interest arbitration provisions of the Connecticut Teacher Negotiation Act were only applicable to the negotiation of a new contract and were not applicable to mid-term collective bargaining disputes.

5. In *Professional Airways Sys. Specialists, MEBA v. FLRA,* 809 F.2d 855 (D.C. Cir. 1986), the Court of Appeals for the District of Columbia rejected the FLRA's per se rule against the award of back pay to remedy a federal agency's failure to bargain over the "impact and implementation" of a decision. The court held that the "Back Pay Act permits a back pay award to affected employees of an agency that has failed to engage in 'impact and implementation' bargaining, so long as the employees meet the initial burden of establishing a causal nexus between the violation and the loss of pay." The court further stated that "it scarcely need[s] to be said that we no wise suggest that every procedural violation ineluctably results in back pay. Far from it, the employer must be afforded the opportunity to demonstrate that the requisite causal nexus under the Back Pay Act did not exist."

3. EFFECT OF CIVIL SERVICE LAWS

The origins of civil service systems can be traced to passage of the Pendleton Act of 1883. This Act was viewed as the modus operandi for protecting federal employees from the spoils system. The core concept underlying the Act and other civil service legislation is that public employees should be selected and retained solely on merit. But over the years these systems have expanded to cover many matters not essential to implementaion of the merit principle.

In many respects the development of civil service systems paralleled the growth of collective bargaining in the private sector. George Shultz observed: "Civil service regulations set forth the law of the public workplace. The governing charter in the private sphere is normally the collective bargaining agreement." GERR No. 319, F-2 (1969). In fact, for many years unions representing public employees staunchly supported the strengthening of civil service systems. The American Federation of State, County and Municipal Employees (AFSCME) was founded in 1934 in Wisconsin in order to lobby against proposed legislation that would have gutted that state's civil service system. See generally L. Kramer, Labor's Paradox 27-38 (1962). As late as its 1960 convention, AFSCME's official position was to "stimulate the growth and extension of civil service and to improve existing merit systems." Proceedings, AFSCME, 12th Int'l Convention, Philadelphia, April 25-29, 1960, p. 341. Increasingly over the past thirty years, however, AFSCME and other unions representing public employees have come to view civil service as an arm of management. More and more they are demanding that matters covered by civil service be made negotiable. The obvious conflict between civil service and collective bargaining has resulted in numerous problems concerning the scope of negotiations.

1967 EXECUTIVE COMMITTEE NATIONAL GOVERNORS' CONFERENCE, REPORT OF TASK FORCE ON STATE AND LOCAL GOVERNMENT LABOR RELATIONS 18-19 (1967)*

A critical issue for many governments is how the merit principle can be preserved and how collective bargaining can be accommodated within the merit system.

Because the two terms, "merit principle" and "merit system" are frequently confused, they should be defined. The merit principle is the concept that public employees should be selected and retained solely on the basis of merit. Political, religious, or racial considerations should play no part in such employment practices as selection, promotion, wages, career progression, assignment, and discharge. The merit principle was originally conceived to minimize the effect of patronage on the efficiency of government operations.

The merit system (or civil service system) is a public employment procedure designed to implement the merit principle. The procedure varies from place to place, but it commonly involves the establishment of a board (civil service commission) with rule-making authority to insure adherence to the merit principle. The essential elements of a merit system are: an impartial recruiting, examining

---

*Reprinted by permission of the International Personnel Management Association.

and selecting program; position classification plans based on duties and responsibilities; promotion on merit; protection against arbitrary disciplinary action.

In practice, many merit systems over the years have come to encompass other aspects of employee relations and personnel management not essentially related to the merit principle. These aspects include the handling of grievances, labor-management relations, employee training, salary administration, safety, morale, and attendance control programs.

In discussing the implications of collective bargaining for the merit system, consideration should be given to the determination of those procedures necessary to the merit principle as compared to procedural aspects of personnel management. Most public administration experts agree that merit system rules on examination, placement and promotion are indispensable to the merit principle and should therefore not be subject to collective bargaining. Many would like to extend the list of exemptions.

Most employee organizations regard every aspect of work as subject to bargaining. They want a voice in all areas that may affect the lives of their members. These areas include position classification, compensation, grievance procedures, discipline, discharge, layoff, and other subjects.

Care should be exercised not to restrict collective bargaining so unreasonably as to nullify the values of the process. Experience has shown that employee organizations denied reasonable scope in bargaining — particularly over the matter of wages — resort to lobbying and political pressure. They attempt a quasi-negotiation of sorts with the group that sets salaries, whether it is a civil service commission or a legislative body.

To the extent that a civil service commission has authority over personnel administration beyond the merit principle, the introduction of collective bargaining raises other problems. One problem is that if an independent civil service commission has authority over bargainable matters, then bargaining responsibility must lie with the commission rather than with the executive department. Conversely, if full authority over personnel matters is vested in an independent commission which is not the bargaining agent, then the scope of negotiation is unduly restricted. In Michigan, for example, a constitutional provision gives the independent commission full authority over salaries, wages, and other conditions of work for state employees.

A possible solution to these problems would be to transfer non-merit functions from a civil service commission to a personnel department under the chief executive. Negotiators would thus have full authority to conclude an agreement. In Canada, a new law gives the Treasury Board, as management's bargaining representative, responsibility for pay, classification, and conditions of employment. The Public Service Commission (formerly the Civil Service Commission) retains authority over examinations, promotions, staffings, and career development of Canadian federal employees.

Attitudes Toward the Civil Service Commission

In this connection it is pertinent to examine how the role of the civil service commission is perceived by different groups. Some public administrators look upon the civil service commission as an arm of management. Others view it as an impartial third party that protects employees from patronage or from excessively arbitrary management.

Unions generally regard the commissioners, who in their eyes represent management, as adversaries. They do not believe that a commission is an impartial third party. Rather, they feel that the duties of the commission should be confined to recruitment, hiring, and the prevention of patronage. Union leaders have asserted that if their unions are to achieve a full, mature relaionship with public employers through collective bargaining, they must be free to negotiate on all matters.

Independent associations tend to take a less hostile position. They speak of "working with" civil service commissions, but they also want a share in decision-making and a change in the traditionally paternalistic method of administration.

Employee organizations often contend that bargaining will have an influence on agencies that are not covered by a merit system or those whose system is weak and does not preserve the merit principle. It is argued that strong employee groups can act as an effective counter to patronage and bring pressure to bear for efficient, impartial administration. Others argue that strong employee organizations may actually reinforce a patronage system.

Legislation in the United States for public employee collective bargaining has attempted in different ways to protect the merit principle and fit collective bargaining into the existing merit system structure....

NOTES

1. In recommending that federal employees be given the right to organize and bargain collectively, President Kennedy's Task Force, headed by then Secretary of Labor Arthur Goldberg, stated:

> The principle of entrance into the career service on the basis of open competition, selection on merit and fitness, and advancement on the same basis, together with the full range of principles and practices that make up the Civil Service system govern the essential character of each individual's employment. Collective dealing cannot vary these principles. It must operate within their framework.

1961 Task Force Report on Employee-Management Cooperation in the Federal Service, in Labor-Management Relations in the Public Service, Pt. 1, at 14 (H. Roberts ed. 1968).

Whereas Executive Order 11491 provided that an agreement between an agency and a labor organization was subject to "existing or future laws and the regulations of appropriate authorities, including policies set forth in the Federal Personnel Manual" (E.O. 11491, § 12(a)), the Federal Service Labor-Management and Employee Relations Law which was enacted as part of Title VII of the Civil Service Reform Act of 1978 provides that "the duty to bargain in good faith shall, to the extent not inconsistent with any federal law or any Government-wide rule or regulation, extend to matters which are the subject of any rule or regulation only if the rule or regulation is not a Government-wide rule or regulation." 5 U.S.C. § 7117(a)(1) (1980).

2. The extent of potential conflict between the civil service laws and collective bargaining agreements is illustrated by the growing popularity of civil service systems. In 1955, only 23 states had civil service laws covering approximately 65 percent of full-time state employees. H. Kaplan, The Law of Civil Service 24, 25

(1958). In 1970, 84 percent of the cities, 83 percent of the counties, and 96 percent of the states in a National Civil Service League survey reported adoption of some form of merit system. Approximately 80 percent of all public employees are now covered by merit systems. National Civil Service League, *Survey of Current Personnel Systems in State and Local Governments,* Good Government 1-28 (Spring 1970). For an excellent treatise on civil service law, see R. Vaughn, Principles of Civil Service Law (1976).

3. Among the many articles examining the relationship between collective bargaining and civil service are Lewin & Horton, *The Impact of Collective Bargaining on the Merit System in Government,* 30 Arb. J. 199 (1975); Comment, *The Civil Service — Collective Bargaining Conflict in the Public Sector: Attempts at Reconciliation,* 38 U. Chi. L. Rev. 826 (1971); Stanley, *What are Unions Doing to Merit Systems?,* 31 Public Personnel Rev. 109 (1970); U.S. Dep't of Labor, Collective Bargaining in Public Employment and the Merit System (1972).

HELBURN & BENNETT, PUBLIC EMPLOYEE BARGAINING AND THE MERIT PRINCIPLE, 23 Lab. L.J. 618, 623-26 (1972)*

Discussion below includes the laws of 20 states which afford general coverage to at least one major category of public employees, state, county, and/or municipal.[14] In general, the laws may be classified into two broad categories with respect to the accommodation of polar views of merit systems: (1). — 11 states with legal provisions related to the problem; and (2). — 10 states with no related provisions.[15]

Accommodation Provisions

The 11 state laws which have provisions bearing on the accommodation problem basically attempt to resolve the conflict by excluding certain matters from the scope of negotiations. This exclusion takes three general forms: (1). — blanket exclusion of all matters covered by law; (2). — specific exclusion of matters covered by merit system laws and regulations; and (3). — selective exclusion only of certain merit-related items.

The statutes of New Hampshire, Vermont, and Pennsylvania exemplify the blanket exclusion approach. The New Hampshire and Pennsylvania laws do not specifically mention the merit system, but appear to limit bargaining to matters not covered by merit system laws. Vermont law includes the blanket exclusion plus the stipulation that bargaining law should not be construed to contravene the spirit and intent of the merit principle. However, since these laws fail to adequately clarify the relationship between merit systems and collective bargain-

---

*This material appeared originally in the October 1972 issue of *Labor Law Journal,* published and copyrighted 1972 by Commerce Clearing House, Inc., Chicago and is reproduced with permission.

[14]The states include California, Connecticut, Delaware, Hawaii, Maine, Massachusetts, Michigan, Minnesota, Missouri, Nevada, New Hampshire, New Jersey, New York, Oregon, Pennsylvania, Rhode Island, South Dakota, Vermont, Washington, and Wisconsin. Joel Seidman has made a general analysis of the public employee labor relations laws of the 16 states which he considers to have the most advanced and comprehensive statutes. Included were all the above except California, Missouri, Nevada, and New Hampshire. See "State Legislation on Collective Bargaining by Public Employees," Labor Law Journal, XXII (January, 1971), pp. 13-22.

[15]Because two sets of Wisconsin laws were considered, the states appear to add to 21. One Wisconsin law was placed in each of the two major groups.

ing, they provide little guidance for a viable approach to the problem of accommodation.

The laws of California, Massachusetts, Rhode Island, and Washington, and the Wisconsin law covering state employees only are of the specific exclusion type. The California statute provides that:

Nothing contained herein shall be deemed to supersede the provisions of existing state law and the charters, ordinances and rules of local public agencies which establish and regulate a merit or civil service system or which provide for other methods of administering employer-employee relations.

The Wisconsin law for state employees is even more specific:

Nothing herein shall require the employer to bargain in relation to statutory and rule provided prerogatives of promotion, layoff, position classification, compensation and fringe benefits, examinations, discipline, merit salary determination policy, and other actions provided for by law and rules governing civil service.

Rhode Island law exempts from bargaining only those matters exclusively reserved for merit systems by law or regulation. The Massachusetts and Washington statutes are least specific of this group, merely exempting matters delegated to civil service and personnel boards. Wellington and Winter note that the Washington statute appears "to subordinate collective bargaining provisions to civil service rules and regulations. However, there is some uncertainty among local officials ... as to which statute takes precedence."

Problems in Definition

While all of these specific exclusion laws provide to some extent a basic framework for accommodation, there still exist problems in defining the merit system-bargaining relationship and in establishing a reasonable scope of bargaining. Merely excluding merit system matters from the scope of bargaining does not necessarily bring about the proper relationship between the merit principle and bargaining, especially if the merit systems involved have authority over personnel matters not essentially related to the merit principle.

Generally the selective exclusion laws manage to avoid this pitfall. By extending bargaining to all matters not deemed essential to the merit principle, they provide a reasonably broad scope of bargaining and at the same time apparently maintain a viable merit system. The statutes of Hawaii, Connecticut, and Maine are in this category.

All three laws remove the appointment and promotion functions from the scope of bargaining, with the Connecticut law providing that:

Nothing herein shall diminish the authority and power of any municipal civil service commission, personnel board, personnel agency or its agents established by statute, charter or special act to conduct and grade merit examinations and to rate candidates in order of their relative excellence from which the appointments or promotions may be made to positions in the competitive division of the classified service of the municipal employer served by such civil service commission or personnel board. The conduct and grading of merit examinations, the rating of candidates and the establishment of lists from such examinations and the appointments from such lists and any provisions of any municipal charter concerning political activity of municipal employees shall not be subject to collective bargaining.

The above law is affected, however, by a previous subsection:

Where there is a conflict between any agreement reached by a municipal employer and an employee organization and approved in accordance with the provisions of [this act] on matters appropriate to collective bargaining, as defined in this act, and any charter, special act, ordinance, rules or regulations adopted by the municipal employer or its agents such as a personnel board or civil service commission ... the terms of such agreement shall prevail."

The Connecticut, as well as the Maine, law permits bargaining over personnel movements other than appointment and promotion, indicating that at least in these states the protection of all personnel movements is not deemed essential to the merit principle. While the Hawaii law does not specifically exclude all personnel movements from bargaining, it does stipulate that agreements cannot contain provisions inconsistent with merit principle[s]. However, "merit principles" are not defined.

Despite problems in specifying the items essential to the merit principle, the above laws confront the problem of accommodation. Unfortunately this is not true of those state laws which have no provisions pertaining to the accommodation of collective bargaining and the merit principle.

The public employee labor relations statutes of Delaware, Michigan, Minnesota, Missouri, Nevada,* ... New York, Oregon, and South Dakota, and the municipal employee law of Wisconsin contain no provisions dealing with accommodation. Although the Oregon bargaining statute does not deal with the problem, the state's civil service law attempts to achieve accommodation by redesignating the state Civil Service Board as the Public Employee Relations Board with the authority to interpret and administer the bargaining statutes. The Board is to make rulings which will preserve the merit principle.

In Michigan, the lack of provisions has resulted in legal conflict between collective bargaining and local merit systems. Since the Michigan Public Employee Relations Act does not specifically exempt the various aspects of merit systems from the scope of bargaining, both the Wayne County and Macomb County Circuit Courts have held that agreements reached through collective bargaining guaranteed by the bargaining statute supersede the provisions of the state civil service law when the two conflict. The Michigan experience suggests a great need for legislation clarifying the relationship between merit systems and public employee bargaining if the merit principle is to be preserved.

---

*Editors' Note: While the Nevada Act does not have a specific provision with respect to civil service, Nev. Rev. Stat. § 288.150(3) provides that "[t]hose subject matters which are not within the scope of mandatory bargaining and which are reserved to the local government employer without negotiation include: (a) The right to hire, direct, assign or transfer an employee, but excluding the right to assign or transfer an employee as a form of discipline." What effect would a provision such as this have on resolving whether the terms of a collective bargaining agreement superseded inconsistent civil service rules and regulations?

NOTES

1. In *Civil Service Comm'n v. Wayne Cty. Bd. of Supvrs.*, 384 Mich. 363, 184 N.W.2d 201 (1971), the case mentioned in the above article, the Michigan Supreme Court had the task of reconciling a direct conflict between provisions of a civil service law enacted in 1941 and provisions of the public sector collective bargaining law enacted in 1965. After noting that it was "left to *guess* what the 1965 legislature would have done had the point come to its attention," the court ruled as follows:

... the purported thrust of the act of 1965, that of prohibiting strikes by public employees and providing collective bargaining, negotiation and enforced mediation of labor disputes arising out of public employment coming within the scope of the act, must be implemented and administered exclusively as provided therein. Hence, the original authority and duty of the plaintiff civil service commission was diminished *pro tanto* by the act of 1965, to the extent of free administration of the latter according to its tenor....

2. The California Assembly Advisory Council on Public Employee Relations made the following recommendations concerning the accommodation between civil service and collective bargaining:

We prefer ... the approach adopted by the State of Connecticut in respect to municipal labor relations, according to which the terms of a negotiated agreement prevail over conflicting laws and regulations, including civil service systems, if the appropriate legislative body approves the agreement. We believe that this approach can be adopted to all public jurisdictions, not only municipal agencies.... [W]e believe a provision should be included in our proposed statute, stating that whenever there is a conflict between any agreement reached by a public employer and an employee organization on matters appropriate to collective bargaining, which is approved in accordance with the provisions of the proposed statute, the terms of such agreement shall prevail over any conflicting statute, charter provision, ordinance, resolution, or regulations adopted by a public employer or its authorized agents.

We also believe that such a provision will minimize the necessity of going to court to resolve negotiability issues involving conflicts with other laws, and that it will, at the same time, enhance the authority of the [Public Employees Relations] Board to deal with impasses over the scope of bargaining. Finally, by leaving the initiative to the parties themselves in expanding the scope of bargaining into areas presently covered by other laws, we believe that active publics will be able to exercise a greater influence than before in shaping the future of bilateral relationships in the public sector.

Assembly Advisory Council on Public Employee Relations, Final Report 175-76 (Cal. 1973).

3. In *Hillsborough Cty. Govtl. Emps. Ass'n v. Hillsborough Cty. Aviation Auth.*, 522 So. 2d 358 (Fla. S. Ct. 1988), the court had to address whether there was any conflict between Article I, Section 6 of the Florida Constitution, which grants public employees the right to bargain collectively, and Section 447.309(3) of the Florida Collective Bargaining Law, which provides that where there is any conflict between a collective bargaining agreement and any rule or regulation "over which the chief executive officer has no amendatory power, the chief executive officer shall submit to the appropriate governmental body having amendatory power a proposed amendment to such law, ordinance, rule or regulation" and that "[u]nless and until such amendment is enacted or adopted

and becomes effective, the conflicting provision of the collective bargaining agreement shall not become effective." After noting that "[t]he right to bargaining collectively is, as a part of the state constitution's declaration of rights, a fundamental right," the court held that application of Section 447.309(3) "unconstitutionally abridges the fundamental right of public employees to bargain collectively." In so ruling, the court stated:

> The art of collective bargaining is one of give and take. It is probable that through the process of negotiation the employees were required to forfeit some benefit to which they were otherwise entitled in order to gain the personal holidays, funeral leave, and seniority benefits which they did receive, and which the Board eventually refused. Were an entity such as a civil service board allowed to strike provisions at will the entire collective bargaining agreement would be of no value. We believe that this is far too great a price to pay for so-called uniform personnel administration.

4. In *AFSCME v. County of Lancaster,* 200 Neb. 301, 263 N.W.2d 471 (1978), the court had to determine what effect, if any, a civil service act passed *after* the public sector collective bargaining law had on the scope of bargaining under the bargaining law. The court held that with respect to such things as hours of work, vacations, wages, transfers, and layoff and recall, "[t]here is nothing in the civil service act which prohibited the county board from bargaining with its employees in regard to these topics." The court noted that there were other matters on which the union presented proposals

> which were controlled by the civil service act to some extent, such as promotions, discipline, grievance procedure, nondiscrimination, and termination. To the extent that the civil service act contains specific and mandatory provisions relating to such matters, the county board is not free to bargain. As an example, the act provides all appointments and promotions shall be based on merit and fitness. The county board has no power or authority to bargain or agree that any appointment or promotion shall be based upon anything other than merit and fitness except as provided in the act.

5. In *Laborers' Int'l Union, Local 1029 v. State,* 310 A.2d 664 (Del. Ch. 1973), *aff'd per curiam,* 314 A.2d 919 (Del. 1974), the court resolved a conflict between the scope of bargaining and the state merit system in favor of the state merit system. The court noted that "where there is uncertainty as to areas where the General Assembly has indicated a clear intention to deny collective bargaining, any doubt should be resolved in favor of the merit system." The court noted that its "decision should not be taken to indicate a negative attitude ... towards the rights of public employees," but rather should be viewed as "an attempt to reconcile conflicts inherent in a public employment program which contemplates both merit system protection as well as collective bargaining for state employees."

LOS ANGELES COUNTY CIVIL SERVICE COMMISSION v. SUPERIOR COURT

23 Cal. 3d 55, 588 P.2d 249, 151 Cal. Rptr. 547 (1978)

NEWMAN, JUSTICE: — In this case we must reconcile two sections of the Meyers-Milias-Brown Act (MMBA). Section 3500 declares that the MMBA shall not supersede local charters, ordinances, and rules that establish civil service systems or other methods of administering employer-employee relations.[2] Section 3505 requires governing bodies of local agencies or their properly designated representatives to meet and confer as to conditions of employment with representatives of employee organizations.

Since we conclude that the Legislature did not intend to exempt counties with civil service systems from the meet-and-confer requirement, we also consider the constitutionality of requiring chartered counties and cities to comply with the MMBA. We rule that the meet-and-confer requirement is not inconsistent with a charter provision that requires a civil service commission to hold public hearings before amending its rules. Therefore requiring Los Angeles County to meet and confer with employee unions before amending its civil service rules does not, we hold, offend the home-rule provisions of the California Constitution.

Article IX of the Los Angeles County Charter provides for civil service. The civil service commission, created by section 30 of the charter, shall "prescribe, amend and enforce rules for the classified service, which shall have the force and effect of law...." (Charter § 34.) Those rules are to provide: "For layoffs or for mandatory reductions in lieu of layoff ... for reasons of economy or lack of work" (§ 34(18)); "For transfer from one position to a similar position in the same class and grade and for reinstatement within one year of persons who without fault or delinquency on their part are separated from the service or reduced" (§ 34(10)); "For the discharge or reduction in rank or compensation after appointment or promotion is complete ..." (§ 34(13)); and "For the adoption and amendment of rules only after public notice and hearing" (§ 34(16)).

In February and March 1976 the commission held hearings concerning amendments to its rules governing layoffs and grade reductions in lieu of layoff. It sent notice of the hearings to several employee unions, but union representatives attended under protest. They claimed that section 3505 of the MMBA required the commission to meet and confer before amending the rules, which the commission refused to do.

Without waiving the asserted right to meet and confer the union representatives expressed their views at the hearings. They supported layoffs based on straight seniority. County management preferred reducing in grade higher ranked employees to displace lower-ranked (though possibly more senior) em-

---

[2]Section 3500 provides: "It is the purpose of this chapter to promote full communication between public employers and their employees by providing a reasonable method of resolving disputes regarding wages, hours, and other terms and conditions of employment between public employers and public employee organizations. It is also the purpose of this chapter to promote the improvement of personnel management and employer-employee relations within the various public agencies in the State of California by providing a uniform basis for recognizing the right of public employees to join organizations of their own choice and be represented by such organizations in their employment relationships with public agencies. Nothing contained herein shall be deemed to supersede the provisions of existing state law and the charters, ordinances, and rules of local public agencies which establish and regulate a merit or civil service system or which provide for other methods of administering employer-employee relations nor is it intended that this chapter be binding upon those public agencies which provide procedures for the administration of employer-employee relations in accordance with the provisions of this chapter. This chapter is intended, instead, to strengthen merit, civil service and other methods of administering employer-employee relations through the establishment of uniform and orderly methods of communication between employees and the public agencies by which they are employed."

ployees. Displaced employees would be laid off. After the hearings the commission adopted amendments supporting management's position.

In April 1976 the unions petitioned the superior court for a writ of mandate to compel the commission to set aside the amended rules and to meet and confer before adopting any rules regarding layoffs or reductions in lieu of layoff. The court issued the writ. In this proceeding we consider the propriety of the lower court's action.

The commission maintains that, because of the nonpreemption language in section 3500, it should not be required to comply with provisions of the MMBA that interfere with its administration of employer-employee relations. Further it asserts that, under article XI, sections 3 and 4 of the California Constitution, the Legislature does not have authority to require bargaining over matters governed by the county charter that, except for the charter, would be within the scope of representation under the MMBA.[6]

The meaning of "meet and confer"

At the outset we note that a meet-and-confer session amounts to much more than the public hearing authorized by the Los Angeles County Charter. Section 3505 of the MMBA requires governing bodies or their representatives to "meet and confer [with employee representatives] in good faith regarding wages, hours, and other terms and conditions of employment" and to "consider fully" such employee presentations. Section 3505.1 provides that, if the representatives successfully reach an agreement, they shall jointly prepare a nonbinding memorandum of understanding.

The meet-and-confer requirement means that "a public agency, or such representatives as it may designate, and representatives of recognized employee organizations, shall have the mutual obligation personally to meet and confer promptly upon request by either party and continue for a reasonable period of time in order to exchange freely information, opinions, and proposals, and to endeavor to reach agreement on matters within the scope of representation prior to the adoption by the public agency of its final budget for the ensuing year" (§ 3505). Thus a public agency must meet with employee representatives (1) promptly on request; (2) personally; (3) for a reasonable period of time; (4) to exchange information freely; and (5) to try to agree on matters within the scope of representation. Though the process is not binding, it requires that the parties seriously "attempt to resolve differences and reach a common ground." (*Placentia Fire Fighters v. City of Placentia* (1976) 57 Cal. App. 3d 9, 25, 92 LRRM 3373.) The public agency must fully consider union presentations; it is not at liberty to grant only a perfunctory review of written suggestions submitted by a union.

---

[6] Article XI, section 3(a) provides: "For its own government, a county or city may adopt a charter by majority vote of its electors voting on the question.... County charters adopted pursuant to this section shall supersede any existing charter and all laws inconsistent therewith. The provisions of a charter are the law of the State and have the force and effect of legislative enactments."

Section 4(g) provides: "Whenever any county has framed and adopted a charter, and the same shall have been approved by the Legislature as herein provided, the general laws adopted by the Legislature in pursuance of Section 1 (b) of this article, shall, as to such county, be superseded by said charter as to matters for which, under this section it is competent to make provision in such charter, and for which provision is made therein, except as herein otherwise expressly provided."

In contrast the character of a public hearing may vary according to "the subject of the hearing, the nature of the board or person holding the hearing and nature of the board or person to be heard." (*Silver Burdett Co. v. State Board of Education* (1940) 36 Cal. App. 2d 714, 718.) It may be only "the opportunity to present statements, arguments, or contentions in writing, with or without opportunity to present the same orally." (§ 11425; see also Davis, Administrative Law (6th ed. 1977) pp. 241-247, 272.) As Justice Kaus pointed out in the Court of Appeal opinion vacated by our hearing this case, "a public hearing by a legislative body is often nothing but an order to show cause why tentatively predetermined action should not be taken."

Are counties with civil service systems exempt from the MMBA's meet-and-confer requirement?

According to its section 3500 the MMBA has two purposes: (1) to promote full communication between public employers and employees; (2) to improve personnel management and employer-employee relations within the various public agencies. Those purposes are to be achieved by establishing methods for resolving disputes over employment conditions and for recognizing the right of public employees to organize and be represented by employee organizations. Section 3500 states, however: "Nothing contained herein shall be deemed to supersede the provisions of existing state law and the charters, ordinances, and rules of local public agencies which establish and regulate a merit or civil service system or which provide for other methods of administering employer-employee relations ..." Those words, the commission asserts, exempt it from the meet-and-confer requirement.[8]

The meaning of those words was discussed in *Huntington Beach Police Officers' Assn. v. City of Huntington Beach* (1976) 58 Cal. App. 3d 492, 500-503, 92 LRRM 2996, and in *Los Angeles County Firefighters Local 1014 v. City of Monrovia* (1972) 24 Cal. App. 3d 289, 294-295, 80 LRRM 2648. Those cases recognize that section 3500 reserves to local agencies the right to pass ordinances and promulgate regulations consistent with the purposes of the MMBA. To extend a broader insulation from MMBA's requirements would allow local rules to undercut the minimum rights that the MMBA guarantees. (See Grodin, *Public Employee Bargaining in California: The Meyers-Milias-Brown Act in the Courts* (1972) 23 Hastings L.J. 719, 724.)

The commission suggests that civil service rules carve out a particular area in employee-employer relations that should remain untouched by the meet-and-confer requirement. It maintains that, since *Huntington* and *Monrovia, supra,* dealt with general regulations and not civil service rules, they are distinguishable. The danger of undermining employee rights, though, is equally apparent

---

[8] After the sentence relied on by the commission, the following sentence appears in section 3500: "This chapter is intended, instead, to strengthen merit, civil service and other methods of administering employer-employee relations through the establishment of uniform and orderly methods of communication between employees and the public agencies by which they are employed." The commission does not adequately explain how this sentence would be interpreted if we were to adopt the view that section 3500 exempts counties with civil service systems from the meet-and-confer requirement. On its face the sentence expresses a legislative view that civil service systems will be strengthened through addition of the communication methods established by the MMBA.

if civil service commissions may freely and without negotiation alter the content of their rules.

The MMBA's stated purpose to guarantee full communication between employers and employees can hardly be met if the commission is not required directly to address employee concerns — concerns that frequently, of course, will be consistent with merit system principles. To carve out for the commission a unilateral authority over civil service rules would place an unjustifiable burden on public employees' right to representation. On the other hand, guaranteeing public employees an opportunity to have their views seriously considered (with the possibility that a nonbinding agreement will be adopted) serves employees' interests without destroying the commission's merit objectives.

Section 3505 extends to all matters "regarding wages, hours, and other terms and conditions of employment." Rules delineating how layoffs will be made clearly fall within the "conditions of employment" phrase of the section. Though section 3504 would permit the commission to consider "the merits, necessity, or organization of any service or activity" without meeting with employee representatives, that exception does not exempt the present rules from the meet-and-confer requirement. As we noted in *Fire Fighters Union v. City of Vallejo* (1974) 12 Cal. 3d 608, 621-622, 87 LRRM 2453, cases under the National Labor Relations Act — persuasive precedents in interpreting the MMBA — indicate that, though an employer has the right unilaterally to decide that a layoff is necessary, he must bargain about such matters as the timing of the layoffs and the number and identity of employees affected. (*NLRB v. United Nuclear Corp.* (10th Cir. 1967) 381 F.2d 972, 66 LRRM 2101.)

The commission also asserts that it is not a public agency within the meaning of section 3501(c) and that it is therefore exempt from the section 3505 meet-and-confer requirement. Section 3501(c) defines public agencies to include all governmental subdivisions, city or county, whether chartered or not "[e]xcept as otherwise provided." Section 3505 imposes the duty to meet and confer on the governing bodies of all public agencies and on such commissions or "other representatives as may be properly designated by law." Because we have ruled above that the nonpreemption language in section 3500 does not exempt counties with civil service systems from the MMBA's requirements, section 3501(c)'s "[e]xcept as otherwise provided" clause does not apply. The commission fits within section 3505 as a representative designated by the county charter to administer rules for the classified service.

The commission contends that, under the charter, the board of supervisors rather than the commission administers salaries and benefits and that the commission therefore is left with little to bargain with in the meet-and-confer process. (See charter § 11(1).) We believe that Los Angeles County's decision to divide decision-making authority in labor matters does not affect bargaining over the content of layoff rules. As Justice Kaus' opinion noted, the commission's poor bargaining position may be reason for reallocating governmental functions but does not excuse noncompliance with section 3505.

Finally the commission argues that a failure to adopt rules tentatively agreed on in the meet-and-confer session would subject it to charges of bad faith. Nothing in the MMBA precludes the commission from altering its rules after the charter-mandated hearing to accommodate more persuasive or previously unexpressed views.[10] A bad faith attack must be supported by specific facts, not simply conclusory statements. (Cf. *Placentia Fire Fighters v. City of Placentia, supra,* 57 Cal. App. 3d at pp. 25-27.)

Constitutionality of the meet-and-confer requirement in chartered counties

We have concluded that the MMBA requires the commission to meet and confer regarding its layoff rules. The commission argues that such a requirement violates the home-rule provisions for charter counties contained in article XI, section 3(a) of the California Constitution, which provides in part: "County charters adopted pursuant to this section shall supersede any existing charter and all laws inconsistent therewith." Further, section 4(g) states: "Whenever any county has framed and adopted a charter ... the general laws adopted by the Legislature in pursuance of Section 1(b) of this article, shall, as to such county, be superseded by said charter as to matters for which, under this section it is competent to make provision in such charter ..." Section 1(b) authorizes the governing body of each county to provide for the number, compensation, tenure, and appointment of employees.

When applicable, those provisions nullify state laws inconsistent with county charters. The commission asserts (1) that to require it to bargain with employee unions irreconcilably conflicts with the charter requirement that it hold a public hearing before amending its rules, and (2) that its unique status as an independent administrator of the merit system would be seriously threatened by requiring it to bargain.

We conclude that the meet-and-confer requirement can coexist with the charter-mandated hearing.[12] We see no reason why the commission's integrity as a neutral administrator of the merit system would be jeopardized by its participating in bargaining sessions with union and management representatives.

The fact that the commission must give notice of what it proposes to do and afford interested parties a chance to be heard does not mean that it must approach the hearing without even a tentative view of what it will do after everyone there has had her or his say. The complexity of matters before rule-making bodies often does not permit their acting only on input received at a hearing. (*California Optometric Assn. v. Lackner* (1976) 60 Cal. App. 3d 500, 508.) We can see no inherent conflict between tentative understandings reached at a meet-and-confer session and an objectively conducted public hearing.

The commission's fear that meet-and-confer sessions will compromise its neutral status appears unfounded. The unions' suggestion that layoffs be based on

---

[10] This case illustrates the kind of views that could be expressed at the hearing by employees not speaking for a union. As we have noted, a group of such employees convinced the commission to add a provision permitting employees whose pay would be greatly decreased by a proposed grade reduction to elect to be laid off instead.

[12] Because we hold that the requirements for a meet-and-confer session and a public hearing do not conflict, we need not decide here if it would be constitutional for the Legislature to require a chartered city or county to comply with a labor law that conflicts with its charter. We note, however, that *Professional Fire Fighters, Inc. v. City of Los Angeles* (1963) 60 Cal. 2d 276, 53 LRRM 2431, expressly held that labor relations is an area of statewide concern in which the Legislature can pass laws to be applied in chartered cities. While that case was decided before the 1970 revision of article XI of the California Constitution, *Huntington Beach Police Officers' Assn. v. City of Huntington Beach, supra,* 58 Cal. App. 3d 492, 92 LRRM 2996, was decided after the revision. *Huntington Beach* adopts the reasoning of *Professional Fire Fighters, Inc.*

seniority appears no less objective than management's view that layoffs should be based on employee grade. The commission's commendable concern for impartiality will be served by a fair application of whichever standard ultimately is adopted. The civil service system's goal of eliminating arbitrary decisions surely can coexist with a good-faith bargaining process.

Conclusion

In sum, we hold that MMBA section 3505 does apply to the layoff rules, that it does govern the commission, and that the meet-and-confer requirement is not satisfied simply by convening the charter-mandated public hearing. The MMBA requires that the commission meet and confer directly with employee representatives.

Further we hold that a meet-and-confer session and a public hearing can coexist and that unions do not relinquish their right to a serious bargaining session merely because they express their views at a hearing. To diminish that right would impair the vitality of the MMBA. We see no constitutional barrier to requiring the county here to meet and confer with employee representatives before amending civil service rules that govern layoff procedures.

The superior court's writ compelling the commission to set aside the amendments and to meet and confer with the unions before adopting rules on layoffs and mandatory reductions in lieu of layoff was properly granted. The commission's petition for our writ is denied.

NOTES

1. In *Pacific Legal Found. v. Brown,* 29 Cal. 3d 168, 624 P.2d 1215, 172 Cal. Rptr. 487 (1981), the California Supreme Court, in an en banc decision, held that the collective bargaining process established by the State Employer-Employee Relations Act (SEERA) does not "on its face" conflict with the general "merit principle" of civil service employment as set forth in the state constitution. In thus upholding the constitutionality of SEERA, the court commented:

As with other basic aspects of the "merit principle" of civil service employment, however, the parties are not free to adopt salary measures that interfere with any fundamental "merit principle" element that the classification system serves. This caveat, of course, in no sense renders SEERA unconstitutional on its face; if any improper measure should be agreed upon by the Governor and approved by the Legislature in the future petitioners or other interested parties will be free to challenge such measures at that time.

After noting that establishment of a collective bargaining law for state employees was "so necessary to the promotion of harmonious understanding between the parties," the court observed that "invalidation of [SEERA] would be a sorrowful step backwards."

2. In *Stephenson Cty.,* 3 PERI ¶ 2021 (Ill. SLRB 1987), the Illinois Board, rejected a union's contention that a merit board established by state statute was a joint employer, observing:

... declaring the Merit Commission to be employer of the employees within its jurisdiction destroys the independence needed for the Merit Commission to operate effectively. As noted earlier, the Merit Commission is designed to accord due process rights to the Sheriff's employees. In order to effectively perform this function, the Merit Commission must maintain the confidence of those who practice before it.... In order to be effective, the Merit Commission must maintain its status as a neutral decisionmaker. If the Merit Commission was aligned with either the employer or the employee, the independence it needs to maintain the confidence of those who practice before it would be destroyed. It would therefore lose its effectiveness in resolving these disputes. Thus, public policy dictates against finding the Merit Commission to be an employer of the employees under its jurisdiction.

See also *AFSCME v. IELRB,* 197 Ill. App. 3d 521, 554 N.E.2d 476 (1990) (State University Civil Service System Merit Board is not a joint employer with its constituent universities where its influence on terms of employment is largely limited to approval of contract terms and the selection of employees in accordance with statutory criteria and its own rules).

CITY OF DECATUR v. AFSCME, LOCAL 268

122 Ill. 2d 353, 522 N.E.2d 1219 (1988)

JUSTICE MILLER delivered the opinion of the court:

Following a complaint by the American Federation of State, County, and Municipal Employees, Local 268, alleging the commission of an unfair labor practice by the City of Decatur, the Illinois State Labor Relations Board entered an order directing the city to bargain over a proposal by the union that would permit employees to submit disciplinary grievances to arbitration. On administrative review, the appellate court reversed the State Board's order and held that the city could not be required to bargain over the union's proposal. (149 Ill. App. 3d 319, 102 Ill. Dec. 680, 500 N.E.2d 573.) We allowed the petitions for leave to appeal filed by Local 268 and the State Board (see 107 Ill. 2d R. 315(a)), consolidated the appeals for purposes of argument and disposition, and now reverse the judgment of the appellate court.

The dispute in this case concerns the scope of bargaining required by the Illinois Public Labor Relations Act (Ill. Rev. Stat. 1985, ch. 48, pars. 1601 through 1627) (the Act). On June 11, 1985, Local 268 of the American Federation of State, County, and Municipal Employees (AFSCME) filed a charge with the Illinois State Labor Relations Board alleging that the City of Decatur was guilty of committing an unfair labor practice under sections 10(a)(1) and 10(a)(4) of the Act (Ill. Rev. Stat. 1985, ch. 48, pars. 1610(a)(1), (a)(4)). The city had previously recognized Local 268 as the exclusive bargaining representative of a certain unit of employees, and, at the time the controversy arose, the parties were negotiating the terms of a new collective-bargaining agreement, their old agreement having expired on April 30, 1985.... The basis for the unfair labor practice charge was the city's refusal to bargain over a union proposal that would permit employees to submit disciplinary grievances to arbitration. The voters of the city had previously adopted, by referendum, a civil service commission under article 10, division 1, of the Illinois Municipal Code (see Ill. Rev. Stat. 1985, ch. 24, pars. 10-1-1 through 10-1-48), and it was the city's view that there was no duty to bargain over disciplinary matters that fell within the scope of the municipal civil service system.

....

The Act imposes on a public employer the duty to bargain collectively with the exclusive bargaining representative designated for an appropriate bargaining unit of public employees. "Collective bargaining" is defined in the Act as "bargaining over terms and conditions of employment, including hours, wages and other conditions of employment, as detailed in Section 7 and which are not excluded by Section 4." (Ill. Rev. Stat. 1985, ch. 48, par. 1603(b).) Section 4 of the Act contains a management rights provision; it excludes from the bargaining duty "matters of inherent managerial policy, which shall include such areas of discretion or policy as the functions of the employer, standards of services, its overall budget, the organizational structure and selection of new employees, examination techniques and direction of employees." (Ill. Rev. Stat. 1985, ch. 48, par. 1604.) The dispute in this case centers on section 7 of the Act, which provides, in pertinent part:

"A public employer and the exclusive representative have the authority and the duty to bargain collectively set forth in this Section.

For the purposes of this Act, 'to bargain collectively' means the performance of the mutual obligation of the public employer or his designated representative and the representative of the public employees to meet at reasonable times, including meetings in advance of the budget-making process, and to negotiate in good faith with respect to wages, hours, and other conditions of employment, not excluded by Section 4 of this Act, or the negotiation of an agreement, or any question arising thereunder and the execution of a written contract incorporating any agreement reached if requested by either party, but such obligation does not compel either party to agree to a proposal or require the making of a concession.

The duty 'to bargain collectively' shall also include an obligation to negotiate over any matter with respect to wages, hours and other conditions of employment, not specifically provided for in any other law or not specifically in violation of the provisions of any law. If any other law pertains, in part, to a matter affecting the wages, hours and other conditions of employment, such other law shall not be construed as limiting the duty 'to bargain collectively' and to enter into collective bargaining agreements containing clauses which either supplement, implement, or relate to the effect of such provisions in other laws." Ill. Rev. Stat. 1985, ch. 48, par. 1607.

The parties here agree that the union's proposal is not excluded from bargaining under the management rights provision of the Act. Moreover, the city acknowledges that the proposal would constitute a mandatory subject of bargaining were it not for the accommodation provision and the city's earlier adoption of the civil service provisions in article 10, division 1, of the Municipal Code. It has been the city's position throughout these proceedings that the scope of its duty to bargain is limited by the language in the third paragraph of section 7: "The duty 'to bargain collectively' shall also include an obligation to negotiate over any matter with respect to wages, hours and other conditions of employment, not specifically provided for in any other law or not specifically in violation of the provisions of any law." (Ill. Rev. Stat. 1985, ch. 48, par. 1607.) The city contends that the union's proposal for final and binding arbitration of disciplinary grievances would supplant certain of the statutory civil service provisions adopted by the city and therefore could constitute a matter that is "specifically provided for" in another law. The city concludes that it has no duty to bargain over the union's proposal.

This argument was rejected by the hearing officer in her recommended decision and order. There the hearing officer said:

"Respondent's [i.e., the city's] refusal to bargain is based on language in Section 7 of the Act, which states that the duty to bargain only applies to 'wages, hours and other conditions of employment, not specifically provided for in any other law ....' Respondent's reliance on this section is incorrect, however. Reading further, Section 7 says that 'if any other law pertains, in part, to a matter affecting the wages, hours and other conditions of employment, such other law shall not be construed as limiting the duty to bargain collectively ....' To adopt Respondent's position is to allow exactly that which Section 7 prohibits. To allow the adoption of a civil service system to eliminate an employer's obligation to bargain over disciplinary matters would clearly limit an employer's duty to bargain collectively. Section 7 specifically prohibits such a finding."

Following the submission of the city's exceptions to the hearing officer's recommended decision and order, and of the union's response to the exceptions, the State Board concluded "that the Hearing Officer properly analyzed all issues presented and that the exceptions are without merit. The Board therefore adopts the Hearing Officer's recommendation as a Decision of the Board."

The appellate court agreed with the city and reversed the State Board's decision. The court believed that the civil service provisions contained in article 10, division 1, of the Municipal Code and adopted by the city were matters "provided for" in other laws, and the court therefore concluded that the city was not required to bargain over the union's proposal that disciplinary matters be resolved by arbitration. Having given broad effect to the accommodation provision in section 7, the appellate court also held that local ordinances are not "laws" within the meaning of that statute. The court was concerned that local units of government might attempt unilaterally to alter or limit the scope of their statutory duty to bargain by passing ordinances on a matter that would otherwise constitute a mandatory subject of bargaining. To prevent that, the appellate court held that local ordinances do not qualify as "other laws" under the accommodation provision of section 7. Apparently the court assumed that the referendum by which the voters of Decatur had adopted the civil service system at issue was itself a law within the meaning of section 7 of the Act.
....

As the appellate court observed, the recommended decision and order, which the State Board later adopted, did not give full effect to the language in section 7 of the Act. (149 Ill. App. 3d at 325, 102 Ill. Dec. 680, 500 N.E.2d 573.) The interpretation adopted by the State Board in this case suggests that the duty to bargain set out in section 7 invariably overrides any contrary statutory command. That reading of the accommodation provision effectively eliminates any potential conflict between another statute and the bargaining duty prescribed by the Act; under that interpretation, no statute would ever limit the duty to bargain. We do not agree that section 7 may be read so broadly. Section 7 requires the parties to bargain over mandatory subjects that are "not specifically provided for in any other law or not specifically in violation of the provisions of any law." This indicates that the bargaining duty may in fact be limited by a law that specifically provides for, or prohibits, a matter that would otherwise be a mandatory subject of bargaining. In addition, section 7 provides that if another statute "pertains, in part," to a mandatory subject, the other law does not limit the duty to bargain over clauses that would "supplement, implement, or relate to the effect of such provisions in other laws." Under that provision, statutes that pertain in part to a mandatory subject do not have preemptive effect, and the parties remain obligated to bargain over supplementary clauses. Contrary to the interpretation adopted by the State Board in this case, the accommodation provision in section 7 allows for laws that will limit the duty to bargain. Although we do not agree with the State Board's interpretation of section 7, our examination of the union's proposal in this case and the law that it would affect leads us to conclude, for the reasons set out below, that the State Board correctly ordered the city to bargain over that proposal.

Section 10-1-18 of the Municipal Code provides, in pertinent part:

> "Except as hereinafter provided in this section, no officer or employee in the classified civil service of any municipality who is appointed under the rules and after examination, may be removed or discharged, or suspended for a period of more than 30 days, except for cause upon written charges and after an opportunity to be heard in his own defense. Such charges shall be investigated by or before the civil service commission, or by or before some officer or board appointed by the commission to conduct that investigation.... Nothing in this Division 1 limits the power of any officer to suspend a subordinate for a reasonable period, not exceeding 30 days except that any employee or officer suspended for more than 5 days or suspended within 6 months after a previous suspension shall be entitled, upon request, to a hearing before the civil service commission concerning the propriety of such suspension." (Ill. Rev. Stat. 1985, ch. 24, par. 10-1-18.)

The parties' previous labor agreement did not attempt to affect the provisions of section 10-1-18 concerning discharges and suspensions, and it expressly left disciplinary suspensions of more than five days, multiple suspensions within a six-month period, and terminations within the exclusive jurisdiction of the municipal civil service commission.

The grievance article in the union's proposed collective-bargaining agreement, at issue here, does not provide an exemption for disciplinary matters. Article V, section 1(a), says:

> "A grievance is defined as any difference, complaint or dispute between the Employer and the Union or any employee regarding the application, meaning, or interpretation of this Agreement or arising out of other circumstances or conditions of employment."

The union's proposal would eliminate disciplinary matters involving terminations, suspensions of five days or more, and multiple suspensions within a six-month period from the jurisdiction of the municipal civil service commission and instead would commit all disciplinary questions to final and binding arbitration.

In other jurisdictions, under a variety of statutory and constitutional schemes, courts facing conflicts between public employee bargaining laws and local civil service systems have opted in favor of granting primacy to the bargaining laws. (See *City of Casselberry v. Orange County Police Benevolent Association* (Fla. 1986), 482 So. 2d 336; *Local 1383 of the International Association of Fire Fighters v. City of Warren* (1981), 411 Mich. 642, 311 N.W.2d 702; *AFSCME Council 75, Local 350 v. Clackamas County* (1984), 69 Or. App. 488, 687 P.2d 1102.) Guiding our analysis of our own State's Act is the fundamental principle that the judicial role in construing a statutory provision is to ascertain and give effect to the legislative intent....

This court has previously noted the broad scope of the Act, with its complex of provisions governing the various aspects of public labor relations. "The Act provides a comprehensive system of collective bargaining for those public employees and employers who fall within its scope." (*County of Kane v. Carlson* (1987), 116 Ill. 2d 186, 196, 107 Ill. Dec. 569, 507 N.E.2d 482.) We do not believe that the legislature intended to make the broad duties imposed by the Act hostage to the myriad of State statutes and local ordinances pertaining to matters of public employment....

... To construe the accommodation provision of section 7 narrowly would, we believe, frustrate the declared policy of the State.

As the language of section 7 indicates, the mere existence of a statute on a subject does not, without more, remove that subject from the scope of the bargaining duty. For example, one type of statute that would not relieve an employer of the duty to bargain over an otherwise mandatory subject of bargaining would be a provision establishing a minimum level of benefit, such as a minimum wage law or minimum salary law. In that case, wages would remain a mandatory subject of bargaining, and the employees' bargaining representative would be free to insist on a level higher—but not lower—than that required by law. (See *Pennsylvania Labor Relations Board v. State College Area School District* (1975), 461 Pa. 494, 509, 337 A.2d 262, 269 (discussing relationship between duty to bargain and accommodation provision in that State's public employee bargaining law); *New Jersey v. State Supervisory Employees Association* (1978), 78 N.J. 54, 80-82, 393 A.2d 233, 246-47 (same).) Thus, in the determination whether the civil service provisions adopted by the city must override the bargaining duty imposed by the Act, it is appropriate to consider the nature of the other law.

Notably, the civil service system provided for in article 10, division 1, of the Municipal Code is an optional scheme and not one imposed by the State on any municipal body. (See Ill. Rev. Stat. 1985, ch. 24, par. 10-1-43.) Moreover, a municipality that has adopted the system may unilaterally alter or amend one of its terms. *Peters v. City of Springfield* (1974), 57 Ill. 2d 142, 311 N.E.2d 107, involved the provision in section 10-1-18 that municipalities "may by ordinance provide an age limit of not less than 63 years as the maximum age for the legal employment of any person employed as a policeman or fireman." (Ill. Rev. Stat. 1971, ch. 24, par. 10-1-18.) In that case the city had passed an ordinance reducing the mandatory retirement age to 60. This court upheld the ordinance as a valid exercise of the municipality's home rule authority (see Ill. Const. 1970, art. VII, § 6). Under *Peters,* a home rule city, such as Decatur, that has adopted the system provided by article 10, division 1, of the Municipal Code is not prohibited from altering its terms. The city could, if it chose to, eliminate those features of the civil service system at issue here.

An additional consideration relevant here is the common role that arbitration plays in resolving labor disputes. The importance of arbitration in private-sector labor relations has long been recognized. (See *United Steelworkers of America v. American Manufacturing Co.* (1960), 363 U.S. 564, 80 S. Ct. 1343, 4 L. Ed. 2d 1403; *United Steelworkers of America v. Warrior & Gulf Navigation Co.* (1960), 363 U.S. 574, 80 S. Ct. 1347, 4 L. Ed. 2d 1409; *United Steelworkers of America v. Enterprise Wheel & Car Corp.* (1960), 363 U.S. 593, 80 S. Ct. 1358, 4 L. Ed. 2d 1424.) With respect to public employees, the legislature has expressed a similar preference for arbitration in section 8 of the Act, which provides:

> "The collective bargaining agreement negotiated between the employer and the exclusive [bargaining] representative shall contain a grievance resolution procedure which shall apply to all employees in the bargaining unit and shall provide for final and binding arbitration of disputes concerning the administration or interpretation of the agreement unless mutually agreed otherwise." (Ill. Rev. Stat. 1985, ch. 48, par. 1608.)

In this case, then, the union's proposal concerns a well-recognized and familiar means for resolving labor disputes.

Given the purpose of the Act, the nature of that part of the civil service system at issue here, and the legislature's express preference for arbitration as a method for resolving disputes during the life of a labor contract, unless mutually agreed otherwise, we conclude that the State Board was correct in ordering the city to bargain over the union's proposal. In these circumstances, we construe the union's proposal as pertaining to a matter not specifically provided for or in violation of another law, and as supplementing, implementing, or relating to the provisions of the civil service scheme adopted by the city. We do not believe that the legislature would have intended that the civil service system it made available, as an optional matter, to municipalities in the Municipal Code would eliminate the duty to bargain over the union's proposal here. Our ruling does not mean that the city must agree to the union's proposal on this, or any other, subject. The duty to bargain collectively does not require a party to reach a particular agreement or make a particular concession; the parties may pursue their views to impasse. The State Board was correct, however, in directing the city to bargain on the matter.

....

For the reasons stated, the judgment of the appellate court is reversed.

Judgment reversed.

NOTES

1. In *Devine v. City of Des Moines,* 366 N.W.2d 580 (Iowa 1985), the Iowa Supreme Court held that a contractual provision providing for arbitration of grievances over employee terminations was not enforceable, since statutory civil service appeal procedures were the sole and exclusive means for reviewing the propriety of terminations of civil service employees. However, in *City of Casselberry v. PBA,* 482 So. 2d 336 (Fla. 1986), the Florida Supreme Court held that a city was required to bargain over a union proposal that would permit police officers to grieve demotions and discharges through the contractual grievance procedure even though the city had previously established a civil service procedure governing demotions and discharges. The court held that "while the city has the authority to enact civil service ordinances, state statutes will take precedence over such ordinances where specific conflicts arise."

2. One of the primary features of the conflict between collective bargaining and the civil service is the philosophical difference between the seniority principle, characteristic of labor contracts, and the merit principle embodied in civil service legislation. Consider the distinction between the merit *principle* and the merit *system*. Should public employers and unions be allowed to substitute seniority provisions for competitive examinations and merit pay raises? In New York, the Supreme Court for Erie County held, in *Kenmore Club, Police Benevolent Ass'n v. Civil Serv. Comm'n,* 61 Misc. 2d 685, 307 N.Y.S.2d 63 (1969) and in *Selover v. Civil Serv. Comm'n,* 61 Misc. 2d 688, 307 N.Y.S.2d 66 (1969), that the petitioning unions, notwithstanding contract provisions, had no right to orders cancelling or regulating the preparation, conduct or rating of competitive examinations. The court said:

> The authority of municipal civil service commissions to prescribe certain minimum qualifications in a promotional examination as here is authority granted by the Civil Service Law. The above agreement although arising from the Taylor Act can take no precedence under the above-mentioned provisions of the Civil Service Law. The Civil Service Law gives to the municipal commission the right to prescribe minimum training and experience qualifications for promotional examinations. No agreement between a municipal corporation and its employees although basically sanctioned by the Taylor Act has any precedence and makes no claim to any precedence over the Civil Service Law.

Accord *Civil Serv. Employees Ass'n, Local 860 v. Town of Harrison,* 407 N.Y.S.2d 627, 99 L.R.R.M. 2742 (App. Div. 1978).

4. EFFECT OF OTHER STATUTORY PROVISIONS

HANSLOWE & OBERER, DETERMINING THE SCOPE OF NEGOTIATIONS UNDER PUBLIC EMPLOYMENT RELATIONS STATUTES (1971), A Special Report Prepared for the New York Public Employment Relations Board

I. General Problem

The general problem examined herein is the relationship of the Taylor Law and of PERB to other laws of the State of New York and to the agencies which administer them, with regard to the determination of the scope of negotiations under the Taylor Law — i.e., the subjects as to which there is a duty to negotiate.

A question within the foregoing question is: What impact, if any, does the Taylor Law have on the pre-existing authority of public employers to determine "terms and conditions of employment" of their employees? In other words is the scope of negotiations under the Taylor Law coterminous with or greater than the scope of the unilateral power held by the particular public employer under pre-existing law, as declared by the Constitution, Legislature, courts, State Comptroller, Attorney General, etc.?

2. A Hypothetical Case: PERB vs. the Comptroller as to Local Government Conditions of Employment

Employee Organization, duly certified representative of certain professional employees, presents to School Board, the public employer, a list of negotiating demands which includes the following item: "Payment of accrued sick leave to the estate of a deceased employee."

School Board refuses to discuss the above item on the ground that inclusion of such a provision in the collective agreement would be illegal, citing 23 Op. State Compt. 649 (1967), #67-735) and Article VIII, § 1 of the State Constitution, prohibiting government entities, including school districts, from giving gifts.

Employee Organization files a charge with PERB under Section 209-a.1 (d), alleging that the above-described action of the School Board constitutes a refusal to negotiate concerning "terms and conditions of employment."

What should PERB do?

Under the 1969 amendments it is clearly PERB's responsibility to determine whether or not the alleged improper practice occurred. Section 205.5, as amended, provides:

> In addition to its powers and functions provided in other sections of this article, the board shall have the following powers and functions: ... (d) To establish procedures for the prevention of improper employer and employee organization practices as provided in section two hundred nine-a of this article.... The board shall exercise exclusive nondelegable jurisdiction of the powers granted to it by this paragraph....

PERB must, therefore, determine whether the unused sick leave demand falls within the scope of "terms and conditions of employment," within the meaning of the Taylor Law.

Concerning the relationship of the above-cited opinion of the State Comptroller to this determination, PERB has three courses of action available: PERB might accept the opinion of the Comptroller as conclusive of the matter and dismiss the charge; PERB might ignore the opinion of the Comptroller as irrelevant; PERB might take into account the opinion of the Comptroller, giving it, however, only such weight as, in the judgment of PERB, its persuasive force merits.

The third course of action is patently the proper one. The decision as to the scope of negotiability is PERB's in the first instance. The first two options — abandonment of decision to the Comptroller and ignoring the opinion of the Comptroller — have little to commend them. As to the first, the Comptroller has no mandate under the law to resolve such questions; his opinions with respect to such local government expenditures are admitted by himself to be "informal and advisory" only.... As to the second, the Comptroller has, by arrogation or otherwise, been in the business of advising local governments as to their powers under a broad body of law for a substantial period of time; in the process he has accumulated considerable experience concerning the legal framework within which local governments of the State of New York operate. For PERB to ignore completely this source of potential guidance would seem unwise.

The burden of demarcating those subjects which are within the scope of the statutory criterion "terms and conditions of employment" is initially PERB's, not merely because PERB has been designated by the State Legislature to make such determinations in the first instance, but because the vitality of the administrative process lives in the development and application of expertise in specially difficult areas of government regulation. The definition of the scope of negotiations under the Taylor Law is such an area.

One way of validating the foregoing position is to consider the matter of judicial review. However the decision as to the scope of negotiability under the Taylor Law is made in the first instance, it is subject to review in the courts. Such review is dependent upon the quality of the record made below and the sophistication of the trial tribunal with regard to the questions before it. Employment relations, as several decades of experience in the private sector demonstrate, is a complex and delicate area in which the adequacy of judicial review is particularly dependent upon the quality of the proceedings, record, and judgment below.

It is instructive to note, in the foregoing regard, that Comptroller opinions are typically rendered on the basis of a mere exchange of letters, without the sharpening of issues through pleadings, the presentation of evidence, confrontation and cross examination of witnesses, oral or written argument. Proceedings before PERB, on the contrary, under sections 209-a and 205.5 (d), entail all of these aids to administrative adjudication and judicial review.

Turning now to the merits of the hypothetical case posed, namely, whether the issue of "payment of accrued sick leave to the estate of a deceased employee" is within the statutory mandate of "terms and conditions of employment," the problems presented to PERB are the following: (1) whether the demand concerning the treatment of accrued sick leave is a term or condition of employment, and (2) whether Article VIII, § 1 of the State Constitution and/or some other state constitutional or legislative provision takes the matter out of the scope of negotiability. The answer to the first question would seem quite clearly to be yes. The real question for the purposes of this memorandum is the second. As to this, PERB must determine, within the limiting context of all relevant constitutional and statutory provisions (i.e., all relevant "law"), whether, as a matter of sound employment relations in the public sector, including such a subject within the scope of negotiability makes sense.

Stated more clearly perhaps, in cases such as the hypothetical one posed, PERB has two questions potentially before it: (1) whether the particular subject should be deemed, as a matter of sound public employment relations, to be within "terms and conditions of employment," (2) whether, even if it should be so deemed, the particular subject has been withheld or withdrawn from negotiability by the operation of some competing provision of law. Where the answer to the second question is unclear by reason of ambiguity in the competing law, the question of negotiability should be decided by PERB on the basis of sound public employment relations.

Whatever the determination of PERB, that determination is of course reviewable in the courts pursuant to Section 210.4 of the Taylor Law....

4. The Relationship of PERB to Other Competing Agencies

What has been said of the Comptroller is dispositive of PERB's relationship with other potentially competing agencies of state government. Whatever the competing agency, the question of negotiability is to be answered by PERB in the first instance. In the process of answering the question, PERB should take into account all pertinent constitutional and statutory provisions; its consideration should not be confined to the Taylor Law alone. Neither the Taylor Law nor PERB exists in a void. (Cf., e.g., *Southern Steamship Co. v. NLRB,* 316 U.S. 31, 47 (1942) ("... the Board has not been commissioned to effectuate the policies of the Labor Relations Act so single-mindedly that it may wholly ignore other and equally important Congressional objectives. Frequently the entire scope of Congressional purpose calls for careful accommodation of one statutory scheme to another, and it is not too much to demand of an administrative body that it undertake this accommodation without excessive emphasis upon its immediate task."); *American News Co.,* 55 NLRB 1302 (1944).

In addition to taking into account other constitutional and statutory provisions, PERB should consider the decisions of tribunals competent to interpret those constitutional and statutory provisions. The weight which PERB gives to any aspect of the foregoing array of law (constitutional, statutory, decisional) should depend on PERB's own interpretation of such of that law as it deems relevant. PERB's interpretation would, of course, be oriented to sound public employment relations as perceived through its own expertise. While PERB cannot and should not ignore clear mandates from the Constitution, the Legislature, or the Court of Appeals, it should deem itself free in the absence of such mandates to exercise its own best judgment, understanding of course that its decisions are themselves subject to judicial review. It would be obviously wasteful for PERB to determine questions of negotiability in the context of the Taylor Law alone, leaving to the reviewing courts in the first instance the questions of the relevance and force of competing law. Such an approach would deny to the reviewing courts the benefit of PERB's developing expertise with respect to the implications of such competing law for sound public employment relations (which is to say, sound public policy in a public employment context) in the State of New York.

Applying the foregoing principles to a concrete case, the decision of the Supreme Court of Nassau County in the *Central High School District No. 3* case (72 LRRM 2858, 305 N.Y.S.2d 724, November, 1969) — to the effect that an arbitration award, granting a sum of money to a deceased employee's estate in lieu of unused sick leave, was unenforceable by reason of the unconstitutional gift provision — should be accorded no more weight by PERB than the persuasive force of the court's reasoning merits. Without repeating again all of the considerations leading to this conclusion, it would seem quite incongruous for important questions of public employment relations to be resolved without any participation in the decisional process by the agency specially constituted by the Legislature to superintend such matters.

5. The Relationship of Scope of Negotiations to the Unit Problem

A somewhat different variety of scope of negotiations question confronts PERB in the following type of situation: where the subject sought to be negotiated is quite clearly within the statutory scope, "terms and conditions of employment," but is not within the authority of management at the unit level. An example of this type of subject is annuities and pensions under the State Employees' Retirement System. (Retirement and Social Security Law, Article 2.) This system applies not only to state employees but also to the employees of "participating" muncipalities and other local government entities. The State Comptroller is declared by § 11 of the Retirement and Social Security Law to be the "administrative head" of the Retirement System, with the express power, among others, to adopt and amend "rules and regulations for the administration and transaction of the business of the retirement system...."

Without delving more deeply into the Retirement and Social Security Law, it may be seen that two sets of potential questions for PERB as to scope of negotiations are presented thereunder. The first set of questions has to do with negotiations in *state* employment; the second set has to do with negotiations in *local* employment.

As to the *state* negotiations, a tug-of-war seems possible between the Office of Employee Relations, on the one hand, and the State Comptroller, on the other. With whom, it may be asked, do state employees have the right to negotiate concerning those aspects of the pension program which the Legislature has expressly placed in the discretionary control of the Comptroller. Those aspects may be said to be (1) not negotiable except with the Comptroller himself (is the Comptroller a "public employer" with regard to employees not employed in the Department of Audit and Control?), (2) negotiable only if the Comptroller *chooses* to negotiate concerning the exercise of his discretionary authority, (3) negotiable only to the extent that the state employer (Office of Employee Relations?) and the employee organization involved may agree upon joint recommendations to be made to the Comptroller and/or to the Legislature.

A possible legislative resolution of the foregoing type of problem may be foreshadowed by a very recent amendment to § 8 of the State Finance Law. The duties of the Comptroller with regard to a related matter have been modified as follows in subdivision 16 thereof:

> Notwithstanding any inconsistent provision of law, no change shall be made in the rate or eligibility standards for state employees' travel, meals, lodging, and other expenses for which the state makes payment (either in advance or by reimbursement), without the approval of the director of employee relations.

As to negotiations over pensions involving *local* governments participating in the State Retirement System, the only practical effect of such would be to produce joint proposals to be presented in the form of requests to the Comptroller and/or the State Legislature. This is an instance of a larger question which will confront PERB in several different contexts. The question is whether PERB should require a particular public employer to negotiate with regard to a subject as to which the employer has no control *except* the power to make recommendations. This question is dealt with in the ensuing section.

6. Subjects of Negotiation: Mandatory, Permissible, Illegal?

The subjects of bargaining in the private sector has been trichotomized into mandatory, permissible, and illegal. Mandatory subjects are those which fall within the meaning of "wages, hours, and other terms and conditions of employment" (National Labor Relations Act, Section 8(d)); as to these, the proposing party may bargain to impasse, and the other party has a duty to bargain in response. Permissible subjects are those not within "wages, hours, and other terms and conditions of employment," but not illegal; as to these, the proponent may propose, but not insist upon, and the other party need not, but may, bargain; if agreement is reached on a permissible subject, that agreement is an enforceable part of the contract. Illegal subjects are those which, even if agreed upon, are unenforceable; of course there is no duty to bargain over such a subject. (See generally, sections 8(a)(5), 8(b)(3), 9(a), and 8(d) of the National Labor Relations Act, and *NLRB v. Wooster Division of Borg-Warner Corporation,* 356 U.S. 342 (1958).)

The situation in public employment is sufficiently different as to impugn the relevance of the trichotomy. The *terminology* may, however, be helpful for purposes of analysis. Assuming a subject to be clearly within "terms and conditions of employment" and at the same time not within the authority of management at the level of the unit, should PERB enforce a duty to negotiate at that level? To put it otherwise, should such a subject be treated as mandatory, permissible, or illegal — i.e., should negotiation be required, permitted, prohibited?

The real choice would seem to lie between the mandatory and permissible approaches; little purpose would be served in *prohibiting* negotiations on such a subject. Even where public management at the level of the unit is without authority to control subject X, it would ordinarily have authority to agree with the employee organization involved to make a joint recommendation to the appropriate higher echelon of authority as to the desired disposition of subject X. Accordingly, subjects found to be within the statutory language "terms and conditions of employment" but not within the authority of management at the unit level might, nonetheless, be treated as mandatory subjects and negotiations over them therefore required. A difficulty with this approach is that it might tend to clutter up negotiations with a laundry list of demands for joint importuning of distant and perhaps intractable holders of pertinent powers. On the other hand, a good deal of negotiations in the public sector concerning the most central of subjects is conducted by "public employers" who lack authority to resolve finally those issues. Examples of this are (1) a dependent school board negotiating teacher salaries and (2) the State Office of Employee Relations negotiating state employee salaries; in the case of the first, the pertinent authority resides in the city council; in the second, it resides in the State Legislature.

Perhaps guidance toward a middle course between the mandatory and permissible approaches is offered by Section 207.1(b) of the Taylor Law when it speaks of *"effective* recommendations." Subjects which the particular employer does not control but as to which he has the power to make *effective* recommendations might be treated as mandatory subjects. On the other hand, subjects as to which the employer could make only *ineffective* recommendations might be treated as permissible subjects only.

7. The Impact of the Taylor Law on the Pre-Existing Authority of Public Employers

The array of positions with regard to the effect of the enactment of the Taylor Law on the pre-existing authority of public employers to confer benefits on their employees ranges from the response of the Comptroller at the right extreme, "nil," to a hypothetical position at the left extreme to the effect that the Taylor Law impliedly repeals all prior inconsistent legislation and judicial and administrative rulings....

The Comptroller's position, "a fundamental premise which underlies every Opinion of the State Comptroller, concerning situations involving Article 14, of the Civil Service Law (known as the Taylor Law)" (see Comptroller's Memorandum of Law in the *Town of Huntington* case, page 4), was stated in 23 Op. State Compt. 316, 318-19 (1967, #67-378):

> The new statutory provisions [the Taylor Law] do not in any way enlarge the legal benefits which public employers may confer on their employees nor has there been any expansion of the authority of such public employers in regard to these benefits. Therefore, it will be necessary for us to consider in order each of the employee demands herein to determine whether, irrespective of collective bargaining, this school district may legally comply with the same.

We disagree with the position thus taken by the Comptroller (and also with the position at the opposite extreme of the spectrum). At least two pertinent changes, both, in our judgment, rather basic, have been produced by the Taylor Law. The effect of these two changes is potentially to expand the scope of negotiations beyond the scope of pre-Taylor *exercise* of employer power. The first change is that a new public agency, PERB, has been created and empowered by the Legislature to deal with and decide issues of public employment relations in the State of New York — issues previously presided over (to the extent they were presided over at all) by other agencies. To the extent that those other agencies lacked authority or occasion to render final decisions on questions of employer power presently falling within the purview of PERB, such questions are still open. This means that the only questions of employer power definitively answered at the time of this writing are those questions which have heretofore been unambiguously resolved by the Constitution of the State of New York, the State Legislature, or the Court of Appeals. Opinions of the State Comptroller, and even decisions of lower state courts never challenged in the ultimate through appellate review to the Court of Appeals, establish no controlling precedents.

A second basic change in the public policy of the State of New York occasioned by the enactment of the Taylor Law is the introduction into public employment relations of the whole new concept of resolving employer-employee disagreements through the institution of collective negotiations. We concede that matters unambiguously resolved by the State Constitution, by statutory enactment, or by Court of Appeals interpretation of either of the foregoing are not affected by the passage of the Taylor Law. Where ambiguity exists, however, or where the source of the competing "law" is of a lower order than Constitution, Legislature, Court of Appeals — i.e., in the gray area of public employer authority over "terms and conditions of employment" — strong reason exists for concluding that the legislative intent was to have such gray-area problems resolved through the process of collective negotiations. Indeed, the Taylor Law declares it to be the public policy of the State of New York to resolve disputes between public employees and public employers by that process. (Section 200) ....

NOTE

Oberer and Hanslowe suggested that a PERB should (1) determine whether a given subject is within the "terms and conditions of employment," and, if it is, (2) determine whether such subject should nevertheless be "withheld or withdrawn from negotiability by the operation of some competing provision of law." Is there, or should there be, any difference in the scope of judicial review with respect to these two determinations? Should the scope of judicial review be greater with respect to the second determination?

CITY OF BROOKFIELD v. WERC

87 Wis. 2d 819, 275 N.W.2d 723 (1979)

COFFEY, JUSTICE. This is an appeal of a July 16, 1976 judgment that reversed an April 16, 1975 order of the Wisconsin Employment Relations Commission (hereinafter WERC). The appellant, WERC, ordered the respondent, City of Brookfield (hereinafter Brookfield) to reinstate and reimburse five city firefighters laid off due to a decrease in the funds allocated to the fire department by the city budget. The ordered remedy was based upon the WERC's finding that Brookfield in the 1973 bargaining agreement had violated its duty to collectively bargain when it refused to negotiate the decision to lay off the five firefighters or the effects of the lay off decision, contrary to sec. 111.70(1)(d), Stats. The circuit court reversed the WERC order and found that Brookfield was not required to negotiate the lay off decision; the WERC conclusion in regard to the duty to bargain the effects of the lay off decision was affirmed and is not at issue in this appeal....

Thus, the two issues presented are:

1. Whether an economically motivated decision to lay off five firefighters as a means to implement a fire department budget reduction is a mandatory subject of collective bargaining pursuant to sec. 111.70(1)(d), Stats., of the Municipal Employment Relations Act?

2. Is the commission's order providing remedies for the respondent's failure to collectively bargain in violation of sec. 111.70(1)(d), Stats., reasonable and appropriate under the circumstances?

This appeal challenges a municipality's decision to lay off five union firefighters due to a cut in the department budget. Local 2051 (firefighter's union) maintains that budget related lay offs are a mandatory subject of bargaining pursuant to sec. 111.70(1)(d), Stats., as a matter affecting wages, hours and conditions of employment. The city of Brookfield contends that the layoff decision is a management prerogative by virtue of its municipal powers vested in ch. 62, Stats. Consequently, this case will be decided upon the statutory interpretation the WERC gave to sec. 111.70(1)(d) and ch. 62, Stats., and whether it was appropriate in the particular fact situation.

In dealing with this subject the court must determine which reviewing standards used to interpret sec. 111.70(1)(d) are appropriate herein. In *Unified School District of Racine County v. WERC,* 81 Wis. 2d 89, 259 N.W.2d 724 (1977) the court discussed the standard of review applicable to WERC decisions dealing with mandatory bargaining and stated:

> "Because the case raised 'very nearly questions of first impression,' this court held that it was 'not bound' by the Commission's interpretation of the statute, although the Commission's decision would have 'great bearing' on the court's decision, and would be accorded 'due weight.' *Beloit Education Asso., supra,* at 68, 242 N.W.2d 231. As in the *Beloit* case, because of the limited experience of the Commission with the questions presented, and their strictly legal nature, it is appropriate for this court to reach an independent determination of the intent and meaning of the statute, giving due weight to the decision of the Commission." *Id.* at 93, 259 N.W.2d at 727.

Thus, in this problem area the court finds it necessary to undertake an independent judicial inquiry into the proper construction of sec. 111.70(1)(d) and its impact on the exercise of municipal powers enumerated in ch. 62. A question of interpretation confronts this court to determine whether or not the commission's competence or expertise extends beyond ch. 111. This court in *Glendale Professional Policemen's Assoc. v. Glendale,* 83 Wis. 2d 90, 264 N.W.2d 594 (1978) dealt with the harmonizing of sec. 111.70(1)(d) Stats., and sec. 62.13, Stats., as to whether a promotion of a police officer within the department was enforceable through the collective bargaining agreement. This court answered the question regarding the commission's expertise in the following language:

> "In the typical case, the application of sec. 111.70-77, Stats., to a particular labor dispute requires the expertise of the Commission, the agency primarily charged with administering it. Here the question does not concern the application of a labor statute but the Commission's power to enforce it in the first instance in the light of another state statute. This issue, for relationship between two state statutes, is within the special competence of the courts rather than the Commission, and therefore this court need not give great weight to the arbitrator's determination of the issue." *Id.* at 100-01, 264 N.W.2d at 600.

We are persuaded by the *Glendale* reasoning that the WERC should not be accorded the authority to interpret the appropriate statutory construction to ch. 62. The general charter law for cities as recited in ch. 62 deals solely with the powers and privileges of municipalities to promote the general welfare, peace, good order and prosperity of its inhabitants. These objectives are accomplished by the enactment of charter and general ordinances dealing with finance, public works, zoning, safety and building codes, annexations, etc. Thus, the exclusive grant of authority to municipalities in ch. 62 is far afield from the powers and limitations in the area of labor relations as enumerated in sec. 111.70-77. Accordingly, a question of a strictly legal nature is presented. This court in *Whitefish Bay v. WERB,* 34 Wis. 2d 432, 149 N.W.2d 662 (1967) eloquently pointed out the limitations on the interpretation of statutes by an administrative agency and the agency's void of legal expertise and knowledge when it stated:

> "'In view of this poverty of administrative experience and of the recent passage of the statute giving rise to this strictly legal question of jurisdiction, perhaps the court ought to examine it afresh as a question of law not especially involving administrative expertise. For such a question the court feels free to substitute its own judgment for that of the administrative agency.' Citing *Pabst v. Department of Taxation* (1963), 19 Wis. 2d 313, 323, 120 N.W.2d 77." *Id.* at 444-45, 149 N.W.2d at 669.

This case is an instance where the circuit court, now with this court's approval, is placing a limitation on the attempt of the WERC to expand its scope of authority beyond the limits of the legislative enactment contained in ch. 111. In like situations, WERC's statutory interpretations beyond the field of labor law will not be entitled to persuasive or substantial weight.

Sec. 111.70(1)(d) is controlling upon the duty to collectively bargain between a municipality and its public employees, and reads:

> "'Collective bargaining' means the performance of the mutual obligation of a municipal employer, through its officers and agents, and the representatives of its employes, to meet and confer at reasonable times, in good faith, with respect to wages, hours and conditions of employment with the intention of reaching an agreement, or to resolve questions arising under such an agreement. The duty to bargain, however, does not compel either party to agree to a proposal or require the making of a concession. Collective bargaining includes the reduction of any agreement reached to a written and signed document. The employer shall not be required to bargain on subjects reserved to management and direction of the governmental unit except insofar as the manner of exercise of such functions affects the wages, hours and conditions of employment of the employees. In creating this subchapter the legislature recognizes that the public employer must exercise its powers and responsibilities to act for the government and good order of the municipality, its commercial benefit and the health, safety and welfare of the public to assure orderly operations and functions within its jurisdiction, subject to those rights secured to public employes by the constitutions of this state and of the United States and by this subchapter."

As stated in sec. 111.70(1)(d) a mandatory subject of bargaining is a matter which affects "wages, hours and conditions of employment." The statute also provides for a public sector "management rights" clause guaranteeing as a management prerogative the exercise of municipal powers and responsibilities in promoting the health, safety and welfare for its citizens. Unless the bargaining topic affects "wages, hours and conditions of employment" a municipality is not compelled to collectively bargain but may choose to if not expressly prohibited by legislative delegation. Obviously, it is not the intent of the legislature to permit the elasticity of the phrase "bargaining topics affecting wages, hours and conditions of employment" to be stretched with each and every labor question.

In *Beloit Education Asso. v. WERC, supra,* 73 Wis. 2d at 54, 242 N.W.2d 231, the court held that a mandatory subject of bargaining was distinguished from a permissive subject of bargaining if the topic "primarily" or "fundamentally" related to wages, hours and conditions of employment, now known as the "primary relation test." The primary relation test reflects substantial change in public sector labor law. Prior to the *Beloit* case, mandatory and permissive subjects were delineated in the private sector "change of direction" test. This rule of law was adopted by the court in 1970 wherein *Libby, McNeil & Libby v. WERC, supra,* recited "... most management decisions which change the direction of the corporate enterprise, involving a change in capital investment, are not bargainable." *Id.* 48 Wis.2d at 282, 179 N.W.2d at 811. In *Unified School Dist. No. 1 of Racine v. WERC, supra,* 81 Wis. 2d at 96, 259 N.W.2d 724, it was reasoned that the primary relation test rather than the change of direction standard better encompassed the inherent differences between public and private sector bargaining. See Weisberger, *The Appropriate Scope of Mandatory Bargaining in the Public Sector: The Continuing Controversy and the Wisconsin Experience,* 1977 Wis. L. Rev. 685, 694-99. The *Racine County* decision emphasized that:

> "[I]n the public sector, the principal limit on the scope of collective bargaining is concern for the integrity of political processes." *Unified School Dist. No. 1 of Racine County v. WERC, supra* at 96, 259 N.W.2d at 730.

We hold that economically motivated lay offs of public employees resulting from budgetary restraints is a matter primarily related to the exercise of municipal powers and responsibilities and the integrity of the political processes of municipal government. The citizens of a community have a vital interest in the continued fiscally responsible operation of its municipal services. Thus, it is imperative that we strike a balance between public employees' bargaining rights and protecting the public health and safety of our citizens within the framework of the political and legislative process.

Ch. 62, Stats., which enumerates a legislatively delegated municipal powers and obligations mandates this result and recites in its relevant portions:

> "(5) POWERS. Except as elsewhere in the statutes specifically provided, the council shall have the management and control of the city property, finances, highways, navigable waters, and the public service, *and shall have power to act for the government and good order of the city, for its commercial benefit, and for the health, safety, and welfare of the public,* and may carry out its powers by license, regulation, suppression, borrowing of money, *tax levy,* appropriation, fine, imprisonment, confiscation and other necessary or convenient means. The powers hereby conferred shall be in addition to all other grants, *and shall be limited only by express language."* Sec. 62.11, Stats. (emphasis supplied).

> "(5m) DISMISSALS AND REEMPLOYMENT. (a) When it *becomes necessary, because of need for economy, lack of work or funds,* or for other just causes, *to reduce the number of subordinates,* the emergency, special, temporary, part-time, or provisional subordinates, if any, shall be dismissed first, and thereafter subordinates shall be dismissed in the order of the shortest length of service in the department, provided that, in cities where a record of service rating has been established prior to January 1, 1933, for the said subordinates, the emergency, special, temporary, part-time provisional subordinates, if any, shall be dismissed first, and thereafter subordinates shall be dismissed in the order of the least efficient as shown by the said service rating." Sec. 62.13(5m)(a), Stats. (emphasis supplied).

This court has held that sec. 111.70 should be harmonized with existing statutes when possible, inasmuch as sec. 111.70 "is presumed to have been enacted with full knowledge of the pre-existing statutes and that construction should give each section force and effect." *Glendale Professional Policemen's Assoc. v. Glendale, supra,* citing *Muskego-Norway C.S.T.S.D. No. 9 v. WERB,* 35 Wis. 2d 540, 556, 151 N.W.2d 617 (1967). In fulfilling the exclusive judicial role of interpreting and harmonizing diverse statutes as ch. 62 and 111.70(1)(d), we adhere when possible to the express legislative policy stated in sec. 62.04, Stats.:

> "INTENT AND CONSTRUCTION. ... For the purpose of giving the cities the largest measure of self-government compatible with the constitution and general law, it is hereby declared that sections 62.01 to 62.26, inclusive, *shall be liberally construed in favor of the rights, powers, and privileges of cities to promote the general welfare, peace, good order and prosperity of such cities and the inhabitants thereof."* (emphasis supplied.)

Ch. 62 requires that the city of Brookfield and other municipalities possess the power to decide when a lay off is necessary in order to secure the policy objectives of the community's citizenry as spoken through the actions of its duly elected representatives. The residents of Brookfield through their elected representatives on the city council requested city budget reductions. Unquestionably, fewer firefighters will reduce the level and quality of services provided, but this is a policy decision by a community favoring a lower municipal tax base. Ch. 62 does not expressly prohibit the topic of economically motivated lay offs from becoming a permissive subject of collective bargaining, but the decision to discuss the topic at a bargaining table is a choice to be made by the electorate as expressed through its designated representatives and department heads.

This court's concern for the maintenance of the municipalities' political processes was forcefully stated in *Unified School Dist. No. 1 of Racine County v. WERC, supra* 81 Wis. 2d at 99-100, 259 N.W.2d at 730.

> "As a public body composed of elected officials, a school board is vested with governmental powers and has a responsibility to act for the public welfare. The United States Supreme Court recognized this responsibility in *Hortonville Jt. School Dist. No. 1 v. Hortonville Ed. Asso.,* 426 U.S. 482, 495, 496, 96 S. Ct. 2308, 49 L. Ed. 2d 1 (1976)....

The court recognizes that unions, such as Local 2051, are not powerless in their ability to formulate and influence the direction of public policy decisions. As demonstrated in this case, unions can and do attend public budget meetings and can and do lobby with legislative bodies and organize and motivate the general public regarding the union's position. The distribution of informational fliers, newsletters and media releases as well as the solicitation of prominent and influential speakers are but a few of the ways in which unions can and do have a significant impact on the political processes. Local 2051 exerted acceptable political pressures upon the Brookfield City Council to halt the lay offs resulting from the budget cut. To decide the issue to be a mandatory subject of bargaining would destroy the equal balance of power that insures the collective bargaining rights of the union and protects the rights of the general public to determine the quality and level of municipal services they consider vital. The legislature has made it clear that a budgetary lay off decision is not a subject of mandatory bargaining. If it were, the right of the public to voice its opinion would be restricted as to matters fundamentally relating to the community's safety, general welfare and budgetary management.

While not at issue in this case, we add that the trial court correctly determined that the issue as to the effects of the lay offs was a mandatory subject of bargaining. A reduction in the total work force caused by the economically motivated lay offs will affect the number of employees assigned to a particular shift and thus alter their individual fire fighting responsibilities. Therefore, there is a primary relation between the impact of the lay off decision and the working conditions of the remaining unit employees. Brookfield, after initially refusing to discuss the issue, made an offer to do so on January 15, 1973. We view with disfavor Local 2051's refusal to bargain the effect of the lay offs unless the five firefighters were returned to work and reimbursed for lost time.

In reaching our decision, we deem it important that the Brookfield City Council made the specific decision that the budget cuts would be implemented by personnel lay offs pursuant to its powers. Our decision does not reinstate the WERC ordered remedy of re-employment for the five laid off firefighters and reimbursement of back wages. Therefore, we do not reach the second issue of whether the award was reasonable and appropriate under the circumstances.

Judgment affirmed.

NOTES

1. In *Glendale Prof. Policemen's Ass'n v. City of Glendale,* 83 Wis. 2d 90, 264 N.W.2d 594 (1978), the Wisconsin Supreme Court was faced with the question of whether a promotion clause in a collective bargaining agreement covering police officers was valid in view of a statutory requirement that all subordinates within a police department be appointed by the police chief. In holding that the promotion clause was a mandatory subject of bargaining and therefore enforceable, the court noted that "[s]pecific contract provisions authorized by MERA must ... be harmonized with the preexisting statutory scheme." In this regard, the court observed that "[a] requirement that the chief promote the most senior qualified applicant merely restricts the discretion that would otherwise exist." The court did note, however, that the clause in question did not require the chief "to promote an unqualified person or a person determined solely by the union."

2. In *Board of Regents, State Univ. Sys.,* 4 FPER ¶ 4319 (Fla. PERC 1978), the Florida Commission held that group health insurance was a prohibited subject of bargaining for the university system since it was specifically covered by state law. In so ruling, the Commission stated:

It recognizes that the law has never required a party to do that which has been rendered impossible by statute.... Requiring the parties to bargain over a subject, knowing in advance that the product of such bargaining cannot lawfully be implemented, would be elevating form over substance. This the Commission will not do.

3. In *Fargo Educ. Ass'n v. Fargo Pub. Sch. Dist. No. 1,* 1979-80 PBC ¶ 36,979 (N.D. 1980), the court held that since the teacher bargaining law contained a provision which stated that nothing in the Act was intended to conflict with or diminish the powers, authority, duties and responsibilities vested in school boards by state law, courts could only mandate negotiations on "(1) salary, (2) hours, (3) formulation of an agreement, (4) binding arbitration, and (5) interpretation of an existing agreement." With respect to other matters that might relate directly or indirectly to terms and conditions of employment, the court stated that "[i]t is up to the parties to negotiate what the 'subjects of negotiation' will be." The court further observed that "[i]f none can be agreed upon, an impasse may be deemed to exist and the matter resolved by mediation, if agreed to, or the [statutory] fact-finding process may be utilized."

4. In *Rollins v. Board of Educ.,* 40 Ohio St. 3d 123, 1988-90 PBC ¶ 35,202 (1988), the Ohio Supreme Court upheld a provision contained in a collective bargaining agreement which added a new requirement in order to obtain tenure, i.e., the teacher's principal had to recommend the teacher for tenure. After noting that the tenure statute was "a teacher-protection statute and not a law pertaining to minimum educational requirements," the court, quoting from a prior decision, ruled that the Ohio collective bargaining law "'was designed to free public employees from conflicting laws which may act to interfere with the newly established right to collectively bargain.'" The court stated:

> ... Collective bargaining is not a one-way street. We are not inclined to emasculate collective bargaining in public school employment. Unless a *minimum educational requirement* is at stake, one side cannot be released from the bargain while the other side is bound. By providing that the contract governs conditions of employment, the General Assembly has indicated its preference for enforcing those terms of an agreement which were arrived at through open negotiation at the bargaining table, regardless of which party is advantaged.

DETROIT POLICE OFFICERS ASSOCIATION v. CITY OF DETROIT
319 Mich. 44, 214 N.W.2d 803 (1974)

SWAINSON, JUSTICE. In 1965, the Legislature passed 1965 P.A. 379 which amended the Public Employment Relations Act (PERA) to allow public employees to select a collective bargaining representative and to enter into collective bargaining negotiations with their public employer. Pursuant to the newly amended PERA the Detroit Police Officers Association (DPOA) gained recognition as the exclusive collective bargaining agent for a unit of Detroit patrolmen and policewomen in January of 1966. Shortly thereafter, extensive collective bargaining negotiations proceeded between the City of Detroit (City) and the DPOA.

The collective bargaining negotiations continued until 1968 without resolving several areas of disagreement. The DPOA in July of 1968 filed an unfair labor practices charge with the Labor Mediation Board, later redesignated the Michigan Employment Relations Commission, (MERC) alleging that the City had refused to bargain in good faith on key issues. A hearing was held and MERC issued a Decision and Order on March 18, 1971 addressing the issues raised by the DPOA. *City of Detroit, Police Department,* 6 MERC Lab. Op. 237 (1971). The conclusions of MERC on the issues relevant to today's appeal can be summarized as follows: ...

3. The City erroneously refused to bargain on changes in the police retirement plan when it initiated and conducted a voter referendum to amend the City Charter provisions controlling the police retirement plan. MERC ordered,

on this issue, "that the City of Detroit shall not require as a condition to any agreement reached regarding retirement provisions for police officers that [such agreement] be approved by a vote of the electorate." ...

[The issue is as follows:]

Does the City have a duty under PERA to bargain in good faith with the DPOA on the subject of police retirement plan changes where retirement provisions are a part of the City Charter and amendable only by a popular vote of the electorate? ...

... We summarily find that MERC was correct in holding that changes in the police retirement plan are mandatory subjects of bargaining. Our primary inquiry, then, must be to determine if the incorporation of the retirement provisions into the City Charter obviates the duty under PERA to bargain in good faith over a mandatory subject of bargaining. Secondarily, we must determine if the City committed an unfair labor practice in 1968 by unilaterally submitting a retirement plan amendment to the electorate and thereby foreclosing bargaining.

To briefly answer the City's argument that retirement provisions are not a mandatory subject of bargaining, we cite the leading federal case of *Inland Steel Co. v. NLRB,* 77 NLRB 1; 21 LRRM 1310, *enforced* 170 F.2d 247 (CA 7, 1948), *cert. den.,* 336 U.S. 960, 69 S. Ct. 887, 93 L.Ed. 1112 (1949), which has firmly established that pension and retirement provisions are mandatory subjects of bargaining under the NLRA. We see no reason to deviate from this well-reasoned and long-established federal precedent in interpreting PERA. As we have discussed above, the scope of bargaining under PERA is patterned after that found under the NLRA. Consequently, we deem that the Legislature intended the courts to view the federal labor case law as persuasive precedent.

Turning to our primary inquiry in this second issue, we are confronted with what was accurately described in *Wayne County Civil Service Commission v. Board of Supervisors,* 384 Mich. 363, 367, 184 N.W.2d 201, 202 (1971), as "... that most difficult of all appellant problems; the ascertainment of legislative intent where there is no evidentiary or other reasonably authoritative guide to pertinent meaning or purpose of the legislators." On the one hand the Legislature has adopted PERA which, as we have explained above, foreseeably placed retirement plan issues on the collective bargaining table. On the other hand, it has allowed cities under the Home Rule Cities Act to incorporate the substance of their retirement plans into their city charters and to make those plans amendable only by a popular vote.

A statutory conflict would result if we were to accept the arguments of all parties to this appeal. The City argues that its present retirement plan was placed in the City Charter pursuant to the authority of M.C.L.A. §§ 117.4i, 117.4j; M.S.A. §§ 5.2082, 5.2083, of the Home Rule Cities Act; furthermore, that under the Act the City may not change any aspect of the retirement plan without first seeking voter approval. The DPOA and MERC argue that sections 11 and 15 of PERA require uninhibited collective bargaining between the employees' representative and the public employer; and, if voter approval is required to effect a change in a mandatory subject of bargaining, the collective bargaining process would be impeded. If the positions of all parties were accepted, we would face direct conflict between that which the City contends the

Legislature intended under the Home Rule Cities Act and that which MERC and the DPOA contend that the Legislature intended under PERA and we would be required to determine which state statute should prevail and which would be impliedly repealed.

After closely examining the statutes, however, we find that no such conflict in state law is present and that the statutes can be reconciled and a purpose found to be served by each. While we agree with the DPOA and MERC that PERA contemplates open negotiations between the parties unless controlled by a specific state law, we disagree with the contentions of the City that the Home Rule Cities Act requires voter approval for changes in the substantive details of the retirement plan.

The Home Rule Cities Act was originally enacted in 1909 (P.A. 279) under authority of the Constitution of 1908. The Act has been modified by various amendments over the years, but it has continued to reflect the position now expressed in Const. 1963, art. 7, § 22 that Michigan is a strong home rule state with basic local authority. The Home Rule Cities Act itself appropriately contains very little substance that the cities must include in their governing document — the city charter. In essential part the Act is enabling legislation that permits the cities to mold local government to the needs of the local populace.

Retirement plans are a "permissible charter provision" adoptable under the broad grant of authority bound in M.C.L.A. §§ 117.4i and 117.4j; M.S.A. §§ 5.2082 and 5.2083 of the Home Rule Cities Act. Nowhere in the Home Rule Cities Act is there a requirement that the charter contain more than a general grant and outline of authority to a city government to implement and maintain a retirement plan. When the City placed the complete detail of its police retirement plan into the City Charter it went beyond the requirement of state law as set forth in the Home Rule Cities Act.

The distinction between incorporating the general outline of the retirement plan and incorporating the total detail of such a plan into the City Charter controls our present analysis. The Home Rule Cities Act, a state law, requires only that the charter grant to the city government the authority to institute and maintain a retirement plan. The substantive details of a retirement plan, such as those now a part of the Detroit City Charter, are contractual and charter provisions only and do not rise to the stature of a state law requirement as the City would have us hold. Accordingly since the substantive details of the retirement plan may be classified only as contractual or charter provisions, they are subject to the duty to bargain found in PERA — a state law. Such an outcome comports with M.C.L.A. § 117.36; M.S.A. § 5.2116 of the Home Rule Cities Act which states:

"No provision of any city charter shall conflict with or contravene the provisions of any general law of the state."

See also, *Geftos v. Lincoln Park*, 39 Mich. App. 644, 654, 198 N.W.2d 169 (1972); *Local Union No. 876, International Brotherhood of Electrical Workers v. State Labor Mediation Board*, supra.

To summarize, the Home Rule Cities Act does not require that the substantive terms of pension plans be voter approved. In this important respect it does not conflict with PERA. The Home Rule Cities Act and PERA can be easily harmonized by reading the Home Rule Cities Act to empower a city to set up the procedures for its pension plan in the charter and to leave the substantive terms of the plan to collective negotiation. We therefore follow the most basic tenet of statutory construction and construe these two independent acts of the Legislature to be consistent with each other.

This statutory analysis fits well with the will of the voters of the City of Detroit as expressed through their adoption of a new City Charter on November 6, 1973 to become effective July 1, 1974. Under Article 11 of the new City Charter only the broad outline of the "retirement plan" is included in the charter with the substantive terms and changes in the plan left to city ordinance. We quote in part from Article 11:

> "11-101(1) The city shall provide, by ordinance, for the establishment and maintenance of retirement plan coverage for city employees....
> "11-102 The retirement plans of the City existing when this charter takes effect, including the existing governing bodies for administering the plan, the benefit schedules for those plans, and the terms for accruing rights to and receiving benefits under those plans shall, in all respects, continue in existence exactly as before until changed by ordinance in accordance with this article."

This change in the method for dealing with police retirement plans is more than coincidental. The commentary accompanying Article 11 expresses the view that this more flexible system of retirement plan change was proposed to meet the requirements of collective bargaining. We quote:

> "The detail contained in chapters 5, 6 and 7 of title 9 of the present charter, dealing with the City's retirement systems, has been eliminated from the new charter.
> "The security of City employees' accrued rights and benefits is in no way dependent upon detailed language in the charter. The employees' best protection is article 9, section 24 of the 1963 Michigan constitution....
> "Thus, the new charter, despite the great reduction in the number of words used, makes no change in the existing rights of active and retired City employees. It does, however, permit the benefit schedules of retirement plans to be changed by ordinance, thereby creating a more flexible system for implementing any agreement concerning retirement benefits resulting from the City's legal obligation to bargain collectively with its employees."

The Detroit electorate, in effect, adopted the new City Charter with the intention of facilitating the collective bargaining process.

Before leaving this portion of the retirement issues, we desire to comment upon Const. 1963, art. 9, § 24 which states in part:

> "The accrued financial benefits of each pension plan and retirement system of the state and its political subdivisions shall be a contractual obligation thereof and shall not be diminished or impaired thereby.
> "Financial benefits arising on account of service rendered in each fiscal year shall be funded during that year and such funding shall not be used for financing unfunded accrued liabilities."

With this paramount law of the state as a protection, those already covered by a pension plan are assured that their benefits will not be diminished by future collective bargaining agreements.

Although we agree with MERC that the City had the duty to bargain over changes in the police retirement plan, we will not grant enforcement of the MERC order to bargain. See p. 807, *supra*. Prior to today's opinion there has been no clear statement by this Court regarding the scope of the duty to bargain under PERA. Under today's holding and the mandate of the City's voters as expressed in Article 11 of the new City Charter, the City will be required to bargain over prospective changes in the police retirement and pension plan. We find this to be an equitable result.

NOTES

1. In *Pontiac Police Officers Ass'n v. City of Pontiac*, 397 Mich. 674, 246 N.W.2d 831, 94 L.R.R.M. 2175 (1976), the Michigan Supreme Court held that even though a city charter provided for a civilian review board to handle citizen complaints with respect to police officers, the subject of a civilian review board is a mandatory subject of bargaining and "that a public employer's collective bargaining obligation prevails over a conflicting 'permissible charter provision.' "

2. Are the various public sector labor relations acts applicable to both the executive and legislative branches of government? This question was raised in a case before the Pennsylvania Labor Relations Board in which the City of Pittsburgh was alleged to have committed an unfair labor practice by subcontracting the work of five meter collectors. *PLRB v. City of Pittsburgh*, 3 PPER 241 (Pa. LRB 1973). Although the Board held that the subcontracting of work which affects bargaining unit employees is a mandatory subject of bargaining, the Board nevertheless held that the unilateral action of the City Council did not violate Act 195. The Board stated:

> The Act consistently indicates and the legislature, it would appear, intended a separation between the executive and legislative branches of the public employer in the operation and application of the act. Unstated, but existing by the very nature of state government, the act exists and remains in existence at the sufferance of the legislature. Certainly an act which is a creature of the legislature cannot restrict or limit legislative discretion in matters of budget, services offered, or services withheld. The act can and does regulate the relationship between the executive branch of government and the States' employees....
>
> The foregoing can only lead to the conclusion that where the executive and legislative branches of the government (whether state or any subdivision thereof) are separate entities, the legislative branch in its considerations and application of its legislative duties cannot be bound by the application of Act 195 which regulates the conduct of the public employer acting in its executive capacity. Thus, the charge of a violation under Section 1201 (a) (5), refusing to bargain cannot be sustained against the Employer, the City of Pittsburgh.

Can the decision of the PLRB be squared with the decision of the Michigan Supreme Court in the principal case?

3. In providing financial assistance to state and local governments Congress frequently specifies certain conditions which must be met as a condition precedent to receiving such assistance. For example, in authorizing the Surgeon General to "make grants to State, health or mental health authorities to assist the States in establishing and maintaining adequate public health services," Congress stipulated that a state must submit a plan which must, inter alia,

Provide such methods of administration (including methods relating to the establishment and maintenance of personnel standards on a merit basis, except that the Surgeon General shall exercise no authority with respect to the selection, tenure of office, and compensation of any individual employed in accordance with such methods) as are found by the Surgeon General to be necessary for the proper and efficient operation of the plan.

42 U.S.C. § 246(a)(2)(F) (1982). To what extent does such a statutory provision affect the scope of bargaining?

The Urban Mass Transportation Act of 1964 provides for grants to states and local agencies for the purpose, among others, of acquiring privately operated transit facilities. As a condition precedent to receiving such a grant, however, the Act requires that there be "fair and equitable arrangements ..., as determined by the Secretary of Labor, to protect the interest of employees affected by such assistance." Among the protective arrangements which must be provided for is "the continuation of collective bargaining rights." Urban Mass Transportation Act § 13(c), 49 U.S.C. § 1609(c) (1976). What effect, if any, does this statutory provision have on the interpretation or application of a public sector bargaining statute which provides for a narrower scope of bargaining than that allowed under the National Labor Relations Act? Would the state act apply? See *Regional Transp. Dist., Inc. v. Local Div. 282 of Amalgamated Transit Union,* 316 N.Y.S.2d 325, 64 Misc. 2d 865 (1970).

4. In Advisory Commission on Intergovernmental Relations, Labor-Management Policies for State and Local Government 111 (1969), the following recommendation is made:

Having assessed [the] various facets of present and potential federal mandating and recognizing that further intervention is quite possible, the Commission adopts the general position that Congress should refrain from any additional mandating of requirements related to the working conditions of State and local employees or the authority of these governments to deal with their personnel in whatever fashion they see fit.

5. EFFECT OF BUDGETARY PROCESS

D. STANLEY, MANAGING LOCAL GOVERNMENT UNDER UNION PRESSURE 112, 115-19 (1972)*

Local government employee unions have added new stresses to the already difficult financial situation of these governments but have not basically altered the budget and finance processes. Department heads still prepare preliminary estimates of expenditures. Budget and finance officers organize and adjust the requests of department heads and estimate available revenues. Chief executives make "final" decisions on the budget to be submitted to the legislative body, and the latter holds hearings, approves the budget, and sets tax rates. All this is familiar. What the unions have done is to assume a greatly strengthened and highly visible role in decisions that ultimately have a major impact on the size of the budget. Their political and emotional effect is heightened by the fact that the larger local governments are generally either in or approaching a condition of financial crisis....

In [the] nineteen localities [studied], as in most fair-sized local governments, budget preparation begins about six months before the start of the new fiscal year when the budget office sends to the various department heads instructions on the format and schedule to be followed in preparing estimates. Departments may or may not be told how rigorously to economize or what programs to emphasize as they look ahead. Generally using the current budget figures as a base, department heads make their estimates, often in consultation with a member of the budget staff. Where it is feasible they use workload figures, past and estimated, to back up their calculations — numbers of fires, miles of streets, cubic yards of rubbish. The department heads do not consult unions at this time and are influenced by union pressures only to the extent that previous union-sponsored changes in work rules or pay provisions have changed the expense outlook. Meanwhile the budget office (or the finance staff if it is a separate organization) is estimating expected revenues. Then both revenue and expenditure sheets go to the chief executive, who, aided by the budge and finance staff, must trim the expense estimates, or plan to seek extra revenues, or both, in order to balance his budget before it goes to the legislative body.

In the days before the unions acquired collective bargaining rights, this budget process readily accommodated changes in pay and benefits. Modifications were proposed by the personnel office or civil service commission, approved by the budget office and chief executive, and ultimately enacted by the legislative body. They were kept within anticipated financial resources and were usually timed to begin at the start of the next fiscal year. In the present era of collective bargaining, even though most of the budget process is unrelated to union activities, the schedule has become less controllable for three reasons. First, the bargaining process is time-consuming. Second, unions may adopt a strategy that calls for bargaining to reach a climax at the time the legislative body is considering the budget. Third, the results of bargaining may require new financing measures involving further legislation locally, or a referendum, or action by the state legislature. However, in situations where there is a multi-year union agreement, without pay reopener provisions, such problems are spaced out and therefore less troublesome.

Cities in New York State (including, among those studied, Binghamton and Buffalo but not New York City) are expected to be kept on schedule by the Taylor Law, which provides that negotiations, including mediation and fact finding, must be concluded sixteen [sic] days before the budget is submitted to the local legislative body.[17] Despite the law, Buffalo ran late in 1968. That city's charter requires the mayor to submit the budget to the council by May 1 for adoption by June 1. However, when the 1968 union negotiations (the first under the law) had not been completed by June 1, the city had to include a lump-sum "salary adjustment fund" in the budget to cover the estimated costs of the union settlements.

---

[17] New York, Public Employees' Fair Employment Act of 1967, sec. 209, as amended, March 4, 1969. Section 212 of the law exempts New York City from this requirement.

Several of the cities and counties in other states try to complete bargaining before legislative body starts work on the budget. Hartford has been successful thus far in concluding negotiations well before the budget is closed, even though state law permits bargaining to run on beyond that time. The city aims to finish bargaining by January 1 and to pass the budget in February; the fiscal year begins April 1. Still another method was found in Detroit, where pay discussions are part of the budget process and separate from union negotiations on other matters. Pay settlements there are not included in agreements, but are recommended by the mayor to the common council along with the budget.

Two governments, Dade County and Philadelphia, bargain while the legislative body has the budget under review but before it completes action.

In a still later category are cities and counties where bargaining continues even after the budget is adopted. This means that if the budget does not contain enough funds to finance the agreement, additional revenues must be obtained. Boston, Dayton, New Castle County, and New York have all been in the position of concluding agreements after the budget has been decided. Boston lacks a fixed schedule for both budget submissions and bargaining. Although the fiscal year there begins in January, departmental estimates trickle in until April, when a supplementary budget request based on bargaining settlements is submitted to the city council. The tax rate is set the following July. New York City's scores of agreements are concluded at different times of the year (usually January or July) and vary in their duration; hence it is virtually impossible to budget realistically for bargaining settlements. Budgeting and bargaining have become two very separate operations.

Turning to the four governments that do not have general collective bargaining, in Los Angeles County, New Orleans, and San Francisco the personnel authorities recommend salaries and benefits for consideration by the legislative bodies before budgets are adopted. St. Louis has found it necessary in the past to consider the salary demands of the unions after the budget is adopted. However, tentative agreement has now been reached between the city and four unions to conduct annual negotiating sessions *before* the budget is drafted.

Reconciling the budget schedule with the bargaining schedule is an annual problem where the agreements are for one year only. Elsewhere these coordination problems have to be faced only in the years when agreements are up for renewal.

What Timing is Best?

Financial management is obviously more efficient when negotiations are finished before the budget goes to the legislature. Under such circumstances the executive branch has considered the unions' demands along with other spending needs and with estimated revenues, reconciled any problems, and prepared a budget package that is fully ready for legislative action. This is hard to achieve for reasons already stated: slow bargaining, union strategies, and authorization of supplementary financing. The experience of the governments studied here suggests that bargaining results can feasibly go to the legislative body *after* it has begun work on the budget. It is even possible for bargaining to be completed after the budget has been approved by the legislature. In either event the budget process becomes more protracted, less businesslike, and less controllable from a management standpoint. The city council may have to enact supplementary appropriations and new revenue measures after the start of the new fiscal period.

Several of the governments studied have adapted themselves to these difficulties. The problems perhaps would be lessened if elected officials, citizens' groups, and the news media brought pressure for timely conclusion of bargaining. The union members too would like to have their uncertainties ended sooner — but not at the cost of lower settlements. It seems inevitable on the whole that rigid bargaining schedules to meet budget deadlines will be viewed with more nostalgia than respect. Delayed and revised budgets are inconvenient and stressful for executives and staffs and are more difficult for citizens to understand, but they can be expected to continue, and local governments will make the necessary adaptions.

Reserves For Settlements

Representatives of all the cities and counties, regardless of their budget schedules, were asked if they budgeted any "cushions" (contingency funds) or if they "hid" any money to pay for union settlements that were higher than they had anticipated. A majority of the governments studied answered in the negative. Buffalo, Hartford, Milwaukee, and New Castle County all reported that they use the contingency funds for this purpose. One other county and three cities, whose identity will not be disclosed, candidly said that they "hid" money in the estimates for various departments. The former method (use of an earmarked fund) is risky. It may become a "sitting duck" for legislators who want to eliminate it or use it for another purpose; or it may become a target for bargaining demands — unions may ask for the total amount and more too. Cincinnati operates under another method, financing settlements out of an "income tax permanent improvement fund," which receives income tax revenues that exceed estimates. The city manager commits part of the fund to capital improvement projects, but it is difficult for the unions to find out how much is uncommitted, thus giving the city some bargaining leeway.

NOTES

1. The impact of bargaining on the budgetary process and on public finance is explored in Hays, *Collective Bargaining and the Budget Director,* in Public Workers and Public Unions 89 (S. Zagoria ed. 1972).

2. Concerning the impact of bargaining on municipal pay plans, Kenneth O. Warner, then Executive Director of the Public Personnel Association, stated:

> The traditional approach to pay plans may have to be tossed out the window. With bargaining there is a good chance that the tidy, systematic, integrated pay plan — designed to give equitable treatment to all employees in a given jurisdiction — will undergo considerable change. The 64-dollar question is how do you maintain fairness and equity when many unions bargain for wages in several different units of an organization. It should be noted that union representatives argue that anything would be an improvement over what now exists. The reason: Pay administration is not really scientific.

Warner, *Financial Implications of Employee Bargaining in the Public Service,* in Sorry ... No Government Today 189, 197 (R. Walsh ed. 1969)

3. Several of the comprehensive public sector collective bargaining statutes contain impasse procedures which are specifically geared to the budget submission date and contemplate that collective bargaining will be concluded prior to said date. Suppose a union is recognized or certified as a bargaining representative subsequent to the budget submission date and the unions requests that the public employer negotiate over wages and fringe benefits for the year covered by the budget. If the public employer refused to negotiate on the ground that the budget submission date had already passed, would it be committing an unfair labor practice? In *Ligonier Valley Sch. Dist.,* 2 PPER 159 (Pa. LRB 1972), the Pennsylvania Labor Relations Board held that an employer had a duty to bargain even though the budget submission date had passed. Cf. *Town of New Canaan,* Decision No. 828 (Conn. SLRB 1968).

In *Garden City Educators' Ass'n v. Vance,* 224 Kan. 732, 585 P.2d 1057 (1978), the court held that negotiations could not be halted prior to exhaustion of the impasse resolution procedures even though this would extend beyond the employer's budget submission date. Although the court recognized that "the issue of salary is the most often disputed item in negotiations," it noted "that redistribution of monies along line items is a common practice in school districts" and that "[t]o the extent of the flexibility of the budget, the issue of salaries of teachers continues to be a negotiable item." This decision should be contrasted with the decision of the Supreme Court of Iowa in *City of Des Moines v. PERB,* 269 N.W.2d 446 (Iowa 1979), in which the court held that the budget submission date for Iowa's political subdivisions constitutes the termination date for all mandated statutory impasse procedures. In giving considerable deference to the statutory budget submission date, the court stated:

> A construction of the Act which failed to recognize the certified budget submission date as a mandatory cutoff for impasse procedures would be inimical to the purpose of the Act. Such a construction would make it impossible for a political subdivision to deal effectively with its duty to formulate a budget and carry out is provisions. The year-round bargaining which could result would only detract from the effective and orderly delivery of governmental services by political subdivisions.

In *Public Emps. Local 71 v. State,* 775 P.2d 1062 (Alaska 1989), the Alaska Supreme Court, in affirming the State Labor Relations Agency dismissal of an unfair labor practice charge alleging a refusal to bargain in good faith, held that the legislature's failure to fund the third year of a collective bargaining agreement was not an unfair labor practice. The court ruled that the monetary terms of a collective bargaining agreement are not effective until the legislature appropriates the necessary funds and that such terms are subject to annual approval by the legislature. Moreover, the court held that the Governor had not refused to bargain in good faith since he had requested funding for the negotiated third-year wage increases.

C. ELEMENTS OF GOOD FAITH BARGAINING

1. GENERALLY

WEST HARTFORD EDUCATION ASSOCIATION v. DECOURCY

162 Conn. 566, 295 A.2d 526 (1972)

RYAN, ASSOCIATE JUSTICE: .... Since [the court has ruled that class size, teacher load, the assignment to and compensation for extracurricular activities, and the submission of grievances to binding arbitration were mandatory subjects of bargaining], the parties ask us to decide whether or not the board violated its duty to negotiate with the plaintiff by: (i) Not making counter-proposals on those topics, or (ii) taking the position that such matters be reserved for unilateral decision by the board, or (iii) taking the position that such matters be included in the "board prerogatives" clause of the contract.

Section 10-153d requires the board to "confer in good faith with respect to salaries and other conditions of employment, or the negotiation of an agreement, or any question arising thereunder and the execution of a written contract incorporating any agreement reached if requested by either party, but such obligation shall not compel either party to agree to a proposal or require the making of a concession." This language is almost identical to the corresponding portion of the National Labor Relations Act.

The duty to negotiate in good faith generally has been defined as an obligation to participate actively in deliberations so as to indicate a present intention to find a basis for agreement. *N.L.R.B. v. Montgomery Ward & Co.,* 133 F.2d 676, 686 (9th Cir.). Not only must the employer have an open mind and a sincere desire to reach an agreement but a sincere effort must be made to reach a common ground. *Ibid.*

This duty does not require an employer to agree to a proposal or require the making of a concession. The National Labor Relations Board has interpreted this provision as freeing an employer from any duty to make counterproposals in the form of concessions, so that the failure to make counterproposals is not a per se violation of the act, but must be tested against the usual standard of good faith. *N.L.R.B. v. Arkansas Rice Growers Assn.,* 400 F.2d 565, 571 (8th Cir.). The answer to question (b)(i) is "No." The board of education does not violate its duty to negotiate by refusing to make counterproposals on the mandatory subjects listed in question (a) as long as it is negotiating in good faith.

Questions (b)(ii) and (b)(iii) should be discussed together. Question (b)(ii) is somewhat vague because there are insufficient facts contained in the stipulation to indicate what is meant by reserving matters for the "unilateral action of the board." If the conduct of the board amounted to a complete refusal to negotiate with the teachers' representatives on mandatory subjects of bargaining, such conduct would, of course, constitute a violation of its statutory duty to negotiate. On the other hand, the board's insistence on a broad "board prerogatives clause," or as it is referred to in nonpublic labor relations cases, a "management rights clause," would not constitute a per se violation of § 10-153d. In *N.L.R.B. v. American National Ins. Co.,* 343 U.S. 395, the Supreme Court of the United States held that employer-bargaining for a clause under which management retains the exclusive right to control what certain conditions of employment will be does not amount to conduct which constitutes a refusal to bargain per se, nor does it alone demonstrate a lack of good faith. In effect, the court was saying that this type of provision is itself a condition of employment, and a mandatory subject of collective bargaining. *Long Lake Lumber Co.,* 185 N.L.R.B., No. 65, 74 L.R.R.M. 1116.

"While it is well established that an employer's insistence upon a management rights clause does not itself violate ... [the act], the nature of the employer's proposals on management's rights ... are material factors in assessing its motivations in approaching negotiations." *Stuart Radiator Core Mfg. Co.,* 173 N.L.R.B., No. 27, 69 L.R.R.M. 1243. Thus, if the employer insisted on retaining for himself absolute unilateral control over wages, hours and other conditions of employment in effect requiring the union to waive practically all of its statutory rights his good faith is suspect. *Stuart Radiator Core Mfg. Co., supra; I.T.T. Corporation, Henze Valve Service Division,* 166 N.L.R.B. No. 65, 65 L.R.R.M. 1654; *East Texas Steel Castings,* 154 N.L.R.B., No. 94, 60 L.R.R.M. 1097; *"M" System, Inc.,* 129 N.L.R.B., No. 64, 47 L.R.R.M. 1017; *Dixie Corporation,* 105 N.L.R.B., No. 49, 32 L.R.R.M. 1259. Where the subject of a dispute is a mandatory bargaining point adamant insistence on a bargaining position is not necessarily a refusal to bargain in good faith. *N.L.R.B. v. Wooster Division, Borg-Warner Corporation,* 356 U.S. 342, 349. To determine the question of good faith the totality of the parties' conduct throughout the negotiations must be considered. *N.L.R.B. v. Alva Allen Industries, Inc.,* 369 F.2d 310, 321 (8th Cir.); *New Canaan v. Connecticut State Board of Labor Relations,* 160 Conn. 285, 293, 278 A.2d 761.

Questions (b)(ii) and (b)(iii) cannot be answered categorically.

Question (c)

The issue in this question is the extent to which the school board may communicate with its teachers about salaries and other conditions of employment while collective bargaining negotiations are being conducted. Section 10-153d makes it unlawful for the board to interfere with, restrain or coerce employees in the exercise of their rights under the Teacher Negotiation Act. A similar prohibition appears in the National Labor Relations Act, 29 U.S.C. § 158(a)(1) which makes it an unfair labor practice to interfere with, restrain or coerce employees who seek to pursue their rights under that act. Thus, we can again turn to cases arising under the federal act for guidance.

The National Labor Relations Act makes it an employer's duty to bargain collectively with the chosen representatives of his employees, and since this obligation is exclusive, it exacts the negative duty to treat with no other. *Medo Photo Supply Corporation v. N.L.R.B.,* 321 U.S. 678; *International Ladies' Garment Workers' Union v. N.L.R.B.,* 108 U.S. App. D.C. 68, 280 F.2d 616, aff'd, 366 U.S. 731. After a duly authorized collective bargaining representative has been selected, the employer cannot negotiate wages or other terms of employment with individual workers. *Medo Photo Supply Corporation v. N.L.R.B., supra, 321 U.S. 684; N.L.R.B. v. United States Sonics Corporation,* 312 F.2d 610 (1st Cir.). Thus, an employer interferes with his employees' right to bargain collectively in violation of 29 U.S.C. § 158(a)(1) when he treats directly with employees and grants them a wage increase in return for their promise to repudiate the union which they have designated as their representative. *N.L.R.B. v. Katz,* 369 U.S. 736. The statutory obligation thus imposed is to deal with the employees through the union rather than dealing with the union through the employees. Attempts to bypass the representative may be considered evidence of bad faith in the duty to bargain. The conduct proscribed in the *Medo* case was direct negotiation with the employees and bypassing the union. The act does not prohibit an employer from communicating in noncoercive terms with his employees while collective negotiations are in progress. *Proctor &*

Gamble Mfg. Co., 160 N.L.R.B., No. 36, 62 L.R.R.M. 1617. The element of negotiation is critical. Another crucial factor in these cases is whether or not the communication is designed to undermine and denigrate the union. *Flambeau Plastics Corporation v. N.L.R.B.,* 401 F.2d 128 (7th Cir.), *cert. denied,* 393 U.S. 1019.

The question in the present case is whether the defendant Richter was engaging in direct negotiation with teachers offering something in return for a consideration, dealing with them in a manner calculated to subvert the union, or merely communicating with them without interfering, restraining or coercing them.

The first situation occurred in March, 1969, while negotiations between the parties were continuing. During that month the defendant board proposed a new work year, vacation schedule and salary schedule for department chairmen, coordinating teachers and subject area specialists. The program involved a substantially different length of work day, length of work year and a salary schedule for the personnel involved, and was to take effect July 1, 1969. Before this program was presented to the plaintiff association the defendant Richter called special meetings on March 5 and 6, 1969, and discussed the plan directly with the staff members who would be affected.

It is proper for an employer to discuss his proposals with his employees and to defend his position. *Tobasco Prestressed Concrete Co.,* 177 N.L.R.B., No. 101, 71 L.R.R.M. 1565. Moreover, it is permissible for an employer to discuss certain items with his employees before he presents them to the union. In *Little Rock Downtowner, Inc.,* 168 N.L.R.B., No. 107, 66 L.R.R.M. 1267, an employer had discussed with two employees the possibility of giving them additional duties and additional compensation before any proposal had been made at the bargaining table. The board found that the communication was for the purpose of exchanging ideas and did not constitute negotiation or a violation of the act where the employees understood that the matter would be determined between the employer and the union at the bargaining table.

The law as to attempts to negotiate with employees for the purpose of bypassing or denigrating the union is clear. On this very limited stipulation of facts, however, we cannot conclude that communicating to these special employees some of the details of a new program was unlawful. There is nothing to indicate that the defendant Richter was engaged in negotiations with the teachers nor that this was an attempt to bypass or subvert the union. The proposed new program was discussed later at the bargaining table with the union.

The plaintiff next alleges that the defendant board violated § 10-153d by communicating directly with the teachers concerning the "resource teacher program." On February 13, 1970, during negotiations, the board proposed that the teaching staff be differentiated into two groups, one working more days and more hours per day than heretofore and the other group continuing to work the same days and hours as in the past. This became known as the "extended plan" or "resource teacher program." Despite failure to reach accord on the working conditions of this plan, the board adopted a resolution resolving to implement the program and directing the superintendent to solicit the advice of the plaintiff association and of individual teachers in order to develop a tentative guide for this position. On April 6, 1970, the defendant Richter, acting as superintendent and with the knowledge and assent of the defendant board, informed the entire teaching staff of the West Hartford school system of the adoption of said resolution by distributing copies of it in the Staff Bulletin.

The defendants contend that this conduct on the part of the board and the defendant Richter did not violate the law because the board was merely implementing a policy decision to employ certain personnel as resource teachers. The decision to create a new type of position is a matter which goes to the heart of educational policy. It is true that the salary and working conditions of the resource teachers were mandatory subjects of negotiation, and these matters were actually being negotiated between the plaintiff and the defendants. The adoption of the resolution in question and the communication of this to the teachers and to the plaintiff association did not involve direct negotiations with employees on mandatory subjects of negotiation nor can it be construed as an attempt to bypass the union.

The answer to question (c) is "No."

Question (d)

The final question presented in this case involves the legality of the board of education's unilateral implementation of their contract proposals after the parties had failed to reach agreement on them. The particular proposals which the board put into effect were those dealing with the salary and working conditions of department chairmen, coordinating teachers and subject area specialists for the school year 1969-70. Contrary to the claims of the plaintiff the stipulated facts do not indicate that the proposals involving the extended program or resource teacher program, first made on February 13, 1970, were "implemented." We have no occasion, therefore, to discuss the subject under question (d).

The duty to bargain under the National Labor Relations Act is similar to the duty to negotiate that is created by our Teacher Negotiation Act. A breach of this duty in the federal area is deemed a refusal to bargain and an unfair labor practice under § 158(a)(5). It is a fundamental tenet of the federal labor law that an employer who unilaterally changes wages and other working conditions which are under negotiation commits a § 158(a)(5) unfair labor practice. *N.L.R.B. v. Katz*, 369 U.S. 736, 743. The employer who engages in such conduct circumvents his duty to deal exclusively with the union and is refusing to bargain in fact with the employee organization. *Id.*, 743.

The defendants contend that there was a legally cognizable impasse in negotiations over these topics such that it had the right to put its plans into operation. There is no acid test for determining whether or not an impasse exists. *N.L.R.B. v. Tex-Tan, Inc.*, 318 F.2d 472 (5th Cir.), describes it as a state of facts in which the parties, despite the best of faith, are simply deadlocked. In most cases, the National Labor Relations Board and the courts have looked at the fact pattern for certain indicia of impasse. Have the parties stopped talking? How many bargaining sessions were held? Have the positions become solidified and the parties intransigent? Was a mediator called in? See *American Ship Building Co. v. N.L.R.B.*, 380 U.S. 300; 44 Tex. L. Rev. 769. Here, although the stipulated facts reveal that the parties had negotiated but were unable to agree on the topics in question, we note that both sides remained at the bargaining table and continued to negotiate on a wide range of topics. Neither party expressed a desire to terminate these discussions. Moreover, the record indicates that mediation was not requested until after the board had suggested implementation of its proposals. It would appear that at this point the parties believed that a continuation of discussions might be fruitful. On this limited statement of facts, we cannot conclude that the parties were "simply deadlocked." *Newspaper Drivers & Handlers', Local No. 372 v. N.L.R.B.,* 404 F.2d 1159 (6th Cir.).

The defendants, however, claim that impasse may exist with reference to a particular issue, and, even though the parties are still negotiating about other topics, the deadlock on the individual issue permits the board to implement its last proposal thereon. This claim is inaccurate. The relevant federal cases deal with the situation where the inability to resolve one or two key issues creates a general impasse, and, despite agreement or willingness to talk about other subjects, it is apparent that further negotiations would not produce a broad meeting of the minds. *American Federation of Television & Radio Artists v. N.L.R.B.,* 129 U.S. App. D.C. 399, 395 F.2d 622; *Dallas General Drivers, Local No. 745 v. N.L.R.B.,* 122 U.S. App. D.C. 417, 355 F.2d 842; *N.L.R.B. v. Intercoastal Terminal, Inc.,* 286 F.2d 954 (5th Cir.). "It cannot be doubted that a deadlock on one critical issue can create as impassable a situation as an inability to agree on several or all issues." *American Federation of Television & Radio Artists v. N.L.R.B., supra,* 395 F.2d 627 n.13. Some bargaining may go on even though the parties are unable to agree on many topics. But, only if the deadlock on the critical issue demonstrates that there is no realistic possibility that further discussions would be fruitful in bringing the parties together generally on salaries and other conditions of employment, can we conclude that there is an impasse.

Even though an impasse had not been reached, however, it does not follow on the facts in the present case that the defendants were in violation of the statute. While *N.L.R.B. v. Katz, supra,* holds "that an employer's unilateral change in conditions of employment under negotiation is … a violation of § 8(a)(5)," because it is circumvention of the duty to negotiate, the court did, however, note that circumstances might justify unilateral employer action. The language of the court, 369 U.S. on page 745, is significant: "Of course there is no resemblance between the situation wherein an employer, after notice and consultation, 'unilaterally' institutes a wage increase identical with one which the union has rejected as too low. See *National Labor Relations Board v. Bradley Washfountain Co.,* 192 F.2d 144, 150-152 [7th Cir.]; *National Labor Relations Board v. Landis Tool Co.,* 193 F.2d 279 [3d Cir.]." In the *Bradley Washfountain* case, the employer, before an impasse had been reached, after notice and consultation with the union, unilaterally instituted a wage increase identical to the one which the union had rejected as too low, it was held that the employer did not violate the statute.

In the case at bar the defendant board, in March, 1969, proposed a new work year, vacation schedule and salary schedule for department chairmen, coordinating teachers and subject area specialists involving changes in work day, work year and salary schedules. During April, 1969, the parties negotiated but were unable to agree as to the salary and conditions of employment for these positions and neither party offered further proposals on these subjects. In May and

June, 1969, the defendant Richter with the approval of the board hired teachers to fill these positions on the basis of the salary schedule and conditions of employment originally proposed by the board but rejected by the plaintiff. During the 1969-70 school year the persons hired to fill these positions performed duties on the basis of the conditions of employment originally proposed, and received salaries based on the salary schedule originally proposed but on which the parties had been unable to agree in their negotiations. A letter appointing the department head of the high school informed the appointee as follows: "Your salary rate cannot be determined precisely until the salary schedule is finally negotiated with the W.H.E.A. I suspect, however, that you may already know the approximate range in which it will fall and that you are informed as to how you will be placed within that range. For your information, this formula is enclosed." A letter from this department head to the superintendent acknowledged receipt of a check for initial services as a department head and informed the superintendent that the employee was cashing the check "with the express understanding and stipulation that it is received on account as part payment and that it does not necessarily constitute my total compensation for my services in the West Hartford schools for the initial pay period of the 1969-70 school year." On these facts it is clear that the defendants did not "interfere, restrain or coerce employees in derogation" of their rights under the statute. There was no attempt to bypass or denigrate the union. We recognize the fact that the terms of the board's proposal embraced not only subjects which are clearly matters of board policy but mandatory subjects of negotiation as well. Our statutes have given the boards of education a clear mandate to "maintain ... good public elementary and secondary schools." § 10-220. It was not the intention of the legislature to permit progress in education to be halted until agreement is reached with the union....

NOTES

1. To what extent, if any, may an employer communicate with his employees concerning the negotiations while negotiations are in progress. In *General Elec. Co.,* 150 N.L.R.B. 192 (1964), *enforced,* 418 F.2d 736 (2d Cir. 1969), *cert. denied,* 397 U.S. 965 (1970), the NLRB held that an employer's communications program, in conjunction with its take it or leave it approach to bargaining, constituted bad faith bargaining. In so ruling, the NLRB stated:

> It is not consistent with ... [the obligation to bargain in good faith] for an employer to mount a campaign, as Respondent did, both before and during negotiations, for the purposes of disparaging and discrediting the statutory representative in the eyes of its employee constituents, to seek to persuade the employees to exert pressure on the representative to submit to the will of the employer, and to create the impression that the employer rather than the union is the true protector of the employees' interest. As the Trial Examiner phrased it, the employer's statutory obligation is to deal with the employees through the union, and not with the union through the employees.

The NLRB, however, has held that it is permissible for an employer to communicate its position on the various issues in negotiations as long as the purpose of such communications does not undermine the union's role as the collective bargaining representative of the employees. *Procter & Gamble Mfg. Co.,* 160

N.L.R.B. 334, 339-41 (1966). In *Grand Haven Bd. of Educ.,* 1973 MERC Lab. Op. 1 (Mich.) the MERC held that an employer did not commit an unfair labor practice when it communicated to bargaining unit employees the offer it had previously presented to the union where such communication was not coercive and did not contain threats or offers of benefit. Accord *Town of Sharon,* Case No. MUP-275 (Mass. LRC 1972); *Ogdensburg City Sch. Dist.,* 11 PERB ¶ 4667 (N.Y. 1978). On the other hand, in *PLRB v. Northern Bedford Sch. Dist.,* 7 PPER 194 (Pa. LRB 1976), the Pennsylvania Board held that a school board committed an unfair labor practice by disseminating to employees minutes of bargaining sessions which were attached to the employer's bargaining position. The Pennsylvania Commission reasoned as follows:

> To afford public employees the full benefit and protection of the collective bargaining rights guaranteed to them by the Act, it is necessary to insulate them from any efforts by the public employer, direct or indirect, to undercut the authority of the employees' duly selected representative, or fragment the unity of the bargaining unit. Any such action by the public employer is considered to be an unfair labor practice.

Accord *Oregon City Educ. Ass'n v. Oregon City Sch. Dist. No. 62,* Case No. C-163-79 (Or. ERB 1980). See also *Reno Police Protective Ass'n v. City of Reno,* Item No. 52 (Nev. LGE-MRB 1976) (placing misleading newspaper advertisement held violation of employer's duty to bargain in good faith).

2. In *NTEU v. FLRA,* 826 F.2d 114 (D.C. Cir. 1987), the Court of Appeals for the District of Columbia held that a federal agency did not commit an unfair labor practice when it distributed questionnaires seeking information about conditions of employment from agency employees without any prior approval or involvement from their union. In so ruling, the court rejected the FLRA's per se rule against agency solicitation of information directly from employees. The court noted that "nowhere does the Act imply that a union's exclusive representation of employees at the bargaining table precludes direct communication between management and its employees for other purposes." Noting that one of the purposes of the Act was to advance governmental effectiveness and efficiency, the court noted that "[i]t should be self-evident that achievement of [this] goal will at times require reliable information and views only employees are in a position to give; and it stands to reason that the reliability of such information will not be enhanced by filtering through a third party such as a Union." On the other hand, the court noted that "a search for reliable information may not be used as a screen behind which to subvert a Union's role as its members' exclusive collective bargaining representative." In upholding the direct solicitation in the instant case, the court specifically noted that it did not occur during the course of collective bargaining.

3. Does a party commit an unfair labor practice by submitting a proposal to the terminal step of a statutory impasse proceeding which was not previously discussed at the bargaining table? In *Police Local 798, AFSCME & Town of Enfield,* Case No. MEPP 3872 & 3946, 723 GERR 22 (Conn. SBLR 1977), the Connecticut Board, after noting that the statutory scheme "contemplates collective bargaining as the normal and preferred way to resolve labor-management differences" and that binding arbitration is provided as "a last resort when all else fails," stated:

> Any practice that would tend to reduce the chances for resolution through bargaining would therefore work against the grand plan of the Act and if a party were free to raise in arbitration a claim that he had not proposed in

bargaining, he might be tempted to withhold claims from bargaining whenever he expected a more favorable resolution of them in arbitration. Such a result would, we believe, run counter to the policies of the Act. If it is shown that a party withheld a claim from collective bargaining with the intent to present it for the first time in arbitration we should probably hold that this constituted a refusal to bargain in good faith.

In this particular case, however, the Connecticut Board held that the issue presented was outside its jurisdiction in that it should be presented to the Board of Mediation and Arbitration for decision. See also *Sunnyside Valley Irrig. Dist.,* Decision No. 314 (Wash. PERC 1977) (union's action in increasing demands and adding new demands violated its duty to bargain in good faith).

4. Is bargaining in good faith a prerequisite to a union's right to request interest arbitration under a state statute which provides for interest arbitration where the parties are at impasse? In rejecting such an employer argument, the Michigan Court of Appeals in *City of Manistee v. MERC,* 168 Mich. App. 422, 425 N.W.2d 168, *leave to appeal denied,* 431 Mich. 882 (1988), held that to require good faith bargaining as a prerequisite would encourage dilatory practices, create delays, and otherwise detract from the expeditious resolution of the impasse through interest arbitration.

5. In *State of N.J. & Council of N.J. State College Locals,* Decision No. 79, 628 GERR 13-22 (N.J. PERC 1975), the New Jersey PERC held that "[a]n adamant position that limits wage proposals to existing levels is not necessarily a failure to negotiate in good faith." The New Jersey PERC further stated:

> Good faith collective negotiations do not require one party to adopt the position of the other; they only require a willingness to negotiate the issue with an open mind and a desire to reach an agreement. The fact that the two parties approach negotiations with different priorities does not mean that either side is not negotiating in good faith.

Accord *PLRB v. Commonwealth of Pa. & State Liquor Control Bd.,* 367 A.2d 738, 94 L.R.R.M. 2346 (Pa. Commw. Ct. 1977).

6. Can one party insist on completing negotiations over non-economic items before commencing negotiations on economic items? In *Town of Rockland,* Case No. MUP-3498 (Mass. LRC 1980), the Massachusetts Commission held that a town committed an unfair labor practice by refusing to negotiate over economic issues until agreement was reached on all non-economic issues. The Commission ruled that a party's unilateral refusal to discuss any major economic items until resolution of non-economic items tended to narrow the range of possible compromise and thereby frustrated the bargaining process. Moreover, the Commission held that even though the union may have initially agreed to attempt to resolve non-economic items first, the Town was obligated to bargain in response to the union's demands in later bargaining sessions to discuss cost items that constituted mandatory bargaining subjects.

7. Does a party's violation of mutually agreed to ground rules for negotiations constitute an unfair labor practice? In *Dover Sch. Comm.,* Decision No. 87-22(A) (N.H. PERB 1987), the New Hampshire Board held that violation of mutually agreed to ground rules constituted bad faith bargaining and therefore constituted an unfair labor practice.

8. Does an employer have an obligation to bargain in good faith following the issuance of a fact finder's recommendations? The MERC in *City of Dearborn,* 1972 MERC Lab. Op. 749 (Mich.), responded affirmatively, stating:

> Statutory fact finding may be invoked only after the parties have bargained and a genuine impasse has occurred. Although the duty to bargain does not mean that parties must engage in futile bargaining in the face of a genuine impasse, changed circumstances may develop, and therefore require compliance with the bargaining requirement.... Even though there may be a strike, the duty to bargain may not necessarily be suspended.... Just as a strike may create conditions in which the parties would be more willing to make concessions to compromise the matters in difference, the fact finder's recommendations may enlighten or persuade them of the reasonableness or unreasonableness of their bargaining position. The fact finder's report, thus, is the functional equivalent of a strike and may change the factual situation regarding "the negotiation of an agreement, or any question arising thereunder." MCLA 423, 215; MSA 17.455(15). It must be given the same serious consideration as the initial bargaining proposals. Therefore, there is an affirmative obligation to bargain in good faith about the substantive recommendations of the report of a statutory fact finder.

Accord *East Hartford Educ. Ass'n v. East Hartford Bd. of Educ.,* 30 Conn. Supp. 63, 299 A.2d 554 (Conn. Super. Ct. 1972).

The MERC further held that "the duty to bargain requires that the employer make a reasonable effort in some direction to close the differences with the union." Does this mean that the employer in order to meet its obligation to bargain in good faith must modify its position on some of the issues? If so, would this be consistent with the statutory provision that the duty to bargain "does not compel either party to agree to a proposal or require the making of a concession"? Would an employer meet its obligation to bargain in good faith if it stated in detail its reasons for rejecting the fact finder's recommendations? In *Lamphere Sch. Dist.,* 1978 MERC Lab. Op. 194 (Mich.), the Michigan Commission stated that "[w]here a party in good faith intends to resolve its differences with its bargaining adversary, although not accepting the fact finder's recommendations, there is no bad-faith refusal to bargain."

INTERNATIONAL ASSOCIATION OF FIREFIGHTERS
v. CITY OF HOMESTEAD

Case No. 72-9285 (Fla. Cir. Ct. 1973), *aff'd,* 291 So. 2d 38
(Fla. Ct. App. 1974)

JUDGE GROSSMAN: ....

I. *Factual Background of This Litigation*

Plaintiff, Local No. 2010 of the International Association of Firefighters, is a labor organization representing a majority of the persons employed as firefighters by the Defendant, City of Homestead. In January, 1971, Plaintiff sent to the City Manager and the City Councilmen of the City of Homestead a letter seeking recognition as collective bargaining agent for the firefighter employees of the City of Homestead. Subsequently, recognition was granted by the City Council and thereafter the council designated Homestead City Manager, Olaf R. Pearson, as the City's bargaining representative. Negotiations between Pearson and Plaintiff commenced with the mutual understanding that any agreement reached between the parties would be subject to the approval of the City Council.

In November, 1971, after more than 50 hours of negotiations, the City Manager and the Plaintiff reached accord on a collective bargaining agreement. This agreement with the recommendations of the City Manager attached was submitted to the Homestead City Council for its approval. The council met with representatives of Plaintiff on January 10th, 1972 for that purpose. At this meeting, however, the City Council proceeded to renegotiate the contract from the beginning and, in fact, changed every provision of the contract brought up before the meeting terminated. Among the changes made, the Council altered the "bargaining unit" clause (which had been agreed to by City Manager Pearson and Plaintiff) by excluding certain members of the Union from the contract's coverage, and proposed that the entire negotiated wage provisions be stricken from the contract and in substitution therefor these wages unilaterally established by the City Council in their budget hearings of the year before be inserted in the contract. In addition, notwithstanding the fact that the City had recognized the Plaintiff and had bargained with their representatives, the Council directed the City Attorney to write an opinion concerning the city's duty to further recognize and bargain with the Plaintiff.

In response to these actions of the City Council, Plaintiff's representatives walked out of the meeting, and on January 27th, 1972, sent a letter to the City Manager invoking the arbitration provisions of the Firefighters Collective Bargaining Act. However, Defendant City failed to respond to said letter except by passing an Ordinance (No. 72-01-4) designed to supersede the Firefighters Collective Bargaining Law....

This action was brought by Plaintiffs to enforce their constitutional right to bargain collectively and to bring the City once again to the bargaining table.

II. *Issues Before This Court*

This litigation presents several issues to the Court for decision. First, the Court must determine whether the City has performed its obligation of negotiating in good faith with its employees under Article I, Section 6 of the Florida Constitution. Second, the Court must determine if the Firefighters Collective Bargaining Law establishes collective bargaining guidelines in support of the Constitutional obligation and, if so, the respective duties of the parties thereunder....

III. *The City Did Not Meet Its Duty to Bargain in Good Faith*

Article I, Section 6 of the Constitution of the State of Florida grants public employees the right of collective bargaining. The Florida Supreme Court and the Circuit Courts of this State have on several occasions held that this Section imposes a duty upon the public employer to negotiate in good faith with their employees through an organization such as Plaintiff Union.

This Court finds that the practices followed by the Defendant City in this case did not constitute good faith collective bargaining. The defendant's conduct in attempting to renegotiate the entire contract after the lengthy negotiations between the Union and the City Manager, indicates that the bargaining between the City Manager and the Union was only surface bargaining and not a good faith effort by the City to reach agreement with Plaintiff Union. This change in the ground rules after the lengthy contract negotiations were completed demonstrates that the City Manager's function was not to negotiate with the Union on behalf of the City, but rather *to induce the Union to compromise some of its demands in the belief that they were reaching an agreement and then present these compromises to the City Council where further concessions from the Union were to be demanded.* The refusal of the City to show any confidence in the preliminary agreement reached by its City Manager (its appointed negotiator) and its attempt to renegotiate the entire agreement and gain further concessions from the Union on almost every provision of the preliminary agreement, is not good faith bargaining and does not fulfill the duty imposed by the Florida Constitution.... [This is] a proper case for the award of punitive damages; this is especially so since the compensatory damages awarded for actual losses to the persons deprived by his conduct are small and difficult to ascertain. The denial of a constitutional right, however, even without any accompanying financial loss, is reprehensible. It is the duty of the Court to protect the constitutional rights of our citizens and to punish those who deliberately subvert these rights. To that end, the Court hereby declares that Councilman Rhodes is a violator of the constitutional rights of the citizens of this State and reprimands him for his unlawful activities which are unbecoming to any American citizen and are even more unworthy in one who purports to be a public servant. There is no higher duty in one who serves in government than obedience to the law. When an elected official acts as Councilman Rhodes has acted, in deliberate violation of his oath of office (that is, to support the Constitutions of this State and of the nation), he sets a shameful and humiliating example of lawlessness.

Since this is the first instance of judicial action upon one of the many recalcitrant public employers who wish to purposely ignore the new collective bargaining mandates of Article I, Section 6 of our State's Constitution this Court will, in addition to the foregoing reprimand, only impose $1.00 as punitive damages upon Councilman Rhodes. Such judgment should, however, be a warning and an indication of the intent of this Court to compel obedience to our laws and to the Constitution of this State in the future, by whatever means may be required....

NOTES

1. Does a PERB have the authority to issue a "make-whole" order where it finds that an employer has failed to bargain in good faith? In *IUE v. NLRB (Tiidee Prods.)*, 426 F.2d 1243 (D.C. Cir.), *cert. denied*, 400 U.S. 950 (1970), the Court of Appeals for the District of Columbia held that where an employer's refusal to bargain constituted "a clear and flagrant violation" of the NLRA, a cease-and-desist order was not sufficient. The court noted "that damages can be awarded on an assessment of the contract terms that would have been in effect if the law had been complied with even though the law-violating employer has not yet entered into the contract." On remand, however, the Board declined to issue a "make-whole" remedy, reasoning as follows:

> We have carefully considered the Union's request for a make-whole remedy in light of the record herein and have decided that it is not practicable. The Union suggests that we determine what the parties *"would* have agreed to" in 1967 and thereafter on the basis of a record which contains only a proposed collective-bargaining agreement submitted by the Union to Respondent on December 18, 1967; a chart comparing the wages then paid by Respondent for certain job classifications with those paid by other employers in comparable industries in the Dayton area who were then under contract with the Union; testimonial evidence of employee wage rates as of the date of the hearing herein and a list thereof as of May 25, 1970; certain testimony about the time required to negotiate a first contract; and several charts and tables depicting nationwide changes in wages and benefits since 1967. We know of no way by which the Board could ascertain with even approximate accuracy from the above what the parties *"would* have agreed to" if they had bargained in good faith. Inevitably, the Board would have to decide from the above what the parties *"should* have agreed to." And this, the court stated, the Board must not do.

Tiidee Prods. Inc., 194 N.L.R.B. 1234 (1972). Nevertheless, the Board devised certain "alternative remedies ... [to] undo some of the baneful effects pointed out by the court as having resulted from Respondent's 'clear and flagrant violation of the law.'" The Board thus ordered the employer to (1) mail copies of the notice to employees to all employees in the unit, (2) give the union reasonable access to the employer's bulletin boards during the period of contract negotiations, and (3) reimburse the union and the NLRB for litigation costs and expenses.

2. In *NTEU v. FLRA,* 856 F.2d 293 (D.C. Cir. 1988), the court held that where an agency unlawfully makes a unilateral change in terms and conditions of employment without meeting its bargaining obligation, the fullest measure of "make whole" relief should normally be ordered, including a retroactive bargaining order (RBO). The court noted that "retroactive remedies are an indispensable means to vindicate the Statute's central goals." The court stated:

> ... A "make whole" remedy compensates individual employees for losses suffered and divests management of the benefits of illegal action. A retroactive bargaining order aims to do the same. The difference is that an RBO requires the Authority, or a grievance committee, to estimate the "make whole" compensation due employees by means of the convenient, albeit somewhat speculative, conceit of assuming that the agreement the parties eventually negotiate approximates the agreement they would have forged in the first instance. The retroactive application of a contract ultimately negotiated by the parties relieves the Authority of the need to speculate on the precise details of a hypothetical contract.

The court noted that "the legislative history shows that Congress contemplated that retroactivity would be routinely ordered as a remedy for straightforward refusal to bargain.

3. In *Duval Teachers United v. Duval Cty. Sch. Bd.,* 3 FPER 96 (Fla. PERC 1977), the Florida PERC held that a school board's flagrant violations of its bargaining obligations under the Florida Act required the issuance of an extraordinary remedy. The Florida PERC stated:

> Due to the flagrant nature of respondent's violation, and length of time during which the employees were deprived of an opportunity to reach an agreement (over a year since the union's request to bargain on March 16, 1976), an extraordinary remedy is required. The Commission will therefore require the respondent to bargain in good faith not only as to wages, hours, and terms and conditions of employment for the future, but also to bargain in good faith with respect to the monetary benefits sought by the employee representative for the employees since March 16, 1976.

4. In *Town of Putnam Valley,* 17 PERB ¶ 3041 (N.Y. 1984), the New York Board held that the failure of members of a union negotiating team to affirmatively support a tentative agreement that had been negotiated constituted a refusal to bargain in good faith where they had failed to notify the employer team in advance.

2. SELECTION AND AUTHORITY OF THE PARTIES' REPRESENTATIVES

NORTH BRUNSWICK TOWNSHIP BOARD OF EDUCATION

6 NJPER ¶ 11095 (N.J. Pub. Emp. Rel. Comm'n 1980)

An Unfair Practice Charge was filed with the Public Employment Relations Commission on February 14, 1980 by the North Brunswick Township Education Association (the "Association") alleging that the North Brunswick Township Board of Education (the "Board") engaged in unfair practices within the meaning of the New Jersey Employer-Employee Relations Act, N.J.S.A. 34:13A-1 et seq. (the "Act"). Specifically, the Education Association alleges that after it designated a negotiating team including members of the teachers' unit, a professional negotiator and other Board employees, the Board, in violation of N.J.S.A. 34:13A-5.4(a)(1), (2) and (5), objected to the makeup of this negotiating team and refused to negotiate with the Association until the members of the other negotiations units were removed from its negotiating team, either as members or observers. On the same date, the Board filed an Unfair Practice Charge against the Association alleging that, after the Association had filed a representation petition to include all certified and non-certified employees in its unit, and after the Board had filed a representation petition for two separate units of certified and non-certified employees, the Association, prior to Commission resolution of these conflicting representation petitions, include[d] as part of its negotiating team representatives from the Secretarial, Custodial, Special Services and Aides units. The Board further alleges that the Association, by insisting on the inclusion of representatives from these other units in its negotiating team, is refusing to negotiate in good faith, destroying the integrity of these other majority representatives, imposing on the Board the unit composition requested in its representation petition, and undermining negotiations between the Board and these various employee negotiations units, all in violation of N.J.S.A. 34:13A-5.4(b)(1) and (3).

It appearing that the allegations of both Unfair Practice Charges, if true, may constitute unfair practices within the meaning of the Act, Complaints and an

Order Consolidating Cases was issued on March 7, 1980. Thereafter, the parties, pursuant to N.J.A.C. 19:14-6.7, agreed to a stipulation of facts in this matter and waived a Hearing Examiner's Recommended Report and Decision....

The Association, in support of its charge, argues that since the Act guarantees employees a free choice to select whomever they wish to represent them in collective negotiations, the Board has violated section (a)(5) by refusing to negotiate with the duly designated negotiating team which it selected. The Association further contends that it is not attempting to destroy the integrity of the other negotiations units. Although the negotiating teams for each unit were composed of members of other units, the Association argues that there is no allegation that at the negotiations for its unit it attempted to also negotiate concerning the terms and conditions of employment for the employees in any of these other units.

The Board, in support of its charge, contends that the Association has committed unfair practices by attempting, through joint negotiating teams and common demands, to consolidate with other certified units during the pendency of conflicting representation petitions, thereby imposing improper coalition negotiations. The Board further argues that the over-all conduct of the Association, as stated in the stipulation of facts, constitutes bad faith negotiations.

N.J.S.A. 34:13A-5.3 states that:

> Representatives designated or selected by public employees for the purposes of collective negotiation by the majority of the employees in a unit appropriate for such purposes or by the majority of the employees voting in an election conducted by the commission as authorized by this Act shall be the exclusive representative for collective negotiations concerning the terms and conditions of employment of the employees in such unit ... and [a] majority representative of public employees in an appropriate unit shall be entitled to act for and to negotiate agreements covering all employees in the unit.

N.J.S.A. 34:13A-6 grants the Commission the authority to: ... decide in each instance which unit of employees is appropriate for collective negotiation....

It is clear from these explicit provisions of the Act that the Board's only obligation is to negotiate with those negotiations units which it has recognized or which have been found appropriate by the Commission. Similarly, under these sections, an employee organization has the authority and obligation to negotiate only for the unit which it represents.

It is well established that parties may voluntarily agree to consolidate or merge separate units for the purpose of collective negotiations. However absent voluntary agreement, neither party may attempt to force upon the other an enlargement or merger of existing units. The Board may lawfully insist on confining negotiations within the parameters of the existing units, i.e., require that each association negotiate solely on behalf of the employees in the unit which it represents. This rule is based on the rationale that, once an appropriate unit has been recognized or certified, the statutory interest in maintaining stability and certainty in the negotiations structure requires adherence to existing unit definitions. Accordingly, during negotiations for the Association's unit, its negotiating representatives: 1) could not demand that the Board also negotiate with regard to contracts covering the terms and conditions of employment for employees in additional units represented by other associations; 2) could not demand that any settlement for its unit must also apply to these other units; 3) could not condition its agreement on the Board's offering of identical terms to these other units; and 4) could not condition its agreement on the Board's settling of contracts with these other units.

. . . .

On the other hand, uniformity of working standards including common expiration dates are legitimate aims of associations. In furtherance of their goal for uniform contracts, associations may consult to prepare a list of common demands, and they may coordinate their negotiations strategies through interlocking or joint negotiating teams, which include members from all of the various employee units. Each of the associations, through its interlocking negotiations team, may then simultaneously, but separately, attempt to negotiate such a common contract for the employees in the unit which it represents. *AFL-CIO Joint Negotiating Committee for Phelps Dodge v. NLRB,* 470 F.2d 722, *Utility Workers, Ohio Power Co., supra; General Electric v. NLRB,* 412 F.2d 512; *Standard Oil Co. v. NLRB,* 50 LRRM 1238, aff'd, 322 F.2d 40; *Minnesota Mining and Manufacturing Company v. NLRB,* 415 F.2d 174.

Accordingly, the Association could lawfully agree on common negotiating demands with the Secretarial, Custodial, Special Services and Aides units, could coordinate negotiating strategies, and could establish joint or interlocking negotiating teams with these other units. Thus, each one of the five associations may be represented by a negotiating team which includes members from all the other associations. During negotiations for the Education Association, its joint negotiating team can demand that the Board agree to certain terms for the employees in its unit; while, for example, during separate negotiations for the Custodial and Maintenance Association, its joint negotiating team can make the same demands for the employees in its unit as appropriate.

It is apparent from the stipulated facts that the Education Association has not attempted to engage in any of the four types of improper coalition negotiations previously enumerated. Rather, it is clear that the Education Association's method of negotiating, as stated in stipulations #24 through #39, is within the permissible negotiations boundaries discussed above. Accordingly, the Education Association has not engaged in any unfair practice and, therefore, the Complaint against it is dismissed in its entirety. However, the Board has violated sections (a)(1) and (5) by refusing to negotiate with the negotiating team selected by the Education Association, due to the inclusion of members from those associations which represent other units of the Board's employees.[5]

NOTES

1. The NLRB has held that a union can include on its bargaining team "observers" from other unions representing an employer's employees. *General*

---

[5] The Commission's conclusion in this regard is not affected by the current pendency of conflicting Board and Education Association representation petitions, either one of which will result in an alteration of the current unit structure. Until the Commission rules on these petitions, the Board, in accordance with the guidelines established herein, is required to negotiate with the units as they currently exist. In addition, the Commission notes that this decision does not in any manner affect the final resolution of these representation petitions.

Elec. Co., 173 N.L.R.B. 253 (1968), *enf'd as modified,* 412 F.2d 512 (2d Cir. 1969). This tactic, commonly referred to as coordinated bargaining, is discussed in Comment, *Coordinated — Coalition Bargaining: Theory, Legality, Practice and Economic Effects,* 55 Minn. L. Rev. 599 (1971). What are the advantages and disadvantages of coordinated bargaining in the public sector? Cf. *City of Reno,* Item #86 (Nev. LGE-MRB 1978) (union could select one bargaining team to represent several bargaining units). Would the same legal principles be applicable to a public employer if it sought to include a taxpayer's representative or a representative of another public employer on its bargaining team?

2. In *Kenosha Cty.,* Decision No. 21130-B (Wis. ERC 1985), the Wisconsin Commission held that a county lawfully refused to bargain with a coalition of five separate bargaining units as a single entity. The Wisconsin Commission held that to hold otherwise would render meaningless the five separate bargaining units that had previously been found to be appropriate. On the other hand, the Wisconsin Commission held that the union's insistence on such coalition bargaining over the employer's objection was a violation of its duty to bargain in good faith.

3. May either party refuse to negotiate with the other party because it objects to the presence of one or more members of the other party's negotiating team? In *City of Superior,* Decision No. 8325 (Wis. ERC 1967), the Wisconsin Employment Relations Commission stated:

> Personal differences arising between the representatives of the parties engaged in negotiations with respect to wages, hours and working conditions of municipal employees do not constitute a valid reason for refusing to bargain in good faith. Both municipal employers and representatives of their employees have the right to designate whomever they choose to represent them at the bargaining table. To allow either or both parties to refuse to bargain with each other because of alleged or actual conflicts between their representatives would be contrary to the intent and purpose of Section 111.70.

In *Fort Jackson Laundry Facility,* A/SLMR Decision No. 242 (1972), the Assistant Secretary of Labor held that with respect to formal discussions under § 10(e) of Executive Order 11491, "The right to choose its representatives at such discussions must be left to the discretion of the exclusive bargaining representative and not to the whim of management." Accord *United States Postal Serv. (Tampa, Fla.),* 202 N.L.R.B. No. 823 (1973); *City of Reno,* Item #86 (Nev. LGE-MRB 1978).

4. In *NFFE v. FLRA,* 652 F.2d 191 (D.C. Cir. 1981), the court held that the Federal Naval Training Center was not required to bargain over a proposal that each party limit their designated representatives to three. In affirming the Federal Labor Relations Authority, the court held that the number of negotiators designated by each party was not a "condition of employment" concerning which the employer must negotiate. See also *Southern Worcester Cty. Reg'l Vocation Sch. Dist. v. Massachusetts Labor Rels. Comm'n,* 387 Mass. 897 389 N.E.2d 389 (1979), the court upheld a determination that it was an unfair labor practice for an employer to condition the commencement of negotiations upon disclosure by the union of the identity of the members of its bargaining team. The court stated that "the selecion of the union negotiating team was an internal union matter, and provided no basis for the employer's refusal to bargain."

5. In most jurisdictions it is an unfair labor practice for a managerial or supervisory employee who is excluded from the bargaining unit to be a member of the union's bargaining team. But see *Commonwealth of Pa. v. PLRB,* 40 Pa.

Commw. 468, 397 A.2d 858 (1979) (participation by first level supervisors as members of rank and file bargaining team not improper under Pennsylvania Act). On the other hand, would it similarily be improper for an employer to have a bargaining unit employee sitting on its bargaining team? In *Department of Health, Education & Welfare, Office of Secretary,* A/SLMR No. 701 (1976), the Assistant Secretary of Labor for Labor-Management Relations held that Executive Order 11491 did not preclude an agency from selecting a bargaining unit employee to participate on the agency's bargaining team. Accordingly, the Assistant Secretary held that an exclusive bargaining representative committed an unfair labor practice "by refusing to negotiate because a bargaining unit employee was serving as a member of the management negotiating team."

The New Hampshire act provides that "persons exercising supervisory authority involving the significant exercise of discretion may not belong to the same bargaining unit as the employees they supervise." In *City of Concord v. PELRB,* 119 N.H. 725, 407 A.2d 363, (1979), the court held that this statutory provision precluded a supervisory bargaining unit of officers in the city's fire department from including members of the rank-and-file fire fighters bargaining unit on its negotiating team. After noting that the legislature intended "to avoid conflicts between the two groups because of the differing duties and relationships which characterize each group," the court held "that the legislature intended not only that the supervisors and the fire fighters were to be in separate bargaining units, but that there should be no commingling of members on their negotiating teams." The court further stated that the intent was "to keep supervisory personnel separate from the rank and file, not only by requiring that their members be in separate bargaining units, but also, as a logical consequence, that they not be allowed to commingle on each other's negotiating teams." Accordingly, the court held that the employer did not commit an unfair labor practice by refusing to negotiate with a bargaining team that was commingled.

6. Section 7131(a) of the Civil Service Reform Act, which covers federal sector labor relations, provides that an employee serving as a representative of an exclusive representative in bargaining "shall be authorized official time for such purposes ... during the time the employee would be in duty status." The Federal Labor Relations Authority (FLRA) held that official time included per diem allowances and travel expenses for union negotiators. However, in *Bureau of Alcohol, Tobacco & Fire Arms v. FLRA,* 104 S. Ct. 439 (1983), the Supreme Court held that federal agencies were not required to pay per diem allowances or travel expenses. In rejecting the union's contention that it was the intent of the Act to provide employee negotiators, like management representatives, with all of the customary forms of compensation, including travel expenses and per diem allowances, the Court stated:

> There is, of course, nothing inconsistent in paying the salaries, but not the expenses, of union negotiators. Congress may well have concluded that, although union representatives should not be penalized by a loss in salary while engaged in collective bargaining, they need not be further subsidized with travel and per diem expenses. The provisions of the Act intended to facilitate the collection of union dues ... certainly suggests that Congress contemplated that unions would ordinarily pay their own expenses.

The Court did observe in a footnote, however, that "unions may presumably negotiate for such payments [per diem allowances and travel expenses] in collective bargaining as they do in the private sector."

7. In reversing a decision of the FLRA which held that a union's proposal with respect to the amount of official time to be allotted union representatives for the purposes of negotiations was negotiable only at the election of the agency, the United States Court of Appeals for the District of Columbia in *AFGE v. FLRA*, 798 F.2d 1525 (D.C. Cir. 1986), ruled that "to the extent that FLRA considers official time nonnegotiable because it would require an agency to hire another employee or change its staffing patterns, its approach is an unreasonable interpretation of the Statute," noting that the FLRA's approach would effectively ignore "the express language of section 7131(d)" of the Civil Service Reform Act which provides that "any employee representing an exclusive representative ... shall be granted official time in any amount the agency and the exclusive representative involved agree to be reasonable, necessary, and in the public interest." The court observed that by this provision Congress "committed the determination of the public interest to the union and agency together, not to the agency alone." In rejecting a prediction of the dire consequences that would follow from a determination that the union's proposal was negotiable, the court commented that "[a] finding of negotiability means only that a proposal is a proper subject of bargaining, not that the proposal ought to be implemented on the merits" and that "[a]n agency has no obligation to abandon what it conceives to be the best interests of the agency merely because it must negotiate on a[n] official time proposal." Finally, the court noted that "the union's obligation to bargain in good faith ... sets some limits on the amount of official time that a union may request and thus to some extent protects the agency's ability to function efficiently."

8. The Tennessee Education Professional Negotiations Act appears to preclude either party from using outside representatives for the purposes of negotiations. Thus Section 49-5-609(9) provides that the term

> ... "negotiator" means that person or persons selected by the board of education and the professional employees' organization to do the negotiating. The board may select the superintendent, any member of the board, or fulltime system-wide employees as prescribed in § 49-5-608. The professional employees' organization may select from among those who are members of the organization. Tenn. Code Ann. § 49-5-602(9) (1990).

Are these restrictions on who may sit as the parties' representatives at the bargaining table constitutional? See *Kenai Peninsula Borough Sch. Dist. v. Kenai Peninsula Borough Sch. Dist. Classification Ass'n*, 590 P.2d 437, 1979-80 PBC ¶ 36,512 (Alaska 1979).

9. The Wyoming Fire Fighter Bargaining Law provides that a city, town, or county is required to negotiate in good faith through its corporate authorities with the bargaining agent chosen by a majority of the firefighters. The law defines the term "corporate authorities" to "mean the council, commission or other proper officials of any city, town, or county, whose duty or duties it is to establish wages, salaries, rates of pay, working conditions, and other conditions of employment of firefighters." Wyo. Stat. § 27-265(b). In *Nation v. State ex rel. Fire Fighters Local 279*, 518 P.2d 931, 86 L.R.R.M. 2574 (Wyo. 1974), the mayor appointed the personnel director, the city treasurer, the assistant city attorney, and the fire chief as the city's representatives for negotiations with the fire fighters local. In upholding the union's contention that these individuals were not "corporate authorities" within the meaning of the Wyoming Act, the Wyoming Supreme Court held that the corporate authorities were required to negotiate in person with the representatives of the fire fighters union and that the corporate authorities could not be represented through agents.

Subsequently, in *City of Casper v. IAFF Local 904,* 713 P.2d 1187 (Wyo. 1986), the court held that no valid collective bargaining agreement had been entered into since the city's negotiators were not "corporate authorities" as required by state law. The court ruled that "[n]either party can enforce an agreement made other than as empowered by the legislature to be made." In reaffirming its earlier decision in *Nation v. Fire Fighters Local 279,* the court further noted that while "[i]t may be time-consuming and perhaps distasteful for a mayor, councilman, city manager or county commissioner to be present and direct negotiations with the bargaining agent of the firefighters, ... such has been mandated by the legislature."

10. Absent unique statutory language such as that contained in the Wyoming law discussed in the preceding note, public employers have the right to designate their representatives for the purposes of collective bargaining. As the Michigan Commission stated in *City of Detroit, Bd. of Fire Comm'rs,* 1970 MERC Lab. Op. 953, 957 (Mich.):

> It is not required that Municipal Councils, Commissions and Boards bargain directly with the representatives of their employees. This may be done by administrative employees or other agents who are clothed with authority to participate in effective collective bargaining but reserving final approval to the governing body. Such is common practice in the private sector, and it is effective and workable.

3. DUTY TO SUPPLY INFORMATION

LOS RIOS COMMUNITY COLLEGE DISTRICT

12 PERC ¶ 19083 (Cal. Pub. Emp. Rel. Bd. 1988)

[The Los Rios Classified Employee Association (Charging Party or Association) requested that the Los Rios Community College District (Respondent or District) provide it with copies of the Position Control Report (PCR) which] contains information about every nonfaculty position in the District including whether or not the position is filled or vacant, the identity of the employee in the position, job classification, budgeted salary for the position, amount of salary expended to date, and the social security number of the employee occupying the position....

... [T]he District responded by expressing its concern over the fact that the requested reports contained names and social security numbers of employees both within and outside the bargaining unit. The District outlined the various costs associated with providing the requested reports without the social security numbers and further indicated that said costs are payable in advance.

....

[Thereafter, the Association filed unfair labor charges alleging that the District refused to bargain in good faith by failing to provide the PCR and by conditioning delivery of the PCR upon the Association's advance payment of an "excessive and burdensome fee." When the charges were dismissed by the Administrative Law Judge, the Association appealed the dismissal to the PERB.]

Good Faith Bargaining

Charging Party excepts to the ALJ's conclusion of law that the District did not fail to bargain in good faith. The exception is based upon the Union's contention that the District refused to provide necessary and relevant information in a timely manner.

Generally, the Association is entitled to all information that is necessary and relevant to discharging its duty to represent unit employees. *Trustees of the California State University* (1987) PERB Decision No. 613-H. An employer's refusal to provide such information evidences bad faith bargaining unless the employer can demonstrate adequate reasons why it cannot supply the information. *Stockton Unified School District* (1980) PERB Decision No. 143. However, the Association is not entitled to demand receipt of the information in a particular form. *Emeryville Research Center* (9th Cir. 1971) 441 F.2d 880, 887 [77 LRRM 2043]; *Soule Glass and Glazing Co. v. NLRB* (1st Cir., 1981) 652 F.2d 1055 [107 LRRM 2781, 2806], denying enf. in part to 246 NLRB 792, (1979) [102 LRRM 1693].

The record shows that the District was willing to provide the PCR to the Association. However it contends that the social security numbers of nonunit employees must first be deleted… [W]e agree with the ALJ's finding of fact that the District timely responded to the Association's request for information. Therefore, the issue must turn on whether the District's assertion of the confidentiality of the social security numbers of nonbargaining unit employees was proper.

The Board has recognized state and federal court decisions in support of the premise that constitutional rights of personal privacy may limit otherwise lawfully authorized demands for the production of personal information. *Modesto City Schools and High School District* (1985) PERB Decision No. 479. The U.S. Supreme Court has determined that where a union seeks relevant information about a mandatory subject of bargaining, the disclosure of which may infringe upon constitutionally protected privacy interests, the NLRB must undertake to balance the conflicting rights. *Detroit Edison Company v. NLRB* (1979) 440 U.S. 301 [100 LRRM 2728].

There is authority in support of recognizing the confidential nature of social security numbers. Section 7 of the Federal Privacy Act of 1974 prohibits federal, state or local agencies from denying rights or benefits to an individual for refusing to disclose his/her social security number unless required by federal statute (P.L. 93-579, section 7 subs. (a)(1), (a)(2); 5 U.S.C. section 552a note). The section further requires any agency requesting disclosure to inform the individual as to whether the disclosure is mandatory or voluntary, pursuant to which statute, and what use will be made of it. (See, *California Housing Finance Agency* (1981) 64 Ops AG 576, 583-584.) The court in *Swisher v. Department of the Air Force* (1980) 660 F.2d 369, 495 F. Supp. 377 held that plaintiff was entitled to a copy of the requested Report of Inquiry; however his motion to compel disclosure of social security numbers listed in the report which identified people other than plaintiff was denied under 5 U.S.C. section 552(b)(6), since release of these "identifying numbers" would "constitute a clearly unwarranted invasion of personal privacy."

Furthermore, where nonexempt materials are not inextricably interwined with exempt materials, segregation is required to serve the objectives of the Public Records Act (PRA). *Northern California Police Practices Project v. Craig* (1979) 90 Cal. App. 3d 116; 153 Cal. Rptr. 173; *Johnson v. Winter* (1982) 127 Cal. App. 3d 435.

Accordingly, we affirm the ALJ's conclusion that the confidentiality of the social security numbers of nonunit employees was properly asserted by the District. The District's subsequent refusal to provde the PCR in its present form and its offer to delete the social security numbers did not, in and of itself, constitute bad faith bargaining.

Obligation to Bargain over Costs

The Association excepts to the ALJ's conclusion that it was obligated to bargain with the District over the cost of providing the PCR. The Association contends that such a request would be futile, and therefore, it was not obligated to bargain, citing *Los Angeles Community College District* (1982) PERB Decision No. 252.

The District raised bona fide objections to the form of the information requested. The District also countered the Association's demand with reasonable proposals designed to satisfy the needs of the Association and achieve a mutually satisfactory resolution. We think, in this instance, the Association's resort to PERB is premature. While the Association is not required to engage the District in extensive negotiations regarding the content of the disclosure, it cannot instantly put the District to the election of immediately supplying everything demanded or defending against an unfair practice charge. The Association must provide the District with the opportunity to provide the requested information on mutually satisfactory terms. Good faith is required on both sides. See, *Emeryville Research Center v. NLRB* (9th Cir. 1971) 441 F.2d 880 at 885 [77 LRRM 2043]; *Soule Glass and Glazing Co. v. NLRB* (1st Cir. 1981) 652 F.2d 1055 [107 LRRM 2781, 2806], *denying enf. in part to* 246 NLRB 792 (1979) [102 LRRM 1693].

The District determined the costs of removing the social security numbers of nonunit employees based upon information from the support staff directly involved in producing the PCR. The ALJ found that such costs were reasonable. If the employer has demonstrated substantial costs involved in compiling the information in the precise form at the intervals requested by the Union, the parties must bargain in good faith as to who shall bear such costs. *Queen Anne Record Sales dba Tower Books* (1984) 273 NLRB 671 [118 LRRM 1113], enf'd, (CA 9, 1985) 772 F.2d 913 [121 LRRM 2048]. While we recognize that the Association did not request deletion of the social security numbers, the District's assertion of confidentiality was proper and therefore resulted in additional costs. There is no evidence that the District was unwilling to meet with the Association to discuss costs. The record does not indicate that Charging Party made any effort to negotiate the costs of supplying the PCR prior to filing the instant unfair practice charge. Therefore, we affirm the ALJ's conclusion that the Association was under the obligation to make a request to bargain over the costs of providing the PCR.

NOTES

1. In *Detroit Edison Co. v. NLRB*, 440 U.S. 301, 99 S. Ct. 1123, 59 L. Ed. 2d 333 (1979), a case relied on by the California Board in the principal case, the Supreme Court held that the NLRB abused its discretion in ordering an employer to provide a union, upon request, with the questions used on an aptitude test battery, as well as the answer sheets. The Court held that the company's interest in maintaining the confidentiality of this information outweighed the union's interest in obtaining it. The Court noted that "[a] union's bare assertion tht it needs information to process a grievance does not automatically oblige the employer to supply all the information in the manner requested." In rejecting the NLRB's contention that the confidentialiy of the information requested would be adequately protected, the Court stated:

> The restrictions barring the Union from taking any action that might cause the test to fall into the hands of employees who have taken or are likely to take them are only as effective as the sanctions available to enforce them. In this instance, there is substantial doubt whether the Union would be subject to a contempt citation were it to ignore the restrictions.... Moreover, the Union ciearly would not be accountable in either contempt or unfair labor practice proceedings for the most realistic vice inherent in the Board's remedy — the danger of inadvertent leaks.

The Court also held that the company could require an employee's consent before releasing an employee's test score to the union "[i]n the light of the sensitive nature of testing information" and "the minimal burden that compliance with the Company's offer would have placed on the Union."

In sharp contrast to the Supreme Court's decision in *Detroit Edison*, the Minnesota Supreme Court in *Operating Eng'rs Local 49 v. City of Minneapolis*, 305 Minn. 364, 233 N.W.2d 748 (1975), after noting that "the duty to meet and negotiate in good faith includes the obligation to provide information which is necessary to intelligent functioning in the bargaining process," held that an employee organization that was challenging the validity of a civil service examination is entitled to access to "the questions and the answer key to the civil service examination." The court noted "that the public interest in protecting the confidentiality of civil service examinations can be adequately served if respondent is directed to refrain from disclosing the requested information to applicants who will take this examination in the future."

2. In *Department of Navy v. FLRA*, 840 F.2d 1131 (3d Cir. 1988), the court upheld an FLRA's decision holding that it was an unfair labor practice for an employer to deny a union's request for the names and addresses of the employees which it represented. The court specifically rejected the Navy's contention "that such release is prohibited by the Privacy Act and that disclosure of such material is not necessary for effective collective bargaining...."

On the other hand, the District of Columbia Court of Appeals, in *FLRA v. Treasury Dep't*, 884 F.2d 1446 (D.C. Cir. 1989), held that the release of the names and addresses of bargaining unit employees by federal agencies would violate the Privacy Act. In reversing a decision of the FLRA, the court rejected the Authority's finding that the union's need for the names and addresses "far outweighs" the privacy interests of federal employees, noting that any public purpose in disclosing the names and addresses was not enough "to outweigh the workers' significant interest in privacy."

3. Does an employer's obligation to provide relevant information to a union extend to a request for information concerning a grievance which is being processed in accordance with the contractual grievance procedure? In *NLRB v. Acme Indus. Co.*, 385 U.S. 432 (1967), the Court answered this question affirmatively, stating that the "duty to bargain unquestionably extends beyond the period of contract negotiations and applies to labor-management relations during the term of an agreement." Accord *Commonwealth of Mass., Dep't of Pub. Works,* Case No. SUP-20 (Mass. LRC 1972); *Joint Sch. Dist. No. 9, Merton Sch.,* Decision No. 15155-D (Wis. ERC 1978) (unfair labor practice to refuse to provide tapes of disciplinary meetings where requested in order to process grievance).

In *AFGE Local 1345 v. FLRA,* 793 F.2d 1360 (D.C. Cir. 1986), the court held that a union's obligations as exclusive bargaining representative entitled the union to information concerning employee dismissals even though the employees had not asked the union for representation with respect to their dismissals. The court noted that in order to fulfill its obligations as the exclusive bargaining representative necessarily meant "that the Union must be able to inform employees of the procedures to which they are entitled and to communicate its willingness to enforce compliance with the bargaining agreement."

4. The Supreme Court in *NLRB v. Truitt Mfg. Co.,* 351 U.S. 149 (1956), held that the employer committed an unfair labor practice under the NLRA when it failed, upon request, to supply financial data in support of its claim that it could not afford to pay higher wages. In so ruling, the Court stated:

> We think that in determining whether the obligation of good faith bargaining has been met, the Board has a right to consider an employer's refusal to give information about its financial status. While Congress did not compel agreement between employer and bargaining representatives, it did require collective bargaining in the hope that agreements would result. Section 204(a)(1) of the Act admonishes both employers and employees to "exert every reasonable effort to make and maintain agreements concerning rates of pay, hours, and working conditions...." In their effort to reach an agreement here, both the union and the company treated the company's ability to pay increased wages as highly relevant. The ability of an employer to increase wages without injury to his business is a commonly considered factor in wage negotiations. Claims for increased wages have sometimes been abandoned because of an employer's unsatisfactory business condition; employees have even voted to accept wage decreases because of such conditions.
>
> Good-faith bargaining necessarily requires that claims made by either bargainer should be honest claims. This is true about an asserted inability to pay an increase in wages. If such an argument is important enough to present in the give and take of bargaining, it is important enough to require some sort of proof of its accuracy. And it would certainly not be farfetched for a trier of fact to reach the conclusion that bargaining lacks good faith when an employer mechanically repeats a claim of inability to pay without making the slightest effort to substantiate the claim. Such has been the holding of the Labor Board since shortly after the passage of the Wagner Act. In *Pioneer Pearl Button Co.,* decided in 1936, where the employer's representative relied on the company's asserted "poor financial condition," the Board said: "He did no more than take refuge in the assertion that the respondent's financial condition was poor; he refused either to prove his statement, or to permit independent verification. This is not collective bargaining." 1 N.L.R.B. 837, 842-843. This was the position of the Board when the Taft-Hartley Act was passed in 1947 and has been its position ever since. We agree with the Board

that a refusal to attempt to substantiate a claim of inability to pay increased wages may support the finding of a failure to bargain in good faith.

Accord *Sergeant Bluff-Luton Community Sch. Dist.,* Case No. 984 (Iowa PERB 1977); *Macomb County Community College,* 1972 MERC Lab. Op. 775 (Mich.) (union's right to financial information dependent on employer's claim of inability to pay).

5. In *Commonwealth of Pa. v. PLRB,* 1986-88 PBC ¶ 35,049 (Pa. Commw. Ct. 1987), the court upheld a Pennsylvania Labor Relations Board order requiring an employer to produce information on non-bargaining unit employees where the union demonstrated a need for the requested information. In addition, the court ruled that the Pennsylvania Board had the authority to require an employer to reduce to writing its reasons for making particular managerial decisions which had not been previously put in written form. See also *Timberlane Regional Educ. Ass'n v. Crompton,* 114 N.H. 315, 319 A.2d 632 (1974) (school board ordered to provide teachers association with names and addresses of all employees, including substitutes employed during strike, in order to permit association to review credentials of substitutes, etc.); *Doolan v. Board of Coop. Educ. Servs.,* 48 N.Y.2d 341, 398 N.E.2d 533, 422 N.Y.S.2d 927 (1979) (union president held entitled to receive copy of comparative salary survey of county school districts which was prepared and distributed to subscribing school districts where there was no showing that the release of the survey would impair negotiations).

4. UNILATERAL ACTION

Once a union has been duly designated as the collective bargaining representative for a given group of employees, the employer is thereafter obligated to negotiate and bargain in good faith with the union with respect to matters that are negotiable. Concomitant with this obligation is the requirement that an employer refrain from taking unilateral action with respect to matters that are subject to negotiation without first offering to negotiate with the union. Thus, in *NLRB v. Katz,* 369 U.S. 736 (1952), the Court stated:

> The duty "to bargain collectively" enjoined by § 8(a)(5) is defined by § 8(d) as the duty to "meet ... and confer in good faith with respect to wages, hours, and other terms and conditions of employment." Clearly, the duty thus defined may be violated without a general failure of subjective good faith; for there is no occasion to consider the issue of good faith if a party has refused even to negotiate *in fact* — "to meet ... and confer" — about any of the mandatory subjects. A refusal to negotiate *in fact* as to any subject which is within § 8(d), and about which the union seeks to negotiate, violates § 8(a)(5) though the employer has every desire to reach agreement with the union upon an overall collective agreement and earnestly and in all good faith bargains to that end. We hold that an employer's unilateral change in conditions of employment under negotiation is similarly a violation under § 8(a)(5), for it is a circumvention of the duty to negotiate which frustrates the objectives of § 8(a)(5) much as does a flat refusal.
>
> ... Unilateral action by an employer without prior discussion with the union does amount to a refusal to negotiate about the affected conditions of employment under negotiation and must of necessity obstruct bargaining, contrary to the congressional policy. It will often disclose an unwillingness to agree with the union. It will rarely be justified by any reason of substance. It

follows that the board may hold such unilateral action to be an unfair labor practice in violation of § 8(a)(5), without also finding the employer guilty of over-all subjective bad faith. While we do not foreclose the possibility that there may be circumstances under which the Board could or should accept as excusing or justifying unilateral action, no such case is presented here.

Citing *Katz*, the Connecticut State Board of Labor Relations in *Town of Stratford*, Decision No. 1069 (1972), observed that "[i]t is well recognized that unilateral employer action upon a matter which is the subject of current collective bargaining between the parties constitutes a failure and refusal to bargain in good faith upon the issue in question." Accord *Borough of Naugatuck*, Conn. State Bd. of Lab. Rel. Decision No. 769 (1967) (unilateral adoption of a new classification plan while negotiations were in progress). See generally *West Hartford Educ. Ass'n v. DeCourcy, supra.*

BOARD OF COOPERATIVE EDUCATIONAL SERVICES v. NEW YORK STATE PERB

41 N.Y.2d 753, 363 N.E.2d 1174 (1977)

COOKE, JUDGE. We hold that, after the expiration of an employment agreement, it is not a violation of a public employer's duty to negotiate in good faith to discontinue during the negotiations for a new agreement the payment of automatic annual salary increments, however, long standing the practice of paying such increments may have been. Accordingly, it was error for the Public Employment Relations Board (PERB) to order the petitioner in this proceeding to negotiate in good faith because of its failure to pay increments after expiration of an employment agreement.

This labor dispute arose between the Board of Cooperative Educational Services of Rockland County (BOCES), a public employer, and the BOCES Staff Council (the Staff Council), the recognized negotiating representative of instructional employees of BOCES. Since 1968, the parties have been signatories to a series of four agreements, the most recent of which covered the period from July 1, 1972 to June 30, 1974. A progression of automatic steps increments for employees in the unit has been provided for in each of these agreements. In addition, in prior years, when a contract between the parties had expired, even if a successor agreement had not yet been reached, BOCES paid the automatic step increments to returning unit employees.

In March, 1974, the Staff Council advised BOCES that it wished to negotiate a successor contract to the 1972-1974 agreements. Prior to the commencement of negotiations, on June 19, 1974, BOCES adopted a resolution which provided that pending the execution of a new agreement or September 1, 1974, whichever came earlier, the provisions of the agreement expiring June 30, 1974 would be recognized, including salary and salary rates in effect on June 30, 1974, for the period herein contemplated. Pursuant to this resolution, which was subsequently extended, BOCES maintained the salaries at the rate in effect on June 30, 1974 during negotiations for the successor agreement, but refused to pay the step increments to returning unit employees. Because of this refusal, the Staff Council filed with PERB an improper practice charge against BOCES alleging that the latter had unilaterally withdrawn a previously enjoyed benefit

— automatic salary increments — while a successor agreement was being negotiated, in violation of section 209-a (subd. 1, par. [d]) of the Civil Service Law (the Public Employees' Fair Employment Act).

At the hearing, BOCES raised an affirmative defense that the right to the salary increments was extinguished when the most recent agreement expired on June 30, 1974. This argument was rejected by the hearing officer, who reasoned that the duty of an employer to maintain the *status quo* during the course of negotiations is not directly concerned with whether or not contractual obligations survive a contract's expiration. Authority for this reasoning was based on PERB's decision in *Matter of Triborough Bridge & Tunnel Auth. (District Council 37 & Local 1396)* (5 PERB 3064 [1972]). In that decision, PERB held that it is a violation of a public employer's duty to negotiate in good faith for it to alter, unilaterally during negotiations, terms and conditions of employment which include a long-standing and continued practice of providing annual salary increments, even though the agreement under which such increments were negotiated has expired. The hearing officer, applying this decision, commonly referred to as the "Triborough Doctrine," found that BOCES had violated its duty to negotiate in good faith and recommended that it be ordered to negotiate in good faith, such order contemplating that it would cease and desist from refusing to pay the increments and would forthwith pay such increments retroactive to the commencement of the 1974-1975 school year.

Thereafter, PERB indorsed the reasoning of the hearing officer and his conclusions of law. It also reasserted the validity of the Triborough "doctrine" or proposition and further noted that it makes no difference under said proposition whether or not the practice of paying increments was ever embodied in any agreement. In addition, while recognizing that it could not compel BOCES to pay the increments, it rejected BOCES' request that it limit its order to a direction that BOCES negotiate in good faith. PERB's order, therefore, stated in relevant part: "we order respondent to negotiate in good faith, such order contemplating that respondent will cease and desist from refusing to pay increments to those of its employees entitled to increments under the recently expired agreement and that it will forthwith pay to such employees increments retroactive to the commencement of the 1974-75 school year".

BOCES thereafter commenced an article 78 proceeding seeking to annul and vacate PERB's order....

... [W]e granted leave ... in order to consider PERB's so-called "Triborough Doctrine". At the outset, it should be noted that the Federal cases involving the private sector relied on by the Staff Council and PERB are not dispositive. That there are problems peculiar to public employers is manifested by the number of cases before this court concerning the financial difficulties of these employers. In addition to financial pressures, other factors enter in the budgetary considerations of such employers (see, e.g., L. 1976, ch. 132, commonly known as the Stavisky-Goodman bill). Perhaps for this reason, the Legislature provided with respect to improper labor practices that "fundamental distinctions between private and public employment shall be recognized, and no body of federal or state law applicable wholly or in part to private employment, shall be regarded as binding or controlling precedent" (Civil Service Law, § 209-a, subd. 3). So mindful, we turn to a consideration of "Triborough".

It has been held that the Triborough proposition is unnecessary where the unilateral conduct of an employer in refusing to grant agreed upon increments occurs before the bargaining agreement expires, because in that instance the evidence of failure to negotiate in good faith is manifested by the failure to live up to the terms of the existing contract.... The proposition, however, is sought to be applied in circumstances where the contract has expired because, it is said, an unilateral failure to pay increments under the expired contract also manifests a lack of good faith. While such a principle may apply where an employer alters unilaterally during negotiations other terms and conditions of employment, it should not apply where the employer maintains the salaries in effect at the expiration of the contract but does not pay increments.

The reasons for not giving effect in these circumstances to the so-called "Triborough Doctrine" should be apparent. Involving a delicate balance between fiscal and other responsibilities, its perpetuation is fraught with problems, equitable and economic in nature. As a reward and by encouraging the retention of experienced personnel in public positions, the concept of increments based on continuance in service, properly exercised, is creditable for the public entity and the citizenry are better served, and time losses suffered because of training periods and inefficiency in performance are likely to be reduced. The concept of continual successive annual increments, however, is tied into either constantly burgeoning growth and prosperity on the part of the public employer, or the territory served by it, or a continuing general inflationary spiral, without admeasurement either of the growth or inflation and without consideration of several other relevant good faith factors such as comparative compensation, the condition of the public fisc and a myriad of localized strengths and difficulties. In thriving periods the increment of the past may not squeeze the public purse, nor may it on the other hand be even fair to employees, but in times of escalating costs and diminishing tax bases, many public employers simply may not be able in good faith to continue to pay automatic increments to their employees.

PERB's counsel takes the position that applying "Triborough", so as, in effect, to require the payment during negotiations of salary increments under an expired contract, does not lock the employees into a guaranteed gain position. Rather, it is argued, payment of such increments merely preserves the existing relationship until different conditions are established through collective bargaining which may include the entire abolition of the incremental structure. Such arguments, though superficially appealing, are not convincing. They are based on the erroneous assumption that it is the "existing relationship" which is being preserved, when, in reality, such payments extend or change the relationship established by the parties. In times either of inflation or depression, employees, quite naturally, will be reluctant to accept abolition of automatic increments which they have been receiving. To the extent that it provides that such increments must be paid even after expiration of contract, the proposition gives an edge and makes negotiation of that point that much more difficult.

To say that the status quo must be maintained during negotiations is one thing; to say that the status quo includes a change and means automatic increases in salary is another. The matter of increments can be negotiated and, if it is agreed that such increments can and should be paid, provision can be made for payment retroactively. The inherent fallacy of PERB's reasoning is that it seeks to make automatic increments a matter of right, without regard to the particular facts and circumstances, by establishing a rule that failure by a public employer to continue such increments during negotiations is a violation of the duty to negotiate in good faith. No such principle appears in the statute, nor should one exist by administrative fiat. Therefore, without expressing complete disapproval of the "Triborough Doctrine", we hold that it was error for PERB to determine that BOCES had violated its duty to negotiate in good faith solely because of its failure to pay increments after the expiration of an employment agreement.

Accordingly, the judgment of the Appellate Division should be modified, without costs, by annulling and vacating PERB's determination in its entirety, and, as so modified, affirmed.

NOTES

1. Accord *Menasha Teachers Union, Local 1166,* Decision No. 16589-B (Wis. ERC 1981).

2. In *Ledyard Bd. of Educ.,* Decision No. 1564 (Conn. St. Bd. Lab. Rel. 1977), the Connecticut SBLR held that a school board committed an unfair labor practice when it unilaterally withheld payment of vertical salary increments, even though the contract which provided for the increments had expired. The Connecticut SBLR held that "[r]egular annual salary increments payable under existing policies or practice constitute an existing condition of employment whether or not the increment was mandated by contract, and a discontinuance of such policy or practice constitutes a change in existing wages and conditions of employment." Accord *Hudson Cty. Bd. of Chosen Free-holders,* 4 NJPER 39 (N.J. PERC 1978); *Detroit Pub. Schs.,* 1984 MERC Lab. Op. 579 (Mich.); *School Bd. of Escambia Cty.,* 10 FPER ¶ 15160 (Fla. PERC 1984); *Calexico Unified Sch. Dist.,* 7 PERC ¶ 14291 (Cal. PERB 1983).

In *Vienna Sch. Dist. No. 55 v. IELRB,* 515 N.E.2d 476, 1986-88 PBC ¶ 35,023 (Ill. App. Ct. 1987), the court held that an employer committed an unfair labor practice by not providing annual step increases to teachers that were provided for by the terms of an expired collective bargaining agreement where it was reasonable for the teachers in question to expect such step increases based upon their education and experience. In distinguishing the New York Court of Appeals decision in the principal case, the court noted that subsequent to that decision the New York legislature "amended its labor provisions to conform to the majority rule." This amendment to the Taylor Law made it an improper practice for a public employer "to refuse to continue all terms of an expired contract until a new agreement is negotiated unless the employee organization which is a party to such agreement has, during such negotiations or prior to such resolution of such negotiations, engaged in [a strike prohibited by the Act]. New York Civil Service Law 209-a(1)(a) (McKinney 1983).

3. In *Maine Dep't of Inland Fisheries & Wildlife v. Maine State Emps. Ass'n,* 503 A.2d 1285 (Me. 1986), the Maine Supreme Judicial Court held that an employer did not commit an unfair labor practice when it unilaterally changed a negotiated policy concerning use of department vehicles in order to comply with a recently enacted state law.

4. In *State of N.Y. & AFSCME Council 82,* 7 PERB ¶ 3009 (N.Y. 1974), the New York PERB held that the Governor's signing of a bill prohibiting negotiations on retirement benefits is legislative action and not subject to challenge

before the Board. In thus dismissing an unfair practice charge filed by AFSCME alleging that the Governor's action interfered with the collective bargaining process, PERB upheld its hearing officer who stated:

> In reaching this conclusion, a distinction must be drawn between the Governor's constitutional role in the lawmaking process and his executive and/or delegated role in the proper implementation of legislation.... Only his proprietary actions in the latter role may be reviewed by this Board.

Since the Governor's role in signing law was legislative in nature, the hearing officer concluded that "it must then follow that the Governor's constitutional mandate to approve or veto legislative bills cannot be abrogated by statute and certainly not by an administrative decision of this tribunal." See also *Oregon State Emps. Ass'n v. State,* Case No. C-6-75 (Or. PERB 1975) (Governor's budget recommendation not an unlawful refusal to bargain in good faith).

GREEN COUNTY

Decision No. 20308-B (Wis. Emp. Relations Comm'n 1984)

BACKGROUND

In its complaint initiating this proceeding, the Union alleged that the County committed a prohibited practice within the meaning of Secs. 111.70(3)(a) 1 and 4 of the Municipal Employment Relations Act (MERA) by unilaterally changing the health insurance plan covering its unit employes. The County denied that it committed any prohibited practice.

THE EXAMINER'S DECISION

The Examiner found applicable herein a rule that an employer may unilaterally implement a change in terms and conditions of employment after having first bargained the same to impasse with the collective bargaining representative. The Examiner found, however, that no such impasse had been reached under the facts of this case. The Examiner concluded that by substituting the Blue Cross-Blue Shield plan for the WPS-HMP plan on April 1, 1982, the County violated Secs. 111.70(3)(a) 1 and 4 of MERA.

In reaching this conclusion the Examiner relied on what he interpreted as the County's relatively late introduction of the proposed change into negotiations, the failure of the County to prove any real urgency as to the issue, the continuing flexibility displayed by the Union and the limited number of face-to-face discussions held by the parties on this issue.

The Examiner also concluded, contrary to the contention of the County, that the Union had not waived its right to bargain on the issue by its responses or nonresponses to the County's offers to bargain on the issue.

Having determined that no impasse existed at the time of the unilateral change, the Examiner found it unnecessary to determine what impact, if any, Sec. 111.77, Stats., has on post-petition unilateral implementation after impasse has been reached.

In his remedial order, the Examiner limited his make-whole order to the period between April 1, 1982, and March 4, 1983, based on the fact that on the latter date the health insurance proposal submitted by the Union in its final offer of that date became identical to that of the County. The Examiner thus concluded that as of that date the parties had effectively reached tentative agreement on the issue such that no further remedial relief was necessary or appropriate.

THE COUNTY'S PETITION FOR REVIEW AND SUPPORTING ARGUMENTS

In its petition for review the County alleges that the Examiner erred in not finding that the parties had reached impasse prior to the County's unilateral implementation of its health insurance proposal, and in his subsequent finding of a violation based on the lack of impasse. The County contends that there is substantial evidence in the record which supports a finding of impasse....

THE UNION'S PETITION FOR REVIEW AND SUPPORTING ARGUMENTS

In its petition for review the Union alleges that the Examiner erred as a matter of law by (1) basing his decision on a rule that an employer can unilaterally implement changes in mandatory subjects of bargaining prior to the completion of final and binding interest arbitration and (2) by limiting his makewhole remedy to the period from April 1, 1982, to March 4, 1983. Rather, the Union contends that Sec. 111.77, Stats., does not allow for unilateral implementation upon impasse and that the Examiner's remedy should be amended to extend its application until such time as either the parties agree to implementation or the balance of the issues outstanding are decided by an interest arbitrator.

In its brief in support of its petition the Union contends that the fact that during the course of the investigatory phase of the interest arbitration procedure it submitted a "final offer" containing a proposal identical to that submitted by the County, does not require it to stay with that proposal. It maintains that the process contemplates package proposals and that in the absence of agreement on the entire package, the County was not entitled to selectively pick from the proposals contained in the Union's package for implementation. The Union points out that it has a statutory right to change the composition of its "final offers" until such time as the WERC investigator certifies the final offers to the Commission. Thus it argues that for remedial purposes it cannot be bound to contents of any of its earlier offers. It further argues that these "early" final offers do not rise to the level of a tentative agreement and the Commission has already ruled that an employer cannot unilaterally select and implement tentative agreements....

DISCUSSION

Existence and Nature of Impasse Defense in Disputes Subject to Sec. 111.77 Arbitration.

It is well established that, absent a valid defense, a unilateral change in a mandatory subject of bargaining constitutes a per se violation of the MERA duty to bargain and hence of Sec. 111.70(3)(a)4, Stats. Clear and unmistakable evidence of waiver of the Complainant's right to bargain has been recognized as a valid defense, and the possible availability of a defense based on necessity has also been mentioned.[6] A number of MERA cases refer to an additional valid defense where the bargaining involved has reached an impasse. The Union's Petition for Review takes issue with the Examiner's premising his decision on the notion that an impasse (as defined in private sector case law) constitutes a valid defense to a unilateral change where, as here, the dispute involved is subject to the Sec. 111.77 impasse resolution procedures.

The Examiner found that since there was no impasse under private sector analysis it was unnecessary for him to determine the effect, if any, of Sec. 111.77 on the rights and obligations of the parties in the instant circumstances. However, the Examiner's application of private sector principles seems necessarily to imply that Sec. 111.77 does not foreclose a defense based on impasse defined in private sector terms.

For that reason, we find it both appropriate and necessary in this case to consider whether an "impasse," however defined, constitutes a valid defense to a unilateral implementation of a previous proposal on a mandatory subject in a contract negotiation dispute subject to the binding interest arbitration (municipal interest arbitration, i.e. MIA) procedures in Sec. 111.77, Stats.

This is essentially a case of first impression for the Commission as a whole. A right to implement at impasse (as defined in the private sector cases) has been recognized in cases arising under MERA, but this appears to be the first in which the Commission is squarely presented in a petition for complaint review with the question of whether such a right exists as regards a dispute subject to final and binding Sec. 111.77, Stats., interest arbitration.

While the waiver and necessity defenses are not, in our view, affected by the availability of compulsory final and binding interest arbitration, the same cannot be said of the impasse defense. The Sec. 111.77 provisions making compellable final and binding arbitration an available statutory procedure for resolving contract negotiation disputes in certain law enforcement and firefighting bargaining units departs radically from the comparatively free exercise of economic strength preserved in the private sector law as available means of resolving bargaining impasses. Therefore, although the general refusal to bargain language introduced into MERA in 1971 parallels its private sector precursors under which an impasse defense has long been recognized, the provisions in Sec. 111.77 warrant a different rule.

Thus, we conclude that the binding interest provisions of Sec. 111.77 make inappropriate an application of the private sector impasse defense principles to disputes subject to that final and binding impasse resolution procedure. In our view, the underlying purposes of MERA and Sec. 111.77 warrant and require the conclusion that there is no available impasse-based defense in disputes subject to compulsory final and binding interest arbitration under Sec. 111.77, Stats.

---

[6]*Racine Schools,* Dec. Nos. 13696-C and 13876-B (Fleischli with final authority for WERC, 4/78) at 56. cf. *Milwaukee Schools,* Dec. No. 15829-D (Yaeger, 3/80) at 5, 13 *aff'd by operation of law,* Dec. No. 15829-E (4/80). In the private sector, see, e.g., *Standard Candy Co.,* 147 NLRB 1070 (1964) (change justified as good faith response to need to conform with minimum wage provisions of the Fair Labor Standards Act); and *AAA Motor Lines,* 215 NLRB 793, 88 LRRM 1253 (1974) (change justified by union's dilatory and unlawful bargaining tactics combined with need to change in order to avoid employe losses of certain fringe benefits after contract expiration.)

We do not agree with the County that Sec. 111.77(1) constitutes an implied authorization of unilateral changes such as those at issue herein or any others.[12] The 60-day limitation provided therein, where applicable,[13] constitutes a pre-condition on termination or modification of an existing agreement. The language of that provision prohibits changes (during the 60-day period specified) in any of the terms and conditions of the parties' existing agreement, not merely those that constitute mandatory subjects of bargaining. Therefore, in our view, the 60-day provision is an additional pre-condition to — rather than a substitute for — the otherwise existing limitations on unilateral changes in mandatory subjects imposed by MERA as regards disputes subject to Sec. 111.77 compulsory final and binding interest arbitration.

The three-year limit on the duration of collective bargaining agreements in Sec. 111.70(3)(a)4 relied upon by the County is not contravened by our holding herein. The duty to refrain from unilateral changes in mandatory subjects after expiration of a predecessor agreement derives from the statutory duty to bargain (and in this case from the implications of the statutory procedure for final and binding contract negotiation dispute resolution), *not* from an extension of the term of the predecessor collective bargaining agreement. Thus, post-expiration unilateral changes in permissive subject agreement provisions are not per se violations of the statutory duty to bargain.[14] The duty to bargain in good faith requires the parties to continue the status quo wages, hours and conditions of employment until the party seeking to change the status quo has a valid defense for doing so, whether or not three years have passed since the effective date of the predecessor agreement. To hold otherwise would, for example, remove any limits on unilateral changes in mandatory subjects immediately after expiration of a three year agreement — an interpretation that would ill serve the underlying purposes of MERA. Nevertheless, as is discussed more fully below, in conforming our outcome herein to the underlying purposes of MERA, we have taken into account the possibility of a prolonged period in which the party seeking change is precluded from implementing that change.

We are also cognizant that — unlike Sec. 111.77 — the separate interest arbitration procedure for Milwaukee Police personnel in Sec. 111.70(4)(jm) contains an express provision prohibiting the parties to such disputes from unilaterally altering any mandatory subject of bargaining from the time either party has filed a petition to initiate the interest arbitration process to the time that the matter is resolved by execution of a successor agreement. We do not, however, view the Legislature's silence on that subject in Sec. 111.77 as an indication that the Legislature made any specific judgment as to the availability

[12] Section 111.77 states that in the relationships to which it applies, the parties "have the duty to bargain collectively in good faith including the duty to ... comply with ... procedures ..." including an express obligation "(1) ... Not to terminate or modify any contract in effect unless the party desiring such termination or modification (*inter alia*) ... (d) Continues in full force and effect ... all terms and conditions of the existing contract for a period of 60 days after (certain) notice is given or until the expiration date of the contract, whichever occurs later."

[13] That provision is addressed only to a subset of unilateral changes, to wit, changes in terms and conditions contained in an agreement. Thus it does not apply to unilateral changes in matters not contained in the expiring agreement.

[14] See, e.g., City of Madison, supra, Dec. No. 17300-C (WERC, 7/83) (Timing of implementation of permissive subject changes can, in some circumstances, contribute to the conclusion that the totality of a party's conduct is not consistent with the requirements of good faith bargaining.)

of an impasse defense in disputes subject to final and binding arbitration under Sec. 111.77.

The Legislature cannot, for example, be deemed by its silence to have intended that disputes subject to Sec. 111.77 interest arbitration would be subject to a rule that is just the opposite of that expressly contained in the Milwaukee Police provision. For that conclusion would mean that either party is free at any time after the petition is filed for municipal interest arbitration under Sec. 111.77 to make any unilateral changes it chooses, whether previously proposed or not, and regardless of the status of the bargaining. Such would obviously be inconsistent with the duty to bargain in good faith and with the underlying purposes of MERA.

... Most other public sector tribunals that have addressed the question have limited impasse-based defenses to situations in which available statutory impasse resolution procedures have been exhausted.[16]

The Legislature has included in Sec. 111.70(6) of MERA an express DECLARATION OF POLICY as follows:

> The public policy of the state as to labor disputes arising in municipal employment is to encourage voluntary settlement through the procedures of collective bargaining. Accordingly, it is in the public interest that municipal employes so desiring be given an opportunity to bargain collectively with the municipal employer through a labor organization or other representative of the employes' own choice. If such procedures fail, the parties should have available to them a fair, speedy, effective and, above all, peaceful procedure for settlement as provided in this subchapter.

Contrary to those express statutory purposes, the Examiner's and County's approach of directly applying private sector impasse defense principles to disputes subject to final and binding Sec. 111.77 interest arbitration would, in our view, create an incentive for parties to render less speedy and less effective the statutory processes for peaceful resolution of disputes that the parties are unable to resolve voluntarily through collective bargaining. For, in the absence of a collective bargaining agreement in force, and after the 60-day period specified in Sec. 111.77, a party could propose any change in the status quo that is unacceptable to the other side, maneuver to an impasse in the private sector sense, implement the propsed change, and simultaneously prevent the immedi-

---

[16] See, e.g., State of Washington Public Employment Relation Commission Rule 391-45-552, WAC (12-1-83) (by rule, agency provides that in disputes involving teachers, employer must exhaust mediation and fact finding prior to unilateral change in *status quo* where specific statute — Ch. 41.56.470, RCW — states that in disputes involving uniformed personnel, neither party may make changes in *status quo* "during pendency of the proceedings before the arbitration panel"). *Pennsylvania Labor Relation Board v. Millcreek School District*, 8 PPER 47 (Pennsylvania L.R.B. 1976); *AFSCME Local No. 2752 v. WASCO County*, 4 PECBR 2397 (Oregon PECBR, 1979) *aff'd* 46 Ore. App. 859 (1980); *School Board of Orange County v. Palowitch*, 367 S.2d 730 (Fla. Ct App, 1979); *In Re Piscataway Township Board of Education*, PERC No. 91 (N.J. PERC, 1975); and *Moreno Valley Unified School District v. Public Employment Relations Board*, 142 Cal. App. 3d 191. See also, *In the matter of Triborough Bridge and Tunnel Authority*, 5 PERB 3064 (N.Y. PERB, 1972) (prior to legislation specifically prohibiting unilateral changes, N.Y. PERB held that employer was prohibited from unilaterally changing mandatory subject of bargaining contained in expired contract prior to exhaustion of statutory conciliation procedures). But see, *Commonwealth of Massachusetts (Unity)*, MLC Case No. Sup.-2497 (1982) and *Southwest Michigan College*, 1979 Michigan ERC Lab OP 908, (citing private sector cases, agencies hold unilateral implementation lawful once parties are deadlocked, i.e., exhaustion of mediation and fact finding not required.)

ate referral of the dispute to an interest arbitrator by filing a petition for a declaratory ruling on the mandatory/non-mandatory status of certain of the other party's proposals. That, in our view, is not a scenario consistent with or promotive of peaceful resolution of disputes.

It could be argued, of course, that the further into the bargaining and Sec. 111.77 process a party must go before it may lawfully implement a previously proposed change in the status quo, the greater the incentives for the party favored by the status quo to (1) avoid or delay reaching that point in the statutory process at which the other party is permitted to implement its proposed change in the status quo; and (2) avoid or delay reaching a voluntary settlement on other, less favorable terms. On that basis it could be argued that to adopt the Union's view that there can be no valid impasse defense to a unilateral change in a dispute subject to Sec. 111.77 might tempt some parties opposed to changes in the status quo to drag out the statutory process. However, in our view, creative retroactivity proposals can be proposed which — if agreed upon or included in the final offer selected by the arbitrator — would eliminate much of the advantage of such delaying tactics.[17] In an extreme case, unlawful abusive delay of the statutory process (not present here) might be sufficient to render lawful a unilateral change previously proposed. We recognize that in many instances where both parties are acting in exemplary good faith the statutory processes continue well beyond expiration of any predecessor agreement and that some changes will be difficult to implement retroactively. Nevertheless, we are persuaded that the underlying purposes of MERA and Sec. 111.77 are better served if the parties focus on achieving solutions to retroactivity problems and the rest of their bargaining objectives through bargaining and the statutory procedures rather than through unilateral action.

Contrary to the County's contention, we find nothing anomalous about an interpretation of the legislative scheme wherein an impasse defense is available as regards in-term unilateral changes in subjects not covered by the existing agreement but not available in post-expiration disputes. The critical difference is the non-availability of a statutory method for resolving such in-term disputes as compared with the availability of such a procedure for resolving negotiation disputes concerning new agreements and arising out of formal reopener provisions contained in existing agreements.

It could be argued that an impasse defense to unilateral changes should be recognized in Sec. 111.77 disputes once the Commission has formally declared that the parties are at impasse and certified their respective final offers to an arbitrator under Sec. 111.77. However, we conclude that it is more consistent

---

[17] For example, the County in the instant case could have made a proposal as follows concerning retroactive implementation of its health insurance modification which, if selected, would have closely approximated the outcome it sought to achieve by its unilateral change herein:

In the event that an agreement containing the foregoing health insurance arrangements is not entered into between the parties prior to April 1, 1982, the foregoing provision shall, to the extent possible, be retroactively implemented so as to charge the employes involved (including those who may have quit or been discharged in the interim) as if the employer had been entitled throughout the period since April 1, 1982, to deduct from their pay the portions of health insurance premium costs attributable to the general employe contribution provided above plus the full costs of incremental premiums attributable to the County's provision of additional insurance benefits provided for in the predecessor agreement but not provided for in the health insurance provision above.

with the final and binding interest arbitration provisions of Sec. 111.77 to require the parties to pursue their bargaining objectives to voluntary agreement and (if necessary) the peaceful statutory interest arbitration procedures, than it would to authorize parties at any point in the process to pursue their bargaining objectives through unilateral action by reason of an impasse.

Thus, we conclude that there is no available impasse-based defense to a unilateral change in a mandatory subject in disputes that are subject to final and binding Sec. 111.77 interest arbitration. That conclusion, in our view, will encourage the parties to utilize the fair and peaceful statutory procedure to achieve proposed changes in the status quo regarding mandatory subjects rather than resort to self-help unilateral action to that end. Making changes in the mandatory subject status quo achievable for the most part[19] only through the procedures provided by law will encourage voluntary agreements and will promote the speed with which such disputes are processed in Sec. 111.77 arbitration, rather than focusing the attention of the parties on potentially less peaceful self-help methods (e.g., unilateral changes) of pursuing their bargaining objectives.[20] ...

The insurance change at issue herein was implemented by the County before the parties either had reached an unconditional agreement concerning that change in health insurance or had received a final and binding Sec. 111.77 arbitration award concerning the terms of their successor agreement. Under our analysis above, the County has no valid defense based on an impasse, however defined. Furthermore, we agree with the Examiner's reasons for rejection of the County's contention that the Union waived its bargaining rights in the circumstances, and the facts do not constitute the sort of circumstances that might justify recognition of a necessity defense to the complaint of unilateral change herein. Thus, the County had no valid defense for its unilateral change in the mandatory subject involved herein.

REMEDY

Contrary to the County's contention, it is our view that the pendency of final offer arbitration concerning the County's proposal for a retroactive contract provision consistent with the health insurance change it implemented on April 1, 1982, does not render moot the instant complaint concerning that implementation and does not bar otherwise appropriate make whole relief....

Neither the potential MIA award nor the collective bargaining agreement that would be entered into pursuant to it could be deemed to be a Union waiver of the Union's rights to a determination of the merits of its allegations and to an order providing a remedy for the violation found. A waiver of statutory rights by contract must be established by clear and unmistakable contract language or bargaining history, and that test is not met herein. Indeed, the Union's final

---

[19] As noted, this decision does not affect the continuing validity of defenses based on waiver or necessity in disputes subject to Sec. 111.77, Stats. (See cases cited in Notes 5 and 6, *supra*), and an extreme case of unlawful abusive delay of the statutory dispute resolution process may be another exception.

[20] Our conclusion above does not affect the municipal employer's right to implement changes in permissive subjects of bargaining recognized expressly by the Commission in *City of Madison (Police)*, *supra*, Note 14.

offer expressly states the Union's intention to pursue a remedy for the unilateral change at issue herein outside of the interest arbitration proceeding.

The Union's allegation of a County prohibited practice would not be answered or otherwise rendered of no consequence by the issuance of a Sec. 111.77 interest arbitration award, and it is not rendered moot by the pendency of the arbitration proceeding. The extant standards for mootness have not been met.

The question of what remedy for a prohibited practice will best effectuate the underlying purposes of MERA is a matter for determination by the Commission pursuant to Sec. 111.07(4), rather than for the interest arbitrator. The interest arbitrator is called upon to determine which of the two final offers is more reasonable in consideration of the statutory criteria. Whether or not the County has fashioned the more reasonable of the two offers is not determinative of whether a prohibited practice has been committed or of what remedy, if any, will best effectuate the underlying purposes of MERA. The County could not mandatorily bargain for the Union's waiver of the Union's complaint and request for remedial relief herein. The Union ought not, therefore, be expected or required to fashion its final offer in such a way as to seek a remedy for the County's unlawful conduct through the interest arbitration process. Nor should the potential outcome in the final offer proceeding be deemed conclusive as to the propriety or availability of make whole relief.

The Commission's remedial authority includes requiring the person complained of to take such affirmative action ... as the Commission deems proper." The MERA Declaration of Policy set forth in Sec. 111.70(6), Stats., calls for the parties to have an opportunity to reach a voluntary settlement through collective bargaining. Unlawful unilateral changes such as that committed by the County herein tend to undercut both the integrity of the statutory bargaining process and the status of the Union as the exclusive collective bargaining representative, thereby interfering with employe rights to bargain collectively through their chosen representative.

The conventional remedy for a unilateral change refusal to bargain includes an order to reinstate the status quo existing prior to the change and to make whole affected employes for losses they experienced by reason of the unlawful conduct. The purposes of reinstatement of the status quo *ante* is to restore the parties to the extent possible to the pre-change conditions in order that they may proceed free of the influences of the unlawful change. In our view, the purposes of make whole relief include preventing the party that committed the unlawful change from benefiting from that wrongful conduct, compensating those affected adversely by the change, and preventing or discouraging such violations in the future.

In our view, relief closely approximating that conventional remedy described above should have been ordered in this case. The fact that the Union had — as of the time of the Examiner hearing in this matter — submitted a contemplated final offer that would have adopted the changes in the status quo proposed by the County is of no consequence. Contemplated final offers are subject to unilateral change by the parties prior to the close of the investigation. Had there been an unconditional agreement reached between the parties that the change should be made and had they further specifically agreed that such change should be put into effect on and after a date certain, then, but only then, would it have been appropriate to expressly limit the back pay period to which the instant remedial order applies. Since there was no such unconditional agreement reached herein, we have ordered the County to make whole the affected employes for the losses they experienced from and after the date of the implementation and throughout the period until a successor agreement was executed. For, by implementing and keeping in effect its change in health insurance from April 1, 1982, through the time the parties either unconditionally agree on the change or receive a Sec. 111.77 award, the County's conduct constituted a prohibited practice.

If the Commission does not make the employes adversely affected by those changes whole for losses caused by the County's unlawful conduct, there would be no meaningful disincentive for the County and other parties to commit similar violations in the future. While making whole the employes in that way may in some circumstances give the employes a benefit they are ultimately unable to achieve through the collective bargaining and final offer arbitration processes, we find that to be the necessary and appropriate consequence of the unlawful conduct involved.

Therefore, we have extended the remedy ordered by the Examiner to cover the period from initial implementation of the change until the earlier of the time the parties reach an unconditional agreement concerning that change or receive an interest arbitration award concerning the terms of a successor agreement. We have added the usual interest applicable to back pay orders to this remedial amount, as well.

NOTE

1. In addition to the principal case and the cases cited in footnote 16, other decisions holding that it is an unfair labor practice for an employer to implement its last offer where the parties have not exhausted the statutory impasse procedure even though the parties are at impasse in negotiations include *County of Wayne,* Case Nos. C83 G-206 et al. (Mich. ERC 1984), and *City of Burlington,* Docket No. 80-72 (Vt. LRB 1981). Contra *Massachusetts Org. of State Eng'rs & Scientists v. Labor Rels. Comm'n,* 389 Mass. 920, 452 N.E.2d 1117 (1983).

2. In *Kewanee Community Unit Sch. Dist. No. 229,* 4 PERI ¶ 1136 (Ill. ELRB 1988), the Illinois Educational Labor Relations board held that where the parties have bargained in good faith and are at legitimate impasse, "... an employer may then unilaterally implement a change in mandatory subjects of bargaining consistent with its pre-impasse proposal, after it has given the union notice of its intent to implement the change." The IELRB noted that there was no requirement that mediation must be exhausted before an employer can unilaterally implement its pre-impasse proposal.

5. DUTY TO EXECUTE AN AGREEMENT
CITY OF SAGINAW
1967 MERC Lab. Op. 465 (Mich. Emp. Relations Comm'n)

TRIAL EXAMINER JAMES McCORMICK: I ... am unable to conclude that the City's announced unwillingness to enter into a signed bilateral labor contract is a breach of the bargaining duty as spelled out in Section 15 of PERA. It is true that, under federal law, the refusal of either party to labor negotiations to enter into a signed contract covering agreements reached constitutes an unlawful failure to bargain in good faith. *H.J. Heinz Company v. N.L.R.B.*, 311 U.S. 514, 7 L.R.R.M. 291 (1941); National Labor Relations Act, as amended, sec. 8(d). As stated by National Labor Relations Board Solicitor William Feldesman in a speech reported in the October 31, 1966, Labor Relations Reporter, 53 L.R.R. 186:

> "Of course the labor contract has always been regarded as the hoped-for product of collective bargaining, as it brings to the industrial community concerned a charter of voluntarily made law and palpably evidences labor relations stability."

Professor Archibald Cox (Cases on Labor Law, p. 2) refers to the basic labor relations statutes as the "constitution" of industrial self-government and views the written collective bargaining agreements as the "statutory law" of the employer-employee relationship. It can be seen from such an analogy how important the written contract is to effective collective bargaining in private enterprise. Local governmental bodies, however, must conduct business in a way appropriate to the making of a proper official record. They may act by ordinance, resolution, motion or order. Fordham, *Local Government Law*, p. 403. (In Michigan practice an ordinance ordinarily prescribes a permanent rule for the conduct of government, while a resolution is of a special or temporary character.) *Kalamazoo Municipal Utilities Assn. v. City of Kalamazoo*, 345 Mich. 318, 76 N.W.2d 1 (1956). Modifications in wages, hours and working conditions have generally been effected by adoption of a resolution approving changes in the governmental body's personnel "plan" or "policy." Even where such action has followed upon, and represented the fruit of, consultation with a union, the resolution of the City Council or other legislative body has not reflected that fact, but has appeared to be a unilateral act.

One of the problems created by incorporating collective bargaining agreements into ordinances or resolutions is the fact that these are subject to being modified or repealed by the body that enacted or adopted them. *City of Saginaw v. Consumers Power Co.*, 213 Mich. 460, 182 N.W. 146 (1921). Imagine the situation which would exist if a private employer could modify or repeal its contracts at will. Enforcement of an ordinance or resolution against the public employer also presents legal difficulties.

In any event, the Michigan legislature has specified in Section 15 of PERA that the "execution of a written contract, ordinance or resolution incorporating any agreement reached if requested by either party" satisfies the bargaining duty. While the language is ambiguous, the more reasonable interpretation is that any of these three ways of evidencing or memorializing the verbal understanding is sufficient, and that either party may lawfully hold out for its preferred way, not being obliged to sign a bilateral written contract if it prefers an ordinance or resolution.

It may be, however, that an ordinance or resolution which represents and incorporates a final meeting of minds on a collective bargaining agreement results in contractual rights in both employees and public employer, and is, in fact, a contract, even though it is, in another sense, the free and unilateral decree of a duly-empowered governing body. In *Dodge v. Board of Education of Chicago,* 302 U.S. 74, 58 S. Ct. 98 (1937) the issue was whether a statute providing for pensions for retired teachers created a contract with the teachers, the obligations of which could not be impaired by a later statute decreasing the annuities. The Court recognized that a state may enter into contracts with citizens, the obligation of which the legislature cannot impair by subsequent enactment, but said "On the other hand, an act merely fixing salaries of officers creates no contract in their favor, and the compensation named may be altered at the will of the legislature.... The presumption is that such a law is not intended to create private contractual or vested rights, but merely declares a policy to be pursued until the legislature shall ordain otherwise. He who asserts the creation of a contract with the state in such a case has the burden of overcoming the presumption." It would appear that where an ordinance or resolution "incorporates" a collective bargaining "agreement," following extensive "negotiations," any presumption against the creation of contractual rights could be rebutted. In either event, the peculiar language used in Section 15 of the PERA precludes the finding of a violation in the City's anticipatory refusal to enter into a written contract.

[The Trial Examiner's decision was adopted by the MERC.]

NOTES

1. If the parties reach agreement on a substantial number of issues in negotiations but are nevertheless at impasse on a number of other issues, is the employer obligated to reduce to writing and execute an agreement on those issues on which the parties have reached agreement? In *Local 1363, Int'l Ass'n of Fire Fighters v. DiPrete,* 103 R.I. 592, 239 A.2d 716 (1968), the union, relying on a statutory provision which imposed on employers "the duty to cause any agreement resulting from negotiations to be reduced to a written contract," alleged that the statute required "that whatever matters may have been agreed upon, even though less than all in issue, shall be embodied in a formal writing which, upon execution, will become the collective bargaining agreement governing the working conditions of the Cranston firefighters." The Rhode Island Supreme Court, noting that the word "agreement" "presumes that the parties have arrived at a mutual understanding on all of the matters in negotiation," held that there was no obligation on the city to execute an incomplete collective bargaining agreement.

2. Where a union is certified as the exclusive bargaining representative for a unit of public employees, can the union limit a ratification vote on a proposed collective bargaining agreement to its members only and exclude non-members from participating? In *Daigle v. Jefferson Parish Sch. Bd.,* 345 So. 2d 583 (La. Ct. App. 1977), the court held that there was no statutory law or constitutional provision which granted employees an absolute right to vote for or against ratification of a collective bargaining agreement and that a policy adopted by a union which permitted only members to vote on ratification was reasonable and rational. Citing *Daigle v. Jefferson Parish Sch. Bd.,* the court in *PLRB v. Eastern Lancaster Cty. Educ. Ass'n,* 427 A.2d 305, 1980-81 PBC ¶ 37,262 (Pa. Commw. Ct. 1981), held that it was not an unfair labor practice for a union to limit voting on ratification of a new collective bargaining agreement to union members only. Accord *Wald v. Civil Serv. Emps. Ass'n,* 72 Misc. 2d 723, 340 N.Y.S.2d 451 (S.

Ct., Nassau Cty., 1973). Contra *National Educ. Ass'n of Shawnee Mission, Inc. v. Board of Educ.,* 212 Kan. 741, 512 P.2d 426 (1973) ("ratification is required by a majority of the entire negotiating unit, not just of the negotiating organization"). See also *City of Detroit,* 1978 MERC Lab. Op. 519 (Mich.) (no exceptions filed to ALJ opinion that membership ratification is not required by the Michigan Act). In *City of Reno,* Item #86 (Nev. LGE-MRB 1978), the Nevada Board held that "the means, methods, and procedures whereby an employee organization ratifies its collective bargaining agreement with an employer are internal concerns of the organizaton into which the employer may have no input." The Nevada Board further stated that "[e]fforts by an employer to attempt to dictate the contract ratification procedure utilized by an employee organization would clearly be an interference in the internal administration of an employee organization."

3. Is a collective bargaining agreement which extends beyond the contracting officials' term of office binding on their successors? In *AFSCME Dist. Council No. 33 v. Philadelphia,* 83 Pa. D. & C. 537 (C.P. 1952), the court held that a collective bargaining agreement was binding on a successor administration. Accord *Malone v. Court of Common Pleas,* 594 GERR B-6 (Ohio App. Ct. 1974).

4. Missouri is one of the few states to have a pure "meet and confer" public sector collective bargaining law. As Harry Edwards noted in *An Overview of the "Meet and Confer" States—Where Are We Going?,* Law Quadrangle Notes, Vol. 16, Winter 1972, at 15, "... under the pure 'meet and confer' model, the outcome of any public employer-employee discussions will depend more on management's determinations than on bilateral decisions by 'equals' at the bargaining table." In *Sumpter v. City of Moberly,* 645 S.W.2d 359 (Mo. 1982) (en banc), the Supreme Court of Missouri held that Missouri law does not authorize a city to enter into a binding and enforceable collective bargaining agreement. While the Missouri public sector labor law sets forth a procedure whereby an exclusive bargaining representative can meet and confer with respect to salaries and other terms and conditions of employment and further provides that "[u]pon the completion of the discussions, the results shall be reduced to writing and be presented to the appropriate administrative, legislative, or other governing body in the form of an ordinance, resolution, bill or other form required for adoption, modification or rejection," the court held that this law only meant that "when a proposal is submitted to a public body ..., it has a duty to consider and act on such proposal" and that the law "says nothing whatsoever about a public body entering into or executing a contract if it decides to adopt the representative's proposal."

6. EFFECT OF ILLEGAL CONCERTED ACTIVITY

WARREN EDUCATION ASSOCIATION

1977 MERC Lab. Op. 818 (Mich. Emp. Relations Comm'n)

On December 29, 1976, this Commission issued its decision and Order in the above-entitled matter, holding that a strike by public employees does not constitute a per se refusal to bargain in good faith violative of Section 10(3)(c) of the Public Employment Relations Act (PERA), 1965 PA 379, as amended by 1973 PA 25, MCLA 423.210; MSA 17.455(10). In so ruling, the Commission adopted the reasoning set forth in *Warren Education Association,* 1975 MERC Lab Op 76, in which the Commission adopted the findings of the Administrative Law Judge but ruled that Respondent's work stoppage on October 8, 1973, did not violate Section 10(3)(c) of the Act. This Commission order was vacated and remanded by the Court of Appeals on other grounds.[2] Thereafter, Charging Party filed a motion requesting oral argument and seeking reconsideration of the Commission decision issued December 29, 1976.

In its brief in support of the motion for reconsideration, Charging Party has withdrawn its exception to the Administrative Law Judge's determination that the Union's refusal to agree in writing to items no longer in dispute is not a refusal to bargain in good faith. Charging Party has confined its argument to the issue of whether a strike by a labor organization during the course of bargaining is a per se refusal to bargain in good faith violative of PERA; and, alternatively, whether for purposes of the instant proceeding the Union refused to bargain in good faith based upon the totality of its conduct at and away from the bargaining table. In his Decision and Recommended Order, the Administrative Law Judge found that the strike of October 8, 1973, and concomitant threat to strike violated Respondent's duty to bargain in good faith mandated by Secton 10(3)(c) of PERA. The Administrative Law Judge reasoned that enacting PERA the legislature did not contemplate public employers bargaining under the duress of a work stoppage. To permit a labor organization to bring to the bargaining table pressure through its strike activity would conflict with the policy and the purpose of PERA. Similarly, Charging Party contends that a strike is by definition inconsistent with good faith bargaining; hence, a work stoppage held violative of Section 2 of PERA constitutes a per se refusal in good faith under the Act.

Charging Party urges this Commission to exercise its discretion to reverse our earlier ruling in *Montrose Community Schools,* 1975 MERC Lab Op 38, and to fashion an unfair labor practice in this matter consistent with the legislative intent to prohibit strikes. Initially, we reject Charging Party's contention that the Union escapes accountability for an unlawful work stoppage in that Section 6 PERA provides a discipline procedure only for individual employees. The attempt to dichotomize the Association and its teacher members was expressly rejected by the Michigan Supreme Court in *Lamphere Schools v Federation of Teachers,* 400 Mich 104, 252 NW2d 818, 95 LRRM 2279 (1977). The Court rejected the notion that PERA, and specifically the Section 6 remedies, in effect applies only to public employees individually but not their collective bargaining agents. Moreover, the Court acknowledged: "The utilization of Section 6 remedies results in a significant sanction against the Federation, as an organization consisting of its public employee members." As such, the argument that a strike authorized by a union must be violative of Section 10(3)(c) because Section 6 applies only to individuals must fail.

Charging Party would have this Commission ignore the results of two Court of Appeals decisions addressing the issue of whether a strike is a refusal to bargain in good faith. In *Lamphere School District v Lamphere Federation of Teachers,* 67 Mich App 485, 241 NW2d 257, 92 LRRM 3182 (1976), *aff'g* 1975 MERC Lab Op 555; *lv to app den,* 396 Mich 842 (1972), the Court of Appeals determined that a strike need not indicate failure to bargain in good faith and accordingly affirmed a Commission refusal to accept as binding a party's stipu-

---

[2] *Warren Consolidated Schools v. MERC,* Mich App 58, 240 NW2d 265, 92 LRRM 3051 (1976).

lation that a teachers strike constituted an unfair labor practice. While the Court determined that the stipulation was properly set aside, it further concluded that the school district should have full opportunity to prove its refusal to bargain allegation and remanded to MERC the determination of whether a strike may be evidentiary of bad faith bargaining.

In its decision the Court excerpted from the Court of Appeals decision in *Detroit Board of Education v Detroit Federation of Teachers,* 55 Mich App 499, 503, 223 NW2d 23, 25, 88 LRRM 2389 (1974). In determining that the Circuit Court had subject matter jurisdicion to enjoin the teachers' strike, the Court of Appeals rejected the Union's argument that a strike is an unfair labor practice, vesting in MERC exclusive jurisdiction. In so holding, the Court of Appeals acknowledged the possibility that a union could both bargain in good faith and still strike. We find these Court of Appeals decisions instructive and supportive of our prior ruling in *Montrose Community Schools, supra.* Charging Party likewise discounts the Court of Appeals rationale in *Detroit Board of Education, supra,* as mere dicta having no authoritative or precedential value. It is clear from a review of the briefs filed in this matter by Charging Party, Respondent, and *amici curiae* that the appellate decision which most directly addresses the issue of whether a strike constitutes a per se refusal to bargain is Presiding Judge Gillis' decision in *Lamphere School District v Lamphere Federation of Teachers,* at 67 Mich App 485 — a decision which Charging Party fails to discuss or distinguish.

As noted by the Court of Appeals in *Detroit Board of Education v Federation of Teachers, supra,* the term "strike" is conspicuously absent from the list of statutory unfair labor practices delineated in Section 10 of PERA.[5] Nonetheless, Charging Party contends that Section 16 of PERA authorizes the Commission to adjudicate and remedy unfair labor practices; and, since no section of the Act explicitly excludes strike activity from the scope of unfair labor practices, the Commission should effectuate legislative intent by recognizing a strike as an unfair labor practice. The force of this argument is diminished in light of the 1973 legislative amendments to PERA, which, while delineating union unfair labor practices and vesting in MERC jurisdiction to adjudicate charges against employee organizations, nonetheless failed to include work stoppage in the enumerated unfair labor practices. The significance of the legislature's failure to categorize a strike as an unfair labor practice stems from the high incidence of strike activity which characterized public sector labor relations at the time the amendment were enacted. Section 16 of PERA does not parallel section 23(2) of the Labor Relations and Mediation Act (LRMA), which expressly authorizes MERC to remedy, as an unfair labor practice, an unauthorized or illegal strike. Moreover, we must conclude that the legislature was not unmindful when it amended PERA of the Michigan Supreme Court decision in *Holland School District,* ... wherein the Court injected traditional prerequisites

---

[5] Some jurisdictions expressly designate strike activity a prohibited or unfair labor practice. See e.g., Florida Stat Ann, § 447.501(2)(e); Kansas Stat Ann, § 75-4333(c)(5); Maine Rev Stat Ann, tit. 26, ch. 9-A § 964(2)(c)(3); Minnesota Stat Ann, § 179.68(3)(11); New Hampshire Rev Stat Ann, § 273-A:5(II)(e); Pennsylvania Stat Ann, tit. 43 § 43, § 1201(b)(6)(7); Vermont Stat Ann, tit. 3, Ch. 27, § 962(5); Wisconsin Stat Ann, § 111.84(2)(e).

for obtaining injunctive relief into equity proceedings which involve public sector work stoppages.

In its brief on reconsideration and at oral argument, Charging Party places a strong emphasis on the applicability of the Administrative Law Judge's decision in *Genesee Intermediate School District,* 1970 MERC Lab Op 261, to the issues in the instant matter. Charging Party even goes so far as to contend that when the legislature amended PERA in 1973 it somehow acknowledged the *Genesee* decision as the authoritative analysis for the proposition that an unlawful strike constitutes a refusal to bargain within the meaning of the amended statute. It is difficult for this Commission to conjecture that the legislature when it amended PERA in 1973 had in mind a decision of an Administrative Law Judge, to which no exceptions were filed with this Commission, and not a decision of this State's highest court requiring public employers to prove more than the mere existence of a strike to obtain injunctive relief.

Assuming arguendo that the legislature did contemplate application of the *Genesee* decision by this Commission to strike activity, we nonetheless conclude that the *Genesee* case is not dispositive of the issues in this matter. As *Genesee Intermediate School District* involves a Decision and Recommended Order of the Administrative Law Judge to which no exceptions were taken, the case's limited precedential value must be noted. More importantly, a careful reading of the Administrative Law Judge's Decision and Recommended Order discloses that he construed PERA's strike prohibition as the basis for prohibiting *offensive* lockouts. Nowhere has this Commission determined that a lockout per se constitutes a refusal to bargain in good faith. As such, this Commission has not been faced with the issue of whether a "bargaining" lockout vis-a-vis an economically-justified lockout is a refusal to bargain in good faith; nor has this Commission flatly recognized that in all bargaining disputes strikes and lockouts are equivalent weapons, as contended in Charging Party's brief. Based upon the foregoing, we reaffirm that portion of our ruling in *Montrose Community Schools,* 1975 MERC Lab Op 38, which holds that a public sector work stoppage does not constitute ipso facto a refusal to bargain violative of Section 10 of PERA.

This ruling of law leaves unresolved the determination of whether Respondent refused to bargain in good faith based upon its total course of conduct surrounding negotiations as developed in the record below. We must address this factual issue and modify our December 29, 1976, Decision and Order based upon our recent ruling in *Kalamazoo Public Schools,* 1977 MERC Lab Op 771. Therein we held that conduct away from the bargaining table can constitute such gross interference with employee rights as to render a sham bargaining table conduct which otherwise appears legitimate. Accordingly, we now hold that while a public sector strike does not constitute a per se refusal to bargain, such strike activity can be evidentiary of bad faith bargaining. This holding challenges that portion of our decision in *Montrose Community Schools* wherein we stated, "We are in agreement with the conclusions and reasoning in *Insurance Agents* and will henceforth limit our inquiry as to 10(3)(c) violations to the actual conduct of the Union with regard to meeting and conferring with the Employer."

In the case at hand, the evidence demonstrates that Respondent's at-the-table conduct fulfilled its obligation to bargain in good faith. We are left with the issue of whether Respondent's conduct away from the bargaining table can amount to a repudiation of that apparent good faith. In the case of an employer, we have held that conduct away from the table can lead to the conclusion that bargaining table conduct is superficial, a sham to cover an underlying intent to undermine the union's representative status and bargaining strength, thus violating the employer's 10(3)(c) obligation. *Kalamazoo Public Schools, supra.* The precise issue remaining here is whether a union's total course of conduct away from the table can lead to a related violation; namely, that the union does not desire agreement except on its own unilaterally-imposed terms.

In briefest summary, Respondent's actions here which Charging Party contends should evidence such a violation are the following:

1. The setting of a strike deadline, including a whole series of well-publicized plans and activities designed to persuade the Board and the community that a strike would take place if agreement was not reached by the deadline date.

2. Refusal to accept the Employer's proffer that the parties seek the recommendation of a neutral factfinder.

3. A written statement that Respondent, once the strike began, would not "initiate negotiations" until Charging Party's proposals for change in the previous collective bargaining agreement were withdrawn.

4. The strike itself, which began on the date which Respondent had set as the deadline.

A decision on whether these acts violate the good faith bargaining obligation set forth in 10(3)(c) requires analysis of the principles underlying the statute (PERA) which this Commission is required to enforce. PERA's language in many respects is akin to National Labor Relations Act, and the Supreme Court of Michigan has approved this Commission's use of federal precedents in construing parties' obligations under the Act. *Detroit Police Officers Association v City of Detroit,* 391 Mich 44, 214 NW2d 803, 85 LRRM 2536 (1974). It was on this basis that the Commission in *Montrose Community Schools* relied on the decision of the U.S. Supreme Court in *NLRB v Insurance Agents Union,* 361 US 477 (1960), that unprotected and even illegal activity away from the bargaining table does not constitute a refusal to bargain in good faith.

But PERA is not identical with NLRA in every respect. One of the most important differences is that PERA declares the strike illegal. Under MERC's administration of PERA the parties are instead provided alternatives to the strike, enabling them to press each other for changes in unacceptable positions when a temporary impasse develops. Initially in negotiations, PERA, like NLRA, requires both parties to bargain in good faith in an effort to reach agreement. If these efforts prove unavailing, neutral and professional mediation services are provided under both statutes to assist the parties in their search for peaceful agreement. But if no agreement is reached during mediation, as will inevitably occur in some situations, parties may invoke factfinding procedures, in contrast to the NLRA, rather than strike.

It is unnecessary here to describe in detail the theory and practice of factfinding. Neither is it necessary that we consider whether factfinding is always adequate to force changes in positions leading to voluntary agreement. It is sufficient to note that the legislature of the State of Michigan has determined that either party, or the Commission on its own motion, may institute the factfinding process as a pressure device alternative to the strike.

During the course of negotiations in the instant proceeding, well prior to the strike, Charging Party suggested to Respondent that they seek factfinding recommendations on the outstanding issues. Respondent refused, initially on the basis that in the past years Charging Party had not always accepted the recommendations of factfinders. Subsequently, Respondent stated that it would accept factfinding only if the results thereof were agreed upon by both parties to be binding upon them. Neither of these counterproposals provide an adequate defense for the failure of Respondent to seek a factfinder's recommendation as the legislature provided. [15] Respondent here did not exhaust, much less indicate a willingness to utilize, the legal remedies set forth in the statute for impasse resolution.[16] Rather, Respondent was more inclined to resort to a work stoppage than to employ available statutory impasse resolution mechanisms.

Based upon the foregoing, we conclude that Respondent's totality of conduct constituted a refusal to bargain in good faith. Specifically, we find that Respondent's rejection of proffered recourse to factfinding, the strike and strike-related activity are evidentiary in determining whether the duty to bargain has been breached.

In light of the circumstances as a whole, including Respondent's conduct away from the table and its circumvention of impasse resolving procedures contemplated by the legislature, we further find that Respondent's action amounted to a refusal to bargain in good faith.

To the extent that the foregoing conflicts with that portion of our decision in *Montrose Community Schools, supra,* regarding the use of economic pressure away from the bargaining table, that rationale is hereby overruled.

Any bargaining dispute involving a total course of conduct alleged to violate the obligation to bargain in good faith must be evaluated in light of its own facts and circumstances. On the record here, Respondent violated its good faith bargaining obligation under 10(3)(c).

NOTES

1. In *City of New Haven,* Decision No. 1555 (Conn. SBLR 1977), the Connecticut SBLR held that a union's boycott of extra duty assignments constituted prohibited economic coercion and that the use of such coercion constituted a refusal to bargain in good faith. After concluding that "the Legislature did not intend in MERA to have both good faith bargaining and economic pressure

---

[15] Charging Party's failure to accept recommendations in the past repudiated no obligation upon it, nor predicted what the result might have been had the parties gone to the factfinding prior to the strike in the instant dispute. Moreover, "binding factfinding," as counterproposed by Respondent, is not the impasse resolution procedure which the legislature provided. Such a counter offer, therefore, does not constitute a satisfactory fulfillment of Respondent's obligation to use the legislative alternatives available.

[16] The parties ultimately did settle the dispute following court-ordered bargaining and resort to factfinding.

devices 'exist side by side' as means available to obtain bargaining objectives," the Connecticut Board stated:

Before the labor statutes the employer was free to change conditions of employment unless that freedom has been restricted by contract. If it is a prohibited practice to introduce economic coercion into bargaining by unilaterally changing these conditions it is hard to see why the Union should be free to resort unilaterally to measures of self-help that exert a similar kind of extraneous coercion on the bargaining process.

2. In *Fresno Unified Sch. Dist.*, 6 PERC ¶ 13110 (Cal. PERB 1982), the California Board held that a union strike which was not provoked by the school district but was rather for the purpose of gaining concessions at the bargaining table constituted an unlawful refusal to bargain.

3. The WERC in *City of Portage*, Decision No. 8378 (1968), in response to the city's assertion that a work stoppage constituted a defense to a prohibited practice charge, noted that it did "not apply the unclean hands' doctrine as a defense to prohibited practices ...." However, in *City of Milwaukee (Dep't of Pub. Works)*, Dec. No. 6575B (Dec. 12, 1963), the WERC held:

The fact finding procedure set forth in the statute is designed to give representatives of municipal employes an opportunity to persuade the municipal employer and the public of the merits of their particular requests with reference to the wages, hours and working conditions of municipal employes. As administrators of this statute we do not believe that labor organizations, who ignore these considerations by engaging in a strike, should at the same time be entitled to the benefits of fact finding or other rights granted to them by statute. The Board as a general policy and in the absence of good cause shown will decline to process any fact finding petition filed by a labor organization which is engaged in a strike.

4. In *Saginaw Twp. Bd. of Educ.*, 1970 MERC Lab. Op. 127 (Mich.), the Michigan Commission in a split decision held that a union's illegal strike did not relieve an employer from the obligation to negotiate during the duration of the strike.

5. In *Cherry Hill Bd. of Educ.*, 4 NJPER 462 (N.J. PERC 1978), the New Jersey Commission held that a board of education "was within its rights to schedule the makeup day without negotiating with the teachers" where this was necessary due to an illegal teacher strike. The New Jersey Commission, however, held that it was an unfair labor practice for the employer to unilaterally reduce teachers' pay by refusing to pay teachers who struck for days of work that were rescheduled.

6. The National Labor Relations Board has held "that it is a defense to a charge of employer bad faith [bargaining], that the union was not itself in good faith." *Roadhome Constr. Corp.*, 170 N.L.R.B. 91 (1968). In *Times Publishing Co.*, 72 N.L.R.B. 676, 682-83 (1947), the NLRB reasoned as follows:

The test of good faith in bargaining that the Act requires of an employer is not a rigid but a fluctuating one, and is dependent in part upon how a reasonable man might be expected to react to the bargaining attitude displayed by those across the table. It follows that ... a union's refusal to bargain in good faith may remove the possibility of negotiation and thus preclude the existence of a situation in which the employer's own good faith can be tested. If it cannot be tested, its absence can hardly be found.

D. THE DUTY TO BARGAIN DURING THE TERM OF A COLLECTIVE BARGAINING AGREEMENT

CITY OF ST. PETERSBURG

6 FPER ¶ 11277 (Fla. Pub. Emp. Rel. Comm'n 1980)

On November 21, 1979, the Pinellas County Police Benevolent Association, Inc., (PBA) filed a timely unfair labor practice charge alleging that the City of St. Petersburg (City) violated Section 447.501(1)(a) and (c), Florida Statutes (1979), by unilaterally revising disciplinary rules governing certain of its employees.

An evidentiary hearing on the allegations set forth in the charge was conducted before Commission Hearing Officer Curtis A. Billingsley on January 14 and 15, 1980, at which the parties were given an opportunity to present evidence and to cross-examine witnesses. On January 30, 1980, the PBA filed proposed findings of fact and conclusions of law, and the City filed a brief to the Hearing Officer. The Hearing Officer's Recommended Order issued on February 29, 1980. The PBA and the City timely filed exceptions to the Recommended Order and argument in support thereof....

In its exceptions, the City also urges the Commission to defer to arbitration, and suggests that the Commission does not have jurisdiction to process the instant unfair labor practice charge until "exhaustion of contractual remedies" has taken place through utilization of the contractual grievance-arbitration process.

The Commission has jurisdiction to process the instant unfair labor practice charge pursuant to Section 447.503, Florida Statutes (1979). The Second District Court of Appeal has held that the Commission and the circuit courts have concurrent jurisdiction over actions which may involve both a breach of a collective bargaining agreement and an unfair labor practice....

Deferral to arbitration is not a matter of right, but is a matter of policy, the application of which is committed to the sound discretion of the Commission. Deferral to arbitration serves to implement the fundamental policy of allowing and encouraging the parties to provide their own solutions to disputes which may be resolved by interpretation or application of the collective bargaining agreement. *Florida PBA, Inc. v. State of Florida,* 4 FPER ¶ 4108 (1978). In such cases, it is preferable that disputes be settled, if possible, "without resort to the sometimes ponderous apparatus of [state] intervention." *T.I.M.E.—DC, Inc. v. NLRB,* 504 F.2d 294, 302 (5th Cir. 1974).

These policy goals would not be furthered by deferral to arbitration where no arbitration proceeding is pending and where there is no indication that, as a practical matter, arbitration will occur. Deferral under such circumstances might very well result only in the reassertion of jurisdiction by the Commission after a wait-and-see period of delay. The Commission will not defer to arbitration when it is uncertain whether deferral is likely to result in the prompt resolution of the dispute....

Review of the record in the instant case reveals that, although the City raised the issue of deferral to arbitration in its Answer filed December 20, 1979, and in its Prehearing Statement filed January 4, 1980, as well as in the exceptions we here discuss, the City has not indicated that grievance-arbitration proceedings are pending or that it is willing to waive any time requirements or other procedural impediments which might bar full and final resolution of the dispute through the contractual grievance-arbitration mechanism. In the absence of such an unconditional submission to arbitration, deferral is inappropriate, especially where, as here, the requested deferral would occur subsequent to the completion of the evidentiary hearing and issuance of the Recommended Order by the Hearing Officer.

We next consider the PBA's exceptions....

The PBA next excepts to the Hearing Officer's failure to find that the contractual managment rights clause (Article 3) and the "zipper" clause (Article 24) contained in the current PBA/City labor agreements were adopted verbatim and carried forward without discussion from previous labor agreements entered into by the parties. Review of the PBA's proposed findings of fact filed with the Hearing Officer reveals that the PBA did not specifically propose a finding of fact to this effect. Nevertheless, such a supplemental finding would aid a full understanding of the dispute in this case, and is supported by substantial competent evidence (Transcript pages 85, 97, 102, 168-169). Therefore, the Commission makes the following finding of fact:

The contractual management rights clause (Article 3) and the "zipper" clause (Article 24) contained in the current PBA/City labor agreements were adopted verbatim and carried forward without discussion from previous collective bargaining agreements.

The PBA also excepts to the Hearing Officer's conclusions of law that the PBA waived its right to negotiate concerning the Police Department's Rules of Conduct, that the unfair labor practice charge be dismissed, and that attorney's fees not be awarded the PBA. Because we agree with the Hearing Officer's recommendation that the unfair labor practice charge be dismissed, for reasons explained below, these exceptions are rejected.

....

It is well established that absent a clear and unmistakable waiver by the certified bargaining representative or exigent circumstances requiring immediate action, a public employer's unilateral alteration of the wages, hours, or other terms and conditions of employment of employees represented by a certified bargaining representative constitutes a *per se* violation of Section 447.501(1)(a) and (c), Florida Statutes (1979).... A clear and unmistakable waiver by the certified bargaining agent of its right to bargain on a specific subject may be demonstrated by a variety of factors, including the precise wording of relevant contractual provisions, evidence of contract negotiations, and the history of collective bargaining between the parties. See *Bancroft-Whitney Co.,* 214 NLRB 57 (1974).

In the instant case, Article 24, the "zipper" clause,[5] functions to "zip up" the collective bargaining agreement. It insulates either party to the agreement from

[5] Article 24, Section 1 provides:

The parties acknowledge that, during the negotiations which resulted in this agreement, each had the right and opportunity to make proposals with respect to subjects or matters not removed by law from the area of collective bargaining. The understandings and agreements arrived at by the parties after the exercise of such right and opportunity are set forth in this agreement.

a demand by the other party that a provision included in the agreement be renegotiated during the term of the agreement. A zipper clause thus shields both parties from a request to reconsider provisions of a collective bargaining agreement during the life of that agreement. Such a zipper clause serves as a defense to an asserted violation of the bargaining obligation arising from a refusal to renegotiate provisions included in an agreement. See e.g., *Local No. 301, LIU v. City of Jacksonville,* 6 FPER ¶ 11047 (1980); *Orange County PBA v. City of Orlando,* 6 FPER ¶ 11016 (1979); *St. Petersburg Association of Fire Fighters, Local 747 v. City of St. Petersburg,* 4 FPER ¶ 4201 (1978).

Nevertheless, the fact that a zipper clause may serve as shield does not imply that it may also be used as a sword to accomplish the unilateral alteration of terms and conditions of employment. The purpose of the zipper clause is only to protect those items upon which the parties have reached agreement. Indeed, the stability of the parties' agreement would be seriously eroded by affording the employer the opportunity to unilaterally alter terms and conditions of employment during the contract term. The finality of the agreement would be destroyed. With such a sword, a public employer could argue that the inclusion of a provision in a collective bargaining agreement, while apparently binding the parties and memorializing their agreement, actually frees the employer to alter the provision. Such an interpretation would transform every substantive provision of a collective bargaining agreement into a matter of employer prerogative, in derogation of that agreement, thus subjecting collective bargaining "agreements" to unilateral alteration at the employer's whim. This interpretation "would effectively gut the life of the statute providing for bargaining by public employees." *School Board of Orange County v. Palowitch,* 367 So. 2d 730, 731 (Fla. 4th DCA 1979).

The fact that the parties in the instant case included a management rights clause (Article 3) as well as a zipper clause (Article 24) in the collective bargaining agreements at issue further demonstrates that the broad reading of the zipper clause urged by the City will not withstand close scrutiny. Had the parties intended the zipper clause to function as a grant of unilateral authority to alter all subjects included in the agreement, the specific management rights clause would be unnecessary surplusage.

Article 3, Section 1(N) of the management rights clause provides that the City retains sole authority to "change, modify or delete any Rule or Regulation." The City's consistent position throughout this proceeding has been that the rule revisions at issue were semantic in nature.[6] The Commission agrees. While the

---

The Employer and the PBA for the duration of this agreement, each voluntarily and unqualifiedly waives the right, and agrees that the other shall not be obliged, to bargain collectively with respect to any subject or matter referred to or covered in this agreement or with respect to any subject or matter not specifically referred to or covered in this agreement, even though such subject matter may not have been within the knowledge or contemplation of either or both parties at the time that they negotiated this agreement, unless otherwise provided for herein.

[6] The previous rule, Group III, Rule 9 of the Rules & Regulations of the Personnel Management System of the City, prohibits:

[I]mmoral, unlawful or improper conduct or indecency, either on or off the job, which would tend to affect the employee's relationship to his job, his fellow workers, his reputation or goodwill in the community.

two rules are obviously not identical, it appears practically impossible to specify conduct which would fall within the scope of one rule and outside the scope of the other. The City's position is that the scope of application of the revised rule is identical to that of the preexisting rule. This case is analogous to a situation where a rule change is in fact a "mere codification" of rules "already known and in force," or where a rule change is only a "more particularized rule on the same subject matter." *NLRB v. Miller Brewing Co.,* 408 F.2d 12, 15-16 (9th Cir. 1969); *NLRB v. Hilton Mobile Homes,* 387 F.2d 7, 11-12 (8th Cir. 1967). *Contrast Murphy Diesel Co. v. NLRB,* 454 F.2d 303, 306-07 (7th Cir. 1971) (violation found where rule changes were not m[e]re clarification of preexisting rules; new formalized procedures constituted substantial changes in rules). Absent application of the revised rules in a specific factual contest, the Commission is precluded from finding that the City will apply the revised rules in such a manner as would constitute a departure from the City's practice under preexisting rules.

Furthermore, the precise wording of Article 3, Section 1(N) authorizes the rule revisions at issue in this case. This conclusion is supported by reading this management rights provision in light of two other contract provisions. First, Article 3, Section 1(g) provides that the City retains the right "[t]o suspend, demote, discharge, or take other disciplinary action against employees *for just cause.*" (Emphasis added.) Second, Article 22, Section 11, Maintenance of Conditions, provides as follows:

A. No employee shall be unfavorably affected by the signing of this agreement as to wages, hours or other conditions of employment. Any written rule, regulation, policy or procedure in conflict with this agreement shall be resolved by modification of such rule, regulation, policy or procedure to be compatible with this agreement. A consultation meeting, as provided in the Article 22, Section 10, shall be deemed appropriate to resolve conflicts arising under this section.

B. Employees covered by this agreement are also, entitled to the benefits and rights of the Personnel Management System of the City. If any conflicts occur between this Labor Agreement and the City's Personnel Management System, the Labor Agreement shall take precedence. The Labor Agreement shall be the governing factor in all cases even though the benefits or rights may be greater or lesser than provided for in the Personnel Management System of the City.

The rule revisions at issue are consistent with and not prohibited by the limiting language contained in Article 3, Section 1(G), and Article 22, Section 11, set forth above.

Express contractual language, when its effect is clear and unmistakable, can "demonstrate a conscious yielding of the Charging Party's right to negotiate prior to alteration of existing working conditions." *Hillsborough County PBA v. City of Tampa,* 6 FPER ¶ 11033 (1980) (Commission determined existence of

---

The revised rule, Section II-A No. 6 of the Police Department Rules of Conduct, provides in full:

Employees shall conduct themselves in a proper manner and with appropriate demeanor. They shall not engage in conduct unbecoming an employee of the Police Department.

As the Hearing Officer noted, the City's general Rules & Regulations and the specific Police Department Rules of Conduct are both applicable to Police Department employees.

waiver from contractual language expressly providing that City retained right to "alter or vary past practices"). It appears from the record in the instant case that there was no discussion during negotiations concerning the provisions at issue which could augment our understanding of the relevant contractual language. Neither the negotiating history nor the practices of the parties under these agreements demonstrates that the interpretation of the agreements urged by the City is incorrect. Examination of the collective bargaining agreement provisions at issue here establishes that the parties addressed the specific subject of the promulgatin of changes in the City's rules, and that the PBA agreed that the City retained sole authority to "change, modify or delete any Rule or Regulation."[8] By agreeing to the inclusion of this provision in the collective bargaining agreement, the PBA waived its right to bargain concerning the City's revision of its disciplinary rules. Under these circumstances, the Commission adopts the Hearing Officer's recommendation that the unfair labor practice charge in this case be dismissed.

For the foregoing reasons, pursuant to Section 447.503(6)(a), Florida Statutes (1979), this case is DISMISSED.

It is so ordered.

NOTES

1. The NLRB has ruled "that an employer's duty to give a union prior notice and an opportunity to bargain normally arises where the employer proposes to take action which will effect some change in existing employment terms or conditions within the range of mandatory bargaining." *Westinghouse Elec. Corp.,* 150 N.L.R.B. 1574 (1965). If the applicable collective bargaining agreement, however, gives the employer the right to take the action in question, then the employer can act unilaterally without bargaining with the union. See, e.g., *United Technologies Corp., Hamilton Standard Div.,* 300 N.L.R.B. No. 122, 136 L.R.R.M. 1049 (1990); *Ador Corp.,* 155 N.L.R.B. 1658 (1965). Finally, the NLRB has consistently held that an employer, in the absence of mutual agreement, cannot modify a condition of employment which is set forth in an agreement during the term of the agreement even though it has given the union advance notice and an opportunity to bargain over the proposed modification. In this regard, the NLRB relies on § 8(d) of the NLRA which provides "[t]hat where there is in effect a collective-bargaining contract ..., the duty to bargain collectively shall also mean that no party to such contract shall terminate or modify such contract." For example, in *Standard Oil Co.,* 174 N.L.R.B. 177 (1969), the NLRB held that an employer violated § 8(d) when it unilaterally increased certain wage rates during the term of the parties' agreement without obtaining the union's consent. The Board observed that the employer "was not free ... to modify the unexpired agreement over the Union's objections, but was

---

[8]Because the question is not presented by this case, we do not here determine whether such contractual language is sufficient to constitute a broad across-the-board waiver of the right to bargain over any change in rules and regulations, regardless of how substantial the departure from previous wages, hours, or other terms and conditions of employment. Compare *Southern Florida Hotel & Motel Association,* 245 NLRB No. 49 at pp. 23-25 (September 28, 1979) (contractual language authorizing employer to "make, continue and change such reasonable rules and regulations as it may deem necessary and proper in the conduct of its business" held to constitute "a broad waiver of the union's right to bargain about changes in working conditions"; such language held *not* to authorize unilateral changes in "tipping practices, meal practices, or similar rules that effect (sic) the wages or compensation received by hotel employees").

obligated to maintain in effect all preexisting contractual commitments for the contract term."

2. In *Grey-New Gloucester Teachers Ass'n v. MSAD 15 Bd. of Dirs.,* Case No. 85-01 (Me. LRB 1984), the Maine Board held that a school board did not unlawfully institute a merit pay plan where the parties' contract provided that contract wages were minimums and that "additional sums could be paid to individual teachers at the discretion of the Board of Directors." Accord *City of Hollywood,* 7 FPER ¶ 12293 (Fla. PERC 1981) (no obligation to negotiate over shift changes where the contract gave the employer the right to take the action in question); *Jackson Cty. Sch. Dist. No. 549C,* 5 PECBR 2911 (Or. ERB 1980).

3. Does a union have a right to engage in mid-term negotiations on issues not covered by an existing collective bargaining agreement and where the employer has not proposed any changes in existing practices? In *NTEU v. FLRA,* 810 F.2d 295 (D.C. Cir. 1987), the court, in reversing a decision of the FLRA, held that "[i]n view of the absence of any statutory distinction between mid-term and basic negotiations," the duty to bargain extended to "mid-term proposals initiated by either management or labor, provided the proposals do not conflict with the existing agreement."

4. In *Rock Falls Elem. Sch. Dist. No. 13,* 2 PERI ¶ 1150 (Ill. ERB 1986), the Illinois Education Labor Relations Board held that while "midterm bargaining is required over mandatory subjects of bargaining which are neither fully negotiated nor the subject of a clause in an existing collective bargaining agreement," where the parties have agreed to a broad waiver or "zipper clause" which provided that the parties waived the right to bargain over subjects that were not contemplated by either or both parties at the time the agreement was entered into constituted a waiver of the union's right to negotiate over the employer's adoption of a new suspension policy, a matter that was not covered by the parties' collective bargaining agreement. The IELRB reasoned as follows:

> In reaching our conclusion, we reject the contention of the Association that our Act or public policy demands that a union should never be allowed to waive its right to bargain. If the waiver takes place, as here, *during* collective bargaining and is itself a negotiated agreement, no diminution in employee or union rights to "collectively bargain" under our statute results.
>
> ... [O]nly by requiring the parties to accept the plain meaning of their agreements can the collective bargaining process be preserved and made meaningful. The Association may now be unhappy that it agreed to this provision in light of subsequent events, but the provision stands as part of the agreement and must be given its full effect if the collective bargaining process is to be meaningful.

5. In *Kent Cty. Educ. Ass'n v. Cedar Springs Pub. Schs.,* 157 Mich. App. 59, 403 N.W.2d 494 (1987), the court held that a "zipper clause" was not sufficient evidence, in and of itself, of a clear and explicit waiver of a union's right to bargain over a school board's change in the number of class periods per school day.

E. PUBLIC SECTOR COLLECTIVE BARGAINING AND THE PUBLIC'S RIGHT TO KNOW

NEW YORK PUBLIC EMPLOYMENT RELATIONS BOARD, SURVEY ON DISCLOSURE DURING PUBLIC SECTOR NEGOTIATIONS, GERR No. 463, D-2 to D-6 (1972)

Introduction

On January 3, 1972, Governor Rockefeller requested that the Public Employment Relations Board give top priority to the problem of public disclosure following negotiations with public employee groups.

For some time the problem of disclosure at various stages of the negotiating process had been discussed by PERB with the parties, the media, and knowledgeable people in the labor relations field. To completely encompass this field, PERB's analysis of the question was broadened beyond the Governor's request to include all stages of the negotiating process. Opinions on disclosure throughout the process were solicited from the media, mediators and fact-finders, and recognized industrial and labor relations experts. In addition, a questionnaire soliciting information on what actually occurred with respect to disclosure during the course of negotiations and their opinions was sent to the parties in impasse situations in which the fact-finding report and recommendations had not been acted upon within 10 days.

For purposes of structuring the analysis, the negotiating process was broken into the following stages:

1. Negotiations prior to the third-party assistance.
2. During the course of mediation.
3. During the course of fact-finding.
4. After the fact-finder has rendered his report and recommendations but before agreement.
5. After agreement has been reached but prior to employee ratification.
6. After agreement has been reached but prior to enactment of legislation required to implement the agreement.

In addition to the above points, the respondents also were requested to recommend whether disclosure should be mandated by statute.

A full discussion of the issue follows PERB's Recommendations.

Recommendations

On the basis of the inquiry and responses from the affected parties and others, PERB recommends that:

No amendments to the Taylor Law are required with respect to disclosure of agreements negotiated between public employers and employee groups.

1. Legislation regarding disclosure is unnecessary because:

(a) Inquiry indicates that the basic details of most such agreements are made public either when agreement is reached or after ratification by the employee groups.

(b) If the negotiations reach the fact-finding stages, the fact-finding report and recommendations are made public by PERB five days after receipt by the parties as required by law. Often the parties themselves release the substance of the report within the five-day period. Subsequent negotiations, if any, take place within the framework of the fact-finder's report.

(c) If a legislative hearing is required, the law mandates a *public* hearing.

(d) In almost all instances the agreement is made available to the public by the employer, and sometimes by the employee organization. Normally, the contract is also available from PERB on request.

(e) A substantial part of all memoranda agreement, including the fiscal aspects, requires legislative implementation. Public sector labor agreements appear to receive essentially the same amount of disclosure as do other government matters.

2. Legislation regarding disclosure is *undesirable* because:

(a) It would deny governments necessary flexibility. Given the diversity of negotiating situations among the 1,100 public employers and 2,500 negotiating units (varying from three-man police departments to units with 30,000 or more employees), it would be difficult to devise legislation which would fit this wide variety of situations.

(b) It subverts the authority of elected officials.

Negotiations under the Taylor Law are, in theory at least, between the Chief Executive and the employee organization on behalf of the public and as the public's agent. The Chief Executive is authorized to pursue his policies, and by entering into the contracts to obligate the government to carry out those policies. If disclosure of an agreement of the Chief Executive is not designed to induce renunciation or modification of that agreement, it is meaningless, adding nothing but costs and delay to ordinary disclosure requirements. If disclosure contemplates renunciation or modification of the agreement, it subverts the authority of the Chief Executive and imperils the negotiation process.

This analysis suggests one caveat. Most employee organizations require disclosure of their agreements to — and ratification by — their members. The possibility of the agreement of labor officials being renounced by their constituency is no less troublesome than the possibility of the agreement of a Chief Executive being renounced under pressure from his constituency. A case could be made for giving to the constituency of the Chief Executive an opportunity to be informed of an agreement before it is executed by the Chief Executive if the employee organization reserves to its members the right of ratification. We would not mandate such disclosure by law but recognize that under such circumstances, the government might choose to disclose the terms of the proposed agreement before executing it.

Discussion

The Study

In making his request of PERB to study the question of disclosure, the Governor said:

"The public has a right to know the full details of agreements reached with public employee groups. More often than not, these agreements involve large sums of public funds. At the same time every effort should be made to avoid interference with the collective negotiating process.

"I have, therefore, called upon the State Public Employment Relations Board to make specific recommendations on this subject, including any necessary amendments to the Taylor law."

As noted earlier in this report, PERB expanded the inquiry to include disclosure at various stages of negotiations. Among those queried were the parties to actual impasses, media representatives and recognized labor relations experts. A discussion of the responses received from each group follows:

Media Responses

In discussion with representatives of the Public Employment Relations Board from time to time throughout the years, representatives of the media have generally taken a strong position that much, if not all, of the negotiating process should be "public." However, responses from media representatives were generally somewhat more conservative.

The following is a representative response:

"While there is one element of even public sector bargaining which concededly should be private — that is, the bargaining session itself (to assure the maximum opportunity for fruitful discussion and expeditious reaching of agreement), it is in the public interest that full and prompt public disclosure be made, presumably by a PERB spokesman, on the following points as they develop:

"1. The issues.

"2. The points of difference, including the sums of public money involved.

"3. Progress or lack of progress in the negotiations.

"4. The basis of agreement, including the amount of public money involved."

Another respondent stated:

"We agree wholeheartedly with the Governor's position that the public has a right to know the full details of agreements reached with public employee groups.

"We also feel that since public money is involved, there should be disclosure from the start of negotiations of what the employees are asking and what the employer is offering...."

Another respondent, a distinguished long-time observer of the labor relations scene, said in part:

"The notion that disclosure interferes with the bargaining process has little validity in my experience. There might be something to be said for it if unions in the public sector clothe their bargainers with full power to conclude an agreement. Then, it could be argued that both sides ought to go in prepared to put their best offers on the table, confident that a final deal can be made.

"But desirable as such a procedure would be in narrow terms of the efficacy of bargaining, it has distinct flaws in a period of institutional upheaval when union leaders are hard pressed to hold their members in line even when the contracts are superb in every respect. Rank and file ratification is a fact of life and must be reckoned with in unions that were once the acme of conservatism.

"By the same token, taxpayers will have every right to rebel if they keep finding themselves stuck with a *fait accompli* that pushes up cost while necessitating reductions in service. Such rebellion is even more likely where the basic issues of public policy affecting schools, hospitals or other vital agencies are determined by union and public management with no direct voice for the neighborhood or other affected groups. Whatever embarrassments disclosing may create, they are vastly preferable in a democracy to shutting the public away from knowledge of things that the community has committed itself to until after the commitment is irrevocable."

The essence of the media response would appear to be that there should be disclosure with respect to the opening position of the parties, limited disclosure during the course of negotiations with periodic progress reports dealing with how far apart the parties are or how near they are, but not necessarily with substance, and full disclosure once agreement has been reached.

Clientele Responses

Public Employers

The responses summarized below are those received from representatives of organizations representing public employers, e.g., Conference of Mayors, N.Y.S. School Boards Association, etc. Answers received from public employers as such are summarized in a later section dealing with questionnaire responses as previously indicated.

There appears to be substantial consensus among public employer representatives that there should be no disclosure until the fact-finder has rendered his report and recommendations. If no third-party assistance is required or if third-party assistance is confined to mediation, there appears to be agreement that disclosure should not take place until the parties have ratified the contract. Response to the specific questions are summarized below:

1. During the course of negotiations without third-party assistance.

Employer representatives felt that the least possible disclosure should be made during the normal course of negotiations. The situation should be kept flexible. When either side makes public pronouncements of its position, it must then answer to its constituents for any deviation from the stated position. This has the effect of prolonging the negotiations and defeats the normal give-and-take which should be available to the negotiating teams.

2. During the course of mediation.

Mediation is an extension of the negotiating process with a third party present in an informal procedure. The considerations discussed under Question 1 were held to apply to Question 2.

3. During the course of fact-finding.

Fact-finding is a more formalized procedure for impasse resolution. However, none of the public employer representatives advocated making the fact-finding proceeding public or for disclosure of the positions of the parties during fact-finding.

4. After the fact-finder has rendered his report and recommendations but before agreement.

Section 209.3(c) provides that a fact-finding report and recommendations shall be made public within five days of its transmission to the parties. Thus, at this point, some disclosure is mandated in that the fact-finding report in some manner is reported to the public. (See section on questionnarie responses below.) Representatives of public employers generally felt that public pressures have little effect upon employee groups. All the respondents agreed that the public does have a right to know prior to the legislative hearing. The opinion was expressed that if agreement had not been reached at this point, it would be difficult to predict when agreement would be reached. Therefore, the public employer, at least, should be free to make such disclosure as he sees fit at the time the fact-finder's report becomes public.

Section 209.3(e) provides that if either party does not accept the fact-finder's recommendations in whole or in part, the chief executive officer shall, within ten days after receipt of the recommendations, submit to the legislative body both the fact-finding report and recommendations and his own recommendations for settling the dispute. The employee organization also is authorized to submit its recommendations.

The legislative body is then directed to "forthwith conduct a public hearing at which the parties shall be required to explain their positions with respect to the report of the fact-finding board." These provisions led to the following comments by one respondent:

"These considerations lead me to conclude that the public's right to know about contracts with public employee groups arises at either of two points: when the contract has been negotiated *and executed,* or when agreement has not been possible and a public hearing is to be held on the fact-finder's report, and public opinion is to play its part in the legislative decision." The respondent added: "This conclusion is consistent with the rights and responsibilities that are a part of our representative system of government."

5. After agreement has been reached, but prior to employee ratification.

This question brought forth a two-part response. Assuming that negotiations have proceeded with no third-party assistance, there was agreement that public disclosure should await ratification by the parties. Full public disclosure should take place, employer associations felt, when ratification is accomplished so that the public may know what its elected representatives are doing and how public funds are being used.

If there has been fact-finding assistance, then the answers to Question 4 pertain — there should be disclosure simultaneously or shortly after the publication of the fact-finder's report and recommendations.

6. After agreement has been reached, but prior to the enactment of legislation required to implement the agreement.

At this point there was some disagreement. All agreed that there would be disclosure, but one respondent had a reservation:

"To reveal all of the details of an agreement and heed public reaction is tantamount to allowing the public to veto the agreement, or, in fact, to be a party to the negotiations. In a representative form of government ... the responsibility rests with the elected official to perform his duty ... and a remedy for the voter who does not approve of his representative's actions is in the ballot box."

This particular respondent felt that the above quote pertained in a situation where the parties had arrived at an agreement without third-party assistance and where the legislature, of course, has not been required to make a determination but to implement an agreement bilaterally negotiated.

The final, but unnumbered question, was:

Should such disclosure as you consider to be appropriate be mandated by statute?

Significantly, none of the respondents felt that disclosure, in the sense of full publication of the text of the contract, should be mandated prior to legislative implementation. Some felt that this was not necessary at all. Others felt that the full text of the agreement should be published in an official newspaper after ratification and after implementation but within a specified period. An alternative would be to print the agreement and to make it available to all interested parties including employees, residents, etc. It was pointed out that to require publication of the full text of an agreement in an official newspaper would be to impose a substantial financial burden upon an employer, particularly if there were several units.

Public Employee Organizations. The views of parent labor organizations representing public employees also were solicited. The views of locals were solicited by questionnaire and are discussed in a later section of this report.

The views of the leadership of parent organizations representing public employees can best be summarized by the following comment:

"I have no quarrel with full disclosure after the contract has been agreed upon or certainly disclosure to the legislative body as legislation is needed.... Only after the contract is consummated and ratified would I give it full public disclosure. Labor relations, like international relations, is much too sensitive and difficult a process without putting it in the glare of public emotion. The public has a right to know — after it's negotiated. The ... legislature should be kept fully informed in terms of the process of negotiations, the goals of negotiations...."

Public employee union leadership was in general agreement that there should be no disclosure until:

1. Agreement has been reached and ratified; or
2. The matter is before the legislative body.

Panel Member Responses

Because of a wide variation in a number of impasses coming to the Public Employment Relations Board at various times of the year — half of the total impasses brought to to the Board come in the second calendar quarter — and because PERB staff members do not engage in fact-finding the Board makes extensive use of panel mediators and fact-finders. These panel members are drawn from a variety of sources and have varying backgrounds and experience. The reactions of a sample of the members of the panel were sought to the same questions submitted to representatives of employer and employee organizations.

One panel respondent summarized the comments of most panel members who were queried.

"1. No disclosure should be required or even encouraged during the stages of negotiations, mediation or fact-finding. Such disclosure would not only inhibit the making of offers and counterproposals *between* the parties, but might also cause serious problems of internal communications within the ranks of the bargainers. Just as one example, when I entered the XYZ school district negotiations last May, the parties had wasted ten entire bargaining sessions engaging in mutual recriminations about releases of information to the press. The minutes of these sessions reflect the progressive animosities which developed over the winter — feelings which had hardened to such an extent that absolutely no discussion had taken place on substantive issues. I was able to get the dispute settled by mediation only after both parties had agreed that no one (including the mediator) would talk to the press until settlement had been achieved, or until the mediator released the parties from their pledge of silence both to the press *and* to their constituents.

"2. After a fact-finding report has been issued and following the expiration of the five-day negotiating period the Law already mandates the release of the report. I see nothing harmful in disclosure of the report at this point.

"3. Once agreement has been reached, the parties themselves should agree on the ground rules for disclosure of the terms to their constituents. Otherwise, the agreement may blow up or be rejected because of mistrust, misunderstandings, or mutual recriminations.

"4. After an agreement has been ratified and signed, I have no objection to its terms being disclosed before implementing legislation is enacted. In fact, such disclosure would seem to be in the public interest.

"5. I am opposed to any form of disclosure being mandated by law. [It] could more appropriately be handled by administrative rule making."

Disagreement with the positions articulated above centered on two factors:
1. The nature of the fact-finding process; and
2. The problem of disclosure itself.

Those panelists who had different views were, nevertheless, in agreement that there should be no disclosure at least until the beginning of fact-finding.

Some of the panelists felt that certain advantages might flow from public fact-finding proceedings, and perhaps more formalized ones. One advocate of public fact-finding hearings, operating on the assumption that only organized public groups would participate, summarized his position this way:

"1. The immediate advantage, it seems to me, would result from allowing parent groups in teacher disputes and general taxpayer groups involving other classes of public employees to get at first hand all the facts relating to the dispute....

"2. Participation by the public in the fact-finding proceeding may alert the disputants to adopt a reasonable and rational approach to the ultimate solution of the dispute.

"3. Since participation should assume a real recognition of the opinions and judgments of the participants, the third parties (taxpayer groups, et al.) will bring to the proceedings evidence of the public interest and thus may affect the positions of the disputants....

"4. Psychologically, public participation may result in public acceptance of the findings and recommendations even when they may be at variance of the opinions of the public participants. The right to participate in itself is a form of due process which in time makes adverse decisions palatable and acceptable....

"5. Exposure of the fact-finding proceedings to the glare of interested public groups may result in a reduction of the many peripheral issues commonly raised by the disputants under existing procedures...."

The problem of *how* to disclose bothered some panelists. One put it this way:

"As you well know, there are at least two ways to multiplying and adding the same set of figures — employer's way and union's way — and at least one more way of doing it objectively ... it may seem possible to avoid all this by merely listing tersely the items in the memorandum of agreement or list of demands without costing or explanation. But what will it mean to the public? Very little....

"I see one possible avenue in the direction of involving the taxpayers. That is, in enlarging the concept of the 'legislative body' as responsive to the community as a whole. Provide that no settlement may be finalized until there is a public hearing on it by the legislative body — similar to the 'show cause' hearing on the fact-finder's report, but for both instances with mandated advance notice to the public — at least 25 days. That is, no settlement may be final until it has been 'shown to the public and an opportunity given to them to react to it.'"

Another panelist, accepting the concept that there should be no disclosure until the fact-finder has reported, commented as follows:

"After the fact-finder has issued his report and recommendations, the rules of the game change. The fact-finder is the voice of the public and his document, once issued, becomes public property. At the same time, however, I am fully aware that a fact-finder's report is subject to modifications and exchanges by the parties and they should be given the opportunity to make these changes within a reasonable time after the report is issued, and a period of five days appears reasonable.

"The activities of the parties starting with the sixth day after the issuance of a fact-finder's report should be given the full public exposure and the element of distortion by the media is substantially reduced because the fact-finder's document contains in written form ... all the ingredients of the dispute and thus it is relatively easier for the media to give accurate, objective information when this document is available as a foundation.

"As a statutory provision for disclosure, I would advise amendment of the existing language on legislative hearing which would require same to be held within a precise and exact time insofar as the public employer is concerned. In order to put an end point to delay by design, I would further recommend that the results of the legislative hearing must be publicly communicated by a time certain after the issuance of the fact-finder's report and failure to so communicate would constitute acceptance of the report as final and binding, that this is also true as to the public employee organization where the employee organization does assert a definitive position within a time certain, and I think 20 days would be ample for the parties. The public employee organization would be deemed to have accepted the report as a final and binding document in the case of failure to declare within the specified time...."

Thus the position of the panelists can be summed up by saying that they were unanimous in holding that there should be no disclosure until the beginning of fact-finding. A few thought that public participation in the fact-finding process might be helpful, but the vast majority did not. All of the panelists appeared to be in agreement with the present provision of the Taylor Law which requires disclosure of the fact-finding report and recommendations five days after receipt by the parties.

There was disagreement, and fairly wide disagreement, among the panelists as to whether some form of disclosure should be mandated by law. Many felt that if such action was required it could be done by administrative rule. They felt that this procedure would allow for some experimentation and less rigidity if whatever was proposed did not work.

Those panelists who felt that some form of disclosure should be mandated after issuance of the fact-finding report coupled such proposals with proposed modifications of the impasse procedure.

"Expert" Respondents

A variety of labor relations "experts" also were canvassed. These included members of the Taylor Committee, heads of public sector labor relations agencies in other states, academic experts, and distinguished practitioners.

In those states which have "anti-secrecy" statutes, the mediation process is either exempt from such laws or the process has escaped being affected by such laws. In Michigan, a school board which insisted that the press be present during negotiations was held to be guilty of bad faith bargaining. In Wisconsin the Supreme Court held, contrary to the ruling of the Labor Relations agency, that a school board did not interfere with the rights of an employee who was a member of a minority organization by denying that individual the opportunity to speak at a public hearing conducted by the school board with reference to the negotiated agreement. All of the heads of the state labor relations agencies with public sector responsibilities canvassed were essentially in agreement. Their position can best be summarized by the following response:

> "It has been our opinion that once the collective bargaining agreement has been tentatively approved by the negotiators for the public employer [and the] union, the details of the agreement should be made known. All three of the Commissioners — as well as our two staff men who do quite a bit of public speaking — have taken this position. We do so on the basis you state in your letter: that the agreements most often involve large sums of public funds and that the public is entitled to know."

The only disagreement among administrators of state agencies is *when* there should be disclosure. Some feel that disclosure should occur at the tentative agreement stage while others contend that disclosure should not occur until after ratification.

Other experts and practitioners canvassed were similarly divided on this point. One stated:

> "... when agreement is reached by negotiators, there are often very delicate situations involved in achieving ratification, sometimes on both sides — by the union's general membership or by the legislative body involved. For

this reason it is probably advisable to guard against premature release of the terms of the contract because of possible interference with the ratification. While I recognize the strength of the argument that the people who pay the bills should be entitled to know the cost of the agreement before it is finalized, I am experienced enough in the bargaining process to realize that such disclosure would make agreement more difficult to achieve. We must rely on the good faith of the municipal negotiators and the power of the public to change them by the process of recall or election, to assure the community that the agreement is a sound one.

"On the other hand, I do believe that a great deal more can be done to inform the public of the actual cost of finalized agreements — after ratification — so that they may be in a better position to judge the correctness of the agreement which has been acted upon. I refer to effective costing out of fringe benefits in general and pensions in particular...."

Other groups of respondents were as concerned with the "how" of disclosure as with the "when" of disclosure. Among the academic-practitioner respondents concerned with this question, the following is a typical comment:

"The 'how' question is even more difficult. Even in the public sector, I have grave reservations about the ability of the general public to digest and appraise complicated issues. Simple publication of the terms usually is somewhat a waste of paper since few people will read a complete agreement. Moreover, even if they do, most people outside of the immediate scene cannot intelligently appraise the terms. Consequently well-written summaries that are interpretive are almost required. Who is to do this job? Good labor reporters are increasingly hard to find. Moreover, whoever prepares a summary can always be accused, sometimes rightly, of 'slanting a story.' I suspect that there is no perfect way of meeting these problems. The mediator, or the fact-finder, or P.R. personnel in the agency can be most helpful in the preparation of an accurate and understandable summary but some risks are involved. Probably the potential values are worth the risk."

Responses of Parties

The comments from the parties generally opposed disclosure citing reasons as inhibiting the negotiations process, creating a fish bowl effect and polarizing the parties.

One employer replied:

"If agreements are made public before ratification, political pressures to turn down negotiated agreements will be brought against the legislative body with the only possible results being the rejection of negotiated agreements in greater numbers than have existed in the past and even greater distrust of the negotiating procedure on the part of employee organizations than at present."

The replies as to the actual amount of disclosure indicate that there was very little public disclosure....

Most of the clients responding did not favor additional disclosure. Majorities ranging from 90 to 60 per cent were opposed to more disclosure. The highest vote for more disclosure was for releasing the fact-finding report to the public and the press at the same time it is released to the parties. Slightly under 40 per cent of the respondents favor this step.

There was slightly less support for public fact-finding hearings. The support for this viewpoint was strongest by employers. More than 44 per cent of them supported this idea. However, it seemed apparent that many of the replies favoring more disclosure were not advocating public policy but were advancing ideas that they thought would have aided their cause in recent negotiations.

In the instances in which there was public disclosure, the side making it often claimed that the "public" supported their side. It seems apparent that public disclosure is not being used as a means of informing the citizens but rather as a means of marshalling support for their respective position. There also were several comments that indicated that disclosure inhibited flexibility and compromise.

In terms of public impact, the comments varied from no impact to support of position by community (on both sides). There were several comments that positions as reported by media were distorted. However, in most cases the impact of the community toward reaching an agreement even after the fact-finder's report was published appeared to be slight. Those who commented on attendance at legislative hearings indicated that the public did not attend.

NOTES

1. Despite the preference of most parties to negotiate in private, several states have enacted legislation which specifically requires that negotiations be conducted in public. For example, Section 11 of the Tennessee Education Professional Negotiations Act provides that "[a]ny negotiations under the provisions of this Act shall be meetings within the provisions of [the Tennessee Open Meetings Law]." Tenn. Code Ann. § 49-5-611(b) (1990). The Florida Act provides that "collective bargaining negotiations between a chief executive officer or his representative and a bargaining agent shall not be exempt from [the Florida Sunshine Law]." However, Florida law does exempt "[a]ll discussions between the chief executive officer of the public employer, or his representative and the legislative body or the public employer relative to collective bargaining." Fla. Stat. Ann. § 447.605 (West 1981).

2. The Texas bargaining law covering firefighters and police officers provides that "[a]ll deliberations pertaining to collective bargaining between an association and a public employer or any deliberation by a quorum of members of an association authorized to bargain collectively or by a member of a public employer authorized to bargaining collectively shall be open to the public and in compliance with the Acts of the State of Texas." Tex. Rev. Civ. Stat. Ann. art. 5154c-1(7)(e) (Vernon 1987). In *Enterprise Co. v. City of Beaumont,* 574 S.W.2d 786 (Tex. Ct. Civ. App. 1978), the court noted that "[t]he legislature has determined that the public's right to know what is going on in the negotiation sessions between its representatives and those representing its firefighters is entitled to statutory protection," even though "[i]t may very well be that such statutorily protected right may inhibit or prevent successful negotiations." The court, however, relying on another section of the Act which permitted a mediator to hold separate conferences with the parties, held that while the public "is entitled to be present and observe the *joint* conferences," it "has no right to see or observe the proceedings in the *separate* conferences with the mediator." See also *Southwestern Or. Pub'g Co. v. Southwestern Or. Community College Dist.,*

28 Or. App. 383, 559 P.2d 1289 (1977) (Oregon Public Meeting Law did not apply to labor negotiations conducted on behalf of a community college by a retained labor negotiator).

3. In the past couple of years several states have enacted legislation which seeks to balance the public's right to know what is happening in negotiations with the parties' normal preference to negotiate in private. For example, a 1977 amendment to the Wisconsin Municipal Employment Relations Act provides that the meetings that are held by the parties "for the purpose of presenting initial bargaining proposals, along with supporting rationale, shall be open to the public." Wis. Stat. Ann. § 111.70(4)(cm)(2) (West 1988). Another example is the following public notice provision in the California Educational Employment Relations Act:

(a) All initial proposals of exclusive representatives and of public school employers, which relate to matters within the scope of representation, shall be presented at a public meeting of the public school employer and thereafter shall be public records.

(b) Meeting and negotiating shall not take place on any proposal until a reasonable time has elapsed after the submission of the proposal to enable the public to become informed and the public has the opportunity to express itself regarding the proposal at a meeting of the public school employer.

(c) After the public has had the opportunity to express itself, the public school employer shall, at a meeting which is open to the public, adopt its initial proposal.

(d) New subjects of meeting and negotiating arising after the presentation of initial proposals shall be made public within 24 hours. If a vote is taken on such subject by the public school employer, the vote thereon by each member voting shall also be made public within 24 hours.

(e) The board may adopt regulations for the purpose of implementing this section, which are consistent with the intent of the section; namely that the public be informed of the issues that are being negotiated upon and have full opportunity to express their views on the issues to the public school employer, and to know of the positions of their elected representatives.

Cal. Gov't Code § 3547 (West 1980).

TALBOT v. CONCORD UNION SCHOOL DISTRICT

114 N.H. 532, 323 A.2d 912, 87 L.R.R.M. 3159 (1974)

KENISON, CHIEF JUSTICE: — The principal question raised by these proceedings is whether the defendant is required under the Right to Know Law (RSA ch. 91-A (Supp. 1973)) to open to the public, including the press, its collective bargaining sessions with the Concord Education Association concerning teacher salary scales, fringe benefits and other related matters. The plaintiffs brought a petition for an injunction pursuant to RSA 91-A:7 (Supp. 1973) to enjoin the defendant from excluding them from such collective bargaining sessions. After an evidentiary hearing, the Trial Court (Keller, C.J.) denied the plaintiffs' request for a temporary injunction on the grounds that such a remedy would disrupt negotiations and delay the adoption of the school budget. The parties subsequently agreed that the hearing for the temporary injunction should be treated as if it had been a hearing for a permanent injunction. The trial court reserved and transferred the plaintiffs' exception to its denial of the petition.

The basic facts of this case are not in dispute. The defendant school district is a corporation organized by special act of the legislature and is empowered by law to conduct the public schools within the geographic boundaries of the district, which includes a major portion of the City of Concord. Laws 1961, ch. 355, as amended Laws 1967, ch. 560 and Laws 1971, ch. 262. All powers of the district are vested in a board of education composed of nine members. The Concord Education Association is a local teachers' organization which is recognized by the board as the bargaining representative of the teachers in the district. The parties entered into a "negotiations contract" which establishes in pertinent part procedures governing negotiations between the parties concerning "salaries and other matters." It provides that the parties shall meet on the written request of either of them at a mutually convenient time to exchange "facts, opinions, proposals and counter-proposals ... freely and in good faith during the meeting or meetings (and between meetings, if advisable) in an effort to reach mutual understanding and agreement." In practice, the negotiations between the parties are conducted in an informal manner by committees appointed by each of them. These committees have no authority to bind the parties to the terms of any collective bargaining agreement, but must return to their principals for approval of their recommendations. Although the bargaining sessions between the committees have been traditionally closed to the public, the recommendations of the committees are received and voted upon by the board in an open meeting.

The present action arose from the board's refusal to permit the plaintiff Roger G. Talbot, a reporter for the Concord Monitor, to attend one or more of the bargaining committees' sessions. The parties have agreed that none of the exceptions to the Right to Know Law (RSA 91-A:3 (Supp. 1973)) are applicable to these facts, and the narrow issue presented by this case is whether the bargaining sessions of the committees are within the purview of the act.

The parties have drawn this court's attention to two legislative policies which bear on this issue. The first policy is that of the Right to Know Law which is to protect the democratic process by making public the decisions and considerations on which government action is based. *Carter v. Nashua,* 113 N.H. 407, 416, 308 A.2d 847, 853 (1973). The second is that of the collective bargaining statute (RSA 31.3) which recognizes the right of public employees to negotiate the terms of their contractual relationship with the government by using the well-established techniques of private sector bargaining. *Timberlane Regional School Dist. v. Timberlane Regional Educ. Ass'n,* 114 N.H. —, —, 317 A.2d 555, 557, 87 LRRM 2015 (1973); *Tremblay v. Berlin Police Union,* 108 N.H. 416, 237 A.2d 668, 68 LRRM 2070 (1966). See also RSA ch. 98-C (Supp. 1973). The plaintiffs urge that the former policy must take precedence over the latter because the broad language used in RSA 91-A:2 (Supp. 1973) requires that all public proceedings of any school district board or subcommittee thereof must be open to the public. The defendant contends in response that the unlimited extension of the former policy would consume the latter because the collective bargaining process cannot operate effectively if exposed to the public eye.

There is nothing in the legislative history of the Right to Know Law to indicate that the legislature specifically considered the impact of its provisions on public sector bargaining. However, it is improbable that the legislature intended the law to apply in such a fashion as to destroy the very process it was attempting to open to the public. See Annot., 38 A.L.R.3d 1070 § 6 (b) (1971). There is substantial authority in support of the defendant's position that the delicate mechanisms of collective bargaining would be thrown awry if viewed prematurely by the public. Bassett v. Braddock, 262 So.2d 425, 80 LRRM 2955 (Fla. 1972); R. Smith, H. Edwards & R. Clark, Jr., Labor Relations Law in the Public Sector 569-594 (1974); Edwards, *The Emerging Duty to Bargain in the Public Sector,* 71 Mich. L. Rev. 885, 901-02 (1973); *Wickham, Let the Sun Shine In! Open-Meeting Legislation Can Be Our Key to Closed Doors in State and Local Government,* 68 Nw. U. L. Rev. 480, 491-92 (1973); see R. Smith, L. Merrifield & D. Rothschild, Collective Bargaining and Labor Arbitration 36-44 (1970). In fact, a number of State labor boards have gone so far as to hold that a party's insistence on bargaining in public constituted a refusal to negotiate in good faith, reasoning that bargaining in the public arena "would tend to prolong negotiations and damage the procedure of compromise inherent in collective bargaining." *Menominee Bd. of Educ.,* MERC Lab. Op. 383, 386 (Mich. 1968); see *Mayor Samuel E. Zoll and the City of Salem,* MLRC Case No. MUP-309 (Mass. 1972); *Bethlehem Area School Directors,* Penn. Lab. Rel. Bd. Case No. PERA-C-2861-C, Gov't Employ Rel. Rep't No. 505, E-1 (1973). See also CAL. GOVT. CODE § 54957.6 (West 1974) (Authorizing school boards to deny public access to "consultations and discussions" with public employee representatives concerning salaries and other matters); Grodin, *Public Employee Bargaining in California: The Meyers-Milias-Brown Act in the Court,* 23 Hast. L. J. 719, 752 (1972); cf. Minn. Stat. Ann. ch. 179, § 179.69 (1971) (Permitting public access to all negotiating sessions *unless* otherwise provided by the director of mediation services).

The record is replete with evidence indicating that the presence of the public and the press at negotiating sessions would inhibit the free exchange of views and freeze negotiators into fixed positions from which they could not recede without loss of face. Moreover, in the opinion of one witness, the opening of such sessions to the public could result in the employment of professional negotiators, thus removing the local representatives from the bargaining process. See Mont. Rev. Code Ann. § 75-6127 (1971) (opening *professional* negotiating sessions but closing preliminary deliberations of school board).

We agree with the Florida Supreme Court "that meaningful collective bargaining in the circumstances here would be destroyed if full publicity were accorded at each step of the negotiations" (*Bassett v. Braddock,* 262 So. 2d 425, 426, 80 LRRM 2955, 2956 (Fla. 1972)) and hold that the negotiation sessions between the school board and union committees are not within the ambit of the Right to Know Law. However, in so ruling, we would emphasize that these sessions serve only to produce recommendations which are submitted to the board for final approval. The board's approval must be given in an open meeting in accordance with RSA 91-A:3 (Supp. 1973), thus protecting the public's right to know what contractual terms have been agreed upon by the negotiators.

Plaintiffs' exception overruled.

All concurred.

NOTES

1. In *Appeal of the Town of Exeter,* 495 A.2d 1288 (N.H. 1985), the New Hampshire Supreme Court upheld a PLRB decision prohibiting an employer from preconditioning negotiations on public bargaining sessions. In so ruling, the court specifically reaffirmed its earlier decision in *Talbot,* noting that there had been no amendments to the Right-to-Know Law which would require a different result. See also *Burlington Community Sch. Dist. v. PERB,* 268 N.W.2d 517, 99 L.R.R.M. 2394 (Iowa 1978) (unfair labor practice for employer to insist that negotiation sessions be conducted in public; negotiation sessions must be closed if the parties reach impasse on question); *County of Saratoga,* 17 PERB ¶ 3033 (N.Y.), *aff'd sub nom. County of Saratoga v. Newman,* 124 Misc. 2d 626, 476 N.Y.S.2d 1020 (S. Ct. 1984) (unfair labor practice for employer to precondition negotiations on the presence of the press and other members of the public without the union's consent).

On the other hand, in *Carroll Cty. Educ. Ass'n v. Board of Educ.,* 294 Md. 144, 448 A.2d 345 (Md. Ct. App. 1982), Maryland's highest court held that under Maryland's Open Meetings Act a school board has the unilateral right to insist that bargaining sessions be held in public. In rejecting the union's argument that the school board's unilateral act constituted a per se violation of its statutory obligation to negotiate in good faith, the court ruled that "a harmonious reading of the two statutes affords an interpretation of the good-faith requirement consistent with the Open Meetings Act—that while the Board must come to the bargaining table with an open mind, prepared to negotiate a contract, it may conduct the bargaining process in public." The court rejected precedent in other jurisdictions holding that neither party in public sector negotiations can unilaterally insist on public bargaining, observing that such decisions were "either inopposite on their facts or unpersuasive in their reasoning."

2. In *Ghiglione v. School Comm. of Southbridge,* 376 Mass. 70, 1977-78 PBC ¶ 36,446 (Mass. 1978), the court held that it was permissible for a school board to meet in closed session to discuss a grievance since the Massachusetts Open Meeting Law permits closed sessions to conduct collective bargaining and since collective bargaining includes resolving grievances under a collective bargaining agreement. Contra *Lebanon Sch. Bd.,* Dec. No. 87-32 (N.H. PELRB 1987) (exception in opening meetings act for negotiations not applicable to a grievance hearing).

3. In sharp contrast to the decision in the principal case, the North Dakota Supreme Court in *Dickinson Educ. Ass'n v. Dickinson Pub. Sch. Dist. No. 1,* 252 N.W.2d 205, 95 L.R.R.M. 2744 (N.D. 1977), held that the North Dakota constitutional and statutory provisions concerning open meetings were violated when the school board and members of the board's bargaining team consulted in private to discuss and adopt bargaining positions. The court stated:

> We find that our constitutional and statutory open meeting provisions require that all school board meetings at which teacher contract offers and school board offers and counter offers are considered shall be open to the public. We further find that our constitutional and statutory open meeting provisions require that all school board-teacher contract negotiating sessions, regardless of negotiating committee composition, shall be open to the public.

Accord *Littleton Educ. Ass'n v. Arapahoe Cty. Sch. Dist.,* 533 P.2d 793 (Colo. 1976).

4. In *City of Ft. Myers v. News-Press Pub'g Co.,* 514 So. 2d 408 (Fla. Dist. Ct. App. 1987), the court held that the state's "Sunshine Law," which requires that negotiations take place in public pursuant to the state's "Sunshine Law," was applicable to private meetings between the attorneys for both sides during the interim between the declaration of impasse and the commencement of special master proceedings. In so ruling the court noted that its "holding that all phases of the public employee collective bargaining process between the contending parties must be held in the sunshine merely reiterates the strong public policy in Florida in place since the enactment of [the] Sunshine Law in 1967."

5. The Minnesota Public Employment Labor Relations Act provides that "all negotiations, mediation sessions, and hearings between public employers and public employees or their respective respresentatives shall be public meetings except when otherwise provided by the director." In *Minnesota Educ. Ass'n v. Bennett,* 321 N.W.2d 395 (Minn. 1982), the court held that once a mediator

takes jurisdiction of the bargaining process, it is only reasonable to conclude that to aid effectively in resolving the issues between the parties, a mediator may meet with both parties together, or with each party separately and may direct, or permit, a party to meet without the mediator being present, nonpublicly at any place within or without the district, the mediator, or permitted party, deems suitable.

Subsequent to the events giving rise to this decision, the Minnesota Legislature amended its Open Meetings Law to provide an exception for the purpose of holding "a closed meeting to consider strategy for labor negotiations, including negotiation strategies or developments or discussion and review of labor negotiation proposals...." This exception provides, however, that any such closed meeting "shall be tape-recorded at the expense of the governing body and shall be preserved by it for two years after the contract is signed and shall be made available to the public after all labor contracts are signed by the governing body for the current budget period." Minn. Stat. § 471.705, subd. 1a (1980). Is the purpose of permitting a governing body to meet in closed session to discuss negotiation strategies furthered or hindered by requiring that the closed meeting be taped and then made available to the public following the conclusion of negotiations?

6. In *Cohalan v. Board of Educ.,* 74 App. Div. 2d 812, 1977-78 PBC ¶ 36,389 (N.Y. 1978), the court held that a taxpayer was not entitled to the proposals and demands made by the parties when they were engaged in mediation and prior to the time that the taxpayers voted on the school budget.

7. Must a public employer make public copies of tentative collective bargaining agreements which have not yet been submitted to the legislative body for ratification and approval? In *Beacon Journal Pub'g Co. v. City of Stow,* 25 Ohio St. 3d 347, 496 N.E.2d 908 (1986), the Ohio Supreme Court held that tentative collective bargaining agreements were public records under Ohio law and that the city's refusal to provide copies of such tentative agreements upon request violated such law.

8. In *Attorney General v. School Comm. of Taunton,* 7, 386 N.E.2d 1295, (1979), the court held that a school committee did not violate the Massachusetts Open Meeting Act when it met in executive session to discuss the salaries and working conditions of non-union employees when such discussions related to the school committee's overall strategy in negotiations with unions representing other school employees. The court reasoned as follows:

There was evidence before the judge that the committee was engaged in active negotiations with the representatives of the teachers', custodians' and cafeteria workers' unions, and that a decision had not been made with respect to the salary proposals that would be offered to the bargaining representatives of these groups. There was ample evidence to support the conclusion that the factors involved in the setting of the salaries for the non-union personnel could, if known to the union groups, have an effect on the wage packages that would be made to the unions and could be detrimental to the ongoing collective bargaining discussions with those groups.... We cannot say that the judge was plainly wrong in his ruling that the Committee had met its burden of establishing that the exemption to discuss strategy with respect to collective bargaining applied to validate the session, since the evidence points to the conclusion that the Committee was engaged in formulating a particular negotiating position in preparation for collective bargaining....

Accord *People v. Bd. of Educ. of Dist. 170,* 140 Ill. App. 3d 819, 353 N.E.2d 147 (1976).

9. See generally Note, *Public Sector Collective Bargaining and Sunshine Laws — Needless Conflict,* 18 Wm. & Mary L. Rev. 159 (1976).

Chapter 5

UNION SECURITY IN PUBLIC EMPLOYMENT

A. INTRODUCTION

There are six basic types of union security provisions — closed shop, union shop, maintenance of membership, agency shop, fair share, and dues checkoff. The general characteristics of each of these forms of union security are as follows:

1. *Closed Shop.* A closed-shop provision requires that an employee as a condition of employment must become a member of the union prior to being employed and must remain a member. The closed shop was lawful under the National Labor Relations Act as originally enacted in 1935, but since 1947 has been prohibited under the Taft-Hartley Amendments. For all intents and purposes the closed shop is illegal in both the public and private sectors.

2. *Union Shop.* A union-shop clause requires that an employee as a condition of employment become a member of the union within a stipulated period, usually thirty days, after being hired or after the effective date of the collective bargaining agreement, whichever is later. The NLRA specifically provides that private sector employers and unions may negotiate union-shop agreements, except where such agreements are prohibited by state right-to-work laws. Sixty-two percent of the collective bargaining agreements negotiated in the private sector include union-shop clauses. BNA, Collective Bargaining Negotiations and Contracts 87:1. In the public sector, five states[1] have legislatively authorized the negotiation of union-shop clauses for some or all categories of public employees.

3. *Maintenance of Membership.* A maintenance of membership clause requires that once an employee becomes a member of a union he or she must continue to be a member as a condition of employment. There is no requirement, however, that an employee initially become a member. Maintenance of membership agreements are permitted under the NLRA, although they are prohibited in those states with right-to-work laws. Only two states — California (teachers and state employees) and Pennsylvania — specifically permit public employers and unions to negotiate maintenance of membership clauses. Presumably, however, maintenance of membership clauses would also be permissible in states that permit the negotiation of union-shop clauses.

4. *Agency Shop.* An agency-shop clause requires that an employee as a condition of employment pay an amount equal to the periodic union dues uniformly required as a condition of acquiring or retaining membership. The agency shop is legal under the NLRA, but is prohibited by most state right-to-work laws. The

---

[1] Alaska, Kentucky (fire fighters, but only applicable to cities over 300,000 or cities petitioning for coverage), Maine (university employees), Vermont (municipal employees), and Washington (state and municipal employees).

negotiation of agency-shop clauses is specifically permitted by law in at least six states[2] and the District of Columbia.

5. *Fair Share.* A fair-share agreement is a variation of the agency shop, which requires that the employee as a condition of employment pay a proportionate share of the cost of collective bargaining activities but not the cost of other union activities. At least eleven states[3] authorize fair-share agreements.

In sharp contrast to the statutory provisions which permit the parties to voluntarily agree upon a fair-share agreement, the Hawaii public sector law requires an employer, wholly independent of negotiations, to deduct from the pay of all employees in the appropriate unit service fees and remit the same to the exclusive representative. Hawaii Rev. Stat. tit. 7, § 89-4 (1985). Similarly, the Minnesota law provides that "[a]n exclusive representative may require employees who are not members of the exclusive representative to contribute a fair share fee for the services rendered" and that "[t]he employer shall deduct the fee from the earnings of the employee and transmit the fee to the exclusive representative...." Minn. Stat. Ann. § 179A.06(3) (West Supp. 1991).

6. *Dues Checkoff.* Although not technically considered as such, the dues checkoff is, as a practical matter, a form of union security and will be so considered for the purposes of this chapter. A dues checkoff clause typically provides that upon receipt of a written authorization from an employee the employer will deduct the periodic union dues from the employee's pay and remit the same directly to the union. Most of the comprehensive public sector collective bargaining laws specifically permit the check off of union dues. In addition, several states that have not enacted public sector bargaining laws have specific statutory provisions that permit the check off of union dues.

Effect of Right to Work Laws. Twenty-one states have adopted constitutional or statutory provisions prohibiting the negotiation of union security clauses.[4] While these enactments were intended primarily for the private sector, they have been interpreted to prohibit the negotiation of union-shop, agency-shop, or fair-share agreements in the public sector. For example, in *Florida Educ. Ass'n v. PERC,* 346 So. 2d 551, 94 L.R.R.M. 2607 (Fla. Dist. Ct. App. 1977), an employee organization petitioned the Florida Commission to adopt a rule which would require that non-members in a certified bargaining unit pay the exclusive bargaining representative "a pro rata share of the specific expenses incurred for services rendered by the representative in relationship to negotiations and administration of grievance procedures." In upholding the Commission's decision that it did not have the authority to adopt such a rule, the court held that the proposed rule was repugnant to the right-to-work provisions of the Florida Constitution "because it would require non-union employees to purchase a right which the Constitution gives them." Accord *Levasseur v. Wheeldon,* 79 S.D. 442, 112 N.W.2d 894 (1964) ("A municipality cannot by legislative action or otherwise require union membership as a prerequisite to employment").

---

[2] Connecticut (state employees and teachers), Michigan, Montana, Rhode Island (teachers and state employees), Vermont (municipal employees), and Washington (teachers).

[3] California (educational and state employees), Hawaii, Illinois, Massachusetts, Minnesota, New Jersey, North Dakota, New York, Ohio, Oregon, and Wisconsin.

[4] Alabama, Arizona, Arkansas, Florida, Georgia, Idaho, Iowa, Kansas, Louisiana, Mississippi, Nebraska, Nevada, North Carolina, North Dakota, South Carolina, South Dakota, Tennessee, Texas, Utah, Virginia, and Wyoming.

B. GENERAL POLICY CONSIDERATIONS

NEW YORK STATE COMMISSION ON THE QUALITY, COST, AND FINANCING OF ELEMENTARY AND SECONDARY EDUCATION, Vol. 3, Appendix 13C, pp. 10-16 (1972)

The Commission has considered whether it ought to recommend to the Legislature that the Taylor Law be amended so as to authorize public employers and employee organizations to negotiate some form of organizational security provision. Since it is unlikely that the Legislature would consider authorizing the union shop because of the serious constitutional questions raised by compulsory membership, our discussion and tentative recommendations will concern only the agency shop.

There have been a number of cogent arguments advanced in support of legislative authorization of the agency shop. Foremost among them is the "free rider" argument: if it is public policy that public employees be granted collective bargaining rights, and that public employers be required to enter into collective agreements with organizations representing these employees, then it follows that those employees benefiting from this new arrangement have some obligation to lend financial support to the organization that wins these benefits. In short, the employee organization, through its authority to participate in the bilateral determination of economic benefits and other quasi policy issues, now serves a public purpose. To require employees to lend financial support to an employee organization is but the counterpart of requiring citizens to pay taxes to support local and state governments.

A second argument often advanced in support of legislative authorization of the agency shop is that those employers granting this provision find generally that their labor relations have become more stabilized. It is usually very difficult for rival organizations to unseat an incumbent organization when all employees in the bargaining unit are already paying dues. This means not only that the employer will be relatively free from the problems posed by frequent changes in bargaining agents, but also that there will be less pressure on the incumbent to outdo the "out" organization by becoming more strident in its pronouncements and more intransigent in its bargaining posture. By the same token, an agency shop allows the employee organization to become somewhat immune from the sometimes unreasonable demands of dissidents within the ranks; such dissidents lack the numerical strength to unseat current leadership, and there is no rival organization to which they can turn.

A third argument in support of legalizing agency shop arrangements is that they provide the employer with a certain amount of sorely needed bargaining leverage, yet at no cost to the taxpayer or to management prerogatives. If school management is determined to bargain hard on this issue — for example, if it refuses to grant the agency shop concession unless the employee organization agrees to remove some undesirable features from the existing contract — it is conceivable that certain gains, particularly in the area of administrative efficiency, will be achieved.

How persuasive are these arguments? To most teacher leaders, and probably to a majority of labor relations experts as well, they are quite persuasive. Yet there are counterarguments, and these too have cogency.

First, an agency shop provision would probably reduce by a significant degree whatever political leverage "satellite" personnel now enjoy within the employee organization. The language of criterion (c) of Section 207 of the Taylor Law, "the unit shall be compatible with the joint responsibilities of the public employer and public employees to serve the public," has generally been construed to mean that it is not in the public interest to fragment or "balkanize" bargaining units. Thus such satellite groups as counselors, nurse teachers, librarians and sometimes department chairmen and assistant principals are deemed to share a community of interest with teachers and are therefore included in the latter's bargaining units. To establish separate bargaining units for each of the above groups would not only invite whipsawing and leapfrogging tactics — to the detriment of both the employer and the public — but also require the employer to spend virtually all his time negotiating with each of the dozen or so bargaining agents representing these various groups.

Consequently, a number of nonteaching school employees are locked into the teacher unit. Relatively few in number, they lack political influence with the teacher organization leadership, which must direct most of its attention to winning benefits for the dominant political majority, the teachers. Thus satellite employees can only hope that when bargaining benefits are distributed the leadership will be generous. If such is not the case, under present circumstances they can threaten to withdraw membership. Thus the employee organization is instructed that even though satellite votes may not have much influence, there are other options open to them.

Under an agency shop arrangement it would not be possible to exercise this kind of leverage. Thus the complaints heard even now from satellite employees about the failure of the teacher organization to represent them fairly, will most assuredly be increased as teacher organizations become more politicized (majoritarian) and budget stringencies more acute.

As for the argument that the agency shop would engender greater stability in employer-employee relations, little can be said in opposition. Certainly the incumbent organization would become relatively immune from raids by rival organizations, just as the leadership of these organizations would enjoy greater insulation from the political machinations of dissident minorities within the ranks. But it can also be said that while stability is a laudable goal in labor relations, so too is freedom of choice. "Unions of their own choosing" was the slogan that accompanied the passage of the Wagner Act, and there is some merit in the argument that industrial democracy is better served if employee organizations are occasionally put to the political test by those whom they represent. This does not mean that the leadership is to be put to the test as there already exists adequate machinery to unseat unresponsive union leaders; it means that the organization itself ought to face the possibility of being voted out of office. Obviously, organizational security tends to reduce the chances of this happening. It is also arguable that a law that obliges an employee organization to win financial support by establishing a record as an effective and responsive bargaining agent, may prove in the long run to be more consistent with the public interest than a statutory provision that in many cases makes a dues collector out of the employer, willing as that employer may be.

The most troublesome feature of the agency shop, however, rests with its enforcement procedures. It was pointed out earlier that the enforcement technique most frequently applied is for the employer to agree to discharge any employee refusing to authorize deductions of the agency fee from his paycheck.... Under New York State's tenure law the only grounds for dismissal of a tenured teacher are "(a) insubordination, immoral character or conduct unbecoming a teacher; (b) inefficiency, incompetency, physical or mental disability or neglect of duty." It would be difficult, unless one put a strained interpretation on the term "insubordination," to so interpret any of the above grounds for dismissal to cover refusal to render funds to a private organization. Surely the tenure law would have to be amended if the Legislature were to authorize the agency shop, particularly if the statute permitted enforcement procedures that included dismissal of noncomplying tenured teachers.

It is anyone's guess as to how many tenured teachers in the state would on grounds of principle refuse to sign an agency fee authorization card, thereby leaving no option to the employer but to initiate dismissal proceedings. Surely there would be several — probably not enough to cause irreparable damage to public education, but enough to give pause to those who value the rights of individuals at least as much as they value employee bargaining power and organizational security.

The question, then, is how to balance the advantages of some form of organizational security against the obvious disadvantages of forcing upon tenured teachers the option of signing an agency shop fee authorization card or face automatic dismissal. A legislative proposal of the New York State Teachers Association (NYSTA) would provide one answer, empowering employers to deduct agency shop fees without individual authorizations. Thus an employee who chose not to join the organization would have his fee deducted anyway, along with income tax and social security deductions, which are also obligatory.

While this arrangement would resolve the dilemma of forced dismissal of recalcitrant tenured teachers, it would also raise certain constitutional issues, particularly those rights that citizens enjoy under the Fourteenth Amendment. It could at least be argued that the state, acting through one of its agencies, the school boards, would be denying individuals their property (agency fees) without due process of law.

What the issue comes down to is whether there is sufficient merit in the agency shop provision for the Legislature to authorize it. While such authorization does not require the parties to incorporate the agency shop into the agreement, it is nevertheless implicit that this provision would not be contrary to the public interest as it is rare that legislatures deliberately act *against* the latter. A secondary consideration is whether the Legislature should allow for enforcement procedures including possible dismissal of tenured teachers refusing to authorize the agency fee deduction.

The arguments allowing for some form of organizational security are persuasive, although they become less so in the concept of statewide collective bargaining. While it is not known what the status of membership in local organizations now is, and while it is certainly not known what level of membership is required before an employee organization can represent it effectively, there is evidence that in a number of cases employee organizations need greater protection than now enjoyed if they are to carry out obligations under the law and at the same time be reasonably immune from those pressures that so frequently provoke irresponsible behavior. In one region, for example, NYSTA affiliates represent over 6,000 teachers, yet membership is slightly more than 3,000. Certainly it is difficult for these employee organizations to carry out their "public purpose" functions under such circumstances.

It does not follow, however, that enforcement by dismissal of those who refuse to comply with the agency shop agreement — or even the denial of options, as NYSTA has proposed — is consistent with public policy. What is needed is a mechanism that, without impeding opportunities to engage volunteer workers and in general attain more flexible staff arrangements, will also provide contractual protection for struggling organizations. In the context of local bargaining, we therefore propose legislative authorization that (1) would allow for contractual provisions requiring newly hired personnel to permit some form of fee deduction to support the collective bargaining activity, but that (2) would render those teachers already on the payroll immune from the provisions. Thus a new teacher would have the option of accepting or rejecting a position in New York State education where the payment of an agency fee was a condition of continuing employment, just as he might refuse employment because he did not like the pay, hours, or course load involved. However, this recommendation does not meet the objections raised by some satellite personnel that an agency shop clause would practically guarantee underrepresentation at the bargaining table. Conceivably, Section 209-a of the Taylor Law (improper practices) could be strengthened so as to provide a remedy for this problem. The proposal would seem, however, to provide a modicum of organizational security without undermining the spirit of the teacher tenure law.

NOTE

Is there any relationship between the policy, espoused by many experts, of encouraging the establishment of broad bargaining units in the public sector and the negotiation of union security agreements? One commentator made the following observation:

> Even if a union succeeds in winning recognition in a large unit employees in that unit are generally not required to become members of the union. The relative lack of union security clauses in the collective bargaining agreements of the public service assures that, to a degree unparalleled in the private sector, dissident small-unit groups are able to maintain their separate identities and to prolong the battle for break-off from the larger group's exclusive bargaining agent.

Rock, *The Appropriate Unit Question in the Public Service: The Problem of Proliferation,* 67 Mich. L. Rev. 1001, 1005 (1969).

GOTBAUM, COLLECTIVE BARGAINING AND THE UNION LEADER, in PUBLIC WORKERS AND PUBLIC UNIONS 77, 84-85 (S. Zagoria ed. 1972)*

The Less Union Security, the More Militant Leadership

In an open shop situation, the percentage of dues-paying members gives you an indication of the labor leader's militancy: the smaller the percentage of membership, the greater the militancy. In a newly organized situation or where organization hovers around the 50 percent area, the union leader knows that he must come up with something new and dramatic or at least look dramatic, in order to increase membership. Where organization approaches the 100 percent level, the union leader can afford the luxury of dealing with issues on their merits.

In one television discussion John DeLury was magnificently stylistic and involved himself in some beautiful rank and file prose. My wife, who watched the program, queried me as to whether this was going to bring the public over to his side. I submitted to her that it would be nice for him to bring the public over to his side, but it was much more important that in an open shop situation the New York City sanitationmen were 99 percent organized. Good public will is of little help to a leader whose union is poorly organized and whose opposition grows troublesome.

In an open shop situation you do not want your contract just ratified: you want it *overwhelmingly* ratified. The opposition does not need a majority, all it needs is to keep the leadership off guard. If you lose a point at the bargaining table it is not considered by the opposition to be a part of normal bargaining. "You sold out" becomes the rallying cry for the opposition. In addition you never know how many members you are going to lose because you did not satisfy their specific desires. So you become an "irresponsible union boss" or a "pirate."

The fight for an agency shop in the public sector is almost ridiculous. Management's insistence on an open shop situation is the most counter-productive imaginable. It is to management's interest that the union be stable and representative of all the people in its unit. This would give the union leader maneuverability and flexibility. It would make him less demanding, less insecure, and less verbose. The agency shop is eminently fair; yet very few governments allow it. This makes little sense and is another example of public administration immaturity. It perhaps should be regarded in the same light as the public administrator who refuses to accept the role of management.

*Copyright © 1972 by The American Assembly, Columbia University. Reproduced by permission of the publisher, Prentice-Hall, Inc. The author, Victor Gotbaum, was the Executive Director of District Council 37 (New York City) of the American Federation of State, County and Municipal Employees, AFL-CIO, from 1957 to 1987.

ZWERDLING, UNION SECURITY IN THE PUBLIC SECTOR, in LABOR RELATIONS IN THE PUBLIC SECTOR 156, 161-63 (A. Knapp ed. 1977)*

Union organization and recognition often come hard, and once achieved are costly to maintain. Under the predominant type of state public employment collective bargaining legislation, the union that is the exclusive representative has a duty of fair representation with reference to *all* bargaining unit employees — union members and non-members alike. Proponents of service fee arrangements argue that if employees cannot be forced to join the union as a condition of continued employment, they should at least be required to share the costs of union representation — the costs of negotiating and administering the collective bargaining agreement which applies equally to them and from which they derive equal benefits.

Unions expend a large amount of financial and other resources in negotiating and administering collective bargaining agreements. Some of these expenses are borne by the respective local affiliates, but many services are provided by the locals' parent organizations. Examples of some of the more costly union functions include:

1) Payment of salaries and expenses for staff engaged in negotiation and administration of the contract;

2) Payment of general office and overhead expenses;

3) Maintenance of a research department which prepares local representatives for contract negotiations, prepares economic data, drafts contract language, and evaluates contract proposals;

4) Maintenance of a legal department or retained counsel which represents employees in arbitration, disciplinary proceedings, and negotiations; communicates significant legal developments in other parts of the country; and assistance in significant legal cases;

5) Provision of training in grievance handling — including arbitration and communication of local employee needs to their immediate employer or relevant government bodies and to their community;

6) Provision of information on activities of affiliates around the country, and their varying solutions to common problems;

7) Provision of assistance in federal and state legislative efforts with respect to public employees — including revenue sharing, civil rights, minimum wage laws, unemployment compensation, pension legislation, health insurance, public jobs programs, and occupational health and safety.

The requirement that all individuals who benefit from union activities contribute their fair share of the costs is but an application of the democratic concept. The service fee arrangement is plainly fair and equitable and consistent with good labor relations policy as well as basic democratic values. It is analogous to all Americans being taxed for the costs of government expenditures and the benefits received therefrom.

---

*Reprinted by permission of the American Bar Association and the Section of Labor Relations Law. The author, A.L. Zwerdling, is a Washington, D.C., attorney who represents public sector unions.

HAY, UNION SECURITY AND FREEDOM OF ASSOCIATION, in LABOR RELATIONS IN THE PUBLIC SECTOR 145, 146-47 (A. Knapp ed. 1977)*

The paramount reason why public employers with whom I have dealt oppose union security is their unwillingness to discharge a good employee for a reason which has absolutely nothing to do with that employee's job performance. That is their compelling objection to union security.

Furthermore, many believe that voluntary as opposed to compulsory unionism limits a union's bargaining strength, and thus may well result in a more tolerable economic package than could otherwise be negotiated against a more cohesive labor organization — certainly a legitimate goal for the public employer. Furthermore, I believe that compulsory unionism increases rather than decreases the number and intensity of public employee strikes — again, a goal which public employers may legitimately seek to avoid.

Another very real concern expressed by many public employers is that increased membership and financial resources for public unions will enable them to make direct political or legislative intrusions into the public sector bargaining process. For example, strong public sector unions have already elected school board members whose first loyalty is to the union rather than to the school board, thereby undermining if not destroying the school board's ability to negotiate effectively.

Similarly, strong public sector unions may secure by political pressures on the legislature laws which distort the collective bargaining process, such as mandatory benefit levels or minimum pay increases or requirements now in existence in California that a school board's initial bargaining proposals must be announced and discussed in public meetings held prior to the first negotiating session — public meetings at which the union brings public and political pressure for a liberalization of the employer's position prior to the first negotiation.

In these and many other ways, strong public sector unions have been able to put themselves on both sides of the bargaining table, in pursuit of their own and their members' interests and to the detriment of the public employer and the public at large.

So there are many very pragmatic reasons why a public employer, on behalf of itself and the society at large, may vigorously and legitimately oppose union security in the public sector. Furthermore, there is a serious question whether compulsory unionism has any advantage for the general public which outweighs its obvious disadvantages.

LARSON, PUBLIC EMPLOYEES AND THEIR "RIGHT TO WORK"**

It is easy to figure out why union officials put compulsory membership at the top of their "want list" when negotiating with public agencies. There are more than twelve million public employees, including nearly three million Federal

---

*Reprinted by permission of the American Bar Association and the Section of Labor Relations Law. The author, Howard Hay, is a California attorney who represents public employers.

**Reprinted by permission of Mr. Reed Larson, The National Right to Work Committee, 1990 M Street, N.W., Washington, D.C., 20036. Mr. Larson is Executive Vice President of the National Right to Work Committee.

employees. If every public employee were under compulsion to pay union dues of $5 a month, the take would amount to $700 million a year — not counting millions in initiation fees!

The stakes are enormous and the union bosses are at work. As Jerry Wurf said, "Our potential is nothing less than fantastic ... right now six out of every ten new jobs being created are jobs in government." He added that his union would have a million members now instead of just 400,000 if all his contracts called for compulsory unionism!

It is obvious to us that union officials, with the help of some politicians who receive campaign support from union treasuries, are making fantastic progress in a massive, coast-to-coast, community-by-community program aimed ultimately at locking every public employee into a contract forcing him to pay dues into a union treasury in order to keep his job.

To us the real threat in the compulsory unionization of government workers lies in the fact that it provides a thinly disguised pipeline diverting enforced salary deductions in the form of union dues to provide campaign funds for union-controlled politicians — politicians who as public officials are the government employee's bosses, and who are the very persons who forced him to pay the union in the first place.

The action of Mayor Lindsay is an excellent example of this problem and graphically illustrates why the AFL-CIO recently made an unprecedented decision at the national level to participate fully in campaigns for mayors and other local officials. In the past this has always been left to the local unions, some of which are effective and some of which are not. Our interpretation of this new emphasis is that it is part of an overall program aimed at obtaining union-controlled public officials at the local level who will — to put it bluntly — roll over and play dead whenever they are confronted by a union organizer representing a handful of militant employees.

The crux of the problem here is the inordinate influence of union political power on public officials charged with the responsibility of setting employee policies. In private industry, the interests of union officials are being served primarily on one side of the bargaining table. But in public employee bargaining we can see what amounts to an agent of union power representing both the employer and the organized employees. The solution, as we see it, is to make compulsory unionism illegal; to take the choice of membership or nonmembership in an employee union out of the hands of the politician and the union professionals, and keep it where it belongs — with the individual employee.

It is the widespread practice of compulsory unionism in private industry that frees union officials from the normal responsibilities of operating a voluntary organization. It is compulsory unionism that releases a major percentage of union resources directly for political action rather than for selling and maintaining membership. According to union spokesmen, retention and expansion of compulsory membership is essential if they are to continue and expand the political activity which they consider necessary and desirable.

Union representative Walter H. Barnes, of the Teamsters Local 636 in New Jersey, let the cat out of the bag last fall after the New Jersey legislature, over the veto of Governor Richard Hughes, passed a Right to Work law covering the state's public employees. Barnes said, "Since we can't get the union shop I have orders from the President of our local to stop trying to organize the Department of Public Works in Englewood because it just isn't worthwhile."

The late President John F. Kennedy clearly recognized the danger involved in the forced unionization of public employees when he insisted that his 1962 Executive Order 10988, authorizing the unionization of Federal employees, also protect the right *not* to join. That order reads: "Employees of the Federal government shall have, and shall be protected in the exercise of the right, freely and without fear of penalty or reprisal, to form, join and assist any employee organization or to refrain from such activity." That part of the Kennedy Executive Order can properly be called the Federal employees' Right to Work law. And as long as it remains in existence compulsory unionism cannot exist for Federal employees.

President Kennedy's Secretary of Labor, Arthur Goldberg, in explaining the order in a speech to members of the American Federation of Government Employees AFL-CIO said,

> I know you will agree with me that the union shop and the closed shop are inappropriate to the Federal government. And because of this, there is a larger responsibility for enlightenment on the part of the government union. In your own organization you have to win acceptance by your own conduct, your own action, your own wisdom, your own responsibility and your own achievements.... So you have an opportunity to bring into your organization people who come in because they want to come in and who will participate, therefore, in the full activity of your organization....

As a single-purpose organization the National Right to Work Committee is concerned only with compulsory versus voluntary unionism. We believe the drive for compulsory dues underlies most of the current turmoil in public employee-management relations. And we believe strongly that any meaningful labor legislation — for industrial as well as public employees — must have as its foundation the elimination of compulsory unionism. It is our firm belief that the record shows that voluntarism will go far to provide the checks and balances necessary to keeping union leadership responsive to the individual member.

K. HANSLOWE, THE EMERGING LAW OF LABOR RELATIONS IN PUBLIC EMPLOYMENT 114-15 (1967)*

[A] democratic political structure has limits as to the amount of organized group pressure it can tolerate. At some point the risk arises of a dangerous dilution of governmental authority by its being squeezed to death by conflicting power blocks. If that point is reached, foreign policy is made by defense industry, agricultural policy by farmers, and public personnel policy by employee organizations, and *not* by government representing the wishes of an electorate consisting of individual voters. If that point is reached, an orderly system of individual liberty under lawful rule would seem to be the victim. For surely it is difficult to conceive of a social order without a governmental repository of authority, which is authoritative for the very reason that it is representative and democratic.

---

*Reprinted by permission of the New York State School of Industrial and Labor Relations, Cornell University.

To illustrate: Problems may arise, if public employee organizations begin to press, as they have already commenced to do, for union security arrangements of one sort or another, making financial support of the employee organization a condition of public employment. On the face of it, this sounds innocent enough, and legal objections of incompatibility with civil service concepts of merit employment are likely to be overridden. If an exclusive bargaining agent is empowered, and is therefore required, to represent all employees in the bargaining unit, it seems fair to require all those benefiting from such representation to contribute to its cost.

But the Supreme Court of the United States has decided, as to the private sector, that the contractual obligation (in the form of the union shop) to contribute to the costs of the representation may not lawfully include, as a condition of employment, coerced support of *political* activities of the organization to which an individual member objects. Support of *collective bargaining activity* is all that may be compelled. Yet, in the public sector, political activity is unavoidably part and parcel of the process of *bargaining with politicians*. Thus there arises the possibility of involuntary contributions to organizational support of politicians who, while ready to improve the working conditions of public employees, on other questions take positions of which such public employees disapprove. Unless careful protections are worked out, enabling individual public employees to "contract out" from compelled support of unwanted political parties, politicians, and public policies, the union shop in public employment has the potential of becoming a neat mutual back-scratching mechanism, whereby public employee representatives and politicians each reinforce the other's interests and domain, with the individual public employee and the individual citizen left to look on, while his employment conditions, and his tax rate, and public policies generally are being decided by entrenched and mutually supportive government officials and collective bargaining representatives over whom the public has diminishing control.

Such dangers are perhaps not immediate. The point needs, however, to be reiterated that there are limits on the amount of stress which a democratic governmental structure can tolerate from organized group pressure. At some point its fibre can be broken, and democratic rule under law be replaced by authoritarian rule by clique.

NOTE

See generally K. Hanslowe, D. Dunn & J. Erstling, *Union Security in Public Employment: Of Free Riding and Free Association,* N.Y. St. Sch. Indus. & Lab. Rel., Inst. Pub. Employment, Monograph No. 8 (1978). For a discussion of the treatment of union security clauses under the National Labor Relations Act, see Cantor, *Uses and Abuses of the Agency Shop,* 50 Notre Dame Law. 61 (1983); Zipp, *Rights and Responsibilities of Parties to a Union-Security Agreement,* 31 Lab. L.J. 202 (1982).

C. CONSTITUTIONAL CONSIDERATIONS

CITY OF CHARLOTTE v. LOCAL 660, INT'L ASS'N OF FIREFIGHTERS

426 U.S. 283, 96 S. Ct. 2036, 48 L. Ed. 2d 636 (1976)

JUSTICE MARSHALL delivered the opinion of the Court.

The city of Charlotte, N.C., refuses to withhold from the paychecks of its firefighters dues owing to their union, Local 660, International Association of Firefighters. We must decide whether this refusal violates the Equal Protection Clause of the Fourteenth Amendment.

I

Local 660 represents some 351 of the 543 uniformed members of the Charlotte Fire Department. Since 1969 the union and individual members have repeatedly requested the city to withhold dues owing to the union from the paychecks of those union members who agree to a checkoff. The city has refused each request. After the union learned that it could obtain a private group life insurance policy for its membership only if it had a dues checkoff agreement with the city, the union and its officers filed suit in federal court alleging, inter alia, that the city's refusal to withhold the dues of union members violated the Equal Protection Clause of the Fourteenth Amendment.[1] The complaint asserted that since the city withheld amounts from its employees' paychecks for payment to various other organizations, it could not arbitrarily refuse to withhold amounts for payment to the union.

On cross-motions for summary judgment, the District Court for the Western District of North Carolina ruled against the city. The court determined that, although the city had no written guidelines, its "practice has been to allow check offs from employees' pay to organizations or programs as required by law or where the check off option is available to all City employees or where the check off option is available to all employees within a single employee unit such as the Fire Department." 381 F. Supp. 500, 502 (1974). The court further found that the city has "not allowed check off options serving only single employees or programs which are not available either to all City employees or to all employees engaged in a particular section of City employment." *Ibid.* Finding, however, that withholding union dues from the paychecks of union members would be no more difficult than processing any other deduction allowed by the city, the District Court concluded that the city had not offered a rational explanation for its refusal to withhold for the union. Accordingly, the District Court held that the city's refusal to withhold moneys when requested to do so by the respondents for the benefit of Local 660 "constitutes a violation of the individual [respondents'] rights to equal protection of laws under the Fourteenth Amendment." *Id.,* at 502-503. The court ordered that so long as the city continued "without clearly stated and fair standards, to withhold moneys from the paychecks of City employees for other purposes," it was enjoined from refusing to withhold union dues from the paychecks of the respondents. *Id.,* at 503. The

---

[1]Respondents brought suit under 42 U.S.C. § 1983, grounding jurisdiction in 28 U.S.C. §§ 1331 and 1343....

Court of Appeals for the Fourth Circuit affirmed, 518 F.2d 83 (1975), and we granted certiorari. 423 U.S. 890 (1975). We reverse.

II

Since it is not here asserted — and this Court would reject such a contention if it were made — that respondents' status as union members or their interest in obtaining a dues checkoff is such as to entitle them to special treatment under the Equal Protection Clause, the city's practice must meet only a relatively relaxed standard of reasonableness in order to survive constitutional scrutiny.

The city presents three justifications for its refusal to allow the dues checkoff requested by respondents. First, it argues, North Carolina law makes it illegal for the city to enter into a contract with a municipal union, N.C. Gen. Stat. § 95-98 (1975), and an agreement with union members to provide a dues checkoff, with the union as a third-party beneficiary, would in effect be such a contract. See 40 N.C. Op. Atty. Gen. 591 (1968-1970). Thus, compliance with the state law, and with the public policy it represents of discouraging dealing with municipal unions, is said to provide a sufficient basis for refusing respondents' request. Second, it claims, a dues checkoff is a proper subject of collective bargaining, which the city asserts Congress may shortly require of state and local governments. Under this theory, the desire to preserve the checkoff as a bargaining chip in any future collective-bargaining process is in itself an adequate basis for the refusal. Lastly, the city contends, allowing withholding only when it benefits all city or departmental employees is a legitimate method for avoiding the burden of withholding money for all persons or organizations that request a checkoff. Because we find that this explanation provides a sufficient justification for the challenged practice, we have no occasion to address the first two reasons proffered.

The city submitted affidavits to show that it would be unduly burdensome and expensive for it to withhold money for every organization or person that requested it, App. 17, 45, 55, and respondents did not contest this showing. As respondents concede, it was therefore reasonable, and permissible under the Equal Protection Clause, for the city to develop standards or restrictions to determine who would be eligible for withholding. *Mathews v. Diaz,* [426 U.S. 67,] at 82-83. See Brief for Respondents 9. Within the limitations of the Equal Protection Clause, of course, the choice of those standards is for the city and not for the courts. Thus, our inquiry is not whether standards might be drawn that would include the union but whether the standards that were drawn were reasonable ones with "some basis in practical experience." *South Carolina v. Katzenbach,* 383 U.S. 301, 331 (1966). Of course, the fact that the standards were drawn and applied in practice rather than pursuant to articulated guidelines is of no import for equal protection purposes.

The city allows withholding for taxes, retirement-insurance programs, savings programs, and certain charitable organizations. These categories, the District Court found, are those in which the checkoff option can, or must, be availed of by all city employees, or those in an entire department. Although the District Court found that this classification did not present a rational basis for rejecting respondents' requests, 381 F. Supp., at 502, we disagree. The city has determined that it will provide withholding only for programs of general interest in which all city or departmental employees can, without more, participate. Employees can participate in the union checkoff only if they join an outside organization — the union. Thus, Local 660 does not fit the category of groups for which the city will withhold. We cannot say that denying withholding to associational or special interest groups that claim only some departmental employees as members and that employees must first join before being eligible to participate in the checkoff marks an arbitrary line so devoid of reason as to violate the Equal Protection Clause. Rather, this division seems a reasonable method for providing the benefit of withholding to employees in their status as employees, while limiting the number of instances of withholding and the financial and administrative burdens attendant thereon.

Given the permissibility of creating standards and the reasonableness of the standards created, the District Court's conclusion that it would be no more difficult for the city to withhold dues for the union than to process other deductions is of no import. We may accept, *arguendo,* that the difficulty involved in processing any individual deduction is neither great nor different in kind from that involved in processing any other deduction. However, the city has not drawn its lines in order to exclude individual deductions, but in order to avoid the cumulative burden of processing deductions every time a request is made; and inherent in such a line-drawing process are difficult choices and "some harsh and apparently arbitrary consequences...." *Mathews v. Diaz,* [426 U.S.,] at 83. See *id.*] at 82-84; *Dandridge v. Williams,* 397 U.S. 471, 485 (1970). Cf. *Schilb v. Kuebel,* 404 U.S. 357, 364 (1971); *Williamson v. Lee Optical Co.,* 348 U.S. 483, 489 (1955).

Respondents recognize the legitimacy of such a process and concede that the city "is free to develop fair and reasonable standards to meet any possible cost problem." Brief for Respondents 9. Respondents have wholly failed, however, to present any reasons why the present standards are not fair and reasonable — other than the fact that the standards exclude them. This fact, of course, is insufficient to transform the city policy into a constitutional violation. Since we find a reasonable basis for the challenged classification, the judgment of the Court of Appeals for the Fourth Circuit must be reversed, and the case remanded for further proceedings consistent with this opinion.

It is so ordered.

MR. JUSTICE STEWART concurs in the judgment upon the ground that the classification challenged in this case is not invidiously discriminatory and does not, therefore, violate the Equal Protection Clause of the Fourteenth Amendment.

NOTES

1. Is it a violation of the equal protection clause for a public employer to deny an employee organization the right to have its dues checked off if the public employer grants another employee organization this right? In *Edwards v. Alhambra Elementary Sch. Dist. No. 63,* 488 P.2d 501 (Ariz. Ct. App. 1971), the court held that a school board's action in granting a dues checkoff to an employee organization representing teachers and denying the same right to an employee organization representing support staff was constitutional on the ground that it constituted a reasonable classification. The court noted that "the classification of teachers vis-à-vis non-teachers for purposes of employment and inducements for employment has long been recognized" and that "[o]ne of the inducements which ... could be held out to teachers and withheld from non-teachers, is the privilege of payroll deductions."

In *South Carolina Educ. Ass'n v. Campbell*, 883 F.2d 1251 (4th Cir. 1989), *cert. denied*, 110 S. Ct. 1129 (1990), the South Carolina Education Association (SCEA) challenged on both first amendment and equal protection grounds a South Carolina law which extended a dues deduction privilege to the State Employees Association but which denied such privilege to the South Carolina Education Association. In upholding the constitutionality of the law, the Fourth Circuit ruled that "the district court's extensive reliance on the testimony of individual members of the General Assembly as to legislative motive [was] an improper intrusion into the legislative function." In rejecting the SCEA's argument that it had been denied equal protection because it was a similarly situated organization, the court held that there was a rational distinction between the State Employees Association, a "general interest" organization open to all State employees without regard to occupation or job classification, and the SCEA, "a 'special interest' association open only to individuals employed in the South Carolina public education system."

On the other hand, in *Teamsters Local 728 v. City of Atlanta*, 468 F. Supp. 620 (N.D. Ga. 1979), the court held that it was a violation of the equal protection clause for a city to refuse to check off union dues for members of its police department when it was withholding union dues from members of its fire department. Although the city attempted to justify its action on the ground that the two departments performed different functions, the court found that this was not a relevant distinction. Accordingly, the court ruled that "so long as the City of Atlanta has unions within both its police and fire departments, and so long as it is willing to withhold union dues from the firemen, it must, under the equal protection clause, make the same option open to police employees."

2. Once a public employer has agreed to check off union dues, is there any constitutional restriction on the right of the employer to cease checking off dues? In *Arkansas State Hwy. Emps., Local 1315 v. Kell*, 628 F.2d 1099 (8th Cir. 1980), the court held that a highway department's action in ceasing its practice of checking off union dues did not violate either the first or fourteenth amendment. With respect to the first amendment, the court held that while the action of discontinuing the dues checkoff might "impair the effectiveness of the union, this type of impairment is not one that the First Amendment prohibits." As for the fourteenth amendment, the court ruled that the union had not satisfied its obligation to demonstrate that the highway department "had no reasonable basis for believing that the burden of withholding union dues outweighed any possible benefits to be derived therefrom by the highway department or its employees as a whole." Accord *Maine State Emps. Ass'n v. University of Me.*, 395 A.2d 829, 1979-80 PBC ¶ 36,492 (Me. 1978).

3. In *Local 995, IAFF v. City of Richmond*, 415 F. Supp. 325 (E.D. Va. 1976), the court held a city did not infringe upon the first amendment rights of union members in refusing to check off union dues. In rejecting the union's argument that without a dues checkoff it would be unable to adequately fund its operations, the court said the city's refusal did not "significantly impair the union's ability to organize and provide services for its members." The court further noted that "while the First Amendment protects the right of American citizens to freely associate, it was never intended to provide an affirmative factor in forcing the state to aid union organizational activities."

4. In *Brown v. Alexander,* 718 F.2d 1417 (6th Cir. 1984), the court rejected various constitutional objections to provisions of a Tennessee dues checkoff statute which (a) conferred dues checkoff privileges on a state employee association but not on nationally affiliated unions, (b) required that the state employees association must have at least 20% of the employees in the executive branch of state government as members in order to obtain dues checkoff privileges, (c) required that the state employee organization must have as one of its objectives the promoting of an efficient and effective work force, and (d) required that the state employee organization must be a wholly domestic organization which was not part of a multistate employee organization. The court said that a "state may differentiate between public employee organizations ... in bestowing benefits as long as there is a reasonable and rational basis in these actions." On the other hand, the Sixth Circuit held that the Tennessee statute's requirement that the state employee organization be an independent organization violated the first amendment, noting that "this subsection directly limits freedom of association between labor organizations, and their members or members of other such organizations, and thus it could restrain or restrict freedom of association, a fundamental first amendment right."

5. In *Bauch v. City of New York,* 21 N.Y.2d 599, 237 N.E.2d 211, 289 N.Y.S.2d 951, *cert. denied,* 393 U.S. 834 (1968), the New York Court of Appeals held that the City of New York did not violate either the first or the fourteenth amendment by granting a union which represented a majority of the municipal employees in an appropriate bargaining unit an exclusive dues checkoff privilege and denying such a privilege to a minority union. After noting that "[t]he requirements of due process are satisfied as long as the challenged measure is reasonably related to the attainment of a permissible objective," the court stated:

> In the case before us, the existence of such a reasonable relationship and basis is apparent. The maintenance of stability in the relations between the city and employee organizations, as well as the avoidance of devastating work stoppages, are major responsibilities of the city administration. The Mayor seeks to further these objectives by introducing into city labor relations a practice which has been commonplace in common industry and in the labor policies of other governmental bodies.... The city program is in accord with the national labor policy, which has been built on the premise that a majority organization is the most effective vehicle for improving wages, hours and working conditions.... Be that as it may, we may not consider the merits or the ultimate wisdom of the policy ... ; it is enough, as already indicated, that a method of implementing union security, so widely utilized and so long tested as the one proposed by the Mayor, may not be said to lack a rational basis or to be unrelated to the city's legitimate purposes.

In rejecting the minority union's contention that withdrawal of the dues checkoff would weaken its organization to the point of threatening its very existence, the court noted:

> Nothing in the city's labor policy denies members of the petitioners' union the right to meet, to speak, to publish, to proselytize and to collect dues by the means employed by thousands of organizations of all kinds, that do not have the benefit of a dues check-off. Neither the First Amendment nor any other

constitutional provision entitles them to the special aid of the city's collection and disbursing facilities.

Finally, the court held that under the Taylor Act "the employer is plainly under no obligation" to check off dues for a minority union not recognized as a bargaining agent. Accord *Sacramento Cty. Emps. Org., Local 22 v. County of Sacramento,* 28 Cal. App. 3d 424, 104 Cal. Rptr. 619 (1972).

6. A number of state statutes provide that once an employee organization is certified or recognized as the exclusive bargaining representative, it has the exclusive right to have its dues deducted. For example, the California Education Employment Relations Act provides that once an employee organization has been recognized as the exclusive representative in an appropriate unit the deduction of membership dues as to any employee in that unit "shall not be permissible except to the exclusive representative." Cal. Gov't Code § 3543.1(d) (West 1980).

7. The Nevada Local Government Employee-Management Relations Board has held that the exclusive bargaining representative has the exclusive right to contract for dues checkoff and that it is not a prohibited practice for an employer to refuse to grant a minority union the privilege of checking off the dues of its members. *Operating Eng's Local No. 3 v. City of Reno,* Item # 7 (Nev. LGE-MRB 1972).

8. The Wisconsin Supreme Court in *Board of Sch. Dirs. v. WERC,* 42 Wis. 2d 637, 168 N.W.2d 92 (1969), held that granting a majority union an exclusive dues checkoff was a prohibited practice. The court approved the WERC's test that "'[t]*hose rights or benefits which are granted exclusively to the majority representative,* and thus denied its minority organizations, *must in some rational manner be related to the functions of the majority organization in its representative capacity,* and must not be granted to entrench such organization as the bargaining representative.'" The court, however, rejected the WERC's conclusion that granting an exclusive dues checkoff was permissible, stating:

> The WERC made no attempt to explain how the granting of exclusive checkoff was rationally related to the functioning of the majority organization *in its representative capacity;* nor can we see any relationship whatsoever. The sole and complete purpose of *exclusive* checkoff is self-perpetuation and entrenchment. While a majority representative may negotiate for checkoff, he is negotiating for all the employees, and, if checkoff is granted for any, it must be granted for all.

In 1971, the Wisconsin law was amended to provide that it is not a prohibited practice for an employer to enter into a fair-share agreement with a certified union. In *Milwaukee Fed'n of Teachers Local 252 v. WERC,* 83 Wis. 2d 588, 266 N.W.2d 314 (1978), the Wisconsin Supreme Court reaffirmed its decision in *Board of Sch. Dirs.* and held that it is a prohibited practice for a municipal employer to refuse to check off dues for a minority organization where such right is extended to the exclusive bargaining representative. The court stated:

> Although ... both fair-share agreements and exclusionary checkoff privileges are union security devices, they differ ... in function and effect. A legislative decision to permit the certified union to recoup some of its bargaining costs from non-union bargaining unit employees is perfectly compatible with this Court's holding that one union may not arrange a checkoff system to the exclusion of other unions. The first negates the possibility that there will be freeloaders who reap the benefits of collective bargaining without paying the

costs; the latter tends to destroy competing unions or at least discourages membership in them. The legislature could very well permit the one without permitting the other.

The court also noted that "it is significant that the amendments to the statute do not expressly provide the certified union with a right to an exclusive checkoff arrangement."

ABOOD v. DETROIT BOARD OF EDUCATION

431 U.S. 209, 97 S. Ct. 1782, 52 L. Ed. 2d 261 (1977)

JUSTICE STEWART delivered the opinion of the Court.

The State of Michigan has enacted legislation authorizing a system for union representation of local governmental employees. A union and a local government employer are specifically permitted to agree to an "agency shop" arrangement, whereby every employee represented by a union — even though not a union member — must pay to the union, as a condition of employment, a service fee equal in amount to union dues. The issue before us is whether this arrangement violates the constitutional rights of government employees who object to public sector unions as such or to various union activities financed by the compulsory service fees.

I

After a secret ballot election, the Detroit Federation of Teachers (Union) was certified in 1967 pursuant to Michigan law as the exclusive representative of teachers employed by the Detroit Board of Education (Board). The Union and the Board thereafter concluded a collective-bargaining agreement effective from July 1, 1969, to July 1, 1971. Among the agreement's provisions was an "agency shop" clause, requiring every teacher who had not become a Union member within 60 days of hire (or within 60 days of January 26, 1970, the effective date of the clause) to pay the Union a service charge equal to the regular dues required of Union members. A teacher who failed to meet this obligation was subject to discharge. Nothing in the agreement, however, required any teacher to join the Union, espouse the cause of unionism, or participate in any other way in Union affairs.

On November 7, 1969 — more than two months before the agency-shop clause was to become effective — Christine Warczak and a number of other named teachers filed a class action in a state court, naming as defendants the Board, the Union, and several Union officials. Their complaint, as amended, alleged that they were unwilling or had refused to pay dues and that they opposed collective bargaining in the public sector. The amended complaint further alleged that the Union "carries on various social activities for the benefit of its members which are not available to non-members as a matter of right," and that the Union is engaged

"in a number and variety of activities and programs which are economic, political, professional, scientific and religious in nature of which Plaintiffs do not approve, and in which they will have no voice, and which are not and will not be collective bargaining activities, i.e., the negotiation and administration of contracts with Defendant Board, and that a substantial part of the sums required to be paid under said Agency Shop Clause are used and will continue to be used for the support of such activities and programs, and not solely for the purpose of defraying the cost of Defendant Federation of its activities as bargaining agent for teachers employed by Defendant Board."

The complaint prayed that the agency-shop clause be declared invalid under state law and also under the United States Constitution as a deprivation of, inter alia, the plaintiffs' freedom of association protected by the First and Fourteenth Amendments, and for such further relief as might be deemed appropriate.

Upon the defendants' motion for summary judgment, the trial court dismissed the action for failure to state a claim upon which relief could be granted. *Warczak v. Board of Education,* 73 L.R.R.M. 2237 (Cir. Ct. Wayne County). The plaintiffs appealed, and while their appeal was pending the Michigan Supreme Court ruled in *Smigel v. Southgate Community School Dist.,* 388 Mich. 531, 202 N.W.2d 305, that state law prohibited an agency shop in the public sector. Accordingly, the judgment in the *Warczak* case was vacated and remanded to the trial court for further proceedings consistent with the *Smigel* decision.

Meanwhile, D. Louis Abood and other named teachers had filed a separate action in the same state trial court. The allegations in the complaint were virtually identical to those in *Warczak,* and similar relief was requested. This second action was held in abeyance pending disposition of the *Warczak* appeal, and when that case was remanded the two cases were consolidated in the trial court for consideration of the defendants' renewed motion for summary judgment.

On November 5, 1973, that motion was granted. The trial court noted that following the *Smigel* decision, the Michigan Legislature had in 1973 amended its Public Employment Relations Act so as expressly to authorize an agency shop. 1973 Mich. Pub. Acts, No. 25, codified as Mich. Comp. Laws § 432.210(1)(c).[7] This amendment was applied retroactively by the trial court to validate the agency-shop clause predating 1973 as a matter of state law, and the court ruled further that such a clause does not violate the Federal Constitution.

The plaintiffs' appeals were consolidated by the Michigan Court of Appeals, which ruled that the trial court had erred in giving retroactive application to the 1973 legislative amendment. The appellate court proceeded, however, to consider the constitutionality of the agency-shop clause, and upheld its facial validity on the authority of this Court's decision in *Railway Employes' Dept. v. Hanson,* 351 U.S. 225, which upheld the constitutionality under the First Amendment of a union-shop clause, authorized by the Railway Labor Act, requiring financial support of the exclusive bargaining representative by every member of the bargaining unit. *Id.,* at 238. Noting, however, that Michigan law also permits union expenditures for legislative lobbying and in support of political candidates, the state appellate court identified an issue explicitly not considered in *Hanson* — the constitutionality of using compulsory service charges to further "political purposes" unrelated to collective bargaining. Although recog-

---

[7]That section provides in relevant part: "[N]othing in this act or in any law of this state shall preclude a public employer from making an agreement with an exclusive bargaining representative as defined in section 11 to require as a condition of employment that all employees in the bargaining unit pay to the exclusive bargaining representative a service fee equivalent to the amount of dues uniformly required of members of the exclusive bargaining representative...."

nizing that such expenditures "could violate plaintiffs' First and Fourteenth Amendment rights," the court read this Court's more recent decisions to require that an employee who seeks to vindicate such rights must "make known to the union those causes and candidates to which he objects." Since the complaints had failed to allege that any such notification had been given, the court held that the plaintiffs were not entitled to restitution of any portion of the service charges. The trial court's error on the retroactivity question, however, led the appellate court to reverse and remand the case. 60 Mich. App. 92, 230 N.W.2d 322. After the Supreme Court of Michigan denied review, the plaintiffs appealed to this Court, 28 U.S.C. § 1257(2), and we noted probable jurisdiction, 425 U.S. 949.

II

A

Consideration of the question whether an agency-shop provision in a collective-bargaining agreement covering governmental employees is, as such, constitutionally valid must begin with two cases in this Court that on their face go far toward resolving the issue. The cases are *Railway Employes' Dept. v. Hanson, supra,* and *Machinists v. Street,* 367 U.S. 740.

In the *Hanson* case a group of railroad employees brought an action in a Nebraska court to enjoin enforcement of a union-shop agreement.[10] The challenged clause was authorized, and indeed shielded from any attempt by a State to prohibit it, by the Railway Labor Act, 45 U.S.C. § 152 Eleventh. The trial court granted the relief requested. The Nebraska Supreme Court upheld the injunction on the ground that employees who disagreed with the objectives promoted by union expenditures were deprived of the freedom of association protected by the First Amendment. This Court agreed that "justiciable questions under the First and Fifth Amendments were presented," 351 U.S., at 231,[12] but reversed the judgment of the Nebraska Supreme Court on the

---

[10] Under a union-shop agreement, an employee must become a member of the union within a specified period of time after hire, and must as a member pay whatever union dues and fees are uniformly required. Under both the National Labor Relations Act and the Railway Labor Act, "[i]t is permissible to condition employment upon membership, but membership, insofar as it has significance to employment rights, may in turn be conditioned only upon payment of fees and dues." *NLRB v. General Motors,* 373 U.S. 734, 742. See 29 U.S.C. § 158(a)(3); 45 U.S.C. § 152 Eleventh, quoted in n. 11, *infra.* Hence, although a union shop denies an employee the option of not formally becoming a union member, under federal law it is the "practical equivalent" of an agency shop, *NLRB v. General Motors, supra,* at 743. See also *Lathrop v. Donohue,* 367 U.S. 820, 828.

Hanson was concerned simply with the requirement of financial support for the union, and did not focus on the question whether the additional requirement of a union-shop arrangement that each employee formally join the union is constitutionally permissible. See *NLRB v. General Motors, supra,* 373 U.S. at 744 ("Such a difference between the union and agency shop may be of great importance in some contexts ...."); cf. *Storer v. Brown,* 415 U.S. 724, 745-746. As the agency shop before us does not impose that additional requirement, we have no occasion to address that question.

[12] Unlike § 14(b) of the National Labor Relations Act, 29 U.S.C. § 164(b), the Railway Labor Act pre-empts any attempt by a State to prohibit a union-shop agreement. Had it not been for that federal statute, the union-shop provision at issue in *Hanson* would have been invalidated under Nebraska law. The *Hanson* Court accordingly reasoned that government action was present: "[T]he federal statute is the source of the power and authority by which any private rights are lost or sacrificed.... The enactment of the federal statute authorizing union shop agreements is the governmental action on which the Constitution operates ...." 351 U.S., at 232. See also *id.,* at 232 n.4.

merits. Acknowledging that "[m]uch might be said *pro* and *con* " about the union shop as a policy matter, the Court noted that it is Congress that is charged with identifying "[t]he ingredients of industrial peace and stabilized labor-management relations ...." *Id.,* at 233-234. Congress determined that it would promote peaceful labor relations to permit a union and an employer to conclude an agreement requiring employees who obtain the benefit of union representation to share its cost, and that legislative judgment was surely an allowable one. *Id.,* at 235.

The record in *Hanson* contained no evidence that union dues were used to force ideological conformity or otherwise to impair the free expression of employees, and the Court noted that "[i]f 'assessments' are in fact imposed for purposes not germane to collective bargaining, a different problem would be presented." *Ibid.* (footnote omitted). But the Court squarely held that "the requirement for financial support of the collective-bargaining agency by all who receive the benefits of its work ... does not violate ... the First Amendmen[t]." *Id.,* at 238.

The Court faced a similar question several years later in the *Street* case, which also involved a challenge to the constitutionality of a union shop authorized by the Railway Labor Act. In *Street,* however, the record contained findings that the union treasury to which all employees were required to contribute had been used "to finance the campaigns of candidates for federal and state offices whom [the plaintiffs] opposed, and to promote the propagation of political and economic doctrines, concepts and ideologies with which [they] disagreed." 367 U.S., at 744.

The Court recognized, *id.,* at 749, that these findings presented constitutional "questions of the utmost gravity" not decided in *Hanson,* and therefore considered whether the Act could fairly be construed to avoid these constitutional issues. 367 U.S., at 749-750.[13] The Court concluded that the Act could be so construed, since only expenditures related to the union's functions in negotiating and administering the collective bargaining agreement and adjusting grievances and disputes fell within "the reasons ... accepted by Congress why authority to make union-shop agreements was justified," *id.,* at 768. The Court ruled, therefore, that the use of compulsory union dues for political purposes violated the Act itself. Nonetheless, it found that an injunction against enforcement of the union-shop agreement as such was impermissible under *Hanson,* and remanded the case to the Supreme Court of Georgia so that a more limited remedy could be devised.

The holding in *Hanson,* as elaborated in *Street,* reflects familiar doctrines in the federal labor laws. The principle of exclusive union representation, which underlies the National Labor Relations Act as well as the Railway Labor Act, is a central element in the congressional structuring of industrial relations. The designation of a single representative avoids the confusion that would result

---

("Once courts enforce the agreement the sanction of government is, of course, put behind them. See *Shelley v. Kraemer,* 334 U.S. 1; *Hurd v. Hodge,* 334 U.S. 24; *Barrows v. Jackson,* 346 U.S. 249").

[13] In suggesting that *Street* "significantly undercut," and constituted a "rethinking" of, *Hanson, post,* at 247, the concurring opinion loses sight of the fact that the record in *Street,* unlike that in *Hanson,* potentially presented constitutional questions arising from union expenditures for ideological purposes unrelated to collective bargaining.

from attempting to enforce two or more agreements specifying different terms and conditions of employment. It prevents inter-union rivalries from creating dissension within the work force and eliminating the advantages to the employee of collectivization. It also frees the employer from the possibility of facing conflicting demands from different unions, and permits the employer and a single union to reach agreements and settlements that are not subject to attack from rival labor organizations.

The designation of a union as exclusive representative carries with it great responsibilities. The tasks of negotiating and administering a collective-bargaining agreement and representing the interests of employees in settling disputes and processing grievances are continuing and difficult ones. They often entail expenditure of much time and money. See *Street,* 367 U.S., at 760. The services of lawyers, expert negotiators, economists, and a research staff, as well as general administrative personnel, may be required. Moreover, in carrying out these duties, the union is obliged "fairly and equitably to represent all employees ..., union and non-union," within the relevant unit. *Id.,* at 761. A union-shop arrangement has been thought to distribute fairly the cost of these activities among those who benefit, and it counteracts the incentive that employees might otherwise have to become "free riders" — to refuse to contribute to the union while obtaining benefits of union representation that necessarily accrue to all employees.

To compel employees financially to support their collective-bargaining representative has an impact upon their First Amendment interests. An employee may very well have ideological objections to a wide variety of activities undertaken by the union in its role as exclusive representative. His moral or religious views about the desirability of abortion may not square with the union's policy in negotiating a medical benefits plan. One individual might disagree with a union policy of negotiating limits on the right to strike, believing that to be the road to serfdom for the working class, while another might have economic or political objections to unionism itself. An employee might object to the union's wage policy because it violates guidelines designed to limit inflation, or might object to the union's seeking a clause in the collective-bargaining agreement proscribing racial discrimination. The examples could be multiplied. To be required to help finance the union as a collective-bargaining agent might well be thought, therefore, to interfere in some way with an employee's freedom to associate for the advancement of ideas, or to refrain from doing so, as he sees fit. But the judgment clearly made in *Hanson* and *Street* is that such interference as exists is constitutionally justified by the legislative assessment of the important contribution of the union shop to the system of labor relations established by Congress. "The furtherance of the common cause leaves some leeway for the leadership of the group. As long as they act to promote the cause which justified bringing the group together, the individual cannot withdraw his financial support merely because he disagrees with the group's strategy. If that were allowed, we would be reversing the *Hanson* case, *sub silentio.*" *Machinists v. Street,* 367 U.S., at 778. (Douglas, J., concurring.)

B

The National Labor Relations Act leaves regulation of the labor relations of state and local governments to the States. See 29 U.S.C. § 152(2). Michigan has chosen to establish for local government units a regulatory scheme which, although not identical in every respect to the NLRA or Railway Labor Act is broadly modeled after federal law. Under Michigan law employees of local government units enjoy rights parallel to those protected under federal legislation: the rights to self-organization and to bargain collectively, Mich. Comp. Laws §§ 423.209, 423.215 (1970); see 29 U.S.C. § 157; 45 U.S.C. § 152 Fourth; and the right to secret-ballot representation elections, Mich. Comp. Laws § 423.212 (1970); see 29 U.S.C. § 159(e)(1); 45 U.S.C. § 152 Ninth.

Several aspects of Michigan law that mirror provisions of the Railway Labor Act are of particular importance here. A union that obtains the support of a majority of employees in the appropriate bargaining unit is designated the exclusive representative of those employees. Mich. Comp. Laws § 423.211 (1970). A union so designated is under a duty of fair representation to all employees in the unit, whether or not union members. And in carrying out all of its various responsibilities, a recognized union may seek to have an agency-shop clause included in a collective-bargaining agreement. Mich. Comp. Laws § 423.210(1)(c) (1970). Indeed, the 1973 amendment to the Michigan law was specifically designed to authorize agency shops in order that "employees in the bargaining unit ... share fairly in the financial support of their exclusive bargaining representative...." § 423.210(2).

The governmental interests advanced by the agency-shop provision in the Michigan statute are much the same as those promoted by similar provisions in federal labor law. The confusion and conflict that could arise if rival teachers' unions, holding quite different views as to the proper class hours, class sizes, holidays, tenure provisions, and grievance procedures, each sought to obtain the employer's agreement, are no different in kind from the evils that the exclusivity rule in the Railway Labor Act was designed to avoid. The desirability of labor peace is no less important in the public sector, nor is the risk of "free riders" any smaller.

Our province is not to judge the wisdom of Michigan's decision to authorize the agency shop in public employment. Rather, it is to adjudicate the constitutionality of that decision. The same important government interests recognized in the *Hanson* and *Street* cases presumptively support the impingement upon associational freedom created by the agency shop here at issue. Thus, insofar as the service charge is used to finance expenditures by the union for the purposes of collective bargaining, contract administration, and grievance adjustment, those two decisions of this Court appear to require validation of the agency-shop agreement before us.

While recognizing the apparent precedential weight of the *Hanson* and *Street* cases, the appellants advance two reasons why those decisions should not control decision of the present case. First, the appellants note that it is *government employment* that is involved here, thus directly implicating constitutional guarantees, in contrast to the private employment that was the subject of the *Hanson* and *Street* decisions. Second, the appellants say that in the public sector collective bargaining itself is inherently "political," and that to require them to give financial support to it is to require the "ideological conformity" that the Court expressly found absent in the *Hanson* case. 351 U.S., at 238. We find neither argument persuasive.

Because it is employment by the State that is here involved, the appellants suggest that this case is governed by a long line of decisions holding that public employment cannot be conditioned upon the surrender of First Amendment rights. But, while the actions of public employers surely constitute "state action," the union shop, as authorized by the Railway Labor Act, also was found to result from governmental action in *Hanson*. The plaintiffs' claims in *Hanson* failed, not because there was no governmental action, but because there was no First Amendment violation.[23] The appellants' reliance on the "unconstitutional conditions" doctrine is therefore misplaced.

The appellants' second argument is that in any event collective bargaining in the public sector is inherently "political" and thus requires a different result under the First and Fourteenth Amendments. This contention rests upon the important and often-noted differences in the nature of collective bargaining in the public and private sectors. A public employer, unlike his private counterpart, is not guided by the profit motive and constrained by the normal operation of the market. Municipal services are typically not priced, and where they are they tend to be regarded as in some sense "essential" and therefore are often price-inelastic. Although a public employer, like a private one, will wish to keep costs down, he lacks an important discipline against agreeing to increases in labor costs that in a market system would require price increases. A public-sector union is correspondingly less concerned that high prices due to costly wage demands will decrease output and hence employment.

The government officials making decisions as the public "employer" are less likely to act as a cohesive unit than are managers in private industry, in part because different levels of public authority — department managers, budgetary officials, and legislative bodies — are involved, and in part because each official may respond to a distinctive political constituency. And the ease of negotiating a final agreement with the union may be severely limited by statutory restrictions, by the need for the approval of a higher executive authority or a legislative body, or by the commitment of budgetary decisions of critical importance to others.

---

[23] Nothing in our opinion embraces the "premise that public employers are under no greater constitutional constraints than their counterparts in the private sector," *post*, at 245 (POWELL, J., concurring in the judgment), or indicates that private collective-bargaining agreements are, without more, subject to constitutional constraints, see *post*, at 252. We compare the union-shop agreement in this case to those executed under the Railway Labor Act simply because the existence of governmental action in both contexts requires analysis of the free expression question.

It is somewhat startling, particularly in view of the concession that *Hanson* was premised on a finding that governmental action was present, see *post*, at 246 (POWELL, J., concurring in the judgment), to read in MR. JUSTICE POWELL's concurring opinion that *Hanson* and *Street* "provide little or no guidance for the constitutional issues presented in this case," *post*, at 254. *Hanson* nowhere suggested that the constitutional scrutiny of the union-shop agreement was watered down because the governmental action operated less directly than is true in a case such as the present one. Indeed, Mr. Justice Douglas, the author of *Hanson*, expressly repudiated that suggestion: "Since neither Congress nor the state legislatures can abridge [First Amendment] rights, they cannot grant the power to private groups to abridge them. As I read the First Amendment, it forbids any abridgement by government whether directly or indirectly." *Street*, 367 U.S., at 777 (concurring opinion).

Finally, decisionmaking by a public employer is above all a political process. The officials who represent the public employer are ultimately responsible to the electorate, which for this purpose can be viewed as comprising three over-lapping classes of voters — taxpayers, users of particular government services, and government employees. Through exercise of their political influence as part of the electorate, the employees have the opportunity to affect the deci-sions of government representatives who sit on the other side of the bargaining table. Whether these representatives accede to a union's demands will depend upon a blend of political ingredients, including community sentiment about unionism generally and the involved union in particular, the degree of taxpayer resistance, and the views of voters as to the importance of the service involved and the relation between the demands and the quality of service. It is surely arguable, however, that permitting public employees to unionize and a union to bargain as their exclusive representative gives the employees more influence in the decisionmaking process than is possessed by employees similarly organized in the private sector.

The distinctive nature of public-sector bargaining has led to widespread dis-cussion about the extent to which the law governing labor relations in the private sector provides an appropriate model. To take but one example, there has been considerable debate about the desirability of prohibiting public em-ployee unions from striking, a step that the State of Michigan itself has taken, Mich. Comp. Laws § 423.202 (1970). But although Michigan has not adopted the federal model of labor relations in every respect, it has determined that labor stability will be served by a system of exclusive representation and the permissive use of an agency shop in public employment. As already stated, there can be no principled basis for according that decision less weight in the constitutional balance than was given in *Hanson* to the congressional judgment reflected in the Railway Labor Act. The only remaining constitutional inquiry evoked by the appellants' argument, therefore, is whether a public employee has a weightier First Amendment interest than a private employee in not being compelled to contribute to the costs of exclusive union representation. We think he does not.

Public employees are not basically different from private employees; on the whole, they have the same sort of skills, the same needs, and seek the same advantages. "The uniqueness of public employment is *not in the employees* nor in the work performed; the uniqueness is in the special character of the em-ployer." Summers, *Public Sector Bargaining: Problems of Governmental Deci-sionmaking,* 44 U. Cin. L. Rev. 669, 670 (1975) (emphasis added). The very real differences between exclusive agent collective bargaining in the public and pri-vate sectors are not such as to work any greater infringement upon the First Amendment interests of public employees. A public employee who believes that a union representing him is urging a course that is unwise as a matter of public policy is not barred from expressing his viewpoint. Besides voting in accordance with his convictions, every public employee is largely free to express his views, in public or private, orally or in writing. With some exceptions not pertinent here, public employees are free to participate in the full range of political activities open to other citizens. Indeed, just this Term we have held that the First and Fourteenth Amendments protect the right of a public school teacher to oppose, at a public school board meeting, a position advanced by the teacher's union. *Madison School Dist. v. Wisconsin Employment Relations Comm'n,* 429 U.S. 167. In so ruling we recognized that the principle of exclusivity cannot constitutionally be used to muzzle a public employee who, like any other citizen, might wish to express his view about governmental decisions concerning labor relations, *id.,* at 174.

There can be no quarrel with the truism that because public employee unions attempt to influence governmental policymaking, their activities — and the views of members who disagree with them — may be properly termed political. But that characterization does not raise the ideas and beliefs of public employees onto a higher plane than the ideas and beliefs of private employees. It is no doubt true that a central purpose of the First Amendment "'was to protect the free discussion of governmental affairs.'" *Post,* at 259, citing *Buckley v. Valeo,* 424 U.S. 1, 14, and *Mills v. Alabama,* 384 U.S. 214, 218. But our cases have never suggested that expression about philosophical, social, artistic, economic, literary, or ethical matters — to take a nonexhaustive list of labels — is not entitled to full First Amendment protection. Union members in both the public and private sector may find that a variety of union activities conflict with their beliefs. Nothing in the First Amendment or our cases discussing its meaning makes the question whether the adjective "political" can properly be attached to those beliefs the critical constitutional inquiry.

The differences between public- and private-sector collective bargaining simply do not translate into differences in First Amendment rights. Even those commentators most acutely aware of the distinctive nature of public-sector bargaining and most seriously concerned with its policy implications agree that "[t]he union security issue in the public sector ... is fundamentally the same issue ... as in the private sector.... No special dimension results from the fact that a union represents public rather than private employees." H. Wellington & R. Winter, The Unions and the Cities 95-96 (1971). We conclude that the Michigan Court of Appeals was correct in viewing this Court's decisions in *Hanson* and *Street* as controlling in the present case insofar as the service charges are applied to collective-bargaining, contract administration, and grievance-adjustment purposes.

C

Because the Michigan Court of Appeals ruled that state law "sanctions the use of nonunion members' fees for purposes other than collective bargaining," 60 Mich. App., at 99, 230 N.W.2d, at 326, and because the complaints allege that such expenditures were made, this case presents constitutional issues not decided in *Hanson* or *Street.* Indeed *Street* embraced an interpretation of the Railway Labor Act not without its difficulties, see 367 U.S., at 784-786 (Black, J., dissenting); *id.,* at 799-803 (Frankfurter, J., dissenting), precisely to avoid facing the constitutional issues presented by the use of union-shop dues for political and ideological purposes unrelated to collective bargaining, *id.,* at 749-750. Since the state court's construction of the Michigan statute is authoritative, however, we must confront those issues in this case.

Our decisions establish with unmistakable clarity that the freedom of an individual to associate for the purpose of advancing beliefs and ideas is protected by the First and Fourteenth Amendments. Equally clear is the proposition that a government may not require an individual to relinquish rights guaranteed him by the First Amendment as a condition of public employment. E.g., *Elrod v. Burns, supra,* at 357-360, and cases cited; *Perry v. Sindermann,* 408 U.S. 593; *Keyishian v. Board of Regents,* 385 U.S. 589. The appellants argue that they fall within the protection of these cases because they have been prohibited, not from actively associating, but rather from refusing to associate. They specifically argue that they may constitutionally prevent the Union's spending a part of their required service fees to contribute to political candidates and to express political views unrelated to its duties as exclusive bargaining representative. We have concluded that this argument is a meritorious one.

One of the principles underlying the Court's decision in *Buckley v. Valeo,* 424 U.S. 1, was that contributing to an organization for the purpose of spreading a political message is protected by the First Amendment. Because "[m]aking a contribution ... enables like-minded persons to pool their resources in further-ance of common political goals," *id.,* at 22, the Court reasoned that limitations upon the freedom to contribute "implicate fundamental First Amendment in-terests," *id.,* at 23.

The fact that the appellants are compelled to make, rather than prohibited from making, contributions for political purposes works no less an infringement of their constitutional rights. For at the heart of the First Amendment is the notion that an individual should be free to believe as he will, and that in a free society one's beliefs should be shaped by his mind and his conscience rather than coerced by the State. See *Elrod v. Burns, supra,* at 356-357; *Stanley v. Georgia,* 394 U.S. 557, 565; *Cantwell v. Connecticut,* 310 U.S. 296, 303-304. And the freedom of belief is no incidental or secondary aspect of the First Amendment's protections:

> "If there is any fixed star in our constitutional constellation, it is that no official, high or petty, can prescribe what shall be orthodox in politics, nation-alism, religion, or other matters of opinion or force citizens to confess by word or act their faith therein." *West Virginia Bd. of Ed. v. Barnette,* 319 U.S. 624, 642.

These principles prohibit a State from compelling any individual to affirm his belief in God, *Torcaso v. Watkins,* 367 U.S. 488, or to associate with a political party, *Elrod v. Burns, supra;* see 427 U.S., at 363-364, n. 17, as a condition of retaining public employment. They are no less applicable to the case at bar, and they thus prohibit the appellees from requiring any of the appellants to contrib-ute to the support of an ideological cause he may oppose as a condition of holding a job as a public school teacher.

We do not hold that a union cannot constitutionally spend funds for the expression of political views, on behalf of political candidates, or towards the advancement of other ideological causes not germane to its duties as collective bargaining representative.[32] Rather, the Constitution requires only that such

---

[32] To the extent that this activity involves support of political candidates, it must, of course, be conducted consistently with any applicable (and constitutional) system of election campaign regula-tion. See generally *Buckley v. Valeo,* 424 U.S. 1; Developments in the Law — Elections, 88 Harv. L. Rev. 1111, 1237-1271 (1975).

expenditures be financed from charges, dues, or assessments paid by employees who do not object to advancing those ideas and who are not coerced into doing so against their will by the threat of loss of governmental employment.

There will, of course, be difficult problems in drawing lines between collective-bargaining activities, for which contributions may be compelled, and ideological activities unrelated to collective bargaining, for which such compulsion is prohibited.[33] The Court held in *Street,* as a matter of statutory construction, that a similar line must be drawn under the Railway Labor Act, but in the public sector the line may be somewhat hazier. The process of establishing a written collective-bargaining agreement prescribing the terms and conditions of public employment may require not merely concord at the bargaining table, but subsequent approval by other public authorities; related budgetary and appropriations decisions might be seen as an integral part of the bargaining process. We have no occasion in this case, however, to try to define such a dividing line. The case comes to us after a judgment on the pleadings, and there is no evidentiary record of any kind. The allegations in the complaint are general ones, see *supra,* at 212-213, and the parties have neither briefed nor argued the question of what specific Union activities in the present context properly fall under the definition of collective bargaining. The lack of factual concreteness and adversary presentation to aid us in approaching the difficult line-drawing questions highlight the importance of avoiding unnecessary decision of constitutional questions. All that we decide is that the general allegations in the complaint, if proven, establish a cause of action under the First and Fourteenth Amendments.

III

In determining what remedy will be appropriate if the appellants prove their allegations, the objective must be to devise a way of preventing compulsory subsidization of ideological activity by employees who object thereto without restricting the Union's ability to require every employee to contribute to the cost of collective-bargaining activities.[35] This task is simplified by the guidance to be had from prior decisions. In *Street,* the plaintiffs had proved at trial that expenditures were being made for political purposes of various kinds, and the Court

---

[33] The appellants' complaints also alleged that the Union carries on various "social activities" which are not open to nonmembers. It is unclear to what extent such activities fall outside the Union's duties as exclusive representative or involve constitutionally protected rights of association. Without greater specificity in the description of such activities and the benefit of adversary argument, we leave those questions in the first instance to the Michigan courts.

[35] It is plainly not an adequate remedy to limit the use of the actual dollars collected from dissenting employees to collective-bargaining purposes. "[Such a limitation] is of bookkeeping significance only rather than a matter of real substance. It must be remembered that the service fee is admittedly the exact equal of membership initiation fees and monthly dues ... and that ... dues collected from members may be used for a 'variety of purposes, in addition to meeting the union's costs of collective bargaining.' Unions 'rather typically' use their membership dues 'to do those things which the members authorize the union to do in their 'interest and on their behalf.' If the union's total budget is divided between collective bargaining and institutional expenses and if nonmember payments, equal to those of a member, go entirely for collective bargaining costs, the nonmember will pay more of these expenses than his pro rata share. The member will pay less and to that extent a portion of his fees and dues is available to pay institutional expenses. The union's budget is balanced. By paying a larger share of collective bargaining costs the nonmember subsidizes the union's institutional activities." *Retail Clerks v. Schermerhorn,* 373 U.S. 746, 753-754.

found those expenditures illegal under the Railway Labor Act. See *supra,* at 219-220. Moreover, in that case each plaintiff had "made known to the union representing his craft or class his dissent from the use of his money for political causes which he opposes." 367 U.S., at 750; see *id.,* at 771. The Court found that "[i]n that circumstance, the respective unions were without power to use payments thereafter tendered by them for such political causes." *Ibid.* Since, however, *Hanson* had established that the union-shop agreement was not unlawful as such, the Court held that to enjoin its enforcement would "[sweep] too broadly." 367 U.S., at 771. The Court also found that an injunction prohibiting the union from expending dues for political purposes would be inappropriate, not only because of the basic policy reflected in the Norris-LaGuardia Act against enjoining labor unions, but also because those union members who do wish part of their dues to be used for political purposes have a right to associate to that end "without being silenced by the dissenters." *Id.,* at 772-773.

After noting that "dissent is not to be presumed" and that only employees who have affirmatively made known to the union their opposition to political uses of their funds are entitled to relief, the Court sketched two possible remedies: First, "an injunction against expenditure for political causes opposed by each complaining employee of a sum, from those moneys to be spent by the union for political purposes, which is so much of the moneys exacted from him as is the proportion of the union's total expenditures made for such political activities to the union's total budget"; and second, restitution of a fraction of union dues paid equal to the fraction of total union expenditures that were made for political purposes opposed by the employee. *Id.,* at 774-775.[38]

The Court again considered the remedial question in *Railway Clerks v. Allen,* 373 U.S. 113. In that case employees who had refused to pay union-shop dues obtained injunctive relief in state court against enforcement of the union-shop agreement. The employees had not notified the union prior to bringing the lawsuit of their opposition to political expenditures, and at trial, their testimony was principally that they opposed such expenditures, as a general matter. *Id.,* at 118-119, n. 5. The Court held that the employees had adequately established their cause of action by manifesting "opposition to *any* political expenditures by the union," *id.,* at 118 (emphasis in original), and that the requirement in *Street* that dissent be affirmatively indicated was satisfied by the allegations in the complaint that was filed, 373 U.S., at 118-119, and n. 6. The Court indicated again the appropriateness of the two remedies sketched in *Street;* reversed the judgment affirming issuance of the injunction; and remanded for determination of which expenditures were properly to be characterized as political and what percentage of total union expenditures they constituted.[40]

---

[38] In proposing a restitution remedy, the *Street* opinion made clear that "[t]here should be no necessity, however, for the employee to trace his money up to and including its expenditure; if the money goes into general funds and no separate accounts of receipts and expenditures of the funds of individual employees are maintained, the portion of his money the employee would be entitled to recover would be in the same proportion that the expenditures for political purposes which he had advised the union he disapproved bore to the total union budget." 367 U.S., at 775.

[40] The Court in *Allen* went on to elaborate: "Since the unions possess the facts and records from which the proportion of political to total union expenditures can reasonably be calculated, basic considerations of fairness compel that they, not the individual employees, bear the burden of proving such proportion. Absolute precision in the calculation of such proportion is not, of course, to be expected or required; we are mindful of the difficult accounting problems that may arise. And

The Court in *Allen* described a "practical decree" that could properly be entered, providing for (1) the refund of a portion of the exacted funds in the proportion that union political expenditures bear to total union expenditures, and (2) the reduction of future exactions by the same proportion. 373 U.S., at 122. Recognizing the difficulties posed by judicial administration of such a remedy, the Court also suggested that it would be highly desirable for unions to adopt a "voluntary plan by which dissenters would be afforded an internal union remedy." *Ibid.* This last suggestion is particularly relevant to the case at bar, for the Union has adopted such a plan since the commencement of this litigation.[41]

Although *Street* and *Allen* were concerned with statutory rather than constitutional violations, that difference surely could not justify any lesser relief in this case. Judged by the standards of those cases, the Michigan Court of Appeals' ruling that the appellants were entitled to no relief at this juncture was unduly restrictive. For all the reasons outlined in *Street,* the court was correct in denying the broad injunctive relief requested. But in holding that as a prerequisite to any relief each appellant must indicate to the Union the *specific* expenditures to which he objects, the Court of Appeals ignored the clear holding of *Allen.* As in *Allen,* the employees here indicated in their pleadings that they opposed ideological expenditures of *any* sort that are unrelated to collective bargaining. To require greater specificity would confront an individual employee with the dilemma of relinquishing either his right to withhold his support of ideological causes to which he objects or his freedom to maintain his own beliefs without public disclosure. It would also place on each employee the considerable burden of monitoring all of the numerous and shifting expenditures made by the Union that are unrelated to its duties as exclusive bargaining representative.

The Court of Appeals thus erred in holding that the plaintiffs are entitled to no relief if they can prove the allegations contained in their complaints, and in depriving them of an opportunity to establish their right to appropriate relief, such, for example, as the kind of remedies described in *Street* and *Allen.* In view of the newly adopted union internal remedy, it may be appropriate under Michigan law, even if not strictly required by any doctrine of exhaustion of remedies, to defer further judicial proceedings pending the voluntary utilization by the parties of that internal remedy as a possible means of settling the dispute.[45]

---

no decree would be proper which appeared likely to infringe the unions' right to expend uniform exactions under the union-shop agreement in support of activities germane to collective bargaining and, as well, to expend nondissenters' such exactions in support of political activities." 373 U.S., at 122.

[41] Under the procedure adopted by the Union, as explained in the appellees' brief, a dissenting employee may protest at the beginning of each school year the expenditure of any part of his agency-shop fee for "activities or causes of a political nature or involving controversial issues of public importance only incidentally related to wages, hours, and conditions of employment." The employee is then entitled to a pro rata refund of his service charge in accordance with the calculation of the portion of total Union expenses for the specified purposes. The calculation is made in the first instance by the Union, but is subject to review by an impartial board.

[45] We express no view as to the constitutional sufficiency of the internal remedy described by the appellees. If the appellants initially resort to that remedy and ultimately conclude that it is constitutionally deficient in some respect, they would of course be entitled to judicial consideration of the adequacy of the remedy.

The judgment is vacated, and the case is remanded for further proceedings not inconsistent with this opinion.

It is so ordered.

[The concurring opinions of JUSTICE REHNQUIST, JUSTICE STEVENS and JUSTICE POWELL are omitted.]

NOTES

1. Can a local political subdivision advance a sufficient governmental interest to uphold the constitutionality of a fair-share agreement in the absence of authorizing state legislation? In *Perry v. IAM Lodge 2569,* 708 F.2d 1258 (7th Cir. 1983), the court, after observing that it knew "of no doctrine or constitutional law that requires cities and other political subdivisions to point to state statutes as the only source evidencing governmental interests," held that "[a] review of *Abood* itself reveals that the constitutionality of an agency shop provision is not contingent upon the existence of a state statute expressing the interests justifying such a provision."

2. The California Educational Employment Relations Act permits the negotiation of either a fair-share agreement or a maintenance of membership clause. Cal. Educ. Code § 3540.1(i) (West Supp. 1991). The latter is defined as follows:

An arrangement pursuant to which a public school employee may decide whether or not to join an employee organization, but which requires him or her, as a condition of continued employment, if he or she does join, to maintain his or her membership in good standing for the duration of the written agreement. However, no such arrangement shall deprive the employee of the right to terminate his or her obligation to the employee organization within a period of 30 days following the expiration of the written agreement.

Id. § 3540.1(i)(1). Is this maintenance of membership provision constitutional in light of the Supreme Court's decision in *Abood?* What difference, if any, does the "escape period" have on this determination?

3. In *Ellis v. Brotherhood of Ry., Airline & S.S. Clerks,* 466 U.S. 435, 104 S. Ct. 1883, 80 L. Ed. 2d 428 (1984), the Supreme Court was called upon to determine whether objecting nonmembers could be required to contribute towards the cost of the following six specified union activities: (a) union conventions, (b) litigation not involving the negotiation of agreements or settlement of grievances, (c) union publications, (d) social activities, (e) death benefits for employees, and (f) general organizing efforts. Rather than directly tackling the constitutional question, the Court said its initial obligation was to determine "whether the statute can be reasonably construed to avoid the constitutional difficulty." After noting that in its prior decisions the Court had not been called upon to "define the line between union expenditures that all employees must help defray and those that are not sufficiently related to collective bargaining to justify their being imposed upon dissenters," the Court stated that:

the test must be whether the challenged expenditures are necessarily or reasonably incurred for the purpose of performing the duties of an exclusive representative of the employees in dealing with the employer on labor-management issues. Under this standard, objecting employees may be compelled to pay their fair share of not only the direct cost of negotiating and administering a collective-bargaining contract and of settling grievances and disputes, but also the expenses of activities or undertakings normally or reasonably employed to implement or effectuate the duties of the union as exclusive representative of the employees in the bargaining unit.

Applying this test, the Court held that the union could charge objecting employees for the following expenses: (a) the cost of the union's convention, (b) social activities, and (c) union publications insofar as the publications reported activities for which the union could charge the dissenting employees. On the other hand, the Court held that the union could not charge objecting employees for expenses incurred in litigation not involving the negotiation of agreements or settlement of grievances or for its general organizing efforts. With respect to the latter, the Court noted that "[u]sing the dues exacted from an objecting employee to recruit members among workers outside the bargaining unit can afford only the most attenuated benefits to collective bargaining on behalf of the dues payer." While the Court found it unnecessary to rule on whether dissenters could be compelled to contribute toward the cost of the union's death benefit, the Court observed that it "would have no hesitation in holding ... that the union lacks authorization under the [Railway Labor Act] to use non-members' fees for death benefits they cannot receive." The Court noted that the union shop provisions of the Railway Labor Act are based on the presumption "that nonmembers benefit equally with members from the uses to which union money is put." See also *Cumero v. PERB*, 49 Cal. 3d 575, 778 P.2d 174, 262 Cal. Rptr. 46 (1989) (the benefits of organizing employees "are too attenuated to cause organizing and recruiting to become a representational obligation chargeable to objecting non-members under an organizational security arrangement").

4. In *Communication Workers of Am. v. Beck,* 108 S. Ct. 2641 (1988), the Supreme Court, in a 5 to 3 decision authored by Justice Brennan, held that a nonmember who objected to payment of an agency fee could not be required "to support union activities beyond those germane to collective bargaining, contract administration, and grievance adjustment." In determining how much could be charged to nonmembers the Court looked to its prior decisions under the Railway Labor Act and held that since the statutory provisions under the RLA and NLRA were "in all material respects identical," it was therefore clear "that Congress intended the same language to have the same meaning in both statutes." After noting that in an earlier case the Court had recognized that "'Congress' decision to allow union-security agreements at all reflects its concern that ... the parties to a collective bargaining agreement be allowed to provide that there be no employees who are getting the benefits of union representation without paying for them,'" the Court held that it was proper to interpret the NLRA, as it had previously interpreted the RLA, "in light of this animating principle." Accordingly, the Court held "that § 8(a)(3), like its statutory equivalent, § 2, Eleventh of the RLA, authorizes the exaction of only those fees and dues necessary to 'performing the duties of an exclusive representative of the employees in dealing with the employer on labor-management issues.'"

5. In *Conley v. MBTA,* 405 Mass. 168, 539 N.E.2d 1024 (1989), the court held that a transportation authority could not enforce a provision in a collective bargaining agreement that required employees to become members of the union. Citing both the Supreme Court's decision in *Abood* and precedent under the NLRA, the court stated that "[i]t is a well-established principle that formal union membership, which necessarily includes supporting, and being associated with, a union's institutional, political, and ideological activities, cannot be required as a condition of employment."

LEHNERT v. FERRIS FACULTY ASSOCIATION

111 S. Ct. 1950 (1991)

JUSTICE BLACKMUN announced the judgment of the Court and delivered the opinion of the Court with respect to Parts I, II, III-B, III-C, IV-B (except for the final paragraph), IV-D, IV-E, and IV-F, and an opinion with respect to Parts III-A and IV-A, the final paragraph of Part IV-B, and Parts IV-C and V, in which THE CHIEF JUSTICE, JUSTICE WHITE, and JUSTICE STEVENS join.

This case presents issues concerning the constitutional limitations, if any, upon the payment, required as a condition of employment, of dues by a non-member to a union in the public sector.

I

Michigan's Public Employment Relations Act (Act), Mich. Comp. Laws §§ 423.201 et seq. (1978), provides that a duly selected union shall serve as the exclusive collective-bargaining representative of public employees in a particular bargaining unit. The Act, which applies to faculty members of a public educational institution in Michigan, permits a union and a government employer to enter into an "agency shop" arrangement under which employees within the bargaining unit who decline to become members of the union are compelled to pay a "service fee" to the union.

Respondent Ferris Faculty Association (FFA), an affiliate of the Michigan Education Association (MEA) and the National Education Association (NEA), serves, pursuant to this provision, as the exclusive bargaining representative of the faculty of Ferris State College in Big Rapids, Mich. Ferris is a public institution established under the Michigan Constitution and is funded by the State. See Mich. Const. Art. VIII, § 4. Since 1975, the FFA and Ferris have entered into successive collective-bargaining agreements containing agency-shop provisions. Those agreements were the fruit of negotiations between the FFA and respondent Board of Control, the governing body of Ferris. See Mich. Comp. Law § 390.802 (1988).

Subsequent to this Court's decision in *Abood v. Detroit Board of Education,* 431 U.S. 209 (1977), in which the Court upheld the constitutionality of the Michigan agency-shop provision and outlined permissible uses of the compelled fee by public-employee unions, Ferris proposed, and the FFA agreed to, the agency-shop arrangement at issue here. That agreement required all employees in the bargaining unit who did not belong to the FFA to pay a service fee equivalent to the amount of dues required of a union member. Of the $284.00 service fee for 1981-1982, the period at issue, $24.80 went to the FFA, $211.20 to the MEA, and $48.00 to the NEA.

Petitioners were members of the Ferris faculty during the period in question and objected to certain uses by the unions of their service fees. Petitioners instituted this action, pursuant to 42 U.S.C. §§ 1983, 1985, 1986, in the United States District Court for the Western District of Michigan, claiming that the use of their fees for purposes other than negotiating and administering a collective-bargaining agreement with the Board of Control violated rights secured to them by the First and Fourteenth Amendments of the United States Constitution. Petitioners also claimed that the procedures implemented by the unions to determine and collect service fees were inadequate.

After a 12-day bench trial, the District Court issued its opinion holding that certain union expenditures were chargeable to petitioners, that certain other expenditures were not chargeable as a matter of law, and that still other expenditures were not chargeable because the unions had failed to sustain their burden of proving that the expenditures were made for chargeable activities. 643 F. Supp. 1306 (1986).

Following a partial settlement, petitioners took an appeal limited to the claim that the District Court erred in holding that the costs of certain disputed union activities were constitutionally chargeable to the plaintiff faculty members. Specifically, petitioners objected to the District Court's conclusion that the union constitutionally could charge them for the costs of (1) lobbying and electoral politics; (2) bargaining, litigation, and other activities on behalf of persons not in petitioners' bargaining unit; (3) public relations efforts; (4) miscellaneous professional activities; (5) meetings and conventions of the parent unions; and (6) preparation for a strike which, had it materialized, would have violated Michigan law.

The Court of Appeals, with one judge dissenting in large part, affirmed. 881 F.2d 1388 (CA6 1989). After reviewing this Court's cases in the area, the court concluded that each of the challenged activities was sufficiently related to the unions' duties as the exclusive bargaining representative of petitioners' unit to justify compelling petitioners to assist in subsidizing it. The dissenting judge concurred with respect to convention expenses but disagreed with the majority's resolution of the other items challenged. *Id.*, at 1394. Because of the importance of the issues, we granted certiorari. — U.S. — (1990).

II

This is not our first opportunity to consider the constitutional dimemsions of union-security provisions such as the agency-shop agreement at issue here. The Court first addressed the question in *Railway Employees v. Hanson*, 351 U.S. 225 (1956), where it recognized the validity of a "union shop" agreement authorized by § 2, Eleventh, of the Railway Labor Act (RLA), as amended, 64 Stat. 1238, 45 U.S.C. § 152, Eleventh, as applied to private employees. As with the Michigan statute we consider today, the RLA provision at issue in *Hanson* was permissive in nature. It was more expansive than the Michigan Act, however, because the challenged RLA provision authorized an agreement that compelled union membership, rather than simply the payment of a service fee by a nonmember employee.

Finding that the concomitants of compulsory union membership authorized by the RLA extended only to financial support of the union in its collective-bargaining activities, the Court determined that the challenged arrangement did not offend First or Fifth Amendment values. It cautioned, however: "If 'assessments' are in fact imposed for purposes not germane to collective bargaining, a different problem would be presented." 351 U.S., at 235 (footnote omitted). It further emphasized that the Court's approval of the statutorily sanctioned agreement did not extend to cases in which compelled membership is used "as a cover for forcing ideological conformity or other action in contravention of the First Amendment." *Id.*, at 238.

Hanson did not directly concern the extent to which union dues collected under a governmentally authorized union-shop agreement may be utilized in support of ideological causes or political campaigns to which reluctant union members are opposed. The Court addressed that issue under the RLA in *Machinists v. Street,* 367 U.S. 740 (1961). Unlike *Hanson,* the record in *Street* was replete with detailed information and specific factual findings that the union dues of dissenting employees had been used for political purposes. Recognizing that, in enacting § 2, Eleventh, of the RLA, Congress sought to protect the expressive freedom of dissenting employees while promoting collective representation, the *Street* Court construed the RLA to deny unions the authority to expend dissenters' funds in support of political causes to which those employees objected.

Two years later in *Railway Clerks v. Allen,* 378 U.S. 113 (1963), another RLA case, the Court reaffirmed that holding. It emphasized the important distinction between a union's political expenditures and "those germane to collective bargaining," with only the latter being properly chargeable to dissenting employees under the statute.

Although they are cases of statutory construction, *Street* and *Allen* are instructive in delineating the bounds of the First Amendment in this area as well. Because the Court expressly has interpreted the RLA "to avoid serious doubt of [the statute's] constitutionality," *Street,* 367 U.S., at 749; see *Ellis v. Railway Clerks,* 466 U.S. 435, 444 (1984), the RLA cases necessarily provide some guidance regarding what the First Amendment will countenance in the realm of union support of political activities through mandatory assessments. Specifically, those cases make clear that expenses that are relevant or "germane" to the collective-bargaining functions of the union generally will be constitutionally chargeable to dissenting employees. They further establish that, at least in the private sector, those functions do not include political or ideological activities.

It was not until the decision in *Abood* that this Court addressed the constitutionality of union-security provisions in the public-employment context. There, the Court upheld the same Michigan statute which is before us today against a facial First Amendment challenge. At the same time, it determined that the claim that a union has utilized an individual agency-shop agreement to force dissenting employees to subsidize ideological activities could establish, upon a proper showing, a First Amendment violation. In so doing, the Court set out several important propositions:

First, it recognized that "[t]o compel employees financially to support their collective-bargaining representative has an impact upon their First Amendment interests." 431 U.S., at 222. Unions traditionally have aligned themselves with a wide range of social, political, and ideological viewpoints, any number of which might bring vigorous disapproval from individual employees. To force employees to contribute, albeit indirectly, to the promotion of such positions implicates core First Amendment concerns. See, e.g., *Wooley v. Maynard,* 430 U.S. 705, 714 (1977) ("[T]he right of freedom of thought protected by the First Amendment against state action includes both the right to speak freely and the right to refrain from speaking at all").

Second, the Court in *Abood* determined that, as in the private sector, compulsory affiliation with, or monetary support of, a public-employment union does not, without more, violate the First Amendment rights of public employees. Similarly, an employee's free speech rights are not unconstitutionally burdened because the employee opposes positions taken by a union in its capacity as collective-bargaining representative. "[T]he judgment clearly made in *Hanson* and *Street* is that such interference as exists is constitutionally justified by the legislative assessment of the important contribution of the union shop to the system of labor relations established by Congress." 431 U.S., at 222.

In this connection, the Court indicated that the considerations that justify the union shop in the private context — the desirability of labor peace and eliminating "free riders" — are equally important in the public-sector workplace. Consequently, the use of dissenters' assessments "for the purposes of collective bargaining, contract administration, and grievance adjustment," *id.,* at 225-226, approved under the RLA, is equally permissible when authorized by a State vis-à-vis its own workers.

Third, the Court established that the constitutional principles that prevent a State from conditioning public employment upon association with a political party, see *Elrod v. Burns,* 427 U.S. 347 (1976) (plurality opinion), or upon professed religious allegiance, see *Torcaso v. Watkins,* 367 U.S. 488 (1961), similarly prohibit a public employer "from requiring [an employee] to contribute to the support of an ideological cause he may oppose as a condition of holding a job" as a public educator. 431 U.S., at 235.

The Court in *Abood* did not attempt to draw a precise line between permissible assessments for public-sector collective-bargaining activities and prohibited assessments for ideological activities. It did note, however, that, while a similar line must be drawn in the private sector under the RLA, the distinction in the public sector may be "somewhat hazier." *Id.,* at 236. This is so because the "process of establishing a written collective-bargaining agreement prescribing the terms and conditions of public employment may require not merely concord at the bargaining table, but subsequent approval by other public authorities; related budgetary and appropriations decisions might be seen as an integral part of the bargaining process." *Ibid.*

Finally, in *Ellis,* the Court considered, among other issues, a First Amendment challenge to the use of dissenters' funds for various union expenses including union conventions, publications, and social events. Recognizing that by allowing union-security arrangements at all, it has necessarily countenanced a significant burdening of First Amendment rights, it limited its inquiry to whether the expenses at issue "involve[d] *additional* interference with the First Amendment interests of objecting employees, and, if so, whether they are nonetheless adequately supported by a governmental interest." 466 U.S., at 456 (emphasis added).

Applying that standard to the challenged expenses, the Court found all three to be properly supportable through mandatory assessments. The dissenting employees in *Ellis* objected to charges relating to union social functions, not because those activities were inherently expressive or ideological in nature, but purely because they were sponsored by the union. Because employees may constitutionally be compelled to affiliate with a union, the Court found that forced contribution to union social events that were open to all imposed no additional burden on their First Amendment rights. Although the challenged expenses for union publications and conventions were clearly communicative in nature, the Court found them to entail little additional encroachment upon freedom of speech, "and none that is not justified by the governmental interests behind the union shop itself." *Ibid.* See also *Keller v. State Bar of California,* — U.S. — (1990), and *Communication Workers v. Beck,* 487 U.S. 735 (1988).

Thus, although the Court's decisions in this area prescribe a case-by-case analysis in determining which activities a union constitutionally may charge to dissenting employees, they also set forth several guidelines to be followed in making such determinations. *Hanson* and *Street* and their progeny teach that chargeable activities must (1) be "germane" to collective-bargaining activity; (2) be justified by the government's vital policy interest in labor peace and avoiding "free riders"; and (3) not significantly add to the burdening of free speech that is inherent in the allowance of an agency or union shop.

III

In arguing that these principles exclude the charges upheld by the Court of Appeals, petitioners propose two limitations on the use by public-sector unions of dissenters' contributions. First, they urge that they may not be charged over their objection for lobbying activities that do not concern legislative ratification of, or fiscal appropriations for, their collective-bargaining agreement. Second, as to nonpolitical expenses, petitioners assert that the local union may not utilize dissenters' fees for activities that, though closely related to collective bargaining generally, are not undertaken directly on behalf of the bargaining unit to which the objecting employees belong. We accept the former proposition but find the latter to be foreclosed by our prior decisions.

A

The Court of Appeals determined that unions constitutionally may subsidize lobbying and other political activities with dissenters' fees so long as those activities are "'pertinent to the duties of the union as a bargaining representative.'" 881 F.2d, at 1392, quoting *Robinson v. New Jersey,* 741 F.2d 598, 609 (CA3 1984), cert. denied, 469 U.S. 1228 (1985). In reaching this conclusion, the court relied upon the inherently political nature of salary and other workplace decisions in public employment. "To represent their members effectively," the court concluded, "public sector unions must necessarily concern themselves not only with negotiations at the bargaining table but also with advancing their members' interests in legislative and other 'political' arenas." 881 F.2d, at 1392.

This observation is clearly correct. Public-sector unions often expend considerable resources in securing ratification of negotiated agreements by the proper state or local legislative body. See Note, *Union Security in the Public Sector: Defining Political Expenditures Related to Collective Bargaining,* 1980 Wis. L. Rev. 134, 150-152. Similarly, union efforts to acquire appropriations for approved collective-bargaining agreements often serve as an indispensable prerequisite to their implementation. See *Developments in the Law: Public Employment,* 97 Harv. L. Rev. 1611, 1732-1733 (1984). It was in reference to these characteristics of public employment that the Court in *Abood* discussed the "somewhat hazier" line between bargaining-related and purely ideological activities in the public sector. 431 U.S., at 236. The dual roles of government as employer and policymaker in such cases make the analogy between lobbying and collective bargaining in the public sector a close one.

This, however, is not such a case. Where, as here, the challenged lobbying activities relate not to the ratification or implementation of a dissenter's collective-bargaining agreement, but to financial support of the employee's profession or of public employees generally, the connection to the union's function as bargaining representative is too attenuated to justify compelled support by objecting employees.

We arrive at this result by looking to the governmental interests underlying our acceptance of union security arrangements. We have found such arrangements to be justified by the government's interest in promoting labor peace and avoiding the "free-rider" problem that would otherwise accompany union recognition. *Chicago Teachers v. Hudson,* 475 U.S. 292, 302-303 (1986); *Abood,* 431 U.S., at 224. Neither goal is served by charging objecting employees for lobbying, electoral, and other political activities that do not relate to their collective-bargaining agreement.

Labor peace is not especially served by allowing such charges because, unlike collective-bargaining negotiations between union and management, our national and state legislatures, the media, and the platform of public discourse are public fora open to all. Individual employees are free to petition their neighbors and government in opposition to the union which represents them in the workplace. Because worker and union cannot be said to speak with one voice, it would not further the cause of harmonious industrial relations to compel objecting employees to finance union political activities as well as their own.

Similarly, while we have endorsed the notion that nonunion workers ought not be allowed to benefit from the terms of employment secured by union efforts without paying for those services, the so-called "free-rider" concern is inapplicable where lobbying extends beyond the effectuation of a collective-bargaining agreement. The balancing of monetary and other policy choices performed by legislatures is not limited to the workplace but typically has ramifications that extend into diverse aspects of an employee's life.

Perhaps most important, allowing the use of dissenters' assessments for political activities outside the scope of the collective-bargaining context would present "additional interference with the First Amendment interests of objecting employees." *Ellis,* 466 U.S., at 456. There is no question as to the expressive and ideological content of these activities. Further, unlike discussion by negotiators regarding the terms and conditions of employment, lobbying and electoral speech is likely to concern topics about which individuals hold strong personal views. Although First Amendment protection is in no way limited to controversial topics or emotionally charged issues, see *Winters v. New York,* 333 U.S. 507, 510 (1948); *Buckley v. Valeo,* 424 U.S. 1, 14 (1976); *Abood,* 431 U.S., at 231, and n. 28, the extent of one's disagreement with the subject of compulsory speech is relevant to the degree of impingement upon free expression that compulsion will effect.

The burden upon freedom of expression is particularly great where, as here, the compelled speech is in a public context. By utilizing petitioners' funds for political lobbying and to garner the support of the public in its endeavors, the union would use each dissenter as "an instrument for fostering public adherence to an ideological point of view he finds unacceptable." *Maynard,* 430 U.S., at 715. The First Amendment protects the individual's right of participation in these spheres from precisely this type of invasion. Where the subject of compelled speech is the discussion of governmental affairs, which is at the core of our First Amendment freedoms, *Roth v. United States,* 354 U.S. 476, 484 (1957); *Mills v. Alabama,* 384 U.S. 214, 218 (1966); *Buckley v. Valeo,* 424 U.S., at 14, the burden upon dissenters' rights extends far beyond the acceptance of the agency shop and is constitutionally impermissible.

Accordingly, we hold that the State constitutionally may not compel its employees to subsidize legislative lobbying or other political union activities outside the limited context of contract ratification or implementation.

B

Petitioners' contention that they may be charged only for those collective-bargaining activities undertaken directly on behalf of their unit presents a closer question. While we consistently have looked to whether nonideological expenses are "germane to collective bargaining," *Hanson,* 351 U.S., at 235, we have never interpreted that test to require a direct relationship between the expense at issue and some tangible benefit to the dissenters' bargaining unit.

We think that to require so close a connection would be to ignore the unified-membership structure under which many unions, including those here, operate. Under such arrangements, membership in the local union constitutes membership in the state and national parent organizations. See 643 F. Supp., at 1308. See also *Cumero v. Public Employment Relations Board,* 49 Cal. 3d 575, 603-604, 778 P. 2d 174, 192 (1989) (noting the inherent "close organizational relationship").

The essence of the affiliation relationship is the notion that the parent will bring to bear its often considerable economic, political, and informational resources when the local is in need of them. Consequently, that part of a local's affiliation fee which contributes to the pool of resources potentially available to the local is assessed for the bargaining unit's protection, even if it is not actually expended on that unit in any particular membership year.

The Court recognized as much in *Ellis.* There it construed the RLA to allow the use of dissenters' funds to help defray the costs of the respondent union's national conventions. It reasoned that "if a union is to perform its statutory functions, it must maintain its corporate or associational existence, must elect officers to manage and carry on its affairs, and may consult its members about overall bargaining goals and policy." 466 U.S., at 448. We see no reason why analogous public-sector union activities should be treated differently.[4]

---

[4] The Michigan Employment Relations Commission — the state agency responsible for administering the Act — has reached the same conclusion in applying the statute to local affiliates of the MEA and the NEA. In determining that the involvement of the NEA and the MEA in local contract administration and grievance adjustment was a legitimate aspect of the local's service fee, the agency explained that "to restrict chargeability to only those activities directly relating to the local bargaining unit is to totally ignore the fact of affiliation." *Bridgeport-Spaulding Community Schools,* 1986 MERC Op. 1024, 1057. See also *Garden City School District,* 1978 MERC Op. 1145, 1155-1156. While the agency's conclusions of law are without effect upon this Court, we find persuasive its factual findings regarding the structure and operation of labor organizations within its jurisdiction.

We therefore conclude that a local bargaining representative may charge objecting employees for their pro rata share of the costs associated with otherwise chargeable activities of its state and national affiliates, even if those activities were not performed for the direct benefit of the objecting employees' bargaining unit. This conclusion, however, does not serve to grant a local union carte blanche to expend dissenters' dollars for bargaining activities wholly unrelated to the employees in their unit. The union surely may not, for example, charge objecting employees for a direct donation or interest-free loan to an unrelated bargaining unit for the purpose of promoting employee rights or unionism generally. Further, a contribution by a local union to its parent that is not part of the local's responsibilities as an affiliate but is in the nature of a charitable donation would not be chargeable to dissenters. There must be some indication that the payment is for services that may ultimately enure to the benefit of the members of the local union by virtue of their membership in the parent organization. And, as always, the union bears the burden of proving the proportion of chargeable expenses to total expenses. *Chicago Teachers v. Hudson,* 475 U.S., at 306; *Abood,* 431 U.S., at 239-240, n. 40; *Railway Clerks v. Allen,* 373 U.S., at 122. We conclude merely that the union need not demonstrate a direct and tangible impact upon the dissenting employee's unit.

C

JUSTICE SCALIA would find "implicit in our cases since *Street,*" the rule that "to be constitutional, a charge must *at least* be incurred in performance of the union's statutory duties." *Post,* at 9. As the preceding discussion indicates, we reject this reading of our cases. This Court never has held that the First Amendment compels such a requirement and our prior decisions cannot reasonably be construed to support his stated proposition. See, e. g., *Ellis,* 466 U.S., at 456 ("Petitioners may feel that their money is not being well-spent, but that does not mean they have a First Amendment complaint"); see also *Keller, supra* (distinguishing between statutory and constitutional duties in the context of integrated state bar membership).

Even if viewed merely as a prophylactic rule for enforcing the First Amendment in the union-security context, JUSTICE SCALIA's approach ultimately must be rejected. As the relevant provisions of the Michigan Act illustrate, state labor laws are rarely precise in defining the duties of public-sector unions to their members. Indeed, it is reasonable to assume that the Michigan provisions relating to collective-bargaining duties were purposefully drafted in broad terms so as to provide unions the flexibility and discretion necessary to accommodate the needs of their constituents. Here, as in the RLA context, "[t]he furtherance of the common cause leaves some leeway for the leadership of the group." *Street,* 367 U.S., at 778 (Douglas, J., concurring), quoted in *Abood,* 431 U.S., at 222-223.

Consequently, the terms of the Act provide a poor criterion for determining which charges violate the First Amendment rights of dissenting employees. The broad language of the Act does not begin to explain which of the specific activities at issue here fall within the union's collective-bargaining function as contemplated by our cases. Far from providing a bright-line standard, JUSTICE

SCALIA's "statutory duties" test fails to afford courts and litigants the guidance necessary to make these particularized distinctions.

More important, JUSTICE SCALIA's rigid approach fails to acknowledge the practicalities of the complex interrelationship between public employers, employees, unions, and the public. The role of an effective representative in this context often encompasses responsibilities that extend beyond those specifically delineated in skeletal state labor law statutes. See *Abood,* 431 U.S., at 236. That an exclusive bargaining representative has gone beyond the bare requirements of the law in representing its constituents through employee contributions does not automatically mean that the Constitution has been violated, at least where the funded activities have not *transgressed* state provisions. "The very nature of the free-rider problem and the governmental interest in overcoming it require that the union have a certain flexibility in its use of compelled funds." *Ellis,* 466 U.S., at 456.

We therefore disagree with JUSTICE SCALIA that any charge that does not relate to an activity expressly authorized by statute is *constitutionally* invalid, irrespective of its impact, or lack thereof, on free expression. In our view, his analysis turns our constitutional doctrine on its head. Instead of interpreting statutes in light of First Amendment principles, he would interpret the First Amendment in light of state statutory law. It seems to us that this proposal bears little relation to the values that the First Amendment was designed to protect. A rule making violations of freedom of speech dependent upon the terms of state employment statutes would sacrifice sound constitutional analysis for the appearance of administrability.

We turn to the union activities at issue in this case.

IV

A

The Court of Appeals found that the union could constitutionally charge petitioners for the costs of a Preserve Public Education (PPE) program designed to secure funds for public education in Michigan, and that portion of the MEA publication, the Teacher's Voice, which reported these activities. Petitioners argue that, contrary to the findings of the courts below, the PPE program went beyond lobbying activity and sought to affect the outcome of ballot issues and "millages" or local taxes for the support of public schools. Given our conclusion as to lobbying and electoral politics generally, this factual dispute is of little consequence. None of these activities was shown to be oriented toward the ratification or implementation of petitioner's collective-bargaining agreement. We hold that none may be supported through the funds of objecting employees.

B

Petitioners next challenge the Court of Appeals' allowance of several activities that the union did not undertake directly on behalf of persons within petitioners' bargaining unit. This objection principally concerns NEA "program expenditures" destined for States other than Michigan, and the expenses of the Teacher's Voice listed as "Collective Bargaining" and "Litigation." Our conclusion that unions may bill dissenting employees for their share of general collective-bargaining costs of the state or national parent union is dispositive as to the bulk of the NEA expenditures. The District Court found these costs to be germane to collective bargaining and similar support services and we decline to disturb that finding. No greater relationship is necessary in the collective-bargaining context.

This rationale does not extend, however, to the expenses of litigation that does not concern the dissenting employees' bargaining unit or, by extension, to union literature reporting on such activities. While respondents are clearly correct that precedent established through litigation on behalf of one unit may ultimately be of some use to another unit. we find extra-unit litigation to be more akin to lobbying in both kind and effect. We long have recognized the important political and expressive nature of litigation. See, e. g., *NAACP v. Button,* 371 U.S. 415, 431 (1963) (recognizing that for certain groups, "association for litigation may be the most effective form of political association"). Moreoever, union litigation may cover a diverse range of areas from bankruptcy proceedings to employment discrimination. See *Ellis,* 466 U.S., at 453. When unrelated to an objecting employee's unit, such activities are not germane to the union's duties as exclusive bargaining representative. Just as the Court in *Ellis* determined that the RLA, as informed by the First Amendment, prohibits the use of dissenters' fees for extra-unit litigation, *ibid.,* we hold that the Amendment proscribes such assessments in the public sector.

C

The Court of Appeals determined that the union constitutionally could charge petitioners for certain public-relations expenditures. In this connection, the court said: "Public relations expenditures designed to enhance the reputation of the teaching profession ... are, in our opinion, sufficiently related to the unions' duty to represent bargaining unit employees effectively so as to be chargeable to dissenters." 881 F.2d, at 1394. We disagree. Like the challenged lobbying conduct, the public-relations activities at issue here entailed speech of a political nature in a public forum. More important, public speech in support of the teaching profession generally is not sufficiently related to the union's collective-bargaining functions to justify compelling dissenting employees to support it. Expression of this kind extends beyond the negotiation and grievance-resolution contexts and imposes a substantially greater burden upon First Amendment rights than do the latter activities.

Nor do we accept the Court of Appeals' comparison of these public-relations expenses to the costs of union social activities held in *Ellis* to be chargeable to dissenters. In *Ellis,* the Court found the communicative content of union social activities, if any, to derive solely from the union's involvement in them. 466 U.S., at 456. "Therefore," we reasoned, "the fact that the employee is forced to contribute does not increase the infringement of his First Amendment rights already resulting from the compelled contribution to the union." *Ibid.* The same cannot be said of the public-relations charges upheld by the Court of Appeals which covered "informational picketing, media exposure, signs, posters and buttons." 643 F. Supp., at 1313.

D

The District Court and the Court of Appeals allowed charges for those portions of the Teachers' Voice that concern teaching and education generally, professional development, unemployment, job opportunities, award programs of the MEA, and other miscellaneous matters. Informational support services such as these are neither political nor public in nature. Although they do not directly concern the members of petitioners' bargaining unit, these expenditures are for the benefit of all and we discern no additional infringement of First Amendment rights that they might occasion. In short, we agree with the Court of Appeals that these expenses are comparable to the *de minimis* social activity charges approved in *Ellis*. See 466 U.S., at 456.

E

The Court of Appeals ruled that the union could use the fees of objecting employees to send FFA delegates to the MEA and the NEA conventions and to participate in the 18E Coordinating Council, another union structure. Petitioners challenge that determination and argue that, unlike the national convention expenses found to be chargeable to dissenters in *Ellis*, the meetings at issue here were those of affiliated parent unions rather than the local, and therefore do not relate exclusively to petitioners' unit.

We need not determine whether petitioners could be commanded to support all the expenses of these conventions. The question before the Court is simply whether the unions may constitutionally require petitioners to subsidize the participation in these events of delegates from the local. We hold that they may. That the conventions were not solely devoted to the activities of the FFA does not prevent the unions from requiring petitioners' support. We conclude above that the First Amendment does not require so close a connection. Moreoever, participation by members of the local in the formal activities of the parent is likely to be an important benefit of affiliation. This conclusion is supported by the District Court's description of the 13E Coordinating Council meeting as an event at which "bargaining strategies and representational policies are developed for the UniServ unit composed of the Ferris State College and Central Michigan University bargaining units." 643 F. Supp., at 1326. As was held in *Ellis*, "[c]onventions such as those at issue here are normal events ... and seem to us to be essential to the union's discharge of its duties as bargaining agent." 466 U.S., at 448-449.

F

The chargeability of expenses incident to preparation for a strike which all concede would have been illegal under Michigan law, Mich. Comp. Laws § 423.202 (1979), is a provocative question. At the beginning of the 1981-1982 fiscal year, the FFA and Ferris were engaged in negotiating a new collective-bargaining agreement. The union perceived these efforts to be ineffective, and began to prepare a "job action" or, in more familiar terms, to go out on strike. These preparations entailed the creation by the FFA and the MEA of a "crisis center" or "strike headquarters." The District Court found that, "whatever label is attached to this facility, prior to a strike it serves as a meeting place for the local's membership, a base from which tactical activities such as informational picketing can be conducted, and serves to apply additional pressure on the employer by suggesting, whether true or not, that the local is prepared to strike if necessary." 643 F. Supp., at 1313.

Had the FFA actually engaged in an illegal strike, the union clearly could not have charged the expenses incident to that strike to petitioners. We can imagine no legitimate governmental interest that would be served by compelling objecting employees to subsidize activity that the State has chosen to disallow. See *Male v. Grand Rapids Education Association,* 98 Mich. App. 742, 295 N.W.2d 918 (1980), *appeal denied,* 412 Mich. 851, — N.W.2d — (1981) (holding that, under Michigan law, compulsory-service fees cannot include money allocated to the support of public-sector strikes). Similarly, one might expect the State to prohibit unions from using dissenters' funds to threaten or prepare for such conduct. The Michigan Legislature, however, has chosen not to impose such a restriction, and we do not find the First Amendment to require that limitation.

Petitioners can identify no determination by the State of Michigan that mere preparation for an illegal strike is itself illegal or against public policy, and we are aware of none. Further, we accept the rationale provided by the Court of Appeals in upholding these charges that such expenditures fall "within the range of reasonable bargaining tools available to a public sector union during contract negotiations." 881 F.2d, at 1394. The District Court expressly credited trial testimony by an MEA representative that outward preparations for a potential strike serve as an effective bargaining tool and that only one out of every seven or eight "job action investigations" actually culminates in a strike. 643 F. Supp., at 1312. The Court of Appeals properly reviewed this finding for clear error. See *Anderson v. Bessemer City,* 470 U.S. 564, 575 (1985).

In sum, these expenses are substantively indistinguishable from those appurtenant to collective-bargaining negotiations. The District Court and the Court of Appeals concluded, and we agree, that they aid in those negotiations and enure to the direct benefit of members of the dissenters' unit. Further, they impose no additional burden upon First Amendment rights. The union may properly charge petitioners for those costs.

V

The judgment of the Court of Appeals is affirmed in part and reversed in part, and the case is remanded for further proceedings consistent with this opinion.

It is so ordered.

JUSTICE MARSHALL, concurring in part and dissenting in part.

The parties in this case dispute the amount that public sector unions may charge as a "service fee" to employees who are not union members. Under an agency-shop provision like the one that covers petitioners, dissenting (*i.e.,* nonunion) employees are generally obliged to share the union's cost of negotiating and administering their collective-bargaining agreement. The key question we confront is whether, consistently with the First Amendment, a union may charge dissenting employees for union activities that are conducted away from the bargaining table but that are also reasonably designed to influence the public employer's position at the bargaining table.

The principal opinion concedes that "'[t]o represent their members effectively, ... public sector unions must necessarily concern themselves not only with negotiations at the bargaining table but also with advancing their members' interests in legislative and other "political" arenas.'" *Ante,* at 10, quoting 881 F.2d 1388, 1392 (CA6 1989). One would expect endorsement of this proposition to lead the principal opinion, as it led both the Court of Appeals and the District Court below, to include within the petitioners' service fee the costs of (1) lobbying legislators (and, where relevant, voters) to increase funding of the public sector in which petitioners work, namely, education, and (2) a public relations campaign to improve the voters' and the public employer's view of petitioners and their fellow teachers. After all, the extent to which public employees may secure favorable terms in a collective-bargaining agreement depends on the availability of funds in the relevant public sector. Similarly, the more favorable the public attitude toward a bargaining unit's members, the more likely that the public employer will accept a given bargaining proposal.

The principal opinion rejects these reasonable implications of the proposition whose truth it concedes, and thus the Court today holds that the respondent teachers' unions — the National Education Association (NEA); its state affiliate, the Michigan Education Association (MEA); and a local affiliate, the Ferris Faculty Association (FFA) at Ferris State College — may not assess FFA's dissenting members for the lobbying and public relations expenses I have just described. I respectfully dissent from these two aspects of today's decision.

I also disagree with the Court's decision that the costs of articles printed in MEA's employee journal about union litigation outside petitioners' bargaining unit are not chargeable. The principal opinion requires the MEA to isolate the expense of each such article and to charge it solely to the bargaining unit involved in the particular suit. Neither precedent nor common sense supports this burdensome accounting procedure — particularly since the publication costs at issue are *de minimis.*

... I otherwise join in Parts I, II, III-B, and C, and IV-B (except the final paragraph), D, E, and F of the principal opinion.

JUSTICE SCALIA, with whom JUSTICE O'CONNOR and JUSTICE SOUTER join, and with whom JUSTICE KENNEDY joins as to all but Part III-C, concurring in the judgment in part and dissenting in part.

While I agree with the Court's disposition of many of the challenged expenditures, I do not agree with the test it proposes. In my view today's opinion both expands and obscures the category of expenses for which a union may constitutionally compel contributions from dissenting nonmembers in an agency shop. I would hold that contributions can be compelled only for the costs of performing the union's statutory duties as exclusive bargaining agent.

I

The Court purports to derive from "*Hanson* and *Street* and their progeny," *ante,* at 9, a proverbial three-part test, whereunder activities are chargeable to nonunion members of the bargaining unit if (1) they are "'germane' to collective-bargaining activity," (2) they are "justified by the government's vital policy interest in labor peace and avoiding "free riders,'" and (3) they do not "significantly add to the burdening of free speech that is inherent in the allowance of an agency or union shop." *Ibid.* As I shall later discuss, I do not find this test set forth in the referenced opinions. Since, moreover, each one of the three "prongs" of the test involves a substantial judgment call (What is "germane"? What is "justified"? What is a "significant" additional burden?) it seems calculated to perpetuate give-it-a-try litigation of monetary claims that are individually insignificant but cumulatively worth suing about, in the style of the present case.

To take but one example, presented by the facts before us: The majority would permit charging nonmembers for an informational newsletter that "concern[s] teaching and education generally, professional development, unemployment, job opportunities, award programs of the MEA, and other miscellaneous matters," *ante,* at 19; but four members of that majority would not permit charging for "informational picketing, media exposure, signs, posters and buttons," *ibid.* As I shall discuss in greater detail later, it seems to be that the former, the allowed charge, fails the "germaneness-to-collective-bargaining" test, and that the latter, the disallowed charge, fares no worse than the former insofar as the asserted basis for its disallowance, the "significant-additional-burden" test, is concerned. Thus, the three-part test, if its application is to be believed, provides little if any guidance to parties contemplating litigation, or to lower courts. It does not eliminate past confusion, but merely establishes new terminology to which, in the future, the confusion can be assigned.

I think this unhelpful test is neither required nor even suggested by our earlier cases, and that a much more administrable criterion is.

II

In past decisions considering both constitutional and statutory challenges to state compulsion of union dues, we have focused narrowly upon the union's role as an exclusive bargaining agent. In *Railway Employees v. Hanson,* 351 U.S. 225 (1956), we upheld the federal union shop provision, § 2, Eleventh of the Railway Labor Act (RLA), 45 U.S.C. § 152 Eleventh, against a First Amendment challenge. We emphasized that the statute sought only to ensure that workers would reimburse unions for the unions' bargaining efforts on their behalf. "We ... hold that the requirement for financial support of the collective-bargaining agency by all who receive the benefits of its work is within the power of Congress ... and does not violate ... the First ... Amendment." *Hanson,* 351 U.S., at 238. We expressly reserved the question whether the Act could, consistent with the Constitution, allow a union to charge expenses other than those related to bargaining. As Justice Black later described the case, "Thus the *Hanson* case held only that workers could be required to pay *their part of the cost of actual bargaining* carried on by a union selected as a bargaining agent under authority of Congress, just as Congress doubtless could have required workers to pay the cost of such bargaining had it chosen to have the bargaining carried on by the Secretary of Labor or any other appropriately selected bargaining agent." *Machinists v. Street,* 367 U.S. 740, 787 (1961) (Black, J., dissenting) (emphasis added).

In *Abood v. Detroit Bd. of Ed.,* 431 U.S. 209 (1977), we reaffirmed that the union's role as bargaining agent gave rise to the state interest in compelling dues:

> "The designation of a union as exclusive representative carries with it great responsibilities. The tasks of negotiating and administering a collective-bargaining agreement and representing the interests of employees in settling disputes and processing grievances are continuing and difficult ones. They often entail expenditure of much time and money. The services of lawyers, expert negotiators, economists, and a research staff, as well as general administrative personnel, may be required. Moreover, in carrying out these duties, the union is obliged fairly and equitably to represent all employees ..., union and non-union, within the relevant unit. A union-shop arrangement has been thought to distribute fairly the cost of *these activities* among those who benefit, and it counteracts the incentive that employees might otherwise have to become free-riders — to refuse to contribute to the union while obtaining benefits of union representation that *necessarily* accrue to all employees." *Id.,* at 221-222 (internal quotations and citations omitted; emphasis added).

As this passage demonstrates, the state interest that can justify mandatory dues arises solely from the union's statutory duties. Mandatory dues allow the cost of "these activities" — i.e., the union's statutory duties — to be fairly distributed; they compensate the union for benefits which "necessarily" — that is, by law — accrue to the nonmembers.

Our statutory cases, construing the mandatory dues provisions of the § 2, Eleventh of the RLA and § 8(a)(3) of the Taft-Hartley Act, 29 U.S.C. § 158(a)(3), are to the same effect....

....

Street, Ellis, and *Beck* were statutory cases, but there is good reason to treat them as merely reflecting the constitutional rule suggested in *Hanson* and later confirmed in *Abood. Street* adopted a construction of the Railway Labor Act nowhere suggested in its language, to avoid "serious doubt of [its] constitutionality." 367 U.S., at 749. As Justice Black argued in dissent, "Neither § 2, Eleventh nor any other part of the Act contains any implication or even a hint that Congress, wanted to limit the purposes for which a contracting union's dues should or could be spent ... [N]o one has suggested that the Court's statutory construction of § 2, Eleventh could possibly be supported without the crutch of its fear of unconstitutionality." *Id.,* at 784, 786 (Black, J., dissenting). See also *Beck,* 487 U.S., at 763 (JUSTICE BLACKMUN, concurring in part and dissenting in part) ("Our accepted mode of resolving statutory questions would not lead to a construction of § 8(a)(3) so foreign to that section's express language and legislative history.").

Our First Amendment jurisprudence therefore recognizes a correlation between the rights and the duties of the union, on the one hand, and the nonunion members of the bargaining unit, on the other. Where the state imposes upon the union a duty to deliver services, it may permit the union to demand reimbursement for them; or, looked at from the other end, where the state creates in the nonmembers a legal entitlement from the union, it may compel them to pay the cost. The "compelling state interest" that justifies this constitutional rule is not simply elimination of the inequity arising from the fact that some union activity redounds to the benefit of "free-riding" nonmembers; private speech often furthers the interests of nonspeakers, and that does not alone empower the state to compel the speech to be paid for. What is distinctive, however, about the "free riders" who are nonunion members of the union's own bargaining unit is that in some respects *they* are free riders whom the law *requires* the union to carry — indeed, requires the union to go *out of its way* to benefit, even at the expense of its other interests. In the context of bargaining, a union *must* seek to further the interests of its nonmembers; it cannot, for example, negotiate particularly high wage increases for its members in exchange for accepting no increases for others. Thus, the free ridership (if it were left to be that) would be not incidental but calculated, not imposed by circumstances but mandated by government decree.

Once it is understood that the source of the state's power, despite the First Amendment, to compel nonmembers to support the union financially, is elimination of the inequity that would otherwise arise from mandated free-ridership, the constitutional limits on that power naturally follow. It does not go beyond the expenses incurred in discharge of the union's "great responsibilities" in "negotiating and administering a collective-bargaining agreement and representing the interests of employees in settling disputes and processing grievances," *Abood,* 431 U.S., at 221; the cost of performing the union's "statutory functions," *Ellis,* 466 U.S., at 447; the expenses "necessary to performing the duties of an exclusive representative," *Beck,* 487 U.S., at 762. In making its other disbursements the union can, like any other economic actor, seek to eliminate inequity by either eliminating the benefit or demanding payment in exchange for not doing so. In a public relations campaign, for example, it can, if nonmembers refuse to contribute, limit the focus of publicity to union members, or even direct negative publicity against nonmembers, or terminate the campaign entirely. There is no reason — and certainly no compelling reason sufficient to survive First Amendment scrutiny — for the state to interfere in the private ordering of these arrangements, for the state itself has not distorted them by compelling the union to perform.

The first part of the test that the Court announces — that the activities for which reimbursement is sought must be "germane" to collective-bargaining activity — could, if properly elaborated, stand for the proposition set forth above. But it is not elaborated, and the manner in which the Court applies it to the expenditures before us here demonstrates that the Court considers an expenditure "germane" to collective bargaining not merely when it is reasonably necessary for the very performance of that collective bargaining, but whenever it is reasonably designed to achieve a more favorable outcome from collective bargaining (e.g., expenditures for strike preparations). That in my view is wrong. The Court adds two further tests, which apparently all expenditures that pass the first one must also meet, but neither of them compensates for the overly broad concept of "germaneness." I think that those two additional tests, which are seemingly derived from Part VI of the *Ellis* opinion, represent a mistaken reading of that case, but since they make no difference to my analysis of the expenditures at issue here I need not contest them.

I would hold that to be constitutional a charge must *at least* be incurred in performance of the union's statutory duties. I would make explicit what has been implicit in our cases since *Street*: a union cannot constitutionally charge nonmembers for any expenses except those incurred for the conduct of activities in which the union owes a duty of fair representation to the nonmembers being charged.

III

A

Applying this test, I readily conclude that a number of the challenged expenses cannot be charged to the nonmembers. Michigan defines the union's duty as that of "be[ing] the exclusive representative[] of all the public employees in [its] unit for the purposes of collective bargaining," Mich. Comp. Laws § 423.211 (1978) and defines collective bargaining as "the performance of the mutual obligation of the employer and the representative of the employees to meet at reasonable times and confer in good faith with respect to wages, hours, and other terms and conditions of employment, or the negotiation of an agreement, or any question arising thereunder," id., § 423.214.[3] Public relations activities, though they may certainly affect the outcome of negotiations, are no part of this collective bargaining process. For the same reason I agree that the challenged lobbying expenses are nonchargeable. I emphatically do not agree that costs of the parts of the union's magazine "that concern teaching and education generally, professional development, unemployment, job opportunities, award programs ... and other miscellaneous matters," ante, at 19, can be charged to nonmembers. As the Court appears to concede, the magazine items challenged here have nothing whatever to do with bargaining, and I cannot understand how they can be upheld even under the Court's own test. The Court suggests that they fall within the de minimis exception of Ellis, see 466 U.S., at 456. But the charges allowed on that basis in Ellis (the cost of refreshments at union business meetings and occasional social functions) were de minimis not only in amount but also in First Amendment impact. They were constitutional because:

> "the communicative content is not inherent in the act, but stems from the union's involvement in it. The objection is that these are union social hours. Therefore, the fact that the employee is forced to contribute does not increase the infringement of his First Amendment rights already resulting from the compelled contribution to the union." Id., at 456.

Here, in contrast, the newsletter is inherently communicative; that the Court thinks what it communicates is "for the benefit of all," ante, at 19, does not lessen the First Amendment injury to those who do not agree.

---

[3] The Court suggests, ante at 16, that this "broad language" fails to provide guidance as to the scope of the union's statutory duties. It seems to me, however, that it makes entirely clear that the union's duties extend only to negotiating an agreement and resolving disputes under it. This demonstrates, coincidentally, the error of the Court's assertion that it will be burdensome for courts to construe the scope of union duties under applicable laws. That assertion is implausible in any event, since courts routinely perform such construction when deciding suits alleging a breach of the union's statutory duty.

B

The Court permits the charging of all expenses of sending delegates to conventions held by the Michigan Educational Association (MEA), the National Educational Association (NEA), and the 13E Coordinating Council. Quoting *Ellis,* 466 U.S., at 449-450, the Court says that "[c]onventions such as those at issue here are normal events ... and seem to us to be essential to the union's discharge of its duties as bargaining agent." *Ante,* at 20. The conventions at issue in *Ellis,* however, were those of the union-bargaining agent *itself*; and the costs were chargeable because "if a union is to perform its statutory functions, it must maintain its corporate or associational existence, must elect officers to manage and carry on its affairs, and may consult its members about overall bargaining goals and policy." 466 U.S., at 448. But that reason obviously does not apply to costs for attendance at the convention of *another* organization with which the union-bargaining agent chooses to affiliate. It is not "essential to [the Ferris Faculty Association's] discharge of its duties as bargaining agent," *id.,* at 448-449, that the MEA, NEA and 13E Coordinating Council "maintain [their] corporate or associational existence, ... elect officers," etc. It may be that attendance at certain meetings of those organizations, where matters specifically relevant to the union's bargaining responsibilities are discussed, are properly chargeable, but attendance at all conventions seems to me clearly not.

Another item relating to affiliated organizations that the Court allows to be charged consists of a pro rata assessment of NEA's costs in providing collective-bargaining services (such as negotiating advice, economic analysis, and informational assistance) to its affiliates nationwide, and in maintaining the support staff necessary for that purpose. It would obviously be appropriate to charge the cost of such services *actually provided* to Ferris *itself,* since they relate directly to performance of the union's collective-bargaining duty. It would also be appropriate to charge to nonunion members an annual fee charged by NEA in exchange for contractually promised availability of such services from NEA on demand. As Ferris conceded at argument, however, there is no such contractual commitment here. The Court nonetheless permits the charges to be made, because "[t]he essence of the affiliation relationship is the notion that the parent will bring to bear its often considerable economic, political, and informational resources when the local is in need of them." *Ante,* at 13. I think that resolution is correct. I see no reason to insist that, in order to be chargeable, on-call services for use in the bargaining process be committed by contract rather than by practice and usage. If and when it becomes predictable that requested assistance from the NEA will not be forthcoming, the nonunion members would presumably have cause to object to the charges, just as they would have cause to object if written contracts for the services would predictably not be honored.

I assuredly do not agree, however, with the other reason that the Court gives for its conclusion on this point — or perhaps it can more accurately be characterized as the general principle that the Court derives from its conclusion: namely, that chargeability does not require "a direct relationship between the expense at issue and some tangible benefit to the dissenters' bargaining unit." *Ante,* at 12-13. It assuredly does, and a tangible benefit relating to the union's performance of its representational duties. It is a tangible benefit, however, to have expert consulting services on call, even in the years when they are not used.

C

The final category of challenged expenses consists of the costs of preparing for a strike. In conducting a strike, a union does not act in its capacity as the government-appointed bargaining agent for all employees. And just as, for that reason, nonmembers cannot be assessed the costs of the strike, neither can they be assessed the costs of preparing for the strike. It may be true, of course, that visible preparations for a strike strengthen the union's position in negotiations. But so does the strike itself, and many other union activities, including lobbying. The test of chargeability, as I have described it, is not whether the activities at issue help or hinder achievement of the union's bargaining objectives, but whether they are undertaken as part of the union's representational duty.

For the foregoing reasons, I concur in part and dissent in part.

JUSTICE KENNEDY, concurring in the judgment in part and dissenting in part.

I join all except for Part III-C of JUSTICE SCALIA's opinion. With respect to the strike preparation activities, I agree with the majority that these are indistinguishable in substance from other expenses of negotiating a collective bargaining agreement. I would find, under JUSTICE SCALIA's test, that it was reasonable to incur these expenditures to perform the duties of an exclusive representative of the employees in negotiating an agreement.

The opinion for the majority discerns an altogether malleable three-part test for the chargeability of expenses. The test is so malleable that, at Part IV-B, JUSTICE BLACKMUN can choose to draw different lines with respect to expenses of affiliates, lines with no principled basis. JUSTICE BLACKMUN removes litigation and lobbying from the scope of the Court's holding that a local bargaining unit may charge employees for their pro rata share of the costs associated with "otherwise chargeable" expenses of affiliate unions. This makes little sense if we acknowledge, as JUSTICE SCALIA articulates, *ante,* at 11-12, that we permit charges for affiliate expenditures because such expenditures do provide a tangible benefit to the local bargaining unit, in the nature of a prepaid but noncontractual consulting or legal services plan. Will a local bargaining unit now be permitted to charge dissenters for collective bargaining-related litigation so long as the unit enters into a contractual arrangement or insurance policy with its affiliate? If so, JUSTICE BLACKMUN's distinction has little meaning. If not, then why not, for I discern no additional burden on free speech from such an arrangement, so long as the litigation is undertaken in the course of the union's duties as exclusive bargaining representative. I would draw the same substantive line for litigation and lobbying, whether it is funded through an arrangement with an affiliate or by an individual unit.

In both the discussion of extra-unit litigation, at Part IV-B, and of conventions, at Part IV-E, JUSTICE BLACKMUN places unfounded reliance upon *Ellis v. Railway Clerks,* 466 U.S. 435 (1984), where we disallowed some expenses for extra-unit litigation, and allowed other expenses for a union convention....We should avoid establishing rigid categories such as conventions (chargeable) and extra-unit litigation (non-chargeable), but rather examine whether each expense was reasonably or necessarily incurred in the performance of the union's statutory duties as exclusive bargaining representative.

NOTES

What role, if any, should a state PERB or PERC play in determining the permissible amount that can be charged against a dissenting fair-share fee payor? In *Browne v. Milwaukee Bd. of Sch. Dirs.*, 83 Wis. 2d 316, 265 N.W.2d 559 (1978), the court, after noting that "[t]he statute itself forbids use of fair-share funds for purposes unrelated to collective bargaining or contract administration," held that it was proper to transfer the case to the Wisconsin Employment Relations Commission to determine "what portion of the fair-share dues are being used for purposes unrelated to contract administration or collective bargaining, in contravention of the statute." The court noted that the use of fair-share funds for purposes unrelated to collective bargaining or contract administration interferes with, restrains, or coerces employees in the exercise of their rights guaranteed under the Wisconsin Act and therefore constitutes a prohibited practice.

In *School Comm. v. Greenfield Educ. Ass'n*, 385 Mass. 70, 431 N.E.2d 180 (1982), the court held that the factual issues concerning the proper amount that could be charged to objecting fair-share fee payors should be resolved by the Massachusetts Labor Relations Commission and that it "would expect the commission to adopt appropriate procedures, including one involving a prompt preliminary determination and payment of that portion of the fee clearly payable to the association, with the balance of the funds in escrow to be held by the commission pending resolution of the dispute."

CHICAGO TEACHERS UNION v. HUDSON

475 U.S. 292, 106 S. Ct. 1066, 89 L. Ed. 2d 232 (1986)

JUSTICE STEVENS delivered the opinion of the Court.

In *Abood v. Detroit Board of Education*, 431 U.S. 209 (1977), "we found no constitutional barrier to an agency shop agreement between a municipality and a teacher's union insofar as the agreement required every employee in the unit to pay a service fee to defray the costs of collective bargaining, contract administration, and grievance adjustment. The union, however, could not, consistently with the Constitution, collect from dissenting employees any sums for the support of ideological causes not germane to its duties as collective-bargaining agent." *Ellis v. Railway Clerks*, 466 U.S. 435, 447 (1984). The *Ellis* case was primarily concerned with the need "to define the line between union expenditures that all employees must help defray and those that are not sufficiently related to collective bargaining to justify their being imposed on dissenters." *Ibid.* In contrast, this case concerns the constitutionality of the procedure adopted by the Chicago Teachers Union, with the approval of the Chicago Board of Education, to draw that necessary line and to respond to nonmembers' objections to the manner in which it was drawn.

I

The Chicago Teachers Union has acted as the exclusive collective-bargaining representative of the Board's educational employees continuously since 1967. Approximately 95% of the 27,500 employees in the bargaining unit are members of the Union. Until December 1982, the Union members' dues financed the entire cost of the Union's collective bargaining and contract administration. Nonmembers received the benefits of the Union's representation without making any financial contribution to its cost.

In an attempt to solve this "free rider" problem, the Union made several proposals for a "fair share fee" clause in the labor contract. Because the Illinois School Code did not expressly authorize such a provision, the Board rejected these proposals until the Illinois General Assembly amended the School Code in 1981. In the following year, the Chicago Teachers Union and the Chicago Board of Education entered into an agreement requiring the Board to deduct "proportionate share payments" from the paychecks of nonmembers. The new contractual provision authorized the Union to specify the amount of the payment; it stipulated that the amount could not exceed the members' dues. The contractual provision also required the Union to indemnify the Board for all action taken to implement the new provision.

For the 1982-83 school year, the Union determined that the "proportionate share" assessed on nonmembers was 95% of union dues. At that time, the union dues were $17.35 per month for teachers and $12.15 per month for other covered employees; the corresponding deduction from the nonmembers' checks thus amounted to $16.48 and $11.54 for each of the 10 months that dues were payable.

Union officials computed the 95% fee on the basis of the Union's financial records for the fiscal year ending on June 30, 1982. They identified expenditures unrelated to collective bargaining and contract administration (which they estimated as $188,549.82). They divided this amount by the Union's income for the year ($4,103,701.58) to produce a percentage of 4.6%; the figure was then rounded off to 5% to provide a "cushion" to cover any inadvertent errors.

The Union also established a procedure for considering objections by nonmembers. Before the deduction was made, the nonmember could not raise any objection. After the deduction was made, a nonmember could object to the "proportionate share" figure by writing to the Union President within 30 days after the first payroll deduction. The objection then would meet a three-stage procedure. First, the Union's Executive Committee would consider the objection and notify the objector within 30 days of its decision. Second, if the objector disagreed with that decision and appealed within another 30 days, the Union's Executive Board would consider the objection. Third, if the objector continued to protest after the Executive Board decision, the Union President would select an arbitrator from a list maintained by the Illinois Board of Education. The Union would pay for the arbitration, and, if there were multiple objections, they could be consolidated. If an objection was sustained at any stage of the procedure, the remedy would be an immediate reduction in the amount of future deductions for all nonmembers and a rebate for the objector.

In October 1982, the Union formally requested the Board to begin making deductions and advised it that a hearing procedure had been established for nonmembers' objections. The Board accepted the Union's 95% determination without questioning its method of calculation and without asking to review any of the records supporting it. The Board began to deduct the fee from the paychecks of nonmembers in December 1982. The Board did not provide the nonmembers with any explanation of the calculation, or of the Union's procedures. The Union did undertake certain informational efforts. It asked its member delegates at all schools to distribute flyers, display posters, inform nonmembers of the deductions, and invite nonmembers to join the Union with an amnesty for past fines. It also described the deduction and the protest procedures in the December issue of the Union newspaper, which was distributed to nonmembers.

Three nonmembers — Annie Lee Hudson, K. Celeste Campbell, and Walter Sherrill — sent identical letters of protest to the Union stating that they believed the Union was using part of their salary for purposes unrelated to collective bargaining and demanding that the deduction be reduced. A fourth nonmember — Beverly Underwood — objected to any deduction from her paycheck. The Union's response to each of the four briefly explained how the proportionate share fee had been calculated, described the objection procedure, enclosed a copy of the Union Implementation Plan, and concluded with the advice that "any objection you may file" would be processed in compliance with that procedure. None of the letters was referred to the Executive Committee. Only Hudson wrote a second letter; her request for detailed financial information was answered with an invitation to make an appointment for an "informational conference" at the Union's office, at which she could review the Union's financial records. The four nonmembers made no further effort to invoke the Union procedures; instead, they challenged the new procedure in court.

II

In March 1983, the four nonmembers, joined by three other nonmembers who had not sent any letters, filed suit in Federal District Court, naming as defendants, the Union, its officials, the Board, and the Board members. They objected to the Union procedure for three principal reasons: it violated their First Amendment rights to freedom of expression and association; it violated their Fourteenth Amendment due process rights; and it permitted the use of their proportionate shares for impermissible purposes.

The District Court rejected the challenges. 573 F. Supp. 1505 (ND Ill. 1983). It first noted that the procedure passed the initial threshold established by an earlier Seventh Circuit opinion on the subject because the procedure itself was fair; it represented a good-faith effort by the Union; and it was not unduly cumbersome. The District Court then rejected the First Amendment objection because it found that the procedure was the "least restrictive means" to protect the nonmembers' First Amendment rights while also protecting the Union's legitimate interest in promptly obtaining service fees from nonmembers. The District Court also rejected the argument that the procedure deprived the plaintiffs of property without due process because it did not accept the plaintiffs' analogy to cases requiring predeprivation hearings. Finally, the District Court refused to reach the contention that the nonmembers' proportionate shares were, in fact, being used for impermissible purposes.[4] The District Court

---

[4] The plaintiffs had challenged, for instance, the Union's 95% calculation because more than half of the Union's income ($2,167,000 of an income of $4,103,701.58) was passed on to affiliated state

found that only two of the plaintiffs (Hudson and Underwood) had validly invoked the union procedures; that only those two were thus entitled to rebates if their objections were sustained; and that any assessment of the permissible use of the funds should await the outcome of the union procedures.

The posture of the case changed significantly in the Court of Appeals. The plaintiffs no longer focused on the claim that particular expenditures were inappropriate; they concentrated their attack on the procedures used by the Union to determine the amount of the deductions and to respond to their objections. The Union also modified its position. Instead of defending the procedure upheld by the District Court, it advised the Court of Appeals that it had voluntarily placed all of the dissenters' agency fees in escrow, and thereby avoided any danger that respondents' constitutional rights would be violated.

The Court of Appeals was unanimous in its judgment reversing the District Court. 743 F.2d 1187 (CA7 1984). All three judges agreed that the Constitution requires the Union to follow a procedure that protects the nonmembers from being compelled to subsidize political or ideological activities not germane to the collective-bargaining process, that the Union's objection procedure was inadequate, and that any rebate which allowed the Union temporary use of money for activities that violate the nonmembers' rights was unconstitutional. In his concurring opinion, however, Judge Flaum declined to reach certain questions discussed by the majority.

Specifically, the majority concluded that the category of impermissible expenditures included all those that were not germane to collective bargaining, even if they might not be characterized as "political or ideological." Judge Flaum found it unnecessary to reach this constitutional issue because the procedure could be deemed inadequate without deciding it and because, in his view, the collective-bargaining agreement and the Illinois statute limited agency shop fees to collective-bargaining and representational expenses. However, the majority believed that its conclusion derived from the fact that the possible infringement on the "liberty" of the nonmembers was not limited to the forced subsidization of political or ideological views, but also included the negative dimension of the freedom of association.

Determining that the Union's existing procedures were constitutionally inadequate, and that the Union "must go back to the drawing board," id., at 1196, the majority suggested that the "constitutional minimum" of any revised procedure must include "fair notice, a prompt administrative hearing before the Board of Education or some other state or local agency — the hearing to incorporate the usual safeguards for evidentiary hearings before administrative agencies — and a right of judicial review of the agency's decision. The combination of an internal union remedy and an arbitration procedure is unlikely to satisfy constitutional requirements given the nature of the issues to be decided and the union's stake in how they are decided." Ibid.

In response to the Union's advice that it had voluntarily placed dissenters' agency fees in escrow, the majority noted that the Union had made no commitment to continue the escrow in the future, had not indicated the terms of the

and national labor organizations. The plaintiffs claimed that some of this money was expended for political or ideological activities.

escrow, and, in all events, "[t]he terms cannot be left entirely up to the Union." *Id.,* at 1197.

The importance of the case, and the divergent approaches of other courts to the issue, led us to grant certiorari, 472 U.S. —, 105 S. Ct. 2700 (1985). We affirm the judgment of the Court of Appeals, but we do not find it necessary to resolve all of the questions discussed in its opinion.

III

In *Abood v. Detroit Board of Education,* 431 U.S. 209 (1977), we recognized that requiring nonunion employees to support their collective-bargaining representative "has an impact upon their First Amendment interests," *id.,* at 222, and may well "interfere in some way with an employee's freedom to associate for the advancement of ideas, or to refrain from doing so, as he sees fit," *ibid.* See also *id.,* at 255 (POWELL, J., concurring in judgment). We nevertheless rejected the claim that it was unconstitutional for a public employer to designate a union as the exclusive collective-bargaining representative of its employees, and to require nonunion employees, as a condition of employment, to pay a fair share of the union's cost of negotiating and administering a collective-bargaining agreement. We also held, however, that nonunion employees do have a constitutional right to "prevent the Union's spending a part of their required service fees to contribute to political candidates and to express political views unrelated to its duties as exclusive bargaining representative." *Id.,* at 234.

The question presented in this case is whether the procedure used by the Chicago Teachers Union and approved by the Chicago Board of Education adequately protects the basic distinction drawn in *Abood.* "[T]he objective must be to devise a way of preventing compulsory subsidization of ideological activity by employees who object thereto without restricting the Union's ability to require every employee to contribute to the cost of collective-bargaining activities." *Abood,* 431 U.S., at 237.

Procedural safeguards are necessary to achieve this objective for two reasons. First, although the government interest in labor peace is strong enough to support an "agency shop" notwithstanding its limited infringement on nonunion employees' constitutional rights, the fact that those rights are protected by the First Amendment requires that the procedure be carefully tailored to minimize the infringement. Second, the nonunion employee — the individual whose First Amendment rights are being affected — must have a fair opportunity to identify the impact of the governmental action on his interests and to assert a meritorious First Amendment claim.

In *Ellis v. Railway Clerks,* 466 U.S. 435, 443 (1984), we determined that, under the Railway Labor Act, a "pure rebate approach is inadequate." We explained that, under such an approach, in which the union refunds to the nonunion employee any money to which the union was not entitled, "the union obtains an involuntary loan for purposes to which the employee objects." *Id.,* at 444. We noted the possibility of "readily available alternatives, such as advance reduction of dues and/or interest-bearing escrow accounts," *ibid.,* but, for purposes of that case, it was sufficient to strike down the rebate procedure.

In this case, we must determine whether the challenged Chicago Teachers Union procedure survives First Amendment scrutiny, either because the procedure upheld by the District Court was constitutionally sufficient, or because the subsequent adoption of an escrow arrangement cured any constitutional defect. We consider these questions in turn.[13]

IV

The procedure that was initially adopted by the Union and considered by the District Court contained three fundamental flaws.[14] First, as in *Ellis*, a remedy which merely offers dissenters the possibility of a rebate does not avoid the risk that dissenters' funds may be used temporarily for an improper purpose. "[T]he Union should not be permitted to exact a service fee from nonmembers without first establishing a procedure which will avoid the risk that their funds will be used, even temporarily, to finance ideological activities unrelated to collective bargaining." *Abood*, 431 U.S., at 244 (concurring opinion). The amount at stake for each individual dissenter does not diminish this concern. For, whatever the amount, the quality of respondents' interest in not being compelled to subsidize the propagation of political or ideological views that they oppose is clear. In *Abood*, we emphasized this point by quoting the comments of Thomas Jefferson and James Madison about the tyrannical character of forcing an individual to contribute even "three pence" for the "propagation of opinions which he disbelieves." A forced exaction followed by a rebate equal to the amount improperly expended is thus not a permissible response to the nonunion employees' objections.

Second, the "advance reduction of dues" was inadequate because it provided nonmembers with inadequate information about the basis for the proportionate share. In *Abood*, we reiterated that the nonunion employee has the burden of raising an objection, but that the union retains the burden of proof: "'Since the unions possess the facts and records from which the proportion of political to total union expenditures can reasonably be calculated, basic considerations of fairness compel that they, not the individual employees, bear the burden of proving such proportion.'" *Abood*, 431 U.S., at 239-240, n. 40, quoting *Railway*

---

[13]Respondents argue that this case should be considered through the prism of the procedural due process protections necessary for deprivations of property. As in *Abood*, we analyze the problem from the perspective of the First Amendment concerns. We are convinced that, in this context, the procedures required by the First Amendment also provide the protections necessary for any deprivation of property.

Moreover, in view of the fact that the First Amendment principles identified in *Abood* require procedural safeguards and in view of the fact that respondents' challenge is to the procedures, not the expenditures, we find it unnecessary to resolve any question concerning non-germane, non-ideological expenditures. Unlike the Seventh Circuit, we are not convinced that resolution of the constitutional non-germaneness question will lead to appreciably different procedural requirements, and we thus find no need to reach that constitutional question. See *Rescue Army v. Municipal Court*, 331 U.S. 549, 568-572 (1947). Cf. *Ellis v. Railway Clerks*, 466 U.S. 435 (1984) (analyzing specific challenged expenditures under the Railway Labor Act and, as necessary, under the First Amendment).

[14]Like the Seventh Circuit, we consider the procedure as it was presented to the District Court. It is clear that "voluntary cessation of allegedly illegal conduct does not moot a case." *United States v. Consolidated Phosphate Export Assn.*, 393 U.S. 199, 203 (1968). See also *City of Mesquite v. Aladdin's Castle, Inc.*, 455 U.S. 283, 289 (1982); *United States v. W.T. Grant Co.*, 345 U.S. 629, 632 (1953). The same concerns — the fear that a defendant would be "free to return to his old ways," *id.*, at 632, and that he would have "a powerful weapon against public law enforcement," *ibid.* — dictate that we review the legality of the practice defended before the District Court.

Clerks v. Allen, 373 U.S. 113, 122 (1963).[16] Basic considerations of fairness, as well as concern for the First Amendment rights at stake, also dictate that the potential objectors be given sufficient information to gauge the propriety of the union's fee. Leaving the nonunion employees in the dark about the source of the figure for the agency fee — and requiring them to object in order to receive information — does not adequately protect the careful distinctions drawn in *Abood.*

In this case, the original information given to the nonunion employees was inadequate. Instead of identifying the expenditures for collective bargaining and contract administration that had been provided for the benefit of nonmembers as well as members — and for which nonmembers as well as members can fairly be charged a fee — the Union identified the amount that it admittedly had expended for purposes that did not benefit dissenting nonmembers. An acknowledgment that nonmembers would not be required to pay any part of 5% of the Union's total annual expenditures was not an adequate disclosure of the reasons why they were required to pay their share of 95%.[18]

Finally, the original Union procedure was also defective because it did not provide for a reasonably prompt decision by an impartial decisionmaker. Although we have not so specified in the past,[19] we now conclude that such a requirement is necessary. The nonunion employee, whose First Amendment rights are affected by the agency shop itself and who bears the burden of objecting, is entitled to have his objections addressed in an expeditious, fair, and objective manner.[20]

The Union's procedure does not meet this requirement. As the Seventh Circuit observed, the "most conspicuous feature of the procedure is that from start

---

[16] The nonmembers' "burden" is simply the obligation to make his objection known. See *Machinists v. Street,* 367 U.S. 740, 774 (1961) ("dissent is not to be presumed — it must affirmatively be made known to the union by the dissenting employee"); *Railway Clerks v. Allen,* 373 U.S. 113, 119 (1963); *Abood, supra,* 431 U.S., at 238.

[18] We continue to recognize that there are practical reasons why "[a]bsolute precision" in the calculation of the charge to nonmembers cannot be "expected or required." *Allen,* 373 U.S., at 122 quoted in *Abood,* 431 U.S., at 239-240, n. 40. Thus, for instance, the Union cannot be faulted for calculating its fee on the basis of its expenses during the preceding year. The Union need not provide nonmembers with an exhaustive and detailed list of all its expenditures, but adequate disclosure surely would include the major categories of expenses, as well as verification by an independent auditor. With respect to an item such as the Union's payment of $2,167,000 to its affiliated state and national labor organizations, see n. 4, *supra,* for instance, either a showing that none of it was used to subsidize activities for which nonmembers may not be charged, or an explanation of the share that was so used was surely required.

[19] Our prior opinions have merely suggested the desirability of an internal union remedy. See *Abood, supra,* at 240, and n. 41; *Allen, supra,* at 122.

[20] We reject the Union's suggestion that the availability of ordinary judicial remedies is sufficient. This contention misses the point. Since the agency shop itself is "a significant impingement on First Amendment rights," *Ellis,* 466 U.S., at 455, the government and union have a responsibility to provide procedures that minimize that impingement and that facilitate a non-union employee's ability to protect his rights. We are considering here the procedural adequacy of the agency shop arrangement itself; we presume that the courts remain available as the ultimate protectors of constitutional rights.

In other First Amendment contexts, of course, we have required swift judicial review of the challenged governmental action. See, e.g., *Southeastern Promotions, Ltd. v. Conrad,* 420 U.S. 546 (1975); *Blount v. Rizzi,* 400 U.S. 410 (1971); *Freedman v. Maryland,* 380 U.S. 51 (1965). In this context, we do not believe that such special judicial procedures are necessary. Clearly, however, if a state chooses to provide extraordinarily swift judicial review for these challenges, that review would satisfy the requirement of a reasonably prompt decision by an impartial decision-maker.

to finish it is entirely controlled by the union, which is an interested party, since it is the recipient of the agency fees paid by the dissenting employees." 743 F.2d, at 1194-1195. The initial consideration of the agency fee is made by Union officials, and the first two steps of the review procedure (the Union Executive Committee and Executive Board) consist of Union officials. The third step — review by a Union-selected arbitrator — is also inadequate because the selection represents the Union's unrestricted choice from the state list.[21]

Thus, the original Union procedure was inadequate because it failed to minimize the risk that nonunion employees' contributions might be used for impermissible purposes, because it failed to provide adequate justification for the advance reduction of dues, and because it failed to offer a reasonably prompt decision by an impartial decisionmaker.

V

The Union has not only created an escrow of 100% of the contributions exacted from the respondents, but has also advised us that it would not object to the entry of a judgment compelling it to maintain an escrow system in the future. The Union does not contend that its escrow has made the case moot. Rather, it takes the position that because a 100% escrow completely avoids the risk that dissenters' contributions could be used improperly, it eliminates any valid constitutional objection to the procedure and thereby provides an adequate remedy in this case. We reject this argument.

Although the Union's self-imposed remedy eliminates the risk that nonunion employees' contributions may be temporarily used for impermissible purposes, the procedure remains flawed in two respects. It does not provide an adequate explanation for the advance reduction of dues, and it does not provide a reasonably prompt decision by an impartial decisionmaker. We reiterate that these characteristics are required because the agency shop itself impinges on the nonunion employees' First Amendment interests, and because the nonunion employee has the burden of objection. The appropriately justified advance reduction and the prompt, impartial decisionmaker are necessary to minimize both the impingement and the burden.[22]

We need not hold, however, that a 100% escrow is constitutionally required. Such a remedy has the serious defect of depriving the Union of access to some escrowed funds that it is unquestionably entitled to retain. If, for example, the

---

[21] We do not agree, however, with the Seventh Circuit that a full-dress administrative hearing, with evidentiary safeguards, is part of the "constitutional minimum." Indeed, we think that an expeditious arbitration might satisfy the requirement of a reasonably prompt decision by an impartial decisionmaker, so long as the arbitrator's selection did not represent the Union's unrestricted choice. In contrast to the Union's procedure here, selection of an arbitrator frequently does not represent one party's unrestricted choice from a list of state-approved arbitrators. See F. Elkouri & E. Elkouri, How Arbitration Works (4th ed. 1985) 135-137; O. Fairweather, Practice and Procedure in Labor Arbitration (2d ed. 1983) 79-90.

The arbitrator's decision would not receive preclusive effect in any subsequent § 1983 action. See McDonald v. City of West Branch, 466 U.S. 284 (1984).

[22] In view of the fact that plaintiffs established a constitutional violation, moreover, the task of fashioning a proper remedy is one that should be performed by the District Court after all interested parties have had an opportunity to be heard. The judicial remedy for a proven violation of law will often include commands that the law does not impose on the community at large. See National Society of Professional Engineers v. United States, 435 U.S. 679, 697-698 (1978); Swann v. Charlotte-Mecklenburg Board of Education, 402 U.S. 1, 15-16 (1971).

original disclosure by the Union had included a certified public accountant's verified breakdown of expenditures, including some categories that no dissenter could reasonably challenge, there would be no reason to escrow the portion of the nonmember's fees that would be represented by those categories.[23] On the record before us, there is no reason to believe that anything approaching a 100% "cushion" to cover the possibility of mathematical errors would be constitutionally required. Nor can we decide how the proper contribution that might be made by an independent audit, in advance, coupled with adequate notice, might reduce the size of any appropriate escrow.

Thus, the Union's 100% escrow does not cure all of the problems in the original procedure. Two of the three flaws remain, and the procedure therefore continues to provide less than the Constitution requires in this context.

VI

We hold today that the constitutional requirements for the Union's collection of agency fees include an adequate explanation of the basis for the fee, a reasonably prompt opportunity to challenge the amount of the fee before an impartial decisionmaker, and an escrow for the amounts reasonably in dispute while such challenges are pending.

The determination of the appropriate remedy in this case is a matter that should be addressed in the first instance by the District Court. The Court of Appeals correctly reversed the District Court's original judgment and remanded the case for further proceedings. That judgment of reversal is affirmed, and those further proceedings should be consistent with this opinion.

It is so ordered.

JUSTICE WHITE, with whom THE CHIEF JUSTICE joins, concurring.

I join the opinion and judgment of the Court with the following observations. First, since the Court, as did Judge Flaum in the Court of Appeals, deems it unnecessary to reach the issue of non-germane, non-ideological expenditures, the panel's remarks on the subject are therefore obvious dicta. Under our cases, they are also very questionable.

Second, as I understand the Court's opinion, the complaining non-member need only complain; he need not exhaust internal union hearing procedures, if any, before going to arbitration. However, if the union provides for arbitration and complies with the other requirements specified in our opinion, it should be entitled to insist that the arbitration procedure be exhausted before resorting to the courts.

NOTES

1. Applying the Supreme Court's decision in *Hudson*, the court in *Gilpin v. AFSCME*, 643 F. Supp. 733 (N.D. Ill. 1986), *aff'd in relevant part*, 875 F.2d 1310 (7th Cir. 1990) established the following three requirements with respect

---

[23] If the Union chooses to escrow less than the entire amount, however, it must carefully justify the limited escrow on the basis of the independent audit, and the escrow figure must itself be independently verified.

to the notification which non-members are entitled to receive concerning their right to object to the amount of the fair share fee:

1. "First, the notice must inform all interested parties of the rationale behind the calculation of the 'fair share.'"
2. "Adequate notice entails information sufficient for an individual, unsophisticated non-union employee to file a written objection without further investigation."
3. "[A]dequate notice requires notification a sufficient time prior to the deprivation so as not to present the deprived party with a *fait accompli*."

2. In *Robinson v. New Jersey*, 806 F.2d 442 (3d Cir. 1986), the court held that a three-member appeal board established by statute to rule on fair share fee cases did not violate the procedural due process rights of fair share fee payors. The appeal board in question consisted of three members appointed by the Governor, of which "one shall be representative of public employers, one shall be representative of public employee organizations and one, as chairman, who shall represent the interest of the public as a strictly impartial member...."

3. In *Andrews v. Education Ass'n of Cheshire*, 829 F.2d 335 (2d Cir. 1987), the court upheld the constitutionality of a union's agency fee collection plan under *Hudson* where it provided a reasonably prompt opportunity to challenge the amount of the fair share fee before an arbitrator experienced in representation fee disputes who was selected by the American Arbitration Association. The court held, however, that the union's agreement with the American Arbitration Association which allowed the union to unilaterally waive the oral hearing provided for by AAA rules was not constitutional, and it therefore enjoined the union from waiving an objector's right to an oral hearing.

Other decisions holding that an arbitrator selected by the American Arbitration Association in accordance with its own internal selection rules without any input from the union satisfies *Hudson*'s impartial decisionmaker requirement include *Ping v. NEA*, 870 F.2d 1369 (7th Cir. 1989); *Damiano v. Matish*, 830 F.2d 1363 (6th Cir. 1987).

4. What constitutes "a reasonably prompt decision" with respect to a constitutional challenge raised by a non-member to the fair share fee or the procedure utilized to collect the fee? In *Kuehn v. AFSCME*, 435 N.W.2d 130 (Minn. Ct. App. 1989), the court held that a five-month period between the filing of an employee's challenge and the holding of the administrative hearing constituted "a reasonably prompt review by an impartial state agency." The court also rejected an objecting non-member's contention that he could not be required to pay fair share fees to organizations that were affiliated with his exclusive representative, but were not actually his exclusive representative. In rejecting this contention, the court held that "AFSCME was an integrated organization and therefore could appropriately include in the calculation of fair share fees payments of other levels of its organization."

5. In *Kuehn v. AFSCME*, 435 N.W.2d 130 (Minn. Ct. App. 1989), the court upheld the constitutionality of the Minnesota Fair Share Fee Statute. One of the grounds on which the statute was attacked was that the independent auditor's verification did not articulate which expenses were related to collective bargaining and which were members-only benefits. In rejecting this contention, the court concluded that the decision in *Hudson* "did not require that an independent auditor categorize expenditures of the union as chargeable and nonchargeable," noting that "[a]n independent auditor would be unfamiliar with the functioning of a union so that categorizing expenditures would be nearly impossible." The court stated that "it is a union's responsibility to present its own categorization of expenditures, not the independent auditor's."

6. In *Lowary v. Lexington Local Bd. of Educ.,* 854 F.2d 131 (6th Cir. 1988), the Sixth Circuit reversed a district court order which permitted a union to continue to collect fair share fees after a lawsuit had been filed as long as the fees were placed in an interest-bearing escrow account pending a decision on the merits. The court reasoned as follows:

> ... We find that once a non-union member has objected to the current procedures in place for the collection of fair-share fees on the ground that these procedures do not satisfy the constitutional requirement set forth in *Hudson,* and the district court has found it likely that the procedures will be found, on the merits of the case, to violate *Hudson,* it constitutes an abuse of discretion for the court to allow fair-share fees to be collected even if the collected fees are placed in an escrow account. Such a remedy is contrary to the Supreme Court's decision in *Hudson* as later interpreted by this court in *Tierney* [824 F.2d 1497].

As a result, the court ordered that "the escrow account is to be disbanded and the fees previously placed therein remitted to plaintiffs." Accord *Gibney v. Toledo Bd. of Educ.,* 40 Ohio St. 3d 152, 532 N.E.2d 1300 (1988).

7. In *Oliver v. Ft. Wayne Educ. Ass'n,* 820 F.2d 913 (7th Cir. 1987), the Seventh Circuit upheld a district court's decision to abstain from hearing a complaint filed by non-union teachers challenging the constitutionality of a fair share fee since the same relief was being sought in state court litigation which had already proceeded to point of judgment.

D. STATUTORY CONSIDERATIONS

CITY OF HAYWARD v. SEIU

54 Cal. App. 3d 761, 126 Cal. Rptr. 710 (1976)

CHRISTIAN, JUSTICE: — The City of Hayward and its city manager appeal from a judgment declaring that an "agency shop" agreement between the City and respondent United Public Employees, Local 390, is lawful.

Respondent (hereinafter "the Union") is a labor organization affiliated with the Service Employees International Union, AFL-CIO; certain employees of the City are members of the Union. On July 11, 1972, the Union and the City entered into a "Memorandum of Understanding," whereby the City recognized the Union as representing a majority of the employees in the City's Maintenance and Operations Unit.

The agreement covered wages, hours, and other terms and conditions of employment, about which there is no controversy. A dispute arose, however, over the validity of section 1.02 of the agreement, which provides that, although employees are not to be required to join the Union, all employees in the Maintenance and Operations Unit, including nonmembers of the Union,

> "shall, as a condition of continued employment, pay to the union an amount of money equal to that paid by other employees in the appropriate unit who are members of the union, which shall be limited to an amount of money equal to the union's usual and customary initiation and monthly dues."

Except as may be authorized by statute, public employees have no right to bargain collectively with the employing agency. (*Sacramento County Employees Organization, Local 22 etc. Union v. County of Sacramento* (1972) 28 Cal. App. 3d 424, 429, 81 LRRM 2841; *City of San Diego v. American Federation of State etc. Employees* (1970) 8 Cal. App. 3d 308, 310, 74 LRRM 2407.) In 1961, California became one of the first states to create a right on the part of government employees to organize and to confer with management as to the terms and conditions of their employment. Another enactment, the Meyers-Milias-Brown Act (Gov. Code, §§ 3500-3510 [hereinafter "MMBA"]) has created certain additional rights of organization in employees of municipalities and local agencies, and authorized representatives of labor and management to enter into written agreements for presentation to the governing body. (Gov. Code, §§ 3505-3505.1.)[2]

The memorandum of understanding entered into by the parties was negotiated by means of procedures which conform to the MMBA. The sole question presented is whether the MMBA permits the creation of an agency shop in an agency of local government. An agency shop agreement is to be distinguished from a union shop agreement, which conditions the continuance of an employee's job on union membership; a union shop is prohibited by statute in public employment. (§ 3502.) In an agency shop, union membership is not a condition of employment, but all employees, including those who do not choose to join the union, must pay union dues. The MMBA does not explicitly refer to agency shop agreements; no reported decision has previously addressed the issue of the legality of this type of agreement.

Section 3502 provides: "Except as otherwise provided by the Legislature, public employees shall have the right to form, join, and participate in the activities of employee organizations of their own choosing for the purpose of representation on all matters of employer-employee relations. Public employees also shall have the right to refuse to join or participate in the activities of employee organizations *and shall have the right to represent themselves individually in their employment relations with the public agency.*"(Emphasis added.)

Section 3506 prohibits both public agencies and employee organizations from interfering with, intimidating, restraining, coercing or discriminating against public employees "because of their exercise of their rights under Section 3502." The freedom of choice provisions of each of these sections must be construed as prohibiting the extraction of union dues, or their equivalent, as a condition of continued employment. Otherwise the statutory right of employees to represent themselves would be defeated.

The trial judge did not address either of these sections; instead, he found that the agency shop provision was a "reasonable rule or regulation" adopted pursuant to the authority conferred by section 3507.

Section 3507 provides:

"A public agency may adopt reasonable rules and regulations after consultation in good faith with representatives of an employee organization or organizations for the administration of employer-employee relations under this chapter (commencing with Section 3500).

---

[2] Unless otherwise indicated, all statutory references hereinafter are to the Government Code.

"Such rules and regulations may include provisions for (a) verifying that an organization does in fact represent employees of the public agency (b) verifying the official status of employee organization officers and representatives (c) recognition of employee organizations (d) exclusive recognition of employee organizations formally recognized pursuant to a vote of the employees of the agency or an appropriate unit thereof, subject to the right of an employee to represent himself as provided in Section 3502 (e) additional procedures for the resolutions of disputes involving wages, hours and other terms and conditions of employment (f) access of employee organization officers and representatives to work locations (g) use of official bulletin boards and other means of communication by employee organizations (h) furnishing nonconfidential information pertaining to employment relations to employee organizations (i) such other matters as are necessary to carry out the purposes of this chapter.

"Exclusive recognition of employee organizations formally recognized as majority representatives pursuant to a vote of the employees may be revoked by a majority vote of the employees only after a period of not less than 12 months following the date of such recognition.

"No public agency shall unreasonably withhold recognition of employee organizations."

The trial judge reasoned that the agency shop provision could be lawfully enacted under section 3507 because "(a) it obligates the Union to represent *all* employees, (b) it requires nonmembers to share the cost of the benefits which such representation is intended to provide, and (c) it clearly relates to the administration of employer-employee relationships." He recognized the inconsistency of the provision with the employees' statutorily guaranteed freedom of choice, but reasoned that the right of the individual should be subordinated to a policy in furtherance of collective bargaining "as a vehicle for improving employment relationships and avoiding the harsh consequences of labor disputes involving public services."

Courts must, if possible, harmonize statutes, reconcile seeming inconsistencies and construe them to give force and effect to all provisions thereof.... A court may not add to or detract from a statute or insert or delete words to accomplish a purpose that does not appear on its face or from its legislative history....

The MMBA was enacted to promote "full communication between public employers and their employees by providing a reasonable method of resolving disputes regarding wages, hours, and other terms and conditions of employment...." (§ 3500.) It was not intended to supersede existing systems for the administration of employer-employee relations in the public sector, but to strengthen such systems by improving communication. (Ibid.)

It is argued that an agency shop agreement is a reasonable method of resolving labor disputes and that, since it is not specifically prohibited, it should be held permissible under the MMBA. But that construction would render the provisions of sections 3502 and 3506 meaningless. Section 3502 implicitly recognizes that employees may choose to join or participate in different organizations. (See, e.g., *Sacramento County Employees Organization, Local 22 etc. Union v. County of Sacramento, supra,* 28 Cal. App. 3d 424, 81 LRRM 2841.) It also confers upon each employee the right not to join or participate in the activities of any employee organization. Section 3506 not only prohibits management from interfering with an employee's section 3502 rights, but also imposes the same ban on employee organizations.

Without common law collective bargaining rights, public employees enjoy only those rights specifically granted by statute. Statutes governing the labor relations of other public employee groups indicate that when the Legislature has authorized union security devices, it has done so with explicit language. Certain public transit district employees have been granted extensive collective bargaining rights, including the right to contract for a closed or union shop. (See, e.g., Pub. Util. Code, §§ 25051-25057.) The labor relations of teachers and other school district employees have been governed by the Winton Act. (Ed. Code, §§ 13080-13090.) Sections 13082 and 13086 of that Act contain provisions paralleling sections 3502 and 3506 of the MMBA. The Winton Act has never been construed to authorize an agency shop. However, legislation recently enacted will repeal the Winton Act as of July 1, 1976, and add section 3540 et seq. to the Government Code. (Stats. 1975, ch. 961.)

Under the new law, school district employees still have the right to refuse to join or participate in the activities of employee organizations and the right to represent themselves in their employment relations with the school district *when no exclusive representative has been recognized.* (§ 3543.) When a majority organization is recognized as the exclusive representative pursuant to the prescribed procedures (§§ 3544-3544.9), employees may no longer represent themselves. (§ 3543.) The agency shop is explicitly authorized as an organizational security device (§ 3540.1, subd. (i)) subject to certain limitations. (§§ 3546-3546.5.) Although the MMBA has been amended from time to time since its enactment, the Legislature has never modified the language of sections 3502 and 3506 nor added provisions limiting or enlarging the rights created therein.

Those rights cannot reasonably be reconciled with an agency shop provision. The forced payment of dues or their equivalent is, at the very least, "participation" in an employee organization. Practically, it would have the effect of inducing union membership on the part of unwilling employees. While increased participation and membership is a legitimate goal of labor organizations, coercion toward that end is forbidden by statute. Such union security devices as the agency shop must await authorization by the Legislature.

The courts of other states having similar statutes recognizing the right of a public employee not to join or participate in an employee organization have held the agency shop to be unlawful. (See *Smigel v. Southgate Community School District* (Mich. S. Ct. 1972), 388 Mich. 531, 202 N.W.2d 305, 81 LRRM 2944; *New Jersey Turnpike Employees' Union, Local 194 v. New Jersey Turnpike Authority* (N.J. Super. Ct. App. Div. 1973) 123 N.J. Super. 461, 303 A.2d 599, 83 LRRM 2250, aff'd (N.J. S. Ct. 1974), 64 N.J. 579, 319 A.2d 224, 86 LRRM 2842; *Farrigan v. Helsby* (S. Ct. 1971), 68 Misc. 2d 952, 327 N.Y.S.2d 909, 68 LRRM 2360, aff'd (S. Ct. App. Div. 1973), 42 A.D. 2d 2653, 346 N.Y.S.2d 39, 83 LRRM 3052; *Pennsylvania Labor Relations Board v. Zelem* (1974), 329 A.2d 477, 88 LRRM 2524.) Apparently, only Rhode Island has held that there is a common law right to include an agency shop provision in a collective bargaining agreement. *(Town of N. Kingstown v. North Kingstown Teach. Assn.* (1972), 110 R.I. 698, 297 A.2d 342, 344-345, 82 LRRM 2010 [statute merely gave teachers the right "to join or to decline to join" any employee organization].)

This conclusion is further supported by a comparison with federal statutes. Recognizing that many state labor enactments have followed federal models, California courts have often looked to interpretations of federal labor legislation when construing similar state statutes.... The National Labor Relations Act, 29 U.S.C. § 151 et seq. (hereinafter "NLRA"), contains provisions similar to sections 3502 and 3506 of the MMBA with one major difference. Section 7 of the federal act provides: "Employees shall have the right to self-organization, to form, join, or assist labor organizations, to bargain collectively through representatives of their own choosing, and to engage in other concerted activities for the purpose of collective bargaining or other mutual aid or protection, and shall have the right to refrain from any or all of such activities except to the extent that such right may be affected by an agreement requiring membership in a labor organization as a condition of employment as authorized in section 158(a)(3) of this title." (29 U.S.C. § 157.) Sections 8(a)(1) and 8(a)(3) make it unfair labor practices for an employer to threaten, restrain, or coerce employees in the exercise of their section 157 rights or to encourage or discourage union activity by discrimination in employment except for union shop agreements. (Id., §§ 158(a)(1), (a)(3).) The Supreme Court has held that, without the express provisos in section 7 and 8(a)(3), conditioning employment upon union membership would be an unfair labor practice. (*Retail Clerks v. Schermerhorn* (1963) 373 U.S. 746, 756, 53 LRRM 2318.) The court has further held that the agency shop is the practical equivalent of the union shop. (*Id.,* 373 U.S. at p. 751; *Labor Board v. General Motors* (1963) 373 U.S. 734, 743, 53 LRRM 2313.)

The provisos permitting union security arrangements were enacted by Congress in 1935 and 1947. Sections 3502 and 3506 of the MMBA were not enacted until 1961, and major revisions were made in 1968. It is reasonable to infer that the California Legislature was aware of the analogous provisions of the NLRA, and the construction thereof, and chose not to permit the agency shop in public employment in California. (Cf. *Fire Fighters Union v. City of Vallejo, supra,* 12 Cal. 3d 608 at pp. 615-617, 87 LRRM 2453.)

The judgment is reversed with directions to enter a new judgment declaring the agency shop provisions of the agreement to be unlawful.

NOTES

1. Accord *Weissenstein v. Burlington Bd. of Sch. Comm'rs,* 149 Vt. 288, 543 A.2d 69 (1988); *Churchill v. School Admin. Dist. No. 49,* 380 A.2d 186 (Me. 1977); *State Employees' Ass'n of New Hampshire, Inc. v. Mills,* 115 N.H. 473, 344 A.2d 6 (1976).

2. In *Rae v. Bay Area Rapid Transit Supervisory & Prof. Ass'n,* 114 Cal. App. 3d 147, 1979-80 PBC ¶ 37,223 (Cal. Ct. App. 1980), the court held that the agency-shop clause included in the collective bargaining agreement between a transit district and a transit workers union was lawful even though the Bay Area Rapid Transit (BART) Act did not expressly permit the negotiation of an agency-shop clause. The court primarily relied on its determination that the term "working conditions" encompassed union security provisions and the act's omission of any explicit guarantee of the right to refrain from union activities. The court distinguished *City of Hayward* on the ground that the court there "was confronted with express language in the MMBA declaring the right of public employees to represent themselves individually, and prohibiting interference with their exercise of that right, among others." The court further stated:

> The court held that in face of those *express* statements, the agency shop was impermissible without explicit authorization. Unlike *Hayward,* the problem here is not reconciling the agency shop with statutory guarantees which seem to forbid that shop.

See also *Tremblay v. Berlin Police Union,* 108 N.H. 416, 237 A.2d 668 (1968) (agency-shop clause valid in absence of statutory prohibition).

3. In sharp contrast to the holding in the principal case, the Rhode Island Supreme Court in *Town of N. Kingstown v. North Kingstown Teachers Ass'n,* 110 R.I. 698, 297 A.2d 342 (1972), upheld the legality of an agency-shop clause even though such clauses were not specifically authorized by the applicable collective bargaining act and even though said law recognized the right of employees "to decline to join any association or organization." After noting that there was nothing in the act's legislative history which "even hint[ed] at an attitudinal approach," the court reasoned as follows:

> In evaluating those considerations which in our judgment would be likely to prompt legislative action, foremost is the argument that a certified labor organization, as sole bargaining agent for all employees in the bargaining unit, is bound by law to negotiate for both unions and nonunion members; that the negotiations are costly; that it would be manifestly inequitable to permit those who see fit not to join the union to benefit from its services without at the same time requiring them to bear a fair and just share of the financial burdens; and that no member of a bargaining unit, be he a joiner or a nonjoiner, should expect or be allowed a "free-ride."
>
> Because this argument is persuasive on the general question of the legitimacy of the agency shop does not mean that it is similarly convincing with respect to the validity of a provision calling for nonunion members to pay more than a just portion of the costs of the benefits conferred upon them. To accept such a provision as valid would, in effect, sanction an inverse "free-rider" situation in which the union member, rather than the nonjoiner, would be the "free-rider."
>
> Accordingly, our approval is expressly limited to that kind of agency shop provision which neither requires a nonjoiner to share in expenditures for benefits he is not entitled to receive, nor exacts from him more than a proportionate share of the costs of securing the benefits conferred upon all members of the bargaining unit. An agency shop provision thus limited has been recognized both judicially and at the bargaining table.

4. In states without laws authorizing public sector negotiations, it has generally been held that union security agreements are invalid. See, e.g., *Foltz v. City of Dayton,* 27 Ohio App. 2d 35, 56 Ohio Op. 2d 213, 272 N.E.2d 169 (1970) (agency fee agreement "conflict[s] with the general laws of Ohio relating to civil service and is invalid"); Mo. Op. Att'y Gen. No. 473, 370 GERR B-8 (1970).

5. State statutory provisions which authorize the deduction of union dues upon the submission of written authorizations but which permit employees to revoke such authorizations at any time have been uniformly interpreted to prohibit union-shop, agency-shop, or fair-share agreements in the absence of legislation specifically permitting these forms of union security. See, e.g., *Farrigan v. Helsby,* 68 Misc. 2d 952, 327 N.Y.S.2d 909 (1971), *aff'd,* 42 App.

Div. 2d 2653, 346 N.Y.S.2d 39 (1973); *Devita v. Scher,* 52 Misc. 2d 138, 276 N.Y.S.2d 913 (Sup. Ct. Monroe Cty. 1966); *Whipley v. Youngstown State Univ.,* 96 L.R.R.M. 3067 (Ohio Ct. C.P. 1977); Ill. Op. Att'y Gen. No. S-804 (1974).

In *Beckman v. St. Louis Cty. Bd. of Comm'rs,* 308 Minn. 129, 241 N.W.2d 302 (1976), the court held that an involuntary dues checkoff clause was invalid since the statutory provision which granted public employees the right to request a dues checkoff "carrie[d] with it by necessary implication the right to refuse such checkoff." In this case the court was interpreting the Minnesota law in effect prior to the 1973 amendments which authorized fair share deductions upon the request of the exclusive bargaining representative.

6. In *Erdreich v. Bailey,* 333 So. 2d 810, 92 L.R.R.M. 3671 (Ala. 1976), the Alabama Supreme Court held that a public employer had the authority to deduct union dues from union members who voluntarily requested that their dues be deducted from their wages. The court reasoned that if employees have the right to present requests to a public employer concerning wages and conditions of employment, "it must necessarily follow that the employer has the legal authority to assent to such request." The court noted that the power of a public employer to decline a "request for a checkoff from wages can be meaningful only in the context of the comparable power of the [public employer] to assent."

WHITE CLOUD EDUCATION ASSOCIATION v. BOARD OF EDUCATION

101 Mich. App. 309, 300 N.W.2d 551 (1980), appeal dismissed for want
of substantial federal question, 105 S. Ct. 236 (1984)

FREEMAN, JUDGE. Defendants appeal as of right from the trial court's order granting summary judgment to plaintiff on June 19, 1979, which provided that defendant Board of Education discharge intervenor-defendant Jibson for failure to pay the mandatory agency shop fee provided for in the collective bargaining agreement between the parties.

Defendant Board and plaintiff entered into a collective bargaining agreement for the 1977-1978 and 1978-1979 school years, requiring teachers to become members of the union or pay an agency shop fee equivalent to union dues as a condition of continued employment. When intervenor-defendant Jibson, a tenured teacher, refused to become a member of the union or pay the agency shop fee, the union asked the Board to hold a tenure hearing and discharge him. Based upon the Michigan Teachers' Tenure Act ("TTA"), 1967 P.A. 216 as amended, M.C.L. § 38.71 et seq.; M.S.A. § 15.1971 et seq., the Board refused to honor the union's request. The union brought this suit demanding that intervenor-defendant Jibson be discharged for failure to pay the agency shop fee.

The critical issue in this case involves a conflict between the TTA, and the Public Employment Relations Act ("PERA"), 1947 P.A. 336 as amended, M.C.L. § 423.201 et seq.; M.S.A. § 17.455(1) et seq. M.C.L. § 38.101; M.S.A. § 15.2001 provides that discharge of a tenured teacher "may be made only for reasonable and just cause, and only after such charges, notice, hearing, and determination thereof, as are hereinafter provided." Jibson argues that nonpayment of an agency shop fee is not "reasonable and just cause" for discharge of a tenured teacher, and that he is thus protected from discharge for failing to pay the fee.

In conflict with Jibson's argument is section 10 of PERA, which provides as follows:

"Provided further, [t]hat nothing in this act or in any law of this state shall preclude a public employer from making an agreement with an exclusive bargaining representative as defined in section [eleven] [footnote omitted] to require as a condition of employment that all employees in the bargaining unit pay to the exclusive bargaining representative a service fee equivalent to the amount of dues uniformly required of members of the exclusive bargaining representative." M.C.L. § 423.210(1)(c); M.S.A. § 17.455(10(1)(c).

Section 10 further provides that:

"It is the purpose of this amendatory act to reaffirm the continuing public policy of this state that the stability and effectiveness of labor relations in the public sector require, if such requirement is negotiated with the public employer, that all employees in the bargaining unit shall share fairly in the financial support of their exclusive bargaining representative by paying to the exclusive bargaining representative a service fee which may be equivalent to the amount of dues uniformly required of members of the exclusive bargaining representative." M.C.L. § 423.210(2); M.S.A. § 17.455(10)(2).

This section was so amended by 1973 P.A. 25, following the Michigan Supreme Court's decision in *Smigel v. Southgate Community School Dist.,* 388 Mich. 531, 543, 202 N.W.2d 305 (1972), that an agency shop provision requiring as a condition of employment that all employees either join the union and pay dues or pay the equivalent agency shop fee was repugnant on its face to the provisions of PERA. The United States Supreme Court has since upheld the validity of union shop clauses in the public employment sector. *Abood v. Detroit Board of Education,* 431 U.S. 209 (1977).

In *Rockwell v. Crestwood School Dist. Board of Education,* 393 Mich. 616, 629-630, 227 N.W.2d 736 (1975), the Michigan Supreme Court stated as follows with regard to conflicts between PERA and the TTA:

"This Court has consistently construed the PERA as the dominant law regulating public employee labor relations. In *Detroit Police Officers Association v. Detroit,* 391 Mich. 44, 214 N.W.2d 803 (1974), we held that residency and retirement benefits are mandatory subjects of collective bargaining under the PERA, although provisions of a city's ordinance and charter, promulgated under the home rule act, would otherwise govern. Earlier, in *Regents of the University of Michigan v. Employment Relations Commission,* 389 Mich. 96, 204 N.W.2d 218 (1973), this Court 'harmonized' the constitutional authority of the Regents to supervise the university and the authority of the Legislature to provide for the resolution of public employee disputes, holding that interns and residents in the University of Michigan Hospital were entitled to engage in collective bargaining. In *Wayne County Civil Service Commission v. Board of Supervisors,* 384 Mich. 363, 374, 184 N.W.2d 201 (1971), this Court held that the original authority and duty of the Wayne County Civil Service Commission 'was diminished *pro tanto*' by the PERA 'to the extent of free administration of the latter.'

"The analysis is the same whether we label this reconciliation repeal by expression or by implication, *pro tanto* diminishing or harmonizing. The supremacy of the provisions of the PERA is predicated on the Constitution

(Const.1963, art. 4, sec. 48) and the apparent legislative intent that the PERA be the governing law for public employee labor relations.

"The teachers' tenure act was not intended, either in contemplation or design, to cover labor disputes between school boards and their employees. The 1937 Legislature in enacting the teachers' tenure act could not have anticipated collective bargaining or meant to provide for the resolution of labor relations disputes in public employment. This Court's observation in *Wayne County Civil Service Commission, supra,* is pertinent: 'In [no] instance could collective bargaining by public employees have been in the minds of the people, or of the [1937] legislators. The thought of strikes by public employees was unheard of. The right of collective bargaining, applicable at the time to private employment, was then in comparative infancy and portended no suggestion that it eventually might enter the realm of *public* employment.' (Emphasis by the Court.)" (Footnotes omitted.)

In a more recent decision, this Court concluded that the PERA provision authorizing agency shop fees superseded both the substantive and procedural protections embodied in the TTA. *Detroit Board of Education v. Parks,* 98 Mich. App. 22, 296 N.W.2d 815 (1980). The *Parks* Court found that a collective bargaining agreement providing for discharge of a nonpaying employee was valid and enforceable, despite the TTA requirement of reasonable and just cause to terminate. The Court also held:

"Unlike section 6 of the PERA, which specifically superseded not only the substantive but also the procedural requirements of the Tenure Act with regard to teachers who are dismissed for striking, section 10 allows an agency shop agreement as a condition of employment but does not provide procedures for dismissal. In light of the legislative intent that the PERA occupy the field of labor relations in the public sector, however, it would be inappropriate to follow the procedures set forth in the Tenure Act." (Footnote omitted.)

Although the *Parks* Court rejected as inapplicable the hearing requirements of the TTA, it still found a pretermination hearing necessary to satisfy procedural due process. The sole issue at such a hearing is to be whether the recalcitrant employee paid the agency shop fee. The Court found that the Board failed to provide Parks with a hearing prior to termination. However, in a factual setting similar to the instant case, the *Parks* Court found the Board's failure to hold a hearing did not constitute reversible error:

"The agency shop clause itself does now and always has required notice of nonpayment of the fees and Parks received such notice, including notice of the possibility of discharge as a result. It would be pointless, however, to require that the Board now hold a hearing for Parks. She has already appealed her discharge to the Tenure Commission and we review its decision now. Furthermore, she has submitted an affidavit stating that she has not paid agency shop fees since 1973-74 and that she paid the fees that year 'under protest.' There is, therefore, no factual dispute to be resolved at a hearing and we hold that it is not necessary to hold one."

We find that the provisions of the TTA are not applicable to the instant dispute. We also find that employee Jibson's admitted refusal to pay requisite agency shop fees precludes the need to hold a hearing to determine the fact of payment. Therefore, the lower court did not err in ordering summary judgment in the plaintiff's favor....

[The concurring opinion of Judge Kelly is omitted.]

NOTES

1. Although the Supreme Court dismissed the appeal in the principal case for want of a substantial federal question, Justices Blackmun, Rehnquist, and Stevens would have "note[d] probable jurisdiction and set the case for oral argument." 105 S. Ct. 236 (1984).

2. Several state courts have held that agency-shop or fair-share fee clauses negotiated pursuant to statutory authorization do not contravene the rights of employees under previously enacted civil service laws. For example, in *Karchmar v. City of Worcester,* 364 Mass. 124, 301 N.E.2d 570 (1973), the Massachusetts Supreme Judicial Court held that if the parties negotiate an agency service fee agreement, "all nonunion members of the particular bargaining unit are liable to the union for the agency service fee provided in that contract," regardless of whether some or all of the employees are covered by the state's civil service law. Accord *Association of Capitol Powerhouse Eng'rs v. State,* 89 Wash. 2d 177, 570 P.2d 1042 (1977).

3. While the Michigan Court of Appeals in *White Cloud Educ. Ass'n* sanctioned discharge as a remedy for non-payment of agency shop fees, the California Supreme Court in *San Lorenzo Educ. Ass'n v. Wilson,* 32 Cal. 3d 841, 654 P.2d 202, 187 Cal. Rptr. 432 (1982), in holding that a union "may enforce through a civil action the agency shop obligations of individual employees," noted that "[r]equiring dismissal of an employee is too drastic a remedy for this court to endorse."

4. In *Anderson Fed'n of Teachers, Local 519 v. Alexander,* 416 N.E.2d 1327 (Ind. Ct. App. 1981), the Indiana Court of Appeals ruled that it was unlawful for a school board to agree to a "fair-share" provision which required the dismissal of non-members who did not pay the contractually mandated fair-share fee. The court held that the provisions of the state's school collective bargaining law "forbid any school corporation to make *any* collective bargaining agreement — for union security purposes or otherwise — in which the schools undertake the mandatory discharge of a given class of employees." (Emphasis in original.)

5. The Illinois Public Labor Relations Act provides that where a public employer and a union agree to a fair share clause, the union "shall certify to the employer the amount constituting each nonmember's employee's proportionate share" and that such amount "shall be deducted by the employer from the earnings of the nonmember employees and paid to the employee organization." Ill. Rev. Stat., ch. 48, ¶ 1606(e) (Supp. 1990). The Illinois Educational Labor Relations Act contains a similar provision. Ill. Rev. Stat., ch. 48 ¶ 1711 (Supp. 1990). These statutory provisions effectively eliminate any need to discharge or take other enforcement action against employees for failure to pay their fair share fees.

6. In *Berns v. Wisconsin Emp. Rels. Comm'n,* 99 Wis. 2d 252, 299 N.W.2d 248 (1980), the court held that it was not an unfair labor practice for a school board and a union to agree to make the fair-share provisions of their agreement retroactive to cover the period between the expiration date of the prior collective bargaining agreement and the date the new agreement was ratified. In so ruling, the court stated:

> The petitioners' position is that the imposition of fair-share fees for the period from January 1 through February 3, 1975, was unlawful, even though they received the benefits of the newly-negotiated successor agreement retroactively to January 1, 1975. This is inconsistent with the obvious aim of fair-share agreements to spread the cost of collective negotiations among all who enjoy the benefits of the bargain. The petitioners enjoyed the benefits of the successor agreement for the period from January 1 through February 3, and thus fair-share deductions for the same period are clearly in furtherance of the cost allocation rationale of fair-share.

Although the court stated that it was "not prepared to establish a maximum limit to the permissible retroactivity of a fair-share agreement," it did state that it did "not see how such an agreement could extend retroactively beyond the effective date of the benefits whose cost the fees are meant to defray."

Chapter 6

UNION COLLECTIVE ACTION—THE RIGHT TO STRIKE AND PICKET IN THE PUBLIC SECTOR

LIKE THEIR PRIVATE SECTOR COUNTERPARTS, LABOR UNION ADHERENTS IN THE public sector have established labor organizations which are not mere fraternal societies or innocuous professional associations. Many public sector unions have become militant groups formed for the primary purpose of advancing the perceived economic interests of their members, and they have not been content to rely exclusively upon the art of persuasion when endeavoring to extract bargaining concessions from public employers. Although concerted activity, in the form of the strike or the picket line, has often been legally proscribed, public sector unions have frequently resorted to "economic action" to gain leverage at the negotiating table.

This chapter deals with this troublesome phase of public sector labor relations. In a sense, the construction of the chapter may be unrealistic, because union collective action is treated as a problem separate and distinct from the issue of impasse resolution. It is surely legitimate to contend that the crucial question is not whether strikes should be prohibited in public sector labor relations, but whether the bargaining process itself and dispute resolution procedures can be made so effective that the need for work stoppages will be obviated. However, given our present state of knowledge, it is unlikely that we can devise a system that would totally supplant the need (or desire) for work stoppages. This chapter deals with some of the considerations surrounding the difficult strike issue which, combined with the various impasse resolution devices discussed in the next chapter, may offer some suggestions as to how to achieve stable and harmonious labor relations in the public sector.

Table 1. Work Stoppages in Government 1958-80[1]
(Workers involved and days idle in thousands)

	Total			Federal Government			State government			Local government		
	Number of stoppages	Workers involved	Days idle during year	Number of stoppages	Workers involved	Days idle during year	Number of stoppages	Workers involved	Days idle during year	Number of stoppages	Workers involved	Days idle during year
1958 ...	15	1.7	7.5	—	—	—	1	(3)	(3)	14	1.7	7.4
1959 ...	25	2.0	10.5	—	—	—	4	.4	1.6	21	1.6	8.8
1960 ...	36	28.6	58.4	—	—	—	3	1.0	1.2	33	27.6	57.2
1961 ...	28	6.6	15.3	—	—	—	—	—	—	28	6.6	15.3
1962 ...	28	31.1	79.1	5	4.2	33.8	2	1.7	2.3	21	25.3	43.1
1963 ...	29	4.8	15.4	—	—	—	2	.3	2.2	27	4.6	13.3
1964 ...	41	22.7	70.8	—	—	—	4	.3	3.2	37	22.5	67.7
1965 ...	42	11.9	146.0	—	—	—	—	—	1.3[2]	42	11.9	145.0
1966 ...	142	105.0	455.0	—	—	—	9	3.1	6.0	133	102.0	449.0
1967 ...	181	132.0	1,250.0	—	—	—	12	4.7	16.3	169	127.0	1,230.0
1968 ...	254	201.8	2,545.2	3	1.7	9.6	16	9.3	42.8	235	190.9	2,492.8
1969 ...	411	160.0	745.7	2	.6	1.1	37	20.5	152.4	372	139.0	592.2
1970 ...	412	333.5	2,023.2	3	155.8	648.3	23	8.8	44.6	388	168.9	1,330.5
1971 ...	329	152.6	901.4	2	1.0	8.1	23	14.5	81.8	304	137.1	811.6
1972 ...	375	142.1	1,257.3	—	—	—	40	27.4	273.7	335	114.7	983.5
1973 ...	387	196.4	2,303.9	1	.5	4.6	29	12.3	133.0	357	183.7	2,166.3
1974 ...	384	160.7	1,404.2	2	.5	1.4	34	24.7	86.4	348	135.4	1,316.3
1975 ...	478	318.5	2,204.4	—	—	—	32	66.6	300.5	446	252.0	1,903.9
1976 ...	378	180.7	1,690.7	1	(3)	(3)	25	33.8	148.2	352	146.8	1,542.6
1977 ...	413	170.2	1,765.7	2	.4	.5	44	33.7	181.9	367	136.2	1,583.3
1978 ...	481	193.7	1,706.7	1	4.8	27.8	45	17.9	180.2	435	171.0	1,498.8
1979 ...	593	254.1	2,982.5	—	—	—	57	48.6	515.5	536	205.5	2,467.1
1980[4] ..	536	223.6	2,347.8	1	.9	7.2	45	10.0	99.7	493	212.7	2,240.9

1. Includes stoppages lasting a full day or shift, or longer, and involving 6 workers or more.
2. Idleness in 1965 resulted from 2 stoppages that began in 1964.
3. Fewer than 100.
4. Last year for which the Bureau of Labor Statistics reported public sector work stoppage data.

A. THE NATURE OF THE PROBLEM

Statistics gathered by the Department of Labor, Bureau of Labor Statistics, illustrate the meteoric rise of the public sector strike from near oblivion in 1958 to substantial proportions by the 1970's.

Table 2. Work Stoppages in Government
by Major Issue, 1960-1980

(Number involved and days idle in thousands)

Year	General Wage Changes and Supplementary Benefits			Union Organization and Security			Job Security		
	Stoppages	Number Involved	Days Idle	Stoppages	Number Involved	Days Idle	Stoppages	Number Involved	Days Idle
1960	19	16.6	40.8	8	6.2	9.6	—	—	—
1965	25	9.8	128.0	12	0.9	11.5	1	0.08	0.08
1970	230	128.9	853.0	59	22.9	411.5	9	2.3	6.1
1975	316	145.3	1,255.2	25	8.2	82.6	54	90.3	449.2
1980	409	146.9	1,478.9	17	6.6	84.8	28	54.4	689.9

Moreover, the increase of strike activity in the public sector vis-à-vis the total economy increased markedly during the same period. Although the percentage of the entire employed work force involved in strikes did not increase substantially from 1958 through 1980, the percentage participating in governmental stoppages rose dramatically from 0.022 in 1958 to 1.4 by 1980.

Many theories have been propounded to explain the cause of strikes in the public sector. Some have attributed this phenomenon to the increased militancy of public sector unions which, for the first time, possess sufficient power to use effectively the traditional methods of economic coercion. Others cite a shift in emphasis in public employment from the traditional concerns over job security to the more difficult issues of wages and conditions of employment. Indeed, statistical evidence seems to support the latter theory, since most of the increase in work stoppages in the public sector between 1958 and 1980 has been caused by disputes over wages and supplementary benefits rather than other items.

Year	Administration Matters			Interunion and Intraunion Matters			Other Working Conditions		
	Stoppages	Number Involved	Days Idle	Stoppages	Number Involved	Days Idle	Stoppages	Number Involved	Days Idle
1960	—	—	—	1	0.01	0.01	8	5.8	8.0
1965	1	0.01	0.05	2	1.0	6.2	—	—	—
1970	71	11.2	32.4	3	0.9	1.8	10	3.4	35.0
1975	47	68.7	399.2	9	2.2	3.2	10	2.2	10.1
1980	44	6.2	26.2	3	3.5	24.3	4	1.0	16.1

Regardless of the causes underlying these strikes, it is noteworthy that they have persisted during a period when, for the most part, work stoppages by public employees have been illegal. Thus, whatever may be said about the causes of public employee strikes, it is apparent that the present methods of dealing with them have not proved adequate to prevent them.

On the basis of these statistics, an ostrich-like approach to the problem is not indicated. If, as in the usual view, public sector strikes are inimical to the public interest and should be eliminated or kept to a minimum, action either in terms of eliminating their causes or in deterring them, or both, is needed. Alternatively, it is arguable that not all public sector work stoppages seriously damage the public interest and that public policy, therefore, should not reflect an absolute condemnation of strike action, but rather, as in the private sector, should accept such service disruptions except where a substantial public interest (such as health or safety) is involved. In facing the problem of strike activity, this overall evaluation must surely constitute a threshold consideration.

NOTES

1. Comprehensive statistical analyses of the problem are contained in Hall, *Work Stoppages in Government,* 91 Monthly Lab. Rev. 53 (July, 1968); Torrence, *City Public Employee Work Stoppages: A Time-Line Analysis for Educational Purposes,* 27 Lab. L.J. 177 (1976); White, *Work Stoppages of Government Employees,* 92 Monthly Lab. Rev. 29 (Dec., 1969); Young & Brewer, *Strikes by State and Local Government Employees,* 9 Ind. Rel. 356 (1970); and U.S. Dep't of Labor, Bureau of Labor Statistics, Work Stoppages in Government, 1980, reprinted in 71 GERR RF 1011.

2. Some commentators have suggested that strikes in the public sector may be reduced by extending private sector recognition and grievance procedures to the public sector. See, e.g., Clark, *Public Employee Strikes: Some Proposed Solutions,* 23 Lab. L.J. 111 (1972); Zack, *Why Public Employees Strike,* 23 Arb. J. 69, 82-83 (1968). Available statistics indicate that the incidence of recognition and grievance strikes has been markedly reduced in those states providing for union recognition and unfair labor practice regulation. See Burton & Krider, *The Role and Consequence of Strikes by Public Employees,* 79 Yale L.J. 418, 439 (1970). But see Pub. Serv. Research Council, Public Sector Bargaining and Strikes (1978), summarized in GERR No. 759, 25, wherein a positive statistical correlation between increased strike activity and the recent enactment of state public employee relations statutes is demonstrated.

B. THEORETICAL CONSIDERATIONS RELATING TO THE RIGHT TO STRIKE

In dealing with theoretical considerations in this area, it might be well to question the assumption that strikes are not a fundamental and necessary part of the American collective bargaining system. Can a labor relations system work in the absence of some compulsion on both parties? If not, are there alternative devices to introduce compulsion into the system which are as effective as the strike yet not so disruptive? If public sector strikes are to be proscribed, what sanctions should be imposed on employees and labor organizations which violate that prohibition?

1. THE PUBLIC/PRIVATE SECTOR DISTINCTION

WELLINGTON & WINTER, STRUCTURING COLLECTIVE BARGAINING IN PUBLIC EMPLOYMENT, 79 Yale L.J. 805, 822 (1970)*

A. The Role of the Strike

We have argued that distortion of the political process is the major, long-run social cost of strikes in public employment. The distortion results from unions obtaining too much power, relative to other interest groups, in decisions affecting the level of taxes and the allocation of tax dollars. This distortion may, therefore, result in a redistribution of income by government, one in which union members are subsidized at the expense of other interest groups. And, where non-monetary issues, such as the decentralization of the governance of schools or the creation of a civilian board to review police conduct, are resolved through bargaining in which the strike or threat thereof is used, the distortion of the political process is no less apparent.

It has been earnestly argued, however, that if public employee unions are successfully denied the strike, they will have too little relative power. To unpack the claims in this argument is crucially important. In the private sector collective bargaining depends upon the strike threat and the occasional strike. It is how deals are made, how collective bargaining works, why employers agree to terms and conditions of employment better than they originally offered. Intuition suggests that what is true of the private sector also is true of the public. Without the strike threat and the strike, the public employer will be intransigent; and this intransigence will, in effect, deprive employees of the very benefits unionization was intended to bring to them. Collective bargaining, the argument goes, will be merely a facade for "collective begging."

Initially, it must be noted that even in the absence of unionism and bargaining the market imposes substantial limitations on the ability of public employers to "take advantage" of their employees. Because they must compete with private employers, and other units of government as well, to hire workers, public employers cannot permit their wages and conditions of employment to be relatively poorer than those offered in the private sector and still get the needed workers. And, as we noted in the *Limits* article [Wellington & Winter, *The Limits of Collective Bargaining in Public Employment,* 78 Yale L.J. 1107 (1969). — Ed.], the fact that most public employees work in areas in which there are numerous alternative employment opportunities reduces the likelihood that many public employers are monopsonists. Even if they are, moreover, the lack of a profit motive reduces the likelihood that government's monopsony power, if it exists, will be exercised.

Much of the argument about the role of the strike is, in any event, overstated. First, it exaggerates the power of the strike weapon in the private sector. As we argued in the *Limits* article, the power of private sector unions to gain comparative advantages, while real, is inherently limited by what we there called the employment-benefit tradeoff.

Second, the very unionization of public employees creates a powerful interest group, at least in large urban centers, that seems able to compete very well with other groups in the political decision-making process. Indeed, collective bargaining (the strike apart) is a method of channeling and underscoring the demands of public employees that is not systematically available to other groups. Public employee unions frequently serve as lobbying agents wielding political power quite disproportionate to the size of their membership. The failure of the Hartford firefighters, mentioned earlier, to seek formal status as a bargaining agent demonstrates how much punch such organizations can wield. And where a strong local labor council exists, association with it can significantly increase the power of public employee unions. This is some assurance, therefore, that public employees, even if prohibited from striking, will not be at a comparative disadvantage in bargaining with their employers.

Thus, on the merits, when one takes the trouble to unpack its claims, the argument for the strike in public employment is hardly inexorable.

BURTON & KRIDER, THE ROLE AND CONSEQUENCES OF STRIKES BY PUBLIC EMPLOYEES, 79 Yale L.J. 418, 424-32 (1970)*

Wellington and Winter's discussion [*The Limits of Collective Bargaining in Public Employment,* 78 Yale L.J. 1107 (1969)] of the cost of substituting collective for individual bargaining in the public sector includes a chain of causation which runs from (1) an allegation that market restraints are weak in the public sector, largely because the services are essential; to (2) an assertion that the public puts pressure on civic officials to arrive at a quick settlement; to (3) a statement that other pressure groups have no weapons comparable to a strike; to (4) a conclusion that the strike thus imposes a high cost since the political process is distorted.

Let us discuss these steps in order:

(1) *Market Restraints:* A key argument in the case for the inappropriateness of public sector strikes is that economic constraints are not present to any meaningful degree in the public sector. This argument is not entirely convincing. First, wages lost due to strikes are as important to public employees as they are to employees in the private sector. Second, the public's concern over increasing tax rates may prevent the decision-making process from being dominated by political instead of economic considerations. The development of multilateral bargaining in the public sector is an example of how the concern over taxes may result in a close substitute for market constraints. In San Francisco, for example, the Chamber of Commerce has participated in negotiations between the city and public employee unions and has had some success in limiting the economic gains of the unions. A third and related economic constraint arises for such services as water, sewage, and, in some instances, sanitation, where explicit prices are charged. Even if representatives of groups other than employees and the employer do not enter the bargaining process, both union and local government are aware of the economic implications of bargaining which leads to higher prices which are clearly visible to the public. A fourth economic constraint on employees exists in those services where subcontracting to the private

---

sector is a realistic alternative. Warren, Michigan, resolved a bargaining impasse with an American Federation of State, County and Municipal Employees (AFSCME) local by subcontracting its entire sanitation service; Santa Monica, California, ended a strike of city employees by threatening to subcontract its sanitation operations. If the subcontracting option is preserved, wages in the public sector need not exceed the rate at which subcontracting becomes a realistic alternative.

An aspect of the lack-of-market-restraints argument is that public services are essential. Even at the analytical level, Wellington and Winter's case for essentiality is not convincing. They argue:

"The Services performed by a private transit authority are neither less nor more essential to the public than those that would be performed if the transit authority were owned by a municipality. A railroad or a dock strike may be much more damaging to a community than 'job action' by teachers. This is not to say that government services are not essential. They are both because they may seriously injure a city's economy and occasionally the physical welfare of its citizens."

This is a troublesome passage. It ends with the implicit conclusion that all government services are essential. This conclusion is important in Wellington and Winter's analysis because it is a step in their demonstration that strikes are inappropriate in all governmental services. But the beginning of the passage, with its example of "job action" by teachers, suggests that essentiality is not an *inherent* characteristic of government services but depends on the specific service being evaluated. Furthermore the transit authority example suggests that many services are interchangeable between the public and private sectors. The view that various government services are not of equal essentiality and that there is considerable overlap between the kinds of services provided in the public and private sectors is reinforced by our field work and strike data from the Bureau of Labor Statistics. Examples include:

1. Where sanitation services are provided by a municipality, such as Cleveland, sanitationmen are prohibited from striking. Yet, sanitationmen in Philadelphia, Portland, and San Francisco are presumably free to strike since they are employed by private contractors rather than by the cities.

2. There were 25 local government strikes by the Teamsters in 1965-68, most involving truck drivers and all presumably illegal. Yet the Teamsters' strike involving fuel oil truck drivers in New York City last winter was legal even though the interruption of fuel oil service was believed to have caused the death of several people.

(2) *Public Pressure:* The second argument in the Wellington and Winter analysis is that public pressure on city officials forces them to make quick settlements. The validity of this argument depends on whether the service is essential. Using as a criterion whether the service is essential in the short run, we believe a priori that services can be divided into three categories: (1) essential services — police and fire — where strikes immediately endanger public health and safety; (2) intermediate services — sanitation, hospitals, transit, water, and sewage — where strikes of a few days might be tolerated; (3) nonessential services — streets, parks, education, housing, welfare and general administra-

tion — where strikes of indefinite duration could be tolerated. These categories are not exact since essentiality depends on the size of the city. Sanitation strikes will be critical in large cities such as New York but will not cause much inconvenience in smaller cities where there are meaningful alternatives to governmental operation of sanitation services.

Statistics on the duration of strikes which occurred in the public sector between 1965 and 1968 provide evidence not only that public services are of unequal essentiality, but also that the a priori categories which we have used have some validity.... [S]trikes in the essential services (police and fire) had an average duration of 4.7 days, while both the intermediate and the nonessential services had an average duration of approximately 10.5 days. It is true that the duration of strikes in the intermediate and nonessential services is only half the average duration of strikes in the private sector during these years. However, this comparison is somewhat misleading since all of the public sector strikes were illegal, and many were ended by injunction, while presumably a vast majority of the private sector strikes did not suffer from these constraints. It would appear that with the exception of police and fire protection, public officials are, to some degree, able to accept long strikes. The ability of governments to so choose indicates that political pressures generated by strikes are not so strong as to undesirably distort the entire decision-making process of government. City officials in Kalamazoo, Michigan, were able to accept a forty-eight day strike by sanitationmen and laborers; Sacramento County, California, survived an eighty-seven day strike by welfare workers. A three month strike of hospital workers has occurred in Cuyahoga County (Cleveland), Ohio.

(3) *The Strike as a Unique Weapon:* The third objection to the strike is that it provides workers with a weapon unavailable to the employing agency or to other pressure groups. Thus, unions have a superior arsenal. The Taylor Committee Report opposes strikes for this reason, among others, arguing that "there can scarcely be a countervailing lockout." Conceptually, we see no reason why lockouts are less feasible in the public than in the private sector. Legally, public sector lockouts are now forbidden, but so are strikes; presumably both could be legalized. Actually, public sector lockouts have occurred. The Social Service Employees Union (SSEU) of New York City sponsored a "work-in" in 1967 during which all of the caseworkers went to their office but refused to work. Instead, union-sponsored lectures were given by representatives of organizations such as CORE, and symposia were held on the problems of welfare workers and clients. The work-in lasted for one week, after which the City locked out the caseworkers.

A similar assertion is made by Wellington and Winter, who claim that no pressure group other than unions has a weapon comparable to the strike. But this argument raises a number of questions. Is the distinctive characteristic of an inappropriate method of influencing decisions by public officials that it is economic as opposed to political? If this is so, then presumably the threat of the New York Stock Exchange to move to New Jersey unless New York City taxes on stock transfers were lowered and similar devices should be outlawed along with the strike.

(4) *Distortion of the Political Process:* The ultimate concern of both the Taylor Committee and Wellington and Winter is that "a strike of government em-

ployees ... introduces an alien force in the legislative process." It is "alien" because, in the words of the Taylor Committee Report:

> "Careful thought about the matter shows conclusively, we believe, that while the right to strike normally performs a useful function in the private enterprise sector (where relative economic power is the final determinant in the making of private agreements), it is not compatible with the orderly functioning of our democratic form of representative government (in which relative political power is the final determinant)."

The essence of this analysis appears to be that certain means used to influence the decision-making process in the public sector — those which are political — are legitimate, while others — those which are economic — are not. For several reasons, we believe that such distinctions among means are tenuous.

First, any scheme which differentiates economic power from political power faces a perplexing definitional task.... The former concept would seem to be encompassed by the latter. The degree of overlap is problematical since there can be economic aspects to many forms of persuasion and pressure. It may be possible to provide an operational distinction between economic power and political power, but we do not believe that those who would rely on this distinction have fulfilled their task.

Second, even assuming it is possible to operationally distinguish economic power and political power, a rationale for utilizing the distinction must be provided. Such a rationale would have to distinguish between the categories either on the basis of characteristics inherent in them as a means of action or on the basis of the ends to which the means are directed. Surely an analysis of ends does not provide a meaningful distinction. The objectives of groups using economic pressure are of the same character as those of groups using political pressure — both seek to influence executive and legislative determinations such as the allocation of funds and the tax rate. If it is impossible effectively to distinguish economic from political pressure groups in terms of their ends, and it is desirable to free the political process from the influence of all pressure groups, then effective lobbying and petitioning should be as illegal as strikes.

If the normative distinction between economic and political power is based, not on the ends desired, but on the nature of the means, our skepticism remains undiminished. Are all forms of political pressure legitimate? Then consider the range of political activity observed in the public sector. Is lobbying by public sector unions to be approved? Presumably it is. What then of participation in partisan political activity? On city time? Should we question the use of campaign contributions or kickbacks from public employees to public officials as a means of influencing public sector decisions? These questions suggest that political pressures, as opposed to economic pressures, cannot *as a class* be considered more desirable.

Our antagonism toward a distinction based on means does not rest solely on a condemnation of political pressures which violate statutory provisions. We believe that perfectly legal forms of political pressure have no automatic superiority over economic pressure. In this regard, the evidence from our field work is particularly enlightening. First, we have found that the availability of political power varies among groups of employees within a given city. Most public administrators have respect for groups which can deliver votes at strategic times. Because of their links to private sector unions, craft unions are invariably in a better position to play this political role than a union confined to the public sector, such as AFSCME. In Chicago, Cleveland and San Francisco, the public sector craft unions are closely allied with the building trades council and play a key role in labor relations with the city. Prior to the passage of state collective bargaining laws such unions also played the key role in Detroit and New York City....

Second, the range of issues pursued by unions relying on political power tends to be narrow. The unions which prosper by eschewing economic power and exercising political power are often found in cities, such as Chicago, with a flourishing patronage system. These unions gain much of their political power by cooperating with the political administration. This source of political power would vanish if the unions were assiduously to pursue a goal of providing job security for their members since this goal would undermine the patronage system. In Rochester, for example, a union made no effort to protect one of its members who was fired for political reasons. For the union to have opposed the city administration at that time on an issue of job security would substantially have reduced the union's influence on other issues. In Chicago, where public sector strikes are rare (except for education) but political considerations are not, the unions have made little effort to establish a grievance procedure to protect their members from arbitrary treatment.

Third, a labor relations system built on political power tends to be unstable since some groups of employees, often a substantial number, are invariably left out of the system. They receive no representation either through patronage or through the union. In Memphis, the craft unions had for many years enjoyed a "working relationship" with the city which assured the payment of the rates that prevailed in the private sector and some control over jobs. The sanitation laborers, however, were not part of the system and were able to obtain effective representation only after a violent confrontation with the city in 1968. Having been denied representation through the political process, they had no choice but to accept a subordinate position in the city or to initiate a strike to change the system. Racial barriers were an important factor in the isolation of the Memphis sanitation laborers. Similar distinctions in racial balance among functions and occupations appear in most of the cities we visited.

C. Conclusions in Regard to Strikes and the Political Process

Wellington and Winter and the Taylor Committee reject the use of the Strike Model in the public sector. They have endorsed the No-Strike Model in order "to ensure the survival of the 'normal' American political process." Our field work suggests that unions which have actually helped their members either have made the strike threat a viable weapon despite its illegality or have intertwined themselves closely with their nominal employer through patronage-political support arrangements. If this assessment is correct, choice of the No-Strike Model is likely to lead to patterns of decision making which will subvert, if not the "normal" American political process, at least the political process which the Taylor Committee and Wellington and Winter meant to embrace. We would not argue that the misuse of political power will be eliminated by legalizing the strike; on balance, however, we believe that, in regard to most governmental functions, the Strike Model has more virtues than the No-Strike Model.

NOTES

1. The literature on the theoretical aspects of the strike ban is voluminous, with the following articles being perhaps the most comprehensive on the point: Anderson, *Strikes and Impasse Resolution in Public Employment,* 67 Mich. L. Rev. 943 (1969); Bilik, *Toward Public Sector Equality: Extending the Strike Privilege,* 21 Lab. L.J. 338 (1970); Comment, *Collective Bargaining for Public Employees and the Prevention of Strikes in the Public Sector,* 68 Mich. L. Rev. 260 (1969); Edwards, *The Developing Labor Relations Law in the Public Sector,* 10 Duq. L. Rev. 357 (1972); Kheel, *Resolving Deadlocks Without Banning Strikes,* 92 Monthly Lab. Rev. 62 (July 1969) and *Strikes and Public Employment,* 67 Mich. L. Rev. 931 (1969); Note, *The Strike and Its Alternatives in Public Employment,* 1966 Wis. L. Rev. 549; Smith, *State and Local Advisory Reports on Public Employment Labor Legislation: A Comparative Analysis,* 67 Mich. L. Rev. 891 (1968); Taylor, *Public Employment: Strikes or Procedures,* 20 Indus. & Lab. Rel. Rev. 617 (1967); Wellington & Winter, The Unions and the Cities (Brookings Institution 1971).

2. Should different treatment be accorded to public employees working in small versus large municipalities? It has been argued that strikes by public employees in smaller towns and cities may be tolerable, especially in nonessential services, but that in a city like New York any strike by public sector employees, because of its political and economic consequences, is too severe to be tolerated. Does it make sense to distinguish between large and small communities? Would such a distinction survive constitutional challenge?

3. In Dripps, *New Directions for the Regulation of Public Employee Strikes,* 60 N.Y.U. L. Rev. 590 (1985), the author rejects the traditional justifications for proscribing public sector strikes and suggests that many governmental work stoppages should be permitted. To prevent unacceptable disruptions of public services, he would require that no bargaining unit contain more than 25 percent of the employees providing a particular service. Would such an approach effectively deprive public employees of a meaningful strike weapon?

4. A very important (and sometimes neglected) factor in the theoretical considerations is that any calculation of the legitimacy of public sector strikes on the basis of "essentiality" may be likely to have considerable spill-over effects in the private sector. See Anderson, *Strikes and Impasse Resolution in Public Employment,* 67 Mich. L. Rev. 943, 950-51 (1969):

> For one thing, the ultimate resolution of public policy toward the strike issue is likely to affect the private as well as the public sector because it is difficult to distinguish between essential public and private services. Resolution of this problem is in turn complicated by the fact that federal law protects the right to strike in private employment, while public employment disputes are a matter for state regulation. The impact of certain critical disputes in the private sector has recently raised the question whether the NLRA machinery is adequate to deal with local emergencies. For example, during the strike against Consolidated Edison Company in the New York City area, the New York City Corporation Counsel considered whether the emergency procedures of the Taft-Hartley Act could be applied. A strike by fuel oil drivers resulted in the declaration by the Emergency Control Board of the City of New York that the city was in a state of imminent peril. The strike, which

occurred during the midst of a flu epidemic, brought severe hardships to apartment dwellers, home owners, and hospital patients. Thus, any test which purports to relate the right to strike to the essentiality of the service involved cannot operate to prohibit strikes in the public sector alone; the private sector also provides countless vital services affecting the health and safety of the public.

See generally Howlett, *The Right to Strike in the Public Sector,* 53 Chi. B. Rec. 108 (1971). Some commentators have noted that the utility of the strike in the private sector is increasingly being questioned. See, e.g., Clark, *Public Employee Strikes: Some Proposed Solutions,* 23 Lab. L.J. 111 (1972). If public sector employees are given the right to strike, will this result in the extension of a right to the public sector which may be of doubtful value in the private sector?

2. APPROPRIATE SANCTIONS FOR VIOLATIONS OF STRIKE PROSCRIPTIONS

REPORT TO GOVERNOR GEORGE ROMNEY BY THE MICHIGAN ADVISORY COMMITTEE ON PUBLIC EMPLOYEE RELATIONS (1966)*

... The question has been raised whether the basic "no-strike" policy expressed in the present law should be revised so as to recognize the right to strike either generally (i.e., without any specific prohibition) or at least in non-critical situations. On this issue there appear to be (or to be developing) highly polarized positions between public employers and most organizations representing public employees. The former insist that the "no-strike" prohibition represents sound public policy, and that it must be applied uniformly and be supported by adequate sanctions. The organizations, for the most part, disagree, although we find a general consensus among them that police officers and firemen should not strike. "Neutral" opinion is divided, although predominantly, so far as our inquiries indicate, accepting the view that for a variety of reasons the strike is inappropriate in public employment. However, there appears to be wide disagreement on the kinds of sanctions which should or can, with effectiveness, be used.

We think the ultimate disposition of the strike issue is far from clear. Experience in the United States and in other countries over the next several years will clarify the underlying considerations and increase the experience necessary for sound evaluation.

We think, however, that existing Michigan policy with respect to the strike issue — which is reflective of state and federal policy generally — should be continued, at least pending further experience. Consistently therewith, certain changes should be made in the law which, on the one hand, will fairly and appropriately implement that policy, and, on the other hand, will clarify it in the important matter of the distinction between group or concerted action and individual employee action.

The legislature, in enacting the amendments of 1965, continued to make strikes by public employees illegal. Controversy exists as to whether it intended

---

*The members of the Advisory Committee included Gabriel N. Alexander, Edward L. Cushman, Ronald W. Haughton, Charles C. Killingsworth and Russell A. Smith, Chairman.

to restrict available sanctions to discipline or discharge action taken by the employer. We think in any event that there should, in addition, be available in appropriate circumstances the remedy of the injunction. We reject, however, the views, variously expressed, that criminal penalties should be applied; that strikers should automatically forfeit all job rights and be denied the opportunity for re-employment; that injunctions should always be sought and, whenever sought, should always be issued, regardless of circumstances, upon a finding that a strike has occurred or is threatened; that an injunction, once issued, should be supported by a fixed scale of fines for violation of the court's order, which may not be "forgiven"; and that other sanctions, such as loss of representation rights, should be used. In our opinion these provisions could be unduly punitive, or impractical, or damaging to the collective bargaining process.

We think that, where strikes are undertaken *before* the required statutory bargaining and other dispute settlement procedures are fully exhausted (and, in the case of police and firefighters, at any time), injunctive relief should be mandatory when requested. In all other cases, the courts should be authorized to exercise their traditional right to make the injunctive remedy available if warranted in terms of the total equities in the particular case (including, of course, as a primary consideration, the impact of a strike on the public) and should retain their traditional right to adapt sanctions imposed for violation of injunctions to the particular situation.

The court, under this approach, would be expected to inquire into all the circumstances pertinent in the case, including any claim made by the defendants that the employer has failed to meet some statutory obligation. This approach assumes that not all strikes will be enjoined, or at least enjoined forthwith, but by the same token it seems to us to be inconceivable that a strike which involved serious damage to the public interest will not be enjoined. It has been argued that the circuit courts should be removed from responsibility in the area of injunctive relief since they are subject to varying "political" pressures and are too close to the scene of the dispute. To the contrary, we believe the very facts that courts are in the locale of the dispute, bear a direct and immediate responsibility for total law enforcement, and are part of the "political" process in the broadest sense, mean that the responsibility for administering the statutory no-strike policy should rest with them whenever this legal remedy is sought....

NEW YORK GOVERNOR'S COMMITTEE ON PUBLIC EMPLOYEE RELATIONS (1969 Taylor Committee Report)

Our emphasis has been, and continues to be, the development of procedures for the resolution of impasses which will assure equitable treatment for public employees and which will constitute an effective substitute for the strike. Notwithstanding the development of these procedures, there is an evident need for effective deterrents against illegal strikes. In our 1968 Interim Report we stated:

> In face of the safeguards set up in the Taylor Law for the employees, it seems indisputable that the interest of the public as a whole deserves at least

the kind of protection reserved in the law as the ultimate method of concluding the most obstinate dispute.

It is safe to say that however carefully the law may undertake to see that public employees are treated fairly and equitably, there will be those who, through impatience or in a desire to achieve more than is fair and equitable, will thoughtlessly advocate and support the use of the strike weapon. Aside from the harm this will inflict on the public and on the labor movement itself, it will promote lawlessness and disrespect for the law and the courts, which can lead to serious consequences. The fact of the matter is that Federal laws prohibiting strikes by public employees have been observed far more scrupulously, and court injunctions against strikes have been given a far higher level of respect and compliance.

It is primarily because we believe that interruption of services will not assure equity for all public employees and the public that we recommended in our 1966 Report that penalties be stipulated. Our hope was that they would serve as additional deterrents to those leaders who believe they are justified in using muscle they uniquely possess, rather than persuasion and orderliness, in advancing the cause of those they represent. The strongest deterrent should, of course, be the realization that justice can be obtained through the techniques set up in the legislation, without use of the public-punishing strike.

a. Union Deterrents

1. Deterrents Related to Contempt Proceedings

At present, the Taylor Law provides that where an employee organization has violated an order of the Court enjoining an illegal public employees' strike, the Court's discretion to levy fines for such criminal contempt is substantially limited. Section 751(2) of the Judiciary Law, as amended by the Taylor Law, limits such fine to one week's dues collections of the respondent organization or $10,000, whichever is less, or a minimum fine of $1,000, for each day that the contempt persists.

In our judgment this is an inequitable limitation and does not serve as an effective deterrent. Some large employee organizations are not deterred from asserting the right to strike because the penalties impose no real economic burden upon them. Less affluent unions may find the provision to be an effective deterrent.

We believe that limits now imposed upon the discretion of the Court in the assessment of fines for criminal contempt of its orders are unwise. We would therefore recommend that such limits as to fines for employee organizations be removed.[2]

---

[2]Our 1968 Interim Report states in part:

We also thought, and recommended, that full discretion in the enforcement of its decrees restraining illegal strikes should be returned to the court. We are of the opinion that the court would be in the best position to determine the appropriate steps to compel compliance with its orders. In the Taylor Law, however, there is a stipulated maximum fine against a defiant labor organization of the lesser of $10,000 per day or one week's dues. To one union this may be very severe; to another it may be brushed off. Indeed, one union advocating the use of the strike publicly announced that it could purchase immunity from violation of the court's injunction for a price of 25 cents per member per day.

We would prefer to leave the appropriate penalties to the court's discretion. Respect for law and the courts should not be sold off at bargain rates. We proposed that there be no limit placed

There seems to be considerable merit, however, in the mandatory and permissive guidelines in the present Taylor Law setting forth the criteria to be applied by the court in the assessment of fines. The provisions in the present law permitting deferral of payment of the fine until the appeal is finally determined and the granting a preference in appellate review of contempt convictions seem to be salutary.

We feel impelled to comment upon the imprisonment of union officials, and others, in consequence of the violation by them of an injunction against an illegal strike. From the standpoint of sound government-employee relations alone we are convinced that the possibility of such imprisonment is not an effective deterrent against engaging in illegal strikes. We have never recommended it. Nor is it a part of the Taylor Law. Indeed, achievement of the objectives of the Taylor Law could very well be enhanced if an imposition of this penalty was not a possibility. On the other hand, whether or not such a penalty is deemed by the courts to be essential for the preservation of the judicial process, upon which all of us depend for the protection of our basic rights, is a question which goes beyond the matter of government-employee relations with which we are here particularly concerned. This is a matter, therefore, for courts to determine.

2. Deterrents Related to Administrative Proceedings

The Taylor Law presently limits the authority of the State Board to suspend the right of check-off of an employee organization found to have been responsible for an illegal strike. There is a similar restriction upon the contempt power of the courts, pursuant to Section 751(2) of the Judiciary Law involving a union in an exempted municipality under Section 212 of the Taylor Law. In each case, the maximum period of suspension is 18 months.

Our belief is that an uncertainty of the extent of this sanction would operate as a more effective deterrent. The limitations which now appear in Section 210(3) of the Taylor Law and Section 751(2) of the Judiciary Law restrict the effectiveness of this approach. We believe, therefore, that the deterrent as limited by the Taylor Law is not completely effective.

We recommend, accordingly, that an illegal strike should subject the responsible employee organization to a loss of the right or privilege of check-off. An employee organization having been denied this right should be accorded an opportunity to petition the State Board or the court and the suspension should be lifted only after the organization has proved that it has conformed to the law prohibiting strikes and has affirmed its readiness, willingness, and ability to conform to such law. In the ordinary case the organization could not be accorded the opportunity to prove its bona fides until there had passed without incident at least one full contract term next succeeding the term in which the

---

on the criminal contempt fines which the court might impose on a non-complying labor organization in order to assure compliance. We have no special comment to make about the permissible punishment that may be inflicted by the courts on individuals who refuse to comply, for if the shield is taken away from the labor organizations, we believe the likelihood is that there will be less non-compliance. In any event we did not suggest any change in the level of punishment that has been customarily imposed by the courts on individuals found to be in criminal contempt. The penalty of imprisonment for individual criminal contempt did not originate in the Taylor Law nor was it discussed in our 1966 Report.

strike occurred. The suspension of check-off by the State Board or the court, therefore, would be open-ended, subject to resumption upon convincing proof of the organization's record and its readiness to conform to the law.

b. Individual Deterrents

Section 210 of the Taylor Law presently provides that a public employee who violates the prohibition against strikes *shall* be subject to certain disciplinary penalties provided by Civil Service Law for misconduct in accordance with procedures established by that law. Notwithstanding the fact that the language is mandatory rather than permissive, it appears that proceedings for individual misconduct under Section 75 of the Civil Service Law have not been undertaken to the extent necessary to serve as an effective deterrent to the participation in an illegal strike. This sanction remains within the control of the public employer. It has often become a negotiable matter in reaching a strike settlement. Where it has not been expressly waived by the public employer as a condition of restoring public services, public employers reportedly have been reluctant to impose these sanctions after a strike. It's easier that way.

In full recognition of these pragmatic considerations, we nonetheless believe that public employers have a responsibility to enforce the law. We believe it would be helpful if the officers or bodies having the power and responsibility to discipline public employees involved in a strike were required to submit to the chief executive officer of the government involved a written report dealing with the carrying out of their responsibilities to enforce disciplinary penalties upon individuals who engage in an illegal strike. Such a report should be submitted within one month after the termination of a strike, should be made public and should provide the following information: (i) the circumstances surrounding the commencement of the strike, (ii) the efforts used to terminate the strike, (iii) the names of those employees whom the officer or body had reason to believe were responsible for causing, instigating or encouraging the strike as well as findings as to their varying degrees of responsibility, and (iv) related to the varying degrees of individual responsibility, the sanctions imposed against such individual employees by such officer or body under the provisions of Section 75 of the Civil Service Law.

NOTES

1. A survey of some of the more inventive state legislation banning strikes shows a wide variety of sanctions being used. Some of the more stringent state laws include Georgia (Ga. Code Ann. ch. 45-19, §§ 1-4, covering state employees providing for five years probation for employees coupled with no pay increase for three years); Nevada (Nev. Rev. Stat. ch. 288, §§ 288.230 to 288.260, covering state and local employees, providing for injunctions, a maximum fine of $50,000 per day against the union, a maximum fine of $1000 per day against union officials coupled with an indeterminate prison sentence, and dismissal or suspension of the union rank and file); and South Dakota (S.D. Comp. Laws ch. 3-18, §§ 3-18-9 to 3-18-14, covering state and local employees, providing for injunctive relief and misdemeanors for inciting or encouraging strikes punishable by a fine up to $50,000 for the union and up to $1000 or one year in prison for the employees). See Schramm, *The Job Rights of Strikers in the Public Sector,* 31 Indus. & Lab. Rel. Rev. 322 (1978); Jackson, *Public Employer Coun-*

termeasures to Union Concerted Activity: An Analysis of Alternatives, 8 J. Law & Educ. 73 (1979); Craver, *Public Sector Impassee Resolution Procedures,* 60 Chi.-Kent L. Rev. 779, 802-11 (1984).

2. For a construction of what constitutes mitigating circumstances under New York's Taylor Act, see *Associated Teachers of Huntington, Inc.,* 1 PERB ¶ 399.84 (1968); compare, *Troy Firemen's Ass'n,* 2 PERB ¶ 3077 (1969), with *Island Free Teachers,* 2 PERB ¶ 3068 (1969).

3. Some statutes provide that reemployment of strikers is forbidden for a certain period following a strike. Should such provisions be subject to waiver at the discretion of the employer? Compare *City of Detroit v. Division 26, A.A.S.S.R. & M.C.E.,* 332 Mich. 237, 51 N.W.2d 228 (1952), with *East Bay Mun. Emps., Local 390 v. County of Alameda,* 83 Cal. Rptr. 503, 3 Cal. App. 3d 578 (1970) (agreement to reinstate strikers is binding regardless of contention that illegality of the strike served to negate consideration for the promise), and *Durkin v. Board of Comm'rs,* 48 Wis. 2d 112, 180 N.W.2d 1 (1970). Should the answer to this question also govern agreements to pay strikers for time missed while they were on strike? See *Head v. Special Sch. Dist. No. 1,* 288 Minn. 496, 182 N.W.2d 887 (1970), *cert. denied,* 404 U.S. 886 (1971). Should a city be allowed to make special overtime payments to non-striking supervisory employees for emergency work performed during a work stoppage? See *Mone v. Pezzano,* 77 L.R.R.M. 2605 (N.Y. Sup. Ct. 1971).

In *Ashcraft v. Board of Educ.,* 404 N.E.2d 983, 108 L.R.R.M. 2415 (Ill. App. Ct. 1980), the court held that teachers who were denied pay for engaging in an unlawful four-day strike were not denied due process or equal protection where the school district authorized four-days' pay to other teachers who signed affidavits indicating that they would have worked the days in question but for the fact the schools were closed due to the strike. Cf. *Bond v. Board of Educ.,* 408 N.E.2d 714, 1979-80 PBC ¶ 36,993 (Ill. 1980).

4. Should an illegal strike constitute a defense to an employer's alleged violation of its statutory duty to bargain? See *Saginaw Twp. Bd. of Educ.,* 1970 MERC Lab. Op. 127.

5. Union decertification is a device which has been prescribed by some states to enforce anti-strike provisions of their laws. See, e.g., Md. Ann. Code, Art. 77, § 160(1). Should such a provision automatically operate, even where parties have negotiated a new agreement following an illegal strike?

Although the Oklahoma teachers statute provides that a striking labor organization "shall cease to be recognized as representative" of the employees involved, the Oklahoma Supreme Court has decided that this non-recognition sanction should only be applied during the duration of the work stoppage. It determined that it would be inappropriate to permit recognition to be withheld after the strike was over, since this would deprive employees of their statutory right to be represented. See *Independent Sch. Dist. No. 89 v. Teachers Local 2309,* 1979-80 PBC ¶ 36,966 (1980). Where a statute does not expressly authorize the revocation of a union's recognized status as a penalty for an unlawful work stoppage, an illegally struck governmental employer may lack the authority to impose such a sanction. See *IBEW, Local 1245 v. City of Gridley,* 1981-83 PBC ¶ 37,823 (Cal. 1983).

6. Federal employees are prohibited from striking under 5 U.S.C. § 7311, which precludes the employment of any person who has engaged in a work stoppage against the federal government. Individuals violating Section 7311 may additionally be fined and/or imprisoned pursuant to 18 U.S.C. § 1918. A strike authorized or supported by a labor organization constitutes an unfair labor practice under 5 U.S.C. § 7116(b)(7), which was added by the Civil Service Reform Act of 1978. A guilty union may forfeit its recognition rights pursuant to 5 U.S.C. § 7120(f), with participating workers losing their "employee" status under Section 7103(a)(2)(B)(5).

Following the unlawful air traffic controllers strike in 1981, the Federal Labor Relations Authority determined that it had discretion to decide the appropriate penalty to be imposed against *PATCO*. Although the FLRA indicated that a decertification order would not necessarily be an appropriate punitive order with respect to all federal employee strikes, it determined that a decertification order was warranted in the PATCO case due to the union's willful and intentional calling and continuing of an unlawful work stoppage. See *PATCO*, F.L.R.A. No. 3-CO-105, 1981 PEB ¶42,517 (1981), *aff'd sub nom. PATCO v. FLRA*, 685 F.2d 547 (D.C. Cir. 1982).

7. Some state public sector labor relations statutes permit local jurisdictions to establish "mini"-public sector labor laws that are "substantially equivalent" to the state enactments. If a local jurisdiction's ordinance were to provide for the discretionary suspension of a striking union's dues checkoff privilege while the state law mandates automatic revocation of that right, would this difference in treatment constitute a denial of equal protection? See *Buffalo Teachers Fed'n v. Helsby*, 515 F. Supp. 215 (S.D.N.Y. 1981), *aff'd*, 676 F.2d 28 (2d Cir. 1982); *Shanker v. Helsby*, 676 F.2d 31 (2d Cir. 1982).

8. In *United States v. Greene*, 697 F.2d 1229 (5th Cir.), *cert. denied*, 463 U.S. 1210 (1983), the court held that the "prosecution of strike leaders or highly visible vocal [supporters], who are also union officials, does not in and of itself indicate impermissible selection or invidious discrimination," since prosecutors enjoy broad discretion which permits them to focus upon the most vocal promoters of unlawful conduct when deciding which people to prosecute. Accord *United States v. Taylor*, 693 F.2d 919 (9th Cir. 1982). Contra *United States v. Haggerty*, 528 F. Supp. 1286 (D. Colo. 1981) (also precluding both criminal strike sanctions and criminal contempt sanctions for same conduct due to double jeopardy considerations). See also *United States v. Hoover*, 115 L.R.R.M. 3495 (5th Cir. 1984) ("very heavy burdens" imposed upon individuals seeking to demonstrate that government prosecutions for illegal strike activity impermissibly selective).

9. A public sector labor organization may not enforce a mandatory assessment against bargaining unit members where the proceeds are to be used to support teachers who engage in illegal work stoppages. See *Male v. Grand Rapids Educ. Ass'n*, 295 N.W.2d 918, 1979-80 PBC ¶37,077 (Mich. Ct. App. 1980). Nor may a labor organization prohibit a member from being nominated and elected to union office because that member refused to participate in an illegal strike. See *Luther E. Allen, Jr. & AFSCME/SEIU*, Mass. L.R.C. Nos. SUPL-2024 & SUPL-2025, GERR No. 949, 19 (1981).

10. Empirical evidence indicates that the consistent enforcement of sanctions against unlawful strike participants reduces the frequency of such work stoppages, while inconsistent enforcement does not. The legalization of public sector stoppages increases strike activity. See Olson, *Strikes, Strike Penalties, and Arbitration in Six States*, 39 Indus. & Lab. Rel. Rev. 539 (1986). See also Comment, *Public Employee Strikes: Legalization Through the Elimination of Remedies*, 72 Cal. L. Rev. 629 (1984).

C. THE DEFINITION OF STRIKES AND OTHER COLLECTIVE ACTIONS SUBJECT TO REGULATION

United Federation of Postal Clerks v. Blount, 325 F. Supp. 879, 884 (D.D.C.), *aff'd,* 404 U.S. 802 (1971). In response to plaintiff's claim that the federal statutory proscriptions against striking and participating in a strike were unconstitutionally vague, the court noted that:

These concepts of "striking" and "participating in a strike" occupy central positions in our labor statutes and accompanying case law, and have been construed and interpreted many times by numerous state and federal courts. "Strike" is defined in § 501(d) of the Taft-Hartley Act to include "any concerted stoppage of work by employees ... and any concerted slow-down or other concerted interruption of operations by employees." On its face this is a straightforward definition. It is difficult to understand how a word used and defined so often could be sufficiently ambiguous as to be constitutionally suspect. "Strike is a term of such common usage and acceptance that 'men of common intelligence' need not guess of its meaning."... The Government ... interprets "participate" to mean "striking," the essence of which is an actual refusal in concert with others to provide services to one's employer. We adopt this construction of the phrase....

IN RE FORESTVILLE TRANSPORTATION ASSOCIATION

4 PERB ¶ 8020 (1971)

Before: I. Markowitz, Hearing Officer, New York State Public Employment Relations Board....

On or about September 25, 1969, the respondent herein entered into an agreement with the Forestville Central School Board of Education. While this agreement is unusually short (1 page), it, in fact, pertains to terms and conditions of employment and was intended by the signatories to be a collective agreement. It was signed by the President of the Board of Education and by Phyllis Swanson who was denominated "President, Bus Drivers' Association." (sic) The agreement ran from July 1, 1969 through June 30, 1970.

During the term of the agreement, the bus drivers became dissatisfied with the maintenance of discipline among the students they were carrying to and from school. As a result of this dissatisfaction, on April 16, 1970, Phyllis Swanson wrote to the Board of Education requesting a meeting with the Board on Monday, April 20th, at 8:30 a.m. The letter was delivered to Dr. Thomas Marshall, supervising principal of the school district. On April 17, Dr. Marshall informed Mrs. Swanson that the Board could not meet at the requested time, but that a meeting could take place on April 22, at 8:00 p.m.

On Monday, April 20, twelve of the district's sixteen bus drivers called in sick. The absence continued through April 24 with the number dropping from 12 to 11 on this date.

On April 21, the school district caused a temporary restraining order to be served on the bus drivers. On the following evening three of the drivers met with three Board members at which time the drivers indicated that a return to work could be effected by the dropping of further injunctive proceedings and the resolution of the disciplinary problems. On April 24, eleven drivers tendered their resignations.

An accord was reached whereby the resignations would not be acted upon and the drivers would return to work Monday morning, April 27, 1970. The return to work accordingly took place.

Unlike most strikes in both the public and private sectors of our economy, the action herein took place not during contract negotiations, but well after the collective agreement had been executed. While such an action is by no means unique, and if proven to be a strike, no less illegal, the defenses of the respondent make this case somewhat extraordinary.

... The respondent asserts that it did not "cause, instigate, encourage, conduct, or engage in a strike." Such a denial suggests two questions. First, was the action complained of a strike, and second, what was the connection of the association with the action?

As to the first question, the respondent claims that the incidents occurring between April 20 and April 24 did not constitute a strike, but were in fact absences due to illness. This mass sickness, it is argued, was occasioned by both disciplinary problems and the emotional strain caused by Dr. Marshall's alleged refusal to deal with these problems. The absences are further justified by the respondent by reference to the *Manual of Instructions of School Bus Drivers* prepared by the New York State Education Department. This manual states at p. 29 "A school bus driver must never drive a school bus when he is ill, emotionally upset or fatigued." Thus it is argued that since an individual driver suffering from emotional upset has a responsibility to call in sick, 12 drivers acting in this manner cannot be considered to be conducting a strike. It is further contended that only an individual driver is capable of determining his emotional fitness for driving, the implication being that if a driver says he is emotionally upset, there is no way to show that he was not.

Under the Taylor Law, a strike is defined to include a "concerted stoppage of work or slowdown by public employees." (CSL § 201.10) It is well established that a mass sick call may not be used as a subterfuge for an illegal strike within this definition. *In the Matter of the City School District of the City of Elmira* 3 PERB 8122 (8124) the hearing officer stated:

"Certainly the subterfuge for an illegal strike by resort to the use of mass illness and the like is not a new phenomenon in labor relations. It has been uniformly held that such employee practices are deemed a strike or concerted stoppage of work." (See also the matter of *Mahopac Civil Service Employees Association* 3 PERB 8130.)

What must now be determined is whether or not the instant sick call constituted a concerted work stoppage or was in actuality the mere coincidence of a large number of employees becoming "emotionally upset" at the same time and for the same duration. In this connection, the testimony has indicated that normal absenteeism due to sickness was no more than two drivers per day. This alone raises serious doubt as to the probability that 12 employees could, independently of each other, get sick or upset at the same time. Additionally, the fact that all employees apparently "recovered" at the same moment increases this doubt.

The testimony of the drivers themselves does little to strengthen their case. By and large those who testified stated that they were upset either because of the summons served upon them or because of specific disciplinary incidents occurring on their respective busses. While it is conceivable that the service of process in conjunction with other difficulties could upset an employee, it is difficult to imagine that all employees would be equally upset and would remain so upset for exactly the same length of time. It is even more difficult to conceive that disciplinary problems were such that employees having them could report for work for several days after the problem occurred, and *then* become so upset that they could not report for work on the very day when a majority of other employees also became emotionally upset.

The sum and substance of respondent's argument is that the Drivers' Manual be interpreted to mean that any time an emotionally upsetting problem occurs in labor relations, drivers (or anyone else dealing with the health or safety of children) be permitted to strike. Thus, not only might a subpoena trigger an emotional upset but a low salary package might as well. This clearly is not the intent of the Taylor Law, nor is it the intent of any instructional or safety manual which the State might issue. The right to strike has been denied the public employee by the legislature and only the legislature may now grant that right. Thus, the Safety Manual notwithstanding, the mass sickness constituted a strike within the definition of the Taylor Law.

We now come to the question of whether or not the respondent caused, instigated, encouraged, condoned or engaged in the strike. To make this determination the Taylor Law sets up two specific guidelines (CSL § 210.3(e)). The first of these is whether the employee organization called the strike or tried to prevent it. The second is whether the employee organization made or was making good faith efforts to terminate the strike.

As has been indicated, the testimony shows that the employee organization has an usually informal structure, and is not often looked to for guidance by the employees. This, of course, makes it somewhat difficult to determine what the respondent effectively did or did not do during the time of the strike.

On the other hand, its responsibilities during a strike are somewhat easier to ascertain. Thus, it has been held that even where there is no strike vote and the consensus to strike is obtained informally

"Where the officers and a majority of the membership of an employee organization engaged in a strike, the employee organization is responsible for such strike. 'As long as the union functions as a union, the union is responsible for the mass action of its members. This means when the members go out and act in a concerted fashion and do an illegal act, the union is responsible.'" *In the Matter of School Bus Drivers' Association, Elmira City School District* 3 PERB 8149 (8152).

Here, as we have indicated, the respondent did, in fact, function as a union, complete with officers and a negotiating team. At least 12 of the 16 drivers employed by the district participated in the strike. Most importantly, the officers of the respondent, as well as the members of its negotiating team did not attempt to prevent the strike, but instead actually participated in it. Lastly, it was only after the strike was a week old that a good faith effort by the respondent was made to terminate it. In short, it is clear that the respondent made no effort at any time between April 20 and April 24 to bring the employees back to work. At best it did nothing; at worst, it caused the strike to continue by the participation of its officers and negotiating team.

... The actions of the respondent from April 20 through April 24, 1970 constituted a strike in defiance of the "no-strike" provision of CSL § 210.1.

NOTES

1. In *City of Dover v. International Ass'n of Firefighters, Local 1312,* 322 A.2d 918, 87 L.R.R.M. 3083 (N.H. 1974), it was held that the refusal of firefighters to respond to bell alarms and mutual aid calls during off-duty hours, in order to enhance their position during the negotiation of a new bargaining agreement, constituted a concerted "slowdown" which could properly be enjoined. The court noted that "it is unlikely that any situation would arise wherein a court would permit firemen to curtail essential services without being enjoined." A similar conclusion was reached in *Kiernan v. Bronstein,* 342 N.Y.S.2d 977, 83 L.R.R.M. 3095 (N.Y. Sup. Ct. 1973), where the court sustained penalties of fines and probation imposed upon police officers who were absent from work on the date when an unlawful strike occurred. The New York Taylor Law provides that "an employee who is absent from work without permission, or who abstains wholly or in part from the full performance of his duties ... on the date or dates when a strike occurs, shall be presumed to have engaged in such strike." The court ruled that this provision did not violate due process because there was "no difficulty in overcoming the presumption and burden of proof by affidavit, ranging from death in the family to donating blood." A similar presumption is applied to federal employees who fail to explain why they are absent from work during an illegal strike. See *Schapansky v. Department of Transp.,* 735 F.2d 477 (Fed. Cir. 1984); *Adams v. Department of Transp.,* 735 F.2d 488 (Fed. Cir. 1984); but cf. *Letenyei v. Department of Transp.,* 735 F.2d 538 (Fed. Cir. 1984) (no proof that employee on leave during strike engaged in *concerted* withholding of services during strike period). For other cases that have considered the definitional problems relating to public sector strikes, see *Board of Educ., Borough of Union Beach v. New Jersey Educ. Ass'n,* 53 N.J. 29, 247 A.2d 867 (1968); *Board of Educ. v. Shanker,* 283 N.Y.S.2d 548, aff'd, 286 N.Y.S.2d 453 (N.Y. App. Div. 1967); *Holland Sch. Dist. v. Holland Educ. Ass'n,* 380 Mich. 314, 157 N.W.2d 206 (1968). In all three cases, the strike prohibition was held to cover the disputed activities. Even more interesting problems arise when police officers, instead of walking off the job, perform their work so strictly as to cause great public annoyance. Should such assiduity be classified as a "strike"? See *Purcell v. Greenwald,* 1981-83 PBC ¶ 37,361 (N.Y. Sup. Ct. 1980). See generally Comment, *Collective Bargaining for Public Employees and the Prevention of Strikes in the Public Sector,* 68 Mich. L. Rev. 260, 263-65 (1969); Kheel, *Strikes and Public Employment,* 67 Mich. L. Rev. 931, 935 (1969); Wortman, *Collective Bargaining Tactics in Federal Civil Service,* 15 Lab. L.J. 482 (1964).

2. A concerted refusal to perform ancillary job functions which have consistently been performed by employees as a group over a sustained period of time will generally be viewed as a "strike." See, e.g., *Palos Verdes Faculty Ass'n v. Palos Verdes Peninsula Unified Sch. Dist.,* Cal. PERB No. LA-CE-361, 1982 PEB ¶ 42,733 (1982); *Lenox Educ. Ass'n v. Massachusetts LRC,* 471 N.E.2d 81 (Mass. 1984) (also indicating that refusal of specific employee to perform tasks

individual to that particular worker and not customarily done by other employees not "strike" action).

3. Where an illegal work stoppage is being conducted and other public employees refuse to accept emergency job assignments necessitated by that strike because of their real fear of physical violence or future retaliation, their assignment refusals do not constitute unlawful condonation of the work stoppage. See *Van Vlack, Jr. v. Ternullo*, 425 N.Y.S.2d 347, 1979-80 PBC ¶ 36,857 (N.Y. App. Div. 1980), *rev'd on other grounds*, 1979-81 PBC ¶ 37,295 (N.Y. 1981). However, where employees unjustifiably and disingenuously refuse to drive allegedly unsafe buses to enhance their bargaining position (*Local 252, TWU v. New York PERB*, 1984-86 PBC ¶ 34,124 (1983)) or stay home because of the psychological pressures preceding an impending strike and to avoid choosing which side to support (*Zaner v. Board of Educ.*, 429 N.Y.S.2d 725, 1979-80 PBC ¶ 36,988 (N.Y. App. Div. 1980)), they will normally be viewed as "strike" participants.

The Merit Systems Protection Board has ruled that a federal employee who contests a post-strike termination based upon the defense of duress must "demonstrate, by a preponderance of the evidence, that his failure to report for work was the result of a threat or other intimidating conduct, directed toward him, sufficient to instill in him a reasonable fear of physical danger to himself or others, which a person of ordinary firmness would not be expected to resist." *Johnson v. Department of Transp.*, MSPB No. DC075281F0998 (11/15/82), GERR No. 988, 6-8. While corroborative evidence of consummated threats upon other nonstrikers is not "absolutely necessary" to a finding of duress, "a showing of actual retaliation against or harm to others ... would constitute a strong indicium of the reasonableness of the employee's fear." Accord *Martel v. Department of Transp.*, 735 F.2d 504 (Fed. Cir. 1984).

4. In *Area Bd. of Vocational, Technical & Adult Educ., Dist. No. 4 v. Wisconsin Dep't of Indus., Labor & Human Rels.*, 1977-78 PBC ¶ 36,013 (Wis. Cir. Ct. 1977), a governmental lockout of employees who were statutorily precluded from striking was found unlawful since "[t]he economic facts of life make it clear that striking and locking out are two sides of the same coin." However, a defensive lockout intended to prevent strikers from returning to work where the employer reasonably feared that they would not fully perform their required tasks was found permissible in *Utility Workers, Local 466 v. MLRC*, 389 Mass. 500, 1984-86 PBC ¶ 34,062 (1983).

BOARD OF EDUCATION v. REDDING

32 Ill. 2d 567, 207 N.E.2d 427 (1965)

DALY, JUSTICE. This action in chancery was brought in the circuit court of Bond County by plaintiff, the Board of Education of Community Unit School District No. 2 of said county, to enjoin defendants from conducting a strike against the board and from picketing its schools in support of such strike. The named defendants were a national union, its local counterpart, officials of the local, and thirteen members of the union who had been custodial employees of the board. After a hearing, the trial court denied injunctive relief and dismissed the complaint. Plaintiff has appealed directly to this court since questions arising under the State and Federal constitutions are involved. More specifically, it is the contention of plaintiff that the strike and picketing interfere with the constitutional duty of our General Assembly to "provide a thorough and efficient system of free schools," (const. of 1870, art. VIII, sec. 1, S.H.A.,) whereas defendants assert the picketing complained of is a valid exercise of free speech under the State and Federal constitutions.

Although the legal issues presented are narrow and well defined, we believe a consideration of those issues requires a statement in some detail of the facts surrounding the controversy. The plaintiff, duly and lawfully organized under the laws of Illinois, operates seven attendance centers, consisting of three grade schools, a junior high school and a senior high school in Greenville, and grade schools in Pocahontas and Sorento. It has approximately 2500 students enrolled at the seven centers, and employs 153 teachers and other personnel. Prior to September 2, 1964, its custodial force consisted of 13 employees, all of whom are defendants in this suit. The latter employees had joined or became affiliated with a local and national "Teamsters, Chauffeurs and Helpers" union and, on August 3, 1964, union officers presented to the plaintiff-board a proposed collective bargaining agreement on behalf of the thirteen employees. Plaintiff refused to sign the agreement for various reasons, the validity or propriety of which form no part of the issues in this proceeding.

On September 2, 1964, a regularly scheduled school day, the thirteen custodial employees did not report for work, but, with the help and financial support of the union, set up picket lines at each of the seven attendance centers. These lines have been maintained at all times pertinent to the case, and it appears that the picketing has been peaceful. In addition, there is no showing in the record that any of the defendants coerced or advised any persons not to cross the picket lines. The pickets carried and paraded with signs, the exact wording of which does not appear in the record; however, as recalled by witnesses, the placards stated in substance that members of "Teamsters Local No. 525" were "on strike" against "Bond County Unit District No. 2."

During the next eight days, except for nonschool days, normal school operations were disrupted as follows: (1) attendance figures were abnormally low, a circumstance which could indirectly affect State aid plaintiff would get on the basis of daily attendance averages; (2) milk and bread deliveries, as well as the deliveries of surplus foods, were not made to the school cafeterias when deliverymen would not cross the picket lines; (3) schools were not cleaned and no personnel were available for such cleaning; (4) the employees of a roofing contractor refused to cross the picket line to complete repairs on a leak in a school roof; (5) the transportation of pupils to schools was affected; and (6) the board closed the schools completely from September 8 through 10.

The complaint for injunctive relief was filed September 8 and, on such date, it appears that local union officials dispatched a telegram to plaintiff stating that the striking employees would "maintain essential sanitary services" upon request, but no such request was made....

Between September 11 and 24 the picketing continued and the schools operated, but with the following deviations from normal: (1) cleaning was done by volunteers and temporary replacements but the cleanliness of the buildings was below standard; (2) no personnel were available to fire furnaces or operate hot water systems; (3) physical education classes had to be curtailed in the junior high school due to lack of hot water; (4) it became necessary to buy a new type water heater for one of the cafeterias in order for dishes to be washed; and (5) principals and other supervisory personnel were forced to perform many duties aside from their regular educational duties. As we interpret the record, union officials advised deliverymen they could cross the picket line if they chose and the delivery of milk and bread was resumed. Some drivers delivering other supplies, however, chose to honor the picket lines, and school personnel used their own cars to go to warehouses for essential supplies. The employees of the roofing contractor continued their refusal to cross the line and, during and after rains, the leak in the roof became worse and plaster fell from the ceiling. Vandalism occurred in one of the schools over a weekend, but there is no showing that it occurred at a time when the regular custodial personnel would have been present.

The trial court refused to enjoin either the strike or the picketing, and its order dismissing the complaint found that plaintiff had failed to show irreparable injury, that the picketing was peaceful and a valid exercise of the constitutional rights of free speech, and that there was no danger of interference with the operations of the schools.... [T]he scope of our review is limited to a consideration of whether such employees may strike against their school board employer, and whether they may picket to support their strike....

[The court went on at length to find that the lower court erred by refusing to enjoin an unlawful strike].

Turning to the matter of picketing, which the trial court also refused to restrain, it is the position of defendants, and was apparently that of the trial court, that the right of working men to communicate their complaints by peaceful picketing is completely inviolable. That is to say, defendants insist that picketing is a form of free speech and when done in a peaceful and truthful manner may not otherwise be regulated or enjoined. However, the premise that peaceful picketing is immune from all regulation and control is a false one. While picketing has an ingredient of communication, the cases make it clear that it cannot be dogmatically equated with constitutionally protected freedom of speech, and that picketing is more than free speech because picket lines are designed to exert, and do exert, influences which produce actions and consequences different from other modes of communication. Indeed, these by-products of picketing which go beyond free speech are self-evident in this case. It is now well established that the latter aspects of picketing may be subject to restrictive regulations. (*Bakery & Pastry Drivers and Helpers Local 802 of Intern. Brotherhood of Teamsters v. Wohl*, 315 U.S. 769) and while the specific situation must control decision, it is more than clear that a State may, without abridging the right of free speech, restrain picketing where such curtailment is necessary to protect the public interest and property rights and where the picketing is for a purpose unlawful under State laws or policies, whether such policies have been expressed by the judicial organ or the legislature of the State. (*Hughes v. Superior Court of State of California, etc.*, 339 U.S. 460; *International Brotherhood of Teamsters Local 695, etc. v. Vogt, Inc.*, 354 U.S. 284; *Building Service Employees International Union, Local 262 v. Gazzam*, 339 U.S. 532; .... As stated by the late Mr. Justice Frankfurter in the Hughes case: "It has been amply recognized that picketing, not being the equivalent of speech as a matter of fact, is not its inevitable legal equivalent. Picketing is not beyond the control of a State if the manner in which picketing is conducted or the purpose which it seeks to effectuate gives ground for its disallowance.... 'A state is not required to tolerate in all places and all circumstances even peaceful picketing by an individual.'" 339 U.S. at 465-66.

The picketing here, though peaceful, was for the purpose of fostering and supporting an unlawful strike against a governmental employer and, being for an unlawful purpose, should have been enjoined for this reason alone. Apart from this, however, the effect of the influences exerted by the picketing was to impede and obstruct a vital and important governmental function — the proper and efficient education of our children — making its curtailment necessary to protect the patently overriding public interest....

Reversed and remanded, with directions.

NOTES

1. Most state courts have followed the view of *Redding* when determining the legality of peaceful public sector picketing conducted in conjunction with an unlawful work stoppage. See, e.g., *City of Minot v. Teamsters, Local 74*, 142 N.W.2d 612 (N.D. 1966); *State v. Heath*, 177 N.W.2d 751 (N.D. 1970); *City & Cty. of San Francisco v. Evankovich*, 69 Cal. App. 3d 41, 137 Cal. Rptr. 883 (1977); *Trustees of Cal. State Colleges v. Local 1352, San Francisco State College Fed'n of Teachers*, 13 Cal. App. 3d 863, 92 Cal. Rptr. 134 (1970). Although the *Redding* court seemed to rely heavily upon the fact that the picketing involved tended to disrupt the orderly functioning of the school, picketing that occurs away from the site of the dispute may also be enjoined. See *City of Wauwatosa v. King*, 49 Wis. 2d 398, 182 N.W.2d 530 (1971); *Petrucci v. Hogan*, 27 N.Y.S.2d 718 (N.Y. Sup. Ct. 1941). But see *Board of Educ., Union Free Sch. Dist. No. 3, Town of Brookhaven v. NEA*, 30 N.Y.2d 938 (1972), where the New York Court of Appeals denied injunctive relief to prevent the teachers' association from distributing statements urging teachers not to work for the school district, since the record did not demonstrate that the school district's operations were so disrupted that the right of free expression could be judicially curtailed. See also *Woodruff v. Board of Trustees, Cabell Huntington Hosp.*, 1984-86 PBC ¶ 34,194 (W. Va. 1984).

2. Peaceful picketing not related to or in furtherance of an illegal strike was permitted in *Regents of Univ. of Wis. v. Teaching Assistants Ass'n*, 74 L.R.R.M. 2049 (Wis. Cir. Ct. 1970), and in *Board of Educ. v. Educ. Ass'n*, 376 N.E.2d 430, 1977-78 PBC ¶ 36,313 (Ill. App. Ct. 1978). See also *School Bd. v. PERC*, 350 So. 2d 819 (Fla. Dist. Ct. App. 1977), wherein an unfair labor practice finding was sustained regarding an employer's photographic surveillance of peaceful picketing that was not connected with any work stoppage. In *Tassin v. Local 832, Nat'l Union of Police Officers*, 311 So. 2d 591 (1975), the Louisiana Court of Appeals held that the aldermen of Westwego, Louisiana, were not entitled to an injunction restraining picketing by police in front of the aldermen's private businesses, since the aldermen (who, with the mayor, embodied the city government) had no government-provided offices at which they might otherwise be effectively petitioned. See generally Staudohar, *Rights and Limitations of Picketing by Public Employees*, 25 Lab. L.J. 632 (1974).

In *Pittsburg Unified Sch. Dist. v. California Sch. Emps. Ass'n*, 166 Cal. App. 3d 875, 1984-86 PBC ¶ 34,560 (1985), the court considered the propriety of peaceful picketing and leafletting by nonstriking school employees in front of the private businesses of school board members in connection with a collective bargaining dispute. The court ruled that the peaceful picketing and leafletting were constitutionally protected speech which could not be enjoined, because they did not constitute an economic boycott or "legislative bribery."

3. *Frisby v. Schultz,* 108 S. Ct. 2495 (1988), concerned the constitutionality of a Brookfield, Wisconsin ordinance making it "unlawful for any person to engage in picketing before or about the residence or dwelling of any individual." The Supreme Court found that the ordinance did not ban all picketing in residential areas, but was limited to picketing directed at a particular residence. Since the Court found that the provision served the significant governmental interest of protecting residential privacy, was narrowly tailored to achieve that objective, and was completely content neutral, it sustained the ordinance.

4. Section 19(b)(4) of E.O. 11491 specifically proscribed the picketing of "an agency in a labor-management dispute." In *NTEU v. Fasser,* 428 F. Supp. 295 (D.D.C. 1976), Judge Gesell indicated that to the extent § 19(b)(4) prohibited all labor picketing by federal workers, including peaceful, informational, and nondisruptive picketing, it contravened the first amendment free speech guarantee. See Note, *First Amendment Challenges by Federal Employees to the Broad Labor Picketing Proscription of Executive Order 11491,* 69 Mich. L. Rev. 957 (1971). The prohibition contained in § 7116(b)(7) of the Civil Service Reform Act of 1978 appears to satisfy Judge Gesell's concern, since it applies only "if such picketing interferes with an agency's operation," and language in § 7116(b) expressly exempts noninterfering, peaceful picketing.

5. If you were asked to draft a statutory provision prohibiting all labor picketing by public employees that may constitutionally be proscribed, what language would you utilize?

D. THE STRIKE UNDER COMMON LAW AND THE CONSTITUTION

1. AT COMMON LAW

Anderson Federation of Teachers, Local 519 v. School City, 252 Ind. 558, 251 N.E.2d 15 (1969), *cert. denied,* 399 U.S. 928 (1970). In upholding a trial court restraining order against a teachers' strike and a finding that the union was in contempt of court for violating the restraining order, the Indiana Supreme Court noted that:

> [B]oth the federal and state jurisdictions and men both liberal and conservative in their political philosophies have uniformly recognized that to allow a strike by public employees is not merely a matter of choice of political philosophies, but is a thing which cannot and must not be permitted if the orderly function of our society is to be preserved. This is not a matter for debate in the political arena for it appears fundamental, as stated by Governor Dewey, public strikes would lead to anarchy, and, as stated by President Roosevelt, the public strike "is unthinkable and intolerable"....

The majority opinion cited a long list of state court opinions to support the proposition "that strikes by public employees are or should be prohibited and that injunctions should be granted to halt or prevent them." Chief Justice DeBruler, in a lengthy dissent, argued that "the majority opinion offers absolutely no justification for its holding that every strike by any public employees, including teachers is illegal, and therefore, enjoinable regardless of how peaceful and non-disruptive the strike is...." Chief Justice DeBruler also argued extensively that since Indiana had an anti-injunction statute, the trial court should be reversed because it did not follow the procedures required by that statute and, therefore, it had no jurisdiction to issue a temporary restraining order or injunction without notice or hearing in a matter involving a labor dispute. On this point, the majority had ruled that Indiana's "Little Norris-LaGuardia Act" was not applicable to disputes concerning public employees.

NOTE

Despite the impassioned exhortations of Chief Justice DeBruler, it has been traditionally recognized that at common law, public employee strikes are illegal. In addition to the extensive list of cases cited in the majority opinion, see *Board of Educ. v. Kankakee Fed'n of Teachers Local 886,* 46 Ill. 2d 439, 264 N.E.2d 18 (1970), *cert. denied,* 403 U.S. 904 (1971); *City of Evanston v. Buick,* 421 F.2d 595 (7th Cir. 1970); *City of San Diego v. AFSCME Local 127,* 8 Cal. App. 3d 308, 87 Cal. Rptr. 258 (1970); *Delaware River & Bay Auth. v. International Org. of Masters, Mates & Pilots,* 45 N.J. 138, 211 A.2d 789 (1965); *Kirker v. Moore,* 308 F. Supp. 615 (1970), *aff'd,* 436 F.2d 423 (4th Cir.), *cert. denied,* 404 U.S. 824 (1971); *State v. Heath,* 177 N.W.2d 751 (N.D. 1970); *Trustees of Cal. State Colleges v. Local 1352, San Francisco State College Fed'n of Teachers,* 13 Cal. App. 3d 863, 92 Cal. Rptr. 134 (1970).

COUNTY SANITATION DISTRICT v. SEIU LOCAL 660

38 Cal. 3d 564, 699 P.2d 835, *cert. denied,* 474 U.S. 995 (1985)

BROUSSARD, JUSTICE: — Defendants appeal from a judgment awarding plaintiff sanitation district damages and prejudgment interest in connection with defendant union's involvement in a labor strike against plaintiff. The case squarely presents issues of great import to public sector labor-management relations, namely whether all strikes by public employees are illegal and, if so, whether the striking union is liable in tort for compensatory damages. After careful review of a long line of case law and policy arguments, we conclude that the common law prohibition against all public employee strikes is no longer supportable. Therefore, the judgment for the plaintiff finding the strike to be unlawful and awarding damages, interest and costs must be reversed.

I. Statement of the Case

Defendants union (Local 660 or the union) is a labor organization affiliated with the Service Employees International Union, AFL-CIO, and has been the certified bargaining representative of the blue collar employees of the Los Angeles Sanitation District since 1973. Plaintiff is one of 27 sanitation districts within Los Angeles County and is charged with providing, operating and maintaining sewage transport and treatment facilities and landfill disposal sites throughout the county. The District employs some 500 workers who are directly or indirectly responsible for the operation and maintenance of its facilities and who are members of, or represented by, Local 660. Since 1973, the District and Local 660 have bargained concerning wages, hours and working conditions pursuant to the Meyers-Milias-Brown Act (MMBA). (Gov. Code §§ 3500-3511.) Each year these negotiations have resulted in a binding labor contract or memorandum of understanding (MOU). (See *Glendale City Employees' Assn. v. City of Glendale* (1975) 15 Cal. 3d 328.)

On July 5, 1976, approximately 75 percent of the District's employees went out on strike after negotiations between the District and the union for a new wage and benefit agreement reached an impasse and failed to produce a new MOU. The District promptly filed a complaint for injunctive relief and damages and was granted a temporary restraining order. The strike continued for approximately 11 days, during which time the District was able to maintain its facilities and operations through the efforts of management personnel and certain union members who chose not to strike. On July 16, the employees voted to accept a tentative agreement on a new MOU, the terms of which were identical to the District's offer prior to the strike.

The District then proceeded with the instant action for tort damages. The trial court found the strike to be unlawful and in violation of the public policy of the State of California and thus awarded the District $246,904 in compensatory damages,[4] prejudgment interest in the amount of $87,615.22 and costs of $874.65.

II. The Traditional Prohibition Against Public Employee Strikes

Common law decisions in other jurisdictions at one time held that no employee, whether public or private, had a right to strike in concert with fellow workers. In fact, such collective action was generally viewed as a conspiracy and held subject to both civil and criminal sanctions.[5] Over the course of the 20th century, however, courts and legislatures gradually acted to change these laws as they applied to private sector employees; today, the right to strike is generally accepted as indispensable to the system of collective bargaining and negotiation, which characterizes labor-management relations in the private sector.[6]

By contrast, American law continues to regard public sector strikes in a substantially different manner. A strike by employees of the United States government may still be treated as a crime,[7] and strikes by state and local employees have been explicitly allowed by courts or statute in only ten states.[8]

---

[4]This figure represents the following strike-related damages: Wages and FICA payments: $304,227; earned compensatory time off valued at $16,040; miscellaneous security, equipment and meal expenses: $55,080; health care benefits paid to striking employees: $6,000; less a $134,443 set off in wages, FICA and retirement benefits that the District did not have to pay out on behalf of striking workers.

[5]See *Commonwealth v. Pullis* (Mayor's Ct. Phil. 91806) reported in 3 Commons, Documentary History of American Industrial Society (1910) p. 59; *Walker v. Cronin* (1871) 107 Mass. 555; *Vegelahn v. Guntner* (1896) 67 Mass. 92 [44 N.E. 1077]; *Loewe v. Lawlor* (1908) 208 U.S. 274.

[6]Congress gradually, through a series of legislative enactments, not only granted private sector employees a right to strike and to engage in other concerted activities, but also deprived employers of their traditional remedies of injunction and damage suits. (See 38 Stat. 730 (1914) [Clayton Antitrust Act], codified as amended at 15 U.S.C. §§ 15, 17, 26 (1970), 29 U.S.C. § 52 (1970); 47 Stat. 70 (1930) [Norris-La Guardia Act], codified at 29 U.S.C. §§ 101-115 (1970); 47 Stat., pt. II 577 (1926) [Railway Labor Act], codified as amended at 45 U.S.C. §§ 151-88 (1970); 49 Stat. 449 (1935) [Wagner Act], codified as amended at 29 U.S.C. §§ 141-197 (1970))

[7]Employees of the federal government are statutorily prohibited from striking under 5 United States Code section 7311 (1976), which prohibits an individual from holding a federal position if he "participates in a strike, or asserts the right to strike against the Government of the United States ...." ...

[8]Those ten states are Alaska, Hawaii, Idaho, Illinois, Minnesota, Montana, Oregon, Pennsylvania, Vermont, and Wisconsin. (See further discussion below.) Interestingly, the United States is

Contrary to the assertions of the plaintiff as well as various holdings of the Court of Appeals, this court has repeatedly stated that the legality of strikes by public employees in California has remained an open question. In *Los Angeles Met. Transit Authority v. Brotherhood of Railroad Trainmen* (1960) 54 Cal. 2d 684, 687-688, this court stated in dictum that "[i]n the absence of legislative authorization public employees in general do not have the right to strike ..." but proceeded to hold that a statute affording public transit workers the right "to engage in other concerted activities for the purpose of collectively bargaining or other mutual aid or protection" granted these employees a right to strike. However, in our very next opinion on the issue, *In re Berry* (1968) 68 Cal. 2d 137, we invalidated an injunction against striking public employees as unconstitutionally overbroad, and *expressly* reserved opinion on "the question whether strikes by public employees can be lawfully enjoined." (*Id.,* p. 151.)

In our next opportunity to examine public employee strikes, *City and County of San Francisco v. Cooper* (1975) 13 Cal. 3d 898, which involved a suit challenging the validity of a strike settlement agreement enacted by the city, we held only that such settlement agreements are valid. After noting the Court of Appeal holding that public employee strikes are illegal and the employees' counterargument that such strikes are impliedly authorized by statute, our unanimous opinion declared that we had no occasion to resolve that controversy in that action. (*Id.,* p. 912.) ...

Before commencing our discussion, however, we must note that the Legislature has also chosen to reserve judgment on the general legality of strikes in the public sector. As Justice Grodin observed in his concurring opinion in *El Rancho Unified School District v. National Education Assn., supra,* 33 Cal. 3d 946, 964, "the Legislature itself has steadfastly refrained from providing clearcut guidance." With the exception of firefighters (Labor Code, § 1962), no statutory prohibition against strikes by public employees in this state exists.[12]

... The MMBA, the statute under which the present controversy arose, does not directly address the question of strikes.

The MMBA sets forth the rights of municipal and county employees in California. (Gov. Code, §§ 3500-3511.) The MMBA protects the right of such employees "to form, join, and participate in the activities of employee organizations ... for the purpose of representation on all matters of employer-employee relations." It also requires public employers to "meet and confer" in good faith with employee representatives on all issues within the scope of representation.

---

virtually alone among Western industrial nations in upholding a general prohibition of public employee strikes. Most European countries have permitted them, with certain limitations, for quite some time as has Canada. See, e.g., Anderson, *Strikes and Impassee Resolution in Public Employment* (1969) 67 Mich. L. Rev. 943, 961-964.

[12]For just one example, the Winton Act (former Ed. Code, § 13080 et seq.), which governed the relationship between local school boards and teachers' unions, neither affirmed nor rejected the teachers' right to strike. In 1975 the Legislature repealed the Winton Act and added new provisions to the Government Code to establish an Education Employment Relations Board (see Gov. Code, § 3540 et seq.); the new enactment also does not prohibit strikes by teachers. It also bears mention that the California Assembly Advisory Council on Public Employee Relations in its final report of March 15, 1973, concluded that, "[s]ubject only to [certain specified] restrictions and limitations ... public employees should have the right to strike" (p. 24) and proposed a statute to carry out these goals (Appen. A). However, this proposed statute was never enacted into law, perhaps further reflecting a legislative decision to leave the ultimate determination of this thorny issue to the judiciary.

As explained in its preamble, one of the MMBA's main purposes is to improve communications between public employees and their employers by providing a reasonable method for resolving disputes. A futher stated purpose is to promote improved personnel relations by "providing a uniform basis for recognizing the right of public employees to join organizations of their own choice."[14]

On its face, the MMBA neither denies nor grants local employees the right to strike. This omission is noteworthy since the Legislature has not hesitated to expressly prohibit strikes for certain classes of public employees. For example, the above-noted prohibitio.. against strikes by firefighters was enacted nine years before the passage of the MMBA and remains in effect today. Moreover, the MMBA includes firefighters within its provisions. Thus, the absence of any such limitation on other public employees covered by the MMBA at the very least implies a lack of legislative intent to use the MMBA to enact a general strike prohibition.

Plaintiffs have suggested that section 3509 of the MMBA must be construed as a general prohibition on the right to strike because its specifically precludes the application of Labor Code section 923[16] to public employees. Labor Code section 923 has been construed by this court to protect the right of private sector employees to strike (see *Petri Cleaners v. Automotive Employees,* Local 88 (1960) 53 Cal. 2d 455; yet, an examination of other California statutes governing public employees makes it perfectly clear that section 3509 was *not* included in the MMBA as a means for prohibiting strikes.

A provision identical to section 3509 is contained in the statutes governing educational employees and firefighters. However, an explicit strike prohibition is included in the firefighters statute *in addition* to this provision. The fact that the Legislature felt it necessary to include this express strike prohibition clearly indicates that it neither intended nor expected its preclusion of section 923 to serve as a blanket prohibition against strikes. Furthermore, in *San Diego Teachers Assn. v. Superior Court, supra,* 24 Cal. 3d at page 13, this court interpreted section 3549 of the EERA, a provision identical to section 3509 of the MMBA, as specifically *not* prohibiting strikes. Therefore, plaintiff's assertion that section 3509 must be read as a legislative prohibition of public employee strike cannot be sustained.

In sum, the MMBA establishes a system of rights and protections for public employees which closely mirrors those enjoyed by workers in the private sector. The Legislature, however, intentionally avoided the inclusion of any provision

---

[14] However, the MMBA contains no clear mechanism for resolving disputes. It merely provides that if the parties fail to reach an agreement they *may* agree to appoint a mediator or use other impasse resolution procedures agreed upon by the parties. Additionally, the MMBA does not authorize the establishment of an administrative agency to resolve controversies arising under its provisions. In contrast, statutes governing other public employees in California authorize the Public Employee Relations Board (PERB) to resolve disputes and enforce the provisions of the legislation. (See Gov. Code § 3541.3 (setting the powers and duties of the PERB under the Educational Employment Relations Act (EERA)); and Gov. Code, § 3513, subd. (g) [making the powers and duties of the PERB under the EERA applicable to the State Employees Relations Act].)

[16] Section 923 provides in pertinent part: "... the individual workman (shall have full freedom of association, self-organization, and designation of representatives of his own choosing, to negotiate the terms and conditions of his employment, and that he shall be free from the interference ... of employers ... in the designation of such representatives or in self-organization or in other concerted activities for the purpose of collective bargaining or other mutual aid or protection.

which could be construed as either a blanket grant or prohibition of a right to strike, thus leaving the issue shrouded in ambiguity. In the absence of clear legislative directive on this crucial matter, it becomes the task of the judiciary to determine whether, under the law, strikes by public employees should be viewed as a prohibited tort.

III. The Common Law Prohibition Against Public Employee Strikes

As noted above, the Court of Appeal and various lower courts in this and other jurisdictions have repeatedly stated that, absent a specific statutory grant, all strikes by public employees are per se illegal. A variety of policy rationales and legal justifications have traditionally been advanced in support of this common law "rule," and numerous articles and scholarly treatises have been devoted to debating their respective merits. The various justifications for the common law prohibition can be summarized into four basic arguments. First — the traditional justification — that a strike by public employees is tantamount to a denial of governmental authority/sovereignty. Second, the terms of public employment are not subject to bilateral collective bargaining, as in the private sector, because they are set by the legislative body through unilateral lawmaking. Third, since legislative bodies are responsible for public employment decision making, granting public employees the right to strike would afford them excessive bargaining leverage, resulting in a distortion of the political process and an improper delegation of legislative authority. Finally, public employees provide essential public services which, if interrupted by strikes, would threaten the public welfare.

Our determination of the legality of strikes by public employees necessarily involves an analysis of the reasoning and current viability of each of these arguments. The first of these justifications, the sovereignty argument, asserts that government is the embodiment of the people, and hence those entrusted to carry out its function may not impede it.[19] This argument was particularly popular in the first half of the 20th century, when it received support from several American Presidents.[20]

---

[19] For example, in *City of Cleveland v. Division 268 of Amalgamated Assn.* (1949) 41 Ohio Op. 236, 239 [90 N.E.2d 711, 715], the court stated that "[i]t is clear that in our system of government, the government is a servant of all people. And a strike against the public, a strike of public employees, has been denominated ... as a rebellion against government. The right to strike, if accorded to public employees ... is one means of destroying government. And if they destroy government, we have anarchy, we have chaos." A California case which relied on this sovereignty argument is *Nutter v. City of Santa Monica* (1946) 74 Cal. App. 2d 292.

[20] Commenting on the Boston police strike, Calvin Coolidge asserted that "[t]here is no right to strike against public safety by anybody, anywhere, at any time" (quoted in *Norwalk Teachers Ass'n v. Board of Educ.* (1951) 138 Conn. 269, 273 [83 A.2d 482, 484,]). Woodrow Wilson, commenting on the same strike, stated that the strike is "an intolerable crime against civilization" (quoted in *id.*, at p. 273 [83 A.2d at p. 484.]).

In another famous pronouncement of the sovereignty argument, President Franklin Roosevelt stated: "[M]ilitant tactics have no place in the functions of any organization of Government employees.... [A] strike of public employees manifests nothing less than an intent on their part to prevent or obstruct the operations of government until their demands are satisfied. Such action, looking toward the paralysis of Government by those who have sworn to support it, is unthinkable and intolerable." (*Id.* at pp. 273-274 [83 A.2d at p. 484] [quoting a letter from President Roosevelt to the president of the National Federation of Federal Employees (Aug. 16, 1937)].)

The sovereignty concept, however, has often been criticized in recent years as a vague and outdated theory based on the assumption that "the King can do no wrong." As Judge Harry T. Edwards has cogently observed, "the application of the strict sovereignty notion — that governmental power can never be opposed by employee organizations — is clearly a vestige from another era, an era of unexpanded government ... With the rapid growth of the government, both in sheer size as well as in terms of assuming services not traditionally associated with the 'sovereign,' government employees understandably no longer feel constrained by a notion that 'The King can do no wrong.' The distraught cries by public unions of disparate treatment merely reflect the fact that, for all intents and purposes, public employees occupy essentially the same position vis-a-vis the employer as their private counterparts." (Edwards, *The Developing Labor Relations Law in the Public Sector* (1972) 10 Duq. L. Rev. 357, 359-60.)

In recent years, courts have rejected the very same concept of sovereignty as a justification for governmental immunity from tort liability. In California, the death knell came in *Muskopf v. Corning Hospital Dist.* (1961) 55 Cal. 2d 211, where this court stated that, "[t]he rule of governmental immunity for tort is an anachronism, without rational basis, and has existed only by the force of inertia." (55 Cal. 2d at p. 216.) As noted by this court in *Muskopf,* perpetuation of the doctrine of sovereign immunity in tort law led to many inequities, and its application effected many incongruous results. Similarly, the use of this archaic concept to justify a per se prohibition against public employee strikes is inconsistent with modern social reality and should be hereafter laid to rest.

The second basic argument underlying the common law prohibition of public employee strikes holds that since the terms of public employment are fixed by the Legislature, public employers are virtually powerless to respond to strike pressure, or alternatively that allowing such strikes would result in "government by contract" instead of "government by law." (See *City of Los Angeles v. Los Angeles etc. Council* (1949) 94 Cal. App. 2d 36, 46. This justification may have had some merit before the California Legislature gave extensive bargaining rights to public employees. However, at present, most terms and conditions of public employment are arrived at through collective bargaining under such statutes as the MMBA.

We have already seen that the MMBA establishes a variety of rights and protections for public employees — including the right to join and participate in union activities and to meet and confer with employer representatives and confer with employer representatives for the purpose of resolving disputed labor management issues. The importance of mandating these rights, particularly the meet and confer requirement, cannot be ignored. The overall framework of the MMBA represents a nearly exact parallel to the private sector system of collective bargaining — a system which sets forth the guidelines for labor-management relations in the private sphere and which protects the right of private employees to strike. By enacting these significant and parallel protections for public employees through the MMBA, the Legislature effectively removed many of the underpinnings of the common law per se ban against public employee strikes. While the MMBA does not directly address the issue of such strikes, its implications regarding the traditional common law prohibition are significant....

The remaining two arguments have not served in this state as grounds for asserting a ban on public employee strikes but have been advanced by commentators and by courts of other states. With the traditional reasons prohibiting such strikes debunked, these additional reasons do not convince us of the necessity of a judicial ukase prohibiting all such strikes.

The first of these arguments draws upon the different roles of market forces in the private and public spheres. This rationale suggests that because government services are essential and demand is generally inelastic, public employees would wield excessive bargaining power if allowed to strike. Proponents of this argument assume that economic constraints are not present to any meaningful degree in the public sector. Consequently, in the absence of such constraints, public employers will be forced to make abnormally large concessions to workers, which in turn will distort our political process by forcing either higher taxes or a redistribution of resources between government services.

There are, however, several fundamental problems with this "distortion of the political process" argument. For one, as will be discussed more fully below, a key assumption underlying the argument — that all government services are essential — is factually unsupportable. Modern governments engage in an enormous number and variety of functions, which clearly vary as to their degree of essentiality. As such, the absence of an unavoidable nexus between most public services and essentiality necessarily undercuts the notion that public officials will be forced to settle strikes quickly and at any cost. The recent case of the air-traffic controllers' strike is yet another example that governments have the ability to hold firm against a strike for a considerable period, even in the face of substantial inconvenience. As this court concluded in *Los Angeles Met. Transit Authority v. Brotherhood of Railroad Trainmen, supra,* "Permitting employees to strike does *not* delegate to them authority to fix their own wages to the exclusion of the employer's discretion. In collective bargaining negotiations, whether or not the employees strike, the employer is free to reject demands if he determines that they are unacceptable." (54 Cal. 2d at p. 693, italics added.)

Other factors also serve to temper the potential bargaining power of striking public employees and thus enable public officials to resist excessive demands: First, wages lost due to strikes are as important to public employees as they are to private employees. Second, the public's concern over increasing tax rates will serve to prevent the decision-making process from being dominated by political instead of economic considerations. A third and related economic constraint arises in such areas as water, sewage and, in some instances, sanitation services, where explicit prices are charged. Even if representatives of groups other than employees and the employer do not formally enter the bargaining process, both union and local government representatives are aware of the economic implications of bargaining which leads to higher prices which are clearly visible to the public. A fourth economic constraint on public employees exists in those services where subcontracting to the private sector is a realistic alternative. For example, Warren, Michigan resolved a bargaining impasse with an American Federation of State, County and Municipal Employees (AFSCME) local by subcontracting its entire sanitation service; Santa Monica, California, ended a strike of city employees by threatening to subcontract its sanitation operations; in fact, San Francisco has chosen to subcontract its entire sanitation system to *private* firms. If this subcontract option is preserved, wages in the public sector clearly need not exceed the rate at which subcontracting becomes a realistic alternative.

The proponents of a flat ban on public employee strikes not only ignore such factors as the availability of subcontracting, but also fail to adequately consider public sentiment towards most strikes and assume that the public will push blindly for an early resolution at any cost. In fact, public sentiment toward a strike often limits the pressure felt by political leaders, thereby reducing the strike's effectiveness....

In sum, there is little, if any empirical evidence which demonstrates that governments generally capitulate to unreasonable demands by public employees in order to resolve strikes. The result of the strike in the instant case clearly suggests the opposite. During the 11-day strike, negotiations resumed, and the parties subsequently reached an agreement on a new MOU, the terms of which were *precisely the same* as the District's last offer prior to the commencement of the strike. Such results certainly do not illustrate a situation where public employees wielded excessive bargaining power and thereby caused a distortion of our political process.

The fourth and final justification for the common law prohibition is that interruption of government services is unacceptable because they are essential. As noted above, in our contemporary industrial society the presumption of essentiality of most government services is questionable at best. In addition, we tolerate strikes by private employees in many of the same areas in which government is engaged, such as transportation, health, education, and utilities; in many employment fields, public and private activity largely overlap.

In a dissenting opinion in *Anderson Federation of Teachers, Local 519 v. School City of Anderson, supra,* Chief Justice DeBruler of Indiana observed that the source and management of most service enterprises is irrelevant to the relative essentiality of the services: "There is no difference in impact on the community between a strike by employees of a public utility and employees of a private utility; nor between employees of a municipal bus company and a privately owned bus company; nor between public school teachers and parochial school teachers. The form of ownership and management of the enterprise does not determine the amount of destruction caused by a strike of the employees of that enterprise. In addition, the form of ownership that is actually employed is often a political and historical accident, subject to future change by political forces. Services that were once rendered by public enterprise may be contracted out to private enterprise, and then by another administration returned to the public sector." (251 N.E.2d at p. 21.) ...

We of course recognize that there are certain "essential" public services, the disruption of which would seriously threaten the public health or safety. In fact, defendant union itself concedes that the law should still act to render illegal any strikes in truly essential services which would constitute a genuine threat to the public welfare. Therefore, to the extent that the "excessive bargaining power" and "interruption of essential services" arguments still have merit, specific health and safety limitations on the right to strike should suffice to answer the concerns underlying those arguments.

In addition to the various legal arguments advanced to persuade the courts to impose a judicial ban on public employee strikes — arguments which, as we have seen, are decidedly unpersuasive in the context of modern jurisprudence and experience — there is the broader concern that permitting public employees to strike may be, on balance, harmful to labor-management relations in the public sector. This is essentially a political argument, best addressed to the Legislature. We review the matter only to point out that the issue is not so clear cut as to justify judicial intervention, since the Legislature could reasonably conclude that recognizing public employees' right to strike may actually enhance labor-management relations.

At least ten states have granted most of their public employees a right to strike; and the policy rationale behind this statutory recognition further undercuts several of the basic premises relied upon by strike-ban advocates. As the aforementioned Pennsylvania Governor's Commission Report concluded: "The collective bargaining process will be strengthened if this qualified right to strike is recognized. It will be some curb on the possible intransigence of an employer; and the limitations on the right to strike will serve notice on the employee that there are limits to the hardships that he can impose." (251 Govt. Empl. Rel. Rep., *supra,* at p. E-3)

It is unrealistic to assume that disputes among public employees and their employers will not occur; in fact, strikes by public employees are relatively frequent events in California. For example, 46 strikes occurred during 1981-1983, which actually marks a significant decline when compared to the number during the five previous years. Although the circumstances behind each individual strike may vary somewhat, commentators repeatedly note that much of the reason for their occurrence lies in the fact that without the right to strike, or at least a credible strike threat, public employees have little negotiating strength. This, in turn, produces frustrations which exacerbate labor-management conflicts and often provoke illegal strikes....

It is universally recognized that in the private sector, the bilateral determination of wages and working conditions through a collective bargaining process, in which both sides possess relatively equal strength, facilitates understanding and more harmonious relations between employers and their employees. In the absence of some means of equalizing the parties' respective bargaining positions, such as a credible strike threat, both sides are less likely to bargain in good faith; this in turn leads to unsatisfactory and acrimonious labor relations and ironically to more and longer strikes. Equally as important, the possibility of a strike often provides the best impetus for parties to reach an agreement at the bargaining table, because *both* parties lose if a strike actually comes to pass. Thus by providing a clear incentive for resolving disputes, a credible strike threat may serve to avert, rather than to encourage, work stoppages....

A final policy consideration in our analysis addresses a more philosophical issue — the perception that the right to strike, in the public sector as well as in the private sector, represents a basic civil liberty.[31] The widespread acceptance

---

[31] Another interesting and related policy argument in support of granting a right to strike to public employees rests on a recognition of the changing shape and values of the American economic system itself. In essence, it focuses on the fact that our market economy has evolved from its classical model into an increasingly mixed and pluralistic form. In this process of increased government intervention, the line between public and private enterprise has become increasingly blurred. At the same time, a concomitant blurring has occurred between traditional political and economic activity, and it is this latter overlap which renders a flat ban on all public sector strikes so difficult to defend.

of that perception leads logically to the conclusion that the right to strike, as an important symbol of a free society, should not be denied unless such a strike would substantially injure paramount interests of the larger community.

Plaintiff's argument that only the Legislature can reject the common law doctrine prohibiting public employee strikes flies squarely in the face of both logic and past precedent. Legislative silence is not the equivalent of positive legislation and does not preclude judicial reevaluation of common law doctrine. If the courts have created a bad rule or an outmoded one, the courts can change it.

This court has long recognized the need to redefine, modify or even abolish a common law rule "when reason or equity demand it" or when its underlying principles are no longer justifiable in light of modern society....

For the reasons stated above, we conclude that the common law prohibition against public sector strikes should not be recognized in this state. Consequently, strikes by public sector employees in this state as such are neither illegal nor tortious under California common law. We must immediately caution, however, that the right of public employees to strike is by no means unlimited. Prudence and concern for the general public welfare require certain restrictions.

The Legislature has already prohibited strikes by firefighters under any circumstances. It may conclude that other categories of public employees perform such essential services that a strike would invariably result in imminent danger to public health and safety, and must therefore be prohibited.

While the Legislature may enact such specific restrictions, the courts must proceed on a case-by-case basis. Certain existing statutory standards may properly guide them in this task. As noted above, a number of states have granted public employees a limited right to strike, and such legislation typically prohibits strikes by a limited number of employees involved in clearly essential services. In addition, several statutes provide for injunctive relief against other types of striking public employees when the state clearly demonstrates that the continuation of such strikes will constitute an imminent threat or "clear and present danger" to public health and safety. Such an approach guarantees that essential public services will not be disrupted so as to genuinely threaten public health and safety, while also preserving the basic rights of public employees.

After consideration of the various alternatives before us, we believe the following standard may properly guide courts in the resolution of future disputes in this area: strikes by public employees are not unlawful at common law unless

---

The argument then analogizes the deviation of the American system from classical economic models and the corresponding reevaluation of public strike prohibitions to the Solidarity-inspired developments in Poland prior to the latest military crackdown. Ironically, the traditional common law argument that public sector bargaining and striking is antidemocratic and inimical to our political process, closely mirrors the Polish government's view that unions and strikes are antisocial — indeed revisionist and reactionary — conduct in a system operated purportedly for the benefit of all. Deviations from classical models and beliefs thus confront both ideological viewpoints. The argument for a right to strike for public employees in a capitalist system clearly gains strength as society evolves away from the classical ideal of a pure market economy where the public and private sectors are clearly separated. Similarly, the case for a right to strike in a socialist system grows stronger as that society deviates from the classical ideals of the socialist model. For a more detailed analysis of this theory, see Hanslowe & Acierno, *The Law and Theory of Strikes by Government Employees*, 67 Cornell L. Rev. 1055, 1072-1073 (1982).

or until it is clearly demonstrated that such a strike creates a substantial and imminent threat to the health and safety of the public. This standard allows exception in certain essential areas of public employment (e.g., the prohibition against firefighters and law enforcement personnel) and also requires the courts to determine on a case-by-case basis whether the public interest overrides the basic right to strike.

Although we recognize that this balancing process may impose an additional burden on the judiciary, it is neither a novel nor unmanageable task.[34] Indeed, an examination of the strike in the instant case affords a good example of how this new standard should be applied. The 11-day strike did not involve public employees, such as firefighters or law enforcement personnel, whose absence from their duties would clearly endanger the public health and safety. Moreover, there was no showing by the District that the health and safety of the public was at any time imminently threatened. That is not to say that had the strike continued indefinitely, or had the availability of replacement personnel been insufficient to maintain a reasonable sanitation system, there could not have been at some point a clear showing of a substantial threat to the public health and welfare.[35] However, such was not the case here, and the legality of the strike would have been upheld under our newly adopted standard.

Defendant union has also urged this court to find that a per se prohibition of all public employee strikes violates the California Constitution's guarantees of freedom of association, free speech and equal protection. They do not contend that such a constitutional infringement is present when a court exercises its equitable authority to enjoin a strike based on a showing that the strike represents a substantial and imminent danger to the public health or safety. Instead, the union argues that in the absence of such a showing, per se prohibition is constitutionally unsupportable.

The right to form and be represented by unions is a fundamental right of American workers that has been extended to public employees through constitutional adjudication as well as by statute; in this case, it is specifically mandated

---

[34]Legislation in several states already requires the courts to make this precise determination. (See e.g., the relevant statutory provisions in Alaska, Ore., Pa. and Wis.) For just one example, under the Pennsylvania Public Employee Relations Act, public employees are not prohibited from striking after they have submitted to mediation and fact finding, unless or until such a strike creates a clear and present danger or threat to the health, safety and welfare of the public. (Pa. Stat. Ann., tit. 43, § 1101.1003.) In such cases, the employer may petition for equitable relief, including injunctions, and is entitled to relief if the court finds that the strike creates the danger or threat. (*Id.*) The Pennsylvania courts have applied this standard to several classes of public employees. (See, e.g., *Bethel Park School Dist. v. Bethel Park Federation of Teachers, Local 1607, Am. Fed'n of Teachers* (1980) 54 P. Commw. 49, 52 [420 A.2d 18] (teacher's strike constituted a clear and present danger to the public's health, safety and welfare and school district entitled to back-to-work order in view of potential losses of state subsidies, instructional days vocational job, higher education opportunities, counseling, social and health services, extracurricular enrichment programs and employees' work opportunities and wages); *Bristol Township Education Ass'n v. School District* (1974) 14 Pa. Commw. 463, 468-470 [322 A.2d 767] (school district entitled to injunction against teacher's strike under similar circumstances); *Highland Sewer and Water Auth. v. Local Union 459, I.E.B.W.* (1973) 67 Pa. D. & C.2d 564, 565-567 (sewer and water authority not entitled to injunction forcing striking employees back to work since there was no clear and present danger in view of the fact that the services provided by the authority could still be performed during the strike, apparently by supervisors, with relatively little inconvenience).

[35]Had such a showing been made, the trial court would then have had the authority to issue an injunction and declare the strike illegal. In cases involving sanitation strikes, it is often the *length* of the strike which will ultimately require issuance of an injunction....

by the provisions of the MMBA itself. In addition, "'[i]t is now settled law that workmen may lawfully combine to exert various forms of economic pressure upon an employer, provided the object sought to be accomplished thereby has a reasonable relation to the betterment of labor conditions, and they act peaceably and honestly. [Citations.] This right is guaranteed by the federal Constitution as an incident of freedom of speech, press and assemblage, [citations] and it is not dependent upon the existence of a labor controversy between the employer and his employee.'" (*In re Blaney* (1947) 30 Cal. 2d 643, 648, quoting *Steiner v. Long Beach Local No. 128* (1942) 19 Cal. 2d 676, 682)

As the union contends, however, the right to unionize means little unless it is accorded some degree of protection regarding its principal aim — effective collective bargaining. For such bargaining to be meaningful, employee groups must maintain the ability to apply pressure or at least threaten its application. A creditable right to strike is one means of doing so. As yet, however, the right to strike has not been accorded full constitutional protection, the prevailing view being that "[t]he right to strike, because of its more serious impact upon the public interest, is more vulnerable to regulation than the right to organize and select representatives for lawful purposes of collective bargaining which this Court has characterized as a 'fundamental right ....'" (*International Union, UAW, Local 232 v. Wisconsin Employment Relations Board* (1949) 336 U.S. 245, 259)

Further, the federal ban on public employee strikes has been specifically upheld as constitutionally permissible. (See *United Federation of Postal Clerks v. Blount, supra,* 325 F. Supp. 879, 884, affd. (1971) 404 U.S. 802) ...

Thoughtful judges and commentators, however, have questioned the wisdom of upholding a per se prohibition of public employee strikes. They have persuasively argued that because the right to strike is so inextricably intertwined with the recognized fundamental right to organize and collectively bargain, some degree of constitutional protection should be extended to the act of striking in both the public and private sectors.

As Judge J. Skelly Wright declared in his concurrence in *United Federation of Postal Clerks v. Blount, supra,* "[i]f the inherent purpose of a labor organization is to bring the workers' interests to bear on management, the right to strike is historically and practically, an important means of effectuating that purpose. A union that never strikes, or which can make no credible threat to strike, may wither away in ineffectiveness. That fact is not irrelevant to the constitutional calculation...."

We are not persuaded that personal freedoms guaranteed by the United States and California Constitutions confer an *absolute right* to strike,[38] but the arguments above may merit consideration at some future date. If the right to strike is afforded some constitutional protection as derivative of the fundamental right of freedom of association, then this right cannot be abridged absent a substantial or compelling justification....

---

[38] As stated in the United States Supreme Court in *Dorchy v. Kansas:* "Neither the common law nor the Fourteenth Amendment confers the absolute right to strike." (*Dorchy v. Kansas* (1926) 272 U.S. 306, 311.) Similarly, we do not find that the comparable personal freedoms guaranteed by the California Constitution confer an absolute right to strike. (See, e.g., *In re Porterfield* (1946) 28 Cal. 2d 91, 114)

As discussed at length above, the traditional justifications espoused in favor of a per se prohibition cannot withstand a significant degree of judicial scrutiny. Indeed, since not all public employee services are essential and many private employees perform services more vital to the public health and safety than do their counterparts in the public sector, the simplistic public/private dichotomy does not constitute a "compelling" justification for a per se prohibition of public employee strikes. Thus the constitutional arguments of defendant union and several amici cannot easily be dismissed, particularly since we will retain the limitation that public strikes may be prohibited when they threaten the public health or safety.[39]

Since we have already concluded that the traditional per se prohibition against public employee strikes can no longer be upheld on common grounds, we do not find it necessary to reach the issue in constitutional terms. Although we are not inclined to hold that the right to strike rises to the magnitude of a fundamental right, it does appear that associational rights are implicated to a substantial degree. As such, the close connection between striking and other constitutionally protected activity adds further weight to our rejection of the traditional common law rationales underlying the per se prohibition.

We conclude that it is not unlawful for public employees to engage in a concerted work stoppage for the purpose of improving their wages or conditions of employment, unless it has been determined that the work stoppage poses an imminent threat to public health or safety. Since the trial court's judgment for damage in this case was predicated upon an erroneous determination that defendant's strike was unlawful, the judgment for damages cannot be sustained.[40]

The judgment is reversed.

Mosk and Grodin, Justices, concur.

---

[39] Contrary to the characterization of our dissenting colleague, we neither applaud nor disapprove of strikes by public employees as a matter of social policy, for in the present state of the law that is not our function. The old rule in this state, to the effect that strikes by public employees are unlawful, rested expressly upon the premise that wages and conditions of employment for public employees may only be set by unilateral action of the public employer, and that collective bargaining for such employees in itself was contrary to public policy. *It is the Legislature which has removed the underpinnings from the old rule, by sanctioning a system of collective bargaining for local government employees.* At the same time, the Legislature has maintained a stony silence regarding the status of public employee strikes under the new statutory scheme. To the extent that we examine alternative justifications which have been asserted in support of a ban on such strikes, we do so only to determine whether there are any such justifications which are so compelling as to require acceptance by the courts even in the absence of legislative action. We find an affirmative answer only as regards those strikes which imperil public health or safety. As to other strikes, we conclude that the policy questions involved are highly debatable, and best left to the legislative branch in the first instance....

The dissent decries also what it perceives to be the ambiguity in our rule prohibiting strikes which threaten public safety or health, and states a preference for those statutes which clearly define classes of employees who may or may not strike. The formulation we have adopted, however, is in accord with the rule in several states, and the dissent points to no evidence that such a rule is incapable of effective judicial administration. On the contrary, such a rule, which depends upon an assessment of public detriment from a particular strike, is entirely in accord with the traditional role of courts in equity. If the Legislature wishes to adopt a different rule, of course it may do so.

[40] The trial court relied upon *Pasadena Unified School District v. Pasadena Federation of Teachers* (1977) 72 Cal. App. 3d 100, which held that the conduct of an illegal strike was a tort for which damages may be recovered. Since we have held that the strike in this case was not illegal, we need not consider the correctness of that decision.

KAUS, JUSTICE: — I concur in the judgment insofar as it holds that a peaceful strike by public employees does not give rise to a tort action for damages against the union. I am aware of nothing in the Meyers-Milias — Brown Act which suggests that the Legislature intended that common law tort remedies should be applied in this context, and without such legislative endorsement I believe it is improper to import tort remedies that were devised for different situations into this sensitive labor relations arena. As this court noted in *City and County of San Francisco v. Cooper* (1975) 13 Cal. 3d 898, 917, "The question as to what sanctions should appropriately be imposed on public employees who engage in illegal strike activity is a complex one which, in itself, raises significant issues of public policy. In the past, several states have attempted to deter public employee strikes by imposing mandatory draconian statutory sanctions on striking employees; experience has all too frequently demonstrated, however, that such harsh, automatic sanctions do not prevent strikes but instead are counterproductive, exacerbating employer-employee friction and prolonging work stoppages." In the absence of a determination by the Legislature that a tort action, resulting in a money damage award determined by a jury many years after the strike, is the appropriate method for dealing with public employee strikes, I do not believe the judiciary should, on its own, embrace this "solution" to the problem....

In concluding that a common law tort action does not lie in these circumstances, it is not necessary to determine whether such a strike is "legal" or "illegal" in an abstract sense, or whether, and under what circumstances, such a strike could properly be enjoined....

REYNOSO, JUSTICE, concurs.

BIRD, CHIEF JUSTICE, concurring: — ....

Today's decision brings the law of public employee strikes into the 20th century and makes the common law contemporary. As the court has explained, the flat prohibition against such strikes was grounded in outmoded notions of sovereignty and unreasoned fears of free labor organization....

The majority opinion suggests that the right to strike may have constitutional dimensions. I write separately to elaborate on this point. Although the right to strike has a long history in American jurisprudence, its textual and theoretical foundations have eluded a comprehensive analysis. Instead, the courts have danced a minuet around the issue. The time has come to make explicit that which has so frequently been presumed. If the right to strike does indeed differentiate this country from those that are not free, then it must be given substance and enforced.

The constitutional right to strike rests on a number of bedrock principles: (1) the basic personal liberty to pursue happiness and economic security through productive labor (U.S. Const., 5th and 14th Amends.; Cal. Const., art. I, §§ 1, 7, subd. (a)); (2) the absolute prohibition against involuntary servitude (U.S. Const., 13th Amend.; Cal. Const., art. I, § 6); and (3) the fundamental freedoms of association and expression (U.S. Const., 1st Amend.; Cal. Const., art. I, §§ 2, subd. (a), 3).

It is beyond dispute that the individual's freedom to withhold personal service is basic to the constitutional concept of "liberty." Without this freedom, working people would be at the total mercy of their employers, unable either to bargain effectively or to extricate themselves from an intolerable situation. Such a condition would make a mockery of the fundamental right to pursue life, liberty and happiness by engaging in the common occupations of the community...

Nevertheless, in the early years of this country, the concerted withholding of labor was outlawed under the doctrine of "criminal conspiracy." (See Frankfurter & Greene, The Labor Injunction (1930) pp. 2-3, and cases cited.) Although workers — with the exception of chattel slaves — enjoyed the right to leave employment as individuals, they were prohibited from doing so as a group. (*Ibid.*) Apparently, the courts assumed that working people could adequately protect their liberty interests by exercising their personal right to terminate employment and compete as individuals in the labor market....

The right to strike was initially regarded as labor's counterpart to the massive economic power concentrated in the corporation. With the rise of monolithic business enterprises, it could no longer be maintained that employees' freedom to compete in the labor market as individuals would be sufficient to protect their liberty interests. In a famous dissenting opinion, Justice Oliver Wendell Holmes observed: "One of the eternal conflicts out of which life is made up is that between the effort of every man to get the most he can for his services, and that of society, disguised under the name of capital, to get his services for the least possible return. Combination on the one side is patent and powerful. Combination on the other is the necessary and desirable counterpart, if the battle is to be carried on in a fair and equal way." (*Vegelahn v. Guntner* (Mass. 1896) 44 N.E. 1077, 1081 (dis. opn. of Holmes, J.).) ...

This theoretical foundation was later adopted by the United States Supreme Court. In an opinion by Chief Justice Taft, the court declared: "[Unions] were organized out of the necessities of the situation. A single employee was helpless in dealing with an employer. He was dependent ordinarily on his daily wage for the maintenance of himself and family. If the employer refused to pay him the wages that he thought fair, he was nevertheless unable to leave the employ and to resist arbitrary and unfair treatment. Union was essential to give laborers opportunity to deal on equality with their employer. They united to exert influence upon him and to leave him in a body in order by this inconvenience to induce him to make better terms with them. They were withholding their labor of economic value to make him pay what they thought it was worth. The right to combine for such a lawful purpose has in many years not been denied by any court." (*Amer. Foundaries v. Tri-City Council, supra,* 257 U.S. at p. 209.) ...

Though these forceful statements suggest that the Supreme Court included the right to strike among those liberties protected by the Constitution, that proposition was never squarely asserted....

The close connection between the right to strike and the prohibition against involuntary servitude derives from the purposes of the 13th Amendment. That amendment guarantees the freedom to terminate employment not for its own sake, but in order to "prohibit[ ] that control by which the personal service of one man is disposed of or coerced for another's benefit which is the essence of involuntary servitude." (*Bailey v. Alabama* (1911) 219 U.S. 219, 241.)

Accordingly, the amendment is concerned not merely with the formal right to quit, but also with the *practical ability of working people to protect their interests in the workplace:* "[I]n general the defense against oppressive hours, pay, working conditions, or treatment is the right to change employers. When the master can compel and the laborer cannot escape the obligation to go on, there is no power below to redress and no incentive above to relieve a harsh overlordship or unwholesome conditions of work." (*Pollock v. Williams* (1944) 322 U.S. 4, 18).

As courts and commentators universally acknowledge, the group right to strike has replaced the individual right to "change employers" as the principal defense of working people against oppressive conditions. The rise of multinational corporations and large-scale government has produced a corresponding decrease in the practical significance of the right to quit for the individual. To withdraw the right to strike is to deprive the worker of his or her only effective bargaining power....

The notion of a 13th Amendment right to strike has been rejected by some lower federal courts and state courts. These courts have relied on two lines of reasoning. First, some have suggested that the prohibition against involuntary servitude protects only the right of employees to withhold personal services as individuals. (See, e.g., *Western Union Tel. Co. v. International B. of E. Workers* (N.D. Ill. 1924) 2 Fed.2d 993, 994-995, *affd.* (7th Cir. 1925) 6 F.2d 444.) However, as explained above, this line of argument cannot justify the total nonprotection of strike activities in an economy dominated by large and powerful employers.

Other courts have held that the 13th Amendment does not protect a *temporary* withholding of labor. (See, e.g., *Dayton Co. v. Carpet, Linoleum and Resilient Fl. D., etc.* (Minn. 1949) 39 N.W.2d 183, 197-198, *app. dism.*, (1950) 339 U.S. 906). However, in view of the purposes of the prohibition on involuntary servitude, "can it matter whether the worker quits permanently or merely leaves the establishment until conditions are changed? In the former case he may be said to be exercising the right to sell his services to the highest bidder, leaving others to take his former job, while in the latter case he is seeking to injure the employer by cutting off the supply of labor. But this reasoning scarcely justifies a constitutional distinction, for in either case the improvement of employment conditions ultimately depends upon withholding of labor from marginal employers until they offer more.... [T]he temporary or permanent character of the quitting seems irrelevant."

More fundamentally, it is not suggested here that the prohibition on involuntary servitude standing alone necessarily guarantees the right to strike. That provision does, however, provide ample support for the proposition that the right to strike must be counted among those constitutionally protected "liberties" that are essential to human freedom.

The concerted withholding of labor warrants protection not only as an exercise of personal liberty, but also as an incident of the fundamental freedoms of association and expression....

Working people enjoy the constitutional right to form and join unions. (See, e.g., *Orr v. Thorpe* (5th Cir. 1070) 427 F.2d 1129, 1131; *American Federation of State, Co., & Mun. Emp. v. Woodward* (8th Cir. 1969) 406 F.2d 137, 139-140.) Without a constitutionally protected right to strike, the use of these freedoms would be "little more than an exercise in sterile ritualism." (*School Committee v. Westerly Teachers Ass'n* (R.I. 1973) 299 A.2d 441, 448 (dis. opn.

of Roberts, C.J.); see also *United Federation of Postal Clerks v. Blount* (D.D.C. 1971) 325 F. Supp. 879, 885 (conc. opn. of Wright, J.), *affd. mem.* 404 U.S. 802.

Recent decisions concerning consumer boycotts provide persuasive authority for the protection of strikes under the guarantees of free association and expression. Consumer boycotts were, like strikes, originally prohibited at common law. (See generally, Note, *Political Boycott Activity and the First Amendment,* 91 Harv. L. Rev. at pp. 676-677.) ...

In *NAACP v. Claiborne Hardware Co.* (1982) 458 U.S. 886, 907-915 (hereafter *Claiborne Hardware*), the United States Supreme Court held that a peaceful, politically motivated boycott constituted an exercise of the constitutional freedoms of association and expression. In that case, black citizens of Port Gibson, Mississippi, boycotted white-owned businesses to pressure those businesses and elected public officials to implement policies of racial equality.... The court rejected the common law view that boycotts were devoid of constitutional value by virtue of their coercive nature. "Speech does not lose its protected character ... simply because it may embarrass others or coerce them into action." (*Id.,* at p. 910.) On the contrary, the boycott was entitled to protection as an effective and nonviolent means of bringing about political, social, and economic change. (*Id.,* at pp. 907-915.) Accordingly, "[t]he right of the States to regulate economic activity could not justify a complete prohibition" against the boycott. (*Id.,* at p. 914.) ...

I see no principled basis for granting protection to "politically motivated" consumer boycotts while withdrawing protection from labor boycotts.... The issues that arise in the workplace rival those addressed in the political process in their actual impact on the breadth of liberty enjoyed by working people. The strike is an essential weapon in the worker's defense against "that control by which the personal service of one man is disposed of or coerced for another's benefit ...." (*Bailey v. Alabama, supra,* 219 U.S. at p. 241.) And, it is a weapon that employs the constitutionally favored methods for promoting change: peaceful association and expression. Surely, the Constitution protects the efforts of working people to preserve and expand their liberties by means of nonviolent — albeit outspoken and impolite — forms of association and expression. (Cf. *Claiborne Hardware, supra,* 458 U.S. at pp. 907-912.)

As the Polish strikers discovered, a free labor organization cannot coexist with political tyranny. The converse is no less true: "Collective bargaining is today, as Brandeis pointed out, the means of establishing industrial democracy as the essential condition of political democracy, the means of providing for the workers' lives in industry the sense of worth, of freedom, and of participation that democratic government promises them as citizens." ...

The right to strike must be guaranteed to public and private employees alike. In accepting public employment, individuals do not thereby sacrifice their constitutional rights. (See, e.g., *Bagley v. Washington Township Hospital Dist.* (1966) 65 Cal. 2d 499, 503-505.) The constitutional guarantees of personal liberty, freedom of association, and freedom of expression are no less important to public workers than to other working people....

It has been argued that public employee strikes lack constitutional protection since they enable public workers to exercise a disproportionate influence on the political process.... However, as the present majority opinion explains, the coercive potential of public employee strikes is sharply limited by economic and political conditions. Many government services can be foregone over substantial periods without serious harm. Others can be contracted out to private industry. Where services are financed by user fees, the users can exert effective pressure against the strikers. Last but not least, the taxpaying public in general frequently mounts effective opposition to public employee strikes....

This court can scarcely deny to working people the protections that are accorded the forms of economic power possessed by other groups. As Justice Traynor once observed, the courts "should not impose ideal standards on one side [of a conflict among groups in society] when they are powerless to impose similar standards upon the other." (*Hughes v. Superior Court, supra,* 32 Cal. 2d at p. 868 (dis. opn. of Traynor, J.).)

It remains only to determine whether the common law's flat prohibition on public employee strikes is necessary to serve a compelling state interest. The majority have convincingly refuted the traditional justifications for that ban. Although the state has a compelling interest in averting immediate and serious threats to the public health and safety, a flat ban on public employee strikes is by no means the least restrictive method for accomplishing that end. Accordingly, today's holding is compelled not only by common law principles but also by the California Constitution.

GRODIN, JUSTICE, concurring: — Though I have signed Justice Broussard's plurality opinion, I write separately in response to the concerns expressed in the concurring opinion by Justice Kaus.

I suggest there is little merit in attempting to distinguish, with regard to strikes by employees covered by the Meyers-Milias-Brown Act, between the availability of an injunction at common law and the availability of a damage action. If an injunction is violated, the violation can give rise to a proceeding in contempt for which monetary sanctions may be imposed. The underlying legal question is whether there exists a common law predicate for either remedy. The plurality opinion holds, and I agree, that the Meyers-Milias-Brown Act has removed the principal theoretical justification which had been advanced in this state for the proposition that all strikes by local government employees are tortious. Finding no alternative justification sufficiently compelling to require acceptance by the courts in the absence of legislative action, except as regards strikes which imperil public health or safety, the opinion properly places the ball in the Legislature's court, where it belongs....

LUCAS, JUSTICE, dissenting: — I respectfully dissent. In my view, public employees in this state neither have the right to strike, nor should they have that right. In any event, in light of the difficulty in fashioning proper exceptions to the basic "no strike" rule, and the dangers to public health and safety arising from even a *temporary* cessation of governmental services, the courts should defer to the Legislature, a body far better equipped to create such exceptions.

The majority paints a glowing picture of the public strike weapon as a means of "enhanc[ing] labor-management relations," "equalizing the parties' respective bargaining positions," assuring "good faith" collective bargaining, and "providing a clear incentive for resolving disputes." Indeed, so enamored is the majority with the concept of the public strike that it elevates this heretofore *illegal* device to a "basic civil liberty." Though wholly unnecessary to its opinion, the majority in dictum even suggests that public employees may have a *constitutional* right to strike which cannot be legislatively abridged absent some "substantial or compelling justification."

Thus, in the face of an unbroken string of Court of Appeal cases commencing nearly 35 years ago which hold that public strikes are illegal, we suddenly announce our finding that public strikes are not only lawful in most cases, but indeed they may constitute a panacea for many of the social and economic ills which have long beset the public sector. One may wonder, as I do, why we kept that revelation a secret for all these years. (See *El Rancho Unified School District v. National Education Assn.* (1983) 33 Cal. 3d 946, 962 [conc. opn. by Richardson, J.].)

Despite the majority's encomiums, the fact remains that public strikes may devastate a city within a matter of days, or even hours, depending on the circumstances. For this reason, among many others, the courts of this state (and the vast majority of courts in other states and the federal government) have declared *all* public strikes illegal....

Justice Couglin's opinion in *City of San Diego v. American Fed'n of State etc. Employees* (1970), 8 Cal. App. 3d 308, offers a cogent analysis of the various rationales underlying the "no strike" rule. He observed that "This California common law rule is the generally accepted common law rule in many jurisdictions. [Citations, including cases from 24 states.]

"The common law rule has been adopted or confirmed statutorily by 20 states and the federal government. [Citations.]

"...The common law rule [that] public employees do not have the right to bargain collectively or to strike is predicated expressly on the necessity for and lack of statutory authority conferring such right. Where a statute authorizes collective bargaining and strikes it includes them within the methods authorized by law for fixing the terms and conditions of employment. *Those who advocate the right of public employees to strike should present their case to the Legislature.* [Italics added.]

"....

"Wherever the issue has been raised, it has been held laws governing the rights of public employees to engage in union activities, collective bargaining, strikes and other coercive practices, not equally applicable to private employees, and vice versa, are premised on a constitutionally approved classification; and, for this reason, are not violative of the constitutional guarantee of equal protection of the law. [Citations.] The reasons for the law denying public employees the right to strike while affording such right to private employees are not premised on differences in types of jobs held by these two classes of employees but upon differences in the employment relationship to which they are parties. The legitimate and compelling state interest accomplished and promoted by the law denying public employees the right to strike is not solely the need for a particular governmental service but the preservation of a system of government in the ambit of public employer-employee relationship. [Citation.]" 8 Cal. App. 3d at pp. 311-315.

The decision to allow public employee strikes requires a delicate and complex balancing process best undertaken by the Legislature, which may formulate a comprehensive regulatory scheme designed to avoid the disruption and chaos which invariably follow a cessation or interruption of governmental sevices. The majority's own proposal, to withhold the strike weapon only where "truly essential" services are involved and a "substantial and imminent threat" is posed, will afford little guidance to our trial courts who must, on a "case-by-case" basis, decide such issues. Nor will representatives of labor or management be able to predict with any confidence or certainty whether a particular strike is a lawful one or, being lawful at its inception, will become unlawful by reason of its adverse effects upon the public health and safety. In short, the majority's broad holding will prove as unworkable as it is unwise.

Of the few states that permit strikes by public employees, virtually all do so by comprehensive statutory provisions. Some of the statutory schemes begin by creating classifications of employees, distinguishing, for example, workers whose services are deemed essential (e.g., police, firefighters), those whose services may be interrupted for short periods of time (e.g., teachers), and those whose services may be omitted for an extended time (e.g., municipal golf course attendants). These schemes typically define various prerequisites to the exercise of the right to strike for those categories of workers permitted that option. The prerequisites include a period of mandatory mediation as well as advance notice to the employer. In addition, some statutory schemes lay out the ground rules for binding arbitration.

In contrast, the majority's new California rule is hopelessly undefined and unstructured. In addtion to the breadth of the majority's "truly essential" standard, the statutes presently provide no systematic classification of employees according to the nature of their work and the degree to which the public can tolerate work stoppages. Only firefighters are expressly prohibited from striking and giving recognition to picket lines. (Lab. Code, § 1962.) Moreover, the four principal statutory schemes regulating other public employees establish widely differing approaches to labor relations for different types and levels of employees. (Compare Gov. Code §§ 3500-3510 [Meyers-Milias-Brown Act, covering local government employees]; 3512-3524 [State Employer-Employee Relations Act, covering state employees]; 3540-3549.3 [Ed. Employment Relations Act, covering public school employees]; 3560-3599 [governing employment in higher education].) Thus, these statutes produce inconsistent results when, as here, the right to strike is given recognition almost across the board.

The Meyers-Milias-Brown Act, for example, provides "no clear mechanism for resolving disputes" between local governments and their workers. In the absence of an administrative agency to settle charges of unfair labor practices and compel such remedies as mediation, presumably all strike-related issues will go to the courts in the first instance, but the courts are poor forums for the resolution of such issues. On the other hand, issues arising out of work stoppages by public school employees are to be resolved by the Public Employee Relations Board (PERB) on the basis of PERB's own set of remedies. Of course, this anomalous situation is in large part the product of this court's tolerance of strikes by teachers (*El Rancho Unified Sch. Dist. v. National Ed. Assn., supra,* 33 Cal. 3d 946; *San Diego Teachers Assn. v. Superior Court* (1979) 24 Cal. 3d 1; and PERB's correlative expansion of its authority so that it may compel mediation or adopt other remedies in labor disputes in public education (see Cal. Admin. Code, tit. 8, § 3600 et seq.).

Finally, nothing in PERB's explicit statutory powers (Gov. Code, § 3541.3) extends to mandatory arbitration, for example, so it remains to be established whether state employees, also under PERB's jurisdiction (*id.*, § 3513, subd. (g)), will be governed by the same ground rules as educational employees, or whether some of them, perhaps deemed "truly essential," will be subject to binding arbitration under rules that do not now exist.

I would affirm the judgment.

NOTES

1. In *Compton Unified Sch. Dist.,* Cal. PERB Order No. IR-50, CCH PEB ¶ 44,793 (1987), a closely divided PERB reversed its *Modesto City Schs.* decision (Cal. PERB Dec. No. 291, CCH PEB ¶ 43,723 (1983)) and held that school teachers do not have a clear right to strike under the Educational Employment Relations Act. Although the statute is silent with respect to this issue, Member Porter emphasized that public employees have not traditionally enjoyed the right to engage in work stoppages. Concurring Member Hesse refused to find that all teacher strikes are unprotected. She indicated that a teacher work stoppage might be warranted under special circumstances. Member Craib dissented. But see *Davis v. Henry,* 1988-90 PBC ¶ 35,504 (La. 1990), in which the court held that since teachers and other public school personnel have the right to organize for collective bargaining purposes, they must necessarily possess the concomitant right to engage in peaceful picketing, work stoppages, and other concerted activity.

2. In *Boston Hous. Auth. v. LRC,* 398 Mass. 715, 500 N.E.2d 802 (1986), the court decided to extend the general public employee strike proscription contained in Mass. Gen. Law Ch. 150E, Sec. 9A to public housing workers, even though a special bargaining law, which did not include an express strike prohibition, covered public housing personnel. The court noted that public employees have traditionally been denied the right to strike, and it found that public policy considerations supported the extension of the general strike ban to public housing employees.

3. In *Local 1494, IAFF v. City of Coeur d'Alene,* 586 P.2d 1346, 1977-78 PBC ¶ 36,427 (1978), the Idaho Supreme Court was asked to decide whether firefighters were permitted to strike following the expiration of their collective bargaining contract. The applicable statute provides:

Strikes prohibited during contract — Upon consummation and during the term of the written contract or agreement, no firefighter shall strike or recognize a picket line of any labor organization while in performance of his official duties. [Idaho Code § 44-1811]

The court majority concluded that by negative implication the specific language of the strike proscription removed work stoppages following the termination of the applicable labor agreement from the legal prohibition. It went on to consider whether the firefighters' limited right to strike includes, as one of its elements, the right not to be discharged in the event such a stoppage occurs. Since there was no legislative indication that such strikers were to be accorded the same protections as are accorded their private sector counterparts under the NLRA, the majority concluded that they are not automatically immune from disciplinary sanctions. However, it did decide that where a work stoppage has been precipitated by the public employer's refusal to bargain in good faith over the terms of a new contract, no good cause for termination would exist under the applicable civil service regulations. But cf. *Oneida Sch. Dist. v. Educ. Ass'n,* 567 P.2d 830, 95 L.R.R.M. 3244 (1977), wherein the Idaho Supreme Court indicated that the absence of a provision in the state education labor relations statute expressly proscribing work stoppages by such personnel did not inferentially provide them with a right to strike.

2. CONSTITUTIONAL ISSUES

UNITED FEDERATION OF POSTAL CLERKS v. BLOUNT

325 F. Supp. 879 (D.D.C.), aff'd, 404 U.S. 802 (1971)

PER CURIAM: This action was brought by the United Federation of Postal Clerks (hereafter sometimes referred to as "Clerks"), an unincorporated public employee labor organization which consists primarily of employees of the Post Office Department, and which is the exclusive bargaining representative of approximately 305,000 members of the clerk craft employed by defendant. Defendant Blount is the Postmaster General of the United States. The Clerks seek declaratory and injunctive relief invalidating portions of 5 U.S.C. § 7311, 18 U.S.C. § 1918, an affidavit required by 5 U.S.C. § 3333 to implement the above statutes, and Executive Order 11491, C.F.R., Chap. II, p. 191. A three-judge court was convened pursuant to 28 U.S.C. § 2282 and § 2284 to consider this issue.

The Statutes Involved

5 U.S.C. § 7311 (3) prohibits an individual from accepting or holding a position in the federal government or in the District of Columbia if he

"(3) participates in a strike ... against the Government of the United States or the government of the District of Columbia...."

Paragraph C of the appointment affidavit required by 5 U.S.C. § 3333, which all federal employees are required to execute under oath, states (POD Form 61):

"I am not participating in any strike against the Government of the United States or any agency thereof, and I will not so participate while an employee of the Government of the United States or any agency thereof."

18 U.S.C. § 1918, in making a violation of 5 U.S.C. § 7311 a crime, provides:

"Whoever violates the provision of section 7311 of title 5 that an individual may not accept or hold a position in the Government of the United States or the government of the District of Columbia if he ...

"(3) participates in a strike, or asserts the right to strike, against the Government of the United States or the District of Columbia ...

"shall be fined not more than $1,000 or imprisoned not more than one year and a day, or both."

Section 2(e) (2) of Executive Order 11491 exempts from the definition of a labor organization any group which:

"asserts the right to strike against the Government of the United States or any agency thereof, or to assist or participate in such a strike, or imposes a duty or obligation to conduct, assist or participate in such a strike...."

Section 19(b) (4) of the same Executive Order makes it an unfair labor practice for a labor organization to:

> "call or engage in a strike, work stoppage, or slowdown; picket an agency in a labor-management dispute; or condone any such activity by failing to take affirmative action to prevent or stop it; ...."

Plaintiff's Contentions

Plaintiff contends that the right to strike is a fundamental right protected by the Constitution, and that the absolute prohibition of such activity by 5 U.S.C. § 7311 (3) and the other provisions set out above thus constitutes an infringement of the employees' First Amendment rights of association and free speech and operates to deny them equal protection of the law. Plaintiff also argues that the language to "strike" and "participates in a strike" is vague and overbroad and therefore violative of both the First Amendment and the due process clause of the Fifth Amendment. For the purposes of this opinion, we will direct our attention to the attack on the constitutionality of 5 U.S.C. § 7311 (3), the key provision being challenged. To the extent that the present wording of 18 U.S.C. § 1918(3) and Executive Order 11491 does not reflect the actions of two statutory courts in *Stewart v. Washington,* 301 F. Supp. 610 (D.C.D.C. 1969) and *N.A.L.C. v. Blount,* 305 F. Supp. 546 (D.C.D.C. 1969), said wording, insofar as it inhibits the *assertion* of the right to strike, is overbroad because it attempts to reach activities protected by the First Amendment and is therefore invalid. With this *caveat,* our treatment of the issue raised by plaintiffs with respect to the constitutionality of 5 U.S.C. § 7311(3) will also apply to 18 U.S.C. § 1918, the penal provision, and to Form 61, the affidavit required by 5 U.S.C. § 3333. For the reasons set forth below, we deny plaintiff's request for declaratory and injunctive relief and grant defendant's motion to dismiss.

I. Public Employees Have No Constitutional Right to Strike

At common law no employee, whether public or private, had a constitutional right to strike in concert with his fellow workers. Indeed, such collective action on the part of employees was often held to be a conspiracy. When the right of private employees to strike finally received full protection, it was by statute, Section 7 of the National Labor Relations Act, which "took this conspiracy weapon away from the employer in employment relations which affect interstate commerce" and guaranteed to employees in the private sector the right to engage in concerted activities for the purpose of collective bargaining. See discussion in *International Union, U.A.W.A., A.F. of L. Local 232 v. Wisconsin Employment Relations Board,* 336 U.S. 245 (1948). It seems clear that public employees stand on no stronger footing in this regard than private employees and that in the absence of a statute, they too do not possess the right to strike. The Supreme Court has spoken approvingly of such a restriction, see *Amell v. United States,* 384 U.S. 158 (1965), and at least one federal district court has invoked the provisions of a predecessor statute, 5 U.S.C. § 118p-r, to enjoin a strike by government employees. *Tennessee Valley Authority v. Local Union No. 110 of Sheet Metal Workers,* 233 F. Supp. 997 (D.C.W.D. Ky. 1962). Likewise, scores of state cases have held that state employees do not have a right to

engage in concerted work stoppages, in the absence of legislative authorization.... It is fair to conclude that, irrespective of the reasons given, there is a
unanimity of opinion on the part of courts and legislatures that government
employees do not have the right to strike. See Moberly, *The Strike and Its
Alternative in Public Employment,* University of Wisconsin Law Review (1966)
pp. 549-50, 554.

Congress has consistently treated public employees as being in a different
category than private employees. The National Labor Relations Act of 1939 and
the Labor Management Relations Act of 1947, (Taft-Hartley) both defined
"employer" as not including any governmental or political subdivisions, and
thereby indirectly withheld the protections of § 7 from governmental employees. Congress originally enacted the no-strike provision separately from
other restrictions on employee activity, i.e., such as those struck down in *Stewart
v. Washington* and *N.A.L.C. v. Blount, supra,* by attaching riders to appropriations bills which prohibited strikes by government employees. See for example
the Third Urgent Deficiency Appropriation Act of 1946, which provided that
no part of the appropriation could be used to pay the salary of anyone who
engaged in a strike against the Government. Section 305 of the Taft-Hartley Act
made it unlawful for a federal employee to participate in a strike, providing
immediate discharge and forfeiture of civil service status for infractions. Section
305 was repealed in 1955 by Public Law 330, and reenacted in 5 U.S.C. § 118p-
r, the predecessor to the present statute.

Given the fact that there is no constitutional right to strike, it is not irrational
or arbitrary for the Government to condition employment on a promise not to
withhold labor collectively, and to prohibit strikes by those in public employment, whether because of the prerogatives of the sovereign, some sense of
higher obligation associated with public service, to assure the continuing functioning of the Government without interruption, to protect public health and
safety or for other reasons. Although plaintiff argues that the provisions in
question are unconstitutionally broad in covering all Government employees
regardless of the type or importance of the work they do, we hold that it makes
no difference whether the jobs performed by certain public employees are
regarded as "essential" or "non-essential," or whether similar jobs are performed by workers in private industry who do have the right to strike protected
by statute. Nor is it relevant that some positions in private industry are arguably
more affected with a public interest than are some positions in the Government
service. While the Fifth Amendment contains no Equal Protection Clause similar to the one found in the Fourteenth Amendment, concepts of Equal Protection do inhere in Fifth Amendment Principles of Due Process. *Bolling v.
Sharpe,* 347 U.S. 497 (1954). The Equal Protection Clause, however, does not
forbid all discrimination. Where fundamental rights are not involved, a particular classification does not violate the Equal Protection Clause if it is not "arbitrary" or "irrational," i.e., "if any state of facts reasonably may be conceived to
justify it." *McGowan v. Maryland,* 366 U.S. 420, 426 (1961). Compare *Kramer
v. Union Free School District,* 395 U.S. 621, 627-628 (1969). Since the right to
strike cannot be considered a "fundamental" right, it is the test enunciated in
McGowan which must be employed in this case. Thus, there is latitude for
distinctions rooted in reason and practice, especially where the difficulty of

drafting a no-strike statute which distinguishes among types and classes of employees is obvious.

Furthermore, it should be pointed out that the fact that public employees may not strike does not interfere with their rights which are fundamental and constitutionally protected. The right to organize collectively and to select representatives for the purposes of engaging in collective bargaining is such a fundamental right.... But, as the Supreme Court noted in *International Union, etc., Local 232 v. Wisconsin Employment Relations Board, supra,* "The right to strike, because of its more serious impact upon the public interest, is more vulnerable to regulation than the right to organize and select representatives for lawful purposes of collective bargaining which this Court has characterized as a 'fundamental right' and which, as the Court has pointed out, was recognized as such in its decisions long before it was given protection by the National Labor Relations Act." 336 U.S. at 259.

Executive Order 11491 recognizes the right of federal employees to join labor organizations for the purpose of dealing with grievances, but that Order clearly and expressly defines strikes, work stoppages and slow-downs as unfair labor practices. As discussed above, that Order is the culmination of a long-standing policy. There certainly is no compelling reason to imply the existence of the right to strike from the right to associate and bargain collectively. In the private sphere, the strike is used to equalize bargaining power, but this has universally been held not to be appropriate when its object and purpose can only be to influence the essentially political decisions of Government in the allocation of its resources. Congress has an obligation to ensure that the machinery of the Federal Government continues to function at all times without interference. Prohibition of strikes by its employees is a reasonable implementation of that obligation.

II. The Provisions are Neither Unconstitutionally Vague nor Overbroad

Plaintiff contends that the word "strike" and the phrase "participates in a strike" used in the statute are so vague that "men of common intelligence must necessarily guess at [their] meaning and differ as to [their] application," *Connally v. General Construction Co.,* 269 U.S. 385, 391 (1926), and are therefore violative of the due process clause of the Fifth Amendment. Plaintiff also contends that the provisions are overly broad. While there is no sharp distinction between vagueness and overbreadth, an overly broad statute reaches not only conduct which the Government may properly prohibit but also conduct which is beyond the reach of governmental regulation. A vague statute is merely imprecise in indicating which of several types of conduct which could be restricted has in fact been prohibited.

These concepts of "striking" and "participating in a strike" occupy central positions in our labor statutes and accompanying caselaw, and have been construed and interpreted many times by numerous state and federal courts. "Strike" is defined in § 501 (2) of the Taft-Hartley Act to include "any strike or other concerted stoppage of work by employees ... and any concerted slowdown or other concerted interruption of operations by employees." On its face this is a straightforward definition. It is difficult to understand how a word used and defined so often could be sufficiently ambiguous as to be constitutionally suspect. "Strike" is a term of such common usage and acceptance that "men of common intelligence" need not guess at its meaning. *Connally v. General Construction Co., supra,* at 391.

Plaintiff complains that the precise parameters of "participation" are so unclear that employees may fail to exercise other, protected First Amendment rights for fear of overstepping the line; and that in any event, "participates" is too broad to withstand judicial scrutiny. Plaintiff urges that Congress is required to more specifically define exactly what activities are to be caught up in the net of illegality.

The Government, however, represented at oral argument that it interprets "participate" to mean "striking," the essence of which is an actual refusal in concert with others to provide services to one's employer. We adopt this construction of the phrase, which will exclude the First Amendment problems raised by the plaintiff in that it removes from the strict reach of these statutes and other provisions such conduct as speech, union membership, fund-raising, organization, distribution of literature and informational picketing, even though those activities may take place in concert during a strike by others. We stress that it is only an actual refusal by particular employees to provide services that is forbidden by 5 U.S.C. § 7311(3) and penalized by 18 U.S.C. § 1918. However, these statutes, as all criminal statutes, must be read in conjunction with 18 U.S.C. §§ 2 (aiding and abetting) and 371 (conspiracy). We express no views as to the extent of their application to cases that might arise thereunder as it is practically impossible to fashion a meaningful declaratory judgment in such a broad area.

This case does not involve a situation where we are concerned with a prior construction by a state supreme court, but rather one in which we are faced with the interpretation to be given a federal statute in the first instance by a federal court. Under such circumstances federal courts have broad latitude, the language of the statute permitting, to construe a statute in such terms as will save it from the infirmities of vagueness and overbreadth. *Kent v. Dulles,* 357 U.S. 116 (1958). This principle of interpretation is equally true of cases which involve rights under the First Amendment. *United States v. C.I.O.,* 335 U.S. 106, 120-122 (1948); *Chaplinsky v. New Hampshire,* 315 U.S. 568, 573-574 (1942); see also *Williams v. District of Columbia,* 136 U.S. App. D.C. 56, 419 F.2d 638 (en banc, 1969). Such construction of the word "strike" and the phrase "participates in a strike" achieves the objective of Congress and, in defining the type of conduct which is beyond the reach of the statute, saves it from the risk of vagueness and overbreadth.

Accordingly, we hold that the provisions of the statute, the appointment affidavit and the Executive Order, as construed above, do not violate any constitutional rights of those employees who are members of plaintiff's union. The Government's motion to dismiss the complaint is granted. Order to be presented.

J. SKELLY WRIGHT, CIRCUIT JUDGE (concurring): I concur in Part II of the majority's opinion and in the result. My following comments are addressed to the main issue raised in Part I of the opinion — the validity of the flat ban on federal employees' strikes under the Fifth Amendment of the Constitution. This question is, in my view, a very difficult one, and I cannot concur fully in the majority's handling of it.

It is by no means clear to me that the right to strike is not fundamental. The right to strike seems intimately related to the right to form labor organizations, a right which the majority recognizes as fundamental and which, more importantly, is generally thought to be constitutionally protected under the First Amendment — even for public employees. See *Melton v. City of Atlanta*, 324 F. Supp. 315 (N.D. Ga. 1971); *Atkins v. City of Charlotte*, 296 F. Supp. 1068 (W.D.N.C. 1969). If the inherent purpose of a labor organization is to bring the workers' interests to bear on management, the right to strike is, historically and practically, an important means of effectuating that purpose. A union that never strikes, or which can make no credible threat to strike, may wither away in ineffectiveness. That fact is not irrelevant to the constitutional calculations. Indeed, in several decisions, the Supreme Court has held that the First Amendment right of association is at least concerned with essential organizational activities which give the particular association life and promote its fundamental purposes. See *Williams v. Rhodes*, 393 U.S. 23 (1968); *United Mine Workers, etc. v. Illinois State Bar Assn.*, 389 U.S. 217 (1967). I do not suggest that the right to strike is co-equal with the right to form labor organizations. Nor do I equate striking with the organizational activities protected in *Williams* (access to the ballot) or *United Mine Workers* (group legal representation). But I do believe that the right to strike is, at least, within constitutional concern and should not be discriminatorily abridged without substantial or "compelling" justification.

Hence the real question here, as I see it, is to determine whether there is such justification for denying federal employees a right which is granted to other employees of private business. Plaintiff's arguments that not all federal services are "essential" and that some privately provided services are no less "essential" casts doubt on the validity of the flat ban on federal employees' strikes. In our mixed economic system of governmental and private enterprise, the line separating governmental from private functions may depend more on the accidents of history than on substantial differences in kind.

Nevertheless, I feel that I must concur in the result reached by the majority in Part I of its opinion. As the majority indicates, the asserted right of public employees to strike has often been litigated and, so far as I know, never recognized as a matter of law. The present state of the relevant jurisprudence offers almost no support for the proposition that the government lacks a "compelling" interest in prohibiting such strikes. No doubt, the line between "essential" and "non-essential" functions is very, very difficult to draw. For that reason, it may well be best to accept the demarcations resulting from the development of our political economy. If the right of public employees to strike — with all its political and social ramifications — is to be recognized and protected by the judiciary, it should be done by the Supreme Court which has the power to reject established jurisprudence and the authority to enforce such a sweeping rule.

NOTES

1. Prohibitions against public employee strikes have been challenged on almost every conceivable basis. To date nearly every court ruling on this question has held that these prohibitions do not violate the Constitution. The case law includes:

(a) *First amendment challenges: Abbott v. Myers,* 20 Ohio App. 2d 65, 251 N.E.2d 869 (1969); *Board of Educ. Community Sch. Dist. No. 2 v. Redding,* 32 Ill. 2d 567, 207 N.E.2d 427 (1965); *City of Wauwatosa v. King,* 49 Wis. 2d 398, 182 N.W.2d 530 (1971); *Jefferson Cty. Teachers Ass'n v. Board of Educ.,* 463 S.W.2d 627 (Ky. 1970), *cert. denied,* 404 U.S. 865 (1971); *Board of Educ. v. Kankakee Fed'n of Teachers Local 886,* 46 Ill. 2d 439, 264 N.E.2d 18 (1970), *cert. denied,* 403 U.S. 904 (1971); *State v. Heath,* 177 N.W.2d 751 (N.D. 1970); *Regents of Univ. of Wis. v. Teaching Assistants' Ass'n,* 74 L.R.R.M. 2049 (Wis. Cir. Ct. 1970); *Rogoff v. Anderson,* 34 App. Div. 2d 154, 310 N.Y.S.2d 174 (1970); *Holland Sch. Dist. v. Holland Educ. Ass'n,* 380 Mich. 314, 157 N.W.2d 206 (1968); *City of Pawtucket v. Pawtucket Teachers Alliance Local 930,* 87 R.I. 364, 141 A.2d 621 (1958).

(b) *Thirteenth amendment challenges: City of Evanston v. Buick,* 421 F.2d 595 (7th Cir. 1970); *In re Block,* 50 N.J. 494, 236 A.2d 592 (1967); *Pinellas Cty. Classroom Teachers Ass'n v. Board of Pub. Instr.,* 214 So. 2d 34 (Fla. 1968); *Holland Sch. Dist. v. Holland Educ. Ass'n, supra.*

(c) *Fourteenth amendment challenges: Abbott v. Myers, supra; City of N.Y. v. DeLury,* 23 N.Y.2d 175, 243 N.E.2d 128 (1968), *appeal dismissed,* 394 U.S. 455 (1969); *Head v. Special Sch. Dist. No. 1,* 288 Minn. 496, 182 N.W.2d 887, *cert. denied,* 404 U.S. 886 (1970); *In re Block, supra; Jefferson Cty. Teachers Ass'n v. Board of Educ., supra; Holland Sch. Dist. v. Holland Educ. Ass'n, supra.*

(d) *Bill of attainder challenges: Abbott v. Myers, supra; DiMaggio v. Brown,* 19 N.Y.2d 283, 225 N.E.2d 871 (1967).

2. The relevant case law to date also appears to support the proposition that strikes by public employees engaged in proprietary as well as governmental functions are illegal. *Delaware River & Bay Auth. v. International Org. of Masters, Mates & Pilots,* 45 N.J. 138, 211 A.2d 789 (1965); *Port of Seattle v. ILWU,* 52 Wash. 2d 317, 324 P.2d 1099 (1958); *City of Alcoa v. IBEW Local 760,* 203 Tenn. 12, 308 S.W.2d 476 (1957); *City of Los Angeles v. Los Angeles Bldg. Constr. Trades Council,* 94 Cal. App. 2d 36, 210 P.2d 305 (1949).

3. Judge Wright in *Blount* claims that "the relevant jurisprudence offers almost no support for the proposition that the government lacks a 'compelling' interest in prohibiting such strikes." What reasons cited by the majority in *Blount* seem most compelling? The court seems to reject out of hand the argument that it is irrational to totally prohibit strikes of municipal librarians, for example, while allowing strikes of telephone workers. Why?

E. ENFORCEMENT DEVICES

1. INJUNCTION

HOLLAND SCHOOL DISTRICT v. HOLLAND EDUCATION ASSOCIATION

380 Mich. 314, 157 N.W.2d 206 (1968)

O'HARA, JUSTICE: — Leave to appeal was granted in this case to review an order of the Court of Appeals. The order denied a stay of proceedings previously granted and denied the prayer of the appellants to dissolve a temporary injunction. The order remanded the cause to the circuit court for hearing on the merits.

This is a chancery case. The constitutional provision (Const. 1963, art. 6, § 5) abolishes the distinctions between law and equity *proceedings*. It did not abolish the historic difference between law and equity. We note this because it is as a Court of Equity we sit in the case at bar. In this, as in all other cases clearly in equity, we hear appeals *de novo*. The reason for this restatement of principle will appear decisionally later in our opinion.

In 1947, the legislature enacted what is generally referred to as the Hutchinson Act. CL 1948, § 423.201 et seq., as amended by PA 1965, No. 379 (Stat. Ann. 1960 Rev. and Stat. Ann. 1968 Cum. Supp. § 17.455[1] et seq.).

We herewith set forth the title to the act as amended by PA 1965, No. 379:

> "An act to prohibit strikes by certain public employees; to provide review from disciplinary action with respect thereto; to provide for the mediation of grievances and the holding of elections; to declare and protect the rights and privileges of public employees; and to prescribe means of enforcement and penalties for the violation of the provisions of this act."

Its first section, as amended by PA 1965, No. 379, defines a strike:

> "As used in this act the word 'strike' shall mean the concerted failure to report for duty, the wilful absence from one's position, the stoppage of work, or the abstinence in whole or in part from the full, faithful and proper performance of the duties of employment, for the purpose of inducing, influencing or coercing a change in the conditions, or compensation, or the rights, privileges or obligations of employment."

The second section specifies the employees affected:

> "No person holding a position by appointment or employment in the government of the state of Michigan, or in the government of any 1 or more of the political subdivisions thereof, or in the public school service, or in any public or special district, or in the service of any authority, commission, or board, or in any other branch of the public service, hereinafter called a 'public employee,' shall strike."

In the late summer of 1967 the teachers in the School District for the City of Holland, Ottawa and Allegan Counties, acting through their duly certified collective bargaining agency, did not resume their teaching duties on the day set by the board of education. If they were employees within the meaning of the statute they were on strike as that term is defined in the statute.

The school district sought an injunction restraining the teachers from withholding their services. A hearing was held and the trial chancellor issued a temporary injunction. The Court of Appeals denied continuation of a stay order previously granted and the prayer to dissolve the injunction. We likewise denied a stay order and declined to dissolve the injunction but granted leave to appeal. The case is before us in that posture. Regrettably, we have a meager record, the pleadings, transcribed colloquies between court and counsel, and oral argument. To the extent possible, in order that our decision be precedentially meaningful, we will discuss those basic issues which relate to the legal concepts which we consider must govern, and will not limit ourselves to the narrow question of the propriety of the issuance of the temporary injunction....

[I]t is argued that if the act be constitutional, as we have here held, it is inapplicable to appellants for 2 reasons: first, because appellants are not "employees" within the meaning of the act, and second, that as to teachers, injunctive relief may not be granted because an alternative exclusive remedy is to be found in the act.

We consider the first. The principal thrust of this argument is that, because no contracts of employment were in force between appellants and appellee school district at the time the injunction issued, the involved teachers cannot be employees as a matter of law. It is contended that the school code, specifically CLS 1961, § 240.569, as amended by PA 1965, No. 14 (Stat. Ann. 1968 Rev. § 15.3569), mandates such conclusion. Appellants refer to this argument as the "keystone issue." ... In finality, we have come to the conclusion that *Garden City School District v. Labor Mediation Board,* 358 Mich. 258, of necessity must control. In that case the positions of the parties herein were reversed. In *Garden City,* the school board sought injunctive restraint against the State labor mediation board in its attempted mediation between teachers and the board. The school board challenged that jurisdiction, in part, on the ground that the school code required written contracts, and that the mediation board had no jurisdiction over the terms thereof. This Court said (pp. 262, 263,...):

"Public school teachers are certainly persons 'holding a position by appointment or employment ... in the public school service.'

"Appellant school board contends, however, that the provisions of the school code of 1955 (CLS 1956, § 340.569 [Stat. Ann. 1959 Rev. § 15.3659]), by providing that teachers shall be hired by written contract, denies jurisdiction to the labor mediation board for mediation as to any terms which might be included in such contracts.

"The written contract provision was first adopted in 1927, and the legislature was certainly familiar with its requirements when it adopted PA 1947, No. 336, which we have quoted. We read these 2 acts together as allowing mediation of salary disputes *in advance* of the determination of the salary provisions of individual teacher contracts." (emphasis supplied.)

Since this Court concluded that there is jurisdiction to mediate grievances *"in advance* of the determination of salary provisions," it follows that such jurisdiction would necessarily attach in advance of the *executing* of the written contracts themselves, which are required in the case of teachers, by the School Code.

If teachers as we have held *are* subject to the provision of the Hutchinson Act dealing with the mediation of grievances *in advance* of signing written contracts, we can hardly hold with consistency that they *are not* subject to the no-strike provision of the same act for the same reason. We are constrained to hold that appellants were "employees" within the terms of the act.

We next turn to the exclusivity of remedy argument. It is based on § 6 of the act, which provides:

"Notwithstanding the provisions of any other law, any person holding such a position who, by concerted action with others, and without the lawful approval of his superior, wilfully absents himself from his position, or abstains in whole or in part from the full, faithful and proper performance of his duties for the purpose of inducing, influencing or coercing a change in the conditions or compensation, or the rights, privileges or obligations of employment shall be deemed to be on strike but the person, upon request, shall be entitled to a determination as to whether he did violate the provisions of this act. The request shall be filed in writing, with the officer or body having power to remove or discipline such employee, within 10 days after regular compensation of such employee has ceased or other discipline has been imposed. In the event of such request the officer or body shall within 10 days commence a proceeding for the determination of whether the provisions of this act have been violated by the public employee, in accordance with the law and regulations appropriate to a proceeding to remove the public employee. The proceedings shall be undertaken without unnecessary delay. The decision of the proceeding shall be made within 10 days. If the employee involved is held to have violated this law and his employment terminated or other discipline imposed, he shall have the right of review to the circuit court having jurisdiction of the parties, within 30 days from such decision, for determination whether such decision is supported by competent, material and substantial evidence on the whole record."

In this regard we find ourselves in harmony with the holding of the Court of Appeals:

"The claim of the defendants that section 6 of the public employees relations act is the only remedy available to the school board cannot be accepted by this Court. Its provisions for discipline of striking public employees and review procedure for them cannot be interpreted to imply removing the historic power of courts to enjoin strikes by public employees. See 31 A.L.R. 2d 1142 and the cases cited therein."

Additionally, we deem it necessary to observe that the whole section deals with after-the-fact remedies by the employee. The withholding of services and the cessation of compensation for services has had to have taken place before the section can operate. It must be said that appellants' position is eminently, indeed inexorably logical in this regard. The section cannot operate within a situation where injunctive restraint of the withholding of such service has already been granted. We would find ourselves in a complete logical self-contradiction if we were to hold as we have here that courts retain their jurisdiction to issue a restraining order against withholding of services by public employees, and at the same time hold § 6 to be an exclusive remedy. The section seems to us to support the conclusion that the legislature intended that injunctive relief could be granted, but that courts are not required to grant it in every case involving a strike by public employees. To attempt to compel legislatively, a court of equity in every instance of a public employee strike to enjoin it would be to destroy the independence of the judicial branch of government.

Having held that the Hutchinson Act is without constitutional infirmity, that appellants are public employees and as such subject to its no-strike provisions, and that the courts have jurisdiction to restrain prohibited strikes by public employees, but are not required to do so in every case, we turn to the question of whether in the case at bar the chancellor had before him that quantum of proof or uncontradicted allegations of fact which would justify the issuance of an injunction in a labor dispute case.

We here hold it is insufficient merely to show that a concert of prohibited action by public employees has taken place and that *ipso facto* such a showing justifies injunctive relief. We so hold because it is basically contrary to public policy in this State to issue injunctions in labor disputes absent a showing of violence, irreparable injury, or a breach of the peace. For a recent discussion of this question, see *Cross Company v. UAW Local No. 155 (AFL-CIO)*, 371 Mich. 184.... We further so hold because such an interpretation of the act would as before noted raise a serious constitutional question....

We recognize that great discretion is allowed the trial chancellor in the granting or withholding of injunctive relief. We do not, in ordinary circumstances, substitute our judgment for his. We hold here, however, that there was a lack of proof which would support the issuance of a temporary injunction.

The order of the Court of Appeals, affirming the circuit court is reversed. Hearing the matter as we do *de novo,* we dissolve the temporary injunction hereinbefore issued, and remand to the circuit court for further proceedings. We suggest that such proceedings inquire into whether, as charged by the defendants, the plaintiff school district has refused to bargain in good faith, whether an injunction should issue at all, and if so, on what terms and for what period in light of the whole record to be adduced. No costs, a public question.

BLACK and ADAMS, JJ., concurred with O'HARA, J.

SOURIS, JUSTICE.

I agree that the temporary injunction should be vacated, but for reasons other than those stated by my Brethren.

It is my judgment that the individual defendants had not become employees of the plaintiff school district when the complaint was filed. None had entered into the contracts of employment with the school district our Legislature saw fit to require "be in writing and signed by a majority of the board in behalf of the district, or by the president and secretary, or by the superintendent of schools when so directed at a meeting of the board." Section 569, school code of 1955, as amended (CLS 1961, § 340.569, as amended by PA 1965, No. 14 [Stat. Ann. 1968 Rev. § 15.3569]). Absent such written contracts of employment, the teachers were not yet employees of the school district subject to the "no-strike" provisions of the Hutchinson Act. The act's definition of "strike" clearly supports my conclusion that the individual defendants, not yet employees of the school district, did not "strike" in violation of the act. Until written contracts of employment were executed, they were under no obligation to report for duty; they could not absent themselves from their positions, for they had none; they could not stop work, for they had not begun yet to work nor had they agreed even to work; and, finally, they could not abstain from performing the duties of employment for any purpose, for they had not assumed yet any such duties....

No employment relationship yet having arisen between the individual defendants and the plaintiff school district when this action was filed, it follows that the injunctive order enjoining defendants from concerted abstention from employment violated the involuntary servitude provisions of the Thirteenth

Amendment of the United States Constitution and Article I, section 9 of our state Constitution.

I note my agreement with the latter part of Mr. Justice O'Hara's opinion regarding the judicial inadequacy of the record to support the injunction issued. In other words, even were these defendants employees, I would agree with Justice O'Hara that the chancellor, on the record then before him, should not have granted injunctive relief.

The injunction should be vacated. Defendants should be allowed to tax their costs.

KAVANAGH, C.J., concurred with SOURIS, J....

BRENNAN, JUSTICE.

The tests for granting an injunction *pendente lite* are different than the criterion used in granting permanent injunctive relief. We said in the case of *Niedzialek v. Barbers Union,* 331 Mich. 296, at page 300, [28 LRRM 2626]:

> "Under the record before us, it appears beyond cavil that when trial on the merits is had the issue will be: Should the picketing by defendants be permitted or should it be enjoined? The final result will depend upon the proof produced at the hearing bearing upon the issue of whether the picketing was pertinent to a lawful labor objective. And the issue may also be presented as to whether or not the picketing was peaceful or otherwise. Neither of these issues can be decided until there is a hearing on the merits. It is also clear, at least reasonably certain, that if in the instant case the picketing is continued in the interim until a hearing on the merits plaintiff will suffer irreparable injury. The contrary cannot be persuasively urged; nor can it reasonably be inferred from the record that enjoining picketing in the interim would result in any permanent or irreparable injury to defendants, even if the ultimate determination should be that the picketing was lawful. It is the settled policy of this Court under such circumstances to grant to a litigant who is threatened with irreparable injury temporary injunctive relief and thereby preserve the original status quo."

The function of an injunction *pendente lite* is to prevent irreparable harm which would result from natural delay in reaching a trial on the merits. It may be argued that in this case the status quo was summer vacation and that the temporary injunction permitted a change in the status quo by permitting schools to open at the usual time. But the maintenance of actual status quo is not the only function of an injunction *pendente lite*. The court can consider whether under all the facts and circumstances of the case the issuance of the temporary injunction will maintain the parties in that status which is least likely to do irreparable injury to the party who ultimately prevails.

In this case, the plaintiff school board will be entitled to a permanent injunction unless at the trial on the merits the circuit judge should conclude that by reason of its failure or refusal to do equity to the school teachers, it has forfeited its claim to equitable relief. Such a judgment cannot be made by the circuit judge until he has heard testimony on the extent of the bargaining and on the position taken by both sides at the bargaining table. If at the hearing on the merits it should appear that the school board's treatment of the teachers has been and is equitable and reasonable, a permanent injunction will issue and the teachers will have no basis for complaint concerning the temporary injunction.

If, on the other hand, it should appear at the trial on the merits that the school board has not offered to do equity and has not taken a reasonable position at the bargaining table, then a permanent injunction will be denied and the temporary injunction will be dissolved. Under such circumstances the temporary injunction will merely have delayed the strike until the justice of the teachers' cause and the necessity for their strike will have been vindicated in a court of equity. Such delay is a benefit, not an injury, to the teachers.

The temporary injunction should be affirmed and the case remanded to the circuit court for a full evidentiary hearing on the question of whether a final injunction should issue. It is further directed that the court proceed with dispatch so that a decision on a final injunction can be made before the end of the present school year.

NOTES

1. In *Timberlane, Reg'l Sch. Dist. v. Timberlane, Reg'l Educ. Ass'n,* 317 A.2d 555, 87 L.R.R.M. 2015 (N.H. 1974), it was held that although the common law of the state made strikes by public employees illegal, the New Hampshire courts should apply equitable principles to determine whether an injunction should lie against such a strike in the absence of any directive from the legislature. The New Hampshire Supreme Court indicated that the trial courts should consider among other factors whether the public health, safety, and welfare would be substantially harmed if the strike were allowed to continue. Accord *Oneida Sch. Dist. v. Oneida Educ. Ass'n,* 567 P.2d 830, 95 L.R.R.M. 3244 (Idaho 1977).

In *Joint Sch. Dist. v. Educ. Ass'n,* 70 Wis. 2d 292, 234 N.W.2d 289 (1975), the Wisconsin Supreme Court held that courts should not enjoin unlawful work stoppages by public employees merely because they are illegal, but should determine in each case whether irreparable harm would result if the particular strike were not enjoined. Nonetheless, the Court affirmed the lower court's issuance of an injunction against a teachers' strike and specifically approved its reliance upon criteria that would appear to indicate that a petitioning school district's burden may not be too substantial.

> The primary issue in this case is whether the facts and circumstances warranted a finding of irreparable harm. In ordering the temporary injunction, the trial court concluded that irreparable harm was shown by the following factors: (1) The illegal nature of the strike; (2) inability of the board to operate the school system and thereby meet its statutory duties and responsibilities to the taxpayers in the school district; (3) inability of the students to obtain the benefits of a tax-supported educational process; (4) possible loss of state aids; (5) inability of parents to comply with statutory responsibility to educate their children; and (6) cancellation of athletic events and other school activities.

2. The majority of courts have followed the more traditional view that injunctive relief against unlawful work stoppages is available to governmental employers without a showing of irreparable harm or clean hands. See, e.g., *Board of Educ. v. Redding,* 32 Ill. 2d 567, 207 N.E.2d 427 (1965); *Board of Educ., Borough of Union Beach v. New Jersey Educ. Ass'n,* 53 N.J. 29, 247 A.2d 867 (1968). However, since temporary injunctive orders are generally considered to be extraordinary remedies, some courts have ruled that they should be issued "only in cases of great emergency and gravity." See, e.g., *City of Rockford v. Firefighters, Local 413,* 98 Ill. App. 2d 36, 240 N.E.2d 705 (1968). See also *School Comm., Town of Westerly v. Teachers Ass'n,* 299 A.2d 441, 82 L.R.R.M. 2567 (R.I. 1973). See generally Appleton, *Standards for Enjoining Teacher Strikes: The Irreparable Harm Test and Its Statutory Analogies,* 69 Iowa L. Rev. 853 (1984).

3. In *San Diego Teachers Ass'n v. Superior Ct.,* 24 Cal. 3d 1, 593 P.2d 838 (1979), the court held that an unlawfully struck school district may not directly petition a court for injunctive relief. It must instead file with PERB an unfair labor practice charge alleging bad faith bargaining and/or failure to comply with impasse procedures. PERB can initially determine whether the strike constitutes an unfair labor practice and then decide whether it should seek injunctive relief. This exhaustion requirement was imposed to protect PERB's exclusive jurisdiction over such disputes. However, in *United States v. PATCO,* 653 F.2d 1134 (7th Cir.), *cert. denied,* 454 U.S. 1083 (1981), the court ruled that a federal agency may directly petition a district court for a strike injunction, despite the fact that the work stoppage also constitutes an unfair labor practice cognizable before the Federal Labor Relations Authority. District courts possess independent authority to enforce the strike proscription contained in 5 U.S.C. § 7311, and their jurisdiction is not preempted by the FLRA's exclusive jurisdiction over unfair labor practices. Accord *City of Manchester v. Firefighters Ass'n,* 1979-80 PBC ¶ 36,879 (N.H. 1980), which also recognized that a court may immediately enjoin a serious strike without first considering union claims that employer provocation precipitated the unlawful work stoppage.

4. In *Allen v. Maurer,* 6 Ill. App. 3d 633, 286 N.E.2d 135 (1972), the court rejected the "public trust" concept in a taxpayer action to enjoin a teachers' union from engaging in an unlawful strike.

> Here, the issue is whether or not taxpayers who have children in the public schools can maintain an action for injunctive relief grounded upon the duty of the State to maintain a free, efficient and high quality system of public education. We are not faced with an alleged misuse of public funds or conveyance of public property. We are concerned with the constitutionally mandated duty of the State to maintain a public school system. Can taxpayer-parents sue to enjoin a teachers strike in order to secure the performance of that constitutional duty under the facts presented by this record? We hold that they cannot.
>
> The Illinois Constitution S.H.A., provides that "a fundamental goal of the People of the State is the educational development of all persons to the limits of their capacities" and that "the State shall provide for an efficient system of high quality public educational institutions and services." Ill. Const., Art. X, Sec. 1. Hence, the State has a constitutional duty to provide and the public has a right to receive an efficient, high quality educational system. This duty is discharged by the State through local boards of education who are primarily responsible for fulfilling this constitutional mandate.
>
> The parties to this appeal have not cited, nor has our research disclosed, any precedent which would confer standing upon individual taxpayer-parents under the situation presented by the facts of this case. We hold that in the circumstances present here, the authority to seek an injunction rests in the State and its official representative, the Board of Education, the members of which are elected by the people to implement the command of the constitution. Any other decision would have the effect of usurping the Board of Education's control of the local educational system.

The Supreme Judicial Court of Massachusetts has similarly refused to permit private citizens to seek injunctive relief against an unlawful governmental work stoppage. See *Allen v. Sch. Comm. of Boston*, 396 Mass. 582, 487 N.E.2d 529 (1986).

5. If parties choose to disobey an injunctive order against strikes and picketing based upon their belief that the order is too broad, they may risk contempt liability, at least where the order is not void on its face. See *Ex parte James R. Purvis*, 382 So. 2d 512, 1979-80 PBC ¶ 36,997 (Ala. 1980).

6. Does a court possess jurisdiction to entertain a complaint in equity to enjoin a strike which is threatened but which has not yet commenced? See *Commonwealth v. Ryan*, 327 A.2d 351, 88 L.R.R.M. 2638 (Pa. 1974).

2. THE EFFECT OF ANTI-INJUNCTION STATUTES

Joint School District v. Education Association, 70 Wis. 2d 292, 234 N.W.2d 289 (1974). The Wisconsin Supreme Court considered the applicability of the Wisconsin anti-injunction statute to public sector labor disputes.

While this court has not previously considered this issue, nearly all courts which have, have concluded that the provisions of state Little Norris-LaGuardia Acts are inapplicable to suits brought by states or their political subdivisions against governmental employees. These decisions follow the rationale of the Supreme Court in *[United States v.] United Mine Workers (1947)*, 330 U.S. 258, 67 S. Ct. 677, 91 L. Ed. 884. In that case, which involved the federal Norris-LaGuardia Act, the court held that a labor dispute under 29 U.S.C.A., p. 53, sec. 113(a) must involve persons who have a certain status or relationship to other persons, and persons does not include the federal government. State courts have held that state copies of the federal act do not apply to public employees in the absence of an express statutory provision that they should so apply.

NOTES

1. State court decisions regarding this issue have generally followed the *United Mine Workers'* reasoning and concluded that state anti-injunction statutes do not apply to governmental labor disputes. See, e.g., *Oneida Sch. Dist. v. Oneida Educ. Ass'n*, 567 P.2d 830, 95 L.R.R.M. 3244 (Idaho 1977); *City of Minot v. Teamsters, Local 74*, 142 N.W.2d 612, 62 L.R.R.M. 2283 (N.D. 1966); *City of Pawtucket v. Pawtucket Teachers Alliance, Local 930*, 87 R.I. 364, 141 A.2d 624 (1958); *Delaware River & Bay Auth. v. International Org. of Masters, Mates & Pilots*, 45 N.J. 138, 211 A.2d 789 (1965); *Hansen v. Commonwealth*, 344 Mass. 214, 181 N.E.2d 843 (1962); *Port of Seattle v. ILWU*, 52 Wash. 2d 317, 324 P.2d 1099 (1958); *Rankin v. Shanker*, 23 N.Y.2d 111, 242 N.E.2d 802 (1968), *appeal dismissed*, 396 U.S. 120 (1969); *City of Los Angeles v. Los Angeles Bldg. & Trades Council*, 94 Cal. App. 2d 36, 210 P.2d 305 (1949); *Anderson Fed'n of Teachers, Local 519 v. School City*, 252 Ind. 558, 251 N.E.2d 15 (1969), *cert. denied*, 399 U.S. 928 (1970).

2. Although the Illinois Supreme Court initially ruled in *County of Peoria v. Benedict*, 47 Ill. 2d 166, 265 N.E.2d 141 (1970), *cert. denied*, 402 U.S. 929 (1971), that the Illinois anti-injunction act did apply to public sector labor disputes, it has since accepted the general view that such enactments are inapplicable to such disputes. See *City of Pana v. Crowe*, 57 Ill. 2d 547, 316 N.E.2d 513 (1974). A similar judicial reversal occurred in Minnesota. Compare *Board of*

Educ. v. Public Sch. Emps. Union, 233 Minn. 141, 45 N.W.2d 797 (1951), with *Minneapolis Fed'n of Teachers v. Obermeyer,* 275 Minn. 347, 147 N.W.2d 358 (1966).

3. In *Davis v. Henry,* 1988-90 PBC ¶ 35,504 (La. 1990), the Louisiana Supreme Court rejected the prevailing view and held that, absent specific statutory language to the contrary, the Louisiana "Little Norris-LaGuardia Act" would be applied to public sector work stoppages. See also *Kansas City v. Carpenters Dist. Council,* 699 P.2d 493, 1984-86 PBC ¶ 34,497 (Kan. 1985), wherein the court held that the provision in the Public Employer-Employee Relations Act (PERA) which specifically exempted public employee strikes from coverage under the state anti-injunction law was not applicable to a municipal employer that exercised its option to forego coverage under the PERA, precluding that municipality from obtaining injunctive relief against peaceful strike activity by its employees.

3. CONTEMPT PROCEEDINGS

STATE v. KING

82 Wis. 2d 124, 262 N.W.2d 80 (1978)

BEILFUSS, CHIEF JUSTICE.

These two cases arise from a labor dispute between the Wisconsin State Employees Union, Council 24, representing the state employees, and the State of Wisconsin. The orders appealed from in both cases deal with contempt of court proceedings for the alleged violations of temporary injunctions which required the employees at two state mental health centers to refrain from picketing and to return to work.

The parties in both cases are the State of Wisconsin, the Union, and certain named officers and employees. The issues in both cases are basically the same and for that reason these issues will be decided in one opinion....

Judge Bardwell, a circuit judge for Dane county, presided over the Central Center case, and Judge Pfiffner, the circuit judge for Chippewa county, presided over the Northern Center case. Central Center is located in Dane county and Northern Center in Chippewa county. Both institutions are state owned and operated by the State for the care, consultation, training and education for developmentally disabled persons.

Because of an unresolved labor dispute between the State and the Wisconsin State Employees Union, a statewide strike of state employees represented by the Union was called in the summer of 1977.

In both cases, during the strike, the State of Wisconsin commenced civil actions against the Wisconsin State Employees Union and some of its officers and agents. The State sought an injunction restraining the defendants from engaging in or encouraging others to engage in the strike at the two centers. These actions were commenced by the Attorney General at the request of the secretary of the Department of Administration and the Acting Governor.

On July 11, 1977, a temporary injunction was issued in the Central Center action enjoining the defendants from engaging in or encouraging others to engage in the strike. On July 8, 1977, a like temporary injunction was issued in the Northern Center case.

The employees in both cases ignored the temporary injunction and continued to strike in defiance of the injunction.

The strike was settled on July 17, 1977, and the employees returned to work forthwith. On July 20, 1977 the Attorney General received instructions from the secretary of the Department of Administration to compromise and discontinue all pending litigation pursuant to a non-recrimination clause agreed to by the Union and the State.

However, earlier in the day, on July 20th, the Attorney General had filed petitions for orders to show cause why the Union and designated employees should not be found in contempt of court for violating the temporary injunction....

In Central Center the Attorney General filed a notice to dismiss. At the July 28th hearing Judge Bardwell denied the motion and issued another order to show cause directing the Union to appear on September 12, 1977, in the contempt proceeding. On August 3d the trial court denied a motion by Thomas King, executive director of the Union, to dismiss the action and all proceedings.

The Attorney General was ordered to serve as special counsel for the September 12th hearing. King's subsequent motion to stay was denied. This court granted a temporary stay on August 31, 1977, and on September 8, 1977 King appealed from the various orders of the trial courts.

The proceedings in the Northern Center case were quite similar, but different in some important aspects. The Attorney General and the Union made motions to dismiss — both motions were denied. Judge Pfiffner announced the contempt hearing would be held and decided to hear the alleged contempt of one of the employees, Norma Chance. Counsel for the Union moved for substitution of judge, which was denied. Judge Pfiffner then proceeded to hear the matter. He called and examined witnesses and found Norma Chance in contempt of court for her violation of the temporary injunction. A fine of $10 per day for six days was imposed. Judge Pfiffner then ordered the Attorney General to represent the court as special counsel in contempt proceedings against other named individuals.

There is no real challenge to the validity of the orders granting the temporary injunctions. The legislature has said it is an unfair labor practice for state employees to strike, — further, the only employees enjoined were those engaged in what may be regarded as essential services for the mentally disadvantaged at Central Center and Northern Center.

The Union and Norma Chance have appealed from the various orders.

The major issue is whether the court can conduct a civil contempt proceeding after the principal action has been settled.

In general there are two categories of contempt: civil and criminal.[2] In some instances the same conduct can constitute civil or criminal contempt. Several general rules have become well accepted. Usually a contempt action which seeks to vindicate the authority and dignity of the court is a criminal contempt, while a contempt which seeks to enforce a private right of one of the parties in an action is a civil contempt. This distinction is often expressed in the results which flow from the particular finding of contempt. If the order is coercive or reme-

---

[2]There are also direct contempts occurring in the presence of or having an effect upon court proceedings, and indirect contempts occurring outside the presence of the court, but these are not involved here.

dial, the contempt is civil. If the order is purely punitive, the contempt is criminal.

When invoked to enforce a right of a party the contempt power manifests itself in fines or imprisonment (usually of an indeterminate duration), which can be purged if the party found in contempt obeys the order which led to the contempt. For example, if a party desires information and another party refuses to give it in spite of a court order commanding that he do so, that party may be held in civil contempt.[5]

The fact that civil contempts are remedial or coercive, *i.e.*, designed to force one party to accede to another's demand, is demonstrated by the statutory requirement that the sentences be purgable. Civil contempt looks to the present and future and the civil contemnor holds the key to his jail confinement by compliance with the order. On the other hand, the criminal contemnor is brought to account for a completed past action, his sentences are not purgable and are determinate. Criminal contempt is punitive. It is not intended to force the contemnor to do anything for the benefit of another party.

The distinction between the two forms of contempt is important because most of the constitutionally required bill of rights procedures and due process protections apply only to criminal contempt. With the major exception of contempt committed in the physical presence of the trial court (direct contempt), a criminal contemnor is entitled to, *inter alia,* an unbiased judge, *In re Murchison,* 349 U.S. 133, 137 (1955), *Mayberry v. Pennsylvania,* 400 U.S. 455 (1971); a presumption of innocence until found guilty beyond a reasonable doubt, a right against self-incrimination, *State ex rel. Rodd v. Verage,* 177 Wis. 295, 317, 187 N.W. 830 (1922), *Gompers v. Bucks Stove & Range Co.,* 221 U.S. 418, 444 (1911); notice of the charges, the right to call witnesses, time to prepare a defense, *Cooke v. United States,* 267 U.S. 517, 537 (1925); and a right to a jury trial if the sentence is for more than six months, *Cheff v. Schnackenberg,* 384 U.S. 373 (1966), *Bloom v. Illinois,* 391 U.S. 194, 210 (1968).

The courts have evidently declined to extend these rights to the civil contemnor, not because he may not serve sentences as long or even longer than those served by a criminal contemnor but on the theory that these rights are unnecessary because he holds the key to his confinement.

In these cases both the parties and both the trial courts agree that the procedures utilized were for civil contempt. In the cases at hand the acts complained of could have been the basis for criminal contempt. Although everyone concerned proclaims this to be a civil contempt, all the indicia of contempt point toward criminal contempt. These cases would have presented no foreseeable problems if they had been brought as criminal contempt.

On July 17, 1977, the strike by the Wisconsin State Employees Union against the State was settled. On July 20, 1977, the Attorney General petitioned the circuit courts for Dane and Chippewa counties to find the Union in contempt. Therefore at the time the contempt proceeding was commenced it was impossible to use it as a tool to enforce the injunction. If the strike had still been ongoing the contempt power could have been used for a coercive or remedial

---

[5] Note however that in refusing to obey an order for the benefit of a party the contemnor also challenges the authority of the court. Thus an element of criminal contempt is evident in some civil contempts.

end, namely to get the workers at the Central and Northern Centers back on their jobs. However, by July 20th the strike had been settled, the workers were back on their jobs, and coercive or remedial action could serve no purpose at that time. The only purpose for a contempt action brought at the time the contempt was sought in these cases was punishment to vindicate the authority of the court.

In *Gompers v. Bucks Stove & Range Co.,* 221 U.S. 418, 31 S. Ct. 492, 55 L. Ed. 797 (1911), the United States Supreme Court held that settlement of the underlying controversy required dismissal of civil contempt grounded in that controversy. Thus, under this rule, civil contempt begun before or, as here, after the settlement of the underlying dispute, is moot because it cannot achieve a coercive or remedial effect.

The State argues that *Gompers* may be distinguished. It cites the following language from *Gompers*:

> "When the main case was settled, every proceeding which was dependent upon it, or a part of it, was also necessarily settled — of course without prejudice to the power and right of the court to punish for contempt by proper proceedings." 221 U.S. at 451.

The State contends that this contempt proceeding is in fact the "proper proceeding" referred to in *Gompers;* that it is a separate and independent proceeding prosecuted by the court on its own motion. The State, however, neglects to include the next sentence from *Gompers,* which provides:

> "If this had been a separate and independent proceeding at law for criminal contempt, to vindicate the authority of the court ... it could not, in any way, have been affected by any settlement which the parties to the equity cause made in their private litigation." 221 U.S. at 451.

The separate proceeding referred to in *Gompers* is one in criminal contempt, not civil contempt as a supplementary proceeding in a civil action.

The State's next response goes to the heart of the issue — Wisconsin has explicitly rejected the *Gompers* holding. *Wisconsin E.R. Board v. Allis-Chalmers Workers' Union,* 249 Wis. 590, 599, 25 N.W.2d 425 (1946); *State ex rel. Rodd v. Verage,* 177 Wis. 295, 312-13, 187 N.W. 830 (1922). In doing so Wisconsin has created a unique third category of contempt — civil contempt with punitive sanctions.

In the *Rodd Case* the contemnor in a civil contempt was given a four month sentence with no opportunity to purge. In spite of the fact that the contemnor did not hold the keys to the jail as is normally required in civil contempt, the court held that the result was permissible in a civil contempt proceeding:

> "So we arrive at the conclusion that where a court in order to protect private rights issues its order restraining the commission of certain acts, and it subsequently is made to appear to the court that one has committed the acts prohibited under circumstances which indicate a purpose on his part to disregard the order of the court and to continue in the performance of the acts prohibited, and that such continued conduct will injuriously affect the rights of a party to the action, the court may, as a remedial measure civil in character and for the purpose of preventing further injury to a suitor, imprison the contemnor; and especially is that so when the court is moved to action on the

application of the aggrieved party. The dominant character of the imprisonment is remedial and coercive, although a punitive effect may also result." 177 Wis. at 314, 187 N.W. at 838.

On its language alone the *Rodd Case* is distinguishable because there is at least a colorable claim in it that the imprisonment is remedial and coercive in that there was a likelihood of continued violation of the court's order. But in these cases the orders — the injunctions — have become ineffectual because the parties have settled. Any sentence here, purgable or not, cannot be remedial because there is no threat nor possibility of continued violation. Any sentence here can only be punitive.

However, language in other cases dealing with this third category of contempt indicates that this court has permitted the imposition of punitive sanctions in civil contempt which have no remedial or coercive attributes. *Emerson v. Huss,* 127 Wis. 215, 106 N.W. 518 (1906); *Wisconsin E.R. Board v. Mews,* 29 Wis. 2d 44, 138 N.W.2d 147 (1965).

If we adhere to the continued existence of this third category then the circuit courts should be affirmed. On the other hand, if the court accepts the Union's position and eliminates this category, then the State may still proceed in contempt but must do so in a new, criminal proceeding. We conclude that the latter course is preferable.

In support of this position is the fact that the legislature no longer recognizes punitive sanctions for civil contempt. Sec. 295.02(5), Stats. (1975), effective June 14, 1976, provides that no person shall be fined or imprisoned for civil contempt except as specified in subs. (1) and (2) which concern remedial and coercive measures and do not mention punitive actions.

The courts of this state and those of many other jurisdictions have long held that they possess an inherent contempt power over their branch of the government to maintain decorum and see that their orders are carried out. *State ex rel. Rodd v. Verage,* 177 Wis. 295, 305-06, 187 N.W. 830 (1922); *In re Hon. Chas. E. Kading,* 70 Wis. 2d 508, 543b, 235 N.W.2d 409, 238 N.W.2d 63, 239 N.W.2d 297 (1975); *Ferris v. State ex rel. Maass,* 75 Wis. 2d 542, 546, 249 N.W.2d 789 (1977); *Anderson v. Dunn,* 19 U.S. (6 Wheat.) 204, 226-27 (1821); *Doyle v. London Guarantee Co.,* 204 U.S. 599, 607 (1907).

However, this court has just as consistently held that this power is subject to reasonable legislative regulation:

"Doubtless, this power may be regulated, and the manner of its exercise prescribed, by statute, but certainly it cannot be entirely taken away, nor can its efficiency be so impaired or abridged as to leave the court without power to compel the due respect and obedience which is essential to preserve its character as a judicial tribunal." *State ex rel. Attorney General v. Circuit Court for Eau Claire County,* 97 Wis. 1, 8, 72 N.W. 193, 194 (1897). See also, *Upper Lakes Shipping v. Seafarers I. Union,* 22 Wis. 2d 7, 17, 125 N.W.2d 324 (1963).

The Union cites the following language from a recent case in support of its claim that punitive sanctions are no longer allowed:

"While this court has reserved its traditional inherent powers in this area.... The differences between civil and criminal contempt are and have been statutorily defined." *Ferris v. State ex rel. Maass, supra,* 75 Wis. 2d at 546, 249 N.W.2d at 791.

This language falls far short of indicating any abdication of the court's inherent powers. We believe the legislative prohibition of punitive civil contempt is a reasonable regulation and should be followed.

Punitive sanctions in civil contempt are contrary to the well recognized opposite natures of civil and criminal contempt. As this court recently stated: "Imprisonment under civil contempt ... is coercive, whereas imprisonment for criminal contempt is punitive." *Ferris, supra,* 75 Wis. 2d at 545, 249 N.W.2d at 791. We now conclude those cases which hold that courts in civil contempt may impose purely punitive sanctions are anomalies and should no longer be considered authority.

This holding will produce uniformity in the Wisconsin decisions which have seen the court declare in the *Rodd Case* that civil contempt may be punitive, while three years later the same court stated:

"While the proceeding is denominated a civil contempt and the procedure is that prescribed by ch. 295, nevertheless it was in the nature of a proceeding for criminal contempt.... The real character of the proceeding is to be determined by the relief sought. The relief sought here was not to enforce a private right but to punish the contemnor for a past offense." *Wetzler v. Glassner,* 185 Wis. 593, 595-96, 201 N.W. 740, 741 (1925).

Another reason for supporting this distinction is as noted above — criminal contemnors have the benefit of a multitude of constitutional procedural rights. The reason that civil contemnors do not possess the same rights is that they hold the keys to their own jails. A civil contemnor in Wisconsin who is fined or imprisoned for purely punitive reasons and does not have the ability to purge probably can make a good case for reversal on the grounds that he is entitled to the constitutional safeguards of the criminal contempt procedure.

The ultimate question in this case is whether the authority and dignity of the circuit courts for Dane and Chippewa counties can be vindicated if the concept of civil contempt with purely punitive sanctions is rejected. Sec. 295.02(6), Stats., declares that:

"Nothing in this section may prohibit the court from imposing punishment of fine or imprisonment for criminal contempt under ss. 256.03 to 256.07."

Although the procedure required in criminal contempt is much more cumbersome, costly and time-consuming, it is not the policy of the law to choose expediency over due process when it should be afforded.

We conclude in the cases before us that the remedy of civil contempt expired when the actions were settled and the parties moved to dismiss the actions. It follows therefore that the civil contempt proceedings in both cases must be dismissed.

Because we have concluded the civil contempt proceedings must be dismissed, the other issues raised in these appeals are not considered.

Orders reversed and remanded for proceedings not inconsistent with the opinion. No costs to be taxed.

SCHOOL COMMITTEE v. DLOUHY

360 Mass. 109, 271 N.E.2d 655 (1971)

QUIRICO, JUSTICE. These are two bills in equity entered in the Superior Court on September 16, 1968, and September 3, 1969, respectively. The plaintiffs in each bill are (a) the school committee of New Bedford (school committee) and (b) the city of New Bedford (city). The defendants in each bill are (a) certain named persons who are made defendants individually and in their representative capacities as officers and members of an unincorporated association (Association) which is the collective bargaining agent for all of the schoolteachers employed by the city, (b) all the members of the Association, and (c) Frederick J. Lambert who is described as the Director of Field Services of the Massachusetts Teachers Association of which the Association in New Bedford is an affiliate.

The plaintiffs seek by each bill to restrain and enjoin the defendants other than Lambert from engaging in a work stoppage or withholding of their services from the city, or engaging in or inducing or encouraging the withholding of services by the teachers of the city's school department. They also seek by each bill to restrain and enjoin the defendant Lambert from inducing or encouraging a work stoppage or withholding of services by these teachers. In each case the court granted such relief in the following stages: by a restraining order, by a preliminary injunction, and by a final decree. The final decree in the 1969 case further held forty-eight defendants, including Lambert, in civil contempt of court and imposed compensatory fines on them, and also held Lambert in criminal contempt of court and imposed a fine on him therefor. The cases are before us on the defendants' appeals from the final decrees in both cases.

1. *Appeal from Final Decree in 1968 Case.* The final decree in the 1968 case permanently enjoined the defendants other than Lambert "from engaging in a work stoppage or withholding of services ... or inducing or encouraging the withholding of services by the teachers of the New Bedford School Department," and it permanently enjoined Lambert "from inducing or encouraging a work stoppage or withholding of services by teachers employed by the City of New Bedford." The decree states that "all parties by counsel in open court" consented to its entry. "The decree appearing to be made by consent, the appeal cannot be sustained." *Winchester v. Winchester,* 121 Mass. 127, 128. See *Evans v. Hamlin,* 164 Mass. 239, 240; *New York Cent. & Hudson River R.R. v. T. Stuart & Son Co.,* 260 Mass. 242, 248; *Fishman v. Alberts,* 321 Mass. 280, 281-82. The final decree in the 1968 case, having been entered by consent of all of the parties, must stand.

2. *Appeal from Final Decree in 1969 Case — Permanent Injunction.* Paragraphs numbered 1 and 2 of the final decree in the 1969 case permanently enjoin the defendants in that case in substantially the same language used in the final decree entered in the 1968 case discussed above. There is a difference in the names of the persons, other than Lambert, who are enjoined, but that difference does not affect our decision.... What we have said above with reference to the final decree in the 1968 case applies equally to them.

3. *Appeal from Final Decree in 1969 Case — Adjudication of Civil Contempt.* On September 3, 1969, a judge of the Superior Court issued a restraining order against the defendants in the 1969 case, using therein the same

language which he later incorporated in the first two numbered paragraphs of the final decree discussed above. On September 4, 1969, the plaintiffs filed a petition alleging that the defendant Lambert and 183 named teachers who were members of the New Bedford Educators' Association had violated the restraining order and asked that Lambert and such teachers be adjudged in contempt for such violation. When this petition was reached for hearing, counsel for the defendants stated to the court: "[M]y clients are all now, each and individually, every one of them, prepared and ready to plead guilty to what they understand is a charge of civil contempt." Thereupon the judge stated: "[T]he clerk will call the name of each person who has been cited for contempt. The clerk will inquire after the name has been called: Do you admit the allegation of contempt, or do you deny it? If you admit it, then I want each defendant as their name is called, to say, 'I admit.' If you deny it, then as your name is called, you say, 'I deny.'" The clerk then called the names of Lambert and of forty-seven other persons who were defendants in the petition for contempt. As each name was called, the person whose name was called replied, "I admit" or "I admit it."

... By reason of their admission of guilt of civil contempt, such defendants cannot now require us to decide the many legal and constitutional, but nonjurisdictional, questions which they raised before the trial judge prior to admitting their guilt....

4. *Appeal from Final Decree in 1969 Case: Amounts of Fines Imposed for Civil Contempt.* As a part of the final decree which adjudged certain defendants guilty of civil contempt, the court also imposed a fine of $50,000 on them and the defendant Lambert. As to each of these fines the decree stated that it was "to compensate the ... [city] for damages as a result of said civil contempt." It also provided that the payment of $50,000 to the city "by one or all of said respondents on the civil contempts shall constitute full compliance with said orders for payment for civil contempts."

After such defendants admitted their guilt of civil contempt and before fixing the amount of the fines therefor, the judge held a hearing to receive evidence on the amount of damages which their contempt had caused to the city. The superintendent of schools testified that despite the work stoppage, many principals, directors, teachers, substitute teachers and cafeteria workers reported for work at schools which had to be closed and those persons had to be paid, that school buses were operated to the schools which had to be closed, that there were charges for utilities serving the schools on the days they had to be closed, and that the days of school thus lost would have to be made up later at which time the same expenditures would be required. He estimated that the total expense to the city for these categories would be about $79,172[4] and that there were some variables and additional items of expense to the city which he could not compute at that time but which he thought would bring the total expense to

---

[4] In arriving at this figure the superintendent said he was including payments of $60 a day to forty principals for eight days each and he computed this item at $11,200. The correct computation should be $19,200. With this correction, the categories of damages to which he testified included the following: $64,000 paid to teachers, $960 for school buses, $19,200 paid to principals, and $4,992 paid to cafeteria workers. These items alone amount to a total of $89,152 instead of the $79,172 stated by the witness.

the city to $100,000. He believed the latter figure to be a "fair figure" and a "conservative figure."

After hearing the evidence and statements by counsel the judge reviewed the background of the controversy and then stated: "It is my judgment that the responsibility for the situation that arose must be shared equally by the ... [plaintiffs] as well as by the ... [defendants].... I find on the evidence that the loss to the ... [city] is $100,000." He then imposed the fines of $50,000. The judge's finding that the loss to the city was $100,000 was supported by the testimony of the superintendent of schools who was the only witness on that subject.

"In cases of civil contempt such as the one before us, a fine may be assessed for the benefit of a party who has suffered injury because of the contempt. As are damages in tort, the fine is designed to compensate the injured party for actual losses sustained by reason of the contumacious conduct of the defendant, i.e., for the pecuniary injury caused by the act of disobedience." *Lyon v. Bloomfield*, 355 Mass. 738, 744; *Root v. MacDonald*, 260 Mass. 344, 361-65. The fine in such a case may also be designed to reimburse the plaintiff for counsel fees and other expenses incurred in enforcing his rights. *Grunberg v. Louison*, 343 Mass. 729, 736; *Parker v. United States*, 126 F.2d 370, 379-80 (1st Cir.)....

5. *Appeal from Final Decree in 1969 Case: Adjudication that Lambert is Guilty of Criminal Contempt.* After the judge heard the evidence from the superintendent of schools on the damages sustained by the city, and before he announced his decision thereon, he asked counsel for the plaintiffs what the evidence he "would have presented to the Court in the event of a trial ... [would disclose] as to the leader in this strike, the guiding influence." Counsel answered in part that "the officers of the Association and Mr. Lambert would have been shown to have influenced the events of the last few days." The judge asked counsel for the defendants for some background information on Lambert and it was given to him. Without further hearing or evidence the judge then announced his finding that "Lambert was the director of the conduct of the other defendants and all the members of the New Bedford Educators Association ... [and] that his directing provided irresponsible leadership." He also stated: "I find Frederick J. Lambert guilty of criminal and civil contempt. On the criminal contempt, I impose a ... fine of $5,000." This finding and fine were incorporated in the final decree, in addition to the findings and fines on civil contempt.

The defendant Lambert's admission of guilt was limited to civil contempt. He was never asked specifically whether he admitted guilt of criminal contempt, and he never specifically admitted such guilt. He was never put to trial on the question of criminal contempt, and no evidence was presented against him on that charge. The burden of proving that charge was on the plaintiffs, and it was not incumbent on Lambert to disprove it. This was not a case of a contempt which had occurred or been committed in the presence of the judge. It was a contempt sometimes referred to or described as an "indirect or constructive" contempt to distinguish it from a "direct" contempt committed in the presence of a judge who may act thereon summarily. *Berlandi v. Commonwealth*, 314 Mass. 424, 445-46.

"The punishment of ... [criminal contempt] is solely for the vindication of public authority and the majesty of the law. In general, the proceedings leading up to the punishment should be in accordance with the principles which govern the practice in criminal cases. In a broad sense, the prosecution of such an offender is a criminal case, and the sentence to punishment is a judgment." *Hurley v. Commonwealth,* 188 Mass. 443, 445. *Woodbury v. Commonwealth,* 295 Mass. 316, 323. *Dolan v. Commonwealth,* 304 Mass. 325, 327. In such a prosecution, "the accused should be advised of the charges and have a reasonable opportunity to meet them by way of defense or explanation." *Cooke v. United States,* 267 U.S. 517, 537; *Garabedian v. Commonwealth,* 336 Mass. 119, 124-25.

The proceedings which concluded with the finding that Lambert was guilty of criminal contempt and the imposition of a fine of $5,000 on him did not comply with the basic requirements applicable to such cases. That adjudication therefore cannot stand.

In summary, (a) the final decree in the 1968 case is affirmed with costs of appeal to the plaintiffs, and (b) the final decree in the 1969 case is modified by striking therefrom so much of paragraph numbered 3 as holds the defendant Lambert guilty of criminal contempt and by striking therefrom paragraph numbered 4 imposing a fine of $5,000 on him for criminal contempt; as thus modified that final decree is affirmed.

So ordered.

NOTES

1. In *Hicks ex rel. Feiock v. Feiock,* 485 U.S. 624 (1988), the Supreme Court succinctly distinguished between "criminal" and "civil" contempt sanctions.

> If the relief provided is a sentence of imprisonment, it is remedial [i.e., "civil"] if "the defendant stands committed unless and until he performs the affirmative act required by the court's order," and is punitive [i.e., "criminal"] if "the sentence is limited to imprisonment for a definite period." [*Gompers v. Bucks Stove & Range Co.,* 221 U.S. 418 (1911)] at 442. If the relief provided is a fine, it is remedial when it is paid to the complainant, and punitive when it is paid to the court, though a fine that would be payable to the court is also remedial when the defendant can avoid paying the fine simply by performing the affirmative act required by the court's order. These distinctions lead up to the fundamental proposition that criminal penalties may not be imposed on someone who has not been afforded the protections that the Constitution requires of such criminal proceedings, including the requirement that the offense be proved beyond a reasonable doubt. See, e.g., *Gompers, supra,* at 444.

See *Hawaii PERB v. AFSCME, Local 646,* 1981-83 PBC ¶ 37,806 (Haw. 1983) ("The significant and essential characteristic of a sanction imposed for civil contempt is that the penalty can be avoided by compliance with the court order."); *Massachusetts LRC v. Fall River Educators' Ass'n,* 416 N.E.2d 1340, 1980-81 PBC ¶ 37,208 (Mass. 1981) (civil contempt fine need not be wholly compensatory, but may be partially coercive).

2. In *City of Wilmington v. General Teamsters, Local 326,* 321 A.2d 123, 86 L.R.R.M. 2959 (Del. 1974), the court considered the nature of contempt proceedings which followed defiance by city dockworkers of a court-ordered injunction. Concluding that the contempt in the case consisted of a combination of civil and criminal elements, the Court held that where the criminal elements predominated, they would control procedure on review, so that the city had no appeal from findings of not guilty with respect to the criminal contempt portion of the case. However, this did not preclude city appeal from the civil aspects of the proceeding. On this issue, the court found the union responsible for the action of its members who had engaged in the unlawful strike, rejecting the union leadership's argument that it had "lost control" of the membership and should thus not be found responsible. Regarding the latter issue, see also *Labor Relations Comm. v. Boston Teachers Union, Local 66,* 371 N.E.2d 761, 97 L.R.R.M. 2507 (Mass. 1977), wherein the court sustained civil contempt citations against union officers who failed to affirmatively endeavor to prevent an enjoined work stoppage.

3. In *Board of Junior College Dist. No. 508 v. Cook Cty. College Teachers Union, Local 1600,* 126 Ill. App. 2d 418, 262 N.E.2d 125 (1970), *cert. denied,* 402 U.S. 998 (1971), the court rejected a joint request made by the employer and the union during criminal contempt proceedings to dismiss the temporary injunction, stating: "Under no theory can a party that obtains an injunction bind the issuing court with condonation of contemptuous or illegal acts of those who violate the lower court's order. To give effect to such a theory would usurp the highest function of our courts." Accord *City of Manchester v. Firefighters Ass'n,* 1979-80 PBC ¶ 36,879 (N.H. 1980).

4. Perhaps the most frequently litigated issue pertaining to the contempt process concerns the right of the charged party to a jury trial. It is established that in the case of purely civil contempt, the right to trial by jury is not constitutionally mandated and arises, if at all, statutorily. *Shillitani v. United States,* 384 U.S. 364 (1966). As was noted in the *King* decision, a jury right attaches to indirect criminal contempt proceedings that are deemed "serious." *Bloom v. Illinois,* 391 U.S. 194 (1968). The seriousness of the offense is usually determined by the penalty actually imposed (due to the plenary power of the court to administer criminal contempt sanctions), and a jury trial is not required for contempts not involving at least six months of incarceration. *Cheff v. Shnackenberg,* 384 U.S. 373 (1966). Where lesser penalties are imposed and there is no statute providing a jury right, most courts have held that a jury trial is not required in criminal contempt cases. See, e.g., *In re Block,* 50 N.J. 494, 236 A.2d 589 (1967); *City of N.Y. v. DeLury,* 23 N.Y.2d 175, 243 N.E.2d 128 (1968), *appeal dismissed,* 391 U.S. 455 (1969); and *State v. Heath,* 177 N.W.2d 751, 75 L.R.R.M. 2204 (N.D. 1970). But cf. *United States v. PATCO,* 678 F.2d 1 (1st Cir. 1982) (finding jury right where $5000 contempt fine imposed on union president).

5. Where a governmental employer decides to terminate unlawfully striking employees and permanently replace them with other workers, a court will generally not continue to assess contempt penalties against the strikers post-dating their date of termination, since they no longer possess the ability to return to work. See *United States v. PATCO,* 524 F. Supp. 160 (D.D.C. 1981); *United States v. PATCO,* 703 F.2d 443 (10th Cir. 1983).

6. A contempt proceeding generally may not be used as a vehicle for contesting the validity of the underlying injunction. See, e.g., *County of Peoria v. Benedict,* 47 Ill. 2d 166, 265 N.E.2d 141 (1970), *cert. denied,* 402 U.S. 929 (1971); *Dade Cty. Classroom Teachers Ass'n v. Rubin,* 238 So. 2d 284 (Fla. 1970), *cert. denied,* 400 U.S. 1009 (1971).

4. DISMISSALS, FINES, DAMAGES, AND TAXPAYER SUITS

HORTONVILLE JOINT SCHOOL DISTRICT NO. 1 v. HORTONVILLE EDUCATION ASSOCIATION

426 U.S. 482, 96 S. Ct. 2308, 49 L. Ed. 2d 1 (1976)

CHIEF JUSTICE BURGER delivered the opinion of the Court.

We granted certiorari in this case to determine whether school board members, vested by state law with the power to employ and dismiss teachers, could, consistent with the Due Process Clause of the Fourteenth Amendment, dismiss teachers engaged in a strike prohibited by state law.

I

The petitioners are a Wisconsin school district, the seven members of its school board, and three administrative employees of the district. Respondents are teachers suing on behalf of all teachers in the district and the Hortonville Education Association (HEA), the collective-bargaining agent for the district's teachers.

During the 1972-1973 school year Hortonville teachers worked under a master collective-bargaining agreement; negotiations were conducted for renewal of the contract, but no agreement was reached for the 1973-1974 school year. The teachers continued to work while negotiations proceeded during the year without reaching agreement. On March 18, 1974, the members of the teachers' union went on strike, in direct violation of Wisconsin law. On March 20, the district superintendent sent all teachers a letter inviting them to return to work; a few did so. On March 23, he sent another letter, asking the 86 teachers still on strike to return, and reminding them that strikes by public employees were illegal; none of these teachers returned to work. After conducting classes with substitute teachers on March 26 and 27, the Board decided to conduct disciplinary hearings for each of the teachers on strike. Individual notices were sent to each teacher setting hearings for April 1, 2, and 3.

On April 1, most of the striking teachers appeared before the Board with counsel. Their attorney indicated that the teachers did not want individual hearings, but preferred to be treated as a group. Although counsel agreed that the teachers were on strike, he raised several procedural objections to the hearings. He also argued that the Board was not sufficiently impartial to exercise discipline over the striking teachers and that the Due Process Clause of the Fourteenth Amendment required an independent, unbiased decisionmaker. An offer of proof was tendered to demonstrate that the strike had been provoked by the Board's failure to meet teachers' demands, and petitioner's counsel asked to cross-examine Board members individually. The Board rejected the request, but permitted counsel to make the offer of proof, aimed at showing that the Board's contract offers were unsatisfactory, that the Board used coercive and illegal bargaining tactics, and that teachers in the district had been locked out by the Board.

On April 2, the Board voted to terminate the employment of striking teachers, and advised them by letter to that effect. However, the same letter invited all teachers on strike to reapply for teaching positions. One teacher accepted the invitation and returned to work; the Board hired replacements to fill the remaining positions.

Respondents then filed suit against petitioners in state court, alleging, among other things, that the notice and hearing provided them by the Board were inadequate to comply with due process requirements. The trial court granted the Board's motion for summary judgment on the due process claim....

On appeal, the Wisconsin Supreme Court reversed, 66 Wis. 2d 469, 225 N.W.2d 658 (1975). On the single issue now presented it held that the Due Process Clause of the Fourteenth Amendment to the Federal Constitution required that the teachers' conduct and the Board's response be evaluated by an impartial decisionmaker other than the Board. The rationale of the Wisconsin Supreme Court appears to be that although the teachers had admitted being on strike, and although the strike violated Wisconsin law, the Board had available other remedies than dismissal, including an injunction prohibiting the strike, a call for mediation, or continued bargaining. Relying on our holding in *Morrissey v. Brewer,* 408 U.S. 471 (1972), the Wisconsin court then held "it would seem essential, even in cases of undisputed or stipulated facts, that an impartial decision maker be charged with the responsibility of determining what action shall be taken on the basis of those facts." 66 Wis. 2d, at 493....

Since it concluded that state law provided no adequate remedy, the Wisconsin Supreme Court fashioned one it thought necessary to comply with federal due process principles. To leave with the Board "[a]s much control as possible ... to set policy and manage the school," the court held that the Board should after notice and hearing make the decision to fire in the first instance. A teacher dissatisfied with the Board's decision could petition any court of record in the county for a *de novo* hearing on *all* issues; the trial court would "resolve any factual disputes and provide the reasonable disposition." 66 Wis. 2d, at 498. The Wisconsin Supreme Court recognized that this remedy was "not ideal because a court may be required to make public policy decisions that are better left to a legislative or administrative body." *Ibid.* But it would suffice "until such time and only until such time as the legislature provides a means to establish a forum that will meet the requirements of due process."...

II ....

The sole issue in this case is whether the Due Process Clause of the Fourteenth Amendment prohibits this school board from making the decision to dismiss teachers admittedly engaged in a strike and persistently refusing to return to their duties. The Wisconsin Supreme Court held that state law prohibited the strike and that termination of the striking teachers' employment was within the Board's statutory authority. 66 Wis. 2d, at 479-481....

A. Respondents argue, and the Wisconsin Supreme Court held, that the choice presented for the Board's decision is analogous to that involved in revocation of parole in *Morrissey v. Brewer, supra,* that the decision could be made only by an impartial decisionmaker, and that the Board was not impartial. In *Morrissey* the Court considered a challenge to state procedures employed in revoking the parole of state prisoners. There we noted that the parole revocation decision involved two steps: First, an inquiry whether the parolee had in fact violated the conditions of his parole; second, determining whether viola-

tions found were serious enough to justify revocation of parole and the consequent deprivation of the parolee's conditional liberty. ... Nothing in this case is
analogous to the first step in *Morrissey,* since the teachers admitted to being on
strike. But respondents argue that the School Board's decision in this case is, for
constitutional purposes, the same as the second aspect of the decision to revoke
parole. The Board cannot make a "reasonable" decision on this issue, the Wisconsin Supreme Court held and respondents argue, because its members are
biased in some fashion that the due process guarantees of the Fourteenth
Amendment prohibit.[3]

Morrissey arose in a materially different context. We recognized there that a
parole violation could occur at a place distant from where the parole revocation
decision would finally be made; we also recognized the risk of factual error,
such as misidentification. To minimize this risk, we held: "[D]ue process requires that after the arrest [for parole violation], the determination that reasonable ground exists for revocation of parole should be made by someone not
directly involved in the case." *Id.,* at 485. But this holding must be read against
our earlier discussion in *Morrissey* of the parole officer's role as counselor and
confidant to the parolee; it is this same officer who, on the basis of preliminary
information, decides to arrest the parolee. A school board is not to be equated
with the parole officer as an arresting officer; the school board is more like the
parole board, for it has ultimate plenary authority to make its decisions derived
from the state legislature. General language about due process in a holding
concerning revocation of parole is not a reliable basis for dealing with the
School Board's power as an employer to dismiss teachers for cause. We must
focus more clearly on, first, the nature of the bias respondents attribute to the
Board, and, second, the nature of the interests at stake in this case.

B. Respondents' argument rests in part on doctrines that have no application
to this case. They seem to argue the Board members had some personal or
official stake in the decision whether the teachers should be dismissed, comparable to the stake the Court saw in *Tumey v. Ohio,* 273 U.S. 510 (1927), or
Ward v. Village of Monroeville, 409 U.S. 57 (1972); see also *Gibson v. Berryhill,*

---

[3]Respondents argue that the requirement that the Board's decision be "reasonable" is in fact a
requirement of state law. From that premise and from the premise that the "reasonableness" determination requires an evaluation of the Board's negotiating stance, they argue that nothing but
decision and review *de novo* by an "uninvolved" party will secure their right to a "reasonable"
decision. See *Withrow v. Larkin,* 421 U.S. 35, n. 25, at 58-59 (1975). It is clear, however, that the
Wisconsin Supreme Court held that the Board's decision must be "reasonable," not by virtue of state
law, but because of its reading of the Due Process Clause of the Fourteenth Amendment. First, the
Wisconsin court relied largely upon cases interpreting the Federal Constitution in this aspect of its
holding. See 66 Wis. 2d, at 493. Second, the only state case the Wisconsin Supreme Court cited for
more than a general statement of federal requirements was *Durkin v. Board of Police & Fire
Commissioners,* 48 Wis. 2d 112, 180 N.W.2d 1 (1970). There the Wisconsin Supreme Court interpreted a state statute that gave firemen and policemen the right to appeal a decision of the Board of
Police and Fire Commissioners to a state court; the statute expressly provided that the court was to
determine whether "upon the evidence the order of the Board was reasonable." 180 N.W.2d, at 3.
See Wis. Stat. Ann. § 62.13(5)(i). There is no comparable statutory provision giving teachers the
right to review by this standard. Finally, to impose a "reasonableness" requirement, or any other test
that looks to evaluation by another entity, makes semantic sense only where review is contemplated
by the statute. Review, and the standard for review, are concepts that go hand in hand. The
Wisconsin Supreme Court concluded both that review of the Board's decision was necessary and
that a "reasonableness" standard was appropriate as a result of its reading of the Due Process Clause
of the Fourteenth Amendment.

411 U.S. 564 (1973), and that the Board has manifested some personal bitterness toward the teachers, aroused by teacher criticism of the Board during the strike, see, e.g., *Taylor v. Hayes,* 418 U.S. 488 (1974); *Mayberry v. Pennsylvania,* 400 U.S. 455 (1971). Even assuming those cases state the governing standards when the decisionmaker is a public employer dealing with employees, the teachers did not show, and the Wisconsin courts did not find, that the Board members had the kind of personal or financial stake in the decision that might create a conflict of interest, and there is nothing in the record to support charges of personal animosity....

The only other factor suggested to support the claim of bias is that the School Board was involved in the negotiations that preceded and precipitated the striking teachers' discharge. Participation in those negotiations was a statutory duty of the Board. The Wisconsin Supreme Court held that this involvement, without more, disqualified the Board from deciding whether the teachers should be dismissed.... Mere familiarity with the facts of a case gained by an agency in the performance of its statutory role does not, however, disqualify a decisionmaker. *Withrow v. Larkin,* 421 U.S. 35, 47 (1975); *FTC v. Cement Institute,* 333 U.S. 683, 700-703 (1948). Nor is a decisionmaker disqualified simply because he has taken a position, even in public, on a policy issue related to the dispute, in the absence of a showing that he is not "capable of judging a particular controversy fairly on the basis of its own circumstances." *United States v. Morgan,* 313 U.S. 409, 421 (1941); see also *FTC v. Cement Institute, supra,* at 701.

Respondents' claim and the Wisconsin Supreme Court's holding reduce to the argument that the Board was biased because it negotiated with the teachers on behalf of the school district without reaching agreement and learned about the reasons for the strike in the course of negotiating. From those premises the Wisconsin court concluded that the Board lost its statutory power to determine that the strike and persistent refusal to terminate it amounted to conduct serious enough to warrant discharge of the strikers. Wisconsin statutes vest in the Board the power to discharge its employees, a power of every employer, whether it has negotiated with the employees before discharge or not. The Fourteenth Amendment permits a court to strip the Board of the otherwise unremarkable power the Wisconsin Legislature has given it only if the Board's prior involvement in negotiating with the teachers means that it cannot act consistent with due process.

C. Due process, as this Court has repeatedly held, is a term that "negates any concept of inflexible procedures universally applicable to every imaginable situation." *Cafeteria Workers v. McElroy,* 367 U.S. 886, 895 (1961). Determining what process is due in a given setting requires the Court to take into account the individual's stake in the decision at issue as well as the State's interest in a particular procedure for making it. See *Mathews v. Eldridge,* 424 U.S. 319 (1976); *Arnett v. Kennedy,* 416 U.S. 134, 168 (1974) (POWELL, J., concurring); *id.,* at 188 (WHITE, J., concurring and dissenting); *Goldberg v. Kelly,* 397 U.S. 254, 263-266 (1970). Our assessment of the interests of the parties in this case leads to the conclusion that this is a very different case from *Morrissey v. Brewer, supra,* and that the Board's prior role as negotiator does not disqualify it to decide that the public interest in maintaining uninterrupted classroom work required that teachers striking in violation of state law be discharged.

The teachers' interest in these proceedings is, of course, self-evident. They wished to avoid termination of their employment, obviously an important interest, but one that must be examined in light of several factors. Since the teachers admitted that they were engaged in a work stoppage, there was no possibility of an erroneous factual determination on this critical threshold issue. Moreover, what the teachers claim as a property right was the expectation that the jobs they had left to go and remain on strike in violation of law would remain open to them. The Wisconsin court accepted at least the essence of that claim in defining the property right under state law, and we do not quarrel with its conclusion. But even if the property interest claimed here is to be compared with the liberty interest at stake in *Morrissey,* we note that both "the risk of an erroneous deprivation" and "the degree of potential deprivation" differ in a qualitative sense and in degree from those in *Morrissey. Mathews v. Eldridge, supra,* 424 U.S. 319, at 335, 341.

The governmental interests at stake in this case also differ significantly from the interests at stake in *Morrissey.* The Board's decision whether to dismiss striking teachers involves broad considerations, and does not in the main turn on the Board's view of the "seriousness" of the teachers' conduct or the factors they urge mitigated their violation of state law. It was not an adjudicative decision, for the Board had an obligation to make a decision based on its own answer to an important question of policy: what choice among the alternative responses to the teachers' strike will best serve the interests of the school system, the interests of the parents and children who depend on the system, and the interests of the citizens whose taxes support it? The Board's decision was only incidentally a disciplinary decision; it had significant governmental and public policy dimensions as well. See Summers, *Public Employee Bargaining: A Political Perspective,* 83 Yale L.J. 1156 (1974).

State law vests the governmental, or policymaking, function exclusively in the School Board and the State has two interests in keeping it there. First, the Board is the body with overall responsibility for the governance of the school district; it must cope with the myriad day-to-day problems of a modern public school system including the severe consequences of a teachers' strike; by virtue of electing them the constituents have declared the Board members qualified to deal with these problems, and they are accountable to the voters for the manner in which they perform. Second, the state legislature has given to the Board the power to employ and dismiss teachers, as a part of the balance it has struck in the area of municipal labor relations; altering those statutory powers as a matter of federal due process clearly changes that balance. Permitting the Board to make the decision at issue here preserves its control over school district affairs, leaves the balance of power in labor relations where the state legislature struck it, and assures that the decision whether to dismiss the teachers will be made by the body responsible for that decision under state law.

III

Respondents have failed to demonstrate that the decision to terminate their employment was infected by the sort of bias that we have held to disqualify other decisionmakers as a matter of federal due process. A showing that the Board was "involved" in the events preceding this decision, in light of the important interest in leaving with the Board the power given by the state legislature, is not enough to overcome the presumption of honesty and integrity in policymakers with decisionmaking power. Cf. *Withrow v. Larkin,* 421 U.S. 35, 47 (1975). Accordingly, we hold that the Due Process Clause of the Fourteenth Amendment did not guarantee respondents that the decision to terminate their employment would be made or reviewed by a body other than the School Board....

JUSTICE STEWART, with whom JUSTICE BRENNAN and JUSTICE MARSHALL join, dissenting.

The issue in this case is whether the discharge of the respondent teachers by the petitioner school board violated the Due Process Clause of the Fourteenth Amendment because the board members were not impartial decisionmakers. It is now well established that "a biased decisionmaker [is] constitutionally unacceptable [and] 'our system of law has always endeavored to prevent even the probability of unfairness.'" *Withrow v. Larkin,* 421 U.S. 35, 47, quoting *In re Murchison,* 349 U.S. 133, 136.

The Court acknowledges, as it must, that it is "bound to accept the interpretation of Wisconsin law by the highest court of the State." *Ante,* at 6. Yet it then proceeds to reverse that court by assuming, as the petitioners urge, that under Wisconsin law the determination to discharge the striking teachers only "involved the [Board's] exercise of its discretion as to what should be done to carry out the duties that law placed on the Board." *Ibid.* It dismisses the respondents' version of Wisconsin law in a footnote. *Ante,* at pp. 7-8, n. 3.

But the fact is that the Wisconsin Supreme Court has not clearly delineated the state law criterion that governs the discharge of striking teachers, and this Court is wholly without power to resolve that issue of state law. I would therefore remand this case to the Wisconsin Supreme Court for it to determine whether, on the one hand, the school board is charged with considering the reasonableness of the strike in light of its own actions, or is, on the other, wholly free, as the Court today assumes, to exercise its discretion in deciding whether to discharge the teachers....

"[U]nder a realistic appraisal of psychological tendencies and human weaknesses," *Withrow v. Larkin, supra,* at 47, I believe that there is a constitutionally unacceptable danger of bias where school board members are required to assess the reasonableness of their own actions during heated contract negotiations that have culminated in a teachers' strike. If, therefore, the respondents' interpretation of the state law is correct, then I would agree with the Wisconsin Supreme Court that "the board was not an impartial decisionmaker in a constitutional sense and that the [teachers] were denied due process of law." 66 Wis. 2d 469, 494, 225 N.W.2d 658, 671.

For the reasons stated, I would vacate the judgment before us and remand this case to the Supreme Court of Wisconsin....

NOTES

1. The issue in *Rockwell v. Crestwood Sch. Dist. Bd. of Educ.,* 393 Mich. 616, 227 N.W.2d 736 (1975), *appeal dismissed,* 427 U.S. 901 (1976), was whether striking school teachers could be disciplined without a prior hearing. Section 6 of Michigan Public Employment Relations Act (PERA) provided for a post-discipline hearing at the employee's request, while the Teachers' Tenure Act provided for a pre-discharge hearing for teachers on continuing tenure. The court applied the PERA, rather than the Teachers' Tenure Act, on the grounds that the latter was designed to cover neither labor disputes nor concerted action by a group of individuals, as was the PERA. Addressing the constitutionality under the due process clause of such discipline, the court relied on *Arnett v. Kennedy,* 416 U.S. 134 (1974), in rejecting the teachers' arguments for a pre-disciplinary hearing, but it emphasized heavily the necessity of personal notice of the impending disciplinary action before the action was taken.

The union, the Crestwood Education Association, had filed unfair labor practice charges with the MERC against the School Board prior to the discharge of the teachers. Relative to this issue, the court said:

> The action of the Crestwood school board in discharging teachers for striking in violation of the provisions of the PERA prior to the hiring of replacements was not violative of that act. It does not necessarily follow, however, that these teachers may not be entitled to reinstatement should MERC determine that the school board engaged in an unfair labor practice....
>
> If MERC should determine that the employing school district committed an unfair labor practice, MERC *may,* despite the illegality of the teachers' strike, order reinstatement.... [Emphasis in the original.]
>
> If the MERC finds that an unfair labor practice or other misconduct was committed by both sides, it should balance the competing equities to reach a result best effectuating the goals of the act.

See *Sanford Hwy. Unit of Local 481, AFSCME v. Town of Sanford,* 411 A.2d 1010, 1979-80 PBC ¶ 36,841 (Me. 1980). See also Aaron, *Unfair Labor Practices and the Right to Strike in the Public Sector: Has the National Labor Relations Act Been a Good Model?,* 38 Stan. L. Rev. 1097 (1986).

In *Steelworkers v. University of Ala.,* 599 F.2d 56 (5th Cir. 1979), public employees who had been discharged for having engaged in an unlawful work stoppage contended that they had been impermissibly deprived of due process. The court indicated that the claimants' rights were substantially dependent upon a finding that they had possessed a "property interest" in their jobs and it determined that this issue had to be resolved by reference to applicable state law. The court concluded that no sufficient property interest had existed.

> We rely primarily upon the fact that these employees were "permanent" employees, defined in [personnel] handbook Section 36 as "individuals who have an indefinite appointment...." Under Alabama law, an employee employed for an indefinite period of time may resign from his employment at any time, and may be terminated therefrom at any time at the will of his employer, provided that the employee furnishes no consideration in addition to the services incident to the employment. See *United Security Life Ins. Co. v. Gregory,* 281 Ala. 264, 201 So. 2d 853 (1967); *Foster Wheeler Corp. v. Zell,* 250 Ala. 146, 33 So. 2d 255 (1948); *Alabama Mills, Inc. v. Smith,* 237 Ala. 296, 186 So. 699 (1939). No assertion of additional consideration has been advanced by plaintiffs. Thus, while Section 3:15 of the handbook would appear in isolation to create a property right, under Alabama law, plaintiffs have no legitimate claim of entitlement.

But cf. *IBEW, Local 1245 v. City of Gridley,* 34 Cal. 3d 191, 666 P.2d 960 (1983).

2. In *Garavalia v. City of Stillwater,* 283 Minn. 354, 168 N.W.2d 336 (1969), the court held that since firefighters who had engaged in an unlawful work stoppage had, by operation of the applicable statute, voluntarily abandoned and terminated their own employment, they were not entitled to a hearing under the Minnesota Veterans Preference Act which only applies to situations where a veteran's employment is involuntarily terminated by a public employer.

3. In *National Educ. Ass'n v. Lee Cty. Bd. of Pub. Instrn.,* 260 So. 2d 206, 80 L.R.R.M. 2368 (1972), the Florida Supreme Court considered the re-employment rights of teachers who had engaged in various work stoppages during 1968. Although the applicable Florida statute specifically precluded the re-employment for one year of any teachers who left their positions without school board approval, the court sustained the right of the state superintendent to circumvent this provision, with respect to those who had merely walked off their jobs, by authorizing the local school boards to grant them emergency, retroactive leaves covering the respective periods they were away from work. This procedure was not available, however, for other teachers who had effectively resigned before leaving their positions. As to them, the court affirmed the power of school boards to condition their re-employment upon the payment of $100 sums as the equivalent of "liquidated damages" covering the losses caused by their disingenuous resignations.

Following the Florida Supreme Court decision, the teachers who were each required to tender $100 to have their resignations revoked had their situation considered by the Fifth Circuit Court of Appeals. In *National Educ. Ass'n v. Lee Cty. Bd. of Pub. Instrn.,* 467 F.2d 447 (5th Cir. 1972), the court ruled:

> Essentially the teachers' theory is that the forced exaction of a $100 payment from each of them in exchange for their returning to work with their pre-resignation status intact amounted to a fine or penalty for a legislatively undefined wrong, violative of their right to procedural due process because they were afforded no hearing or other opportunity to protest the payments or to contest their legality....
>
> Concededly it is now established to a point beyond all dispute that "public employment, including academic employment, may [not] be conditioned upon the surrender of constitutional rights which could not be abridged by direct governmental action." *Keyishian v. Board of Regents,* 1967, 385 U.S. 589....
>
> However, none of these cases has any application here unless the teachers were in fact compelled to forgo the exercise of a Federal constitutional right in return for re-employment. The critical flaw in their argument is the uncritical (and, on this record, insupportable) assumption that the $100 payments constituted a *deprivation* of property without due process of law within the prohibition of the fourteenth amendment. The agreement clearly provided that the teachers would receive a benefit to which concededly they were not otherwise entitled — re-employment with full tenure rights and other accompanying privileges which they had enjoyed before their resignations — in return for a payment of $100. In substance, they were offered an opportunity to surrender one "property right" in order to acquire another "property right" that was plainly of greater value to them. Such a mutually advantageous exchange cannot be characterized as a *deprivation* of property, regardless of whether the teachers' payments are pejoratively denominated as "fines" and regardless of whether the subjective intention of the Board members who voted for it was to "punish" alleged past misconduct.... [W]e may concede that the teachers here were involuntarily subjected to choosing be-

tween paying consideration for an employment benefit of at least equivalent value and foregoing employment altogether. The choice between these options was admittedly coerced. But regardless of whether it was accepted or rejected the Board's offer did not entail a deprivation of property. Accordingly, the payment of the $100 could not have involved the surrender of the right to protection of that property guaranteed by the due process clause of the fourteenth amendment.

Obviously the teachers would be in an entirely different position if they were somehow able to establish that they were legally entitled to tenure without payment of $100 and were therefore unilaterally deprived of that money without due process. Instead they are forced to concede that they had effectively resigned their positions and that the Board was not even legally obligated to rehire them at all. In such circumstances their claim fares no better than that of a teacher who, having neither de facto tenure nor an objective expectancy of re-employment, is discharged for unspecified reasons without notice or a hearing.

Since school teachers do not have a constitutionally protected right to receive the full salaries stated in their individual employment contracts for the school year, a school board has the right to reduce those salaries in connection with the adoption of a shortened school calendar necessitated by an unlawful teachers' strike. See *Ash v. Board of Educ.*, 699 F.2d 822 (6th Cir. 1983).

4. A federal employee who contests a post-strike termination based upon a duress defense must "demonstrate, by a preponderance of the evidence, that his failure to report for work was the result of a threat or other intimidating conduct, directed toward him, sufficient to instill in him a reasonable fear of physical danger to himself or others, which a person of ordinary firmness would not be expected to resist." *Johnson v. Department of Transp.*, MSPB No. DC075281F0998 (11/15/82), GERR No. 988, 6-8. Although corroborative evidence of consummated threats upon other nonstrikers is not "absolutely necessary" to a finding of duress, such evidence "would constitute a strong indicium of the reasonableness of the employee's fear." Accord *Martel v. Dep't of Transp.*, 735 F.2d 504 (Fed. Cir. 1984). See also 21 GERR 967 (1983) (summarizing 7 MSPB decisions regarding the imposition of penalties upon striking PATCO personnel). The authority of the federal government to discharge striking PATCO personnel was sustained in *Schapansky v. Department of Transp.*, 735 F.2d 477 (Fed. Cir.), *cert. denied*, 469 U.S. 1018 (1984); *Campbell v. Department of Transp.*, 735 F.2d 497 (Fed. Cir.), *cert. denied*, 469 U.S. 881 (1984). But cf. *Fitzgerald v. Dep't. of Transp.*, 798 F.2d 461 (Fed. Cir. 1986), *cert. denied*, 480 U.S. 934 (1987) (FAA improperly terminated PATCO negotiators on authorized leave as union agents during 1981 strike, since they could not be considered strike participants while on official leave). See generally *Meltzer & Sunstein, Public Employee Strikes, Executive Discretion, and the Air Traffic Controllers*, 50 U. Chi. L. Rev. 731 (1983); Northrup, *The Rise and Demise of PATCO*, 37 Indus. & Lab. Rel. Rev. 167 (1984); Fox, *PATCO and the Courts: Public Sector Labor Law as Ideology*, 1985 U. Ill. L. Rev. 245 (1985).

5. Section 210 of the Taylor Law authorizes a public employer who determines that an employee has engaged in a strike to place the employee on probation for one year and to deduct from his pay twice his daily rate of pay for each day the worker was on strike. In *Sanford v. Rockefeller*, 35 N.Y.2d 547, 324 N.E.2d 113 (1974), the New York Court of Appeals, relying upon *Arnett v. Kennedy*, 416 U.S. 134 (1974), and *Mitchell v. W.T. Grant Co.*, 416 U.S. 600

(1974), found no due process violation regarding this penalty procedure, even though the affected worker could not obtain a hearing on his objections to the employer's determination until after the imposition of the statutory sanctions. See also *Wolkenstein v. Reville*, 694 F.2d 35 (2d Cir. 1982). In *Phillips v. New York City Health Corp.*, 44 N.Y.2d 807, 377 N.E.2d 742 (1978), the court held that the Taylor Law strike penalty consists of twice each violator's gross wage, rather than net, after-taxes compensation. Furthermore, the court in *Mineola Sch. Dist. v. Teachers Ass'n*, 97 L.R.R.M. 2144 (N.Y. Sup. Ct. 1977), permitted the school district to include daily pay earned by employees for extracurricular activities when computing their strike assessments.

In *Tucker v. Commissioner*, 69 T.C. No. 54, GERR No. 748, 28 (U.S. Tax Ct. 1978), the Tax Court ruled that amounts withheld from a public employee's wages as a penalty for illegal strike activity constitutes taxable income and may not be deducted as an employee business expense since I.R.C. § 162(f) expressly precludes the deduction of "any fine or similar penalty paid to a government for the violation of any law."

6. Where public employees have participated in an impermissible work stoppage, may the affected governmental employer discharge some of the strikers while retaining other similarly situated participants without violating equal protection or due process principles? See *Battle v. Illinois Civil Serv. Comm'n*, 103 L.R.R.M. 2790 (Ill. App. Ct. 1979).

7. Employees who participate in an illegal strike may be deprived of seniority for the period of their work stoppage despite the fact that their union and employer have agreed that no retaliation would be taken against any reinstated striker, where such seniority deprivation is consistent with the practice generally followed with respect to any employees who go on leave without pay. See *Hawaii State Teachers Ass'n v. PERB*, 590 P.2d 993, 101 L.R.R.M. 2323 (Haw. 1979). However, *San Diego Unified Sch. Dist.*, Cal. PERB No. LA-CE-194, 1979-80 PEB ¶ 41,974 (1980), recognized that where such a no-reprisals agreement has been executed, a governmental employer may not place commendation letters in the personnel files of the employees who did not participate in the work stoppage.

BURNS, JACKSON, MILLER, SUMMIT & SPITZER v. LINDNER

59 N.Y.2d 314, 451 N.E.2d 459 (1983)

MEYER, JUDGE: ....

I

This appeal involves separate action by two New York City law firms to recover damages resulting from the April, 1980 transit strike. The first, begun in Queens County by Burns Jackson Miller Summit & Spitzer ("Burns Jackson"), is a class action against the Transport Workers Union of America, AFL-CIO (TWU), the Amalgamated Transit Union, AFL-CIO (ATU), Local 100 of TWU, Locals 726 and 1056 of ATU and their respective officers. It alleges that the strike was intentional and in violation of both section 210 of the Civil Service Law and of a preliminary injunction issued March 31, 1980 by the Supreme Court and seeks damages of $50,000,000 per day for each day of the strike. The complaint sets forth two causes of action: prima facie tort and public nuisance.

The second action, begun in New York County by Jackson, Lewis, Schnitzler and Krupman ("Jackson, Lewis"), likewise alleges an intentional strike in violation of the statute and preliminary injunction. It was, however, brought only against the TWU and its Local 100, and officers of both, sought but $25,000 in damages, and did not ask class action status. It declared on six causes of action: for violation of the Taylor Law, prima facie tort, intentional interference with plaintiff's business, willful injury, conspiracy and breach of plaintiff's rights as third-party beneficiary of the contract between defendant unions and the New York City Transit Authority (NYCTA) and the Manhattan and Bronx Surface Transit Operating Authority (MABSTOA).

... We conclude (1) that the Taylor Law was neither intended to proscribe private damage actions by persons caused injury by a strike by public employees nor to establish a new private right of action for such damages, and (2) that the complaints fail to state a cause of action for (a) prima facie tort, (b) public nuisance, (c) intentional interference with business, or (d) breach of plaintiffs' rights as third-party beneficiary of defendants' contracts with NYCTA or MABSTOA. We, therefore, affirm.

II

The effect of the Taylor Law, whether as preemptive of previously permissible private damage actions or as initiating a new form of private action for damages resulting from a strike in violation of its provisions, turns on what the Legislature intended. The general rule is and long has been that "when the common law gives a remedy, and another remedy is provided by statute, the latter is cumulative, unless made exclusive by the statute" (*Candee v. Hayward,* 37 N.Y. 653, 656) ....

The far better course is for the Legislature to specify in the statute itself whether its provisions are exclusive and, if not, whether private litigants are intended to have a cause of action for violation of those provisions. Absent explicit legislative direction, however, it is for the courts to determine, in light of those provisions, particularly those relating to sanctions and enforcement, and their legislative history, and of existing common-law and statutory remedies, with which legislative familiarity is presumed, what the Legislature intended (see *Merrill Lynch, Pierce, Fenner & Smith v. Curran,* 456 U.S. 353, 374-383; *Middlesex County Sewerage Auth. v. National Sea Clammers Assn.,* 453 U.S. 1, 13). Whether a private cause of action was intended will turn in the first instance on whether the plaintiff is "one of the class for whose especial benefit the statute was enacted" (*Motyka v. City of Amsterdam,* 15 N.Y.2d 134, 139; *Cort v. Ash,* 422 U.S. 66, 78; *Texas & Pacific Ry. Co. v. Rigsby,* 241 U.S. 33, 39). But the inquiry does not, as plaintiffs suggest, end there, for to do so would consider but one of the factors involved in the Legislature's determination. Important also are what indications there are in the statute or its legislative history of an intent to create (or conversely to deny) such a remedy and, most importantly, the consistency of doing so with the purposes underlying the legislative scheme (*Cort v. Ash, supra,* at 78 ....)

Analysis begins, of course, with the statute itself. It contains no explicit statement as to either exclusivity or intent to create a private cause of action. Examination of the history and genesis of the Taylor Law leads us to conclude, however, that it is cumulative, not exclusive, and was not intended to establish a new cause of action.

New York's first statutory proscription against strikes by public employees was the Condon-Wadlin Act, passed in 1947 as a result of a strike by public school teachers in Buffalo (L 1947 ch. 391; Civil Service Law, former § 108). It punished violation by automatic termination, and imposed severe restrictions on re-employment, precluding salary increases for a re-employed striker for three years and requiring that the re-employed person be treated as probationary for five years (Wolk, *Public Employees Strikes — A Survey of the Condon-Wadlin Act,* 13 NY L. Forum 69, 70-71). Although held constitutional (*Matter of Di Maggio v. Brown,* 19 N.Y.2d 283), the harshness of its penalties resulted in their being enforced but twice over a period of 20 years (*id.,* at p. 289), and in widespread criticism and agitation for revision....

On January, 15, 1966, prompted by a massive strike of New York City transit workers which began January 1, 1966, Governor Rockefeller appointed a Committee on Public Employee Relations, chaired by Professor George W. Taylor. The committee was charged "to make legislative proposals for protecting the public against the disruption of vital public services by illegal strikes, while at the same time protecting the rights of public employees".... With respect to illegal strikes, the committee noted the lack of success of the Condon-Wadlin provisions and proposed instead three deterrents: the injunctive power of the courts, but without monetary limit on the fine imposable for violation; the misconduct provisions of section 75 of the Civil Service Law as concerned individual employees; and as concerns the unions, suspension of privileges or decertification, as determined after hearing by the Public Employment Relations Board (Final Report, part 4).

... The Taylor Law (officially the Public Employees' Fair Employment Act) was finally adopted in April, 1967, effective September 1, 1967 (L 1967, ch 392). It declared it to be "the public policy of the state and the purpose of this act to promote harmonious and cooperative relationships between government and its employees and to protect the public by assuring, at all times, the orderly and uninterrupted operations and functions of government" (Civil Service Law, § 200), granted public employees the rights of organization and representation (§§ 202, 203), empowered public employers to recognize employee organizations and provided for their certification (§ 204), created the Public Employment Relations Board to oversee employee relations (§ 205), and established other objective provisions governing the rights of public employees and their unions. Following the recommendations of the Taylor Committee, it continued the prohibition against public employee strikes (§ 210) but replaced Condon-Wadlin's harsh penalties with provisions for injunction without limitation on the fire [sic] for violation (§ 211; Judiciary Law, § 751) and for discipline of individual strikers under section 75 of the Civil Service Law. It subjected the employee organization, however, only to forfeiture of dues checkoff for a period limited to 18 months (§ 210, subd 3, former par [f]), but significantly did not implement the Taylor Committee's decertification recommendation (Collins, *1967 Survey of N.Y. Law-Labor Relations Law,* 19 Syracuse L. Rev. 308, 309).

[A] number of changes were made in the act in 1969 (L 1969, ch 24). Striking employees became subject not only to disciplinary action but also to a one-year probationary period and the deduction of two days' pay for each day of violation was reinstated (Civil Service Law, § 210, subd 2). The imposition of penalties against employees and employee organizations was made mandatory (§ 210, subds 2, 3) and the failure to seek their imposition was made subject to article 78 review at the instance of any taxpayer (originally § 210, subd 4; now § 213, subd e).

The same act made clear, however, the Legislature's intent to protect employee organizations from destruction, even though they may have participated in an illegal strike. Thus, although the 18-month limitation on forfeiture of the union's dues deduction privilege was removed, both that provision (Civil Service Law, § 210, subd 3, par [f]) and section 751 (subd 2, par [a]) of the Judiciary Law (dealing with the fines imposable for criminal contempt) were amended to make the union's ability to pay a factor in the determination of the penalty to be assessed.

Against that background, for a number of reasons, legislative intent to provide a private remedy cannot be discerned. Although Jackson, Lewis is "one of the class for whose especial benefit the statute was enacted" and a right of action in a member of the class may be implied when clearly in furtherance of the legislative purpose ... the provisions of the present statute and the history of their enactment strongly suggest that a private action based upon the statute was not intended. True such an action would be a powerful deterrent to public employee strikes, but it would also, as the claim for damages in the Burns Jackson complaint suggests, impose a crushing burden on the unions and each of the employees participating in the strike, who could be held jointly and severally liable with the union for the damages resulting from violation.... It would do so, moreover, notwithstanding that the penalties of the Condon-Wadlin Act were repealed "precisely because that was a statute punitive rather than constructive in nature," notwithstanding the "unusually elaborate enforcement provisions, conferring authority to sue for this purpose both on government officials and private citizens" which strongly suggest that the Legislature "provided precisely the remedies it considered appropriate," ... and notwithstanding the 1966 decision in *Jamur Prods. Corp. v. Quille,* (51 Misc. 2d 501) which had held that a private cause of action could not be implied from the Condon-Wadlin Act.

Implication of a private action is, moreover, inconsistent with the purposes of the Taylor Law. Its primary purposes, as both Taylor Committee reports emphasize, was to defuse the tensions in public employer-employee relations by reducing the penalties and increasing reliance on negotiation and the newly created Public Employment Relations Board as a vehicle toward labor peace.... A private action, which would impose per se liability without any of the limitations applicable to the common-law forms of action hereafter considered, would inevitably upset the delicate balance established after 20 years of legislative pondering. As the Washington Supreme Court has noted, "the schemes created by statute for collective bargaining and dispute resolution must be allowed to function as intended, without the added coercive power of the courts being thrown into the balance on one side or the other" (*Burke & Thomas v. International Organization of Masters, Mates & Pilots,* 92 Wn. 2d 762, 772; accord *Lamphere Schools v. Lamphere Federation of Teachers,* 400 Mich. 104, 131). Having explicitly directed that in assessing penalties PERB and the courts consider the union's ability to pay and refused to enact a decertification provision, the Legislature must be deemed to have negated the unlimited liability, not only to third parties but to public employers as well, and the consequent demise of public employee unions, that would result from recognition of a new statutory cause of action.

That no new per se action was contemplated by the Legislature does not, however, require us to conclude that the traditional, though more limited, forms of action are no longer available to redress injury resulting from violation of the statute. The penalties imposable by PERB and the courts for such a violation provide some solace, but no recompense, for those injured by acts which not only violate the statute but also constitute a breach of duty, independent of the statute, which common-law remedies made compensable. Although it is within the competence of the Legislature to abolish common-law causes of action (*Montgomery v. Daniels,* 38 N.Y.2d 41), there is no express provision to that effect in the statute, notwithstanding numerous amendments of the Taylor Law after the decision by the Second Department in *Caso v. District Council 37, Amer. Federation of State, County & Municipal Employees AFL-CIO* (43 A.D.2d 159, 160-162; see, also, *People v. Vizzini,* 78 Misc. 2d 1040, 1043-1044), holding that law nonexclusive and a public nuisance action maintainable. It is one thing to conclude that limitation of penalties payable to the public treasury and denial of a decertification sanction are inconsistent with the imposition of a new strict liability cause of action, and quite another to conclude that persons damaged by action tortious before public strikes were declared illegal should be denied the recompense to which they would be otherwise entitled in the interest of labor peace. That indemnification against such liability may become a union demand in the bargaining process and prolong an illegal strike must be recognized ... but is, in our view, an insufficient basis, absent clearer indication of legislative intent, to hold the statute pre-emptive of all common-law causes of action and thus, as the Supreme Court has said in another context, "permit the result, extraordinary in our jurisprudence, of a wrongdoer shifting responsibility for the consequences of his [actions] onto his victim" (*Wyandotte Co. v. United States,* 389 U.S. 191, 204). We are fortified in that conclusion by similar decisions of courts of other States (*Fulenwider v. Firefighters Assn. Local Union 1784,* 649 S.W.2d 268 [Tenn]; ... *Burke & Thomas v. International Organization of Masters, Mates & Pilots,* 92 Wn. 2d 762, supra; see *Pasadena Unified School Dist. v. Pasadena Federation of Teachers,* 72 Cal. App. 3d 100; *State ex rel. Danforth v. Kansas City Firefighters Local No. 42, AFL-CIO,* 585 S.W.2d 94 [Mo.]; cf. *Lamphere Schools v. Lamphere Federation of Teachers,* 400 Mich. 104, supra).

III

The conclusion that the statute is not exclusive requires that we consider the common-law causes of action asserted in the two complaints,...

A. The cause of action common to the two complaints is that in prima facie tort. The elements of such a cause of action as stated in prior New York cases are (1) intentional infliction of harm, (2) resulting in special damages, (3) without excuse or justification, and (4) by an act or series of acts that would otherwise be lawful.... Plaintiff suggests, however, that it is anomalous to deny a cause of action on the ground that the injury-causing act was *unlawful* and the balancing analysis espoused in Comment *e* of section 870 of the Restatement of Torts, Second, lends some credence to that argument.

It can be argued that unlawful acts are not covered by prima facie tort because they will normally be compensable in traditional tort forms of action, unless the policy underlying the traditional tort excludes such an act. But it can also be argued that the reference to "lawful" acts was a result of the genesis of prima facie tort, which was conceived as a means of avoiding a "hardening of ... categories" (*Morrison v. National Broadcasting Co.,* 24 A.D.2d 284, 287 [Breitel, J.], *revd on other grounds* 19 N.Y.2d 453), by providing redress for an act, even though otherwise lawful and not encompassed by a traditional tort, done solely for an improper or evil motive....

We need not now decide whether an unlawful act can be the predicate for prima facie tort, for there is no recovery in prima facie tort unless malevolence is the sole motive for defendant's otherwise lawful act or, in Justice Holmes' characteristically colorful language, unless defendant acts from "disinterested malevolence" (*American Bank & Trust Co. v. Federal Bank,* 256 U.S. 350, 358; see *Squire Records v. Vanguard Recording Soc.,* 25 A.D.2d 190, aff'd 19 N.Y.2d 797; *Morrison v. National Broadcasting Co., supra,* at p. 287; 2 N.Y. P.J.I. 624), by which is meant "that the genesis which will make a lawful act unlawful must be a malicious one unmixed with any other and exclusively directed to injury and damage of another" (*Beardsley v. Kilmer,* 236 N.Y. 80, 90).

Here the prima facie tort causes of action cannot stand because, although they allege intentional and malicious action they do not allege that defendants' sole motivation was "disinterested malevolence."

B. The Burns Jackson complaint alleges in its second cause of action that the strike in by defendants "caused widespread economic dislocation and damage and substantial interference with the public health, safety, comfort and convenience within the New York City metropolitan area, thereby creating a nuisance." Although the allegation of substantial interference with the common rights of the public at large is a sufficient predicate for a private action based on public nuisance (see *Caso v. District Council 37, Amer. Federation of State, County & Municipal Employees, AFL-CIO,* 43 A.D.2d 159, *supra;* ... and additional expense in the performance of a specific contract can constitute the "private and peculiar injury" required for a private action (*Wakeman v. Wilbur,* 147 N.Y. 657, 663; *Callanan v. Gilman,* 107 N.Y. 360, 370; Restatement, Torts 2d, § 821C, Comment *i*), it is, nevertheless, true that the harm suffered must be "of a different kind from that suffered by other persons, exercising the same public right" and that "invasions of rights common to all of the public should be left to be remedied by action by public officials" (Restatements, Torts 2d, § 821C, Comment *b;* see, also, Comment *h;* Prosser, *Private Action For Public Nuisance,* 52 Va. L. Rev. 997, 1008; 2 N.Y. P.J.I. 671).

The damages here alleged are for additional out-of-pocket expenses resulting from defendants' conduct and for loss of business profits. Such damages, though differing as to the nature of the expense or the particular contract from which greater profit was expected, were, as the Appellate Division noted (88 A.D.2d, at p. 71), suffered by every person, firm and corporation conducting his or its business or profession in the City of New York. Indeed, the class as envisioned by plaintiff's complaint consists of "professional and business entities conducted for profit ... that rely on the public transportation system serving the City of New York to enable them to practice their profession and to operate their businesses and that have been damaged as a consequence of the defendants' disruption of the service provided by that system."

When the injury claimed to be peculiar is of the same kind suffered by all who are affected, when it "is common to the entire community" (*Francis v. Schoellkopf,* 53 N.Y. 152, 154), or, as Prosser put it (52 Va. L. Rev., p. 1015), "it becomes so general and widespread as to affect a whole community," the injury is not peculiar and the action cannot be maintained. Cases such as *Francis v. Schoellkopf (supra),* and *Lansing v. Smith* (4 Wend. 9) are not to the contrary, for the injuries they involved were not common to the entire community, though the argument made was that a number of persons had been damaged in the same way. The economic loss which results from a transit strike is not recoverable in a private action for public nuisance because the class includes all members of the public who are affected by the strike (Prosser, 52 Va. L. Rev., p. 1009; Note, 91 Harv. L. Rev., p. 1331).

C. The two remaining causes of action may be dealt with more summarily. Jackson, Lewis' brief devotes but a two-sentence footnote to its third cause of action for intentional interference with business. The complaint alleges that defendants "intentionally and maliciously interfered with the business of the plaintiff" to plaintiff's special damage in that the productivity of partners and employees was reduced and extra expense incurred. What is apparently sought to be pleaded, therefore, is a claim within section 766A of the Restatement of Torts, Second, for causing plaintiff's performance of its contracts with its clients to be more expensive or burdensome.

No New York case recognizing such a cause of action has been cited or has been found by us. We need not, however, now decide whether such a cause of action should be recognized by us in other situations. The interference here alleged was but an incidental result of defendants' conduct and, although that conduct was in violation of the Taylor Law, we conclude that as a matter of policy we should not recognize a common-law cause of action for such incidental interference when the Legislature has, in establishing an otherwise comprehensive labor plan for the governance of public employer-employee relations, failed to do so (*De Angelis v. Lutheran Med. Center,* 58 N.Y.2d 1053; *Albala v. City of New York,* 54 N.Y.2d 269; *Donohue v. Copiague Union Free School Dist.,* 47 N.Y.2d 440; *Drago v. Buonaugurio,* 46 N.Y.2d 778; cf. Restatement, Torts 2d, § 766A, Comment *e;* and § 767, Comments *d, h*).

The Jackson, Lewis contract cause of action alleges that contracts existed between defendant unions and NYCTA and MABSTOA up to and including March 31, 1980, that they continued by operation of law until negotiation of successor agreements ended, that between April 1 and April 11, 1980, defendants and their members engaged in a strike against NYCTA and MABSTOA in violation of the contracts, that plaintiff is a third-party beneficiary of the contracts and that plaintiff was damaged by their breach.

A third party may be the beneficiary of a public as well as a private contract (see *Kornblut v. Chevron Oil Co.,* 62 A.D.2d 831, affd 48 N.Y.2d 853; 22 N.Y. Jur. 2d, Contracts, § 280). He may recover, however, only by establishing (1) the existence of a valid and binding contract between other parties, (2) that the contract was intended for his benefit and (3) that the benefit to him is sufficiently immediate, rather than incidental, to indicate the assumption by the contracting parties of a duty to compensate him if the benefit is lost (*Port Chester Elec. Constr. Corp. v. Atlas*, 40 N.Y.2d 652, 655; *Associated Flour Haulers & Warehousemen v. Hoffman*, 282 N.Y. 173; *Moch Co. v. Rensselaer Water Co.*, 247 N.Y. 160).

Existence of a valid and binding contract is, thus, a *sine qua non* (see *Dunning v. Leavitt*, 85 N.Y. 30, 35; 2 Williston, Contracts [3d ed.], §§ 347, 394; 22 N.Y. Jur. 2d, Contracts, § 281). Here, however, the complaint itself states that the contracts expired on March 31, 1980, ... The contracts having expired before the strike, any rights of plaintiff as a third-party beneficiary of them expired with it (*Fulenwider v. Firefighters Assn. Local Union 1784*, 649 S.W.2d 268 [Tenn.], *supra*).

Further reason why Jackson, Lewis' contract cause of action cannot succeed is that plaintiff is but an incidental beneficiary of the collective bargaining agreement (*Isbrandtsen Co. v. Local 1291 of Int. Longshoremen's Assn.*, 204 F.2d 495), the "intention to assume an obligation of indefinite extension to every member of the public ... [being] the more improbable when we recall the crushing burden that the obligation would impose" (*Moch Co. v. Rensselaer Water Co.*, 247 N.Y. 160, 165, *supra;* see, also, *Kornblut v. Chevron Oil Co., supra*).

For the foregoing reasons, the order of the Appellate Division should be affirmed, with costs.

NOTES

1. In *Burke & Thomas v. IOMM & P*, 92 Wash. 2d 762, 600 P.2d 1282 (1979), the court refused to permit island resort owners and operators who had been significantly injured by a Labor Day weekend strike by state ferry workers in violation of a contractual no-strike clause to sue the participating labor organization for damages. Since there was no evidence that the bargaining parties had intended to create rights for the benefit of the resort entrepreneurs, the plaintiffs could not rely upon a third party beneficiary theory. The absence of any demonstration that the strikers had directly intended to injure the resort operators precluded recovery for tortious interference with business relationships. The court finally declined to recognize a new cause of action to apply to such strike situations, on the ground that such a judicial remedy would unduly interfere with the state labor board's exclusive authority and impermissibly alter the labor relations balance which the legislature had established through the enactment of the comprehensive state public employee bargaining statute. See *Fulenwider v. Firefighters Local 1784*, 649 S.W.2d 268, 1981-83 PBC ¶ 37,630 (Tenn. 1982), wherein the court declined to permit an individual property owner injured by an illegal firefighter strike to sue for damages on the ground that the work stoppage constituted an actionable public nuisance. Cf. *Jackson v. Byrne*, 738 F.2d 1443 (7th Cir. 1984) (finding no constitutional deprivation of property rights regarding citizens adversely affected by firefighter strike). See generally Note, *Private Damage Actions Against Public Sector Unions for Illegal Strikes*, 91 Harv. L. Rev. 1309 (1978), wherein three independent theories for providing damage relief to private parties injured by unlawful public employee work stoppages are explored: (1) Right of action emanating from statutory strike proscription; (2) Right of public as third party beneficiaries to recover for breach of contractual no-strike obligation; and (3) Cause of action based upon contention that illegal strike constitutes public nuisance. See also Waldman, *Damage Actions and Other Remedies in the Public Employee Strike,* 20th Ann. N.Y.U. Conf. on Labor Law 259 (T. Christensen ed. 1968); Note, *Statutory and Common Law Considerations in Defining the Tort Liability of Public Employee Unions to Private Citizens for Damages Inflicted by Illegal Strikes,* 80 Mich. L. Rev. 1271 (1982).

2. In *Rivard v. Chicago Fire Fighters Union Local 2,* 122 L.R.R.M. 2493 (Ill. App. Ct. 1986), the court held that families of individuals who died in fires during the illegal 1980 Chicago fire fighters strike could sue the responsible labor organization for damages. The court ruled that a 1983 statute which authorized suits against unions as legal entities could be retroactively applied to the 1980 work stoppage. A similar result was reached in *Boyle v. Anderson Fire Fighters Ass'n Local 1262,* 1986-88 PBC ¶ 34,711 (Ind. Ct. App. 1986), which found that individual fire fighters and their local union could be held liable for the property damages caused by their unlawful work stoppage. The court noted that the strikers had initially interfered with the fire fighting efforts of others, and it decided that such public safety employees had an affirmative obligation to combat the fire in question.

3. In *Lamphere Schs. v. Federation of Teachers,* 252 N.W.2d 818, 95 L.R.R.M. 2279 (1977), the Michigan Supreme Court utilized alternative theories to support its determination that a school district could not prosecute a tort action against a union for damages caused by a strike conducted in violation of state law.

> ... The PERA was intended to occupy the public employee labor relations field completely; no viable distinction exists between the constituent public employees and their unions in this context. Therefore, along with the equitable relief of injunction, the § 6 remedies of the PERA are presently the exclusive remedies available to plaintiff School District in the case at bar when confronted by an illegal, though peaceful, strike by the teachers, even if such strike was precipitated by defendant Federations....
>
> If this Court permitted plaintiff School District to pursue any of the three civil tort actions pled (causing teachers to breach a duty, tortious interference with existing individual contractual relationships, civil conspiracy), such a result would necessarily circumvent the authority of MERC to determine charges of unfair labor practices. This becomes apparent since the defendant Federations, as representatives of the teachers, would inevitably defend proposed civil actions by alleging unfair labor practices. Then the determination of whether or not an unfair labor practice occurred would inexorably fall to the forum in which the tort action was brought — the circuit court....
>
> Plaintiff School District correctly relies on the *Detroit* case [*Detroit v. Division 26 of Amalgamated Ass'n of Street, Electric Railway & Motor Coach Employees of America,* 332 Mich. 237 (1952)] for the proposition that strikes by public employees are unlawful at common law. However, that case falls far short of creating the classic "duty", "breach of duty", therefore, "monetary damages" triad of traditional tort law. The *Detroit* case stands for the limited proposition that strikes by public employees are against public policy *and are therefore subject to injunction.* There is no precedent establishing a common-law tort duty owed by the Federation or its teachers to the School Board regarding peaceful strike activities....
>
> Furthermore, the ultimate legislative goal is to achieve a prompt, fair resolution of disputes while avoiding the disruption of the educational process.

To recognize alternative tort remedies would result in a substantial negative impact upon such purposes. It would encourage future school board inaction. Eventual settlements could be prolonged pending the resolution of multiple tort claims and counterclaims. The inevitable result would be to create labor law logjams in our courts and, at the same time, to exacerbate labor-management disputes.

The California Supreme Court reached a similar conclusion in *San Francisco v. Local 38,* 42 Cal. 3d 810, 726 P.2d 538 (1986).

Compare *City of Fairmont v. RWDSU,* 1979-80 PBC ¶ 37,157 (W.Va. 1980), with *Missouri v. Kansas City Firefighters Local 42,* 1984-86 PBC ¶ 34,181 (Mo. Ct. App. 1984).

4. Taxpayer suits under statutory provisions prohibiting strikes usually have taken the form of mandamus actions or suits to prevent waste of public treasury moneys. Suits to specifically enforce the penalty provisions of the state no-strike law were upheld in *In re Weinstein,* 267 N.Y.S.2d 111, 61 L.R.R.M. 2323 (N.Y. Sup. Ct. 1966), and *Head v. Special Sch. Dist. No. 1,* 288 Minn. 496, 182 N.W.2d 887 (1970) (joint suit by Attorney General and private individuals). See also *City of Cincinnati v. Cincinnati Dist. Council 51, AFSCME,* 35 Ohio St. 2d 197, 299 N.E.2d 686 (1973), *cert. denied,* 415 U.S. 994 (1974). However, it has been held that where strike penalties are discretionary, rather than mandatory, no such private remedy is available. *Markowski v. Backstrom,* 39 Ohio Op. 2d 247, 226 N.E.2d 825 (Ohio Misc. 1967). Similarly, overtime payments to non-strikers is a proper municipal function that may not be enjoined. *Mone v. Pezzano,* 77 L.R.R.M. 2605 (N.Y. Sup. Ct. 1971). On the question of individual actions for injunctive relief, see *Dade Cty. Classroom Teachers Ass'n v. Rubin,* 238 So. 2d 284 (Fla. 1970), *cert. denied,* 400 U.S. 1009 (1971). Compare *Durkin v. Board of Police & Fire Comm'rs,* 48 Wis. 2d 112, 180 N.W.2d 1 (1970) (city elector could sue director of firefighters' union which had struck, notwithstanding amnesty agreement between city and strikers), with *Shanks v. Donovan,* 32 App. Div. 2d 1037, 303 N.Y.S.2d 783 (1969), and *Shanks v. Procaccino,* 70 L.R.R.M. 2741 (N.Y. Sup. Ct. 1968), *aff'd,* 306 N.Y.S.2d 416 (App. Div. 1969). See also *Fire Fighters v. Board of Supvrs.,* 75 Cal. App. 3d 807; 97 L.R.R.M. 2265 (1977).

5. In *San Francisco v. Cooper,* 13 Cal. 3d 898, 534 P.2d 403 (1975), the California Supreme Court ruled that a city ordinance and a school board resolution granting salary increases to public employees could not be invalidated on the ground that they were enacted as a result of an illegal work stoppage. The court rejected a taxpayer's argument that the duly enacted provisions were invalid because they had been adopted "as a result of" and "under the coercion of" an illegal strike. The court concluded that since California has no constitutional, statutory, or charter provisions prohibiting a city or school board from enacting legislation as a result of an unlawful strike, the court had no authority to nullify the ordinance or resolution merely because individual legislators may have been subjected to improper influences. See also *Legman v. Sch. Dist.,* 438 Pa. 157, 263 A.2d 370 (1970).

710 LABOR RELATIONS LAW IN THE PUBLIC SECTOR

F. THE STATUTORY RIGHT TO STRIKE IN THE PUBLIC SECTOR

EDWARDS, THE DEVELOPING LABOR RELATIONS LAW IN THE PUBLIC SECTOR, 10 Duquesne L. Rev. 357, 376-78 (1972)*

The last group of states — those with a legislatively granted limited right to strike — is certainly the most daring of the four. The problem in granting such a limited right to strike, in general, has been to define precisely the tolerable degree of pressure which the government and the public can withstand. Almost invariably, this is done by attempting to draw a line between essential services (wherein a strike is impermissible) and non-essential services where a strike may be tolerated. However, in most laws this line is very imprecisely delineated — usually by a formula based on some variant of "the public health, safety, or welfare" standard. Such a definition, while admirably flexible, may not be a sufficiently precise formulation to give meaningful guidance.

Another problem with the essential/non-essential calculus is that, in general, it fails to take into account the temporal dimension. A strike, for example, in a highly automated industry, such as the telephone system, may be tolerable for a time. As it endures and the machines begin to break down, it may become intolerable. Other problems of a practical nature — such as who is to make the decision as to essentiality, when this decision is to be made, and whether the strike ban should be mandatory or imposed at the employer's option — are also involved in any partial strike programs.

While the difficulties are legion, there are four states — Hawaii, Pennsylvania, Montana, and Vermont — which have given public employees a limited right to strike. [Alaska, California, Idaho, Illinois, Louisiana, Minnesota, Ohio and Oregon have now extended the right to strike to at least some public employees (Eds.)]. Of the four states, the most limited right is found in Montana, where a nurses law permits strikes, provided that another health care facility within a radius of 150 miles has not simultaneously been shut down. Of more general applicability is the Vermont Act covering municipal employees, which provides that "no public employee may strike or recognize a picket line of a labor organization while performing his official duties, if the strike or recognition of a picket line will endanger the health, safety or welfare of the public." Vermont totally prohibits strikes by "state employees," but it appears to insulate teachers' strikes from injunctive orders in the absence of a showing of a "clear and present danger to a sound program of school education."

Neither of these states has shown the creativity of Hawaii and Pennsylvania in responding to the problem. The Hawaii law, covering all public employees, conditions the right to strike upon:

    (1) Good faith compliance with statutory impasse procedures;
    (2) Passage of sixty days after findings and recommendations of a fact-finding board are made public; and
    (3) The giving of 10 days' notice of desire to strike PERB and employer.

---

*Reprinted by permission of the Duquesne Law Review.

And while all categories of public employees are covered by the act, the Hawaii law also provides:

> When the strike occurring, or is about to occur, endangers the public health or safety, the public employer concerned may petition the board to make an investigation. If the board finds that there is imminent a present danger to the health and safety of the public, the board shall set requirements that must be complied with to avoid or remove any such imminent or present danger.

Pennsylvania has adopted a slightly different approach. First, the law prohibits strikes by guards at mental hospitals or prisons or personnel necessary to functioning of the courts. (Police/Fire workers are covered by a separate compulsory arbitration statute.) For all other personnel, strikes are permitted if:

> (a) Mediation and fact-finding procedures "have been completely utilized and exhausted"; and
> (b) "[U]nless or until such a strike creates a clear and present danger or threat to the health, safety, or welfare of the public."

The basic difference between the Hawaii and Pennsylvania approaches is that when a strike endangers the public health, safety, or welfare, Hawaii's law allows the PERB to make adjustments as it sees fit to eliminate the dangerous aspects of the strike (such as requiring essential employees to work), while Pennsylvania presumably would ban the strike in toto. In the first court decision on record, Pennsylvania's judiciary has indicated the unsoundness of leaving the decision as to the tolerable limits of public employee strikes entirely to the courts. In *SEPTA v. Transport Workers of Philadelphia*,[3] the question of whether a strike of municipal transportation workers was prohibited by the threat to public welfare was answered affirmatively. The court based its holding on some rather tenuous findings that the strike caused increased traffic congestion. The court said that congestion was more than mere inconvenience since it caused a distinct threat to the safety and welfare of those travelling by car as well as pedestrians. It also increased the risk of crime and fire, prevented the aged from obtaining required medical assistance, and markedly interfered with the operation of job training programs, the school system, and the economic welfare in general. Under the rationale of the court in *SEPTA*, few if any public sector strikes will be held to be protected under the new state law....

NOTES

1. Most state enactments granting government personnel the right to strike have distinguished between "essential" and "non-essential" workers, with only "non-essential" employees being permitted to strike. The Alaska Public Employment Relations Act has established three separate categories of employees: (1) "essential" police, fire, correctional, and hospital workers who may not lawfully strike; (2) "semi-essential" public utility, snow removal, sanitation, and educational workers who may strike for a limited period that is "determined by the interests of the health, safety or welfare of the public"; and (3) "non-essential" workers who may strike for extended periods without seriously affecting the public. See Alaska Stat. §§ 23.40.200(b), (c) & (d). The struck employer or the

---

[3] 77 L.R.R.M. 2489 (1971). But see *Hazelton Area School Dist. v. Education Ass'n*, 2 CCH State Lab. Cases ¶ 52,684 (Pa. Comm. Pleas 1971).

state labor relations agency may petition a court to enjoin any stoppage or threatened stoppage by "essential" personnel or any stoppage by "semi-essential" employees that threatens public health, safety, or welfare. Do such statutory gradations dilute the strike privilege by effectively precluding continued work stoppages that meaningfully inconvenience the public? What groups of government workers would you permit to strike? Under what circumstances, if any, would you allow courts to enjoin a peaceful work stoppage?

2. Empirical data indicate that the legalization of public employee strikes increases the frequency of such stoppages. See Olson, *Strikes, Strike Penalties, and Arbitration in Six States,* 39 Indus. & Lab. Rel. Rev. 539 (1986).

JERSEY SHORE AREA SCHOOL DIST. v. EDUCATION ASS'N

519 Pa. 398, 548 A.2d 1202 (1988)

JUSTICE STOUT: This appeal is brought by the members of the Jersey Shore Education Association, which represents the teachers of the Jersey Shore Area School District. In it we are asked to reconcile that provision of the Public Employees Relations Act (PERA), 43 Pa. Stat. Ann. § 1101.101-.2301 (Purdon Supp. Pamph. 1988), which gives teachers the right to strike, with that provision of the Public School Code, 24 Pa. Stat. Ann. §§ 15-1501 to 16-1613 (Purdon 1962 & Supp. 1988), which mandates that school districts provide 180 days of pupil instruction. Specifically, PERA provides:

> If a strike by public employes occurs after the collective bargaining processes set forth in Sections 801 and 802 of Article VIII of this act have been completely utilized and exhausted, it shall not be prohibited unless or until such a strike creates *a clear and present danger or threat* to the health, safety or welfare of the public.

43 Pa. Stat. Ann. § 1101.1003 (emphasis added). On the other hand, the Public School Code provides: "All public kindergartens, elementary and secondary schools shall be kept open each school year for at least one hundred eighty (180) days of instruction for pupils." 24 Pa. Stat. Ann. § 15-1501.

On September 10, 1984, after only four days of pupil instruction, the teachers struck against appellee, Jersey Shore Area School District. On October 8, 1984, the school district filed for an injunction in the Court of Common Pleas of Lycoming County, in an effort to force the teachers back to work. A hearing was held on October 10, 1984, following which the Chancellor issued an injunction ordering the teachers back to work on October 11. The Association filed for reconsideration and an additional hearing was held on October 23, 1988. The Chancellor refused to lift the injunction. The Association appealed to the Commonwealth Court, which affirmed solely on the basis of the Chancellor's finding that the school district's impending inability to schedule 180 days of instruction presented a clear and present danger to the public because of a threatened loss of state subsidies. 99 Pa. Commw. 163, 512 A.2d 163 (1986). See *School District of Pittsburgh v. Commonwealth Dept. of Educ.,* 492 Pa. 140, 422 A.2d 1054 (1980). While we disagree with the Commonwealth Court that the threatened loss of state subsidies alone would support the issuance of an injunction, we nonetheless affirm on the record as a whole...

Ordinarily, a Chancellor's findings of fact will not be disturbed absent "an abuse of discretion or a capricious disbelief of the evidence or a lack of evidentiary support on the record for such findings." *Shapiro v. Shapiro,* 424 Pa. 120, 127, 224 A.2d 164, 168 (1966). A Chancellor's conclusions of law bear stricter scrutiny, see id. at 127, 224 A.2d at 168. This Court has stated that it will not reverse a grant of injunctive relief "unless ... the rules of law relied on are palpably wrong or clearly inapplicable." *Lindenfelser v. Lindenfelser,* 385 Pa. 342, 343-44, 123 A.2d 626, 627 (1956) (citations omitted). Bearing in mind this standard of review, we turn to the evidence.

At the first hearing the superintendent for the school district testified that he had prepared a revised school calendar. Allowing for six snow days and two non-mandatory holidays, the superintendent had concluded that October 15, 1984, would be the last date upon which the teachers could return to the classroom while still ensuring an educationally-sound schedule. In addition, the superintendent testified extensively as to the financial impact of the strike. He stated that the school district stood to lose $26,637.00 per day in state subsidies for each day it fell short of 180 days of instruction. At the time of the hearing the superintendent estimated that the strike had cost the school district $65,944.00 in unemployment compensation, additional salaries and other costs incidental to the strike.

With respect to the students, the superintendent stated that the strike placed the seniors at a competitive disadvantage in terms of SAT testing. Seniors also faced deadlines with respect to scholarship applications and were bereft of guidance counseling services. The longer the strike, the more deleterious its effect on the future of the seniors.

With respect to other grades, students would be at a competitive disadvantage in taking state-mandated tests to determine remedial needs. With only four days of instruction, some students could be placed in remedial courses which they would not otherwise have needed. Moreover, in the event the school district could not administer these tests due to the continuation of the strike, it would lose state funding for the remedial courses themselves.

The superintendent stated that interference with a regular pattern of study, as had occurred in this strike, results in a loss of learning capacity, which increases with the length of the interruption. In support of this hypothesis he cited test scores from a previous year showing a drop in student aptitudes following a strike.

Finally, the superintendent expressed his concern that the strike deprived eligible students of a free, hot lunch, possibly the only such meal they received, while working parents were experiencing difficulties with interim babysitting arrangements.

The school teachers presented the testimony of two experts. The first disputed the superintendent's interpretation of prior test scores insofar as their reflecting a decrease in pupil learning due to the previous strike. This expert opined that it was inappropriate to compare different student groups for such a purpose. The second expert testified that, as of the date of the hearing, the school district would actually have a net savings in salaries and benefits of $24,199.00 over the potentially lost subsidy.

Having heard this evidence, the Chancellor issued the injunction on the basis of his conclusion that all of the evidence had demonstrated the existence of a clear and present danger to the health and welfare of the community.[7]

At the reconsideration hearing, little additional evidence was presented except that two officials of the Department of Education testified as to departmental policy with regard to withholding subsidies and as to their calculations with regard to the last possible date upon which the teachers would have to return to the classroom in order to ensure a 180-day calendar. Following this testimony, the Chancellor refused to lift the injunction.

Since this is an issue of first impression for this Court, we shall begin our legal analysis with a brief review of the decisions of the Commonwealth Court that have addressed it. In *Armstrong School Dist. v. Armstrong Educ. Ass'n,* 5 Pa. Commw. 378, 291 A.2d 120 (1972), Commonwealth Court grappled with the definition of "clear and present danger or threat" in analogizing it to First Amendment, free speech and association cases. *Id.* at 383, 291 A.2d at 123. The Court concluded:

> In this light, the determination of whether or not a strike presents a clear and present danger to the health, safety or welfare of the public must, therefore, require the court to find that the danger or threat is real or actual and that a strong likelihood exists that it will occur. Additionally, it seems to us that the "danger" or "threat" concerned must not be one which is normally incident to a strike by public employees. By enacting [PERA] which authorizes such strikes, the Legislature may be understood to have indicated its willingness to accept certain inconveniences, for such are inevitable, but it obviously intended to draw the line at those which pose a danger to the public health, safety or welfare.

Id. at 383-84, 291 A.2d at 124. In reversing the issuance of an injunction, the Court stated that the disruption of routine administrative procedures and the cancellation of extracurricular activities were inconveniences inherent in a teachers' strike, inconveniences envisioned by the legislature which, if considered a "clear and present danger or threat," would virtually nullify the right to strike. *Id.* at 385, 291 A.2d at 124. In dicta the Court also stated that if a strike lasted so long as to make the 180-day calendar an impossibility, and the cessation of subsidies a possibility, it properly could be enjoined.

In *Philadelphia Fed. of Teachers v. Ross,* 8 Pa. Commw. 204, 301 A.2d 405 (1973), the Court affirmed the issuance of an injunction where the board presented evidence of sharply increased gang activity that necessitated $133,000.00 per day in increased police protection, endemic student underachievement, possible loss of state subsidies, and the disqualification of seniors from entering college. The Court opined:

> It is neither possible nor prudent to state with precision that any one or more given circumstances surrounding a strike by school teachers will constitute a threat to the health, safety or welfare of the public. Nor do we decide that any

---

[7] In announcing his decision to issue the injunction, the Chancellor referred primarily to the potential subsidy loss. His opinion, however, makes it clear that he relied equally upon the evidence of harm to the students themselves.

particular number of days of lost instruction caused by a strike produces such a threat.

Id. at 215, 301 A.2d at 411. See also *Bethel Park School Dist. v. Bethel Park Fed. of Teachers,* 54 Pa. Commw. 49, 52, 420 A.2d 18, 19 (1980) (loss of state subsidies, instructional days, vocational job training, higher education and special education opportunities, counseling, social and health services, extracurricular programs and employees' work and wage opportunities constituted a clear and present danger to the community).

In *Bellefonte Area School Bd. v. The Bellefonte Area Educ. Ass'n,* 9 Pa. Commw. 210, 304 A.2d 922 (1973), the Court reversed the issuance of an injunction in concluding that the facts did not support a finding of "clear and present danger or threat." Since in that case sufficient make-up days remained to replace the thirteen strike days, therefore, the loss of state subsidies was not imminent. Moreover, the possible loss of participation in an educational quality assessment program was not deemed harmful enough to justify the injunction. See also *Wilkes-Barre Educ. Ass'n v. Wilkes-Barre Area School Dist.,* 105 Pa. Commw. 165, 523 A.2d 1183 (1987), *cert. denied,* 516 Pa. 645, 533 A.2d 715 (1987) (issuance of injunction prohibiting selective strikes resulting in only short periods of lost instruction yet possibly usurping school district's managerial prerogatives, reversed for insufficient evidence of a threat or danger to the students' health, safety or welfare). In a vigorous concurring opinion, Judge Kramer inveighed in *Bellefonte:*

All of the parties to this case and the majority opinion blithely speak of using "summer vacations" or holidays as a means of making up teachers' strike days to preserve state education subsidy funds. Not one word of concern is expressed for those school students who work on holidays and vacation days to stay in school. Not one word is utilized to protect high school seniors who must attend college summer school to gain admittance to college in the fall. Not one word is devoted to what happens if high school [senior's] grades are not ready for timely submission to college for the fall admission. Not one word is said because the school children are not represented. They are pawns in an adult game of economics. If the teachers and the school district agree to use all legal holidays, all weekends and all vacation time to make up for the lost days of a strike, does that mean the students will have no rest? Do they have any rights?

9 Pa. Commw. at 220, 304 A.2d at 926 (Kramer, J., concurring).

In *Bristol Twp. Educ. Ass'n v. School Dist. of Bristol,* 14 Pa. Commw. 463, 322 A.2d 767 (1974), although the findings of fact reflected lost educational programs, lost salaries, lost community programs and services, disadvantages for college-bound seniors, the deprivation of free lunches to students, and difficulties for working parents, the Court affirmed the enjoining of a twenty-six day strike solely because the Court determined that the potential loss of state subsidies created a danger or threat to the health, safety or welfare of the public.

More recently, in *Scanlon v. Mount Union Area Bd. of School Directors,* 51 Pa. Commw. 83, 415 A.2d 96 (1980), *aff'd,* 499 Pa. 215, 452 A.2d 1016 (1982), Commonwealth Court held that the scheduling of 180 days by school districts was mandatory, not discretionary....

Finally, in *Armstrong School Dist. v. Armstrong Educ. Ass'n,* 116 Pa. Commw. 571, 542 A.2d 1047 (1988), Commonwealth Court, citing the case *sub judice,* affirmed the issuance of an injunction where a strike threatened to foreshorten the 180-day instructional calendar.

This brief history reflects judicial difficulty, and at times divergence, in reconciling the right to strike with the requirement of 180 instructional days. While some cases have looked at a plethora of factors, including the loss of state subsidies, others have looked only at the loss of state subsidies in determining that it per se creates a clear and present danger or threat. We do not believe that the language of PERA necessitates judicial hand-wringing or hair-pulling. We hold that the loss of state educational subsidies for failure of a school district to schedule 180 days of instruction for pupils, alone, does not constitute a "clear and present danger or threat to the health, safety or welfare of the public."[9] In this case the school district demonstrated beyond peradventure the existence of a "clear and present danger or threat to the health, safety or welfare of the public." Without focusing on any one of the myriad economic and other facts upon which the school board relied, without weighing the interests of seniors as weightier that those of kindergartners, we conclude that, in conjunction, these factors created a school district which, although perhaps able to "make up" a day or two of instruction, could not "make up" the actual, the impending and the ever-increasing harm which was being wrought upon its students. On this record, the health and welfare of the students, who cannot and must not be treated as a category separate from the public at large, was clearly endangered and threatened.

The order of the Commonwealth Court is affirmed.

Justice Larsen, dissenting: When the legislature granted school teachers and other public employees the right to strike in 1970, it was fully cognizant of the provisions in the Public School Code mandating that school districts provide 180 days of pupil instruction and fully aware that such strikes could infringe upon the 180 day mandate. Nevertheless, the legislature granted that right to strike in Act 195 of July 23, 1970, as amended, 43 Pa. Stat. Ann. § 1101.101-.2301 (the Public Employees Relations Act, or PERA), and restricted the possibility of intervention by the courts in providing that a strike occurring after the collective bargaining procedures of Act 195 have been utilized and exhausted "shall not be prohibited unless or until such a strike creates a clear and present danger or threat to the health, safety or welfare of the public." 43 Pa. Stat. Ann. § 1101.1003. This legislative restriction on a court's authority to intervene by injunction against a strike is strong and explicit — a strike "shall not be prohibited" in the absence of a "clear and present danger or threat" to the public's health, safety or welfare. Surely, clear and present danger or threat to the health, safety or welfare of the community requires much more than the myriad inevitable and expected inconveniences and disruptions that are the normal

---

[9] We resist the facile temptation to legislate judicially a 180-day limit to the teachers' right to strike. We leave it to the legislature, well aware of the requisites of the Public School Code when it enacted PERA, to decide whether such a limit should be imposed. Until that time, we shall consider the length of the instructional calendar and the loss of state funding as but one factor in the proper issuance of an injunction.

consequences of any school strike, even one which impinges on the mandatory 180 days of pupil instruction of which the legislature was well aware....

In the instant case, ... there is no evidence on the record of any clear and present danger or threat to the health, safety or welfare of the public other than evidence of the normal disruptions and inconveniences associated with any strike of public school teachers. These types of harms usually associated with a public school teachers' strike were not unknown or unimaginable when the legislature prohibited courts from interfering with such strikes unless or until a clear and present danger or threat to the public health, safety or welfare were presented, and the legislature could not have equated the former harm with the latter clear and present danger or threat. The record, therefore, falls far short of justifying the "extraordinary remedy" of injunctive relief prohibiting the continuation of the strike, and the Chancellor should be reversed.

Unfortunately, the majority opinion seriously undermines the right to strike granted school teachers and other public employees. In fact, the majority transforms the ordinary into the extraordinary and renders the right to strike almost illusory for ... school boards will be able to negotiate with recalcitrance secure in the knowledge that, as soon as the magic 180 day period is actually or nearly threatened, the board will be able to trot out the standard laundry list of inconveniences and disruptions normally associated with any strike by school teachers to obtain an injunction....

PAPADAKOS, JUSTICE, joins in this Dissenting Opinion.

JUSTICE ZAPPALA, dissenting: I agree with the majority that the risk of loss of state educational subsidies due to a school district's failure to schedule 180 days of instruction for pupils is not a "clear and present danger or threat to the health, safety or welfare of the public." But while the majority professed to resist any temptation to judicially legislate a 180-day limitation to the right to strike, it has in fact succumbed to that temptation. By focusing its attention on the inconveniences to the students which accompany the shortened duration of the school year caused by a teachers' strike, the majority has effectively created a per se rule that the inability to schedule 180 days of instruction constitutes a clear and present danger to the health, safety or welfare of the public....

I do not equate the inconveniences to students with a "clear and present danger or threat to the health, safety or welfare of the public." Nor do I agree with the majority that the health and welfare of the student is not a concern separate from the legislative concern for the public at large. The disruptive effect of a teachers' strike upon students is properly a matter for concern. In enacting the Public Employee Relations Act, (PERA), 43 P.S. §§ 1101.101-1101.2301, however, the Legislature weighed the competing interests which would be affected by the legislation in favor of permitting teachers to strike.

The student population was directly affected by that legislation. But it was the clear mandate of the Legislature that a strike by public employes "shall not be prohibited unless or until the strike creates a clear and present danger or threat to the health, safety, or welfare of the public." 43 P.S. § 1101.1003. The public at large does not share the individualized and personalized concerns of the student population. Nor are the terms synonymous. Nevertheless, the majority super imposes student inconveniences upon public welfare. In doing so, the majority places student inconveniences in a preeminent position and relegates the teachers' right to strike to a secondary concern. This is contrary to the legislative intent....

NOTES

1. Although the labor relations statutes in Alaska, Hawaii, Illinois, Minnesota, Ohio, Oregon, Pennsylvania, and Vermont expressly authorize work stoppages by at least some generally nonessential government personnel, the Montana law does not. Nonetheless, in *Montana v. Public Emps. Craft Council,* 529 P.2d 785, 88 L.R.R.M. 2012 (1974), the Montana Supreme Court interpreted that portion of the Public Employees Collective Bargaining Act which protects "concerted activity" as implicitly providing public employees with a strike right similar to that enjoyed by private sector workers under the NLRA. See also *Local 266, IBEW v. Salt River Project,* 78 Ariz. 30, 275 P.2d 393 (1954), sustaining the right of public employees to strike where their employer was engaged in propri-etary and not governmental functions.

In *County San. Dist. v. SEIU Local 660, supra,* the California Supreme Court held that the failure of the state legislature in the Myers-Milias-Brown Act to specifically prohibit strikes by county and municipal employees, as it did for firefighters, indicates that work stoppages by such personnel are not similarly prohibited. The court thus decided that strikes to enhance bargaining demands may be conducted by such governmental employees, unless they "pose an immi-nent threat to public health or safety." Rejecting the prior common-law deci-sions pertaining to this subject, the court said that "the right to strike, as an important symbol of a free society, should not be denied unless such a strike would substantially injure paramount interests of the larger community." See *Davis v. Henry,* 1988-90 PBC ¶ 35,504 (La. 1990) (recognizing right of teachers to strike in absence of specific statutory prohibition); *Local 1494, IAFF v. City of Coeur d'Alene,* 586 P.2d 1346, 1977-78 PBC ¶ 36,427 (Idaho 1978) (finding right of firefighters to strike following expiration of their collective contract, since statute only proscribes strikes "during the term of the written contract").

2. In *Billings Bd. of Trustees v. State,* 604 P.2d 778, 103 L.R.R.M. 2285 (Mont. 1979), the court ruled that a school district improperly interfered with the right of teachers to strike in support of union efforts to obtain a new collective bargaining agreement where it notified the striking teachers that they would be replaced unless they executed individual employment contracts and returned to work by a specified date, since the district had been primarily motivated by a desire to prevent the continuation of the lawful work stoppage rather than by an intention simply to keep the schools open. See also *Board of Trustees v. State,* 604 P.2d 770, 103 L.R.R.M. 3090 (Mont. 1979) (unlawful to fail to renew contract of nontenured teacher because of lawful strike activity).

Missoula Cty. High Sch. Dist. v. Board of Pers. Appeals, 727 P.2d 1327, 1986-88 PBC ¶ 34,744 (Mont. 1986), involved a lawful teachers' strike. When the school district feared that it would lose state aid if it failed to provide a 180-day school year, it offered salary incentives to teachers who would return to work for the necessary 18 days. Twenty individuals agreed to return to work. The school district reopened for only one day and then closed for the remain-der of the year. When the twenty teachers who had agreed to return to work threatened to sue the school district for the 18 days of pay they claimed to be owed, the district agreed to pay them for all 18 days. Since the school district's legitimate reason for settling their claims rebutted any inference of anti-union animus, the court found no unfair labor practice even though none of the striking teachers received any pay for the 18 days in question.

Regarding the right of public employers to replace lawfully striking employees, see Pietrzak, *Some Reflections on Mackay's Application to Legal Economic Strikes in the Public Sector: An Analysis of State Collective Bargaining Statutes,* 68 Ore. L. Rev. 87 (1989); Schooley, *The Reinstatement Rights of Striking Public Employees,* 9 Indus. & Lab. Rel. L.J. 283 (1987); Wilson, *The Replacement of Lawful Economic Strikers in the Public Sector in Ohio,* 46 Ohio St. L.J. 639 (1985).

3. A 1979 amendment to the Oregon public employee bargaining statute regarding the prerequisites to the enjoining of a strike by non-essential government personnel specifically provides that economic or financial inconvenience to the public or to the governmental employer normally incident to work stoppages does not constitute the required "danger or threat to the health, safety or welfare of the public." See Or. Rev. Stat. tit. 22, ch. 243, § 726(6).

4. The Minnesota Public Employment Relations Act generally proscribes public sector work stoppages. However, nonessential government workers are provided with a defense against the statute's strike sanctions where their employer either refuses to submit to binding impasse arbitration or fails to comply with the provisions of a valid interest arbitration award. If one group of nonessential employees may strike with impunity where their public employer has rejected the interest arbitration option, should nonessential personnel in other bargaining units be able to engage in a sympathy stoppage in support of the initial strikers without being liable for strike penalties? See *Teamsters, Local 120 v. City of St. Paul,* 270 N.W.2d 877, 1977-78 PBC ¶ 36,397 (Minn. 1978). See also Comment, *Labor Law: Sympathy Strikes Under the Minnesota Public Employment Relations Act,* 63 Minn. L. Rev. 1023 (1979).

5. Under the Illinois Public Labor Relations Act, an injunction against a public employee strike which constitutes "a clear and present danger to the health and safety of the public" may only be issued against those employees whose services are necessary to prevent or eliminate any such health and safety danger. Cf. *Haw. PERB v. AFSCME, Local 646,* 667 P.2d 783, 1981-83 PBC ¶ 37,806 (Hawaii 1983) (sustaining power of PERB to impose same requirement). Section 18 of the Illinois statute further requires a court issuing a strike injunction to order the parties to participate in interest arbitration procedures. This will force adversely affected public employers to decide whether they would prefer to be inconvenienced by a continued work stoppage or to have their employment terms submitted to by an outside arbiter.

6. Where a public employer's unlawful conduct converts an economic strike into an unfair labor practice strike, the state labor board may order the offending government entity to offer reinstatement to those unfair labor practice strikers who have unconditionally offered to return to work. See *Chittenden South Educ. Ass'n v. Hinesburg Sch. Dist.,* 514 A.2d 1065, 1986-88 PBC ¶ 34,698 (Vt. 1986).

7. In *Pennsylvania Labor Bd. v. New Castle Area Sch. Dist.,* PLRB Case No. PERA-C-4217-W, GERR No. 567, B-2 (1974), the PLRB held that a lockout of local government employees for the purpose of enhancing the public employer's economic position at the bargaining table was lawful. The PLRB indicated, however, that if the lockout had been intended to undermine the union, it would have been impermissible. The PLRB's decision parallels in large part the Supreme Court's reasoning in *American Shipbuilding Co. v. NLRB,* 380 U.S. 300 (1965).

BERNSTEIN, ALTERNATIVES TO THE STRIKE IN PUBLIC LABOR RELATIONS, 85 Harv. L. Rev. 459, 469-75 (1971)*

... It is reasonably clear that in public employment, the strike ban does not work; yet in most jurisdictions legalization of the strike is not a real possibility. And, I submit, the strike as it is known in the private sector would not function in the same way in the public sector and does not fit the peculiarities of public collective bargaining — diffuse responsibility and the consequent need for longer periods of time to reach settlements than in the private sector. Compulsory arbitration has serious drawbacks, not the least of which are its unacceptability to large segments of public management and unions and the likely instability of its results.

Therefore I suggest[4] that we explore the possibilities of two other arrangements which have never been considered in the public sector[5] but which, I suggest, fit the needs of *all* the parties more adequately than either present practices or the currently proposed alternatives.

It will help to give a rough sketch of the functioning of these two arrangements before I go into them in detail. In a nonstoppage strike, operations would continue as usual, but both the employees and the employer would pay to a special fund an amount equal to a specified percentage of total cash wages. Thus, while both parties would be under pressure to settle, there would be no disruption of service. In a graduated strike, employees would stop working during portions of their usual workweek and would suffer comparable reductions of wages. Here, there would be pressure not only on employees and employer but also on the community; however, the decrease in public service would not be as sudden or complete as in the conventional strike. I believe that these two new types of strike substitutes would work best in tandem.

---

*Reprinted by permission of The Harvard Law Review Association and Professor Merton C. Bernstein, Washington University School of Law.

[4]I want to emphasize that the proposed procedures should be part of a comprehensive public labor relations scheme which provides protection of employees against reprisal for collective activity, procedures for ascertaining appropriate bargaining units, elections to determine employee preferences, recognition and mandatory bargaining, sanctions against improper union activity, mediation procedures for bargaining disputes, and factfinding with recommendations in the case of bargaining deadlock. Such procedures are necessary conditions to the proper functioning of the nonstoppage and graduated strikes. Happily, it is also the case that these procedures will work more effectively if the pressure devices I propose are available.

[5]Several proposals for "nonstoppage" or "statutory" (because imposed by statute) strikes were made for the private sector starting in the late 1940's. They were, in chronological order, Marceau & Musgrave, *Strikes in Essential Industries: A Way Out,* 27 Harv. Bus. Rev. 287 (1949); Goble, *The Non-Stoppage Strike,* 2 Lab. L.J. 105 (1951); N. Chamberlain & J. Schilling, Social Responsibility and Strikes 279-86 (1952); Gregory, *Injunctions, Seizure and Compulsory Arbitration,* 26 Temp. L.Q. 397, 402 (1953). The major variations are summarized and assessed in McCalmont, *The Semi-Strike,* 15 Ind. & Lab. Rel. Rev. 191 (1962); Marshall & Marshall, *Nonstoppage Strike Proposals — A Critique,* 7 Lab. L.J. 299 (1956).

All of these proposals envisioned that employees continue at work and that the employer lose some income; and most involved a reduction of pay between declaration of the nonstoppage and settlement. All were limited to the private sector. The proposal I make here is the first to suggest application to the public sector and differs in several respects from each of the earlier versions.

The graduated strike is, to the best of my knowledge, original with me.

A. The Nonstoppage Strike

Under my proposal, a public employee union would be free to declare a nonstoppage strike after all other bargaining procedures failed to produce a settlement. Employees would be obliged to continue to work full time but would forego a portion of their take-home pay. I suggest that, initially, ten percent would suffice. This money would be paid by the public employer directly into a special fund (more fully discussed below). In addition to paying the equivalent of regular wages, the employer would also put into the fund an extra amount equal to what the employees have given up; this latter sum would constitute a loss to the employer. The union would have the option periodically to increase the amount of the foregone wages and employer payment, perhaps by increments of ten percent every two weeks. The public employer would have the option to require the union to switch to a graduated strike. If the employer did this, the employees would continue to lose the same rate of pay, but the employer would forego services rather than pay out additional funds.

I believe that exercise of the option to initiate the nonstoppage strike and increase the percentage can be limited to the union. The union has little other leverage, since the conventional strike would still be prohibited. Also, were the public employer able to initiate a procedure under which employees would work without pay, questions of involuntary servitude might arise. In any event, the employer would still have the strategic bargaining advantage of instituting, after a deadlock in negotiations, certain changes in pay or other terms of employment which have been offered to the union and rejected.

The nonstoppage strike would accommodate the peculiarities of public labor relations. It would attract the attention of and put pressure on both the public officials who deal directly with the union involved and other members of the executive branch whose own budgets might be affected, the local legislature, and state officials. And while a stoppage strike would not precipitate a crisis, its pressure would be steady and increasable. Thus, it may provide the necessary incentive for the various bodies of government to act, while allowing them the time they need to do so effectively. Moreover, it does not disturb consideration of the merits of the dispute with the hysteria and histrionics now typical of illegal strikes.

While nonstoppage strikes would create additional expense for public employers — many of whom are hard pressed as it is — they should also put an end to the present practice of paying the employees at overtime rates when a strike ends to reduce the backlog of work accumulated during the strike. Also, hopefully, the expense should be only temporary, and, as will be explained below, the money will not go to waste. In any event, the price does not seem too high to pay for a substantially improved process of bargaining.

Nonstoppage strikes offer significant advantages to employees, perhaps even more than would legalization of conventional strikes. In the first place, their rate of loss of pay would be lower at any given time than if there were an all-out strike. For employees with mortgage and other installment obligations to meet, this continuity of income is highly desirable. And, to the extent that the nonstoppage strike encourages more responsive bargaining without any stoppages, the total loss of pay may be less. In addition, in a full-scale strike, especially one of long duration, the employer is not liable for fringe benefit payments. Thus, life insurance policies may lapse or require payment by employees at a time when their income is interrupted, and group medical care insurance may have to be kept in force at the higher-cost individual rates. In a nonstoppage strike these benefits should continue.

Second, in actual strikes employees run the risk of losing their jobs. A common sanction in illegal strikes is to fire strikers. In the private strike, too, replacement of economic strikers has long been permitted, and while I have seen no data on public employer activity of this sort, I think it highly probable that permanent, nondiscriminatory replacement of strikers will become a feature of the legal public employee strike. In nonstoppage strikes, of course, jobs would be secure. Moreover, the absence of even temporary replacements would eliminate a traditionally potent source of violence, which everyone has a stake in averting.

Third, long-run employee and union interests are best served by a method that is legal and discomfits the community as little as possible. As union leadership knows from its post-World War II experience, unpopular strikes lead to distasteful legislation. And, by the same token, strikers, even if they feel their conduct justified, often must incur the disapproval of friends, neighbors, and others in the community. A peaceful method of pursuing demands seems clearly preferable.

The public employer would need some means of assuring union and employee compliance with the ground rules. Obviously, working full time for less than full pay might encourage some employees to slow down or "call in sick" — a favored device in strike-ban jurisdictions. Two procedures would minimize violations. First, the unions must see that it is to their advantage to persuade members that it is to *their* advantage to abide by the rules. That is, all must be made aware that the "struck" employer is indeed under strike-like pressure. Second, the statute should provide for an expedited (and I mean quick) unfair labor practice procedure to hear and determine charges of slowdown or improper absence. However, these areas are so sensitive and have such a potential for emotional overreaction that employer discipline of employees should be limited to those cases where impartial hearing officers make a finding that the improper action has taken place.

One serious problem with the nonstoppage strike is finding a suitable use for the special fund to which the public employer and employees have contributed. In order to insure that the loss will actually discipline the parties' conduct in bargaining, the fund would have to be placed effectively beyond their recapture.[6] I recommend that the fund be put at the disposal of a tripartite Public Purposes Committee in which respected community figures outnumber the total number of union and government members. This committee would be charged with the task of applying the money to publicly desirable, preferably short term projects that are not currently in the public budget — creation of scholarships or construction of public recreation facilities, for example. Certainly public employees would get little direct advantage from such a use of the

---

[6] It might, however, be worthwhile to experiment with partial recapture as an incentive to rapid settlement. Thus, the amounts lost by the parties in the week in which they reach a settlement might be returned to them.

money. Moreover, since these projects would not be currently funded, the committee's action would not discharge any of the government's present obligations; and since such contributions would occur irregularly, the government could not count on being relieved of any future burdens. Consequently, given public officialdom's abhorrence of losing control over money, this use of the funds should also provide an incentive for public employers to bargain.

Finally, I would like to dispel what may perhaps be a lingering doubt about nonstoppage strikes. Although they were initially proposed for use in the private sector more than two decades ago, they have had little acceptance by private parties. There are a number of reasons for this. First, although strikes have been the subject of some academic disapproval and periodic editorial dismay, they remain an acceptable device in the private sector. There has been, therefore, little real pressure for a substitute. Second, for a nonstoppage strike in the private sector to be as effective as the conventional strike, the contributions of the employer to the fund must be geared to the amount of profits it is spared from losing. Because of the obvious difficulty of calculating this figure, achieving a formula for employer contribution which is satisfactory to both parties could easily be more formidable an obstacle than resolving their basic economic differences. Third, any statutory imposition of a nonstoppage plan would, while solving in a crude way the complexities of computing the formula, raise the claim by employers of deprivation of property without due process and the analogous employee claim of involuntary servitude.

Clearly the first reason does not apply in the public sector, for strikes are not currently acceptable. Nor does the second carry much weight. There is no need in the public sector to base a formula on profits because there are no profits; what should be required by the employees is that there be sufficient pressure on the public employer, and I believe my proposal provides that. The third, too, is inapplicable. Government may of course impose conditions on itself; and since it is constitutional totally to deprive public employees of the right to strike, it should be permissible to provide them with a halfway measure, especially when it is the union which voluntarily initiates its use. In short, no significant barriers to adoption of nonstoppage strikes exist in the public sector.

B. The Graduated Strike

A nonstoppage strike may be insufficient to induce responsive bargaining. More direct pressure may be required, and the graduated strike would provide it.

In a graduated strike the union would call work to a halt in stages. During the first week or two of the strike the employees would not work for half a day; during the next period, if the union so chose, they would not work for one full day per week; and so on, until they reached some floor short of total stoppage. Employees' take-home pay would be cut proportionately.

The effect of a graduated strike would be to give the public a taste of reduced service without the shock of immediate and total deprivation. This would start in motion the political machinery I described earlier, but would not overload it. Citizens would make complaints about their inconvenience known to their elected representatives. Local officials, both executive and legislative, would thus be under pressure to *do* something, but would nevertheless be able to consult with each other and with the officials at higher levels of government. They would therefore be able to negotiate with the union in a reasonably coordinated and authoritative manner. Free of resentment and of posturing over illegality, the complicated political process of sorting out preferences between higher costs and fewer services and among competing demands could then work itself out.

To insure that employees really suffer proportionate loss of wages would require, first, that they be unable, after the strike, to reduce backlogs at overtime rates. This could probably be accomplished simply by a limitation on overtime pay for some period following the strike. It does not seem necessary to do more: to the extent the employees ultimately recoup their lost wages, the public will have the lost service restored; and in any case it is unlikely that either side's losses will ever be totally recovered. Second, it would be necessary that the shutdown not exceed the announced level. While enforcement of this requirement would not be easy, it would probably be satisfactory for an impartial body with an expedited hearing procedure to determine the actual extent of the employee stoppage and to mete out appropriate penalties, including reduction of wages. In addition, there would be another strong inducement to proper observance of the ground rules: union and employee recognition that they have an effective, fair, and acceptable weapon to encourage good faith bargaining.

As I stated before, I think that the graduated strike and nonstoppage strike would work best in tandem. Because a nonstoppage strike would cause the public less disruption, we should perhaps require that unions try it for at least four weeks; they would then have the option of instituting a graduated strike. However, since both types of strikes are certain to put pressure on the public employer, I think we should give the employer some limited options. If it feels itself financially hard pressed, it can select the graduated strike, which would result in no additional expense. If it believed that the service performed by the employees was so essential to the public that cessation could not be tolerated — for example, fire and police protection — it should have the opportunity to persuade an impartial, preferably expert, tribunal that the services are in reality so indispensable. If successful, it could limit the union to the ever- more-expensive nonstoppage strike.

V. Conclusion

A blanket ban on strikes by public employees does not work. Illegal strikes are bad for labor relations and even worse for the rule of law. However, conventional strikes, if legalized, would be ill adapted to the complex procedures of public labor relations. Yet the public must accord its employees reasonable procedures that produce responsible bargaining. Under my proposals, bargaining could perform its salutary function, but without the disruption caused by the conventional strike and in ways adapted to the peculiarities of the public's needs and the government's intricate procedures for allocating resources.

Our federal system is complex and often awkward, but it enables us to experiment with various means of regulating public labor-management relations so that neither the public nor public employees are victimized. We should test the nonstoppage strike, the graduated strike, and indeed any other promising arrangement as we grope in this old field mined with so many new problems.

NOTE

See generally *Exploring Alternatives to the Strike,* 96 Monthly Lab. Rev. 33-66 (Sept., 1973). See also Donn, *Alternative Impasse Procedures in the Public Sector,* 32 Lab. L.J. 460 (1981).

Chapter 7

SETTLEMENT OF COLLECTIVE BARGAINING IMPASSES

A. INTRODUCTION

1. IMPASSE DISPUTES

Three kinds of impasse disputes arise in the course of labor-management relations in the public and private sectors. These are customarily referred to as "representational," "grievance" (or "rights"), and "collective bargaining" (or "interest") disputes, respectively. "Representational" disputes concern efforts by one or more labor organizations to obtain bargaining rights. These types of disputes constitute the subject matter of Chapter 3. "Grievance" ("rights") disputes arise subsequent to the negotiation of a collective bargaining agreement and ordinarily concern the interpretation or administration of the agreement. These controversies are generally resolved in accordance with contractually negotiated grievance procedures, which are discussed in Chapter 8.

"Interest" disputes arise during the parties' attempt to negotiate the terms of a bargaining agreement. This chapter is devoted to a consideration of the various methods or procedures which have been employed or advocated for use in the public sector to resolve these types of bargaining disputes. With respect to the problem of the settlement of public sector bargaining impasses, the Taylor Report warned:

> The design of dispute settlement procedures must constantly avoid at least two serious pitfalls. The first is that impasse procedures often tend to be overused; they may become too accessible and as a consequence, the responsibility and problem-solving virtues of constructive negotiations are lost. Dispute settlement procedures can become habitforming, and then negotiations become only a ritual. The second pitfall is that a standardized dispute settlement procedure is not ideally suited to all parties and to all disputes. Procedures work best which have been mutually designed, are mutually administered, and have been mutually shaped to the particular problem at hand.*

2. A SURVEY OF IMPASSE PROCEDURES AND THEIR RATIONALE

D. BOK & J. DUNLOP, LABOR AND THE AMERICAN COMMUNITY 333-34, 337-38 (1970)**

Once a negotiating relationship has been established, the concern shifts to the resolution of disputes over the terms of employment. The settlement of these disputes calls for the design of procedures to govern collective negotiation and

---

*Governor's Committee on Public Employee Relations, Final Report to Governor Nelson Rockefeller, State of New York, March 31, 1966, p. 33.
**Reprinted by permission of Simon & Schuster, Inc.

to provide effective alternatives to conflict. In the first instance, it is probably wise to ask the parties involved to design their own machinery. Employee organizations differ widely in their objectives and methods: Governmental units are of varying size and confront diverse budgetary restraints and procedures. The scope of civil-service regulations and collective negotiations are far from uniform, and great differences appear in the nature of government operations and the authority of government negotiators. The influence of employee organizations and the labor movement in the community also varies sharply. It stands to reason, therefore, that no one procedure, imposed legislatively, will suit all the situations to which it would apply.

There are already a variety of procedures available in the public sector, and inventiveness in this field is at an early stage. The parties may develop some variant of the prevailing-wage approach and identify the procedures and the comparable sectors to be used in making these determinations. They may establish various study committees to operate during the term of the agreement, particularly on difficult prospective issues, with resort to fact finding and recommendations before a body of their own design and choice. They may design a system of public hearings with settlement through normal political processes. As George Meany has observed, "Perhaps the best answer in this field is some system of voluntary arbitration."

In the absence of procedures agreed to by the parties to resolve disputes over provisions of an agreement, or in the event that such machinery fails, the government involved in the dispute has an obligation to provide a general procedure. There is wide agreement that provision should be made for mediation between the employee organization and the governmental unit if the parties fail to resolve the dispute by direct negotiations. But what should happen in the event that the dispute remains unresolved and the parties have reached a serious impasse?

There are three groups of major contending views on impasse procedures: 1) Government employees should be allowed to strike except when the public health or safety is in jeopardy. 2) If the impasse cannot otherwise be settled, no strike of public employees is permissible and the dispute should be resolved by compulsory arbitration binding on both the governmental employer and the employee organization. 3) Recommendations should be made by a fact-finding body, and in the event further mediation around these recommendations does not resolve the dispute, the appropriate legislative body should review the dispute and enact a statute prescribing the terms and conditions of employment. The recommendations of the fact finders should have presumptive validity, but should not be binding on the legislature....

The third alternative impasse procedure is fact finding with final resolution to be made, if necessary, by the legislative body. This procedure provides a role for both expert opinion of neutrals and for legislative judgment on questions beyond the province of the labor-management specialist.

Where it works well, fact finding can be a useful and even a powerful device. It seems to focus public opinion and to economize on the legislators' time, while providing them with the guidance they need. Fact finding is also a flexible procedure; it provides maximum opportunity for mediation, before, during, and after recommendations made privately or publicly. The exposure to hard facts also helps to deflate extreme positions; it allows neutrals to develop and "try on for size" possible accommodations, while permitting the parties to modify a recommendation to their mutual advantage. The uncertainty of the ultimate legislative action may stimulate a settlement, and the parties can preserve the opportunity for reaching such an agreement even after recommendations have been made.

In some instances, of course, the legislative body will unwisely reject the recommendations of a fact-finding board. Thus, critics may argue that the procedure is inherently unfair, since the employer — that is, the government — has the ultimate power to decide, even unfairly, in its own case. But what is the alternative? Some observers will suggest that the union be allowed to strike whenever the government refuses to accept the recommendations of the fact-finding body. But fact finders can make egregious errors, and surely they are not qualified to weigh the added labor costs of a settlement against tax increases and competing public programs and expenditures. Decisions of this kind may be more appropriately resolved by political processes and elected officials than by strikes or labor arbitrators. If so, the union is not without recourse, for it can bring political pressure to bear through its constituents and lobbyists. In this respect, the union occupies a very different position vis-à-vis the government than it would vis-à-vis a private employer with final power to fix the terms of employment. It is true that the union may have very little political influence and some legislative bodies may disregard its pleas for this reason. But similar drawbacks will exist in any system; if strikes were allowed, for example, many public employees would also have too little power to protect their legitimate interests. As a result, considering all the interests at stake, the wisest course may lie in letting the legislative body decide on the recommendations of a neutral panel. If the legislature disregards the recommendations too freely and too unfairly, strikes are likely to occur, regardless of the law, to bring home the interests of the employees. Short of this, the strike seems an inappropriate way to resolve the impasse.

HILDEBRAND, THE RESOLUTION OF IMPASSES, in THE ARBITRATOR, THE NLRB, AND THE COURTS, PROCEEDINGS OF THE TWENTIETH ANNUAL MEETING OF THE NATIONAL ACADEMY OF ARBITRATORS 289-92 (D. Jones ed. 1967)*

[The author first discusses impasse procedures used in the private sector and rejects as unworkable a full assimilation of those procedures to the public sector. After deciding that the public sector provides very special and necessary services, as a monopoly enterprise, which demands continuity of operations, the author continues:]

If these judgments are correct, then the government sector is indeed a special case. Accordingly, the critical task becomes that of designing a set of procedures that will accomplish three major objectives. The first one is to develop as fully as possible a role for collective bargaining as a method for achieving accommodation and mutual consent. The second is to protect the integrity of the bargaining process by insuring the independence of public management so that the

---

*Reprinted by permission of the Bureau of National Affairs, Inc.

process will not become transformed into a type of machine politics, hence political bargaining. Political bargaining is not collective bargaining. Whatever may be its own rationale, it carries real dangers to collective bargaining in the public service, and it cannot be defended by arguments in behalf of collective bargaining as such. If we seek the latter, we must insure the independence of public managements, and we must make it possible for such managements to sign binding agreements.

Third, the basic procedure must recognize the need to preserve continuity of operations, but, more than this, it should restrain reliance upon coercion as much as possible, so that bargained settlements can become the rule rather than the exception.

The first objective can be served best by provision for an independent public agency to deal with questions of representation and unfair labor practices. In addition, the enabling statute should provide the parties with incentive to devise their own procedures for resolving impasses, failing which one will be mandated by law.

Treatment of Impasses

The second objective is self-evident, and needs no elaboration. The third refers to the treatment of impasses, about which the rest of my paper will be concerned.

Because the budget-making activities of public bodies are controlled by the calendar, the timing of negotiations becomes critical. They must begin early enough to permit the incorporation of settlements in the budget, and the negotiating period must allow for the possibility of intervention if voluntary agreement cannot be reached. Clearly, too, the whole process must provide sufficient opportunity for legislative consideration, open hearings, and clearance with civil service officials.

Because timing is so important, the procedure should make mediation available whenever serious conflict develops, at the option of either side or of the top public official within the jurisdiction. Obviously, too, this official must be kept continuously informed regarding the progress of negotiations. Furthermore, in my judgment it may well be desirable to provide for preventive mediation at the initiative of the independent agency charged with dealing with representation issues and unfair practices.

But suppose mediation fails. Then what? Here two alternative remedies are possible — compulsory arbitration and fact-finding without compulsory arbitration at its terminus. Recourse to either assumes, of course, that the parties have not built in their own procedure for resolving impasses, a procedure that in turn must be compatible with the fundamental policy laid down by statute.

To my mind, there are two basic weaknesses in the method of compulsory arbitration for dealing with disputes in the public service. One is that the certainty that it can be invoked constitutes an open invitation to extremist strategies. Ask for all you can, because you stand a chance of getting part of it. The insidious consequence is that this will vitiate the very process of collective bargaining. The pressures will then be shifted to what in fact is a juridical mechanism. What begins as collective bargaining ends in something quite different.[2] In the second place, compulsory arbitration amounts to a delegation of the responsibilities of public management and of the lawmakers to outsiders. In my view, this is incompatible with the basic principles of representative government. In fact, it can become a most convenient way to duck hard issues by passing them on to a board that is only temporarily in office and that is not responsible to the electorate. The result is likely to be labor policies that are unsound, because they will be more responsive to power relations than to the equitable accommodation of all interests — those of taxpayers, the citizens who use the service, management, and the whole body of public employees viewed collectively.

The Fact-Finding Approach

The second technique for dealing with impasses is that of fact-finding, following, of course, negotiations and mediation. In my view, and for the reasons just stated, this method should be an open-ended one. That is, if it issues in ultimate failure, compulsory arbitration should not be available at its terminus. I shall submit my reasons for leaving the process open-ended for subsequent consideration.

As I see the matter, fact-finding begins when mediation fails. I favor an all-public tripartite board for this purpose, to increase the likelihood of unanimity. Recourse to such a board should be at the initiative of either party or of the top public official, after the mediation period has run out. Precise time limits are required for hearing the dispute and rendering a report. It also seems to me desirable to provide that the recommendations of the board first should be submitted privately to the parties, coupled with a final mediatory effort by the board itself. If this step proves unsuccessful, the recommendations then should be made public, in hopes of building up public opinion in their behalf. If acceptance still cannot be gained, there may be some merit in having the chief executive assemble a carefully selected private committee to attempt quietly to persuade the intractable side to settle on the basis of these recommendations.

There is much to be said for the fact-finding approach. It is a logical extension of the process of collective bargaining because it continuously keeps open the possibility of voluntary settlement. I know of no other method that would serve this end as well. Moreover, it leaves the ultimate responsibility of the lawmakers intact, and, even more, it can produce a set of guidelines to a fair resolution of the dispute at their hands. In turn, this latter feature reduces the disabilities of attempting to legislate in a context of crisis, by men mostly lacking in the necessary expertise.

---

[2]This danger might be reduced if the arbitration proceeding were made very costly to the parties, and its availability were made uncertain by provision of a choice-of-weapons approach.

KHEEL, STRIKES AND PUBLIC EMPLOYMENT, 67 Mich. L. Rev. 931, 940-41 (1969)*

[After concluding that most compulsory arbitration procedures are unsatisfactory, because of issue framing difficulties and the lack of binding effect on the legislature, Mr. Kheel states:]

The simple lesson is that compulsory arbitration for all disputes and all issues is neither legally sound nor practically feasible. It would be a great mistake to adopt this procedure as the usual method prescribed in advance for all disputes in the expectation that it would signal an end to labor strife in public employment.

I believe, rather, that we should acknowledge the failure of unilateral determination, and turn instead to true collective bargaining, even though this must include the possibility of a strike. We would then clearly understand that we must seek to improve the bargaining process and the skill of the negotiators to prevent strikes. For in the end, the solution to the wide range of labor problems involving the many aspects of a dynamic and complicated human relationship must depend on the human factor. The most elaborate machinery is no better than the people who man it. It cannot function automatically. With skillful and responsible negotiators, no machinery, no outsiders, and no fixed rules are needed to settle disputes. For too long our attention has been directed to the mechanics and penalties rather than to the participants and the process. It is now time to change that, to seek to prevent strikes by encouraging collective bargaining to the fullest extent possible.

For the few strikes that might jeopardize public health or safety, I would favor legislation authorizing the governor of a state to seek an injunction for a specified period through procedures similar to those for emergency disputes under the Taft-Hartley Act. During the cooling-off period, the parties could continue their search for the basis of accommodation to end the dispute. If these procedures prove unavailing, then the legislature could consider means, but not the specific terms, of settlement, including the possibility of submitting the remaining issues to arbitration within specified bounds. In a particular situation, with issues sharply limited and defined through bargaining, arbitration imposed as a last resort by the legislature can effectively protect the public interest without making a sham of the bargaining process. Our primary reliance would then be placed, as I believe it must if we are to prevent strikes, on joint determination by parties in a true bargaining atmosphere.

I suggest, in short, that there is no workable substitute for collective bargaining — even in government — and that our best chance to prevent strikes against the public interest lies in improving the practice of bargaining. In an environment conducive to real bargaining, strikes will be fewer and shorter than in a system where employees are in effect invited to defy the law in order to make real the promise of joint determination. In a real bargaining environment, the employee representatives, I am convinced, can more effectively meet their dual responsibility to negotiate and to lead. Only if leaders do both can there be constructive labor relationships in place of the chaos resulting when agreements

---

*Reprinted by permission of the Michigan Law Review.

reached in negotiations are rejected by angry rank and file or defied by subterfuge forms of strikes such as working to the rule.

NOTES

1. The preceding excerpts emphasize the need for impasse settlement procedures to provide a substitute for strike action. Is the theory, then, that such procedures will or must involve pressure tactics roughly the equivalent of those which would be generated by a strike or lockout? Alternatively, is the theory that settlement procedures properly designed and skillfully used can or should obviate the need for resort to or availability of the strike or lockout? Given that impasse resolution procedures in the public sector are usually mediation and fact-finding with recommendations, or, in some instances binding arbitration, does the question whether specific procedures are appropriate depend upon which of the suggested underlying theories is sound? Are such theories relevant to the determination of mediation and fact-finding methodology (e.g., with respect to the role of the mediator, and the question whether fact-finding recommendations are to be made public)? See Anderson, *Strikes and Impasse Resolution in Public Employment,* 67 Mich. L. Rev. 943, 947-48 (1969) (contending that strikes are not essential to effective dispute settlement given skilled bargainers and sound impasse resolution procedures); R. Doherty & W. Oberer, Teachers, School Boards and Collective Bargaining: A Changing of the Guard 96-113 (1967) (favoring binding arbitration to replace the need for strikes); and Taylor, *Using Factfinding and Recommendation in Impasses,* 92 Monthly Lab. Rev. 63 (July, 1969) (suggesting that the strike must be replaced by other equally effective processes for inducing equitable settlements).

2. If regardless of the de jure prohibition of strikes, strikes in fact occur to the point that there is really a de facto recognition of them as a part of the collective bargaining process, is it not obvious that an evaluation of existing or proposed dispute settlement procedures poses different theoretical and analytical considerations than if it were assumed that strikes are not only illegal, but because illegal will not occur? Does the situation then become roughly comparable to that obtaining in the private sector? If so, is Hildebrand wrong in rejecting the private sector "model"? To put the matter in different terms, is there any justification for structuring dispute settlement procedures as typically now done, mandating mediation and, in addition, fact-finding (or arbitration) for all disputes? For discussions of these questions and alternatives to the no strike ban, see Garber, *Compulsory Arbitration in the Public Sector: A Proposed Alternative,* 26 Arb. J. 226 (1971) (proposing "final last offer arbitration," but permitting the arbitrator to choose the more reasonable solution offered by the parties on each disputed issue); Bernstein, *Alternatives to the Strike in Public Labor Relations,* 85 Harv. L. Rev. 459, 470-75 (1971) (finding strikes inevitable and proposing the use of the graduated strike and the nonstoppage strike, as necessary to give employees sufficient bargaining strength, while not totally disrupting society); Clark, *Public Employee Strikes: Some Proposed Solutions,* 23 Lab. L.J. 111 (1972) (questioning whether any categories of public employees should have the right to strike); Note, *The Strike and Its Alternatives in Public Employment,* 1966 Wis. L. Rev. 549, 554-59 (reasons for denying right to strike). For a criticism of even a partial right to strike, see Foegan, *The Partial Strike: A Solution in Public Employment?* 30 Pub. Personnel Rev. 83 (1969).

3. Should impasse resolution procedures in the public sector be designed to assure "equitable" settlements irrespective of the relative bargaining strength or weakness of the particular group of employees or the public employer; or, alternatively, should impasse procedures be primarily designed to induce settlements and avoid strikes? The 1966 report by the Michigan Advisory Committee on Public Employee Relations suggested that:

> We think the primary objectives of the law should be to maximize the opportunities for equitable settlement of employee relations disputes in the public sector while rejecting, at this juncture, both resort to the strike and (except in the case of police and firefighters) compulsory third party determination of unresolved new contract issues.

Report to Governor George Romney by the Advisory Committee on Public Employee Relations (1966), reprinted in Collective Bargaining in the Public Service 100, 104 (D. Kruger and C. Schmidt eds. 1969).

For two different proposals of procedures which might increase chances of equitable solutions, see Lev, *Strikes by Government Employees: Problems and Solutions,* 57 A.B.A. J. 771 (1971) (suggesting the creation of a Federal Public Employee Mediation Board with mediators designated to issue awards in public sector impasse disputes and, in addition, federal contributions to assist local legislatures to meet monetary terms of awards); and Cole, *Devising Alternatives to the Right to Strike,* 92 Monthly Lab. Rev. 60 (July 1969) (suggesting a public employment advisory council, which could recommend an appropriate level of increased labor costs to be absorbed by each governmental unit in each fiscal year). See also Hogler & Kriksciun, *Impasse Resolution in Public Sector Collective Negotiations: A Proposed Procedure,* 6 Indus. Rel. L.J. 481 (1984); Craver, *Public Sector Impasse Resolution Procedures,* 60 Chi.-Kent L. Rev. 779, 780-801 (1984); *Exploring Alternatives to the Strike,* 96 Monthly Lab. Rev. 33-66 (Sept. 1973).

4. In Gerhart & Drotning, *Do Uncertain Cost/Benefit Estimates Prolong Public Sector Disputes?,* 103 Monthly Lab. Rev. 26 (Sept. 1980), the authors demonstrated that when negotiating parties are more uncertain about the future costs and benefits associated with continued disagreement, they are more likely to reach an impasse. Does this suggest the need for impasse resolution procedures that will provide fairly predictable results to encourage greater reliance upon the bargaining process?

B. EXISTING LEGISLATIVE APPROACHES

1. FEDERAL LEVEL

CIVIL SERVICE REFORM ACT OF 1978*

Sec. 7114(c)(1). An agreement between any agency and an exclusive representative shall be subject to approval by the head of the agency.

(2) The head of the agency shall approve the agreement within 30 days from the date the agreement is executed if the agreement is in accordance with the provisions of this chapter and any other applicable law, rule, or regulation (unless the agency has granted an exception to the provision).

(3) If the head of the agency does not approve or disapprove the agreement within the 30-day period, the agreement shall take effect and shall be binding on the agency and the exclusive representative subject to the provisions of this chapter and any other applicable law, rule, or regulation.

---

*The full text of Title VII of the Civil Service Reform Act of 1978 which pertains to federal sector labor-management relations is reprinted in the *Statutory Appendix.*

(4) A local agreement subject to a national or other controlling agreement at a higher level shall be approved under the procedures of the controlling agreement or, if none, under regulations prescribed by the agency.

Sec. 7119. Negotiation impasses; Federal Service Impasses Panel. — (a) The Federal Mediation and Conciliation Service shall provide services and assistance to agencies and exclusive representatives in the resolution of negotiation impasses. The Service shall determine under what circumstances and in what manner it shall provide services and assistance.

(b) If voluntary arrangements, including the services of the Federal Mediation and Conciliation Service or any other third-party mediation, fail to resolve a negotiation impasse —

(1) either party may request the Federal Service Impasses Panel to consider the matter, or

(2) the parties may agree to adopt a procedure for binding arbitration of the negotiation impasse, but only if the procedure is approved by the Panel.

(c)(1)......

(5)(A) The Panel or its designee shall promptly investigate any impasse presented to it under subsection (b) of this section. The Panel shall consider the impasse and shall either — (i) recommend to the parties procedures for the resolution of the impasse; or (ii) assist the parties in resolving the impasse through whatever methods and procedures, including factfinding and recommendations, it may consider appropriate to accomplish the purpose of this section. (B) If the parties do not arrive at a settlement after assistance by the Panel under subparagraph (A) of this paragraph, the Panel may — (i) hold hearings; (ii) administer oaths, take the testimony or deposition of any person under oath, and issue subpoenas as provided in section 7132 of this title; and (iii) take whatever action is necessary and not inconsistent with this chapter to resolve the impasse. (C) Notice of any final action of the Panel under this section shall be promptly served upon the parties, and the action shall be binding on such parties during the term of the agreement, unless the parties agree otherwise.

NOTES

1. The two bodies involved with federal labor-management relations which have primary responsibility for assisting parties with contract negotiations are the Federal Mediation and Conciliation Service (FMCS) and the Federal Service Impasses Panel (FSIP). The FSIP consists of seven members appointed by the President for five-year terms. A similar impasse resolution procedure existed under Executive Order 11491, which regulated federal labor-management relations before the enactment of the Civil Service Reform Act of 1978. The FSIP will generally not intervene in a bargaining dispute unless the services of the FMCS have been utilized.

One of five determinations can be made by the FSIP: (1) that it has no jurisidiction; (2) that negotiations should be resumed; (3) that negotiations should be resumed with more mediation; (4) that other voluntary arrangements such as arbitration should be utilized; or (5) that advisory or binding fact-finding be conducted. When binding recommendations are made by the FSIP, the parties must either accept them or negotiate their own settlement of the disputed issues. Orders of the FSIP are not subject to direct judicial review. However, a dissatisfied party may indirectly obtain judicial review of an FSIP order by refusing to comply with it, thus exposing itself to unfair labor practice liability under § 7116. It can then challenge the propriety of the antecedent FSIP directive while appealing the FLRA's unfair labor practice determination. See *Council of Prison Locals v. Brewer*, 735 F.2d 1497 (D.C. Cir. 1984).

2. In *AFGE v. FLRA*, 778 F.2d 850 (D.C. Cir. 1985), the court held that the head of a federal agency possessed the statutory authority to invalidate an agreement containing a term that, in his opinion, was contrary to law, rule or regulation, even where the challenged contract term was imposed by the Federal Service Impasses Panel. Since such agency action is tantamount to a determination that the term in question is nonnegotiable, the matter must be resolved by the FLRA and is thus not subject to grievance arbitration procedures. Accord *Department of Defense Dependents Schs. v. FLRA*, 852 F.2d 779 (4th Cir. 1988). In *Dep't. of Agriculture Food & Nutrition Serv. v. FLRA*, 879 F.2d 655 (9th Cir. 1989), however, the court held that an agency head may not review the propriety of contract terms imposed through interest arbitration procedures which the parties have themselves voluntarily agreed to utilize.

3. The major criticism of the impasse resolution procedures which existed under E.O. 11491 concerned their alleged inability to cope with emergency situations. Since § 7119 of the Civil Service Reform Act has adopted the same basic procedures which were previously used, this problem may continue. Some experts have contended that conditioning FSIP intervention upon the request of a party, and thereafter FSIP discretion, reduces the effectiveness of the impasse resolution procedures. However, others have argued that flexibility and uncertainty should be part of any impasse resolution scheme. In this regard, compare the impasse resolution procedures under the Civil Service Reform Act with the more rigid formula adopted under the Postal Reorganization Act, which is reprinted in the *Statutory Appendix*. See generally *Bargaining and Impasse Resolution in the Federal Sector*, 2 Lab. Law. 299 (1986); Willoughby, *The FMCS and Dispute Mediation in the Federal Government*, 92 Monthly Lab. Rev. 27 (May, 1969); Hampton, *The Framework of E.O. 11491, Labor-Management Relations in the Federal Service*, 17 Fed. B. News 70 (1970); and Note, *Federal Services Impasses Panel: Procedural Flexibility and Uncertainty*, 9 Harv. J. Legis. 694 (1972).

4. The substantial differences between the Postal Reorganization Act impasse procedures and those prescribed in the Civil Service Reform Act may be more attributable to historical development than to any inherent differences regarding the negotiation problems likely to arise under the two schemes. The postal strike of 1970 provided the impetus for special legislation which was designed to prevent further strikes and, presumably, to eliminate the need for strikes by providing specific procedures to produce contract settlements. The various steps in the postal impasse procedures, which include binding arbitration, are mandatory. However, it is not clear that the procedures will adequately cope with a work stoppage if one were to occur. What fail-safe mechanisms can be incorporated in a statutory impasse procedure to deal with unlawful strikes? See Kennedy, *The Postal Reorganization Act of 1970: Heading Off Future Postal Strikes?* 59 Geo. L.J. 305 (1970). See also Cohn, *Labor Features of the Postal Reorganization Act*, 22 Lab. L.J. 44 (1971).

2. STATE AND LOCAL LEVELS

a. A Survey of Legislation

DISPUTE SETTLEMENT IN THE PUBLIC SECTOR: THE STATE-OF-THE-ART, REPORT SUBMITTED TO THE DEPARTMENT OF LABOR, DIVISION OF PUBLIC EMPLOYEE LABOR RELATIONS 8-15 (T. Gilroy & A. Sinicropi eds. 1972 — updated to 1990)*

By October of 1990, at least forty-one states had enacted legislation dealing with interest dispute procedures in public employment. These states were: Alaska, California, Connecticut, Delaware, Florida, Georgia, Hawaii, Idaho, Illinois, Indiana, Iowa, Kansas, Kentucky, Maine, Maryland, Massachusetts, Michigan, Minnesota, Missouri, Montana, Nebraska, Nevada, New Hampshire, New Jersey, New Mexico, New York, North Dakota, Ohio, Oklahoma, Oregon, Pennsylvania, Rhode Island, South Carolina, South Dakota, Tennessee, Texas, Utah, Vermont, Washington, Wisconsin, and Wyoming.

Public employee statutes in the above states range in employee coverage from one specific occupational group, such as teachers or firefighters, to statutes with comprehensive coverage of most public employees in the state. Moreover, a number of states have separate statutes for different types of employees, such as state and municipal employees, teachers, and police and fire personnel.

In addition to variations in coverage, state legislation presents a diversified pattern of impasse procedures such as voluntary systems devised by the parties, mediation, factfinding, arbitration, and "show cause" hearings. Individual statutes often call for one or a combination of the above mentioned procedures. It should be noted that most of the state legislation which includes interest dispute procedures has been passed since 1967....

The following is a summary of the pattern of impasse procedures in state law.

Mediation

At least thirty-six states provide in some way for mediation of negotiation disputes. These states are: Alaska, California, Connecticut, Delaware, Florida, Georgia, Hawaii, Idaho, Illinois, Indiana, Iowa, Kansas, Kentucky, Maine, Maryland, Massachusetts, Michigan, Minnesota, Montana, Nebraska, Nevada, New Hampshire, New Jersey, New Mexico, New York, North Dakota, Ohio, Oregon, Pennsylvania, Rhode Island, South Dakota, Tennessee, Texas, Vermont, Washington, and Wisconsin.

The provisions for mediation differ among and within states with respect to how the procedure is initiated, who provides the service, the use of one mediator or a panel, the relationship of mediation to other impasse procedures, and provisions for payment of costs.

In most states, mediation can be requested by either party. However, under statutes in a few states (e.g., California, North Dakota), both parties must request the service. In some states, such as Kansas and New York, the Public Employment Relations Board will intervene either by request or on its own initiative.

---

*Updated to 1990 by the editors of this casebook.

The agencies providing the mediation services vary among states and in some cases within a state for different groups of employees. Some states, such as New Jersey, provide mediation services through a public employment relations board or commission. Other states use an agency previously established to handle private sector disputes....

While most states provide for a single mediator, several states provide for a panel. Frequently, a tripartite panel is utilized in which each party selects one member of the panel, with the partisan members agreeing on a third panel member....

With respect to the costs of mediation, in the private sector the costs are generally borne by the mediation agency. However, in the public sector, there is often an implication or requirement that the parties pay part of the mediation costs.

Factfinding

Unlike the private sector, where factfinding is limited primarily to so-called national emergency disputes, the public sector relies more heavily on this technique in negotiation impasse resolution. At least thirty-six states authorize the use of factfinding. These states are: Alaska, California, Connecticut, Delaware, Florida, Georgia, Hawaii, Idaho, Illinois, Indiana, Iowa, Kansas, Kentucky, Maine, Maryland, Massachusetts, Michigan, Missouri, Montana, Nebraska, Nevada, New Hampshire, New Jersey, New Mexico, New York, North Dakota, Ohio, Oklahoma, Oregon, Pennsylvania, Rhode Island, South Dakota, Tennessee, Vermont, Washington, and Wisconsin.

The normal procedure is that factfinding may be initiated by either party, a tripartite or neutral panel is utilized, and recommendations for settlement are made by that panel. These recommendations are either made public following the decision, or delayed pending further negotiation based on those recommendations....

In most states, factfinders are not specifically authorized to attempt to mediate the dispute. However, a few states (e.g., Connecticut) make specific provisions for factfinders to attempt mediation.

Several states detail criteria for use in making factfinding reports.... For example, Florida requires a factfinder to consider: (1) the salaries paid for comparable jobs by local private employers; (2) the salaries paid public employees by public employers of comparable size within the state; (3) the interest and welfare of the public; and (4) the peculiarities of employment as compared with other occupations.

Arbitration

Twenty-eight states have legislation authorizing voluntary or compulsory arbitration for the resolution of some or all outstanding issues in certain public sector disputes. These states are: Alaska, Connecticut, Delaware, Hawaii, Illinois, Indiana, Iowa, Maine, Massachusetts, Michigan, Minnesota, Montana, Nebraska, Nevada, New Hampshire, New Jersey, New York, North Dakota, Ohio, Oklahoma, Oregon, Pennsylvania, Rhode Island, Texas, Vermont, Washington, Wisconsin, and Wyoming.

In some of the states the decisions are only advisory, in others they are binding, and in a few states the nature of the decision is left to the agreement of the parties. Several states provide for more than one type of arbitration decision under different statutes or in the same law....

Some arbitration statutes cover only "essential" employees, while other laws provide more inclusive coverage. In some jurisdictions arbitration awards for certain workers (e.g., police and fire personnel) are binding, while those pertaining to other employees are merely advisory.

In states which provide for compulsory arbitration, the dispute is referred to an arbitration board rather than an individual arbitrator. Kansas and New York provide for hearings by the legislative body which may take such action as it deems to be in the public interest, including the interest of the involved public employees. In Nebraska, the dispute is resolved by the State Court of Industrial Relations.

Most of the states authorizing arbitration either impose no limit on the issues which may be resolved through this device or are silent on the matter. In Delaware, a limit is specified, while in Louisiana, one is implied. On the other hand, the Maine statute does not appear to limit the scope of arbitration when its use is voluntary, but does provide that determinations shall be advisory concerning salaries, pensions, and insurance, and binding regarding other issues, when compulsory arbitration is utilized. In Rhode Island, which authorizes compulsory arbitration, there is no limit with respect to issues in the case of police and firefighters, whereas arbitration determinations for municipal employees and teachers are binding except on matters involving the expenditure of money.

In some states, specific criteria for arbitration awards have been established.... The Michigan statute includes such criteria as the authority of the employer, the financial ability of the employer, the interests of the public, consumer prices, and comparable wages.

Some statutes, notably those in Michigan and Wyoming, specifically provide for appeal of arbitration awards. Michigan permits appeals if the order is unsupported by competent, material, and substantial evidence on the whole record. Wyoming permits appeals to vacate an award for such reasons as corruption, fraud, or partiality, or if the arbitrators exceed their authority. A court may modify or correct an award when there is miscalculation or mistakes, the arbitrators decided an issue not submitted to them, or the award is imperfect in form....

County and Municipal

While these jurisdictions are in many cases covered by the state legislation previously referred to, in many other instances their labor relations activities take place within the framework of local resolutions or ordinances. In some cases, negotiations take place without any clear legislated guidelines. This is particularly true of larger cities in states without public employment statutes and also in local school districts....

Local ordinances vary widely with respect to both employees covered and impasse resolution procedures adopted, with their variations being similar to those noted previously regarding the different state enactments.

NOTE

See Armbrust, *Impasse Resolution Procedures in Public Employment Negotiations,* 8 Urb. Law. 449 (1976). See also Impasse and Grievance Resolution (H. Kershen ed. 1977).

b. Some Specific Models

WISCONSIN MUNICIPAL EMPLOYMENT LAW — WIS. STAT. ANN. § 111.70(4)(c). See *Statutory Appendix.*

NOTE

There are three statutes covering three separate categories of public employees in Wisconsin: state, municipal, and municipal police and firefighters. The Wisconsin Employment Relations Commission supervises impasse procedures under all three statutes.

There are two separate statutory impasse procedures for police and firefighters disputes. One covers police and firefighters in cities with populations of 2500 to 500,000 and provides for compulsory arbitration of interest disputes at the request of either party. Wis. Stat. Ann. ch. 247, § 111.77. (The statute specifies "final offer" arbitration, unless the parties jointly elect otherwise.) The other covers only the Milwaukee police force and it, too, provides for compulsory arbitration of interest disputes. However, the statute covering Milwaukee police does not adopt the "final offer" approach. Wis. Stat. Ann. § 111.70 (4)-(jm) 1-13.

PENNSYLVANIA PUBLIC EMPLOYEE RELATIONS ACT — PA. STAT. ANN. tit. 43, ch. 19, §§ 1101.801-1101.807, 1101.1002-1101.1003. See *Statutory Appendix.*

NOTE

Pennsylvania requires binding arbitration of disputes involving prison and mental hospital guards and court personnel if an impasse is reached. See *Statutory Appendix,* Pa. Stat. Ann. § 1101.805. A different statute, Pa. Stat. Ann. §§ 217.1-217.10, provides for compulsory arbitration to resolve disputes involving police and firefighters. All other public employees may strike after statutory dispute resolution procedures have been exhausted, unless or until the strike endangers the public health, safety, or welfare.

ILLINOIS PUBLIC LABOR RELATIONS ACT — §§ 12-14, 17-18. See *Statutory Appendix.*

NOTE

The IPLRA covers state and municipal employees, but excludes school personnel who are provided similar rights under the Illinois Educational Labor Relations Act. Although interest arbitration is mandated for "essential" personnel who are not permitted to strike, it is optional with respect to other disputants who may jointly consent to its use. Where other techniques fail to produce a bargaining agreement, nonessential employees are authorized to utilize strike action. See generally Craver, *Public Sector Impasse Resolution Procedures,* 60 U. Chi-Kent L. Rev. 779 (1984).

HAWAII PUBLIC EMPLOYMENT RELATIONS ACT — HAW. REV. STAT. §§ 89-11, 89-12. See *Statutory Appendix.*

NOTE

In allowing strike action after resort to the prescribed impasse procedures, Hawaii's statute departs sharply from the norm. Yet it encompasses features of other states in providing for mediation and fact-finding, and it also includes a detailed procedure for voluntary binding arbitration. Is the right to strike sufficiently restricted to minimize probable resort to strike action? See Pendleton, *Collective Bargaining in the Public Sector,* Report of the Industrial Relations Center, Univ. of Hawaii (May, 1971).

NEW YORK EMPLOYEES' FAIR EMPLOYMENT ACT (TAYLOR LAW) — § 209 OF THE TAYLOR LAW. See *Statutory Appendix.*

NOTE

Some have criticized the New York approach since it places the task of ultimate dispute resolution in the legislative body after fact-finding. The suggestion is that this may decrease serious bargaining efforts in the expectation that more favorable treatment will come from the legislature. Are there countervailing arguments? Statistics released by the New York PERB indicate that most disputes in which mediation or fact-finding are used are resolved short of legislative action. Note that a legislatively imposed impasse resolution may not deprive employees of benefits that existed under the expired contract, since it is unlawful for an employer "to refuse to continue all the terms of an expired agreement until a new agreement is negotiated." See *County of Niagara v. Newman,* 1984-86 PBC ¶ 34,392 (N.Y. Sup. Ct., App. Div. 1984).

For general discussions of the Taylor Act, see Anderson, MacDonald & O'Reilly, *Impasse Resolution in Public Sector Collective Bargaining — An Examination of Compulsory Interest Arbitration in New York,* 51 St. John's L. Rev. 453, 457-481 (1977); Doering, *Impasse Issues in Teacher Disputes Submitted to Fact Finding in New York,* 27 Arb. J. 1 (1972); Drotning & Lipsky, *The Outcome of Impasse Procedures in New York Schools Under the Taylor Law,* 26 Arb J. 87 (1971); Yaffe & Goldblatt, *Factfinding in Public Employment Disputes in New York State: More Promise Than Illusion,* ILR Paperback No. 10 (1971).

NEW YORK CITY COLLECTIVE BARGAINING LAW — §§ 1173-5.0a, 1173-7.0 IN ADMINISTRATIVE CODE, CH. 54, LOCAL LAW 53-1967, AS AMENDED BY LOCAL LAWS 1 & 2 of 1972. See *Statutory Appendix.*

NOTES

1. The New York City scheme evolved during the period when the Taylor Act was being developed. The Office of Collective Bargaining (OCB), which commenced operations on January 2, 1968, was the result of a 1967 agreement between the City and most of the municipal unions with which it bargained. See generally Raskin, *Politics Up Ends the Bargaining Table,* in Public Workers and Public Unions 122 (S. Zagoria ed. 1972); Anderson, *Strikes and Impasse Resolution in Public Employment,* 67 Mich. L. Rev. 943 (1969); Gotbaum, *Finality in Collective Bargaining Disputes: The New York Experience,* 21 Catholic U.L.

Rev. 589 (1972); Schilian, *The Taylor Law, The O.C.B. and the Public Employee,* 35 Brooklyn L. Rev. 214 (1969).

2. It was hoped by city officials and union leaders that the ordinance and OCB structure would prevent strikes. Strikes were not specifically prohibited, but the strike proscription and sanctions of the Taylor Act remained applicable. There have been some problems, especially in the bargaining dispute settlement area. The 1968 sanitation worker strike, followed by police sick-ins and a large backlog of unresolved cases placed the OCB under stress. The ordinance was finally amended in 1972 to empower the OCB Board of Collective Bargaining to appoint Impasse Panels to resolve bargaining disputes. An Impasse Panel is authorized to take whatever action it considers necessary to end a dispute, including mediation or final and binding settlement recommendations. See § 1173-7.0c of the New York City ordinance. See also GERR No. 435, B-10.

C. MEDIATION AND FACT-FINDING

PICKETS AT CITY HALL, REPORT AND RECOMMENDATIONS OF THE TWENTIETH CENTURY FUND TASK FORCE ON LABOR DISPUTES IN PUBLIC EMPLOYMENT 21-24 (1970)*

Mediation

The function of mediation, as it works for an agreement that the negotiators could not find themselves, is to maintain communication between the parties, who may believe they have said everything they have to say and done everything they are able to do; to inject a neutral presence into what, because of the impasse, has become an adversary situation; to strip away the nonessential matters and frame the core issues in dispute; and to propose suggestions for settlement.

Mediation works best when it is jointly sought by the disagreeing parties. Each is acknowledging that outside help may be useful, a posture that launches the mediation effort under the most favorable auspices. But if one, or both, of the parties refuse to invite mediation, it should be initiated anyway, preferably by the labor agency we recommend be established.

Mediation has no power to compel. It is fruitful only through logic and persuasion. The parties may freely accept or reject a mediator's suggestions if he chooses to make them; they abdicate none of their sovereignty. Mediation has, nevertheless, been the most effective process for the resolution of labor disputes. Only if it is employed to its limit and fails should other processes be invoked.

The quality of the mediator, his experience and skills, may mean the difference between success and failure. The parties must believe that he has no bias against them. He must have a broad knowledge of labor relations, knowing all of the formulas that have been used to settle issues such as the one he confronts, and he must be able to articulate them. He should be inventive in producing new formulas if the situation requires. Above all he must be patient and persevering in his effort to bring the alienated parties into agreement, meanwhile keeping their confidence.

---

*Copyright © 1970 by the Twentieth Century Fund, New York. Reprinted by permission.

A cadre of professional mediators with experience in the private sector is attached to the Federal Conciliation and Mediation Service, to various state agencies and to some local governments. In some disputes nonprofessionals who seem to have the necessary qualities are enlisted as mediators. In communities which do not have mediation resources, access to an established mediation service should be established, or such a service of their own should be created. It will have a central role in labor relations policy.

But while much private sector mediation expertness is readily transferable to use in public employment disputes, working with government as a party in negotiations and with a union proscribed from striking requires special techniques that must, in many instances, still be acquired. One example of a problem a mediator is likely to face in the public sector is the question of who, on behalf of the employer, can make and effectuate a final decision on disputed issues. Those who represent government in the negotiations may not have such authority. The mediator may have to work to persuade them, then seek and find the true locus of authority — governor, mayor, legislature, council or board — and persuade still further. In any agency, department or subdivision of government, that locus can vary. As the mediator in the private sector must operate with an awareness that the position taken by union representatives in the negotiations is influenced by whether or not they think their membership will ratify any agreement reached, the public sector mediator must be aware that not only is this same factor present but there is also the need for ratification on the employer side at a higher authority level than is often represented in the negotiations.

Fact-Finding

If mediation should fail to achieve agreement in a dispute, there should follow, as a link in a chain, the process of fact-finding. It will be best initiated through appointive action by the independent agency, the establishment of which we have recommended. If such an agency does not exist, it should be initiated by a high level public official who has had no involvement in the dispute.

Fact-finding has been most effective in both the private and public sector where it has been conducted by an individual or by a panel (usually three in number) qualified as impartial, judicious-minded experts in labor relations whose standing and character attest to their competence and lack of bias. Such men start their work with the advantage of being acceptable to the parties in dispute.

The degree of formality in fact-finding proceedings is usually determined by the fact-finders themselves, depending on what manner appears most promising. In any event, full opportunity will be provided for both the disputing parties to make their case. This may include the testimony of witnesses, the submission of documents and statistics, the presentation of briefs, arguments and rebuttals. The fact-finders may want information beyond that presented and may undertake their own research and call witnesses on their own motion. Their first objective is to establish the true facts which, in the normal dispute, are inevitably in controversy.

Once the sifting and winnowing have disclosed the true facts to the panel's satisfaction — as opposed to what the parties may have alleged during negotiations — the fact-finders will frequently essay a mediatory role. They will try to disabuse one or the other or both parties of false notions or assertions and try to get the parties themselves to agree on settlement terms. In many instances the fact-finding process has succeeded at this point in bringing the disputants into agreement and this has completed its work.

Should the dispute still persist after such an effort, it is incumbent upon the panel to exercise its own judgment as to what the settlement terms should be.

A multiplicity of considerations are to be taken into account and weighed as the fact-finders formulate their conclusions. If disputes involve labor costs, as most do, the panel will have heard or studied cost of living figures, rates paid by other employers for comparable work, the historical trend of wage adjustments for the instant employees, non-wage benefit levels and, among much other data, the employer's ability or inability to meet union demands.

Virtually all of the matters that come under the fact-finders' scrutiny in a private industry dispute will be within the purview of a panel sitting on a government employee case. But if labor costs are involved, the fact-finders in public employment will most likely have to be concerned with another factor indigenous to public employment: where and how the incidence of increased labor costs will fall. Will it require the imposition of new or higher taxes? Will it have to be paid by curtailing some public service not involved in the case before the panel? Will an upward wage adjustment deprive some other group of public employees who are bound under the same limited budget appropriation of a deserved increase?

Fair-minded and conscientious men, assuming the responsibility of making a judgment on behalf of the whole community, which includes employees, government-as-employer and the public at large, will ponder these implications. For their conclusions to be as fair as humanly possible to all interests concerned, they will have to find some balance between the competing needs and equities.

When it has formulated the terms it will endorse, the panel may decide it will be most effective by not immediately making them public but communicating them privately to the parties. When this technique is followed, a revival of direct negotiations often occurs. The disputants learn the fact-finders' conclusions and have some sense of the public pressure they will be under to accept them when the conclusions of the impartial body that has made a careful study of the issues become widely known.

In this advanced stage of resumed negotiations, focused on the fact-finders' decision, concessions by one or the other or both sides may be offered and agreement may be reached. Or willingly or reluctantly, they may submit to the panel's terms as being the best possible way out of their dispute.

If, however, the time allotted for such further negotiations does not bring results, the fact-finders must make their conclusions public and hope that public opinion will make the unwilling party or parties accept them.

SIMKIN, FACT-FINDING: ITS VALUES AND LIMITATIONS, in ARBITRATION AND THE EXPANDING ROLE OF NEUTRALS, PROCEEDINGS OF THE TWENTY-THIRD ANNUAL MEETING OF THE NATIONAL ACADEMY OF ARBITRATORS 165-72 (G. Somers ed. 1970)*

The principal theme of this paper is that the words — fact-finding — should be substantially eliminated from the labor relations vocabulary or, more accurately, that they should be relegated to more limited usefulness. This has happened already in the private sector. Some day — but not soon — I predict it will also occur in the public sector.

The words fact-finding — conjure up notions of preciseness, of objectivity, of virtue. They even have a godlike quality. Who can disagree with facts? In contrast, the word — mediation — that I do espouse, tends to have an aura of compromise, of slipperiness, of connivance and of furtiveness. Since these are frequent impressions, why prefer the vulgar to the sublime?

There is a problem of semantics. Close examination of the actual functioning of Fact-Finding Boards and of mediators or of Mediation Boards shows that the labels are quite secondary. The abilities and proclivities of the individuals named to those Boards and — more important — the reactions of the parties to the process determine what really happens. Fact-finders do or do not mediate. Some fact-finders who mediate find no facts. Persons appointed as mediators frequently do not mediate in any meaningful way but may announce some real or alleged facts and conclusions....

Fact-Finding Without Recommendations

The basic notion about this type of fact-finding is that somebody does not know the real facts and that establishment and proclamation of the facts will somehow assist in settlement.

Who is that somebody who is ignorant of the facts? Is it the parties — the general public — or the public opinion makers?

Experienced negotiators will seldom be surprised or influenced very much by the results of such fact-finding.

In a limited number of situations, publications of unpleasant facts may bring pressure on the negotiators by their constituencies. Facts that are damaging to a union, published during a long strike, may result in diminished strike morale and more willingness of employees to compromise. Or, publicized facts detrimental to a company position may bring pressure on the company negotiators from the Board of Directors. However, these results are infrequent for a simple reason. Most labor disputes are so complicated that a mere portrayal of facts does not provide a "handle" for action or even suggest clear directional signals towards a likely settlement area.

Publication of facts will be of some minor interest to the general public but will not usually provide an adequate basis for translation into an informed opinion about the total dispute.

---

*Reprinted by permission of the Bureau of National Affairs, Inc.

The opinion makers (columnists, editorial writers, etc.) may welcome such a report. They will make fewer goofs of factual content and have a new reason for writing something. But the facts will seldom change any preconceived ideas they may have already expressed.

On a few occasions, fact-finders not empowered to make recommendations on the issues have indulged in assessing blame on one of the parties. This device seldom accomplishes anything. It is much more likely to exacerbate the dispute.

In short, fact-finding without recommendations is likely to be an exercise in futility.

These observations may require modification in some current public employee disputes. Bargainers in the public sector sometimes lack some of the sophistication that is more typical in the private sector. Moreover, since the taxpayers are the employers, however far removed from the bargaining table, their appraisal of facts can assume more significance than is the case in a private dispute.

There is a potential and sometimes utilized variety of this general type of fact-finding that is seldom discussed. It is the use of impartial technicians — long in advance of negotiations — to work with the parties to develop pertinent background facts on such issues as pensions and insurance.

Fact-Finding with Recommendations

When fact-finders are given the responsibility to make specific recommendations on the issues in dispute, the process becomes very familiar to an arbitrator.... It is arbitration with two major points to distinguish it from grievance arbitration. (1) Recommendations are not final and binding decisions. Either or both parties can reject. (2) The recommendations do not develop out of a contractual framework. They are legislative value judgments. Recommendations are not facts, nor are they based exclusively or even primarily on facts.

Many of you will disagree honestly with the last statement. One concept of this type of fact-finding is that the recommendations flow almost automatically out of the facts. In my considered opinion, this notion has little or no validity....

In arms length fact-finding, where is the fact-finder to find a basis for his value judgments? In the last analysis, all he can do is to exercise his best intellectual powers and search his own soul. He has no adequate opportunity to gauge acceptability by the parties. No hearings can ever meet that need adequately.

This is especially true because the parties have known that recommendations will be forthcoming. During the interval between the appointment of the fact-finder and the issuance of his report, any bargaining that may have occurred is almost certain to stop. All efforts of the parties have been directed to getting the best possible set of recommendations. Nor is it an adequate refuge to conclude — as is sometimes the case — that the exposure of the parties to the fact-finder so frightens them that they will reach agreement to avoid recommendations.

We come now to the receipt of the recommendations. Either or both parties can say: "No." If that is not the situation, it is de facto arbitration and should be so labeled. If a "No" is voiced, the dispute has not been settled. The fact-finder has been rebuffed and usually he has no place to go. If he reacts defensively as he is likely to do, the dispute may be exacerbated. What has been a two-way dispute up to that point may become a three-way controversy....

Where fact-finding has been successful, I would suggest — but cannot prove — that the fact-finder has mediated — deliberately, instructively or surreptitiously. When fact-finding without mediation has succeeded in the public sector, I would suspect that it is a transitory phenomenon. Until recently and even now in some jurisdictions, public employees have been so far behind that fact-finders have a broad target range. I would predict that the range will narrow in the years immediately ahead of us.

What do I mean by mediation? Time does not permit analysis of the remarkably wide spectrum of mediation activity — things that a mediator can do — or not do. At one end, the spectrum begins by a decision not to intervene at all — to provide no third party assistance. At the other end of the band, the mediator can issue public recommendations. A major principle is to maximize bargaining and minimize the role of the mediator — to exercise enough patience to let bargaining work. But the mediator must also be able and willing to "grasp the nettle" — to recognize when patience is not a virtue and to act accordingly. Most mediation decisions are decisions as to strategy and timing — not decisions on the specific issues.

In the hands of a skilled mediator, facts are potent tools. It is seldom that publication of facts is either necessary or desirable. But they can be most useful in hard-hitting deflation of extreme positions. This is accomplished in separate head-to-head conferences or meetings, absent the embarrassment of the other side's presence and certainly not in the press. Public reference to the facts, if required at all, comes after a settlement to help save face.

The mediator has unusual opportunities to explore a wide variety of solutions — to "try them on for size." Thus, he acquires a strong intuitive sense, if not the certainty, of the vital element of acceptability.

Package recommendations are a last resort device, to be utilized only if all else fails and maybe not issued even then. The mediator is never committed to the use of that device and he will steadfastly refuse to take such action unless he is convinced or has a strong hunch that it may be productive.

DOERING, IMPASSE ISSUES IN TEACHER DISPUTES SUBMITTED TO FACT FINDING IN NEW YORK, 27 Arbitration J. 1, 12-16 (March 1972)*

What ... are the criteria upon which fact finders base their recommendations? There seem to be two major considerations involved, and one or both may be operative in any one situation. The standards of "acceptability" (what the parties will agree to) and of "equity" (the requirements of the fact finder's notions of fairness and good labor relations) appear to be determinative.

The weighting of these criteria will depend to some extent upon the fact finder's view of his own role: whether he sees his primary function as making proposals which will produce a settlement, or as a neutral third party whose major role is to make public the facts of the dispute and try to suggest an "equitable" (not merely "acceptable") resolution of issues. Actually both of these functions are part of the fact finder's role, and they need not necessarily be

---

*Reprinted by permission of the American Arbitration Association, Inc.

conflicting. If, however, they are not entirely compatible, the fact finder must choose which criterion to modify in light of the other.

Acceptability

"Acceptability" as an abstract criterion by which to decide the issues in dispute is fairly self evident — " to the lion shall go the lion's share." It means convincing the parties that the recommendations represent the best bargain they could have gotten based upon the power balance between them in free collective bargaining if stoppages were not illegal.

While the concept of "acceptability" is easily defined in the abstract, specific definition of the "acceptable" solution for any set of circumstances is often difficult. The neutral party must get the sense of the situation from the parties themselves and from that try to gauge the area of possible settlement. In addition to correctly judging what the area of settlement is, he must convince the parties that his interpretation is accurate and that the recommendations based upon it represent the best they will be able to get.

Sometimes the problem of persuasion becomes part of the criterion itself. A recalcitrant individual on one of the negotiating teams may have to be taken into consideration in defining the area of settlement, and the criterion of "acceptability" may end up relating as much to personalities and emotions around the bargaining table as to the facts in the case. The situation is peculiar to public sector bargaining. In a private sector strike situation, the personalities and rhetoric of the negotiators soon give way to a test of economic strength. In public employment, impasse procedures are designed to avoid such tests, and it is more difficult to call a bluff. Personalities and emotions creep into the process and cannot be ignored if settlement is the object. Another factor which may make the neutral person's job more difficult is the fact that in the public sector there are politics on both sides of the table. Management as well as union spokesmen are elected officials.

Although some pressure can be brought to bear through publication of the fact finder's report, research indicated that attempts to arouse public interest have had only minimal effects on the actual settlement of the dispute. Thus the fact finder looking for a settlement is pretty well limited to the facts, both economic and political, and the personalities at the table.

Equity

In addition to his appraisal of acceptability, the fact finder usually arrives at some notion of the "equity" involved before making his recommendations. The term equity here denotes considerations by the neutral party which are not influenced by the power balance between the parties, but by the arguments put forward and such abstract standards of justice as the fact finder may have.

From the presentations made by the parties the fact finder usually obtains several indications as to the equity of their proposals. Perhaps the most useful of these indicators are past practice within the district, and present practice in other neighboring and/or similar districts, with emphasis usually on the latter. Past practice within the district, except where a district has been a leader in a certain field, is usually de-emphasized because it is no longer current. Furthermore, the practices may be in dispute. Comparison with similar and neighboring districts has the advantage of being both an outside standard and a current one.

Through comparisons with neighboring and similar districts the fact finder can ascertain the level of settlements (or at least the relative positions of the parties if bargaining is incomplete) in other districts faced with the same geography, similar tax problems and the same increases in the cost of living. From this the fact finder gains an idea of the "going rate" and also of the competitive recruiting salaries. If neighboring districts are dissimilar in terms of size or tax-base, the fact finder may modify or weight the criterion of comparability accordingly.

In addition to comparability, past practice, and other arguments presented by the parties, the fact finder himself has professional standards from his training and experience in labor relations which may influence his findings. Certain issues may be handled from the point of view of good labor relations rather than on a basis of comparability, past practice, or even acceptability.

The Weighting of the Criteria

Acceptability and equity are most likely to conflict when acceptability is less dependent on economics, and more a matter of personalities or politics. If agreement is to be achieved, such needs and individuals must be accommodated, sometimes at the expense of equity. Where acceptability is measured in economic terms it usually produces contracts similar to those negotiated in comparable districts if only because those districts also had to find acceptable solutions.

In mediation, which precedes fact finding, settlements (if they are achieved) are achieved on the basis of acceptability. If the mediator is successful in convincing the parties of his impression of the "acceptable" solution, there is no need to go on to fact finding. The disputes most likely to be carried further are those in which acceptability depends upon the personalities at the bargaining table, or on political rather than economic factors; in these disputes there is the greatest conflict between acceptability and equity and one party will undoubtedly feel aggrieved. One or both of the parties may opt for fact finding in hopes of finding someone with a different appraisal of acceptability, or someone who will modify what has already been identified as the "acceptable solution" in light of some higher equity. That is, teachers sometimes feel that if a position is morally right and equitable it should prevail even if the power balance in the community would not support such a position. They occasionally go to fact finding in the hope that the fact finder will lend his support to their position.

Fact finding gives the parties a second neutral interpretation of the "acceptable solution" and often an opinion of the equity as well. Having thus identified acceptability and equity as the major criteria, and having suggested that acceptability may be the more important since fact finding is a dispute settlement procedure, it would be interesting to know with what accuracy fact finders judge the area of settlement. If fact finders cannot be reasonably sure of correctly assessing acceptability, it would suggest that they ought not to place inordinate weight on this criterion, or that they should at least give equity the benefit of the doubt in situations where they perceive a conflict between the two criteria.

GOULD, PUBLIC EMPLOYMENT: MEDIATION, FACT-FINDING AND ARBITRATION, 55 A.B.A. J. 835, 837-38 (1969)*

Is the fact finder's position ... that of a judge or arbitrator, who makes a determination predicated upon purely objective criteria? Or is he more akin to the mediator, whose function is to be acceptable to the parties so that he may bring them together on an amicable basis? It is easy to see that the weight given to either of these functions may depend on the statutory timetable or lack of one.

Chairman Robert Howlett of the Michigan Labor Mediation Board has recently expressed his board's hostility toward mediation efforts by fact finders....

In my judgment, the fact-finding process necessarily partakes of both the mediatory and judicial disciplines. While the process is a fluid one about which the drawing of hard and fast lines is still an audacious act, I am convinced that Chairman Howlett's analogy to "in chambers" settlements is a good one. For it seems difficult for the fact finder to introduce himself as a mediator, gain the parties' confidence and trust and then — having failed to bring them together without recommendations — to put on his judicial robes and hear formal testimony on the issues in dispute. The parties are bound to feel confused and betrayed by this role switching, which can result in a "judge's" reliance on information obtained through informal and frank off-the-record mediation sessions.

On the other hand, the skillful fact finder may be able to find a stage of the proceeding when, in his opinion, a settlement is near and when it is therefore propitious to adjourn the hearing for a limited period of time. Sometimes the opportunity is presented through the appearance of misunderstandings by one side of the other's position. An attempt to obtain clarification concerning the differences between the parties may give the fact finder the chance to don his mediator's hat. But, at this "in chambers" stage — as distinguished from the beginning of the hearing — the parties should have acquired some measure of respect for and confidence in the fact finder. If not, his request to adjourn for clarification or for anything else will be met with a refusal or lack of enthusiasm.

However, even when the fact finder is proceeding down the "in chambers" route, the parties are very often inclined to hold back, anticipating the possible resumption of formal hearings. The fact finder must convince the parties that he will keep the two procedures separate in his own mind. It is an understatement to note that this is not always the easiest feat to carry off.

---

*Reprinted by permission of the American Bar Association.

HOWLETT, COMMENT, in ARBITRATION AND THE EXPANDING ROLE OF NEUTRALS, PROCEEDINGS OF THE TWENTY-THIRD ANNUAL MEETING OF THE NATIONAL ACADEMY OF ARBITRATORS 175, 179-80 (G. Somers ed. 1970)*

We are convinced, however, that if there has been effective mediation, the role of the fact-finder is primarily judicial. If the mediator has performed his role with excellence, a second mediator is generally not helpful. In our 1970 fact-finders' education seminar, two lawyers representing the Michigan Education Association and the Michigan Federation of Teachers, a lawyer representing school districts, and the executive secretary of the Michigan Association of School Boards were in accord that the role of a fact-finder should be judicial and not mediatory. As one lawyer said: "Fact-finding should not be super mediation. If it is used by the fact-finder to club a settlement, the value of the process will be destroyed."

After our initial wandering in the wilderness, we announced that we will not appoint fact-finders until the mediator assigned to the negotiations certifies that mediation has been exhausted and that every effort has been made to narrow the issues to those two or three key items which may make the difference between settlement and failure. Failure may result in a strike. The "strike" is a factor in settlement, as public employees retain the power to strike, even though they do not have that privilege. We do not authorize a fact-finder to return to the dispute after the issuance of his report. We require that our mediators re-enter each case after the fact-finding report if the report is not accepted immediately. Reports have been instrumental in mediated settlements, even though the fact-finder's report was not, per se, accepted.

The debate over whether to combine mediation and fact-finding appears to arise principally from those jurisdictions that do not have an established, competent mediation staff, as we do have in Michigan. I can understand a combination of mediation and fact-finding in those states that use ad hoc mediation and ad hoc fact-finding, with the same person performing both services. In Michigan, ad hoc mediation is seldom needed.

Nor have we found that our fact-finders react defensively if employer and union do not accept their recommendations. Perhaps this is because our fact-finders do not return to the bargaining scene, but are succeeded by a mediator. My knowledge of the ability and balance of our fact-finders, however, leads me to conclude that even though these men should engage in post-fact-finding mediation, few of them would react defensively or be unduly concerned at the failure of employer and union to accept their recommendations. Possibly Michigan fact-finders are more thick-skinned than fact-finders in other states, but I doubt it. Contacts with my "opposite numbers" in other states lead me to conclude that they, too, have able fact-finders who perform a significant role in resolving impasses and who are neither prima donnas nor live in a world of fantasy in which they believe that their dictates will, ipso facto, be accepted.

Bill Simkin opines that the fact-finder "has no adequate opportunity to gauge acceptability by the parties." Our experience denies the validity of this criticism *if the fact-finder is competent*. He has greater flexibility than the arbitrator, for

---

*Reprinted by permission of the Bureau of National Affairs, Inc.

he may meet with the parties separately because — in spite of our jaundiced view of mediation by fact-finders — fact-finders do engage in the "search for a solution." A fact-finder, unlike an arbitrator, may discuss the case with each party separately. The arbitrator, who renders a "legal" and binding solution, may not "trim." The fact-finder may, because his primary task is to find *an* equitable — not necessarily *the most* equitable — settlement.

NOTES

1. Is access to fact-finding without an evaluation of prior negotiation efforts undesirable? The Wisconsin and Connecticut statutes provide for a review of prior negotiations to determine whether a genuine impasse has been reached. If there should be such review, should it be by the fact-finder or by the agency administering the basic collective bargaining law? See McKelvey, *Fact-Finding in Public Employment Disputes: Promise or Illusion?* 22 Indus. & Lab. Rel. Rev. 528, 535 (1969), suggesting that in those two states fact-finding has not been as addictive as in New York where the statute does not provide for such review. But see Yaffe & Goldblatt, *Factfinding in Public Employment in New York State: More Promise Than Illusion,* ILR Paperback No. 10, 25 (1971).

2. A party's failure to comply in good faith with applicable fact-finding procedures may constitute an unfair labor practice. See *Sanford Teachers Ass'n v. Sanford Sch. Comm.,* Me. L.R.B., Case No. 77-36, 1977-78 PEB ¶ 40,216 (1977); *In re E. Iowa Community College,* Iowa P.E.R.B., Case No. 973, 1977-78 PEB ¶ 40,016 (1977). See also *Association of Classroom Teachers v. Independent Sch. Dist. No. 89,* 540 P.2d 1171 (1975), wherein the Oklahoma Supreme Court found it improper for a party to refuse to agree upon the impartial third member of a fact-finding panel. Finding the statutorily prescribed selection procedure to be mandatory, and not merely permissive, the court ordered the school district to cooperate with the teachers' association in selecting the third panel member through the strike-off method.

3. *Massachusetts Org. of State Eng'rs & Scientists v. MLRC,* 389 Mass. 920, 452 N.E.2d 1117 (1983), recognized that a public employer could lawfully make unilateral changes in working conditions following a good faith bargaining impasse but prior to the completion of the fact-finding process. Does such a rule diminish the effectiveness of fact-finding procedures?

4. Fact-finders under the Iowa PERA have discretion to report that they are unable on the record presented to choose between the parties' stated positions or to recommend some better resolution of their impasse, but they are not empowered to recommend that no provision be included in the resulting contract with respect to a mandatory topic covered by different party proposals. See *Iowa State Educ. Ass'n v. PERB,* 369 N.W.2d 793, 1984-86 PBC ¶ 34,494 (Iowa 1985).

5. Some commentators have argued that the availability of fact-finding impairs the effectiveness of mediation and impedes the bargaining process. See, e.g., Zack, *Impasses, Strikes, and Resolutions,* in Public Workers and Public Unions 101 (S. Zagoria ed. 1972). For other views, see A. Anderson, *The Use of Fact-Finding in Dispute Settlement,* and Saxton, *The Employers View,* in Arbitration and Social Change, Proceedings of the Twenty-Second Annual Meeting of the National Academy of Arbitrators 107, 127 (G. Somers ed. 1970); Friedman & Mukamal, *Wisconsin's Mediation-Arbitration Law: What Has It Done to Bargaining?,* 13 J. Coll. Negot. Pub. Sector 171 (1984).

6. The states are laboratories for experimentation with the fact-finding process. Variations exist as to a variety of incidentals of procedure including (1) who may invoke the process (whether a party or only the public labor relations law administrative agency), (2) how the tribunal is chosen, (3) who pays for its services, (4) time limitations on its functioning, (5) whether its procedures are to be public or private, (6) how "evidence" is to be presented, (7) which party is required to proceed first at the hearing, (8) what is the "burden of proof," if any, and where does it rest, (9) whether an official record of the "hearing" is to be taken, and, if so, who pays for it, (10) whether the tribunal is restricted to that record as the basis for its conclusions of fact, and (11) whether the tribunal's report and recommendations are to be made public. Differences in approach also exist, as must be apparent at this point, with respect to the question whether there is a "next step" (beyond additional bargaining) after the tribunal issues its report.

7. See generally Craver, *Public Sector Impasse Resolution Procedures*, 60 Chi.-Kent L. Rev. 779 (1984); Hoh, *The Effectiveness of Mediation in Public Sector Arbitration Systems: The Iowa Experience*, 39 Arb. J. 30 (1984); Wolkinson & Stieber, *Michigan Fact-finding Experience in Public Sector Disputes*, 31 Arb. J. 225 (1976); Wheeler, *Is Compromise the Rule in Fire Fighter Arbitration?*, 29 Arb. J. 176 (1974); Stern, *The Wisconsin Public Employee Factfinding Procedure*, 20 Ind. & Lab. Rel. Rev. 3 (1966); Zack, *Improving Mediation and Fact-Finding in the Public Sector*, 21 Lab. L. J. 264 (1970); Zack, *Impasses, Strikes and Resolutions*, in Public Workers and Public Unions 111 (S. Zagoria ed. 1972); Anderson, *The Use of Fact-Finding in Dispute Settlement*, in Arbitration and Social Change, Proceedings of the Twenty-Second Annual Meeting of the National Academy of Arbitrators 107 (G. Somers ed. 1970); McKelvey, *Fact Finding in Public Employment Disputes: Promise or Illusion?*, 22 Indus. & Lab. Rel. Rev. 528 (1969); Yaffe & Goldblatt, *Factfinding in Public Employment in New York State: More Promise Than Illusion*, ILR Paperback No. 10 (1971); Doering, *Impasse Issues in Teacher Disputes Submitted to Fact Finding in New York*, 27 Arb. J. 1 (1972); Drotning & Lipsky, *The Outcome of Impasse Procedures in New York Schools Under the Taylor Law*, 26 Arb. J. 87 (1971); Gould, *Public Employment: Mediation, Fact-Finding and Arbitration*, 55 A.B.A. J. 835 (1969); *Dispute Settlement in the Public Sector: The State-of-the-Art*, Report Submitted to U.S. Dep't of Labor, Div. of Public Employee Labor Relations (T. Gilroy & A. Sinicropi, eds. 1972).

D. BINDING INTEREST ARBITRATION

What mechanisms should be used to resolve interest disputes in the public sector in the event that negotiation, mediation, and fact-finding have failed to produce a settlement? In the private sector, if an impasse is reached, the union has two basic options: (1) accept the employer's last offer and settle; or (2) strike in an effort to gain leverage at the bargaining table.

Since strikes by most public employees are statutorily proscribed, the weapon of economic coercion is presumably removed as a bargaining stratagem. In the public sector, therefore, the issue arises as to whether there are any legitimate and viable substitutes for the strike weapon which can produce settlements of interest disputes on terms which are reasonable and are not necessarily limited to the public employer's last offer. In an effort to deal with this problem, numerous municipal, state, and federal jurisdictions have adopted a variety of legislative schemes aimed at achieving finality in the resolution of public sector bargaining disputes. The most popular among these legislative schemes may be summarized as follows:

(1) *Fact-Finding Recommendations Backed by Show Cause Procedures* — This approach addresses the problem of how to make fact-finding with recommendations work well in providing a final solution to bargaining impasses. In a typical situation, only one party will accept the fact-finder's recommendations. The other party, for a number of reasons, rejects them in whole or in part. In the event this occurs, some have suggested that the rejecting party be required, in a quasi-judicial proceeding, to justify its failure to accept the terms of the proposed settlement. See Davey, *Dispute Settlement in Public Employment,* in Dispute Settlement in the Public Sector 12, 21 (T. Gilroy ed. 1972).

(2) *Legislative Determination* — Under this approach, the failure of either party to accept a fact-finder's recommendations, in whole or in part, leads to hearings before the governing legislative body which, after receiving input from all of the interested parties, decides the terms of the final settlement. This scheme is typified by Section 209.3(e) of the New York Taylor Act, which is set forth in the *Statutory Appendix. See Florida State Lodge, FOP v. City of Hialeah,* 815 F.2d 631 (11th Cir. 1987) (finding no due process problem concerning legislative determination provision).

(3) *Executive Declaration of Finality* — Nevada provides that prior to the submission of an interest dispute to fact-finding, either party may request that the governor exercise his emergency powers and declare that the recommendations shall be binding. Fact-finding then proceeds as usual, observing the criteria set out in the statute. See 9 Nev. Rev. Stat. § 288.200. A somewhat different approach is taken under the New York City law, which makes the recommendations of an Impasse Panel final and binding as accepted or modified by the Board of Collective Bargaining. The details of the New York City scheme are set forth in the *Statutory Appendix* in § 1173-7.0c of the New York City Collective Bargaining Law.

(4) *Right to Strike* — Several states, including Hawaii, Illinois, and Pennsylvania, have sought to resolve the finality problem by granting a right to strike to certain categories of public employees. The right to strike is discussed in Part F of Chapter Six.

(5) *"Advisory" Arbitration* — Several states have made "advisory" (i.e., nonbinding) arbitration an alternative or a sequel to fact-finding. The Maine law provides for both binding and advisory arbitration, depending upon the issues involved. Arbitration may be requested by either party, with a tripartite panel made up of one member selected by each side and a neutral third member selected by the other two members or by the American Arbitration Association. The recommendations of the arbitration panel are advisory with respect to salaries, pensions, and insurance. See Me. Rev. Stat. Ann. tit. 26, § 965(4).

Rhode Island statutes covering municipal employees and teachers also provide for voluntary arbitration, which is merely advisory with respect to matters involving the expenditure of money. See R.I. Gen. Laws Ann. §§ 28-9.4-10 to 28-9.4-15 and 28-9.3-9 to 28-9.3-14. Conversely, the Rhode Island laws covering police and fire personnel make compulsory arbitration mandatory and binding as to all issues. See R.I. Gen. Laws Ann. §§ 28-9.2-7 to 28-9.2-11 and 28-9.1-7 to 28-9.1-11.

The Pennsylvania law covering guards at prisons and mental hospitals and court personnel provides that all bargaining impasses "shall be submitted to a panel of arbitrators whose decision shall be final and binding ... with the proviso that the decisions of the arbitrators which would require legislative enactment to be effective shall be considered advisory only." See Pa. Stat. Ann. § 1101.805, set forth in the *Statutory Appendix.* A separate statutory provision requires binding arbitration, at the request of either party, covering all bargaining issues in dispute regarding police and fire personnel. Pa. Stat. Ann. tit. 43, §§ 217.4-.8. It is also noteworthy that the Pennsylvania Public Employee Relations Act provides for "voluntary binding arbitration" of public employee interest disputes which are not otherwise covered by the compulsory arbitration provisions of Pennsylvania law. See Pa. Stat. Ann. § 1101.804. Voluntary binding arbitration arises only pursuant to an agreement by the parties and, if it is utilized, "the decisions of the arbitrator which ... require legislative enactment to be effective shall be considered advisory only."

In Oklahoma, either party may request advisory arbitration to resolve a police or firefighter bargaining dispute. However, if the award is accepted by the municipality involved, it becomes binding. See Okla. Sess. Laws, ch. 14, §§ 7-11.

Some commentators believe that advisory arbitration is more likely to encourage antecedent negotiations than is binding arbitration, since a party may think it has a good chance of receiving more favorable treatment through binding arbitration than through negotiations, whereas advisory arbitration is less stultifying of the bargaining process because the award can be rejected. For good discussions of the use of advisory arbitration in the telegraph and wire service industries, see Bryan, *Avoiding Confrontation by Advisory Arbitration,* and Groner, *Why Advisory Arbitration of New Contracts?* in Arbitration and the Expanding Role of Neutrals, Proceedings of the Twenty-Third Annual Meeting, Nat'l Academy of Arb. 55 (G. Somers ed. 1970). Is there any meaningful difference between advisory arbitration and fact-finding with recommendations?

(6) *Voluntary, Binding Arbitration* — At least twenty-one states (Connecticut, Delaware, Hawaii, Illinois, Indiana, Iowa, Maine, Massachusetts, Minnesota, Montana, Nevada, New Hampshire, New Jersey, New York, Ohio, Oregon, Pennsylvania, Rhode Island, Texas, Vermont and Wisconsin) permit voluntary, binding arbitration of interest disputes involving some categories of public sector employees. The Postal Reorganization Act of 1970, which is set forth in the *Statutory Appendix,* provides for voluntary, binding arbitration, but also for compulsory arbitration if a voluntary arrangement is not reached. Under the Civil Service Reform Act of 1978, binding interest arbitration for federal workers may be used when authorized by the Federal Service Impasses Panel.

(7) *Compulsory, Binding Arbitration* — At least twenty-three states (Alaska, Connecticut, Hawaii, Illinois, Iowa, Maine, Massachusetts, Michigan, Minnesota, Montana, Nebraska, Nevada, New Jersey, New York, North Dakota, Ohio, Oklahoma, Oregon, Pennsylvania, Rhode Island, Washington, Wisconsin, and Wyoming) provide for compulsory, binding arbitration of interest disputes for at least some groups of government employees. This alternative is most fre-

quently employed with respect to "essential" personnel who are absolutely forbidden to strike.

1. COMMENTARY

H. WELLINGTON & R. WINTER, THE UNIONS AND THE CITIES 178-80 (1971)*

Compulsory and binding arbitration seeks to prevent strikes in two ways, neither of which is completely successful. First, it attempts to enforce a settlement by application of legal sanctions. Ordinarily this will be enough for all but the aberrational case. And the occasional strikes that still occur sometimes may be prevented if the law responds with very harsh penalties. Such penalties, however, often do not have the support of the community and may stir a feeling of revulsion. In those circumstances they are unlikely to be effective and, in any event, workers willing to accept such penalties can still make a strike effective. Legal sanctions, therefore, do not provide total protection.

Compulsory and binding arbitration, however, seeks to prevent strikes in a second way. Because the strike in private employment is viewed by many as a fundamental right located well within the foothills of the Constitution, there is in some places a corresponding sense that laws against strikes in the public sector are unfair. This attitude — which survives in a fierce state of tension with counter attitudes — emboldens public employees to break the law. A procedure that offers public employees a seemingly fair alternative to the strike, however, may change the community's sense of the propriety of the strike and may in the long run influence the attitude of public employees. They may in time reach that desirable state of accepting an award that they find less than totally fair. This is the goal of compulsory arbitration, and is what differentiates it from nonfinality procedures. No moral imperative, above and beyond the preexisting moral imperative of not breaking the no-strike law, is generated by nonfinality procedures such as fact-finding with recommendations. They are advisory only. An aim of arbitration binding on both parties is to generate just such an imperative. Again, however, total success cannot be expected.

The second factor limiting the effectiveness of arbitration is that it deters collective bargaining. The point is simple enough. Either the public employer or the union will reckon that an arbitration award will be more advantageous than a negotiated settlement. That party will then employ tactics to ensure arbitration by bargaining without a sincere desire to reach agreement.

It is almost impossible wholly to solve this problem; but the route to partial and perhaps satisfactory resolution is to fashion a procedure sufficiently diverse and uncertain as to make a negotiated settlement more attractive to the parties than arbitration.

The composition of an arbitration panel can importantly influence its award. Honest men acting disinterestedly often see things differently. The behaviorists are surely right in thinking that results are influenced by the perspectives of decision makers. Thus, to the extent that the composition of an arbitration panel is unknown beforehand and is outside the control of the parties, some

---

uncertainty will exist. On the other hand, the parties are more likely to have confidence in an award rendered by arbitrators they have chosen. This tension can be eased by allowing each party to select one member of a three-man panel.

G. TAYLOR, IMPASSE PROCEDURES — THE FINALITY QUESTION, GOVERNOR'S CONFERENCE ON PUBLIC EMPLOYMENT RELATIONS 5-6 (New York City, October 15, 1968)

There is considerable wishful thinking that the involvement of the legislative and executive branches of government can be minimized — or even avoided altogether — by having a board of impartial labor relations experts make a final and binding decision to resolve an impasse. While recognizing the apparent simplicity of compulsory arbitration, one should not be unaware of the consquences of the broad delegation of governmental authority which is entailed. An arbitration board would become a powerful arm of government acting without the checks and balances upon which we depend in the fashioning of our laws. Some additional difficult questions have to be faced. Is it sound and wise to consider the claims of one particular group of employees for their share of limited public funds in isolation from the claims of other employees? Or, to do so without regard to the leap-frogging effect upon the total wage bill of a decision made in narrow context? What effect would all this have upon the allocations of limited resources for other sorely needed services to the public? And, if a legislative body cannot or will not do what it takes to carry out an award by the impartial arbitrators, is it intended that a court will compel them to do so? Bringing such questions into the appraisal of compulsory arbitration transforms an apparently easy answer into a very doubtful one.

A. ANDERSON, COMPULSORY ARBITRATION IN PUBLIC SECTOR DISPUTE SETTLEMENT — AN AFFIRMATIVE VIEW, in DISPUTE SETTLEMENT IN THE PUBLIC SECTOR 3-3 (T. Gilroy ed. 1972)*

[I]mpasse panel procedures may prove to be an interim step on the road to a system which features binding arbitration of contract terms in the public sector. In some cases, the parties have taken the additional step of agreeing to be bound by the recommendations of the impasse panel. In other instances, the parties have, in effect, requested the arbitrator to confirm their bargain by taking the responsibility of making an award confirming the agreement of the parties. There has also been an increase in the use of voluntary arbitration of contract terms in the public sector. Such arbitration is authorized by the Taylor Law.

President George Meany of the AFL-CIO, while expressing strong reservations about the use of arbitration in the private sector for resolving bargaining impasses, has suggested the use of binding arbitration in some circumstances in the public sector. The procedure for binding arbitration of contract terms under the new Postal Corporation Act was endorsed by the AFL-CIO. Mr. Meany, in supporting the Postal Corporation Act, stated that any procedure which preserves workers' rights without strikes is acceptable. Labor leaders who en-

---

*Reprinted by permission of the Center for Labor and Management, College of Business Administration, University of Iowa.

dorse the right to strike in public employment have at times qualified such advocacy by supporting binding arbitration of disputes for employees engaged in essential services such as law enforcement and fire fighting. In addition to the new laws and changed attitudes, the number of cases already submitted to arbitration in police and fire disputes in Pennsylvania and Michigan make an examination of compulsory arbitration procedures worthwhile.

The traditional attitudes of labor relations experts toward the binding arbitration process is that it's bad because it won't work and because it will destroy free collective bargaining. Arbitration of contract terms in public employment has been considered to be illegal in some jurisdictions because the process results in the unconstitutional delegation of responsibility to a third party, who is a private person of legislative and executive authority, to fix the terms and conditions of employment and the resulting budget changes and tax rates. Furthermore, it is charged that arbitration will not work because it will not prevent strikes or bring about settlements and will destroy the free collective bargaining process and the willingness of the parties to solve their own disputes. It is argued that compulsory arbitration will result in the piling up of all kinds of disputes to be submitted for resolution to a third party who neither understands the problems nor has a continuing responsibility for the results of the settlement....

The adoption of compulsory and binding arbitration statutes in such jurisdictions as Michigan, Pennsylvania, Rhode Island, Maine and Wyoming for police and fire disputes is based on the premise that since the right to strike is legally denied and cannot be realistically conferred on employees engaged in vital services, then a substitute bargaining balancer, the right to invoke binding arbitration by a neutral third party, is an effective and equitable substitute as a dispute settlement procedure. Arbitration transfers some of the powers of decision making about contract terms from the economic and political power of the parties involved to neutral arbitrators. Therefore, I don't accept the premise that the right to strike is the *sine qua non* to make the bargaining process work in the public sector. I think arbitration can work and has worked effectively for public employees as a substitute for the strike weapon.

NOTES

1. Is it undemocratic for an individual who is not accountable to the electorate to make quasi-legislative budgetary determinations that may significantly affect the fiscal policies of a governmental entity? See Grodin, *Political Aspects of Public Sector Interest Arbitration,* 64 Calif. L. Rev. 678 (1976); Bornstein, *Interest Arbitration in Public Employment: An Arbitrator Views the Process,* 29 Lab. L.J. 77 (1978); Barr, *The Public Arbitration Panel as an Administrative Agency: Can Compulsory Interest Arbitration Be an Acceptable Dispute Resolution Method in the Public Sector?,* 39 Albany L. Rev. 377 (1975).

2. Does compulsory interest arbitration insulate elected officials from the difficult political pressures they would encounter if they had to make the final decisions regarding the employment conditions of their public employees? Does this fact actually inure to the benefit of the public by minimizing the impact of special interest groups over this important area?

2. LEGALITY

DIVISION 540, AMALGAMATED TRANSIT UNION v. MERCER COUNTY IMPROVEMENT AUTHORITY

386 A.2d 1290, 98 L.R.R.M. 2526 (N.J. 1978)

SULLIVAN, J.: This is a labor dispute in the public sector. The Mercer County Improvement Authority (Mercer Metro Division) is the operator of a public transportation facility in Mercer County. Division 540, Amalgamated Transit Union, AFL-CIO, an unincorporated association, plaintiff herein, represents the drivers, garage personnel and clerical workers of Mercer Metro.

During the spring of 1975 plaintiff and defendant met to negotiate the terms and conditions of a collective bargaining agreement to replace an existing agreement between the parties which was due to expire on March 31, 1975. Upon failure to reach agreement, primarily over the issue of wages including a cost of living allocation, plaintiff-union demanded that the dispute be submitted to binding arbitration in accordance with N.J.S.A. 40:37A-96. When defendant refused, the union filed the present suit which, inter alia, sought to compel defendant to comply with the statutory provision which requires defendant to offer to submit the dispute to binding arbitration. Defendant, on its part, challenged the constitutionality of such provision.

The Superior Court, Chancery Division, upheld the constitutionality of N.J.S.A. 40:37A-96 and entered final judgment ordering the defendant to submit the labor dispute between it and plaintiff to final and binding arbitration pursuant to the statute. On appeal by defendant, the Appellate Division affirmed the Chancery Division ruling. Certification was granted by this Court on defendant's petition, solely on the issue of the constitutionality of N.J.S.A. 40:37A-96.71 N.J. 518 (1976). We affirm....

Capitol Transit, Inc. was a privately owned transportation facility operating bus lines in Mercer County. In the 1960s, it began to sustain increasingly heavy financial losses. During this period Mercer County tried to sustain the operation by providing subsidies, but by 1968 Capitol Transit's condition had worsened to a point where it faced bankruptcy and gave notice that it intended to cease operations.

At this point the New Jersey Legislature, by L. 1968, c. 66, adopted amendments to N.J.S.A. 40:37A-44 et seq. so as to permit a county improvement authority to acquire a privately owned transportation system and operate the same as a public transportation facility. Defendant Improvement Authority thereupon purchased the assets of Capitol Transit and took over its operations through its Mercer Metro Division.

The principal financing for this acquisition came from a federal grant made under the Urban Mass Transportation Act of 1964, 49 U.S.C. § 1601 et seq. However, federal assistance under this act is conditioned on fair and equitable arrangements being made to protect the interests of employees affected by such assistance....

The New Jersey Legislature in empowering a county improvement authority to acquire a private transportation system and operate it, has specified protective conditions and benefits for the employees of a transportation system so acquired and operated. N.J.S.A. 40:37A-94 and -95. These include continuation of employment rights, privileges and benefits.

Another section, N.J.S.A. 40:37A-96 calls for arbitration of labor disputes as follows:

> In the case of any labor dispute between a county improvement authority operating a public transportation facility and its employees where collective bargaining does not result in agreement, irrespective of whether such dispute relates to the making or maintaining of collective bargaining agreements, the terms to be included in such agreements, the interpretation or application of such agreements, the adjustment of any grievance or any difference or any question that may arise between the authority and the labor organization representing its employees concerning wages, salaries, hours, working conditions or benefits including health and welfare, sick leave, insurance or pension or retirement provisions, the authority shall offer to submit such dispute to final and binding arbitration by a single arbitrator or by a tripartite board of arbitrators. Upon acceptance by the labor organization of such arbitration proposal, ... [an arbitrator is then selected or tripartite board of arbitrators appointed in accordance with specified procedures]. The arbitration proceeding shall take place in the manner provided by the rules of the New Jersey State Board of Mediation applicable to arbitration of labor disputes and the decision of the arbitrator or board of arbitrators shall be final and binding upon the parties.

The foregoing section provides for arbitration of labor disputes involving the terms in collective bargaining agreements (interest arbitration). It is also to be noted that the requirement to submit to arbitration is imposed only on the Authority.

Other provisions of the statute emphasize the uniqueness of the authority's relationship with its transportation system employees. A county improvement authority is a public body corporate and politic. N.J.S.A. 40:37A-46. Nevertheless, if it operates a public transportation facility its employees in that facility have the right to "bargain collectively" through their union as to terms and conditions of employment. N.J.S.A. 40:37A-92. The Authority has the power to enter into a closed shop agreement with the union and to have a check-off system for the payment of union dues and assessments. N.J.S.A. 40:37A-97. As heretofore noted, the Authority is subject to compulsory and binding arbitration of labor disputes that arise between it and its transportation facility employees where collective bargaining does not result in agreement. N.J.S.A. 40:37A-96. The constitutionality of this latter provision is the issue in this case.

There can be no doubt but that under the provisions of the Urban Mass Transportation Act of 1965 and the implementing statutory provisions of L. 1968, c. 66 enacted by our Legislature, employees of a transportation facility taken over by a county improvement authority and operated by it, have some rights which are consistent with private employment. However, in the overall picture, they must be considered as public employees in the sense that they are employed by a public body corporate and politic. Counsel for plaintiff-union in his supplemental brief filed with this Court concedes that as employees of such a public body, they do not presently have the right to strike, a right they formerly enjoyed as employees of Capitol Transport.

We find the provisions for compulsory and binding arbitration contained in N.J.S.A. 40:37A-96 to be constitutional. The proliferation of labor disputes in the public sector and the resultant disruption of essential public services has caused many state legislatures to try to formulate new approaches to the resolution of these disputes. In the past, in New Jersey, statutory provisions for binding arbitration of labor disputes in the public area merely authorized the parties to enter into an agreement to submit the labor dispute to binding arbitration. N.J.S.A. 34:13A-5.3. However, this required mutual agreement and often did not provide resolution of the problem.

The concept of compulsory and binding arbitration of labor negotiation as well as grievance disputes in the public sector has been coming more and more into favor. See McAvoy, "Binding Arbitration of Contractual Terms: A New Approach to the Resolution of Disputes in the Public Sector," 72 Colum. L. Rev. 1192 (1972). The New Jersey Legislature has not only adopted this procedure in the statutory section under consideration, but also has recently imposed compulsory arbitration for resolution of such disputes between municipal bodies and their police and firemen, N.J.S.A. 34:13A-14 to 21.

The principal objection made to compulsory and binding arbitration of labor negotiation disputes in the public sector is that it constitutes an unlawful delegation of public authority and responsibility to a private person or persons. However, most of the cases that have dealt with the question have sustained the concept as an innovative way to avoid the morass of deadlocked labor disputes in the public sector. Nevertheless, in doing so, there must be excluded from the arbitration process matters involving governmental policy determinations which involve an exercise of delegated police power.

Some of the cases reason that there is no improper delegation involved as the arbitrator is deemed a public official when performing functions which are public in nature. *Town of Arlington v. Board of Council. & Arbit.,* — Mass. —, 352 N.E. 2d 914, 93 L.R.R.M. 2494 (Sup. Jud. Ct. 1976); *City of Warwick v. Warwick Regular Firemen's Ass'n,* 106 R.I. 109, 256 A.2d 206, 71 L.R.R.M. 3192 (Sup. Ct. 1969). Others hold that legislative delegation is not illegal as long as adequate standards and safeguards are provided. *City of Amsterdam v. Helsby,* 37 N.Y.2d 19, 332 N.E.2d 290, 89 L.R.R.M. 2871 (Ct. App. 1975). Still other decisions hold that statutory provisions for compulsory arbitration of labor disputes in the public sector do not really entail the delegation of a governmental function at all, but rather in the exercise of that function, merely utilize a well-established procedure for the resolution of deadlocked labor disputes. *State v. City of Laramie,* 437 P.2d 295, 68 L.R.R.M. 2038 (Wyo. Sup. Ct. 1968). See generally Annotation, "Validity and construction of statutes or ordinances providing for arbitration of labor disputes involving public employees," 68 A.L.R.3d 885 (1976). Some authorities are critical of the standards rule as applied to delegation of power. They suggest that procedural safeguards and judicial review are more important than a requirement of standards. See 1 Davis, Administrative Law Treatise, § 2.15 at 148-151 (1958).

There are decisions to the contrary, such as *Greeley Police Union v. City Council of Greeley,* 553 P.2d 790 (Colo. Sup. Ct. 1976); *Dearborn Firefighters, Local 412 v. City of Dearborn,* 394 Mich. 229, 231 N.W.2d 226, 90 L.R.R.M. 2002 (Sup. Ct. 1975); *City of Sioux Falls v. Sioux Falls Firefighters,* 234 N.W.2d

35, 90 L.R.R.M. 2945 (S.D. Sup. Ct. 1975). However, most of them have been decided on the basis of specific constitutional provisions or statutory language.

In the instant case, defendant, citing *Van Riper v. Traffic Tel. Workers Fed. of N.J.*, 2 N.J. 335 (1949), suggests that the arbitration clause under consideration is invalid because it lacks standards to govern the arbitrator in the exercise of the power delegated to him. *Van Riper* was decided almost thirty years ago.[3] In the interim, the widening use of arbitration in labor disputes, particularly in the public sector, has resulted in the development of standards and criteria which are inherent in the present-day process.

Thus, the arbitrator must act within the scope of the authority delegated to him. He must consider the public interest and the impact of his decision on the public welfare. He must act fairly and reasonably to the end that labor peace between the public employer and its employees will be stabilized and promoted. He must make findings which are adequate, and sufficient to support the award. N.J.S.A. 40:37A-96 should be construed as incorporating these inherent standards and criteria in its provisions for compulsory arbitration. See *Avant v. Clifford,* 67 N.J. 496, 549-554 (1976).

In addition to these implied standards, these are explicit standards set forth in the statute. N.J.S.A. 40:37A-92 confines the scope of the collective bargaining to wages, hours, working conditions and welfare, pension and retirement provisions. As heretofore noted, N.J.S.A. 40:37A-94 and -95 specify protective conditions and benefits such as continuation of employment rights, privileges and benefits. Under N.J.S.A. 40:37A-96 the procedural rules and practices of the State Board of Mediation, promulgated pursuant to N.J.S.A. 34:13A-11, govern the arbitration. See N.J.A.C. 12:105-5.1 to -5.12 and N.J.A.C. 12:105-6.1 to -6.6, which establish procedures governing stenographic recording of hearings, representation, evidence, briefs and the form of award. The method of selection of the arbitrator or arbitrators is also provided for in N.J.S.A. 40:37A-96.

Although N.J.S.A. 40:37A-96 has no express requirement for judicial review of the arbitrator's award, we conclude that such review must be available if the statutory provision is to be sustained. The statute subjects the development Authority to compulsory and binding arbitration. Because it is compulsory, principles of fairness, perhaps even due process, require that judicial review be available to ensure that the award is not arbitrary or capricious and that the arbitrator has not abused the power and authority delegated to him.

Also, because the arbitration process is imposed by law, the judicial oversight available should be more extensive than the limited judicial review had under N.J.S.A. 2A:24-8 to parties who voluntarily agree to submit their dispute to binding arbitration. See *Daly v. Komline-Sanderson Engineering Corp.,* 40 N.J. 175, 178 (1963). We conclude that when, as here, the arbitration process is compulsory,[4] the judicial review should extend to consideration of whether the award is supported by substantial credible evidence present in the record. This

---

[3] The original statute declared invalid for lack of standards in *Van Riper,* was amended by L. 1949, c. 308 so as to include specific standards. See N.J.S.A. 34:13B-27(b). As amended, the statute was upheld in *N.J. Bell Tel. Co. v. Communications Workers, etc.,* 5 N.J. 354 (1950).

[4] Although the arbitration process herein is compulsory only as to defendant-Authority, the union and the Authority should stand on equal terms insofar as the right to judicial review and scope thereof are concerned.

is the test normally applied to the review of administrative agency decisions and is particularly appropriate here. See *City of Amsterdam v. Helsby, supra,* 37 N.Y.2d at 38-41, 332 N.E.2d at 300-302 (Fuchsberg, J., concurring).

We find no merit in defendant-Authority's equal protection argument. Even assuming its standing to raise an equal protection issue, it is clear that the unique status of employees of a transportation facility taken over and operated by a County Improvement Authority serves as a rational basis for the statutory classification made and the imposition of unilateral compulsory arbitration.

In short, we uphold N.J.S.A. 40:37A-96 as a constitutional expression of legislative policy. We find therein, and in its companion statutory sections, standards, express and implied, to guide the arbitrator in the exercise of his authority. Adequate procedural safeguards have been established. We also conclude that the arbitrator's decision is subject to judicial review, the scope of such review being the same as that normally had in appeals from decisions of administrative agencies. Affirmed.

NOTES

1. Most state courts have sustained the constitutionality of compulsory and binding interest arbitration laws, where legislatively defined or judicially recognized safeguards and standards were present to adequately guide the arbitrators when they reached their decisions. See, e.g., *Rocky River v. State Emp. Rels. Bd.,* 43 Ohio St. 3d 1, 539 N.E.2d 103 (1989); *City of Richfield v. Firefighters Local 1215,* 276 N.W.2d 42, 1979-80 PBC ¶ 36,501 (Minn. 1979); *Arlington v. Board of Conciliation & Arbitration,* 352 N.E.2d 914, 93 L.R.R.M. 2494 (Mass. 1976); *Spokane v. Spokane Police Guild,* 553 P.2d 1316, 93 L.R.R.M. 2373 (Wash. 1976); *City of Amsterdam v. Helsby,* 37 N.Y.2d 19, 332 N.E.2d 290, 89 L.R.R.M. 2871 (1975); *City of Biddeford v. Biddeford Teachers Ass'n,* 304 A.2d 387, 83 L.R.R.M. 2098 (Me. 1973). However, several courts have struck down such interest arbitration provisions as constituting unconstitutional delegations of legislative authority. See, e.g., *Transit Auth., Lexington-Fayette Urban Cty. Gov't v. ATU,* 698 S.W.2d 520, 1984-86 PBC ¶ 34,546 (Ky. 1985); *Salt Lake City v. International Ass'n of Firefighters,* 563 P.2d 786, 95 L.R.R.M. 2383 (Utah 1977); *City of Aurora v. Aurora Firefighters' Protective Ass'n,* 556 P.2d 1356, 96 L.R.R.M. 2252 (Colo. 1977); *Greeley Police Union v. City Council,* 553 P.2d 790, 93 L.R.R.M. 2382 (Colo. 1976); *City of Sioux Falls v. Sioux Falls Firefighters' Local 814,* 234 N.W.2d 35, 90 L.R.R.M. 2945 (S.D. 1975). In *Dearborn Firefighters' Union Local 412 v. City of Dearborn,* 324 Mich. 229, 231 N.W.2d 226, 90 L.R.R.M. 2002 (1975), the court divided equally on the issue, affirming a lower court ruling that the Michigan compulsory arbitration law was constitutional. Nevertheless, a majority of the court concluded that the legislation's delegation to an arbitration panel selected only by the parties, instead of through the statutory alternative of appointment by the chairman of the state mediation board, was unconstitutional. In *City of Detroit v. Detroit Police Officers Ass'n,* 294 N.W.2d 68, 1979-80 PBC ¶ 36,959 (Mich. 1980), *appeal dismissed,* 450 U.S. 903 (1981), the court sustained the constitutionality of the Michigan Police-Firefighter Arbitration Act since adequate standards were provided to guide the arbitrators and the impartial chairs of the arbitral panels were to be appointed by the Michigan Employment Relations Commission chairperson from a permanent panel of qualified neutrals. Accord

School Comm. v. Education Ass'n, 433 A.2d 383, 1981-83 PBC ¶ 37,319 (Me. 1981).

2. In *Carofano v. City of Bridgeport,* 495 A.2d 1011, 1984-86 PBC ¶ 34,518 (Conn. 1985), the court sustained the constitutionality of a broad compulsory interest arbitration statute. It found sufficient statewide interest to support application of the enactment to all municipalities, thus avoiding problems under the "home rule" charter in the state constitution. Accord, *City of Roseburg v. Firefighters, Local 1489,* 639 P.2d 90, 1981-83 PBC ¶ 37,500 (Or. 1981).

3. In *Firefighters Union, Local 1186 v. City of Vallejo,* 12 Cal. 3d 608, 526 P.2d 971 (1974), the California Supreme Court sustained the constitutionality of a city charter provision that prescribed compulsory arbitration in the event of a bargaining impasse regarding wages, hours, or working conditions. However, where such a dispute resolution procedure was merely established through the parties' negotiated memorandum of understanding instead of in a charter provision, a California Court of Appeal found it to constitute an impermissible delegation of legislative authority, since it was not effectuated through the constitutionally recognized charter amendment process. *Firefighters v. San Francisco,* 68 Cal. App. 3d 896, 95 L.R.R.M. 2835, *petition for hearing denied,* 95 L.R.R.M. 3069 (Cal. Sup. Ct. 1977).

4. See generally Note, *Binding Interest Arbitration in the Public Sector: Is It Constitutional?,* 18 Wm. & Mary L. Rev. 787 (1977); Staudohar, *Constitutionality of Compulsory Arbitration Statutes in Public Employment,* 27 Lab. L.J. 670 (1976); Weisberger, *Constitutionality of Compulsory Public Sector Interest Arbitration Legislation: A 1976 Perspective,* in Labor Relations Law in the Public Sector 35 (A. Knapp ed. 1977). See also Petro, *Sovereignty and Compulsory Public Sector Bargaining,* 10 Wake Forest L. Rev. 25, 103-12 (1974); Craver, *The Judicial Enforcement of Public Sector Interest Arbitration,* 21 B.C.L. Rev. 557, 561-68 (1980).

3. SURVEY OF LEGISLATION; PRACTICE AND PROCEDURE

McAVOY, BINDING ARBITRATION OF CONTRACT TERMS: A NEW APPROACH TO THE RESOLUTION OF DISPUTES IN THE PUBLIC SECTOR, 72 Colum. L. Rev. 1192, 1194-1205 (1972)*

I. Statutory Provisions

[As of 1990, the states authorizing compulsory ("c") or voluntary ("v") interest arbitration for at least some categories of public employees were: Alaska (c); Connecticut (c & v); Delaware (v); Hawaii (c & v); Illinois (c & v); Indiana (v); Iowa (c & v); Maine (c & v); Massachusetts (c & v); Michigan (c); Minnesota (c & v); Montana (c & v); Nebraska (c); Nevada (c & v); New Hampshire (v); New Jersey (c & v); New York (c & v); North Dakota (c); Ohio (c & v); Oklahoma (c); Oregon (c & v); Pennsylvania (c & v); Rhode Island (c & v); Texas (v); Vermont (v); Washington (c); Wisconsin (c & v); and Wyoming (c). Binding interest arbitration is mandated under the Postal Reorganization Act and may be authorized for federal employees by the FSIP under the Civil Service Reform Act of 1978. Eds.]

---

*Reprinted by permission of Columbia Law Review.

A. Employees Covered

The present pattern of coverage of arbitration statutes seems to reflect a degree of uncertainty as to the wisdom or desirability of such measures. The applicability of the few state statutes that mandate arbitration if agreement is not reached within a stated time period is usually limited to firefighters or police. Both the number and scope of the statutes increase as the parties are granted a voice in the implementation of the arbitration procedure. [Some of the statutes in the] states that require arbitration when requested by one party cover, in addition to firemen and police, hospital and public transportation workers, Port Authority employees, and others. The largest category of statutes, which covers "public employees generally," applies only when both parties agree to the arbitration procedure....

B. Timing of Award

Submission to arbitration deprives the public employer of the power to determine the proportion of its budget it will allocate for employee salaries. As a result, reallocation of previously budgeted funds may be required to satisfy the terms of an award. Many statutes, including the majority of those authorizing arbitration upon agreement of both parties, do not attempt to deal with the problem....

Most statutes that look to completion of arbitration prior to a budget appropriation date provide a detailed timetable, specifying dates for the commencement of bargaining, submission to arbitration, selection of arbitrators, holding of hearings, and issuance of the award. Although most statutes mandating arbitration contain such a schedule, only Minnesota's statute expressly requires the issuance of an award before a date related to appropriations....

C. Composition of the Panel

Although most statutes authorizing arbitration upon the agreement of both parties permit an ad hoc determination of the size of the panel, the great majority of arbitration laws provide for a tripartite panel composed of one member selected by each party plus a chairman chosen by the two appointees. This type of panel carries the collective bargaining process over into arbitration, since the first two appointees are likely to maintain a partisan stance. In justification of such an approach, it is argued that the labor and employer members will be more familiar with the issues and their sponsors' positions and thus able to help the neutral arbitrator avoid any serious error that might result in an award completely unacceptable to one side. In contrast, statutes in Minnesota and Denver remove collective bargaining procedures from the arbitration process by providing that the parties select the entire tripartite panel from a list of seven names submitted by an independent, neutral board.

D. Dissenting Opinions

Most statutes providing for tripartite panels permit a decision by majority vote, thus creating the possibility of a dissent, either in whole or in part, by one of the arbitrators. Undoubtedly, in jurisdictions that require each party to appoint an arbitrator, the dissenter will most probably be a partisan, rather than the neutral chairman. Present experience is inadequate to indicate what effect such dissents will have on the use of arbitration procedures. A dissenting opinion by the employee-arbitrator may cause the union membership to reject the settlement, while an employer might seek repeal of the arbitration statute following too many dissents by its panel member. Tripartite panels are in fact not mandated in New York City because of apprehension concerning the dissents in other jurisdictions. On the other hand, after a dissent, a party may pursue collective bargaining more aggressively in an attempt to avoid arbitration. Such a result might lead to smoother negotiation of subsequent contracts.

E. Residency Requirement

The majority of statutes have no residency requirement for panel members, although a few impose such a requirement on a judge-appointed chairman of a tripartite panel selected when the two other members, who normally select a chairman, are unable to agree. Only Minnesota's law directs that the names of the arbitrators submitted to the parties contain "whenever possible ... names of persons from the geographical area in which the public employer is located."

When a city must lay off employees and reduce city services to comply with a binding arbitration award, a likely result is public resentment against an "outside" arbitrator who need not live with the consequences of his award....

F. Criteria for Award

Most statutes mandating arbitration establish some criteria for the arbitrators to follow in making their award.... [Some provide only general standards, instructing the arbitration panel to consider such factors as the types of employment involved, the public interest, and the relative equities of the parties.] The Rhode Island Policemen's Arbitration Act typifies the use of longer and more specific criteria:

> The factors, among others, to be given weight by the arbitrators in arriving at a decision shall include:
>   (a) Comparison of wage rates or hourly conditions of employment of the police department in question with prevailing wage rates or hourly conditions of employment of skilled employees of the building trades and industry in the local operating area involved.
>   (b) Comparison of wage rates or hourly conditions of employment of the police department in question with wage rates or hourly conditions of employment of police departments in cities or towns of comparable size.
>   (c) Interest and welfare of the public.
>   (d) Comparison of peculiarities of employment in regard to other trades or professions, specifically:
>   (1) Hazards of employment
>   (2) Physical qualifications
>   (3) Educational qualifications
>   (4) Mental qualifications
>   (5) Job training and skills.

In contrast to the statutes mandating arbitration, there are no criteria in seven of the eleven statutes that require arbitration upon the request of one party, and there are no criteria in most of the statutes that authorize arbitration upon the consent of both parties.

Among the statutes with standards, few attempt to deal with the complex question of the employer's ability to pay, which may be computed by reference to either revenues presently available or the community's capacity to tax and its utilization of its fiscal resources as compared to other communities. As public employers increasingly claim inability to provide higher compensation and to cover the costs of non-salary demands, arbitrators, in the absence of specific guidelines, will probably tend to base awards on the jurisdiction's potential ability to increase its revenues.

Nevada's statute provides the clearest standard concerning an employer's ability to pay. The arbitrators must first determine that there is

> a current financial ability to grant monetary benefits based on all existing available revenues as established by the local government employer, and with due regard for the obligation of the local government employer to provide facilities and services....

Once that finding has been made, "normal criteria for interest disputes" may be employed. Such a formulation avoids the possibility of an award that would necessitate increased taxes, employee lay-offs or reduced municipal services.

When a statute does not prescribe rules for decision, arbitrators will presumably apply "general standards." In these circumstances, articulation of the rationale underlying the award is important to forestall a charge of arbitrariness by a disgruntled party. Similarly, decisions that demonstrably correspond to prevailing wages, terms, and conditions of employment in comparable jurisdictions will be more readily accepted by the parties.

G. Terms of an Award

All but four jurisdictions permit arbitrators wide latitude in the selection of settlement terms. Minnesota, Wisconsin, Michigan, and Eugene, Oregon, however, limit awards to either of the parties' final offers. The Michigan statute provides for a choice on each economic issue, while the others mandate a selection of a "package" deal. The primary effect of these provisions is to encourage reasonable bargaining positions at the negotiation stage, since an unreasonable offer will probably lead to adoption of the other party's position in the arbitration award.

The Michigan approach, termed "last offer" arbitration, is favored by at least one commentator who would allow the arbitrator to

> make a choice between the final offers of the parties on an issue-by-issue basis. In this way, the arbitrator would have the prerogative of considering each issue on its merits and of accepting the "most reasonable" offer.

It would thus not be necessary to choose between two packages, each possibly containing some unreasonable demands, and intransigence would never be rewarded....

H. Limitations on an Award

Although it seems clear that an arbitrator cannot require either party to act illegally or beyond its authority, a few statutes contain provisions explicitly dealing with the possibility of a conflict between an arbitrator's award and existing law. The Vallejo law seeks to avoid any conflict ab initio by defining the efficacy of an award by reference to "applicable law." An after-the-fact approach is taken by provisions in Vermont and Minnesota that void portions of an award found to contravene pre-existing statutes. In contrast to these absolute provisions, the New York City ordinance and a Pennsylvania statute adopt a median course. When a term of an award would require enabling legislation, New York City stays its effect "until the appropriate legislative body enacts such [a] law," while Pennsylvania considers the term "advisory only." In such a case the employer's obligation is probably limited to sponsoring and supporting the necessary legislation.

A unique provision of the Pennsylvania statute covering firemen and police attempts to guarantee the binding effect of any award:

> Such determination shall constitute a mandate to the head of the political subdivision which is the employer, or to the appropriate officer of the Commonwealth, if the Commonwealth is the employer, with respect to matters which can be remedied by administrative action, and to the lawmaking body of such political subdivision or of the Commonwealth with respect to matters which require legislative action, to take the action necessary to carry out the determination of the board of arbitration.

Despite the vigor of this language, the Pennsylvania Supreme Court has limited its scope by ruling that in the case of direct conflict, existing laws need not be altered, and the offending terms of the award are therefore void. [*City of Washington v. Police Dep't,* 436 Pa. 168, 179, 259 A.2d 437, 443 (1969).]

Five statutes limit an arbitration panel's power to affect a jurisdiction's taxing or budgeting operations by rendering advisory terms relating to monetary expenditures. Practical assessment of the significance of these provisions is difficult. A public employer may feel great pressure to accept what is technically a recommendation when it is part of an award containing other binding terms. The pressure will be especially intense if the award fails to distinguish nonbinding from binding provisions and thus raises the expectation of employees that the employer must accept the entire package. In addition arbitrators may well make less costly determinations knowing their decisions are only advisory. Such a result is probably intended by the statutes, which implicitly warn the parties that excessively costly terms may be rejected.

I. Judicial Review

The majority of statutes are silent on the question of appeal from an award, and while no reported decisions have considered the issue as to them, the absence of a specific provision usually will not preclude judicial review on grounds such as fraud, lack of impartiality or wrongful assumption of power by the panel. Ten statutes, however, do explicitly provide for a right to appeal to the courts. South Dakota allows the broadest "appeal de novo"; Michigan permits review on the grounds, inter alia, that "the order is unsupported by competent, material and substantial evidence on the whole record." Other laws authorize review of questions of law, and, more narrowly, allegations of fraud, misconduct, and wrongful assumption of power. Consistent with the legislative intent that awards covering firemen and police be absolutely binding, a Pennsylvania statute denies any right to appeal from an award. The Pennsylvania Supreme Court, however, has held that this provision allows review to determine if the panel has exceeded its authority.

J. Expenses

Since a right to arbitrate at the expense of the other party may lead to obstinacy at the bargaining table, who must compensate the arbitrators is a question of some importance. Most statutes require the parties to share the costs of arbitration. The majority of the laws authorizing arbitration by mutual consent are silent on the question, in keeping with the statutory purpose of permitting, but not requiring, the parties to work out their own arrangements.

NOTES

1. The Pennsylvania, Michigan, and Wisconsin compulsory interest arbitration statutes are representative of the variations indigenous to such enactments. Pennsylvania allows the arbitration panel to make its own determination with respect to the different issues without being bound by the positions of the parties. In Michigan, the panel must select from the parties' respective positions on an issue-by-issue basis, while in Wisconsin, the more reasonable total package must be chosen. For excellent evaluations of the procedures and experiences under these three schemes, see J. Stern, C. Rehmus, J. Loewenberg, H. Kasper & B. Dennis, Final-Offer Arbitration (1975). See also R. Lester, Labor Arbitration in State and Local Government (1984). Concerning the Massachusetts experience, see Lipsky & Barocci, *Public Employees in Massachusetts and Final-Offer Arbitration,* 101 Monthly Lab. Rev. 34 (April, 1978). Regarding the application of compulsory arbitration to disputes involving protective employees, see Feuille & Delaney, *Collective Bargaining, Interest Arbitration, and Police Salaries,* 39 Indus. & Lab. Rel. Rev. 228 (1986) (empirical comparison of negotiated police salaries and salaries established through interest arbitration); Loewenberg, *Compulsory Arbitration for Police and Fire Fighters in Pennsylvania in 1968,* 23 Indus. & Lab. Rel. Rev. 367 (1969) (containing excellent statistical breakdowns by size of cities, location, salary, and the experience of the negotiators); Anderson, *A Survey of Statutes with Compulsory Arbitration Provisions for Fire and Police,* in Arbitration of Police and Firefighters Disputes, Proceedings of a Conference on Arbitration of New Contract Terms for the Protective Services, Am. Arb. Ass'n, New York (March 9, 1971) (discussing the various state approaches and evaluating their effectiveness). See also Newman, *Interest Arbitration — Practice and Procedures,* in Labor Relations Law in the Public Sector 44 (A. Knapp ed. 1977); Zack, *Final Offer Selection — Panacea or Pandora's Box?,* 19 N.Y.L. Found. 567 (1974); Clark, *Public Employee Strikes: Some Proposed Solutions,* 23 Lab. L.J. 111, 68 Lab. Arb. 454 (Witney, Arb. 1977); *City of Rialto,* 67 Lab. Arb. 654 (Gentile, Arb. 1976); Sector 25 (T. Gilroy ed. 1972); Garber, *Compulsory Arbitration in the Public Sector: A Proposed Alternative,* 26 Arb. J. 226 (1971); Stevens, *The Management of Labor Disputes in the Public Sector,* 51 Or. L. Rev. 191 (1971).

2. If a public employer improperly refuses to submit unresolved issues to binding arbitration after a bargaining impasse has been reached, this could constitute an unfair labor practice. See *St. Paul Prof. Emps. Ass'n v. City of St. Paul,* 226 N.W.2d 311, 88 L.R.R.M. 2861 (Minn. 1975).

The FLRA will not seek judicial enforcement of a federal interest arbitration award until unfair labor practice procedures have been exhausted. See *Air Force Logistics Command & AFGE,* FLRA No. 96, Case No. 0-MC-6, GERR No. 895, 6 (1980). Compare *Geriot v. Borough of Darby,* 417 A.2d 1144, 1979-80 PBC ¶ 37,027 (Pa. 1980), permitting direct judicial action to enforce an interest arbitration award since such a dispute was not within the exclusive jurisdiction of the PLRB.

3. In *Milwaukee Deputy Sheriffs Ass'n v. Milwaukee Cty.,* 221 N.W.2d 673, 88 L.R.R.M. 2169 (Wis. 1974), a case involving "final offer" arbitration, the Court held that an arbitrator could not adopt a final offer that was never discussed by the parties during their collective negotiations. However, the arbitrator may be able to accept revisions of the parties' "final offers" until the close of the proceedings. See *Newark Firemen's Mut. Benevolent Ass'n v. City of Newark,* 447 A.2d 130, 1981-83 PBC ¶ 37,596 (N.J. 1982).

4. Where a statute provides for an "issue-by-issue" arbitral determination based upon the final offers of the parties, how should the term "issue" be defined? If the parties have disagreed about four separate aspects of the grievance procedure, should this be considered a dispute over a single issue, or should each point of contention be regarded as a separate impasse item? See *West Des Moines Educ. Ass'n v. PERB,* 266 N.W.2d 118, 1977-78 PBC ¶ 36,284 (Iowa 1978). Regarding the demarcation between Pennsylvania interest arbitration awards that cover binding, non-monetary items, as opposed to advisory, monetary subjects, see *Franklin Cty. Prison Bd. v. PLRB,* 417 A.2d 1138, 1979-80 PBC ¶ 36,995 (Pa. 1980). See also *School Comm., City of Bangor v. Education Ass'n,* 433 A.2d 383, 1981-83 PBC ¶ 37,319 (Me. 1981).

5. Under the Iowa PERA, interest arbitrators do not possess the discretion to render a decision which leaves a submitted issue that pertains to a mandatory topic for bargaining unresolved. They must make an award with respect to each mandatory item. See *Iowa State Educ. Ass'n v. PERB,* 369 N.W.2d 793, 1984-86 PBC ¶ 34,494 (Iowa 1985).

6. In *Township of Moon v. Police Officers,* 498 A.2d 1305, 1984-86 PBC ¶ 34,562 (Pa. 1985), the court held that a grievance arbitration procedure may be awarded by an interest arbitrator, even though the arbitral statute does not specifically mention this topic, since it is a term or condition of employment which could be agreed upon voluntarily by the parties. Accord, *Commonwealth of Pa. v. State Conf. of Police Lodges,* 1986-88 PBC ¶ 34,766 (Pa. 1987) (sustaining power of interest arbitrator to award agency shop provision).

The Washington Supreme Court has decided that an interest arbitrator may not direct parties to include in their contract an interest arbitration provision which would apply to future bargaining disputes. Such a "permissive" topic may only be included by agreement of the parties themselves. *Klauder v. San Juan Cty. Deputy Sheriff's Guild,* 728 P.2d 1044, 1986-88 PBC ¶ 34,808 (Wash. 1986).

7. Where a "mixed" bargaining unit contains some employees subject to binding interest arbitration and personnel not covered by that statutory procedure, arbitral jurisdiction is limited to the covered workers. See *Alaska Pub. Emps. Ass'n v. City of Fairbanks,* 753 P.2d 725, 1986-88 PBC ¶ 35,092 (Alaska 1988).

8. In *Maquoketa Valley Community Sch. Dist. v. Education Ass'n,* 279 N.W.2d 510, 102 L.R.R.M. 2056 (Iowa 1979), the court ruled that where the state public employee bargaining statute mandates the issuance of an interest arbitration decision within fifteen days after the first meeting of the arbitral panel, an award issued following the expiration of that period would be invalid, unless the parties had previously agreed to extend or waive the statutory time limit.

9. Since party-appointed arbitrators on a tripartite panel are expected to represent the interests of their respective parties, their impartiality is not required and they may be permitted to consult with their appointive entities during the arbitral proceedings. See *Borough of New Cumberland v. Police Emps.,* 467 A.2d 1294, 1984-86 PBC ¶ 34,001 (Pa. 1983).

4. DECISIONAL STANDARDS

DISTRICT OF COLUMBIA METROPOLITAN POLICE DEPARTMENT and FRATERNAL ORDER OF POLICE

84 Lab. Arb. 809 (1985)

ROTHSCHILD, DONALD, Chairman: The facts regarding the parties' negotiations on compensation issues are slim and in dispute.... There is even dispute as to how many negotiation sessions were held between the parties. The District claimed that "there have been approximately eight (8) bargaining sessions with the first four (4) consumed primarily with clarification of proposals." The Union has claimed there were only four.... The Chairman and the Executive Director of PERB observed bargaining personally "to determine if in fact the parties were at impasse," found them to be, and ordered final and binding interest arbitration. From the evidence adduced, it is doubtful that any progress was made on compensation issues, or for that matter that much bargaining actually took place. It appears that only in the area of working conditions involving discipline was there constructive progress....

Management's Last Best Offer

Wages

I. Fiscal Year 1985

A. Each employee who is a member of the bargaining unit and is in a pay status for the pay period that contains the date of the Council approval of this Agreement (or the passage of sixty (60) days after submission to the Council without action being taken thereon) shall receive within two (2) pay periods thereafter, a one-time lump sum payment of three percent (3%), which:

1. Shall be computed on the Police Service Salary Schedule in effect on September 30, 1984, and

2. Shall be in addition to basic pay and shall not constitute an increase to an employee's basic pay nor be construed to constitute an employee's basic pay for any purpose.

B. The Police Service Salary Schedule in effect on September 30, 1984 shall continue in effect on a grade for grade and step by step basis.

II. Fiscal Year 1986

Effective the first pay period that begins on or after October 1, 1985, the Police Service Salary Schedule then in effect shall be adjusted by four percent (4%) in accordance with past methods of increasing the Fire Service Salary Schedule.

III. Fiscal Year 1987

A. Effective the first pay period that begins on or after October 1, 1986, the Police Service Salary Schedule then in effect shall be adjusted by four percent (4%) in accordance with past methods of increasing the Fire Service Salary Schedule.

B. Effective the first day of the pay period that contains September 30, 1987, the Police Service Schedule then in effect shall be adjusted by dollar value of one and one-half percent (1½%) base increase computed on the FY 1986 Police Service Salary Schedule in accordance with past methods of increasing the Police Service Salary Schedule.

Technicians Pay

Throughout the period this Agreement is in effect, each Technician shall receive $1,010 per annum in addition to his/her scheduled rate of basic compensation.

Optical and Dental Benefits

1. Commencing the first full pay period after the effective date of this agreement, the Employer agrees to continue to pay for each bargaining unit member up to $4.75 per month as the premium for self and self/family coverage in an approved optical plan.

2. Commencing the first full pay period after the effective date of this Agreement the Employer agrees to pay $6.50 per month for single coverage or $13.00 per month for self/family coverage for each participating bargaining unit member in an approved dental plan.

3. The optical and dental plans shall be contracted for by the Union with the Employer's approval prior to implementation. The Employer shall be held harmless from any liability arising out of the implementation and administration of the optical and dental plans (provided that the Employer transmits each month to the carriers payments in the amounts described above). If for any reason the carrier remits any part of the premium paid by the Employer, those funds shall be paid over to the Employer.

4. The benefit provider(s) shall be responsible for program administration and shall bear all such administrative costs.

5. The benefit provider for dental services shall be responsible for identifying to the Employer, after surveying the unit employees, the names and number of employees to be carried under individual and family status.

6. The Employer shall not make dual premium payments for employees who are married and are both in the bargaining unit, and the benefit provider(s) shall be responsible for identifying to the employer the name of each designated employee for whom the premium is to be paid.

7. If, during the period this collective bargaining agreement is in effect, the Employer contracts with a carrier that provides equal or better optical and/or dental benefits, the Union will review its option to participate in each program.

Uniform and Plain Clothes Maintenance Allowance

Effective for Fiscal Years 1985, 1986 and 1987, the Employer agrees to provide a Uniform and Plain Clothes Maintenance Allowance which shall be paid in lump sum during the first full pay period in May of each year to employees who are bargaining unit members on April 30th of each year in the following amounts:

FY 1985: $200
FY 1986: $200
FY 1987: $200

Eligible employees in plain clothes shall receive that sum in addition to the existing allowance of $300 per year for the purchase of plain clothes.

Court Time Pay

Each Officer present in court performing court duty on his/her off duty time shall be compensated at the rate of 1.5 x his/her basic rate of hourly pay for each hour spent on court duty. A minimum of two (2) hours overtime pay will be guaranteed for each day of court duty on the officer's scheduled day off or on any off duty time that does not immediately precede or follow the employee's regular scheduled tour of duty.

Reimbursement for Use of Personal Vehicles

The maximum monthly amount to be reimbursed to an employee who uses his personal vehicle for authorized police work shall be increased by $25 from the current $75 to $100, subject to supervisory approval in accordance with existing Department procedures.

Union's Last Best Offer

Pay Raise

1) Effective retroactively to the first pay period on or after October 1, 1984, the Employer will increase unit employees' base salaries by 4.5% in each step of each class in the bargaining unit.

2) Effective the first pay period on or after October 1, 1985, the Employer will increase unit employees' base salaries by an additional 5.0% in each step of each class in the bargaining unit.

3) Effective the first pay period on or after October 1, 1986, the Employer will increase unit employees' base salaries an additional 5.5% in each step of each class in the bargaining unit.

Shift Differential

Effective the first pay period on or after June 1, 1985, all employees covered by this agreement are entitled to pay at their scheduled rate plus a differential of 3% for regularly scheduled non-overtime work when the majority of their work hours occur between 3 p.m. and midnight; or 4% of their scheduled rate if the majority of their work hours occur between 11 p.m. and 8 a.m.

Clothing Allowance

The clothing allowance for Officers and Detectives assigned to plain clothes, effective the first pay period on or after June 1, 1985, shall increase to $450 per year, payable in two payments in December and June of each year. The clothing allowance for casual clothes officers shall be $225.00 per year, also payable twice yearly in December and June.

Insurance Benefits — Dental, Vision, Legal and Health

Dental: Effective the first pay period on or after the new effective contract date, the employer pays to union 100% of premium to cover cost of pre-paid dental plan for members. The employer's contribution will be $8.50 per month per member for single coverage and $18.25 per month per member for family coverage. This payment level will be maintained through the contract duration.

Optical: Effective the first pay period on or after the new effective contract date, the employer pays to union 100% of premium for each member. Employer's contribution shall be $6.00 per month per member throughout the contract duration.

Pre-Paid Legal Plan: Effective the first pay period on or after June 1, 1985, the employer pays to union $6.00 per member per month towards legal insurance premium for each member. Employer's contribution shall be $6.00 per month per member throughout the contract duration. This pre-paid legal plan includes non-duty related issues.

Health: The City shall continue to pay the maximum amount allowable contribution of health premiums pursuant to federal law for both single and family coverage.

Tech Pay and Other Current Special Duty and Skill Premiums

Effective the first pay period on or after June 1, 1985, Tech pay will increase to $950. Effective the first pay period on or after October 1, 1985, Tech pay will be $1,150 per year. Effective the first pay period on or after October 1, 1986, Tech pay will be $1,250 per year.

October current special duty and skill premiums shall increase by $140 effective the first pay period on or after June 1, 1985; shall increase by $340 effective the first pay period on or after October 1, 1985; and shall increase by $440 effective the first pay period on or after October 1, 1986.

Issues

1. What procedure is mandated by the Statute and PERB for resolution of the Parties' impasse on compensation issues?

2. Does the Union have the burden of proof to show a compelling reason by clear and convincing evidence that a departure from its traditional wage relationship and bargaining patterns is warranted?

3. What criteria is appropriate for selecting the last best offer of either the Fraternal Order of Police (FOP) or Metropolitan Police Department (MPD)?

4. Which parties' last best offer presents the most suitable compensation package under the appropriate criteria and why?

Analysis

1. ... Under last best offer (final offer) arbitration, "the last best offer of each party shall be the basis for such impasse arbitration." PERB Rule 104.6. Simply, this means that "the Panel is permitted to select only one or the other of the parties' final offers, with no power to make a choice anywhere in between." See Rehmus, *Interest Arbitration* in Public Employment Relations Services, Portrait of a Process: Collective Negotiations in Public Employment 218 (Gibbons, Helsby, Lefkowitz, Tener eds. 1979) [hereinafter cited as "Rehmus, *Interest Arbitration*"]....

The theory is that this inflexible procedure would force negotiating parties to continue to move closer together in negotiations so that each of their last best offers would elicit an arbitrator's sympathy. In the present situation, PERB in ordering the impasse procedures, found that:

> The parties' dealings have been characterized for over eight months by exchanges, occasionally across the table, frequently in writing, or acrimonious charges and counter-charges. *Whatever actual bargaining has taken place has moved them further away from final settlement than toward it.* (emphasis added) PERB Case No. 85-I-06, Opinion No. 103, p. 2.

Indeed, the record is replete with evidence that fruitful bargaining never took place. Accordingly, this Panel is faced with the draconian choice of choosing between two compensation packages that do *not* result from bargaining or movement toward each other. As the distinguished former chair of the Michigan Employment Relations Commission pointed out,

> This harsh or risky form of final-offer arbitration discourages *but does not eliminate it.* One concern of critics is that when recourse to arbitration nevertheless ensues, arbitrators *may be forced to choose not the best or most suitable package, but that which is the least inequitable.* Hence, injustice to a greater or lesser degree may result. (emphasis added) [Rehmus, *Interest Arbitration* p. 218.]

2. In its closing argument, Counsel for the District asked the Panel to impose the burden of proof on the Union to show by "clear and convincing evidence" why FOP's members should be compensated differently from other public safety employees in the District. Specifically, Counsel contends:

> ... [W]here a traditional wage relationship or bargaining pattern has existed for some time, the burden is on the party wishing to change that, to show some compelling reason by clear and convincing evidence that such a departure is warranted, and we would refer you to Factfinder Block's decision in IAFF Local 1285, which is an unreported decision. However, it is quoted in Edwards, Clark, and Craver, Labor Relations Law in the Public Sector, Bobbs-Merrill, Second Edition, Page 637....

The Panel does not agree that it should impose the burden of proof on the Union by clear and convincing evidence to show a compelling reason for departure from a traditional wage relationship or bargaining pattern in the instant case....

The Panel does not believe that last best offer arbitration imposes a burden of proof on the *Union alone,* even on issues as important as parity. The Panel believes last best offer arbitration imposes *on both parties* a burden to show by statute, by rule, and/or by traditional criteria that their final offer is best....

[W]e reject the proposition that once a non-statutory issue of parity in compensation between police and firefighters is raised, the burden of proof, as distinguished from the burden of presenting evidence, shifts to the party wishing to change the status quo to prove their case by an extraordinary quantum of proof — i.e. different from that quantum required from either party to persuade the Panel of its case in chief. The Panel does *not reject* the issue of "comparability" raised by the District, and particularly that issue as it relates to the compensation of "Police and Fire Pay" or with "Other Unions," or with "Other Local Jurisdictions." The issue of "comparability" is a traditional and important criteria applied in compensation arbitration. However, this issue goes to the merits of each parties' final offer, and is not a procedural issue. Insofar as the procedural issue raised by the District is concerned, we disagree with both the burden of proof and the quantum of proof cited by the District....

3. The point of departure required of the Panel in considering each parties' last best compensation offer is dictated by the D.C. Code. Section 1-618.2(d) provides in pertinent part that:

> Where deemed appropriate, impasse resolution machinery may be invoked by either party or on application to the Board. The choice of the form(s) of impasse resolution machinery to be utilized in a particular instance shall be the prerogative of the Board, after appropriate consultation with the interested parties. *In considering the appropriate award for each impasse item to be resolved, any third party shall consider at least the following criteria:*
> (1) Existing laws and rules and regulations which bear on the item in dispute;
> (2) Ability of the District to comply with the terms of the award;
> (3) The need to protect and maintain the public health, safety and welfare; and
> (4) The need to maintain personnel policies that are fair, reasonable and consistent with the objectives of this chapter.

... Section 1-612.3 indicates that:

> (a) Compensation for all employees in the Career, Educational and the Excepted Services shall be fixed in accordance with the following policy:
> (1) Compensation shall be competitive with that provided to *other public sector employees* having *comparable duties,* responsibilities, qualifications, and working conditions *by occupational groups.* For purposes of this paragraph, *compensation shall be deemed to be competitive if it falls reasonably within* the range of *compensation prevailing in the* Washington, D.C. Standard Metropolitan Statistical Area (SMSA): Provided, that *compensation levels may be examined* for *public and/or private employees outside the*

area and/or for federal government employees when necessary to establish a reasonably representative statistical basis for compensation comparisons, or when conditions in the local labor market require a larger sampling of prevailing compensation levels;

(2) *Pay for the various occupations and groups of employees shall be to the maximum extent practicable, interrelated and equal for substantially equal work;*

(3) *Differences in pay shall be maintained* in keeping *with differences in level of work and quality of performance....* (emphasis added)

Thus, the D.C. Code mandates that compensation, even when set through impasse procedures selected by the Board, as in the instant case, be set in accordance with existing laws. The D.C. Code instructs the Panel that to make such determinations compensation shall be competitive with other public sector employees having comparable duties, responsibilities, qualifications, and working conditions by occupational groups. Compensation will be deemed competitive if it falls reasonably within the range prevailing in the Washington, D.C. SMSA. The Code provides for looking at public and/or private employees outside the SMSA area when necessary to establish a representative statistical basis for comparison. It further provides that pay for occupational groups be interrelated and equal for substantially equal work; and that differences be maintained in keeping with differences in level of work and quality of performance. The Code mandates that the Board authorize broad units in order to minimize the number of different pay systems. Finally, the Code directs that the above compensation considerations take into account the District's ability to pay, the public interest, and result in personnel policies that are fair and reasonable....

Records and Studies

Before proceeding with an examination of this evidence, it is again important to note that the D.C. Code Section 1-618.17(c) provides, *inter alia,* that in the process of collective bargaining concerning compensation:

No earlier than 150 days before the expiration of any existing negotiated agreement between the parties [Fiscal 1984], *management shall begin a thorough study of the compensation being paid to comparable occupational groups of employees in other jurisdictions in the Washington Standard Metropolitan Statistical Area and the nation's 30 largest cities by population.* The annual study *may include hours of work, health benefits and vacation time.* The annual study *shall also include the current percentage change in the Consumer Price Index for the Washington Metropolitan Area published by the Bureau of Labor Statistics,* United States Department of Labor.

... [N]one of the reports or studies submitted by either the Union or the District proceed from the same data elements or survey universe — and this includes the submission of each party in regard to the CPI and SMSA.... The parties not only differ on the composition of the Washington Standard Metropolitan Statistical Area (SMSA), but also on the meaning of "compensation being paid," as well as the definition of comparable occupational groups of employees. For example, the Union's Table VI in Exhibit 11D lists Arlington, Fairfax, Montgomery County, and Prince George's County in comparison with the District, while the District's Chart 5A in Exhibit 8 lists Howard County, Arlington County, Montgomery County, Fairfax County, Anne Arundel County, Baltimore County, Prince George's County and Baltimore City in comparison with the District. Union Tables I through V in Exhibit 11D list minimum pay for Police Officers in progression of classifications through a 20 year career in each SMSA jurisdiction, while the Distict's Table 2 in Exhibit 8 lists entry and maximum salaries paid for Police Officers and Sergeants but, with the exception of Montgomery County, differs on progression classification....

4. After carefully examining the over 900 pages of the official compensation record and over 80 exhibits containing hundreds of pages of documentary evidence, it is the considered opinion of the majority of the Panel that the Union's last best offer is the most suitable total compensation package to be included in the FY 1985 to FY 1987 Collective Bargaining Agreement.

a. The Total Compensation Packages

(1) The Washington Standard Metropolitan Statistical Area (SMSA)

... Section 1-612.3 in dealing with "compensation policy" provides in subsection (1) that compensation shall be competitive with that provided other public sector employees "having comparable duties, responsibilities, qualifications, and working conditions by occupational groups." As the District points out, "[i]n many cases strong reason exists for using the prevailing practice of the same class of employers within the locality or area for the comparison." [Quoting F. Elkouri & E. Elkouri, How Arbitration Works 750 (3d ed. 1979).] Thus, SMSA is a relevant criteria for comparison, albeit not controlling, and the D.C. Code requires that salaries at least be competitive with those paid within the Washington SMSA.

There are a number of problems associated with making this comparison, as the parties' data indicates. First, each party has picked different local jurisdictions that should be considered within the Washington, SMSA. Secondly, each party has made different assumptions of what economic benefits should be included within the term compensation. Thirdly, there is the problem of determining which police forces within the local jurisdictions (if any) have "comparable duties, responsibilities, qualifications and working conditions" with MPD police officers. Fourthly, the parties used different levels of salary — entry, maximum, weighted or some other level, as the best indicator to measure the relative compensation between the different departments. Fifthly, the parties took an entirely different approach to "wage improvements" in SMSA. The obvious conclusion to be drawn from this evidence is that it is virtually impossible to have an exact comparison of SMSA compensation, since the compensation systems for each jurisdiction contain many different factors, and salary schedules are implemented at different times and in such different manners that comparison is quite difficult. However, it is possible to draw some conclusions from the conflicting data regarding the SMSA comparison.

From the District's vantage, whether one accepts the Union argument that entry level pay for Police Officers in Washington, D.C. is fourth out of five SMSA jurisdictions or third out of ten SMSA jurisdictions it cannot be concluded that the District is not competitive at entry level at this point in time (FY

1984) under D.C. Code 1-612.3, because the difference between the second and fourth salary levels, accepting the Union's figures, is less than $550, and the recruitment figures adduced by the District do not indicate a loss of qualified applicants even with the District's residency requirement. Moreover, it would be difficult to hold that career opportunities in the District, at the present time are not competitive....

Nevertheless, a majority of the Panel finds that when the SMSA comparable pay criteria is applied to last best offers of each party for FY 1985 through FY 1987, there is a significant difference. It is important to note in reviewing both parties' massive documentary evidence, that the evidence on the record addresses MPD compensation in the past, present and future. Although all three are relevant, it is the Panel's task to utilize the relevant criteria (including SMSA statistics) to analyse the last best offers on the compensation package which analysis requires future projections to cover FY 1985 through FY 1987. Union Exhibit 39 is revealing in these projections. Prince George's police received a 4% pay raise in July 1984, Arlington and Fairfax County police will receive a 4% pay raise in July, 1985, and Montgomery County will receive a 5.3% pay raise in July, 1985. These are pay raises which will increase the pay rates of SMSA police officers on an annualized basis (subsequent raises will be on top of the increased pay rates). Under the District's proposal, MPD officers will receive a non-annualized, one-time only bonus of 3%, but no increase in their pay rate during the period October, 1984 through October, 1985. While under the FOP last best offer, the District's police would receive a 4.5% pay rate raise retroactive from October, 1984 (FY 1985).

Although future pay raises for the Arlington and Fairfax police officers are unknown, since there is no collective bargaining in these SMSA jurisdictions and raises are set by the County, Prince George's County police will receive a 6% pay raise in October, 1985, and Montgomery County will receive a 5.4% pay raise in July 1986. Under the District's proposal, MPD officers would receive 4% in October, 1935, while under the FOP last best offer, they would receive 5%.

In July 1986, Prince George's County police will receive another 6% pay raise, and in July 1987, Montgomery County police will receive another 5.3%. Under the District's proposal, MPD officers would receive 4% in October 1986 (the 1½% pay raise from September, 1987 ["kicker"] included in the District's last best offer will be discussed subsequently); while under the FOP proposal, they will receive 5.5%.

Thus, looking at the District's last best offer, the MPD would be the only local SMSA jurisdiction in the immediate vicinity (which has acted) that would not receive a pay rate raise in FY 1985. Instead, they would receive a non-annualized bonus of 3%. This is compounded by the fact that the second year pay raise under the District's proposal (FY 1986), which would relate back to FY 1984 pay rates, and the third year pay raise (FY 1987) are significantly less than those being paid to officers in Prince George's and Montgomery [Counties]. In sum, the evidence indicates that the competitive comparable SMSA wages which now exist will be substantially eroded by the District's last best compensation offer....

(2) Consumer Price Index (CPI)

D.C. Code 1-618.17(c) indicates that the management study of compensation "shall also include the current percentage change in the Consumer Price Index for the Washington Metropolitan Area published by the Bureau of Labor Statistics, United States Department of Labor." Although this index, like SMSA comparisons, is not a legally determinative factor and "[t]he Bureau of Labor Statistics does not hold that its index is an exact measurement of changes in the cost of living ... arbitrators can be expected to give it considerable weight." [F. Elkouri & E. Elkouri, How Arbitration Works 762 (3d ed. 1979).] ...

It has an obvious appearance of fairness, because it provides a fixed basis of prices in the Washington, D.C. Metropolitan (SMSA) area against which wages can be compared. Even though the District does not use it as a major criteria, it does use it to provide one of the factors that it used as a "foundation for pay-setting in the District of Columbia." Further, Management uses the Cost-of-Living criteria to support its contention that what occurred between FY 1982 and FY 1984 in its Collective Bargaining Agreement with Police Officers "show[s] what happened and why we [the District] believe that what we have offered in the first year [the bonus of 3%] makes sense, as well as the succeeding years." Using the CPI, the District points out that the D.C. Metropolitan Police Base Pay Adjustments exceeded the CPI-W, Washington SMSA index by 5.4%. Following this logic, the District reasons that the excess of 5.4% D.C. Police adjustments over the contract period justifies it giving a bonus which does not annualize over the term of the next contract period rather than a pay rate adjustment that would annualize. The majority of the Panel disagrees with this contention....

It is necessary to take a broader perspective of CPI than just three years of low inflation. Indeed, the District when necessary to support its argument takes the position that the Panel must consider the historic connection between police and fire pay relationship ("for over sixty years") in judging their last best offer, which will be discussed later in detail. In other words, when it supports their case the District urges we consider Congressional and District action, when it does not, the pay relationship to CPI should begin with the collective bargaining phase. However, this argument is unpersuasive, because, as the Union points out, the "Comprehensive Merit System of Personal Management for the Government of the District of Columbia" was entered prior to January 2, 1980. D.C. Code 1-601.1. This period (two three-year bargaining cycles) includes periods of both high and low inflation. The Union's constant dollar purchasing power review of this period using CPI indicates that by 1984, the purchasing power for D.C. police officers had eroded 7.4%, instead of the surplus of 5.4% indicated by the District. The Panel finds as a matter of fact that the District's use of only three years of the pay relationship to CPI in order to arrive at a surplus is not justified. Whether one uses the more reasonable Union history or not, the point is that the concept of a "surplus" is statistical rather than actual. More importantly, when the Union uses the broader six year perspective, under the City's pay proposal, by 1987 D.C. police officers' salary will have eroded 12.1%, because using the District's own figures, their last best offer is less than their CPI projections. The District's estimate is that "prices are expected to rise by 4.3

percent in 1984 and 4.6% in 1985. For this budget, it is assumed that Washington area consumer prices will rise by 5.5 percent in 1985 and by 6.0 percent in 1986." ...

It is reasonable to assume that over the three year life of the FY 1985 — FY 1987 Agreement, the CPI will increase between 16-17%. The District's *wage rate* increase (excluding the one-time bonus and the one-month "kicker") is 8.0%. Thus, without a surplus of 5.4%, the District's pay raise does not come close to the anticipated price increases in the Washington, D.C. Metropolitan Area as measured by CPI. When one uses the Union's broader CPI perspective, there is a substantial erosion of D.C. Police Officer's pay. On the other hand, the Union's proposal will give police officers a cumulative increase in wages of 15.8% over the FY 1985 — FY 1987 contract, which is close to the projected price increases of CPI....

(3) Other Studies

The D.C. Code authorizes the use of other studies, and indeed the parties agreed to this procedure, as previously indicated. However, for reasons which will be stated later, a majority of the Panel believes that these studies are corroborative rather than independent criteria such as SMSA or CPI. The dissenting member of the Panel believes that the Union studies are less than persuasive. The Union utilizes a number of studies: The Chicago Study; its own 30 City Study, and a 10 City Study. The Chicago Study is a "management study," which the Union's economic consultant testified "has often been used in impasse resolution and in binding interest arbitration." [Its] methodology also served as a basis for the Union's own 30 City Study. Although it does a disservice to the massive amount of information presented by the two studies to characterize their findings briefly, their findings are that the 30 city universe utilized by them (and the "Bonner Study") over a six year period of 1/1/79 to 1/1/85 indicate[s] that Police Officer Pay increased dramatically more in the other cities than in Washington, D.C. The Union characterizes this as a "trend that is severely impacting police officers." The dissenting member of the Panel disagrees with the universe used by these studies, the assumptions about compensation, and the figures themselves.... While the majority of the Panel agrees that the Union's 10 City Study is probably irrelevant since the District of Columbia is "1483 miles from the closest city [being compared to the District], which is Houston," the majority does not agree that the Chicago Study or the FOP 30 City Study is unverifiable or incorrect. The majority of the Panel agrees with Mr. Galleher, the economic consultant who testified on behalf of FOP, that the differences alluded to by Mr. Levitt are the result of different methodology as well as assumptions.... [T]he Panel is also impressed with the District's statistics showing that insofar as "entry salary" as of Fiscal 1984 is concerned, the MPD rates well among East Coast Cities both on the private and sergeant level. In other words, a majority of the Panel finds as a matter of fact that the other statistics used by the Union corroborate the argument that the District's last best offer for its wage package from FY 1985 — FY 1987 would erode D.C. Police Officer's salary, but do not establish that these salaries are not competitive now. The Panel agrees with the District that its FY 1982 — FY 1984 package was not unreasonable; but a majority of the Panel believes that its last best offer for FY

1985 — FY 1987 will result in an erosion of D.C. police officer pay. The majority further finds as a matter of fact that the Union's studies (other than the 10 City Study) support this conclusion. The Chicago and 30 City Studies indicate that the D.C. police officers require a substantial wage rate raise in order to keep pace with police officers wage rates for FY 1985 and beyond in SMSA as well as predicted price increases (CPI).

(4) Parity and/or Wage Comparability

This issue is of extreme importance to the District in justifying its compensation package. As Director Weinberg indicated:

> [The] "historical relationship that we have been able to maintain between police officers and firefighters. Now, this is the relationship that has existed for six decades. It has been for the most part an identical, and it has been a special relationship between police and fire....
> We believe that it requires the most compelling reasons to separate these two groups of employees.

Indeed, the District raised this issue as a procedural issue relating to burden of proof in this arbitration proceeding. Although the Panel rejected this contention, it stated that ...

> [n]o discussion of the issues arising in collective bargaining with uniformed personnel would be complete without some reference to the problems that arise out of the concent of parity. While it is possible to question the legitimacy of the concept as a rationale for bargaining with law enforcement and fire fighting personnel, its importance to the process cannot be disputed." [Slavney, The Uniformed Services p. 416.]

However, the Panel finds as a matter of law and fact that parity does not exist between the police and firefighters in the District of Columbia. First, as a matter of law, D.C. Code Section 1-618.16(b) provides:

> The provisions of this section shall become effective on January 1, 1980, and shall apply to all employees.... In determining appropriate bargaining units for negotiations concerning compensation, *the Board shall authorize broad units of occupational groups so as to minimize the number of different pay systems* or schemes. The Board may authorize bargaining by multiple employer or employee groups as may be appropriate. (emphasis added.)

It is very clear as a matter of statutory construction that the D.C. Code authorizes the Board (PERB) to determine appropriate units on a case by case basis. The Code directs the Board to establish units of like organization and operation, which historically has included the uniformed services. [See M. Moscow, J. Loewenberg & E. Koziara, Collective Bargaining in Public Employment 184-87 (1969).] Further, the Code directs the Board to establish broad units to minimizing the number of different pay systems or schemes, which is precisely what Director Weinberg is asking this Panel to do. However, the PERB Board by Order dated February 6, 1981 in Case No. 80-R-08 established fourteen different compensation bargaining units for D.C. government employees and placed the members of the Metropolitan Police Department in Compensation Unit 3 *with no other D.C. government employees....* [D]esignating the police and fire-fighters as separate bargaining units indicates a thorough understanding of the difference in the operation and compensation needs of the police and fire-fighter departments.

It is very important to understand that no one who is party to this arbitration has or is indicating that either the police or the firefighters are not important to the District of Columbia as members of the uniformed services. Nor is anyone indicating that one is more or less important than the other. What is being acknowledged, which is also being acknowledged on a national level, is that their organization, duties and skills are different. Indeed, as the evidence indicates, as early as 1967 the President's Commission on Law Enforcement and Adminis-tration of Justice stated that identical pay scales for police and firefighters was unfair and unwise because of their widely differing functions, and recom-mended that salary proposals for each department within local government should be considered on their own merits and should not be joined with the demands of other departments within a city. Further, the Chicago Study indi-cates that although in 1979 only 12 of 30 cities practiced parity, the number dropped by 1984 to 6 out of 30....

The Panel finds as a matter of fact that wage comparability/parity does not exist at the present time between the Police and Firefighters *even if the Panel accepts the District's FY 1985 — FY 1987 compensation package.* For example, with respect to salary, the $1\frac{1}{2}\%$ "kicker" does not come into effect until Septem-ber 30, 1987, in the District's Police Wage proffer, while it comes into effect April 1, 1987, for the firefighters. For all intents and purposes, it has very little positive effect on the proposed wage package for the police as will be discussed later. With respect to the dental plan, the City's last best offer to the police is $6.50 per month for single coverage or $13.00 per month for self/family cover-age. Fire personnel are to receive $13.00 per month for single coverage or $26.00 per month for self/family coverage — exactly double that to be paid police personnel. With respect to uniform allowances, firefighters are to receive $325.00 in fiscal year 1985, and $400.00 in fiscal years 1986 and 1987, for a total of $1,125.00 over the three-year period. Police officers are to receive $200.00 in each of the three years, for a total of $600.00. Thus, firefighters are to receive almost twice as much in uniform allowance as police officers. Fire-fighters are to receive a personal leave day for their birthday. Police officers will not receive such a personal leave day. Firefighters are guaranteed pay at one and one-half times the regular hourly rate for all overtime, to include call-back, work on assigned days off, or court appearances on off-duty time. (Continua-tion of duty shall be compensated by compensatory time on an hour-for-hour basis.) Police officers are guaranteed time and one-half for overtime only for court duty. Firefighters are guaranteed a minimum of four hours overtime pay for call-backs; police officers receive no such guarantee....

[T]he comparability argument is based on historic relationships that arise from a pattern of bargaining with a single employer, as the District argues in its brief in support of its compensation offer. The Panel finds as a matter of fact, that the District has chosen to break this pattern with the firefighters, and is not committed to it with other unions or local jurisdictions, except when it chooses to do so....

(5) The District Budget and Ability to Pay

The City has disavowed raising an ability to pay issue. Specifically, its Counsel stated "[w]e have said that we are not making an inability to pay argument." An examination of the City's Bond Prospectus and the Market Trends Forecast for April 1985, as well as the testimony of Mr. Fennel and Ms. Reveal establish that virtually all of the economic indicators for the District's economy are positive. However, the District indicated that Congress is requiring it to reduce the large deficit that occurred when Congress was administering the District's finances. The District has had a balanced budget for the past several years, and has shown a significant revenue surplus notwithstanding the retirement of the debt. Although Ms. Reveal indicated that she was only projecting a revenue growth between FY 1985 and FY 1986 of 5.8%, she acknowledged that the actual revenue growths for the two preceeding years were 9.7% between FY 1983 and FY 1984 and 9.7% between FY 1984 and FY 1985. Personal services are estimated to be 6.8% of the total budget, and the Police Department's total budget is 7.2% of the personnel budget. When asked if they had calculated the difference between the Union last best offer and the District's, she replied that it was approximately 1% of the total D.C. budget over three years, or approximately ³/₁₀ths of 1% per year. On the basis of these facts, a majority of the Panel found that the District could comply with the terms of the award under D.C. Code Section 1-618.2(d)(2)....

b. The Parties' Last Best Offers

(1) Fair and Reasonable Personnel Policies

Wage Proposals: As previously indicated, a majority of the Panel found that the District's wage proposals would result in an erosion of Police Officer's pay rates over FY 1985 — FY 1987. The reason for this finding can be found in the 3% non-annualized, one-time only bonus to be paid in FY 1985 and the 1.5% base pay raise occurring in September 1987....

By offering a 3% pay "enhancement" (bonus) during the first year, employees are not only being denied an adequate pay raise to keep up with the inflation rate of 4.5% for the first year, they are also being shortchanged in the subsequent two years when they would also receive inadequate raises, because there is no compounding of the first year bonus raise. The FY 1986 pay rate raise is applied to the FY 1984 pay rate. This inadequacy is "compounded" by the fact that there is no improvement in retirement benefits, insurance or overtime calculations.... Further, the 1½% "kicker" on September 30th of FY 1987 ($139,398 estimated cost) does not seem to be as much of an advantage as it is a disadvantage....

The Chair asked,

> Isn't that also a negative, in the sense that what it does in terms of our analysis and comparison is that it puts the rate of pay of the District at a percent and a half higher, while giving the employees who have been serving over the term of this contract one thirty-sixth of that benefit during the term of the contract or one-twelfth over the last year?...

... [I]t shows an artifically high rate of pay from which to negotiate a new contract, because it shows a rate which is one and a half percent above what has actually been earned by the employees in the unit.

Mr. Levitt replied,

It absolutely does. The employees do not get the one and a half percent during, let's say during any of the fiscal years. What it does for them, though, is that for FY 1988 and forevermore they will be getting one and a half percent on top of their base pay.

As indicated, the District's wage package would make the District the only SMSA jurisdiction (that has acted) that is not giving a pay rate raise. Thus, the D.C. police officers would neither keep apace of CPI or SMSA. A majority of the Panel found as a matter of fact that this compensation package is not a fair or reasonable personnel policy.

As previously indicated, the Union compensation package has been found by a majority of the Panel to be appropriate in light of SMSA and CPI. The District has suggested that if the police get a pay raise beyond what the District now considers to be comparable (the District's proposal), the other unions will seize this opportunity to whipsaw the District in the next negotiations. The fact is that the other unions (other than the nurses) have concluded negotiations with the District for the next three year period. The majority of the Panel submits that the negotiations to be conducted in FY 1987 will be influenced far more by the prevailing circumstances in 1987 than by what occurred early in 1985....

Shift Differential: The Union proposes that on or after June 1, 1985, officers who work the evening shift shall receive a 3% pay differential, and those who work the midnight shift shall receive a 4% pay differential. The District proposes no shift differentials, and argues that since the only D.C. police officers permanently assigned to the 11:00 p.m. to 7:00 a.m. shift are volunteers, "it would be anomalous to pay them more for work schedule than they apparently prefer. Since all other officers rotate equitably among the other shifts (or, in the case of the 5th District, among all shifts) ... no shift differential is justified." Yet, shift differentials are a traditional aspect of police compensation, and are a mandatory subject for negotiation pursuant to D.C. Code 1-618.17(b), which specifically mentions "shift differential."...

[T]he Union adduced evidence that all four of the neighboring comparable police jurisdictions pay shift differentials (Arlington, Fairfax, Montgomery [County] and Prince George's County). The shift differential in the Union proposal is not inconsistent with that paid in the surrounding comparable jurisdictions or the 30 Cities. Although the District cites *City of Renton,* 71 LA 271 (Snow, Green, & Glenn 1978), an impasse interest arbitration as precedent for disallowing this compensation proposal, it is obvious that the *City of Renton* panel had jurisdiction to consider individual compensation items while we do not. Accordingly, a majority of the Panel finds as a matter of fact that the shift differential is a fair and reasonable personnel policy consistent with the objectives of the chapter.

Clothing Allowance: In 1973 Congress enacted legislation authorizing the Chief of Police to provide a clothing allowance not to exceed $300 in any one year to any officer or member assigned to perform duty in plain clothes. D.C.

Code 4-128(b). Since this legislation was enacted, the MPD has paid $300 per year to officers assigned to duties which normally require them to wear "plain clothes," which in practice has been business attire. The Union proposal seeks to increase the $300 "plain clothes" allowance to $450 per year, and the $100 "casual clothes" allowance to $225 per year, commencing June 1, 1985. The Union justifies this proposal by inflation figures. The District offers a uniform maintenance allowance of $200 to every uniformed bargaining unit member, which the Union has not requested in its final offer. The District inadvertently omitted an increase in the allowance for casual clothes officers (about 10% of the bargaining unit). Both parties conceded that the District's last best offer is more generous than the Union's, and could, therefore, probably have been resolved in negotiations. However, in last best offer compensation package interest arbitration, this Panel is not free to pick and choose from among the various proposals. A majority of the Panel finds as a matter of fact that the Union proposal is a fair and reasonable personnel policy since it is a means of restoring the purchasing power of those officers who must wear their own clothing to perform police services....

[The panel majority next found that the Union proposals pertaining to Dental Insurance, Optical Insurance, and Health Benefits constituted "fair and reasonable personnel policies."]

Legal Services Plan: The Union proposes that commencing June 1, 1985, the District should pay the Union $6.00 per member per month towards the premium for a prepaid legal plan for non-duty related legal matters for the members of the bargaining unit. Testimony by the Chairman of the Labor Committee of the Union established that the Union currently has such a plan in effect for its members to cover family law, probate, wills, traffic and criminal, landlord and tenant and other litigation. Its proposal would eliminate the deductible in the present plan with Robert Ades & Associates. He further testified that the need for outside legal services is peculiar to police officers. The District contends that "[t]his is one aspect of the Union's proposal [that] is so unreasonable that it alone should warrant rejection of the Union's entire compensation package by the Arbitration Board." However, its rationale for this serious contention appears to be: (1) that D.C. police officers are already entitled to representation by the Corporation Counsel's Office for matters related to the performance of their official duties; (2) a survey of other jurisdictions reveals that none provide legal insurance to cover other than duty-related services; and (3) why should D.C. taxpayers be required to pay for police officers' divorces? Although it may well be that this proposal would not result from collective bargaining negotiations at this time, it does not appear that the stated objections are serious enough to disqualify the Union's compensation package. Clearly this plan does not interfere with nor duplicate Corporation Counsel representation. Although this plan may not be common, it is currently in use by Union members on their own. Further, it does not seem radically different from employer paid optical and dental plans. To the question why should D.C. taxpayers pay for divorces, one might respond with the rhetorical question, why should they pay for any services provided the District's employees? Is the provision of legal services to police officers more offensive than those provided through the District's other legal services programs? This is a form of wage supplements commonly called a fringe benefit. The District may have objected to its inclusion in a contract in collective bargaining, but the majority of the Panel finds it to be a fair and reasonable personnel policy.

Technician Pay: Additional compensation for members of the Department who perform certain duties was originally authorized by Congress in 1973, and was carried over by the City Council in subsequent salary schedules. D.C. Code Sections 4-411, 4-408, and 4-406. Pay for technician positions was established at $810.00 per year. This pay has not been increased in the intervening twelve years. The special duty pay pursuant to D.C. Code 4-408 was set at $2,270.00, and has also not been increased.

The Union proposes that technician's pay be increased from $810.00 per year to $950.00 effective June 1, 1985; and to $1,250.00 effective October 1, 1986. The Union proposes that special duty pay be increased by $140.00 effective June 1, 1985; by $340.00 effective October 1, 1985; and by $440.00 effective October 1, 1986. Thus, by 1986, tech pay would have been increased from $2,270.00 to $2,710.00 per year. Once again, the Union's proposal is designed to maintain the approximate level of purchasing power that was in effect at the time the additional compensation was originally awarded. Since tech pay was established in 1973, inflation in the Washington, D.C. Metropolitan Area has increased 138.7%. In order to maintain the same level of purchasing power that $810.00 provided in 1973, it would be necessary to raise tech pay to $1,934.00 as of March 1985. Obviously, the Union proposal does not go nearly so far. It seeks merely to restore to a partial extent the purchasing power that officers had when they originally received technician pay and special duty pay....

Court Pay: The District proposes to compensate officers at a guaranteed minimum pay of two hours' overtime pay for appearances in Court on off-duty days. As the District states, "[p]reviously, pursuant to law, first appearances in court, even on the officer's day off, was only compensated by 'compensatory time'. D.C. Code Section 4-1104(e)." Under the District's proposal, police officers still would receive compensatory time, rather than overtime pay, for all first appearances in court which either immediately precede or follow a regular scheduled tour of duty. However, the District's proposal, with respect to this item has been preempted by *Garcia v. San Antonio Metropolitan Transit Authority,* 105 S.Ct. 1005 (1985). *Garcia* reimposes the FLSA overtime provisions pertaining to law enforcement agencies on state and local governments, and the District of Columbia is specifically included in the definition of a state. 29 USC 203. As indicated, these provisions apply to those employed by a state in law enforcement activities, 29 USC 207(k), and so these provisions would apply to MPD. Accordingly, the Panel finds that the District proposal must comply with this decision under federal law and D.C. Code 1-618.2(d)(1), and no evidence was adduced that it does. On the basis of the Supreme Court decision, the Panel finds this District compensation proposal unacceptable without further documentation.

Personal Vehicle Use: The District offers an increase in the "cap" on mileage reimbursement to officers who use their personal vehicles in the line of duty from the current $75.00 a month to $100.00 a month. The Union has no such provision in its last best offer. Although this proposal might have been accepted in negotiations, it is part of the compensation package that a majority of the

Panel has rejected, and, therefore, cannot be made part of the FY 1985 — FY 1987 Collective Bargaining Agreement.

Retirees' Equalization: In costing the last best offers, the District has included an item for retiree's equalization, while the Union has not. However, the Panel considers this item to be a very important factor in the selection of the last-best offer compensation package of the parties.

First, it is significant that neither party has made a last best offer proposal pertaining to retirement, because retirement benefits are established by law. Thus, retirement benefits are literally not part of this interest arbitration. The District's inclusion of almost 8 million dollars as a contribution for this item in costing its proposal is quite revealing insofar as its compensation package is concerned. It is necessitated because the District's FY 1985 wage proposal contains a bonus, rather than a wage pay rate raise. Under the amended retirement provisions, annuities who retired prior to the effective date of the amendment — 1980, receive an increase in their annuities that is proportional to *any increase in salary for active members,* while those who retire after the effective date of the amendment receive a cost of living increase based on CPI. D.C. Code 4-605.... [P]olice retirees who retired prior to 1980 are tied to salary increases and thus are affected by whether the District gives a salary wage increase or a bonus. It is for those retirees that the District has included a provision of almost 8 million dollars since, under the District's wage proposal, they would receive nothing for FY 1985. Recognizing this, the District costed an item to equalize retiree's benefits with the bonus, but this equalization is not contained in its last best wage offer and so is also beyond the jurisdiction of the panel....

(2) Costing and Ability to Pay

The District estimates that its last best offer has a three year cost of $34,317,167, while the Union's is $57,397,570. The Union's estimate is that the District's last best offer has a three year cost of $19,308,167 while its last best offer has a cost of $38,948,921 for a difference of $19,640,754. The differences between the two costing estimates turns on inclusions and exclusions of compensation proposals. A majority of the Panel finds as a matter of fact that the Union estimate is a more reasonable approximation of the cost of the FY 1985 to FY 1987 compensation proposals.

First, and most significantly, the District cannot include $7,985,560 (almost 8 million dollars) for retirees' equalization, because it has no such proposal in its last best offer. Indeed, the Panel does not believe this item should appear as a last best offer by either side since neither side has made a proposal about statutorily mandated retirees' contributions. Secondly, inclusion of $3,669,882 (over 3½ million dollars) for Court Pay in light of the imposition of FLSA on the District due to the *Garcia* decision, is unsupported by documentation. Thirdly, the Union alleges that the District's calculation of shift differential is short by approximately $577,723 (½ million dollars) bringing the Union estimate to $3,022,891, and the Panel would prefer to use the more conservative figure in its estimate.

Beyond this there is a dispute of whether additional costs for existing items in the FY 1984 budget should be included in the costing of the FY 1985 last best offer compensation proposals. In other words, the argument centers on whether costing should be based on "increases" or "total costs". The Panel believes this is a dispute between statisticians, not unlike others presented in this arbitration, and since it applies to both parties and does not greatly affect the difference between the two proposals. It is not of the importance of the approximately 12 million dollars worth of items that the Panel finds should not be represented in the costing estimates. [*supra*]. Accordingly, the Panel finds that the difference between the two proposals' is approximately $19,501,000, resulting from the difference between an approximate cost of the Union's compensation package of $42,162,725 as opposed to the District's compensation package costing approximately $22,661,725. This brings the differences between the two packages closer to the Union compensation package estimates of approximately 19½ million dollars, which has been selected by a majority of the Panel. A majority of the Panel finds as a matter of fact that the District is able to comply with the terms of the award as specified under D.C. Code 1-618.2(d)(2).(3).

(3) Public Health, Safety and Welfare

In addition to the minimal criteria of existing laws and rules and regulations, the need to maintain personnel policies that are fair, reasonable and consistent with the District Merit System, and the ability of the District to comply with the terms of an arbitration award, D.C. Code Section 1-618.3(d)(3) requires this Panel to consider "The need to protect and maintain the public health, safety, and welfare." This is a totally appropriate criteria to apply in an interest arbitration involving a contract between the District, the MPD, and a Union representing approximately 4,000 police officers.

The Panel is impressed with the responsibilities generally imposed on Police Department's and police officers to protect the public health, safety and welfare of citizens in an urban center in today's society. Perhaps nowhere in this country are the demands more complex or more important than in this nation's capital where concepts of a free society are constantly being challenged....

It is necessary ... to attract, train, and maintain personnel of extraordinary sensitivity and ability in order protect the public health, safety and welfare. A majority of the Panel believes that the Union's compensation package selected in this arbitration will, to the best of the alternatives available to the Panel, achieve these obejectives, and thus satisfy this important criteria. Specifically, a majority of the Panel finds, as previously indicated that the package: (1) satisfies all existing laws and rules and regulations which bear on the items in dispute; (2) is not beyond the District's ability to comply with its proposals; (3) enables the MPD to continue to protect and maintain the public health, safety and welfare; and (4) provides the employees with the unit it covers with fair and reasonable personnel policies that are consistent with the objectives of the merit system. D.C. Code criteria provided in Section 1-618.2(d)(1-4)....

Award

The Panel directs that the Union's last best compensation offers be entered as a package into the Labor Agreement between the Government of the District of Columbia, Employer, the Metropolitan Police Department, Agency, and the Fraternal Order of Police MPD/Labor Committee for the effective period Fiscal

Years 1985-1987 for approval by the appropriate officials in the District of Columbia Government.

[Employer Panel Member Robert Klotz dissented.]

NOTES

1. Probably the most perplexing consideration raised in most interest arbitration proceedings concerns the financial capacity of the public employer in question.

In the 1971-72 compulsory arbitration involving the City of Detroit and the Detroit Police Officers Ass'n, the Panel was confronted with an assertion that the City was "sinking into a financial quagmire." In evaluating the evidence regarding the City's ability to pay, Panel Chairman Gabriel N. Alexander observed:

> The evidence establishes that the City has been unable to extricate itself from a steadily increasing year to year deficit for several years, and that it is powerless to do anything by way of increasing revenues without additional legislation from other governments, state or federal. I am convinced to a depressing certainty that the City cannot survive as an independent unit of government as that concept was understood, say, a decade ago.
>
> DPOA argues, and I agree, that the "financial ability" criterion set forth in Section 9(c) is not controlling. If it were, I might well conclude that there should be no salary increases, or even (considering what has happened on some occasions in private employment) that salaries should be reduced. But this is beside the point. The city acknowledges that some increase is appropriate. The statute commands us to take into account other criteria, in addition to financial ability, and what I have asserted as the ruling is a reflection of the amalgam of all the considerations pro and con which bear upon the ultimate point in issue. As DPOA points out, Detroit cannot buy coal for its generating plants or salt for its streets for less than the "going rate" because it is impoverished. Why then should it be able to "buy" the labor of its policemen for less than the "going rate" because it is impoverished? Of course the answer lies in the statute which defines the "going rate" (in statutory words "just and reasonable") as that rate which shall be fixed by the Panel after taking into account, among other things, the "financial ability of the unit of government to meet those costs."

2. How much financial destitution must be documented by a municipality before it significantly influences an arbitration decision? See *Sioux Cty. & AFSCME, Local 1774*, 68 Lab. Arb. 1258, 1262 (Gruenberg, Arb. 1978), wherein the arbitrator stated: "While both the County and the fact finder made much of [the ability to pay] factor, the arbitrator is of the opinion that changing priorities in the public sector facilitate payment of reasonable wage increases to employees. Unless the fiscal situation of the public employer is verging on bankruptcy, ability to pay is a flexible standard."

3. For some excellent discussions of the problem of ability to pay, see generally Zack, *Ability to Pay in Public Sector Bargaining*, in Proceedings of New York University Twenty-Third Annual Conference on Labor (Christenson ed. 1970); Minami, Clark & Fallon, *Interest Arbitration: Can the Public Sector Afford It? Developing Limitations on the Process*, in Arbitration Issues for the 1980s, Proceedings of the Thirty-Fourth Annual Meeting of the National Academy of Arbitrators 241, 248, 259 (J. Stern & B. Dennis eds. 1982) (three papers); Ross, *The Arbitration of Public Employee Wage Disputes,* 23 Indus. & Lab. Rel. Rev. 3 (1969); Block, *Criteria in Public Sector Interest Disputes,* in Arbitration and the Public Interest, Proceedings of the Twenty-Fourth Annual Meeting of the National Academy of Arbitrators 171 (G. Somers ed. 1971). See also Dell 'Omo, *Wage Disputes in Interest Arbitration: Arbitrators Weigh the Criteria,* 44 Arb. J. 4 (June 1989).

4. On the question of the competence of arbitrators to deal with issues arising pursuant to a government employer's claim of "inability to pay," see Smith, *Comment,* in Arbitration and the Public Interest, Proceedings of the Twenty-Fourth Annual Meeting of the National Academy of Arbitrators 180, 184-87 (G. Somers ed. 1971). Professor Smith argues that "inability to pay" is not a difficult issue in a case where the employer is "utterly without financial resources to fund *any* increase in labor costs"; however, he makes the following additional observations with respect to the problem:

> [T]hese simplistic remarks dodge a whole series of problems for the neutral ranging from the factual to the basic questions of principle. I suggest that among the very serious questions are several that are not within the realm of expertise of labor dispute arbitrators on the basis solely of their private sector experience. The initial question is in a sense factual only. It is: What is the public body's actual fiscal position in terms of its ability to absorb *any* increased operating costs? Any sound analysis of this matter often requires an exhaustive and knowledgeable inquiry into budget allocations, revenue sources, transferability of appropriations, borrowing capability, and the like. The second question is whether, if the public body's ability to absorb increased operating costs is limited (which is probably the typical situation), the neutral should attempt to determine the gross amount of increased labor costs, if any, which the public body can finance. This in itself may turn out to be a fairly complicated problem. But, assuming this gross amount can be determined, the next and crucial question is whether the neutral should assume that this fund is all that can be provided, by way of increases, for any and all groups of employees — given the repercussionary effects of an increase awarded to the group before him — or should act on the basis that this fund can be enlarged by the public body by reductions in force or rearrangements of priorities. Obviously related is the question whether the neutral should attempt to determine the impact his award will have in terms of affecting the economic demands of other groups of employees and their ultimate settlement. Bear in mind, of course, that it is assumed that these other groups of employees, and their bargaining representatives, if any, are not parties to his proceeding or represented in it.

Now I submit that inquiries of these kinds pose problems which are so serious and difficult as to make the criterion ability to pay or, more realistically, alleged inability to pay, one which, if deemed to be relevant or required by law to be taken into consideration, is likely to be taken less seriously than others, such as comparison data. One of Howard Block's observations is that he "is inclined to agree with those who insist that when a neutral rules out inability to pay as a valid defense, he should also assume some responsibility for finding the funds to implement his award," although he also adds, apparently as a proviso, "if the parties have authorized him to do so." I interpret this remark as implying that Howard not only regards ability to pay as a proper criterion for consideration, where advanced by a party, but further as stating that the neutral does, indeed, have the full responsibility, somehow, of dealing with the series of problems which, I have suggested, then must be addressed. But I doubt very much that he can or should attempt any assignment of that magnitude except perhaps in a situation where all parties concerned, including other unions, have deliberately vested in him what would be tantamount to the full authority of the public body with respect to its budget, allocations, and priorities.

What, then, is the likely result where ability to pay is accepted by the neutral, or by law forced upon him, as a factor to be taken into account? Only a searching analysis of arbitral decisions would provide anything like an accurate answer. I have knowledge of some, however, including several in which I have participated. My impression is that a number of arbitrators, absent any statutory compulsion to take fiscal matters into account, tend to regard them as substantially irrelevant. But my impression, further, is that where, as under the Michigan police and firefighter compulsory arbitration law, this is one of the several factors specified for consideration as applicable, there has been a more or less valiant effort to analyze the public body's fiscal position, and, upon finding a very tight situation, to make an award on economic issues which would be somewhat less, or stated as being somewhat less, than otherwise would have been considered justified, but yet not to let the fiscal factor predominate.

5. Regarding the impact of appropriations act and cap law limitations on the interest arbitration process, compare *Association of Pa. State College Faculties v. State,* 436 A.2d 1386, 1981-83 PBC ¶ 37,402 (Pa. 1981) (arbitral authority not restricted since only applicable to *negotiated* increases), with *City of Atlantic City v. Laezza,* 403 A.2d 465, 1979-80 PBC ¶ 36,596 (N.J. 1979) (arbitrator must consider impact of cap law upon employer's financial capacity).

5. JUDICIAL REVIEW

CASO v. COFFEY

41 N.Y.2d 153, 359 N.E.2d 683 (1976)

FUCHSBERG, JUDGE. In these two cases we confront directly the question of the manner and scope of judicial review of awards made by public arbitration panels acting pursuant to subdivision 4 of section 209 of the Civil Service Law in their determination of disputes arising from failures of local governments and their employees to reach collective bargaining agreements.

The County of Nassau and its police and the City of Albany and its firefighters, after exhausting all intermediate steps in negotiating new contracts, submitted their controversies to binding, compulsory arbitration pursuant to the mandate of the Taylor Law (Civil Service Law, § 209, subd. 4). Each arbitration panel reached a determination and made an award which reflected in part the requests of the government and in part those of the employees.

In the first case, the Appellate Division dismissed an article 78 proceeding [Pertaining to review of administrative action. Eds.] (with a request for relief in the alternative under article 75) brought by Ralph Caso, the County Executive of Nassau County, against the Nassau County Public Relations Board to review and annul a panel's award of a wage increase to the police and granted the cross motion of the board to confirm the award, holding that article 78 is the proper procedural vehicle for its review and that on such review the appropriate standard is whether the award is supported by substantial evidence (CPLR 7803, subd. 4). The county had joined the collective bargaining agent for the police, Nassau County Patrolmen's Benevolent Association, as a respondent.

In the second case, a proceeding pursuant to CPLR article 75 (CPLR 7510) [Pertaining to review of arbitration awards. Eds.] brought by the Albany Permanent Professional Firefighters Association to confirm a panel's award was consolidated by the Appellate Division with an article 78 proceeding brought by the city against both the Albany Public Employment Relations Board (PERB) and the members of the arbitration panel to annul that award. The firefighters were intervenors in the latter proceeding. The Appellate Division unanimously affirmed judgments of the Supreme Court which confirmed the award in the firefighters' proceeding and dismissed the city's article 78 proceeding, holding that article 75 was the proper procedural vehicle, but "broadened in scope" by our decision in *Mount St. Mary's Hosp. v. Catherwood,* 26 N.Y.2d 493, 260 N.E.2d 508 to make applicable on review the test as to whether the determination "was arbitrary or capricious". (51 A.D.2d 386, 390, 381 N.Y.S.2d 699, 702.)

Preliminarily, we note that subdivision 4 of section 209 of the Taylor Law, applicable when local governments and their police or firefighters cannot reach agreement on a new contract, does not specify either the procedure or the standard by which the arbitrations it mandates are to be tested. Indeed, it does not expressly provide for any review. But such legislative silence does not mean that the actions of the arbitrators are therefore unreviewable (see *Matter of Guardian Life Ins. Co. v. Bohlinger,* 308 N.Y. 174, 183, 124 N.E.2d 110, 113). At least since our decision in *Mount St. Mary's Hosp. v. Catherwood (supra),* a case that arose under a different statute, it has been clear that, in New York, when arbitration has been made compulsory rather than consensual, availability of review sufficient to meet due process standards is required (*Mount St. Mary's Hosp. v. Catherwood, supra,* 26 N.Y.2d pp. 501, 508, 260 N.E.2d pp. 511, 516).

We therefore focus first on the proper procedural path for review of compulsory Taylor Law arbitrations, a question which, though it has previously invited judicial concern (see *City of Amsterdam v. Helsby,* 37 N.Y.2d 19, 38-41, 332 N.E.2d 290, 300-302; *Matter of Buffalo Police Benevolent Ass'n v. City of Buffalo,* 81 Misc. 2d 172, 364 N.Y.S.2d 362), is met head on by us for the first time today. We now decide that the appropriate vehicle for review is article 75.

A number of considerations dictate that view. Section 209, in denominating "arbitration" as the final step in resolving these disputes, makes unqualified use of that word; article 75 is our only statutory vehicle for the enforcement of arbitration. It is structured to provide the procedural and practical guidance most useful to both courts and parties in obtaining review in an orderly fashion (see, e.g., CPLR 7511). Perhaps most importantly, it is not the PERB or the arbitration panel but the local governments and their employees who are the real parties in interest; it is under article 75 procedure, and not under that provided by article 78, that both parties in interest will be brought face to face with one another as advocates of their respective positions. In contrast, the PERB, which itself possesses no power to review the arbitration award, after having completed its role in facilitating the mediational and negotiational steps the statute requires of the parties preceding arbitration (Civil Service Law, § 209, subd. 4, pars. [a], [b]), and after setting up the arbitration itself (§ 209, subd. 4, par. [c], cls. [i], [ii]), plays no part in the actual conduct or decision-making of the arbitration panel and, as a consequence, will not be possessed of the knowledge relevant to facilitate review. There is no logical reason to call upon the PERB to defend a decision which, for all that appears, may be different from the one it would itself have reached.

For its part, the arbitration panel, as pointed out in the Albany case by Mr. Justice Larkin at the Appellate Division, Third Department, is an ad hoc body composed of three citizens (§ 209, subd. 4, par. [c], cl. [ii]); by the time of review, it will already have made its views available to the court in its decision and on the record in the case. It is called into existence only to decide the dispute before it. It represents neither of the parties. Moreover, a requirement that those who serve on such panels be prepared to defend their awards in court, perhaps even at their own expense, could only work to discourage qualified and competent persons from serving as arbitrators and, perhaps, even to frustrate the flexible design of the arbitral process itself.

We turn next to the question of whether the arbitration awards made under subdivision 4 of section 209 are to be treated as quasi-judicial or as quasi-legislative for purposes of review.

In that connection, we note first that, though the statute itself pointedly directs the attention of the panel to such vital factors as the comparability of the benefits received by the employees before it with those of similar employees in public and private employment in comparable communities, the financial ability of the public employer to pay, and the public interest (§ 209, subd. 4, par. [c], cl. [v], subcls. a-d), it mandates that they be taken into "consideration" only "so far as it deems them applicable" (§ 209, subd. 4, par. [c], cl. [v]). Similarly, the precatory language that the "panel shall make a just and reasonable determination of the matters in dispute", an injunction expressly intended for the panel and not reviewing courts, bespeaks a like elasticity. (§ 209, subd. 4, par. [c], cl. [v].) The latitude with which these phrases are to be applied is suggested also by the fact that the essential function of these compulsory arbitration panels is to "write collective bargaining agreements for the parties" (*Mount St. Mary's Hosp. v. Catherwood,* 26 N.Y.2d 493, 503, 260 N.E.2d 508, 513, *supra*). It follows that such awards, on judicial review, are to be measured according to whether they are rational or arbitrary and capricious in accordance with the principles articulated in *Mount St. Mary's Hosp. v. Catherwood (supra)* (see CPLR 7803, subd. 3, for parallel language).

Of course, the presence of evidence pertaining to any or all of the specific criteria which are to be "considered" is a factor to be taken into account when determining whether the award itself is founded on a rational basis (see *Matter of Pell v. Board of Educ.,* 34 N.Y.2d 222, 313 N.E.2d 321; *Matter of Graziani v. Rohan,* 10 A.D.2d 154, 198 N.Y.S.2d 383, aff'd, 8 N.Y.2d 967, 169 N.E.2d 8). An award may be found on review to be rational if any basis for such a conclusion is apparent to the court (*Matter of Pell v. Board of Educ., supra;* see *Matter of Campo Corp. v. Feinberg,* 279 App. Div. 302, 110 N.Y.S.2d 250, aff'd, 303 N.Y. 995, 106 N.E.2d 70). And it need only appear from the decision of the arbitrators that the criteria specified in the statute were "considered" in good faith and that the resulting award has a "plausible basis" (*Matter of Caruci v. Dulan,* 41 Misc.2d 859, 862, 246 N.Y.S.2d 727, 730, *rev'd on other grounds,* 24 A.D.2d 529, 261 N.Y.S.2d 677).Though the presence of evidence which could have met a substantial evidence test may serve to meet the test of rationality, the substantial evidence test as such is not the criterion here (*Mount St. Mary's Hosp. v. Catherwood, supra,* 26 N.Y.2d 493, p. 508, 260 N.E.2d p. 516).

In point of fact, in each of the cases before us, the records and the opinions of the arbitrators indicate that the panels gave careful consideration to the criteria enumerated by subdivision 4 of section 209 and were alert to the ravages which rising inflation and economic stress are now visiting on local governments and their employees alike. In the Albany case, voluminous and detailed exhibits and its Mayor's vigorous amplification of the city's written and detailed presentation of its tax resource limitations and over-all costs were presented; in juxtaposition the firefighters presented their own economic and comparative scale proof in great detail. The panel there, obviously selective in its award, while allowing a wage increase equal to that earlier recommended by the impartial fact finder, rejected the firefighters' economic benefit demands relating, among other things, to pension, longevity, vacation, overtime, personal leave and release time. In the *Caso* case, Mr. Justice Hopkins, writing for the Appellate Division, Second Department, went so far as to describe the extended evidence presented there as "monumental" and specifically found that "serious and close attention was devoted to all of the matters mandated for consideration by the statute". (53 A.D.2d 373, 379, 385 N.Y.S.2d 593, 597.)

Nevertheless, we comment on two subsidiary issues raised by the parties. First is the county's contention, in the *Caso* case, that the burden of proof to show that it has the ability to pay the award should be placed upon the employees under a kind of presumption that the county's best offer during bargaining prior to arbitration represented its good faith statement of the most it could afford. But our statutes and case law indicate plainly that the burden to show invalidity of any arbitral award is upon the party who brings a proceeding to set it aside (see *Korein v. Rabin,* 29 A.D.2d 351, 287 N.Y.S.2d 975; *Matter of Brill [Muller Bros.],* 40 Misc. 2d 683, 243 N.Y.2d 905, *rev'd on other grounds,* 17 A.D.2d 804, 232 N.Y.2d 806, *aff'd,* 13 N.Y.2d 776, 192 N.E.2d 34, *cert. denied,* 376 U.S. 927; see, generally, 16 Williston, Contracts [3d ed.], § 1923A, p. 650) and, for that matter, in a proceeding brought to review a quasi-legislative determination made by an agency, the burden again is on the party who challenges to show that the determination lacks rational basis (see *Matter of Pell v. Board of Educ.,* 34 N.Y.2d 222, 313 N.E.2d 321, *supra; Matter of Mallen v. Morton,* 199 Misc. 805, 99 N.Y.S.2d 521; 1 N.Y. Jur., Administrative Law, § 182, and cases cited therein).

The second subsidiary issue was raised by the City of Albany. It contends that, as no "record" of the proceedings before the arbitration panel was made, proper review cannot be had here. It is undisputed that neither party in the Albany case made advance written request for a reporter for the purpose of making a verbatim transcript (see PERB's rules, 4 NYCRR 205.7[d]), not even when the chairman of the panel made particular inquiry of both sides at the outset of the hearings.

Finally, the fact that the *Caso* proceeding was brought solely under article 78 and was adjudicated on review by the Appellate Division under the substantial evidence test is no bar to our upholding that court's confirmation of the arbitral award in this instance. Although in a proceeding brought in form under article

78 the governmental or administrative agency rather than the employees or their collective bargaining agent would be expected to be the respondent, here the collective bargaining agent was joined and has submitted a brief on this appeal in which it is made clear that confirmation is exactly what the employees seek; thus, they are not prejudiced by an affirmance. Moreover, the opinion in the Appellate Division, in detailing its reasons for confirming the award, more than adequately shows that the panel had a rational basis for the result it reached.

Accordingly, the determination of the Appellate Division in each case should be affirmed.

NOTES

1. It is relatively difficult for public employers to successfully challenge terms contained in interest arbitration awards. See, e.g., *Guthrie v. Borough of Wilkinsburg,* 499 A.2d 570, 1984-86 PBC ¶ 34,577 (Pa. 1985) (award of additional compensation to police officers who perform "detective" work did not impermissibly create separate rank for such police officers in violation of borough ordinance). See also *Boulder City v. Teamsters Local 14,* 694 P.2d 498, 121 L.R.R.M. 2462 (Nev. 1985). But see *Transit Union Local 589 v. MBTA,* 467 N.E.2d 87, 120 L.R.R.M. 3136 (Mass. 1984), wherein the court invalidated that portion of an interest arbitration award which impermissibly restricted the public employer's inherent managerial authority to hire and schedule part-time personnel.

2. In *City of Buffalo v. Rinaldo,* 41 N.Y.2d 764, 364 N.E.2d 817 (1977), the New York Court of Appeals recognized that while the financial ability of the public employer to pay the increases requested is one of the relevant criteria for consideration by the arbitrator, it is not necessarily the dispositive factor. So long as there is support for the award based upon the statutorily prescribed criteria, it is entitled to enforcement. But cf. *Nebraska City Educ. Ass'n v. School Dist.,* 267 N.W.2d 530, 98 L.R.R.M. 3228 (Neb. 1978), wherein the court found that the employer's ability to finance the requested wage increases was not a relevant factor, since it was not one of the criteria specified in the statute to guide the court of industrial relations when it resolved impasse disputes.

The Iowa Supreme Court has indicated that since interest arbitration proceedings are conducted pursuant to authority delegated through the PERB, reviewing courts should use the same standards when examining challenged arbitral orders as they would to evaluate the propriety of determinations made by the PERB itself. See *Maquoketa Valley Community Sch. Dist. v. Education Ass'n,* 279 N.W.2d 510, 102 L.R.R.M. 2056 (1979).

3. Where the applicable interest arbitration statute mandates the arbitral consideration of certain specified factors, the failure to consider all of the relevant criteria may render the resulting award unenforceable. See, e.g., *City of Detroit v. Detroit Police Officers Ass'n,* 294 N.W.2d 68, 1979-80 PBC ¶ 36,959 (Mich. 1980), *appeal dismissed,* 450 U.S. 903 (1981).

4. Where an interest arbitration award directs a public employer to increase the insurance premiums for certain workers in violation of a state statute requiring equal insurance premiums for all municipal employees, *Watertown Firefighters, Local 1347 v. Town of Watertown,* 383 N.E.2d 494, 100 L.R.R.M. 2375 (Mass. 1978), or orders a city to provide overtime compensation to police officers who work hours in excess of a limit statutorily prescribed for such employees regardless of their compensation level, *Conley v. Joyce,* 393 A.2d 654,

100 L.R.R.M. 2471 (Pa. 1978), the award will not be enforced. Cf. *Town of Tiverton v. Police Lodge 23*, 372 A.2d 1273, 95 L.R.R.M. 2993 (R.I. 1977) (voiding award directing implementation of pension plan following the one-year period covered by award).

5. In *Superintending Sch. Comm. v. Winslow Educ. Ass'n*, 363 A.2d 229, 93 L.R.R.M. 2398 (Me. 1976), the court held that a school committee could not be compelled through interest arbitration to broaden the teachers' rights clause of a contract by imposing a "just cause" requirement on the employer's disciplinary actions. Deciding whether a matter is subject to interest arbitration involves a two-step inquiry: (1) is the matter within the statutorily-defined scope of bargaining, and, if so, (2) is it limited by any other existing statutory enactments. The court focused on the conflict between interest arbitration and other laws governing the rights and duties of school committees. Since pre-existing education laws provided school committees with exclusive authority over dismissals and the non-renewal of teacher contracts, the court concluded, without deciding whether the issue would otherwise constitute a mandatory bargaining subject, that this power could not be diminished by an interest arbitration award. Compare *Boston Sch. Comm. v. Teachers Local 66*, 363 N.E.2d 485, 95 L.R.R.M. 2855 (Mass. 1977), wherein the court held that where no statutory provision expressly or impliedly restricted the scope of interest arbitration and the parties had contractually agreed to submit bargaining impasses to binding arbitration, permissive as well as mandatory topics may be presented for arbitral resolution. Would the latter approach allow a party to obtain through interest arbitration a benefit or privilege that it could not insist upon at the bargaining table? See also *Patterson Police Local 1 v. City of Patterson*, 432 A.2d 847, 112 L.R.R.M. 2205 (N.J. 1981); *AFSCME, Local 1277 v. City of Center Line*, 1981-83 PBC ¶ 37,656 (Mich. 1982).

6. In *Local 66, Boston Teachers Union v. School Comm.*, 363 N.E.2d 492, 95 L.R.R.M. 3126 (Mass. 1977), the court ruled that where an employer failed to comply with the terms of a bargaining agreement obtained through an interest arbitration award that had been judicially enforced, the proper recourse was through the contractual grievance-arbitration procedure and not through a civil contempt proceeding, since the judicial enforcement of the interest arbitration award could not be viewed as having incorporated the provisions of the sustained agreement into the injunctive order of the enforcing court.

The Oregon Supreme Court has ruled that the State Employment Relations Board has primary jurisdiction over claims arising from noncompliance with wage determinations contained in interest arbitration awards. Courts should thus hold wage suits in abeyance until the ERB has considered the matter. See *Tracy v. Lane Cty.*, 305 Or. 378, 1986-88 PBC ¶ 35,089 (1988).

7. *Chirico v. Board of Supvrs.*, 1984-86 PBC ¶ 34,216 (Pa. 1984), recognized that even where a losing party has not filed a timely appeal from an interest arbitration award, it may still challenge the legality of a particular term in a subsequent enforcement action prosecuted by the prevailing party, to insure that a court will not be required to direct the performance of an unlawful act.

8. Individual employees who challenge particular parts of interest arbitration determinations will rarely prevail. See, e.g., *Carofano v. City of Bridgeport*, 495 A.2d 1011, 1984-86 PBC ¶ 34,518 (Conn. 1985) (sustaining power of interest arbitrator to impose residency requirement for police officers). But see *In re Appeal of Police Lodge 27*, 526 A.2d 315, 127 L.R.R.M. 2627 (Pa. 1987) (voiding interest arbitration award which eliminated post-retirement hospital and

medical benefits, since it impermissibly reduced retirement benefits of former and present employees).

   9. See generally Anderson & Krause, *Interest Arbitration: The Alternative to the Strike,* 56 Fordham L. Rev. 153 (1987); Craver, *The Judicial Enforcement of Public Sector Interest Arbitration,* 21 B.C.L. Rev. 557, 568-77 (1980); Grodin, *Judicial Response to Public-Sector Arbitration,* in Public Sector Arbitration 241-250 (B. Aaron, J. Grodin & J. Stern eds. 1979).

Chapter 8

ENFORCEMENT OF THE COLLECTIVE BARGAINING AGREEMENT

A. PRIVATE SECTOR CONCEPTS CONCERNING THE LEGAL STATUS OF THE COLLECTIVE AGREEMENT

The Legal Status of the Collective Agreement*

Early common-law decisions advanced at least three separate theories to explain the legal nature of the collective agreement:

1. The labor agreement establishes local customs or usages, which are then incorporated into the individual employee's contract of hire. This seems to have been the orthodox view of the American courts, at least prior to the era of the labor relations acts. See Rice, *Collective Labor Agreements in American Law*, 44 Harv. L. Rev. 572, 582 (1931). For a historical overview, see Symposium, *Origins of the Union Contract*, 33 Lab. L.J. 512 (1982). Under the original form of this theory, the collective agreement itself was not regarded as a contract. It had legal effect only as its terms were absorbed into individual employment contracts. Somewhat similar is the traditional English concept that collective agreements are merely "gentlemen's agreements" or moral obligations not enforceable by the courts. *Young v. Canadian N. Ry.*, [1931] A.C. 83 (P.C.); K. Wedderburn, The Worker and the Law 105-11 (1965). Some American scholars also have voiced an occasional plea that court litigation over collective agreements should be rejected as detrimental to the parties' continuing relationship. See Shulman, *Reason, Contract, and Law in Labor Relations*, 68 Harv. L. Rev. 999 (1955). Nevertheless, judicial enforcement at the behest of either employers or unions became generally accepted in this country well before the passage of the LMRA in 1947 and was confirmed by that Act.

2. The collective agreement is a contract that is negotiated by the union as the agent for the employees, who become the principals on the agreement. *Barnes & Co. v. Berry*, 169 F. 225 (6th Cir. 1909); *Maisel v. Sigman*, 123 Misc. 714, 205 N.Y.S. 807 (N.Y. Sup. Ct. 1924). This so-called agency theory was adopted by a few courts that could not rationalize the enforceability of an instrument executed by an unincorporated association lacking juristic personality. Suits between individual employees and employers were maintainable, however, on the theory the union had merely served as the employees' agent in negotiations.

3. The collective agreement is a third-party beneficiary contract, with the employer and union the mutual promisors and promisees, and with the employees the beneficiaries. *Marranzano v. Riggs Nat'l Bank*, 184 F.2d 349 (D.C. Cir. 1950); *Yazoo & M.V.R.R. v. Sideboard*, 161 Miss. 4, 133 So. 669 (1931); *H. Blum & Co. v. Landau*, 23 Ohio App. 426, 155 N.E. 154 (1926). Despite argu-

---

*From L. Merrifield, T. St. Antoine & C. Craver, Labor Relations Law; Cases and Materials (8th ed. 1989).

able shortcomings (is the employer to be left without recourse against the employee beneficiary, who has made no promises?), the third-party beneficiary theory became rather widely accepted as the best explanation of the collective agreement in terms of traditional common-law concepts. See C. Gregory & H. Katz, Labor and the Law 481 (3d ed. 1979).

Today, collective bargaining agreements in industries affecting commerce are enforced as a matter of federal law under § 301 of the LMRA. This means that the Supreme Court's views on the nature of the labor contract are now of primary concern. Two characteristics of the Court's thinking stand out. First, the Court is eclectic in its approach to common-law doctrines; it refuses to confine itself to any single theory, but draws upon whatever elements may be helpful in a variety of theories. Second, the Court has emphasized what may be described as the "constitutional" or "governmental" quality of the labor agreement. Thus, the collective agreement has been described as "not an ordinary contract" but rather a "generalized code" for "a system of industrial self-government." See *John Wiley & Sons v. Livingston,* 376 U.S. 543, 550 (1964); *United Steelworkers v. Warrior & Gulf Nav. Co.,* 363 U.S. 574, 578-80 (1960).

The Supreme Court's eclectic approach to the nature of the labor contract is reflected in the following well-known comments by Justice Jackson in *J.I. Case Co. v. NLRB,* 321 U.S. 332, 334-35 (1944):

> Collective bargaining between employer and the representatives of a unit, usually a union, results in an accord as to terms which will govern hiring and work and pay in that unit. The result is not, however, a contract of employment except in rare cases; no one has a job by reason of it and no obligation to any individual ordinarily comes into existence from it alone. The negotiations between union and management result in what often has been called a trade agreement, rather than in a contract of employment. Without pushing the analogy too far, the agreement may be likened to the tariffs established by a carrier, to standard provisions prescribed by supervising authorities for insurance policies, or to utility schedules of rates and rules for service, which do not of themselves establish any relationships but which do govern the terms of the shipper or insurer or customer relationship whenever and with whomever it may be established....
>
> [H]owever engaged, an employee becomes entitled by virtue of the Labor Relations Act somewhat as a third party beneficiary to all benefits of the collective trade agreement, even if on his own he would yield to less favorable terms. The individual hiring contract is subsidiary to the terms of the trade agreement and may not waive any of its benefits, any more than a shipper can contract away the benefit of filed tariffs, the insurer the benefit of standard provisions, or the utility customer the benefit of legally established rates.

NOTES

1. Much has been written on the legal nature of the collective agreement, with most commentators noting its unique characteristics and the difficulties and dangers of adopting traditional doctrines developed in other fields of contract law. See Burstein, *Enforcement of Collective Agreements by the Courts,* in N.Y.U. Sixth Annual Conference on Labor 31 (1953); Chamberlain, *Collective Bargaining and the Concept of Contract,* 48 Colum. L. Rev. 829 (1948); Cox, *Rights Under a Labor Agreement,* 69 Harv. L. Rev. 601 (1956); Cox, *The Legal*

Nature of Collective Bargaining Agreements, 57 Mich. L. Rev. 1 (1958); Feller, *A General Theory of the Collective Bargaining Agreement,* 61 Calif. L. Rev. 663 (1973); Gregory, *The Law of the Collective Agreement,* 57 Mich. L. Rev. 635 (1959); Gregory, *The Collective Bargaining Agreement: Its Nature and Scope,* 1949 Wash. U.L.Q. 3; Rice, *Collective Labor Agreements in American Law,* 44 Harv. L. Rev. 572 (1931); Shulman, *Reason, Contract, and Law in Labor Relations,* 68 Harv. L. Rev. 999 (1955); Warns, *The Nature of the Collective Bargaining Agreement,* 3 U. Miami L.Q. 235 (1949); Witmer, *Collective Labor Agreements in the Courts,* 48 Yale L.J. 195 (1938).

2. Although private sector employers certainly possess the innate authority to enter into collective bargaining agreements, it has not always been clear whether governmental entities are empowered to execute collective contracts in the absence of specific labor relations statutes. Most courts which confronted this question found that public employers had the inherent right to negotiate such agreements. See, e.g., *Local 2238, AFSCME v. Stratton,* 769 P.2d 76, 1988-90 PBC ¶ 35,254 (N.M. 1989); *Dayton Teachers Ass'n v. Board of Educ.,* 41 Ohio St. 2d 127, 323 N.E.2d 714 (1975); *Local 598, AFSCME v. City of Huntington,* 1984-86 PBC ¶ 34,346 (W.Va. 1984). In *Commonwealth v. County Bd.,* 217 Va. 558, 232 S.E.2d 30 (1977), however, the Virginia Supreme Court reached a contrary conclusion. It held that agreements negotiated by school districts with teacher unions were invalid, since such districts possessed no statutory authority to enter into collective contracts. The vast majority of states have rendered this issue moot through the enactment of public sector bargaining laws.

B. THE ENFORCEMENT OF THE COLLECTIVE AGREEMENT THROUGH GRIEVANCE-ARBITRATION PROCEDURES

PICKETS AT CITY HALL: REPORT AND RECOMMENDATIONS OF THE TWENTIETH CENTURY FUND TASK FORCE ON LABOR DISPUTES IN PUBLIC EMPLOYMENT 17-18 (1970)*

In any agreement negotiated, the public employer and the union should be strongly encouraged to provide a system for the presentation and disposition of grievances as they may be alleged by employees. One of the most positive values to be found in a union-employer relationship is that it establishes a formal process through which complaints that might otherwise be unknown and unattended by management are brought into the light.

No matter how detailed the agreement between union and management may be, it cannot take into account all of the problems that will arise during its term. Nor can it anticipate what differences there may be over interpreting provisions in the agreement and their application. Hence the grievance procedure is a safety valve. Rather than let a difference that arises while the agreement is in force develop into a deadlock which might disrupt the work place or lead to a strike, formal grievance machinery should be established. As it functions, the individual employee has assurance that he will not suffer from management arbitrariness while the union has assurance that it will be heard and management has assurance that employee claims will not be supported by coercive pressures.

The lack of formal grievance machinery has led to public employee disputes, as employees have no alternative method of pressing a claim against unfair treatment, real or imagined. Established grievance procedures, leading ultimately to arbitration, have proved essential in achieving peaceful resolution of disputes in the private sector. Such procedures are equally essential for public employment.

Giving an outsider (the arbitrator) power to render a binding decision on a grievance involving internal organizational or operational matters may appear to be a momentous step for the responsible administrator of a government agency. His protection is that despite any ruling by an arbitrator, he cannot be required to do something beyond his legal authority or contrary to law. Against this hazard he will be protected by the courts. If his interpretation or application of the terms of an agreement seem wrong to his employees, with no opportunity to appeal they cannot escape a frustration that can seriously damage employee relations.

Unless specifically proscribed by law from agreeing to binding arbitration — and where such laws exist they should be repealed — a government agency should accept the arbitration of grievance matters in its own protection against unresolved and potentially explosive disputes. In jurisdictions where binding arbitration remains impermissible, the arbitrator's award should be taken as advisory and, if necessary, referred for implementation to the body or official with authority to order it.

1. THE GRIEVANCE PROCEDURE

One of the most significant accomplishments of labor law in the private sector has been the development of a system of industrial jurisprudence, a system whereby the parties themselves establish the machinery for the resolution of day-to-day disputes over the interpretation and application of the collective bargaining agreement. Almost all of the these disputes are settled by means of this machinery; few disputes get as far even as the last step in the process, which is usually some form of arbitration.

The essence of a grievance procedure is to provide a means by which an employee, without jeopardizing his job, can express a complaint about his work or working conditions and obtain a fair hearing through progressively higher levels of management. Under collective bargaining, four important and related features have been added to this concept. First, the collective bargaining contract, while it drastically limits the area of legitimate complaints by establishing the basic conditions of employment and rules for day-to-day administration deemed to be fair by mutual agreement, at the same time may create a source of grievances and disagreements through ambiguities of language and omissions, as do changing circumstances and violations. Second, the union is recognized and accepted as the spokesman for the aggrieved worker, and an inability to agree on a resolution of the issue becomes a dispute between union and management. Third, because an unresolved grievance becomes a union-management dispute, a way ultimately must be found to reach settlements short of a strike or lockout or substitutes for such actions. Final and binding arbitration is the principal means to this end. Fourth, the process of adjusting grievances and grievance disputes is itself defined in the agreement, and, along with other aspects of collective bargaining, tends to become increasingly formal.

U.S. Bureau of Labor Statistics Bull. No. 1425-1, Major Collective Bargaining Agreements: Grievance Procedures 1 (1964).

Private sector grievance procedures typically consist of a series of steps, with the employee-grievant and the management seeking to resolve the dispute at successively higher levels. The employee normally takes his grievance first to his foreman or to his union steward. If the union steward is consulted first, he will present the grievance on behalf of the employee to the foreman. Normally, the employee is entitled to union representation at each step. If no resolution is achieved, the matter may be taken to a higher company official, often the foreman's immediate superior; this is the second step. If no solution is found here, the matter may then go to a still higher company official or to a hearing before a union shop committee and certain company officials who have been designated to meet regularly with this committee. If the grievance is denied at this level, but the union continues to deem it meritorious, it may go to a conference of regional union officials and high company officers. Failure to settle the grievance at this step may result in a union demand that the matter be arbitrated. The number of steps in the procedure will of course vary from contract to contract, and the nature of the proceedings at each step may differ, but the pattern is fairly well established in the private sector.

Public sector grievance procedures in the past have generally not followed the private sector pattern. There are two major reasons for this. First, the sovereignty doctrine led many public employers to conclude that they were powerless to negotiate any kind of procedure which would result in the sharing of decision-making authority or its transfer to any third party. Second, a negotiated grievance procedure was thought to be superfluous; often, a grievance procedure already existed in the form of a civil service appeals system. See Ullman & Begin, *The Structure and Scope of Appeals Procedures for Public Employees,* 23 Indus. & Lab. Rel. Rev. 323 (1970).

There are major differences, however, between civil service appeals procedures in the public sector and a private sector model grievance procedure. See Amundson, *Negotiated Grievance Procedures in California Public Employment: Controversy and Confusion,* 6 Cal. Pub. Empl. Rel. 2 (August 1970). A civil service procedure is normally established unilaterally by the public employer or through the legislative process, though employee organizations are generally consulted. In contrast, a negotiated grievance procedure is by definition established bilaterally through collective bargaining; it exists by virtue of the effort and approval of both parties. Processing a grievance is usually an individual matter in a civil service procedure, though the individual is generally allowed union representation at some stage of the proceedings; in a negotiated procedure, however, it is a union matter, the union taking up the cudgel for the employee and determining how far and how fast to process the grievance dispute. A civil service procedure is an "appeals" procedure; the employee is seen as appealing to higher authority from the decision of a public official. A negotiated grievance procedure, however, is less an appeal than a continuation of the collective bargaining process, a method by which the rights and responsibilities of the parties are continually clarified in the developing "common law of the shop."

Further distinctions between civil service appeal procedures and grievance procedures are detailed in Massey, *Employee Grievance Procedures,* in Developments in Public Employee Relations 64-65 (1965):

> [A] civil service commission is not like an arbitrator. An arbitrator, hopefully at least, is a disinterested party. On the other hand, when a commission is hearing an appeal, it is passing on the application by an operating agency of regulations issued by the commission pursuant to law. It is enforcing its own regulations.
>
> Also, a civil service commission is not an integral part of management, as is the personnel department of a private business. While many commissions have taken a positive role in personnel administration and have become to a degree an arm of management, they are not in a position to be an integral part of management. They have a legal existence independent of management. Moreover, historically, they were established as the protector of job applicants and employees against political favoritism by management, and they are now regarded by employees as the protector of a number of employee rights. Incidentally, some unions of government employees seem to consider it an advantage to apply more-or-less continuous pressure on the commissions. Of course, some other organizations with a considerable population of government employees as members — veterans' organizations, for example — do the same. Thus, civil service commissioners are likely to have a dual loyalty — to management, on the one hand, and to employees, on the other. This arrangement has endured for many years and may have its advantages. It is, however, a different arrangement than is found in private business.

Conceptually, there is also a great difference in the subject matter covered by the two types of procedures. A grievance procedure, as a matter of contract, may cover such subjects as wages, fringe benefits, working conditions, and other matters not normally covered by civil service appeals procedures. The scope of a civil service appeals procedure, on the other hand, depends on the applicable statute or city ordinance; typically, civil service laws deal almost exclusively with the manner of appointment, promotions, discharges and changes of status of employees. Civil service regulations in these areas have historically been considered non-negotiable.

As a practical matter, however, there is often a considerable overlap of grievance and appeals procedures. Indeed, employees sometimes may have a choice of procedures, or the procedure may be mandated by the type of incident that has occurred. An "adverse action," for example — an official reprimand, suspension or discharge — may require an appeal to the civil service commission or supervisory political body rather than a grievance within the management structure.

In the last few years there has been increasing reliance on the private sector model in the formulation of public sector grievance procedures. See Begin, *The Private Grievance Model in the Public Sector,* 10 Indus. Rel. 21 (1971); Lewin, *Collective Bargaining Impacts on Personnel Administration in the American Public Sector,* 27 Lab. L.J. 426 (1976). In part, this is due to the trend away from viewing the doctrine of sovereignty as a complete bar to the adoption and enforcement of public sector collective bargaining agreements concerning grievance procedures, even those that culminate in binding arbitration. See, e.g., *Tremblay v. Berlin Police Union*, 108 N.H. 416, 237 A.2d 668 (1968); *Board of Educ. v. Associated Teachers*, 30 N.Y.2d 122, 282 N.E.2d 109 (1972). See also Note, *Legality and Propriety of Agreements to Arbitrate Major and Minor Disputes in Public Employment*, 54 Cornell L. Rev. 129 (1968). In part, too, it is due to the recognition that negotiated grievance procedures are capable of coexisting with or supplanting civil service appeals procedures. See Ullman & Begin, *The Structure and Scope of Appeals Procedures for Public Employees*, 23 Indus. & Lab. Rel. Rev. 323 (1970). See, e.g., Fla. Stat. § 447.401, which requires public sector bargaining agreements to contain grievance machinery culminating in binding arbitration. See also *Township of W. Windsor v. PERC*, 393 A.2d 255 (N.J. 1978), wherein the court indicated that while the public sector statute requires parties to provide grievance procedures covering all employment disputes, it does not obligate them to provide for arbitration of all such matters.

NOTES

1. Though a method for handling grievances is a nearly universal feature of collective bargaining agreements in both the public and private sectors, not all contracts define "grievance" in the same way. Some contracts, in fact, detail the procedure without defining the term at all. The language outlining the scope of the grievance procedure may be very broad, or it may detail the matters which are subject to the procedure in very specific terms. Other provisions generally exclude certain subjects from the grievance procedure as matters of management prerogative.

2. The scope of the grievance procedure should not be confused with the scope of arbitration. The two are not necessarily coextensive. Some disputes may be grievable even though they concern matters which the parties have not agreed to submit to arbitration. In most cases, however, the scope of the grievance procedure and the scope of arbitration coincide.

2. NEGOTIATING THE GRIEVANCE PROCEDURE

In the private sector, the most important element in negotiating a grievance procedure is the intent of the parties as to what should and what should not be a grievable dispute. In the public sector, other factors are also important. Principal among those other factors is the intent of the legislature. Did the state legislature or city council, in enacting a public employee bargaining law, intend that the area in question be subject to the grievance procedure, or did they intend that it be left to the unbridled discretion of the public employer? Also relevant is the effect of past or existing civil service systems. In addition to the procedures they establish, civil service appeals procedures also create customs and attitudes as to the proper way to do things. How are the procedures and their attendant customs to be accommodated?

In negotiating a grievance procedure, the following questions are likely to be of concern to the parties:

1. Is the procedure to culminate in final and binding arbitration?

2. How extensively is the employee organization to be involved in the procedure? Are stewards or other union representatives to be present from the initial
stages of their grievance? Will the individual employee or the organization have
the final say as to whether the grievance is processed through the succeeding
stages of the procedure, settled, or dropped? Unions typically want control of
the procedure to insure uniformity in its operation and to facilitate the development of informal channels of communication, customs, practices and settlement
mechanisms. On the other hand, the individual in civil service systems has
always been responsible for processing his own appeals, with union advice but
not control; the practice is not easily supplanted.

3. What are the time limits to be for filing and processing grievances? Should
time limits begin to run from the time of a grievable occurrence or from the
time the employee realizes he has a grievance?

4. Should the union have the right to file general "policy" grievances or
should it be restricted to filing specific grievances on behalf of designated employee grievants?

5. What should be considered a grievable dispute? What type of complaints is
the grievance procedure designed to handle? Generally, employee organizations seek to broaden the scope of the procedure to include as many specific
subjects as possible and to open the door to new grievable matters by adding
"past practices" and other open-ended clauses. Management, just as in the private sector, seeks to reserve as much as possible to its own discretion by the
insertion of a broad "management rights" clause. Of course, the scope is often
circumscribed by the legislature.

6. Should employees be required to exhaust available grievance procedures
before seeking redress for the same conduct through external procedures?
Should they be subject to discipline if they do not do so?

NOTES

1. Where the applicable labor relations statute provides that the labor organization selected by the majority of employees in an appropriate bargaining unit
shall constitute the workers' exclusive representative, it is generally recognized
that an aggrieved employee may not be represented by a rival minority union.
See, e.g., *Diablo Valley Fed'n of Teachers & Mt. Diablo Unified Sch. Dist.,* Cal.
PERB Case No. SF-CE-88, 1977-78 PEB ¶ 40,452 (1977); *Bayonne Bd. of Educ.
& Bayonne Fed'n of Teachers,* N.J. PERC, Case No.78-60, GERR No. 765, 11
(1978). See generally R. Gorman, Basic Text on Labor Law 394-95 (1976).
However, in the absence of such statutory recognition of the "exclusivity" prin-
ciple, a bargaining agent may not always be permitted to act as the sole bargain-
ing representative for nonconsenting employees. See *Dade Cty. Classroom
Teachers Ass'n v. Ryan,* 225 So. 2d 903, 71 L.R.R.M. 2958 (Fla. 1969).

2. Should an employer be permitted to insist that all grievances be initiated
only by individual employees, or should a representative labor organization
possess the inherent right to file grievances on behalf of unit workers? See *Red
Bank Reg'l Educ. Ass'n v. High Sch. Bd. of Educ.,* 393 A.2d 267 (N.J. 1978).
Why would a union desire the right to institute grievances where no individual
has done so? Where only those who have suffered "personal loss or injury" may
file a grievance, the president of the representative union may lack standing to
file a grievance on behalf of the employees directly affected by the action being

challenged. See *In re Berlin Bd. of Educ.*, 413 A.2d 312, 106 L.R.R.M. 2558 (N.H. 1980).

3. For an early in-depth study of public employee grievance procedures, see Berger, *Grievance Process in the Philadelphia Public Service,* 13 Indus. & Lab. Rel. Rev. 568 (1960). Later studies may be found in Ullman & Begin, *The Structure and Scope of Appeals Procedures for Public Employees,* 23 Indus. & Lab. Rel. Rev. 323 (1970), and Begin, *The Private Grievance Model in the Public Sector,* 10 Indus. Rel. 21 (1971). See generally M. Bowers, Contract Administration in the Public Sector (1976); U.S. Bureau of Labor Statistics, Bull. No. 1661, Negotiation Impasse, Grievance, and Arbitration in Federal Agreements (1970); Koretz, *Labor Relations Law,* 22 Syracuse L. Rev. 133, 136-39 (1971); Wolf, *Grievance Procedures for School Employees,* in Employer-Employee Relations in the Public Schools 133 (R. Doherty ed. 1967).

3. GRIEVANCE ARBITRATION

Almost universally in the private sector and increasingly in the public sector, negotiated grievance procedures are capped by an arbitration provision. Grievance arbitration involves the adjudication of disputes which the parties have been unable to settle among themselves by a neutral third party or panel. The neutral may be a single arbitrator or a multi-member (either tripartite or all-neutral) panel; an arbitrator or panel may be ad hoc (temporary, invited by the parties to hear one or a series of cases) or permanent (as an umpire who is hired to hear all disputes between the parties). The arbitrator's decision may be final and binding on the parties or advisory only.

In the private sector, grievance arbitration performs a number of very important functions. First, it provides a relatively speedy and inexpensive means of settling disputes. Secondly, it gives the employee the security of knowing that the ultimate recourse for the resolution of any grievance he may have lies with a neutral and not with his employer. Thirdly, it helps conserve judicial resources by providing a means to settle most disputes without court action. Fourthly, and most importantly, it serves national labor policy as a mechanism for the maintenance of industrial peace, providing an alternative to the strike in the resolution of day-to-day disputes.

Arbitration of grievances is a method of industrial self-regulation, a private rather than a governmental proceeding. Yet, private sector arbitration enjoys the sanction and support of law. Section 203(e) of the Labor Management Relations Act of 1947 (29 U.S.C. § 173(d)) states: "Final adjustment by a method agreed upon by the parties is hereby declared to be the desirable method for settlement of grievance disputes arising over the application or interpretation of an existing collective-bargaining agreement." In the 1957 case of *Textile Workers Union v. Lincoln Mills,* 353 U.S. 448 (1957), the Supreme Court held that arbitration agreements were specifically enforceable in the federal courts under § 301(a) of the LMRA (29 U.S.C. § 185(a)); and in the 1960 *Steelworkers' Trilogy* cases, the Court determined that arbitration agreements and awards should be reviewable by the courts only according to a very narrowly prescribed standard, thus discouraging both refusals to arbitrate and appeals from arbitration awards. See *United Steelworkers v. American Mfg. Co.,* 363 U.S. 564 (1960); *United Steelworkers v. Warrior & Gulf Nav. Co.,* 363 U.S. 574 (1960); *United Steelworkers v. Enterprise Wheel Car Corp.,* 363 U.S. 593 (1960).

The reasons for enforcing arbitration agreements and awards in the private sector are frequently applicable in the public sector too. Some objection has been voiced against the legality of grievance arbitration on the ground that it is in derogation of the power of legislatures to determine public policy. However, the judicially created principle that an agreement to arbitrate constitutes an unlawful delegation of governmental authority has lost much of its force, and most courts have evidenced an inclination to follow the enforcement rules developed in *Lincoln Mills* and the *Steelworkers' Trilogy* when dealing with public sector grievance arbitration. See, e.g., *City & Cty. of Denver v. Denver Firefighters Local No. 858,* 663 P.2d 1032, 1981-83 PBC ¶ 37,731 (Colo. 1983). Nonetheless, some courts have continued to demonstrate either a reluctance to adopt entirely the private sector precedents or an outright hostility toward doctrines they believe are inapposite with respect to public sector grievance disputes.

There are two quite different types of labor arbitration: grievance arbitration, or "arbitration of rights," and impasse arbitration, or "arbitration of interests." In dealing with public sector labor relations, it is particularly important to be aware of the differences between the two. In the private sector, impasse arbitration is seldom used; references to "arbitration" almost always mean grievance arbitration. But in the public sector, where strikes by public employees are usually illegal, impasse arbitration is important and occasionally mandated by statute. Grievance arbitration involves the determination of rights under an *existing* contract by an arbitrator acting in a judicial capacity. Impasse arbitration, on the other hand, is utilized when the parties are unable to agree to the provisions of a labor contract at the bargaining table; it is a substitute for the economic weaponry of strikes and lockouts in the determination of what the contract rights of the parties *shall be.* The impasse arbitrator is a combination policy-maker, administrator, and chancellor at equity; in contrast to the grievance arbitrator, he is a formulator, rather than a follower of the parties' contract.

NOTE

Concerning the general subject of grievance arbitration, see D. Rothschild, L. Merrifield & C. Craver, Collective Bargaining and Labor Arbitration (1988); F. Elkouri & E. Elkouri, How Arbitration Works (1973); R. Fleming, The Labor Arbitration Process (1965). Regarding grievance arbitration in the public sector, see Frazier, *Labor Arbitration in the Federal Service,* 45 Geo. Wash. L. Rev. 712 (1977); Rock, *The Role of the Neutral in Grievance Arbitration in Public Employment,* in Collective Bargaining in Government 141 (J. Loewenberg & M. Moskow eds. 1972); U.S. Bureau of Labor Statistics, Bull. No. 1661, Negotiation Impasse, Grievance, and Arbitration in Federal Agreements (1970); Note, *Legality and Propriety of Agreements to Arbitrate Major and Minor Disputes in Public Employment,* 54 Cornell L. Rev. 129 (1968); Krislov & Schmulowitz, *Grievance Arbitration in State and Local Government Units,* 18 Arb. J. 171 (1963); Killingsworth, *Grievance Adjudication in Public Employment,* 13 Arb. J. 3 (1958). See also Granof & Moe, *Grievance Arbitration in the U.S. Postal Service: The Postal Service View,* 29 Arb. J. 1 (1974); Cohen, *Grievance Arbitration in the United States Postal Service,* 28 Arb. J. 258 (1973).

C. ENFORCEMENT OF GRIEVANCE ARBITRATION AGREEMENTS

1. THE PRIVATE SECTOR PRECEDENTS: *LINCOLN MILLS* AND THE "TRILOGY"

H. WELLINGTON, LABOR AND THE LEGAL PROCESS 99-100 (1968)*

Textile Workers v. Lincoln Mills [, 353 U.S. 448 (1957),] ... was decided by the Supreme Court in 1957, and it grew out of the effort of a union to compel an employer to submit grievances to arbitration. The union brought suit in a federal district court under section 301. It asserted that the employer had promised in the collective agreement to arbitrate grievances which arose during contract time; that he had broken this promise, and that, therefore, the court should order specific performance of the promise to arbitrate.... At common law in most states the promise to arbitrate was not enforceable by an order of specific performance.[37] This was so whether the promise was contained in a commercial contract or in a collective agreement. Theoretically one might recover damages for breach of this promise, but practically one could never show damages. This state rule was also the federal rule.[38] Some states,[39] and the federal government,[40] had legislation which, for some types of contracts at least, changed the common law rule. But the law of the relevant state apparently could not help the union in *Lincoln Mills,* and there was serious doubt whether the United States Arbitration Act applied to arbitration promises in collective bargaining agreements.[41]

Moreover, it was unclear which body of law governed a suit brought under section 301. The statute appeared to be no more than a grant of jurisdiction to the federal courts. It said nothing about the substantive rights of the parties. The early law — what there was of it — on the subject of rights under the collective agreement was, as noted, of state, not federal, origin. Nor was it clear whether the law governing the availability of the equitable remedy of specific performance was the law of the forum or the law which created the cause of action....

The Court held that section 301 was a charter to the courts to develop a federal "common law" of the collective bargaining agreement, and that section 301 itself empowered the courts to grant specific performance of the promise to arbitrate.

---

*Reprinted by permission of the Yale University Press.

[37]See, e.g., *Roe v. Williams,* 97 Mass. 163 (1867). Cf. *Cogswell v. Cogswell,* 70 Wash. 178, 126 P. 431 (1912).

[38]See *Red Cross Line v. Atlantic Fruit Co.,* 264 U.S. 109, 120-22 (1924).

[39]The statutes are collected in 4 BNA Labor Relations Reporter.

[40]9 U.S.C. §§ 1-14 (1964).

[41]Compare *United Furniture Workers v. Colonial Hardwood Flooring Co.,* 168 F.2d 33 (4th Cir. 1948), with *Mercury Oil Refining Co. v. Oil Workers Int'l Union,* 187 F.2d 980 (10th Cir. 1951) and *Tenney Eng'g, Inc. v. United Elec. Workers,* 207 F.2d 450 (3d Cir. 1953).

R. SMITH & D. JONES, THE SUPREME COURT AND LABOR DISPUTE ARBITRATION: THE EMERGING FEDERAL LAW, 63 Mich. L. Rev. 751, 755-60 (1965)*

The so-called "Trilogy" of 1960 consisted of three cases in which, in each instance, the union involved was the United Steelworkers of America. The cases have been stated, dissected, and critically examined to the point that we now have a wealth of literature concerning them. A brief review of the issues presented and the decisions is, nevertheless, desirable as part of our background recital.

In *Warrior & Gulf*,[42] the grievances brought by the Union protested the contracting out of certain maintenance work clearly encompassed by the bargaining unit. There was a layoff situation at the time the grievances were filed which, in part, was due to the contracting out of such work. The labor agreement was silent on the subject of contracting out; however, it undoubtedly contained recognition, wage, and seniority provisions. The agreement also contained a no-strike provision. Excluded from the arbitration process were matters that were "strictly a function of management," but otherwise the arbitration clause was unusually broad. It stated:

> "Should differences arise between the Company and the Union or its members ... as to the meaning and application of the provisions of this Agreement, or should any local trouble of any kind arise, there shall be no suspension of work on account of such differences, but an earnest effort shall be made to settle such differences in the following manner [referring to the grievance and arbitration procedure]."

In a suit by the Union under section 301 to compel arbitration, the district court granted the Company's motion to dismiss, holding that the agreement did not confide in an arbitrator the right to review the defendant's business judgment in contracting out work and that contracting out was strictly a function of management within the meaning of the exclusionary language of the arbitration clause. The court of appeals affirmed, but the Supreme Court reversed and the Company was forced to arbitrate.

In *American Manufacturing*,[43] the question was whether the Company was required to submit to arbitration a grievance based on its refusal to reinstate an employee who had suffered an industrial injury. In a consent decree settlement of a workmen's compensation claim, the employee had been awarded a lump-sum payment plus costs on the basis that he had incurred a permanent partial disability of twenty-five per cent. His subsequent demand for reinstatement was predicated on a statement by his physician (who had supported the earlier claim of permanent partial disability) that the employee "is now able to return to his former duties without danger to himself or to others." Contractually, the demand was based on a provision in the seniority article of the labor agreement which recognized "the principle of seniority as a factor in the selection of employees for promotion, transfer, layoff, re-employment, and filling of vacancies, where ability and efficiency are equal." The arbitration clause was standard in

---

*Reprinted by permission of the Michigan Law Review.
[42] *United Steelworkers v. Warrior & Gulf Nav. Co.*, 363 U.S. 574 (1960).
[43] *United Steelworkers v. American Mfg. Co.*, 363 U.S. 564 (1960).

that it permitted arbitration of "any disputes, misunderstandings, differences or grievances rising between the parties as to the meaning, interpretation and application of the provisions of this agreement." The district court and court of appeals refused to require the Company to arbitrate, although they disagreed on the basis of decision. The district court used an estoppel theory; the court of appeals held that estoppel did not go to the question of arbitrability, but it examined the cited seniority provisions and concluded that the grievance was "a frivolous, patently baseless one" and hence not within the arbitration clause. Again, the Supreme Court reversed and ordered arbitration.

In *Enterprise*,[44] the grievance sought the reinstatement of certain employees who had been discharged because they had left their jobs in protest against the discharge of a fellow employee. The Company refused to arbitrate the grievance, but was ordered to do so by a federal district court. The arbitrator's decision reduced the penalty of discharge to a ten-day disciplinary layoff and ordered the grievants reinstated with back pay adjusted for the ten-day penalty. The decision was handed down five days after the labor agreement had expired, and the Company refused to comply with the award on the ground, inter alia, that the arbitrator lacked the authority either to order back pay for any period subsequent to the expiration date of the labor agreement or to order reinstatement. The district court directed the Company to comply with the award, but the court of appeals reversed on the ground urged by the Company. The Supreme Court, however, once more upheld the authority of the arbitrator.

Seven Justices concurred in these decisions. Mr. Justice Whitaker dissented, and Mr. Justice Black did not participate. The principal opinion for the majority was written by Mr. Justice Douglas. Mr. Justice Frankfurter did not join in this opinion, but concurred in the results in each case. Justices Brennan and Harlan, while joining the Douglas opinion in each case, also added "a word" in *Warrior & Gulf* and *American Manufacturing*.

The decisions have been viewed as indicating a strong federal policy favoring the arbitration process as a means of resolving disputes concerning the interpretation or application of collective bargaining agreements and as restricting the role of the courts in this area. This interpretation, we think, is correct, although it derives its principal support from the content of the opinions, especially the opinion by Mr. Justice Douglas, rather than from the specific dispositions of the issues presented....

Considering at this point only the 1960 decisions, the following propositions seem to have been declared as a matter of federal substantive law with respect to labor agreements subject to enforcement under section 301 of the Labor Management Relations Act of 1947:

> (1) The existence of a valid agreement to arbitrate, and the arbitrability of a specific grievance sought to be arbitrated under such an agreement, are questions for the courts ultimately to decide (if such an issue is presented for judicial determination) unless the parties have expressly given an arbitrator the authority to make a binding determination of such matters.

---

[44] *United Steelworkers v. Enterprise Wheel & Car Corp.*, 363 U.S. 593 (1960).

(2) A court should hold a grievance non-arbitrable under a valid agreement to use arbitration as the terminal point in the grievance procedure only if the parties have clearly indicated their intention to exclude the subject matter of the grievance from the arbitration process, either by expressly so stating in the arbitration clause or by otherwise clearly and unambiguously indicating such intention.

(3) Evidence of intention to exclude a claim from the arbitration process should not be found in a determination that the labor agreement could not properly be interpreted in such manner as to sustain the grievance on its merits, for this is a task assigned by the parties to the arbitrator, not the courts.

(4) An award should not be set aside as beyond the authority conferred upon the arbitrator, either because of claimed error in interpretation of the agreement or because of alleged lack of authority to provide a particular remedy, where the arbitral decision was or, if silent, might have been the result of the arbitrator's interpretation of the agreement; if, however, it was based not on the contract but on an obligation found to have been imposed by law, the award should be set aside unless the parties have expressly authorized the arbitrator to dispose of this as well as any contract issue.[45]

NOTES

1. *AT&T Technologies v. CWA,* 475 U.S. 643 (1986), involved a contractual dispute over the propriety of layoffs. When the CWA sought arbitration, AT&T claimed that the grievance was not arbitrable, on the ground the layoffs had been effectuated pursuant to the non-arbitrable authority it possessed under the management prerogative clause. The district court found that the CWA's suggested contractual interpretation was "arguable," and it held that the arbitrator should determine whether that interpretation was in fact meritorious. It thus directed the parties to have the arbitrator decide the arbitrability dispute. The Supreme Court rejected such judicial deference to arbitral authority. After the Court reaffirmed the principles articulated in the *Steelworkers Trilogy,* it emphasized that district courts, and not arbitrators, are required to resolve substantive arbitrability questions. "[T]he question of arbitrability — whether a collective-bargaining agreement creates a duty for the parties to arbitrate the particular grievance — is undeniably an issue for judicial determination. Unless

---

[45] See also *Report of Special Warrior & Gulf Committee,* in 1963 Proceedings of the ABA Section of Labor Relations Law 196-97, in which the following six general propositions with respect to arbitration under collective bargaining agreements were said to have been established by the Trilogy: "(1) Arbitration is a matter of contract, not of law; parties are required to arbitrate only if, and to the extent that, they have agreed to do so. (2) The question of arbitrability under a collective bargaining agreement is a question for the courts, not for the arbitrator, unless the parties specifically provide otherwise in their agreement. (3) Since arbitration under a collective bargaining agreement is an alternative to strike, rather than to litigation, as in commercial arbitration, the traditional judicial reluctance toward compelling parties to arbitrate is not applicable to labor arbitration. (4) When the parties have provided for arbitration of all disputes as to the application or interpretation of a collective bargaining agreement, the courts should order arbitration of any grievance which claims that management has violated the provisions of the agreement, irrespective of the courts' views as to the merits of the claim. (5) When the parties have coupled with a provision for arbitration of all disputes a clause specifically excepting certain matters from arbitration, the courts should order arbitration of a claim that the employer has violated the agreement unless it may be said with positive assurance that the subject matter falls within the exception clause. (6) An arbitral award should be enforced (absent fraud or similar vitiating circumstance) unless it is clear that the arbitrator has based that award upon matters outside the contract he is charged with interpreting and applying."

the parties clearly and unmistakably provide otherwise, the question of whether the parties agreed to arbitrate is to be decided by the court, not the arbitrator."

2. In *United Paperworkers Int'l Union v. Misco, Inc.,* 484 U.S. 29 (1987), the Supreme Court indicated that judges may not refuse to enforce private sector arbitral decisions simply because they believe that the awards contravene their personal notions of "public policy."

[A] court's refusal to enforce an arbitrator's *interpretation* of [collective bargaining] contracts is limited to situations where the contract as interpreted would violate "some explicit public policy" that is "well defined and dominant, and is to be ascertained by reference to the laws and legal precedents and not from general considerations of supposed public interests."

2. COMPELLING ARBITRATION

AFSCME, LOCAL 1226, RHINELANDER CITY EMPLOYEES v. CITY OF RHINELANDER

35 Wis. 2d 209, 151 N.W.2d 30 (1967)

HANLEY, JUSTICE. On December 10, 1964, the plaintiff, Frances Bischoff, was discharged from her job as an administrative assistant in the water department of the city by order of the city mayor. At that time Mrs. Bischoff was a member of the union. The local union was the exclusive bargaining agent for city employees in several city departments, including the water department. The city and the union had a written collective bargaining agreement which in Article X provided [for a grievance procedure concluding in binding arbitration]....

Mrs. Bischoff felt that by her discharge her rights and privileges under the collective bargaining agreement had been violated, and submitted the problem to the union grievance committee. The union determined that a grievance existed and processed Mrs. Bischoff's grievance through the first four steps of the Article X proceeding without solution satisfactory to both sides. Thereupon the union chose its member of the arbitration panel as provided in Article X of the collective bargaining agreement. The city refused to choose its member of the arbitration board and refused to follow the procedure set out in the agreement for choosing the third member chairman of the arbitration board.

Mrs. Bischoff and the union commenced this action for specific performance of the arbitration clause of the agreement for Mrs. Bischoff's grievance on her discharge. The city demurred upon the ground that the plaintiffs' complaint failed to state facts sufficient to constitute a cause of action. The trial court sustained the demurrer, basically upon the ground that the city had no statutory authority to enter into a binding arbitration agreement, and that therefore no cause of action will lie to specifically enforce such an agreement. From the judgment sustaining the demurrer, the plaintiffs appeal....

The following issues are presented on this appeal:

1. Is the arbitration clause contained in the collective bargaining agreement binding on the city?

2. If the clause is binding, is it specifically enforceable in the courts?

3. Is the question of whether Mrs. Bischoff was discharged for just cause an arbitrable issue under the agreement?

1. Binding effect of the agreement to arbitration.

At the conclusion of the agreement, prior to the signatures of the officials of the city and the union, is the following provision:

"This Agreement shall be binding upon both the Employer and the Union."

The initial question is whether that part of the "agreement," Article X, which provides an arbitration procedure as a final step in the processing of grievances is binding upon the city.

We think it is binding. By sec. 111.70(4)(i), Stats., the legislature has decreed that written collective bargaining agreements between municipal employers and labor organizations "shall be binding" if they contain express language to that effect. Here we have such an agreement which contains such express language. Thus the contract comes exactly within the provision of the statute and is binding.

2. Specific enforceability of the agreement to arbitrate grievances.

In the leading case on the point of enforceability, *Local 1111 of United Electrical, Radio & Machine Workers of America v. Allen-Bradley Co.* (1951), 259 Wis. 609, 49 N.W.2d 720, this court held that a collective bargaining contract containing provisions for the arbitration of grievances was legal and in full force in Wisconsin, but that without some statutory basis the courts have no power to order an employer to perform its agreement to arbitrate. The basis of the court's opinion was that courts may specifically enforce agreements to arbitrate differences arising under an existing contract only under sec. 298.01, Stats. Since sec. 298.01 specifically does not apply to contracts between employers and employees, except as provided in sec. 111.10, Stats., the court reasoned that the union was not entitled to a judgment requiring the employer to arbitrate.

It should be noted that in *Local 1111, etc. v. Allen-Bradley, supra,* the court was divided. Mr. Justice Currie, joined by Mr. Justice Broadfoot, dissented on the grounds that Wisconsin courts are not so impotent as to be unable to enforce valid and lawful agreements and that the declaratory judgment statute under which the action was brought authorized the court to grant supplementary relief when necessary and proper.

Mr. Justice Currie in his dissenting opinion, at page 618, 49 N.W.2d at page 725, stated:

> "I cannot subscribe to the theory that the common law is an inflexible instrument which does not permit growth and adjustment to meet the social needs of the times. This court in the past has repudiated this very theory. Mr. Justice Nelson in his opinion in *Schwanke v. Garlt,* 219 Wis. 367, 371, 263 N.W. 176, 178, declared:
>
> "'While we are at all times bound to uphold the Constitution of this state and to give due effect to its paramount provisions, we may not ignore the fact "that the common law is susceptible of growth and adaptation to new circumstances and situations, and that the courts have power to declare and effectuate what is the present rule in respect of a given subject without regard to the old rule.... The common law is not immutable, but flexible, and upon its own principles adapts itself to varying conditions." *Dimick v. Schiedt,* 293 U.S. 474. To the same effect is *Funk v. United States,* 290 U.S. 371.'"

We believe the rule that the enforcement of an arbitration provision in a collective bargaining agreement is not enforceable at common law should be repudiated.

The very purpose of grievance arbitration is to prevent individual problems from blossoming into labor disputes which cause strikes and lockouts and which require collective bargaining to restore peace and tranquility.

We now adopt the view expressed by Mr. Justice CURRIE in his dissent in *Local 1111, supra,* and concluded that it is illogical to hold in this case that the arbitration provisions are valid but the court is powerless to enforce them by compelling the city to arbitrate Mrs. Bischoff's grievance, especially in the light of the legislative enactment in sec. 111.70(4) (i), Stats., that "... Such agreements shall be binding...."

The city and the trial court in its decision contend that the legislative history of sec. 111.70(4), Stats., demonstrates that the legislature rejected the use of grievance arbitration as a means of settling disagreements which arise under collective bargaining agreements with municipal employees. Actually, if the legislative history demonstrates anything, it is that the legislature rejected the idea of extending the jurisdiction to the Wisconsin Employment Relations Board to handle or enforce arbitration agreements in municipal employment relations....

3. Arbitrability of the discharge.

The city contends that even if Article X of the collective bargaining agreement is binding upon the city, Mrs. Bischoff's discharge is not a grievance subject to arbitration under the terms of that article. The trial court did not consider this question, but the parties have argued it and it is a question of law which the court will consider in order to avoid additional appeals.

According to Article X of the agreement, the following matters are subject to the grievance procedure:

"... differences [which may] arise between the Employer and the Union as to the meaning and application of the provisions of this agreement or as to any question relating to wages, hours, and conditions of employment...."

Article IV of the agreement provides the following with respect to probationary employment:

"Section 1. New employees without prior service shall be employed on a six (6) months probationary basis, and during said period may be discharged for cause without recourse through the Union."

Mrs. Bischoff was apparently a permanent employee who claims that this section of the agreement, at least by implication, protects her from discharge without cause, and that she was discharged without cause. It would thus seem that Mrs. Bischoff's grievance, processed by the union, can fairly be said to be a difference "as to the meaning and application of the provisions" of the agreement, if not a "question relating to wages, hours, and conditions of employment." Moreover, Mrs. Bischoff felt that her rights and privileges under the agreement were violated by her discharge. The question of her discharge would seem to be arbitrable under sec. 2 of Article X, which in part provides:

"Should an employee feel that his rights and privileges under this Agreement have been violated he shall first submit the problem to the Union Grievance Committee. If it is determined after investigation by the Union that a grievance does exist it shall be processed in the manner described below:...."

4. Arbitration is not an unlawful infringement on the legislative power of the city.

The city has contended that to require the city to submit to binding arbitration is an unlawful infringement upon the legislative power of the city council and a violation of its home rule powers. Yet in all of its arguments the city is talking about arbitration in the collective bargaining context — arbitration to set the terms of a collective bargaining agreement. Such is not this case, which involves arbitration to resolve a grievance arising under an existing agreement to which the city is a party. The legislature has passed statutes doubtless of statewide concern, which provide that the city's agreement to arbitrate grievances is binding on the city.

We conclude that the arbitration clause contained in the collective bargaining agreement is binding upon the city and is specifically enforceable in the courts and that Mrs. Bischoff's discharge is an arbitrable issue under the agreement.

Judgment reversed and cause remanded for further proceedings in conformity with the opinion.

BOARD OF EDUCATION v. ROCKAWAY TOWNSHIP EDUCATION ASSOCIATION

81 L.R.R.M. 2462 (N.J. Super. Ct. 1972)

STAMLER, JUDGE: — Plaintiff is The Board of Education of the Township of Rockaway in Morris County. Defendants are Rockaway Township Education Association (hereinafter RTEA) and Joseph Youngman, a teacher in the employ of the Board. The Board asks that defendants be enjoined from proceeding before the American Arbitration Association on the question of interference with the "academic freedom" of the teacher in violation of a contract between the Board and RTEA....

On June 23, 1971, the Board and RTEA entered into a contract which provided for the terms and conditions of employment of teachers in the Rockaway Township School District. In February 1972, Youngman, a teacher of Humanities, was directed by the Superintendent of the school district not to conduct in his 7th grade class a previously announced "debate" on the subject of abortion. The 7th grade class is composed of eleven and twelve year old children....

Defendants contend that the preclusion decision of the Superintendent and its affirmance by the Board was a denial of "academic freedom" to defendants and a violation of Article XXVII, Paragraph C of the collective bargaining contract between the parties.

Paragraph C reads as follows:

"The Board and the Association agree that academic freedom is essential to the fulfillment of the purposes of the Rockaway Township School District. Free discussion of controversial issues is the heart of the democratic process. Through the study of such issues, political, economic or social, youth develops those abilities needed for functional citizenship in our democracy. *Whenever appropriate for the maturation level of the group,* controversial issues may be studied in an unprejudiced and dispassionate manner. It shall be the duty of the teacher to foster the study of an issue and not to teach a particular viewpoint in regard to it." (Emphasis supplied.)

Defendants demanded of the Board that the issue of the alleged violation of Article XXVII, Par. C as well as the issue of academic freedom of a member of the teaching staff be processed as a "grievance" before the American Arbitration Association as provided in the contract. Notice of its intention to proceed before the Arbitration Association was given to the Board. The Board filed its complaint seeking an injunction, asserting that the appropriate forum is a proceeding before the Commissioner of Education....

Article III, Paragraph A (1) of the contract defines "grievance" as:

"The term 'grievance' means a complaint by an employee of the Association that, as to him, there has been a personal loss or injury because of an administrative decision affecting said employee, or an unjust application, interpretation or violation of a policy, or agreement. The term 'grievance' and the procedure relative thereto shall not apply to a complaint of a non-tenure teacher which arises by reason of his not being re-employed after only two years on probation."

It is clear that both the Board and RTEA agreed that "academic freedom" is essential to the fulfillment of the purposes of the School District. The heart of the problem is the fourth sentence in the quoted section of Article XXVII (C):

"Whenever appropriate for the maturation level of the group, controversial issues may be studied in an unprejudiced and dispassionate manner."...

To determine "maturation level" requires expertise in education. One proposition upon which the authors of the articles cited above agree: a trial court is not so qualified.

This then places the obligation on either the teacher or the Board or both. When disagreement arises, shall it be settled before a panel selected from the American Arbitration Association or before the Commissioner of Education with review by the State Board of Education and thereafter the Appellate Courts?

The New Jersey Employer-Employee Relations Act, P.L., 1968, Ch. 303, requires a public employer, including a board of education, to negotiate with the majority representative of an appropriate unit of its employees concerning the terms and conditions of employment. Specifically to be negotiated is a grievance procedure. N.J.S.A. 34:13A-53. In N.J.S.A. 34:13A-10 the following appears:

"Nothing in this act shall be construed to annul or modify, or to preclude the renewal or continuation of any agreement heretofore entered into between any public employer and any employee organization, *nor shall any provision hereof annul or modify any statute or statutes of the state.*" (Emphasis added.)

It cannot be argued, therefore, that Title 18 "Education" insofar as it is concerned with relationship between Boards, teachers *and* pupils has been superseded. Even were this language eliminated from Chapter 303, our Supreme Court has held that the general rule of statutory construction, in the absence of clear legislative direction to the contrary, requires a determination that a later statute will not be deemed to repeal or modify an earlier one, but all existing statutes pertaining to the same subject matter "are to be construed together as a unitary and harmonious whole, in order that each may be fully effective." *Clifton v. Passaic County Board of Taxation,* 28 N.J. 411, 421 (1958). Thus, the provisions of both Title 18A and Chapter 303 must be read together so that both are harmonized and each is given its appropriate role.

The selection of courses to be presented to students and the subjects to be presented or discussed cannot be a "term or condition of employment." Defendants argue "there can be no doubt that the methods of selecting courses and even more clearly, the procedures and methods by which these courses are to be presented, may be negotiated at least in broad terms." This proposition is untenable.

The Board is responsible for the production of a "thorough and efficient" school system (N.J. Constitution, Art. 8 Sec. 4 P.1) and particularly the statutory obligation to provide "courses of study suited to the ages and attainments of all pupils." N.J.S. 18A:33-1. The Board has a continuing obligation placed upon it by the Legislature to adopt and alter courses of study....

In *Porcelli v. Titus,* 108 N.J. Super. 301, 2 FEP Cases 344 (App. Div. 1970), *cert. denied,* 55 N.J. 310 (1970), the following appears at p. 312, 2 FEP Cases at 348:

"'The public schools were not created, nor are they supported for the benefit of the teachers therein, ... but for the benefit of the pupils, and the resulting benefit to their parents and the community at large.'"

The courts have recognized that public employees cannot make contracts with public agencies that are contrary to the dictates of the Legislature. *Lullo v. International Association of Fire Fighters,* 55 N.J. 409, 73 LRRM 2680 (1970). Nor can public agencies such as a board of education "abdicate or bargain away their continuing legislative or executive obligations or discretion." *Lullo, supra,* 440, 73 LRRM at 2693.

It is concluded therefore that if the contract is read to delegate to a teacher or to a teacher's union the subject of courses of study, the contract in that respect is *ultra vires* and unenforceable. It must follow therefore that the American Arbitration Association cannot be the subdelegee of the Board and of the teachers. Additionally, it is to be noted that the American Arbitration Association may be well qualified to "arbitrate" compensation, hours of work, sick leave, fringe-benefits and the like, but they and their panels possess no expertise in arbitrating the maturation level of a 7th grade student in the elementary schools of Rockaway Township.

However, defendants who were dissatisfied with the action of the Superintendent and the Board are not without a remedy. N.J.S. 18A:6-9 provides that the Commissioner of Education "shall have jurisdiction to hear and determine, without cost to the parties, all controversies and disputes arising under the school laws...." On subsequent appeal, our appellate courts will have the benefit of the special experience of the administrative agencies operating in the vital area of education, especially of the young....

NOTES

1. In *PLRB v. Williamsport Sch. Dist.*, 406 A.2d 239, 103 L.R.R.M. 2299 (1979), the Pennsylvania Supreme Court held that the fact a union seeking an order to compel grievance arbitration had engaged in two short work stoppages, which were finally enjoined by a lower court, prior to its request for arbitration did not ipso facto preclude an order from the P.L.R.B. presently directing arbitration.

2. In *Grand Forks Educ. Ass'n v. Grand Forks Pub. Sch. Dist. No. 1*, 285 N.W.2d 578, 103 L.R.R.M. 2945 (N.D. 1979), the court recognized that the proper recourse for a labor organization aggrieved by a governmental employer's unilateral modification of working conditions during the term of a bargaining agreement is to proceed under the contractual grievance-arbitration machinery rather than to commence a direct court action seeking injunctive relief until the parties are able to negotiate a resolution of the contractual dispute. If a union initially seeks judicial intervention regarding such a controversy, might it be found to have waived its right thereafter to obtain arbitration of the matter? See *City of Yonkers v. Cassidy*, 44 N.Y.2d 784, 377 N.E.2d 475 (1978). But cf. *Bernalillo Cty. Medical Center Emps. Ass'n v. Cancelosi*, 587 P.2d 960, 99 L.R.R.M. 3469 (N.M. 1978); *Doers v. Golden Gate Bridge Transp. Dist.*, 588 P.2d 1261, 100 L.R.R.M. 2877 (Cal. 1979).

3. When governmental employers which have purchased private transit systems with federal financial assistance fail to honor their bargaining agreements, the aggrieved unions may not prosecute contract enforcement actions in federal court under Section 13(c) of the Urban Mass Transportation Act, 49 U.S.C. § 1609(c). They must instead sue in state court, since Congress intended such negotiated agreements to be regulated by applicable state law, not federal standards. See *Jackson Transit Auth. v. Local Div. 1285, Amalgamated Transit Union*, 457 U.S. 15 (1982).

In *Local Div. 732, ATU v. MARTA*, 303 S.E.2d 1, 1981-83 PBC ¶ 37,735 (Ga. 1983), the court held that since under Georgia law general agreements to submit contractual disputes to arbitration may be revoked by either party prior to the issuance of an arbitral award, MARTA had the right, even under a Section 13(c) bargaining agreement, to withdraw its previous consent to submit grievances to arbitration. Is such a result consistent with the Congressional intent underlying Section 13(c)?

4. See generally Note, *Legality and Propriety of Agreements to Arbitrate Major and Minor Disputes in Public Employment*, 54 Cornell L. Rev. 129 (1968); Killingsworth, *Grievance Adjudication in Public Employment*, 13 Arb. J. 3 (1958); Howlett, *Arbitration in the Public Sector*, Proceedings of the Southwestern Legal Foundation 15th Annual Institute on Labor Law 231 (1969).

3. DECIDING QUESTIONS OF ARBITRABILITY

POLICEMEN'S & FIREMEN'S RETIREMENT BOARD v. SULLIVAN

173 Conn. 1, 376 A.2d 399 (1977)

Longo, Associate Justice. Since these cases arise from the same factual situation and since they have been treated as companion cases throughout the course of their development we shall treat them in a single opinion. In the first case the plaintiffs, the Policemen's and Firemen's Retirement Board of the city of New Haven and the city of New Haven, sought an injunction, which was granted by the Superior Court (*Mulvey, J.*), restraining and prohibiting the defendants from initiating or proceeding with arbitration. In the second case, the plaintiffs, New Haven Police Union Local 530 et al., sought an order, which was denied, directing the defendant to proceed with arbitration. The union appealed from both judgments, along with Donald R. Sullivan and James Jackson who appealed with it from the former judgment.

The parties filed a stipulation of facts applicable to both cases from which the following summary may be drawn: Donald R. Sullivan and James Jackson are city of New Haven police officers who suffered injuries in the course of their employment whereupon they applied for disability retirement and were rejected by the Policemen's and Firemen's Retirement Board. Instead, they were offered less strenuous duty, which they refused. The New Haven Police Union Local 530, of which Sullivan and Jackson were members, initiated a grievance pursuant to the procedure provided in an agreement between the city of New Haven and the New Haven Police Union Local 530 and Council 15, AFSCME, AFL-CIO, hereinafter referred to as the agreement, and claimed that the dispute should go to arbitration under the terms of the agreement. The Policemen's and Firemen's Retirement Board of the city of New Haven and the city of New Haven instituted an action in Superior Court seeking an injunction restraining Officers Sullivan and Jackson, the union and the Connecticut Board of Mediation and Arbitration from proceeding with arbitration. The union, on the same date, filed an action to compel the city to proceed with arbitration. The issues posed by these appeals are whether the court erred in ruling that the union was not entitled to an order directing the city to proceed with arbitration and in ruling that the union et al. were enjoined from seeking arbitration.

The first question requiring resolution is whether the issue of the arbitrability of the grievance is a question for the court or for the arbitrator to decide. The determination of this issue requires a preliminary examination of the agreement and the grievance procedure provided therein. The grievance procedure established by article 3 of the agreement consists of a four-step process, the last step of which provides: "If the complainant and his representative, if represented, are not satisfied with the decision rendered, he or his representative may submit the grievance to the Connecticut State Board of Mediation and Arbitration, and the decision rendered by the arbitrator(s) shall be final and binding upon both parties." In order to invoke article 3, the claimant must have a grievance, which is defined by article 3(b) as follows: "A grievance for the purpose of this procedure shall be considered to be an employee or Union complaint concerned with: (1) Discharge, suspension or other disciplinary action. (2) Charge of favoritism or discrimination. (3) Interpretation and application of rules and regulations and policies of the Police Department. (4) *Matters relating to the interpretation and application of the Articles and Sections of this Agreement.*" (Emphasis supplied.) The union et al. seek to reach arbitration through the application of part 4 of article 3(b). They contend that the dispute involves the interpretation or application of the agreement since it involves a determination of the applicability and interpretation of article 15 of the agreement. Article 15 states: "Section 1. Police Pension Plan # 1, and all amendments thereto, shall continue to be the Police Pension for all members of the Department employed prior to December 31, 1957. Section 2. Police Pension Plan # 2, and all amendments thereto, shall continue to be the Police Pension for all members of the Department employed on or after January 1, 1958." If article 15 were intended by the parties to the agreement to incorporate the provisions of the pension plans in the agreement, then it would appear that the determination of the pension claims of Sullivan and Jackson would be matters relating to the interpretation and application of the articles and sections of the agreement. This final issue, however, need not be reached if we decide that the question of arbitrability is enough to send the dispute to arbitration.

The agreement sets forth the boundaries of the disputes the parties have agreed to submit to arbitration in article 3, step 4(e), which states in part: "The arbitrator(s) jurisdiction to make an award shall be limited by the submission and confined to the interpretation and/or application of the provisions of this Agreement." It is clear that by using the broad language of this provision the parties intended to allow submission of legal, as well as factual, questions to the arbitrators. The authority to allow arbitrators to resolve legal questions is clearly established in our law. *United Electrical, Radio & Machine Workers v. Union Mfg. Co.,* 145 Conn. 285, 141 A.2d 479; *Colt's Industrial Union v. Colt's Mfg. Co.,* 137 Conn. 305, 77 A.2d 301. Granting the arbitrator's authority to resolve legal questions, however, does not automatically require that the issue of arbitrability go to arbitration. As we stated in the leading case of *Connecticut Union of Telephone Workers v. Southern New England Telephone Co.,* 148 Conn. 192, 197, 169 A.2d 646: "Whether the parties have agreed to submit to arbitration not only the merits of the dispute but the very question of arbitrability, as well, depends upon the intention manifested in the agreement they have made. No one is under a duty to submit any question to arbitration except to the extent that he has signified his willingness." We stated further (p. 198, 169 A.2d p. 649): "Whether a dispute is an arbitrable one is a legal question for the court rather than for arbitrators, in the absence of a provision in the agreement giving arbitrators such jurisdiction. The parties may manifest such a purpose by an express provision or by the use of broad terms." Such broad terms were found to exist in a case where the contract called for the submission to arbitration of "'[a]ny dispute that cannot be adjudicated between the Employer and Union'"; *International Brotherhood v. Trudon & Platt Motor Lines, Inc.,* 146 Conn. 17, 20, 147 A.2d 484, 487; and where arbitration was required of "[a]ll questions in dispute and all claims arising out of said contract"; *Liggett v. Torrington Building Co.,* 114 Conn. 425, 430, 158 A. 917, 918. Shortly after we decided *Connecticut Union of Telephone Workers v. Southern New England Telephone Co., supra,* we decided *International Union v. General Electric Co.,*

148 Conn. 693, 174 A.2d 298, in which we applied the controlling federal law as declared in *United Steelworkers of America v. American Mfg. Co.*, 363 U.S. 564, and *United Steelworkers of America v. Warrior & Gulf Navigation Co.*, 363 U.S. 574, to a dispute involving interstate commerce. We quoted from *Warrior, supra,* 582, the rule that "the judicial inquiry [as to the scope of an arbitration clause in a labor management contract] ... must be strictly confined to the question whether the reluctant party did agree to arbitrate the grievance.... An order to arbitrate the particular grievance should not be denied unless it may be said with positive assurance that the arbitration clause is not susceptible of an interpretation that covers the asserted dispute. Doubts should be resolved in favor of coverage." *International Union v. General Electric Co., supra,* 148 Conn. 700-701, 174 A.2d 302. Though it was our duty in that case, and in *Hudson Wire Co. v. Winsted Brass Workers Union,* 150 Conn. 546, 191 A.2d 557, to apply the federal rule; *Textile Workers Union v. Lincoln Mills,* 353 U.S. 448, 456; this court has subsequently indicated its approval of application of the *Warrior* rule to situations in which Connecticut law applied. In the recent case of *Board of Police Commissioners v. Maher,* 171 Conn. 613, 621, 370 A.2d 1076, 1080, in ruling that the board of mediation and arbitration was authorized by the agreement presently under consideration to arbitrate a grievance concerning disciplinary action against a New Haven police officer, this court stated: "[T]he trial court correctly concluded that the bargaining agreement conferred on the defendant board the authority to arbitrate disciplinary grievances. *International Brotherhood v. Trudon & Platt Motor Lines, Inc.,* 146 Conn. 17, 21, 147 A.2d 484; *Pratt, Read & Co. v. United Furniture Workers,* 136 Conn. 205, 209, 70 A.2d 120. This is especially true since any '[d]oubts [concerning arbitrability] should be resolved in favor of coverage.' *United Steelworkers of America v. Warrior & Gulf Navigation Co.,* 363 U.S. 574, 583; *International Union v. General Electric Co.,* 148 Conn. 693, 701, 702, 174 A.2d 298." Despite our acceptance of the federal rule favoring arbitration, we are unpersuaded that the language of this agreement requires that we send the question of the arbitrability of the dispute to arbitration. The question of arbitrability is not one which requires a court to interject its presence into the merits of a labor dispute. Rather, the question of arbitrability is purely a question of contract interpretation in which courts have expertise and an historically established role to play. Indeed, in discussing the leading federal case of *United Steelworkers of America v. Warrior & Gulf Navigation Co., supra,* the United States Supreme Court stated that pursuant to a grievance procedure submitting to arbitration "all disputes between the parties 'as to the meaning, interpretation and application of the provisions of this agreement'"; *United Steelworkers of America v. American Mfg. Co., supra,* 363 U.S. 565; the question of arbitrability should be resolved by the court. The court stated in *Warrior, supra,* 583 n. 7: "It is clear that under both the agreement in this case and that involved in [*United Steelworkers of America v.*] *American Manufacturing Co.* [363 U.S. 564], the question of arbitrability is for the courts to decide. Cf. Cox, *Reflections Upon Labor Arbitration,* 72 Harv. L. Rev. 1482, 1508-1509. Where the assertion by the claimant is that the parties excluded from court determination not merely the decision of the merits of the grievance but also the question of its arbitrability, vesting power to make both decisions in the arbitrator, the claim-

ant must bear the burden of a clear demonstration of that purpose." We can find no such clear demonstration in the present case where the arbitrator's power is "limited by the submission and confined to the interpretation and/or application of the provisions of this Agreement."

Having determined that the court was correct in ruling that it had the authority to decide whether the dispute should go to arbitration, we must now turn to the issue whether it properly decided that issue against sending the dispute to arbitration. By requesting the lower court to issue an injunction restraining the union et al. from proceeding with arbitration, the plaintiffs were, in effect, asking the court to interpret the substantive provisions of the agreement. As the court stated in *United Steelworkers of America v. Warrior & Gulf Navigation Co., supra,* 363 U.S. 585: "[T]he court should view with suspicion an attempt to persuade it to become entangled in the construction of the substantive provisions of a labor agreement." We are also mindful of the court's distinction in *Warrior, supra,* 578, between arbitration of commercial and labor disputes. The court stated: "In the commercial case, arbitration is the substitute for litigation. Here arbitration is the substitute for industrial strife. Since arbitration of labor disputes has quite different functions from arbitration under an ordinary commercial agreement, the hostility evinced by courts toward arbitration of commercial agreements has no place here. For arbitration of labor disputes under collective bargaining agreements is part and parcel of the collective bargaining process itself." This court must, therefore, look carefully at any order which seeks to interject a judicial body into the functioning of the collective bargaining process. As we stated in *Waterbury Board of Education v. Waterbury Teachers Assn.,* 168 Conn. 54, 64, 357 A.2d 466, 471: "Arbitration is a creature of contract. *Connecticut Union of Telephone Workers v. Southern New England Telephone Co.,* 148 Conn. 192, 197, 169 A.2d 646. The continued autonomy of that process can be maintained only with a minimum of judicial intrusion."

Under the grievance procedure established by the agreement "[m]atters relating to the interpretation and application of the Articles and Sections of this Agreement" are considered grievances subject to arbitration under step four of the grievance procedure. Since there is no claim that the parties have not complied with the procedural requirements of the grievance procedure, the only question confronting us is whether there is doubt that the dispute should not go to arbitration. If there is any doubt, the issue must be resolved in favor of arbitration. *Board of Police Commissioners v. Maher, supra.*

We conclude that the trial court did not err in deciding that the parties did not intend that disputes involving disability retirement should be the subject of arbitration under the procedure established by article 3 of the agreement. Those seeking arbitration argue that the parties to the agreement, by agreeing to article 15 of the agreement, intended to incorporate the provisions of the two police pension plans mentioned therein into the agreement. We do not agree. Article 15 merely states which pension plans shall apply to which employees and states nothing about the provisions of either. Further, the pension plans were not established by the agreement, but were created by Special Act. The police officers, Sullivan and Jackson, fall into the category of employees covered by Special Acts 1957, No. 531, entitled "An Act Establishing a Pension Fund for New Haven Policemen and Firemen Employed after December 31, 1957." Section 2 of No. 531 of the 1957 Special Acts states, in part: "The management and administration of the pension plan are hereby vested in a pension board, which shall consist of seven members." The pension board is a distinct entity which was not made a party to the agreement and could not, therefore, have agreed to grant its powers to an arbitrator, who derives his powers from the agreement. Further, the provisions of article 15 of the agreement may be compared to those of article 17, § 1, of the agreement by which "[t]he City agrees to continue to provide for the member and his enrolled dependents, at no cost to the employee, the Blue Cross Semi-Private Room Plan with the Maternity Care Rider, Major Medical insurance coverage and the CMS Community Plan." Clearly, the parties, by agreeing to article 17, did not intend to allow the submission to arbitration of claims by covered employees which had been disallowed by Blue Cross, CMS or the major medical carrier. The pension plans are not incorporated by reference nor are they set forth verbatim in the agreement. It is, therefore, impossible to say that the substantive provisions of the pension plans were made part of the agreement or that the parties signified their willingness to submit pension disputes to arbitration. As stated before: "No one is under a duty to submit any question to arbitration except to the extent that he has signified his willingness." *Connecticut Union of Telephone Workers v. Southern New England Telephone Co., supra,* 148 Conn. 197, 169 A.2d 649. Therefore, since the city did not signify its willingness to submit such disputes to arbitration, the court properly denied the application of Local 530 and Council 15 for an order directing the city to proceed with arbitration....

[The final portion of the opinion sustained the lower court's order enjoining the parties from proceeding with arbitration of the dispute.]

LOISELLE, ASSOCIATE JUSTICE (dissenting): These consolidated appeals present two questions. The first is: Does the contract at issue here assign to the arbitrators the duty of *deciding* which disputes are arbitrable, or is that decision one for the courts? I agree with the majority opinion that this contract does not assign that duty to the arbitrators. The arbitration clause requires arbitration of "[m]atters relating to the interpretation and application of the Articles and Sections of this Agreement." I understand that we have decided to follow the United States Supreme Court in arbitration matters. The language of this arbitration clause tracks that of a contract which the United States Supreme Court held left the *decision* as to which disputes are arbitrable to the courts. The language in that contract required arbitration of all disputes "'as to the meaning, interpretation and application of the provisions of this agreement.'" *United Steelworkers of America v. American Mfg. Co.,* 363 U.S. 564, 565.

Once the decision as to which disputes are arbitrable has been determined to be one for the court to make, the second question arises: Is *this* dispute arbitrable? It is in answering this question that I disagree with the majority. If we follow the United States Supreme Court, and apply the same test it applied in *United Steelworkers of America v. American Mfg. Co., supra,* this dispute is arbitrable.

United Steelworkers of America v. American Mfg. Co., supra, involved a grievance which the Court of Appeals had determined to be frivolous and patently baseless, thus not subject to arbitration. The Supreme Court reversed, holding that even frivolous, baseless claims must go to arbitration if "the party seeking arbitration is making a claim which on its face is governed by the contract." *Id.*, 568. The Court explained: "The courts ... have no business weighing the merits of the grievance, considering whether there is equity in a particular claim, or determining whether there is particular language in the written instrument which will support the claim.... The processing of even frivolous claims may have therapeutic values of which those who are not a part of the plant environment may be quite unaware." *Ibid.* I submit that the majority opinion weighs the merits and looks for language in the written instrument to support the claim.

The grievance in this case is a claim by the union that the "contract provided for a review of the orders and decision of the Policemen's and Firemen's Retirement Board." The majority tests the arbitrability of the dispute by asking whether the agreement incorporated the provisions of the police pension plans, or whether the parties signified their willingness to submit *pension disputes* to arbitration. I think those are the wrong yardsticks. The contract clearly indicates the willingness of the parties to submit to arbitration disputes concerning the application and interpretation of the contract, and one party has asserted that the contract should be interpreted to provide for review of the decision of the pension board. This is a dispute concerning interpretation of the contract, and it must go to arbitration.

Applying the test of *United Steelworkers of America v. American Mfg. Co.,* *supra,* "whether the party seeking arbitration is making a claim which on its face is governed by the contract," it is clear that this claim, that the contract provides for review, is determined *by the contract.* The fact that examination of the contract shows that no review is provided for does not make the dispute less arbitrable, but more arbitrable. This is a claim not governed by statute, by general contract law or, indeed, by any authority other than the contract itself. Only by looking *to the contract* may its validity or lack of validity be seen....

ACTING SUPERINTENDENT v. UNITED LIVERPOOL FACULTY ASSOCIATION

42 N.Y.2d 509, 369 N.E.2d 746 (1977)

JONES, JUDGE: We hold that in arbitrations which proceed under the authority of the Taylor Law, the scope of the particular arbitration clause, and thus whether the question sought to be submitted to arbitration is within or without the ambit of that clause, is to be determined by the courts. In making such determinations the courts are to be guided by the principle that the agreement to arbitrate must be express, direct and unequivocal as to the issues or disputes to be submitted to arbitration; anything less will lead to a denial of arbitration.

In this case Liverpool Central School District and the United Liverpool Faculty Association entered into a collective bargaining agreement which provided a grievance procedure, the fourth and final step of which called for submission of an unresolved grievance to arbitration. Tracking the provisions of subdivision 4 of section 682 of the General Municipal Law, the school district and the faculty association defined a grievance as follows: "*Grievance* shall mean any claimed violation, misinterpretation, or inequitable application of the existing laws, rules, procedures, regulations, administrative orders or work rules of the

District, which relates to or involves Teachers' health or safety, physical facilities, materials or equipment furnished to teachers or supervision of Teachers; provided, however, that such term shall not include any matter involving a Teacher's rate of compensation, retirement benefits, disciplinary proceeding or any matter which is otherwise reviewable pursuant to law or any rule or regulation having the force and effect of law."

In November, 1974, Mrs. Lorraine Gargiul, an elementary school teacher, was obliged to take sick leave due to illness. In February, 1975 she notified the school district that she would be able to return to her teaching duties the following month. On February 26 she was advised that pursuant to the provisions of section 913 of the Education Law she would be required to submit to a complete medical examination by the school district physician, Dr. Paul Day, before being permitted to return to the classroom. The teacher took the position that she would participate only in an examination by a female physician. Following further correspondence of similar tenor, on March 17, 1975 the board of education passed a resolution directing her to be examined by Dr. Day before returning to her teaching responsibilities, if, after reviewing her health history, he determined that such examination was necessary. On the same day, based on the teacher's refusal to be examined by Dr. Day, she was placed on leave of absence without pay until the matter was resolved.

On April 10, 1975 the faculty association instituted grievance procedures on behalf of Mrs. Gargiul. When the issue was not resolved, the faculty association demanded arbitration in accordance with the provisions of the collective bargaining agreement. The school district promptly applied for a stay of arbitration which was granted at Special Term. The Appellate Division reversed. We now reverse the determination of that court and reinstate the disposition of Special Term.

It will be useful to place this case, and indeed all arbitration under the Taylor Law, in a broader context. Generally speaking, as the law of arbitration between private parties has developed and progressed, a difference in perspective and approach has evolved between arbitration in commercial matters and arbitration in labor relations. In the former it is the rule that the parties will not be held to have chosen arbitration as the forum for the resolution of their disputes in the absence of an express, unequivocal agreement to that effect; absent such an explicit commitment neither party may be compelled to arbitrate (*Gangel v. DeGroot,* 41 N.Y.2d 840, 841, 362 N.E.2d 249, 250; *Riverdale Fabrics Corp. v. Tillinghast-Stiles Co.,* 306 N.Y. 288, 289, 292, 118 N.E.2d 104, 105, 106). In the field of labor relations, by contrast, the general rule is the converse. Because of the recognition that arbitration has been demonstrated to be a salutary method of resolving labor disputes, because of the public policy (principally expressed in the Federal cases) which favors arbitration as a means of resolving such disputes, and because of the associated available inference that the parties to a collective bargaining agreement probably intended to resolve their differences by arbitration, the courts have held that controversies arising between the parties to such an agreement fall within the scope of the arbitration clause unless the parties have employed language which clearly manifests an intent to exclude a particular subject matter (*Howard & Co. v. Daley,* 27 N.Y.2d 285, 289-290,

265 N.E.2d 747, 749-751; *Long Island Lumber Co. v. Martin,* 15 N.Y.2d 380, 385, 207 N.E.2d 190, 193).[1]

Arbitration agreements that derive their vitality from the Taylor Law (Civil Service Law, art. 14) are sufficiently different that they cannot properly be categorized under either of these headings. Initially we observe that our court has never held that boards of education, unless authorized by specific legislation, are free to delegate to arbitrators the resolution of issues for which the boards have official responsibility. The enactment of the Taylor Law, establishing authority for the use of voluntary arbitration, confirmed rather than vitiated the principle of the nondelegable responsibility of elected representatives in the public sector. Hence, we approach consideration of the scope of arbitration clauses in public employment from this perspective.

When challenge is raised to the submission to arbitration of a dispute between employer and employee in the public sector the threshold consideration by the courts as to whether there is a valid agreement to arbitrate (CPLR 7503, subd. [a]) must proceed in sequence on two levels. Initially it must be determined whether arbitration claims with respect to the particular subject matter are authorized by the terms of the Taylor Law. The permissible scope of arbitration under that law is variously limited (*Susquehanna Valley Central School Dist. at Conklin v. Susquehanna Valley Teacher's Ass'n,* 37 N.Y.2d 614, 616-617, 339 N.E.2d 132, 133-134; *Syracuse Teachers Ass'n v. Board of Educ.,* 35 N.Y.2d 743, 744, 320 N.E.2d 646; *Board of Educ. v. Associated Teachers of Huntington,* 30 N.Y.2d 122, 130, 282 N.E.2d 109, 113). If, of course, the subject matter of the dispute between the parties falls outside the permissible scope of the Taylor Law, there is no occasion further to consider the language or the reach of the particular arbitration clause (*Candor Central School Dist. v. Candor Teachers Ass'n,* 42 N.Y.2d 266, 366 N.E.2d 826; *Cohoes City School Dist. v. Cohoes Teachers Ass'n,* 40 N.Y.2d 774, 358 N.E.2d 878).

If it is concluded, however, that reference to arbitration is authorized under the Taylor Law, inquiry then turns at a second level to a determination of whether such authority was in fact exercised and whether the parties did agree by the terms of their particular arbitration clause to refer their differences in this specific area to arbitration. In the field of public employment, as distinguished from labor relations in the private sector, the public policy favoring arbitration — of recent origin — does not yet carry the same historical or general acceptance, nor, as evidenced in part by some of the litigation in our court, has there so far been a similar demonstration of the efficacy of arbitration as a means for resolving controversies in governmental employment. Accordingly, it cannot be inferred as a practical matter that the parties to collective bargaining agreements in the public sector always intend to adopt the broadest permissible arbitration clauses. Indeed, inasmuch as the responsibilities of the elected representatives of the tax-paying public are overarching and fundamentally nondelegable, it must be taken, in the absence of clear, unequivocal agree-

---

[1] In our view the not infrequent reference to a "presumption of arbitrability," while understandable, does not advance analysis and indeed in some instances serves rather to obfuscate. In the field of labor relations, however, experience has demonstrated that an inference may usually be drawn that the signatories to a collective bargaining agreement between private parties intended to submit their differences to arbitration.

ment to the contrary, that the board of education did *not* intend to refer differences which might arise to the arbitration forum. Such reference is not to be based on implication.

We turn then to the appeal now before us to make the necessary judicial determinations both with respect to Taylor Law authorization and as to the scope of this arbitration clause, i.e., whether Mrs. Gargiul's present complaint falls within the contract definition of grievance. We have no difficulty at the first level in concluding that there is nothing in statute, decisional law or public policy which would preclude the board of education, acting in behalf of the district, and the association, should they agree to do so, from referring disputes of the present nature to arbitration.

At the second level, we address the particular language employed by the parties for the articulation of their agreement to arbitrate. Surely their definition of grievances does not approach the breadth of provisions which in other contexts are referred to as "broad arbitration clauses." This clause is explicitly a limited one. Indeed in form it expresses two separate agreements. First, the parties agree that certain disputes ("claimed violation, misinterpretation or inequitable application of existing laws, rules, procedures, regulations, administrative orders or work rules of the District which relate to or involve Teachers' health or safety, physical facilities, materials or equipment furnished to teachers or supervision of Teachers") shall be submitted to arbitration. In the same paragraph they then agree that other disputes shall not be referred to arbitration ("any matter involving a Teacher's rate of compensation, retirement benefits, disciplinary proceeding"). Thus, the question is not to determine the outer boundaries of a single definition: the problem is rather to determine into which of two different classifications the present dispute falls, or more precisely in this instance, how it shall be treated when it may reasonably be included within both groups.

As is evident from the arguments pressed by the parties, as well as from the decisions in the courts below, the present controversy could be classified both in surface description and substantive context in either category. On the one hand, although contending principally that the issue of arbitrability is for the arbitrator and not for the courts, the faculty association has labeled the board's action a claimed violation or inequitable application of existing laws and rules relating to the teacher's health, thus in the included category. On the other hand, the school district classifies the dispute as a matter involving disciplinary proceedings, in the excluded category. The labels attached by the parties, each evidently for its own advantage, can never be determinative. A very reasonable assertion can be made that this particular controversy falls within both the included and the excluded categories.

In this circumstance, we cannot conclude that the present dispute falls clearly and unequivocally within the class of claims agreed to be referred to arbitration. Accordingly, the application of the school district for a stay of arbitration was properly granted.

For the reasons stated, the order of the Appellate Division should be reversed, without costs, and the order of Supreme Court, Onondaga County, reinstated.

[The concurring opinion of Gabrielli, J., is omitted.]

NOTES

1. Courts appear to be more willing to declare a dispute non-arbitrable in the public sector than in the private sector. This phenomenon has probably resulted because governmental employers are generally considered to retain broader discretion and "management rights" to control the employment relationship than are their private sector counterparts. In addition, collective agreements in the public sector are likely to exclude in specific terms more subjects from arbitration, and statutes and public policy considerations often reserve other areas for final decision by management alone. See generally Toole, *Judicial Activism in Public Sector Grievance Arbitration: A Study of Recent Developments*, 33 Arb. J. 6 (1978); Abrams, *The Power Issue in Public Sector Grievance Arbitration*, 67 Minn. L. Rev. 261 (1982); Craver, *The Judicial Enforcement of Public Sector Grievance Arbitration*, 58 Tex. L. Rev. 329, 331-41 (1980).

2. In *Mineola Sch. Dist. v. Teachers Ass'n*, 46 N.Y.2d 568, 389 N.E.2d 111 (1979), the New York Court of Appeals reaffirmed its *Liverpool* arbitrability standard precluding the arbitral resolution of grievances where the result might contravene public policy, but it emphasized that an order to arbitrate would only be denied on this ground where it would contravene "a strong public policy, almost invariably involving an important constitutional or statutory duty or responsibility." Mere incantations of "public policy" will not be permitted to prevent the arbitration of every grievance that may impair the unfettered flexibility of management. Contrast this view with the more extreme position taken in *Bargaining Comm. v. City of Pittsburgh*, 391 A.2d 1318, 99 L.R.R.M. 3278 (1978), wherein the Pennsylvania Supreme Court informed governmental entities that arbitration will almost never be withheld based upon the claim that the public employer's delegation of authority over the matter in dispute to an outside arbiter contravenes public policy.

> To permit an employer to enter into agreements and include terms such as grievance arbitration which raise the expectations of those concerned, and then to subsequently refuse to abide by those provisions on the basis of its lack of capacity would invite discord and distrust and create an atmosphere wherein a harmonious relationship would virtually be impossible to maintain.
>
> Good faith bargaining would require that questions as to the legality of the proposed terms of a collective bargaining agreement should be resolved by the parties to the agreement at the bargaining stage.

See also *Lakeland Bd. of Educ. v. Barni*, 49 N.Y.2d 311, 401 N.E.2d 912 (1980), and *Wyandanch Sch. Dist. v. Teachers Ass'n*, 48 N.Y.2d 669, 397 N.E.2d 384 (1979), wherein the New York Court of Appeals indicated that a court should not deny arbitrability merely because the contractual language in dispute is ambiguous, since it is the function of the arbitrator, and not the court, to interpret such ambiguous language.

3. In *Kaleva-Norman-Dickson Sch. Dist. v. Teachers Ass'n*, 227 N.W.2d 500, 89 L.R.R.M. 2078 (1975), the Michigan Supreme Court adopted the private sector presumption of arbitrability in holding that even though a school board in a negotiated agreement had reserved to itself without limitation all statutory powers vested in it, including the right to hire all employees and to determine the conditions of their continued employment or their dismissal, where the contract required the arbitration of claims concerning the violation or misinterpretation of any provision and provided that no teacher could be reduced in rank or compensation without just cause, a probationary teacher's claim that the nonrenewal of her contract violated the agreement was subject to arbitration. The Pennsylvania Supreme Court has similarly ruled that just cause for the dismissal of a non-tenured teacher is arbitrable and that such a contractual provision does not constitute an impermissible delegation of school board authority to the arbitrator. *Philadelphia Bd. of Educ. v. Teachers Local 3,* 346 A.2d 35, 90 L.R.R.M. 2879 (1975).

But cf. *Neshaminy Fed'n of Teachers v. School Dist.,* 462 A.2d 629, 1981-83 PBC ¶ 37,761 (Pa. 1983), wherein the court found a dismissal grievance nonarbitrable under a contract which provided that employees would not be "disciplined, reprimanded, reduced in rank, contractual compensation or contractual advantage without just cause" and further indicated that the agreement would not supercede the provisions of the Public School Code, since the omission of the word "dismissal" was found to evidence an intent not to include such actions within the scope of the term "discipline" in light of the specific School Code procedures available for dismissal appeals. See also *AFSCME, Local 1905 v. Recorder's Court Judges,* 248 N.W.2d 220, 94 L.R.R.M. 2392 (Mich. 1976) (holding that specific procedures of probation officer removal statute take precedence over contractual arbitration procedures). Other courts have determined that since decisions regarding the retention or nonrenewal of non-tenured teachers fall within the exclusive competence of school boards, public policy considerations dictate that disagreements concerning such judgments are not subject to grievance arbitration. See, e.g., *Mindemann v. Indep. Sch. Dist. No. 6 of Caddo Cty.,* 771 P.2d 996, 1988-90 PBC ¶ 35,274 (Okla. 1989); *Moravek v. Davenport Community Sch. Dist.,* 262 N.W.2d 797, 1977-78 PBC ¶ 36,182 (Iowa 1978); *Chassie v. School Dist.,* 356 A.2d 708, 92 L.R.R.M. 3359 (Me. 1976). See also *Wibaux Educ. Ass'n v. Wibaux High Sch.,* 573 P.2d 1162, 97 L.R.R.M. 2592 (1978), wherein the Montana Supreme Court indicated that while decisions regarding the continuation of probationary teachers would not themselves be arbitrable, a claim that a school district failed to comply properly with contractually specified evaluation or hearing procedures would be subject to arbitration. Accord *Bear Lake Educ. Ass'n v. Board of Trustees,* 776 P.2d 452, 1988-90 PBC ¶ 35,307 (Idaho 1989); *New York Bd. of Educ. v. Federation of Teachers,* 46 N.Y.2d 1018, 389 N.E.2d 1057 (1979); *Professional Assembly v. University of Hawaii,* 659 P.2d 717, 113 L.R.R.M. 3201 (Haw. 1983).

Even where a public employer does not possess the authority to permit an arbitrator to finally resolve a matter within its exclusive managerial prerogative, it may agree to *advisory* arbitration, and a court will enforce such a contractual obligation despite the non-binding character of the resulting award. See *Board of Educ., Twp. of Bernards v. Education Ass'n,* 399 A.2d 620, 101 L.R.R.M. 2251 (N.J. 1979); *Teaneck Bd. of Educ. v. Teaneck Teachers Ass'n,* 462 A.2d 137, 1981-83 PBC ¶ 37,785 (N.J. 1983).

4. A school district's decision not to renew a teacher's extra-curricular assignment may well be arbitrable, but some courts require a more substantial demonstration of arbitrability than do others. Compare *Westbrook Sch. Comm. v. Westbrook Teachers Ass'n,* 404 A.2d 204, 1979-80 PBC ¶ 36,623 (Me. 1979) (arbitrable), with *Albert Lea Educ. Ass'n v. Independent Sch. Dist.,* 284 N.W.2d 1, 103 L.R.R.M. 2378 (Minn. 1979) (not arbitrable). Can the two decisions be logically distinguished or do they simply reflect differing judicial philosophies regarding arbitrability? See also *Cloquet Educ. Ass'n v. Independent Sch. Dist.,* 1984-86 PBC ¶ 34,170 (Minn. 1984).

5. When a permissive subject for bargaining is included in a negotiated agreement that contains a broad grievance-arbitration provision, the representative labor organization may be able to obtain arbitration of disputes pertaining to that non-mandatory topic. See, e.g., *Minneapolis Fed'n of Teachers Local 59 v. Minneapolis Sch. Dist. 1*, 258 N.W.2d 802, 96 L.R.R.M. 2706 (Minn. 1977) (teacher transfers); *Susquehanna Valley Cent. Sch. Dist. v. Susquehanna Valley Teachers Ass'n*, 37 N.Y.2d 614, 339 N.E.2d 132 (1975) (staff reduction). However, other courts have indicated that contractual disputes relating to such non-mandatory items are not arbitrable, particularly where matters of basic government policy are involved. See, e.g., *Ridgefield Park Educ. Ass'n v. Ridgefield Park Bd. of Educ.*, 393 A.2d 278, 98 L.R.R.M. 3285 (N.J. 1978); *Dunellen Bd. of Educ. v. Dunellen Educ. Ass'n*, 64 N.J. 17, 311 A.2d 737 (1973).

6. In *PLRB v. Bald Eagle Area Sch. Dist.*, 451 A.2d 671, 1981-83 PBC ¶ 37,636 (Pa. 1982), teachers sought arbitration of a dispute concerning the number of school days for which they were contractually entitled to pay during a year which had involved a strike. Although state law prohibited compensation for days teachers were on strike, the court ruled that the dispute was arbitrable, since "arbitration is not an improper remedy simply because an arbitrator might possibly fashion an invalid award." The court found that there was no reason to assume that arbitrators would ignore the law and issue decisions based upon contract interpretations that conflict with legislative mandates. See also *Arbor Park Sch. Dist. v. Ballweber*, 1981-83 PBC ¶ 37,763 (Ill. 1983).

7. Where a court can find no express contractual provision remotely regulating the issue in dispute, it will usually conclude that the grievance is not arbitrable. See, e.g., *City of Brooklyn Center v. Minnesota Teamsters, Local 320*, 271 N.W.2d 315, 1977-78 PBC ¶ 36,429 (Minn. 1978); *AFSCME, Local 66 v. St. Louis Cty. Bd. of Comm'rs*, 281 N.W.2d 166, 1979-80 PBC ¶ 36,593 (Minn. 1979). Do you think that courts should permit public sector arbitrators to interpret collective contracts as implicitly imposing some enforceable restrictions upon management freedom? If yes, what sources of arbitral law would be available to guide the arbitrators?

8. In the private sector, issues concerning "procedural arbitrability" are generally held to be matters to be decided by the arbitrator, not the court. See *John Wiley & Sons v. Livingston*, 376 U.S. 543 (1964). Such arbitral deference regarding procedural arbitrability issues is generally followed in the public sector too. See, e.g., *West Fargo Sch. Dist. v. West Fargo Educ. Ass'n*, 259 N.W.2d 612, 97 L.R.R.M. 2361 (N. Dak. 1977); *Duquesne School Dist. v. Educ. Ass'n*, 380 A.2d 353, 97 L.R.R.M. 2011 (Pa. 1977); *Minnesota Fed'n of Teachers, Local 331 v. School Dist.*, 310 N.W.2d 482, 113 L.R.R.M. 2279 (Minn. 1981).

9. Should a grievance arising *after* the expiration date of the relevant agreement be arbitrable? Compare *Machinists Lodge 264 v. Massachusetts Bay Transp. Auth.*, 452 N.E.2d 1155, 116 L.R.R.M. 2283 (Mass. 1983) (arbitrable), with *City of White Plains v. Professional Fire Fighters Ass'n*, 95 L.R.R.M. 3150 (N.Y. Sup. Ct. 1977) (not arbitrable). In *County of Ottawa v. Jaklinski*, 377 N.W.2d 668, 1984-86 PBC ¶ 34,601 (Mich. 1985), the court held that while the right to arbitrate survives contractual expiration when the dispute concerns rights that can accrue or vest during the life of the agreement, an employee's contractual right not to be discharged except for just cause does not survive expiration of the contract. See also *Nolde Bros. v. Local 358, Bakery & Confectionery Workers Union*, 430 U.S. 243 (1977), wherein the Supreme Court held arbitrable a private sector severance pay dispute that did not arise until after the expiration of the controlling contract. Can a stronger argument be made to support post-expiration arbitrability in the public sector, since most governmental employees, unlike their private sector counterparts, cannot strike to enhance their claims even after the bargaining agreement has expired?

10. *City of Grand Rapids v. Police Lodge 97,* 330 N.W.2d 52, 1981-83 PBC ¶ 37,678 (Mich. 1982), involved a collective contract that provided for the termination of grievance proceedings where the underlying employee complaint was submitted to a court or administrative agency for resolution. The court sustained the authority of a labor organization to agree to such an election of remedies clause and held that such a provision precluded arbitration of a grievance that had become the basis for legal proceedings. In the absence of such a provision, an employee who has unsuccessfully sought redress through external procedures, such as those provided under a veteran's preference act, may still be able to have his dispute taken to arbitration. See *Bay City Sch. Dist. v. Bay City Educ. Ass'n,* 390 N.W.2d 159, 1986-88 PBC ¶ 34,678 (Mich. 1986); *AFSCME, Council 96 v. Arrowhead Reg'l Cors. Bd.,* 356 N.W.2d 295 (Minn. 1984).

11. Once a bargaining agreement has been executed, statutorily prescribed impasse resolution procedures will generally not be applicable to disputes that arise with respect to the interpretation of the negotiated contract. See *AFSCME, Local 1518 v. Meharg,* 281 N.W.2d 313, 1979-80 PBC ¶ 36,642 (Mich. 1979); *Transportation Workers v. Omaha Transit Auth.,* 286 N.W.2d 102, 1979-80 PBC ¶ 36,787 (Neb. 1979).

4. JUDICIAL REVIEW OF ARBITRATION AWARDS

JACINTO v. EGAN

391 A.2d 1173, 100 L.R.R.M. 2138 (R.I. 1978)

KELLEHER, JUSTICE: This is an appeal by the Cumberland Teachers' Association (the association) from a judgment of the Superior Court vacating an arbitration award made pursuant to the terms of a collective bargaining agreement effective during the years 1974-76 (the agreement) between the Cumberland School Committee (the school committee) and the association. The arbitrator had approved a request by a Cumberland teacher for a 1-year leave of absence without pay which had been previously denied by the school committee.

In March 1975, Paula McKeown, a chemistry teacher with 3 years' experience in the Cumberland school system, applied to the Superintendent of Schools (the superintendent) for a leave of absence without remuneration for the 1975-76 academic year. The leave was sought to pursue a graduate degree in Molecular Biology at the University of Connecticut, a program which requires full-time study and is not offered either part-time or at night. The advanced academic credits were necessary for further certification as a teacher by the State Department of Education when her provisional certification expired at the end of 5 years.

The agreement contains detailed provisions setting forth the conditions under which Cumberland schoolteachers could be granted leaves of absence. Article XX, entitled "Sabbatical Leave," provides for 1-year leaves with pay for advanced study in an approved college or university program. Leaves under this provision are reserved for teachers with at least 5 years' teaching experience in the Cumberland system. Article XXI, entitled "Long-Term Leaves of Absence," provides for leaves due to a teacher-exchange program, the Peace

Corps, Vista, military duty, and pregnancy. Article XIX is entitled "Leaves of Absence" and lists seven different categories, including section "E. Temporary Leaves of Absence." This section authorizes absence for a variety of events, including such occurrences as religious holidays, educational conferences, and participation in any legal proceeding which is related to the teacher's employment. Section E contains a catchall provision which reads: "2. Teachers may be allowed additional time off for other personal reasons when such requests are considered valid by the Superintendent." Ms. McKeown sought her leave pursuant to this latter provision.

When the school committee denied the request, the association invoked the grievance procedure set forth in Article XXII of the agreement on behalf of Ms. McKeown. Article XXII was described as the "exclusive remedy" for the resolution of grievances.[2] Binding arbitration, before an arbitrator selected by the American Arbitration Association, was the final process for the disposition of grievances.

After a hearing on the merits in July 1975, the arbitrator made the following award:

"That the grievance is arbitrable.
"That Miss McKeown be granted a year's leave without remuneration to attend the University of Connecticut for Advanced Studies.
"In addition, the School Committee has no obligation to keep the teacher(s) after the return of Miss McKeown in September, 1976."

Thereupon, the school committee brought a complaint in the Superior Court for a declaratory judgment to determine the rights of all the parties involved under the agreement and a motion to vacate the award pursuant to G.L. 1956 (1968 Reenactment) § 28-9-18. In a decision dated September 23, 1976, the trial justice held that the arbitrator had, in effect, amended the agreement by granting Ms. McKeown a leave to which she was not entitled. Accordingly, he vacated the award on the ground that the arbitrator exceeded his authority.

The association is now before us on an appeal from the Superior Court judgment, contending that the trial justice exceeded his authority in vacating the arbitrator's award and in refusing to confirm it....

Judicial authority to review or vacate arbitration awards is statutorily prescribed. Section 28-9-18 authorizes the judiciary to vacate an arbitration award only in three limited instances:

"(a) When the award was procured by fraud.
"(b) Where the arbitrator or arbitrators exceeded their powers, or so imperfectly executed them, that a mutual, final and definite award upon the subject matter submitted was not made.
"(c) If there was no valid submission or contract, and the objection has been raised under the conditions set forth in § 28-9-13."

The trial justice, in vacating the award, ruled that the arbitrator "exceeded his powers." He relied in particular on a provision of the agreement (Article XXII) which prohibited the arbitrator from making any decision "amending, modify-

---

[2] A grievance was defined broadly to include any claim by any party to the agreement that there has been a "violation, misinterpretation or inequitable application of the provisions of the agreement."

ing, adding to or subtracting from the provisions of this agreement." In his view the arbitrator, in effect, created a "new classification of leave."

In *Belanger v. Matteson,* 115 R.I. 332, 355, 346 A.2d 124, 137-38, 91 LRRM 2003 (1975), *cert. denied,* 424 U.S. 968, 91 LRRM 2916 (1976), we noted that the judicial branch must not overlook the fact that an arbitration award is the decision of an extra-judicial tribunal which the parties themselves have created and by whose judgment they have mutually agreed to abide. The fact that the arbitrator misconstrued the contract or the law is no ground for striking down his award.

"A judicial reversal of an arbitration award based solely on the reviewing court's disagreement with the arbitrators' interpretation of the contract would not only nullify the bargain made by the parties but also threaten the strong public policy that favors private settlement of grievance disputes arising from collective bargaining agreements." *Id.* at 355-56, 346 A.2d at 138.

The statutory authority to vacate an arbitration award where the arbitrators "exceeded their powers" does not authorize a judicial re-examination of the relevant contractual provisions. *National Railroad Passenger Corp. v. Chesapeake & Ohio Railway,* 551 F.2d 136 (7th Cir. 1977); *Amicizia Societa Navegazione v. Chilean Nitrate & Iodine Sales Corp.,* 274 F.2d 805 (2d Cir.), *cert. denied,* 363 U.S. 843 (1960). The courts are in agreement that an alleged misconstruction of the contract is not a sufficient basis for vacating an arbitration award. *National Railroad Passenger Corp. v. Chesapeake & Ohio Railway,* 551 F.2d at 142. Indeed, awards premised on "clearly erroneous" interpretations of the contract have been affirmed where the result was rationally based upon the contract. *I/S Stavborg v. National Metal Converters, Inc.,* 500 F.2d 424, 432 (2d Cir. 1974). The proper role for the courts in this regard is to determine whether the arbitrator has resolved the grievance by considering the proper sources — "the contract and those circumstances out of which comes the 'common law of the shop'" — but not to determine whether the arbitrator has resolved the grievance correctly. Gorman, Labor Law 585 (1976), quoting *Safeway Stores v. American Bakery & Confectionery Workers International Union, Local 111,* 390 F.2d 79, 82, 67 LRRM 2646 (5th Cir. 1968). As long as the award "draws its essence" from the contract and is based upon a "passably plausible" interpretation of the contract, it is within the arbitrator's authority and our review must end. *United Steelworkers of America v. Enterprise Wheel & Car Corp.,* 363 U.S. 593, 597, 46 LRRM 2423, 34 LA 569 (1960); *Safeway Stores v. American Bakery & Confectionery Workers International Union, Local 111,* 390 F.2d at 83.

The arbitrator basically relied upon three provisions of the contract in finding that certain provisions of the collective bargaining agreement had been violated when the grievant was denied a 1-year leave of absence without pay. First, Article XIX (Leaves of Absence), section E(2), of the agreement provides that "[t]eachers may be allowed additional time off for other personal reasons when such requests are considered valid by the Superintendent." Second, the opening paragraph of Article XIX recognizes the right of the school committee to make and enforce reasonable rules to ensure that there is no abuse of leave benefits. The committee agreed to discuss these rules with the teachers' association prior to their promulgation and agreed that they would be subject to a test in arbitration concerning their reasonableness and their fair and impartial administration in individual cases.[4] Finally, the arbitrator relied upon Article XXV of the agreement, which provides that the regulations and practices in effect relating to conditions of employment shall continue in force, unless the agreement provides for the contrary. The arbitrator found that the committee had not promulgated any rules relating to leaves but had established a pattern and practice of arbitrarily granting leaves (to coach a football team, to run a political campaign, etc.). The arbitrator apparently accepted the association's argument that the arbitrary granting of leaves without any rules or regulations violated the reasonableness requirement of Article XIX. Accordingly, he granted the grievant a 1-year leave without remuneration.

We believe the decision of the arbitrator "draws its essence" from the contract and is sufficiently "grounded in the contract" to be within the scope of his authority. *United Steelworkers of America v. United States Gypsum Co.,* 492 F.2d 713, 731-32, 85 LRRM 2962 (5th Cir.), *cert. denied,* 419 U.S. 998, 87 LRRM 2658 (1974). Absent a manifest disregard of the contractual provisions, or a completely irrational result, the courts have no authority to vacate the arbitrator's award. *Belanger v. Matteson,* 115 R.I. at 356, 346 A.2d at 138. The trial justice erred in ruling that the arbitrator exceeded his authority by deciding the precise issue submitted to him. *Oinoussian Steamship Corp. v. Sabre Shipping Corp.,* 224 F. Supp. 807, 809 (S.D.N.Y. 1963).

The trial justice and my Brother Weisberger place particular reliance on the contractual provision which bars the arbitrator from adding to, subtracting from, or "modifying" the terms of the contract. To be sure, at least one case has seized upon this common provision to support or justify the reversal of an arbitrator's interpretation. *Torrington Co. v. Metal Products Workers Union Local 1645,* 362 F.2d 677, 62 LRRM 2495 (2d Cir. 1966). This result has been severely criticized by the commentators[5] and with good cause. By reviewing the arbitrator's decision on the merits, in order to implement the rather vague restrictions of a "no addition or modification" clause, the courts would appear to be overstepping the limitations imposed upon them by statute. Gorman, Labor Law 589-90 (1976). "This legerdemain, by which a judicial determination of arbitral error is transformed into an arbitral amendment of the agreement, is an indefensible inroad into contractual finality." Dunau, *Three Problems in Labor Arbitration,* 55 Va. L. Rev. 427, 454 (1969).

Accordingly, the *Torrington* case has been, for the most part, rejected. *Amoco Oil Co. v. Oil Chemical & Atomic Workers International Union, Inc.,* 548 F.2d 1288, 94 LRRM 2518 (7th Cir.), *cert. denied,* 431 U.S. 905, 95 LRRM 2144 (1977); *Holly Sugar Corp. v. Distillery, Rectifying, Wine & Allied Workers*

---

[4] This paragraph of Article XIX provides: "The Association recognizes the right of the Committee to make and enforce reasonable rules to ensure that there is no abuse of leave benefits. The Committee agrees to discuss any such proposed rules with the Association prior to their implementation. It is understood and agreed that the rules promulgated by the Committee are subject to a test in arbitration as to their reasonableness, if challenged by the Association, and as to their fair and impartial administration in individual cases."

[5] Gorman, Labor Law 589-93 (1976); Dunau, *Three Problems in Labor Arbitration,* 55 Va. L. Rev. 427, 454 (1969); Feller, *A General Theory of the Collective Bargaining Agreement,* 61 Cal. L. Rev. 663, 802 n. 538 (1973); Christensen, *Labor Arbitration and Judicial Oversight,* 19 Stan. L. Rev. 671, 690-93 (1967).

International Union, 412 F.2d 899, 71 LRRM 2841 (9th Cir. 1969); *Textile Workers Union of America v. Textile Paper Products, Inc.*, 405 F.2d 397, 69 LRRM 2578 (5th Cir. 1968); *Dallas Typographical Union, No. 173 v. A. H. Belo Corp.*, 372 F.2d 577, 64 LRRM 2491 (5th Cir. 1967); *Yakima Newspaper Guild Local No. 27 v. Republic Publishing Co.*, 375 F. Supp. 945, 86 LRRM 2725 (E.D. Wash. 1974).

The school committee argues, and the trial justice agreed, that the specificity of Articles XIX, XX, and XXI with respect to conditions under which leaves of absence and sabbaticals could be granted "completely cover the types of leaves upon which the parties had agreed." Both the committee and the trial justice took the position that since Ms. McKeown did not qualify for any of the specified leaves, the arbitrator, by granting her a year's unpaid leave, had modified the contract and added a new provision. This argument misses the mark. As noted above, neither the trial justice nor this court has any authority to make such inferences of contractual intent.[6] While we are reluctant to enter into the interpretive areas, we would point out that Article XIX of the agreement, wherein the teachers recognize the school committee's right to promulgate further rules relating to leaves, disputes any suggestion that the parties intended to cover completely the types of leaves which could be granted. Furthermore, Ms. McKeown did not apply for one of the specifically enumerated leaves, but applied under the catchall provision which allowed teachers additional time off "for other personal reasons when such requests are considered valid by the Superintendent."

In short, the parties did not completely cover the occasions under which teachers could be absent from their pedagogical duties. A large measure of discretion was vested in the school committee and the superintendent regarding the granting of leaves of absence. The arbitrator did not "modify" the agreement by granting the requested leave, for there was sufficient evidence before him to indicate that, by arbitrarily granting and denying leaves in the past, without any accompanying rules or regulations, the school committee had breached the reasonableness requirement of the agreement.

Here, Cumberland's teachers and its school committee had agreed to submit all disputes concerning the interpretation of their contract to binding arbitration. The trial justice, through his reliance on the "no modification" clause, and without statutory authority, has reversed the arbitrator's interpretation. Judicial reversal of an arbitration award based solely upon a disagreement with the arbitrator's interpretation of the contract nullifies the bargain of the parties and threatens the strong public policy that favors private settlement of grievance disputes arising from collective bargaining agreements. *Belanger v. Matteson*,

---

[6] The United States Supreme Court in the Steelworkers trilogy sought to put a halt to the practice of the judiciary's usurping the arbitrator's responsibilities under the guise of ruling on the arbitrability of a dispute. *United Steelworkers of America v. Enterprise Wheel & Car Corp.*, 363 U.S. 593, 46 LRRM 2423, 34 LA 569 (1960); *United Steelworkers of Am. v. Warrior & Gulf Navigation Co.*, 363 U.S. 574, 46 LRRM 2416, 34 LA 561 (1960); *United Steelworkers of Am. v. American Mfg. Co.*, 363 U.S. 564, 46 LRRM 2414, 34 LA 559 (1960). In its trilogy the Court stressed that all doubts as to arbitration were to be resolved in favor of arbitration and observed that courts had no business weighing the merits of a grievance. Parenthetically, it should be noted that the collective bargaining agreement in the *American Mfg.* case and the Cumberland contract contain the identical boilerplate about the arbitrator's inability to add to, delete from, or modify. 363 U.S. at 565.

115 R.I. at 355-56, 346 A.2d at 138. If the loser in arbitration has even modest prospects of winning in court, litigation is encouraged and the essence of arbitration — the conclusiveness of the award — is thereby defeated. Dunau, *Three Problems in Labor Arbitration,* 55 Va. L. Rev. 427, 461-62 (1969); Note, *Judicial Review of Arbitration Awards on the Merits,* 63 Harv. L. Rev. 681-82 (1950). If the bargain of the parties is to be effectuated and the policy of the Rhode Island Arbitration Act to be adhered to, the following admonition should be our guide:

"The arbiter was chosen to be the judge. That Judge has spoken. There it ends." *Safeway Stores v. American Bakery & Confectionery Workers International Union, Local 111,* 390 F.2d 79, 84, 67 LRRM 2646 (5th Cir. 1968).

Before concluding, a brief comment should be made about the views expressed by my Brother Weisberger. In his dissent he has detailed a series of cases in which he believes the arbitrator has misconstrued the contract or reached the wrong conclusion. If such a misconception occurred while the arbitrator was attempting to resolve a grievance dispute which arose in the public sector, my Brother would hold that the erring arbitrator had exceeded his power.

Such a view is totally inconsistent with the unanimous view expressed in other jurisdictions, and it completely nullifies the bargain of the parties. More importantly, nothing in chapter 9 of title 28 suggests or implies that the General Assembly ever intended that there be dual standards of judicial review under § 28-9-18, one for the public sector and another for the private sector. If, as my brother contends, the public interest would be served by closer judicial scrutiny of the merits of an arbitration award made in the public sector, this service is to be afforded at the statehouse and not the courthouse.

The association's appeal is sustained, the judgment appealed from is reversed, and the case is remitted to the Superior Court for the entry of a judgment confirming the award.

WEISBERGER, JUSTICE, with whom DORIS, JUSTICE, joins, dissenting: — The majority have in effect determined that an arbitration award, even where clearly erroneous and based upon substantial amendments to a collective bargaining agreement, will be insulated from judicial review unless utterly irrational in nature. In coming to this conclusion, my brothers have embraced a distinguished line of federal cases which generally support the finality of arbitration in the private sector.

In applying the principles of these cases to arbitration of labor disputes in the public sector, we must consider certain lurking perils. The "common law of the shop" or past practice may include the application of elaborate statutory schemes for the government of state and municipal employees, and an arbitrator can be called upon to adjudicate disputes which may involve the interpretation of such statutes. Should the arbitrator under such circumstances be substantially insulated from judicial review? My position in this matter may be helpfully illustrated if a brief analysis of the case law in this area is given....

In spite of language indicating that an arbitrator may not dispense his own brand of industrial justice, the federal courts have refused to disturb arbitration awards even in situations where one might argue that the arbitrator had exceeded his powers or that the results required an amendment of the contract. For example, in *Amoco Oil Co. v. Oil, Chemical & Atomic Workers International Union, Local 7-1, Inc.,* 548 F.2d 1288, 94 LRRM 2518 (7th Cir. 1977), the court of appeals declined to overturn an arbitrator's award under circumstances which might be termed extreme....

A few cases have recognized that a court may review and set aside an award if the arbitrator exceeds his contractual authority. *Cannon v. Consolidated Freightways Corp.,* 524 F.2d 290, 90 LRRM 2996 (7th Cir. 1975); *Torrington Co. v. Metal Products Workers Union Local 1645,* 362 F.2d 677, 62 LRRM 2495 (2d Cir. 1966). The weight of authority has been in support of the proposition that an arbitrator's determination will not be reviewed for error of law on the theory that for all practical purposes, save for utterly irrational conduct, the arbitrator's determination is completely insulated from review. *Safeway Stores v. American Bakery & Confectionery Workers International Union, Local 111,* 390 F.2d 79, 67 LRRM 2646 (5th Cir. 1968). The rationale of these cases has been rather succinctly expressed by Professor Bernard Dunau in *Three Problems in Labor Arbitration,* 55 Va. L. Rev. 427, 461, as follows: "The ordinary judge has ordinarily nothing to teach the ordinary arbitrator in the adjudication of an ordinary grievance under an ordinary collective bargaining agreement." The theory seems to be that the arbitrator's normal expertise is so great, and a judge's lack of expertise is so dangerous to the whole process, that it is better to suffer an occasional egregious error than to submit the outcome of arbitration to the dangers even of limited judicial review.

The principal cases which follow this theory have dealt with grievances in the private sector. Only in *Belanger v. Matteson, supra,* did we touch upon a grievance relating to a public employee. We must now decide whether the rigors of the rule suggested in the plethora of federal and state cases should be applied to arbitration of grievances in the public sector. The School Teachers' Arbitration Act, G.L. 1956 (1968 Reenactment) chapter 9.3 of title 28, adopted in 1966, was superimposed upon a very extensive statutory scheme which had previously governed the operation and management of the public school system....

Thus, it may be necessary for an arbitrator in determining a grievance and in supplementing the contract with past practice to consider and interpret the contract in the light of Rhode Island educational law.

If this court should choose to abdicate from any meaningful function in the review of such determinations, the practical enforcement of a large body of public law would be left to the untrammeled and unreviewable discretion of arbitrators. I think that the interest of the people of this state in the enforcement and application of laws relating to education and the rights and responsibilities of those who carry out the educational function is far too compelling in nature to warrant such abstention on our part. Even the most rudimentary demands of consistency and consonance would be set at nought by such a system, since arbitrators have no obligation even to provide reasons for their determinations.

In the private sector, to a great extent, it was thought by Mr. Justice Douglas and his colleagues in *United Steelworkers of America v. Enterprise Wheel & Car Corp., supra,* that industrial peace and the giving up of the right to strike would best be served by making an arbitrator's decision to all intents and purposes final. In the public sector in Rhode Island there is no right to strike.

I would respectfully suggest that the appropriate rule to follow in respect to enforcement or review of an arbitrator's decision might be derived from a literal reading of the statute. The statute now provides that an award may be vacated "[w]here the arbitrator or arbitrators exceeded their powers." Section 28-9-18(b). I would also suggest that we should enforce contract provisions which preclude an arbitrator from making any decision amending, modifying, adding to or subtracting from the provisions of the agreement, as in the case at bar. I would urge that such cases as *Torrington Co. v. Metal Products Workers Union Local 1645, supra,* provide a much more workable rule in respect to arbitration in the public sector than do the majority of private employment arbitration cases which in effect furnish no review at all. Perhaps it would not be wholly inappropriate to limit arbitrators to the agreement or submission of the parties as was the rule of the earlier cases....

I submit that when dealing with the sovereign power of the state and its subdivisions, clear expression of willingness should be essential to the submission of matters of magnitude to a third party for determination. Indeed, the Supreme Court of New Hampshire observed in *Tremblay v. Berlin Police Union,* 108 N.H. 416, 237 A.2d 668, 68 LRRM 2070 (1968), that a requirement for arbitration in a labor contract to be subordinated to the provisions of state law might well be constitutionally required. For a number of useful concepts see Note, *Legality and Propriety of Agreements to Arbitrate Major and Minor Disputes in Public Employment,* 54 Cornell L. Rev. 129 (1968).

As public sector bargaining grows apace in our nation, new techniques must be devised to meet the ever increasing problems. See Anderson, *The Impact of Public Sector Bargaining,* 1973 Wis. L. Rev. 986.

In the instant case, I am of the opinion that the arbitrator exceeded his contractual authority by adding a dimension to the contract in an area where the parties had set forth comprehensive terms governing all types of leaves of absence. I would therefore affirm the judgment as rendered in the Superior Court.

NOTES

1. Courts reviewing public sector grievance arbitration awards have generally followed the private sector practice of according substantial deference to the arbitrators' grievance resolutions, with awards being denied affirmance only where the arbitrators have clearly exceeded their contractual authority or issued decisions contravening law or public policy. See, e.g., *State v. Berthiaume,* 259 N.W.2d 104, 96 L.R.R.M. 3240 (Minn. 1977) (also placing burden of proof on party challenging award); *International Bhd. of Firemen v. School Dist.,* 350 A.2d 804, 91 L.R.R.M. 2710 (Pa. 1976); *Caribou Bd. of Educ. v. Caribou Teachers Ass'n,* 404 A.2d 212, 102 L.R.R.M. 2402 (Me. 1979); *Sergeant Bluff-Luton Educ. Ass'n v. Sergeant Bluff-Luton Community Sch. Dist.,* 282 N.W.2d 144, 103 L.R.R.M. 2247 (Iowa 1979). Doubts regarding the propriety of an award are usually resolved in favor of enforcement. See, e.g., *Community College v. Community College Soc'y of Faculty,* 375 A.2d 1267, 96 L.R.R.M. 2375 (Pa. 1977); *Darien Educ. Ass'n v. Board of Educ.,* 374 A.2d 1081, 94 L.R.R.M. 2895 (Conn. 1977). Even where arbitrators do not explain the bases underlying their decisions, their awards will generally be enforced if they appear to draw their essence from the applicable agreement. See *Virgin Islands Nursing Ass'n Bargaining Unit v. Schneider,* 668 F.2d 221 (3d Cir. 1981). Nevertheless, if an arbitrator exercises jurisdiction over an issue that is expressly excluded from the coverage of the grievance-arbitration procedures, *School Comm. v. Portland Teachers Ass'n,* 338 A.2d 155, 90 L.R.R.M. 2597 (Me. 1975), or issues an award contrary to law, *Board of Trustees, Conn. State Technical Colleges v. Teamsters, Local 1942,* 425 A.2d 1247, 103 L.R.R.M. 2597 (Conn. 1979), enforcement will be denied. See also *Board of Trustees, Community College Dist. No. 508 v. Cook Cty. College Teachers Union, Local 1600,* 386 N.E.2d 47, 1979-80 PBC ¶ 36,497 (Ill. 1979) (vacating an arbitration award that had effect of providing teachers who had engaged in illegal work stoppage with extra work assignment preference over teachers who had not, since found to contravene public policy); *Board of Directors v. Maine Sch. Admin. Dist. No. 36 Teachers Ass'n,* 428 A.2d 419, 1980-81 PBC ¶ 37,240 (Me. 1981), and *Milwaukee Bd. of Sch. Dirs. v. Milwaukee Teachers Educ. Ass'n,* 287 N.W.2d 131, 1979-80 PBC ¶ 36,802 (Wis. 1980) (refusing to enforce awards directly infringing upon statutorily recognized prerogative of government officials to make personnel appointments).

Where losing parties seek to vacate awards based upon alleged improprieties committed by the presiding arbitrators, their efforts are generally unsuccessful. See, e.g., *Lodge 1296, UAFF v. City of Kennewick,* 542 P.2d 1252, 92 L.R.R.M. 2118 (Wash. 1976). See also *City of Hartford v. Local 308, Int'l Bhd. of Police Officers,* 370 A.2d 996, 93 L.R.R.M. 2321 (Conn. 1976). But see *School Dist. of Spooner v. Northwest United Educators,* 401 N.W.2d 578, 1986-88 PBC ¶ 34,789 (Wis. 1987) (arbitrator's failure to disclose his prior employment by union representing grievant constituted "evident partiality").

See generally Craver, *The Judicial Enforcement of Public Sector Grievance Arbitration,* 58 Tex. L. Rev. 329, 341-53 (1980); Hodges, *The Steelworkers Trilogy in the Public Sector,* 67 Chi.-Kent L. Rev. — (1991).

2. *School Comm. of Boston v. Teachers Union, Local 66,* 479 N.E.2d 645, 1984-86 PBC ¶ 34,521 (Mass. 1985), concerned the enforceability of a job security provision contained in a three-year bargaining agreement. Since the court found that such a severe restriction upon managerial authority could not legally bind the school committee for more than one year, it refused to enforce an arbitral award of back pay to 710 teachers who were found to have been laid off — at the beginning of the second year of the contract — in violation of that job security clause. See also *School Comm. of Holbrook v. Education Ass'n,* 481 N.E.2d 484, 1984-86 PBC ¶ 35,571 (Mass. 1985) (finding that arbitrator lacked authority to order recall of laid-off instructor to fill position she had never held and for which she lacked requisite statutory approval). But cf. *Lake Washington Sch. Dist. v. Educ. Ass'n,* 745 P.2d 504, 127 L.R.R.M. 2478 (Wash. 1987) (upholding arbitral award enforcing provision permitting teachers to transfer from part-time to full-time positions, since such procedure did not impermissibly interfere with school board's authority to employ teaching personnel).

3. In *Bremen Community High Sch. Dist. v. Joint Faculty Ass'n,* 461 N.E.2d 406, 1984-86 PBC ¶ 34,129 (Ill. 1984), the court held that while the arbitrator was not empowered to review the school board's nondelegable right to determine whether an "economic necessity" which precipitated the nonrenewal of several teacher contracts actually existed, he did have the right to decide whether the nonrenewal actions taken were based upon that necessity and he possessed the authority to review the board's compliance with a provision requiring the holding of a public hearing prior to such nonrenewals. However, the court found that the arbitrator lacked the power to order the reinstatement of the teachers whose contracts had been terminated without the requisite hearing. See also *Public Serv. Union v. City of Duluth*, 336 N.W.2d 68, 116 L.R.R.M. 2187 (Minn. 1983), wherein the court held that even where the arbitrator lacked the authority to require the city to demonstrate the financial necessity underlying its decision to lay off personnel, he did possess the power to decide whether it had followed the contractually prescribed layoff procedures. Accord *Township of Oldbridge Bd. of Educ. v. Education Ass'n*, 1984-86 PBC ¶ 34,447 (N.J. 1985).

Regarding the authority of arbitrators to review sabbatical decisions made by school districts, compare *Rochester City Sch. Dist. v. Rochester City Teachers Ass'n*, 41 N.Y.2d 578, 362 N.E.2d 977 (1977), and *Board of Educ. v. Bridgeport Educ. Ass'n*, 377 A.2d 323, 96 L.R.R.M. 2567 (Conn. 1967) (sustaining expansive arbitral authority), with *South Stickney Bd. of Educ. v. Murphy*, 372 N.E.2d 899, 97 L.R.R.M. 2441 (Ill. Ct. App. 1978). See also *Iowa City Community Sch. Dist. v. Iowa City Educ. Ass'n*, 343 N.W.2d 139, 116 L.R.R.M. 2832 (Iowa 1983) (sustaining power of arbitrator to review school performance evaluations which affect wage increases).

4. Challenges to arbitral awards based upon claims that public policy has been impermissibly infringed continue to cause courts some difficulty. Nonetheless, where the arbitrator's decision does not substantially contravene a vital public policy, it will usually receive judicial respect. See, e.g., *School Comm. v. Teachers Union, Local 66*, 389 N.E.2d 970, 103 L.R.R.M. 2303 (Mass. 1979) (requiring administrators to consult teachers union before implementing new policy of giving exams to elementary school students); *Teachers Ass'n v. Brookhaven Sch. Dist.*, 45 N.Y.2d 898, 383 N.E.2d 553 (1978) (restricting authority of school district to assign specialist teachers to positions outside their respective areas of specialization); *Niagara Wheatfield Adm'rs Ass'n v. Wheatfield Cent. Sch. Dist.*, 44 N.Y.2d 68, 375 N.E.2d 37 (1978) (sustaining contractual provision that tied school administrator salaries to teacher salary levels). To avoid the difficulties presented by such public policy challenges to arbitral determinations, some courts will endeavor to construe the relevant grievance-arbitration provision as not covering the dispute in question. See, e.g., *Maine Sch. Dist. No. 33 v. Teachers Ass'n*, 395 A.2d 461, 99 L.R.R.M. 3301 (Me. 1978). Does the latter approach really invade the province of the arbitrator to a lesser degree than where the arbitral award is simply found to be in conflict with some important government policy?

5. Courts have not always agreed upon the authority arbitrators possess to review disciplinary decisions of public employers. In *Gresham Sch. Dist. v. ERB*, 570 P.2d 682, 97 L.R.R.M. 2143 (Or. Ct. App. 1977), the court upheld an arbitrator's award that reinstated a probationary teacher, thereby affording her tenure, where she had been terminated in reprisal for having previously utilized the grievance procedure. Accord *University of Haw. Prof. Ass'y v. University of Haw.*, 659 P.2d 720, 1981-83 PBC ¶ 37,834 (Hawaii 1983). Other arbitral decisions ordering the re-employment of improperly terminated employees have been similarly sustained. See, e.g., *Shenandoah Educ. Ass'n v. Shenandoah Community Sch. Dist.*, 337 N.W.2d 477, 114 L.R.R.M. 2699 (Iowa 1983); *Cape Elizabeth Sch. Bd. v. Cape Elizabeth Teachers Ass'n*, 459 A.2d 166, 116 L.R.R.M. 2812 (Me. 1983); *State v. Berthiaume*, 259 N.W.2d 104, 96 L.R.R.M. 3240 (Minn. 1977); *Middlesex Cty. Comm'rs v. AFSCME*, 362 N.E.2d 523, 95 L.R.R.M. 2864 (Mass. 1977) (requiring employer to follow "progressive discipline" concept). See also *Binghamton Civil Serv. Forum v. Binghamton*, 44 N.Y.2d 23, 374 N.E.2d 380 (1978), where the court sustained an arbitration award reducing the penalty imposed upon a worker who accepted bribes from dismissal to a six-month suspension, since the court did not believe that the public policy of the state automatically required the discharge of any employee who accepted a bribe. Accord *Taylor v. Crane*, 595 P.2d 129, 101 L.R.R.M. 3060 (Cal. 1979). But cf. *PLBC v. Indep. State Stores Union*, 553 A.2d 948, 130 L.R.R.M. 2780 (Pa. 1989), and *United States Postal Serv. v. American Postal Workers Union*, 736 F.2d 822 (1st Cir. 1984) (vacating arbitral awards that directed reinstatement of employees guilty of embezzlement); *County College of Morris Staff Ass'n v. County College of Morris*, 495 A.2d 865, 1984-86 PBC ¶ 34, 572 (N.J. 1985), and *In re Gage*, 398 A.2d 297, 100 L.R.R.M. 2827 (Vt. 1979) (progressive discipline not inherent element of discharge procedures).

Other courts have indicated that while any contractual provision restricting the unfettered right of public employers to terminate probationary personnel would conflict with public policy and thus be unenforceable, they would enforce arbitration awards ordering the reinstatement of discharged workers where necessary to allow employers to provide the grievants with their procedural right under their contract to a proper evaluation or a fair hearing before dismissal. See, e.g., *School Comm. v. Korbut*, 369 N.E.2d 1148, 97 L.R.R.M. 2447 (Mass. 1977); *Candor Cent. Sch. Dist. v. Candor Teachers Ass'n*, 42 N.Y.2d 266, 366 N.E.2d 826 (1977); *Cohoes City Sch. Dist. v. Cohoes Teachers Ass'n*, 40 N.Y.2d 774, 358 N.E.2d 878 (1976). See also *Board of Directors v. Merrymeeting Educators Ass'n*, 354 A.2d 169, 92 L.R.R.M. 2268 (Me. 1976), wherein the court upheld an arbitrator's decision to reinstate a nonprobationary teacher where the school principal had failed to provide the teacher with the assistance that had been recommended by her evaluators and the superintendent. In deciding that the arbitrator had not exceeded his authority under the contract, the court implied a reciprocal obligation on the part of school administrators to correct deficiencies in teacher performance, if possible, before resorting to discharge.

6. In *Niagara Bd. of Educ. v. Teachers Ass'n*, 46 N.Y.2d 553, 389 N.E.2d 104 (1979), the court indicated that arbitrators possess broad discretion when formulating compensatory remedies.

> Merely because an arbitrator's award is not arrived at by precise mathematical computations does not make it punitive. Indeed, much of the laudatory value of arbitration lies in the arbitrator's power to construct a remedy best suited to the situation without regard to the restrictions on traditional relief in a court of law.... Merely because the computation of damages may be so speculative as to be unsupportable if awarded by a court does not make the award infirm, for, as we have firmly stated, arbitrators are not bound by rules of substantive law or, indeed, rules of evidence.

See also *Board of Educ., Fairbanks N. Star Borough Sch. Dist. v. Ewig*, 609 P.2d 10, 1979-80 PBC ¶ 36,874 (Alaska 1980).

There is reason to believe that some courts will be more active in reviewing the merits of public sector arbitration awards that require the granting of economic benefits than they will be with respect to non-monetary awards. In the private sector, there is usually no question regarding the power of an arbitrator to order back pay or other "make whole" relief in appropriate cases; nor is there any question concerning the authority of an employer to comply with such an award. In the public sector, however, public policy considerations may raise special problems with respect to the enforcement of such "make whole" remedies. For example, in *Boston Teachers Union v. School Comm.*, 350 N.E.2d 707, 93 L.R.R.M. 2205 (1976), the Massachusetts Supreme Judicial Court held that an arbitrator exceeded his authority when he directed the school board to pay $52,000 to a teachers union scholarship fund as damages that allegedly resulted when the board violated its bargaining agreement with the teachers union by refusing to hire substitute teachers to replace regular teachers during absences.

7. Where the parties have included nothing in their bargaining agreement concerning past practices which have been observed and an arbitration award orders the continuation of such established practices on the ground they have been implicitly incorporated in the contract, the award may be denied enforcement as being beyond the authority of the arbitrator to merely apply and interpret the actual terms of the agreement. See *County of Allegheny v. County Prison Emps. Indep. Union*, 381 A.2d 849, 96 L.R.R.M. 3396 (Pa. 1977); *Milwaukee Professional Firefighters, Local 215 v. Milwaukee*, 253 N.W.2d 481, 95 L.R.R.M. 2684 (Wis. 1977). But see *Ramsey Cty. v. AFSCME, Council 91*, 309 N.W.2d 785, 1981-83 PBC ¶ 37,342 (Minn. 1981) (sustaining award based upon past practice).

8. *Board of Educ. v. Woodstown-Pilesgrove Reg'l Educ. Ass'n*, 410 A.2d 1131, 1979-80 PBC ¶ 36,848 (N.J. 1980), considered a grievance clause providing that the failure of the school district to issue a decision regarding a pending grievance within a five-day period would result in a final settlement in favor of the grievant. The court ruled that where the school administration did not provide a timely response, an arbitrator could appropriately determine that it would be bound by the position stated in the grievance. What if the resulting settlement were contrary to law or public policy?

Many state labor arbitration statutes provide that a reviewing court shall confirm an arbitral award if no motion to vacate, modify, or correct the award has been filed within the prescribed time limit. May a losing party that failed to file a timely motion to vacate, modify, or correct an arbitration decision nonetheless challenge its validity in response to the prevailing party's request for judicial confirmation? Compare *Milwaukee Police Ass'n v. City of Milwaukee*, 285 N.W.2d 119, 1979-80 PBC ¶ 36,735 (Wis. 1979) (yes), with *Charles Cty. Bd. of Educ. v. Education Ass'n*, 408 A.2d 89, 103 L.R.R.M. 2187 (Md. Ct. App. 1979) (no).

9. Although arbitral decisions enforcing contract provisions covering merely "permissive" bargaining topics may be enforced in some circumstances (see *Iowa City Community Sch. Dist. v. Iowa City Community Educ. Ass'n*, 343 N.W.2d 139, 1984-86 PBC ¶ 34,097 (Iowa 1983)), enforcement will be denied where the result would interfere with nondelegable management prerogatives. See *Police Officers Local 1 v. City of Patterson*, 432 A.2d 847, 1981-83 PBC ¶ 37,306 (N.J. 1981).

10. Section 7122 of the Civil Service Reform Act of 1978 defines the limited grounds upon which a party may challenge a federal grievance arbitration award. The FLRA may only sustain a party's objection to an award where either the decision is contrary to some law, rule, or regulation, or is otherwise invalid for reasons similar to those utilized by federal courts to evaluate the propriety of private sector arbitral determinations. Where an award is reviewed by the FLRA which does not concern any alleged unfair labor practice, the FLRA's decision is not subject to judicial review. See *AFGE v. FLRA*, 675 F.2d 612 (4th Cir. 1982). When a federal agency does not voluntarily comply with an arbitral award, the proper forum in which to seek enforcement is the FLRA, not a district court, since such agency conduct constitutes an unfair labor practice under Section 7116(a)(8) and is within the exclusive jurisdiction of the FLRA. See *Columbia Power Trades Council v. United States Dep't of Energy*, 671 F.2d 325 (9th Cir. 1982).

Where a federal employee exercises the option to challenge an adverse personnel action through the contractual grievance procedure instead of through procedures available under the Civil Service Reform Act, the arbitrator must apply the same substantive statutory standards, including the "harmful error" rule, that would be applied by an administrative law judge or hearing officer if the case were processed before the Merit Systems Protection Board under the procedures contained in the Civil Service Reform Act. Furthermore, only errors "harmful" to the individual grievant, and not those merely affecting the labor organization, may provide the basis for a modification of the adverse action. See *Cornelius v. Nutt*, 472 U.S. 648 (1985).

In *AFGE, Local 2578 v. GSA*, 711 F.2d 261 (D.C. Cir. 1983), the court ruled that arbitrators are not to provide federal agencies with complete discretion regarding the penalties imposed in adverse action cases, but are instead expected to exercise some degree of independent judgment with respect to this area. However, in *Devine v. Pastore*, 732 F.2d 213 (D.C. Cir. 1984), the same court indicated that such arbitrators are not empowered under the Civil Service Reform Act to make entirely de novo assessments. They are instead obliged to determine merely if the penalties involved were arbitrarily or capriciously imposed.

Where an arbitrator orders the reinstatement of a federal employee who has engaged in an unlawful work stoppage, that award will not be entitled to enforcement, since 5 U.S.C. § 7311 precludes the continued employment of individuals who have engaged in strikes against the federal government. See *American Postal Workers Union v. United States Postal Serv.*, 682 F.2d 1280 (9th Cir. 1982). See also *National Post Office Mailhandlers v. United States Postal Serv.*, 751 F.2d 834 (6th Cir. 1985).

See generally F. Elkouri & E. Elkouri, Legal Status of Federal-Sector Arbitration (1980); Craver, *The Regulation of Federal Sector Labor Relations: Overlapping Administrative Responsibiliites*, 39 LAB. L.J. 387 (1988); Note, *Arbitration Awards in Federal Sector Public Employment: The Compelling Need Standard of Appellate Review*, 1977 B.Y.U. L. Rev. 429 (1977). See also Kagel, *Grievance Arbitration in the Federal Service: Still Hardly Final and Binding* in Arbitration Issues for the 1980s, Proceedings of the Thirty-Fourth Annual Meeting of the National Academy of Arbitrators 178 (J. Stern & B. Dennis eds., 1982) (discussing extent to which Comptroller General reviews monetary awards contained in arbitral decisions).

D. INDIVIDUAL RIGHTS UNDER THE COLLECTIVE BARGAINING AGREEMENT

1. INTRODUCTION

H. WELLINGTON & R. WINTER, THE UNIONS AND THE CITIES 162-64 (1971)*

The interest of the individual employee is generally well served in the grievance procedure by his representative, the union. Typically, it is the union that brings the grievance and pursues it through the several steps spelled out in the contract, and, if necessary, on to arbitration. But, as we have learned from experience in the private sector, it would be a terrible mistake to assume that congruity of interests between union and individual always exists. Divergence is possible because of a reasonable disagreement as to what the contract provides, because the interests of the individual and those of a majority of employees do not coincide, because the individual is a political rival of the union president, because he is black and a majority of the union is white, because he is disliked, against union policy, unwilling to do what he is told to do, and so forth. And divergence of interests may occur at any stage of the grievance procedure. The union may decline to process a grievance at all, take it through some steps and drop it, or refuse to go to arbitration.

While potential conflict between individual and union exists at the precontract negotiation stage as well, it is most troublesome during contract administration. This may be because at that stage the employee is viewed as having rights that grow out of an existing agreement, rather than amorphous and hard-to-define interests in a yet to be achieved contractual settlement.

Be that as it may, the private sector has developed a bewilderingly complicated and relatively unsatisfactory body of law to deal with the problem. The law is complicated largely because of the complexities in the underlying problem. On the one hand, if collective bargaining is to be an orderly, efficient process that brings stability to labor relations, it is desirable to place the employer in a position where he is able to work out binding settlements with the union, and the union alone. On the other hand, the individual needs protection from the union that fails adequately to represent his interests.

One approach to the problem is to give the individual employee a cause of action against the union if it fails to represent him fairly; but to give him no redress against the employer. Indeed, the duty of fair representation exists in the private sector under federal law. It has, however, been much hedged about. The other approach is to give the employee a direct and individual right in the collective agreement, recognize the fact that this right may undercut efficiency and stability, but recognize also that the effect of this can be grossly overestimated and that institutions have ways of adapting themselves. Federal law recognizes individual rights in the contract. It also hedges them about.

Whatever one's position as to what the law should be in the private sector, it seems clear that in municipal collective bargaining the individual should have access, as an individual, to the grievance procedure, arbitration, and the courts. Without collective bargaining, there is no comparable right in private employ-

---

*Copyright 1971 by the Brookings Institution, Washington, D.C. Reprinted by permission.

ment. In public employment such a right generally does obtain and is administered by civil service commissions. While it has been argued that these commissions have no legitimate role in the resolution of grievances where collective bargaining is established, the protection afforded the individual under civil service should not be lost with their demise. Such protection may be retained by giving the employee generous individual rights in the collective agreement.

Of course, the union's interests must be protected. It should be able to argue for its interpretation of the contract at each level of the grievance procedure, in arbitration, and before the court. Nor, where its antagonistic position is reasonable, should it have to bear the costs of the individual's case. But these are minor and easily resolved difficulties when compared to some of the ... problems that must be faced when techniques of contract administration are transplanted from the private to the public sector.

NOTE

The view expressed by Professors Wellington and Winter regarding rights which should be enjoyed by individual grievants was accepted by the New Jersey Supreme Court in *Saginario v. New Jersey*, 435 A.2d 1134, 1981-83 PBC ¶ 37,391 (1981):

> In summary we hold that where a public employee has a substantial interest arising out of the agreement entered into between the State and the majority representative of the employees as a result of collective negotiations and the agreement provides for a grievance mechanism to resolve disputes arising out of the agreement including the particular dispute of the public employee, then the public employee is entitled to be heard within that dispute mechanism either through his majority representative or, if his position is in conflict with the majority representative, then through his personal representative or *pro se.*

The New Jersey Court has thus resurrected the rule it had previously applied to private sector grievance disputes in *Donnelly v. United Fruit*, 40 N.J. 61 (1963), despite the fact that the *Donnelly* approach had been subsequently rejected by the United States Supreme Court in *Vaca v. Sipes*, 386 U.S. 171 (1967). Do the differences between public and private employment warrant a different rule providing governmental employees with rights which transcend those enjoyed by their private sector counterparts? Should grievants under the *Saginario* doctrine be permitted to ask rival labor organizations to represent their interests despite the objections of the exclusive bargaining agents? If individual grievants are allowed to participate in arbitral proceedings through their own representatives, should this relieve the exclusive bargaining agents of their duty of fair representation toward such grievants? For a view contrary to that expressed in *Saginario*, see *Galbreath v. School Bd.*, 446 So. 2d 1045, 1984-86 PBC ¶ 34,043 (Fla. 1984). Should an individual grievant possess standing to seek judicial review of an adverse arbitral determination? Compare *Racine v. Alaska Dep't of Transp.*, 663 P.2d 555, 1981-83 PBC ¶ 37,801 (Alaska 1983) (yes), with *McNair v. Postal Serv.*, 768 F.2d 730 (5th Cir. 1985), and *Eisen v. Minnesota Dep't of Pub. Welfare*, 352 N.W.2d 731 (Minn. 1984) (no).

2. EXHAUSTION OF CONTRACTUAL REMEDIES AS PREREQUISITE TO JUDICIAL ENFORCEMENT ACTION BY INDIVIDUAL EMPLOYEES

KAUFMAN v. GOLDBERG

64 Misc. 2d, 524, 315 N.Y.S.2d 35 (1970)

LIEBOWITZ, JUSTICE. [Petitioner Kaufman, an employee of the New York City Department of Social Services, complained that he had been punitively transferred and demoted from Resource Consultant to Caseworker, with a loss of seniority. In accordance with procedures established in a collective bargaining agreement between the City and the Social Service Employees Union, Local 371, the petitioner filed a grievance alleging violation of the agreement on the part of the Department of Social Services. The grievance was denied at Steps I, II, and III of the grievance procedure. Kaufman claimed he then requested that the union take the grievance to Step IV by demanding arbitration, but that the request was refused because of Kaufman's non-membership in the union. The petitioner then brought this action against the Commissioner of the Department of Social Services, the Director of the Office of Labor Relations, and the City Civil Service Commission, seeking an order to vacate the determinations which denied the grievance at each step of the procedure and to direct the Civil Service Commission to reinstate his seniority and restore his title of Resource Consultant. After determining that the petitioner had failed to establish any contractual violation on the part of the Department of Social Services, the court went on to discuss whether Kaufman had in fact demanded arbitration and whether the union had wrongfully refused to proceed to arbitration on his behalf.]

If petitioner had established that his "transfer" was in violation of the contract, there would remain the issue as to whether petitioner could resort to direct action in face of the Step IV provision for arbitration which, pursuant to the contract, could be prosecuted only by the Union, and whether there was truth in his statement that his request for arbitration was rejected by the Union because of his non-membership.

The law is well established that by union membership an employee indicates he "has entrusted his rights to his union representative" and ordinarily has no individual right to demand or control the arbitration procedures (*Parker v. Borock*, 5 N.Y.2d 156, 182 N.Y.S.2d 577, 156 N.E.2d 297; *Matter of Soto* [*Goldman*], 7 N.Y.2d 397, 198 N.Y.S.2d 282, 165 N.E.2d 855; *Chupka v. Lorenz-Schneider*, 12 N.Y.2d 1, 233 N.E.2d 929, 186 N.E.2d 191). There is however, a line of cases in other jurisdictions which imposes on a union the duty of fair representation to its members and that the violation of that duty permits the employee to proceed directly against the employer. The authorities are exhaustively researched and discussed in *Jenkins v. Schluderberg-T, etc., Co.*, 217 Md. 556, 144 A.2d 88 (see 45 Corn. L.Q. 25). In *Jenkins*, the court held that where the union acted in an arbitrary and discriminatory manner in failing to proceed on behalf of the employee against the employer, the employee may proceed directly. The court quoted (at pp. 564-565, 144 A.2d at p. 93) from the article by Professor Cox in 69 Harvard Law Review 601, 652:

> "'While the rule which bars an individual employee from bringing an action on the contract when the union is unwilling to take the case to arbitration is sound if the union has made an adjustment or is satisfied that the grievance lacks merit, nevertheless it would work injustice in situations where the union is unwilling to press the claim because of indifference or reluctance to suffer the expense. Both factors come into play under open-shop contracts when a grievance having no precedent value is filed by a nonmember, whose failure to pay dues means that he contributes nothing to the cost of acting as his representative. One solution would be to open arbitration proceedings to individual grievants. Another alternative is to allow the employees to bring suit against the employer and union as codefendants upon analogy to the bill in equity which the beneficiary of a trust may maintain against the trustee who fails to press a claim against a third person. The suit would fail on the merits if it appeared that the collective bargaining representative had dropped the grievance for *lack of merit or had negotiated a reasonable adjustment.*'"

The court also quoted (p. 565, 144 P.2d p. 93) from Professor Cox's article, "Individual Enforcement of Collective Bargaining Agreements," (8 Lab. L.J. 850, 858), which is most pertinent to a situation where the employee is a nonmember of the union, as follows:

> "'In my opinion the presumption should be against individual enforcement of a collective bargaining agreement *unless the union has unfairly refused* to act.... The bargaining representative would be guilty of a breach of duty if it refused to press a justifiable grievance either because of laziness, prejudice or *unwillingness to expend* money *on behalf of employees who were not members of the union.* Individual enforcement would then become appropriate....' (Emphasis added.)"

The broad authority of the union as exclusive bargaining agent, even where it springs from statute, in the negotiation and administration of a collective bargaining agreement, is accompanied by the responsibility of fair representation (*Humphrey v. Moore,* 375 U.S. 335, 342; *Vaca v. Sipes,* 386 U.S. 171, 177[)]. In *Vaca,* the court, in firm dictum, stated (pp. 184-186):

> "However, if the wrongfully discharged employee himself resorts to the courts before the grievance procedures have been fully exhausted, the employer may well defend on the ground that the exclusive remedies provided by such a contract have not been exhausted. Since the employee's claim is based upon breach of the collective bargaining agreement, he is bound by terms of that agreement which govern the manner in which contractual rights may be enforced. For this reason, it is settled that the employee must at least attempt to exhaust exclusive grievance and arbitration procedures established by the bargaining agreement. *Republic Steel Corp. v. Maddox,* 379 U.S. 650. However, because these contractual remedies have been devised and are often controlled by the union and the employer, they may well prove unsatisfactory or unworkable for the individual grievant. The problem then is to determine under what circumstances the individual employee may obtain judicial review of his breach-of-contract claim despite his failure to secure relief through the contractual remedial procedures.

....

"We think that another situation when the employee may seek judicial enforcement of his contractual rights arises if, as is true here, the union has sole power under the contract to invoke the higher stages of the grievance procedure, *and* if, as is alleged here, the employee-plaintiff has been prevented from exhausting his contractual remedies by the union's *wrongful* refusal to process the grievance. It is true that the employer in such a situation may have done nothing to prevent exhaustion of the exclusive contractual remedies to which he agreed in the collective bargaining agreement. But the employer has committed a wrongful discharge in breach of that agreement, a breach which could be remedied through the grievance process to the employee-plaintiff's benefit were it not for the union's breach of its statutory duty of fair representation to the employee. To leave the employee remediless in such circumstances would, in our opinion, be a great injustice. We cannot believe that Congress, in conferring upon employers and unions the power to establish exclusive grievance procedures, intended to confer upon unions such unlimited discretion to deprive injured employees of all remedies for breach of contract. Nor do we think that Congress intended to shield employers from the natural consequences of their breaches of bargaining agreements by wrongful union conduct in the enforcement of such agreements. Cf. *Richardson v. Texas & N.O.R. Co.*, 242 F.2d 230, 235-236 (C.A. 5th Cir.).

For these reasons, we think the wrongfully discharged employee may bring an action against his employer in the face of a defense based upon the failure to exhaust contractual remedies, provided the employee can prove that the union as bargaining agent breached its duty of fair representation in its handling of the employee's grievance...."

(See, also, Thomas P. Lewis, "Fair Representation in Grievance Administration: *Vaca v. Sipes*" in the Supreme Court Review [1967], p. 81; see, also, dictum in *Bilinski v. Delco Appliance Corporation*, 23 A.D.2d 805, 258 N.Y.S.2d 61, *lv. to app. den.* 16 N.Y.2d 482, 261 N.Y.S.2d 1026, 209 N.E.2d 563, citing *Humphrey v. Moore*, 375 U.S. 335).

The authority of the Social Service Employees Union in the case at bar arises from statute (N.Y.C. Collective Bargaining Law, Administrative Code, Chap. 54; Local Law 53-1967; and implemented by the Mayor's Executive Order No. 52). The Union by its contract undertook to represent *all* Caseworkers as their "sole and exclusive" agent (Art. I). As such it was under a duty to entertain and consider petitioner's alleged grievance on the merits so as to determine whether to prosecute it to arbitration if, in fact, a demand had been made upon it for such relief. The court determines, however, that the Union did not violate this duty since it finds as a fact that petitioner at no time made a request of the Union to demand arbitration of his alleged grievances. Under the circumstances, it may not be said that petitioner has fully exhausted his contractual grievance procedures, since, as expressed in *Vaca v. Sipes* (*supra,* [(]citing *Republic Steel Corp. v. Maddox*, 379 U.S. 650), the employee must at least *attempt* to exhaust exclusive grievance and arbitration procedures established by the bargaining agent as a condition precedent to proceeding against the employer. (See also, *Bilinski v. Delco Appliance Division, General Motors Corporation*, 23 A.D.2d 805, 258 N.Y.S.2d 61, *lv. to app. den.* 16 N.Y.2d 482, 261 N.Y.S.2d

1026, 209 N.E.2d 563, *supra,* but cf. *Pattenge v. Wagner Iron Works,* 275 Wis. 495, 82 N.W.2d 172).

Assuming, therefore, that the petitioner was transferred in violation of the collective bargaining agreement (which the court found earlier not to be the case), it is, nonetheless, clear that the petitioner would not be entitled to relief, even under the theory of "Jenkins," "Vaca" and allied cases, because petitioner failed to first exhaust his contractual remedies.

Accordingly, judgment is directed dismissing the petition on the merits.

NOTES

1. Although individual employees will usually be unable to seek judicial enforcement of contract rights until they have endeavored to exhaust available grievance procedures provided in their bargaining agreement, courts continue to recognize exceptions to this doctrine. A failure to exhaust contractually specified procedures will be excused if the employee alleges that the representative labor organization has breached its duty of fair representation. See, e.g., *Ford v. University of Mont.,* 598 P.2d 604, 102 L.R.R.M. 2927 (Mont. 1979). Exhaustion of contractual grievance-arbitration procedures will not be required where the sued government employer has repudiated those very procedures. See *Cabarga Cruz v. Fundacion Educativa Ana G. Mendez,* 822 F.2d 188 (1st Cir. 1987). A sued governmental entity may waive its right to demand the exhaustion of available grievance procedures by simply not raising the matter in a timely fashion before the court. See *Ellerbrook v. Special Sch. Dist.,* 269 N.W.2d 858, 99 L.R.R.M. 3304 (Minn. 1978); *North Smithfield Teachers Ass'n v. North Smithfield Sch. Comm.,* 461 A.2d 930, 1981-83 PBC ¶ 37,826 (R.I. 1983). Furthermore, where statutorily prescribed notice and hearing rights pertain to the issue in dispute and the contractual grievance-arbitration procedures do not effectively protect those rights, judicial action to guarantee their effectuation may be permitted without prior resort to arbitration. See *Jerviss v. Sch. Dist. No. 294,* 273 N.W.2d 638, 100 L.R.R.M. 2068 (Minn. 1978).

2. Where the gravamen of an individual's suit concerns rights under the applicable bargaining agreement, ancillary allegations of constitutional deprivations will not be sufficient to render the usual exhaustion doctrine inapplicable where resort to the grievance-arbitration procedures would be likely to resolve the basic dispute. However, application of the exhaustion doctrine does not authorize the arbitrator to decide the constitutional issues raised, since the arbiter's authority only covers the interpretation and application of the contract. See *McGrath v. State,* 309 N.W.2d 54, 1981-83 PBC ¶ 37,318 (Minn. 1981). Such exhaustion will not be required with respect to a constitutional claim where resort to contractual procedures would likely be futile. See *Casey v. City of Fairbanks,* 670 P.2d 1133, 1984-86 PBC ¶ 34,066 (Alaska 1983); *Browne v. Milwaukee Bd. of Sch. Dirs.,* 230 N.W.2d 704, 90 L.R.R.M. 2412 (Wis. 1975).

3. Although many courts in fair representation and breach of contract actions will award reinstatement and backpay to impermissibly terminated employees whose union did not represent them fairly, others will only refer the underlying controversy to arbitration. See *Martino v. Transport Workers Union, Local 234,* 1984-86 PBC ¶ 34,222 (Pa. 1984).

4. *Smith v. Daws,* 614 F.2d 1069 (5th Cir.), *cert. denied,* 449 U.S. 1011 (1980), recognized that a postal employee aggrieved by an arbitral determination could only challenge that award in court by demonstrating that the representative union had breached its duty of fair representation with respect to its presentation of the worker's case before the arbitrator. This rule is consistent with that applied to similar private sector controversies. See *Hines v. Anchor Motor Freight, Inc.*, 424 U.S. 554 (1976).

5. *Mail Handlers, Local 305 v. United States Postal Serv.*, 594 F.2d 988 (4th Cir. 1979), involved a suit to enforce grievance settlements that had been agreed upon but which the employer had declined to honor. The court rejected the argument of the Postal Service that the dispute should first be sent through the grievance-arbitration procedures, since it concluded that such an effort would likely be futile, given the employer's unwillingness to comply with settlements that had earlier been achieved through those same procedures.

3. THE UNION'S DUTY OF FAIR REPRESENTATION

BELANGER v. MATTESON

346 A.2d 124 (R.I. 1975), *cert. denied*, 424 U.S. 968 (1976)

KELLEHER, JUSTICE: — This is an appeal from a Superior Court judgment vacating an arbitration award which had been granted under the terms of a collective bargaining agreement between the Warwick Teachers' Union Local 915, AFT, AFL-CIO (Union) and the Warwick School Committee (School Committee).

The Union is the exclusive bargaining agent of all the teachers employed by the School Committee.... The controversy in this case concerns, in part, the provisions of the contract which was in force from February 1, 1972 to January 31, 1973.

On June 22, 1972, the School Committee posted a notice of a vacancy for the position of Business Department Head at Warwick Veterans' Memorial High School. The vacancy was a "promotional position" within the terms of the contract, and the notice was posted in compliance with its terms. Four teachers applied for the position, including plaintiff and one of the named defendants, Arthur B. Matteson. The candidates were interviewed, and their credentials reviewed by a committee of school administrators .... This committee unanimously recommended the appointment of Belanger to the vacant position. Its recommendation was in turn reviewed by the superintendent, who concurred in its decision. Finally, the matter was put before the School Committee who voted to appoint Belanger to the post.

Upon learning that he had been unsuccessful in his bid for the promotion, Matteson met with Mr. Venditto, the Assistant Superintendent in Charge of Personnel to discuss his dissatisfaction. This was his right under art. V, sec. 4(d) of the agreement. He did not obtain satisfaction from this discussion, and thereafter wrote to his union representative and requested the Union to invoke on his behalf the grievance procedures provided in the collective bargaining agreement. The core of Matteson's grievance rested with his belief that the School Committee had violated the agreement by appointing Belanger. Article V, sec. 4(b) provides that, "[c]andidates shall be recommended on the basis of qualifications for the position. Where qualifications are considered equal, seniority in the Warwick School System shall prevail." It is undisputed that Matteson has more seniority than Belanger. Throughout this controversy, Matteson and the Union have insisted that since Matteson was at least as equally qualified for the position as Belanger, the appointment should have been given to the senior person.

The School Committee appointed Belanger on August 1, 1972. On August 7, 1972, the Union filed a written notice of Matteson's grievance with the Assistant Superintendent in Charge of Personnel. The Assistant Superintendent met with Matteson and a union representative in early September. On October 11, 1972, he sent Matteson a letter notifying him that his decision was to retain Belanger in the post of department head. The Union followed the grievance procedures set forth in the agreement. It first placed Matteson's cause before the Superintendent and then went before the School Committee. Matteson, having had no success at the administrative level, requested the Union to take his complaint to arbitration. The Union met in executive committee and voted to initiate the arbitration.

A hearing was held on April 6, 1973, before three arbitrators....

The issue submitted to the arbitrators by both sides was: "Has the Committee violated Article V, Section 4(b) of the collective bargaining agreement by not appointing Mr. Arthur Matteson as Business Department Head at Veterans' Memorial High School? If so, what shall the remedy be?"

[O]n August 16, 1973 the arbitrators rendered a decision. They ruled that Matteson was entitled to the appointment as head of the Business Department.

After a full year on the job, Belanger found himself deprived of his promotion and back in the classroom. He wrote to his principal and the Union and requested that a grievance be filed on his behalf as he wished to challenge this demotion.

The Union president responded that, although the Union would be happy to file a grievance for him alleging that the School Committee had not adequately represented or protected his interest in his former position as department head, it would not ask for his reinstatement in that position because: "We [the Union] cannot, at this time, however, ask for a remedy which in effect would reverse a decision which was a result of a grievance filed by the Union. This would be illogical and inconsistent with our role as bargaining agent and our obligation under the contract. We have, after all, agreed to make binding arbitration the final step in our grievance procedure."

Thereafter, Belanger instituted this ligitation in the Superior Court. He named as defendants Matteson, the Union, the arbitrators, and the School Committee and asked the court to overturn the arbitrators' decision and reinstate him. His suit was based on 2 grounds: (1) that the arbitrators exceeded their jurisdiction, and (2) that the Union breached its duty to fairly represent his interests when it decided to pursue Matteson's grievance.

The trial justice found that there existed a duty of fair representation which the Union had breached, and that the award was in excess of the arbitrators' power and thus void. He vacated the award, and reinstated Belanger. Matteson and the Union appealed. We will first consider the duty of fair representation facet of this appeal .... The question of the duty owed by a union to its members is one of first impression in this court. It has, however, been extensively litigated in other jurisdictions, most notably in the federal courts, in cases arising under the National Labor Relations Act, 29 U.S.C.A. § 151 et seq. (1973), the Labor

Management Relations Act, 1947, 29 U.S.C.A. § 141 et seq. (1973), and the Railway Act, 45 U.S.C.A. § 151 et seq. (1972).

The first of what has become a long line of cases was *Steele v. Louisville & Nashville R.R.,* 323 U.S. 192, 15 LRRM 708 (1944). There, the Court held that the Railway Labor Act, in providing that an organization chosen by the majority of employees would be the exclusive representative of all the employees within its class, mandated a concomitant duty "to act for and not against those whom it represents," and "to exercise fairly the power conferred upon it in behalf of all those for whom it acts ...." [Citing cases.] By taking away the right of individual employees to further their interests individually or to organize into numerous small units to deal with their employer, Congress has given a union power and control over the working lives of each of its members. A corollary of such power is the duty to act for the benefit of its members.

Our Legislature has created a structure of labor regulations which parallels in many significant respects the federal scheme. Our focus here is G.L. 1956 (1968 Reenactment) § 28-9.3-1 et seq., entitled Arbitration of School Teacher Disputes...." Section 28-9.3-3 mandates that the school committee recognize the labor organization chosen by the teachers to be their "sole and exclusive" bargaining agent. Thus, a labor organization representing teachers of this state has the same broad authority in the negotiation, administration, and enforcement of the collective bargaining agreement as does a union regulated by federal law. We find ourselves in agreement with the persuasive logic of the *Steele* opinion and its progeny, and, therefore hereby recognize, as implicit in our Act, a statutory duty on the part of an exclusive bargaining agent to fairly and adequately represent the interests of all of those for whom it negotiates and contracts, not only those who are members, but all those who are part of the bargaining unit.

The union and its bargaining unit are necessarily composed of many individuals with diverse views and oft-times conflicting employment demands. The whole purpose behind the creation of the union is, however, to present a solid, unified front to the employer. "In unity there is strength," went the old organizing slogan, and it was the truth. In dealing with the employer, the union gains its negotiating power from the fact that it speaks with one voice for all the employees.

That we find a duty on the part of the union does not, however, solve the controversy before us. We must define the parameters of the duty, and then apply it to the facts as found by the Superior Court....

In the negotiation process, we hold that a union must make an honest effort to serve the interest of all of its members, without hostility to any, and its power must be exercised in complete good faith and with honesty of purpose. *Ford Motor Co. v. Huffman, supra.*

Where the union and the employer have provided by contract for the internal settlement of disputes by means of grievance and arbitration procedures, and where these settlement procedures can be initiated and continued solely by the union, the union is likewise subject to a duty of fair representation in its handling of employee grievances. As in contract negotiations, the union as it deals with grievances must often take a position which is detrimental to some employees as it is helpful to others. The duty upon the Union here is to "... in good faith and in a nonarbitrary manner, make decisions as to the merits of particular grievances," *Vaca v. Sipes*, 386 U.S. 171, 194, 64 LRRM 2369, 2378 (1967), and, if it decides to pursue a grievance, it must not do so in a perfunctory manner.

Applying these standards of conduct to the facts of this case, we are faced with a clear breach by the Union of the duty it owed to Belanger. The testimony was undisputed, and the trial justice found that throughout the grievance procedure, the Union and its representatives acted without ever contacting Belanger or considering his qualifications for the position; the Union aligned itself with Matteson in seeking Belanger's removal; and at the arbitration hearing the union representatives attempted to demonstrate that Matteson, rather than Belanger, was entitled to the position....

We have said a union may, and often must, take sides. But we wish to make it clear that it must act, when it does, in a nonarbitrary, nonperfunctory manner. Here the Union chose sides totally on the fortuitous circumstances of who the School Committee did not hire. It is true, in a very simplistic sense, that Matteson, being the only member of the bargaining unit with "a grievance," is therefore the only individual in need of Union support. But one would require blinders to accept this view. It should have been apparent to the Union that Matteson's grievance, although theoretically against the School Committee, was in reality against Belanger. Any action the Union took on Matteson's behalf threatened Belanger's job.

The Union had as much of an obligation to support Belanger as it had to support Matteson until such time as it had examined the qualifications of both candidates, and it believed that the seniority clause would control the selection process.

This was clearly a situation that was akin to the situations found in *Humphrey, Huffman,* and *Vaca* where a union faced with conflicting loyalties must make a choice as to which member it will support. To enforce a requirement of neutrality on the union in cases such as this would not, in our opinion, further the purposes of the statute which was designed to strengthen the power of teachers in controlling their employment situation by allowing them all to speak through a single, but strong voice. Neutrality could only weaken the power of employees to deal with their employer. Even if in any particular grievance procedure neutrality would not be harmful, the [cumulative] effect of such a stance taken over a period of time would undermine the position of the union as employee advocate in its dealings with the employer.

Also, by remaining neutral, the union would lose the ability to control the scope and focus of the arguments made on behalf of the employees. Professor Cox has argued that the settlement of an individual employee grievance involves more than the individual because precedent is established which will control the course of future employer-employee relations. This distinguished educator also points out that any time the parties do battle over their contract, they are also engaging in a process of negotiation over its terms.

The Union must choose its side in a nonarbitrary manner, based on its good-faith judgment as to the merits of the conflicting claims. In the present case the Union never offered Belanger an opportunity to present his case to them. It never recognized its duty to independently determine whether Matteson or

Belanger was entitled to the job. It seems to us that the only fair procedure in this type of a conflict is for the Union, at the earliest stages of the grievance procedure, to investigate the case for both sides, to give both contestants an opportunity to be heard, and to submit their qualifications to the Union. We are not mandating a full-blown hearing, replete with strict rules of procedure and adversary proceedings. If the Union investigates in an informal manner, this would be sufficient so long as its procedure affords the two employees the ability to place all the relevant information before the Union. See *Bures v. Houston Symphony Soc'y,* 503 F.2d 842, 87 LRRM 3124 (5th Cir. 1974); *Waiters' Union, Local 781 v. Hotel Ass'n,* 498 F.2d 998, 86 LRRM 2001 (1974).

For a union to make a decision affecting its members without investigating the underlying factual situation is a clear breach of the duty of fair representation. *De Arroyo v. Sindicato De Trabajadores Packinghouse,* AFL-CIO, 425 F.2d 281, 74 LRRM 2028 (1st Cir. 1970). In an examination of the union's conduct in its discharge of its duty to the members of the bargaining unit, there are three possible foci for our analysis; the union's motives, its decision making procedures, and the reasons for its acting as it did. A court's investigation into the first two questions is proper and necessary. We will, however, be more careful in any review of the merits of the Union's decision. An inquiry into the merits would open the way for our substituting our judgment for that of the Union, and that is not our role. It will be enough protection for an employee represented by a union if we inquire into motives and ensure that the union has fairly considered both sides before taking a stand.

[The balance of the court's opinion limits the scope of the proper remedy for the breach of the duty of fair representation under the facts of this case, and holds that the panel of arbitrators did not exceed its authority in its decision to replace Belanger with Matteson.]

NOTES

1. A labor organization will usually not be found to have breached its duty of fair representation unless it acted in bad faith or capriciously. See, e.g., *Ford v. University of Mont.,* 598 P.2d 604, 102 L.R.R.M. 2927 (Mont. 1979). Substantial discretion is normally given to representative unions. Thus, a union does not necessarily breach its duty when it decides to furnish legal counsel to one worker who is involved in a seniority dispute with another member of the same bargaining unit. See *Jacobs v. Board of Educ., East Meadow Union Free Sch. Dist.,* 1979, PBC ¶ 36,465 (N.Y. Sup. Ct., App. Div. 1978). See also *Goolsby v. City of Detroit,* 358 N.W.2d 856, 1984-86 PBC ¶ 34,378 (Mich. 1984), indicating that while "mere negligence" would not constitute a breach of the fair representation duty, "inept conduct undertaken with little care or with indifference to the interests of those affected" might. Thus arbitrary or perfunctory action involving "impulsive, irrational, or unreasoned conduct; or inept conduct" might be found to constitute a fair representation breach.

2. In *McGrail v. Detroit Fed'n of Teachers,* 82 L.R.R.M. 2623 (Mich. Cir. Ct. 1973), substitute teachers sued the union which represented them and regular teachers for allegedly breaching its duty of fair representation for failing to obtain a pay increase for them during the 1967-68 year when raises were procured for regular personnel. The court quoted from *Ford Motor Co. v.*

Huffman, 345 U.S. 330 (1953), and then proceeded to reject the plaintiffs' contention:

"The mere existence of ... differences does not make them invalid. The complete satisfaction of all who are represented is hardly to be expected. A wide range of reasonableness must be allowed a statutory bargaining representative in serving the unit it represents subject always to complete good faith and honesty of purpose in the exercise of its discretion.

"Compromises on a temporary basis, with a view to long range advantages are natural incidents of negotiation. Differences in wages, hours and conditions of employment reflect countless variables." (Emphasis added.)

....

In the present case before the court the plaintiff has simply alleged a breach of a duty to fair representation and bases this solely on the fact that the classes he represents did not receive a raise during a certain period covered under a contract. This in itself does not constitute arbitrary or discriminatory action, bad faith or fraud. At most, the facts plaintiff shows amount to a temporary compromise for the benefit of all, which the union is entitled to make.

What if substitutes were denied such increases for three consecutive years while regular teachers were obtaining annual raises?

3. *Rouse v. Anchorage Sch. Dist.,* 613 P.2d 263, 1979-80 PBC ¶36,972 (Alaska 1980), held that where the exclusive representative acted in good faith, it could lawfully bargain away a contractual longevity pay increase during negotiations for a new collective agreement, even though some of the employees in the bargaining unit had already completed the service requirement which entitled them to the increase under the old contract. See also *Civil Serv. Bar Ass'n, Local 237 v. City of N.Y.,* 64 N.Y.2d 188, 474 N.E.2d 587 (1984), wherein the court recognized the right of a labor organization that had prevailed in an arbitral proceeding to enter into a good faith settlement agreement which somewhat diminished the benefits which some employees would have enjoyed under the prior arbitral award.

4. Even where breach of a union's fair representation duty constitutes an unfair labor practice cognizable before the public employment relations commission, courts will generally have concurrent jurisdiction to entertain judicial actions alleging a fair representation breach. See *Leahy v. AFSCME, Local 1526,* 399 Mass. 341, 504 N.E.2d 602 (1987); *Teamsters, Local 45 v. State,* 635 P.2d 1310, 1981-83 PBC ¶37,490 (Mont. 1981); *Fetterman v. University of Conn.,* 473 A.2d 1176, 1984-86 PBC ¶34,264 (Conn. 1984). But see *Bodensack v. AFSCME, Local 587,* 81 L.R.R.M. 2639 (Wis. Cir. Ct. 1972).

5. In *Karahalios v. National Fed'n of Fed. Emps., Local 1263,* 109 S. Ct. 1282 (1989), the Supreme Court held that the FLRA has exclusive jurisdiction over claims by federal employees that labor organizations have breached their duty of fair representation, since such conduct constitutes an unfair labor practice. The Court thus found that Title VII of the Civil Service Reform Act does not provide federal personnel with a private cause of action for such fair representation breaches.

6. The New Jersey Supreme Court has ruled that an individual employee whose contractual interests conflict with the position being asserted by the exclusive bargaining agent in a grievance-arbitration proceeding has the right to participate in the proceeding either *pro se* or through a personal representative. See *Saginario v. New Jersey,* 435 A.2d 1134, 1981-83 PBC ¶37,391 (1981).

7. Where a representative labor organization requires bargaining unit employees who are not union members to pay a special representation fee prior to the processing of their grievances, it will generally be found to have breached its fair representation duty. See *Deglow v. Los Rios College Fed'n of Teachers, Local 2279,* Cal. PERB No. HO-U-147, PEB ¶ 43,052 (1982). A union similarly breaches its fair representation duty where it automatically provides legal counsel to represent members during grievance-arbitration proceedings but usually provides only nonlawyer representatives for nonmembers. See *NTEU v. FLRA,* 721 F.2d 1402 (D.C. Cir. 1983). A violation will also be found where union members are given a contractual preference over nonmembers with respect to involuntary transfers. See *Bowman v. TVA,* 744 F.2d 1207 (6th Cir. 1984), *cert. denied,* 470 U.S. 1084 (1985).

Although a labor organization breaches its fair representation duty when it provides legal counsel to represent union members during grievance-arbitration proceedings but only nonlawyer representatives for most nonmember grievances, it does not breach that duty when it provides legal representation to terminated members invoking statutorily prescribed review procedures but does not provide such legal assistance to discharged nonmembers. Since such statutory review procedures are separate and distinct from negotiated contractual grievance procedures which all employees could alternatively elect to pursue through their representative union, the duty of fair representation does not require a labor organization to treat employees who invoke such external procedures the same regardless of their membership status. See *NTEU v. FLRA,* 800 F.2d 1165 (D.C. Cir. 1986); *AFGE, Local 916 v. FLRA,* 812 F.2d 1326 (10th Cir. 1987).

8. In *Allen v. Seattle Police Officers Guild,* 670 P.2d 246, 1981-83 PBC ¶ 37,898 (1983), the Washington Supreme Court found that a labor organization which prosecuted a legal challenge to an employer-initiated affirmative action program which modified certain seniority rights did not ipso facto breach the fair representation duty owed to the minority workers being benefited by the affirmative action plan, particularly where the union had historically acted diligently to insure reliance upon seniority rights with respect to worker advancement.

9. The United States Supreme Court has decided that where an employee has been wrongfully terminated by his employer and his union has impermissibly refused to prosecute his grievance, backpay liability must be apportioned between the employer and the union. The employer will be held liable for the period following the discharge until the worker would presumably have been reinstated had the union represented him properly, with the labor organization being primarily liable — and the employer secondarily liable — for the period following that date. See *Bowen v. United States Postal Serv.,* 459 U.S. 212 (1983).

10. It would appear that a public sector employee may not obtain punitive damages from a labor union which has breached its duty of fair representation. See *Santos v. AFSCME, Council 82,* 1980-81 PBC ¶ 37,206 (N.Y. App. Div. 1981). Cf. *IBEW v. Foust,* 442 U.S. 42 (1979) (no punitive damages for fair representation breach under Railway Labor Act).

11. See Note, *Federal Employees Federal Unions, and Federal Courts: The Duty of Fair Representation in the Federal Sector,* 64 Chi-Kent L. Rev. 271 (1988); Note, *Public Sector Grievance Procedures, Due Process, and the Duty of Fair Representation,* 89 Harv. L. Rev. 752 (1976). See generally Aaron, *Some Aspects of the Union's Duty of Fair Representation,* 22 Ohio St. L.J. 39 (1961);

Clark, *The Duty of Fair Representation: A Theoretical Structure,* 51 Texas L. Rev. 1119 (1973); Cox, *The Duty of Fair Representation,* 2 Vill. L. Rev. 151 (1957); Gould, *Labor Arbitration of Grievances Involving Racial Discrimination,* 118 Pa. L. Rev. 40 (1969); Wellington, *Union Democracy and Fair Representation: Federal Responsibility in a Federal System,* 67 Yale L.J. 1327 (1958); Note, *Union Discretion and the Abridgement of Employee Rights,* 51 Or. L. Rev. 248 (1971).

E. BREACH OF CONTRACT AS AN UNFAIR LABOR PRACTICE

1. CONTRACT DISPUTES BEFORE A STATE AGENCY

BOARD OF EDUCATION, UNION FREE SCHOOL DISTRICT NO. 3 & EAST MEADOW TEACHERS ASSOCIATION

4 PERB ¶ 4-4018 (N.Y. 1971)

The East Meadow Teachers Association (EMTA) filed an improper practice charge against the Board of Education, Union Free School District No. 3, Town of Hempstead, Nassau County (respondent).

The charge alleged a violation of § 209-a.1 (d)[1] of the Public Employees' Fair Employment Act (Act) in that the respondent unilaterally changed the terms and conditions relating to sabbatical leaves by requiring all applicants for such leaves to agree to return to the employment of respondent for a period of two years following the termination of the sabbatical leave.

EMTA and respondent entered into a written agreement in July, 1969 setting forth the terms and conditions of employment for teaching personnel. The agreement became effective on September 1, 1969, and terminated on August 31, 1970.

The agreement provided in ¶ 5.1:

"Sabbatical Leave — The existing practices, policies and procedures respecting sabbatical leaves to teaching personnel are confirmed and shall remain in effect except that (a) a teacher eligible for sabbatical may select a half-year sabbatical at full pay for full-time study or its equivalent upon approval of the Superintendent of Schools, either in the United States or abroad and (b) in selecting among applicants for sabbatical leave, length of service in the District shall be one of the prime considerations."

In April, 1970 the respondent changed its policy relating to sabbatical leave to require, as a condition to the granting thereof, an agreement to work for respondent for a two-year period following the leave. It is conceded that in effecting this change respondent did not negotiate with EMTA.

The hearing officer concluded that procedures and policies relating to sabbatical leave are a mandatory subject of collective negotiations and that there is an obligation on the part of the respondent to negotiate with EMTA "prior to implementing a change in its sabbatical leave policy."

---

[1]"to refuse to negotiate in good faith with the duly recognized or certified representatives of its public employees."

The hearing officer, after giving consideration to several affirmative defenses asserted by respondent and finding them lacking in merit, thereupon found that respondent violated § 209-a.1 (d) of the Act.

Respondent has excepted to the decision and recommended order of the hearing officer.

The arguments in defense of the position of respondent may be summarized as (1) Sabbatical Leave is not a term or condition of employment under the Act; (2) The conduct of respondent alleged as the basis of the charge herein would constitute a breach of the agreement between the parties and, therefore, the grievance procedure set forth in the contract is the sole remedy available to EMTA; (3) The question has become moot in that in the subsequent agreement between the parties there is a contractual provision covering sabbatical leave, the point at issue....

First, we agree with the hearing officer that the issue of sabbatical leave is a term and condition of employment and thus is a proper subject of collective negotiations. The provisions of § 1709, subdivision 16 of the Education Law does not negate this conclusion.

Therefore, either party has the duty to negotiate concerning this subject if requested by the other. This duty to negotiate, of course, does not compel one party to agree to the proposal of the other. Rather, this duty requires each party to negotiate in good faith on all mandatory subjects of negotiations.

As to respondent's second contention that the respondent's conduct herein should be relegated to the grievance procedure agreed upon by the parties in their negotiated agreement, the hearing officer reasoned that the "claim here does not relate to the interpretation of any clause of the collective agreement." The hearing officer concluded that, "this dispute is not one of contract interpretation but of statutory obligation" and, therefore, EMTA could properly invoke the improper practice section of the Act, rather than the grievance procedures in the negotiated agreement.

This issue raised by respondent is one of first impression before this Board and raises some basic questions. The first question is: Does this Board have general jurisdiction to police and enforce negotiated agreements between public employers and employee organizations within this state?

We conclude that it does not. The legislature of this state has not dealt explicitly with this problem, as have the legislatures of Wisconsin,[2] or Hawaii,[3] in making the breach of a collective bargaining agreement an unfair labor practice. While the legislature of this state has stated that, in the administration of improper practices, decisions in the private sector shall not be binding or controlling precedent[4] nevertheless such statutory mandate does not by its terms preclude this Board from considering the vast reservoir of experience in the private sector.

In decisions construing the National Labor Relations Act, it appears to be well-settled that the National Labor Relations Board does not have general jurisdiction over alleged violations of collective bargaining agreements.[5] In

---

[2] State Employment Labor Relations Act, § 111.84(I)(e).

[3] State of Hawaii, Act 171, L. 1970, § 13(a)(8).

[4] CSL § 209-a.8.

[5] NLRB v. C & C Plywood Corp., 385 U.S. 421; NLRB v. M & M Oldsmobile Inc., 377 F.2d 712.

reaching this conclusion, the Supreme Court relied upon the legislative history of the enactment of the Taft-Hartley Act[6] and concluded that Congress "deliberately chose to leave the enforcement of collective agreements to the usual processes of law."[7]

There is no such legislative history as to the Act herein. Nevertheless, we find the conclusion reached by the Supreme Court in the private sector to be a salutary approach, particularly since the legislature of this state did not provide that a breach of a negotiated agreement would constitute an improper practice. However, this is not dispositive of the issue raised by respondent, for all that has been concluded so far is that a breach of contract is not per se an improper labor practice.

A second question arises whether conduct which constitutes a breach of contract may also constitute an improper practice. This question requires an affirmative answer in the light of facts of this case.

Respondent herein agreed, in the negotiated agreement, to maintain existing policies, practices and procedures relating to sabbatical leave. Respondent unilaterally changed such practices, policies and procedures without negotiating such change with the representative of its employees. This constitutes a violation of § 209-a.1 (d) of the Act in that it violates respondent's obligation "to negotiate in good faith" with such representative.

The fact that respondent, in effecting such change, contends that it acted in the public interest, does not cure the violation herein. The Act mandates that a public employer negotiate terms and conditions of employment with the certified or recognized representative of its employees. This obviously precludes the unilateral imposition of terms and conditions of employment.

We do not reach the question here of whether, in such circumstances, this Board should defer to the grievance and arbitration procedures in an agreement because the subject contract does not provide for binding arbitration.

The third defense, to wit, the allegation that the question has become moot, is not a defense at all; rather, its relevance in this case is only to the nature of the remedial order to be issued by this Board....

NOTE

If a party refuses to comply with its contractual obligation to participate in the selection of a grievance arbitrator, it may be found guilty of an unfair refusal to bargain, since the administration of a collective agreement is generally considered to constitute part of the bargaining process. See *Blackhawk Sch. Dist.*, Pa. LRB Case No. PERA-C-10, 466-W, 1977-78 PEB ¶ 40,390 (1977). However, where a party simply declines to honor an adverse arbitration award, the prevailing party may be required to seek judicial enforcement, with no redress being available through unfair labor practice proceedings. See *West Bloomfield Bd. of Educ.*, Mich. BER Case No. C76E-148, 1977-78 PEB ¶ 40,033 (1977). Is this distinction logical?

---

[6] *NLRB v. C & C Plywood Corp., supra,* footnote 5.
[7] *Charles Dowd Box Co. v. Courtney,* 368 U.S. 518.

2. DEFERENCE TO ARBITRATION

CITY OF WILMINGTON v. WILMINGTON FIREFIGHTERS, LOCAL 1590

385 A.2d 720 (Del. 1978)

DUFFY, JUSTICE: This appeal involves a controversy between the City of Wilmington and a union representing Wilmington firemen over the proper forum for resolving the union's complaint that the City, by amending a medical plan covering its firefighters, violated both a State statute and the contract between the parties.

I

The facts are these:

The City (defendant) made a collective bargaining agreement with Wilmington Firefighters Local 1590, International Association of Firefighters (plaintiff) governing wages and other terms of employment. The official personnel rules and regulations of the Wilmington Bureau of Fire were incorporated in the contract. Thereafter, the City abolished the position of Fire Physician and adopted a revised medical plan for its firemen. The Association then filed an action in the Court of Chancery alleging that the City had, by so doing, violated 19 Del. C. ch. 13 and the collective bargaining agreement. The Union sought injunctive relief which would eliminate the alleged violations.

The City moved to dismiss the complaint on jurisdictional grounds, arguing that the collective bargaining agreement, which created a grievance and arbitration procedure for resolving disputes, was the Union's exclusive remedy. The parties agreed to a stay until the Court decided a then pending action brought by Wilmington policemen against the City and involving the same issues. *Fraternal Order of Police, Lodge No. 1 v. City of Wilmington,* Del. Ch., C.A. No. 4783. The latter case was decided by an unpublished opinion, dated December 23, 1975, in which the then Chancellor stayed the action on condition that the City agree to certain modifications in the grievance procedure established by the contract between the City and the Union.[2] Relying on the stipulation of the parties and the principle of *stare decisis,* the Court, in this case, denied the City's motion to dismiss and imposed the same conditions as those fixed in *Fraternal Order of Police, Lodge No. 1.* The City filed this appeal. We reverse.

II

The ultimate question before us concerns the action which should be taken by a Delaware Court when it is asked to award relief on grounds that allegedly violate both a State statute and a labor relations contract in which the parties established a binding and final settlement procedure for disputes.

---

[2] The Court's order included the following conditions: (1) that the grievance procedure begin with a written complaint which must be discussed with the Director of Personnel and the Commissioner of Public Safety; (2) that the City must supply at its expense the means of securing a verbatim record in any Grievance Appeal Board proceeding; (3) that depositions can be taken by plaintiff of persons noticed (not exceeding 3) between the filing of the complaint and the discussion required by (1), *supra.*

In considering the question and in formulating an opinion, we emphasize that the alleged violation concerns a refusal-to-bargain. That is important in limiting the impact of this ruling on judicial determinations of future labor disputes in which public employees are involved.

The Union argues that the Court should proceed to determine the merits of the case, that the arbitration clause in a labor agreement is an optional remedy for breach of contract and, in any event, that the procedure adopted by the Trial Court is reasonable and should be approved.

The City, on the other hand, contends that the Court of Chancery should have abstained from exercising its jurisdiction until contract arbitration had been completed and that the Court erred by imposing terms which amount to an amendment of the contract without the City's consent.

The statutory sections allegedly violated by the City, 19 Del. C. ch. 13, concern a public employer's duty to engage in collective bargaining with an exclusive bargaining representative.[3] And the contract provisions allegedly violated are the Bureau of Fire rules and regulations incorporated into the collective bargaining agreement. As we have noted, the violations are said to result from the City's independent or unilateral abolition of the Fire Physician position and implementation of a revised medical plan. The charge is that such actions constitute a refusal-to-bargain, and interference, restraint and coercion of protected labor rights, and a violation of contractually agreed-upon medical programs.

III

The appropriate point of entry for a Delaware Court into this kind of controversy is an issue of first impression. In beginning our review, we assume that the City's actions constitute both a statutory and a contractual violation. This kind of controversy has been litigated elsewhere and so we look for guidance to the procedure adopted in the Federal forums and by the Courts and administrative tribunals in other States for dealing with such situations.

First, as to Federal precedent: Section 10 of the National Labor Relations Act (Act), 29 U.S.C. § 151, et seq., authorizes the National Labor Relations Board (NLRB) to adjudicate statutory violations constituting unfair labor practices arising under the Act. However, the existence of a claimed contract violation and the availability of a contract remedy — arbitration, for example — does not divest the NLRB of jurisdiction to adjudicate an alleged statutory violation for the same conduct. *NLRB v. Acme Industrial Co.,* 385 U.S. 432 (1967). NLRB jurisdiction continues but, if the labor dispute involves both allegations (that is, statutory as well as contract violations) and if it is at a pre-arbitral stage, the NLRB will defer to the contractually agreed-upon arbitration procedures when the issue is a refusal-to-bargain. *Collyer Insulated Wire,* 192 NLRB 837, 77 LRRM 1931 (1971).

---

[3] 19 Del. C. ch. 13, which became effective on June 15, 1965, confers rights on public employees, including the right to organize, § 1302; to be free from restraint, coercion or discrimination in the free exercise of any rights under chapter 13, § 1303; to have bargaining units established and exclusive bargaining representatives elected, §§ 1304 — 1306; and the right to bargain collectively with the public employer, § 1309.

Speaking of the NLRB policy with approval, the United States Supreme Court in *William E. Arnold Co. v. Carpenters District Council,* 417 U.S. 12 (1974), said this:

"... Board policy is to refrain from exercising jurisdiction in respect of disputed conduct arguably both an unfair labor practice and a contract violation when, as in this case, the parties have voluntarily established by contract a binding settlement procedure. See, e.g., *The Associated Press,* 199 N.L.R.B. 1110 (1972); *Eastman Broadcasting Co.,* 199 N.L.R.B. 434 (1972); *Laborers Local 423,* 199 N.L.R.B. 450 (1972); *Collyer Insulated Wire,* 192 N.L.R.B. 837 (1971). The Board said in *Collyer,* 'an industrial relations dispute may involve conduct which, at least arguably, may contravene both the collective agreement and our statute. When the parties have contractually committed themselves to mutually agreeable procedures for resolving their disputes during the period of the contract, we are of the view that those procedures should be afforded full opportunity to function .... We believe it to be consistent with the fundamental objectives of Federal law to require the parties ... to honor their contractual obligations rather than, by casting [their] dispute in statutory terms, to ignore their agreed-upon procedures.' *Id.,* at 842-843. The Board's position harmonizes with Congress' articulated concern that, '[f]inal adjustment by a method agreed upon by the parties is ... the desirable method for settlement of grievance disputes arising over the application or interpretation of an existing collective-bargaining agreement ...' § 203(d) of the LMRA, 29 U.S.C. § 173(d)."

When the NLRB does defer, it retains jurisdiction to consider an application for additional relief on a showing that either: (1) the dispute has not been resolved or submitted to arbitration with reasonable promptness, or (2) the arbitration procedures have been unfair or have rendered a result repugnant to the Act. *Collyer Insulated Wire, supra.*

The Federal Courts of Appeal have consistently upheld the *Collyer* deferral policy. See, e.g., *Local Union No. 2188, Int'l Bhd. of Elec. Workers v. NLRB,* 494 F.2d 1087 (Fed. Cir. 1974), *cert. denied,* 419 U.S. 835 (1974); *Provision House Workers Union Local 274 v. NLRB,* 493 F.2d 1249 (9th Cir. 1974), *cert. denied,* 419 U.S. 828 (1974); *Nabisco, Inc. v. NLRB,* 479 F.2d 770 (2d Cir. 1973). And, as we have indicated, the United States Supreme Court noted its approval by saying that the pre-arbitral deferral policy "harmonizes" with a Legislative preference for voluntary settlement procedures in labor disputes. *William E. Arnold Co. v. Carpenters District Council, supra.*

A number of State labor commissions, including those in Massachusetts, Michigan, New Jersey and New York, have adopted deferral doctrines in public employee refusal-to-bargain situations. 1 *Pub. Empl. Barg.* (CCH) ¶ 5015. For example, the Michigan Employment Relations Commission has expressly approved and cited the *Collyer* deferral doctrine. Deferral has been held appropriate in Michigan public employee cases where there is a contractual provision for arbitration and the dispute can arguably be resolved under the contract language; and allegations of unilateral changes in terms and conditions of employment in violation of Michigan's Public Employment Relations Act have frequently prompted deferral to arbitration. See 1 *Pub. Empl. Barg.* (CCH) Michigan ¶ 5015 and cases cited therein.

We conclude from this brief review that a deferral policy is widely followed and has much to commend it in practice.

IV

Returning now to the present dispute, when it was placed before the Court of Chancery, that Court had several options available. We know, of course, what the Court did. But, it could have taken jurisdiction and adjudicated the dispute. Or, it could have dismissed the action as premature and left the parties to pursue their contract remedies. Or, the Court could have followed the *Collyer* practice by taking jurisdiction and then staying the action until after the parties had followed the contract procedure.

We conclude that the *Collyer* deferral to arbitration is a sound and sensible policy for Delaware to follow. Other States, many of them with large populations and complex governments have followed the Federal lead. And there is similarity between the Federal Labor Act and 19 Del. C. ch. 13, as expressly noted by Judge Stapleton in *Cofrancesco v. City of Wilmington*, 419 F. Supp. 109 (D. Del. 1976):

> "Delaware law extends to State, county and municipal employees many of the same rights to ... bargain collectively that the [federal labor law] affords to employees in the private sector. 19 Del. C. § 1301, et seq. In cases where the problems raised under Delaware's labor law are similar to those that arise under the [federal law], Delaware could be expected to consider and, in all likelihood, follow federal law."

Id., at 111.

And our holding is supported by the long-accepted view that a settlement in a labor dispute is often best achieved through use of the parties' voluntary agreement to arbitrate. *United Steelwkrs. of Amer. v. American Mfg. Co.*, 363 U.S. 564 (1960); *United Steelwkrs. of Am. v. Warrior & Gulf N. Co.*, 363 U.S. 574 (1960); *United Steelwkrs. of A. v. Enterprise W. & Co. Corp.*, 363 U.S. 593 (1960) — Steelworkers Trilogy. For that reason, the arbitral process is sometimes viewed as superior to the judicial process because of an arbitrator's greater knowledge and experience regarding the parties, and because he has been selected by them. Along the same line, we note that Title 19 of the Delaware Code indicates a strong State policy favoring voluntary mediation as a means to promote industrial peace in Delaware. See 19 Del. C. §§ 110, 111(a), 1310. And pre-arbitral deferral will "require the parties here to honor their contractual obligations rather than, by casting this dispute in statutory terms, to ignore their agreed-upon procedures." *Collyer Insulated Wire, supra.* Finally, in this case, the parties' own agreement reveals a preference for the grievance-arbitration procedure by stating in Article III-A, Section 1:

> "The grievance procedures set forth in this section are established in order to provide adequate opportunity for members of the Department of Public Safety to bring forth their views relating to any unfair or improper aspect of their employment situation and to seek correction thereof."

It follows that the Court of Chancery was correct in accepting jurisdiction while ordering the parties to arbitrate, but that the Court erred in requiring modifications to the contractually agreed-upon grievance procedures. Undoubtedly the Court wanted to be helpful but, under the circumstances, that constituted unwarranted judicial meddling in the parties' contractual relations. See *John Wiley & Sons, Inc. v. Livingston,* 376 U.S. 543 (1964); and compare *Safe Harbor Fishing Club v. Safe Harbor Realty Co.,* 34 Del. Ch. 28, 107 A.2d 635 (1953). The case should have been stayed and the parties directed to proceed under the contract. And jurisdiction should have been retained by the Court to consider any application for relief on the ground that the dispute is not being resolved by arbitration with reasonable promptness, or that the arbitral process had been unfair, or that it resulted in an award repugnant to 19 Del. C. ch. 13, or that it failed to resolve the statutory claim. But, otherwise the Court should not have encumbered the agreement which the parties had made with its own notion of what was fair....

In adopting a pre-arbitral deferral policy, we emphasize that while the parties are a public employer and public employees, the present dispute is grounded in a nonpublic interest, private sector-type issue which arises in a refusal-to-bargain context. The case involves only that kind of controversy and our ruling and comments are limited to it. In other words, nothing said herein applies to an action which affects the public interest — a strike by public employees, for example. In that kind of situation the issues are different and so is the Court's responsibility. Nor are we here concerned with a post-arbitral dispute between the parties....

Reversed and remanded for further proceedings consistent herewith.

NOTES

1. Compare the *City of Wilmington* rationale with *Fire Fighters, Local 344 v. City of Detroit,* 293 N.W.2d 278, 1979-80 PBC ¶ 36,971 (1980), wherein the Michigan Supreme Court ruled that arbitral deferral of unfair labor practice cases was inappropriate under the Michigan Public Employment Relations Act. The court simply found no legislative intent to permit such a substantial delegation of statutorily established unfair labor practice authority to private arbitrators. The Oregon PERB has similarly indicated that it will not permit an arbitrator's resolution of a purely statutory question to supplant its exclusive jurisdiction over such interpretive matters. See *Eugene Educ. Ass'n. v. School Dist. 4J,* PERB Case No. C-141-78 (Or. 1980), and *Willamina Educ. Ass'n v. School Dist. 30J,* PERB Case No. C-93-78 (Or. 1980), both noted in GERR No. 856, 16-17.

2. The Massachusetts Labor Relations Commission has ruled that it will not refer an unfair labor practice charge to arbitration for resolution where the underlying issue concerns the respondent's willingness to comply with the very contractual grievance-arbitration procedures that would have to be used, *In re Bellingham Sch. Comm.,* MLRC Case No. MUP-2893, 1979-80 PEB ¶ 40,767 (1978), or where the respondent employer refuses to waive the fact that no timely grievance has been filed concerning the matter in dispute, *City of Everett,* MLRC Case No. MUP-2893, 1979-80 PEB ¶ 41,891 (1980). A similar result may occur where neither party to the unfair labor practice proceeding requests arbitral deferral. See *Appleton Professional Policemen's Ass'n v. City of Appleton,* WERC Case No. 20446 MP-615, 1977-78 PEB ¶ 40,143 (1978). Deferral to a prior arbitral award will likely be rejected where the party seeking deferral has initiated judicial action challenging that arbitral decision. See *County of Suffolk*, MLRC Case No. MUP-4466, 1981 PEB ¶ 42,755 (1981).

3. In *Olin Corp.*, 268 N.L.R.B. 573 (1984), the Labor Board modified its *Spielberg Mfg. Co.*, 112 N.L.R.B. 1080 (1955), standards as it indicated that it would henceforth defer to prior arbitral determinations where the proceedings were fair and regular, the parties had agreed to be bound by the arbitral decision, the contractual issue was factually parallel to the unfair labor practice question, the arbitrator had been presented generally with the facts relevant to the resolution of the unfair labor practice issue, and the award is not clearly repugnant to the policies of the NLRA. The Board further noted that it would honor awards that are not entirely consistent with NLRB precedent, so long as they are not "palpably wrong." The party seeking rejection of a previous award will have the burden of demonstrating some defect in that decision.

4. When an unfair labor practice issue that could be resolved through the grievance-arbitration process is initially presented to a labor relations board for determination and the board is deciding whether to defer the matter to arbitration, should a distinction be made between refusal to bargain charges that directly affect the status of the representative labor organization, with deferral of such cases being appropriate, and those charges pertaining to the restraint or coercion of individual employees, where it might be preferable to have the board itself hear the case to best insure the full protection of individual rights? Compare *United Techs. Corp.*, 268 N.L.R.B. 557 (1984) (no distinction), with *Young v. City of Great Falls*, 646 P.2d 512, 112 L.R.R.M. 2988 (Mont. 1982) (drawing such distinction).

5. See generally Cowden, *Deferral to Arbitration by the Pennsylvania Labor Relations Board*, 80 Dick. L. Rev. 666 (1976); Hayford & Wood, *Deferral to Grievance Arbitration in Unfair Labor Practice Matters: The Public Sector Treatment*, 32 Lab. L.J. 679 (1981).

F. LEGALLY IMPOSED FINANCIAL LIMITATIONS ON PUBLIC EMPLOYERS

SONOMA COUNTY ORGANIZATION OF PUBLIC EMPLOYEES v. COUNTY OF SONOMA

23 Cal. 3d 296, 591 P.2d 1 (1979)

MOSK, JUSTICE. On June 6, 1978, an initiative measure was passed by the electorate adding article XIIIA to the California Constitution. The provision, designated on the ballot as Proposition 13, placed significant limitations upon the taxing power of local and state government; the amount of revenue which local entities could raise by means of property taxes was sharply reduced. In order to mitigate the effects of this reduction, the Legislature determined to distribute surplus funds which had been accumulated in the state treasury to local agencies.

By enactment of section 16280 of the Government Code, the Legislature prohibited the distribution of state surplus or loan funds to any local public agency granting to its employees a cost-of-living wage or salary increase for the 1978-1979 fiscal year which exceeded the cost-of-living increase provided for state employees. In addition, the section declares null and void any agreement by a local agency to pay a cost-of-living increase in excess of that granted to state employees.

The primary issues raised in these five original proceedings for writs of mandate are whether section 16280 impairs the obligation of contracts in violation of article I, section 10, of the United States Constitution and article I, section 9, of the California Constitution, and whether the statute violates the home rule provisions of the California Constitution. (Art. XI, §§ 4, 5.) ...

Each of the local entities entered into a Memorandum of Understanding (agreement) to pay to the employees represented by the petitioner labor organizations a wage increase for the 1978-1979 fiscal year. These agreements were ratified by resolution or ordinance adopted by the local governing bodies. Although the Legislature provided in the 1978-1979 budget for a 2½ percent salary increase for state employees, the Governor vetoed the increase. Thereafter, the local entities failed or refused to authorize the additional wages called for in the agreements which they had previously ratified.

Petitioners seek writs of mandate to compel the local agencies to grant the increases called for in the agreements and to prohibit the state from enforcing the condition for payment of state funds set forth in section 16280. We granted alternative writs of mandate in order to consider the important issues raised.

I

We consider, first, whether the provision of section 16280 invalidating agreements calling for wage increases by local public agencies violates the state and federal constitutional prohibitions against impairing the obligations of contracts.... Section 16281 provides that limiting wage increases for local employees will "allow essential local government services to be maintained at a higher level than would otherwise be the case, and will promote full employment and prevent layoffs," and that the limitation of local employee salaries is designed "to alleviate the current fiscal crisis created by the passage of Proposition 13 ... and to provide for maintaining essential services which would otherwise be lost."

We note as a preliminary matter that the agreements between the respondent local entities and petitioners are binding contracts. Under the Meyers-Milias-Brown Act (§ 3500 et seq.) local governmental entities may enter into collective bargaining contracts with authorized employee organizations....

There can be no doubt that section 16280 impairs the obligations entered into under these agreements. The Legislature could hardly have expressed itself more clearly in this regard, for it declared *null and void* any provision of "a contract, agreement, or memorandum of understanding between a local public agency and an employee organization or an individual employee which provides for a cost of living wage or salary increase" in excess of the increase provided for state employees.

But the fact that the state has impaired the obligations of these agreements by enactment of section 16280 is the beginning rather than the end of our analysis, for it has long been settled that although the constitutional provision, literally read, proscribes "any" impairment of contract it is "not an absolute one and is not to be read with literal exactness like a mathematical formula." (*Home Building & Loan Assn. v. Blaisdell* (1934) 290 U.S. 398, 428.) The state's police power remains paramount, for a legislative body "cannot 'bargain away the public health or the public morals.'" (*Id.* at p. 436.) Obviously, however, if the contract clause is to have any effect, it must limit the exercise of the police power to some degree. Our inquiry, then, concerns not whether the state may in some cases impair the obligation of contracts, but the circumstances under which such impairment is permissible.

In *Home Building & Loan Association v. Blaisdell, supra,* 290 U.S. 398, the United States Supreme Court comprehensively reviewed the history and application of the contract clause. It upheld the constitutionality of a Minnesota mortgage moratorium law designed to provide relief to landowners whose property was threatened with foreclosure. The legislation did not entirely abrogate a mortgagee's right to foreclose as provided in the contract, but, rather, for two years from the enactment of the law, the period of redemption from foreclosure sales was extended. During the extension period, the mortgagee was entitled to the rental value of the property.

The high court identified four factors which impelled it to hold that the Minnesota law did not amount to an unconstitutional impairment of the mortgage contract. First, Minnesota had declared an emergency as the justification for the law and in the Great Depression that declaration did not lack an adequate basis. Second, the legislation was enacted not for the advantage of particular individuals, but for the protection of a basic interest of society. Third, the law was appropriate to the emergency and the conditions it imposed were reasonable: the redemption period was extended upon reasonable conditions; the integrity of the mortgage indebtedness was not impaired; interest continued to run, and the right of the mortgagee to buy the property or to obtain a deficiency judgment remained inviolate. Finally, the legislation was temporary and limited to the exigency which provoked the legislative response....

Similar factors have been applied in California decisions. In *Brown v. Ferdon* (1936) 5 Cal. 2d 226, 54 P.2d 712 and *Hales v. Snowden* (1937) 19 Cal. App. 2d 366, 65 P.2d 847, statutes providing relief to defaulting mortgagors were held to violate the constitutional prohibition against impairment of contracts because they were not limited to debtors who needed or desired relief.

Two recent cases decided by the United States Supreme Court are particularly instructive. In *Allied Structural Steel Company v. Spannaus* (1978) 438 U.S. 234, a corporation challenged a Minnesota law which substantially increased the liabilities of certain corporations for the payment of pensions to employees. The high court held that the statute constituted an unlawful impairment of contract because it retroactively modified the compensation the company had agreed to pay its employees. The court opined that, although minimal alteration of contractual obligations would call for a lesser standard of inquiry, a severe impairment "will push the inquiry to a careful examination of the nature and purpose of the state legislation."...

Perhaps the decision which is most useful in resolving the problem at hand is *United States Trust Co. v. New Jersey* (1977) 431 U.S. 1. In that case, as here, the government attempted to impair not obligations entered into between private parties, but the obligations of the public entity itself. New York and New Jersey had entered into a bistate compact to coordinate transportation facilities at the port of New York by establishment of the Port Authority. Under a 1962 statutory covenant, the two states agreed with the holders of bonds issued to finance activities of the Port Authority that, so long as the bonds remained outstanding, the revenues pledged as security would not be used for certain purposes. In 1974, the states repealed the covenant in order to facilitate the financing of mass transit improvements.

The repeal was held an unconstitutional impairment of contract because it eliminated an important security provision for the protection of the bond-holders and was neither reasonable nor necessary to serve an important state interest. The court held that a less drastic modification of the bondholders' security rights would have sufficed, that alternative means of achieving the state's goals could have been adopted, and that changed circumstances did not justify the impairment because the need for mass transit in the New York metropolitan area had been known by the state as early as 1922.

The court recognized that the contract clause was not an absolute bar to subsequent modification of a state's own financial obligations, but held that in determining whether such a modification is justified, complete deference to a legislative assessment of reasonableness and necessity is not required because the government's self-interest is at stake. It stated, "[A] governmental entity can always find a use for extra money, especially when taxes do not have to be raised. If a State could reduce its financial obligations whenever it wanted to spend the money for what it regarded as an important public purpose, the Contract Clause would provide no protection at all.... [A] State cannot refuse to meet its legitimate financial obligations simply because it would prefer to spend the money to promote the public good rather than the private welfare of its creditors.... [A] State is not completely free to consider impairing the obligations of its own contracts on a par with other policy alternatives. Similarly, a State is not free to impose a drastic impairment when an evident and more moderate course would serve its purposes equally well." (431 U.S. at pp. 26, 29, 30-31.)

In applying these standards to the impairment of petitioners' contracts, we assess, first, the severity of the impact of section 16280 upon the contract rights of petitioners. Respondents urge that the impairment is not substantial because it affects only a single contract provision for salary increases in the 1978-1979 fiscal year, and by its express terms does not invalidate contract provisions dealing with fringe benefits and other matters. We reject this assertion. An increase in wages is frequently the very heart of an employment contract; other provisions, including those relating to fringe benefits, are inextricably interwoven with those relating to wages, since employees may surrender various employment benefits in exchange for a wage increase. And, unlike the situation in the cases cited above, in which contractual benefits were either postponed (*Blaisdell*) or enforcement remedies were altered (*El Paso* [*v. Simmons,* 379 U.S. 497 (1965)]), in the present case the right of petitioners to a wage increase for the 1978-1979 fiscal year is irretrievably lost. Thus here, as in *Allied Structural Steel,* there was a "severe, permanent, and immediate change" in petitioners rights under the contract (438 U.S. at p. 250) and it cannot be said that "[t]he measure taken ... was a mild one ... hardly burdensome" to petitioners (*El Paso v. Simmons, supra,* 379 U.S. at pp. 516-517.)

Since the statute accomplishes a severe impairment of petitioners' contractual rights, the "height of the hurdle the state legislation must clear" is elevated and "a careful examination of ... [its] nature and purpose" is required. (*Allied Structural Steel Company v. Spannaus, supra,* 438 U.S. at p. 245.)

As we have seen, section 16281 declares that the salary limitation was intended by the Legislature to alleviate the "fiscal crisis" created by the passage of Proposition 13, and to provide for maintaining essential services, and that the measure would allow local government to continue services at a higher level than would otherwise be the case, would promote full employment, and prevent layoffs.

Respondents contend that this declaration of a fiscal emergency was justified. They rely in this connection upon a report prepared by the legislative analyst in May 1978, prior to the time the initiative measure was passed and section 16280 was enacted. The analysis, compiled for the Legislature, predicted the following: If Proposition 13 was enacted, local entities would lose $7 billion in property tax revenues, representing an average reduction of 57 percent of such revenues previously projected. As a result, local agencies would suffer an average 22 percent reduction in the overall revenue which had been anticipated for the 1978-1979 fiscal year. Such a reduction would not only require curtailment of essential services, but (assuming expenditure reductions were proportionately distributed between personnel costs and all other costs) an estimated 270,000 local employees would be laid off, increasing the state's projected 1978 unemployment rate from 7½ percent to 10 percent.

In view of these and other dire consequences from the loss of revenue by local agencies as a result of the passage of Proposition 13, the Legislature was faced with a fiscal crisis of severe magnitude, assert respondents, and this emergency justified the limitation of wage increases to local government employees.

In assessing this contention, we must recall the admonition in *United States Trust Company* that complete deference to a legislative assessment of reasonableness and necessity is not required where, as here, government is attempting to modify governmental financial obligations. Here respondents rely upon the existence of a fiscal crisis as justification for the impairment, but they have not met their burden of establishing that such a crisis existed. The estimate of an average 22 percent reduction in local government revenue in the legislative analyst's report assumes that the property tax revenues lost by local agencies as a result of Proposition 13 will not be replaced. But the Legislature almost immediately returned $5 billion accumulated in the state's surplus to local agencies to alleviate the potential — but not realized — effects of Proposition 13 (Gov.Code, § 16250 et seq.). Since five-sevenths of the revenues lost by the local entities was replaced by state funds, the loss to local entities amounts not to the 22 percent upon which respondents' claim of emergency is based, but, rather, to a loss of approximately 6 percent. Respondents do not claim that a 6 percent loss of revenue would justify the invalidation of wage increases called for in the agreements between petitioners and the local entities.... Thus, the asserted "fiscal emergency" relied upon by respondents as justification for the salary limitation was largely alleviated by the very same bill which contains the limitation. But even if these events had not occurred simultaneously, we would not be precluded from considering matters which followed the enactment of section 16280 for, as *Blaisdell* makes clear, "a law 'depending upon the existence of an emergency ... to uphold it may cease to operate if the emergency ceases or the facts change even though valid when passed'" and "[i]t is always open to judicial inquiry whether the exigency still exists upon which the continued operation of the law depends." (290 U.S. at p. 442.)

Respondents rely upon *Subway-Surface Supervisors Association v. New York City Transit Authority* (1978) 44 N.Y.2d 101, 404 N.Y.S.2d 323, 375 N.E.2d 384, which held that a statute deferring a wage increase in a collective bargaining agreement with a public agency did not violate the United States Constitution. There are several important distinctions between *Subway-Surface* and the present case. It was conceded there by the petitioner employee organization that the fiscal emergency was so severe that the city could be forced to cease operating if the crisis was not relieved. Here, by contrast, local government entities lost approximately 6 percent of their anticipated revenues. Moreover, in the New York case, the wage increase was deferred rather than completely eliminated, as in the present case.

Subway-Surface, like the present case, involved a multi-year contract, and the employees had performed services for the city for a substantial period prior to the wage freeze. Respondents rely upon the conclusion of the New York court that the impairment was reasonable because the contract was still executory at the time the freeze took effect. The court, after finding that the deferment was justified by the fiscal emergency, proceeded to consider whether the steps taken to meet the emergency were reasonable. In concluding that they were, it determined that since the employees had not rendered services for the second year of the two-year contract at the time of the freeze, the impairment as to them was prospective only. (44 N.Y.2d 101, 404 N.Y.S.2d at p. 328 n. 3, 375 N.E.2d 384, 389 n. 3).

Here, of course, we do not reach the issue of whether the elimination of wage increases was a reasonable measure to resolve the problems engendered by Proposition 13 since, unlike the grave circumstances which existed in New York, the government has failed to meet its threshold burden of establishing that an emergency existed.

Even if respondents were not faced with this fundamental defect, we seriously question the New York court's rationale. A contract must be viewed as a whole; it cannot be fractured into isolated components. The anticipated wage increases during the second year thereof may have affected the employees' wage demands for the first year of the contract, and undoubtedly many employees rendered their services in the first year in anticipation of their contractual right to the second year increase. It is doubtful, therefore, that the New York court was correct in its conclusion that the employees had not rendered consideration for the second year of the contract when the freeze was imposed....

Petitioners make an appealing argument that even if an emergency was created by Proposition 13, it would not justify the impairment of their contracts. The contention goes as follows: The passage of Proposition 13 by initiative was an action of the state. Thus, any emergency which existed subsequent to its enactment was created by the state itself, and a contract may not be impaired because of a crisis created by the state's voluntary conduct. They rely in this connection upon cases which hold that a state unconstitutionally impairs the obligation of its contracts if it limits its taxing power so as to disable itself from fulfilling its obligations. (See, e.g., *Hubert v. New Orleans* (1909) 215 U.S. 170,

Wolff v. New Orleans (1880) 103 U.S. 358.) We need not decide the merits of this argument, however appealing it may be, since it is clear, as we conclude above, that respondents have not demonstrated that Proposition 13 created an emergency warranting the invalidation of salary increases called for in petitioners' contracts....

Thus we conclude that the provision of section 16280 which invalidates agreements granting cost-of-living wage increases to local public agency employees is invalid as an impairment of contract, in violation of both the state and federal Constitutions.

II

[The court went on to hold that the § 16280 limitation also violated the Home Rule provision of the California Constitution. It finally determined that since the state could not impair the rights of public employees covered by collective contracts, Equal Protection and Due Process principles precluded the application of the state wage limitation to public employees not covered by existing bargaining agreements.]

NOTES

1. Compare the *Sonoma Cty.* decision with *Washington Educ. Ass'n v. State,* 652 P.2d 1347, 116 L.R.R.M. 2360 (Wash. 1982), which sustained the constitutionality of reduction-in-force legislation passed by the State of Washington during a financial emergency.

2. In *Providence Teachers Union, Local 953 v. McGovern,* 319 A.2d 358, 86 L.R.R.M. 2899 (R.I. 1974), it was decided that money due to retired teachers under the terms of an arbitration award interpreting the severance pay provisions of a bargaining agreement constituted a debt of the city which had to be satisfied by the city treasurer. See *Mendes v. City of Taunton,* 366 Mass. 109, 315 N.E.2d 865 (1974). See also *Providence Teachers Union Local 958 v. School Comm.,* 276 A.2d 762, 77 L.R.R.M. 2530 (R.I. 1971) (alleged unavailability of appropriated funds not defense to enforcement of arbitration award); *District Council 33, AFSCME v. City of Philadelphia,* 81 L.R.R.M. 2539 (Pa. C.P., Phila. County 1971) (exhaustion of municipal funds does not relieve city of obligations under bargaining agreement).

3. In *City of Passaic v. Local Fin. Bd.,* 441 A.2d 737, 1981-83 PBC ¶ 37,475 (N.J. 1982), the court directed the local finance board to approve a city's request for an emergency appropriation to cover the salary increases necessitated by interest arbitration awards issued after the regular budget had been adopted. Although the arbitral awards could not be viewed as "sudden, unexpected or unanticipated circumstances," they were found to constitute the type of occurrence for which an "emergency appropriation" was statutorily authorized. See also *International Bhd. of Firemen & Oilers, Local 1201 v. Philadelphia Bd. of Educ.,* 457 A.2d 1269, 1981-83 PBC ¶ 37,705 (Pa. 1983); *Board of Educ., Yonkers City Sch. Dist. v. Yonkers Fed'n of Teachers,* 40 N.Y.2d 268, 353 N.E.2d 569 (1976); *Patrolmen's Benevolent Ass'n v. City of N.Y.,* 41 N.Y.2d 205, 359 N.E.2d 1338 (1976).

4. In *Board of Educ. v. Teachers Union, Local 1,* 430 N.E.2d 1111, 1981-83 PBC ¶ 37,465 (Ill. 1981), the court ruled that the school board lawfully cancelled the last day of the contractually specified thirty-nine week school calendar and refused to remunerate teachers for that day, thereby reducing the annual sala-

ries provided in the collective agreement. The school board contended that its need to insure a balanced budget permitted it to take the action in question, and the Court agreed. It noted that the board possessed the nondelegable right to determine the length of the school year, and it found that the board's decision to end the year one day early due to extreme budget constraints was neither arbitrary nor unreasonable. But cf. *Piro v. Bowen,* 1979-80 PBC ¶ 37,026 (N.Y. App. Div. 1980) (damages for breach of contractual job security clause must be paid despite financial crisis).

5. Where unilateral changes have been made by a public employer because of financial considerations, most of the resulting union complaints have been processed as refusal-to-bargain changes. See Ch. 4, secs. C and D *supra.*

6. Public employers have had some success in effectuating staff reductions to save money as a management prerogative, although courts have carefully scrutinized contract language for any employment guarantees and have usually given effect to employment security provisions that have been negotiated by employers and unions. See, e.g., *Burke v. Bowen,* 40 N.Y.2d 264, 353 N.E.2d 567 (1976). Courts have also sustained arbitration awards enforcing such contractual provisions. See, e.g., *Yonkers Fed'n of Teachers v. Board of Educ.,* 44 N.Y.2d 752, 376 N.E.2d 1326 (1978). However, where a bargaining agreement containing a job security provision expires, previously laid off employees who may still be entitled to damages for breach of the prior contract may lose their right to reinstatement. See *Schwab v. Bowen,* 41 N.Y.2d 907, 363 N.E.2d 341 (1977).

7. What recourse does a municipality have if it lacks sufficient financial resources to satisfy its obligations under collective bargaining agreements? See Note, *Executory Labor Contracts and Municipal Bankruptcy,* 85 Yale L.J. 957 (1976). See also Miscimarra, *Inability to Pay: The Problem of Contract Enforcement in Public Sector Collective Bargaining,* 43 U. Pitt. L. Rev. 703 (1982).

Chapter 9

THE POLITICAL AND CIVIL RIGHTS OF PUBLIC EMPLOYEES

NO STUDY OF LABOR RELATIONS LAW IN THE PUBLIC SECTOR WOULD BE COMPLETE without some analysis of the political and civil rights of public employees. The line that divides the "public" and the "private" employment sectors is frequently obscure. Nevertheless, partly because of certain overriding constitutional principles, the history of regulation of employment relations in the public sector in the United States has posed many special problems that have not been seen in the private sector. As Robert M. O'Neil so aptly noted:

> Much of what government can do *for* its own work force, it can also require private employers to do for their workers. The harder question remains, and will be the crux of this chapter: What can government do *to* its employees — what conditions and restrictions can it impose upon them — which it could not do to employees of private firms?

The Price of Dependency: Civil Liberties in the Welfare State 61-62 (1970).

On the one hand, history has demonstrated that public employees in the United States may be made subject to rigid conditions of employment. The most familiar general restrictions on public employment relate to political activities and associations. However, several other types of employment restrictions have also proved to be controversial in the public service; among these have been loyalty oaths, bans on partisan political activities, reprisals for criticizing government officials or policies, and employment disabilities created by criminal records, personal appearance, sexual activity, private associations, and deviant conduct.

On the other hand, although it is clear that the public employee may be burdened by special job conditions and restrictions, it is likewise clear that, as a public servant, the government worker cannot be saddled with unconstitutional conditions or restrictions of employment. Public workers, therefore, enjoy certain constitutional protections, privileges, and rights, which provide a framework for the regulation of employment relations in the government service. For example, constitutional issues concerning freedom of association and expression, the privilege against self incrimination, due process as a protection against dismissal, and protections against discrimination on the basis of race, sex, national origin, or religion have an important and direct bearing on employment relations law in the public sector.

Since these constitutional issues and related statutory applications are matters transcending labor relations law and collective bargaining in the public sector, they cannot be ignored. With this in mind, the following materials are presented to help the student comprehend some of the important legal principles, both constitutional and statutory, that affect the political and civil rights of public employees.

McAuliffe v. Mayor of New Bedford, 155 Mass. 216, 29 N.E. 517 (1892). In a decision written by Justice Oliver Wendell Holmes, the Massachusetts court upheld a city rule that prohibited policemen from joining labor unions. In reaching this conclusion, the court rendered its now famous dictum that:

> The petitioner may have a constitutional right to talk politics, but he has no constitutional right to be a policeman. There are few employments for hire in which the servant does not agree to suspend his constitutional right of free speech, as well as of idleness, by the implied terms of his contract. The servant cannot complain, as he takes the employment on the terms which are offered him.

O'NEIL, THE PRIVATE LIVES OF PUBLIC EMPLOYEES, 51 Or. L. Rev. 70, 82-83 (1971)*

The public employee's legal status is vastly better today than at the time when Justice Holmes remarked that Officer McAuliffe might "have a constitutional right to talk politics, but ... no right to be a policeman." If it is true that the Supreme Court has never squarely relieved the government worker of Holmes' dilemma, one who enters the public service may still (save in California[2] and Oregon[3]) be compelled to steer clear of partisan politics.[4] But that is one of the few lacunae remaining from a time when public employment and other government benefits were classed as "privileges which could be conditioned, denied, or terminated as agency heads or legislators saw fit."

All that has changed. The principal catalyst for reform has been the recent development of the doctrine of unconstitutional conditions, applied with particular force to government employment.[5] Courts have consistently repudiated the notion that because government was under no legal obligation to offer employment to any person, it might therefore withhold such employment on arbitrary or discriminatory grounds or encumber public service with onerous and intrusive conditions. In a host of recent decisions, the Supreme Court has cautioned that "public employment ... may [not] be conditioned upon the surrender of constitutional rights which could not be abridged by direct government action."[6]

---

*Reprinted by permission. Copyright by the University of Oregon.

[2] *Bagley v. Washington Township Hosp. Dist.,* 65 Cal. 2d 499, 421 P.2d 409, 55 Cal. Rptr. 401 (1966); *Fort v. Civil Serv. Comm'n,* 61 Cal. 2d 331, 392 P.2d 385, 38 Cal. Rptr. 625 (1964).

[3] *Minielly v. State,* 242 Ore. 490, 411 P.2d 69 (1966).

[4] *United Public Workers v. Mitchell,* 330 U.S. 75 (1947). Despite a constant barrage from scholars and critics and growing pressures for reform within the civil service, the Hatch Act survives. See, e.g., Esman, *The Hatch Act: A Reappraisal,* 60 Yale L.J. 986 (1951); Nelson, *Public Employees and the Right to Engage in Political Activity,* 9 Vand. L. Rev. 27 (1955); Rose, *A Critical Look at the Hatch Act,* 75 Harv. L. Rev. 510 (1962); Note, *The Public Employee and Political Activity,* 3 Suffolk L. Rev. 380 (1969).

[5] See especially the works of the two most thoughtful commentators on this development, Linde, *Justice Douglas on Liberty in the Welfare State: Constitutional Rights in the Public Sector,* 40 Wash. L. Rev. 10 (1965); and Van Alstyne, *The Constitutional Rights of Public Employees: A Comment on the Inappropriate Uses of an Old Analogy,* 16 U.C.L.A.L. Rev. 751 (1969). For more specialized comments on a particular application of the doctrine, see O'Neil, *Public Employment, Antiwar Protest and Preinduction Review,* 17 U.C.L.A.L. Rev. 1028 (1970).

[6] *Keyishian v. Board of Regents,* 385 U.S. 589, 605-06, 87 S. Ct. 675, 17 L. Ed. 2d 629 (1967).

A. RESTRICTIONS AND PRIVILEGES OF PUBLIC EMPLOYMENT

1. LOYALTY OATHS

COLE v. RICHARDSON

405 U.S. 676, 92 S. Ct. 1332, 31 L. Ed. 2d 593 (1972)

CHIEF JUSTICE BURGER delivered the opinion of the Court.

In this appeal we review the decision of the three-judge District Court holding a Massachusetts loyalty oath unconstitutional.

[Appellee], Mrs. Richardson, was asked to subscribe to the oath required of all public employees in Massachusetts. The oath is as follows:

> "I do solemnly swear (or affirm) that I will uphold and defend the Constitution of the United States of America and the Constitution of the Commonwealth of Massachusetts and that I will oppose the overthrow of the government of the United States of America or of this Commonwealth by force, violence or by any illegal or unconstitutional method."

[Appellee was advised that she could not continue as an employee of the Boston State Hospital unless she subscribed to the oath. When she refused to comply, her employment was terminated.] ...

A three-judge District Court held the oath statute unconstitutional and enjoined the appellant from applying the statute to prohibit Mrs. Richardson from working for Boston State Hospital. The District Court found the attack on the "uphold and defend" clause, the first part of the oath, foreclosed by *Knight v. Board of Regents,* 269 F. Supp. 339 (S.D.N.Y. 1967), *affirmed,* 390 U.S. 36 (1968). But it found that the "oppose and overthrow" clause was "fatally vague and unspecific," and therefore a violation of First Amendment rights. The court granted the requested injunction but denied the claim for damages....

We conclude that the Massachusetts oath is constitutionally permissible ....

A review of the oath cases in this Court will put the instant oath into context. We have made clear that neither federal nor state governments may condition employment on taking oaths which impinge rights guaranteed by the First and Fourteenth Amendments respectively, as for example those relating to political beliefs. Nor may employment be conditioned on an oath that one has not engaged, or will not engage, in protected speech activities such as the following: criticizing institutions of government; discussing political doctrine that approves the overthrow of certain forms of government; and supporting candidates for political office. *Keyishian v. Board of Regents,* 385 U.S. 589 (1967); *Baggett v. Bullitt,* 377 U.S. 360 (1964); *Cramp v. Board of Public Instruction,* 368 U.S. 278 (1961). Employment may not be conditioned on an oath denying past, or abjuring future, associational activities within constitutional protection; such protected activities include membership in organizations having illegal purposes unless one knows of the purpose and shares a specific intent to promote the illegal purpose. *Whitehill v. Elkins,* 389 U.S. 54 (1967); *Keyishian v. Board of Regents, supra; Elfbrandt v. Russell,* 384 U.S. 11 (1966); *Wieman v. Updegraff,* 344 U.S. 183 (1952).... And, finally, an oath may not be so vague that " 'men of common intelligence must necessarily guess at its meaning and differ as to its application, [because such an oath] violates the first essential of due process of law.'" *Cramp v. Board of Public Instruction,* 368 U.S., at 287....

An underlying, seldom articulated concern running throughout these cases is that the oaths under consideration often required individuals to reach back into their pasts to recall minor, sometimes innocent, activities. They put the government into "the censorial business of investigating, scrutinizing, interpreting, and then penalizing or approving the political viewpoint" and past activities of individuals. *Law Students Research Council v. Wadmond,* 401 U.S., at 192 (MARSHALL, J., dissenting).

Several cases recently decided by the Court stand out among our oath cases because they have upheld the constitutionality of oaths, addressed to the future, promising constitutional support in broad terms. These cases have begun with a recognition that the Constitution itself prescribes comparable oaths in two articles. Article II, § 1, cl. 7, provides that the President shall swear that he will "faithfully execute the office ... and will to the best of my ability preserve, protect and defend the Constitution of the United States." Article VI, cl. 3, provides that all state and federal officers shall be bound by an oath "to support this Constitution."...

Bond v. Floyd, 385 U.S. 116 (1966), involved Georgia's statutory requirement that state legislators swear to "support the Constitution of this State and of the United States," a paraphrase of the constitutionally required oath. The Court there implicitly concluded that the First Amendment did not undercut the validity of the constitutional oath provisions. Although in theory the First Amendment might have invalidated those provisions, approval of the amendment by the same individuals who had included the oaths in the Constitution suggested strongly that they were consistent. The Court's recognition of this consistency did not involve a departure from its many decisions striking down oaths which infringed First and Fourteenth Amendment rights. The Court read the Georgia oath as calling simply for an acknowledgment of a willingness to abide by "constitutional processes of government." 385 U.S., at 135. Although disagreeing on other points, in *Wadmond, supra,* all members of the Court agreed on this point. MR. JUSTICE MARSHALL noted there, while dissenting as to other points,

> "The oath of constitutional support requires an individual assuming public responsibilities to affirm ... that he will endeavor to perform his public duties lawfully." 401 U.S., at 192.

The Court has further made clear that an oath need not parrot the exact language of the constitutional oaths to be constitutionally proper. Thus in *Ohlson v. Phillips,* 397 U.S. 317 (1970), we sustained the constitutionality of a state requirement that teachers swear to "uphold" the Constitution....

The District Court in the instant case properly recognized that the first clause of the Massachusetts oath, in which the individual swears to "uphold and defend" the constitutions of the United States and the Commonwealth, is indistinguishable from the oaths this Court has recently approved. Yet the District Court applied a highly literalistic approach to the second clause to strike it down. We view the second clause of the oath as essentially the same as the first.

The second clause of the oath contains a promise to "oppose the overthrow of the government of the United States of America or of this Commonwealth by force, violence or by any illegal or unconstitutional method." The District Court sought to give a dictionary meaning to this language and found "oppose" to raise the specter of vague, undefinable responsibilities actively to combat a potential overthrow of the government. That reading of the oath understandably troubled the court because of what it saw as vagueness in terms of what threats would constitute sufficient danger of overthrow to require the oath-giver to actively oppose overthrow, and exactly what actions he would have to take in that respect.

... We have rejected such rigidly literal notions and recognized that the purpose leading legislatures to enact such oaths, just as the purpose leading the Framers of our Constitution to include the two explicit constitutional oaths, was not to create specific responsibilities but to assure that those in positions of public trust were willing to commit themselves to live by the constitutional processes of our system as MR. JUSTICE MARSHALL suggested in *Wadmond,* 401 U.S., at 192. Here the second clause does not require specific action in some hypothetical or actual situation. Plainly "force, violence or ... any illegal or unconstitutional method" modifies "overthrow" and does not commit the oath taker to meet force with force. Just as the connotatively active word "support" has been interpreted to mean simply a commitment to abide by our constitutional system, the second clause of this oath is merely oriented to the negative implication of this notion; it is a commitment not to use illegal and constitutionally unprotected force to change the constitutional system. The second clause does not expand the obligation of the first; it simply makes clear the application of the first clause to a particular issue. Such repetition, whether for emphasis or cadence, seems to be the wont of authors of oaths. That the second clause may be redundant is no ground to strike it down; we are not charged with correcting grammar but with enforcing a constitution.

The purpose of the oath is clear on its face. We cannot presume that the Massachusetts legislature intended by its use of such general terms as "uphold," "defend," and "oppose" to impose obligations of specific, positive action on oath takers. Any such construction would raise serious questions whether the oath was so vague as to amount to a denial of due process.

Nor is the oath as interpreted void for vagueness.... It is punishable only by a prosecution for perjury and, since perjury is a knowing and willful falsehood, the constitutional vice of punishment without fair warning cannot occur here. Nor here is there any problem of the punishment inflicted by mere prosecution. See *Cramp v. Board of Public Instruction,* 368 U.S., at 284. There has been no prosecution under this statute since its 1948 enactment, and there is no indication that prosecutions have been planned or begun. The oath "triggered no serious possibility of prosecution" by the Commonwealth. Were we confronted with a record of actual prosecutions or harassment through threatened prosecutions, we might be faced with a different question....

Appellee mounts an additional attack on the Massachusetts oath program in that it does not provide for a hearing prior to the determination not to hire the individual based on the refusal to subscribe to the oath. All of the cases in this Court which require a hearing before discharge for failure to take an oath involved impermissible oaths. In *Slochower v. Board of Education,* 350 U.S. 551 (1956) (not an oath case), the State sought to dismiss a professor for claiming the Fifth Amendment privilege in a United States Senate committee hearing; the Court held the State's action invalid because the exercise of the privilege was a constitutional right from which the State could not draw any rational inference of disloyalty. Appellee relies on *Nostrand v. Little,* 362 U.S. 474 (1960), and *Connell v. Higginbotham,* 403 U.S. 207 (1971), but in those cases the Court held only that the mere refusal to take the particular oath was not a constitutionally permissible basis for termination. In the circumstances of those cases only by holding a hearing, showing evidence of disloyalty, and allowing the employee an opportunity to respond might the State develop a permissible basis for concluding that the employee was to be discharged.

Since there is no constitutionally protected right to overthrow a government by force, violence, or illegal or unconstitutional means, no constitutional right is infringed by an oath to abide by the constitutional system in the future. Therefore there is no requirement that one who refuses to take the Massachusetts oath be granted a hearing for the determination of some other fact before being discharged.

The judgment of the District Court is reversed and the case is remanded for further proceedings consistent with this opinion.

[The dissenting opinions of Justice Douglas and Justice Marshall, joined by Justice Brennan, have been omitted.]

NOTE

For some useful comments on the general subject of loyalty oaths and related topics, see Bruff, *Unconstitutional Conditions upon Public Employment: New Departures in the Protection of First Amendment Rights,* 21 Hastings L.J. 129 (1969); Leahy, *Loyalty and the First Amendment — A Concept Emerges,* 43 N.D.L. Rev. 53 (1966); Leahy, *The Public Employee and the First Amendment — Must He Sacrifice His Civil Rights To Be a Civil Servant,* 4 Cal. W.L. Rev. 1 (1968); Van Alstyne, *The Constitutional Rights of Public Employees: A Comment on the Inappropriate Use of an Old Analogy,* 16 U.C.L.A. L. Rev. 751 (1969); Israel, *Elfbrandt v. Russell — The Demise of the Oath?* 1966 Sup. Ct. Rev. 193; Van Alstyne, *The Demise of the Right-Privilege Distinction in Constitutional Law,* 81 Harv. L. Rev. 1439 (1968).

2. PRIVILEGE AGAINST SELF-INCRIMINATION AND THE DUTY OF DISCLOSURE

GARRITY v. NEW JERSEY

385 U.S. 493, 87 S. Ct. 616, 17 L. Ed. 2d 562 (1967)

JUSTICE DOUGLAS delivered the opinion of the Court.

Appellants were police officers in certain New Jersey boroughs. The Supreme Court of New Jersey ordered [an investigation of] alleged fixing of traffic tickets.

Before being questioned, each appellant was warned (1) that anything he said might be used against him in any state criminal proceeding; (2) that he had the privilege to refuse to answer if the disclosure would tend to incriminate him; but (3) that if he refused to answer he would be subject to removal from office.

Appellants answered the questions. No immunity was granted .... Over their objections, some of the answers given were used in subsequent prosecutions for conspiracy to obstruct the administration of the traffic laws. Appellants were convicted and their convictions were sustained over their protests that their statements were coerced, by reason of the fact that, if they refused to answer, they could lose their positions with the police department.

We postponed the question of jurisdiction to a hearing on the merits. 383 U.S. 941. The statute whose validity was sought to be "drawn in question," 28 U.S.C. § 1257(2), was the forfeiture statute.[3] But the New Jersey Supreme Court refused to reach that question (44 N.J., at 223, 207 A.2d, at 697), deeming the voluntariness of the statements as the only issue presented. *Id.*, at 220-222, 207 A.2d, at 695-696. The statute is therefore too tangentially involved to satisfy 28 U.S.C. § 1257(2), for the only bearing it had was whether, valid or not, the fear of being discharged under it for refusal to answer on the one hand and the fear of self-incrimination on the other was "a choice between the rock and the whirlpool" which made the statements products of coercion in violation of the Fourteenth Amendment. We therefore dismiss the appeal, treat the papers as a petition for certiorari (28 U.S.C. § 2103), grant the petition and proceed to the merits.

We agree with the New Jersey Supreme Court that the forfeiture-of-office statute is relevant here only for the bearing it has on the voluntary character of the statements used to convict petitioners in their criminal prosecutions....

The choice given petitioners was either to forfeit their jobs or to incriminate themselves. The option to lose their means of livelihood or to pay the penalty of self-incrimination is the antithesis of free choice to speak out or to remain silent. That practice, like interrogation practices we reviewed in *Miranda v. Arizona,* 384 U.S. 436, 464-465, is "likely to exert such pressure upon an individual as to disable him from making a free and rational choice." We think the statements were infected by the coercion inherent in this scheme of questioning and cannot be sustained as voluntary under our prior decisions....

In these cases ... though petitioners succumbed to compulsion, they preserved their objections, raising them at the earliest possible point. The cases are therefore quite different from the situation where one who is anxious to make a clean breast of the whole affair volunteers the information.

---

[3]"Any person holding or who has held any elective or appointive public office, position or employment (whether state, county or municipal), who refuses to testify upon matters relating to the office, position or employment in any criminal proceeding wherein he is a defendant or is called as a witness on behalf of the prosecution, upon the ground that his answer may tend to incriminate him or compel him to be a witness against himself or refuses to waive immunity when called by a grand jury to testify thereon or who willfully refuses or fails to appear before any court, commission or body of this state which has the right to inquire under oath upon matters relating to the office, position or employment of such person or who, having been sworn, refuses to testify or to answer any material question upon the ground that his answer may tend to incriminate him or compel him to be a witness against himself, shall, if holding elective or public office, position or employment, be removed therefrom or shall thereby forfeit his office, position or employment and any vested or future right of tenure or pension granted to him by any law of this state provided the inquiry relates to a matter which occurred or arose within the preceding five years. Any person so forfeiting his office, position or employment shall not thereafter be eligible for election or appointment to any public office, position or employment in this state." N.J. Rev. Stat. § 2A:81-17.1 (Supp. 1965).

Mr. Justice Holmes in *McAuliffe v. New Bedford,* 155 Mass. 216, 29 N.E. 517, stated a dictum on which New Jersey heavily relies:

"The petitioner may have a constitutional right to talk politics, but he has no constitutional right to be a policeman. There are few employments for hire in which the servant does not agree to suspend his constitutional right of free speech, as well as of idleness, by the implied terms of his contract. The servant cannot complain, as he takes the employment on the terms which are offered him. On the same principle, the city may impose any reasonable condition upon holding offices within its control." *Id.,* at 220, 29 N.E., at 517-518.

The question in this case, however, is not cognizable in those terms. Our question is whether a State, contrary to the requirement of the Fourteenth Amendment, can use the threat of discharge to secure incriminatory evidence against an employee.

We held in *Slochower v. Board of Education,* 350 U.S. 551, that a public school teacher could not be discharged merely because he had invoked the Fifth Amendment privilege against self-incrimination when questioned by a congressional committee:

"The privilege against self-incrimination would be reduced to a hollow mockery if its exercise could be taken as equivalent either to a confession of guilt or a conclusive presumption of perjury.... The privilege serves to protect the innocent who otherwise might be ensnared by ambiguous circumstances." *Id.,* at 557-558.

We conclude that policemen, like teachers and lawyers, are not relegated to a watered-down version of constitutional rights....

Reversed.

JUSTICE HARLAN, whom JUSTICE CLARK and JUSTICE STEWART join, dissenting....

The majority is apparently engaged in the delicate task of riding two unruly horses at once: it is presumably arguing simultaneously that the statements were involuntary as a matter of fact, in the same fashion that the statements in *Chambers v. Florida,* 309 U.S. 227, and *Haynes v. Washington,* 373 U.S. 503, were thought to be involuntary, and that the statements were inadmissible as a matter of law, on the premise that they were products of an impermissible condition imposed on the constitutional privilege. These are very different contentions and require separate replies, but in my opinion both contentions are plainly mistaken, for reasons that follow....

As interrogation commenced, each of the petitioners was sworn, carefully informed that he need not give any information, reminded that any information given might be used in a subsequent criminal prosecution, and warned that as a police officer he was subject to a proceeding to discharge him if he failed to provide information relevant to his public responsibilities....

All of the petitioners testified at trial, and gave evidence essentially consistent with the statements taken from them....

The issue remaining is whether the statements were inadmissible because they were "involuntary as a matter of law," in that they were given after a warning that New Jersey policemen may be discharged for failure to provide information pertinent to their public responsibilities. What is really involved on this score, however, is not in truth a question of "voluntariness" at all, but rather whether the condition imposed by the State on the exercise of the privilege against self-incrimination, namely dismissal from office, in this instance serves in itself to render the statements inadmissible. Absent evidence of involuntariness in fact, the admissibility of these statements thus hinges on the validity of the consequence which the State acknowledged might have resulted if the statements had not been given. If the consequence is constitutionally permissible, there can surely be no objection if the State cautions the witness that it may follow if he remains silent. If both the consequence and the warning are constitutionally permissible, a witness is obliged, in order to prevent the use of his statements against him in a criminal prosecution, to prove under the standards established since *Brown v. Mississippi,* 297 U.S. 278, that as a matter of fact the statements were involuntarily made. The central issues here are therefore identical to those presented in *Spevack v. Klein:* whether consequences may properly be permitted to result to a claimant after his invocation of the constitutional privilege, and if so, whether the consequence in question is permissible. For reasons which I have stated in *Spevack v. Klein,* in my view nothing in the logic or purposes of the privilege demands that all consequences which may result from a witness' silence be forbidden merely because that silence is privileged. The validity of a consequence depends both upon the hazards, if any, it presents to the integrity of the privilege and upon the urgency of the public interests it is designed to protect.

It can hardly be denied that New Jersey is permitted by the Constitution to establish reasonable qualifications and standards of conduct for its public employees. Nor can it be said that it is arbitrary or unreasonable for New Jersey to insist that its employees furnish the appropriate authorities with information pertinent to their employment. Cf. *Beilan v. Board of Education,* 357 U.S. 399; *Slochower v. Board of Education,* 350 U.S. 551. Finally, it is surely plain that New Jersey may in particular require its employees to assist in the prevention and detection of unlawful activities by officers of the state government. The urgency of these requirements is the more obvious here, where the conduct in question is that of officials directly entrusted with the administration of justice....

NOTES

1. The companion cases *Gardner v. Broderick,* 392 U.S. 273 (1968), and *Uniformed San. Men Ass'n v. Commissioner of San.,* 392 U.S. 280 (1968), involved the validity of the terminations of public employees who refused to waive immunity from prosecution or testify at grand jury hearings concerning alleged bribery and corruption. The Court, in striking down the employee dismissals as unconstitutional, stressed the fact that in neither case were the dismissals based on the employees' refusal to answer pertinent questions about their official duties, but instead were for their refusal to waive their constitutionally protected privilege against self-incrimination. The Court, per Justice Fortas, concluded that "if New York had demanded that petitioners answer questions specifically, directly and narrowly relating to the performance of their official duties in pain of dismissal from public employment without requiring relinquishment of the benefits of the constitutional privilege, and if they had refused to do so, this case would be entirely different," but that in the instant case they had instead been presented with a choice between waiving their constitutional rights or losing their jobs. All of the employees had been terminated in accordance with a New York City Charter provision that required the discharge of public servants who invoked the privilege against self-incrimination during authorized investigations of public employees' conduct or who refused to waive immunity against prosecution prompted by their testimony.

2. Broadly applying the standard set out in *Uniformed San. Men Ass'n* that the privilege against self-incrimination is not infringed if an employee is discharged for failure to answer questions "specifically, directly and narrowly" related to the job, the First Circuit upheld a Boston Police Department requirement that police officers submit copies of their state and federal income tax forms along with other financial information, including a list of significant assets of all household members. The court found that the questions about the officers' personal finances were sufficiently closely related to their jobs because "[e]ven a hint of police corruption endangers respect for the law." *O'Brien v. DiGrazia,* 544 F.2d 543 (1st Cir. 1976), *cert. denied,* 431 U.S. 914 (1977).

3. In a subsequent case, *Lefkowitz v. Turley,* 414 U.S. 70 (1973), the Court extended the privilege against self-incrimination to government contractors, declaring unconstitutional a provision of New York law that permitted cancellation of existing contracts and disqualification from future contracts if the contractor refused to waive the privilege if called upon to testify concerning his or her state contracts. In clarifying its actions in past cases, the Court stated:

We should make clear, however, what we have said before. Although due regard for the Fifth Amendment forbids the State to compel incriminating answers from its employees and contractors that may be used against them in criminal proceedings, the Constitution permits that very testimony to be compelled if neither it nor its fruits are available for such use. *Kastigar v. United States, supra.* Furthermore, the accommodation between the interest of the State and the Fifth Amendment requires that the State have means at its disposal to secure testimony if immunity is supplied and testimony is still refused. This is recognized by the power of the courts to compel testimony, after a grant of immunity, by use of civil contempt and coerced imprisonment. *Shillitani v. United States,* 384 U.S. 364 (1966). Also, given adequate immunity, the State may plainly insist that employees either answer questions under oath about the performance of their job or suffer the loss of employment. By like token, the State may insist that the architects involved in this case either respond to relevant inquiries about the performance of their contracts or suffer cancellation of current relationships and disqualification from contracting with public agencies for an appropriate time in the future. But the State may not insist that appellees waive their Fifth Amendment privilege against self-incrimination and consent to the use of the fruits of the interrogation in any later proceedings brought against them. Rather, the State must recognize what our cases hold: that answers elicited upon the threat of the loss of employment are compelled and inadmissible in evidence. Hence, if answers are to be required in such circumstances States must offer to the witness whatever immunity is required to supplant the privilege and may not insist that the employee or contractor waive such immunity.

414 U.S. 84-85. See also *Lefkowitz v. Cunningham,* 431 U.S. 801 (1977) (New York statute unconstitutional where it required termination of office of political

party official who refused to answer potentially incriminating questions at grand jury investigation of the conduct of his office).

5. The earlier decision of *Slochower v. Board of Higher Educ.,* 350 U.S. 551 (1956), held invalid the summary dismissal of a teacher pursuant to a section of the Charter of the City of New York that provided for dismissal of any city employee who invoked the privilege against self-incrimination and thereby refused to answer questions of a legislative committee. The appellant, a teacher in a college maintained by the city, had been summarily discharged from his position when he refused to answer certain questions asked by a Senate Sub-committee regarding his alleged membership in the Communist party some eleven years prior to the hearing. He had stated, however, that he was not currently a member of the Communist party and would answer all questions relating to the eleven-year period subsequent to his alleged membership. In upholding appellant's dismissal the state's highest court construed the charter section as providing that "the assertion of the privilege against self-incrimination is equivalent to a resignation" thereby attempting to avert conflict with the state law which allowed for discharge of a person in appellant's position "only for cause, and after notice, hearing, and appeal." The Supreme Court, in overturning the dismissal, stated that "[t]he privilege against self-incrimination would be reduced to a hollow mockery if its exercise could be taken as equivalent either to a confession of guilt or a presumption of perjury." Since no inference of guilt was permissible from appellant's assertion of privilege the Court held the dismissal arbitrary, and therefore a denial of fourteenth amendment due process of law.

6. May a public employer discipline employees who refuse to submit to polygraph examinations concerning alleged misconduct? See *Texas State Emps. Union v. Texas Dep't of Mental Health & Mental Retardation,* 746 S.W.2d 203 (Tex. 1987); *Kaske v. City of Rockford,* 96 Ill. 2d 298, 450 N.E.2d 314, *cert. denied,* 464 U.S. 960 (1983). See also *Anderson v. Philadelphia,* 845 F.2d 1216 (3d Cir. 1988).

3. PROTECTION AGAINST UNREASONABLE SEARCHES

NATIONAL TREASURY EMPLOYEES UNION v. von RAAB

489 U.S. 656, 109 S. Ct. 1384, 103 L. Ed. 2d 685 (1989)

JUSTICE KENNEDY delivered the opinion of the Court.

We granted certiorari to decide whether it violates the Fourth Amendment for the United States Customs Service to require a urinalysis test from employees who seek transfer or promotion to certain positions.

I

A. The United States Customs Service, a bureau of the Department of the Treasury, is the federal agency responsible for processing persons, carriers, cargo, and mail into the United States, collecting revenue from imports, and enforcing customs and related laws. See Customs USA, Fiscal Year 1985, p. 4. An important responsibility of the Service is the interdiction and seizure of contraband, including illegal drugs. *Ibid.* In 1987 alone, Customs agents seized drugs with a retail value of nearly 9 billion dollars. See Customs USA, Fiscal Year 1987, p. 40. In the routine discharge of their duties, many Customs employees have direct contact with those who traffic in drugs for profit. Drug import operations, often directed by sophisticated criminal syndicates, *United*

States v. Mendenhall, 446 U.S. 544, 561-562 (1980) (Powell, J., concurring), may be effected by violence or its threat. As a necessary response, many Customs operatives carry and use firearms in connection with their official duties.

In December 1985, respondent, the Commissioner of Customs, established a Drug Screening Task Force to explore the possibility of implementing a drug screening program within the Service. After extensive research and consultation with experts in the field, the Task Force concluded "that drug screening through urinalysis is technologically reliable, valid and accurate." Citing this conclusion, the Commissioner announced his intention to require drug tests of employees who applied for, or occupied, certain positions within the Service. The Commissioner stated his belief that "Customs is largely drug-free," but noted also that "unfortunately no segment of society is immune from the threat of illegal drug use." Drug interdiction has become the agency's primary enforcement mission, and the Commissioner stressed that "there is no room in the Customs Service for those who break the laws prohibiting the possession and use of illegal drugs."

In May 1986, the Commissioner announced implementation of the drug-testing program. Drug tests were made a condition of placement or employment for positions that meet one or more of three criteria. The first is direct involvement in drug interdiction or enforcement of related laws, an activity the Commissioner deemed fraught with obvious dangers to the mission of the agency and the lives of customs agents. The second criterion is a requirement that the incumbent carry firearms, as the Commissioner concluded that "[p]ublic safety demands that employees who carry deadly arms and are prepared to make instant life or death decisions be drug free." The third criterion is a requirement for the incumbent to handle "classified" material, which the Commissioner determined might fall into the hands of smugglers if accessible to employees who, by reason of their own illegal drug use, are susceptible to bribery or blackmail.

After an employee qualifies for a position covered by the Customs testing program, the Service advises him by letter that his final selection is contingent upon successful completion of drug screening. An independent contractor contacts the employee to fix the time and place for collecting the sample. On reporting for the test, the employee must produce photographic identification and remove any outer garments, such as a coat or a jacket, and personal belongings. The employee may produce the sample behind a partition, or in the privacy of a bathroom stall if he so chooses. To ensure against adulteration of the specimen, or substitution of a sample from another person, a monitor of the same sex as the employee remains close at hand to listen for the normal sounds of urination. Dye is added to the toilet water to prevent the employee from using the water to adulterate the sample.

Upon receiving the specimen, the monitor inspects it to ensure its proper temperature and color, places a tamper-proof custody seal over the container, and affixes an identification label indicating the date and the individual's specimen number. The employee signs a chain-of-custody form, which is initialed by the monitor, and the urine sample is placed in a plastic bag, sealed, and submitted to a laboratory.

The laboratory tests the sample for the presence of marijuana, cocaine, opiates, amphetamines, and phencyclidine. Two tests are used. An initial screening test uses the enzyme-multiplied-immunoassay technique (EMIT). Any specimen that is identified as positive on this initial test must then be confirmed using gas chromatography/mass spectrometry (GC/MS). Confirmed positive results are reported to a "Medical Review Officer," "[a] licensed physician ... who has knowledge of substance abuse disorders and has appropriate medical training to interpret and evaluate the individual's positive test result together with his or her medical history and any other relevant biomedical information." HHS Reg. § 1.2, 53 Fed. Reg. 11980 (1988); HHS Reg. § 2.4(g), *id.*, at 11983. After verifying the positive result, the Medical Review Officer transmits it to the agency.

Customs employees who test positive for drugs and who can offer no satisfactory explanation are subject to dismissal from the Service. Test results may not, however, be turned over to any other agency, including criminal prosecutors, without the employee's written consent.

B. Petitioners, a union of federal employees and a union official, commenced this suit in the United States District Court for the Eastern District of Louisiana on behalf of current Customs Service employees who seek covered positions. Petitioners alleged that the [Customs] Service drug-testing program violated, inter alia, the Fourth Amendment. The District Court agreed. 649 F. Supp. 380 (1986). The court acknowledged "the legitimate governmental interest in a drug-free work place and work force," but concluded that "the drug testing plan constitutes an overly intrusive policy of searches and seizures without probable cause or reasonable suspicion, in violation of legitimate expectations of privacy." *Id.*, at 387. The court enjoined the drug testing program, and ordered the Customs Service not to require drug tests of any applicants for covered positions.

A divided panel of the United States Court of Appeals for the Fifth Circuit vacated the injunction. 816 F.2d 170 (1987). The court agreed with petitioners that the drug screening program, by requiring an employee to produce a urine sample for chemical testing, effects a search within the meaning of the Fourth Amendment. The court held further that the searches required by the Commissioner's directive are reasonable under the Fourth Amendment....

We granted certiorari. 485 U.S. — (1988). We now affirm so much of the judgment of the court of appeals as upheld the testing of employees directly involved in drug interdiction or required to carry firearms. We vacate the judgment to the extent it upheld the testing of applicants for positions requiring the incumbent to handle classified materials, and remand for further proceedings.

II

In *Skinner v. Railway Labor Executives Assn.*, 109 S. Ct. 1402, 1412-1413, decided today, we hold that federal regulations requiring employees of private railroads to produce urine samples for chemical testing implicate the Fourth Amendment, as those tests invade reasonable expectations of privacy. Our earlier cases have settled that the Fourth Amendment protects individuals from unreasonable searches conducted by the Government, even when the Government acts as an employer, *O'Connor v. Ortega*, 480 U.S. 709, 717 (1987) (plurality opinion); see *id.*, at 731 (Scalia, J., concurring in judgment), and, in view of our holding in *Railway Labor Executives* that urine tests are searches, it follows that the Customs Service's drug testing program must meet the reasonableness requirement of the Fourth Amendment.

While we have often emphasized, and reiterate today, that a search must be supported, as a general matter, by a warrant issued upon probable cause, see, e.g., *Griffin v. Wisconsin,* 483 U.S. 868, — (1987); *United States v. Karo,* 468 U.S. 705, 717 (1984), our decision in *Railway Labor Executives* reaffirms the longstanding principle that neither a warrant nor probable cause, nor, indeed, any measure of individualized suspicion, is an indispensable component of reasonableness in every circumstance. See also *New Jersey v. T.L.O.,* 469 U.S. 325, 342, n.8 (1985); *United States v. Martinez-Fuerte,* 428 U.S. 543, 556-561 (1976). As we note in *Railway Labor Executives,* our cases establish that where a Fourth Amendment intrusion serves special governmental needs, beyond the normal need for law enforcement, it is necessary to balance the individual's privacy expectations against the Government's interests to determine whether it is impractical to require a warrant or some level of individualized suspicion in the particular context.

It is clear that the Customs Service's drug testing program is not designed to serve the ordinary needs of law enforcement. Test results may not be used in a criminal prosecution of the employee without the employee's consent. The purposes of the program are to deter drug use among those eligible for promotion to sensitive positions within the Service and to prevent the promotion of drug users to those positions. These substantial interests, no less than the Government's concern for safe rail transportation at issue in *Railway Labor Executives,* present a special need that may justify departure from the ordinary warrant and probable cause requirements.

A. Petitioners do not contend that a warrant is required by the balance of privacy and governmental interests in this context, nor could any such contention withstand scrutiny. We have recognized before that requiring the Government to procure a warrant for every work-related intrusion "would conflict with 'the common-sense realization that government offices could not function if every employment decision became a constitutional matter.'" *O'Connor v. Ortega, supra,* 480 U.S., at 722, quoting *Connick v. Myers,* 461 U.S. 138, 143 (1983). See also *id.,* 480 U.S., at 732 (SCALIA, J., concurring in judgment); *New Jersey v. T.L.O., supra,* 469 U.S., at 340 (noting that "[t]he warrant requirement ... is unsuited to the school environment: requiring a teacher to obtain a warrant before searching a child suspected of an infraction of school rules (or of the criminal law) would unduly interfere with the maintenance of the swift and informal disciplinary procedures needed in the schools"). Even if Customs Service employees are more likely to be familiar with the procedures required to obtain a warrant than most other Government workers, requiring a warrant in this context would serve only to divert valuable agency resources from the Service's primary mission. The Customs Service has been entrusted with pressing responsibilities, and its mission would be compromised if it were required to seek search warrants in connection with routine, yet sensitive, employment decisions.

Furthermore, a warrant would provide little or nothing in the way of additional protection of personal privacy. A warrant serves primarily to advise the citizen that an intrusion is authorized by law and limited in its permissible scope and to interpose a neutral magistrate between the citizen and the law enforcement officer "engaged in the often competitive enterprise of ferreting out crime." *Johnson v. United States,* 333 U.S. 10, 14 (1948). But in the present context, "the circumstances justifying toxicological testing and the permissible limits of such intrusions are defined narrowly and specifically ..., and doubtless are well known to covered employees." Under the Customs program, every employee who seeks a transfer to a covered position knows that he must take a drug test, and is likewise aware of the procedures the Service must follow in administering the test. A covered employee is simply not subject "to the discretion of the official in the field." *Camara v. Municipal Court,* 387 U.S. 523, 532 (1967). The process becomes automatic when the employee elects to apply for, and thereafter pursue, a covered position. Because the Service does not make a discretionary determination to search based on a judgment that certain conditions are present, there are simply "no special facts for a neutral magistrate to evaluate." *South Dakota v. Opperman,* 428 U.S. 364, 383 (1976) (Powell, J., concurring).

B. Even where it is reasonable to dispense with the warrant requirement in the particular circumstances, a search ordinarily must be based on probable cause. Our cases teach, however, that the probable-cause standard "'is peculiarly related to criminal investigations.'" *Colorado v. Bertine,* 479 U.S. 367, 371 (1987), quoting *South Dakota v. Opperman,* 428 U.S. 364, 370, n. 5 (1976). In particular, the traditional probable-cause standard may be unhelpful in analyzing the reasonableness of routine administrative functions, *Colorado v. Bertine, supra,* 479 U.S., at 371; see also *O'Connor v. Ortega,* 480 U.S., at 723, especially where the Government seeks to *prevent* the development of hazardous conditions or to detect violations that rarely generate articulable grounds for searching any particular place or person. Cf. *Camara v. Municipal Court,* 387 U.S., at 535-536 (noting that building code inspections, unlike searches conducted pursuant to a criminal investigation, are designed "to prevent even the unintentional development of conditions which are hazardous to public health and safety"); *United States v. Martinez-Fuerte,* 428 U.S., at 557 (noting that requiring particularized suspicion before routine stops on major highways near the Mexican border "would be impractical because the flow of traffic tends to be too heavy to allow the particularized study of a given car that would enable it to be identified as a possible carrier of illegal aliens"). Our precedents have settled that, in certain limited circumstances, the Government's need to discover such latent or hidden conditions, or to prevent their development, is sufficiently compelling to justify the intrusion on privacy entailed by conducting such searches without any measure of individualized suspicion. We think the Government's need to conduct the suspicionless searches required by the Customs program outweighs the privacy interests of employees engaged directly in drug interdiction, and of those who otherwise are required to carry firearms.

The Customs Service is our Nation's first line of defense against one of the greatest problems affecting the health and welfare of our population. We have adverted before to "the veritable national crisis in law enforcement caused by smuggling of illicit narcotics." *United States v. Montoya de Hernandez,* 473 U.S. 531, 538 (1985). See also *Florida v. Royer,* 460 U.S. 491, 513 (BLACKMUN, J., dissenting). Our cases also reflect the traffickers' seemingly inexhaustible repertoire of deceptive practices and elaborate schemes for importing narcotics, e.g., *United States v. Montoya de Hernandez, supra,* 473 U.S., at 538-539 *United States v. Ramsey,* 431 U.S. 606, 608-609 (1977). The record in this case confirms that, through the adroit selection of source locations, smuggling routes, and increasingly elaborate methods of concealment, drug traffickers have managed to bring into this country increasingly large quantities of illegal drugs. The record also indicates, and it is well known, that drug smugglers do not hesitate to use violence to protect their lucrative trade and avoid apprehension.

Many of the Service's employees are often exposed to this criminal element and to the controlled substances they seek to smuggle into the country. Cf. *United States v. Montoya de Hernandez, supra,* 473 U.S., at 543. The physical safety of these employees may be threatened, and many may be tempted not only by bribes from the traffickers with whom they deal, but also by their own access to vast sources of valuable contraband seized and controlled by the Service. The Commissioner indicated below that "Customs [o]fficers have been shot, stabbed, run over, dragged by automobiles, and assaulted with blunt objects while performing their duties." At least nine officers have died in the line of duty since 1974. He also noted that Customs officers have been the targets of bribery by drug smugglers on numerous occasions, and several have been removed from the Service for accepting bribes and other integrity violations....

It is readily apparent that the Government has a compelling interest in ensuring that front-line interdiction personnel are physically fit, and have unimpeachable integrity and judgment. Indeed, the Government's interest here is at least as important as its interest in searching travelers entering the country. We have long held that travelers seeking to enter the country may be stopped and required to submit to a routine search without probable cause, or even founded suspicion, "because of national self protection reasonably requiring one entering the country to identify himself as entitled to come in, and his belongings as effects which may be lawfully brought in." *Carroll v. United States,* 267 U.S. 132, 154 (1925). See also *United States v. Montoya de Hernandez, supra,* 473 U.S., at 538; *United States v. Ramsey, supra,* 431 U.S., at 617-619. This national interest in self protection could be irreparably damaged if those charged with safeguarding it were, because of their own drug use, unsympathetic to their mission of interdicting narcotics. A drug user's indifference to the Service's basic mission or, even worse, his active complicity with the malefactors, can facilitate importation of sizable drug shipments or block apprehension of dangerous criminals. The public interest demands effective measures to bar drug users from positions directly involving the interdiction of illegal drugs.

The public interest likewise demands effective measures to prevent the promotion of drug users to positions that require the incumbent to carry a firearm, even if the incumbent is not engaged directly in the interdiction of drugs. Customs employees who may use deadly force plainly "discharge duties fraught with such risks of injury to others that even a momentary lapse of attention can have disastrous consequences." We agree with the Government that the public should not bear the risk that employees who may suffer from impaired perception and judgment will be promoted to positions where they may need to employ deadly force. Indeed, ensuring against the creation of this dangerous risk *balancing test* [handwritten annotation]

will itself further Fourth Amendment values, as the use of deadly force may violate the Fourth Amendment in certain circumstances. See *Tennessee v. Garner,* 471 U.S. 1, 7-12 (1985).

Against these valid public interests we must weigh the interference with individual liberty that results from requiring these classes of employees to undergo a urine test. The interference with individual privacy that results from the collection of a urine sample for subsequent chemical analysis could be substantial in some circumstances. We have recognized, however, that the "operational realities of the workplace" may render entirely reasonable certain work-related intrusions by supervisors and co-workers that might be viewed as unreasonable in other contexts. See *O'Connor v. Ortega,* 480 U.S., at 717 (SCALIA, J., concurring in judgment). While these operational realities will rarely affect an employee's expectations of privacy with respect to searches of his person, or of personal effects that the employee may bring to the workplace, *id.,* at 716, 725, it is plain that certain forms of public employment may diminish privacy expectations even with respect to such personal searches. Employees of the United States Mint for example, should expect to be subject to certain routine personal searches when they leave the workplace every day. Similarly, those who join our military or intelligence services may not only be required to give what in other contexts might be viewed as extraordinary assurances of trustworthiness and probity, but also may expect intrusive inquiries into their physical fitness for those special positions. Cf. *Snepp v. United States,* 444 U.S. 507, 509, n. 3 (1980); *Parker v. Levy,* 417 U.S. 733, 758 (1974); *Committee for GI Rights v. Callaway,* 171 U.S. App. D.C. 73, 84, 518 F.2d 466, 477 (1975).

We think Customs employees who are directly involved in the interdiction of illegal drugs or who are required to carry firearms in the line of duty likewise have a diminished expectation of privacy in respect to the intrusions occasioned by a urine test. Unlike most private citizens or government employees in general, employees involved in drug interdiction reasonably should expect effective inquiry into their fitness and probity. Much the same is true of employees who are required to carry firearms. Because successful performance of their duties depends uniquely on their judgment and dexterity, these employees cannot reasonably expect to keep from the Service personal information that bears directly on their fitness. Cf. *In re Caruso v. Ward,* 72 N.Y.2d 433, 441, 534 N.Y.S.2d 142, 146-148, 530 N.E.2d 850, 854-855 (1988). While reasonable tests designed to elicit this information doubtless infringe some privacy expectations, we do not believe these expectations outweigh the Government's compelling interests in safety and in the integrity of our borders.[2]

_____

[2] The procedures prescribed by the Customs Service for the collection and analysis of the requisite samples do not carry the grave potential for "arbitrary and oppressive interference with the privacy and personal security of individuals," *United States v. Martinez-Fuerte,* 428 U.S. 543, 554 (1976), that the Fourth Amendment was designed to prevent. Indeed, these procedures significantly minimize the program's intrusion on privacy interests. Only employees who have been tentatively accepted for promotion or transfer to one of the three categories of covered positions are tested, and applicants know at the outset that a drug test is a requirement of those positions. Employees are also notified in advance of the scheduled sample collection, thus reducing to a minimum any "unsettling show of authority," *Delaware v. Prouse,* 440 U.S. 648, 657 (1979), that may be associated with unexpected intrusions on privacy. Cf. *United States v. Martinez-Fuerte, supra,* 428 U.S., at 559 (noting that the intrusion on privacy occasioned by routine highway checkpoints is minimized by the fact that motorists "are not taken by surprise as they know, or may obtain

Without disparaging the importance of the governmental interests that support the suspicionless searches of these employees, petitioners nevertheless contend that the Service's drug testing program is unreasonable in two particulars. First, petitioners argue that the program is unjustified because it is not based on a belief that testing will reveal any drug use by covered employees. In pressing this argument, petitioners point out that the Service's testing scheme was not implemented in response to any perceived drug problem among Customs employees, and that the program actually has not led to the discovery of a significant number of drug users. Counsel for petitioners informed us at oral argument that no more than 5 employees out of 3,660 have tested positive for drugs. Second, petitioners contend that the Service's scheme is not a "sufficiently productive mechanism to justify [its] intrusion upon Fourth Amendment interests," *Delaware v. Prouse,* 440 U.S., at 648, 658-659, because illegal drug users can avoid detection with ease by temporary abstinence or by surreptitious adulteration of their urine specimens. These contentions are unpersuasive.

Petitioners' first contention evinces an unduly narrow view of the context in which the Service's testing program was implemented. Petitioners do not dispute, nor can there be doubt, that drug abuse is one of the most serious problems confronting our society today. There is little reason to believe that American workplaces are immune from this pervasive social problem, as is amply illustrated by our decision in *Railway Labor Executives.* See also *Masino v. United States,* 589 F.2d 1048, 1050, 218 Ct. Cl. 531 (1978) (describing marijuana use by two Customs Inspectors). Detecting drug impairment on the part of employees can be a difficult task, especially where, as here, it is not feasible to subject employees and their work-product to the kind of day-to-day scrutiny that is the norm in more traditional office environments. Indeed, the almost unique mission of the Service gives the Government a compelling interest in ensuring that many of these covered employees do not use drugs even off-duty, for such use creates risks of bribery and blackmail against which the Government is entitled to guard. In light of the extraordinary safety and national security hazards that would attend the promotion of drug users to positions that require the carrying of firearms or the interdiction of controlled substances, the Service's policy of deterring drug users from seeking such promotions cannot be deemed unreasonable.

The mere circumstance that all but a few of the employees tested are entirely innocent of wrongdoing does not impugn the program's validity. The same is likely to be true of householders who are required to submit to suspicionless

---

knowledge of, the location of the checkpoints and will not be stopped elsewhere"); *Wyman v. James,* 400 U.S. 309, 320-321 (1971) (providing a welfare recipient with advance notice that she would be visited by a welfare caseworker minimized the intrusion on privacy occasioned by the visit). There is no direct observation of the act of urination, as the employee may provide a specimen in the privacy of a stall.

Further, urine samples may be examined only for the specified drugs. The use of samples to test for any other substances is prohibited. See HHS Reg. § 2.1(c), 53 Fed. Reg. 11980 (1988). And, as the court of appeals noted, the combination of EMIT and CC/MS tests required by the Service is highly accurate, assuming proper storage, handling, and measurement techniques. 816 F.2d, at 181. Finally, an employee need not disclose personal medical information to the Government unless his test result is positive, and even then any such information is reported to a licensed physician. Taken together, these procedures significantly minimize the intrusiveness of the Service's drug screening program.

housing code inspections, see *Camara v. Municipal Court,* 387 U.S. 523 (1967), and of motorists who are stopped at the checkpoints we approved in *United States v. Martinez-Fuerte,* 428 U.S. 543 (1976). The Service's program is designed to prevent the promotion of drug users to sensitive positions as much as it is designed to detect those employees who use drugs. Where, as here, the possible harm against which the Government seeks to guard is substantial, the need to prevent its occurrence furnishes an ample justification for reasonable searches calculated to advance the Government's goal.[3]

We think petitioners' second argument — that the Service's testing program is ineffective because employees may attempt to deceive the test by a brief abstention before the test date, or by adulterating their urine specimens — overstates the case. As the Court of Appeals noted, addicts may be unable to abstain even for a limited period of time, or may be unaware of the "fadeaway effect" of certain drugs. 816 F.2d, at 180. More importantly, the avoidance techniques suggested by petitioners are fraught with uncertainty and risks for those employees who venture to attempt them. A particular employee's pattern of elimination for a given drug cannot be predicted with perfect accuracy, and in any event, this information is not likely to be known or available to the employee. Petitioners' own expert indicated below that the time it takes for particular drugs to become undetectable in urine can vary widely depending on the individual, and may extend for as long as 22 days. Thus, contrary to petitioners' suggestion, no employee reasonably can expect to deceive the test by the simple expedient of abstaining after the test date is assigned. Nor can he expect attempts at adulteration to succeed, in view of the precautions taken by the sample collector to ensure the integrity of the sample. In all the circumstances, we are persuaded that the program bears a close and substantial relation to the Service's goal of deterring drug users from seeking promotion to sensitive positions.

In sum, we believe the Government has demonstrated that its compelling interests in safeguarding our borders and the public safety outweigh the privacy expectations of employees who seek to be promoted to positions that directly involve the interdiction of illegal drugs or that require the incumbent to carry a firearm. We hold that the testing of these employees is reasonable under the Fourth Amendment.

C. We are unable, on the present record, to assess the reasonableness of the Government's testing program insofar as it covers employees who are required

---

[3]The point is well illustrated also by the Federal Government's practice of requiring the search of all passengers seeking to board commercial airliners, as well as the search of their carry-on luggage, without any basis for suspecting any particular passenger of an untoward motive. Applying our precedents dealing with administrative searches, see, e.g., *Camara v. Municipal Court,* the lower courts that have considered the question have consistently concluded that such searches are reasonable under the Fourth Amendment. As Judge Friendly explained in a leading case upholding such searches:

"When the risk is the jeopardy to hundreds of human lives and millions of dollars of property inherent in the pirating or blowing up of a large airplane, that danger *alone* meets the test of reasonableness, so long as the search is conducted in good faith for the purpose of preventing hijacking or like damage and with reasonable scope and the passenger has been given advance notice of his liability to such a search so that he can avoid it by choosing not to travel by air." *United States v. Edwards,* 498 F.2d 496, 500 (CA2 1974) (emphasis in original). See also *United States v. Skipwith,* 482 F.2d 1272, 1275-1276 (CA5 1973); *United States v. Davis,* 482 F.2d 893, 907-912 (CA9 1973)....

"to handle classified material." We readily agree that the Government has a compelling interest in protecting truly sensitive information from those who, "under compulsion of circumstances or for other reasons, ... might compromise [such] information." *Department of the Navy v. Egan,* 484 U.S. 518, 528 (1988). See also *United States v. Robel,* 389 U.S. 258, 267 (1967) ("We have recognized that, while the Constitution protects against invasions of individual rights, it does not withdraw from the Government the power to safeguard its vital interests.... The Government can deny access to its secrets to those who would use such information to harm the Nation"). We also agree that employees who seek promotions to positions where they would handle sensitive information can be required to submit to a urine test under the Service's screening program, especially if the positions covered under this category require background investigations, medical examinations, or other intrusions that may be expected to diminish their expectations of privacy in respect of urinalysis test. Cf. *Department of the Navy v. Egan, supra,* 484 U.S., at 528 (noting that the Executive branch generally subjects those desiring a security clearance to "a background investigation that varies according to the degree of adverse effect the applicant could have on the national security").

It is not clear, however, whether the category defined by the Service's testing directive encompasses only those Customs employees likely to gain access to sensitive information. Employees who are tested under the Service's scheme include those holding such diverse positions as "Accountant," "Accounting Technician," "Animal Caretaker," "Attorney (All)," "Baggage Clerk," "Co-op Student (All)," "Electric Equipment Repairer," "Mail Clerk/Assistant," and "Messenger." We assume these positions were selected for coverage under the Service's testing program by reason of the incumbent's access to "classified" information, as it is not clear that they would fall under either of the two categories we have already considered. Yet it is not evident that those occupying these positions are likely to gain access to sensitive information, and this apparent discrepancy raises in our minds the question whether the Service has defined this category of employees more broadly than necessary to meet the purposes of the Commissioner's directive.

We cannot resolve this ambiguity on the basis of the record before us, and we think it is appropriate to remand the case to the court of appeals for such proceedings as may be necessary to clarify the scope of this category of employees subject to testing. Upon remand the court of appeals should examine the criteria used by the Service in determining what materials are classified and in deciding whom to test under this rubric. In assessing the reasonableness of requiring tests of these employees, the court should also consider pertinent information bearing upon the employees' privacy expectations, as well as the supervision to which these employees are already subject.

III

Where the Government requires its employees to produce urine samples to be analyzed for evidence of illegal drug use, the collection and subsequent chemical analysis of such samples are searches that must meet the reasonableness requirement of the Fourth Amendment. Because the testing program adopted by the Customs Service is not designed to serve the ordinary needs of law enforcement, we have balanced the public interest in the Service's testing program against the privacy concerns implicated by the tests, without reference to our usual presumption in favor of the procedures specified in the Warrant Clause, to assess whether the tests required by Customs are reasonable.

We hold that the suspicionless testing of employees who apply for promotion to positions directly involving the interdiction of illegal drugs, or to positions which require the incumbent to carry a firearm, is reasonable. The Government's compelling interests in preventing the promotion of drug users to positions where they might endanger the integrity of our Nation's borders or the life of the citizenry outweigh the privacy interests of those who seek promotion to these positions, who enjoy a diminished expectation of privacy by virtue of the special, and obvious, physical and ethical demands of those positions. We do not decide whether testing those who apply for promotion to positions where they would handle "classified" information is reasonable because we find the record inadequate for this purpose.

The judgment of the Court of Appeals for the Fifth Circuit is affirmed in part and vacated in part, and the case is remanded for further proceedings consistent with this opinion.

It is so ordered.

JUSTICE MARSHALL, with whom JUSTICE BRENNAN joins, dissenting.

For the reasons stated in my dissenting opinion in *Skinner v. Railway Labor Executives Association,* 109 S. Ct., at 1422, I also dissent from the Court's decision in this case. Here, as in *Skinner,* the Court's abandonment of the Fourth Amendment's express requirement that searches of the person rest on probable cause is unprincipled and unjustifiable. But even if I believed that balancing analysis was appropriate under the Fourth Amendment, I would still dissent from today's judgment, for the reasons stated by JUSTICE SCALIA in his dissenting opinion, and for the reasons noted by the dissenting judge below relating to the inadequate tailoring of the Customs Service's drug-testing plan. See 816 F.2d 170, 182-184 (CA5 1987) (Hill, J.).

JUSTICE SCALIA, with whom JUSTICE STEVENS joins, dissenting.

The issue in this case is not whether Customs Service employees can constitutionally be denied promotion, or even dismissed, for a single instance of unlawful drug use, at home or at work. They assuredly can. The issue here is what steps can constitutionally be taken to *detect* such drug use. The Government asserts it can demand that employees perform "an excretory function traditionally shielded by great privacy," *Skinner v. Railway Labor Executives Assn.,* 109 S. Ct., at 1418, while "a monitor of the same sex ... remains close at hand to listen for the normal sounds," *ante,* at 1388, and that the excretion thus produced be turned over to the Government for chemical analysis. The Court agrees that this constitutes a search for purposes of the Fourth Amendment — and I think it obvious that it is a type of search particularly destructive of privacy and offensive to personal dignity.

Until today this Court had upheld a bodily search separate from arrest and without individualized suspicion of wrongdoing only with respect to prison inmates, relying upon the uniquely dangerous nature of that environment. See *Bell v. Wolfish,* 441 U.S. 520, 558-560 (1979). Today, in *Skinner,* we allow a less intrusive bodily search of railroad employees involved in train accidents. I joined the Court's opinion there because the demonstrated frequency of drug and alcohol use by the targeted class of employees, and the demonstrated connection between such use and grave harm, rendered the search a reasonable means of protecting society. I decline to join the Court's opinion in the present case because neither frequency of use nor connection to harm is demonstrated or even likely. In my view the Customs Service rules are a kind of immolation of privacy and human dignity in symbolic opposition to drug use.

The Fourth Amendment protects the "right of the people to be secure in their persons, houses, papers, and effects, against unreasonable searches and seizures." While there are some absolutes in Fourth Amendment law, as soon as those have been left behind and the question comes down to whether a particular search has been "reasonable," the answer depends largely upon the social necessity that prompts the search. Thus, in upholding the administrative search of a student's purse in a school, we began with the observation (documented by an agency report to Congress) that "[m]aintaining order in the classroom has never been easy, but in recent years, school disorder has often taken particularly ugly forms: drug use and violent crime in the schools have become major social problems." *New Jersey v. T.L.O.*, 469 U.S. 325, 339 (1985). When we approved fixed checkpoints near the Mexican border to stop and search cars for illegal aliens, we observed at the outset that "the Immigration and Naturalization Service now suggests there may be as many as 10 or 12 million aliens illegally in the country," and that "[i]nterdicting the flow of illegal entrants from Mexico poses formidable law enforcement problems." *United States v. Martinez-Fuerte*, 428 U.S. 543, 551-552 (1976). And the substantive analysis of our opinion today in *Skinner* begins, "[t]he problem of alcohol use on American railroads is as old as the industry itself," and goes on to cite statistics concerning that problem and the accidents it causes, including a 1979 study finding that "23% of the operating personnel were 'problem drinkers.'" *Skinner, ante.*

The Court's opinion in the present case, however, will be searched in vain for real evidence of a real problem that will be solved by urine testing of Customs Service employees. Instead, there are assurances that "[t]he Customs Service is our Nation's first line of defense against one of the greatest problems affecting the health and welfare of our population," *ante;* that "[m]any of the Service's employees are often exposed to [drug smugglers] and to the controlled substances they seek to smuggle into the country"; that "Customs officers have been the targets of bribery by drug smugglers on numerous occasions, and several have been removed from the Service for accepting bribes and other integrity violations"; that "the Government has a compelling interest in ensuring that front-line interdiction personnel are physically fit, and have unimpeachable integrity and judgment"; that the "national interest in self protection could be irreparably damaged if those charged with safeguarding it were, because of their own drug use, unsympathetic to their mission of interdicting narcotics"; and that "the public should not bear the risk that employees who may suffer from impaired perception and judgment will be promoted to positions where they may need to employ deadly force." To paraphrase Churchill, all this contains much that is obviously true, and much that is relevant; unfortunately, what is obviously true is not relevant, and what is relevant is not obviously true. The only pertinent points, it seems to me, are supported by nothing but speculation, and not very plausible speculation at that. It is not apparent to me that a Customs Service employee who uses drugs is significantly more likely to be bribed by a drug smuggler, any more than a Customs Service employee who wears diamonds is significantly more likely to be bribed by a diamond smuggler — unless, perhaps, the addiction to drugs is so severe, and requires so much money to maintain, that it would be detectable even without benefit of a urine test. Nor is it apparent to me that Customs officers who use drugs will be appreciably less "sympathetic" to their drug-interdiction mission, any more than police officers who exceed the speed limit in their private cars are appreciably less sympathetic to their mission of enforcing the traffic laws....

What is absent in the Government's justifications — notably absent, revealingly absent, and as far as I am concerned dispositively absent — is the recitation of *even a single instance* in which any of the speculated horribles actually occurred: an instance, that is, in which the cause of bribetaking, or of poor aim, or of unsympathetic law enforcement, or of compromise of classified information, was drug use....

... In *Skinner, Bell, T.L.O.,* and *Martinez-Fuerte,* we took pains to establish the existence of special need for the search or seizure — a need based not upon the existence of a "pervasive social problem" combined with speculation as to the effect of that problem in the field at issue, but rather upon well known or well demonstrated evils *in that field,* with well known or well demonstrated consequences. In *Skinner,* for example, we pointed to a long history of alcohol abuse in the railroad industry, and noted that in an 8-year period 45 train accidents and incidents had occurred because of alcohol- and drug-impaired railroad employees, killing 34 people, injuring 66, and causing more than $28 million in property damage. In the present case, by contrast, not only is the Customs Service thought to be "largely drug-free," but the connection between whatever drug use may exist and serious social harm is entirely speculative. Except for the fact that the search of a person is much more intrusive than the stop of a car, the present case resembles *Delaware v. Prouse,* 440 U.S. 648 (1979), where we held that the Fourth Amendment prohibited random stops to check drivers' licenses and motor vehicle registration. The contribution of this practice to highway safety, we concluded, was "marginal at best" since the number of licensed drivers that must be stopped in order to find one unlicensed one "will be large indeed." *Id.,* at 660.

Today's decision would be wrong, but at least of more limited effect, if its approval of drug testing were confined to that category of employees assigned specifically to drug interdiction duties. Relatively few public employees fit that description. But in extending approval of drug testing to that category consisting of employees who carry firearms, the Court exposes vast numbers of public employees to this needless indignity. Logically, of course, if those who carry guns can be treated in this fashion, so can all others whose work, if performed under the influence of drugs, may endanger others — automobile drivers, operators of other potentially dangerous equipment, construction workers, school crossing guards. A similarly broad scope attaches to the Court's approval of drug testing for those with access to "sensitive information."[1] Since this category is not limited to Service employees with drug interdiction duties, nor to "sensitive information" specifically relating to drug traffic, today's holding apparently approves drug testing for all federal employees with security clearances — or, indeed, for all federal employees with valuable confidential information to impart. Since drug use is not a particular problem in the Customs Service, employees throughout the government are no less likely to violate the public trust by taking bribes to feed their drug habit, or by yielding to blackmail. Moreover, there is no reason why this super-protection against harms arising from drug use must be limited to public employees; a law requiring similar testing of private citizens who use dangerous instruments such as guns or cars, or who have access to classified information would also be constitutional.

There is only one apparent basis that sets the testing at issue here apart from all these other situations — but it is not a basis upon which the Court is willing to rely. I do not believe for a minute that the driving force behind these drug-testing rules was any of the feeble justifications put forward by counsel here and accepted by the Court. The only plausible explanation, in my view, is what the Commissioner himself offered in the concluding sentence of his memorandum to Customs Service employees announcing the program: "Implementation of the drug screening program would set an important example in our country's struggle with this most serious threat to our national health and security." Or as respondent's brief to this Court asserted: "if a law enforcement agency and its employees do not take the law seriously, neither will the public on which the agency's effectiveness depends." What better way to show that the Government is serious about its "war on drugs" than to subject its employees on the front line of that war to this invasion of their privacy and affront to their dignity? To be sure, there is only a slight chance that it will prevent some serious public harm resulting from Service employee drug use, but it will show to the world that the Service is "clean," and — most important of all — will demonstrate the determination of the Government to eliminate this scourge of our society! I think it obvious that this justification is unacceptable; that the impairment of individual liberties cannot be the means of making a point; that symbolism, even symbolism for so worthy a cause as the abolition of unlawful drugs, cannot validate an otherwise unreasonable search....

NOTES

1. Courts have generally sustained the power of government employers to require persons in safety-sensitive positions to submit to urinalysis where there is a reasonable basis to suspect drug use. See, e.g., *Copeland v. Philadelphia Police Dep't,* 840 F.2d 1139 (3d Cir. 1988), *cert. denied,* 109 S. Ct. 1636 (1989) (police officers); *Everett v. Napper,* 833 F.2d 1507 (11th Cir. 1987) (firefighters). See also *Seelig v. Koehler,* 76 N.Y.2d 87, 556 N.E.2d 125 (1990), and *McDonell v. Hunter,* 809 F.2d 1302 (8th Cir. 1987) (sustaining uniform and random urinalysis of prison employees). Random testing of non-safety-sensitive

---

[1] The Court apparently approves application of the urine tests to personnel receiving access to "sensitive information." *Ante,* at 1396. Since, however, it is unsure whether "classified material" is "sensitive information," it remands with instructions that the court of appeals "examine the criteria used by the Service in determining what materials are classified and in deciding whom to test under this rubric."...

public employees has normally not been permitted. See, e.g., *NFFE v. Weinberger*, 818 F.2d 935 (D.C. Cir. 1987); *Patchoque-Medford Congress of Teachers v. Board of Educ.*, 70 N.Y.2d 57, 510 N.E.2d 325 (1987). In *NTEU v. Bush*, 891 F.2d 99 (5th Cir. 1989), the court refused to find that an executive order which subjects more than one million federal employees to random drug testing is facially unconstitutional. The propriety of such tests will thus have to be determined on a case-by-case basis. Compare *Willner v. Thornburgh*, — F.2d — (D.C. Cir. 1991) (sustaining suspicionless drug testing of all applicants for Department of Justice attorney positions), with *NTEU v. Yeutter*, 918 F.2d 968 (D.C. Cir. 1990) (voiding portion of Department of Agriculture drug testing program that mandated testing of workers not involved with safety or sensitive information).

The Department of Transportation subjects employees to random drug testing where their positions have "a direct and immediate impact on public health and safety, the protection of life and property, law enforcement, or national security." In *AFGE v. Skinner*, 885 F.2d 884 (D.C. Cir. 1989), the court sustained the constitutionality of such suspicionless, random testing based upon compelling safety considerations. See also *National Fed'n of Fed. Emps. v. Cheney*, 884 F.2d 603 (D.C. Cir. 1989), wherein the court upheld the propriety of random drug testing of U.S. Army civilian personnel occupying "critical" positions.

See generally Note, *Alternative Challenges to Drug Testing of Government Employees: Options After Von Raab*, 58 Geo. Wash. L. Rev. 148 (1989); Note, *A Proposal for Mandatory Drug Testing of Federal Civilian Employees*, 62 N.Y.U. L. Rev. 322 (1987).

2. In *O'Connor v. Ortega*, 480 U.S. 709 (1987), a divided Supreme Court considered the right of public employers to conduct warrantless searches of employee offices and desks. Chief Justice Rehnquist and Justices O'Connor, White, and Powell acknowledged that searches by government supervisors of the private property of their employees are subject to fourth amendment restraints. Although they noted that some government offices may be so open to fellow workers or the public that there would be no reasonable employee expectation of privacy, they recognized that other workers may well have a reasonable expectation of privacy with respect to their desks and file cabinets. They nonetheless reasoned that one "must balance the invasion of the employees' legitimate expectations of privacy against the government's need for supervision, control and the efficient operation of the workplace." A warrant and probable cause requirement for supervisory personnel would be inappropriate, since such employer agents "most frequently need to enter the offices and desks of their employees for legitimate work-related reasons wholly unrelated to illegal conduct." These four Justices thus found that "public employer intrusions on the constitutionally protected privacy interests of government employees for noninvestigatory, work-related purposes, as well as for investigations of work-related misconduct, should be judged by the standard of reasonableness under all the circumstances." Under their standard, both the inception and the scope of the intrusion must be reasonable. They concluded that "a search of an employee's office by a supervisor will [ordinarily] be 'justified at its inception' when there are reasonable grounds for suspecting that the search will turn up evidence that the employee is guilty of work-related misconduct, or that the search is necessary for a noninvestigatory work-related purpose such as to retrieve a needed file.... The search will be permissible in its scope when 'the measures adopted are reasonably related to the objectives of the search and not exces-

sively intrusive in light of ... the nature of the [misconduct].'" Justice Scalia indicated that while government searches of public employee offices and files are subject to fourth amendment constraints, supervisory searches to retrieve work-related material or to investigate work-related misconduct must be regarded as reasonable under that Amendment when they are conducted in a manner regarded as normal and appropriate when carried out by private sector employers. Justices Blackmun, Brennan, Marshall, and Stevens dissented. They believed that the actual search conducted of Dr. Ortega's desk and files transcended any reasonable employer need and thus violated his Fourth Amendment rights. See also *Schowengerdt v. General Dynamics Corp.*, 823 F.2d 1328 (9th Cir. 1987); *American Postal Workers Union v. Postal Serv.*, 871 F.2d 556 (6th Cir. 1989).

4. FREEDOM OF ASSOCIATION

SHELTON v. TUCKER

364 U.S. 479, 81 S. Ct. 247, 5 L. Ed. 2d 231 (1960)

JUSTICE STEWART delivered the opinion of the Court.

An Arkansas statute compels every teacher, as a condition of employment in a state-supported school or college, to file annually an affidavit listing without limitation every organization to which he has belonged or regularly contributed within the preceding five years. At issue in these two cases is the validity of that statute under the Fourteenth Amendment to the Constitution....

... The provisions of the Act are summarized in the opinion of the District Court as follows:

"Act 10 provides in substance that no person shall be employed or elected to employment as a superintendent, principal or teacher in any public school in Arkansas, or as an instructor, professor or teacher in any public institution of higher learning in that State until such person shall have submitted to the appropriate hiring authority an affidavit listing all organizations to which he at the time belongs and to which he has belonged during the past five years, and also listing all organizations to which he at the time is paying regular dues or is making regular contributions, or to which within the past five years he has paid such dues or made such contributions. The Act further provides, among other things, that any contract entered into with any person who has not filed the prescribed affidavit shall be void; that no public moneys shall be paid to such person as compensation for his services; and that any such funds so paid may be recovered back either from the person receiving such funds or from the board of trustees or other governing body making the payment. The filing of a false affidavit is denounced as perjury, punishable by a fine of not less than five hundred nor more than one thousand dollars, and, in addition, the person filing the false affidavit is to lose his teaching license." 174 F. Supp. 353-354....

The plaintiffs in the Federal District Court (appellants here) were B.T. Shelton, a teacher employed in the Little Rock Public School System, suing for himself and others similarly situated, together with the Arkansas Teachers Association and its Executive Secretary, suing for the benefit of members of the Association. Shelton had been employed in the Little Rock Special School District for twenty-five years. In the spring of 1959 he was notified that, before he could be employed for the 1959-1960 school year, he must file the affidavit required by Act 10, listing all his organizational connections over the previous five years. He declined to file the affidavit, and his contract for the ensuing school year was not renewed. At the trial the evidence showed that he was not a member of the Communist Party or of any organization advocating the overthrow of the Government by force, and that he was a member of the National Association for the Advancement of Colored People. The court upheld Act 10, finding the information it required was "relevant," and relying on several decisions of this Court, particularly *Garner v. Board of Public Works of Los Angeles,* 341 U.S. 716; *Adler v. Board of Education,* 342 U.S. 485; *Beilan v. Board of Education,* 357 U.S. 399; and *Lerner v. Casey,* 357 U.S. 468.

The plaintiffs in the state court proceedings (petitioners here) were Max Carr, an associate professor at the University of Arkansas, and Ernest T. Gephardt, a teacher at Central High School in Little Rock, each suing for himself and others similarly situated. Each refused to execute and file the affidavit required by Act 10.... Both were advised that their failure to comply with the requirements of Act 10 would make impossible their re-employment as teachers for the following school year. The Supreme Court of Arkansas upheld the constitutionality of Act 10, on its face and as applied to the petitioners. 231 Ark. 641, 331 S.W.2d 701.

I

It is urged here, as it was unsuccessfully urged throughout the proceedings in both the federal and state courts, that Act 10 deprives teachers in Arkansas of their rights to personal, associational, and academic liberty, protected by the Due Process Clause of the Fourteenth Amendment from invasion by state action. In considering this contention, we deal with two basic postulates.

First. There can be no doubt of the right of a State to investigate the competence and fitness of those whom it hires to teach in its schools, as this Court before now has had occasion to recognize....

This controversy is thus not of a pattern with such cases as *N.A.A.C.P. v. Alabama,* 357 U.S. 449, and *Bates v. Little Rock,* 361 U.S. 516. In those cases the Court held that there was no substantially relevant correlation between the governmental interest asserted and the State's effort to compel disclosure of the membership lists involved. Here, by contrast, there can be no question of the relevance of a State's inquiry into the fitness and competence of its teachers.

Second. It is not disputed that to compel a teacher to disclose his every associational tie is to impair that teacher's right of free association, a right closely allied to freedom of speech and a right which, like free speech, lies at the foundation of a free society. *DeJonge v. Oregon,* 299 U.S. 353, 364; *Bates v. Little Rock, supra,* at 522-523. Such interference with personal freedom is conspicuously accented when the teacher serves at the absolute will of those to whom the disclosure must be made — those who any year can terminate the teacher's employment without bringing charges, without notice, without a hearing, without affording an opportunity to explain.

The statute does not provide that the information it requires be kept confidential. Each school board is left free to deal with the information as it wishes. The record contains evidence to indicate that fear of public disclosure is neither theoretical nor groundless. Even if there were no disclosure to the general public, the pressure upon a teacher to avoid any ties which might displease those who control his professional destiny would be constant and heavy. Public exposure, bringing with it the possibility of public pressures upon school boards to discharge teachers who belong to unpopular or minority organizations, would simply operate to widen and aggravate the impairment of constitutional liberty....

II

The question to be decided here is not whether the State of Arkansas can ask certain of its teachers about all their organizational relationships. It is not whether the State can ask all of its teachers about certain of their associational ties. It is not whether teachers can be asked how many organizations they belong to, or how much time they spend in organizational activity. The question is whether the State can ask every one of its teachers to disclose every single organization with which he has been associated over a five-year period. The scope of the inquiry required by Act 10 is completely unlimited. The statute requires a teacher to reveal the church to which he belongs, or to which he has given financial support. It requires him to disclose his political party, and every political organization to which he may have contributed over a five-year period. It requires him to list, without number, every conceivable kind of associational tie — social, professional, political, avocational, or religious. Many such relationships could have no possible bearing upon the teacher's occupational competence or fitness.

In a series of decisions this Court has held that, even though the governmental purpose be legitimate and substantial, that purpose cannot be pursued by means that broadly stifle fundamental personal liberties when the end can be more narrowly achieved. The breadth of legislative abridgment must be viewed in the light of less drastic means for achieving the same basic purpose....

The unlimited and indiscriminate sweep of the statute now before us brings it within the ban of our prior cases. The statute's comprehensive interference with associational freedom goes far beyond what might be justified in the exercise of the State's legitimate inquiry into the fitness and competency of its teachers. The judgments in both cases must be reversed.

It is so ordered.

JUSTICE FRANKFURTER, dissenting.

As one who has strong views against crude intrusions by the state into the atmosphere of creative freedom in which alone the spirit and mind of a teacher can fruitfully function, I may find displeasure with the Arkansas legislation now under review. But in maintaining the distinction between private views and constitutional restrictions, I am constrained to find that it does not exceed the permissible range of state action limited by the Fourteenth Amendment. By way of emphasis I therefore add a few words to the dissent of MR. JUSTICE HARLAN, in which I concur....

Where state assertions of authority are attacked as impermissibly restrictive upon thought, expression, or association, the existence *vel non* of other possible less restrictive means of achieving the object which the State seeks is, of course, a constitutionally relevant consideration. This is not because some novel, particular rule of law obtains in cases of this kind. Whenever the reasonableness and fairness of a measure are at issue — as they are in every case in which this Court must apply the standards of reason and fairness, with the appropriate scope to be given those concepts, in enforcing the Due Process Clause of the Fourteenth Amendment as a limitation upon state action — the availability or unavailability of alternative methods of proceeding is germane. Thus, a State may not prohibit the distribution of literature on its cities' streets as a means of preventing littering, when the same end might be achieved with only slightly greater inconvenience by applying the sanctions of the penal law not to the pamphleteer who distributes the paper but to the recipient who crumples it and throws it away. *Hague v. C.I.O.,* 307 U.S. 496; *Schneider v. State,* 308 U.S. 147; *Jamison v. Texas,* 318 U.S. 413.... But the consideration of feasible alternative modes of regulation in these cases did not imply that the Court might substitute its own choice among alternatives for that of a state legislature, or that the States were to be restricted to the "narrowest" workable means of accomplishing an end....

In the present case the Court strikes down an Arkansas statute requiring that teachers disclose to school officials all of their organizational relationships, on the ground that "Many such relationships could have no possible bearing upon the teacher's occupational competence or fitness." Granted that a given teacher's membership in the First Street Congregation is, standing alone, of little relevance to what may rightly be expected of a teacher, is that membership equally irrelevant when it is discovered that the teacher is in fact a member of the First Street Congregation *and* the Second Street Congregation *and* the Third Street Congregation *and* the 4-H Club *and* the 3-H Club *and* half a dozen other groups? Presumably, a teacher may have so many divers associations, so many divers commitments, that they consume his time and energy and interest at the expense of his work or even of his professional dedication. Unlike wholly individual interests, organizational connections — because they involve obligations undertaken with relation to other persons — may become inescapably demanding and distracting. Surely, a school board is entitled to inquire whether any of its teachers has placed himself, or is placing himself, in a condition where his work may suffer....

If I dissent from the Court's disposition in these cases, it is not that I put a low value on academic freedom. See *Wieman v. Updegraff,* 344 U.S. 183, 194 (concurring opinion); *Sweezy v. New Hampshire,* 354 U.S. 234, 255 (concurring opinion). It is because that very freedom, in its most creative reaches, is dependent in no small part upon the careful and discriminating selection of teachers. This process of selection is an intricate affair, a matter of fine judgment, and if it is to be informed, it must be based upon a comprehensive range of information. I am unable to say, on the face of this statute, that Arkansas could not reasonably find that the information which the statute requires — and which may not be otherwise acquired than by asking the question which it asks — is germane to that selection. Nor, on this record, can I attribute to the State a purpose to employ the enactment as a device for the accomplishment of what is constitutionally forbidden. Of course, if the information gathered by the required affidavits is used to further a scheme of terminating the employment of teachers solely because of their membership in unpopular organizations, that use will run afoul of the Fourteenth Amendment. It will be time enough, if such use is made, to hold the application of the statute unconstitutional....

I am authorized to say that MR. JUSTICE CLARK, MR. JUSTICE HARLAN and MR. JUSTICE WHITTAKER agree with this opinion.

JUSTICE HARLAN, whom JUSTICE FRANKFURTER, JUSTICE CLARK and JUSTICE WHITTAKER join, dissenting....

The legal framework in which the issue must be judged is clear. The rights of free speech and association embodied in the "liberty" assured against state action by the Fourteenth Amendment (see *DeJonge v. Oregon,* 299 U.S. 353, 364; *Gitlow v. New York,* 268 U.S. 652, 672, dissenting opinion of Holmes, J.) are not absolute. *Near v. Minnesota,* 283 U.S. 697, 708; *Whitney v. California,* 274 U.S. 357, 373 (concurring opinion of Brandeis, J.). Where official action is claimed to invade these rights, the controlling inquiry is whether such action is justifiable on the basis of a superior governmental interest to which such individual rights must yield. When the action complained of pertains to the realm of investigation, our inquiry has a double aspect: first, whether the investigation relates to a legitimate governmental purpose; second, whether, judged in the light of that purpose, the questioned action has substantial relevance thereto. See *Barenblatt v. United States,* 360 U.S. 109; *Uphaus v. Wyman,* 360 U.S. 72.

In the two cases at hand, I think both factors are satisfied. It is surely indisputable that a State has the right to choose its teachers on the basis of fitness. And I think it equally clear, as the Court appears to recognize, that information about a teacher's association may be useful to school authorities in determining the moral, professional, and social qualifications of the teacher, as well as in determining the type of service for which he will be best suited in the educational system....

Despite these considerations this statute is stricken down because, in the Court's view, it is too broad, because it asks more than may be necessary to effectuate the State's legitimate interest. Such a statute, it is said, cannot justify the inhibition on freedom of association which so blanket an inquiry may entail. Cf. *N.A.A.C.P. v. Alabama, supra; Bates v. Little Rock, supra.*

I am unable to subscribe to this view because I believe it impossible to determine *a priori* the place where the line should be drawn between what would be permissible inquiry and overbroad inquiry in a situation like this. Certainly the Court does not point that place out. There can be little doubt that much of the associational information called for by the statute will be of little or no use whatever to the school authorities, but I do not understand how those authorities can be expected to fix in advance the terms of their inquiry so that it will yield only relevant information....

NOTES

1. In *Curle v. Ward,* 46 N.Y.2d 1049, 389 N.E.2d 1070 (1979), the court held that a state could not automatically preclude the employment of people as correction officers simply because of their membership in the Ku Klux Klan. But see *McMullen v. Carson,* 568 F. Supp. 937 (M.D. Fla. 1983). What would a state have to demonstrate before it could disqualify such individuals from service as prison guards or police officers?

2. In *Cybyske v. Independent Sch. Dist.*, 347 N.W.2d 256 (Minn. 1984), the court ruled that if a teacher were denied employment because of the political views of her husband, she could prosecute an action challenging the impermissible deprivation of her first amendment right to freedom of association.

3. *Norbeck v. Davenport Community Sch. Dist.*, 545 F.2d 63 (8th Cir., 1976), *cert. denied,* 431 U.S. 917 (1977), held that a high school principal had no constitutional right to negotiate on behalf of a teachers' union that represented teachers whom the principal supervised. The Davenport school board did not violate the school principal's first amendment rights when it refused to renew the principal's contract, because the board's interest in efficient school administration outweighed any right the principal might have had to associate freely with the teachers' union.

4. *McDonald v. City of W. Branch,* 466 U.S. 284 1799 (1984), involved a police officer who had unsuccessfully challenged his discharge through contractual grievance-arbitration procedures. He subsequently brought suit under 42 U.S.C. § 1983 claiming that he had been terminated because of his exercise of first amendment rights of free speech, free association, and freedom to petition the government for redress of grievances. The city argued that the prior adverse arbitral decision should preclude litigation under § 1983. However, the Supreme Court held that a federal court should not afford res judicata or collateral estoppel effect to such a previous arbitration determination, since such a plaintiff has the right to have his constitutional claims decided in a judicial proceeding. Compare *Migra v. Warren Sch. Dist. Bd. of Educ.,* 465 U.S. 75 (1984), wherein the Supreme Court held that a prior state court judgment has the same claim preclusive effect in federal court in a subsequent § 1983 action as it would have in state court, even though the § 1983 claim was not litigated in the prior state court case.

5. FREEDOM OF EXPRESSION

RANKIN v. McPHERSON

483 U.S. 378, 107 S. Ct. 2891, 97 L. Ed. 2d 315 (1987)

JUSTICE MARSHALL delivered the opinion of the Court.

The issue in this case is whether a clerical employee in a county constable's office was properly discharged for remarking, after hearing of an attempt on the life of the President, "If they go for him again, I hope they get him."

I

On January 12, 1981, respondent Ardith McPherson was appointed a deputy in the office of the constable of Harris County, Texas. The constable is an elected official who functions as a law enforcement officer.[1] At the time of her appointment, McPherson, a black woman, was 19 years old and had attended college for a year, studying secretarial science. Her appointment was conditional for a 90-day probationary period.

---

[1]While the constable's office is a law enforcement agency, Constable Rankin testified that other law enforcement departments were charged with the day-to-day enforcement of criminal laws in the county and that more than 80% of the budget of his office was devoted to service of civil process, service of process in juvenile delinquency cases, and execution of mental health warrants. The involvement of his office in criminal cases, he testified, was in large part limited to warrants in bad check cases. ("Most of our percentage is with civil papers and hot check warrants.")

Although McPherson's title was "deputy constable," this was the case only because all employees of the constable's office, regardless of job function, were deputy constables. She was not a commissioned peace officer, did not wear a uniform, and was not authorized to make arrests or permitted to carry a gun. McPherson's duties were purely clerical. Her work station was a desk at which there was no telephone, in a room to which the public did not have ready access. Her job was to type data from court papers into a computer that maintained an automated record of the status of civil process in the county. Her training consisted of two days of instruction in the operation of her computer terminal.

On March 30, 1981, McPherson and some fellow employees heard on an office radio that there had been an attempt to assassinate the President of the United States. Upon hearing that report, McPherson engaged a co-worker, Lawrence Jackson, who was apparently her boyfriend, in a brief conversation, which according to McPherson's uncontroverted testimony went as follows:

"Q: What did you say?
"A: I said I felt that that would happen sooner or later.
"Q: Okay. And what did Lawrence say?
"A: Lawrence said, yeah, agreeing with me.
"Q: Okay. Now, when you — after Lawrence spoke, then what was your next comment?
"A: Well, we were talking — it's a wonder why they did that. I felt like it would be a black person that did that, because I feel like most of my kind is on welfare and CETA, and they use medicaid, and at the time, I was thinking that's what it was.
"... But then after I said that, and then Lawrence said, yeah, he's cutting back medicaid and food stamps. And I said, yeah, welfare and CETA. I said, shoot, if they go for him again, I hope they get him."

McPherson's last remark was overheard by another deputy constable, who, unbeknownst to McPherson, was in the room at the time. The remark was reported to Constable Rankin, who summoned McPherson. McPherson readily admitted that she had made the statement, but testified that she told Rankin, upon being asked if she made the statement, "Yes, but I didn't mean anything by it."[4] After their discussion, Rankin fired McPherson.

McPherson brought suit in the United States District Court for the Southern District of Texas under 42 U.S.C. § 1983, alleging that petitioner Rankin, in discharging her, had violated her constitutional rights under color of state law. She sought reinstatement, back pay, costs and fees, and other equitable relief. The District Court held a hearing, and then granted summary judgment to Constable Rankin, holding that McPherson's speech had been unprotected and

---

[4] Rankin testified that, when he asked McPherson whether she meant the remark, she replied, "I sure do." In neither of its opinions in this case did the District Court make an explicit finding regarding which version of this conflicting testimony it found credible. See also 736 F.2d 175, 177, and n.3 (CA5 1984).

We note that the question whether McPherson "meant" the statement is ambiguous. Assuming that McPherson told Rankin she "meant it," McPherson might think she had said that she "meant" that she disliked the President and would not mind if he were dead, while Rankin might believe that McPherson "meant" to indicate approval of, or in any event hope for, political assassination. This ambiguity makes evident the need for carefully conducted hearings and precise and complete findings of fact.

that her discharge had therefore been proper. The Court of Appeals for the Fifth Circuit vacated and remanded for trial, 736 F.2d 175 (1984), on the ground that substantial issues of material fact regarding the context in which the statement had been made precluded the entry of summary judgment.

On remand, the District Court held another hearing and ruled once again, this time from the bench, that the statements were not protected speech. Again, the Court of Appeals reversed. 786 F.2d 1233 (CA5 1986). It held that McPherson's remark had addressed a matter of public concern, requiring that society's interest in McPherson's freedom of speech be weighed against her employer's interest in maintaining efficiency and discipline in the workplace. *Id.,* at 1236. Performing that balancing, the Court of Appeals concluded that the Government's interest did not outweigh the First Amendment interest in protecting McPherson's speech. Given the nature of McPherson's job and the fact that she was not a law enforcement officer, was not brought by virtue of her job into contact with the public, and did not have access to sensitive information, the Court of Appeals deemed her "duties ... so utterly ministerial and her potential for undermining the office's mission so trival" as to forbid her dismissal for expression of her political opinions. *Id.,* at 1239. "However ill-considered Ardith McPherson's opinion was," the Court of Appeals concluded, "it did not make her unfit" for the job she held in Constable Rankin's office. *Ibid.* The Court of Appeals remanded the case for determination of an appropriate remedy.

We granted certiorari, 479 U.S. — (1986), and now affirm.

II

It is clearly established that a State may not discharge an employee on a basis that infringes that employee's constitutionally protected interest in freedom of speech. *Perry v. Sindermann,* 408 U.S. 593, 597 (1972). Even though McPherson was merely a probationary employee, and even if she could have been discharged for any reason or for no reason at all, she may nonetheless be entitled to reinstatement if she was discharged for exercising her constitutional right to freedom of expression. See *Mt. Healthy City Board of Education v. Doyle,* 429 U.S. 274, 284-285 (1977); *Perry v. Sindermann, supra,* at 597-598.

The determination whether a public employer has properly discharged an employee for engaging in speech requires "a balance between the interests of the [employee], as a citizen, in commenting upon matters of public concern and the interest of the State, as an employer, in promoting the efficiency of the public services it performs through its employees." *Pickering v. Board of Education,* 391 U.S. 563, 568 (1968); *Connick v. Myers,* 461 U.S. 138, 140 (1983). This balancing is necessary in order to accommodate the dual role of the public employer as a provider of public services and as a government entity operating under the constraints of the First Amendment. On one hand, public employers are *employers,* concerned with the efficient function of their operations; review of every personnel decision made by a public employer could, in the long run, hamper the performance of public functions. On the other hand, "the threat of dismissal from public employment is ... a potent means of inhibiting speech." *Pickering,* 391 U.S., at 574. Vigilance is necessary to ensure that public employers do not use authority over employees to silence discourse, not because it hampers public functions but simply because superiors disagree with the content of employees' speech.

A. The threshold question in applying this balancing test is whether McPherson's speech may be "fairly characterized as constituting speech on a matter of public concern." *Connick*, 461 U.S. at 146.[7] "Whether an employee's speech addresses a matter of public concern must be determined by the content, form, and context of a given statement, as revealed by the whole record." *Id.*, at 147-148. The District Court apparently found that McPherson's speech did not address a matter of public concern.[8] The Court of Appeals rejected this conclusion, finding that "the life and death of the President are obviously matters of public concern." 786 F.2d, at 1236. Our view of these determinations of the courts below is limited in this context by our constitutional obligation to assure that the record supports this conclusion: "we are compelled to examine for ourselves the statements in issue and the circumstances under which they [were] made to see whether or not they ... are of a character which the principles of the First Amendment, as adopted by the Due Process Clause of Fourteenth Amendment, protect.'" *Connick, supra*, at 150, n.10, quoting *Pennekamp v. Florida*, 328 U.S. 331, 335 (1946) (footnote omitted).

Considering the statement in context, as *Connick* requires, discloses that it plainly dealt with a matter of public concern. The statement was made in the course of a conversation addressing the policies of the President's administration. It came on the heels of a news bulletin regarding what is certainly a matter of heightened public attention: an attempt on the life of the President.[11] While a statement that amounted to a threat to kill the President would not be protected by the First Amendment, the District Court concluded, and we agree, that McPherson's statement did not amount to a threat punishable under 18 U.S.C. § 871(a) or 18 U.S.C. § 2385, or, indeed, that could properly be criminalized at all. See 786 F.2d, at 1235 ("A state would ... face considerable constitutional obstacles if it sought to criminalize the words that were uttered by McPherson on the day the President was shot"); see also Brief for United States as *Amicus Curiae* 8 ("we do not think that respondent's remark could be criminalized"); cf. *Watts v. United States*, 394 U.S. 705 (1969) (*per curiam*). The inappropriate or controversial character of a statement is irrelevant to the question whether it deals with a matter of public concern. "[D]ebate on public issues should be uninhibited, robust, and wide-open, and ... may well include vehement, caustic, and sometimes unpleasantly sharp attacks on government and

---

[7] Even where a public employee's speech does not touch upon a matter of public concern, that speech is not "totally beyond the protection of the First Amendment," *Connick v. Myers*, 461 U.S., at 147, but "absent the most unusual circumstances a federal court is not the appropriate forum in which to review the wisdom of a personnel decision taken by a public agency allegedly in reaction to the employee's behavior." *Ibid*.

[8] The District Court, after its second hearing in this case, delivered its opinion from the bench and did not explicitly address the elements of the required balancing test. It did, however, state that the case was "not like the *Myers* case where Ms. Myers was trying to comment upon the internal affairs of the office, or matters upon public concern. I don't think it is a matter of public concern to approve even more to the second attempt at assassination." ...

[11] The private nature of the statement does not, contrary to the suggestion of the United States, Brief for United States as *Amicus Curiae* 18, vitiate the status of the statement as addressing a matter of public concern. See *Givhan v. Western Line Consolidated School Dist.*, 439 U.S. 410, 414-416 (1979).

public officials." *New York Times Co. v. Sullivan,* 376 U.S. 254, 270 (1964); see also *Bond v. Floyd,* 385 U.S. 116, 136 (1966): "Just as erroneous statements must be protected to give freedom of expression the breathing space it needs to survive, so statements criticizing public policy and the implementation of it must be similarly protected."

B. Because McPherson's statement addressed a matter of public concern, *Pickering* next requires that we balance McPherson's interest in making her statement against "the interest of the State, as an employer, in promoting the efficiency of the public services it performs through its employees." 391 U.S., at 568. The State bears a burden of justifying the discharge on legitimate grounds. *Connick,* 461 U.S., at 150.

In performing the balancing, the statement will not be considered in a vacuum; the manner, time, and place of the employee's expression are relevant, as is the context in which the dispute arose. See *Connick, supra,* at 152-153; *Givhan v. Western Line Consolidated School Dist.,* 439 U.S. 410, 415, n.4 (1979). We have previously recognized as pertinent considerations whether the statement impairs discipline by superiors or harmony among coworkers, has a detrimental impact on close working relationships for which personal loyalty and confidence are necessary, or impedes the performance of the speaker's duties or interferes with the regular operation of the enterprise. *Pickering,* 391 U.S., at 570-573.

These considerations, and indeed the very nature of the balancing test, make apparent that the state interest element of the test focuses on the effective functioning of the public employer's enterprise. Interference with work, personnel relationships, or the speaker's job performance can detract from the public employer's function; avoiding such interference can be a strong state interest. From this perspective, however, petitioner fails to demonstrate a state interest that outweighs McPherson's First Amendment rights. While McPherson's statement was made at the workplace, there is no evidence that it interfered with the efficient functioning of the office. The constable was evidently not afraid that McPherson had disturbed or interrupted other employees — he did not inquire to whom respondent had made the remark and testified that he "was not concerned who she had made it to." In fact, Constable Rankin testified that the possibility of interference with the functions of the Constable's office had *not* been a consideration in his discharge of respondent and that he did not even inquire whether the remark had disrupted the work of the office.

Nor was there any danger that McPherson had discredited the office by making her statement in public. McPherson's speech took place in an area to which there was ordinarily no public access; her remark was evidently made in a private conversation with another employee. There is no suggestion that any member of the general public was present or heard McPherson's statement. Nor is there any evidence that employees other than Jackson who worked in the room even heard the remark. Not only was McPherson's discharge unrelated to the functioning of the office, it was not based on any assessment by the constable that the remark demonstrated a character trait that made respondent unfit to perform her work.

While the facts underlying Rankin's discharge of McPherson are, despite extensive proceedings in the District Court, still somewhat unclear, it is undisputed that he fired McPherson based on the *content* of her speech. Evidently because McPherson had made the statement, and because the constable believed that she "meant it," he decided that she was not a suitable employee to have in a law enforcement agency. But in weighing the State's interest in discharging an employee based on any claim that the content of a statement made by the employee somehow undermines the mission of the public employer, some attention must be paid to the responsibilities of the employee within the agency. The burden of caution employees bear with respect to the words they speak will vary with the extent of authority and public accountability the employee's role entails. Where, as here, an employee serves no confidential, policymaking, or public contact role, the danger to the agency's successful function from that employee's private speech is minimal. We cannot believe that every employee in Constable Rankin's office, whether computer operator, electrician, or file clerk, is equally required, on pain of discharge, to avoid any statement susceptible of being interpreted by the Constable as an indication that the employee may be unworthy of employment in his law enforcement agency.[17] At some point, such concerns are so removed from the effective function of the public employer that they cannot prevail over the free speech rights of the public employee.

This is such a case. McPherson's employment-related interaction with the Constable was apparently negligible. Her duties were purely clerical and were limited solely to the civil process function of the constable's office. There is no indication that she would ever be in a position to further — or indeed to have any involvement with — the minimal law enforcement activity engaged in by the constable's office. Given the function of the agency, McPherson's position in the office, and the nature of her statement, we are not persuaded that Rankin's interest in discharging her outweighed her rights under the First Amendment.

Because we agree with the Court of Appeals that McPherson's discharge was improper, the judgment of the Court of Appeals is

Affirmed.

JUSTICE POWELL, concurring....

There is no dispute that McPherson's comment was made during a private conversation with a co-worker who happened also to be her boyfriend. She had no intention or expectation that it would be overheard or acted on by others. Given this, I think it is unnecessary to engage in the extensive analysis normally required by *Connick v. Myers,* 461 U.S. 138 (1983), and *Pickering v. Board of Education,* 391 U.S. 563 (1968). If a statement is on a matter of public concern, as it was here, it will be an unusual case where the employer's legitimate interests will be so great as to justify punishing an employee for this type of private speech that routinely takes place at all levels in the workplace. The risk that a single, offhand comment directed to only one other worker will lower morale, disrupt the work force, or otherwise undermine the mission of the office borders on the fanciful. To the extent that the full constitutional analysis of the competing interests is required, I generally agree with the Court's opinion....

---

[17] We therefore reject the notion, expressed by petitioner's counsel at oral argument, that the fact that an employee was deputized meant, regardless of that employee's job responsibility, that the Constable could discharge the employee for any expression inconsistent with the goals of a law enforcement agency....

JUSTICE SCALIA, with whom the THE CHIEF JUSTICE, JUSTICE WHITE, and JUSTICE O'CONNOR join, dissenting.

I agree with the proposition, felicitously put by Constable Rankin's counsel, that no law enforcement agency is required by the First Amendment to permit one of its employees to "ride with the cops and cheer for the robbers." The issue in this case is whether Constable Rankin, a law enforcement official, is prohibited by the First Amendment from preventing his employees from saying of the attempted assassination of President Reagan — on the job and within hearing of other employees — "If they go for him again, I hope they get him." The Court, applying the two-prong analysis of *Connick v. Myers,* 461 U.S. 138 (1983), holds that McPherson's statement was protected by the First Amendment because (1) it "addressed a matter of public concern," and (2) McPherson's interest in making the statement outweighs Rankin's interest in suppressing it. In so doing, the Court significantly and irrationally expands the definition of "public concern"; it also carves out a new and very large class of employees — i.e., those in "nonpolicymaking" positions — who, if today's decision is to be believed, can never be disciplined for statements that fall within the court's expanded definition. Because I believe the Court's conclusions rest upon a distortion of both the record and the Court's prior decisions, I dissent.

I

. . . .

Specifically, we have held that the First Amendment's protection against adverse personnel decisions extends only to speech on matters of "public concern," *Connick, supra,* at 147-149, which we have variously described as those matters dealing in some way with "the essence of self-government," *Garrison v. Louisiana,* 379 U.S. 64, 74-75 (1964), matters as to which "free and open debate is vital to informed decisionmaking by the electorate," *Pickering, supra,* at 571-572, and matters as to which "debate ... [must] be uninhibited, robust, and wide-open,'" *Dun & Bradstreet, Inc. v. Greenmoss Builders, Inc.,* 472 U.S. 749, 755 (1985) (plurality) (quoting *New York Times Co. v. Sullivan,* 376 U.S. 254, 270 (1964)). In short, speech on matters of public concern is that speech which lies "at the heart of the First Amendment's protection," *First Nat'l Bank v. Bellotti,* 435 U.S. 765, 776 (1978). If, but only if, an employee's speech falls within this category, a public employer seeking to abridge or punish it must show that the employee's interest is outweighed by the government's interest, "as an employer, in promoting the efficiency of the public services it performs through its employees." *Pickering, supra,* at 568.

McPherson fails this threshold requirement.... The District Judge rejected McPherson's argument that her statement was "mere political hyperbole," finding, to the contrary, that it was, "in context," "violent words." *McPherson v. Rankin,* 786 F.2d 1233, 1235 (CA5 1986). "This is not," he said, "the situation where one makes an idle threat to kill somone for not picking them [sic] up on time, or not picking up their [sic] clothes. It was more than that." *Ibid.* He ruled against McPherson at the conclusion of the second hearing because "I don't think it is a matter of public concern to approve even more to [sic] the second attempt at assassination."...

Given the meaning of the remark, there is no basis for the Court's suggestion that McPherson's criticisms of the President's policies that immediately preceded the remark can illuminate it in such fashion as to render it constitutionally protected. Those criticisms merely reveal the speaker's *motive* for expressing the desire that the next attempt on the President's life succeed, in the same way that a political assassin's remarks to his victim before pulling the trigger might reveal a motive for that crime. The majority's magical transformation of the *motive* for McPherson's statement into its *content* is as misguided as viewing a political assassination preceded by a harangue as nothing more than a strong denunciation of the victim's political views.

That McPherson's statement does not constitute speech on a matter of "public concern" is demonstrated by comparing it with statements that have been found to fit that description in prior decisions involving public employees. McPherson's statement is a far cry from the question by the assistant district attorney in *Connick* whether her co-workers "ever [felt] pressured to work in political campaigns," *Connick*, at 149; from the letter written by the public school teacher in *Pickering* criticizing the board of education's proposals for financing school construction, *Pickering*, at 556; from the legislative testimony of a state college teacher in *Perry v. Sindermann*, 408 U.S. 593, 595 (1972), advocating that a particular college be elevated to 4-year status; from the memorandum given by a teacher to a radio station in *Mt. Healthy City Board of Ed. v. Doyle*, 429 U.S. 274, 282 (1977), dealing with teacher dress and appearance; and from the complaints about school board policies and practices at issue in *Givhan v. Western Line Consolidated School Dist.*, 439 U.S. 410, 413 (1979). See *Connick*, at 145-146.

McPherson's statement is indeed so different from those that it is only one step removed from statements that we have previously held entitled to no First Amendment protection even in the nonemployment context — including assassination threats against the President (which are illegal under 18 U.S.C. § 871), see *Frohwerk v. United States*, 249 U.S. 204, 206 (1919); "'fighting words,'" *Chaplinsky v. New Hampshire*, 315 U.S. 568, 572 (1942); epithets or personal abuse, *Cantwell v. Connecticut*, 310 U.S. 296, 309-310 (1940); and advocacy of force or violence, *Harisiades v. Shaughnessy*, 342 U.S. 580, 591-592 (1952). A statement lying so near the category of completely unprotected speech cannot fairly be viewed as lying within the "heart" of the First Amendment's protection; it lies within the category of speech that can neither be characterized as speech on matters of public concern nor properly subject to criminal penalties, see *Connick*, at 147. Once McPherson stopped explicitly criticizing the President's policies and expressed a desire that he be assassinated, she crossed the line....

II

Even if I agreed that McPherson's statement was speech on a matter of "public concern," I would still find it unprotected. It is important to be clear on what the issue is in this part of the case. It is not, as the Court suggests, whether "Rankin's interest *in discharging* [McPherson] outweighed her rights under the First Amendment." (emphasis added). Rather, it is whether his interest in preventing the expression of such statements in his agency outweighed her First Amendment interest in making the statement....

The Constable testified that he "was very concerned that this remark was made." Rightly so. As a law enforcement officer, the Constable obviously has a strong interest in preventing statements by any of his employees approving, or expressing a desire for, serious, violent crimes — regardless of whether the statements actually interfere with office operations at the time they are made or demonstrate character traits that made the speaker unsuitable for law enforcement work. In *Connick,* we upheld the dismissal of an assistant district attorney for circulating among her co-workers a questionnaire implicitly criticizing her superiors. Although we held that one of the questions — dealing with pressure in the office to participate in political campaigns — satisfied the "public concern" requirement, we held that the discharge nonetheless did not violate the First Amendment because the questionnaire itself "carrie[d] the clear potential for undermining office relations."...

The Court's sweeping assertion (and apparent holding) that where an employee "serves no confidential, policymaking, or public contact role, the danger to the agency's successful function from that employee's private speech is minimal," is simply contrary to reason and experience. Nonpolicymaking employees (the assistant district attorney in *Connick,* for example) can hurt working relationships and undermine public confidence in an organization every bit as much as policymaking employees. I, for one, do not look forward to the new First Amendment world the Court creates, in which nonpolicymaking employees of the Equal Employment Opportunity Commission must be permitted to make remarks on the job approving of racial discrimination, nonpolicymaking employees of the Selective Service System to advocate noncompliance with the draft laws, and (since it is really quite difficult to contemplate anything more absurd than the present case itself), nonpolicymaking constable's deputies to express approval for the assassination of the President....

NOTES

1. John Germann was a fire captain and IAFF local union president. In May of 1973, the fire chief sent him a letter objecting to the union's alleged attempt "to obstruct and alter the operation of the fire department." Germann replied in a letter which said that no one had "done as much as [the fire chief] to tear the fire department to shreds." It further suggested that the fire chief was a "liar" who had a "pitifully twisted outlook toward the employees in the department." The fire chief subsequently refused to promote Germann to battalion chief because of this bitter exchange. This decision was judicially sustained. Although Germann had addressed a matter of "public interest" in his letter to the fire chief, he had done so with such personal animosity that the fire chief could reasonably have questioned Germann's "loyalty and respect for him as fire chief and whether [Germann] would promote and implement department policy." *Germann v. Kansas City,* 776 F.2d 761 (8th Cir. 1985), *cert. denied,* 479 U.S. 813 (1986). See also *Boals v. Gray,* 775 F.2d 686 (6th Cir. 1985). Compare *Rode v. Dellarciprete,* 845 F.2d 1195 (3d Cir. 1988) (government employee's personal stake in employment dispute that involved matter of public concern did not cause loss of first amendment protection), with *Callaway v. Hafeman,* 832 F.2d 414 (7th Cir. 1987) (oral complaint to government employer regarding alleged sexual harassment not protected speech since not attempt to speak as citizen about matter of public concern). See also *American Postal Wkrs.*

Union v. Postal Serv., 830 F.2d 294 (D.C. Cir. 1987) (Postal Service interest in public confidence in confidentiality of mail did not outweigh union steward's protected interest in commenting upon political content of third class mail).

2. *Roberts v. Van Buren Pub. Schs.,* 773 F.2d 949 (8th Cir. 1985), concerned teacher grievances which expressed dissatisfaction with the manner in which parental complaints regarding student seating arrangements on a field trip had been handled. The court determined that these grievances did not involve speech protected by the first amendment, since they pertained to the internal relationship between the school principal and the teachers, as supervisor and subordinates, rather than to the school district's discharge of the public function of education. But cf. *Cox v. Dardanelle Pub. Sch. Dist.,* 790 F.2d 668 (8th Cir. 1986) (teacher grievance criticism of school policies pertaining to matter of public concern protected by first amendment); *Zamboni v. Stamler,* 847 F.2d 73 (3d Cir.), *cert. denied,* 109 S. Ct. 245 (1988) (employee statements opposing changes in personnel policies of county prosecutor's office constitute comments on matter of public concern protected by first amendment). See also *Johnsen v. Independent Sch. Dist. No. 3,* 891 F.2d 1485 (10th Cir. 1989) (comments on matter of public concern unprotected when needlessly disruptive of government authority).

3. In *James v. Board of Educ.,* 461 F.2d 566 (2d Cir.), *cert. denied,* 409 U.S. 1042 (1972), the court ruled that a school district could not constitutionally discipline a high school English teacher who wore a black armband in class as a symbolic protest against the Vietnam conflict, since the teacher's conduct did not disrupt classroom activities or engender student unrest. See also *Leonard v. City of Columbus,* 705 F.2d 1299 (11th Cir. 1983), extending first amendment protection to police officers who removed the flag from their uniform sleeves in violation of a city ordinance as a symbolic protest against racially discriminatory police department practices.

4. In *Tygrett v. Barry,* 627 F.2d 1279 (D.C. Cir. 1980), the court decided that the District of Columbia could not discharge a police officer who merely advocated the use of "blue flu" tactics by police personnel, since such discipline impermissibly infringed the employee's free speech privilege. But cf. *Brown v. Department of Transp.,* 735 F.2d 543 (Fed. Cir. 1984), which found that a Federal Aviation Administration supervisor's remarks at a PATCO meeting in support of illegally striking PATCO members were not constitutionally protected, since the interest of the FAA in promoting efficient public service during a national emergency outweighed the supervisor's free speech rights. See also *Federacion de Empleados v. Torres,* 747 F.2d 35 (1st Cir. 1984) (sustaining discipline of court employees who engaged in demonstration for higher pay during working hours in front of courthouse).

5. INS regulations require border inspectors to wear official uniforms and prohibit "all ornaments which are not part of the uniform." In *Immigration & Nat'n Serv. v. FLRA,* 855 F.2d 1454 (9th Cir. 1988), the court upheld the right of the INS to enforce this rule to preclude the wearing of union insignia on official uniforms.

6. While a statute may authorize the discharge of teachers who engage in public acts of homosexuality, it may not constitutionally permit the termination of teachers for "advocating, ... encouraging and promoting" public or private homosexual activity. See *NGTF v. Oklahoma City Bd. of Educ.,* 729 F.2d 1270 (10th Cir. 1984), *aff'd by an equally divided Court,* 470 U.S. 903 (1985). But cf. *Rowland v. Mad River Local Sch. Dist.,* 730 F.2d 444 (6th Cir. 1984), *cert. denied,* 105 S. Ct. 1373 (1985), which held that a school district had the right to terminate a high school counselor who disclosed the fact that she was bisexual, since her wholly personal disclosure, which involved no public concern, did not constitute protected speech.

7. In *Byrd v. Gain*, 558 F.2d 553 (9th Cir. 1977), *cert. denied*, 434 U.S. 1087 (1978), the court denied relief to two police officers who had received written reprimands following their issuance of a press release criticizing the police department's stop-and-frisk procedure because of its disparate impact upon Black male citizens. The court distinguished *Pickering* and related cases, stating that "substantial differences between the public interest in education and the public interest in safety and order justify a difference in the standards by which the respective institutions may protect themselves from attempted destruction by their employees." See *Hanneman v. Breier*, 528 F.2d 750 (7th Cir. 1976); *Gasparinetti v. Kerr*, 568 F.2d 311 (3d Cir. 1977), *cert. denied*, 436 U.S. 903 (1978). See also *Snepp v. United States*, 444 U.S. 507 (1980), wherein the Supreme Court recognized that employees of the CIA can have greater restrictions placed upon their freedom of expression than might be constitutionally appropriate with respect to government employees occupying less sensitive positions.

8. *Bush v. Lucas*, 462 U.S. 367 (1983), involved a NASA engineer who had been demoted as a result of public statements that were critical of his federal employer. Through Civil Service Commission review procedures, Bush had his demotion rescinded and obtained backpay. The Supreme Court decided that he could not prosecute a separate damage action against the supervisor who had demoted him in violation of his first amendment rights, since that claim arose out of an employment relationship that was governed by comprehensive procedural and substantive civil service provisions which provided federal personnel with meaningful remedies. The Court thus concluded that it would be inappropriate to supplement that congressionally established regulatory scheme with a new nonstatutory damage remedy. See also *Chappell v. Wallace*, 462 U.S. 296 (1983); *Spagnola v. Mathis*, 859 F.2d 223 (D.C. Cir. 1988).

9. In *Memphis Community Sch. Dist. v. Stachura*, 477 U.S. 299 (1986), the Court considered the scope of compensatory damages which may be awarded in a § 1983 action to an employee whose first amendment rights have been violated by his governmental employer.

> [C]ompensatory damages may include not only out-of-pocket loss and other monetary harms, but also such injuries as "impairment of reputation ..., personal humiliation, and mental anguish and suffering."... [However,] the abstract value of a constitutional right may not form the basis for § 1983 damages.

The Court thus ruled that a trial judge had erred when he instructed the jury to consider the abstract "value" and "importance" of the constitutional rights involved when it determined the amount of compensatory damages to award. See also *Vasbinder v. Almbach*, 926 F.2d 133 (2d Cir. 1991) (permitting punitive damages in egregious speech suppression cases).

In *Texas State Teachers Ass'n v. Garland Indep. Sch. Dist.*, 109 S. Ct. 1486 (1989), the Court held that a plaintiff in a section 1983 action need not prevail on the "central issue" to be entitled to an award of attorney fees under section 1988. The plaintiff need only prevail on "any significant issue" that materially alters the legal relationship between the parties. See also *Venegas v. Mitchell*, 110 S. Ct. 1679 (1990) (section 1988 does not invalidate contingent fee contract requiring plaintiff to pay attorney more than statutory award entered against defendant). In *Kay v. Ehrler*, 111 S. Ct. __ (1991), the Court held that lawyers who represent themselves in section 1983 actions are not entitled to attorney fee awards.

10. See generally J. Nowak, R. Rotunda & N. Young, Constitutional Law 1001-03 (1983); Allred, *From Connick to Confusion: The Struggle to Define Speech on Matters of Public Concern,* 64 Ind. L. J. 43 (1988); Note, *Nonpartisan Speech in the Police Department: The Aftermath of Pickering,* 7 Hastings Const. L.Q. 1001 (1980); Kaufman, *The Medium, the Message and the First Amendment,* 45 N.Y.U. L. Rev. 761 (1970).

MT. HEALTHY CITY SCHOOL DISTRICT BOARD OF EDUCATION v. DOYLE

429 U.S. 274, 97 S. Ct. 568, 50 L. Ed. 2d 471 (1977)

JUSTICE REHNQUIST delivered the opinion of the Court.

Respondent Doyle sued petitioner Mt. Healthy Board of Education in the United States District Court for the Southern District of Ohio. Doyle claimed that the Board's refusal to renew his contract in 1971 violated his rights under the First and Fourteenth Amendments to the United States Constitution. After a bench trial the District Court held that Doyle was entitled to reinstatement with backpay. The Court of Appeals for the Sixth Circuit affirmed the judgment, 529 F.2d 524, and we granted the Board's petition for certiorari, 425 U.S. 933, to consider an admixture of jurisdictional and constitutional claims....

[The Court initially disposed of several procedural questions.]

III

The District Court found it unnecessary to decide whether the Board was entitled to immunity from suit in the federal courts under the Eleventh Amendment, because it decided that any such immunity had been waived by Ohio statute and decisional law. In view of the treatment of waiver by a State of its Eleventh Amendment immunity from suit in *Ford Motor Co. v. Dept. of Treasury,* 323 U.S. 459, 464-466 (1945), we are less sure than was the District Court that Ohio had consented to suit against entities such as the Board in the federal courts. We prefer to address instead the question of whether such an entity had any Eleventh Amendment immunity in the first place, since if we conclude that it had none it will be unnecessary to reach the question of waiver.

The bar of the Eleventh Amendment to suit in federal courts extends to States and state officials in appropriate circumstances, *Edelman v. Jordan,* 415 U.S. 651 (1974); *Ford Motor Co. v. Dept. of Treasury, supra,* but does not extend to counties and similar municipal corporations. See *Lincoln County v. Luning,* 133 U.S. 529, 530 (1890); *Moore v. County of Alameda,* 411 U.S. 693, 717-721 (1973). The issue here thus turns on whether the Mt. Healthy Board of Education is to be treated as an arm of the State partaking of the State's Eleventh Amendment immunity, or is instead to be treated as a municipal corporation or other political subdivision to which the Eleventh Amendment does not extend. The answer depends, at least in part, upon the nature of the entity created by state law. Under Ohio law the "State" does not include "political subdivisions," and "political subdivisions" do include local school districts. Ohio Rev. Code Ann. § 2743.01 (Page Supp. 1975). Petitioner is but one of many local school boards within the State of Ohio. It is subject to some guidance from the State Board of Education, Ohio Rev. Code Ann. § 3301.07 (Page 1972 and Supp. 1975), and receives a significant amount of money from the State. Ohio Rev. Code Ann. § 3317 (Page 1972 and Supp. 1975). But local school boards have extensive powers to issue bonds, Ohio Rev. Code Ann. § 133.27 (Page 1969), and to levy taxes within certain restrictions of state law. Ohio Rev. Code Ann. §§ 5705.02, 5705.03, 5705.192, 5705.194 (Page 1973 and Supp. 1975). On balance, the record before us indicates that a local school board such as petitioner is more like a county or city than it is like an arm of the State. We therefore hold that it was not entitled to assert any Eleventh Amendment immunity from suit in the federal courts.

IV

Having concluded that respondent's complaint sufficiently pleaded jurisdiction under 28 U.S.C. § 1331, that the Board has failed to preserve the issue whether that complaint stated a claim upon which relief could be granted against the Board, and that the Board is not immune from suit under the Eleventh Amendment, we now proceed to consider the merits of respondent's claim under the First and Fourteenth Amendments.

Doyle was first employed by the Board in 1966. He worked under one-year contracts for the first three years, and under a two-year contract from 1969 to 1971. In 1969 he was elected president of the Teachers' Association, in which position he worked to expand the subjects of direct negotiation between the Association and the Board of Education. During Doyle's one-year term as president of the Association, and during the succeeding year when he served on its executive committee, there was apparently some tension in relations between the Board and the Association.

Beginning early in 1970, Doyle was involved in several incidents not directly connected with his role in the Teachers' Association. In one instance, he engaged in an argument with another teacher which culminated in the other teacher's slapping him. Doyle subsequently refused to accept an apology and insisted upon some punishment for the other teacher. His persistence in the matter resulted in the suspension of both teachers for one day, which was followed by a walkout by a number of other teachers, which in turn resulted in the lifting of the suspensions.

On other occasions, Doyle got into an argument with employees of the school cafeteria over the amount of spaghetti which had been served him; referred to students, in connection with a disciplinary complaint, as "sons of bitches"; and made an obscene gesture to two girls in connection with their failure to obey commands made in his capacity as cafeteria supervisor. Chronologically the last in the series of incidents which respondent was involved in during his employment by the Board was a telephone call by him to a local radio station. It was the Board's consideration of this incident which the court below found to be a violation of the First and Fourteenth Amendments.

In February 1971, the principal circulated to various teachers a memorandum relating to teacher dress and appearance, which was apparently prompted by the view of some in the administration that there was a relationship between teacher appearance and public support for bond issues. Doyle's response to the receipt of the memorandum — on a subject which he apparently understood was to be settled by joint teacher-administration action — was to convey the substance of the memorandum to a disc jockey at WSAI, a Cincinnati radio station, who promptly announced the adoption of the dress code as a news item. Doyle subsequently apologized to the principal, conceding that he should have made some prior communication of his criticism to the school administration.

Approximately one month later the superintendent made his customary annual recommendations to the Board as to the rehiring of nontenured teachers. He recommended that Doyle not be rehired. The same recommendation was made with respect to nine other teachers in the district, and in all instances, including Doyle's, the recommendation was adopted by the Board. Shortly after being notified of this decision, respondent requested a statement of reasons for the Board's actions. He received a statement citing "a notable lack of tact in handling professional matters which leaves much doubt as to your sincerity in establishing good school relationships." That general statement was followed by references to the radio station incident and to the obscene-gesture incident.[1]

The District Court found that all of these incidents had in fact occurred. It concluded that respondent Doyle's telephone call to the radio station was "clearly protected by the First Amendment," and that because it had played a "substantial part" in the decision of the Board not to renew Doyle's employment, he was entitled to reinstatement with backpay. Pet. for Cert., App. 12a-13a. The District Court did not expressly state what test it was applying in determining that the incident in question involved conduct protected by the First Amendment, but simply held that the communication to the radio station was such conduct. The Court of Appeals affirmed in a brief *per curiam* opinion. 529 F.2d 524.

Doyle's claims under the First and Fourteenth Amendments are not defeated by the fact that he did not have tenure. Even though he could have been discharged for no reason whatever, and had no constitutional right to a hearing prior to the decision not to rehire him, *Board of Regents v. Roth,* 408 U.S. 564 (1972), he may nonetheless establish a claim to reinstatement if the decision not to rehire him was made by reason of his exercise of constitutionally protected First Amendment freedoms. *Perry v. Sindermann,* 408 U.S. 593 (1972).

That question of whether speech of a government employee is constitutionally protected expression necessarily entails striking "a balance between the interests of the teacher, as a citizen, in commenting upon matters of public concern and the interest of the State, as an employer, in promoting the efficiency of the public services it performs through its employees." *Pickering v. Board of Education,* 391 U.S. 563, 568 (1968). There is no suggestion by the

---

[1]"I. You have shown a notable lack of tact in handling professional matters which leaves much doubt as to your sincerity in establishing good school relationships.

"A. You assumed the responsibility to notify W.S.A.I. Radio Station in regards to the suggestion of the Board of Education that teachers establish an appropriate dress code for professional people. This raised much concern not only within this community, but also in neighboring communities.

"B. You used obscene gestures to correct students in a situation in the cafeteria causing considerable concern among those students present.

"Sincerely yours,
"Rex Ralph
"Superintendent"

Board that Doyle violated any established policy, or that its reaction to his communication to the radio station was anything more than an *ad hoc* response to Doyle's action in making the memorandum public. We therefore accept the District Court's finding that the communication was protected by the First and Fourteenth Amendments. We are not, however, entirely in agreement with that court's manner of reasoning from this finding to the conclusion that Doyle is entitled to reinstatement with backpay.

The District Court made the following "conclusions" on this aspect of the case:

"1) If a non-permissible reason, e.g., exercise of First Amendment rights, played a substantial part in the decision not to renew — even in the face of other permissible grounds — the decision may not stand (citations omitted).

"2) A non-permissible reason did play a substantial part. That is clear from the letter of the Superintendent immediately following the Board's decision, which stated two reasons — the one, the conversation with the radio station clearly protected by the First Amendment. A court may not engage in any limitation of First Amendment rights based on 'tact' — that is not to say that the 'tactfulness' is irrelevant to other issues in this case." Pet. for Cert., App. 12a-13a.

At the same time, though, it stated that

"[i]n fact, as this Court sees it and finds, both the Board and the Superintendent were faced with a situation in which there did exist in fact reason ... independent of any First Amendment rights or exercise thereof, to not extend tenure." *Id.*, at 12a.

Since respondent Doyle had no tenure, and there was therefore not even a state-law requirement of "cause" or "reason" before a decision could be made not to renew his employment, it is not clear what the District Court meant by this latter statement. Clearly the Board legally *could* have dismissed respondent had the radio station incident never come to its attention. One plausible meaning of the court's statement is that the Board and the Superintendent not only could, but in fact *would* have reached that decision had not the constitutionally protected incident of the telephone call to the radio station occurred. We are thus brought to the issue whether, even if that were the case, the fact that the protected conduct played a "substantial part" in the actual decision not to renew would necessarily amount to a constitutional violation justifying remedial action. We think that it would not.

A rule of causation which focuses solely on whether protected conduct played a part, "substantial" or otherwise, in a decision not to rehire, could place an employee in a better position as a result of the exercise of constitutionally protected conduct than he would have occupied had he done nothing. The difficulty with the rule enunciated by the District Court is that it would require reinstatement in cases where a dramatic and perhaps abrasive incident is inevitably on the minds of those responsible for the decision to rehire, and does indeed play a part in that decision — even if the same decision would have been reached had the incident not occurred. The constitutional principle at stake is sufficiently vindicated if such an employee is placed in no worse a position than if he had not engaged in the conduct. A borderline or marginal candidate should not have the employment question resolved against him because of constitutionally protected conduct. But that same candidate ought not to be able, by engaging in such conduct, to prevent his employer from assessing his performance record and reaching a decision not to rehire on the basis of that record, simply because the protected conduct makes the employer more certain of the correctness of its decision.

This is especially true where, as the District Court observed was the case here, the current decision to rehire will accord "tenure." The long-term consequences of an award of tenure are of great moment both to the employee and to the employer. They are too significant for us to hold that the Board in this case would be precluded, because it considered constitutionally protected conduct in deciding not to rehire Doyle, from attempting to prove to a trier of fact that quite apart from such conduct Doyle's record was such that he would not have been rehired in any event.

In other areas of constitutional law, this Court has found it necessary to formulate a test of causation which distinguishes between a result caused by a constitutional violation and one not so caused. We think those are instructive in formulating the test to be applied here.

In *Lyons v. Oklahoma,* 322 U.S. 596 (1944), the Court held that even though the first confession given by a defendant had been involuntary, the Fourteenth Amendment did not prevent the State from using a second confession obtained 12 hours later if the coercion surrounding the first confession had been sufficiently dissipated as to make the second confession voluntary. In *Wong Sun v. United States,* 371 U.S. 471, 491 (1963), the Court was willing to assume that a defendant's arrest had been unlawful, but held that "the connection between the arrest and the statement [given several days later] had 'become so attenuated as to dissipate the taint.' *Nardone v. United States,* 308 U.S. 338, 341." *Parker v. North Carolina,* 397 U.S. 790, 796 (1970), held that even though a confession be assumed to have been involuntary in the constitutional sense of the word, a guilty plea entered over a month later met the test for the voluntariness of such a plea. The Court in *Parker* relied on the same quoted language from *Nardone, supra,* as did the Court in *Wong Sun, supra.* While the type of causation on which the taint cases turn may differ somewhat from that which we apply here, those cases do suggest that the proper test to apply in the present context is one which likewise protects against the invasion of constitutional rights without commanding undesirable consequences not necessary to the assurance of those rights.

Initially, in this case, the burden was properly placed upon respondent to show that his conduct was constitutionally protected, and that this conduct was a "substantial factor" — or, to put it in other words, that it was a "motivating factor"[2] in the Board's decision not to rehire him. Respondent having carried that burden, however, the District Court should have gone on to determine whether the Board had shown by a preponderance of the evidence that it would have reached the same decision as to respondent's reemployment even in the absence of the protected conduct.

---

[2]See *Village of Arlington Heights v. Metropolitan Housing Development Corp.* [429 U.S.], at 270-271, n. 21.

We cannot tell from the District Court opinion and conclusions, nor from the opinion of the Court of Appeals affirming the judgment of the District Court, what conclusion those courts would have reached had they applied this test. The judgment of the Court of Appeals is therefore vacated, and the case remanded for further proceedings consistent with this opinion.

So ordered.

NOTES

1. The Court's opinion in *Mt. Healthy* does not consider the possible chilling effect that a public employer's action might have on other employees. Should it matter that other employees might be inhibited in exercising their first amendment rights in the future? How can this danger be mitigated?

2. Where an employee's protected conduct is inextricably linked to allegedly unprotected behavior, it will frequently be difficult for the affected governmental employer to demonstrate satisfactorily that it would have discharged the worker even in the absence of the protected activity. See *Hickman v. Valley Local Sch. Dist.,* 619 F.2d 606 (6th Cir. 1980). But cf. *Reichert v. Draud,* 701 F.2d 1168 (6th Cir. 1983) (finding that defendant school board satisfied *Mt. Healthy* standard).

6. REGULATION OF THE PRIVATE LIVES OF PUBLIC EMPLOYEES

PADULA v. WEBSTER

822 F.2d 97 (D.C. Cir. 1987)

SILBERMAN, CIRCUIT JUDGE:

Appellant Margaret A. Padula alleges that the Federal Bureau of Investigation ("FBI" or "Bureau") refused to employ her as a special agent because of her homosexuality, in violation of both Bureau policy and the equal protection guarantee of the Constitution....

The FBI's policy towards employing homosexuals has been in some flux. Eight years ago, the Bureau formally represented to this court that it "has always had an absolute policy of dismissing proven or admitted homosexuals from its employ." *Ashton v. Civiletti,* 613 F.2d 923, 926 (D.C. Cir. 1979). Two months later, FBI Director Webster issued a somewhat different formulation of the Bureau's position toward homosexuality:

> Now we treat it as a factor, and I must say in candor, it's a significant factor. It's a troublesome thing; I hope that the particular case will be handled with fairness and justice and I hope that at some point we will have a better understanding of the problem and the policy that should be addressed to it.

Id. at 927 n. 5.

Several law schools, concerned with possible discrimination toward their homosexual students during the job recruitment season, requested clarification of the FBI's policy. John Mintz, an Assistant Director of the FBI and the FBI's Legal Counsel, assumed responsibility for answering these queries. On July 31,

1980, he wrote to Professor Marina Angel of the Temple University School of Law that:

> The FBI's focus in personnel matters has been and continues to be on conduct rather than status or preference and we carefully consider the facts in each case to determine whether the conduct may affect the employment. At the same time, we recognize individual privacy rights of applicants and employees.

In other letters to law school officials, Mintz stated that "individual sexual orientation, whether homosexual or heterosexual, may involve secret conduct that is relevant to employment in the FBI in that it increases employee susceptibility to compromise or breach of trust." He added, however, that "we are confident that the FBI has not engaged in improper discrimination regarding sexual orientation." Mintz also assured one law school dean that administrative action is taken not "simply because of ... sexual orientation" but homosexual conduct is a significant factor in such decisions. When pressed for clarification, Mintz conceded that

> in fairness ... based upon experience, I can offer no specific encouragement that a homosexual applicant will be found who satisfies all of the requirements.... In any event, each case is reviewed independently for an objective determination of suitability.

In the summer of 1982, Padula applied for a position as a special agent with the FBI. On the basis of a written examination and an interview, the FBI ranked her 39th out of 303 qualified female applicants and 279th out of 1273 male and female applicants. Following these screening tests, the FBI conducted a routine background check. In addition to revealing favorable information about the applicant's abilities and character, the background investigation disclosed that appellant is a practicing homosexual. At a follow-up interview, Padula confirmed that she is a homosexual — explaining that although she does not flaunt her sexual orientation, she is unembarrassed and open about it and it is a fact well known to her family, friends and co-workers.

On October 19, 1983, the Bureau notified Padula that it was unable to offer her a position; her subsequent attempt to obtain reconsideration of the decision was denied. It was explained to her that her application had been evaluated in the same manner as all others, but had been rejected due to intense competition. Seventeen months later, Padula filed suit in the United States District Court for the District of Columbia. She alleged the FBI's decision not to hire her was based solely on the fact that she was a homosexual and that this decision violated the Bureau's "stated policy" not to discriminate on the basis of an applicant's sexual orientation. She also charged that the decision violated her constitutional rights to privacy, equal protection and due process under the first, fourth, fifth and ninth amendments to the Constitution.

In a memorandum opinion and order issued on November 15, 1985, the district court granted the FBI's motion for summary judgment. The court found that the FBI had not adopted a binding policy regarding the hiring of homosexuals and that it therefore was free to determine on a case-by-case basis whether to hire a particular homosexual applicant. In reaching this decision, the court examined various FBI memoranda and letters unearthed by Padula during discovery. Addressing the constitutional claim, the court found that the challenged classification of homosexuals need only satisfy a "minimum standard of rationality," a standard the court held was "clearly met in this case."...

Padula alleges that the FBI refused to hire her solely because of her homosexuality and that this action denied her the equal protection of the law guaranteed by the fourteenth amendment.[5] She urges us to recognize homosexuality as a suspect or quasi-suspect classification. A suspect classification is subjected to strict scrutiny and will be sustained only if "suitably tailored to serve a compelling state interest." *City of Cleburne v. Cleburne Living Center,* 473 U.S. 432 (1985), whereas under heightened scrutiny given to a quasi-suspect class, the challenged classification must be "substantially related to a legitimate state interest." *Mills v. Habluetzel,* 456 U.S. 91, 99 (1982).

We perceive ostensible disagreement between the parties as to the description of the class in question. The government insists the FBI's hiring policy focuses only on homosexual conduct, not homosexual status. By that, we understand the government to be saying that it would not consider relevant for employment purposes homosexual orientation that did *not* result in homosexual conduct. Plaintiff rejects that distinction, suggesting that "homosexual status is accorded to people who engage in homosexual conduct, and people who engage in homosexual conduct are accorded homosexual status." But whether or not homosexual status attaches to someone who does not — for whatever reason — engage in homosexual conduct, appellant does not claim those circumstances apply to her. The parties' definitional disagreement is therefore irrelevant to this case. The issue presented us is only whether homosexuals, when defined as persons who engage in homosexual conduct, constitute a suspect or quasi-suspect classification and accordingly whether the FBI's hiring decision is subject to strict or heightened scrutiny.

The Supreme Court has used several explicit criteria to identify suspect and quasi-suspect classifications. In *San Antonio School Dist. v. Rodriguez,* 411 U.S. 1 (1973), the Court stated that a suspect class is one "saddled with such disabilities, or subjected to such a history of purposeful unequal treatment, or relegated to such a position of political powerlessness as to command extraordinary protection from the majoritarian political process." *Id.* at 28. The immutability of the group's identifying trait is also a factor to be considered. *See Frontiero v. Richardson,* 411 U.S. 677, 686 (1973). However, the Supreme Court has recognized only three classifications as suspect: race, *Loving v. Virginia,* 388 U.S. 1, 11 (1967), alienage, *Graham v. Richardson,* 403 U.S. 365, 372 (1971); but see *Ambach v. Norwick,* 441 U.S. 68, 72-75 (1979), and national origin, *Korematsu v. United States,* 323 U.S. 214, 216 (1944); and two others as quasi-suspect: gender, *Mississippi University for Women v. Hogan,* 458 U.S. 718, 723-24 (1982), and illegitimacy, *Lalli v. Lalli,* 439 U.S. 259, 265 (1978). Appellant, asserting that homosexuals meet all the requisite criteria, would have us add homosexuality to that list. Appellees, on the other hand, contend that two re-

---

[5] The equal protection component of the fourteenth amendment is binding upon the federal government as part of the fifth amendment's due process clause. See *Bolling v. Sharpe,* 347 U.S. 497, 499 (1954). Our analysis is governed by the Supreme Court's general approach of treating "Fifth Amendment equal protection claims ... precisely the same as equal protection claims under the Fourteenth Amendment." *Weinberger v. Wiesenfeld,* 420 U.S. 636, 638 n.2 (1975).

cent cases, *Bowers v. Hardwick,* — U.S. —, 106 S. Ct. 2841 (1986) and *Dronenburg v. Zech,* 741 F.2d 1388 (D.C. Cir. 1984), are insurmountable barriers to appellant's claim. We agree.

In *Dronenburg,* a naval petty officer claimed violation of his constitutional rights to privacy and to equal protection of the laws because he was discharged from the Navy for engaging in homosexual conduct. A panel of this court rejected the claim, holding that "we can find no constitutional right to engage in homosexual conduct and, … as judges, we have no warrant to create one." *Id.* at 1397. Although the court's opinion focused primarily on whether the constitutional right to privacy protected homosexual conduct, the court reasoned that if the right to privacy did not provide protection "then appellant's right to equal protection is not infringed unless the Navy's policy is not rationally related to a permissible end." *Id.* at 1391. The unique needs of the military, the court concluded, justified discharge for homosexual conduct. *Id.* at 1398.

Dronenburg anticipated by two years the Supreme Court's decision in *Hardwick,* in which the Court upheld a Georgia law criminalizing sodomy against a challenge that it violated the due process clause. In *Hardwick,* the Court explained that the right to privacy as defined in its previous decisions inheres only in family relationships, marriage and procreation and does not extend more broadly to all kinds of private sexual conduct between consenting adults. 106 S. Ct. at 2844. Putting the privacy precedent aside, the Court further concluded that a right to engage in consensual sodomy is not constitutionally protected as a fundamental right since it is neither "implicit in the concept of ordered liberty," *id.* at 2844 (quoting *Palko v. Connecticut,* 302 U.S. 319, 325-26 (1937)), nor "deeply rooted in this Nation's history and tradition." *Id.* (quoting *Moore v. East Cleveland,* 431 U.S. 494, 503 (1977) (opinion of Powell, J.)). Accordingly, the Court's review of the Georgia statute inquired only whether a rational basis for the law existed. And the Court determined that the presumed beliefs of the Georgia electorate that sodomy is immoral provide an adequate rationale for criminalizing such conduct. *Id.* at 2846.

Padula argues that both *Dronenburg* and *Hardwick* are inapposite because they addressed only the scope of the privacy right, not what level of scrutiny is appropriate under equal protection analysis. But as we have noted, *Dronenburg* did involve an equal protection claim. Although the court did not explicitly consider whether homosexuals should be treated as a suspect class, it seemed to regard that question settled by its conclusion that the Constitution does not afford a privacy right to engage in homosexual conduct. See 741 F.2d at 1391, 1398. In *Hardwick,* to be sure, plaintiffs did not rely on the equal protection clause, but after the Court rejected an extension of the right to privacy, it responded to plaintiffs' alternate argument that the Georgia law should be struck down as without rational basis (under the due process clause) since it was predicated merely on the moral judgment of a majority of the Georgia electorate. The Court summarily rejected that position, refusing to declare the Georgian majoritarian view "inadequate" to meet a rational basis test. *Hardwick,* 106 S. Ct. at 2846. We therefore think the courts' reasoning in *Hardwick* and *Dronenburg* forecloses appellant's efforts to gain suspect class status for practicing homosexuals. It would be quite anomolous, on its face, to declare status defined by conduct that states may constitutionally criminalize as deserving of strict scrutiny under the equal protection clause. More importantly, in all those cases in which the Supreme Court has accorded suspect or quasi-suspect status to a class, the Court's holding was predicated on an unarticulated, but necessarily implicit, notion that it is plainly unjustifiable (in accordance with standards not altogether clear to us) to discriminate invidiously against the particular class. E.g. compare *Frontiero v. Richardson,* 411 U.S. 677, 686-87 (1973) (statutory distinctions between the sexes often invidiously relegate women to inferior positions); with *Massachusetts Board of Retirement v. Murgia,* 427 U.S. 307, 313 (1976) (aged have not been subject to invidious discrimination justifying extra protection from the political process). If the Court was unwilling to object to state laws that criminalize the behavior that defines the class, it is hardly open to a lower court to conclude that state sponsored discrimination against the class is invidious. After all, there can hardly be more palpable discrimination against a class than making the conduct that defines the class criminal. Accord *Baker v. Wade,* 769 F.2d 289, 292 (5th Cir. 1985); *Rich v. Secretary of the Army,* 735 F.2d 1220, 1229 (10th Cir. 1984).

That does not mean, however, that any kind of negative state action against homosexuals would be constitutionally authorized. Laws or government practices must still, if challenged, pass the rational basis test of the equal protection clause. A governmental agency that discriminates against homosexuals must justify that discrimination in terms of some government purpose. Appellants did not specifically argue that the FBI's practices challenged here failed that lesser examination — perhaps because the Supreme Court in *Hardwick* rejected a similar rational basis argument under the due process clause. But assuming the argument is implicit in their equal protection challenge, we think it was squarely rejected in *Dronenburg.* In *Dronenburg,* the court held that it was rational for the Navy to conclude that homosexual conduct was detrimental to the maintenance of morale and discipline. 741 F.2d at 1398. The court observed that homosexuality "generate[s] dislike and disapproval among many ... who find it morally offensive," and, moreover, is criminalized in many states. *Id.*

The FBI, as the Bureau points out, is a national law enforcement agency whose agents must be able to work in all the states of the nation. To have agents who engage in conduct criminalized in roughly one-half of the states would undermine the law enforcement credibility of the Bureau. Perhaps more important, FBI agents perform counterintelligence duties that involve highly classified matters relating to national security. It is not irrational for the Bureau to conclude that the criminalization of homosexual conduct coupled with the general public opprobrium toward homosexuality exposes many homosexuals, even "open" homosexuals, to the risk of possible blackmail to protect their partners, if not themselves. We therefore conclude the Bureau's specialized functions, like the Navy's in *Dronenburg,* rationally justify consideration of homosexual conduct that could adversely affect that agency's responsibilities. The judgment of the district court is hereby

Affirmed.

NOTES

1. Contrast the *Padula v. Webster* holding with *Norton v. Macy,* 417 F.2d 1161 (D.C. Cir. 1969), wherein the court found that NASA had acted improperly when it terminated a GS-14 budget analyst who had made a homosexual advance to another individual. To sustain a discharge based upon homosexual conduct, a "reviewing court must at least be able to discern some reasonably foreseeable specific connection between [the] employee's potentially embarrassing conduct and the efficiency of the service." The court found no such employment nexus in the *Norton* case. In *Morrison v. State Bd. of Educ.,* 1 Cal. 3d 214, 461 P.2d 375 (1969), the court held that a school teacher could not be dismissed for a single homosexual act. The court noted that broad proscriptions against "immoral acts" would raise serious constitutional questions. "[S]chool officials concerned with enforcing such broad prohibitions might be inclined to probe into the private life of each and every teacher, no matter how exemplary his classroom conduct. Such prying might all too readily lead school officials to search for 'telltale signs' of immorality in violation of the teacher's constitutional rights." But cf. *NGTF v. Oklahoma City Bd. of Educ.,* 729 F.2d 1270 (10th Cir. 1984), *aff'd. by equally divided court,* 470 U.S. 903 (1985), indicating that a regulation may authorize the termination of teachers who engage in public homosexual acts.

2. In *Ben-Shalom v. Marsh,* 881 F.2d 454 (7th Cir. 1989), *cert. denied,* 110 S. Ct. 1296 (1990), the court sustained the constitutionality of an Army regulation precluding the re-enlistment of soldiers who are admitted homosexuals. See also *High Tech Gays v. Defense Indus. Sec. Clearance Office,* 895 F.2d 563 (9th Cir. 1990), wherein the court upheld a Defense Department policy subjecting homosexual applicants for secret and top secret industrial security clearance to more expansive investigations than other applicants, due to the legitimate governmental objective of reducing security risks.

3. Would it be unconstitutional for a government employer to refuse to hire or to discharge an individual who has undergone a sex change operation? See *Holloway v. Arthur Andersen & Co.,* 566 F.2d 659 (9th Cir. 1977) (finding no equal protection or due process violation).

4. See generally Sunstein, *Sexual Orientation and the Constitution: A Note on the Relationship Between Due Process and Equal Protection,* 55 U. Chi. L. Rev. 1161 (1988); Friedman, *Constitutional and Statutory Challenges to Discrimination in Employment Based on Sexual Orientation,* 64 Iowa L. Rev. 527 (1979). See also La Morte, *Legal Rights and Responsibilities of Homosexuals in Public Education,* 4 J.L. & Educ. 449 (1975).

CARTER v. UNITED STATES

407 F.2d 1238 (D.C. Cir. 1968)

LEVENTHAL, CIRCUIT JUDGE: Appellant Carter brought an action asserting that his discharge from Government service deprived him of statutory and constitutional rights. He appeals to this court on the ground that the District Court erred when it granted judgment in favor of the Government without a trial.

The facts shown on the record before us are these. Carter was hired by the Federal Bureau of Investigation (FBI) in 1960 as a clerk in its identification division. His employment with the Bureau was interrupted by his enlistment in the Air Force. After completing his military service in 1965 he was reinstated at his old job. In August 1965, the FBI received an anonymous letter complaining that Carter was "sleeping with young girls and carrying on." When questioned about the matter by his supervisor, Carter admitted that a female friend had twice stayed overnight at his apartment. He admitted that they slept together, although not nude, in the same bed, but insisted that they did not have sexual relations. He told his supervisor that the lady had been visiting Washington from out of town for a period of three days, that they had been going together for several years, and that he was seriously considering marriage. On one occasion she had visited at his home in Kentucky and stayed with his brother and sister-in-law....

Carter was dismissed by the FBI for "conduct unbecoming an employee of this Bureau." ... Carter sued for reinstatement and backpay, and served interrogatories. Without answering, the Government pressed a motion for summary judgment, which the District Court granted, holding that appellant was not entitled to a trial.

We affirm the District Court's ruling that Carter had no statutory rights to employment under the Civil Service laws or the Veterans Preference Act. However we cannot agree with the District Court's conclusion that Carter was not entitled to a trial to determine whether the discharge violated Section 9(c) of the Universal Military Training and Service Act, 50 U.S.C. App. § 459(c) (1964). We do not rule on appellant's claim of unconstitutional arbitrariness.[4]

Because of the exemption of the FBI from the civil service laws, the Bureau is generally free to discharge its employees for any reasons it chooses, subject only to constitutional limitations. Obviously, however, that discretion is subject to any specific limitations that Congress has chosen to impose. This much is conceded by appellee. Thus, like any other employer, the FBI is subject to the provisions of § 9(c) of the Universal Military Training and Service Act by which Congress granted special rights and protections to the returning veteran: the right to reinstatement in the civilian job he held prior to military service; the right to be free in the first year after resumption of civilian life from discharge for other than "cause."

The law giving a returning veteran a right to be free of discharge except for "cause" puts on the employer the burden of coming forward with a cause sufficient to justify the discharge....

2. The FBI asserts that it had "cause" to dismiss Carter. Essentially the contention is that any FBI employee would be fired for this conduct, and the application of a general FBI personnel policy which does not discriminate against veterans must be upheld unless so arbitrary as to violate due process.

A private employer may have the right, in the absence of statute or contract to the contrary, to fire an employee for personal reasons, unrelated to job function, that appeal to the employer, the color of hair, a dislike of men who smoke, or have a tattoo, etc. That does not mean that the employer can fire a returning veteran for the same reason as constituting "cause." ...

3. The "cause" provision was inserted by Congress to provide the reemployed veteran with a protection of reasonableness similar to that enjoyed by a union

[4] It seems plain to us that no discharge could be for "cause" within the meaning of § 9(c) if it were so arbitrary and unreasonable as to violate due process. We therefore need not reach constitutional questions in this case.

member protected by provisions in a collective bargaining agreement limiting discharge to cause. The ultimate criterion, whether the employer acted reasonably, is the one generally applied where an employment contract is terminated by an employer because of employee misconduct, and that standard is appropriate under this Federal statute. *Kemp v. John Chattillon & Sons,* 169 F.2d 203 (3rd Cir. 1948). We think a discharge may be upheld as one for "cause" only if it meets two criteria of reasonableness: one, that it is reasonable to discharge employees because of certain conduct, and the other, that the employee had fair notice, express or fairly implied, that such conduct would be ground for discharge....

... The District Judge granted summary judgment on the ground that regardless of whether Carter's action was moral or immoral, he had been indiscreet in carrying on his relationship. The Government's brief also treats the nexus of the case as including: "that appellant's sexual misadventures had become sufficiently public knowledge to cause an anonymous complaint to the FBI" (p. 15).

That theory is not maintainable on the present record so as to support summary judgment without a trial. The only conduct before us on this record was limited to two occasions, and in Carter's own apartment. There is no suggestion here that Carter was notoriously promiscuous, consorted with prostitutes or anything of that sort. Certainly Carter's admitted conduct cannot be equated with that generally "loose" conduct likely to become a matter of public notoriety. The only basis for inferences as to the extent to which Carter's conduct was known outside the circle of his roommates — also employed by the FBI — is an anonymous letter. The letter does not indicate how the writer came to know of Carter's acts....

The FBI may well have made an informed appraisal, or investigation, that permitted it to ascertain that Carter so conducted himself as to turn a private relationship into a public affront. But that is a question of fact and Carter is entitled to a trial of that fact.

We turn to the issue whether "cause" for discharge was established as a matter of law by Carter's admitted overnight "necking" and "petting" with his young lady in his apartment on two occasions....

Appellant's counsel point out that Carter did nothing more than the "bundling" condoned in Puritan New England. As for more modern precedent, the law is clear that an unmarried man does not have an "immoral" character for purposes of exclusion from citizenship even if he goes beyond necking and engages in heterosexual relations. Judge Learned Hand pointed out, "we have answered in the negative the question whether an unmarried man must live completely celibate, or forfeit his claim to a 'good moral character.'" *Schmidt v. United States,* 177 F.2d 450, 452 (2d Cir. 1949).

3. The Government's motion put before the court, as an exhibit, the Handbook for FBI Employees, distributed to all FBI employees. We consider whether that Handbook shows that Carter was put on notice that his admitted conduct was prohibited. The Handbook is a description of the FBI and its work, as well as a "guide" to "help you refrain from doing anything which would in any way detract from the Bureau's reputation or embarrass it in any manner." The sole relevant passage is one stating — "personal misbehavior of Bureau

employees reflecting unfavorably upon them or the Bureau, and neglect of duty cannot be tolerated."

The Government invokes the standard of the lady from Dubuque and argues that as the FBI relies on the cooperation of the citizenry it is reasonable to compel moral standards for all employees — clerks as well as agents — that would satisfy that most upright lady. Pretermitting the issue whether the standard of the lady from Dubuque would have been reasonable if announced, there is a threshold problem, whether the employees have adequate notice of such a standard. The FBI employees are expressly told in the Handbook that legal gambling is permitted, as is off-duty use of intoxicants, yet these sit poorly with many upright citizens. We do not think a court can deny an employee a trial of the issue on the ground that this Handbook clearly puts FBI employees on notice that they must meet not only the general standards of their own community, but also the special standards of the lady from Dubuque....

... The question is whether the limitation on private life now asserted to apply to all FBI employees is something the average FBI clerical employee should and does know as contemplated by "ordinarily expected standards of personal conduct." We cannot say that the answer is so clear that Carter is not even entitled to a trial....

The order of the District Court is vacated and the case remanded for further proceedings.

So ordered.

DANAHER, CIRCUIT JUDGE (dissenting): ...

This court on many occasions has recognized the principle that the power to remove inferior Government employees is an incident of the power to appoint them, following the statement in *Myers v. United States,* 272 U.S. 52, 161 (1925). Put another way the interest of a Government employee in retaining his job can be summarily denied. "It has become a settled principle that government employment, in the absence of legislation, can be revoked at the will of the appointing officer." *Cafeteria and Restaurant Workers, etc. v. McElroy,* 367 U.S. 886, 896 (1961); *Vitarelli v. Seaton,* 359 U.S. 535, 539 (1959). No matter who has stated the law, no one has said it better than Mr. Justice Reed speaking for the Court of Claims in *Batchelor v. United States,* 169 Ct. Cl. 180, 183, *cert. denied,* 382 U.S. 870 (1965), where we read:

> "The Supreme Court in *Keim v. United States,* 177 U.S. 290 (1900), considered the question of whether or not the courts may supervise the acts of an executive department head in discharging an employee. The Court's decision in that case clearly placed the removal of executive department employees within the ambit of executive discretion, and ruled that until Congress, by 'special and direct legislation makes provisions to the contrary,' the courts cannot review the soundness or propriety of the exercise of the department head's discretion. This case stands as a solid milestone in a long line of unbroken authorities holding that where there are no established procedures or statutes to be followed, removal of an employee is solely within the discretion of agency officials and accordingly may be effected without giving reason. See *Cafeteria Workers v. McElroy,* 367 U.S. 886, 896-97 (1961) and cases cited therein."...

It has been suggested that the Handbook for FBI Employees is not sufficiently specific in pointing out that the Bureau cannot tolerate personal misbehavior of its employees "reflecting unfavorably upon them or the Bureau." It is true that the Handbook does not say that an FBI employee may not use profane and obscene language in denouncing his superiors in the presence of others. A fingerprint clerk is not enjoined against mocking or vilifying a police officer who brings in a "lifted" fingerprint for classification in furtherance of cooperation with the Bureau. Myriad examples of unspecified misbehavior will suggest themselves. Something is lacking, it is argued, in that the Handbook did not particularize with respect to any such illustration, or by way of denouncing the very conduct under discussion here, admitted by Carter who "told exactly what happened." If an employee of the Bureau did not know that he was expected to comply satisfactorily with "ordinarily accepted standards of personal conduct," I would suppose he did not belong in the Bureau in the first place. Were I required to do so, I would rule that the Director had ample cause for dismissing Carter....

ANDREWS v. DREW MUNICIPAL SCHOOL DISTRICT

507 F.2d 611 (5th Cir. 1975), *cert. dismissed*, 425 U.S. 559 (1976)

SIMPSON, CIRCUIT JUDGE: This suit attacking the validity of the Drew Municipal School District's rule against employing parents of illegitimate children was initiated by two such parents, both mothers, against whom the rule militated. Named as defendants were the Drew Municipal School District (the District), George Ferris Pettey, its Superintendent, and the individual members of the District's Board of Trustees (the Board).

The complaint sought declaratory and injunctive relief to "redress the deprivation of rights and privileges and immunities of the plaintiffs guaranteed by the (sic) 42 U.S.C. 1981, 1983 et seq., Title VI of the Civil Rights Act of 1964, 42 U.S.C. Section 2000d et seq., the Fifth and Fourteenth Amendments to the United States Constitution. Plaintiffs further asked for declaratory relief under 28 U.S.C. Sections 2201, 2202." Jurisdiction was invoked under Title 28 U.S.C. Section 1343.

Following a series of hearings the district court decided the case on the merits, holding that the rule violated both the Equal Protection Clause and the Due Process Clause of the Fourteenth Amendment. We affirm for reasons stated below.

In the Spring of 1972, Superintendent Pettey learned that there were some teacher aides presently employed in the District who were parents of illegitimate children. Disturbed by this knowledge, Pettey immediately implemented an unwritten edict to the effect that parenthood of an illegitimate child would automatically disqualify an individual, whether incumbent or applicant, from employment with the school system.[2] ...

---

[2] Pettey in testimony indicated confusion as to the expanse of the policy he had promulgated. He was positive that the rule should apply to all instructional personnel. Upon questioning, he expanded the list to include not only teachers and teacher aides, but also secretaries, librarians, dieticians, cafeteria operators, nurses, social workers, school principals, school volunteers and even PTA presidents. Although he was not positive, he did not think the rule should apply to bus drivers, janitors or maids.

Mrs. Fred McCorkle is one of the administrators responsible for implementing the unwed parent policy. As Coordinator of Elementary Instruction for the school district, she is in charge of the teacher aide program and recommends to Pettey who shall be hired to fill teacher aide vacancies....

Both plaintiffs-appellees, Lestine Rogers and Katie Mae Andrews, were victims of the unwed parent policy. Lestine Rogers was hired as a teacher aide in the Fall preceding the initiation of the rule, although her application stated that she was single and had a child. After the Pettey policy rule was announced, Mrs. McCorkle informed Ms. Rogers that because she was the parent of an illegitimate child, she would not be re-hired for the following year. Katie Mae Andrews, on the other hand, knew about the Pettey rule prior to applying for a teacher aide position. Although she too was the mother of an illegitimate child, she did not so indicate on her application. Mrs. McCorkle learned of Ms. Andrews' illegitimate child in the course of her investigation of the application....

From the beginning, unwed mothers only, not unwed fathers, were adversely affected by the rule. This factor coupled with the conclusion that the policy, by its nature, could only be applied against females, led the district court to hold alternatively that "assuming a rational relation does exist between the Drew policy and legitimate educational objectives, the rule creates an inherently suspect classification based on sex, i.e. single women, which cannot survive strict scrutiny mandated by the Fourteenth Amendment." 371 F. Supp. at 35. The district court's primary holding was that the rule "has no rational relation to the objectives ostensibly sought to be achieved by the school officials and is fraught with invidious discrimination; thus it is constitutionally defective under the traditional, and most lenient, standard of equal protection and violative of due process as well." *Ibid.* at 31. Thus this appeal concerns a policy or rule that has not only been held to violate equal protection for alternative reasons, but has also been held to violate due process. On the basis relied upon by the district court of traditional notions of equal protection, because the policy created an irrational classification, we affirm.[5]

"Traditional" equal protection analysis requires that legislative classifications must be sustained as long as the classification itself is rationally related to a legitimate governmental interest. To find the governmental objective ostensibly served by the rule, we turn to the testimony of Superintendent Pettey, the rule's originator and explicator. Pettey's avowed objective was to create a scholastic environment which was conducive to the moral development as well as the intellectual development of the students. Certainly this objective is not without legitimacy. Schools have the right, if not the duty, to create a properly moral scholastic environment. See *Beilan v. Board of Education,* 1958, 357 U.S. 399. But the issue is not simply whether the objective itself is legitimate, but rather whether the Pettey rule "advances that objective in a manner consistent with the Equal Protection Clause," *Reed v. Reed,* 1971, 404 U.S. 71, 76. We hold that it does not.

The District offers three possible rationales through which it asserts that its rule under attack furthers the creation of a properly moral scholastic environ-

---

[5]Because we affirm upon traditional equal protection grounds, we do not consider the district court's alternative finding of a sex based classification or its legal conclusion that such classifications are inherently suspect.

ment: (1) unwed parenthood is prima facie proof of immorality; (2) unwed parents are improper communal role models, after whom students may pattern their lives; (3) employment of an unwed parent in a scholastic environment materially contributes to the problem of school-girl pregnancies.

The first of these postulates violates not only the Equal Protection Clause, but the Due Process Clause as well. The law is clear that due process interdicts the adoption by a state of an irrebuttable presumption, as to which the presumed fact does not necessarily follow from the proven fact. See *Cleveland Board of Education v. LaFleur*, 1974, 414 U.S. 632; *Vlandis v. Kline*, 1973, 412 U.S. 441; *Stanley v. Illinois*, 1972, 405 U.S. 645. Thus, unless the presumed fact here, present immorality, necessarily follows from the proven fact, unwed parenthood, the conclusiveness inherent in the Pettey rule must be held to violate due process. We agree with the district court that the one does not necessarily follow the other:

> By the rule, a parent, whether male or female, who has had such a child, would be forever precluded from employment. Thus no consideration would be given to the subsequent marriage of the parent or to the length of time elapsed since the illegitimate birth, or to a person's reputation for good character in the community. A person could live an impeccable life, yet be barred as unfit for employment for an event, whether the result of indiscretion or not, occurring at any time in the past. But human experience refutes the dogmatic attitude inherent in such a policy against unwed parents. Can it be said that an engaged woman, who has premarital sex, becomes pregnant, and whose fiance dies or is killed prior to their marriage, is morally depraved for bearing the posthumous child? The rule allows no compassion for the person who has been unwittingly subjected to sexual relations through force, deceptive design or while under the influence of drugs or alcohol, yet chooses to have the child rather than to abort it. The rules makes no distinction between the sexual neophyte and the libertine. In short, the rule leaves no consideration for the multitudinous circumstances under which illegitimate childbirth may occur and which may have little, if any, bearing on the parent's present moral worth. A past biological event like childbirth out of wedlock, even if relevant to the issue, may not be controlling; and that it may be considered more conventional or circumspect for the infant to be surrendered to others for upbringing rather than be reared by the natural parent is hardly determinative of the matter. Furthermore, the policy, if based on moral judgment, has inherent if unintended defects or shortcomings. While obviously aimed at discouraging prematerial (sic) sex relations, the policy's effect is apt to encourage abortion, which is itself staunchly opposed by some on ethical or moral grounds. It totally ignores, as a disqualification, the occurrence of extra-marital sex activity, though thought of by many as a more serious basis for moral culpability. Indeed, the superintendent's fiat, altogether unsupported by sociological data, equates the single fact of illegitimate birth with irredeemable moral disease. Such a presumption is not only patently absurd, it is mischievous and prejudicial, requiring those who administer the policy to "investigate" the parental status of school employees and prospective applicants. Where no stigma may have existed before, such inquisitions by overzealous officialdom can rapidly create it. 371 F. Supp. at 33-34 (footnotes deleted)....

The school district urges a second rationale for its rule based upon the holding in *McConnell v. Anderson,* 8 Cir. 1971, 451 F.2d 193:

"What the school board looks at is whether, moral considerations aside, proper educational growth can be furthered and respect for marriage ingrained by employing unwed parents. The question then becomes whether the open and notorious existence of the status as an unwed parent would injure the affected students." Reply Brief of Defendants/Appellants, p. 5....

We do not consider *McConnell* supportive of the District's position. The record before us contains no evidence of proselytizing of pupils by the plaintiffs and reveals instead that each plaintiff, along with her illegitimate offspring, is living under the same roof as her parents, brothers and sisters. It would be a wise child indeed who could infer knowledge of either plaintiff's unwed parent status based on the manner of plaintiffs' existence....

The third rationale proffered by the school district in hopes of salvaging the Pettey rule, that the presence of unwed parents in a scholastic environment materially contributes to school-girl pregnancies is without support, other than speculation and assertions of opinion, in the record before us.

Because we hold that the Board rule under attack violated traditional concepts of equal protection, we find it unnecessary to discuss numerous other issues urged on appeal by appellees or in their behalf by *amici curiae;* for example, whether the rule creates a suspect classification based upon race or sex, or whether it infringes upon some constitutionally protected interest such as the right to privacy or the right to procreation....

NOTES

1. *Bonet v. United States Postal Serv.,* 712 F.2d 213 (5th Cir. 1983), concerned a postal worker who had been terminated following his indictment for indecency involving his eleven-year-old stepdaughter. The indictment had been ultimately dismissed due to his wife's refusal to prosecute. The court indicated that a federal agency seeking to sustain the discharge of an employee for off-duty misconduct said to have affected the efficiency of the service must be able to demonstrate three things: (1) the misconduct affected efficiency; (2) the misconduct reasonably could be expected to cause that sort of adverse reaction; and (3) the discharge did not violate any other legal policy. Since the court found that the MSPB had made all three showings in this case, its decision to sustain the employee's termination was upheld. See also *Hayes v. Department of Navy,* 727 F.2d 1535, 401 (Fed. Cir. 1984) (upholding removal of employee who had been convicted for off-duty child molestation since his work provided him with access to government housing projects in which children would be present). In *Allred v. Dep't of Health & Human Servs.,* 786 F.2d 1128 (Fed. Cir. 1986), the court indicated that removal of an employee convicted of an off-duty sex offense involving a minor child would be appropriate whenever the misconduct was sufficient to undermine public confidence in the government agency, without the need for proof of specific harm to the individual's capacity to perform his actual job.

2. In *Shawgo v. Spradlin,* 701 F.2d 470 (5th Cir.), *cert. denied,* 464 U.S. 965 (1983), the court sustained the right of a city to suspend two unmarried police officers who had engaged in an off-duty affair. Cf. *Thorne v. City of El Segundo,* 726 F.2d 455 (9th Cir. 1983) (finding impermissible a police depart-

ment policy which punished female police personnel for off-duty affairs but which did not similarly punish male personnel for similar conduct). See also *Potter v. Murray City*, 760 F.2d 1065 (10th Cir. 1985) (finding that police department's termination of officer because of his practice of plural marriage violated neither his right of privacy nor his right to the free exercise of religion).

3. May a school district constitutionally refuse to permit a teacher to breast-feed her child during her lunch period? See *Dike v. Sch. Bd.*, 650 F.2d 783 (5th Cir. 1981).

4. In O'Neil, *The Private Lives of Public Employees,* 51 Or. L. Rev. 70, 105-106 (1971), the author suggests that the courts must evaluate the following factors in weighing the substantiality of governmental interests against infringement of personal freedoms in cases involving the regulation of the private lives of public employees: What is the effect, if any, upon the individual's job performance? What is the effect, if any, upon the efficiency of the agency? What is the effect, if any, on the image of and public confidence in the agency? O'Neil concludes that "judgments about governmental interests cannot be made in the abstract ... [and that] the following factors ... have been deemed pertinent by courts in passing upon recent public employment dismissals: (a) How sensitive is the position held or sought? ... (b) Have other members of the agency or institution been involved? ... (c) Was the behavior recent and is it recurrent? ... (d) What is the probability of repetition? ... (e) How does the transgression relate to the employee's entire record? ... What is the status of the behavior outside the public service? ... How clear and specific is the standard of conduct? ... What less onerous alternatives are available to the agency? ... What procedures are provided within the agency?"

KELLEY v. JOHNSON

425 U.S. 238, 96 S. Ct. 1440, 47 L. Ed. 2d 708 (1976)

JUSTICE REHNQUIST delivered the opinion of the Court.

The District Court for the Eastern District of New York originally dismissed respondent's complaint seeking declaratory and injunctive relief against a regulation promulgated by petitioner limiting the length of a policeman's hair. On respondent's appeal to the Court of Appeals for the Second Circuit, that judgment was reversed, and on remand the District Court took testimony and thereafter granted the relief sought by respondent. The Court of Appeals affirmed, and we granted certiorari, 421 U.S. 987 (1975), to consider the constitutional doctrine embodied in the rulings of the Court of Appeals. We reverse.

I

In 1971 respondent's predecessor, individually and as president of the Suffolk County Patrolmen's Benevolent Association, brought this action under the Civil Rights Act of 1871, 42 U.S.C. § 1983, against petitioner's predecessor, the Commissioner of the Suffolk County Police Department. The Commissioner had promulgated Order No. 71-1, which established hair-grooming standards applicable to male members of the police force.[1] ... The regulation was

---

[1] "2/75.1 Hair: Hair shall be neat, clean, trimmed, and present a groomed appearance. Hair will not touch the ears or the collar except the closely cut hair on the back of the neck. Hair in front will be groomed so that it does not fall below the band of properly worn headgear. In no case will the bulk or length of the hair interfere with the proper wear of any authorized headgear. The accept-

attacked as violative of respondent patrolman's right of free expression under the First Amendment and his guarantees of due process and equal protection under the Fourteenth Amendment, in that it was "not based upon the generally accepted standard of grooming in the community" and placed "an undue restriction" upon his activities therein.

The Court of Appeals held that cases characterizing the uniform civilian services as "para-military," and sustaining hair regulations on that basis, were not soundly grounded historically. It said the fact that a police force is organized "with a centralized administration and a disciplined rank and file for efficient conduct of its affairs" did not foreclose respondent's claim, but instead bore only upon "the existence of a legitimate state interest to be reasonably advanced by the regulation." *Dwen v. Barry,* 483 F.2d 1126, 1128-1129 (1973). The Court of Appeals went on to decide that "choice of personal appearance is an ingredient of an individual's personal liberty" and is protected by the Fourteenth Amendment. It further held that the police department had "failed to make the slightest showing of the relationship between its regulation and the legitimate interest it sought to promote." *Id.,* at 1130-1131. On the basis of this reasoning it concluded that neither dismissal nor summary judgment in the District Court was appropriate, since the department "has the burden of establishing a genuine public need for the regulation." *Id.,* at 1131.

Thereafter the District Court, under the compulsion of the remand from the Court of Appeals, took testimony on the question of whether or not there was a "genuine public need." The sole witness was the Deputy Commissioner of the Suffolk County Police Department, petitioner's subordinate, who testified as to the police department's concern for the safety of the patrolmen, and the need for some standards of uniformity in appearance. The District Court held that "no proof" was offered to support any claim of the need for the protection of the police officer, and that while "proper grooming" is an ingredient of a good police department's "esprit de corps," petitioner's standards did not establish a public need because they ultimately reduced to "[u]niformity for uniformity's sake." The District Court granted the relief prayed for by respondent, and on petitioner's appeal that judgment was affirmed without opinion by the Court of Appeals.

II

Section I of the Fourteenth Amendment to the United States Constitution provides in pertinent part:

"[No State] shall ... deprive any person of life, liberty, or property, without due process of law."

This section affords not only a procedural guarantee against the deprivation of "liberty," but likewise protects substantive aspects of liberty against unconstitutional restriction by the State. *Board of Regents v. Roth,* 408 U.S. 564, 572 (1972); *Griswold v. Connecticut,* 381 U.S. 479, 502 (1965) (WHITE, J., concurring).

---

ability of a member's hair style will be based upon the criteria in this paragraph and not upon the style in which he chooses to wear his hair."

The "liberty" interest claimed by respondent here, of course, is distinguishable from those protected by the Court in *Roe v. Wade,* 410 U.S. 113 (1973); *Eisenstadt v. Baird,* 405 U.S. 438 (1972); *Stanley v. Illinois,* 405 U.S. 645 (1972); *Griswold v. Connecticut, supra;* and *Meyer v. Nebraska,* 262 U.S. 390 (1923). Each of those cases involved a substantial claim of infringement on the individual's freedom of choice with respect to certain basic matters of procreation, marriage, and family life. But whether the citizenry at large has some sort of "liberty" interest within the Fourteenth Amendment in matters of personal appearance is a question on which this Court's cases offer little, if any, guidance. We can, nevertheless, assume an affirmative answer for purposes of deciding this case, because we find that assumption insufficient to carry the day for respondent's claim.

Respondent has sought the protection of the Fourteenth Amendment not as a member of the citizenry at large, but on the contrary as an employee of the police force of Suffolk County, a subdivision of the State of New York. While the Court of Appeals made passing reference to this distinction, it was thereafter apparently ignored. We think, however, it is highly significant. In *Pickering v. Board of Education,* 391 U.S. 563, 568 (1968), after noting that state employment may not be conditioned on the relinquishment of First Amendment rights, the Court stated that "[a]t the same time it cannot be gainsaid that the State has interests as an employer in regulating the speech of its employees that differ significantly from those it possesses in connection with regulation of the speech of the citizenry in general." More recently, we have sustained comprehensive and substantial restrictions upon activities of both federal and state employees lying at the core of the First Amendment. *Civil Serv. Comm'n v. Letter Carriers,* 413 U.S. 548 (1973); *Broadrick v. Oklahoma,* 413 U.S. 601 (1973). If such state regulations may survive challenges based on the explicit language of the First Amendment, there is surely even more room for restrictive regulations of state employees where the claim implicates only the more general contours of the substantive liberty interest protected by the Fourteenth Amendment.

The hair-length regulation here touches respondent as an employee of the county and, more particularly, as a policeman. Respondent's employer has, in accordance with its well-established duty to keep the peace, placed myriad demands upon the members of the police force, duties which have no counterpart with respect to the public at large. Respondent must wear a standard uniform, specific in each detail. When in uniform he must salute the flag. He cannot take an active role in local political affairs by way of being a party delegate or contributing or soliciting political contributions. He cannot smoke in public. All of these and other regulations of the Suffolk County Police Department infringe on respondent's freedom of choice in personal matters, and it was apparently in view of the Court of Appeals that the burden is on the State to prove a "genuine public need" for each and every one of these regulations....

The promotion of safety of persons and property is unquestionably at the core of the State's police power, and virtually all state and local governments employ a uniformed police force to aid in the accomplishment of that purpose. Choice of organization, dress, and equipment for law enforcement personnel is a decision entitled to the same sort of presumption of legislative validity as are state choices designed to promote other aims within the cognizance of the State's police power. *Day-Brite Lighting, Inc. v. Missouri,* 342 U.S. 421, 423 (1952); *Prince v. Massachusetts,* 321 U.S. 158, 168-170 (1944); *Olsen v. Nebraska,* 313 U.S. 236, 246-247 (1941). Having recognized in other contexts the wide latitude accorded the Government in the "dispatch of its own internal affairs," *Cafeteria Workers v. McElroy,* 367 U.S. 886, 896 (1961), we think Suffolk County's police regulations involved here are entitled to similar weight. Thus the question is not, as the Court of Appeals conceived it to be, whether the State can "establish" a "genuine public need" for the specific regulation. It is whether respondent can demonstrate that there is no rational connection between the regulation, based as it is on respondent's method of organizing its police force, and the promotion of safety of persons and property. *United Public Workers v. Mitchell,* 330 U.S. 75, 100-101 (1947); *Jacobson v. Massachusetts,* 197 U.S. 11, 30-31, 35-37 (1905).

We think the answer here is so clear that the District Court was quite right in the first instance to have dismissed respondent's complaint. Neither this Court, the Court of Appeals, or the District Court is in a position to weigh the policy arguments in favor of and against a rule regulating hairstyles as a part of regulations governing a uniformed civilian service. The constitutional issue to be decided by these courts is whether petitioner's determination that such regulations should be enacted is so irrational that it may be branded "arbitrary," and therefore a deprivation of respondent's "liberty" interest in freedom to choose his own hair style. *Williamson v. Lee Optical Co.,* 348 U.S. 483, 487-488 (1955). The overwhelming majority of state and local police of the present day are uniformed. This fact itself testifies to the recognition by those who direct those operations, and by the people of the States and localities who directly or indirectly choose such persons, that similarity in appearance of police officers is desirable. This choice may be based on a desire to make police officers readily recognizable to the members of the public, or a desire for the esprit de corps which such similarity is felt to inculcate within the police force itself. Either one is a sufficiently rational justification for regulations so as to defeat respondent's claim based on the liberty guaranty of the Fourteenth Amendment....

The regulation challenged here did not violate any right guaranteed respondent by the Fourteenth Amendment to the United States Constitution, and the Court of Appeals was therefore wrong in reversing the District Court's original judgment dismissing the action. The judgment of the Court of Appeals is

Reversed.

NOTES

1. A board of education dress code requiring male teachers to wear neckties was held to be unconstitutional in that it interfered with a teacher's constitutional rights without significantly furthering the board's stated objectives. The plaintiff teacher claimed that somewhat less formal dress would help him achieve a better rapport with the students and thus enhance his teaching ability. The court held that there was a liberty interest involved in personal dress, and that a first amendment academic freedom concern was raised by the teacher's contention that his teaching was impeded by the dress code. The board's countervailing interests in establishing a professional image for teachers, promoting

good grooming in students, and maintaining decorum in the classroom were insufficient to outweigh the intrusion on both first and fourteenth amendment rights. *East Hartford Educ. Ass'n v. Board of Educ.*, 562 F.2d 838 (2nd Cir. 1977).

2. In *Keckeisen v. Independent Sch. Dist. No. 612,* 509 F.2d 1062 (8th Cir. 1975), *cert. denied,* 423 U.S. 833 (1975), a Minnesota public school board policy prohibiting employment of a husband and wife in an administrator/teacher relationship "where a conflict of interest could arise" was held not to be an unconstitutional violation of the right to marry. Accord *Cutts v. Fowler,* 692 F.2d 138 (D.C. Cir. 1982). See *Parsons v. County of Del Norte,* 728 F.2d 1234 (9th Cir.), *cert. denied,* 105 S. Ct. 158 (1984) (sustaining rule precluding employment of spouses in same department). See also *Littlejohn v. Rose,* 768 F.2d 765 (6th Cir. 1985), *cert. denied,* 475 U.S. 1045 (1986) (government entity may not terminate employees who become divorced).

3. Some municipalities require that public employees reside within city limits while employed by the city. Challenges to such regulations as violative of the individual employee's right to travel have not been sustained. See, e.g., *McCarthy v. Philadelphia Civil Serv. Comm'n,* 424 U.S. 645 (1976); *Winkler v. Spinnato,* 72 N.Y.2d 402, 530 N.E.2d 835 (1988).

Some governmental entities have established rules requiring that a certain minimum percentage of workers employed by contractors performing public works projects consist of residents of the contracting municipality. In *White v. Massachusetts Council of Constr. Emps.,* 460 U.S. 204 (1983), the Court sustained such a requirement by recognizing that where a state or local government enters the market as a participant, rather than as a mere regulator, it is not subject to the restraints of the commerce clause. However, in *United Bldg. & Constr. Trades Council v. Mayor & Council, City of Camden,* 465 U.S. 208 (1984), the Court held that such residency requirements for contractors working on public projects may violate the privileges and immunities clause, since they affect the fundamental right of out-of-state people to obtain employment on municipal construction projects. Cities will have to demonstrate a "substantial reason" for such requirements if they are to be sustained. See also *Robison v. Francis,* 713 P.2d 259 (Alaska 1985).

4. In *Price v. United States,* GERR No. 818, 6 (not published in F.2d) (5th Cir. 1979), the court sustained the dismissal of a probationary inspector for the Treasury Department's Bureau of Alcohol, Tobacco and Firearms, where the Department had discovered that he had been previously arrested on three occasions for drug violations. The court noted that the inspector's criminal reputation would make it easy for parties to challenge his credibility in administrative and judicial proceedings and agreed that this would be an intolerable situation for an employee engaged in law enforcement activities. See also *Johnson v. United States,* 628 F.2d 187 (D.C. Cir. 1980) (sustaining discharge of Alcohol, Tobacco and Firearms special agent for private misuse of personal firearm); *Borsari v. Federal Aviation Admin.,* 699 F.2d 106 (2d Cir.), *cert. denied,* 104 S. Ct. 115 (1983) (sustaining discharge of air traffic controller for off-duty possession of drugs). But cf. *Gloster v. GSA,* 720 F.2d 700 (D.C. Cir. 1983) (finding insufficient nexus between person's conviction for welfare fraud and her job as custodial worker); *Young v. Hampton,* 568 F.2d 1253 (7th Cir. 1977) (finding marijuana conviction insufficient cause for termination of senior employee).

5. In *New York City Transit Auth. v. Beazer,* 440 U.S. 568 (1979), the Supreme Court found that the Transit Authority's exclusion of all current drug users, including those individuals participating in methadone maintenance treatment programs, from all jobs did not violate the fourteenth amendment equal protection clause. The possibility that such drug users might pose a danger to the public or to other employees was found to constitute a rational concern of the Transit Authority. Furthermore, while a more narrow exclusionary policy might have been formulated, the Court concluded that the blanket exclusion rule was neither unprincipled nor invidious. If such a personnel policy were to disqualify a greater percentage of minority applicants than nonminority applicants, should more than a rational basis be required to sustain it?

6. In *Yacavone v. Bolger,* 645 F.2d 1028 (D.C. Cir.), *cert. denied,* 454 U.S. 844 (1981), the court sustained the termination of a small town postmaster whose conviction for shoplifting was widely publicized, despite the fact that the state governor had granted him a "full and unconditional" pardon while his removal appeal was still being administratively processed. See also *Rotolo v. Merit Sys. Protection Bd.,* 636 F.2d 6 (1st Cir. 1980) (sustaining removal of IRS clerical employee whose improper understatement of her income had resulted in wrongful tax avoidance); *Book v. United States Postal Serv.,* 675 F.2d 158 (8th Cir. 1982) (sustaining termination of postmaster for unauthorized possession and unofficial use of postal property); *Wild v. HUD,* 692 F.2d 1129 (7th Cir. 1982) (upholding discharge of HUD employee whose publicized "slumlord" operations conflicted with agency's stated objective of achieving improved housing).

7. In *Abrams v. Department of Navy,* 714 F.2d 1219 (1983), the Third Circuit sustained the validity of the MSPB's "presumed nexus" rule which indicates that there are some forms of off-duty behavior that are so egregious that damage to a federal employee's continued ability or fitness to perform his job can be presumed, thus shifting to the employee the burden of rebutting this presumption. The Ninth Circuit, however, has refused to accept this doctrine, since it concluded that this doctrine impermissibly shifts the burden of proof to the affected employee in violation of the burden Congress placed on federal agencies under sections 7513(a) and 2302(b)(10) of the Civil Service Reform Act. See *D.E. v. Department of Navy,* 21 GERR 1377 (not published in F.2d) (1983). Does such a burden shifting rule violate due process principles? See *In re Grievance of Muzzy,* 449 A.2d 970, 1981-83 PBC ¶37,907 (Vt. 1982).

B. PROCEDURAL DUE PROCESS AS A PROTECTION AGAINST DISMISSAL FROM PUBLIC EMPLOYMENT

BOARD OF REGENTS v. ROTH

408 U.S. 564, 92 S. Ct. 2701, 33 L. Ed. 2d 548 (1972)

JUSTICE STEWART delivered the opinion of the Court.

In 1968 the respondent, David Roth, was hired for his first teaching job as assistant professor of political science at Wisconsin State University-Oshkosh. He was hired for a fixed term of one academic year. The notice of his faculty appointment specified that his employment would begin on September 1, 1968, and would end on June 30, 1969. The respondent completed that term. But he was informed that he would not be rehired for the next academic year.

The respondent had no tenure rights to continued employment. Under Wisconsin statutory law a state university teacher can acquire tenure as a "permanent" employee only after four years of year-to-year employment. Having acquired tenure, a teacher is entitled to continued employment "during efficiency and good behavior." A relatively new teacher without tenure, however, is under Wisconsin law entitled to nothing beyond his one-year appointment. There are no statutory or administrative standards defining eligibility for re-employment. State law thus clearly leaves the decision whether to rehire a nontenured teacher for another year to the unfettered discretion of university officials.

... Rules promulgated by the Board of Regents provide that a nontenured teacher "dismissed" before the end of the year may have some opportunity for review of the "dismissal." But the Rules provide no real protection for a nontenured teacher who simply is not re-employed for the next year. He must be informed by February 1 "concerning retention or non-retention for the ensuing year." But "no reason for non-retention need be given. No review or appeal is provided in such case."

In conformance with these Rules, the President of Wisconsin State University-Oshkosh informed the respondent before February 1, 1969, that he would not be rehired for the 1969-1970 academic year. He gave the respondent no reason for the decision and no opportunity to challenge it at any sort of hearing.

The respondent then brought this action in a federal district court alleging that the decision not to rehire him for the next year infringed his Fourteenth Amendment rights. He attacked the decision both in substance and procedure. First, he alleged that the true reason for the decision was to punish him for certain statements critical of the University administration, and that it therefore violated his right to freedom of speech.[5] Second, he alleged that the failure of University officials to give him notice of any reason for nonretention and an opportunity for a hearing violated his right to procedural due process of law.

The District Court granted summary judgment for the respondent on the procedural issue, ordering the University officials to provide him with reasons and a hearing. 310 F. Supp. 972. The Court of Appeals, with one judge dissenting, affirmed this partial summary judgment. 446 F.2d 806. We granted certiorari. 404 U.S. 909. The only question presented to us at this stage in the case is whether the respondent had a constitutional right to a statement of reasons and a hearing on the University's decision not to rehire him for another year.[6] We hold that he did not.

I

The requirements of procedural due process apply only to the deprivation of interests encompassed within the Fourteenth Amendment's protection of liberty and property. When protected interests are implicated the right to some kind of

---

[5]While the respondent alleged that he was not rehired because of his exercise of free speech, the petitioners insisted that the nonretention decision was based on other, constitutionally valid grounds. The District Court came to no conclusion whatever regarding the true reason for the University President's decision....

[6]The courts that have to decide whether a nontenured public employee has a right to a statement of reasons or a hearing upon nonrenewal of his contract have come to varying conclusions. Some have held that neither procedural safeguard is required. E.g., Orr v. Trinter, 444 F.2d 128 (CA6); Jones v. Hopper, 410 F.2d 1323 (CA10); Freeman v. Gould Special School District, 405 F.2d 1153 (CA8). At least one court has held that there is a right to a statement of reasons but not a hearing. Drown v. Portsmouth School District, 435 F.2d 1182 (CA1). And another has held that both requirements depend on whether the employee has an "expectancy" of continued employment. Ferguson v. Thomas, 430 F.2d 852, 856 (CA5).

prior hearing is paramount.[7] But the range of interests protected by procedural due process is not infinite.

... Undeniably, the respondent's re-employment prospects were of major concern to him — concern that we surely cannot say was insignificant. And a weighing process has long been a part of any determination of the *form* of hearing required in particular situations by procedural due process. But, to determine whether due process requirements apply in the first place, we must look not to the "weight" but to the *nature* of the interest at stake. See *Morrissey v. Brewer,* [405 U.S.], at 481. We must look to see if the interest is within the Fourteenth Amendment's protection of liberty and property.

"Liberty" and "property" are broad and majestic terms. They are among the "[g]reat [constitutional] concepts ... purposely left to gather meaning from experience.... [T]hey relate to the whole domain of social and economic fact, and the statesmen who founded this Nation knew too well that only a stagnant society remains unchanged." *National Mutual Ins. Co. v. Tidewater Transfer Co.,* 337 U.S. 582, 646 (Frankfurter, J., dissenting). For that reason the Court has fully and finally rejected the wooden distinction between "rights" and "privileges" that once seemed to govern the applicability of procedural due process rights.[9] The Court has also made clear that the property interests protected by procedural due process extend well beyond actual ownership of real estate, chattels, or money.[10] By the same token, the Court has required due process protection for deprivations of liberty beyond the sort of formal constraints imposed by the criminal process.

Yet, while the Court has eschewed rigid or formalistic limitations on the protection of procedural due process, it has at the same time observed certain boundaries. For the words "liberty" and "property" in the Due Process Clause of the Fourteenth Amendment must be given some meaning.

II ....

The State, in declining to rehire the respondent, did not make any charge against him that might seriously damage his standing and associations in his community. It did not base the nonrenewal of his contract on a charge, for example, that he had been guilty of dishonesty, or immorality. Had it done so, this would be a different case. For "[w]here a person's good name, reputation, honor, or integrity is at stake because of what the government is doing to him, notice and an opportunity to be heard are essential." In such a case, due process would accord an opportunity to refute the charge before University officials. In

---

[7] Before a person is deprived of a protected interest, he must be afforded opportunity for some kind of a hearing, "except for extraordinary situations where some valid governmental interest is at stake that justifies postponing the hearing until after the event."...

[9] In a leading case decided many years ago, the Court of Appeals for the District of Columbia Circuit held that public employment in general was a "privilege," not a "right," and that procedural due process guarantees therefore were inapplicable. *Bailey v. Richardson,* 86 U.S. App. D.C. 248, 182 F.2d 46, *aff'd by an equally divided Court,* 341 U.S. 918. The basis of this holding has been thoroughly undermined in the ensuing years. For, as Mr. Justice Blackmun wrote for the Court only last year, "this Court now has rejected the concept that constitutional rights turn upon whether a governmental benefit is characterized as a 'right' or as a 'privilege.'" *Graham v. Richardson,* 403 U.S. 365, 374.

[10] See, e.g., *Connell v. Higginbotham,* 403 U.S. 207, 208; *Bell v. Burson,* 402 U.S. 535; *Goldberg v. Kelly,* 397 U.S. 254.

the present case, however, there is no suggestion whatever that the respondent's interest in his "good name, reputation, honor or integrity" is at stake.

Similarly, there is no suggestion that the State, in declining to re-employ the respondent, imposed on him a stigma or other disability that foreclosed his freedom to take advantage of other employment opportunities. The State, for example, did not invoke any regulations to bar the respondent from all other public employment in State universities. Had it done so, this, again, would be a different case....

To be sure, the respondent has alleged that the nonrenewal of his contract was based on his exercise of his right to freedom of speech. But this allegation is not now before us. The District Court stated proceedings on this issue, and the respondent has yet to prove that the decision not to rehire him was, in fact, based on his free speech activities.[14]

Hence, on the record before us, all that clearly appears is that the respondent was not rehired for one year at one University. It stretches the concept too far to suggest that a person is deprived of "liberty" when he simply is not rehired in one job but remains as free as before to seek another. *Cafeteria Workers v. McElroy,* 367 U.S. at 895-896.

III

The Fourteenth Amendment's procedural protection of property is a safeguard of the security of interests that a person has already acquired in specific benefits. These interests — property interests — may take many forms.

Thus, the Court has held that a person receiving welfare benefits under statutory and administrative standards defining eligibility for them has an interest in continued receipt of those benefits that is safeguarded by procedural due process. *Goldberg v. Kelly,* 397 U.S. 254. Similarly, in the area of public employment, the Court has held that a public college professor dismissed from an office held under tenure provisions, *Slochower v. Board of Education,* 350 U.S. 551, and college professors and staff members dismissed during the terms of their contracts, *Wieman v. Updegraff,* 344 U.S. 183, have interests in continued employment that are safeguarded by due process. Only last year, the Court held that this principle "proscribing summary dismissal from public employment without hearing or inquiry required by due process" also applied to a teacher recently hired without tenure or a formal contract, but nonetheless with a

---

[14] See n. 5, *infra.* The Court of Appeals, nonetheless, argued that opportunity for a hearing and a statement of reasons were required here "as a *prophylactic* against non-retention decisions improperly motivated by exercise of protected rights." 446 F.2d, at 810 (emphasis supplied). While the Court of Appeals recognized the lack of a finding that the respondent's nonretention was based on exercise of the right of free speech, it felt that the respondent's interest in liberty was sufficiently implicated here because the decision not to rehire him was made "with a background of controversy and unwelcome expressions of opinion." *Ibid.*

When a State would directly impinge upon interests in free speech or free press, this Court has on occasion held that opportunity for a fair adversary hearing must precede the action, whether or not the speech or press interest is clearly protected under substantive First Amendment standards....

In the respondent's case, however, the State has not directly impinged upon interests in free speech or free press in any way comparable to a seizure of books or an injunction against meetings. Whatever may be a teacher's rights of free speech, the interest in holding a teaching job at a state university, *simpliciter,* is not itself a free speech interest.

clearly implied promise of continued employment. *Connell v. Higginbotham,* 403 U.S. 207, 208.

Certain attributes of "property" interests protected by procedural due process emerge from these decisions. To have a property interest in a benefit, a person clearly must have more than an abstract need or desire for it. He must have more than a unilateral expectation of it. He must, instead, have a legitimate claim of entitlement to it. It is a purpose of the ancient institution of property to protect those claims upon which people rely in their daily lives, reliance that must not be arbitrarily undermined. It is a purpose of the constitutional right to a hearing to provide an opportunity for a person to vindicate those claims.

Property interests, of course, are not created by the Constitution. Rather they are created and their dimensions are defined by existing rules or understandings that stem from an independent source such as state law — rules or understandings that secure certain benefits and that support claims of entitlement to those benefits. Thus the welfare recipients in *Goldberg v. Kelly, supra,* had a claim of entitlement to welfare payments that was grounded in the statute defining eligibility for them. The recipients had not yet shown that they were, in fact, within the statutory terms of eligibility. But we held that they had a right to a hearing at which they might attempt to do so.

Just as the welfare recipients' "property" interest in welfare payments was created and defined by statutory terms, so the respondent's "property" interest in employment at the Wisconsin State University-Oshkosh was created and defined by the terms of his appointment. Those terms secured his interest in employment up to June 30, 1969. But the important fact in this case is that they specifically provided that the respondent's employment was to terminate on June 30. They did not provide for contract renewal absent "sufficient cause." Indeed, they made no provision for renewal whatsoever.

Thus the terms of the respondent's appointment secured absolutely no interest in re-employment for the next year. They supported absolutely no possible claim of entitlement to re-employment. Nor, significantly, was there any state statute or University rule or policy that secured his interest in re-employment or that created any legitimate claim to it.[16] In these circumstances, the respondent surely had an abstract concern in being rehired, but he did not have a *property* interest sufficient to require the University authorities to give him a hearing when they declined to renew his contract of employment.

IV ....

We must conclude that the summary judgment for the respondent should not have been granted, since the respondent has not shown that he was deprived of liberty or property protected by the Fourteenth Amendment. The judgment of the Court of Appeals, accordingly, is reversed and the case is remanded for further proceedings consistent with this opinion.

It is so ordered.

---

[16] To be sure, the respondent does suggest that most teachers hired on a year-to-year basis by the Wisconsin State University-Oshkosh are, in fact, rehired. But the District Court has not found that there is anything approaching a "common law" of re-employment, see *Perry v. Sindermann,* [405 U.S.], at 602, so strong as to require University officials to give the respondent a statement of reasons and a hearing on their decision not to rehire him.

JUSTICE DOUGLAS, dissenting.

... Though Roth was rated by the faculty as an excellent teacher, he had publicly criticized the administration for suspending an entire group of 94 Black students without determining individual guilt. He also criticized the university's regime as being authoritarian and autocratic. He used his classroom to discuss what was being done about the Black episode; and one day, instead of meeting his class, he went to the meeting of the Board of Regents....

When a violation of First Amendment rights is alleged, the reasons for dismissal or for nonrenewal of an employment contract must be examined to see if the reasons given are only a cloak for activity or attitudes protected by the Constitution. A statutory analogy is present under the National Labor Relations Act, 29 U.S.C. § 151 et seq. While discharges of employees for "cause" are permissible (*Fibreboard Paper Products Corp. v. National Labor Relations Board,* 379 U.S. 203, 217), discharges because of an employee's union activities is [sic] banned by § 8(a)(3), 29 U.S.C. § 158(c)(3). So the search is to ascertain whether the stated ground was the real one or only a pretext. See *J.P. Stevens & Co. v. National Labor Relations Board,* 380 F.2d 292, 300....

There is sometimes a conflict between a claim for First Amendment protection and the need for orderly administration of the school system, as we noted in *Pickering v. Board of Education,* 391 U.S. 563, 569. That is one reason why summary judgments in this class of cases are seldom appropriate. Another reason is that careful factfinding is often necessary to know whether the given reason for nonrenewal of a teacher's contract is the real reason or a feigned one.

... In *Wieman v. Updegraff,* 344 U.S. 183, we held that an applicant could not be denied the opportunity for public employment because he had exercised his First Amendment rights. And in *Speiser v. Randall,* 357 U.S. 513, we held that a denial of a tax exemption unless one gave up his First Amendment rights was an abridgement of Fourteenth Amendment rights.

As we held in *Speiser v. Randall, supra,* when a State proposes to deny a privilege to one who it alleges has engaged in unprotected speech, Due Process requires that the State bear the burden of proving that the speech was not protected. "The 'protection of the individual against arbitrary action' ... [is] the very essence of due process." *Slochower v. Board of Higher Education,* 350 U.S. 551, 559 (1956), but where the State is allowed to act secretly behind closed doors and without any notice to those who are affected by its actions, there is no check against the possibility of such "arbitrary action." ...

JUSTICE MARSHALL, dissenting....

... I would go further than the Court does in defining the terms "liberty" and "property."

The prior decisions of this Court, discussed at length in the opinion of the Court, established a principle that is as obvious as it is compelling — *i.e.,* federal and state governments and governmental agencies are restrained by the Constitution from acting arbitrarily with respect to employment opportunities that they either offer or control. Hence, it is now firmly established that whether or not a private employer is free to act capriciously or unreasonably with respect to employment practices, at least absent statutory or contractual controls, a government employer is different. The government may only act fairly and reasonably.

This Court has long maintained that "the right to work for a living in the common occupations of the community is of the very essence of the personal freedom and opportunity that it was the purpose of the [Fourteenth] Amendment to secure." *Truax v. Raich,* 239 U.S. 33, 41 (1915) (Hughes, J.). See also *Meyer v. Nebraska,* 262 U.S. 390, 399 (1923)....

In my view, every citizen who applies for a government job is entitled to it unless the government can establish some reason for denying the employment. This is the "property" right that I believe is protected by the Fourteenth Amendment and that cannot be denied "without due process of law." And it is also liberty — liberty to work — which is the "very essence of the personal freedom and opportunity" secured by the Fourteenth Amendment.

This Court has often had occasion to note that the denial of public employment is a serious blow to any citizen. See, e.g., *Joint Anti-Fascist Refugee Committee v. McGrath,* 341 U.S. 123, 185 (1951) (Jackson, J., concurring); *United States v. Lovett,* 328 U.S. 303, 316-317 (1946). Thus, when an application for public employment is denied or the contract of a government employee is not renewed, the government must say why, for it is only when the reasons underlying government action are known that citizens feel secure and protected against arbitrary government action.

Employment is one of the greatest, if not the greatest, benefits that governments offer in modern-day life. When something as valuable as the opportunity to work is at stake, the government may not reward some citizens and not others without demonstrating that its actions are fair and equitable. And it is procedural due process that is our fundamental guarantee to fairness, our protection against arbitrary, capricious, and unreasonable government action....

We have often noted that procedural due process means many different things in the numerous contexts in which it applies. See, e.g., *Goldberg v. Kelly,* 397 U.S. 254, 262 (1970); *Bell v. Burson,* 402 U.S. 535 (1971). Prior decisions have held that an applicant for admission to practice as an attorney before the United States Board of Tax Appeals may not be rejected without a statement of reasons and a chance for a hearing on disputed issues of fact; [4] that a tenured teacher could not be summarily dismissed without notice of the reasons and a hearing; [5] that an applicant for admission to a state bar could not be denied the opportunity to practice law without notice of the reasons for the rejection of his application and a hearing; [6] and even that a substitute teacher who had been employed only two months could not be dismissed merely because she refused to take a loyalty oath without an inquiry into the specific facts of her case and a hearing on those in dispute.[7] I would follow these cases and hold that respondent was denied due process when his contract was not renewed and he was not informed of the reasons and given an opportunity to respond.

It may be argued that to provide procedural due process to all public employees or prospective employees would place an intolerable burden on the

---

[4] *Goldsmith v. United States Board of Tax Appeals,* 270 U.S. 117 (1926).
[5] *Slochower v. Board of Higher Education,* 350 U.S. 551 (1956).
[6] *Willner v. Committee on Character,* 373 U.S. 96 (1963).
[7] *Connell v. Higginbotham,* 403 U.S. 207 (1972).

machinery of government. Cf. *Goldberg v. Kelly, supra.* The short answer to that argument is that it is not burdensome to give reasons when reasons exist. Whenever an application for employment is denied, an employee is discharged, or a decision not to rehire an employee is made, there should be some reason for the decision. It can scarcely be argued that government would be crippled by a requirement that the reason be communicated to the person most directly affected by the government's action.

Where there are numerous applicants for jobs, it is likely that few will choose to demand reasons for not being hired. But, if the demand for reasons is exceptionally great, summary procedures can be devised that would provide fair and adequate information to all persons. As long as the government has a good reason for its actions it need not fear disclosure. It is only where the government acts improperly that procedural due process is truly burdensome. And that is precisely when it is most necessary.

... Moreover, proper procedures will surely eliminate some of the arbitrariness that results not from malice, but from innocent error.... When the government knows it may have to justify its decisions with sound reasons, its conduct is likely to be more cautious, careful, and correct....

CHIEF JUSTICE BURGER, concurring.

I concur in the Court's judgments and opinions in *Sindermann* and *Roth,* but there is one central point in both decisions that I would like to underscore since it may have been obscured in the comprehensive discussion of the cases. That point is that the relationship between a state institution and one of its teachers is essentially a matter of state concern and state law. The Court holds today only that a state-employed teacher who has a right to re-employment under state law, arising from either an express or implied contract, has, in turn, a right guaranteed by the Fourteenth Amendment to some form of prior administrative or academic hearing on the cause for nonrenewal of his contract. Thus whether a particular teacher in a particular context has any right to such administrative hearing hinges on a question of state law....

PERRY v. SINDERMANN

408 U.S. 593, 92 S. Ct. 2694, 33 L. Ed. 2d 570 (1972)

JUSTICE STEWART delivered the opinion of the Court.

From 1959 to 1969 the respondent, Robert Sindermann, was a teacher in the state college system of the State of Texas. After teaching for two years at the University of Texas and for four years at San Antonio Junior College, he became a professor of Government and Social Science at Odessa Junior College in 1965. He was employed at the college for four successive years, under a series of one-year contracts. He was successful enough to be appointed, for a time, the cochairman of his department.

During the 1968-1969 academic year, however, controversy arose between the respondent and the college administration. The respondent was elected president of the Texas Junior College Teachers Association. In this capacity, he left his teaching duties on several occasions to testify before committees of the Texas Legislature, and he became involved in public disagreements with the policies of the college's Board of Regents. In particular, he aligned himself with a group advocating the elevation of the college to four-year status — a change opposed by the Regents. And, on one occasion, a newspaper advertisement appeared over his name that was highly critical of the Regents.

Finally, in May 1969, the respondent's one-year employment contract terminated and the Board of Regents voted not to offer him a new contract for the next academic year. The Regents issued a press release setting forth allegations of the respondent's insubordination.[1] But they provided him no official statement of the reasons for the nonrenewal of his contract. And they allowed him no opportunity for a hearing to challenge the basis of the nonrenewal....

The Court of Appeals reversed the judgment of the District Court. 430 F.2d 939. First, it held that, despite the respondent's lack of tenure, the nonrenewal of his contract would violate the Fourteenth Amendment if it in fact was based on his protected free speech. Since the actual reason for the Regents' decision was "in total dispute" in the pleadings the court remanded the case for a full hearing on this contested issue of fact. *Id.,* at 942-943. Second, the Court of Appeals held that, despite the respondent's lack of tenure, the failure to allow him an opportunity for a hearing would violate the constitutional guarantee of procedural due process if the respondent could show that he had an "expectancy" of re-employment. It, therefore, ordered that this issue of fact also be aired upon remand....

I

The first question presented is whether the respondent's lack of a contractual or tenure right to re-employment, taken alone, defeats his claim that the nonrenewal of his contract violated the First and Fourteenth Amendments. We hold that it does not.

For at least a quarter-century, this Court has made clear that even though a person has no "right" to a valuable governmental benefit and even though the government may deny him the benefit for any number of reasons, there are some reasons upon which the government may not act. It may not deny a benefit to a person on a basis that infringes his constitutionally protected interests — especially, his interest in freedom of speech. For if the government could deny a benefit to a person because of his constitutionally protected speech or associations, his exercise of those freedoms would in effect be penalized and inhibited. This would allow the government to "produce a result which [it] could not command directly." *Speiser v. Randall,* 357 U.S. 513, 526. Such interference with constitutional rights is impermissible.

... We have applied the principle regardless of the public employee's contractual or other claim to a job. Compare *Pickering v. Board of Education, supra,* with *Shelton v. Tucker, supra.*

Thus, the respondent's lack of a contractual or tenure "right" to re-employment for the 1969-1970 academic year is immaterial to his free speech claim. Indeed, twice before, this Court has specifically held that the nonrenewal of a nontenured public school teacher's one-year contract may not be predicated on

---

[1] The press release stated, for example, that the respondent had defied his superiors by attending legislative committee meetings when college officials had specifically refused to permit him to leave his classes for that purpose.

his exercise of First and Fourteenth Amendment rights. *Shelton v. Tucker, supra; Keyishian v. Board of Regents, supra.* We reaffirm those holdings here.

In this case, of course, the respondent has yet to show that the decision not to renew his contract was, in fact, made in retaliation for his exercise of the constitutional right of free speech. The District Court foreclosed any opportunity to make this showing when it granted summary judgment. Hence, we cannot now hold that the Board of Regents' action was invalid.

But we agree with the Court of Appeals that there is a genuine dispute as to "whether the college refused to renew the teaching contract on an impermissible basis — as a reprisal for the exercise of constitutionally protected rights." 430 F.2d, at 943. The respondent has alleged that his nonretention was based on his testimony before legislative committees and his other public statements critical of the Regents' policies. And he has alleged that this public criticism was within the First and Fourteenth Amendment's protection of freedom of speech. Plainly, these allegations present a bona fide constitutional claim. For this Court has held that a teacher's public criticism of his superiors on matters of public concern may be constitutionally protected and may, therefore, be an impermissible basis for termination of his employment. *Pickering v. Board of Education, supra.*

For this reason we hold that the grant of summary judgment against the respondent, without full exploration of this issue, was improper.

II

The respondent's lack of formal contractual or tenure security in continued employment at Odessa Junior College, though irrelevant to his free speech claim, is highly relevant to his procedural due process claim. But it may not be entirely dispositive.

We have held today in *Board of Regents v. Roth,* [408 U.S.], p. 564, that the Constitution does not require opportunity for a hearing before the nonrenewal of a nontenured teacher's contract, unless he can show that the decision not to rehire him somehow deprived him of an interest in "liberty" or that he had a "property" interest in continued employment, despite the lack of tenure or a formal contract. In *Roth* the teacher had not made a showing on either point to justify summary judgment in his favor.

Similarly, the respondent here has yet to show that he has been deprived of an interest that could invoke procedural due process protection. As in *Roth,* the mere showing that he was not rehired in one particular job, without more, did not amount to a showing of a loss of liberty.[5] Nor did it amount to a showing of a loss of property.

But the respondent's allegations — which we must construe most favorably to the respondent at this stage of the litigation — do raise a genuine issue as to his interest in continued employment at Odessa Junior College. He alleged that this interest, though not secured by a formal contractual tenure provision, was secured by a no less binding understanding fostered by the college administra-

---

[5] The Court of Appeals suggested that the respondent might have a due process right to some kind of hearing simply if he *asserts* to college officials that their decision was based on his constitutionally protected conduct. 430 F.2d at 944. We have rejected this approach in *Board of Regents v. Roth,* [408 U.S.] at 575 n. 14.

tion. In particular, the respondent alleged that the college had a *de facto* tenure program, and that he had tenure under that program. He claimed that he and others legitimately relied upon an unusual provision that had been in the college's official Faculty Guide for many years:

> "*Teacher Tenure:* Odessa College has no tenure system. The Administration of the College wishes the faculty member to feel that he has a permanent tenure as long as his teaching services are satisfactory and as long as he displays a cooperative attitude toward his co-workers and his superiors, and as long as he is happy in his work."

Moreover, the respondent claimed legitimate reliance upon guidelines promulgated by the Coordinating Board of the Texas College and University System that provided that a person, like himself, who had been employed as a teacher in the state college and university system for seven years or more has some form of job tenure. Thus, the respondent offered to prove that a teacher, with his long period of service, at this particular State College had no less a "property" interest in continued employment than a formally tenured teacher at other colleges, and had no less a procedural due process right to a statement of reasons and a hearing before college officials upon their decision not to retain him.

We have made clear in *Roth* that "property" interests subject to procedural due process protection are not limited by a few rigid, technical forms. Rather, "property" denotes a broad range of interests that are secured by "existing rules or understandings." A person's interest in a benefit is a "property" interest for due process purposes if there are such rules or mutually explicit understandings that support his claim of entitlement to the benefit and that he may invoke at a hearing.

A written contract with an explicit tenure provision clearly is evidence of a formal understanding that supports a teacher's claim of entitlement to continued employment unless sufficient "cause" is shown. Yet absence of such an explicit contractual provision may not always foreclose the possibility that a teacher has a "property" interest in re-employment. For example, the law of contracts in most, if not all, jurisdictions long has employed a process by which agreements, though not formalized in writing, may be "implied." 3 A. Corbin on Contracts, §§ 561-572A (1960). Explicit contractual provisions may be supplemented by other agreements implied from "the promisor's words and conduct in the light of the surrounding circumstances." *Id.,* at § 562. And, "[t]he meaning of [the promisor's] words and acts is found by relating them to the usage of the past." *Ibid.*

A teacher, like the respondent, who has held his position for a number of years, might be able to show from the circumstances of this service — and from other relevant facts — that he has a legitimate claim of entitlement to job tenure. Just as this Court has found there to be a "common law of a particular industry or of a particular plant" that may supplement a collective-bargaining agreement, *Steelworkers v. Warrior & Gulf Co.,* 363 U.S. 574, 579, so there may be an unwritten "common law" in a particular university that certain employees shall have the equivalent of tenure. This is particularly likely in a college or university, like Odessa Junior College, that has no explicit tenure system even for senior members of its faculty, but that nonetheless may have created such a system in practice. See C. Byse & L. Joughin, Tenure in American Higher Education 17-28 (1959).

In this case, the respondent has alleged the existence of rules and understandings, promulgated and fostered by state officials, that may justify his legitimate claim of entitlement to continued employment absent "sufficient cause." We disagree with the Court of Appeals insofar as it held that a mere subjective "expectancy" is protected by procedural due process, but we agree that the respondent must be given an opportunity to prove the legitimacy of his claim of such entitlement in light of "the policies and practices of the institution." 430 F.2d, at 942. Proof of such a property interest would not, of course, entitle him to reinstatement. But such proof would obligate college officials to grant a hearing at his request, where he could be informed of the grounds for his nonretention and challenge their sufficiency.

Therefore, while we do not wholly agree with the opinion of the Court of Appeals, its judgment remanding this case to the District Court is

Affirmed.

BISHOP v. WOOD

426 U.S. 341, 96 S. Ct. 2074, 48 L. Ed. 2d 684 (1976)

JUSTICE STEVENS delivered the opinion of the Court.

Acting on the recommendation of the Chief of Police, the City Manager of Marion, N.C., terminated petitioner's employment as a policeman without affording him a hearing to determine the sufficiency of the cause for his discharge. Petitioner brought suit contending that since a city ordinance classified him as a "permanent employee," he had a constitutional right to a pretermination hearing.[1] During pretrial discovery petitioner was advised that his dismissal was based on a failure to follow certain orders, poor attendance at police training classes, causing low morale, and conduct unsuited to an officer. Petitioner and several other police officers filed affidavits essentially denying the truth of these charges. The District Court granted defendants' motion for summary judgment. The Court of Appeals affirmed and we granted certiorari, 423 U.S. 890.

The questions for us to decide are (1) whether petitioner's employment status was a property interest protected by the Due Process Clause of the Fourteenth Amendment, and (2) assuming that the explanation for his discharge was false, whether that false explanation deprived him of an interest in liberty protected by that clause.

I

Petitioner was employed by the city of Marion as a probationary policeman on June 9, 1969. After six months he became a permanent employee. He was

---

[1] He relied on 42 U.S.C. § 1983, invoking federal jurisdiction under 28 U.S.C. § 1343(3). He sought reinstatement and backpay. The defendants were the then City Manager, Chief of Police, and the city of Marion. Since the city is not a "person" within the meaning of the statute, it was not a proper defendant. *Monroe v. Pape,* 365 U.S. 167, 187-192.

dismissed on March 31, 1972. He claims that he had either an express or an implied right to continued employment.

A city ordinance provides that a permanent employee may be discharged if he fails to perform work up to the standard of his classification, or if he is negligent, inefficient or unfit to perform his duties.[5] Petitioner first contends that even though the ordinance does not expressly so provide, it should be read to prohibit discharge for any other reason, and therefore to confer tenure on all permanent employees. In addition, he contends that his period of service, together with his "permanent" classification, gave him a sufficient expectancy of continued employment to constitute a protected property interest.

A property interest in employment can, of course, be created by ordinance, or by an implied contract. In either case, however, the sufficiency of the claim of entitlement must be decided by reference to state law. The North Carolina Supreme Court has held that an enforceable expectation of continued public employment in that State can exist only if the employer, by statute or contract, has actually granted some form of guarantee. *Still v. Lance,* 275 N.C. 254, 182 S.E.2d 403 (1971). Whether such a guarantee has been given can be determined only by an examination of the particular statute or ordinance in question.

On its face the ordinance on which petitioner relies may fairly be read as conferring such a guarantee. However, such a reading is not the only possible interpretation; the ordinance may also be construed as granting no right to continued employment but merely conditioning an employee's removal on compliance with certain specified procedures.[8] We do not have any authoritative interpretation of this ordinance by a North Carolina state court. We do, however, have the opinion of the United States District Judge who, of course, sits in North Carolina and practiced law there for many years. Based on his understanding of state law, he concluded that petitioner "held his position at the will and pleasure of the city."[9] This construction of North Carolina law was upheld

---

[5] Article II, § 6, of the Personnel Ordinance of the city of Marion, reads as follows: *"Dismissal.* A permanent employee whose work is not satisfactory over a period of time shall be notified in what way his work is deficient and what he must do if his work is to be satisfactory. If a permanent employee fails to perform work up to the standard of the classification held, or continues to be negligent, inefficient, or unfit to perform his duties, he may be dismissed by the City Manager. Any discharged employee shall be given written notice of his discharge setting forth the effective date and reasons for his discharge if he shall request such a notice."

[8] This is not the construction which six Members of this Court placed on the federal regulations involved in *Arnett v. Kennedy,* 416 U.S. 134. In that case the Court concluded that because the employee could only be discharged for cause, he had a property interest which was entitled to constitutional protection. In this case, a holding that as a matter of state law the employee "held his position at the will and pleasure of the city" necessarily establishes that he had no property interest. The Court's evaluation of the federal regulations involved in *Arnett* sheds no light on the problem presented by this case.

[9] "Under the law in North Carolina, nothing else appearing, a contract of employment which contains no provision for the duration or termination of employment is terminable at the will of either party irrespective of the quality of performance by the other party. By statute, G.S. 115-142(b), a County Board of Education in North Carolina may terminate the employment of a teacher at the end of the school year without filing charges or giving its reasons for such termination, or granting the teacher an opportunity to be heard. *Still v. Lance,* 279 N.C. 254, 182 S.E.2d 403 (1971).

"It is clear from Article II, Section 6, of the City's Personnel Ordinance, that the dismissal of an employee does not require a notice or hearing. Upon request of the discharged employee, he shall be given written notice of his discharge setting forth the effective date and the reasons for the discharge. It thus appears that both the city ordinance and the state law have been complied with.

by the Court of Appeals for the Fourth Circuit, albeit by an equally divided Court. In comparable circumstances, the Court has accepted the interpretation of state law in which the District Court and the Court of Appeals have concurred even if an examination of the state law issue without such guidance might have justified a different conclusion.

In this case, as the District Court construed the ordinance, the City Manager's determination of the adequacy of the grounds for discharge is not subject to judicial review; the employee is merely given certain procedural rights which the District Court found not to have been violated in this case. The District Court's reading of the ordinance is tenable; it derives some support from a decision of the North Carolina Supreme Court, *Still v. Lance, supra;* and it was accepted by the Court of Appeals for the Fourth Circuit. These reasons are sufficient to foreclose our independent examination of the state-law issue.

Under that view of the law, petitioner's discharge did not deprive him of a property interest protected by the Fourteenth Amendment.

II

Petitioner's claim that he has been deprived of liberty has two components. He contends that the reasons given for his discharge are so serious as to constitute a stigma that may severely damage his reputation in the community; in addition, he claims that those reasons were false.

In our appraisal of petitioner's claim we must accept his version of the facts since the District Court granted summary judgment against him. His evidence established that he was a competent police officer; that he was respected by his peers; that he made more arrests than any other officer on the force; that although he had been criticized for engaging in high speed pursuits, he had promptly complied with such criticism; and that he had a reasonable explanation for his imperfect attendance at police training sessions. We must therefore assume that his discharge was a mistake and based on incorrect information.

In *Board of Regents v. Roth,* 408 U.S. 564, we recognized that the nonretention of an untenured college teacher might make him somewhat less attractive to other employers, but nevertheless concluded that it would stretch the concept too far "to suggest that a person is deprived of 'liberty' when he simply is not retained in one position but remains as free as before to seek another." *Id.,* at 575. This same conclusion applies to the discharge of a public employee whose position is terminable at the will of the employer when there is no public disclosure of the reasons for the discharge.

In this case the asserted reasons for the City Manager's decision were communicated orally to the petitioner in private and also were stated in writing in answer to interrogatories after this litigation commenced. Since the former communication was not made public, it cannot properly form the basis for a claim that petitioner's interest in his "good name, reputation, honesty, or integrity" was thereby impaired. And since the latter communication was made in the course of a judicial proceeding which did not commence until after petitioner had suffered the injury for which he seeks redress, it surely cannot provide

---

"It further appears that the plaintiff held his position at the will and pleasure of the city." 377 F. Supp., at 504.

retroactive support for his claim. A contrary evaluation of either explanation would penalize forthright and truthful communication between employer and employee in the former instance, and between litigants in the latter.

Petitioner argues, however, that the reasons given for his discharge were false. Even so, the reasons stated to him in private had no different impact on his reputation than if they had been true. And the answers to his interrogatories, whether true or false, did not cause the discharge. The truth or falsity of the City Manager's statement determines whether or not his decision to discharge the petitioner was correct or prudent, but neither enhances nor diminishes petitioner's claim that his constitutionally protected interest in liberty has been impaired.[13] A contrary evaluation of his contention would enable every discharged employee to assert a constitutional claim merely by alleging that his former supervisor made a mistake.

The federal court is not the appropriate forum in which to review the multitude of personnel decisions that are made daily by public agencies.[14] We must accept the harsh fact that numerous individual mistakes are inevitable in the day-to-day administration of our affairs. The United States Constitution cannot feasibly be construed to require federal judicial review for every such error. In the absence of any claim that the public employer was motivated by a desire to curtail or to penalize the exercise of an employee's constitutionally protected rights, we must presume that official action was regular and, if erroneous, can best be corrected in other ways. The Due Process Clause of the Fourteenth Amendment is not a guarantee against incorrect or ill-advised personnel decisions.

The judgment is affirmed.

So ordered.

JUSTICE BRENNAN, with whom JUSTICE MARSHALL concurs, dissenting.

Petitioner was discharged as a policeman on the grounds of insubordination, "causing low morale," and "conduct unsuited to an officer." *Ante,* at 343. It is difficult to imagine a greater "badge of infamy" that could be imposed on one following petitioner's calling; in a profession in which prospective employees are invariably investigated, petitioner's job prospects will be severely constricted by the governmental action in this case. Although our case law would appear to require that petitioner thus be accorded an opportunity "to clear his name" of this calumny, see, e.g., *Board of Regents v. Roth,* 408 U.S. 564, 573 and n. 12

---

[13] Indeed, the impact on petitioner's constitutionally protected interest in liberty is no greater even if we assume that the City Manager deliberately lied. Such fact might conceivably provide the basis for a state-law claim, the validity of which would be entirely unaffected by our analysis of the federal constitutional question.

[14] The cumulative impression created by the three dissenting opinions is that this holding represents a significant retreat from settled practice in the federal courts. The fact of the matter, however, is that the instances in which the federal judiciary has required a state agency to reinstate a discharged employee for failure to provide a pretermination hearing are extremely rare. The reason is clear. For unless we were to adopt MR. JUSTICE BRENNAN's remarkably innovative suggestion that we develop a federal common law of property rights, or his equally far reaching view that almost every discharge implicates a constitutionally protected liberty interest, the ultimate control of state personnel relationships is, and will remain, with the States; they may grant or withhold tenure at their unfettered discretion. In this case, whether we accept or reject the construction of the ordinance adopted by the two lower courts, the power to change or clarify that ordinance will remain in the hands of the City Council of the city of Marion.

(1972); *Arnett v. Kennedy,* 416 U.S. 134, 157 (1974) (opinion of REHNQUIST, J.), the Court condones this governmental action and holds that petitioner was deprived of no liberty interest thereby....

JUSTICE WHITE, with whom JUSTICE BRENNAN, JUSTICE MARSHALL, and JUSTICE BLACKMUN join, dissenting.

I dissent because the decision of the majority rests upon a proposition which was squarely addressed and in my view correctly rejected by six Members of this Court in *Arnett v. Kennedy,* 416 U.S. 134 (1974).

Petitioner Bishop was a permanent employee of the Police Department of the City of Marion, N.C. The city ordinance applicable to him provides:

> "*Dismissal.* A permanent employee whose work is not satisfactory over a period of time shall be notified in what way his work is deficient and what he must do if his work is to be satisfactory. *If a permanent employee fails to perform work up to the standard of the classification held, or continues to be negligent, inefficient, or unfit to perform his duties, he may be dismissed by the City Manager.* Any discharged employee shall be given written notice of his discharge setting forth the effective date and reasons for his discharge if he shall request such a notice." (Emphasis added.)

The second sentence of this ordinance plainly conditions petitioner's dismissal on cause — i.e., failure to perform up to standard, negligence, inefficiency, or unfitness to perform the job. The District Court below did not otherwise construe this portion of the ordinance. In the only part of its opinion rejecting petitioner's claim that the ordinance gave him a property interest in his job, the District Court said, in an opinion predating this Court's decision in *Arnett v. Kennedy, supra:*

> "It is clear from Article II, Section 6, of the City's Personnel Ordinance, that the dismissal of an employee does not require a notice or hearing. Upon request of the discharged employee, he shall be given written notice of his discharge setting forth the effective date and the reasons for the discharge. It thus appears that both the city ordinance and the state law have been complied with." 377 F. Supp. 501, 504 (WDNC 1973).

Thus in concluding that petitioner had no "property interest" in his job entitling him to a hearing on discharge and that he held his position "at the will and pleasure of the city," the District Court relied on the fact that the ordinance described its own *procedures* for determining cause which procedures did not include a hearing. The majority purports, *ante,* at 345, and n. 8, to read the District Court's opinion as construing the ordinance *not* to condition dismissal on cause, and, if this is what the majority means, its reading of the District Court's opinion is clearly erroneous for the reasons just stated.[1] However, later

---

[1] The Court accepts the District Court's conclusion that the city employee holds his position at the will and pleasure of the city. If the Court believes that the District Court's conclusion did not rest on the procedural limitations in the ordinance, then the Court must construe the District Court's opinion — and the ordinance — as permitting, but not limiting, discharges to those based on the causes specified in the ordinance. In this view, discharges for other reasons or for no reason at all could be made. Termination of employment would in effect be within the complete discretion of the city; and for this reason the employee would have no property interest in his employment which would call for the protections of the Due Process Clause. As indicated in the text, I think this construction of the ordinance and of the District Court's opinion is in error.

in its opinion the majority appears to eschew this construction of the District Court's opinion and of the ordinance. In the concluding paragraph of its discussion of petitioner's property interest, the majority holds that since neither the ordinance nor state law provides for a hearing, or any kind of review of the City Manager's dismissal decision, petitioner had no enforceable property interest in his job. The majority concludes:

"In this case, as the District Court construed the ordinance, the City Manager's *determination of the adequacy of the grounds for discharge* is not subject to judicial review; the employee is merely given certain procedural rights which the District Court found not to have been violated in this case. The District Court's reading of the ordinance is tenable ...." *Ante,* at 347. (Emphasis added.)

The majority thus implicitly concedes that the ordinance supplies the "grounds" for discharge and that the City Manager must determine them to be "adequate" before he may fire an employee. The majority's holding that petitioner had no property interest in his job in spite of the unequivocal language in the city ordinance that he may be dismissed only for certain kinds of cause rests, then, on the fact that state law provides no *procedures* for assuring that the City Manager dismiss him only for cause. The right to his job apparently given by the first two sentences of the ordinance is thus redefined, according to the majority, by the procedures provided for in the third sentence and as redefined is infringed only if the procedures are not followed.

This is precisely the reasoning which was embraced by only three and expressly rejected by six Members of this Court in *Arnett v. Kennedy, supra....*

CLEVELAND BOARD OF EDUCATION v. LOUDERMILL

470 U.S. 532, 105 S. Ct. 1487, 84 L. Ed. 2d 494 (1985)

JUSTICE WHITE delivered the opinion of the Court.

In these cases we consider what pretermination process must be accorded a public employee who can be discharged only for cause.

I

In 1979 the Cleveland Board of Education, petitioner in No. 83-1362, hired respondent James Loudermill as a security guard. On his job application, Loudermill stated that he had never been convicted of a felony. Eleven months later, as part of a routine examination of his employment records, the Board discovered that in fact Loudermill had been convicted of grand larceny in 1968. By letter dated November 3, 1980, the Board's Business Manager informed Loudermill that he had been dismissed because of his dishonesty in filling out the employment application. Loudermill was not afforded an opportunity to respond to the charge of dishonesty or to challenge his dismissal. On November 13, the Board adopted a resolution officially approving the discharge.

Under Ohio law, Loudermill was a "classified civil servant." Ohio Rev. Code Ann. § 124.11 (1984). Such employees can be terminated only for cause, and may obtain administrative review if discharged. Section 124.34 (1984). Pursuant to this provision, Loudermill filed an appeal with the Cleveland Civil Service Commission on November 12. The Commission appointed a referee, who held a hearing on January 29, 1981. Loudermill argued that he had thought that his 1968 larceny conviction was for a misdemeanor rather than a felony. The referee recommended reinstatement. On July 20, 1981, the full Commission heard argument and orally announced that it would uphold the dismissal. Proposed findings of fact and conclusions of law followed on August 10, and Loudermill's attorneys were advised of the result by mail on August 21.

Although the Commission's decision was subject to judicial review in the state courts, Loudermill instead brought the present suit in the Federal District Court for the Northern District of Ohio. The complaint alleged that § 124.34 was unconstitutional on its face because it did not provide the employee an opportunity to respond to the charges against him prior to removal. As a result, discharged employees were deprived of liberty and property without due process. The complaint also alleged that the provision was unconstitutional as applied because discharged employees were not given sufficiently prompt post-removal hearings.

Before a responsive pleading was filed, the District Court dismissed for failure to state a claim on which relief could be granted. See Fed. Rule Civ. Proc. 12(b)(6). It held that because the very statute that created the property right in continued employment also specified the procedures for discharge, and because those procedures were followed, Loudermill was, by definition, afforded all the process due. The post-termination hearing also adequately protected Loudermill's liberty interests. Finally, the District Court concluded that, in light of the Commission's crowded docket, the delay in processing Loudermill's administrative appeal was constitutionally acceptable.

The other case before us arises on similar facts and followed a similar course. Respondent Richard Donnelly was a bus mechanic for the Parma Board of Education. In August 1977, Donnelly was fired because he had failed an eye examination. He was offered a chance to retake the exam but did not do so. Like Loudermill, Donnelly appealed to the Civil Service Commission. After a year of wrangling about the timeliness of his appeal, the Commission heard the case. It ordered Donnelly reinstated, though without backpay. In a complaint essentially identical to Loudermill's, Donnelly challenged the constitutionality of the dismissal procedures. The District Court dismissed for failure to state a claim, relying on its opinion in *Loudermill*.

The District Court denied a joint motion to alter or amend its judgment,[2] and the cases were consolidated for appeal. A divided panel of the Court of Appeals for the Sixth Circuit reversed in part and remanded. 721 F.2d 550 (1983). After rejecting arguments that the actions were barred by failure to exhaust administrative remedies and by res judicata — arguments that are not renewed here — the Court of Appeals found that both respondents had been deprived of due process. It disagreed with the District Court's original rationale. Instead, it concluded that the compelling private interest in retaining employment, combined with the value of presenting evidence prior to dismissal, out-

---

[2] In denying the motion, the District Court no longer relied on the principle that the state legislature could define the necessary procedures in the course of creating the property right. Instead, it reached the same result under a balancing test based on JUSTICE POWELL's concurring opinion in *Arnett v. Kennedy*, 416 U.S. 134, 168-169 (1974), and the Court's opinion in *Mathews v. Eldridge*, 424 U.S. 319 (1976).

weighed the added administrative burden of a pretermination hearing. *Id.,* at 561-562. With regard to the alleged deprivation of liberty, and Loudermill's 9-month wait for an administrative decision, the court affirmed the District Court, finding no constitutional violation. *Id.,* at 563-564.

The dissenting Judge argued that respondents' property interests were conditioned by the procedural limitations accompanying the grant thereof. He considered constitutional requirements satisfied because there was a reliable pretermination finding of "cause," coupled with a due process hearing at a meaningful time and in a meaningful manner. *Id.,* at 566.

Both employers petitioned for certiorari. Nos. 83-1362 and 83-1363. In a cross-petition, Loudermill sought review of the rulings adverse to him. No 83-6392. We granted all three petitions, 467 U. S. — (1984), and now affirm in all respects.

II

Respondents' federal constitutional claim depends on their having had a property right in continued employment. *Board of Regents v. Roth,* 408 U.S. 564, 576-578 (1972); *Reagan v. United States,* 182 U.S. 419, 425 (1901). If they did, the State could not deprive them of this property without due process. See *Memphis Light, Gas & Water Div. v. Craft,* 436 U.S. 1, 11-12 (1978); *Goss v. Lopez,* 419 U.S. 565, 573-574 (1975).

Property interests are not created by the Constitution, "they are created and their dimensions are defined by existing rules or understandings that stem from an independent source such as state law ...." *Board of Regents v. Roth, supra,* at 577. See also *Paul v. Davis,* 424 U.S. 693, 709 (1976). The Ohio statute plainly creates such an interest. Respondents were "classified civil service employees," Ohio Rev. Code Ann. § 124.11 (1984), entitled to retain their positions "during good behavior and efficient service," who could not be dismissed "except ... for ... misfeasance, malfeasance, or nonfeasance in office," § 124.34.[4] The statute plainly supports the conclusion, reached by both lower courts, that respondents possessed property rights in continued employment. Indeed, this question does not seem to have been disputed below.[5]

The Parma Board argues, however, that the property right is defined by, and conditioned on, the legislature's choice of procedures for its deprivation. The Board stresses that in addition to specifying the grounds for termination, the

---

[4] The relevant portion of § 124.34 provides that no classified civil servant may be removed except "for incompetency, inefficiency, dishonesty, drunkenness, immoral conduct, insubordination, discourteous treatment of the public, neglect of duty, violation of such sections or the rules of the director of administrative services or the commission, or any other failure of good behavior, or any other acts of misfeasance, malfeasance, or nonfeasance in office."

[5] The Cleveland Board of Education now asserts that Loudermill had no property right under state law because he obtained his employment by lying on the application. It argues that had Loudermill answered truthfully he would not have been fired. He therefore lacked a "legitimate claim of entitlement" to the position.

For several reasons, we must reject this submission. First, it was not raised below. Second, it makes factual assumptions — that Loudermill lied, and that he would not have been hired had he not done so — that are inconsistent with the allegations of the complaint and inappropriate at this stage of the litigation, which has not proceeded past the initial pleadings stage. Finally, the argument relies on a retrospective fiction inconsistent with the undisputed fact that Loudermill was hired and did hold the security guard job. The Board cannot escape its constitutional obligations by rephrasing the basis for termination as a reason why Loudermill should not have been hired in the first place.

statute sets out procedures by which termination may take place. The procedures were adhered to in these cases. According to petitioner, "[t]o require additional procedures would in effect expand the scope of the property interest itself."

This argument, which was accepted by the District Court, has its genesis in the plurality opinion in *Arnett v. Kennedy*, 416 U.S. 134 (1974). *Arnett* involved a challenge by a former federal employee to the procedures by which he was dismissed. The plurality reasoned that where the legislation conferring the substantive right also sets out the procedural mechanism for enforcing that right, the two cannot be separated:

"The employee's statutorily defined right is not a guarantee against removal without cause in the abstract, but such a guarantee as enforced by the procedures which Congress has designated for the determination of cause.

"... [W]here the grant of a substantive right is inextricably intertwined with the limitations on the procedures which are to be employed in determining that right, a litigant in the position of appellee must take the bitter with the sweet." *Id.,* at 152-154.

This view garnered three votes in *Arnett,* but was specifically rejected by the other six Justices. See *id.,* at 166-167 (POWELL, J., joined by BLACKMUN, J.,); *id.,* at 177-178, 185 (WHITE, J.,); *id.,* at 211 (MARSHALL, J., joined by DOUGLAS and BRENNAN, JJ.). Since then, this theory has at times seemed to gather some additional support. See *Bishop v. Wood,* 426 U.S. 341, 355-361 (1976) (WHITE, J., dissenting); *Goss v. Lopez,* 419 U.S., at 586-587 (POWELL, J., joined by BURGER, C.J., and BLACKMUN and REHNQUIST, JJ., dissenting). More recently, however, the Court has clearly rejected it. In *Vitek v. Jones,* 445 U.S. 480, 491 (1980), we pointed out that "minimum [procedural] requirements [are] a matter of federal law, they are not diminished by the fact that the State may have specified its own procedures that it may deem adequate for determining the preconditions to adverse official action." This conclusion was reiterated in *Logan v. Zimmerman Brush Co.,* 455 U.S. 422, 432 (1982), where we reversed the lower court's holding that because the entitlement arose from a state statute, the legislature had the prerogative to define the procedures to be followed to protect that entitlement.

In light of these holdings, it is settled that the "bitter with the sweet" approach misconceives the constitutional guarantee. If a clearer holding is needed, we provide it today. The point is straightforward: the Due Process Clause provides that certain substantive rights — life, liberty, and property — cannot be deprived except pursuant to constitutionally adequate procedures. The categories of substance and procedure are distinct. Were the rule otherwise, the Clause would be reduced to a mere tautology. "Property" cannot be defined by the procedures provided for its deprivation any more than can life or liberty. The right to due process "is conferred, not by legislative grace, but by constitutional guarantee. While the legislature may elect not to confer a property interest in [public] employment, it may not constitutionally authorize the deprivation of such an interest, once conferred, without appropriate procedural safeguards." *Arnett v. Kennedy, supra,* at 167 (POWELL, J., concurring in part and concurring in result in part); see *id.,* at 185 (WHITE, J., concurring in part, and dissenting in part).

In short, once it is determined that the Due Process Clause applies, "the question remains what process is due." *Morrissey v. Brewer,* 408 U.S. 471, 481 (1972). The answer to that question is not to be found in the Ohio statute.

III

An essential principle of due process is that a deprivation of life, liberty, or property "be preceded by notice and opportunity for hearing appropriate to the nature of the case." *Mullane v. Central Hanover Bank & Trust Co.,* 339 U.S. 306, 313 (1950). We have described "the root requirement" of the Due Process Clause as being "that an individual be given an opportunity for a hearing *before* he is deprived of any significant property interest." *Boddie v. Connecticut,* 401 U.S. 371, 379 (1971) (emphasis in original); see *Bell v. Burson,* 402 U.S. 535, 542 (1971). This principle requires "some kind of a hearing" prior to the discharge of an employee who has a constitutionally protected property interest in his employment. *Board of Regents v. Roth,* 408 U.S., at 569-570; *Perry v. Sinderman,* 408 U.S. 593, 599 (1972). As we pointed out last Term, this rule has been settled for some time now. *Davis v. Scherer,* 468 U.S. —, —, n. 10 (1984); *id.,* at — (BRENNAN, J., concurring in part and dissenting in part). Even decisions finding no constitutional violation in termination procedures have relied on the existence of some pretermination opportunity to respond. For example, in *Arnett* six Justices found constitutional minima satisfied where the employee had access to the material upon which the charge was based and could respond orally and in writing and present rebuttal affidavits. See also *Barry v. Barchi,* 443 U.S. 55, 65 (1979) (no due process violation where horse trainer whose license was suspended "was given more than one opportunity to present his side of the story").

The need for some form of pretermination hearing, recognized in these cases, is evident from a balancing of the competing interests at stake. These are the private interest in retaining employment, the governmental interest in the expeditious removal of unsatisfactory employees and the avoidance of administrative burdens, and the risk of an erroneous termination. See *Mathews v. Eldridge,* 424 U.S. 319, 335 (1976).

First, the significance of the private interest in retaining employment cannot be gainsaid. We have frequently recognized the severity of depriving a person of the means of livelihood. See *Fusari v. Steinberg,* 419 U.S. 379, 389 (1975); *Bell v. Burson, supra,* at 539; *Goldberg v. Kelly,* 397 U.S. 254, 264 (1970); *Sniadach v. Family Finance Corp.,* 395 U.S. 337, 340 (1969). While a fired worker may find employment elsewhere, doing so will take some time and is likely to be burdened by the questionable circumstances under which he left his previous job. See *Lefkowitz v. Turley,* 414 U.S. 70, 83-84 (1973).

Second, some opportunity for the employee to present his side of the case is recurringly of obvious value in reaching an accurate decision. Dismissals for cause will often involve factual disputes. Cf. *Califano v. Yamasaki,* 442 U.S. 682, 686 (1979). Even where the facts are clear, the appropriateness or necessity of the discharge may not be; in such cases, the only meaningful opportunity to invoke the discretion of the decisionmaker is likely to be before the termination takes effect. See *Goss v. Lopez,* 419 U.S., at 583-584; *Gagnon v. Scarpelli,* 411 U.S. 778, 784-786 (1973).[8]

The cases before us illustrate these considerations. Both respondents had plausible arguments to make that might have prevented their discharge. The fact that the Commission saw fit to reinstate Donnelly suggests that an error might have been avoided had he been provided an opportunity to make his case to the Board. As for Loudermill, given the Commission's ruling we cannot say that the discharge was mistaken. Nonetheless, in light of the referee's recommendation, neither can we say that a fully informed decisionmaker might not have exercised its discretion and decided not to dismiss him, notwithstanding its authority to do so. In any event, the termination involved arguable issues,[9] and the right to a hearing does not depend on a demonstration of certain success. *Carey v. Piphus,* 435 U.S. 247, 266 (1978).

The governmental interest in immediate termination does not outweigh these interests. As we shall explain, affording the employee an opportunity to respond prior to termination would impose neither a significant administrative burden nor intolerable delays. Furthermore, the employer shares the employee's interest in avoiding disruption and erroneous decisions; and until the matter is settled, the employer would continue to receive the benefit of the employee's labors. It is preferable to keep a qualified employee on than to train a new one. A governmental employer also has an interest in keeping citizens usefully employed rather than taking the possibly erroneous and counter-productive step of forcing its employees onto the welfare rolls. Finally, in those situations where the employer perceives a significant hazard in keeping the employee on the job, it can avoid the problem by suspending with pay.

IV

The foregoing considerations indicate that the pretermination "hearing," though necessary, need not be elaborate. We have pointed out that "[t]he formality and procedural requisites for the hearing can vary, depending upon the importance of the interests involved and the nature of the subsequent proceedings." *Boddie v. Connecticut,* 401 U.S., at 378. See *Cafeteria Workers v. McElroy,* 367 U.S. 886, 894-895 (1961). In general, "something less" than a full evidentiary hearing is sufficient prior to adverse administrative action. *Mathews v. Eldridge,* 424 U.S., at 343. Under state law, respondents were later entitled to

---

[8]This is not to say that where state conduct is entirely discretionary the Due Process Clause is brought into play. See *Meachum v. Fano,* 427 U.S. 215, 228 (1976). Nor is it to say that a person can insist on a hearing in order to argue that the decisionmaker should be lenient and depart from legal requirements. See *Dixon v. Love,* 431 U.S. 105, 114 (1977). The point is that where there is an entitlement, a prior hearing facilitates the consideration of whether a permissible course of action is also an appropriate one. This is one way in which providing "effective notice and informal hearing permitting the [employee] to give his version of the events will provide a meaningful hedge against erroneous action. At least the [employer] will be alerted to the existence of disputes about facts and arguments about cause and effect.... [H]is discretion will be more informed and we think the risk of error substantially reduced." *Goss v. Lopez,* 419 U.S. 565, 583-584 (1975).

[9]Loudermill's dismissal turned not on the objective fact that he was an ex-felon or the inaccuracy of his statement to the contrary, but on the subjective question whether he had lied on his application form. His explanation for the false statement is plausible in light of the fact that he received only a suspended 6-month sentence and a fine on the grand larceny conviction.

a full administrative hearing and judicial review. The only question is what steps were required before the termination took effect.

In only one case, *Goldberg v. Kelly,* 397 U.S. 254 (1970), has the Court required a full adversarial evidentiary hearing prior to adverse governmental action. However, as the *Goldberg* Court itself pointed out, see *id.,* at 264, that case presented significantly different considerations than are present in the context of public employment. Here, the pretermination hearing need not definitively resolve the propriety of the discharge. It should be an initial check against mistaken decisions — essentially, a determination of whether there are reasonable grounds to believe that the charges against the employee are true and support the proposed action. See *Bell v. Burson,* 402 U.S., at 540.

The essential requirements of due process, and all that respondents seek or the Court of Appeals required, are notice and an opportunity to respond. The opportunity to present reasons, either in person or in writing, why proposed action should not be taken is a fundamental due process requirement. See Friendly, "Some Kind of Hearing," 123 U. Pa. L. Rev. 1267, 1281 (1975). The tenured public employee is entitled to oral or written notice of the charges against him, an explanation of the employer's evidence, and an opportunity to present his side of the story. See *Arnett v. Kennedy,* 416 U.S., at 170-171 (opinion of POWELL, J.); *id.,* at 195-196 (opinion of WHITE, J.); see also *Goss v. Lopez,* 419 U.S., at 581. To require more than this prior to termination would intrude to an unwarranted extent on the government's interest in quickly removing an unsatisfactory employee.

V

Our holding rests in part on the provisions in Ohio law for a full post-termination hearing. In his cross-petition Loudermill asserts, as a separate constitutional violation, that his administrative proceedings took too long. The Court of Appeals held otherwise, and we agree. The Due Process Clause requires provision of a hearing "at a meaningful time." E.g., *Armstrong v. Manzo,* 380 U.S. 545, 552 (1965). At some point, a delay in the post-termination hearing would become a constitutional violation. See *Barry v. Barchi,* 443 U.S., at 66. In the present case, however, the complaint merely recites the course of proceedings and concludes that the denial of a "speedy resolution" violated due process. This reveals nothing about the delay except that it stemmed in part from the thoroughness of the procedures. A 9-month adjudication is not, of course, unconstitutionally lengthy per se. Yet Loudermill offers no indication that his wait was unreasonably prolonged other than the fact that it took nine months. The chronology of the proceedings set out in the complaint, coupled with the assertion that nine months is too long to wait, does not state a claim of a constitutional deprivation.[13]

---

[13] The cross-petition also argues that Loudermill was unconstitutionally deprived of liberty because of the accusation of dishonesty that hung over his head during the administrative proceedings. As the Court of Appeals found, 721 F.2d, at 563, n. 18, the failure to allege that the reasons for the dismissal were published dooms this claim. See *Bishop v. Wood,* 426 U.S. 341, 348 (1976).

VI

We conclude that all the process that is due is provided by a pre-termination opportunity to respond, coupled with post-termination administrative procedures as provided by the Ohio statute. Because respondents allege in their complaints that they had no chance to respond, the District Court erred in dismissing for failure to state a claim. The judgment of the Court of Appeals is affirmed, and the case is remanded for further proceedings consistent with this opinion.

So ordered.

JUSTICE MARSHALL, concurring in Part II and concurring in the judgment.

I agree wholeheartedly with the Court's express rejection of the theory of due process, urged upon us by the petitioners, that a public employee who may be discharged only for cause may be discharged by whatever procedures the legislature chooses. I therefore join Part II of the opinion for the Court. I also agree that, before discharge, the respondents were entitled to the opportunity to respond to the charges against them (which is all they requested), and that the failure to accord them that opportunity was a violation of their constitutional rights. Because the Court holds that the respondents were due all the process they requested, I concur in the judgment of the Court.

I write separately, however, to reaffirm my belief that public employees who may be discharged only for cause are entitled, under the Due Process Clause of the Fourteenth Amendment, to more than respondents sought in this case. I continue to believe that *before the decision is made to terminate an employee's wages,* the employee is entitled to an opportunity to test the strength of the evidence "by confronting and cross-examining adverse witnesses and by presenting witnesses on [their] own behalf, whenever there are substantial disputes in testimonial evidence," *Arnett v. Kennedy,* 416 U.S. 134, 214 (1974) (MARSHALL, J., dissenting). Because the Court suggests that even in this situation due process requires no more than notice and an opportunity to be heard before wages are cut off, I am not able to join the Court's opinion in its entirety.

To my mind, the disruption caused by a loss of wages may be so devastating to an employee that, whenever there are substantial disputes about the evidence, additional pre-deprivation procedures are necessary to minimize the risk of an erroneous termination. That is, I place significantly greater weight than does the Court on the public employee's substantial interest in the accuracy of the pre-termination proceeding. After wage termination, the employee often must wait months before his case is finally resolved, during which time he is without wages from his public employment. By limiting the procedures due prior to termination of wages, the Court accepts an impermissibly high risk that a wrongfully discharged employee will be subjected to this often lengthy wait for vindication, and to the attendant and often traumatic disruptions to his personal and economic life....

Were there any guarantee that the post-deprivation hearing and ruling would occur promptly, such as within a few days of the termination of wages, then this minimal pre-deprivation process might suffice. But there is no such guarantee. On a practical level, if the employer had to pay the employee until the end of the proceeding, the employer obviously would have an incentive to resolve the issue expeditiously. The employer loses this incentive if the only suffering as a result of the delay is borne by the wage earner, who eagerly awaits the decision on his livelihood. Nor has this Court grounded any guarantee of this kind in the Constitution. Indeed, this Court has in the past approved, at least implicitly, an average 10- or 11-month delay in the receipt of a decision on Social Security benefits, *Mathews v. Eldridge,* 424 U.S. 319, 341-342 (1976), and, in the case of respondent Loudermill, the Court gives a stamp of approval to a process that took nine months. The hardship inevitably increases as the days go by, but nevertheless the Court countenances such delay. The adequacy of the pre- and post-deprivation procedures are inevitably intertwined, and only a constitutional guarantee that the latter will be immediate and complete might alleviate my concern about the possibility of a wrongful termination of wages....

JUSTICE BRENNAN, concurring in part and dissenting in part....

I

First, the Court today does not prescribe the precise form of required pretermination procedures in cases where an employee disputes the *facts* proffered to support his discharge. The cases at hand involve, as the Court recognizes, employees who did not dispute the facts but had "plausible arguments to make that might have prevented their discharge." In such cases, notice and an "opportunity to present reasons," are sufficient to protect the important interests at stake....

The Court acknowledges that what the Constitution requires prior to discharge, in general terms, is pretermination procedures sufficient to provide "an initial check against mistaken decisions — essentially, a determination of whether there are reasonable grounds to believe that the charges against the employee are *true* and support the proposed action." (emphasis added). When factual disputes are involved, therefore, an employee may deserve a fair opportunity before discharge to produce contrary records or testimony, or even to confront an accusor in front of the decisionmaker. Such an opportunity might not necessitate "elaborate" procedures, but the fact remains that in some cases only such an opportunity to challenge the source or produce contrary evidence will suffice to support a finding that there are "reasonable grounds" to believe accusations are "true."

Factual disputes are not involved in these cases, however, and the "very nature of due process negates any concept of indexible procedures universally applicable to every imaginable situation." *Cafeteria Workers v. McElroy,* 367 U.S. 886, 895 (1961). I do not understand Part IV to foreclose the views expressed above or by JUSTICE MARSHALL, with respect to discharges based on disputed evidence or testimony. I therefore join parts I-IV of the Court's opinion.

II

The second issue not resolved today is that of administrative delay. In holding that Loudermill's administrative proceedings did not take too long, the Court plainly does *not* state a flat rule that nine-month delays in deciding discharge appeals will pass constitutional scrutiny as a matter of course. To the contrary, the Court notes that a full post-termination hearing and decision must be provided at "a meaningful time" and that "[a]t some point, a delay in the post-termination hearing would become a constitutional violation." For example, in *Barry v. Barchi,* 443 U.S. 55 (1979), we disapproved as "constitutionally infirm" the shorter administrative delays that resulted under a statute that required "prompt" postsuspension hearings for suspended racehorse trainers with decision to follow within thirty days of the hearing. *Id.,* at 61, 66. As JUSTICE MARSHALL demonstrates, when an employee's wages are terminated pending administrative decision, "hardship inevitably increases as the days go by." ...

III

Recognizing the limited scope of the holding in Part V, I must still dissent from its result, because the record in this case is insufficiently developed to permit an informed judgment on the issue of overlong delay. Loudermill's complaint was dismissed without answer from the respondent Cleveland Civil Service Commission. Allegations at this early stage are to be liberally construed, and "[i]t is axiomatic that a complaint should not be dismissed unless 'it appears beyond doubt that the plaintiff can prove no set of facts in support of his claim which would entitle him to relief.'" *McLain v. Real Estate Bd. of New Orleans, Inc.,* 444 U.S. 232, 246 (1980) (citation omitted). Loudermill alleged that it took the Commission over two and one-half months simply to hold a hearing in his case, over two months *more* to issue a non-binding interim decision, and more than three and one-half months after *that* to deliver a final decision. The Commission provided no explanation for these significant gaps in the administrative process; we do not know if they were due to an overabundance of appeals, Loudermill's own foot-dragging, bad faith on the part of the Commission, or any other of a variety of reasons that might affect our analysis. We do know, however, that under Ohio law the Commission is obligated to hear appeals like Loudermill's "within thirty days." Ohio Rev. Code Ann. § 124.34 (1984). Although this statutory limit has been viewed only as "directory" by Ohio courts, those courts have also made it clear that when the limit is exceeded, "[t]he burden of proof [is] placed on the [Commission] to illustrate to the court that the failure to comply with the 30-day requirement ... was reasonable." *In re Bronkar,* 53 Ohio Misc. 13, 17, 372 N.E.2d 1345, 1347 (Ct. Comm. Pleas 1977). I cannot conclude on this record that Loudermill could prove "no set of facts" that might have entitled him to relief after nine months of waiting....

JUSTICE REHNQUIST, dissenting.

In *Arnett v. Kennedy,* 416 U.S. 134 (1974), six Members of this Court agreed that a public employee could be dismissed for misconduct without a full hearing prior to termination. A plurality of Justices agreed that the employee was entitled to exactly what Congress gave him, and no more. THE CHIEF JUSTICE, JUSTICE STEWART, and I said:

"Here appellee did have a statutory expectancy that he not be removed other than for 'such cause as will promote the efficiency of [the] service.' But the very section of the statute which granted him that right, a right which had previously existed only by virtue of administrative regulation, expressly provided also for the procedure by which 'cause' was to be determined, and expressly omitted the procedural guarantees which appellee insists are mandated by the Constitution. Only by bifurcating the very sentence of the Act of Congress which conferred upon appellee the right not to be removed save for cause could it be said that he had an expectancy of that substantive right without the procedural limitations which Congress attached to it. In the area of federal regulation of government employees, where in the absence of statutory limitation the governmental employer has had virtually uncontrolled latitude in decisions as to hiring and firing, *Cafeteria Workers v. McElroy,* 367 U.S. 886, 896-897 (1961), we do not believe that a statutory enactment such as the Lloyd-La Follette Act may be parsed as discretely as appellee urges. Congress was obviously intent on according a measure of statutory job security to governmental employees which they had not previously enjoyed, but was likewise intent on excluding more elaborate procedural requirements which it felt would make the operation of the new scheme unnecessarily burdensome in practice. Where the focus of legislation was thus strongly on the procedural mechanism for enforcing the substantive right which was simultaneously conferred, we decline to conclude that the substantive right may be viewed wholly apart from the procedure provided for its enforcement. The employee's statutorily defined right is not a guarantee against removal without cause in the abstract, but such a guarantee as enforced by the procedures which Congress has designated for the determination of cause." *Id.,* at 151-152.

In this case, the relevant Ohio statute provides in its first paragraph that

"[t]he tenure of every officer or employee in the classified service of the state and the counties, civil service townships, cities, city health districts, general health districts, and city school districts thereof, holding a position under this chapter of the Revised Code, shall be during good behavior and efficient service and no such officer or employee shall be reduced in pay or position, suspended, or removed, except ... for incompetency, inefficiency, dishonesty, drunkenness, immoral conduct, insubordination, discourteous treatment of the public, neglect of duty, violation of such sections or the rules of the director of administrative services or the commission, or any other failure of good behavior, or any other acts of misfeasance, malfeasance, or nonfeasance in office." Ohio Rev. Code Ann. § 124.34 (1981).

The very next paragraph of this section of the Ohio Revised Code provides that in the event of suspension of more than three days or removal the appointing authority shall furnish the employee with the stated reasons for his removal. The next paragraph provides that within ten days following the receipt of such a statement, the employee may appeal in writing to the State Personnel Board of Review or the Commission, such appeal shall be heard within 30 days from the time of its filing, and the Board may affirm, disaffirm, or modify the judgment of the appointing authority.

Thus in one legislative breath Ohio has conferred upon civil service employees such as respondents in this case a limited form of tenure during good behavior, and prescribed the procedures by which that tenure may be terminated. Here, as in *Arnett,* "[t]he employee's statutorily defined right is not a guarantee against removal without cause in the abstract, but such a guarantee as enforced by the procedures which [the Ohio legislature] has designated for the determination of cause." 416 U.S., at 152 (opinion of REHNQUIST, J.). We stated in *Board of Regents v. Roth,* 408 U.S. 564, 577 (1972):

> "Property interests, of course, are not created by the Constitution. Rather, they are created and their dimensions are defined by existing rules or understandings that stem from an independent source such as state law — rules or understandings that secure certain benefits and that support claims of entitlement to those benefits."

We ought to recognize the totality of the State's definition of the property right in question, and not merely seize upon one of several paragraphs in a unitary statute to proclaim that in that paragraph the State has inexorably conferred upon a civil service employee something which it is powerless under the United States Constitution to qualify in the next paragraph of the statute. This practice ignores our duty under *Roth* to rely on state law as the source of property interests for purposes of applying the Due Process Clause of the Fourteenth Amendment. While it does not impose a federal definition of property, the Court departs from the full breadth of the holding in *Roth* by its selective choice from among the sentences the Ohio legislature chooses to use in establishing and qualifying a right....

NOTES

1. In *Codd v. Velger,* 429 U.S. 624 (1977), the Court recognized that a mere claim that a discharged employee has been stigmatized by his accusers does not ipso facto establish his right to a due process hearing:

> Assuming all of the other elements necessary to make out a claim of stigmatization under *Roth* and *Bishop,* the remedy mandated by the Due Process Clause of the Fourteenth Amendment is "an opportunity to refute the charge." 408 U.S., at 573. "The purpose of such notice and hearing is to provide the person an opportunity to clear his name," *id.,* at 573 n. 12. But if the hearing mandated by the Due Process Clause is to serve any useful purpose, there must be some factual dispute between an employer and a discharged employee which has some significant bearing on the employee's reputation. Nowhere in his pleadings or elsewhere has respondent affirmatively asserted that the report of the apparent suicide attempt was substantially false. Neither the District Court nor the Court of Appeals made any such finding. When we consider the nature of the interest sought to be protected, we believe the absence of any such allegation or finding is fatal to respondent's claim under the Due Process Clause that he should have been given a hearing.

429 U.S. at 627. In *Siegert v. Gilley,* 111 S. Ct. — (1991), the Supreme Court refused to permit a federal employee to sue a former supervisor who provided a reference that characterized him as inept, unethical, and untrustworthy, since the Court majority concluded that injury to one's reputation is not a constitutionally protected "liberty" interest.

2. In *Lake Mich. College Fed'n of Teachers v. Lake Mich. Community College,* 518 F.2d 1091 (1975), *cert. denied,* 427 U.S. 904 (1976), the Sixth Circuit applied the standards of *Roth* and *Arnett* to find that Michigan college teachers who participated in an illegal strike had been properly discharged since neither that state's Public Employment Relations Act nor the collective bargaining agreement between the parties granted any property interest in continued employment to the teachers. The court also held that the teachers' fourteenth amendment liberty interests were not automatically implicated when they were accused of breaking the law absent a showing that (1) the allegations discredited the teachers' honesty, morality, and integrity; (2) their reputations were seriously damaged in the community; or (3) a definite range of opportunities was no longer open to them.

3. In *Soni v. Board of Trustees,* 513 F.2d 347 (6th Cir. 1975), *cert. denied,* 426 U.S. 919 (1976), a nontenured university professor who had been terminated claimed a violation of his due process rights. The court there held that the existence of a formal tenure system would not automatically foreclose a determination that a nontenured professor has acquired a property interest in his employment. Where the university objectively acted toward the plaintiff in such a manner as to lead the professor reasonably to believe his employment was relatively permanent, a lower court finding that he had acquired a property interest that could not be terminated without procedural due process was not clearly erroneous and would not be overturned. Cf. *Cusumano v. Ratchford,* 507 F.2d 980 (8th Cir.), *cert. denied,* 423 U.S. 829 (1975), where professors hired under "term appointments" as opposed to continuous or tenured appointments were held to have acquired no tenure, de facto or otherwise, under the University of Missouri's academic tenure regulations and had no constitutional or contractual right to a statement of reasons for nonreappointment or a hearing. Compare *Jordan v. City of Lake Oswego,* 734 F.2d 1374 (9th Cir. 1984) (city attorney appointed to four-year term entitled to due process hearing before discharge), with *Osman v. Hialeah Hous. Auth.,* 785 F.2d 1550 (11th Cir. 1986) (outside counsel retained for three-year period not entitled to due process hearing before termination of that part-time arrangement). See also *Bigby v. City of Chicago,* 766 F.2d 1053 (7th Cir. 1985), *cert. denied,* 474 U.S. 1056 (1986) (mere expectation interest of police sergeants seeking promotion to lieutenant insufficient to entitle them to due process rights prior to their rejection); *Griffith v. FLRA,* 842 F.2d 487 (D.C. Cir. 1988) (employees have insufficient property interest in annual within-grade increases to warrant due process protection).

4. Although a municipal employee may be entitled to a due process hearing prior to his discharge, he may not have to be afforded such formal protection before a disciplinary suspension of no more than five days, since the consequences of an erroneous short-term suspension are not nearly as significant as the ramifications of a wrongful termination. See *Civil Serv. Ass'n v. San Francisco,* 22 Cal. 3d 552, 586 P.2d 162 (1978). Cf. *Brown v. Brienen,* 722 F.2d 360 (7th Cir. 1983) (no right to hearing for employees denied compensatory time off for overtime work); *APWU v. United States Postal Serv.,* 707 F.2d 548 (D.C. Cir. 1983), *cert. denied,* 104 S. Ct. 1594 (1984) (no right to hearing regarding change in method of computing nonvested pension benefits for current employees).

5. In *Hostrop v. Board of Junior College Dist. No. 515,* 523 F.2d 569 (7th Cir. 1975), *cert. denied,* 425 U.S. 963 (1976), termination of the president of a public junior college without notice and impartial hearing was held actionable despite the trial court finding that his conduct in withholding information from the board constituted just cause for dismissal. Damages, however, were limited to those that were attributable only to the failure to afford due process and not for the termination of employment itself. On a theory of recovery for tortious injury, such an award could include damages for constitutional deprivation, as well as mental distress, humiliation, and any other injury caused as a result of being deprived of federally protected rights, but not attorneys' fees.

6. Where minimal procedural safeguards are provided in contractual grievance-arbitration provisions, that avenue of relief may provide an acceptable substitute for constitutionally mandated procedural protections. See *Gorham v. City of Kansas City,* 590 P.2d 1051, 101 L.R.R.M. 2290 (Kan. 1979). Cf. *Winston v. United States Postal Serv.,* 585 F.2d 198 (7th Cir. 1978). See also *Stephens v. Postmaster Gen.,* 623 F.2d 594 (9th Cir. 1980), finding no due process violation where the postal service and the representative union cancelled a scheduled arbitration of a discharged employee's grievance on the ground he had waived his access to the grievance procedure under the collective contract by virtue of his appeal to the Civil Service Commission, even though his CSC appeal had been dismissed as untimely during the period his grievance was being processed. A similar result was reached in *Jackson v. Temple Univ.,* 721 F.2d 931 (3d Cir. 1983), wherein the court found that a discharged employee who possessed the right to utilize contractual grievance-arbitration procedures, but whose union chose not to invoke the arbitration step on his behalf, had been provided with adequate due process.

Some courts will require employees to exhaust available grievance-arbitration procedures before litigating constitutional claims, where it appears likely that resort to those procedures would resolve the issues in dispute. See *McGrath v. State,* 309 N.W.2d 54, 1981-83 PBC ¶ 37,318 (Minn. 1981). See also *Carter v. Kurzejeski,* 706 F.2d 835 (8th Cir. 1983). But cf. *McDonald v. City of W. Branch,* 104 S. Ct. 1799 (1984), wherein the Court held that a prior adverse arbitral decision did not have a preclusive effect in a subsequent first amendment suit under § 1983, since the plaintiff had the right to have such a constitutional claim decided in a judicial proceeding. See generally Wallace, *Union Waiver of Public Employees' Due Process Rights,* 8 Indus. Rel. L.J. 583 (1986); Finkin, *The Limits of Majority Rule in Collective Bargaining,* 64 Minn. L. Rev. 183, 239-73 (1980).

7. In *Johnson v. United States,* 628 F.2d 187 (D.C. Cir. 1980), the court held that due process does not preclude administrative reliance upon hearsay evidence in a removal hearing. The court also found that the legal inability of the CSC to issue subpoenas requested by the discharged employee did not deprive him of procedural due process. See also *Rodgers v. Norfolk Sch. Bd.,* 755 F.2d 59 (4th Cir. 1985), where the court found no due process violation where the board refused to provide a discharged bus driver with the right to confront and cross-examine children who had accused her of engaging in an altercation, which involved the brandishing of a knife, with her sister on their bus, due to the obvious countervailing risk of emotional trauma for the children involved. However, see *Hoska v. Dep't of Army,* 677 F.2d 131 (D.C. Cir. 1982), indicating that an employee's termination cannot be based entirely upon unsubstantiated hearsay.

Where a government hearing officer arbitrarily limited the length of a pretermination hearing and demanded that the grievant's attorney expedite his presentation of the case, the court found that the employee had been deprived of a fair hearing. *Frampton v. Department of Interior,* 811 F.2d 1486 (Fed. Cir. 1987). See also *Swank v. Smart,* 898 F.2d 1247 (7th Cir. 1990) (failure to provide police officer with opportunity at pretermination hearing to respond to written statements by accuser and police chief regarding his alleged misconduct deprived him of due process).

In *Banks v. Federal Aviation Admin.*, 687 F.2d 92 (5th Cir. 1982), the court held that the discharges of air traffic controllers for alleged drug usage could not be sustained where the principal evidence relied upon by the government, voluntarily submitted urine samples, had been destroyed and was thus not available for independent testing, and where other available evidence was insufficient to provide an independent basis to support the terminations.

8. When an employee is terminated for alleged misconduct, due process requires that he receive clear notification of the charges against him, so that he has the opportunity to reply to them effectively. See *Knuckles v. Bolger,* 654 F.2d 25 (8th Cir. 1981). However, even where a discharged school employee is not formally advised of his right to a hearing before the school board and none is conducted, there may be no due process violation if the employee actually knew about his right to have such a hearing and simply failed to request one. See *Pedersen v. Williamsport Sch. Dist.,* 677 F.2d 312 (3d Cir. 1982), *cert. denied,* 459 U.S. 972 (1982). See also *Coleman v. Department of Pers. Admin.,* — Cal. 3d —, 805 P.2d 300 (1991) (state must provide notice and opportunity to respond before terminating person's employment under statute that treats five consecutive days of unexcused absence as "automatic resignation").

9. *Webster v. Doe,* 486 U.S. 592 (1988), involved a Central Intelligence Agency (CIA) employee who was discharged after he voluntarily informed the CIA that he was a homosexual. He sought review of his termination under the Administrative Procedure Act (APA) and the due process clause of the fifth amendment. The Supreme Court found that APA review was unavailable due to the statutory exception pertaining to "action committed to agency discretion by law," since section 102(c) of the National Security Act of 1947 (NSA) provides the CIA Director with broad discretion over such employment determinations. Nonetheless, the Court went on to find that district court review of the discharged employee's constitutional claims was not precluded by section 102(c) of the NSA. While the CIA Director enjoys substantial discretion with respect to such decisions, he is not authorized to ignore applicable constitutional doctrines. See also *Doe v. Cheney,* 885 F.2d 898 (D.C. Cir. 1989), wherein the court held that, since no one has a "right" to a security clearance, there is no need for the National Security Agency to provide a hearing before it revokes an individual's security clearance.

10. Regarding the consistency of Supreme Court decisions in the due process area, compare Van Alstyne, *The Demise of the Right-Privilege Distinction in Constitutional Law,* 81 Harv. L. Rev. 1439 (1968), with Smolla, *The Reemergence of the Right-Privilege Distinction in Constitutional Law: The Price of Protesting Too Much,* 35 Stan. L. Rev. 69 (1982). See also Van Alstyne, *Cracks in "The New Property": Adjudicative Due Process in the Administrative State,* 62 Corn. L. Rev. 445 (1977); Monaghan, *Of "Liberty" and "Property,"* 62 Corn. L. Rev. 401 (1977).

C. REGULATION OF PARTISAN POLITICAL ACTIVITIES OF PUBLIC EMPLOYEES

1. THE HATCH ACT

COMMENT, THE HATCH ACT — A CONSTITUTIONAL RESTRAINT OF FREEDOM? 33 Alb. L. Rev. 345-47 (1969)*

The Hatch Act was the product of two Congressional enactments and was intended to prevent what Congress deemed to be "pernicious political activities" among certain federal, state and local employees. In the opinion of one author, the purpose of the act was to insure the political neutrality of federal and state bureaucracies because "political neutrality among career civil servants is a necessary corollary to efficient and responsible administration." It has been claimed that the Hatch Act, by eliminating partisan political activity among federal employees, combats four evils: the act prevents the bureaucracy from becoming a united political power bloc; it prevents the party in power from using government workers to promote the continued dominance of the party; it prevents competition between the party and the department head for the employee's loyalty; and it prevents employee demoralization which results from promotions and rewards based on politics rather than merit.

With regard to political activity, the act prohibits specified employees of the federal executive department from either affecting the result of an election or from actively participating in political management or political campaigns.[13] Generally, every employee in the executive branch of the federal government falls within the prohibition of the act. However, there are several notable exceptions. The prohibition against political management and political campaigns does not apply to any person employed as the head or assistant head of an executive department, or paid from the appropriations of the President's office, or appointed as a member of the executive department, by the President with the advice and consent of the Senate.[14] Likewise, not all political activities are prohibited. Section 7326 exempts nonpartisan political activities from the scope of the act.[15] Penalties for violations of the act range from thirty days suspension without pay to removal from office.

---

*Reprinted by permission of the Albany Law Review.

[13] 5 U.S.C. § 7324 provides: "(a) An employee in an Executive agency or an individual employed by the government of the District of Columbia may not —

(1) use his official authority or influence for the purpose of interfering with or affecting the result of an election; or

(2) take an active part in political management or in political campaigns."

This language was adopted from Executive Order No. 642 (June 3, 1907). This order became a rule of the Civil Service Commission until 1939 when it was adopted as § 9(a), 53 Stat. 1147. See also 5 C.F.R. § 4.1 (1968).

[14] 5 U.S.C. § 7324 (d) (Supp. III, 1968): "Subsection (a)(2) of this section does not apply to —

(1) an employee paid from the appropriation for the office of the President;

(2) the head or the assistant head of an Executive department or military department;

(3) an employee appointed by the President, by and with the advice and consent of the Senate, who determines policies to be pursued by the United States in its relations with foreign powers or in the nationwide administration of Federal laws; ...."

[15] 5 U.S.C. § 7326 (Supp. III, 1968) provides: "Section 7324(a) (2) of this title does not prohibit political activity in connection with —

With respect to state and local government employees, the act seeks to regulate the political conduct of only those employees who work for state or local agencies and whose activities are "financed in whole or in part by loans or grants made by the United States or Federal agency."[17] Thus, for example, most employees of a state department of social welfare come within the act since this department probably receives federal funds under the categorical assistance programs of the Social Security Act.[18] One important exception to the act's restrictions involves those individuals "employed by an educational or research institution, establishment, agency or system which is supported in whole or in part by a State or political subdivision thereof."[19] Similar to the provisions for federal employees, various non-partisan activities of state and local government employees are exempt.[20] Employees who violate the act are liable for removal from office. Additionally, should the state or local government either fail to remove the offending employee or reappoint the employee to another state agency, the Civil Service Commission may direct the appropriate federal agency to withhold from the state agency a sum equal to two years' salary of the employee charged with the violation.[22]

---

(1) an election and the preceding campaign if none of the candidates is to be nominated or elected at that election as representing a party any of whose candidates for presidential elector received votes in the last preceding election at which presidential electors were selected; or

(2) a question which is not specifically identified with a National or State political party or political party of a territory or possession of the United States.

For the purpose of this section, questions relating to constitutional amendments, referendums, approval of municipal ordinances, and others of a similar character, are deemed not specifically identified with a National or State political party or political party of a territory or possession of the United States."

[17] 5 U.S.C. § 1502 (Supp. III, 1968) provides: "(a) A State or local officer or employee may not —

(1) use his official authority or influence for the purpose of interfering with or affecting the result of an election or a nomination for office;

(2) ...

(3) take an active part in political management or in political campaigns."

5 U.S.C. § 1501 (4) (Supp. III, 1968) defines a state or local officer or employee as "an individual employed by a State or local agency whose principal employment is in connection with an activity which is financed in whole or in part by loans or grants made by the United States or Federal Agency...."

[18] E.g., Title IV (Aid to Dependent Children) 42 U.S.C. §§ 601-09 (1964); Title XIX (Medical Assistance) 42 U.S.C. §§ 1396-96d (Supp. I, 1965); Title I (Aid to the Aged) 42 U.S.C. §§ 301-06 (1964). The same applies to employees of state labor departments which receive grants under Title III (Unemployment Compensation) of the Social Security Act. 42 U.S.C. §§ 501-03 (1964).

[19] 5 U.S.C. § 1501(4)(B) (Supp. III, 1968). In addition, § 1502(c)(1) specifically exempts the governor and lieutenant governor from the provisions of § 1502(a)(3).

[20] 5 U.S.C. § 1503 (Supp. III, 1968) provides: "Section 1502(a)(3) of this title does not prohibit political activity in connection with —

(1) an election and the preceding campaign if none of the candidates is to be nominated or elected at that election as representing a party any of whose candidates for presidential elector received votes in the last preceding election at which presidential electors were selected; or

(2) a question which is not specifically identified with a National or State political party.

For the purpose of this section, questions relating to constitutional amendments, referendums, approval of municipal ordinances, and others of a similar character, are deemed not specifically identified with a National or State political party."

[22] 5 U.S.C. § 1506 (Supp. III, 1968). For a more thorough analysis of the provisions of the Hatch Act, see Clark, *Federal Regulation of Campaign Activities*, 6 Fed. B.J. 5 (1944): Friedman and Klinger, *The Hatch Act: Regulation by Administrative Action of Political Activities of Governmental Employees*, 7 Fed. B.J. 5 (1945); Howard, *Federal Restrictions upon Political Activity of Government Employees*, 35 Am. Pol. Sci. Rev. 470 (1941). For a comprehensive list of those activities which are barred by the Hatch Act see Friedman and Klinger, *supra*, at 9-13.

United Public Workers of America v. Mitchell, 330 U.S. 75, 67 S. Ct. 556, 91 L. Ed. 754 (1947). The constitutionality of the Hatch Act was challenged by a roller at the Federal Mint who wanted to engage in proscribed political activity. The Supreme Court rejected this challenge and indicated that Congress possessed the authority to regulate the political actions of federal personnel:

[T]he practice of excluding classified employees from party offices and personal political activity at the polls has been in effect for several decades. Some incidents similar to those that are under examination here have been before this Court and the prohibition against certain types of political activity by officeholders has been upheld. The leading case was decided in 1882. *Ex parte Curtis,* 106 U.S. 371. There a subordinate United States employee was indicted for violation of an act that forbade employees who were not appointed by the President and confirmed by the Senate from giving or receiving money for political purposes from or to other employees of the government on penalty of discharge and criminal punishment. Curtis urged that the statute was unconstitutional. This Court upheld the right of Congress to punish the infraction of this law. The decisive principle was the power of Congress, within reasonable limits, to regulate, so far as it might deem necessary, the political conduct of its employees. A list of prohibitions against acts by public officials that are permitted to other citizens was given. This Court said, p. 373:

"The evident purpose of Congress in all this class of enactments has been to promote efficiency and integrity in the discharge of official duties, and to maintain proper discipline in the public service. Clearly such a purpose is within the just scope of legislative power, and it is not easy to see why the act now under consideration does not come fairly within the legitimate means to such an end." ...

... The provisions of § 9 of the Hatch Act and the Civil Service Rule I are not dissimilar in purpose from the statutes against political contributions of money. The prohibitions now under discussion are directed at political contributions of energy by government employees. These contributions, too, have a long background of disapproval. Congress and the President are responsible for an efficient public service. If, in their judgment, efficiency may be best obtained by prohibiting active participation by classified employees in politics as party officers or workers, we see no constitutional objection....

The argument that political neutrality is not indispensable to a merit system for federal employees may be accepted. But because it is not indispensable does not mean that it is not desirable or permissible. Modern American politics involves organized political parties. Many classifications of government employees have been accustomed to work in politics — national, state and local — as a matter of principle or to assure their tenure. Congress may reasonably desire to limit party activity of federal employees so as to avoid a tendency toward a one-party system. It may have considered that parties would be more truly devoted to the public welfare if public servants were not overactive politically.

... Congress may regulate the political conduct of government employees "within reasonable limits," even though the regulation trenches to some extent upon unfettered political action. The determination of the extent to which political activities of governmental employees shall be regulated lies primarily with Congress. Courts will interfere only when such regulation passes beyond the generally existing conception of governmental power. That conception develops from practice, history, and changing educational, social and economic conditions....

330 U.S. at 96-102.

NOTES

1. In *Oklahoma v. United States Civil Serv. Comm'n,* 330 U.S. 127 (1947), decided the same day as *Mitchell,* the Supreme Court upheld the constitutionality of those provisions of the Hatch Act that limited the right of certain state employees to participate in partisan politics. Oklahoma brought suit to review a determination of the CSC that a member of the state's highway commission had, by acting as chairman of the Democratic State Central Committee, violated the Hatch Act. The CSC directed the state to remove this member.

The state contended that the Hatch Act was unconstitutional because it regulated the internal affairs of a state and intruded upon state sovereignty in violation of the tenth amendment. While concluding that the federal government could not directly regulate the political activities of state or local employees, the Court held that the federal government could do so indirectly by fixing the terms and conditions upon which federal moneys would be allotted to the states. The Court held that the tenth amendment did not deprive the federal government of its power to use any necessary and proper means in the exercise of a granted power to attain a permissible goal. The Court defined the permissible goal as "better public service," which was to be attained by "requiring those who administered funds for national needs to abstain from active political partisanship."

2. The holding in *Mitchell* has been soundly criticized over the years. For example, in *Hobbs v. Thompson,* 448 F.2d 456, 457 (5th Cir. 1971), the court considered the constitutionality of a city ordinance that provided that no employee of the fire department

> shall take an active part in any primary or election, and all [such] employees are hereby prohibited from contributing any money to any candidate, soliciting votes or prominently identifying themselves in a political race with or against any candidate for office.

The court rejected the argument that the constitutionality of the ordinance should be determined by the *Mitchell* "rational basis" balancing test. Instead, the court ruled that the treatment in *Mitchell* of first amendment rights was inconsistent with other first amendment cases decided in the same time period, as well as those decided subsequently, and that the "privilege theory" of public employment, seemingly adopted by the Court in *Mitchell,* was no longer tenable. The court applied traditional overbreadth principles to the ordinance and held it to be "fatally overbroad and vague" because it "failed to focus narrowly upon a substantial state interest which might justify some proscription of the political activity of ... firemen." 448 F.2d at 475.

3. For a good discussion of many of the court decisions since *Mitchell* dealing with state and federal legislation, see Shartsis, *The Federal Hatch Act and Related State Court Trends — A Time for a Change?* 25 Bus. Law. 1381 (1970). See also Comment, *"Un-Hatching" Federal Employee Political Endorsements,* 134 U. Pa. L. Rev. 1497 (1986); Esman, *The Hatch Act — A Reappraisal,* 60 Yale L.J. 986 (1954); Bruff, *Unconstitutional Conditions upon Public Employ-*

ment: New Departures in the Protection of First Amendment Rights, 21 Hastings L.J. 129 (1969); Note, *The First Amendment and Public Employees — An Emerging Constitutional Right to Be a Policeman?* 37 Geo. Wash. L. Rev. 409 (1968); Van Alstyne, *The Constitutional Rights of Public Employees: A Comment on the Inappropriate Use of an Old Analogy,* 16 U.C.L.A. L. Rev. 751 (1969).

4. A federal government Commission on Political Activity of Government Personnel concluded that the existing political restrictions imposed on public servants are far in excess of what appears to be needed. See Jones, *Reevaluating the Hatch Act: A Report on the Commission on Political Activity of Government Personnel,* 29 Pub. Admin. Rev. 249 (1969). The Commission indicated that there should become clear a relationship between the dangers feared and the corrective measures used to regulate political activities. For cases that have tended to adopt this view, see *Fort v. Civil Serv. Comm'n,* 61 Cal. 2d 331, 392 P.2d 385 (1964); *Bagley v. Washington Twp. Hosp. Dist.,* 65 Cal. 2d 449, 421 P.2d 409 (1966); *Minielly v. State,* 242 Or. 490, 411 P.2d 69 (1966); *De Stefano v. Wilson,* 96 N.J. Super. 592, 233 A.2d 682 (1967); *Gray v. City of Toledo,* 323 F. Supp. 1281 (N.D. Ohio 1971) (upholding a state statute restricting policeman's right to engage in political activity, but indicating that only partisan political action that directly and adversely affected the employee's ability to perform his job efficiently could be constitutionally prohibited).

UNITED STATES CIVIL SERVICE COMMISSION v. NATIONAL ASSOCIATION OF LETTER CARRIERS

413 U.S. 548, 93 S. Ct. 2880, 37 L. Ed. 2d 796 (1973)

JUSTICE WHITE delivered the opinion of the Court.

On December 11, 1972, we noted probable jurisdiction of this appeal, 409 U.S. 1058, based on a jurisdictional statement presenting the single question whether the prohibition in § 9(a) of the Hatch Act, now codified in 5 U.S.C. § 7324(a)(2), against federal employees taking "an active part in political management or in political campaigns," is unconstitutional on its face. Section 7324(a) provides:

"An employee in an Executive agency or an individual employed by the government of the District of Columbia may not —
"(1) use his official authority or influence for the purpose of interfering with or affecting the result of an election; or
"(2) take an active part in political management or in political campaigns.
"For the purpose of this subsection, the phrase 'an active part in political management or in political campaigns' means those acts of political management or political campaigning which were prohibited on the part of employees in the competitive service before July 19, 1940, by determinations of the Civil Service Commission under the rules prescribed by the President."

A divided three-judge court sitting in the District of Columbia had held the section unconstitutional. 346 F. Supp. 578 (1972). We reverse the judgment of the District Court.

I

The case began when the National Association of Letter Carriers, six individual federal employees and certain local Democratic and Republican political committees filed a complaint, asserting on behalf of themselves and all federal employees that 5 U.S.C. § 7324(a)(2) was unconstitutional on its face and seeking an injunction against its enforcement.

Each of the plaintiffs alleged that the Civil Service Commission was enforcing, or threatening to enforce, the Hatch Act's prohibition against active participation in political management or political campaigns with respect to certain defined activity in which that plaintiff desired to engage. The Union, for example, stated among other things that its members desired to campaign for candidates for public office. The Democratic and Republican Committees complained of not being able to get federal employees to run for state and local offices. Plaintiff Hummel stated that he was aware of the provision of the Hatch Act and that the activities he desired to engage in would violate that Act as, for example, his participating as a delegate in a party convention or holding office in a political club.

A three-judge court was convened, and the case was tried on both stipulated evidence and oral testimony. The District Court then ruled that § 7324(a)(2) was unconstitutional on its face and enjoined its enforcement. The court recognized the "well-established governmental interest in restricting political activities by federal employees which [had been] asserted long before enactment of the Hatch Act," 346 F. Supp., at 579, as well as the fact that the "appropriateness of this governmental objective was recognized by the Supreme Court of the United States when it endorsed the objective of the Hatch Act. *United Public Workers v. Mitchell,* 330 U.S. 75 ... (1947) ...." *Id.,* at 580. The District Court ruled, however, that *United Public Workers v. Mitchell,* 330 U.S. 75 (1947), left open the constitutionality of the statutory definition of "political activity," 346 F. Supp., at 580, and proceeded to hold that definition to be both vague and overbroad, and therefore unconstitutional and unenforceable against the plaintiffs in any respect. The District Court also added, *id.,* at 585, that even if the Supreme Court in *Mitchell* could be said to have upheld the definitional section in its entirety, later decisions had so eroded the holding that it could no longer be considered binding on the District Court.

II

As the District Court recognized, the constitutionality of the Hatch Act's ban on taking an active part in political management or political campaigns has been here before. This very prohibition was attacked in the *Mitchell* case by a labor union and various federal employees as being violative of the First, Ninth, and Tenth Amendments and as contrary to the Fifth Amendment as being vague and indefinite, arbitrarily discriminatory, and a deprivation of liberty.... As to the plaintiff Poole [in *Mitchell*], the court noted that "[h]e was a ward executive committeeman of a political party and was politically active on election day as a worker at the polls and a paymaster for the services of other party workers." 330 U.S., at 94. Plainly, the Court thought, these activities fell within the prohibition of § 9(a) of the Hatch Act against taking an active part in political management or political campaigning; and "[t]hey [were] also covered by the prior determinations of the [Civil Service] Commission," *id.,* at 103 (footnote omitted), as incorporated by § 15 of the Hatch Act[4] the Court relying on a Civil Service Commission publication, Political Activity and Political Assessments, Form 1236, Sept. 1939, for the latter conclusion. *Id.*, at 103 n. 38. Poole's complaint thus presented a case or controversy for decision, the question being solely whether the Hatch Act "without violating the Constitution, [could make this conduct] the basis for disciplinary action." *Id.*, at 94. The court held that it could....

We unhesitatingly reaffirm the *Mitchell* holding that Congress had, and has, the power to prevent Mr. Poole and others like him from holding a party office, working at the polls and acting as party paymaster for other party workers. An Act of Congress going no farther would in our view unquestionably be valid. So would it be if, in plain and understandable language, the statute forbade activities such as organizing a political party or club; actively participating in fund-raising activities for a partisan candidate or political party; becoming a partisan candidate for, or campaigning for, an elective public office; actively managing the campaign of a partisan candidate for public office; initiating or circulating a partisan nominating petition or soliciting votes for a partisan candidate for public office; or serving as a delegate, alternate or proxy to a political party convention. Our judgment is that neither the First Amendment nor any other provision of the Constitution invalidates a law barring this kind of partisan political conduct by federal employees.

A. Such decision on our part would no more than confirm the judgment of history, a judgment made by this country over the last century that it is in the best interest of the country, indeed essential, that federal service should depend upon meritorious performance rather than political service, and that the political influence of federal employees on others and on the electoral process should be limited....

The original Civil Service rules were promulgated on May 7, 1883, by President Arthur. Civil Service Rule I repeated the language of the Act that no one in the executive service should use his official authority or influence to coerce any other person or to interfere with an election, but went no further in restricting the political activities of federal employees. 8 Richardson, Messages and Papers of the Presidents 161 (1899). Problems with political activity continued to arise, Twenty-fourth Annual Report of the Civil Service Commission, 7-9 (1908), and one form of remedial action was taken in 1907 when in accordance with Executive Order 642 issued by President Theodore Roosevelt, 1 Report of Commission on Political Activity, *supra*, at 9, § 1 of Rule I was amended to read as follows:

"No person in the Executive civil service shall use his official authority or influence for the purpose of interfering with an election or affecting the results thereof. *Persons who, by the provisions of these rules are in the competitive classified service, while retaining the right to vote as they please and to express privately their opinions on all political subjects, shall take no active*

---

[4]Section 15 of the Hatch Act, now codified in 5 U.S.C. § 7324(a)(2), see n. 1, *supra*, defined the prohibition against taking "an active part in political management or in political campaigns" as proscribing those activities that the Civil Service Commission had determined up to the time of the passage of the Hatch Act were prohibited for classified civil service employees. The role and scope of § 15 are discussed in the text, *infra*.

part in political management or in political campaigns." Twenty-fourth Annual Report of the Civil Service Commission, *supra,* at 104 (emphasis added).

It was under this rule that the Commission thereafter exercised the authority it had to investigate, adjudicate, and recommend sanctions for federal employees thought to have violated the rule. See Howard, *Federal Restrictions on the Political Activity of Government Employees,* 35 Am. Pol. Sci. Rev. 470, 475 (1941). In the course of these adjudications, the Commission identified and developed a body of law with respect to the conduct of federal employees that was forbidden by the prohibition against taking an active part in political management or political campaigning. Adjudications under Civil Service Rule I spelled out the scope and meaning of the rule in the mode of the common law, 86 Cong. Rec. 2341-2342; and the rules fashioned in this manner were from time to time stated and restated by the Commission for the guidance of the federal establishment. Civil Service Form 1236 of September 1939, for example, purported to publish and restate the law of "Political Activity and Political Assessments" for federal office holders and employees.

Civil Service Rule I covered only the classified service. The experience of the intervening years, particularly that of the 1936 and 1938 political campaigns, convinced a majority in Congress that the prohibition against taking an active part in political management and political campaigns should be extended to the entire federal service. 84 Cong. Rec. 4304, 9595, 9604, and 9610. A bill introduced for this purpose, S. 1871, "to prevent pernicious political activities," easily passed the Senate, 84 Cong. Rec. 4191-4192; but both the constitutionality and the advisability of purporting to restrict the political activities of employees were heatedly debated in the House. *Id.,* at 9594-9639. The bill was enacted, however, 53 Stat. 1147. This was the so-called Hatch Act, named after the Senator who was its chief proponent....

Section 9(a), which provided the prohibition against political activity now found in 5 U.S.C. § 7324(a)(2), with which we are concerned in this case, essentially restated Civil Service Rule I, with an important exception. It made it

"unlawful for any person employed in the executive branch of the Federal Government, or any agency or department thereof, to use his official authority or influence for the purpose of interfering with an election or affecting the result thereof. No officer or employee of the executive branch of the Federal Government, or any agency or department thereof, shall take any part in political management or in political campaigns. All such persons shall retain the right to vote as they may choose and to express their opinions on all political subjects." ...

Section 9 differed from Civil Service Rule I in important respects. It applied to all persons employed by the Federal Government, with limited exceptions; it made dismissal from office mandatory upon an adjudication of a violation; and, whereas Civil Service Rule I had stated that persons retained the right to express their private opinions on all political subjects, the statute omitted the word "private" and simply privileged all employees "to express their opinions on all political subjects."

On the day prior to signing the bill, President Franklin Roosevelt sent a message to Congress stating his conviction that the bill was constitutional and recommending that Congress at its next session consider extending the Act to state and local government employees. 84 Cong. Rec. 10745-10747 and 10875. This, Congress quickly proceeded to do. The Act of July 19, 1940, c. 640, 54 Stat. 767, extended the Hatch Act to officers and employees of state and local agencies "whose principal employment is in connection with any activity which is financed in whole or in part by loans or grants made by the United States ...." The Civil Service Commission was empowered under § 12(b) to investigate and adjudicate violations of the Act by state and local employees. Also relevant for present purposes, § 9(a) of the Hatch Act was amended so that all persons covered by the Act were free to "express their opinions on all political subjects *and candidates.*" (Emphasis added.) Moreover, § 15 defined § 9(a)'s prohibition against taking an active part in political management or in political campaigns as proscribing "the same activities on the part of such persons as the United States Civil Service Commission has heretofore determined are at the time this section takes effect prohibited on the part of employees in the classified Civil Service of the United States by the provisions of the civil service rules prohibiting such employees from taking any active part in political management or in political campaigns." ...

In 1966, Congress determined to review the restrictions of the Hatch Act on the partisan political activities of public employees. For this purpose, the Commission on Political Activity of Government Personnel was created. 80 Stat. 868. The Commission reported in 1968, recommending some liberalization of the political-activity restrictions on federal employees, but not abandoning the fundamental decision that partisan political activities by government employees must be limited in major respects. 1 Report of Commission on Political Activity of Government Personnel, *supra.* Since that time, various bills have been introduced in Congress, some following the Commission's recommendations and some proposing much more substantial revisions of the Hatch Act. In 1972, hearings were held on some proposed legislation; but no new legislation has resulted.

This account of the efforts by the Federal Government to limit partisan political activities by those covered by the Hatch Act should not obscure the equally relevant fact that all 50 States have restricted the political activities of their own employees.

B. Until now, the judgment of Congress, the Executive, and the country appears to have been that partisan political activities by federal employees must be limited if the Government is to operate effectively and fairly, elections are to play their proper part in representative government, and employees themselves are to be sufficiently free from improper influences. E.g., 84 Cong. Rec. 9598, 9603; 86 Cong. Rec. 2360, 2621, 2864, 9376. The restrictions so far imposed on federal employees are not aimed at particular parties, groups, or points of view, but apply equally to all partisan activities of the type described. They discriminate against no racial, ethnic, or religious minorities. Nor do they seek to control political opinions or beliefs, or to interfere with or influence anyone's vote at the polls.

But as the Court held in *Pickering v. Board of Education,* 391 U.S. 563, 568 (1968), the government has an interest in regulating the conduct and "the speech of its employees that differ[s] significantly from those it possesses in connection with regulation of the speech of the citizenry in general. The problem in any case is to arrive at a balance between the interest of the [employee], as a citizen, in commenting upon matters of public concern and the interest of the [government], as an employer, in promoting the efficiency of the public services it performs through its employees." Although Congress is free to strike a different balance than it has, if it so chooses, we think the balance it has so far struck is sustainable by the obviously important interests sought to be served by the limitations on partisan political activities now contained in the Hatch Act....

III

But however constitutional the proscription of identifiable partisan conduct in understandable language may be, the District Court's judgment was that § 7324(a)(2) was both unconstitutionally vague and fatally overbroad....

Section 7324(a)(2) provides that an employee in an executive agency must not take "an active part in political management or in political campaigns" and goes on to say that this prohibition refers to "those acts of political management or political campaigning which were prohibited on the part of employees in the competitive service before July 19, 1940, by determinations of the Civil Service Commission under the rules prescribed by the President." Section 7324(b) privileges an employee to vote as he chooses and to express his opinion on political subjects and candidates, and §§ 7324(c) and (d), as well as § 7326, also limit the applicability of § 7324(a)(2).[15] The principal issue with respect to this statutory scheme is what Congress intended when it purported to define "an active part in political management or in political campaigns," as meaning the prior interpretations by the Civil Service Commission under Civil Service Rule I which contained the identical prohibition.

Earlier in this opinion it was noted that this definition was contained in § 15 of the 1940 Act. As recommended by the Senate Committee, S. Rep. No. 1236, 76th Cong., 3d Sess., 2, 4, § 15 conferred broad rulemaking authority on the Civil Service Commission to spell out the meaning of "an active part in political management and political campaigns." There were, in any event, strong objections to extending the Hatch Act to those state employees working in federally financed programs, see, e.g., 86 Cong. Rec. 2486, 2793-2794, 2801-2802, and to § 15, in particular, as being an unwise and invalid delegation of legislative power to the Commission. See, e.g., *id.*, at 2352, 2426-2427, 2579, 2794, 2875. The matter was vigorously debated; and ultimately Senator Hatch, the principal proponent and manager of the bill, offered a substitute for § 15, *id.*, at 2928 and 2937, limiting the reach of the prohibition to those same activities that the

---

[15] 5 U.S.C. § 7324 provides:

"(a) An employee in an Executive agency or an individual employed by the government of the District of Columbia may not —

"(1) use his official authority or influence for the purpose of interfering with or affecting the result of an election; or

"(2) take an active part in political management or in political campaigns.

"For the purpose of this subsection, the phrase 'an active part in political management or in political campaigns' means those acts of political management or political campaigning which were prohibited on the part of employees in the competitive service before July 19, 1940, by determinations of the Civil Service Commission under the rules prescribed by the President.

"...."

Commission "has heretofore determined are at the time of the passage of this Act prohibited on the part of employees" in the classified service by the similar provision in Civil Service Rule I. The matter was further debated, and the amendment carried. *Id.,* at 2958-2959.

The District Court and appellees construe § 15, now part of § 7324(a)(2), as incorporating each of the several thousand adjudications of the Civil Service Commission under Civil Service Rule I, many of which are said to be undiscoverable, inconsistent, or incapable of yielding any meaningful rules to govern present or future conduct. In any event, the District Court held the prohibition against taking an active part in political management and political campaigns to be itself an insufficient guide to employee behavior and thought the definitional addendum of § 15 only added additional confusion by referring the concerned employees to an impenetrable jungle of Commission proceedings, orders, and rulings. 346 F. Supp., at 582-583, 585.

We take quite a different view of the statute. As we see it, our task is not to destroy the Act if we can, but to construe it, if consistent with the will of Congress, so as to comport with constitutional limitations. With this in mind and having examined with some care the proceedings surrounding the passage of the 1940 Act and adoption of the substitute for § 15, we think it appears plainly enough that Congress intended to deprive the Civil Service Commission of rulemaking power in the sense of exercising a subordinate legislative role in fashioning a more expansive definition of the kind of conduct that would violate the prohibition against taking an active part in political management or political campaigns. But it is equally plain, we think, that Congress accepted the fact that the Commission had been performing its investigative and adjudicative role under Civil Service Rule I since 1907 and that the Commission had, on a case-by-case basis, fleshed out the meaning of Rule I and so developed a body of law with respect to what partisan conduct by federal employees was forbidden by the rule. 86 Cong. Rec. 2342, 2353. It is also apparent, in our view, that the rules that had evolved over the years from repeated adjudications were subject to sufficiently clear and summary statement for the guidance of the classified service. Many times during the debate on the floor of the Senate, Senator Hatch and others referred to a summary list of such prohibitions, see, e.g., *id.,* at 2929, 2937-2938, 2942-2943, 2949, 2952-2953, the Senator's ultimate reference being to Civil Service Form No. 1236 of September 1939, the pertinent portion of which he placed in the Record, *id.,* at 2938-2940,[18] and which was the Commis-

---

[18]See Appendix to this opinion, *infra,* p. 581. Senator Hatch did not have Form 1236 with him on the floor during debate on § 15 and provided the pertinent portion from the Form for insertion into the Congressional Record after debate had been completed on the section. 86 Cong. Rec. 2938, 2940. However, the Senator had provided the Senate with a card listing 18 rules which were described as the Civil Service Commission's construction of Civil Service Rule I, *id.,* at 2937-2938, 2943. The card, prepared by Senator Hatch with assistance from the Commission, was a summary of pertinent portions of Form 1236, *id.,* at 2937-2938, and was inserted into the Congressional Record, *id.,* at 2943. It provided:

"The pertinent language in section 9 is practically a duplication of the civil-service rule prohibiting activity of employees under the classified civil service.

"The section provides in substance, among other things, that no such officer or employee shall take any active part in political management or in political campaigns.

"The same language of the civil-service rule has been construed as follows:

"1. Rule prohibits participation not only in national politics but also in State, county, and municipal politics.

sion's then-current effort to restate the prevailing prohibitions of Civil Service Rule I, as spelled out in its adjudications to that date. It was this administrative restatement of Civil Service Rule I law, modified to the extent necessary to reflect the provisions of the 1939 and 1940 Acts themselves, that, in our view, Congress intended to serve as its definition of the general proscription against partisan activities. It was within the limits of these rules that the Civil Service Commission was to proceed to perform its role under the statute.

Not only did Congress expect the Commission to continue its accustomed role with respect to federal employees, but also in § 12(b) of the 1940 Act Congress expressly assigned the Commission the enforcement task with respect to state employees now covered by the Act. The Commission was to issue notice, hold hearings, adjudicate and enforce. This process, inevitably and predictably, would entail further development of the law within the bounds of, and necessarily no more severe than, the 1940 rules and would be productive of a more refined definition of what conduct would or would not violate the statutory prohibition of taking an active part in political management and political campaigns.

It is thus not surprising that there were later editions of Form 1236, or that in 1970 the Commission again purported to restate the law of forbidden political activity and, informed by years of intervening adjudications, again sought to

---

"2. Temporary employees, substitutes, and persons on furlough or leave of absence with or without pay are subject to the regulation.

"3. Whatever an official or employee may not do directly he may not do indirectly or through another.

"4. Candidacy for or service as delegate, alternate, or proxy in any political convention is prohibited.

"5. Service for or on any political committee is prohibited.

"6. Organizing or conducting political rallies or meetings or taking any part therein except as a spectator is prohibited.

"7. Employees may express their opinions on all subjects, but they may not make political speeches.

"8. Employees may vote as they please, but they must not solicit votes; mark ballots for others; help to get out votes; act as checkers, marker or challenger for any party or engage in other activity at the polls except the casting of his own ballot.

"9. An employee may not serve as election official unless his failure or refusal so to do would be a violation of State laws.

"10. It is political activity for an employee to publish or be connected editorially, managerially, or financially with any political newspaper. An employee may not write for publication or publish any letter or article signed or unsigned in favor of or against any political party, candidate, or faction.

"11. Betting or wagering upon the results of a primary or general election is political activity.

"12. Organization or leadership of political parades is prohibited but marching in such parades is not prohibited.

"13. Among other forms of political activity which are prohibited are distribution of campaign literature, assuming political leadership, and becoming prominently identified with political movements, parties, or factions or with the success or failure of supporting any candidate for public office.

"14. Candidacy for nomination or for the election to any National, State, county, or municipal office is within the prohibition.

"15. Attending conventions as spectators is permitted.

"16. An employee may attend a mass convention or caucus and cast his vote, but he may not pass this point.

"17. Membership in a political club is permitted, but employees may not be officers of the club nor act as such.

"18. Voluntary contributions to campaign committees and organizations are permitted. An employee may not solicit, collect, or receive contributions. Contributions by persons receiving remuneration from funds appropriated for relief purposes are not permitted."

define those acts which are forbidden and those which are permitted by the Hatch Act. These regulations, 5 CFR pt. 733, are wholly legitimate descendants of the 1940 restatement adopted by Congress and were arrived at by a process that Congress necessarily anticipated would occur down through the years. We accept them as the current and, in most respects, the long-standing interpretations of the statute by the agency charged with its interpretation and enforcement. It is to these regulations purporting to construe § 7324 as actually applied in practice, as well as to the statute itself, with its various exclusions, that we address ourselves in rejecting the claim that the Act is unconstitutionally vague and overbroad.

Whatever might be a difficulty with a provision against "taking active part in political management or in political campaigns," the Act specifically provides that the employee retains the right to vote as he chooses and to express his opinion on political subjects and candidates. The Act exempts research and educational activities supported by the District of Columbia or by religious, philanthropic or cultural organizations, 5 U.S.C. § 7324(c); and § 7326 exempts nonpartisan political activity: questions, that is, that are not identified with national or state political parties are not covered by the Act, including issues with respect to constitutional amendments, referendums, approval of municipal ordinances and the like. Moreover, the plain import of the 1940 amendment to the Hatch Act is that the proscription against taking an active part in the proscribed activities is not open-ended but is limited to those rules and proscriptions that had been developed under Civil Service Rule I up to the date of the passage of the 1940 Act. Those rules, as refined by further adjudications within the outer limits of the 1940 rules, were restated by the Commission in 1970 in the form of regulations specifying the conduct that would be prohibited or permitted by § 7324 and its companion sections.

We have set out these regulations in the margin.[21] We see nothing impermissibly vague in 5 CFR § 733.122, which specifies in separate paragraphs the

---

[21]The pertinent regulations, appearing in 5 CFR Part 733, provide:

"PERMISSIBLE ACTIVITIES

"§ 733.111 Permissible activities.

"(a) All employees are free to engage in political activity to the widest extent consistent with the restrictions imposed by law and this subject. Each employee retains the right to —

"(1) Register and vote in any election;

"(2) Express his opinion as an individual privately and publicly on political subjects and candidates;

"(3) Display a political picture, sticker, badge, or button;

"(4) Participate in the nonpartisan activities of a civic, community, social, labor, or professional organization, or of a similar organization;

"(5) Be a member of a political party or other political organization and participate in its activities to the extent consistent with law;

"(6) Attend a political convention, rally, fund-raising function, or other political gathering;

"(7) Sign a political petition as an individual;

"(8) Make a financial contribution to a political party or organization;

"(9) Take an active part, as an independent candidate, or in support of an independent candidate, in a partisan election covered by § 733.124;

"(10) Take an active part, as a candidate or in support of a candidate, in a nonpartisan election;

"(11) Be politically active in connection with a question which is not specifically identified with a political party, such as a constitutional amendment, referendum, approval of a municipal ordinance or any other question or issue of a similar character;

various activities deemed to be prohibited by § 7324(a)(2). There might be quibbles about the meaning of taking an "active part in managing" or about "actively participating in ... fund-raising" or about the meaning of becoming a "partisan" candidate for office; but there are limitations in the English language with respect to being both specific and manageably brief, and it seems to us that although the prohibitions may not satisfy those intent on finding fault at any cost, they are set out in terms that the ordinary person exercising ordinary common sense can sufficiently understand and comply with, without sacrifice to the public interest....

The Act permits the individual employee to "express his opinion on political subjects and candidates," 5 U.S.C. § 7324(b); and the corresponding regulation, 5 CFR § 733.111(a)(2), privileges the employee to "[e]xpress his opinion as an individual privately and publicly on political subjects and candidates." The section of the regulations which purports to state the partisan acts that are proscribed, *id.*, § 733.122, forbids in subparagraph (a)(10) the endorsement of "a

---

"(12) Serve as an election judge or clerk, or in a similar position to perform nonpartisan duties as prescribed by State or local law; and

"(13) Otherwise participate fully in public affairs, except as prohibited by law, in a manner which does not materially compromise his efficiency or integrity as an employee or the neutrality, efficiency, or integrity of his agency.

"(b) Paragraph (a) of this section does not authorize an employee to engage in political activity in violation of law, while on duty, or while in a uniform that identifies him as an employee. The head of an agency may prohibit or limit the participation of an employee or class of employees of his agency in an activity permitted by paragraph (a) of this section, if participation in the activity would interfere with the efficient performance of official duties, or create a conflict or apparent conflict of interests.

"Prohibited Activities

"§ 733.121 Use of official authority; prohibition.

"An employee may not use his official authority or influence for the purpose of interfering with or affecting the result of an election.

"§ 733.122 Political management and political campaigning; prohibitions.

"(a) An employee may not take an active part in political management or in a political campaign, except as permitted by this subpart.

"(b) Activities prohibited by paragraph (a) of this section include but are not limited to—

"(1) Serving as an officer of a political party, a member of a National, State, or local committee of a political party, an officer or member of a committee of a partisan political club, or being a candidate for any of these positions;

"(2) Organizing or reorganizing a political party organization or political club;

"(3) Directly or indirectly soliciting, receiving, collecting, handling, disbursing, or accounting for assessments, contributions, or other funds for a partisan political purpose;

"(4) Organizing, selling tickets to, promoting, or actively participating in a fund-raising activity of a partisan candidate, political party, or political club;

"(5) Taking an active part in managing the political campaign of a partisan candidate for public office or political party office;

"(6) Becoming a partisan candidate for, or campaigning for, an elective public office;

"(7) Soliciting votes in support of or in opposition to a partisan candidate for public office or political party office;

"(8) Acting as recorder, watcher, challenger, or similar officer at the polls on behalf of a political party or partisan candidate;

"(9) Driving voters to the polls on behalf of a political party or partisan candidate;

"(10) Endorsing or opposing a partisan candidate for public office or political party office in a political advertisement, a broadcast, campaign literature, or similar material;

"(11) Serving as a delegate, alternate, or proxy to a political party convention;

"(12) Addressing a convention, caucus, rally, or similar gathering of a political party in support of or in opposition to a partisan candidate for public office or political party office; and

"(13) Initiating or circulating a partisan nominating petition."

partisan candidate for public office or political party office in a political advertisement, a broadcast, campaign literature or similar material," and in subparagraph (a)(12), prohibits "[a]ddressing a convention, caucus, rally or similar gathering of a political party in support of or in opposition to a partisan candidate
for public office or political party office." Arguably, there are problems in
meshing § 733.111(a)(2) with §§ 733.122(a)(10) and (12), but we think the latter
prohibitions sufficiently clearly carve out the prohibited political conduct from
the expressive activity permitted by the prior section to survive any attack on the
grounds of vagueness or in the name of any of those policies that doctrine may
be deemed to further.

It is also important in this respect that the Commission has established a
procedure by which an employee in doubt about the validity of a proposed
course of conduct may seek and obtain advice from the Commission and
thereby remove any doubt there may be as to the meaning of the law, at least
insofar as the Commission itself is concerned.

Neither do we discern anything fatally overbroad about the statute when it is
considered in connection with the Commission's construction of its terms represented by the 1970 regulations we now have before us. The major difficulties in
this respect again relate to the prohibition in §§ 733.122(a)(10) and (12) on
endorsements in advertisements, broadcasts, and literature and on speaking at
political party meetings in support of partisan candidates for public or party
office. But these restrictions are clearly stated, they are political acts normally
performed only in the context of partisan campaigns by one taking an active
role in them, and they are sustainable for the same reasons that the other acts of
political campaigning are constitutionally proscribable. They do not, therefore,
render the remainder of the statute vulnerable by reason of overbreadth.

Even if the provisions forbidding partisan campaign endorsements and
speech making were to be considered in some respects unconstitutionally overbroad, we would not invalidate the entire statute as the District Court did. The
remainder of the statute, as we have said, covers a whole range of easily identifiable and constitutionally proscribable partisan conduct on the part of federal
employees, and the extent to which pure expression is impermissibly threatened, if at all, by §§ 733.122(a)(10) and (12), does not in our view make the
statute substantially overbroad and so invalid on its face.

For the foregoing reasons, the judgment of the District Court is reversed.

So ordered.

[The dissenting opinion of Justice Douglas, concurred in by Justices Brennan
and Marshall, is omitted.]

NOTES

1. In *Broadrick v. Oklahoma,* 413 U.S. 601 (1973), decided the same day as
the principal case, the Supreme Court upheld the constitutionality of the Oklahoma state merit system act, which prohibited any state classified employee
from being "an officer or member" of a "partisan political club" or a candidate
for "any paid public office." The law also forbade the solicitation of contributions "for any political organization, candidacy or other political purpose" and
the taking part "in the management or affairs of any political party or in any
political campaign." Appellants argued that the statute was unconstitutionally

vague and that its prohibitions were too broad in their sweep, failing to distinguish between conduct that may be proscribed and conduct that must be permitted. In rejecting these arguments, the Court ruled that

> where conduct and not merely speech is involved, we believe that the overbreadth of a statute must not only be real, but substantial as well, judged in relation to the statute's plainly legitimate sweep. It is our view that § 818 is not substantially overbroad and that whatever overbreadth may exist should be cured through case-by-case analysis of the fact situations to which its sanctions, assertedly, may not be applied.
>
> Unlike ordinary breach-of-the-peace statutes or other broad regulatory acts, § 818 is directed, by its terms, at political expression which if engaged in by private persons would plainly be protected by the First and Fourteenth Amendments. But at the same time, § 818 is not a censorial statute, directed at particular groups or viewpoints. Cf. *Keyishian v. Board of Regents, supra.* The statute, rather, seeks to regulate political activity in an even-handed and neutral manner.... Under the decision in *Letter Carriers,* there is no question that § 818 is valid at least insofar as it forbids classified employees from: soliciting contributions for partisan candidates, political parties, or other partisan political purposes; becoming members of national, state, or local committees of political parties, or officers or committee members in partisan political clubs, or candidates to any paid public office; taking part in the management or affairs of any political party's partisan political campaign; serving as delegates or alternates to caucuses or conventions of political parties; addressing or taking an active part in partisan political rallies or meetings; soliciting votes or assisting voters at the polls or helping in a partisan effort to get voters at the polls; participating in the distribution of partisan campaign literature; initiating or circulating partisan nominating petitions; or riding in caravans for any political party or partisan political candidate.
>
> These proscriptions are taken directly from the contested paragraphs of § 818, the Rules of the State Personnel Board and its interpretive circular, and the authoritative opinions of the State Attorney General....
>
> ... Appellants further point to the Board's interpretive rules purporting to restrict such allegedly protected activities as the wearing of political buttons or the use of bumper stickers. It may be that such restrictions are impermissible and that § 818 may be susceptible of some other improper applications. But, as presently construed, we do not believe that § 818 must be discarded *in toto* because some persons' arguably protected conduct may or may not be caught or chilled by the statute. Section 818 is not substantially overbroad and is not, therefore, unconstitutional on its face.

413 U.S. at 615-18.

2. In *Bolin v. Minnesota,* 313 N.W.2d 381 (Minn. 1981), the court held that it was impermissible to require state troopers to resign if they wished to seek election to the office of county sheriff. While the state could place reasonable restrictions upon troopers desiring to become sheriffs, to promote cooperation between state troopers and county sheriffs, the court found that it could accomplish its fundamental objective through the less burdensome approach of simply requiring such troopers to take unpaid leaves of absence. However, in *Clements v. Fashing,* 457 U.S. 957 (1982), a closely divided Supreme Court sustained the constitutionality of two provisions of the Texas Constitution restricting the right of public officeholders to seek other elective positions during the remaining terms of their current offices. One provision prohibited certain officials from being elected or appointed to the state legislature during their existing terms of office, while the other provided that officeholders who have more than one year remaining on their present terms of office and who seek election to other public positions shall be considered to "automatically resign" their current positions. These restrictions were found to have only a de minimis impact upon present officeholders and to serve bona fide state interests by encouraging officials to serve out their remaining terms of office.

3. In 1974, following the *National Letter Carriers* and *Broadrick* decisions, Congress passed the Federal Election Campaign Act Amendments, 5 U.S.C. § 1502, which deleted the prohibition against state and local employees principally employed in federally funded activities taking "an active part in political management or in political campaigns," substituting a prohibition against being "a candidate for public office." The amendments, however, did permit state and local government employees to be non-partisan candidates for public office. 5 U.S.C. § 1594.

4. In *American Postal Workers Union v. U.S. Postal Serv.*, 764 F.2d 858 (D.C. Cir. 1985), *cert. denied*, 474 U.S. 1055 (1986), the court strongly suggested that since the Hatch Act only precludes employee participation in partisan political activity, the Postal Service acted improperly when it sought to enforce a regulation which banned employee participation in nonpartisan voter registration drives conducted in public areas of Postal Service premises.

5. Federal union presidents who were on leave from their federal agency positions did not violate the Hatch Act's prohibition against active participation in "political management or in political campaigns" when they wrote various articles in union publications supporting Walter Mondale's 1984 candidacy for President. There was no showing that the union officials acted "in concert" with any political party. *See Blaylock v. MSPB*, 851 F.2d 1348 (11th Cir. 1988); *Biller v. MSPB*, 863 F.2d 1079 (2d Cir. 1988).

6. All fifty States have passed statutes modeled on the Hatch Act that limit the political activities of state employees. These statutes are listed in *Broadrick v. Oklahoma*, 413 U.S. 601, 604 n.2 (1973). See generally Vaughan *Restrictions on the Political Activities of Public Employees: The Hatch Act and Beyond*, 44 Geo. Wash. L. Rev. 516 (1976).

RUTAN v. REPUBLICAN PARTY OF ILLINOIS

497 U.S. —, 110 S. Ct. 2729, 111 L. Ed. 2d 52 (1990)

JUSTICE BRENNAN delivered the opinion of the Court.

To the victor belong only those spoils that may be constitutionally obtained. *Elrod v. Burns*, 427 U.S. 347 (1976), and *Branti v. Finkel*, 445 U.S. 507 (1980), decided that the First Amendment forbids government officials to discharge or threaten to discharge public employees solely for not being supporters of the political party in power, unless party affiliation is an appropriate requirement for the position involved. Today we are asked to decide the constitutionality of several related political patronage practices — whether promotion, transfer, recall, and hiring decisions involving low-level public employees may be constitutionally based on party affiliation and support. We hold that they may not.

I

The petition and cross-petition before us arise from a lawsuit protesting certain employment policies and practices instituted by Governor James Thompson of Illinois. On November 12, 1980, the Governor issued an executive order proclaiming a hiring freeze for every agency, bureau, board, or commission subject to his control. The order prohibits state officials from hiring any employee, filling any vacancy, creating any new position, or taking any similar action. It affects approximately 60,000 state positions. More than 5,000 of these become available each year as a result of resignations, retirements, deaths, expansion, and reorganizations. The order proclaims that "*no* exceptions" are permitted without the Governor's "express permission after submission of appropriate requests to [his] office." Governor's Executive Order No. 5 (Nov. 12, 1980) (emphasis added).

Requests for the Governor's "express permission" have allegedly become routine. Permission has been granted or withheld through an agency expressly created for this purpose, the Governor's Office of Personnel (Governor's Office). Agencies have been screening applicants under Illinois' civil service system, making their personnel choices, and submitting them as requests to be approved or disapproved by the Governor's Office. Among the employment decisions for which approvals have been required are new hires, promotions, transfers, and recalls after layoffs.

By means of the freeze, according to petitioners, the Governor has been using the Governor's Office to operate a political patronage system to limit state employment and beneficial employment-related decisions to those who are supported by the Republican Party. In reviewing an agency's request that a particular applicant be approved for a particular position, the Governor's Office has looked at whether the applicant voted in Republican primaries in past election years, whether the applicant has provided financial or other support to the Republican Party and its candidates, whether the applicant has promised to join and work for the Republican Party in the future, and whether the applicant has the support of Republican Party officials at state or local levels.

Five people (including the three petitioners) brought suit against various Illinois and Republican Party officials in the United States District Court for the Central District of Illinois. They alleged that they had suffered discrimination with respect to state employment because they had not been supporters of the State's Republican Party and that this discrimination violates the First Amendment. Cynthia B. Rutan has been working for the State since 1974 as a rehabilitation counselor. She claims that since 1981 she has been repeatedly denied promotions to supervisory positions for which she was qualified because she had not worked for or supported the Republican Party. Franklin Taylor, who operates road equipment for the Illinois Department of Transportation, claims that he was denied a promotion in 1983 because he did not have the support of the local Republican Party. Taylor also maintains that he was denied a transfer to an office nearer to his home because of opposition from the Republican Party chairmen in the counties in which he worked and to which he requested a transfer. James W. Moore claims that he has been repeatedly denied state employment as a prison guard because he did not have the support of Republican Party officials.

The two other plaintiffs, before the Court as cross-respondents, allege that they were not recalled after layoffs because they lacked Republican credentials. Ricky Standefer was a state garage worker who claims that he was not recalled, although his fellow employees were, because he had voted in a Democratic primary and did not have the support of the Republican Party. Dan O'Brien, formerly a dietary manager with the mental health department, contends that he was not recalled after a layoff because of his party affiliation and that he later obtained a lower paying position with the corrections department only after receiving support from the chairman of the local Republican Party.

The District Court dismissed the complaint with prejudice, under Federal Rule of Civil Procedure 12(b)(6), for failure to state a claim upon which relief could be granted. 641 F. Supp. 249 (C.D. Ill. 1986). The United States Court of Appeals for the Seventh Circuit initially issued a panel opinion, 848 F.2d 1396 (1988), but then reheard the appeal en banc. The court affirmed the District Court's decision in part and reversed in part. 868 F.2d 943 (1989). Noting that this Court had previously determined that the patronage practice of discharging public employees on the basis of their political affiliation violates the First Amendment, the Court of Appeals held that other patronage practices violate the First Amendment only when they are the "substantial equivalent of a dismissal." *Id.*, at 954. The court explained that an employment decision is equivalent to a dismissal when it is one that would lead a reasonable person to resign. *Id.*, at 955. The court affirmed the dismissal of Moore's claim because it found that basing hiring decisions on political affiliation does not violate the First Amendment, but remanded the remaining claims for further proceedings.[3]

... We granted certiorari, 493 U.S. — (1989), to decide the important question whether the First Amendment's proscription of patronage dismissals recognized in *Elrod,* 427 U.S. 347 (1976), and *Branti,* 445 U.S. 507 (1980), extends to promotion, transfer, recall, or hiring decisions involving public employment positions for which party affiliation is not an appropriate requirement.

II

A. In *Elrod, supra,* we decided that a newly elected Democratic sheriff could not constitutionally engage in the patronage practice of replacing certain office staff with members of his own party "when the existing employees lack or fail to obtain requisite support from, or fail to affiliate with, that party." *Id.*, at 351, and 373 (plurality opinion) and 375 (Stewart, J., with BLACKMUN, J., concurring in judgment). The plurality explained that conditioning public employment on the provision of support for the favored political party "unquestionably inhibits protected belief and association." *Id.*, at 359. It reasoned that conditioning employment on political activity pressures employees to pledge political allegiance to a party with which they prefer not to associate, to work for the election of political candidates they do not support, and to contribute money to be used to further policies with which they do not agree. The latter, the plurality noted, had been recognized by this Court as "tantamount to coerced belief." *Id.*, at 355 (citing *Buckley v. Valeo,* 424 U.S. 1, 19 (1976)). At the same time, employees are constrained from joining, working for or contributing to the political party and

---

[3] The Seventh Circuit explained that Standefer's and O'Brien's claims might be cognizable if there were a formal or informal system of rehiring employees in their positions, 868 F.2d, at 956-957, but expressed considerable doubt that Rutan and Taylor would be able to show that they suffered the "substantial equivalent of a dismissal" by being denied promotions and a transfer. *Id.*, at 955-956.

candidates of their own choice. *Elrod, supra,* at 355-356. "[P]olitical belief and association constitute the core of those activities protected by the First Amendment," the plurality emphasized. 427 U.S., at 356. Both the plurality and the concurrence drew support from *Perry v. Sindermann,* 408 U.S. 593 (1972), in which this Court held that the State's refusal to renew a teacher's contract because he had been publicly critical of its policies imposed an unconstitutional condition on the receipt of a public benefit. See *Elrod, supra,* at 359 (plurality opinion) and 375 (Stewart, J., concurring in judgment); see also *Branti, supra,* at 514-516.

The Court then decided that the government interests generally asserted in support of patronage fail to justify this burden on First Amendment rights because patronage dismissals are not the least restrictive means for fostering those interests. See *Elrod, supra,* at 372-373 (plurality opinion) and 375 (Stewart, J., concurring in judgment). The plurality acknowledged that a government has a significant interest in ensuring that it has effective and efficient employees. It expressed doubt, however, that "mere difference of political persuasion motivates poor performance" and concluded that, in any case, the government can ensure employee effectiveness and efficiency through the less drastic means of discharging staff members whose work is inadequate. 427 U.S., at 365-366. The plurality also found that a government can meet its need for politically loyal employees to implement its policies by the less intrusive measure of dismissing, on political grounds, only those employees in policymaking positions. *Id.,* at 367. Finally, although the plurality recognized that preservation of the democratic process "may in some instances justify limitations on First Amendment freedoms," it concluded that the "process functions as well without the practice, perhaps even better." Patronage, it explained, "can result in the entrenchment of one or a few parties to the exclusion of others" and "is a very effective impediment to the associational and speech freedoms which are essential to a meaningful system of democratic government." *Id.,* at 368-370.[4]

Four years later, in *Branti, supra,* we decided that the First Amendment prohibited a newly appointed public defender, who was a Democrat, from discharging assistant public defenders because they did not have the support of the Democratic Party. The Court rejected an attempt to distinguish the case from *Elrod,* deciding that it was immaterial whether the public defender had attempted to coerce employees to change political parties or had only dismissed them on the basis of their private political beliefs. We explained that condition-

---

[4] JUSTICE SCALIA's lengthy discussion of the appropriate standard of review for restrictions the government places on the constitutionally protected activities of its employees to ensure efficient and effective operations is not only questionable, it offers no support for his conclusion that patronage practices pass muster under the First Amendment. The interests that JUSTICE SCALIA regards as potentially furthered by patronage practices are not interests that the government has in its capacity as an employer. JUSTICE SCALIA describes the possible benefits of patronage as follows: "patronage stabilizes political parties and prevents excessive political fragmentation;" patronage is necessary to strong, disciplined party organizations; patronage "fosters the two-party system;" and patronage is "a powerful means of achieving the social and political integration of excluded groups." These are interests the government might have in the structure and functioning of society as a whole. That the government attempts to use public employment to further such interests does not render those interests employment-related. Therefore, even were JUSTICE SCALIA correct that less-than-strict scrutiny is appropriate when the government takes measures to ensure the proper functioning of its internal operations, such a rule has no relevance to the restrictions on freedom of association and speech at issue in this case.

ing continued public employment on an employee's having obtained support from a particular political party violates the First Amendment because of "the coercion of belief that necessarily flows from the knowledge that one must have a sponsor in the dominant party in order to retain one's job." 445 U.S., at 516. "In sum," we said, "there is no requirement that dismissed employees prove that they, or other employees, have been coerced into changing, either actually or ostensibly, their political allegiance." *Id.,* at 517. To prevail, we concluded, public employees need show only that they were discharged because they were not affiliated with or sponsored by the Democratic Party. *Ibid.*[5]

B. We first address the claims of the four current or former employees. Respondents urge us to view *Elrod* and *Branti* as inapplicable because the patronage dismissals at issue in those cases are different in kind from failure to promote, failure to transfer, and failure to recall after layoff. Respondents initially contend that the employee petitioners' First Amendment rights have not been infringed because they have no entitlement to promotion, transfer, or rehire. We rejected just such an argument in *Elrod,* 427 U.S., at 359-360 (plurality opinion) and 375 (Stewart, J., concurring in judgment), and *Branti,* 445 U.S., at 514-515, as both cases involved state workers who were employees at will with no legal entitlement to continued employment. In *Perry,* 408 U.S., at 596-598, we held explicitly that the plaintiff teacher's lack of a contractual or tenure right to re-employment was immaterial to his First Amendment claim. We explained the viability of his First Amendment claim as follows:

> "For at least a quarter-century, this Court has made clear that even though a person has no 'right' to a valuable governmental benefit and even though the government may deny him the benefit for any number of reasons, there are some reasons upon which the government may not rely. It may not deny a benefit to a person on a basis that infringes his constitutionally protected interests — especially, his interest in freedom of speech. For if the government could deny a benefit to a person because of his constitutionally protected speech or associations, his exercise of those freedoms would in effect be penalized and inhibited. This would allow the government to 'produce a result which [it] could not command directly.' *Speiser v. Randall,* 357 U.S. 513, 526 [1958]. Such interference with constitutional rights is impermissible." *Perry, id.,* at 597 (emphasis added).

Likewise, we find the assertion here that the employee petitioners had no legal entitlement to promotion, transfer, or recall beside the point.

Respondents next argue that the employment decisions at issue here do not violate the First Amendment because the decisions are not punitive, do not in any way adversely affect the terms of employment, and therefore do not chill the exercise of protected belief and association by public employees. This is not credible. Employees who find themselves in dead-end positions due to their

---

[5] *Branti v. Finkel,* 445 U.S. 507 (1980), also refined the exception created by *Elrod v. Burns,* 427 U.S. 347 (1976), for certain employees. In *Elrod,* we suggested that policymaking and confidential employees probably could be dismissed on the basis of their political views. *Elrod, supra,* at 367 (plurality), and 375 (Stewart, J., concurring in judgment). In *Branti,* we said that a State demonstrates a compelling interest in infringing First Amendment rights only when it can show that "party affiliation is an appropriate requirement for the effective performance of the public office involved." *Branti, supra,* at 518. The scope of this exception does not concern us here as respondents concede that the five employees who brought this suit are not within it.

political backgrounds are adversely affected. They will feel a significant obligation to support political positions held by their superiors, and to refrain from acting on the political views they actually hold, in order to progress up the career ladder. Employees denied transfers to workplaces reasonably close to their homes until they join and work for the Republican Party will feel a daily pressure from their long commutes to do so. And employees who have been laid off may well feel compelled to engage in whatever political activity is necessary to regain regular paychecks and positions corresponding to their skill and experience.

The same First Amendment concerns that underlay our decisions in *Elrod, supra,* and *Branti, supra,* are implicated here. Employees who do not compromise their beliefs stand to lose the considerable increases in pay and job satisfaction attendant to promotions, the hours and maintenance expenses that are consumed by long daily commutes, and even their jobs if they are not rehired after a "temporary" layoff. These are significant penalties and are imposed for the exercise of rights guaranteed by the First Amendment. Unless these patronage practices are narrowly tailored to further vital government interests, we must conclude that they impermissibly encroach on First Amendment freedoms. See *Elrod, supra,* at 362-363 (plurality opinion) and 375 (Stewart, J., concurring in judgment); *Branti, supra,* at 515-516.

We find, however, that our conclusions in *Elrod, supra,* and *Branti, supra,* are equally applicable to the patronage practices at issue here. A government's interest in securing effective employees can be met by discharging, demoting or transferring staff members whose work is deficient. A government's interest in securing employees who will loyally implement its policies can be adequately served by choosing or dismissing certain high-level employees on the basis of their political views. See *Elrod, supra,* at 365-368; *Branti, supra,* at 518, and 520, n.14. Likewise, the "preservation of the democratic process" is no more furthered by the patronage promotions, transfers, and rehires at issue here than it is by patronage dismissals. First, "political parties are nurtured by other, less intrusive and equally effective methods." *Elrod, supra,* at 372-373. Political parties have already survived the substantial decline in patronage employment practices in this century. See *Elrod,* 427 U.S., at 369, and n.23; see also L. Sabato, Goodbye to Good-time Charlie 67 (2d ed. 1983) ("The number of patronage positions has significantly decreased in virtually every state").... Second, patronage decidedly impairs the elective process by discouraging free political expression by public employees. See *Elrod,* 427 U.S., at 372 (explaining that the proper functioning of a democratic system "is indispensably dependent on the unfettered judgment of each citizen on matters of political concern"). Respondents, who include the Governor of Illinois and other state officials, do not suggest any other overriding government interest in favoring Republican Party supporters for promotion, transfer, and rehire. We therefore determine that promotions, transfers, and recalls after layoffs based on political affiliation or support are an impermissible infringement on the First Amendment rights of public employees. In doing so, we reject the Seventh Circuit's view of the appropriate constitutional standard by which to measure alleged patronage practices in government employment. The Seventh Circuit proposed that only those employment decisions that are the "substantial equivalent of a dismissal" violate a public employee's rights under the First Amendment. 868 F.2d, at 954-957. We find this test unduly restrictive because it fails to recognize that there are deprivations less harsh than dismissal that nevertheless press state employees and applicants to conform their beliefs and associations to some state-selected orthodoxy. See *Elrod, supra,* at 356-357 (plurality opinion); *West Virginia Bd. of Education v. Barnette,* 319 U.S. 624, 642 (1943). The First Amendment is not a tenure provision, protecting public employees from actual or constructive discharge. The First Amendment prevents the government, except in the most compelling circumstances, from wielding its power to interfere with its employees' freedom to believe and associate, or to not believe and not associate. Whether the four employees were in fact denied promotions, transfers, or rehire for failure to affiliate with and support the Republican Party is for the District Court to decide in the first instance. What we decide today is that such denials are irreconcilable with the Constitution and that the allegations of the four employees state claims under 42 U.S.C. § 1983 (1982 ed.) for violations of the First and Fourteenth Amendments. Therefore, although we affirm the Seventh Circuit's judgment to reverse the District Court's dismissal of these claims and remand them for further proceedings, we do not adopt the Seventh Circuit's reasoning.

C. Petitioner James W. Moore presents the closely related question whether patronage hiring violates the First Amendment. Patronage hiring places burdens on free speech and association similar to those imposed by the patronage practices discussed above. A state job is valuable. Like most employment, it provides regular paychecks, health insurance, and other benefits. In addition, there may be openings with the State when business in the private sector is slow. There are also occupations for which the government is a major (or the only) source of employment, such as social workers, elementary school teachers, and prison guards. Thus, denial of a state job is a serious privation.

Nonetheless, respondents contend that the burden imposed is not of constitutional magnitude. Decades of decisions by this Court belie such a claim. We premised *Torcaso v. Watkins,* 367 U.S. 488 (1961), on our understanding that loss of a job opportunity for failure to compromise one's convictions states a constitutional claim. We held that Maryland could not refuse an appointee a commission for the position of notary public on the ground that he refused to declare his belief in God, because the required oath "unconstitutionally invades the appellant's freedom of belief and religion." *Id.,* at 496. In *Keyishian v. Board of Regents of Univ. of New York,* 385 U.S. 589, 609-610 (1967), we held a law affecting appointment and retention of teachers invalid because it premised employment on an unconstitutional restriction of political belief and association. In *Elfbrandt v. Russell,* 384 U.S. 11, 19 (1966), we struck down a loyalty oath which was a prerequisite for public employment.

Almost half a century ago, this Court made clear that the government "may not enact a regulation providing that no Republican ... shall be appointed to federal office." *Public Workers v. Mitchell,* 330 U.S. 75, 100 (1947). What the First Amendment precludes the government from commanding directly, it also precludes the government from accomplishing indirectly. See *Perry,* 408 U.S., at 597 (citing *Speiser v. Randall,* 357 U.S. 513, 526 (1958)). Under our sustained precedent, conditioning hiring decisions on political belief and association plainly constitutes an unconstitutional condition, unless the government has a vital interest in doing so. See *Elrod,* 427 U.S., at 362-363 (plurality opinion), and 375 (Stewart, J., concurring in judgment); *Branti,* 445 U.S., at 515-516; see also *Sherbert v. Verner,* 374 U.S. 398 (1963) (unemployment benefits); *Speiser v. Randall, supra* (tax exemption). We find no such government interest here, for the same reasons that we found the government lacks justification for patronage promotions, transfers or recalls. See *supra.*

The court below, having decided that the appropriate inquiry in patronage cases is whether the employment decision at issue is the substantial equivalent of a dismissal, affirmed the trial court's dismissal of Moore's claim. See 868 F.2d, at 954. The Court of Appeals reasoned that "rejecting an employment application does not impose a hardship upon an employee comparable to the loss of [a] job." *Ibid.,* citing *Wygant v. Jackson Bd. of Education,* 476 U.S. 267 (1986) (plurality opinion). Just as we reject the Seventh Circuit's proffered test, we find the Seventh Circuit's reliance on *Wygant* to distinguish hiring from dismissal unavailing. The court cited a passage from the plurality opinion in *Wygant* explaining that school boards attempting to redress past discrimination must choose methods that broadly distribute the disadvantages imposed by affirmative action plans among innocent parties. The plurality said that race-based layoffs placed too great a burden on individual members of the nonminority race, but suggested that discriminatory hiring was permissible, under certain circumstances, even though it burdened white applicants because the burden was less intrusive than the loss of an existing job. *Id.,* at 282-284. See also *id.,* at 294-295 (WHITE, J., concurring in judgment).

Wygant has no application to the question at issue here. The plurality's concern in that case was identifying the least harsh means of remedying past wrongs. It did not question that some remedy was permissible when there was sufficient evidence of past discrimination. In contrast, the Governor of Illinois has not instituted a remedial undertaking. It is unnecessary here to consider whether not being hired is less burdensome than being discharged because the government is not pressed to do either on the basis of political affiliation. The question in the patronage context is not which penalty is more acute but whether the government, without sufficient justification, is pressuring employees to discontinue the free exercise of their First Amendment rights.

If Moore's employment application was set aside because he chose not to support the Republican Party, as he asserts, then Moore's First Amendment rights have been violated. Therefore, we find that Moore's complaint was improperly dismissed.

III

We hold that the rule of *Elrod* and *Branti* extends to promotion, transfer, recall, and hiring decisions based on party affiliation and support and that all of the petitioners and cross-respondents have stated claims upon which relief may be granted. We affirm the Seventh Circuit insofar as it remanded Rutan's, Taylor's, Standefer's, and O'Brien's claims. However, we reverse the Circuit Court's decision to uphold the dismissal of Moore's claim. All five claims are remanded for proceedings consistent with this opinion.

It is so ordered.

JUSTICE STEVENS, concurring.

While I join the Court's opinion, these additional comments are prompted by three propositions advanced by JUSTICE SCALIA in his dissent. First, he implies that prohibiting imposition of an unconstitutional condition upon eligibility for government employment amounts to adoption of a civil service system. Second, he makes the startling assertion that a long history of open and widespread use of patronage practices immunizes them from constitutional scrutiny. Third, he assumes that the decisions in *Elrod v. Burns,* 427 U.S. 347 (1976), and *Branti v. Finkel,* 445 U.S. 507 (1980), represented dramatic departures from prior precedent.

Several years before either *Elrod* or *Branti* was decided, I had occasion as a judge on the Court of Appeals for the Seventh Circuit to evaluate each of these propositions. *Illinois State Employees Union, Council 34, Am. Fed. of State, County, and Municipal Emp., AFL-CIO v. Lewis,* 473 F.2d 561 (1972), *cert. denied,* 410 U.S. 928 (1973). With respect to the first, I wrote:

> Neither this court nor any other may impose a civil service system upon the State of Illinois. The General Assembly has provided an elaborate system regulating the appointment to specified positions solely on the basis of merit and fitness, the grounds for termination of such employment, and the procedures which must be followed in connection with hiring, firing, promotion, and retirement. A federal court has no power to establish any such employment code.
>
> However, recognition of plaintiffs' claims will not give every public employee civil service tenure and will not require the state to follow any set procedure or to assume the burden of explaining or proving the grounds for every termination. It is the former employee who has the burden of proving that his discharge was motivated by an impermissible consideration. It is true, of course, that a prima facie case may impose a burden of explanation on the State. But the burden of proof will remain with the plaintiff employee and we must assume that the trier of fact will be able to differentiate between those discharges which are politically motivated and those which are not. There is a clear distinction between the grant of tenure to an employee — a right which cannot be conferred by judicial fiat — and the prohibition of a discharge for a particular impermissible reason. The Supreme Court has plainly identified that distinction on many occasions, most recently in *Perry v. Sindermann,* 408 U.S. 593 (1972)....

Denying the Governor of Illinois the power to require every state employee, and every applicant for state employment, to pledge allegiance and service to the political party in power is a far cry from a civil service code. The question in this case is simply whether a Governor may adopt a rule that would be plainly unconstitutional if enacted by the General Assembly of Illinois.

Second, JUSTICE SCALIA asserts that "when a practice not expressly prohibited by the text of the Bill of Rights bears the endorsement of a long tradition of open, widespread, and unchallenged use that dates back to the beginning of the Republic, we have no proper basis for striking it down." (A "clear and continuing tradition of our people" deserves "dispositive effect"). The argument that traditional practices are immune from constitutional scrutiny is advanced in two plurality opinions that JUSTICE SCALIA has authored, but not by any opinion joined by a majority of the Members of the Court.

In the *Lewis* case, I noted the obvious response to this position: "if the age of a pernicious practice were a sufficient reason for its continued acceptance, the constitutional attack on racial discrimination would, of course, have been doomed to failure." 473 F.2d, at 568, n.14. See, e.g., *Brown v. Board of Education*, 347 U.S. 483 (1954)....

With respect to JUSTICE SCALIA's view that until *Elrod v. Burns* was decided in 1976, it was unthinkable that patronage could be unconstitutional, it seems appropriate to point out again not only that my views in *Lewis* antedated *Elrod* by several years, but, more importantly, that they were firmly grounded in several decades of decisions of this Court. As explained in *Lewis*:

> [In 1947] a closely divided Supreme Court upheld a statute prohibiting federal civil service employees from taking an active part in partisan political activities. *United Public Workers v. Mitchell*, 330 U.S. 75. The dissenting Justices felt that such an abridgment of First Amendment rights could not be justified. The majority, however, concluded that the government's interests in not compromising the quality of public service and in not permitting individual employees to use their public offices to advance partisan causes were sufficient to justify the limitation on their freedom.
>
> There was no dispute within the Court over the proposition that the employees' interests in political action were protected by the First Amendment....
>
> In 1952 the Court quoted that dicta in support of its holding that the State of Oklahoma could not require its employees to profess their loyalty by denying past association with Communists. *Wieman v. Updegraff*, 344 U.S. 183, 191-192. That decision did not recognize any special right to public employment; rather, it rested on the impact of the requirement on the citizen's First Amendment rights. We think it unlikely that the Supreme Court would consider these plaintiffs' interest in freely associating with members of the Democratic Party less worthy of protection than the Oklahoma employees' interest in associating with Communists or former Communists....
>
> In 1968 the Court held that "a teacher's exercise of his right to speak on issues of public importance may not furnish the basis for his dismissal from public employment." *Pickering v. Board of Education*, 391 U.S. 563, 574....
>
> In 1972 the Court reaffirmed the proposition that a nontenured public servant has no constitutional right to public employment, but nevertheless may not be dismissed for exercising his First Amendment rights. *Perry v. Sindermann*, 408 U.S. 593....

JUSTICE SCALIA argues that distinguishing "inducement and compulsion" reveals that a patronage system's impairment of the speech and associational rights of employees and would-be employees is insignificant. This analysis contradicts the harsh reality of party discipline that is the linchpin of his theory of patronage (emphasizing the "link between patronage and party discipline, and between that and party success"). More importantly, it rests on the long-rejected fallacy that a privilege may be burdened by unconstitutional conditions. See, e.g., *Perry v. Sindermann*, 408 U.S. 593, 597 (1972).... [T]here are many jobs for which political affiliation is relevant to the employee's ability to function effectively as part of a given administration. In those cases — in other words, cases in which "the efficiency of the public service," *Public Workers v. Mitchell,* 330 U.S. 75, 101 (1947), would be advanced by hiring workers who are loyal to the Governor's party — such hiring is permissible under the holdings in *Elrod* and *Branti....*

JUSTICE SCALIA, with whom THE CHIEF JUSTICE and JUSTICE KENNEDY join, and with whom JUSTICE O'CONNOR joins as to Parts II and III, dissenting.

Today the Court establishes the constitutional principle that party membership is not a permissible factor in the dispensation of government jobs, except those jobs for the performance of which party affiliation is an "appropriate requirement." It is hard to say precisely (or even generally) what that exception means, but if there is any category of jobs for whose performance party affiliation is not an appropriate requirement, it is the job of being a judge, where partisanship is not only unneeded but positively undesirable. It is, however, rare that a federal administration of one party will appoint a judge from another party. And it has always been rare. See *Marbury v. Madison,* 1 Cranch 137 (1803). Thus, the new principle that the Court today announces will be enforced by a corps of judges (the Members of this Court included) who overwhelmingly owe their office to its violation. Something must be wrong here, and I suggest it is the Court.

The merit principle for government employment is probably the most favored in modern America, having been widely adopted by civil-service legislation at both the state and federal levels. But there is another point of view ....

The choice between patronage and the merit principle — or, to be more realistic about it, the choice between the desirable mix of merit and patronage principles in widely varying federal, state, and local political contexts — is not so clear that I would be prepared, as an original matter, to chisel a single, inflexible prescription into the Constitution. Fourteen years ago, in *Elrod v. Burns,* 427 U.S. 347 (1976), the Court did that. *Elrod* was limited, however, as was the later decision of *Branti v. Finkel,* 445 U.S. 507 (1980), to patronage firings, leaving it to state and federal legislatures to determine when and where political affiliation could be taken into account in hirings and promotions. Today the Court makes its constitutional civil-service reform absolute, extending to all decisions regarding government employment. Because the First Amendment has never been thought to require this disposition, which may well have disastrous consequences for our political system, I dissent.

I

The restrictions that the Constitution places upon the government in its capacity as lawmaker, i.e., as the regulator of private conduct, are not the same as the restrictions that it places upon the government in its capacity as employer. We have recognized this in many contexts, with respect to many different constitutional guarantees. Private citizens perhaps cannot be prevented from wearing long hair, but policemen can. *Kelley v. Johnson,* 425 U.S. 238, 247 (1976). Private citizens cannot have their property searched without probable cause, but in many circumstances government employees can. *O'Connor v. Ortega,* 480 U.S. 709, 723 (1987) (plurality opinion); *id.,* at 732 (SCALIA, J., concurring in judgment). Private citizens cannot be punished for refusing to provide the government information that may incriminate them, but government employees can be dismissed when the incriminating information that they refuse to provide relates to the performance of their job. *Gardner v. Broderick,* 392 U.S. 273, 277-278 (1968). With regard to freedom of speech in particular: Private citizens cannot be punished for speech of merely private concern, but government employees can be fired for that reason. *Connick v. Myers,* 461 U.S. 138, 147 (1983). Private citizens cannot be punished for partisan political activity, but federal and state employees can be dismissed and otherwise punished for that reason. *Public Workers v. Mitchell,* 330 U.S. 75, 101 (1947); *CSC v. Letter Carriers,* 413 U.S. 548, 556 (1973); *Broadrick v. Oklahoma,* 413 U.S. 601, 616-617 (1973).

Once it is acknowledged that the Constitution's prohibition against laws "abridging the freedom of speech" does not apply to laws enacted in the government's capacity as employer the same way it does to laws enacted in the government's capacity as regulator of private conduct, it may sometimes be difficult to assess what employment practices are permissible and what are not. That seems to me not a difficult question, however, in the present context. The provisions of the Bill of Rights were designed to restrain transient majorities from impairing long-recognized personal liberties. They did not create by implication novel individual rights overturning accepted political norms. Thus, when a practice not expressly prohibited by the text of the Bill of Rights bears the endorsement of a long tradition of open, widespread, and unchallenged use that dates back to the beginning of the Republic, we have no proper basis for striking it down....

II

Even accepting the Court's own mode of analysis, however, and engaging in "balancing" a tradition that ought to be part of the scales, *Elrod, Branti,* and today's extension of them seem to me wrong.

A. The Court limits patronage on the ground that the individual's interest in uncoerced belief and expression outweighs the systemic interests invoked to justify the practice. The opinion indicates that the government may prevail only if it proves that the practice is "narrowly tailored to further vital government interests."

That strict-scrutiny standard finds no support in our cases. Although our decisions establish that government employees do not lose all constitutional rights, we have consistently applied a lower level of scrutiny when "the governmental function operating ... [is] not the power to regulate or license, as lawmaker, an entire trade or profession, or to control an entire branch of private business, but, rather, as proprietor, to manage [its] internal operatio[ns]...." *Cafeteria & Restaurant Workers v. McElroy,* 367 U.S. 886, 896 (1961). When dealing with its own employees, the government may not act in a manner that is "patently arbitrary or discriminatory," *id.*, at 898, but its regulations are valid if they bear a "rational connection" to the governmental end sought to be served, *Kelley v. Johnson,* 425 U.S., at 247.

In particular, restrictions on speech by public employees are not judged by the test applicable to similar restrictions on speech by nonemployees. We have said that "[a] governmental employer may subject its employees to such special restrictions on free expression as are reasonably necessary to promote effective government." *Brown v. Glines*, 444 U.S. 348, 356, n.13 (1980). In *Public Workers v. Mitchell*, 330 U.S., at 101, upholding provisions of the Hatch Act which prohibit political activities by federal employees, we said that "it is not necessary that the act regulated be anything more than an act reasonably deemed by Congress to interfere with the efficiency of the public service." We reaffirmed *Mitchell* in *CSC v. Letter Carriers*, 413 U.S., at 556, over a dissent by Justice Douglas arguing against application of a special standard to government employees, except insofar as their "job performance" is concerned, *id.*, at 597....

Because the restriction on speech is more attenuated when the government conditions employment than when it imposes criminal penalties, and because "government offices could not function if every employment decision became a constitutional matter," *Connick v. Myers*, 461 U.S., at 143, we have held that government employment decisions taken on the basis of an employee's speech do not "abridg[e] the freedom of speech," U.S. Const., Amdt. 1, merely because they fail the narrow-tailoring and compelling-interest tests applicable to direct regulation of speech. We have not subjected such decisions to strict scrutiny, but have accorded "a wide degree of deference to the employer's judgment" that an employee's speech will interfere with close working relationships. 461 U.S., at 152.

When the government takes adverse action against an employee on the basis of his political affiliation (an interest whose constitutional protection is derived from the interest in speech), the same analysis applies.... Since the government may dismiss an employee for political speech "reasonably deemed by Congress to interfere with the efficiency of the public service," *Public Workers v. Mitchell, supra,* at 101, it follows *a fortiori* that the government may dismiss an employee for political affiliation if "reasonably necessary to promote effective government." *Brown v. Glines, supra,* at 356, n.13....

B. ... The Court holds that the governmental benefits of patronage cannot reasonably be thought to outweigh its "coercive" effects (even the lesser "coercive" effects of patronage hiring as opposed to patronage firing) not merely in 1990 in the State of Illinois, but at any time in any of the numerous political subdivisions of this vast country. It seems to me that that categorical pronouncement reflects a naive vision of politics and an inadequate appreciation of the systemic effects of patronage in promoting political stability and facilitating the social and political integration of previously powerless groups.

The whole point of my dissent is that the desirability of patronage is a policy question to be decided by the people's representatives; I do not mean, therefore, to endorse that system. But in order to demonstrate that a legislature could reasonably determine that its benefits outweigh its "coercive" effects, I must describe those benefits as the proponents of patronage see them: As Justice Powell discussed at length in his *Elrod* dissent, patronage stabilizes political parties and prevents excessive political fragmentation — both of which are results in which States have a strong governmental interest. Party strength requires the efforts of the rank-and-file, especially in "the dull periods between elections," to perform such tasks as organizing precincts, registering new voters, and providing constituent services. *Elrod*, 427 U.S., at 385 (dissenting opinion).

Even the most enthusiastic supporter of a party's program will shrink before such drudgery, and it is folly to think that ideological conviction alone will motivate sufficient numbers to keep the party going through the off-years. "For the most part, as every politician knows, the hope of some reward generates a major portion of the local political activity supporting parties." *Ibid....*

The Court simply refuses to acknowledge the link between patronage and party discipline, and between that and party success. It relies (as did the plurality in *Elrod,* 427 U.S., at 369, n.23) on a single study of a rural Pennsylvania county by Professor Sorauf — a work that has been described as "more persuasive about the ineffectuality of Democratic leaders in Centre County than about the generalizability of [its] findings." Wolfinger, *Why Political Machines Have Not Withered Away and Other Revisionist Thoughts,* 34 J. Politics 365 (1972), at 384, n.39. It is unpersuasive to claim, as the Court does, that party workers are obsolete because campaigns are now conducted through media and other money-intensive means. Those techniques have supplemented but not supplanted personal contacts. See D. Price, Bringing Back the Parties (1984), at 25. Certainly they have not made personal contacts unnecessary in campaigns for the lower-level offices that are the foundations of party strength, nor have they replaced the myriad functions performed by party regulars not directly related to campaigning. And to the extent such techniques have replaced older methods of campaigning (partly in response to the limitations the Court has placed on patronage), the political system is not clearly better off. See *Elrod, supra,* at 384 (Powell, J., dissenting); *Branti,* 445 U.S., at 528 (Powell, J., dissenting). Increased reliance on money-intensive campaign techniques tends to entrench those in power much more effectively than patronage — but without the attendant benefit of strengthening the party system. A challenger can more easily obtain the support of party-workers (who can expect to be rewarded even if the candidate loses — if not this year, then the next) than the financial support of political action committees (which will generally support incumbents, who are likely to prevail)....

The patronage system does not, of course, merely foster political parties in general; it fosters the two-party system in particular. When getting a job, as opposed to effectuating a particular substantive policy, is an available incentive for party-workers, those attracted by that incentive are likely to work for the party that has the best chance of displacing the "ins," rather than for some splinter group that has a more attractive political philosophy but little hope of success. Not only is a two-party system more likely to emerge, but the differences between those parties are more likely to be moderated, as each has a relatively greater interest in appealing to a majority of the electorate and a relatively lesser interest in furthering philosophies or programs that are far from the mainstream. The stabilizing effects of such a system are obvious....

Equally apparent is the relatively destabilizing nature of a system in which candidates cannot rely upon patronage-based party loyalty for their campaign support, but must attract workers and raise funds by appealing to various interest-groups. See M. Tolchin & S. Tolchin, To the Victor (1971), at 127-130. There is little doubt that our decisions in *Elrod* and *Branti,* by contributing to the decline of party strength, have also contributed to the growth of interest-group politics in the last decade. See, e.g., Fitts, *The Vice of Virtue,* 136 U. Pa.

L. Rev. 1567, 1603-1607 (1988). Our decision today will greatly accelerate the trend. It is not only campaigns that are affected, of course, but the subsequent behavior of politicians once they are in power. The replacement of a system firmly based in party discipline with one in which each office-holder comes to his own accommodation with competing interest groups produces "a dispersion of political influence that may inhibit a political party from enacting its programs into law." *Branti, supra,* at 531 (Powell, J., dissenting).

Patronage, moreover, has been a powerful means of achieving the social and political integration of excluded groups. See, e.g., *Elrod, supra,* at 379 (Powell, J., dissenting); Cornwell, *Bosses, Machines and Ethnic Politics,* in Ethnic Group Politics 190, 195-197 (H. Bailey, Jr., & E. Katz eds. 1969). By supporting and ultimately dominating a particular party "machine," racial and ethnic minorities have — on the basis of their politics rather than their race or ethnicity — acquired the patronage awards the machine had power to confer....

While the patronage system has the benefits argued for above, it also has undoubted disadvantages. It facilitates financial corruption, such as salary kickbacks and partisan political activity on government-paid time. It reduces the efficiency of government, because it creates incentives to hire more and less-qualified workers and because highly qualified workers are reluctant to accept jobs that may only last until the next election. And, of course, it applies some greater or lesser inducement for individuals to join and work for the party in power....

What the patronage system ordinarily demands of the party worker is loyalty to, and activity on behalf of, the organization itself rather than a set of political beliefs. He is generally free to urge within the organization the adoption of any political position; but if that position is rejected he must vote and work for the party nonetheless. The diversity of political expression (other than expression of party loyalty) is channeled, in other words, to a different stage — to the contests for party endorsement rather than the partisan elections. It is undeniable, of course, that the patronage system entails some constraint upon the expression of views, particularly at the partisan-election stage, and considerable constraint upon the employee's right to associate with the other party. It greatly exaggerates these, however, to describe them as a general "'coercion of belief,'" *ante,* quoting *Branti,* 445 U.S., at 516; see also *Elrod,* 427 U.S., at 355 (plurality opinion). Indeed, it greatly exaggerates them to call them "coercion" at all, since we generally make a distinction between inducement and compulsion. The public official offered a bribe is not "coerced" to violate the law, and the private citizen offered a patronage job is not "coerced" to work for the party. In sum, I do not deny that the patronage system influences or redirects, perhaps to a substantial degree, individual political expression and political association. But like the many generations of Americans that have preceded us, I do not consider that a significant impairment of free speech or free association.

In emphasizing the advantages and minimizing the disadvantages (or at least minimizing one of the disadvantages) of the patronage system, I do not mean to suggest that that system is best. It may not always be; it may never be. To oppose our *Elrod-Branti* jurisprudence, one need not believe that the patronage system is *necessarily* desirable; nor even that it is always and everywhere *arguably* desirable; but merely that it is a political arrangement that may sometimes be a reasonable choice, and should therefore be left to the judgment of the people's elected representatives....

C. ... *Elrod* and *Branti* should be overruled, rather than merely not extended. Even in the field of constitutional adjudication, where the pull of *stare decisis* is at its weakest, see *Glidden Co. v. Zdanok,* 370 U.S. 530, 543 (1962) (opinion of Harlan, J.), one is reluctant to depart from precedent. But when that precedent is not only wrong, not only recent, not only contradicted by a long prior tradition, but also has proved unworkable in practice, then all reluctance ought to disappear. In my view that is the situation here. Though unwilling to leave it to the political process to draw the line between desirable and undesirable patronage, the Court has neither been prepared to rule that no such line exists (i.e., that all patronage is unconstitutional) nor able to design the line itself in a manner that judges, lawyers, and public employees can understand. *Elrod* allowed patronage dismissals of persons in "policymaking" or "confidential" positions. 427 U.S., at 367 (plurality opinion); *id.,* at 375 (Stewart, J., concurring). *Branti* retreated from that formulation, asking instead "whether the hiring authority can demonstrate that party affiliation is an appropriate requirement for the effective performance of the public office involved." 445 U.S., at 518. What that means is anybody's guess. The Courts of Appeals have devised various tests for determining when "affiliation is an appropriate requirement." See generally Martin, *A Decade of Branti Decisions: A Government Officials' Guide to Patronage Dismissals,* 39 Am. U. L. Rev. 11, 23-42 (1989). These interpretations of *Branti* are not only significantly at variance with each other; they are still so general that for most positions it is impossible to know whether party affiliation is a permissible requirement until a court renders its decision.

A few examples will illustrate the shambles *Branti* has produced. A city cannot fire a deputy sheriff because of his political affiliation,[5] but then again perhaps it can,[6] especially if he is called the "police captain."[7] A county cannot fire on that basis its attorney for the department of social services,[8] nor its assistant attorney for family court,[9] but a city can fire its solicitor and his assistants,[10] or its assistant city attorney,[11] or its assistant state's attorney,[12] or its corporation counsel.[13] A city cannot discharge its deputy court clerk for his political affiliation,[14] but it can fire its legal assistant to the clerk on that basis.[15]

The examples could be multiplied, but this summary should make obvious that the "tests" devised to implement *Branti* have produced inconsistent and

---

[5] *Jones v. Dodson,* 727 F.2d 1329, 1338 (CA 4 1984).

[6] *McBee v. Jim Hogg County, Texas,* 730 F.2d 1009, 1014-1015 (CA 5 1984) (en banc).

[7] *Joyner v. Lancaster,* 553 F. Supp. 809, 818 (M.D.N.C. 1982), *later proceeding,* 815 F.2d 20, 24 (CA 4), *cert. denied,* 484 U.S. 830 (1987).

[8] *Layden v. Costello,* 517 F. Supp. 860, 862 (N.D.N.Y. 1981).

[9] *Tavano v. County of Niagara, New York,* 621 F. Supp. 345, 349-350 (W.D.N.Y. 1985), *aff'd mem.,* 800 F.2d 1128 (CA 2 1986).

[10] *Ness v. Marshall,* 660 F.2d 517, 521-522 (CA 3 1981); *Montaquila v. St. Cyr,* 433 A.2d 206, 211 (R.I. 1981).

[11] *Finkelstein v. Barthelemy,* 678 F. Supp. 1255, 1265 (E.D. La. 1988).

[12] *Livas v. Petka,* 711 F.2d 798, 800-801 (CA 7 1983).

[13] *Bavoso v. Harding,* 507 F. Supp. 313, 316 (S.D.N.Y. 1980).

[14] *Barnes v. Bosley,* 745 F.2d 501, 508 (CA 8 1984), *cert. denied,* 471 U.S. 1017 (1985).

[15] *Bauer v. Bosley,* 802 F.2d 1058, 1063 (CA 8 1986), *cert. denied,* 481 U.S. 1038 (1987).

unpredictable results. That uncertainty undermines the purpose of both the nonpatronage rule and the exception. The rule achieves its objective of preventing the "coercion" of political affiliation, only if the employee is confident that he can engage in (or refrain from) political activities without risking dismissal. Since the current doctrine leaves many employees utterly in the dark about whether their jobs are protected, they are likely to play it safe. On the other side, the exception was designed to permit the government to implement its electoral mandate. *Elrod, supra,* at 367 (plurality opinion). But unless the government is fairly sure that dismissal is permitted, it will leave the politically uncongenial official in place, since an incorrect decision will expose it to lengthy litigation and a large damage award, perhaps even against the responsible officials personally.

This uncertainty and confusion are not the result of the fact that *Elrod,* and then *Branti,* chose the wrong "line." My point is that there is no right line — or at least no right line that can be nationally applied and that is known by judges.... The appropriate "mix" of party-based employment is a political question if there ever was one, and we should give it back to the voters of the various political units to decide, through civil-service legislation crafted to suit the time and place, which mix is best.

III

Even were I not convinced that *Elrod* and *Branti* were wrongly decided, I would hold that they should not be extended beyond their facts, viz., actual discharge of employees for their political affiliation. Those cases invalidated patronage firing in order to prevent the "restraint it places on freedoms of belief and association." *Elrod,* 427 U.S., at 355 (plurality opinion); see also *id.,* at 357 (patronage "compels or restrains" and "inhibits" belief and association). The loss of one's current livelihood is an appreciably greater constraint than such other disappointments as the failure to obtain a promotion or selection for an uncongenial transfer. Even if the "coercive" effect of the former has been held always to outweigh the benefits of party-based employment decisions, the "coercive" effect of the latter should not be....

NOTES

1. In *Avery v. Jennings,* 786 F.2d 233 (6th Cir.), *cert. denied,* 477 U.S. 905 (1986), the court held that the practice by local elected officials of hiring job applicants who were their friends or were referred by political allies, which led to a disproportionate number of employees of one political affiliation, did not violate the first amendment rights of applicants who were not seriously considered because of their lack of such personal connections. The challenged practice did not preclude the employment of individuals because of their political affiliation. It was merely designed to locate good employees who could work comfortably with the elected officials and to maintain advantageous political relationships.

2. *Conklin v. Lovely,* 834 F.2d 543 (6th Cir. 1987), involved an individual who worked half-time for the county clerk and half-time for the county treasurer, both of whom were Republicans. She campaigned openly for the incumbent prosecuting attorney, a Democrat, who lost the election. Ms. Conklin was subsequently discharged. The court held that her termination violated the first amendment, since it impermissibly chilled her free speech rights.

3. *Dickeson v. Quarberg,* 844 F.2d 1435 (10th Cir. 1988), involved the right of a newly-elected sheriff to dismiss the head jailer and an administrative assistant because of their political association with the defeated sheriff. The court indicated that the determinative question is whether party affiliation is an appropriate requirement for effective performance of the public office involved, and it noted that the defendant bears the burden of demonstrating that party affiliation is a proper requirement. See also *Kurowski v. Krajewski,* 848 F.2d 767 (7th Cir.), *cert. denied,* 109 S. Ct. 309 (1988), finding that political affiliation is not an appropriate criterion for the employment of assistant public defenders.

4. See generally Martin, *A Decade of Branti Decisions: A Government Official's Guide to Patronage Dismissals,* 39 Am. U.L. Rev. 11 (1989); Comment, *First Amendment Limitations on Patronage Employment Practices,* 49 U. Chi. L. Rev. 181 (1982); Note, *Patronage and the First Amendment After Elrod v. Burns,* 78 Colum. L. Rev. 468 (1978).

2. POLITICAL ACTIVITY BY UNIONS REPRESENTING EMPLOYEES IN THE PUBLIC SECTOR

H. WELLINGTON & R. WINTER, THE UNIONS AND THE CITIES 24-25, 28-31 (1971)*

Although the market does not discipline the union in the public sector to the extent that it does in the private, the municipal employment paradigm, nevertheless, would seem to be consistent with what Robert A. Dahl has called the "'normal' American political process," which is "one in which there is a high probability that an active and legitimate group in the population can make itself heard effectively at some crucial stage in the process of decision," for the union may be seen as little more than an "active and legitimate group in the population." With elections in the background to perform, as Mr. Dahl notes, "the critical role ... in maximizing political equality and popular sovereignty," all seems well, at least theoretically, with collective bargaining and public employment.

But there is trouble even in the house of theory if collective bargaining in the public sector means what it does in the private. The trouble is that if unions are able to withhold labor — to strike — as well as to employ the usual methods of political pressure, they may possess a disproportionate share of effective power in the process of decision. Collective bargaining would then be so effective a pressure as to skew the results of the "'normal' American political process."

One should straightway make plain that the strike issue is not simply the importance of public services as contrasted with services or products produced in the private sector. This is only part of the issue, and in the past the partial truth has beclouded analysis. The services performed by a private transit authority are neither less nor more important to the public than those that would be performed if the transit authority were owned by a municipality. A railroad or a dock strike may be more damaging to a community than "job action" by police. This is not to say that governmental services are not important. They

---

*Copyright 1971 by The Brookings Institution, Washington, D.C. Reprinted by permission.

are, both because the demand for them is inelastic and because their disruption may seriously injure a city's economy and occasionally impair the physical welfare of its citizens. Nevertheless, the importance of governmental services is only a necessary part of, rather than a complete answer to, the question: Why be more concerned about strikes in public employment than in private?

The answer to the question is simply that, because strikes in public employment disrupt important services, a large part of a mayor's political constituency will, in many cases, press for a quick end to the strike with little concern for the cost of settlement. This is particularly so where the cost of settlement is borne by a different and larger political constituency, the citizens of the state or nation. Since interest groups other than public employees, with conflicting claims on municipal government, do not, as a general proposition, have anything approaching the effectiveness of the strike — or at least cannot maintain that relative degree of power over the long run — they may be put at a significant competitive disadvantage in the political process....

The strike and its threat, moreover, exacerbate the problems associated with the scope of bargaining in public employment. This seems clear if one attends in slightly more detail to techniques of municipal decision making.

Few students of our cities would object to Herbert Kaufman's observation that:

> Decisions of the municipal government emanate from no single source, but from many centers; conflicts and clashes are referred to no single authority, but are settled at many levels and at many points in the system: no single group can guarantee the success of any proposal it supports, the defeat of every idea it objects to. Not even the central governmental organs of the city — the Mayor, the Board of Estimate, the Council — individually or in combination, even approach mastery in this sense.
>
> Each separate decision center consists of a cluster of interested contestants, with a "core group" in the middle, invested by the rules with the formal authority to legitimize decisions (that is to promulgate them in binding form) and a constellation of related "satellite groups" seeking to influence the authoritative issuances of the core group.

Nor would many disagree with Nelson W. Polsby when, in discussing community decision making that is concerned with an alternative to a "current state of affairs," he argues that the alternative "must be politically palatable and relatively easy to accomplish; otherwise great amounts of influence have to be brought to bear with great skill and efficiency in order to secure its adoption."

It seems probable that such potential subjects of bargaining as school decentralization and a civilian police review board are, where they do not exist, alternatives to the "current state of affairs," which are not "politically palatable and relatively easy to accomplish." If a teachers' union or a police union were to bargain with the municipal employer over these questions, and were able to use the strike to insist that the proposals not be adopted, how much "skill and efficiency" on the part of the proposals' advocates would be necessary to effect a change? And, to put the shoe on the other foot, if a teachers' union were to insist through collective bargaining (with the strike or its threat) upon major changes in school curriculum, would not that union have to be considerably less skillful and efficient in the normal political process than other advocates of community change? The point is that with respect to some subjects, collective bargaining may be too powerful a lever on municipal decision making, too effective a technique for changing or preventing the change of one small but important part of the "current state of affairs."

Unfortunately, in this area the problem is not merely the strike threat and the strike. In a system where impasse procedures involving third parties are established in order to reduce work stoppages — and this is common in those states that have passed public employment bargaining statutes — third party intervention must be partly responsive to union demands. If the scope of bargaining is open-ended, the neutral part, to be effective, will have to work out accommodations that inevitably advance some of the union's claims some of the time. And the neutral, with his eyes fixed on achieving a settlement, can hardly be concerned with balancing all the items on the community agenda or reflecting the interests of all relevant groups....

Collective bargaining by public employees and the political process cannot be separated. The costs of such bargaining, therefore, cannot be fully measured without taking into account the impact on the allocation of political power in the typical municipality. If one assumes, as here, that municipal political processes should be structured to ensure "a high probability that an active and legitimate group in the population can make itself heard effectively at some crucial stage in the process of decision," then the issue is how powerful unions will be in the typical municipal political process if a full transplant of collective bargaining is carried out.

The conclusion is that such a transplant would, in many cases, institutionalize the power of public employee unions in a way that would leave competing groups in the political process at a permanent and substantial disadvantage....

A teachers' strike may not endanger public health or welfare. It may, however, seriously inconvenience parents and other citizens who, as voters, have the power to punish one of the parties — and always the same party, the political leadership — to the dispute. How can anyone any longer doubt the vulnerability of a municipal employer to this sort of pressure? Was it simply a matter of indifference to Mayor Lindsay in September 1969 whether another teachers' strike occurred on the eve of a municipal election? Did the size and the speed of the settlement with the United Federation of Teachers (UFT) suggest nothing about one first-rate politician's estimate of his vulnerability? And are the chickens now coming home to roost because of extravagant concessions on pensions for employees of New York City the result only of mistaken actuarial calculations? Or do they reflect the irrelevance of long-run considerations to politicians vulnerable to the strike and compelled to think in terms of short-run political impact?

RASKIN, POLITICS UP-ENDS THE BARGAINING TABLE, in PUBLIC WORKERS AND PUBLIC UNIONS 122, 142-43 (S. Zagoria ed. 1972)*

It is in this area of the scope of bargaining that bitter battles lie ahead for New York City's ultra-political labor movement. Every union contract is a limit on

* A.H. Raskin, *Politics Up-Ends the Bargaining Table,* in Public Workers and Public Unions (Sam Zagoria ed.). Copyright © 1972 by The American Assembly, Columbia University. Reprinted by permission of Prentice-Hall, Inc.

management's freedom, and nowhere is that tug-of-war more difficult to resolve than in governmental service. Everything a teachers' union does affects the quality of education, and in New York the cross-over from straight bread-and-butter concerns to the nature of the educational system is profound. The United Federation of Teachers was not only dominant in the legislative hassle over school decentralization but it incorporated into its contracts a provision for double-manned "More Effective Schools" as the chief vehicle for educational reform. The extent to which such incursions into policy determination would be prohibited by the proposed curbs in Albany has already prompted the UFT to fuse its strength with that of other teacher groups all over the state to mount a militant counteroffensive next year.

Realistically, no legal walls are going to keep civil service unions from moving increasingly into the policy field. Private industry learned many years ago that unions are ingenious enough to find a hundred expedients for punching holes in "management's rights" clauses. Manpower is so much a bedrock of all municipal services that public unions will find ways to tie considerations of job security or working conditions into every policy issue they want to have a voice in.

NOTE

Wellington and Winter argue that if traditional collective bargaining is transplanted in the public sector, "such a transplant would, in many cases, institutionalize the power of public employee unions in a way that would leave competing groups in the political process at a permanent and substantial disadvantage." Assuming that this view is correct, can the dangers and problems posed be effectively protected against by strict enforcement of the Hatch Act or comparable legislation? Does the Hatch Act purport to deal with the kind of problems posed by Wellington and Winter? See generally Masters, *Federal Employee Unions and Political Action,* 38 Indus. & Lab. Rel. Rev. 612 (1985), and Love & Sulzner, *Political Implications of Public Employee Bargaining,* 11 Indus. Rel. 18 (Feb. 1972).

3. THE RIGHT TO PETITION

Section 7102 of the statute governing employee relations in the federal service provides that:

> The right of employees individually or collectively, to petition Congress, or a Member of Congress, or to furnish information to either House of Congress, or to a Committee or Member thereof, may not be interfered with or denied. [5 U.S.C. § 7102 (Supp. IV 1969)]

This section, which first appeared as part of the Lloyd-LaFollette Act of 1912 (37 Stat. 555), was specifically directed at the "gag rule" initiated by President Theodore Roosevelt in 1902. As first instituted, the "gag rule" absolutely prohibited employees of the executive department from petitioning Congress to remedy job grievances. (Exec. Order No. 163, Jan. 31, 1902, *reprinted in* 48 Cong. Rec. 5223 (1912)). Later, in 1909, President Taft issued a similar executive order. The Taft "gag rule" (Exec. Order 1142, Nov. 26, 1909, *reprinted in* 48 Cong. Rec. 4513 (1912)), broadly prohibited employee petitions seeking "congressional action of any kind," however, it did allow employees to present petitions with the "consent and knowledge" of their department heads.

The "gag rule" was severely criticized, especially by postal employees who comprised the largest block of civil servants affected by the rule and against whom the rule was strictly enforced. As a consequence, Congress passed section 6 of the 1912 Act, which read as follows:

The right of persons employed in the civil service of the United States, either individually or collectively, to petition Congress, or any Member thereof, or to furnish information to either House of Congress, or to any Committee or member thereof, shall not be denied or interfered with.

This section subsequently appeared as 5 U.S.C. § 652(d) [62 Stat. 356 (1948)], which is the forerunner of the current provision in 5 U.S.C. § 7102. An excellent review of the legislative history of the act may be found in Comment, *Dismissals of Public Employees for Petitioning Congress: Administrative Discipline and 5 U.S.C. Section 652(d),* 74 Yale L.J. 1156, 1161 (1965), where it is reported that:

The dominant theme in the House and Senate debates seems to have been that the act was designed to insure that unjust treatment of government employees would promptly and effectively be brought to the attention of Congress. Many Congressmen felt that redress of job grievances could not be satisfactorily obtained by employee appeals to superiors; the gag rule "instead of promoting discipline and efficiency, produces the worst kind of tyranny" by department heads....

It is apparent, then, that section 652(d) was intended to encompass job grievance petitions. It also seems clear that Congress meant to prevent the *act* of petitioning from being used as grounds for discipline or dismissal.... [citations omitted]

See also Note, *The Right of Government Employees to Furnish Information to Congress: Statutory and Congressional Aspects,* 57 Va. L. Rev. 885 (1971), which gives the following summary of the leading judicial opinions construing section 7102:

The judicial history of section 7102 is confined to seven cases,[23] of which only two have examined the scope of the protection afforded petitions submitted to Congress. In *Steck v. Connally,* Judge Holtzoff of the District Court for the District of Columbia ordered the reinstatement of a federal employee who had been dismissed on charges that he had circulated among his fellow employees a petition which he forwarded to a member of Congress. The Court explained that section 7102 guaranteed to all civil servants the right to furnish information to Congress "free from *any restriction* or interference on the part of their superior officers." It further found that a department head could not censor the contents of the petition or dismiss the petitioner even if

---

[23] Of the five cases that did not examine the legislative history of section 7102 to determine its scope, four involved statements made either to both Congress and the public, or solely to the public: *Meehan v. Macy,* 392 F.2d 822 (D.C. Cir.), *modified,* 425 F.2d 469 (1968), *vacated,* 425 F.2d 472 (1969) (en banc, per curiam); *Levine v. Farley,* 107 F.2d 186 (D.C. Cir. 1939), *cert. denied,* 308 U.S. 622 (1940); *Eustace v. Day,* 198 F. Supp. 233 (D.D.C. 1961); *Ruderer v. United States,* 412 F.2d 1285 (Ct. Cl. 1969), *cert. denied,* 398 U.S. 914 (1970). In each of these cases, the court held that the right to petition Congress under section 7102 did not encompass the right to direct statements at the public to induce others to write to their Congressmen. In *Swaaley v. United States,* 376 F.2d 857 (Ct. Cl. 1967), the court cited section 7102 as analogous protection of the right of government employees to petition their department head.

the statements in the petition were untrue. In response to the argument that administrative efficiency, discipline, and morale required that the statute be narrowly construed, the court noted: "[t]o be sure an activity of this kind can adversely affect the morale of a Government department. It can be vexatious and annoying at times if the employee acts unreasonably, but the statute contains no limitation."

Despite this broad holding, in *Turner v. Kennedy,* the District Court for the District of Columbia rendered summary judgment against an FBI agent who asked the court to overturn a Civil Service Commission's finding that letters he wrote to several members of Congress were false, irresponsible, and unjustified, and therefore demonstrated his unsuitability for continued employment in the FBI. The court did not discuss the scope of protection guaranteed by section 7102, and seemingly assumed that it did not protect the plaintiff's activities. In a four-line per curiam decision — which alluded neither to the statutory history nor to *Steck v. Connally* — the Court of Appeals affirmed.

Circuit Judge Fahy dissented, relying on the broad language of section 7102 and citing *Steck* with approval. After examining the legislative history, he concluded that the tenor of the debate indicated Congressional intent "that full First Amendment rights were to be extended to a Civil Service employee by Section [7102]." Nevertheless, Judge Fahy went on to reason that "perhaps his right is conditioned to a degree by the circumstance that he is in government service." He therefore proposed to limit the protection of section 7102 in the same way that the Supreme Court, in *New York Times Co. v. Sullivan,* had limited the right of freedom of the press. Adapting the *New York Times* rules to the *Turner* case, Fahy would have excluded from the protection of section 7102 all statements "made with actual malice, that is, with knowledge that they were false or with reckless disregard of whether [they were] false or not." In a footnote he cautioned that he did not reach such questions as whether "the contents of a petition furnishing classified information or confidential information of a nature that is in the public interest not to disclose is privileged."

The significance of *Turner v. Kennedy* lies not so much in its holding as in the suggestion, implicit in the District Court's opinion and in the per curiam and dissenting opinions of the Court of Appeals, that section 7102 is susceptible of limitation despite its sweeping language and its legislative history. In the future courts confronted with the issue of the statute's scope of protection are faced with two alternatives. On the one hand, they may leave to the executive branch the decision whether the information in question is of "a nature that is in the public interest not to [be] disclosed" or constitutes activity that "causes the agency immediate and substantial harm."[29] There is considerable precedent for this course. As early as 1840, the Supreme Court asserted that "interference of the courts with the performance of the ordinary duties of the executive departments of the government, would be productive of nothing but mischief." The consequences of this abdication are twofold.

---

[29] The Civil Service Commission used the latter standard in *Turner.* In *Meehan v. Macy,* 392 F.2d 822, 830 (D.C. Cir. 1968), the Court of Appeals for the District of Columbia stated its standard of review: "[I]n general the courts defer to the agency as the appropriate judge of what is an appropriate cause for discharge as needed to promote efficiency of the service, provided its decision is not arbitrary or capricious." See also *De Fino v. McNamara,* 287 F.2d 339 (D.C. Cir.), *cert. denied,* 366 U.S. 976 (1961) (agency is not required to consider the employee's entire performance record in applying its standard); *Taylor v. Macy,* 252 F. Supp. 1021 (S.D. Cal. 1966) (dismissal based on criminal convictions that had been expunged).

First, the fate of the federal employee who furnished information to Congress would be placed in the hands of his department head or other superior officers — the precise situation Congress sought to change. Second, as the ultimate arbiter, the executive branch could effectively foreclose to Congress an important source of its information.

On the other hand, courts that seek to safeguard the civil servant's right to petition may adopt a strict standard in reviewing executive action. They would then face the difficult task of striking a balance among conflicting interests. In determining whether a civil servant has the right to furnish information to Congress, the courts would have to decide what information must not be disclosed in the public interest, and under what circumstances the agency's interest in discipline, morale, and efficiency overrides the right of the federal employee to consult his representatives. Clearly, these questions could be resolved more effectively if the legislative and executive branches could agree upon a precise statute that would balance their conflicting interests.

57 Va. L. Rev. at 893-95.*

Swaaley v. United States, 376 F.2d 857 (Ct. Cl. 1967), gives definition to the "right of petition" enjoyed by government employees under the first amendment:

We think the freedom of the press to criticize and it may be, defame, public officials has no better support than the freedom of petition here involved. We agree with Judge Fahy's suggestion that the doctrine of *New York Times Co. v. Sullivan, supra,* applies to federal employee's petitions. See *Turner v. Kennedy,* 118 U.S. App. D.C. 104, 332 F.2d 304, 307, *cert. denied,* 379 U.S. 901 (1964) (dissenting opinion). These suggestions, it is true, relate to petitions to Congress. But, it would seem that whatever rights a civil service employee has under the First Amendment include petitions to the head of his own department as well as those to Congress. Mr. Justice Story, in his Commentaries on the Constitution, Vol. II, Section 1895, at 645, note b (5th ed. 1891), said of the right to petition:

The statements made in petitions addressed to the proper authority, in a matter within its jurisdiction, are so far privileged that the petitioner is not liable, either civilly or criminally, for making them, though they prove to be untrue and injurious, unless he has made them maliciously.

This statement was also quoted with approval in *Turner v. Kennedy, supra,* 332 F.2d at 307 (dissenting opinion). In *Bridges v. State of California,* 314 U.S. 252, 277 (1941), a telegram to the Secretary of Labor was held to be a First Amendment petition.

Therefore, we hold that a petition by a federal employee to one above him in the executive hierarchy is covered by the First Amendment and if it includes defamation of any Federal official, protection is lost only under the circumstances in which a newspaper article would lose such protection if it defamed such official. "Criticism of ... official conduct does not lose its constitutional protection merely because it is effective criticism and hence dimin-

---

*Reprinted by permission of the Virginia Law Review and Fred B. Rothman & Co.

ishes ... official reputations. If neither factual error nor defamatory content suffices to remove the constitutional shield from criticism of official conduct, the combination of the two elements is no less inadequate." *New York Times Co. v. Sullivan, supra,* 376 U.S. at 273.

376 F.2d at 862-63.

NOTES

1. Can it be argued that the *New York Times* doctrine should have full application to government employees who criticize superiors "through channels," as in *Swaaley, supra,* but that some lesser standard should apply in cases involving appeals to the public? Compare *Los Angeles Teachers Union, Local 1021 v. Los Angeles City Bd. of Educ.,* 71 Cal. 2d 551, 455 P.2d 827 (1969), and *Hudson v. Gray,* 285 Ala. 546, 234 So. 2d 564 (1970), with the holding in *Meehan v. Macy,* 425 F.2d 469 (D.C. Cir. 1968), *aff'd after rehearing en banc,* 425 F.2d 472 (D.C. Cir. 1969).

2. In T. Emerson, The System of Freedom of Expression 590 (1970), the author argues that:

Restriction on the political conduct of government employees does not abridge their freedom of expression to the extent that it is indispensably required as part of the employment relation; that is to say, is essential to the government's power to carry out its functions through engaging the services of its citizens. Controls are permissible at the point where the expression can be shown to relate to job performance, either by way of indicating the employee's competence, interfering with his capacity to carry out orders, or impairing his relationship with the rest of the organization. Hence regulations concerned with the making of deliberately false statements that may reflect on competence, carrying on political activities during working hours, campaigning against or running for office against an immediate superior, would be justified. So also would controls aimed at eliminating a direct conflict of interest between an employee's political activity and his government position. In addition, needless to say, prohibition of political activities that are no expression at all, such as using official authority for partisan political coercion of subordinates, or refusal to comply with the merit system in promotion, would raise no First Amendment problems.

3. Military regulations require members of the armed forces to obtain the approval of their commanders before they circulate petitions on military bases. However, the regulations specifically preclude commanders from interfering with the circulation of materials other than those posing a clear danger to military loyalty, discipline, or morale. In *Brown v. Glines,* 444 U.S. 348 (1980), a divided Supreme Court sustained this pre-circulation approval requirement against a two-pronged attack. No impermissible first amendment infringement was discerned, since the regulations were found to protect a substantial government interest unrelated to the suppression of free expression — the need to maintain respect for discipline and duty, critical aspects of military effectiveness. Furthermore, although 10 U.S.C. § 1034 proscribes unwarranted restrictions upon the right of military personnel to communicate with members of Congress, this provision was interpreted as protecting only a service member's right to directly communicate with elected representatives, but not that individual's right to circulate protest petitions on a military base. See also *Secretary of Navy v. Huff,* 444 U.S. 453 (1980).

4. POLITICAL LOBBYING

Political lobbying is, to some extent, subsumed under the more general heading of the right to petition. Lobbying by public employees is frequently a supplement to or replacement for traditional collective bargaining. Many of the statutes and executive orders regulating collective bargaining in the public sector have narrowly limited the scope of bargaining; for example, section 7106 of the Civil Service Reform Act (see Statutory Appendix) specifically excludes from bargaining "the authority of any management official of any agency — (1) to determine the mission, budget, organization, number of employees, and internal security practices of the agency."
Thus unions representing employees in the federal service are frequently forced to make direct appeals to Congress to achieve bargaining goals.

Even when a public agency or department is authorized to negotiate and agree to certain substantive items, there may remain the requirement of legislative approval of some parts of the agreement. The New York Taylor Law, for example, includes the following requirement:

> Any written agreement between a public employer and an employee organization determining the terms and conditions of employment of public employees shall contain the following notice in type not smaller than the largest type used elsewhere in such agreement.
> "It is agreed by and between the parties that any provision of this agreement requiring legislative action to permit its implementation by amendment of law or by providing the additional funds therefor, shall not become effective until the appropriate legislative body has given approval." [New York Civil Service Law § 204-a]

The Wisconsin State Employment Labor Relations Act, requires that agreements involving state employees must be sent to a joint legislative committee for approval once they have been approved by the union representative. A public hearing must then be held. If the committee approves the agreement, it introduces bills in both legislative houses to implement those portions of the agreement, such as wage adjustments, which require legislative approval. If the committee rejects the agreement, or if it approves but the legislature rejects the resultant bills, the agreement is sent back to the parties for further negotiation. Wis. Stat. Ann. § 111.92.

Given these types of legislative enactments, it would appear that unions in the public sector must necessarily become involved in the "political process" in order to achieve legislative ratification of negotiated benefits.

For a series of articles discussing the lobbying problem, see Moskow, Loewenbery & Koziara, *Lobbying* 216; Nilan, *Union Lobbying at the Federal Level* 221; McLennan & Moskow, *Multilaterial Bargaining in the Public Sector* 227; and Belasco, *Municipal Bargaining and Political Power* 235, all of which appear in Collective Bargaining in Government (Loewenberg & Moskow eds. 1972).

D. CONSTITUTIONAL PROTECTIONS AGAINST EMPLOYMENT DISCRIMINATION ON THE BASIS OF RACE, SEX, NATIONAL ORIGIN AND AGE

Since the publication of the first edition of the casebook, there has been a literal explosion in the law dealing with equal employment opportunity, most notably under title VII of the Civil Rights Act of 1964. As a consequence, the authors have decided that it is not possible to give adequate treatment to this subject in a book dealing with labor relations law in the public sector. Employment discrimination is now the subject of several entire books, see, e.g., Smith, Craver & Clark, Employment Discrimination Law (Michie 1988), and it is plainly too broad a topic for coverage here. Therefore, employment discrimination materials here will be limited to those cases arising under the United States Constitution, i.e., primarily under the fifth and fourteenth amendments. There will be no coverage of cases arising under title VII, the Equal Pay Act, 42 U.S.C. § 1981, Executive Order 11246, or other like enactments.

1. RACE

WASHINGTON v. DAVIS

426 U.S. 229, 96 S. Ct. 2040, 48 L. Ed. 2d 597 (1976)

Justice White delivered the opinion of the Court.

This case involves the validity of a qualifying test administered to applicants for positions as police officers in the District of Columbia Metropolitan Police Department. The test was sustained by the District Court but invalidated by the Court of Appeals. We are in agreement with the District Court and hence reverse the judgment of the Court of Appeals.

I

This action began on April 10, 1970, when two Negro police officers filed suit against the then Commissioner of the District of Columbia, the Chief of the District's Metropolitan Police Department and the Commissioners of the United States Civil Service Commission. An amended complaint, filed December 10, alleged that the promotion policies of the Department were racially discriminatory and sought a declaratory judgment and an injunction. The respondents Harley and Sellers were permitted to intervene, their amended complaint asserting that their applications to become officers in the Department had been rejected, and that the Department's recruiting procedures discriminated on the basis of race against black applicants by a series of practices including, but not limited to, a written personnel test which excluded a disproportionately high number of Negro applicants. These practices were asserted to violate respondents' rights "under the due process clause of the Fifth Amendment to the United States Constitution, under 42 U.S.C. § 1981 and under D.C. Code § 1-320." ...

According to the findings and conclusions of the District Court, to be accepted by the Department and to enter an intensive 17-week training program, the police recruit was required to satisfy certain physical and character standards, to be a high school graduate or its equivalent, and to receive a grade of at least 40 out of 80 on "Test 21," which is "an examination that is used generally throughout the federal service," which "was developed by the Civil Service Commission, not the Police Department," and which was "designed to test verbal ability, vocabulary, reading and comprehension." [348 F. Supp.], at 16.

The validity of Test 21 was the sole issue before the court on the motions for summary judgment. The District Court noted that there was no claim of "an intentional discrimination or purposeful discriminatory acts" but only a claim that Test 21 bore no relationship to job performance and "has a highly discriminatory impact in screening out black candidates." *Ibid.* Respondents' evidence, the District Court said, warranted three conclusions: "(a) The number of black police officers, while substantial, is not proportionate to the population mix of the city. (b) A higher percentage of blacks fail the Test than whites. (c) The Test has not been validated to establish its reliability for measuring subsequent job performance." *Ibid.* This showing was deemed sufficient to shift the burden of proof to the defendants in the action, petitioners here; but the court nevertheless concluded that on the undisputed facts respondents were not entitled to relief. The District Court relied on several factors. Since August 1969, 44% of new police force recruits had been black; that figure also represented the proportion of blacks on the total force and was roughly equivalent to 20- to 29-year-old blacks in the 50-mile radius in which the recruiting efforts of the Police Department had been concentrated. It was undisputed that the Department had systematically and affirmatively sought to enroll black officers many of whom passed the test but failed to report for duty. The District Court rejected the assertion that Test 21 was culturally slanted to favor whites and was "satisfied that the undisputable facts prove the test to be reasonably and directly related to the requirements of the police recruit training program and that it is neither so designed nor operates [*sic*] to discriminate against otherwise qualified blacks." ...

Having lost on both constitutional and statutory issues in the District Court, respondents brought the case to the Court of Appeals claiming that their summary judgment motion, which rested on purely constitutional grounds, should have been granted. The tendered constitutional issue was whether the use of Test 21 invidiously discriminated against Negroes and hence denied them due process of law contrary to the commands of the Fifth Amendment. The Court of Appeals, addressing that issue, announced that it would be guided by *Griggs v. Duke Power Co.,* 401 U.S. 424 (1971), a case involving the interpretation and application of Title VII of the Civil Rights Act of 1964, and held that the statutory standards elucidated in that case were to govern the due process question tendered in this one. 168 U.S. App. D.C. 42, 512 F.2d 956 (1975). The court went on to declare that lack of discriminatory intent in designing and administering Test 21 was irrelevant; the critical fact was rather that a far greater proportion of blacks — four times as many — failed the test than did whites. This disproportionate impact, standing alone and without regard to whether it indicated a discriminatory purpose, was held sufficient to establish a constitutional violation, absent proof by petitioners that the test was an adequate measure of job performance in addition to being an indicator of probable success in the training program, a burden which the court ruled petitioners had failed to discharge. That the Department had made substantial efforts to recruit blacks was held beside the point and the fact that the racial distribution of recent hirings and of the Department itself might be roughly equivalent to the racial makeup of the surrounding community, broadly conceived, was put aside as a "comparison [not] material to this appeal." ...

II

Because the Court of Appeals erroneously applied the legal standards applicable to Title VII cases in resolving the constitutional issue before it, we reverse its judgment in respondents' favor. Although the petition for certiorari did not present this ground for reversal, our Rule 40(1)(d)(2) provides that we "may notice a plain error not presented"; and this is an appropriate occasion to invoke the rule.

As the Court of Appeals understood Title VII,[10] employees or applicants proceeding under it need not concern themselves with the employer's possibly discriminatory purpose but instead may focus solely on the racially differential impact of the challenged hiring or promotion practices. This is not the constitutional rule. We have never held that the constitutional standard for adjudicating claims of invidious racial discrimination is identical to the standards applicable under Title VII, and we decline to do so today.

The central purpose of the Equal Protection Clause of the Fourteenth Amendment is the prevention of official conduct discriminating on the basis of race. It is also true that the Due Process Clause of the Fifth Amendment contains an equal protection component prohibiting the United States from invidiously discriminating between individuals or groups. *Bolling v. Sharpe,* 347 U.S. 497 (1954). But our cases have not embraced the proposition that a law or other official act, without regard to whether it reflects a racially discriminatory purpose, is unconstitutional *solely* because it has a racially disproportionate impact....

... *Wright v. Rockefeller,* 376 U.S. 52 (1964), upheld a New York congressional apportionment statute against claims that district lines had been racially gerrymandered. The challenged districts were made up predominantly of whites or of minority races, and their boundaries were irregularly drawn. The challengers did not prevail because they failed to prove that the New York Legislature "was either motivated by racial considerations or in fact drew the districts on racial lines"; the plaintiffs had not shown that the statute "was the product of a state contrivance to segregate on the basis of race or place of origin." *Id.,* at 56, 58. The dissenters were in agreement that the issue was whether the "boundaries ... were purposefully drawn on racial lines." *Id.,* at 67.

The school desegregation cases have also adhered to the basic equal protection principle that the invidious quality of a law claimed to be racially discriminatory must ultimately be traced to a racially discriminatory purpose. That

---

[10]Although Title VII standards have dominated this case, the statute was not applicable to federal employees when the complaint was filed, and although the 1972 amendments extending the Title to reach government employees were adopted prior to the District Court's judgment, the complaint was not amended to state a claim under that Title, nor did the case thereafter proceed as a Title VII case. Respondents' motion for partial summary judgment, filed after the 1972 amendments, rested solely on constitutional grounds; and the Court of Appeals ruled that the motion should have been granted.

....

there are both predominantly black and predominantly white schools in a community is not alone violative of the Equal Protection Clause. The essential element of *de jure* segregation is "a current condition of segregation resulting from intentional state action." *Keyes v. School Dist. No. 1,* 413 U.S. 189, 205 (1973). "The differentiating factor between *de jure* segregation and so-called *de facto* segregation ... is *purpose* or *intent* to segregate." *Id.,* at 208. See also *id.,* at 199, 211, 213. The Court has also recently rejected allegations of racial discrimination based solely on the statistically disproportionate racial impact of various provisions of the Social Security Act because "[t]he acceptance of appellant's constitutional theory would render suspect each difference in treatment among the grant classes, however lacking the racial motivation and however rational the treatment might be." *Jefferson v. Hackney,* 406 U.S. 535, 548 (1972).

This is not to say that the necessary discriminatory racial purpose must be express or appear on the face of the statute, or that a law's disproportionate impact is irrelevant in cases involving Constitution-based claims of racial discrimination. A statute, otherwise neutral on its face, must not be applied so as invidiously to discriminate on the basis of race. *Yick Wo v. Hopkins,* 118 U.S. 356 (1886). It is also clear from the cases dealing with racial discrimination in the selection of juries that the systematic exclusion of Negroes is itself such an "unequal application of the law ... as to show intentional discrimination." *Akins v. Texas, supra,* at 404. *Smith v. Texas,* 311 U.S. 128 (1940); *Pierre v. Louisiana,* 306 U.S. 354 (1939); *Neal v. Delaware,* 103 U.S. 370 (1881).... With a prima facie case made out, "the burden of proof shifts to the State to rebut the presumption of unconstitutional action by showing that permissible racially neutral selection criteria and procedures have produced the monochromatic result."

Necessarily, an invidious discriminatory purpose may often be inferred from the totality of the relevant facts, including the fact, if it is true, that the law bears more heavily on one race than another. It is also not infrequently true that the discriminatory impact — in the jury cases for example, the total or seriously disproportionate exclusion of Negroes from jury venires — may for all practical purposes demonstrate unconstitutionality because in various circumstances the discrimination is very difficult to explain on nonracial grounds. Nevertheless, we have not held that a law, neutral on its face and serving ends otherwise within the power of government to pursue, is invalid under the Equal Protection Clause simply because it may affect a greater proportion of one race than of another. Disproportionate impact is not irrelevant, but it is not the sole touchstone of an invidious racial discrimination forbidden by the Constitution. Standing alone, it does not trigger the rule, *McLaughlin v. Florida,* 379 U.S. 184 (1964), that racial classifications are to be subjected to the strictest scrutiny and are justifiable only by the weightiest of considerations.

[Here follows a discussion of *Palmer v. Thompson,* 403 U.S. 217 (1971), and *Wright v. Council of City of Emporia,* 407 U.S. 451 (1972), which indicate that in certain circumstances racial impact of a law, rather than discriminatory purpose, may be the critical factor invalidating the law.]

Both before and after *Palmer v. Thompson,* however, various Courts of Appeals have held in several contexts, including public employment, that the substantially disproportionate racial impact of a statute or official practice standing alone and without regard to discriminatory purpose, suffices to prove racial discrimination violating the Equal Protection Clause absent some justification going substantially beyond what would be necessary to validate most other legislative classifications. The cases impressively demonstrate that there is another side to the issue: but, with all due respect, to the extent that those cases rested on or expressed the view that proof of discriminatory racial purpose is unnecessary in making out an equal protection violation, we are in disagreement.

As an initial matter, we have difficulty understanding how a law establishing a racially neutral qualification for employment is nevertheless racially discriminatory and denies "any person equal protection of the laws" simply because a greater proportion of Negroes fail to qualify than members of other racial or ethnic groups. Had respondents, along with all others who had failed Test 21, whether white or black, brought an action claiming that the test denied each of them equal protection of the laws as compared with those who had passed with high enough scores to qualify them as police recruits, it is most unlikely that their challenge would have been sustained. Test 21, which is administered generally to prospective government employees, concededly seeks to ascertain whether those who take it have acquired a particular level of verbal skill; and it is untenable that the Constitution prevents the Government from seeking modestly to upgrade the communicative abilities of its employees rather than to be satisfied with some lower level of competence, particularly where the job requires special ability to communicate orally and in writing. Respondents, as Negroes, could no more successfully claim that the test denied them equal protection than could white applicants who also failed. The conclusion would not be different in the face of proof that more Negroes than whites had been disqualified by Test 21. That other Negroes also failed to score well would, alone, not demonstrate that respondents individually were being denied equal protection of the laws by the application of an otherwise valid qualifying test being administered to prospective police recruits.

Nor on the facts of the case before us would the disproportionate impact of Test 21 warrant the conclusion that it is a purposeful device to discriminate against Negroes and hence an infringement of the constitutional rights of respondents as well as other black applicants. As we have said, the test is neutral on its face and rationally may be said to serve a purpose the government is constitutionally empowered to pursue. Even agreeing with the District Court that the differential racial effect of Test 21 called for further inquiry, we think the District Court correctly held that the affirmative efforts of the Metropolitan Police Department to recruit black officers, the changing racial composition of the recruit classes and of the force in general, and the relationship of the test to the training program negated any inference that the Department discriminated on the basis of race or that "a police officer qualifies on the color of his skin rather than ability." 348 F. Supp., at 18.

Under Title VII, Congress provided that when hiring and promotion practices disqualifying substantially disproportionate numbers of blacks are challenged, discriminatory purpose need not be proved, and that it is an insufficient response to demonstrate some rational basis for the challenged practices. It is necessary, in addition, that they be "validated" in terms of job performance in any one of several ways, perhaps by ascertaining the minimum skill, ability or potential necessary for the position at issue and determining whether the qualifying tests are appropriate for the selection of qualified applicants for the job in question. However this process proceeds, it involves a more probing judicial review of, and less deference to, the seemingly reasonable acts of administrators and executives than is appropriate under the Constitution where special racial impact, without discriminatory purpose, is claimed. We are not disposed to adopt this more rigorous standard for the purposes of applying the Fifth and the Fourteenth Amendments in cases such as this.

A rule that a statute designed to serve neutral ends is nevertheless invalid, absent compelling justification, if in practice it benefits or burdens one race more than another would be far reaching and would raise serious questions about, and perhaps invalidate, a whole range of tax, welfare, public service, regulatory, and licensing statutes that may be more burdensome to the poor and to the average black than to the more affluent white.

Given that rule, such consequences would perhaps be likely to follow. However, in our view, extension of the rule beyond those areas where it is already applicable by reason of statute, such as in the field of public employment, should await legislative prescription.

[Part III of the Court's opinion holds that statutory standards similar to those under Title VII were also satisfied in this case. The district court's conclusion that Test 21 was directly related to the requirements of the police training program and that a positive relationship between the test and the program was sufficient to validate the test was fully supported by the record, so that no remand to establish further validation would be appropriate.]

The judgment of the Court of Appeals accordingly is reversed.

So ordered.

JUSTICE STEWART joins Parts I and II of the Court's opinion.

JUSTICE BRENNAN, with whom JUSTICE MARSHALL joins, dissenting.
[Justice Brennan would affirm the court of appeals ruling on the basis that petitioners failed to prove Test 21 satisfies applicable statutory standards under either applicable Civil Service Commission rules or EEOC guidelines.]

JUSTICE STEVENS, concurring.
While I agree with the Court's disposition of this case, I add these comments on the constitutional issue discussed in Part II and the statutory issue discussed in Part III of the Court's opinion.

The requirement of purposeful discrimination is a common thread running through the cases summarized in Part II. These cases include criminal convictions which were set aside because blacks were excluded from the grand jury, a reapportionment case in which political boundaries were obviously influenced to some extent by racial considerations, a school desegregation case, and a case involving the unequal administration of an ordinance purporting to prohibit the operation of laundries in frame buildings. Although it may be proper to use the same language to describe the constitutional claim in each of these contexts, the burden of proving a prima facie case may well involve differing evidentiary considerations. The extent of deference that one pays to the trial court's determination of the factual issue, and indeed, the extent to which one characterizes the intent issue as a question of fact or a question of law, will vary in different contexts.

Frequently the most probative evidence of intent will be objective evidence of what actually happened rather than evidence describing the subjective state of mind of the actor. For normally the actor is presumed to have intended the natural consequences of his deeds. This is particularly true in the case of governmental action which is frequently the product of compromise, of collective decisionmaking, and of mixed motivation. It is unrealistic, on the one hand, to require the victim of alleged discrimination to uncover the actual subjective intent of the decisionmaker or, conversely, to invalidate otherwise legitimate action simply because an improper motive affected the deliberation of a participant in the decisional process. A law conscripting clerics should not be invalidated because an atheist voted for it.

My point in making this observation is to suggest that the line between discriminatory purpose and discriminatory impact is not nearly as bright, and perhaps not quite as critical, as the reader of the Court's opinion might assume. I agree, of course, that a constitutional issue does not arise every time some disproportionate impact is shown. On the other hand, when the disproportion is as dramatic as in *Gomillion v. Lightfoot,* 364 U.S. 339, or *Yick Wo v. Hopkins,* 118 U.S. 356, it really does not matter whether the standard is phrased in terms of purpose or effect. Therefore, although I accept the statement of the general rule in the Court's opinion, I am not yet prepared to indicate how that standard should be applied in the many cases which have formulated the governing standard in different language.

My agreement with the conclusion reached in Part II of the Court's opinion rests on a ground narrower than the Court describes. I do not rely at all on the evidence of good-faith efforts to recruit black police officers. In my judgment, neither those efforts nor the subjective good faith of the District administration, would save Test 21 if it were otherwise invalid.

There are two reasons why I am convinced that the challenge to Test 21 is insufficient. First, the test serves the neutral and legitimate purpose of requiring all applicants to meet a uniform minimum standard of literacy. Reading ability is manifestly relevant to the police function, there is no evidence that the required passing grade was set at an arbitrarily high level, and there is sufficient disparity among high schools and high school graduates to justify the use of a separate uniform test. Second, the same test is used throughout the federal service. The applicants for employment in the District of Columbia Police Department represent such a small fraction of the total number of persons who have taken the test that their experience is of minimal probative value in assessing the neutrality of the test itself. That evidence, without more, is not sufficient to overcome the presumption that a test which is this widely used by the Federal Government is in fact neutral in its effect as well as its "purpose" as that term is used in constitutional adjudication.

My study of the statutory issue leads me to the same conclusion reached by the Court in Part III of its opinion....

NOTES

1. In *Batson v. Kentucky,* 476 U.S. 79 (1986), a case questioning the use of peremptory challenges by prosecutors to exclude prospective jurors because of their race, the Supreme Court indicated that a general practice of discrimination need not be demonstrated to establish impermissible discrimination with respect to a particular situation.

[U]nder some circumstances, proof of discriminatory impact "may for all practical purposes demonstrate unconstitutionality because in various circumstances the discrimination is very difficult to explain on nonracial grounds." For example, "total or seriously disproportionate exclusion of Negroes from jury venires is itself such an 'unequal application of the law ... as to show intentional discrimination'".... Once the [party alleging impermissible discrimination] makes the requisite showing, the burden shifts to the State to explain adequately the racial exclusion. The State cannot meet this burden on mere general assertions that its officials did not discriminate or that they properly performed their official duties. Rather, the State must demonstrate that "permissible racially neutral selection criteria and procedures have produced the monochromatic result." ... [A challenging party] may make a prima facie showing of purposeful racial discrimination in selection of the venire by relying solely on the facts concerning its selection *in his case....* [A] consistent pattern of official racial discrimination is not "a necessary predicate to a violation of the Equal Protection Clause. A single invidiously discriminatory governmental act" is not "immunized by the absence of such discrimination in the making of other comparable decisions." For evidentiary requirements to dictate that "several must suffer discrimination" before one could object would be inconsistent with the promise of equal protection to all.

2. A black female medical technologist who had satisfactorily performed her job for years was demoted because she did not have a college degree, pursuant to a recently imposed prerequisite to taking a competitive examination for the position of medical technologist. The Second Circuit rejected the district court's finding of discrimination based on a statistical showing that a college degree requirement had a disparate effect on blacks and on the failure of the employer to show job-relatedness. The circuit court, citing *Washington v. Davis,* said that the plaintiff failed to show any intentional discrimination on the part of the employer. The court also held that statistics relating to the general population rather than the employment practices of the particular defendant were not enough to raise a presumption against the requirement of a college degree. *Townsend v. Nassau Cty. Med. Center,* 558 F.2d 117 (2nd Cir. 1977), *cert. denied,* 434 U.S. 1015 (1978). Compare *Barnes v. Yellow Freight Sys.,* 778 F.2d 1096 (5th Cir. 1985), wherein the court recognized that a presumption of discriminatory intent is raised when a white supervisor treats white employees more favorably than similarly-situated black employees under essentially identical circumstances.

3. *Hamilton v. Rodgers,* 791 F.2d 439 (5th Cir. 1986), concerned a black fire department radio technician who had been subjected to racial harassment by fellow employees. Although his two immediate supervisors had contributed to his harassment, the court decided that the fire department could not be held liable under section 1983. The number of racial incidents was too few to constitute a pattern that would warrant the imputation of constructive knowledge to high-ranking department officers, and those officials had acted promptly to discourage further racial incidents when they learned of them. Compare *Trigg*

v. *Ft. Wayne Schools,* 766 F.2d 299 (7th Cir. 1985) (holding public employer liable for harassment of black woman by her supervisor).

4. In a summary disposition, the Court affirmed a lower court opinion upholding the use of standardized tests to hire teachers in South Carolina, despite the fact that the tests had a strong disparate effect on black applicants. The tests were challenged under Title VII and the Constitution because they disqualified 83 percent of black applicants, but only 17.5 percent of white applicants. The lower court had emphasized the requirement in *Washington v. Davis* that discriminatory intent be proved under the fourteenth amendment and said that state officials had no such intent. *National Educ. Ass'n v. South Carolina,* 434 U.S. 1026 (1978).

5. As in *Washington v. Davis,* many constitutional claims of employment discrimination have been brought against governmental bodies under the Civil Rights Act of 1871, 42 U.S.C. § 1983, which incorporates the fourteenth amendment equal protection clause. Section 1983 reads as follows:

> Every person who, under color of any statute, ordinance, regulation, custom, or usage, of any State or Territory, subjects, or causes to be subjected, any citizen of the United States or other person within the jurisdiction thereof to the deprivation of any rights, privileges, or immunities secured by the Constitution and laws, shall be liable to the party injured in an action at law, suit in equity, or other proper proceeding for redress.

In *Patsy v. Board of Regents,* 457 U.S. 496 (1972), the Supreme Court recognized that plaintiffs filing section 1983 suits in federal district courts alleging unconstitutional race or sex discrimination by state employers are not required to exhaust available state administrative procedures as a prerequisite to judicial consideration of their section 1983 claims. However, in *Migra v. Warren Sch. Dist. Bd. of Educ.,* 465 U.S. 75 (1984), the Court held that prior state court judgments shall be given the same preclusive effect in federal courts in subsequent section 1983 actions as they would enjoy in state court, even where the section 1983 claims were not litigated in the previous state court cases. But cf. *McDonald v. City of W. Branch,* 466 U.S. 284 (1984), holding that prior arbitral decisions under contractual grievance-arbitration procedures are generally not to be accorded res judicata or collateral estoppel effect in subsequent section 1983 suits, since such plaintiffs have the right to have their constitutional claims decided in judicial proceedings.

Since *Patsy* recognized that litigants need not exhaust available state administrative procedures before prosecuting section 1983 claims, a party who opts to resort to such state procedures prior to the filing of a section 1983 suit will generally not be entitled to an award of attorney fees under section 1988. Such an award is only permitted with respect to previous legal work that was both "useful and of a type ordinarily necessary" to advance the section 1983 litigation. See *Webb v. Board of Educ.,* 471 U.S. 234 (1985).

6. In *City of Riverside v. Rivera,* 477 U.S. 561 (1986), the Court ruled that an award of attorney's fees under section 1988 should not be considered excessive merely because it exceeds the amount of damages awarded to the plaintiffs in the underlying section 1983 action. "[R]easonable attorney's fees under section 1988 are not conditioned upon and need not be proportionate to an award of money damages." The Court thus sustained an attorney's fees award of $245,456, even though the jury had awarded only $33,350 to the plaintiffs. See also *Texas State Teachers Ass'n v. Garland Indep. Sch. Dist.,* 109 S. Ct. 1486 (1989) (section 1983 plaintiff need not prevail on the "critical issue" to be entitled to an award of attorney fees under section 1988, but need only prevail on "any significant issue" that materially alters the legal relationship between the parties); *Missouri v. Jenkins,* 109 S. Ct. 2463 (1989) (party prevailing in Reconstruction Era Civil Rights Act suit entitled to an award of fees under section 1988 covering reasonable cost of paralegals, law clerks, and recent law graduates); *Venegas v. Mitchell,* 110 S. Ct. 1679 (1990) (section 1988 does not invalidate contingent fee contract requiring plaintiff to pay attorney more than statutory award entered against defendant).

7. The enforcement provisions applicable to section 1983 claims provide no statute of limitations period. Courts have thus been instructed to apply the state statutory period applicable to personal injury actions. See *Wilson v. Garcia,* 471 U.S. 261 (1985). Where state law provides multiple statutes of limitations for personal injury actions, courts are to apply the general or residual personal injury limitations period. See *Owens v. Okure,* 109 S. Ct. 573 (1989).

WYGANT v. JACKSON BOARD OF EDUCATION
476 U.S. 267, 106 S. Ct. 1842, 90 L. Ed. 2d 260 (1986)

JUSTICE POWELL announced the judgment of the Court and delivered an opinion in which THE CHIEF JUSTICE and JUSTICE REHNQUIST joined, and which JUSTICE O'CONNOR joined in parts I, II, III-A, III-B, and V.

This case presents the question whether a school board, consistent with the Equal Protection Clause, may extend preferential protection against layoffs to some of its employees because of their race or national origin.

I

In 1972 the Jackson Board of Education, because of racial tension in the community that extended to its schools, considered adding a layoff provision to the Collective Bargaining Agreement (CBA) between the Board and the Jackson Education Association (the Union) that would protect employees who were members of certain minority groups against layoffs.[1] The Board and the Union eventually approved a new provision, Article XII of the CBA, covering layoffs. It stated:

"In the event that it becomes necessary to reduce the number of teachers through layoff from employment by the Board, teachers with the most seniority in the district shall be retained, except that at no time will there be a greater percentage of minority personnel laid off than the current percentage of minority personnel employed at the time of the layoff. In no event will the number given notice of possible layoff be greater than the number of positions to be eliminated. Each teacher so affected will be called back in reverse order for positions for which he is certificated maintaining the above minority balance."

When layoffs became necessary in 1974, it was evident that adherence to the CBA would result in the layoff of tenured nonminority teachers while minority

---

[1]Prior to bargaining on this subject, the Minority Affairs Office of the Jackson Public Schools sent a questionnaire to all teachers, soliciting their views as to a layoff policy. The questionnaire proposed two alternatives: continuation of the existing straight seniority system, or a freeze of minority layoffs to ensure retention of minority teachers in exact proportion to the minority student population. Ninety-six percent of the teachers who responded to the questionnaire expressed a preference for the straight seniority system.

teachers on probationary status were retained. Rather than complying with Article XII, the Board retained the tenured teachers and laid off probationary minority teachers, thus failing to maintain the percentage of minority personnel that existed at the time of the layoff. The Union, together with two minority teachers who had been laid off, brought suit in federal court, *id.,* at 30, (*Jackson Education Assn. v. Board of Education,* (*Jackson I*) (mem. op.)), claiming that the Board's failure to adhere to the layoff provision violated the Equal Protection Clause of the Fourteenth Amendment and Title VII of the Civil Rights Act of 1964. They also urged the District Court to take pendent jurisdiction over state law contract claims. In its answer the Board denied any prior employment discrimination and argued that the layoff provision conflicted with the Michigan Teacher Tenure Act. Following trial, the District Court *sua sponte* concluded that it lacked jurisdiction over the case, in part because there was insufficient evident to support the plaintiffs' claim that the Board had engaged in discriminatory hiring practices prior to 1972, and in part because the plaintiffs had not fulfilled the jurisdictional prerequisite to a Title VII claim by filing discrimination charges with the Equal Employment Opportunity Commission. After dismissing the federal claims, the District Court declined to exercise pendent jurisdiction over the state law contract claims.

Rather than taking an appeal, the plaintiffs instituted a suit in state court, *Jackson Education Assn. v. Board of Education,* (Jackson County Circuit Court, 1979) (*Jackson II*), raising in essence the same claims that had been raised in *Jackson I.* In entering judgment for the plaintiffs, the state court found that the Board had breached its contract with the plaintiffs, and that Article XII did not violate the Michigan Teacher Tenure Act. In rejecting the Board's argument that the layoff provision violated the Civil Rights Act of 1964, the state court found that it "ha[d] not been established that the board had discriminated against minorities in its hiring practices. The minority representation on the faculty was the result of societal racial discrimination." The state court also found that "[t]here is no history of overt past discrimination by the parties to this contract." Nevertheless, the court held that Article XII was permissible, despite its discriminatory effect on nonminority teachers, as an attempt to remedy the effects of societal discrimination.

After *Jackson II,* the Board adhered to Article XII. As a result, during the 1976-1977 and 1981-1982 school years, nonminority teachers were laid off, while minority teachers with less seniority were retained. The displaced nonminority teachers, petitioners here, brought suit in Federal District Court, alleging violations of the Equal Protection Clause, Title VII, 42 U.S.C. § 1983, and other federal and state statutes. On cross motions for summary judgment, the District Court dismissed all of petitioners' claims. With respect to the equal protection claim, the District Court held that the racial preferences granted by the Board need not be grounded on a finding of prior discrimination. Instead, the court decided that the racial preferences were permissible under the Equal Protection Clause as an attempt to remedy societal discrimination by providing "role models" for minority schoolchildren, and upheld the constitutionality of the layoff provision.

The Court of Appeals for the Sixth Circuit affirmed, largely adopting the reasoning and language of the District Court. 746 F.2d 1152 (1984). We granted certiorari, 471 U.S. — (1985), to resolve the important issue of the constitutionality of race-based layoffs by public employers. We now reverse.

II

Petitioners' central claim is that they were laid off because of their race in violation of the Equal Protection Clause of the Fourteenth Amendment. Decisions by faculties and administrators of public schools based on race or ethnic origin are reviewable under the Fourteenth Amendment. This Court has "consistently repudiated '[d]istinctions between citizens solely because of their ancestry' as being 'odious to a free people whose institutions are founded upon the doctrine of equality,'" *Loving v. Virginia,* 388 U.S. 1, 11 (1967) quoting *Hirabayashi v. United States,* 320 U.S. 81, 100 (1943). "Racial and ethnic distinctions of any sort are inherently suspect and thus call for the most exacting judicial examination." *Regents of University of California v. Bakke,* 438 U.S. 265, 291 (1978) (opinion of POWELL, J., joined by WHITE, J.).

The Court has recognized that the level of scrutiny does not change merely because the challenged classification operates against a group that historically has not been subject to governmental discrimination. *Mississippi University for Women v. Hogan,* 458 U.S. 718, 724 n. 9 (1982); *Bakke,* 438 U.S., at 291-299; see *Shelley v. Kraemer,* 334 U.S. 1, 22 (1948); see also A. Bickel, The Morality of Consent 133 (1975). In this case, Article XII of the CBA operates against whites and in favor of certain minorities, and therefore constitutes a classification based on race. "Any preference based on racial or ethnic criteria must necessarily receive a most searching examination to make sure that it does not conflict with constitutional guarantees." *Fullilove v. Klutznick,* 448 U.S. 448, 491 (1980) (opinion of BURGER, C.J.). There are two prongs to this examination. First, any racial classification "must be justified by a compelling governmental interest." *Palmore v. Sidoti,* 466 U.S. 429, 432 (1984); see *Loving v. Virginia,* 388 U.S. 1, 11 (1967); cf. *Graham v. Richardson,* 403 U.S. 365, 375 (1971) (alienage). Second, the means chosen by the State to effectuate its purpose must be "narrowly tailored to the achievement of that goal." *Fullilove,* 448 U.S., at 480. We must decide whether the layoff provision is supported by a compelling state purpose and whether the means chosen to accomplish that purpose are narrowly tailored.

III

A. The Court of Appeals, relying on the reasoning and language of the District Court's opinion, held that the Board's interest in providing minority role models for its minority students, as an attempt to alleviate the effects of societal discrimination, was sufficiently important to justify the racial classification embodied in the layoff provision. 746 F.2d, at 1156-1157. The court discerned a need for more minority faculty role models by finding that the percentage of minority teachers was less than the percentage of minority students. *Id.,* at 1156.

This Court never has held that societal discrimination alone is sufficient to justify a racial classification. Rather, the Court has insisted upon some showing of prior discrimination by the governmental unit involved before allowing limited use of racial classifications in order to remedy such discrimination. This Court's reasoning in *Hazelwood School District v. United States,* 433 U.S. 299 (1977), illustrates that the relevant analysis in cases involving proof of discrimination by statistical disparity focuses on those disparities that demonstrate such prior governmental discrimination. In *Hazelwood* the Court concluded that, absent employment discrimination by the school board, "'nondiscriminatory hiring practices will in time result in a work force more or less representative of the racial and ethnic composition of the population in the community from which the employees are hired.'" *Id.,* at 307, quoting *Teamsters v. United States,* 431 U.S. 324, 340, n. 20 (1977). See also *Wygant, supra,* 746 F.2d, at 1160 (Wellford, J., concurring) ("Had the plaintiffs in this case presented data as to the percentage of qualified minority teachers in the relevant labor market to show that defendant Board's hiring of black teachers over a number of years had equalled that figure, I believe this court may well have been required to reverse...."). Based on that reasoning, the Court in *Hazelwood* held that the proper comparison for determining the existence of actual discrimination by the school board was "between the racial composition of [the school's] teaching staff and the racial composition of the qualified public school teacher population in the relevant labor market." 433 U.S., at 308. *Hazelwood* demonstrates this Court's focus on prior discrimination as the justification for, and the limitation on, a State's adoption of race-based remedies. See also *Swann v. Charlotte-Mecklenburg Board of Education,* 402 U.S. 1 (1971).

Unlike the analysis in *Hazelwood,* the role model theory employed by the District Court has no logical stopping point. The role model theory allows the Board to engage in discriminatory hiring and layoff practices long past the point required by any legitimate remedial purpose. Indeed, by tying the required percentage of minority teachers to the percentage of minority students, it requires just the sort of year-to-year calibration the Court stated was unnecessary in *Swann,* 402 U.S., at 31-32:

> "At some point these school authorities and others like them should have achieved full compliance with this Court's decision in *Brown I....* Neither school authorities nor district courts are constitutionally required to make year-by-year adjustments of the racial composition of student bodies once the affirmative duty to desegregate has been accomplished and racial discrimination through official action is eliminated from the system."

See also *id.,* at 24.

Moreover, because the role model theory does not necessarily bear a relationship to the harm caused by prior discriminatory hiring practices, it actually could be used to escape the obligation to remedy such practices by justifying the small percentage of black teachers by reference to the small percentage of black students. See *United States v. Hazelwood School District,* 392 F. Supp. 1276, 1286-1287 (ED Mo. 1975), *rev'd,* 534 F.2d 805 (CA8 1976), *rev'd and remanded,* 433 U.S. 299 (1977). Carried to its logical extreme, the idea that black students are better off with black teachers could lead to the very system the Court rejected in *Brown v. Board of Education,* 347 U.S. 483 (1954) (*Brown I*).

Societal discrimination, without more, is too amorphous a basis for imposing a racially classified remedy. The role model theory announced by the District

Court and the resultant holding typify this indefiniteness. There are numerous explanations for a disparity between the percentage of minority students and the percentage of minority faculty, many of them completely unrelated to discrimination of any kind. In fact, there is no apparent connection between the two groups. Nevertheless, the District Court combined irrelevant comparisons between these two groups with an indisputable statement that there has been societal discrimination, and upheld state action predicated upon racial classifications. No one doubts that there has been serious racial discrimination in this country. But as the basis for imposing discriminatory *legal* remedies that work against innocent people, societal discrimination is insufficient and over expansive. In the absence of particularized findings, a court could uphold remedies that are ageless in their reach into the past, and timeless in their ability to affect the future.

B. Respondents also now argue that their purpose in adopting the layoff provision was to remedy prior discrimination against minorities by the Jackson School District in hiring teachers. Public schools, like other public employers, operate under two interrelated constitutional duties. They are under a clear command from this Court, starting with *Brown v. Board of Education,* 349 U.S. 294 (1955), to eliminate every vestige of racial segregation and discrimination in the schools. Pursuant to that goal, race-conscious remedial action may be necessary. *North Carolina State Board of Education v. Swann,* 402 U.S. 43, 46 (1971). On the other hand, public employers, including public schools, also must act in accordance with a "core purpose of the Fourteenth Amendment" which is to "do away with all governmentally imposed distinctions based on race." *Palmore v. Sidoti,* 466 U.S., at 432. These related constitutional duties are not always harmonious; reconciling them requires public employers to act with extraordinary care. In particular, a public employer like the Board must ensure that, before it embarks on an affirmative action program, it has convincing evidence that remedial action is warranted. That is, it must have sufficient evidence to justify the conclusion that there has been prior discrimination.

Evidentiary support for the conclusion that remedial action is warranted becomes crucial when the remedial program is challenged in court by nonminority employees. In this case, for example, petitioners contended at trial that the remedial program — Article XII — had the purpose and effect of instituting a racial classification that was not justified by a remedial purpose. 546 F. Supp. 1195, 1199 (E.D. Mich. 1982). In such a case, the trial court must make a factual determination that the employer had a strong basis in evidence for its conclusion that remedial action was necessary. The ultimate burden remains with the employees to demonstrate the unconstitutionality of an affirmative action program. But unless such a determination is made, an appellate court reviewing a challenge to remedial action by nonminority employees cannot determine whether the race-based action is justified as a remedy for prior discrimination.

Despite the fact that Article XII has spawned years of litigation and three separate lawsuits, no such determination ever has been made. Although its litigation position was different, the Board in *Jackson I* and *Jackson II* denied the existence of prior discriminatory hiring practices. This precise issue was litigated in both those suits. Both courts concluded that any statistical disparities were the result of general societal discrimination, not of prior discrimination by the Board. The Board now contends that, given another opportunity, it could establish the existence of prior discrimination. Although this argument seems belated at this point in the proceedings, we need not consider the question since we conclude below that the layoff provision was not a legally appropriate means of achieving even a compelling purpose.[5]

IV

The Court of Appeals examined the means chosen to accomplish the Board's race-conscious purposes under a test of "reasonableness." That standard has no support in the decisions of this Court. As demonstrated in Part II above, our decisions always have employed a more stringent standard — however articulated — to test the validity of the means chosen by a state to accomplish its race-conscious purposes. See, e.g., *Palmore,* 466 U.S., at 432 ("to pass constitutional muster, [racial classifications] must be necessary ... to the accomplishment of their legitimate purpose") (quoting *McLaughlin v. Florida,* 379 U.S. 184, 196 (1964); *Fullilove,* 448 U.S., at 480 (opinion of BURGER, C. J.) ("We recognize the need for careful judicial evaluation to assure that any ... program that employs racial or ethnic criteria to accomplish the objective of remedying the present effects of past discrimination is narrowly tailored to the achievement of that goal").[6] Under strict scrutiny the means chosen to accomplish the State's asserted purpose must be specifically and narrowly framed to accomplish that purpose. *Fullilove,* 448 U.S., at 480 (opinion of BURGER, C. J.). "Racial classifications are simply too pernicious to permit any but the most exact connection between justification and classification." *Id.,* at 537 (STEVENS, J., dissenting).

We have recognized, however, that in order to remedy the effects of prior discrimination, it may be necessary to take race into account. As part of this Nation's dedication to eradicating racial discrimination, innocent persons may be called upon to bear some of the burden of the remedy. "When effectuating a limited and properly tailored remedy to cure the effects of prior discrimination, such a 'sharing of the burden' by innocent parties is not impermissible." *Id.,* at

---

[5] JUSTICE MARSHALL contends that "the majority has too quickly assumed the absence of a legitimate factual predicate for affirmative action in the Jackson schools." In support of that assertion, he engages in an unprecedented reliance on non-record documents that respondent has "lodged" with this Court. This selective citation to factual materials not considered by the District Court or the Court of Appeals below is unusual enough by itself. My disagreement with JUSTICE MARSHALL, however, is more fundamental than any disagreement over the heretofore unquestioned rule that this Court decides cases based on the record before it. JUSTICE MARSHALL does not define what he means by "legitimate factual predicate," nor does he demonstrate the relationship of these non-record materials to his undefined predicate. If, for example, his dissent assumes that general societal discrimination is a sufficient factual predicate, then there is no need to refer to respondents' lodgings as to its own employment history. No one disputes that there has been race discrimination in this country. If that fact alone can justify race-conscious action by the State, despite the Equal Protection Clause, then the dissent need not rely on non-record materials to show a "legitimate factual predicate." If, on the other hand, JUSTICE MARSHALL is assuming that the necessary factual predicate is prior discrimination by the Board, there is no escaping the need for a factual determination below — a determination that does not exist....

[6] The term "narrowly tailored," so frequently used in our cases, has acquired a secondary meaning. More specifically, as commentators have indicated, the term may be used to require consideration whether lawful alternative and less restrictive means could have been used. Or, as Professor Ely has noted, the classification at issue must "fit" with greater precision than any alternative means. Ely, *The Constitutionality of Reverse Racial Discrimination,* 41 U. Chi. L. Rev. 723, 727, n. 26 (1974) (hereinafter Ely)....

484, quoting *Franks v. Bowman Transportation Co.*, 424 U.S. 747 (1976).[8] In *Fullilove*, the challenged statute required at least 10 percent of federal public works funds to be used in contracts with minority-owned business enterprises. This requirement was found to be within the remedial powers of Congress in part because the "actual burden shouldered by nonminority firms is relatively light." 448 U.S., at 484.

Significantly, none of the cases discussed above involved layoffs.[10] Here, by contrast, the means chosen to achieve the Board's asserted purposes is that of laying off nonminority teachers with greater seniority in order to retain minority teachers with less seniority. We have previously expressed concern over the burden that a preferential layoffs scheme imposes on innocent parties. See *Firefighters v. Stotts*, 467 U.S. 561, 574-576, 578-579 (1984); see also *Weber*, n. 9, *supra* this page, at 208 ("The plan does not require the discharge of white workers and their replacement with new black hirees"). In cases involving valid *hiring* goals, the burden to be borne by innocent individuals is diffused to a considerable extent among society generally. Though hiring goals may burden some innocent individuals, they simply do not impose the same kind of injury that layoffs impose. Denial of a future employment opportunity is not as intrusive as loss of an existing job.

Many of our cases involve union seniority plans with employees who are typically heavily dependent on wages for their day-to-day living. Even a temporary layoff may have adverse financial as well as psychological effects. A worker may invest many productive years in one job and one city with the expectation

---

[8]Of course, when a state implements a race-based plan that requires such a sharing of the burden, it cannot justify the discriminatory effect on some individuals because other individuals had approved the plan. Any "waiver" of the right not to be dealt with by the government on the basis of one's race must be made by those affected. Yet JUSTICE MARSHALL repeatedly contends that the fact that Article XII was approved by a majority vote of the Union somehow validates this plan. He sees this case not in terms of individual constitutional rights, but as an allocation of burdens "between two racial groups." Thus, Article XII becomes a political compromise that "avoided placing the entire burden of layoffs on either the white teachers as a group or the minority teachers as a group." But the petitioners before us today are not "the white teachers as a group." They are Wendy Wygant and other individuals who claim that they were fired from their jobs because of their race. That claim cannot be waived by petitioners' more senior colleagues. In view of the way union seniority works, it is not surprising that while a straight freeze on minority layoffs was overwhelmingly rejected, a "compromise" eventually was reached that placed the entire burden of the compromise on the most junior union members. The more senior union members simply had nothing to lose from such a compromise. ("To petitioners, at the bottom of the seniority scale among white teachers, fell the lot of bearing the white group's proportionate share of layoffs that became necessary in 1982.") The fact that such a painless accommodation was approved by the more senior union members six times since 1972 is irrelevant. The Constitution does not allocate constitutional rights to be distributed like bloc grants within discrete racial groups; and until it does, petitioners' more senior union colleagues cannot vote away petitioners' rights.

JUSTICE MARSHALL also attempts to portray the layoff plan as one that has no real invidious effect, stating that "within the confines of constant minority proportions, it preserves the heirarchy of seniority in the selection of individuals for layoff." That phrase merely expresses the tautology that layoffs are based on seniority except as to those nonminority teachers who are displaced by minority teachers with less seniority. This is really nothing more than group-based analysis: "each group would shoulder a portion of [the layoff] burden equal to its portion of the faculty." The constitutional problem remains: the decision that petitioners would be laid off was based on their race.

[10]There are cases involving alteration of strict seniority layoffs, see, e.g., *Ford Motor Co. v. Huffman*, 345 U.S. 330 (1953); *Aeronautical Industrial District Lodge 727 v. Campbell*, 337 U.S. 521 (1949), but they do not involve the critical element here — layoffs based on race. The Constitution does not require layoffs to be based on strict seniority. But it does require the state to meet a heavy burden of justification when it implements a layoff plan based on race.

of earning the stability and security of seniority. "At that point, the rights and expectations surrounding seniority make up what is probably the most valuable capital asset that the worker 'owns,' worth even more than the current equity in his home." Fallon & Weiler, *Conflicting Models of Racial Justice*, 1984 S. Ct. Rev. 1, 58. Layoffs disrupt these settled expectations in a way that general hiring goals do not.

While hiring goals impose a diffuse burden, often foreclosing only one of several opportunities, layoffs impose the entire burden of achieving racial equality on particular individuals, often resulting in serious disruption of their lives. That burden is too intrusive. We therefore hold that, as a means of accomplishing purposes that otherwise may be legitimate, the Board's layoff plan is not sufficiently narrowly tailored. Other, less intrusive means of accomplishing similar purposes — such as the adoption of hiring goals — are available. For these reasons, the Board's selection of layoffs as the means to accomplish even a valid purpose cannot satisfy the demands of the Equal Protection Clause.[13]

V

We accordingly reverse the judgment of the Court of Appeals for the Sixth Circuit.

JUSTICE O'CONNOR, concurring in part and concurring in the judgment.

The Equal Protection Clause standard applicable to racial classifications that work to the disadvantage of "nonminorities" has been articulated in various ways. JUSTICE POWELL now would require that: (1) the racial classification be justified by a "'compelling governmental interest,'" and (2) the means chosen by the State to effectuate its purpose be "narrowly tailored." This standard reflects the belief, apparently held by all members of this Court, that racial classifications of any sort must be subjected to "strict scrutiny," however defined.... JUSTICES MARSHALL, BRENNAN, and BLACKMUN, however, seem to adhere to the formulation of the "strict" standard that they authored, with JUSTICE WHITE, in *Bakke*: "remedial use of race is permissible if it serves 'important governmental objectives' and is 'substantially related to achievement of those objectives.'"

I subscribe to JUSTICE POWELL's formulation because it mirrors the standard we have consistently applied in examining racial classifications in other contexts. In my view,

"the analysis and level of scrutiny applied to determine the validity of [a racial] classification do not vary simply because the objective appears acceptable to individual Members of the Court. While the validity and importance of the objective may affect the outcome of the analysis, the analysis itself does not change." *Mississippi University for Women v. Hogan*, 458 U.S. 718, 724, n. 9 (1982).

---

[13]The Board's definition of minority to include blacks, Orientals, American Indians, and persons of Spanish descent, further illustrates the undifferentiated nature of the plan. There is no explanation of why the Board chose to favor these particular minorities or how in fact members of some of the categories can be identified. Moreover, respondents have never suggested — much less formally found — that they have engaged in prior, purposeful discrimination against members of each of these minority groups.

Although JUSTICE POWELL's formulation may be viewed as more stringent than that suggested by JUSTICES BRENNAN, WHITE, MARSHALL, and BLACKMUN, the disparities between the two tests do not preclude a fair measure of consensus. In particular, as regards certain state interests commonly relied upon in formulating affirmative action programs, the distinction between a "compelling" and an "important" governmental purpose may be a negligible one. The Court is in agreement that, whatever the formulation employed, remedying past or present racial discrimination by a state actor is a sufficiently weighty state interest to warrant the remedial use of a carefully constructed affirmative action program. This remedial purpose need not be accompanied by contemporaneous findings of actual discrimination to be accepted as legitimate as long as the public actor has a firm basis for believing that remedial action is required. Additionally, although its precise contours are uncertain, a state interest in the promotion of racial diversity has been found sufficiently "compelling," at least in the context of higher education, to support the use of racial considerations in furthering that interest. See, e.g., *Bakke,* 438 U.S., at 311-315 (opinion of POWELL, J.). And certainly nothing the Court has said today necessarily forecloses the possibility that the Court will find other governmental interests which have been relied upon in the lower courts but which have not been passed on here to be sufficiently "important" or "compelling" to sustain the use of affirmative action policies.

It appears, then, that the true source of disagreement on the Court lies not so much in defining the state interests which may support affirmative action efforts as in defining the degree to which the means employed must "fit" the ends pursued to meet constitutional standards. Yet even here the Court has forged a degree of unanimity; it is agreed that a plan need not be limited to the remedying of specific instances of identified discrimination for it to be deemed sufficiently "narrowly tailored," or "substantially related," to the correction of prior discrimination by the state actor.

In the final analysis, the diverse formulations and the number of separate writings put forth by various members of the Court in these difficult cases do not necessarily reflect an intractable fragmentation in opinion with respect to certain core principles. Ultimately, the Court is at least in accord in believing that a public employer, consistent with the Constitution, may undertake an affirmative action program which is designed to further a legitimate remedial purpose and which implements that purpose by means that do not impose disproportionate harm on the interests, or unnecessarily trammel the rights, of innocent individuals directly and adversely affected by a plan's racial preference.

Respondent School Board argues that the governmental purpose or goal advanced here was the School Board's desire to correct apparent prior employment discrimination against minorities while avoiding further litigation. The Michigan Civil Rights Commission determined that the evidence before it supported the allegations of discrimination on the part of the Jackson School Board, though that determination was never reduced to formal findings because the School Board, with the agreement of the Jackson Education Association (Union), voluntarily chose to remedy the perceived violation. Among the measures the School Board and the Union eventually agreed were necessary to remedy the apparent prior discrimination was the layoff provision challenged here; they reasoned that without the layoff provision, the remedial gains made under the ongoing hiring goals contained in the collective bargaining agreement could be eviscerated by layoffs.

The District Court and the Court of Appeals did not focus on the School Board's unquestionably compelling interest in remedying its apparent prior discrimination when evaluating the constitutionality of the challenged layoff provision. Instead, both courts reasoned that the goals of remedying "societal discrimination" and providing "role models" were sufficiently important to withstand equal protection scrutiny. I agree with the Court that a governmental agency's interest in remedying "societal" discrimination, that is, discrimination not traceable to its own actions, cannot be deemed sufficiently compelling to pass constitutional muster under strict scrutiny. I also concur in the Court's assessment that use by the courts below of a "role model" theory to justify the conclusion that this plan had a legitimate remedial purpose was in error. Thus, in my view, the District Court and the Court of Appeals clearly erred in relying on these purposes and in failing to give greater attention to the School Board's asserted purpose of rectifying its own apparent discrimination.... The courts below ruled that a particularized, contemporaneous finding of discrimination was not necessary and upheld the plan as a remedy for "societal" discrimination, apparently on the assumption that in the absence of a specific, contemporaneous finding, any discrimination addressed by an affirmative action plan could only be termed "societal." See, e.g., 546 F. Supp., at 1199. I believe that this assumption is false and therefore agree with the Court that a contemporaneous or antecedent finding of past discrimination by a court or other competent body is not a constitutional prerequisite to a public employer's voluntary agreement to an affirmative action plan.

A violation of federal statutory or constitutional requirements does not arise with the making of a finding; it arises when the wrong is committed. Contemporaneous findings serve solely as a means by which it can be made absolutely certain that the governmental actor truly is attempting to remedy its own unlawful conduct when it adopts an affirmative action plan, rather than attempting to alleviate the wrongs suffered through general societal discrimination. See, e.g., *Fullilove v. Klutznick,* 448 U.S., at 498 (POWELL, J., concurring). Such findings, when voluntarily made by a public employer, obviously are desirable in that they provide evidentiary safeguards of value both to nonminority employees and to the public employer itself, should its affirmative action program be challenged in court. If contemporaneous findings were *required* of public employers in every case as a precondition to the constitutional validity of their affirmative action efforts, however, the relative value of these evidentiary advantages would diminish, for they could be secured only by the sacrifice of other vitally important values.

The imposition of a requirement that public employers make findings that they have engaged in illegal discrimination before they engage in affirmative action programs would severely undermine public employers' incentive to meet voluntarily their civil rights obligations. See, e.g., *Bakke, supra,* at 364 (opinion of BRENNAN, WHITE, MARSHALL, and BLACKMUN, JJ.). Cf. *Steelworkers v. Weber,* 443 U.S. 193, 210-211 (1979) (BLACKMUN, J., concurring). This result would clearly be at odds with this Court's and Congress' consistent emphasis on "the value of voluntary efforts to further the objectives of the law." *Bakke, supra,* at 364 (opinion of BRENNAN, WHITE, MARSHALL, and BLACKMUN, JJ.). The value of voluntary compliance is doubly important when it is a public employer that acts, both because of the example its voluntary assumption of responsibility sets and because the remediation of governmental discrimination is of unique importance. See S. Rep. No. 92-415, p. 10 (1971) (accompanying the amendments extending coverage of Title VII to the States) ("Discrimination by government ... serves a doubly destructive purpose. The exclusion of minorities from effective participation in the bureaucracy not only promotes ignorance of minority problems in that particular community, but also creates mistrust, alienation, and all too often hostility toward the entire process of government"). Imposing a contemporaneous findings requirement would produce the anomalous result that what private employers may voluntarily do to correct apparent violations of Title VII, *Steelworkers v. Weber, supra,* public employers are constitutionally forbidden to do to correct their statutory and constitutional transgressions.

Such results cannot, in my view, be justified by reference to the incremental value a contemporaneous findings requirement would have as an evidentiary safeguard. As is illustrated by this case, public employers are trapped between the competing hazards of liability to minorities if affirmative action *is not* taken to remedy apparent employment discrimination and liability to nonminorities if affirmative action *is* taken. Where these employers, who are presumably fully aware both of their duty under federal law to respect the rights of *all* their employees and of their potential liability for failing to do so, act on the basis of information which gives them a sufficient basis for concluding that remedial action is necessary, a contemporaneous findings requirement should not be necessary.

This conclusion is consistent with our previous decisions recognizing the States' ability to take voluntary race-conscious action to achieve compliance with the law even in the absence of a specific finding of past discrimination. See, e.g., *United Jewish Organizations of Williamsburgh, Inc. v. Carey,* 430 U.S. 144, 165-166 (1977) (reapportionment); *McDaniel v. Barresi,* 402 U.S. 39 (1971) (school desegregation). Indeed, our recognition of the responsible state actor's competency to take these steps is assumed in our recognition of the States' constitutional *duty* to take affirmative steps to eliminate the continuing effects of past unconstitutional discrimination. See, e.g., *Swann v. Charlotte-Mecklenburg Board of Education,* 402 U.S. 1, 15 (1971); *Green v. New Kent County School Board,* 391 U.S. 430, 437-438 (1968).

Of course, as the Court notes, the public employer must discharge this sensitive duty with great care; in order to provide some measure of protection to the interests of its nonminority employees and the employer itself in the event that its affirmative action plan is challenged, the public employer must have a firm basis for determining that affirmative action is warranted. Public employers are not without reliable benchmarks in making this determination. For example, demonstrable evidence of a disparity between the percentage of qualified blacks on a school's teaching staff and the percentage of qualified minorities in the relevant labor pool sufficient to support a prima facie Title VII pattern or practice claim by minority teachers would lend a compelling basis for a competent authority such as the School Board to conclude that implementation of a voluntary affirmative action plan is appropriate to remedy apparent prior employment discrimination.

To be sure, such a conclusion is not unassailable. If a voluntary affirmative action plan is subsequently challenged in court by nonminority employees, those employees must be given the opportunity to prove that the plan does not meet the constitutional standard this Court has articulated. However, as the Court suggests, the institution of such a challenge does not automatically impose upon the public employer the burden of convincing the court of its liability for prior unlawful discrimination; nor does it mean that the court must make an actual finding of prior discrimination based on the employer's proof before the employer's affirmative action plan will be upheld. In "reverse discrimination" suits, as in any other suit, it is the plaintiffs who must bear the burden of demonstrating that their rights have been violated.... [T]hey continue to bear the ultimate burden of persuading the court that the Board's evidence did not support an inference of prior discrimination and thus a remedial purpose, or that the plan instituted on the basis of this evidence was not sufficiently "narrowly tailored." Only by meeting this burden could the plaintiffs establish a violation of their constitutional rights, and thereby defeat the presumption that the Board's assertedly remedial action based on the statistical evidence was justified....

Although the constitutionality of the hiring goal as such is not before us, it is impossible to evaluate the necessity of the layoff provision as a remedy for the apparent prior employment discrimination absent reference to that goal. In this case, the hiring goal that the layoff provision was designed to safeguard was tied to the percentage of minority students in the school district, not to the percentage of qualified minority teachers within the relevant labor pool. The disparity between the percentage of minorities on the teaching staff and the percentage of minorities in the student body is not probative of employment discrimination; it is only when it is established that the availability of minorities in the relevant labor pool substantially exceeded those hired that one may draw an inference of deliberate discrimination in employment. See *Hazelwood School District v. United States*, 433 U.S. 299, 308 (1977) (Title VII context). Because the layoff provision here acts to maintain levels of minority hiring that have no relation to remedying employment discrimination, it cannot be adjudged "narrowly tailored" to effectuate its asserted remedial purpose.

I therefore join in parts I, II, III-A, III-B, and V of the Court's opinion, and concur in the judgment.

JUSTICE WHITE, concurring in the judgment.

The school board's policy when layoffs are necessary is to maintain a certain proportion of minority teachers. This policy requires laying off non-minority teachers solely on the basis of their race, including teachers with seniority, and retaining other teachers solely because they are black, even though some of them are in probationary status. None of the interests asserted by the board, singly or together, justify this racially discriminatory layoff policy and save it from the strictures of the Equal Protection Clause. Whatever the legitimacy of hiring goals or quotas may be, the discharge of white teachers to make room for blacks, none of whom has been shown to be a victim of any racial discrimination, is quite a different matter. I cannot believe that in order to integrate a work force, it would be permissible to discharge whites and hire blacks until the latter comprised a suitable percentage of the work force. None of our cases suggest that this would be permissible under the Equal Protection Clause. Indeed, our cases look quite the other way. The layoff policy in this case — laying off whites who would otherwise be retained in order to keep blacks on the job — has the same effect and is equally violative of the Equal Protection Clause. I agree with the plurality that this official policy is unconstitutional and hence concur in the judgment.

JUSTICE MARSHALL, with whom JUSTICE BRENNAN and JUSTICE BLACKMUN join, dissenting.

When this Court seeks to resolve far-ranging constitutional issues, it must be especially careful to ground its analysis firmly in the facts of the particular controversy before it. Yet in this significant case, we are hindered by a record that is informal and incomplete. Both parties now appear to realize that the record is inadequate to inform the Court's decision. Both have lodged with the Court voluminous "submissions" containing factual material that was not considered by the District Court or the Court of Appeals....

I

The record and extra-record materials that we have before us persuasively suggest that the plurality has too quickly assumed the absence of a legitimate factual predicate, even under the plurality's own view, for affirmative action in the Jackson schools. The first black teacher in the Jackson Public Schools was hired in 1954. In 1969, when minority representation on the faculty had risen only to 3.9%, the Jackson branch of the NAACP filed a complaint with the Michigan Civil Rights Commission, alleging that the Board had engaged in various discriminatory practices, including racial discrimination in the hiring of teachers. Respondents' Lodging No. 6 (complaint). The Commission conducted an investigation and concluded that each of the allegations had merit.[2]

In settlement of the complaint, the Commission issued an order of adjustment, under which the Jackson Board of Education (Board) agreed to numerous measures designed to improve educational opportunities for black public-school students. Among them was a promise to "[t]ake affirmative steps to recruit, hire and promote minority group teachers and counselors as positions bec[a]me available ...." As a result of the Board's efforts to comply with the order over the next two years, the percentage of minority teachers increased to 8.8%.

In 1971, however, faculty layoffs became necessary. The contract in effect at that time, between the Board and the Jackson Education Association (Union), provided that layoffs would be made in reverse order of seniority. Because of

[2]... This conclusion is supported by extra-record materials suggesting that the shortage of minority teachers was the result of past discrimination in teacher hiring. For example, the then-Superintendent of Schools testified that "an administrator ... told me she had tried to get a position in Jackson in the early 1950's and was told that they didn't hire colored people." This was the "type of thing," he stated, that led to adoption of Article XII.

the recent vintage of the school system's efforts to hire minorities, the seniority scheme led to the layoff of a substantial number of minority teachers, "literally wip[ing] out all the gain" made toward achieving racial balance. Once again, minority teachers on the faculty were a rarity.

By early 1972, when racial tensions in the schools had escalated to violent levels, school officials determined that the best course was full integration of the school system, including integration of the faculty. But they recognized that, without some modification of the seniority layoff system, genuine faculty integration could not take place. The Minority Affairs Office of the Jackson Public Schools submitted a questionnaire to all teachers, asking them to consider the possibility of abandoning the "last hired, first fired" approach to layoffs in favor of an absolute freeze on layoffs of minority teachers. The teachers overwhelmingly voted in favor of retaining the straight seniority system. Negotiations ensued between the two camps — on the one hand, the Board, which favored a freeze of minority layoffs and, on the other, the Union, urging straight seniority — and the negotiators ultimately reached accord. One union leader characterized the development of the layoff compromise as the most difficult balancing of equities that he had ever encountered.

The compromise avoided placing the entire burden of layoffs on either the white teachers as a group or the minority teachers as a group. Instead, each group would shoulder a portion of that burden equal to its portion of the faculty. Thus, the overall percentage of minorities on the faculty would remain constant. Within each group, seniority would govern which individuals would be laid off. This compromise was the provision at issue here, subsequently known as Article XII....

The Board and the Union leadership agreed to the adoption of Article XII. The compromise was then presented to the teachers, who ratified it by majority vote. Each of the six times that the contract has been renegotiated, Article XII has been presented for reconsideration to the members of the Union, at least 80% of whom are white, and each time it has been ratified....

II

....

The sole question posed by this case is whether the Constitution prohibits a union and a local school board from developing a collective-bargaining agreement that apportions layoffs between two racially determined groups as a means of preserving the effects of an affirmative hiring policy, the constitutionality of which is unchallenged.

III

Agreement upon a means for applying the Equal Protection Clause to an affirmative-action program has eluded this Court every time the issue has come before us. In *University of California Regents v. Bakke,* 438 U.S. 265 (1978), four Members of the Court concluded that, while racial distinctions are irrelevant to nearly all legitimate state objectives and are properly subjected to the most rigorous judicial scrutiny in most instances, they are highly relevant to the one legitimate state objective of eliminating the pernicious vestiges of past discrimination; when that is the goal, a less exacting standard of review is appropriate. We explained at length our view that, because no fundamental right was involved and because whites have none of the immutable characteristics of a suspect class, the so-called "strict scrutiny" applied to cases involving either fundamental rights or suspect classifications was not applicable. *Id.,* at 357 (opinion of BRENNAN, WHITE, MARSHALL, and BLACKMUN, JJ.). Nevertheless, we eschewed the least rigorous, "rational basis" standard of review, recognizing that any racial classification is subject to misuse. We determined that remedial use of race is permissible if it serves "important governmental objectives" and is "substantially related to achievement of those objectives." *Id.,* at 359; see also *id.,* at 387 (opinion of MARSHALL, J.); *id.,* at 402 (opinion of BLACKMUN, J.). This standard is genuinely a "strict and searching" judicial inquiry, but is "not '"strict" in theory and fatal in fact.'" *Id.,* at 362 (opinion of BRENNAN, WHITE, MARSHALL, and BLACKMUN, JJ.) (quoting Gunther, The Supreme Court, 1971 Term — Foreward: *In Search of Evolving Doctrine on a Changing Court: A Model for a Newer Equal Protection,* 86 Harv. L. Rev. 1, 8 (1972)). The only other Justice to reach the constitutional issue in *Bakke* suggested that, remedial purpose or no, any racial distinctions "call for the most exacting judicial examination." *Id.,* at 291 (opinion of POWELL, J.)....

IV

The principal state purpose supporting Article XII is the need to preserve the levels of faculty integration achieved through the affirmative hiring policy adopted in the early 1970's. Brief for Respondents 41-43. Justification for the hiring policy itself is found in the turbulent history of the effort to integrate the Jackson Public Schools — not even mentioned in the majority opinion — which attests to the bona fides of the Board's current employment practices.

The record and lodgings indicate that the Commission, endowed by the State Constitution with the power to investigate complaints of discrimination and the duty to secure the equal protection of the laws, Mich. Const., Art. V, § 29, prompted and oversaw the remedial steps now under attack. When the Board agreed to take specified remedial action, including the hiring and promotion of minority teachers, the Commission did not pursue its investigation of the apparent violations to the point of rendering formal findings of discrimination.

Instead of subjecting an already volatile school system to the further disruption of formal accusations and trials, it appears that the Board set about achieving the goals articulated in the settlement. According to the then-Superintendent of Schools, the Board was aware, at every step of the way, that "[t]he NAACP had its court suit ready if either the Board postponed the [integration] operation or abandoned the attempts. They were willing to — they were ready to go into Federal court and get a court order, as happened in Kalamazoo." Rather than provoke the looming lawsuit, the Board and the Union worked with the committees to reach a solution to the racial problems plaguing the school system....

The real irony of the argument urging mandatory, formal findings of discrimination lies in its complete disregard for a longstanding goal of civil rights reform, that of integrating schools without taking every school system to court. Our school desegregation cases imposed an affirmative duty on local school boards to see that "racial discrimination would be eliminated root and branch." *Green v. County School Board,* 391 U.S. 430, 437-438 (1968); see *Brown v. Board of Education,* 349 U.S. 294, 299 (1955). Petitioners would now have us inform the Board, having belatedly taken this Court's admonitions to heart, that it should have delayed further, disputing its obligations and forcing the aggrieved parties to seek judicial relief. This result would be wholly inconsistent with the national policies against overloading judicial dockets, maintaining groundless defenses, and impeding good-faith settlement of legal disputes. Only last Term, writing for the Court, THE CHIEF JUSTICE reaffirmed that civil rights litigation is no exception to the general policy in favor of settlements: "Indeed, Congress made clear its concern that civil rights plaintiffs not be penalized for 'helping to lessen docket congestion' by settling their cases out of court.... In short, settlements rather than litigation will serve the interests of plaintiffs as well as defendants." *Marek v. Chesny,* 473 U.S. —, — (1985). It would defy equity to penalize those who achieve harmony from discord, as it would defy wisdom to impose on society the needless cost of superfluous litigation. The Court is correct to recognize, as it does today, that formal findings of past discrimination are not a necessary predicate to the adoption of affirmative-action policies, and that the scope of such policies need not be limited to remedying specific instances of identifiable discrimination....

V

The second part of any constitutional assessment of the disputed plan requires us to examine the means chosen to achieve the state purpose. Again, the history of Article XII, insofar as we can determine it, is the best source of assistance.

A. Testimony of both Union and school officials illustrates that the Board's obligation to integrate its faculty could not have been fulfilled meaningfully as long as layoffs continued to eliminate the last hired. In addition, qualified minority teachers from other States were reluctant to uproot their lives and move to Michigan without any promise of protection from imminent layoff. The testimony suggests that the lack of some layoff protection would have crippled the efforts to recruit minority applicants. Adjustment of the layoff hierarchy under these circumstances was a necessary corollary of an affirmative hiring policy.

B. Under JUSTICE POWELL's approach, the community of Jackson, having painfully watched the hard-won benefits of its integration efforts vanish as a result of massive layoffs, would be informed today, simply, that preferential layoff protection is never permissible because hiring policies serve the same purpose at a lesser cost. As a matter of logic as well as fact, a hiring policy achieves no purpose at all if it is eviscerated by layoffs. JUSTICE POWELL's position is untenable.

JUSTICE POWELL has concluded, by focusing exclusively on the undisputed hardship of losing a job, that the Equal Protection Clause always bars race-conscious layoff plans. This analysis overlooks, however, the important fact that Article XII does not cause the loss of jobs; someone will lose a job under any layoff plan and, whoever it is, that person will not deserve it. Any *per se* prohibition against layoff protection, therefore, must rest upon a premise that the

tradition of basing layoff decisions on seniority is so fundamental that its modification can never be permitted. Our cases belie that premise.

The general practice of basing employment decisions on relative seniority
may be upset for the sake of other public policies. For example, a court may
displace innocent workers by granting retroactive seniority to victims of employment discrimination. *Franks v. Bowman Transportation Co.,* 424 U.S. 747, 775
(1976). Further, this Court has long held that "employee expectations arising
from a seniority system agreement may be modified by statutes furthering a
strong public policy interest." *Id.,* at 778. And we have recognized that collective-bargaining agreements may go further than statutes in enhancing the seniority of certain employees for the purpose of fostering legitimate interests.
See *Ford Motor Co. v. Huffman,* 345 U.S. 330, 339-340 (1953)....

C. Article XII is a narrow provision because it allocates the impact of an
unavoidable burden proportionately between two racial groups. It places no
absolute burden or benefit on one race, and, within the confines of constant
minority proportions, it preserves the hierarchy of seniority in the selection of
individuals for layoff. Race is a factor, along with seniority, in determining
which individuals the school system will lose; it is not alone dispositive of any
individual's fate. Cf. *Bakke,* 438 U.S., at 318 (opinion of POWELL, J.). Moreover,
Article XII does not use layoff protection as a tool for *increasing* minority
representation; achievement of that goal is entrusted to the less severe hiring
policies. And Article XII is narrow in the temporal sense as well. The very
bilateral process that gave rise to Article XII when its adoption was necessary
will also occasion its demise when remedial measures are no longer required.
Finally, Article XII modifies contractual expectations that do not themselves
carry any connotation of merit or achievement; it does not interfere with the
"cherished American ethic" of "[f]airness in individual competition," *Bakke,
supra,* at 319, n. 53, depriving individuals of an opportunity that they could be
said to deserve. In all of these important ways, Article XII metes out the hardship of layoffs in a manner that achieves its purpose with the smallest possible
deviation from established norms.

The Board's goal of preserving minority proportions could have been
achieved, perhaps, in a different way. For example, if layoffs had been determined by lottery, the ultimate effect would have been retention of current racial
percentages. A random system, however, would place every teacher in equal
jeopardy, working a much greater upheaval of the seniority hierarchy than that
occasioned by Article XII; it is not at all a less restrictive means of achieving the
Board's goal. Another possible approach would have been a freeze on layoffs of
minority teachers. This measure, too, would have been substantially more burdensome than Article XII, not only by necessitating the layoff of a greater
number of white teachers, but also by erecting an absolute distinction between
the races, one to be benefited and one to be burdened, in a way that Article XII
avoids. Indeed, neither petitioners nor any Justice of this Court has suggested
an alternative to Article XII that would have attained the stated goal in any
narrower or more equitable a fashion. Nor can I conceive of one.

VI

It is no accident that this least burdensome of all conceivable options is the very provision that the parties adopted. For Article XII was forged in the crucible of clashing interests. All of the economic powers of the predominantly white teachers' union were brought to bear against those of the elected Board, and the process yielded consensus....

The perceived dangers of affirmative action misused, therefore, are naturally averted by the bilateral process of negotiation, agreement, and ratification. The best evidence that Article XII is a narrow means to serve important interests is that representatives of all affected persons, starting from diametrically opposed perspectives, have agreed to it — not once, but six times since 1972.

VII

The narrow question presented by this case, if indeed we proceed to the merits, offers no occasion for the Court to issue broad proclamations of public policy concerning the controversial issue of affirmative action. Rather, this case calls for calm, dispassionate reflection upon exactly what has been done, to whom, and why. If one honestly confronts each of those questions against the factual background suggested by the materials submitted to us, I believe the conclusion is inescapable that Article XII meets, and indeed surpasses, any standard for ensuring that race-conscious programs are necessary to achieve remedial purposes. When an elected school board and a teachers' union collectively bargain a layoff provision designed to preserve the effects of a valid minority recruitment plan by apportioning layoffs between two racial groups, as a result of a settlement achieved under the auspices of a supervisory state agency charged with protecting the civil rights of all citizens, that provision should not be upset by this Court on constitutional grounds....

JUSTICE STEVENS, dissenting.

In my opinion, it is not necessary to find that the Board of Education has been guilty of racial discrimination in the past to support the conclusion that it has a legitimate interest in employing more black teachers in the future. Rather than analyzing a case of this kind by asking whether minority teachers have some sort of special entitlement to jobs as a remedy for sins that were committed in the past, I believe that we should first ask whether the Board's action advances the public interest in educating children for the future. If so, I believe we should consider whether that public interest, and the manner in which it is pursued, justifies any adverse effects on the disadvantaged group.

I

The Equal Protection Clause absolutely prohibits the use of race in many governmental contexts. To cite only a few: the government may not use race to decide who may serve on juries,[2] who may use public services,[3] who may

---

[2] *Batson v. Kentucky,* 476 U.S. — (1986); *Vasquez v. Hillery,* 474 U.S. — (1985); *Rose v. Mitchell,* 443 U.S. 545 (1979); *Strauder v. West Virginia,* 100 U.S. 303 (1880).

[3] *Turner v. City of Memphis,* 369 U.S. 350 (1962) *(per curiam); Burton v. Wilmington Parking Authority,* 365 U.S. 715 (1961).

marry,[4] and who may be fit parents.[5] The use of race in these situations is "utterly irrational" because it is completely unrelated to any valid public purpose; moreover, it is particularly pernicious because it constitutes a badge of oppression that is unfaithful to the central promise of the Fourteenth Amendment.

Nevertheless, in our present society, race is not always irrelevant to sound governmental decisionmaking. To take the most obvious example, in law enforcement, if an undercover agent is needed to infiltrate a group suspected of ongoing criminal behavior — and if the members of the group are all of the same race — it would seem perfectly rational to employ an agent of that race rather than a member of a different racial class. Similarly, in a city with a recent history of racial unrest, the superintendent of police might reasonably conclude that an integrated police force could develop a better relationship with the community and thereby do a more effective job of maintaining law and order than a force composed only of white officers.

In the context of public education, it is quite obvious that a school board may reasonably conclude that an integrated faculty will be able to provide benefits to the student body that could not be provided by an all white, or nearly all white, faculty. For one of the most important lessons that the American public schools teach is that the diverse ethnic, cultural, and national backgrounds that have been brought together in our famous "melting pot" do not identify essential differences among the human beings that inhabit our land. It is one thing for a white child to be taught by a white teacher that color, like beauty, is only "skin deep"; it is far more convincing to experience that truth on a day to day basis during the routine, ongoing learning process.

In this case, the collective-bargaining agreement between the Union and the Board of Education succinctly stated a valid public purpose — "recognition of the desirability of multi-ethnic representation on the teaching faculty," and thus "a policy of actively seeking minority group personnel." Nothing in the record — not a shred of evidence — contradicts the view that the Board's attempt to employ, and to retain, more minority teachers in the Jackson public school system served this completely sound educational purpose. Thus, there was a rational and unquestionably legitimate basis for the Board's decision to enter into the collective-bargaining agreement that petitioners have challenged, even though the agreement required special efforts to recruit and retain minority teachers.

II

It is argued, nonetheless, that the purpose should be deemed invalid because, even if the Board of Education's judgment in this case furthered a laudable goal, some other boards might claim that their experience demonstrates that segregated classes, or segregated faculties, lead to better academic achievement. There is, however, a critical difference between a decision to *exclude* a member of a minority race because of his or her skin color and a decision to *include* more members of the minority in a school faculty for that reason.

---

[4] *Loving v. Virginia*, 388 U.S. 1 (1967).
[5] *Palmore v. Sidoti*, 466 U.S. 429 (1984).

The exclusionary decision rests on the false premise that differences in race, or in the color of a person's skin, reflect real differences that are relevant to a person's right to share in the blessings of a free society. As noted, that premise is "utterly irrational," and repugnant to the principles of a free and democratic society. Nevertheless, the fact that persons of different races do, indeed, have differently colored skin, may give rise to a belief that there is some significant difference between such persons. The inclusion of minority teachers in the educational process inevitably tends to dispel that illusion whereas their exclusion could only tend to foster it....

III

Even if there is a valid purpose to the race consciousness, however, the question that remains is whether that public purpose transcends the harm to the white teachers who are disadvantaged by the special preference the Board has given to its most recently hired minority teachers. In my view, there are two important inquiries in assessing the harm to the disadvantaged teacher. The first is an assessment of the procedures that were used to adopt, and implement, the race-conscious action. The second is an evaluation of the nature of the harm itself.

In this case, there can be no question about either the fairness of the procedures used to adopt the race-conscious provision, or the propriety of its breadth. As JUSTICE MARSHALL has demonstrated, the procedures for adopting this provision were scrupulously fair. The Union that represents the petitioners negotiated the provision and agreed to it; the agreement was put to a vote of the membership, and overwhelmingly approved....

Finally, we must consider the harm to the petitioners. Every layoff, like every refusal to employ a qualified applicant, is a grave loss to the affected individual. However, the undisputed facts in this case demonstrate that this serious consequence to the petitioners is not based on any lack of respect for their race, or on blind habit and stereotype. Rather, petitioners have been laid off for a combination of two reasons: the economic conditions that have led Jackson to lay off some teachers, and the special contractual protections intended to preserve the newly integrated character of the faculty in the Jackson schools. Thus, the same harm might occur if a number of gifted young teachers had been given special contractual protection because their specialties were in short supply and if the Jackson Board of Education faced a fiscal need for layoffs. A Board decision to grant immediate tenure to a group of experts in computer technology, an athletic coach, and a language teacher, for example, might reduce the pool of teachers eligible for layoffs during a depression and therefore have precisely the same impact as the racial preference at issue here. In either case, the harm would be generated by the combination of economic conditions and the special contractual protection given a different group of teachers — a protection that, as discussed above, was justified by a valid and extremely strong public interest.[14]...

---

[14] The fact that the issue arises in a layoff context, rather than a hiring context, has no bearing on the equal protection question. For if the Board's interest in employing more minority teachers is sufficient to justify providing them with an extra incentive to accept jobs in Jackson, Michigan, it is

NOTES

1. In *Fullilove v. Klutznick,* 448 U.S. 448 (1980), a similarly divided Supreme Court sustained the portion of the Public Works Employment Act of 1977 that required ten percent of the federal funds being granted for local public works projects to be used to procure the services of "minority business enterprises" primarily owned by "Negroes, Spanish-speaking, Orientals, Indians, Eskimos, and Aleuts." Under the challenged provision, each governmental grant recipient and its private prime contractor were obligated to satisfy the ten percent minority set-aside figure, unless the grant recipient was able to obtain a total or partial waiver of that requirement by demonstrating that the ten percent goal could not be achieved through the best efforts of the relevant parties.

Chief Justice Burger, in an opinion concurred in by Justices White and Powell, indicated that the validity of such a race-conscious program had to be ascertained through the application of a two-pronged inquiry. The Court must initially determine the propriety of the *objective* being sought by Congress through the establishment of the program. Since Chief Justice Burger found a rational basis for the congressional decision that the uncorrected subcontracting practices of prime contractors would likely perpetuate the effects of prior discriminatory impediments to access by minority businesses to public contract opportunities, a constitutionally bona fide "remedial" objective was sustained. The Chief Justice then noted that the *means* selected to achieve such an objective had to be properly devised. Through the exercise of its commerce power or its spending authority, Congress could appropriately regulate the subcontracting practices of private prime contractors involved in federally funded public works projects. The governmental grant recipients could permissibly be regulated in the manner accomplished by the ten percent minority set-aside provision through the power of Congress to enforce the equal protection clause of the fourteenth amendment.

Chief Justice Burger went on to note that whether or not the discriminatory impediments to minority business participation in public works contracting had been intentionally established or were merely the inadvertent consequence of seemingly neutral practices, the congressional use of race-conscious criteria for the limited remedial purpose of enhancing the economic rights of minority businesses that had traditionally failed to enjoy equal access to public works contracts was an appropriate means narrowly tailored to guarantee to such entrepreneurs the equal protection of the law. Since the ten percent "target" could be waived in cases where its attainment could not be practically achieved, and the impact of the limited duration program upon non-minority contractors would be slight, the Chief Justice concluded that the enactment of the set-aside provision did not violate the equal protection principles embodied in the due

---

also sufficient to justify their retention when the number of available jobs is reduced. JUSTICE POWELL's suggestion that there is a distinction of constitutional significance under the Equal Protection Clause between a racial preference at the time of hiring and an identical preference at the time of discharge is thus wholly unpersuasive. He seems to assume that a teacher who has been working for a few years suffers a greater harm when he is laid off than the harm suffered by an unemployed teacher who is refused a job for which he is qualified. In either event, the adverse decision forecloses "only one of several opportunities" that may be available to the disappointed teacher. Moreover, the distinction is artificial, for the layoff provision at issue in this case was included as part of the terms of the *hiring* of minority and other teachers under the collective-bargaining agreement.

process clause of the fifth amendment, just as race-conscious school desegregation plans had been found in prior decisions to satisfy constitutional constraints.

Here we deal, as we noted earlier, not with the limited remedial powers of a
federal court, for example, but with the broad remedial powers of Congress.
It is fundamental that in no organ of government, state or federal, does there
repose a more comprehensive remedial power than in the Congress, expressly charged by the Constitution with competence and authority to enforce
equal protection guarantees. Congress not only may induce voluntary action
to assure compliance with existing federal statutory or constitutional antidis-
crimination provisions, but also, where Congress has authority to declare
certain conduct unlawful, it may, as here, authorize and induce state action to
avoid such conduct....

The Congress has not sought to give select minority groups a preferred
standing in the construction industry, but has embarked on a remedial program to place them on a more equitable footing with respect to public contracting opportunities. There has been no showing in this case that Congress
has inadvertently effected an invidious discrimination by excluding from coverage an identifiable minority group that has been the victim of a degree of
disadvantage and discrimination equal to or greater than that suffered by the
groups encompassed by the MBE program. It is not inconceivable that on
very special facts a case might be made to challenge the congressional decision
to limit MBE eligibility to the particular minority groups identified in the
Act....

Congress, after due consideration, perceived a pressing need to move forward with new approaches in the continuing effort to achieve the goal of
equality of economic opportunity. In this effort, Congress has necessary latitude to try new techniques such as the limited use of racial and ethnic criteria
to accomplish remedial objectives; this especially so in programs where voluntary cooperation with remedial measures is induced by placing conditions on
federal expenditures. That the program may press the outer limits of congressional authority affords no basis for striking it down.

448 U.S. at 483-90. Although Justice Powell concurred in the opinion of Chief
Justice Burger, he filed a separate opinion expressly indicating that he continued to adhere to his view that such race-conscious remedial programs had to
comport with the standards he had enunciated in his separate *Bakke* opinion.
He noted that Congress possessed the clear authority to enact legislation aimed
at ameliorating the present effects of past discrimination. Since he concluded
that there was sufficient evidence to indicate that Congress had reasonably
found that improper discriminatory practices had previously prevented minority businesses from enjoying their fair share of public works contracts, that
legislative body possessed the constitutional power to enact a carefully drawn,
race-conscious remedial provision that was of appropriately limited duration.

Justice Marshall, joined by Justices Brennan and Blackmun, followed the
views that had been articulated in their joint *Bakke* opinion. They found that
the use of racial classifications in this program was substantially related to the
compelling congressional objective of remedying the continuing effects of past
racial discrimination, and they thus concluded that the remedial set-aside plan
was permissibly established.

Justices Stewart and Rehnquist dissented, because they continued to believe
that "[o]ur Constitution is color-blind, and neither knows nor tolerates classes

among citizens" even where designed to alleviate the effects of past discrimination.

Justice Stevens filed a separate dissenting opinion challenging the imprecise manner in which he thought Congress was granting preferential rights in response to minimally articulated findings of actual discriminatory treatment regarding the particular groups in question. "[I]f that history can justify such a random distribution of benefits on racial lines as that embodied in this statutory scheme, it will serve not merely as a basis for remedial legislation, but rather as a permanent source of justification for grants of special privileges."

2. In *United States v. Paradise,* 480 U.S. 149 (1987), a closely divided Supreme Court sustained the constitutionality of race-conscious relief formulated by a district court to rectify the effects of long-term, open, and pervasive employment discrimination practiced by the Alabama Department of Public Safety. In 1972, the district court found that the Department had, for almost four decades, systematically excluded blacks from employment as state troopers in violation of the fourteenth amendment, and it issued an affirmative action hiring quota. Although some black troopers were subsequently hired, by 1979 not one black had been promoted to an upper rank. The court then approved a partial consent decree which required the Department to develop a promotional procedure which would have no adverse impact on blacks. When no such procedure was implemented by 1981, the court approved a second consent decree which permitted the Department's proposed corporal promotion test to be administered, subject to the court's review of the results for possible bias. Of the sixty blacks who took the test, only five were listed in the top half of the promotional register.

The district court then found that the promotional test had a disparate impact on blacks, and it decided to establish a limited affirmative action plan. It ordered that "for a limited period of time," at least 50% of those people promoted to corporal and higher must be black, so long as qualified black candidates were available. Its affirmative action directive was to become inoperative for any rank composed of 25% black officers or at such time as the Department developed and implemented an acceptable promotion program which did not adversely affect black candidates.

Justices Brennan, Marshall, Blackmun, and Powell found that the race-conscious promotional order was justified by a compelling government interest in eradicating the Department's pervasive, systematic, and obstinate discriminatory exclusion of blacks from both entry and upper level trooper positions.

> In determining whether race-conscious remedies are appropriate, we look to several factors, including the necessity for the relief and the efficacy of alternative remedies; the flexibility and duration of the relief, including the availability of waiver provisions; the relationship of the numerical goals to the relevant labor market; and the impact of the relief on the rights of third parties.

These four Justices decided that no other remedial order would effectively rectify the Department's discrimination. The one-for-one promotional requirement was "narrowly tailored," since it was temporary, it only applied to necessary promotions and did not require any gratuitous promotions, it only directed the promotion of qualified blacks, and the overall 25% numerical goal for each rank bore a proper relation to the 25% labor force participation rate for blacks in the relevant labor market. The 50% promotion figure was an appropriate means of expanding the upper trooper ranks to the 25% objective within a reasonable period of time. The order did not impose an unacceptable burden upon white candidates. It did not preclude the promotion of white officers, but only postponed the advancement of some. No white troopers were to be laid off or terminated as in *Wygant*.

Justice Stevens concurred in the result. He indicated that the more expansive doctrine established in *Swann v. Charlotte-Mecklenburg Bd. of Educ.*, 402 U.S. 1 (1971), to remedy the effects of school segregation should be applied to cases of employment discrimination by government entities. He found that race-conscious relief was needed to rectify the Department's egregious history of hiring and promotional discrimination.

Chief Justice Rehnquist and Justices O'Connor, White, and Scalia dissented. They thought that judicial relief short of race-conscious promotional quotas could have been employed to minimize the adverse impact upon white employees, and they found the one-to-one promotional quota to be excessive.

3. In *Hammon v. Barry*, 813 F.2d 412 (D.C. Cir. 1987), *cert. denied*, 486 U.S. 1036 (1988), the court found that a Washington, D.C. affirmative action plan which required 60% of new fire department employees to be black violated the fifth amendment due process clause. Without evidence of prior employment discrimination, the declared goal of achieving a racially balanced work force was held to be constitutionally invalid. See also *Janowiak v. Corporate City of S. Bend*, 836 F.2d 1034 (7th Cir. 1987), *cert. denied*, 109 S. Ct. 1310 (1989).

4. In *City of Richmond v. J.A. Croson Co.*, 109 S. Ct. 706 (1989), a divided Supreme Court struck down a thirty percent set-aside program which had been adopted by the City of Richmond. A majority of the Court held, for the first time, that since governmental race-conscious affirmative action programs involve "inherently suspect" classifications, such plans may only be sustained when a compelling state interest can be demonstrated. *Fullilove v. Klutznick*, 448 U.S. 448 (1980), was distinguished because of the special power of Congress to enact legislation enforcing the fourteenth amendment equal protection clause.

Metro Broadcasting, Inc. v. FCC, 110 S. Ct. 2997 (1990), concerned the constitutionality of two race-conscious FCC policies: (1) an enhancement for minority-owned firms weighted with other factors when comparing mutually exclusive applications for new radio and television licenses and (2) a "distress sale" rule which permits a broadcaster whose qualifications to hold a license have been challenged to transfer that license, before the FCC resolves the license issue, to a qualified minority enterprise. The five-Justice majority noted that the FCC policies had been adopted pursuant to a congressional mandate in favor of broadcasting diversity. It then indicated that *congressionally directed* benign race-conscious measures will survive an equal protection challenge if they: (1) serve important governmental objectives and (2) are substantially related to the achievement of those objectives. Since the majority found that broadcasting diversity constituted an important governmental objective and that empirical evidence suggested that a benign preference in favor of minority-owned licensees was substantially related to the attainment of that goal, it sustained the FCC policies. Chief Justice Rehnquist and Justices Kennedy, O'Connor, and Scalia dissented.

5. See generally Rutherglen & Ortiz, *Affirmative Action Under the Constitution and Title VII: From Confusion to Convergence*, 35 U.C.L.A. L. Rev. 467 (1988); Van Alstyne, *Rites of Passage: Race, the Supreme Court, and the Constitution*, 46 U. Chi. L. Rev. 775 (1979); Edwards, *Preferential Remedies and Affirmative Action in Employment in the Wake of Bakke*, 1979 Wash. U.L.Q. 113; Note, *The Constitutionality of Affirmative Action in Public Employment:*

Judicial Deference to Certain Politically Responsible Bodies, 67 Va. L. Rev. 1235 (1981).

2. GENDER

CLEVELAND BOARD OF EDUCATION v. LaFLEUR

414 U.S. 632, 94 S. Ct. 791, 39 L. Ed. 2d 52 (1974)

JUSTICE STEWART delivered the opinion of the Court.

The respondents in No. 72-777 and the petitioner in No. 72-1129 are female public school teachers. During the 1970-1971 school year, each informed her local school board that she was pregnant; each was compelled by a mandatory maternity leave rule to quit her job without pay several months before the expected birth of her child. These cases call upon us to decide the constitutionality of the school boards' rules.

I

Jo Carol LaFleur and Ann Elizabeth Nelson, the respondents in No. 72-777, are junior high school teachers employed by the Board of Education of Cleveland, Ohio. Pursuant to a rule first adopted in 1952, the school board requires every pregnant school teacher to take a maternity leave without pay, beginning five months before the expected birth of her child. Application for such leave must be made no later than two weeks prior to the date of departure. A teacher on maternity leave is not allowed to return to work until the beginning of the next regular school semester which follows the date when the child attains the age of three months. A doctor's certificate attesting to the health of the teacher is a prerequisite to return; an additional physical examination may be required. The teacher on maternity leave is not promised re-employment after the birth of the child; she is merely given priority in reassignment to a position for which she is qualified. Failure to comply with the mandatory maternity leave provisions is grounds for dismissal.

Neither Mrs. LaFleur nor Mrs. Nelson wished to take an unpaid maternity leave; each wanted to continue teaching until the end of the school year. Because of the mandatory maternity leave rule, however, each was required to leave her job in March of 1971. The two women then filed separate suits in the United States District Court for the Northern District of Ohio under 42 U.S.C. § 1983, challenging the constitutionality of the maternity leave rule. The District Court tried the cases together, and rejected the plaintiffs' arguments. 326 F. Supp. 1208. A divided panel of the United States Court of Appeals for the Sixth Circuit reversed, finding the Cleveland rules in violation of the Equal Protection Clause of the Fourteenth Amendment. 465 F.2d 1184.

The petitioner in No. 72-1129, Susan Cohen, was employed by the School Board of Chesterfield County, Virginia. That school board's maternity leave regulation requires that a pregnant teacher leave work at least four months prior to the expected birth of her child. Notice in writing must be given to the school board at least six months prior to the expected birth date. A teacher on maternity leave is declared re-eligible for employment when she submits written notice from a physician that she is physically fit for re-employment, and when she can give assurances that care of the child will cause minimal interferences with her job responsibilities. The teacher is guaranteed re-employment no later than the first day of the school year following the date upon which she is declared re-eligible.

Mrs. Cohen informed the Chesterfield County School Board in November 1970, that she was pregnant and expected the birth of her child about April 28, 1971. She initially requested that she be permitted to continue teaching until April 1, 1971. The school board rejected the request, as it did Mrs. Cohen's subsequent suggestion that she be allowed to teach until January 21, 1971, the end of the first school semester. Instead, she was required to leave her teaching job on December 18, 1970. She subsequently filed this suit under 42 U.S.C. § 1983 in the United States District Court for the Eastern District of Virginia. The District Court held that the school board regulation violates the Equal Protection Clause, and granted appropriate relief. 326 F. Supp. 1159. A divided panel of the Fourth Circuit affirmed, but, on rehearing *en banc,* the Court of Appeals upheld the constitutionality of the challenged regulation in a 4-3 decision. 474 F.2d 395....

II

This court has long recognized that freedom of personal choice in matters of marriage and family life is one of the liberties protected by the Due Process Clause of the Fourteenth Amendment. As we noted in *Eisenstadt v. Baird,* 405 U.S. 438, 453, there is a right "to be free from unwarranted governmental intrusion into matters so fundamentally affecting a person as the decision whether to bear or beget a child."

By acting to penalize the pregnant teacher for deciding to bear a child, overly restrictive maternity leave regulations can constitute a heavy burden on the exercise of these protected freedoms. Because public school maternity leave rules directly affect "one of the basic civil rights of man," *Skinner v. Oklahoma,* [316 U.S.], at 541, the Due Process Clause of the Fourteenth Amendment requires that such rules must not needlessly, arbitrarily, or capriciously impinge upon this vital area of a teacher's constitutional liberty. The question before us in these cases is whether the interests advanced in support of the rules of the Cleveland and Chesterfield County School Boards can justify the particular procedures they have adopted.

The school boards in these cases have offered two essentially overlapping explanations for their mandatory maternity leave rules. First, they contend that the firm cut-off dates are necessary to maintain continuity of classroom instruction, since advance knowledge of when a pregnant teacher must leave facilitates the finding and hiring of a qualified substitute. Secondly, the school boards seek to justify their maternity rules by arguing that at least some teachers become physically incapable of adequately performing certain of their duties during the latter part of pregnancy. By keeping the pregnant teacher out of the classroom during these final months, the maternity leave rules are said to protect the health of the teacher and her unborn child, while at the same time assuring that students have a physically capable instructor in the classroom at all times.[9]

---

[9] The records in these cases suggest that the maternity leave regulations may have originally been inspired by other, less weighty, considerations. For example, Dr. Mark C. Schinnerer, who served as

It cannot be denied that continuity of instruction is a significant and legitimate educational goal. Regulations requiring pregnant teachers to provide early notice of their condition to school authorities undoubtedly facilitate administrative planning toward the important objective of continuity. But, as the Court of Appeals for the Second Circuit noted in *Green v. Waterford Board of Education,* 473 F.2d 629, 635:

> "Where a pregnant teacher provides the Board with a date certain for commencement of leave, however, that value [continuity] is preserved; an arbitrary leave date set at the end of the fifth month is no more calculated to facilitate a planned and orderly transition between the teacher and a substitute than is a date fixed closer to confinement. Indeed, the latter ... would afford the Board more, not less, time to procure a satisfactory long-term substitute." (Footnote omitted.)

Thus, while the advance notice provisions in the Cleveland and Chesterfield County rules are wholly rational and may well be necessary to serve the objective of continuity of instruction, the absolute requirements of termination at the end of the fourth or fifth month of pregnancy are not....

In fact, since the fifth or sixth months of pregnancy will obviously begin at different times in the school year for different teachers, the present Cleveland and Chesterfield County rules may serve to hinder attainment of the very continuity objectives that they are purportedly designed to promote. For example, the beginning of the fifth month of pregnancy for both Mrs. LaFleur and Mrs. Nelson occurred during March of 1971. Both were thus required to leave work with only a few months left in the school year, even though both were fully willing to serve through the end of the term....

We thus conclude that the arbitrary cutoff dates embodied in the mandatory leave rules before us have no rational relationship to the valid state interest of preserving continuity of instruction. As long as the teacher is required to give substantial advance notice of her condition, the choice of firm dates later in pregnancy would serve the boards' objectives just as well, while imposing a far lesser burden on the women's exercise of constitutionally protected freedom.

The question remains as to whether the fifth and sixth month cutoff dates can be justified on the other ground advanced by the school boards — the necessity of keeping physically unfit teachers out of the classroom. There can be no doubt that such an objective is perfectly legitimate, both on educational and safety grounds. And, despite the plethora of conflicting medical testimony in these cases, we can assume, *arguendo,* that at least some teachers become physi-

---

Superintendent of Schools in Cleveland at the time the leave rule was adopted, testified in the District Court that the rule had been adopted in part to save pregnant teachers from embarrassment at the hands of giggling schoolchildren: the cut-off date at the end of the fourth month was chosen because this was when the teacher "began to show." Similarly, at least several members of the Chesterfield County School Board thought a mandatory leave rule was justified in order to insulate schoolchildren from the sight of conspicuously pregnant women. One member of the school board thought that it was "not good for the school system" for students to view pregnant teachers, "because some of the kids say, my teacher swallowed a water melon, things like that."

The school boards have not contended in this Court that these considerations can serve as a legitimate basis for a rule requiring pregnant women to leave work; we thus note the comments only to illustrate the possible role of outmoded taboos in the adoption of the rules. Cf. *Green v. Waterford Board of Education,* 473 F.2d, at 635 ("Whatever may have been the reaction in Queen Victoria's time, pregnancy is no longer a dirty word").

cally disabled from effectively performing their duties during the latter stages of pregnancy.

The mandatory termination provisions of the Cleveland and Chesterfield County rules surely operate to insulate the classroom from the presence of potentially incapacitated pregnant teachers. But the question is whether the rules sweep too broadly. See *Shelton v. Tucker,* 364 U.S. 479. That question must be answered in the affirmative, for the provisions amount to a conclusive presumption that every pregnant teacher who reaches the fifth or sixth month of pregnancy is physically incapable of continuing. There is no individualized determination by the teacher's doctor — or the school board's — as to any particular teacher's ability to continue at her job. The rules contain an irrebuttable presumption of physical incompetency, and that presumption applies even when the medical evidence as to an individual woman's physical status might be wholly to the contrary.

As the Court noted last Term in *Vlandis v. Kline,* 412 U.S. 441, 446, "permanent irrebuttable presumptions have long been disfavored under the Due Process Clause of the Fifth and Fourteenth Amendments." In *Vlandis,* the Court declared unconstitutional, under the Due Process Clause, a Connecticut statute mandating an irrebuttable presumption of nonresidency for the purposes of qualifying for reduced tuition rates at a state university. We said in that case, *id.,* at 452:

> "[I]t is forbidden by the Due Process Clause to deny an individual the resident rates on the basis of a permanent and irrebuttable presumption of nonresidence, when that presumption is not necessarily or universally true in fact, and when the State has reasonable alternative means of making the crucial determination."

Similarly, in *Stanley v. Illinois,* 405 U.S. 645, the Court held that an Illinois statute containing an irrebuttable presumption that unmarried fathers are incompetent to raise their children violated the Due Process Clause....

These principles control our decision in the cases before us. While the medical experts in these cases differed on many points, they unanimously agreed on one — the ability of any particular pregnant woman to continue at work past any fixed time in her pregnancy is very much an individual matter. Even assuming, *arguendo,* that there are some women who would be physically unable to work past the particular cutoff dates embodied in the challenged rules, it is evident that there are large numbers of teachers who are fully capable of continuing work for longer than the Cleveland and Chesterfield County regulations will allow. Thus, the conclusive presumption embodied in these rules, like that in *Vlandis,* is neither "necessarily nor universally true," and is violative of the Due Process Clause....

While it might be easier for the school boards to conclusively presume that all pregnant women are unfit to teach past the fourth or fifth month or even the first month of pregnancy, administrative convenience alone is insufficient to make valid what otherwise is a violation of due process of law.[13] The Four-

---

[13] This is not to say that the only means for providing appropriate protection for the rights of pregnant teachers is an individualized determination in each case and in every circumstance. We are not dealing in these cases with maternity leave regulations requiring a termination of employment at

teenth Amendment requires the school boards to employ alternative administrative means, which do not so broadly infringe upon basic constitutional liberty, in support of their legitimate goals.

We conclude, therefore, that neither the necessity for continuity of instruction nor the state interest in keeping physically unfit teachers out of the classroom can justify the sweeping mandatory leave regulations that the Cleveland and Chesterfield County School Boards have adopted....

III

In addition to the mandatory termination provisions, both the Cleveland and Chesterfield County rules contain limitations upon a teacher's eligibility to return to work after giving birth....

[Under] [t]he Cleveland rule, ... the school board requires the mother to wait until her child reaches the age of three months before the return rules begin to operate. The school boards have offered no reasonable justification for this supplemental limitation, and we can perceive none. To the extent that the three-month provision reflects the school board's thinking that no mother is fit to return until that point in time, it suffers from the same constitutional deficiencies that plague the irrebuttable presumption in the termination rules.[15] The presumption, moreover, is patently unnecessary, since the requirement of a physician's certificate or a medical examination fully protects the school's interests in this regard. And finally, the three-month provision simply has nothing to do with continuity of instruction, since the precise point at which the child will reach the relevant age will obviously occur at a different point throughout the school year for each teacher.

Thus, we conclude that the Cleveland return rule, insofar as it embodies the three-month age provision, is wholly arbitrary and irrational, and hence violates the Due Process Clause of the Fourteenth Amendment....

We perceive no such constitutional infirmities in the Chesterfield County rule. In that school system, the teacher becomes eligible for re-employment upon submission of a medical certificate from her physician; return to work is guaranteed no later than the beginning of the next school year following the eligibility determination. The medical certificate is both a reasonable and narrow method of protecting the school board's interest in teacher fitness, while the possible deferring of return until the next school year serves the goal of preserving continuity of instruction....

....

[The concurring opinion of Justice Powell and the dissenting opinion of Justice Rehnquist, with whom Chief Justice Burger joined, are omitted.]

---

some firm date during the last few weeks of pregnancy. We therefore have no occasion to decide whether such regulations might be justified by considerations not presented in these records....

[15] It is clear that the factual hypothesis of such a presumption — that no mother is physically fit to return to work until her child reaches the age of three months — is neither necessarily nor universally true.

Of course, it may be that the Cleveland rule is based upon another theory — that new mothers are too busy with their children within the first three months to allow a return to work. Viewed in that light, the rule remains a conclusive presumption, whose underlying factual assumptions can hardly be said to be universally valid.

NOTES

1. The Supreme Court has adopted a standard for gender-based discrimination that falls at some point between "rational basis" and "strict scrutiny." A gender-based classification must serve important governmental objectives and be substantially related to the achievement of those objectives. In adopting this standard in *Craig v. Boren,* 429 U.S. 190, 197-99 (1976), the Court traced the recent development of equal protection in the area of sex discrimination:

> Analysis may appropriately begin with the reminder that *Reed* [*v. Reed,* 404 U.S. 71 (1971)], emphasized that statutory classifications that distinguish between males and females are "subject to scrutiny under the Equal Protection Clause." 404 U.S., at 75. To withstand constitutional challenge, previous cases establish that classifications by gender must serve important governmental objectives and must be substantially related to achievement of those objectives. Thus, in *Reed,* the objectives of "reducing the workload on probate courts," *id.,* at 76, and "avoiding intra-family controversy," *id.,* at 77, were deemed of insufficient importance to sustain use of an overt gender criterion in the appointment of intestate administrators. Decisions following *Reed* similarly have rejected administrative ease and convenience as sufficiently important objectives to justify gender-based classifications. See, e.g., *Stanley v. Illinois,* 405 U.S. 645, 656 (1972); *Frontiero v. Richardson,* 411 U.S. 677, 690 (1973); cf. *Schlesinger v. Ballard,* 419 U.S. 498, 506-507 (1975). And only two Terms ago, *Stanton v. Stanton,* 421 U.S. 7 (1975), expressly stating that *Reed v. Reed* was "controlling," 421 U.S., at 13, held that *Reed* required invalidation of a Utah differential age-of-majority statute, notwithstanding the statute's coincidence with and furtherance of the State's purpose of fostering "old notions" of role typing and preparing boys for their expected performance in the economic and political worlds. 421 U.S., at 14-15.[6]
>
> *Reed v. Reed* has also provided the underpinning for decisions that have invalidated statutes employing gender as an inaccurate proxy for other, more germane bases of classification. Hence, "archaic and overbroad" generalizations, *Schlesinger v. Ballard, supra,* at 508, concerning the financial position of service-women, *Frontiero v. Richardson, supra,* at 689 n. 23, and working women, *Weinberger v. Wiesenfeld,* 420 U.S. 636, 643 (1975), could not justify use of a gender line in determining eligibility for certain governmental entitlements. Similarly, increasingly outdated misconceptions concerning the role of females in the home rather than in the "marketplace and world of ideas" were rejected as loose-fitting characterizations incapable of supporting state statutory schemes that were premised upon their accuracy. *Stanton v. Stanton, supra; Taylor v. Louisiana,* 419 U.S. 522, 535 n. 17 (1975). In light of the weak congruence between gender and the characteristic or trait that gender purported to represent, it was necessary that the legislatures choose either to realign their substantive laws in a gender-neutral fashion, or to adopt procedures for identifying those instances where the sex-centered generalization

---

[6] *Kahn v. Shevin,* 416 U.S. 351 (1974) and *Schlesinger v. Ballard,* 419 U.S. 498 (1975), upholding the use of gender-based classifications, rested upon the Court's perception of the laudatory purposes of those laws as remedying disadvantageous conditions suffered by women in economic and military life. See 416 U.S., at 353-354; 419 U.S., at 508. Needless to say, in this case Oklahoma does not suggest that the age-sex differential was enacted to ensure the availability of 3.2% beer for women as compensation for previous deprivations.

actually comported to fact. See, e.g., *Stanley v. Illinois, supra,* at 658; cf. *Cleveland Board of Education v. LaFleur,* 414 U.S. 632, 650 (1974).

2. In *Geduldig v. Aiello,* 417 U.S. 484, 496-97 n.20 (1974), the Court upheld the constitutionality of a California disability insurance program that excluded coverage for pregnancy in order to maintain the self-supporting nature of the insurance program. The Court distinguished *Reed* and *Frontiero* in a footnote:

> The dissenting opinion to the contrary, this case is thus a far cry from cases like *Reed v. Reed,* 404 U.S. 71 (1971), and *Frontiero v. Richardson,* 411 U.S. 677 (1973), involving discrimination based upon gender as such. The California insurance program does not exclude anyone from benefit eligibility because of gender but merely removes one physical condition — pregnancy — from the list of compensable disabilities. While it is true that only women can become pregnant, it does not follow that every legislative classification concerning pregnancy is a sex-based classification like those considered in *Reed, supra,* and *Frontiero, supra.* Normal pregnancy is an objectively identifiable physical condition with unique characteristics. Absent a showing that distinctions involving pregnancy are mere pretexts designed to effect an invidious discrimination against the members of one sex or the other, lawmakers are constitutionally free to include or exclude pregnancy from the coverage of legislation such as this on any reasonable basis, just as with respect to any other physical condition.
>
> The lack of identity between the excluded disability and gender as such under this insurance program becomes clear upon the most cursory analysis. The program divides potential recipients into two groups — pregnant women and nonpregnant persons. While the first group is exclusively female, the second includes members of both sexes. The fiscal and actuarial benefits of the program thus accrue to members of both sexes.

DAVIS v. PASSMAN

442 U.S. 228, 99 S. Ct. 2264, 60 L. Ed. 2d 846 (1979)

JUSTICE BRENNAN delivered the opinion of the Court.

Bivens v. Six Unknown Fed. Narcotics Agents, 403 U.S. 388 (1971), held that a "cause of action for damages" arises under the Constitution when Fourth Amendment rights are violated. The issue presented for decision in this case is whether a cause of action and a damages remedy can also be implied directly under the Constitution when the Due Process Clause of the Fifth Amendment is violated. The Court of Appeals for the Fifth Circuit, en banc, concluded that "no civil action for damages" can be thus implied. 571 F.2d 793, 801 (1978). We granted certiorari, 439 U.S. 925 (1978), and we now reverse.

I

At the time this case commenced, respondent Otto E. Passman was a United States Congressman from the Fifth Congressional District of Louisiana. On February 1, 1974, Passman hired petitioner Shirley Davis as a deputy administrative assistant. Passman subsequently terminated her employment, effective July 31, 1974, writing Davis that, although she was an "able, energetic and a very hard worker," he had concluded "that it was essential that the understudy to my Administrative Assistant be a man."[3] App. at 6.

Davis brought suit in the United States District Court for the Western District of Louisiana, alleging that Passman's conduct discriminated against her "on the basis of sex in violation of the United States Constitution and the Fifth Amendment thereto." Id., at 4. Davis sought damages in the form of backpay. Id., at 5.[4] Jurisdiction for her suit was founded on 28 U.S.C. § 1331(a), which provides in pertinent part that federal "district courts shall have original jurisdiction of all civil actions wherein the matter in controversy exceeds the sum or value of $10,000 ... and arises under the Constitution ... of the United States ...."

Passman moved to dismiss Davis' action for failure to state a claim upon which relief can be granted, Fed. Rule Civ. Proc. 12(b)(6), arguing, inter alia, that "the law affords no private right of action" for her claim.[5] App. 8. The District Court accepted this argument, ruling that Davis had "no private right of action." Id., at 9.[6] A panel of the Court of Appeals for the Fifth Circuit reversed. 544 F.2d 865 (1977). The panel concluded that a cause of action for damages arose directly under the Fifth Amendment; that, taking as true the allegations

---

[3] The full text of Passman's letter is as follows:

Dear Mrs. Davis:

My Washington staff joins me in saying that we miss you very much. But, in all probability, inwardly they all agree that I was doing you an injustice by asking you to assume a responsibility that was so trying and so hard that it would have taken all of the pleasure out of your work. I must be completely fair with you, so please note the following:

You are able, energetic and a very hard worker. Certainly you command the respect of those with whom you work; however, on account of the unusually heavy work load in my Washington Office, and the diversity of the job, I concluded that it was essential that the understudy to my Administrative Assistant be a man. I believe you will agree with this conclusion.

It would be unfair to you for me to ask you to waste your talent and experience in my Monroe office because of the low salary that is available because of a junior position. Therefore, and so that your experience and talent may be used to advantage in some organization in need of an extremely capable secretary, I desire that you be continued on the payroll at your present salary through July 31, 1974. This arrangement gives you your full year's vacation of one month, plus one additional month. May I further say that the work load in the Monroe office is very limited, and since you would come in as a junior member of the staff at such a low salary, it would actually be an offense to you.

I know that secretaries with your ability are very much in demand in Monroe. If an additional letter of recommendation from me would be advantageous to you, do not hesitate to let me know. Again, assuring you that my Washington staff and your humble Congressman feel that the contribution you made to our Washington office has helped all of us.

With best wishes.

Sincerely,
/s/Otto E. Passman
OTTO E. PASSMAN
Member of Congress

App., at 6-7.

[4] Davis also sought equitable relief in the form of reinstatement, as well as a promotion and salary increase. App., at 4-5. Since Passman is no longer a Congressman, however, these forms of relief are no longer available.

[5] Passman also argued that his alleged conduct was "not violative of the Fifth Amendment to the Constitution," and that relief was barred "by reason of the sovereign immunity doctrine and the official immunity doctrine." App. 8.

[6] The District Court also ruled that, although "the doctrines of sovereign and official immunity" did not justify dismissal of Davis' complaint, "the discharge of plaintiff on alleged grounds of sex discrimination by defendant is not violative of the Fifth Amendment to the Constitution." Id., at 9.

in Davis' complaint, Passman's conduct violated the Fifth Amendment; and that Passman's conduct was not shielded by the Speech or Debate Clause of the Constitution, Art. 1, § 6, cf. 1.[7]

The Court of Appeals for the Fifth Circuit, sitting en banc, reversed the decision of the panel. The en banc Court did not reach the merits, nor did it discuss the application of the Speech or Debate Clause. The Court instead held that "no right of action may be implied from the Due Process Clause of the fifth amendment." 571 F.2d, at 801. The Court reached this conclusion on the basis of the criteria that had been set out in *Cort v. Ash,* 422 U.S. 66 (1975), for determining whether a private cause of action should be implied from a federal statute.[8] Noting that Congress had failed to create a damages remedy for those in Davis' position, the Court also concluded that "the proposed damage remedy is not constitutionally compelled" so that it was not necessary to "countermand the clearly discernible will of Congress" and create such a remedy. 571 F.2d, at 800.

II

In *Bivens v. Six Unknown Fed. Narcotics Agents,* federal agents had allegedly arrested and searched Bivens without probable cause, thereby subjecting him to great humiliation, embarrassment, and mental suffering. *Bivens* held that the Fourth Amendment guarantee against "unreasonable searches and seizures" was a constitutional right which Bivens could enforce through a private cause of action, and that a damages remedy was an appropriate form of redress. Last Term, *Butz v. Economou,* 438 U.S. 478 (1978), reaffirmed this holding, stating that "the decision in *Bivens* established that a citizen suffering a compensable injury to a constitutionally protected interest could invoke the general federal-

---

[7] The panel also held that, although sovereign immunity did not bar a damages award against Passman individually, he was entitled at trial to a defense of qualified immunity.

[8] The criteria set out in *Cort v. Ash* are:

"First, is the plaintiff 'one of the class for whose *especial* benefit the statute was enacted,' *Texas & Pacific R. Co. v. Rigsby,* 241 U.S. 33, 39 (1916) (emphasis supplied) — that is does the statute create a federal right in favor of the plaintiff? Second, is there any indication of legislative intent, explicit or implicit, either to create such a remedy or to deny one? See, e.g., *National Railroad Passenger Corp. v. National Assn. of Railroad Passengers,* 414 U.S. 453, 458, 460 (1974) (*Amtrak*). Third, is it consistent with the underlying purposes of the legislative scheme to imply such a remedy for the plaintiff? See, e.g., *Amtrak, supra; Securities Investor Protection Corp. v. Barbour,* 421 U.S. 412, 423 (1975); *Calhoon v. Harvey,* 379 U.S. 134 (1964). And finally, is the cause of action one traditionally relegated to state law, in an area basically the concern of the States, so that it would be inappropriate to infer a cause of action based solely on federal law? See *Wheeldin v. Wheeler,* 373 U.S. 647, 652 (1963); cf. *J. I. Case Co. v. Borak,* 377 U.S. 426, 434 (1964); *Bivens v. Six Unknown Federal Narcotics Agents,* 403 U.S. 388, 394-395 (1971); *id.,* at 400 (Harlan, J., concurring in judgment)." 422 U.S., at 78.

The Court of Appeals had some difficulty applying these criteria to determine whether a cause of action should be implied under the Constitution. It eventually concluded, however, (1) that although "the fifth amendment right to due process certainly confers a right upon Davis, the injury alleged here does not infringe this right as directly as" the violation of the Fourth Amendment rights alleged in *Bivens,* 571 F.2d, at 797; (2) that "[c]ongressional remedial legislation for employment discrimination has carefully avoided creating a cause of action for money damages for one in Davis' position," *id.,* at 798; (3) that, unlike violations of the Fourth Amendment, "the breadth of the concept of due process indicates that the damage remedy sought will not be judicially manageable," *id.,* at 799; and (4) that implying a cause of action under the Due Process Clause would create "the danger of deluging federal courts with claims otherwise redressable in state courts or administrative proceedings ...." *Id.,* at 800.

question jurisdiction of the district courts to obtain an award of monetary damages against the responsible federal official." *Id.,* at 504.

Today we hold that *Bivens* and *Butz* require reversal of the holding of the en banc Court of Appeals. Our inquiry proceeds in three stages. We hold first that, pretermitting the question whether respondent's conduct is shielded by the Speech or Debate Clause, petitioner asserts a constitutionally protected right; second, that petitioner has stated a cause of action which asserts this right; and third, that relief in damages constitutes an appropriate form of remedy.

A. The Fifth Amendment provides that "[n]o person shall be ... deprived of life, liberty, or property, without due process of law ...." In numerous decisions, this Court "has held that the Due Process Clause of the Fifth Amendment forbids the Federal Government to deny equal protection of the laws. E.g., *Hampton v. Mow Sun Wong,* 426 U.S. 88, 100 (1976); *Buckley v. Valeo,* 424 U.S. 1, 93 (1976); *Weinberger v. Wiesenfeld,* 420 U.S. 636, 638 n. 2 (1975); *Bolling v. Sharpe,* 347 U.S. 497, 500 (1954)." *Vance v. Bradley,* 440 U.S. 93, 95 n. 1 (1979). "To withstand scrutiny under the equal protection component of the Fifth Amendment's Due Process Clause, 'classifications by gender must serve important governmental objectives and must be substantially related to achievement of those objectives.' *Craig v. Boren,* 429 U.S. 190, 197 (1976)."[9] *Califano v. Webster,* 430 U.S. 313, 316-317 (1977). The Equal Protection Component of the Due Process Clause thus confers on petitioner a federal constitutional right[10] to be free from gender discrimination which cannot meet these requirements.[11] We inquire next whether petitioner has a cause of action to assert this right.

---

[9]Before it can be determined whether petitioner's Fifth Amendment right has been violated, therefore, inquiry must be undertaken into what "important governmental objectives," if any, are served by the gender-based employment of congressional staff. We express no views as to the outcome of this inquiry.

[10]This right is personal; it is petitioner, after all, who must suffer the effects of such discrimination. See *Cannon v. University of Chicago,* 441 U.S. 677, 690-693, n. 13 (1979); cf. *Monongahela Navigation Co. v. United States,* 148 U.S. 312, 326 (1893).

[11]Respondent argues that the subject matter of petitioner's suit is nonjusticiable because judicial review of congressional employment decisions would necessarily involve a "lack of the respect due coordinate branches of government." *Baker v. Carr,* 369 U.S. 186, 217 (1962). We disagree. While we acknowledge the gravity of respondent's concerns, we hold that judicial review of congressional employment decisions is constitutionally limited only by the reach of the Speech or Debate Clause of the Constitution, Art. I, § 6, cl. 1. The Clause provides that Senators and Representatives, "for any Speech or Debate in either House, ... shall not be questioned in any other Place." It protects Congressmen for conduct necessary to perform their duties "within the 'sphere of legitimate legislative activity.'" *Eastland v. United States Servicemen's Fund,* 421 U.S. 491, 501 (1975). The purpose of the Clause is "to protect the integrity of the legislative process by insuring the independence of individual legislators." *United States v. Brewster,* 408 U.S. 501, 507 (1972). Thus "[i]n the American governmental structure the clause serves the ... function of reinforcing the separation of powers so deliberately established by the Founders. " *United States v. Johnson,* 383 U.S. 169, 178 (1966). The Clause is therefore a paradigm example of "a textually demonstrable constitutional commitment of [an] issue in a coordinate political department." *Baker v. Carr, supra,* at 217. Since the Speech or Debate Clause speaks so directly to the separation of powers concerns raised by respondent, we conclude that if respondent is not shielded by the Clause, the question whether his dismissal of petitioner violated her Fifth Amendment rights would, as we stated in *Powell v. McCormack,* 395 U.S. 486, 548-549 (1969), "require no more than an interpretation of the Constitution. Such a determination falls within the traditional role accorded courts to interpret the law, and does not involve a 'lack of respect due [a] coordinate branch of government,' nor does it involve an 'initial policy determination of a kind clearly for non-judicial discretion.' *Baker v. Carr,* 369 U.S. 186, at 217."

B. It is clear that the District Court had jurisdiction under 28 U.S.C., § 1331(a) to consider petitioner's claim. *Bell v. Hood,* 327 U.S. 678 (1946). It is equally clear, and the en banc Court of Appeals so held, that the Fifth Amendment confers on petitioner a constitutional right to be free from illegal discrimination.[12] Yet the Court of Appeals concluded that petitioner could not enforce this right because she lacked a cause of action. The meaning of this missing "cause of action," however, is far from apparent....[16]

In cases such as these, the question is which class of litigants may enforce in court legislatively created rights or obligations. If a litigant is an appropriate party to invoke the power of the courts, it is said that he has a "cause of action" under the statute, and that this cause of action is a necessary element of his "claim." So understood, the question whether a litigant has a "cause of action" is analytically distinct and prior to the question of what relief, if any, a litigant may be entitled to receive. The concept of a "cause of action" is employed specifically to determine who may judicially enforce the statutory rights or obligations.[18]

It is in this sense that the Court of Appeals concluded that petitioner lacked a cause of action. The Court of Appeals reached this conclusion through the application of the criteria set out in *Cort v. Ash,* 422 U.S. 66 (1975), for ascertaining whether a private cause of action may be implied from "a statute not expressly providing one." *Id.,* at 78. The Court of Appeals used these criteria to

---

The en banc Court of Appeals did not decide whether the conduct of respondent was shielded by the Speech or Debate Clause. In the absence of such a decision, we also intimate no view on the question. We note, however, that the Clause shields federal legislators with absolute immunity "not only from the consequences of litigation's results, but also from the burden of defending themselves." *Dombrowski v. Eastland,* 387 U.S. 82, 82 (1967). Defenses based upon the Clause should thus ordinarily be given priority, since federal legislatures should be exempted from litigation if their conduct is in fact protected by the Clause. We nevertheless decline to remand this case to the en banc Court of Appeals before we have decided whether petitioner's complaint states a cause of action, and whether a damages remedy is an appropriate form of relief. These questions are otherwise properly before us and may be resolved without imposing on respondent additional litigative burdens. Refusal to decide them at this time may actually increase these burdens.

[12] The restraints of the Fifth Amendment reach far enough to embrace the official actions of a Congressman in hiring and dismissing his employees. That respondent's conduct may have been illegal does not suffice to transform it into merely private action. "[P]ower, once granted, does not disappear like a magic gift when it is wrongfully used." *Bivens, supra,* at 392. See *Home Tel. & Tel. Co. v. Los Angeles,* 227 U.S. 278, 287-289 (1913).

[16] The Court of Appeals apparently found that petitioner lacked a "cause of action" in the sense that a cause of action would have been supplied by 42 U.S.C. § 1983. *Chapman v. Houston Welfare Rights Org.,* 441 U.S. 600 (1979), holds this Term that, although § 1983 serves "to ensure that an individual [has] a cause of action for violations of the Constitution," the statute itself "does not provide any substantive rights at all." *Id.,* at 617, 618. Section 1983, of course, provides a cause of action only for deprivations of constitutional rights that occur "under color of any statute, ordinance, regulation, custom, or usage, of any State or Territory," and thus has no application to this case. [Footnote [16] relocated from original position. — Ed.]

[18] Thus it may be said that *jurisdiction* is a question of whether a federal court has the power, under the Constitution or laws of the United States, to hear a case, see *Mansfield, C. & L.M.R. Co. v. Swan,* 111 U.S. 379, 384 (1884); *Montana-Dakota Utilities Co. v. Northwestern Public Serv. Co.,* 341 U.S. 246, 249 (1951); *standing* is a question of whether a plaintiff is sufficiently adversary to a defendant to create an Art. III case or controversy, or at least to overcome prudential limitations on federal court jurisdiction, see *Warth v. Seldin,* 422 U.S. 490, 498 (1975); cause of action is a question of whether a particular plaintiff is a member of the class of litigants that may, as a matter of law, appropriately invoke the power of the court; and *relief* is a question of the various remedies a federal court may make available. A plaintiff may have a cause of action even though he be entitled to no relief at all, as, for example, when a plaintiff sues for declaratory or injunctive relief although his case does not fulfill the "preconditions" for such equitable remedies. See *Trainor v. Hernandez,* 431 U.S. 434, 440-443 (1977)....

determine that those in petitioner's position should not be able to enforce the Fifth Amendment's Due Process Clause, and that petitioner therefore had no cause of action under the Amendment. This was error, for the question of who may enforce a *statutory* right is fundamentally different than the question of who may enforce a right that is protected by the Constitution.

Statutory rights and obligations are established by Congress, and it is entirely appropriate for Congress, in creating these rights and obligations, to determine in addition who may enforce them and in what manner....

The Constitution on the other hand does not "partake of the prolixity of a legal code." *McCulloch v. Maryland,* 4 Wheat. 316, 407 (1819). It speaks instead with a majestic simplicity. One of "its important objects," *ibid.,* is the designation of rights. And in "its great outlines," *ibid.,* the judiciary is clearly discernible as the primary means through which these rights may be enforced....

At least in the absence of "a textually demonstrable constitutional commitment of [an] issue to a coordinate political department," *Baker v. Carr,* 369 U.S. 186, 217, we presume that justiciable constitutional rights are to be enforced through the courts. And, unless such rights are to become merely precatory, the class of those litigants who allege that their own constitutional rights have been violated, and who at the same time have no effective means other than the judiciary to enforce these rights, must be able to invoke the existing jurisdiction of the courts for the protection of their justiciable constitutional rights.... Indeed, this Court has already settled that a cause of action may be implied directly under the Equal Protection Component of the Due Process Clause of the Fifth Amendment in favor of those who seek to enforce his constitutional right. The plaintiffs in *Bolling v. Sharpe,* 347 U.S. 497 (1954), for example, claimed that they had been refused admission into certain public schools in the District of Columbia solely on account of their race. They rested their suit directly on the Fifth Amendment and on the general federal question jurisdiction of the district courts, 28 U.S.C. § 1331. The District Court dismissed their complaint for failure "to state a claim upon which relief can be granted." Fed. Rule Civ. Proc. 12(b)(6). This Court reversed. Plaintiffs were clearly the appropriate parties to bring such a suit, and this Court held that equitable relief should be made available. 349 U.S. 294 (1955).

Like the plaintiffs in *Bolling v. Sharpe, supra,* petitioner rests her claim directly on the Due Process Clause of the Fifth Amendment. She claims that her rights under the Amendment have been violated, and that she has no effective means other than the judiciary to vindicate these rights. We conclude, therefore, that she is an appropriate party to invoke the general federal question jurisdiction of the District Court to seek relief. She has a cause of action under the Fifth Amendment.

Although petitioner has a cause of action, her complaint might nevertheless be dismissed under Rule 12(b)(6) unless it can be determined that judicial relief is available. We therefore proceed to consider whether a damages remedy is an appropriate form of relief.

C. We approach this inquiry on the basis of established law. "[I]t is ... well settled that where legal rights have been invaded, and a federal statute provides for a general right to sue for such invasion, federal courts may use any available remedy to make good the wrong done." *Bell v. Hood,* 327 U.S., at 684. *Bivens,*

403 U.S., at 396, holds that in appropriate circumstances a federal district court may provide relief in damages for the violation of constitutional rights if there are "no special factors counselling hesitation in the absence of affirmative action by Congress." See *Butz v. Economou,* 438 U.S., at 504.

First, a damages remedy is surely appropriate in this case. "Historically, damages have been regarded as the ordinary remedy for an invasion of personal interests in liberty." *Bivens, supra,* at 395. Relief in damages would be judicially manageable, for the case presents a focused remedial issue without difficult questions of valuation or causation. See 403 U.S., at 409 (Harlan, J., concurring in judgment). Litigation under Title VII of the Civil Rights Act of 1964 has given federal courts great experience evaluating claims for backpay due to illegal sex discrimination. See 42 U.S.C. § 2000e-5(g). Moreover, since respondent is no longer a Congressman, see n. 1, *supra,* equitable relief in the form of reinstatement would be unavailing. And there are available no other alternative forms of judicial relief. For Davis, as for Bivens, "it is damages or nothing." *Bivens, supra,* at 410 (Harlan, J., concurring in judgment).

Second, although a suit against a Congressman for putatively unconstitutional actions taken in the course of his official conduct does raise special concerns counselling hesitation, we hold that these concerns are coextensive with the protections afforded by the Speech or Debate Clause.[24] *See* n. 11, *supra.* If respondent's actions are not shielded by the Clause, we apply the principle that "legislators ought ... generally to be bound by [the law] as are ordinary persons." *Gravel v. United States,* 408 U.S. 606, 615 (1972). Cf. *Doe v. McMillan,* 412 U.S. 306, 320 (1973). As *Butz v. Economou* stated only last Term:

> "Our system of jurisprudence rests on the assumption that all individuals, whatever their position in government, are subject to federal law:
> "'No man in this country is so high that he is above the law. No officer of the law may set that law at defiance with impunity. All officers of the government, from the highest to the lowest, are creatures of the law, and are bound to obey it.' *United States v. Lee,* 106 U.S. [196,] 220 [(1882)]." 438 U.S., at 506.[25]

Third, there is in this case "no *explicit* congressional declaration that persons" in petitioner's position injured by unconstitutional federal employment discrimination "may not recover money damages from" those responsible for the injury. *Bivens, supra,* at 397. (Emphasis supplied.) The Court of Appeals apparently interpreted § 717 of Title VII of the Civil Rights Act of 1964, 86 Stat. 111, 42 U.S.C. § 2000e-16, as an explicit congressional prohibition against judicial remedies for those in petitioner's position. When § 717 was added to Title VII to protect federal employees from discrimination, it failed to extend this protection to congressional employees such as petitioner who are not in the competi-

---

[24] The reasoning and holding of *Bivens* is pertinent to the determination whether a federal court may provide a damages remedy. The question of the appropriateness of equitable relief in the form of reinstatement is not in this case, and we consequently intimate no view on that question.

[25] The decision of the panel of the Court of Appeals for the Fifth Circuit found that respondent was not foreclosed "from asserting the same qualified immunity available to other government officials. See generally *Wood v. Strickland,* 420 U.S. 308 (1975); *Scheuer v. Rhodes,* 416 U.S. 232 (1974)." 544 F.2d, at 881. The en banc Court of Appeals did not reach this issue, and accordingly we express no view concerning the disposition by the panel.

tive service.[26] See 42 U.S.C. § 2000-16 (a). There is no evidence, however, that Congress meant § 717 to foreclose alternative remedies available to those not covered by the statute. Such silence is far from "the clearly discernible will of Congress" perceived by the Court of Appeals. 571 F.2d, at 800. Indeed, the Court of Appeals' conclusion that § 717 permits judicial relief to be made available only to those who are protected by the statute is patently inconsistent with *Hampton v. Mow Sun Wong,* 426 U.S. 88 (1976), which held that equitable relief was available in a challenge to the constitutionality of Civil Service Commission regulations excluding aliens from federal employment. That § 717 does not prohibit discrimination on the basis of alienage[27] did not prevent *Hampton* from authorizing relief. In a similar manner, we do not now interpret § 717 to foreclose the judicial remedies of those expressly unprotected by the statute. On the contrary, § 717 leaves undisturbed whatever remedies petitioner might otherwise possess.

Finally, the Court of Appeals appeared concerned that, if a damages remedy were made available to petitioner, the danger existed "of deluging federal courts with claims ...." 571 F.2d, at 800. We do not perceive the potential for such a deluge. By virtue of 42 U.S.C. § 1983, a damages remedy is already available to redress injuries such as petitioner's when they occur under color of state law. Moreover, a plaintiff seeking a damages remedy under the Constitution must first demonstrate that his constitutional rights have been violated. We do not hold that every tort by a federal official may be redressed in damages. See *Wheeldin v. Wheeler,* 373 U.S. 647 (1963). And, of course, were Congress to create equally effective alternative remedies, the need for damages relief might be obviated. See *Bivens,* 403 U.S., at 397. But perhaps the most fundamental answer to the concerns expressed by the Court of Appeals is that provided by Justice Harlan concurring in *Bivens:*

> "Judicial resources, I am well aware, are increasingly scarce these days. Nonetheless, when we automatically close the courthouse door solely on this basis, we implicitly express a value judgment on the comparative importance of classes of legally protected interests. And current limitations upon the effective functioning of the courts arising from budgetary inadequacies should not be permitted to stand in the way of the recognition of otherwise sound constitutional principles." *Id.,* at 411.

We conclude, therefore, that in this case, as in *Bivens,* if petitioner is able to prevail on the merits, she should be able to redress her injury in damages, a "remedial mechanism normally available in the federal courts." *Id.,* at 397.

III

We hold today that the Court of Appeals for the Fifth Circuit, en banc, must be reversed because petitioner has a cause of action under the Fifth Amendment, and because her injury may be redressed by a damages remedy. The

---

[26] Since petitioner was not in the competitive service, the remedial provisions of § 717 of Title VII are not available to her. In *Brown v. GSA,* 425 U.S. 820 (1976), we held that the remedies provided in § 717 are exclusive when those federal employees covered by the statute seek to redress the violation of rights guaranteed by the statute.

[27] Section 717 prohibits discrimination on the basis of "race, color, religion, sex, or national origin." 42 U.S.C. § 2000-16(a).

Court of Appeals did not consider however, whether respondent's conduct was shielded by the Speech or Debate Clause of the Constitution. Accordingly, we do not reach this question. And, of course, we express no opinion as to the merits of petitioner's complaint.

The judgment of the Court of Appeals is reversed and the case is remanded for further proceedings consistent with this opinion.

So ordered.

CHIEF JUSTICE BURGER, with whom JUSTICE POWELL and JUSTICE REHNQUIST join, dissenting.

I dissent because, for me, the case presents very grave questions of separation of powers, rather than Speech or Debate Clause issues, although the two have certain common roots. Congress could, of course, make *Bivens*-type remedies available to its staff employees — and to other congressional employees — but it has not done so. On the contrary. Congress has historically treated its employees differently from the arrangements for other Government employees. Historically, staffs of Members have been considered so intimately a part of the policy-making and political process that they are not subject to being selected, compensated or tenured as others who serve the Government. The vulnerability of employment on congressional staffs derives not only from the hazards of elections but from the imperative need for loyalty, confidentiality and political compatibility — not to a political party, an institution, or an administration, but to the individual Member.

A Member of Congress has a right to expect that every person on his or her staff will give total loyalty to the political positions of the Member, total confidentiality and total support. This may, on occasion, lead a Member to employ a particular person on a racial, ethnic, religious, or gender basis thought to be acceptable to the constituency represented, even though in other branches of government — or in the private sector — such selection factors might be prohibited. This might lead a Member to decide that a particular staff position should be filled by a Catholic or a Presbyterian or a Mormon, a Mexican-American or an Oriental-American — or a woman rather than a man. Presidents consciously select — and dispense with — their appointees on this basis and have done so since the beginning of the Republic. The very commission of a Presidential appointee defines the tenure as "during the pleasure of the President."

Although Congress altered the ancient "spoils system" as to the Executive Branch and prescribed standards for some limited segments of the Judicial Branch, it has allowed its own Members, Presidents, and Judges to select their personal staffs without limit or restraint — in practical effect their tenure is "during the pleasure" of the Member.

At this level of government — staff assistants of Members — long-accepted concepts of separation of powers dictate, for me, that until Congress legislates otherwise as to employment standards for its own staffs, judicial power in this area is circumscribed. The Court today encroaches on that barrier. Cf. *Sinking-Fund Cases,* 99 U.S. 700, 718 (1878)....

[Dissenting opinions of Stewart, J., concurred in by Rehnquist, J., and of Powell, J., concurred in by Burger, C.J., and Rehnquist, J., are omitted.]

NOTES

1. In *Walker v. Jones,* 733 F.2d 923, 1097 (D.C. Cir., *cert. denied,* 469 U.S. 1036 (1984), the court considered the issue that was not resolved in *Passman,* and it held that a congressman's allegedly discriminatory termination of a congressional worker who only performed auxiliary, nonlegislative services (manager of House restaurant system) did not fall within the scope of the immunity provided by the speech or debate clause. The court reserved the question regarding the immunity that might be available with respect to the hiring and firing of congressional staff members who do have "meaningful input" into legislative decisionmaking.

In *Browning v. Clerk, House of Representatives,* 789 F.2d 923 (D.C. Cir.), *cert. denied,* 479 U.S. 996 (1986), the court distinguished *Walker v. Jones,* as it determined that the speech or debate clause barred a suit filed under the fifth amendment due process clause by a former official reporter of House proceedings who claimed to have been terminated because of her race. The court noted that House reporters who prepare verbatim transcripts of House proceedings are very different from House restaurant employees, since reporters perform a role that is an "integral part" of the legislative process. "[T]he standard for determining Speech or Debate Clause immunity is ... whether the employee's duties were directly related to the due functioning of the legislative process.... There can be little doubt that Browning's duties as an official reporter were directly related to the legislative process." Compare *Forrester v. White,* 484 U.S. 219 (1988) (no absolute judicial immunity for judge who discriminatorily terminated female probation officer, since work of probation officer does not meaningfully implicate judicial decision-making process).

2. Where a government employee is discharged as a result of her request for information concerning the scope of her employer's arguably discriminatory maternity leave policy, she may be entitled to first amendment protection. See *Hanson v. Hoffman,* 628 F.2d 42 (D.C. Cir. 1980).

3. Does the equal protection clause require state and local governments to provide employees in traditionally female occupations with wages equal to those paid by them for traditionally male occupations that, while not being substantially equal in job content, are found to be of "comparable worth"? See *Lemons v. City of Denver,* 620 F.2d 228 (10th Cir.), *cert. denied,* 449 U.S. 888 (1980).

4. *Trigg v. Ft. Wayne Schs.,* 766 F.2d 299 (7th Cir. 1985), held that a black female who claimed that she had been harassed and discharged because her employer did not like to work with black women could sue her former public employer under 42 U.S.C. § 1983. *Bohen v. City of East Chicago,* 799 F.2d 1180 (7th Cir. 1986), similarly recognized the right of a female employee who was the victim of "general, on-going, and accepted" sexual harassment from her co-workers and her supervisors to sue her public employer under the fourteenth amendment for intentional gender discrimination. In *Poe v. Haydon,* 853 F.2d 418 (6th Cir. 1988), *cert. denied,* 109 S. Ct. 788 (1989), the court held that section 1983 liability could not be imposed upon supervisors who were merely aware of sexual harassment and failed to take appropriate corrective action. The plaintiff must show that such supervisors either actively participated in or authorized the harassment.

3. RELIGION

GOLDMAN V. WEINBERGER

475 U.S. 503, 106 S. Ct. 1310, 89 L. Ed. 2d 478 (1986)

[This case involved an Air Force officer who was a clinical psychologist and an Orthodox Jew. Air Force Regulation (AFR) 35-10 provides that "[h]eadgear will not be worn ... [w]hile indoors except by armed security police in the performance of their duties." When this regulation was interpreted to preclude Goldman from wearing his religious yarmulke while he was working in the base hospital, he challenged that interpretation under the free exercise clause of the first amendment.]

REHNQUIST, J. delivered the opinion of the court....

Petitioner argues that AFR 35-10, as applied to him, prohibits religiously motivated conduct and should therefore be analyzed under the standard enunciated in *Sherbert v. Verner,* 374 U.S. 398, 406 (1963). See also *Thomas v. Review Board,* 450 U.S. 707 (1981); *Wisconsin v. Yoder,* 406 U.S. 205 (1972). But we have repeatedly held that "the military is, by necessity, a specialized society separate from civilian society." *Parker v. Levy,* 417 U.S. 733, 743 (1974). See also *Chappell v. Wallace,* 462 U.S. 296, 300 (1983); *Schlesinger v. Councilman,* 420 U.S. 738, 757 (1975); *Orloff v. Willoughby,* 345 U.S. 83, 94 (1953). "[T]he military must insist upon a respect for duty and a discipline without counterpart in civilian life," *Schlesinger v. Councilman, supra,* at 757, in order to prepare for and perform its vital role. See also *Brown v. Glines,* 444 U.S. 348, 354 (1980).

Our review of military regulations challenged on First Amendment grounds is far more deferential than constitutional review of similar laws or regulations designed for civilian society. The military need not encourage debate or tolerate protest to the extent that such tolerance is required of the civilian state by the First Amendment; to accomplish its mission the military must foster instinctive obedience, unity, commitment, and esprit de corps. See, e.g., *Chappell v. Wallace, supra,* at 300; *Greer v. Spock,* 424 U.S. 828, 843-844 (1976) (POWELL, J., concurring); *Parker v. Levy, supra,* at 744. The essence of military service "is the subordination of the desires and interests of the individual to the needs of the service." *Orloff v. Willoughby, supra,* at 92.

These aspects of military life do not, of course, render entirely nugatory in the military context the guarantees of the First Amendment. See, e.g., *Chappell v. Wallace, supra,* at 304. But "within the military community there is simply not the same [individual] autonomy as there is in the larger civilian community." *Parker v. Levy, supra,* at 751. In the context of the present case, when evaluating whether military needs justify a particular restriction on religiously motivated conduct, courts must give great deference to the professional judgment of military authorities concerning the relative importance of a particular military interest. See *Chappell v. Wallace, supra,* at 305; *Orloff v. Willoughby, supra,* 93-94. Not only are courts "ill-equipped to determine the impact upon discipline that any particular intrusion upon military authority might have,'" *Chappell v. Wallace, supra,* at 305, quoting Warren, The Bill of Rights and the Military, 37 N.Y.U. L. Rev. 181, 187 (1962), but the military authorities have been charged by the Executive and Legislative Branches with carrying out our

Nation's military policy. "Judicial deference ... is at its apogee when legislative action under the congressional authority to raise and support armies and make rules and regulations for their governance is challenged." *Rostker v. Goldberg,* 453 U.S. 57, 70 (1981)....

Petitioner Goldman contends that the Free Exercise Clause of the First Amendment requires the Air Force to make an exception to its uniform dress requirements for religious apparel unless the accoutrements create a "clear danger" of undermining discipline and esprit de corps. He asserts that in general, visible but "unobtrusive" apparel will not create such a danger and must therefore be accommodated. He argues that the Air Force failed to prove that a specific exception for his practice of wearing an unobtrusive yarmulke would threaten discipline. He contends that the Air Force's assertion to the contrary is mere *ipse dixit,* with no support from actual experience or a scientific study in the record, and is contradicted by expert testimony that religious exceptions to AFR 35-10 are in fact desirable and will increase morale by making the Air Force a more humane place.

But whether or not expert witnesses may feel that religious exceptions to AFR 35-10 are desirable is quite beside the point. The desirability of dress regulations in the military is decided by the appropriate military officials, and they are under no constitutional mandate to abandon their considered professional judgment. Quite obviously, to the extent the regulations do not permit the wearing of religious apparel such as yarmulke, a practice described by petitioner as silent devotion akin to prayer, military life may be more objectionable for petitioner and probably others. But the First Amendment does not require the military to accommodate such practices in the face of its view that they would detract from the uniformity sought by the dress regulations. The Air Force has drawn the line essentially between religious apparel which is visible and that which is not, and we hold that those portions of the regulations challenged here reasonably and evenhandedly regulate dress in the interest of the military's perceived need for uniformity. The First Amendment therefore does not prohibit them from being applied to petitioner even though their effect is to restrict the wearing of the headgear required by his religious beliefs.

NOTES

1. *Cooper v. Eugene Sch. Dist. No. 4J,* 723 P.2d 298 (Or. 1986), *appeal dismissed for want of substantial federal question,* 480 U.S. 942 (1987), determined that the revocation of Ms. Cooper's state teaching certificate because she had violated a religious dress statute by wearing Sikh religious garb — white clothes and turban — in her sixth and eighth grade classes did not violate her free exercise rights. The court found that the revocation was based upon conduct by Ms. Cooper that was incompatible with her teaching function and was not a "sanction" evidencing hostility toward her exercise of religious beliefs.

2. It violates the free exercise clause for states to deny unemployment benefits to persons whose religious convictions preclude their acceptance of Saturday work. *Sherbert v. Verner,* 374 U.S. 398 (1963); *Hobbie v. Florida Unemp. Appeals Comm'n,* 480 U.S. 136 (1987).

Frazee v. Illinois Dep't of Emp. Sec., 109 S. Ct. 1514 (1989), concerned an individual who was denied unemployment compensation benefits because he refused a temporary position which would have required him to work on Sundays. The Illinois Court of Appeals had sustained the denial of benefits, since

Mr. Frazee had failed to demonstrate that he was a member of an established religious sect and that his refusal to accept Sunday work resulted from a tenet of an established religion. The Supreme Court unanimously rejected the notion that one must be responding to the commands of a particular religion to claim the protection of the free exercise clause. The critical inquiry is simply whether Mr. Frazee sincerely believed that religion required him to refrain from Sunday work and not whether he was a member of a particular religious sect which had tenets against such work.

4. AGE

MASSACHUSETTS BOARD OF RETIREMENT v. MURGIA

427 U.S. 307, 96 S. Ct. 2562, 49 L. Ed. 2d 520 (1976)

PER CURIAM.

This case presents the question whether the provision of Mass. Gen. Laws Ann. c. 32, § 26(3)(a) (1969), that a uniformed state police officer "shall be retired ... upon his attaining age fifty," denies appellee police officer equal protection of the laws in violation of the Fourteenth Amendment.

Appellee Robert Murgia was an officer in the Uniformed Branch of the Massachusetts State Police. The Massachusetts Board of Retirement retired him upon his 50th birthday. Appellee brought this civil action in the United States District Court for the District of Massachusetts, alleging that the operation of § 26(3)(a) denied him equal protection of the laws and requesting the convening of a three-judge court under 28 U.S.C. §§ 2281, 2284....

The primary function of the Uniformed Branch of the Massachusetts State Police is to protect persons and property and maintain law and order. Specifically, uniformed officers participate in controlling prison and civil disorders, respond to emergencies and natural disasters, patrol highways in marked cruisers, investigate crime, apprehend criminal suspects, and provide backup support for local law enforcement personnel. As the District Court observed, "service in this branch is, or can be, arduous." 376 F. Supp., at 754. "[H]igh versatility is required, with few, if any, backwaters available for the partially superannuated." *Ibid.* Thus, "even [appellee's] experts concede that there is a general relationship between advancing age and decreasing physical ability to respond to the demands of the job." *Id.,* at 755.

These considerations prompt the requirement that uniformed state officers pass a comprehensive physical examination biennially until age 40. After that, until mandatory retirement at age 50, uniformed officers must pass annually a more rigorous examination, including an electrocardiogram and tests for gastro-intestinal bleeding. Appellee Murgia had passed such an examination four months before he was retired, and there is no dispute that, when he retired, his excellent physical and mental health still rendered him capable of performing the duties of a uniformed officer.

The record includes the testimony of three physicians: that of the State Police Surgeon, who testified to the physiological and psychological demands involved in the performance of uniformed police functions; that of an associate professor of medicine, who testified generally to the relationship between aging and the ability to perform under stress; and that of a surgeon, who also testified to aging and the ability safely to perform police functions. The testimony clearly established that the risk of physical failure, particularly in the cardiovascular system, increases with age, and that the number of individuals in a given age group incapable of performing stress functions increases with the age of the group. App. 77-78, 174-176. The testimony also recognized that particular individuals over 50 could be capable of safely performing the functions of uniformed officers. The associate professor of medicine, who was a witness for the appellee, further testified that evaluating the risk of cardiovascular failure in a given individual would require a number of detailed studies. *Id.*, at 77-78.

In assessing appellee's equal protection claim, the District Court found it unnecessary to apply a strict-scrutiny test, see *Shapiro v. Thompson*, 394 U.S. 618 (1969), for it determined that the age classification established by the Massachusetts statutory scheme could not in any event withstand a test of rationality, see *Dandridge v. Williams*, 397 U.S. 471 (1970). Since there had been no showing that reaching age 50 forecasts even "imminent change" in an officer's physical condition, the District Court held that compulsory retirement at age 50 was irrational under a scheme that assessed the capabilities of officers individually by means of comprehensive annual physical examinations. We agree that rationality is the proper standard by which to test whether compulsory retirement at age 50 violates equal protection. We disagree, however, with the District Court's determination that the age 50 classification is not rationally related to furthering a legitimate state interest.

I

We need state only briefly our reasons for agreeing that strict scrutiny is not the proper test for determining whether the mandatory retirement provision denies appellee equal protection. *San Antonio School District v. Rodriguez*, 411 U.S. 1, 16 (1973), reaffirmed that equal protection analysis requires strict scrutiny of a legislative classification only when the classification impermissibly interferes with the exercise of a fundamental right[3] or operates to the peculiar disadvantage of a suspect class.[4] Mandatory retirement at age 50 under the Massachusetts statute involves neither situation.

This Court's decisions give no support to the proposition that a right of governmental employment *per se* is fundamental. See *San Antonio School District v. Rodriguez, supra; Lindsey v. Normet*, 405 U.S. 56, 73 (1972); *Dandridge v. Williams, supra*, at 485. Accordingly, we have expressly stated that a standard less than strict scrutiny "has consistently been applied to state legislation restricting the availability of employment opportunities." *Ibid.*

Nor does the class of uniformed state police officers over 50 constitute a suspect class for purposes of equal protection analysis. *Rodriguez, supra*, at 28, observed that a suspect class is one "saddled with such disabilities, or subjected to such a history of purposeful unequal treatment, or relegated to such a posi-

---

[3] E.g., *Roe v. Wade*, 410 U.S. 113 (1973) (right of a uniquely private nature); *Bullock v. Carter*, 405 U.S. 134 (1972) (right to vote); *Shapiro v. Thompson*, 394 U.S. 618, 89 S.Ct. 1322, 22 L.Ed.2d 600 (1969) (right of interstate travel); *Williams v. Rhodes*, 393 U.S. 23 (1968) (rights guaranteed by the First Amendment); *Skinner v. Oklahoma ex rel. Williamson*, 316 U.S. 535 (1942) (right to procreate).

[4] E.g., *Graham v. Richardson*, 403 U.S. 365 (1971) (alienage); *McLaughlin v. Florida*, 379 U.S. 184 (1964) (race); *Oyama v. California*, 332 U.S. 633 (1948) (ancestry).

tion of political powerlessness as to command extraordinary protection from the majoritarian political process." While the treatment of the aged in this Nation has not been wholly free of discrimination, such persons, unlike, say, those who have been discriminated against on the basis of race or national origin, have not experienced a "history of purposeful unequal treatment" or been subjected to unique disabilities on the basis of stereotyped characteristics not truly indicative of their abilities. The class subject to the compulsory retirement feature of the Massachusetts statute consists of uniformed state police officers over the age of 50. It cannot be said to discriminate only against the elderly. Rather, it draws the line at a certain age in middle life. But even old age does not define a "discrete and insular" group, *United States v. Carolene Products Co.*, 304 U.S. 144, 152-153, n. 4 (1938), in need of "extraordinary protection from the majoritarian political process." Instead, it marks a stage that each of us will reach if we live out our normal span. Even if the statute could be said to impose a penalty upon a class defined as the aged, it would not impose a distinction sufficiently akin to those classifications that we have found suspect to call for strict judicial scrutiny.

Under the circumstances, it is unnecessary to subject the State's resolution of competing interests in this case to the degree of critical examination that our cases under the Equal Protection Clause recently have characterized as "strict judicial scrutiny."

II

We turn then to examine this state classification under the rational-basis standard. This inquiry employs a relatively relaxed standard reflecting the Court's awareness that the drawing of lines that create distinctions is peculiarly a legislative task and an unavoidable one. Perfection in making the necessary classifications is neither possible nor necessary. *Dandridge v. Williams, supra,* at 485. Such action by a legislature is presumed to be valid.[5]

In this case, the Massachusetts statute clearly meets the requirements of the Equal Protection Clause, for the State's classification rationally furthers the purpose identified by the State: Through mandatory retirement at age 50, the legislature seeks to protect the public by assuring physical preparedness of its uniformed police. Since physical ability generally declines with age, mandatory retirement at 50 serves to remove from police service those whose fitness for uniformed work presumptively has diminished with age. This clearly is rationally related to the State's objective. There is no indication that § 26(3)(a) has the effect of excluding from service so few officers who are in fact unqualified as to render age 50 a criterion wholly unrelated to the objective of the statute.

That the State chooses not to determine fitness more precisely through individualized testing after age 50 is not to say that the objective of assuring physical fitness is not rationally furthered by a maximum-age limitation. It is only to say that with regard to the interest of all concerned, the State perhaps has not chosen the best means to accomplish this purpose. But where rationality is the test, a State "does not violate the Equal Protection Clause merely because the

---

[5]See, e.g., *San Antonio School District v. Rodriguez,* 411 U.S. 1, 40-41 (1973); *Madden v. Kentucky,* 309 U.S. 83, 88 (1940); *Lindsley v. Natural Carbonic Gas Co.,* 220 U.S. 61, 78-79 (1911).

classifications made by its laws are imperfect." *Dandridge v. Williams,* 397 U.S., at 485.

We do not make light of the substantial economic and psychological effects premature and compulsory retirement can have on an individual; nor do we denigrate the ability of elderly citizens to continue to contribute to society. The problems of retirement have been well documented and are beyond serious dispute. But "[w]e do not decide today that the [Massachusetts statute] is wise, that it best fulfills the relevant social and economic objectives that [Massachusetts] might ideally espouse, or that a more just and humane system could not be devised." *Id.,* at 487. We decide only that the system enacted by the Massachusetts Legislature does not deny appellee equal protection of the laws.

The judgment is reversed.

JUSTICE STEVENS took no part in the consideration or decision of this case. [Justice Marshall dissented.]

NOTES

1. In *Vance v. Bradley,* 440 U.S. 93 (1979), the Supreme Court sustained the age sixty retirement rule for foreign service officers, since it agreed that the early retirement policy increased the efficiency of younger officers by providing them with a reasonable expectation of promotion and it eliminated the problems that might be caused to older personnel facing the physical rigors of overseas assignments. The age limitation was thus found to satisfy the *Murgia* rationality standard.

2. In *Palmer v. Ticcione,* 576 F.2d 459 (7th Cir. 1978), *cert. denied,* 440 U.S. 945 (1979), the court upheld the legality of a policy requiring the retirement of school teachers at age seventy. Other courts have similarly sustained the constitutionality of age sixty-five retirement rules for public employees. See, e.g., *Kuhar v. Greensburg-Salem Sch. Dist.,* 616 F.2d 676 (3d Cir. 1980) (school personnel); *Martin v. Tamaki,* 607 F.2d 307 (9th Cir. 1979) (municipal water & power workers); *DeShon v. Bettendorf Sch. Dist.,* 284 N.W.2d 329, 21 F.E.P. Cas. 644 (Iowa 1979) (school teachers).

3. In *Doyle v. Suffolk Cty.,* 786 F.2d 523 (2d Cir.), *cert. denied,* 479 U.S. 825 (1986), the court sustained the constitutionality of a New York statute precluding the employment of persons 29 or older as police officers, since the limit was found to serve "the obvious state interest" of assuring the hiring of individuals who are "physically able" to perform the requisite police tasks.

4. In *Zombro v. Baltimore City Police Dep't,* 868 F.2d 1364 (4th Cir.), *cert. denied,* 110 S. Ct. 147 (1989), the court held that government employees covered by the Age Discrimination in Employment Act (ADEA) may not prosecute age discrimination claims under section 1983. It found that the comprehensive rights and procedures created by the ADEA were intended to provide the exclusive means of addressing age discrimination claims by covered public employees.

5. ALIENAGE

CABELL v. CHAVEZ-SALIDO

454 U.S. 432, 102 S. Ct. 735, 70 L. Ed. 2d 677 (1982)

JUSTICE WHITE delivered the opinion of the Court.

In this case we once again consider a citizenship requirement imposed by a state on those seeking to fill certain governmental offices. California Government Code § 1031(a) requires "public officers or employees declared by law to be peace officers" to be citizens of the United States. California Penal Code § 830.5 provides that probation officers and deputy probation officers are "peace officers." A three judge District Court of the Central District of California held the California requirement unconstitutional both on its face and as applied to the appellees, who sought positions as Deputy Probation Officers.

I

Appellees were, at the time the complaint was filed, lawfully admitted permanent resident aliens living in Los Angeles County, California. Each applied unsuccessfully for positions as Deputy Probation Officers with the Los Angeles County Probation Department. With respect to two of the three appellees, the parties stipulated that the failure to obtain the positions sought was the result of the statutory citizenship requirement.

Appellees filed a complaint in the United States District Court for the Central District of California challenging the constitutionality of the citizenship requirement under the equal protection clause of the Fourteenth Amendment and 42 U.S.C. §§ 1981 and 1983. Named as defendants were certain individual county officials, in their official capacity, and the County of Los Angeles.

Appellees alleged unconstitutional discrimination against aliens, impermissible infringement upon their constitutional right to travel, and unconstitutional interference with Congress' plenary power to regulate aliens. They sought declaratory and injunctive relief, as well as attorneys' fees and damages for two of the plaintiffs.

In February 1977, the District Court concluded that the statutory citizenship requirement was unconstitutional both on its face and as applied. 427 F. Supp. 158 (CD Cal. 1977). That decision rested entirely on appellees' arguments under the equal protection clause; it did not reach the right to travel and federal preemption claims. This Court vacated and remanded that judgment for further consideration in light of *Foley v. Connelie,* 435 U.S. 291 (1978), which upheld a New York statute requiring state troopers to be United States citizens. On remand, the District Court reconsidered its previous position in light of both *Foley, supra,* and *Ambach v. Norwick,* 441 U.S. 68 (1979), which held that a state may refuse to employ as elementary and secondary school teachers aliens who are eligible for United States citizenship but fail to seek naturalization. With Judge Curtis dissenting, the court found its prior views still valid and convincing. It, therefore, came to the identical conclusion that the California statutory scheme was constitutionally invalid both facially and as applied.

We noted probable jurisdiction, — U.S. — (1981), and now reverse.

II

Over the years, this Court has many times considered state classifications dealing with aliens. See, e.g., *Ambach v. Norwick, supra; Nyquist v. Mauclet,* 432 U.S. 1 (1977); *Foley v. Connelie, supra; Examining Board v. Flores de Otero,* 426 U.S. 572 (1976); *In re Griffiths,* 413 U.S. 717 (1973); *Sugarman v.*

Dougall, 413 U.S. 634 (1973); *Graham v. Richardson*, 403 U.S. 365 (1971); *Takahashi v. Fish & Game Comm'n*, 334 U.S. 410 (1948); *Crane v. New York*, 239 U.S. 195 (1915); *Heim v. McCall*, 239 U.S. 175 (1915); *Truax v. Raich*, 239 U.S. 33 (1915); *Yick Wo v. Hopkins*, 118 U.S. 356 (1886). As we have noted before, those cases "have not formed an unwavering line over the years." *Ambach v. Norwick, supra*, at 72. But to say that the decisions do not fall into a neat pattern is not to say that they fall into no pattern. In fact, they illustrate a not unusual characteristic of legal development: broad principles are articulated, narrowed when applied to new contexts, and finally replaced when the distinctions they rely upon are no longer tenable.

In *Yick Wo v. Hopkins, supra,* the Court held both that resident aliens fall within the protection of the equal protection clause of the Fourteenth Amendment and that the state could not deny to aliens the right to carry on a "harmless and useful occupation" available to citizens. Although *Yick Wo* proclaimed that hostility toward aliens was not a permissible ground for a discriminatory classification, it dealt only with a situation in which government had actively intervened in the sphere of private employment. In a series of later cases it became clear that *Yick Wo* did not mean that the state had to be strictly neutral as between aliens and citizens: The Court continued to uphold the right of the state to withhold from aliens public benefits and public resources. *Terrace v. Thompson*, 263 U.S. 197 (1923) (ownership of land); *Heim v. McCall, supra* (employment on public works projects); *Patsone v. Pennsylvania*, 232 U.S. 139 (1914) (taking of wild game).

This distinction between government distribution of public resources and intervention in the private market was clearly established as the principle by which state regulations of aliens were to be evaluated in *Truax v. Raich*, 239 U.S. 33 (1915), which struck down a state statute requiring all employers of more than five workers to employ "not less than eighty per cent, qualified electors or native born citizens of the United States." ...

This public/private distinction, the "special public interest" doctrine, see *Graham v. Richardson, supra*, at 372, 374; *Sugarman v. Dougall, supra*, at 643, 644, was challenged in *Takahashi v. Fish & Game Comm'n*, 334 U.S. 410 (1948), which held that California could not bar lawfully resident aliens from obtaining commercial fishing licenses.... As the principle governing analysis of state classifications of aliens, who are lawful residents, the distinction was further eroded in *Graham v. Richardson*, 403 U.S. 365 (1971), which read *Takahashi* as "[casting] doubt on the continuing validity of the special public-interest doctrine in all contexts," *id.,* at 374, and held that a state could not distinguish between lawfully resident aliens and citizens in the distribution of welfare benefits. Returning to *Yick Wo*'s holding that lawfully present aliens fall within the protection of the Equal Protection Clause and citing the more recent theory of a two-tiered equal protection scrutiny, *Graham* implied that there would be very few — if any — areas in which a state could legitimately distinguish between its citizens and lawfully resident aliens:

"Aliens as a class are a prime example of a 'discrete and insular' minority ... for whom ... heightened judicial solicitude is appropriate. Accordingly, it was said in *Takahashi*, 334 U.S., at 420, that 'the power of a state to apply its laws

exclusively to its alien inhabitants as a class is confined within narrow limits.'"
Id., at 372.

The cases through *Graham* dealt for the most part with attempts by the states to retain certain economic benefits exclusively for citizens. Since *Graham,* the Court has confronted claims distinguishing between the economic and sovereign functions of government. This distinction has been supported by the argument that although citizenship is not a relevant ground for the distribution of economic benefits, it is a relevant ground for determining membership in the political community. "We recognize a State's interest in establishing its own form of government, and in limiting participation in that government to those who are within 'the basic conception of a political community.'" *Sugarman v. Dougall,* 413 U.S. 634, 642 (1973). While not retreating from the position that restrictions on lawfully resident aliens that primarily affect economic interests are subject to heightened judicial scrutiny, *Sugarman v. Dougall, supra,* at 642; *In re Griffiths,* 413 U.S. 717 (1973); *Examining Board v. Flores de Otero,* 426 U.S. 572 (1976), we have concluded that strict scrutiny is out of place when the restriction primarily serves a political function: "[O]ur scrutiny will not be so demanding where we deal with matters resting firmly within a State's constitutional prerogatives [and] constitutional responsibility for the establishment and operation of its own government, as well as the qualifications of an appropriately designated class of public office holders." *Sugarman v. Dougall, supra,* at 648. We have thus "not abandoned the general principle that some state functions are so bound up with the operation of the State as a governmental entity as to permit the exclusion from those functions of all persons who have not become part of the process of self government." *Ambach v. Norwick,* 441 U.S. 68, 73-74 (1979). And in those areas the state's exclusion of aliens need not "clear the high hurdle of 'strict scrutiny,' because [that] would 'obliterate all the distinctions between citizens and aliens, and thus depreciate the historic value of citizenship." *Foley v. Connelie,* 435 U.S. 291, 295 (1978) (citations omitted).

The exclusion of aliens from basic governmental processes is not a deficiency in the democratic system but a necessary consequence of the community's process of political self-definition. Self-government, whether direct or through representatives, begins by defining the scope of the community of the governed and thus of the governors as well: Aliens are by definition those outside of this community. Judicial incursions in this area may interfere with those aspects of democratic self-government that are most essential to it. This distinction between the economic and political functions of government has, therefore, replaced the old public/private distinction. Although this distinction rests on firmer foundations than the old public/private distinction, it may be difficult to apply in particular cases.

Sugarman advised that a claim that a particular restriction on legally resident aliens serves political and not economic goals is to be evaluated in a two-step process. First, the specificity of the classification will be examined: a classification that is substantially over or underinclusive tends to undercut the governmental claim that the classification serves legitimate political ends. The classification in *Sugarman* itself—all members of the competitive civil service — could not support the claim that it was an element in "the State's broad power to define its political community," 413 U.S. at 643, because it indiscriminately swept in menial occupations, while leaving out some of the state's most important political functions. Second, even if the classification is sufficiently tailored, it may be applied in the particular case only to "persons holding state elective or important nonelective executive, legislative, and judicial positions," those officers who "participate directly in the formulation, operation, or review of broad public policy" and hence "perform functions that go to the heart of representative government." *Id.,* at 647.[7] We must therefore inquire whether the "position in question ... involves discretionary decisionmaking, or execution of policy, which substantially affects members of the political community." *Foley v. Connelie, supra,* at 296.

The restriction at issue in this case passes both of the *Sugarman* tests.

III

Appellees argue, and the District Court agreed, that California Government Code § 1031(a), which requires all state "peace officers" to be citizens, is unconstitutionally over-inclusive: "Section 1031(a), is void as a law requiring citizenship which 'sweeps too broadly.'" 490 F. Supp. 984, 986. The District Court failed to articulate any standard in reaching this conclusion. Rather, it relied wholly on its belief that of the more than seventy positions included with the statutory classification of "peace officer," some undefined number of them "cannot be considered members of the political community no matter how liberally that category is viewed." *Id.,* at 987. The District Court's entire argument on this point consisted of just one sentence: "There appears to be no justification whatever for excluding aliens, even those who have applied for citizenship, from holding public employment as cemetery sextons, furniture and bedding inspectors, livestock identification inspectors and toll service employees." *Id.,* at 986. In believing this sufficient, the District Court applied a standard of review far stricter than that approved in *Sugarman* and later cases.

We need not hold that the District Court was wrong in concluding that citizenship may not be required of toll service employees, cemetery sextons, and inspectors to hold that the District Court was wrong in striking down the statute on its face.[9] The District Court assumed that if the statute was overinclusive at

---

[7]The full quotation from *Sugarman* is as follows: "'Each State has the power to prescribe the qualifications of its officers and the manner in which they shall be chosen.' *Boyd v. Thayer,* 134 U.S. 135, 161 (1892). See *Luther v. Borden,* 7 How. 1, 41 (1849); *Pope v. Williams,* 193 U.S. 621, 632-633 (1904). Such power inheres in the State by virtue of its obligation, already noted above, 'to preserve the basic conception of a political community.' *Dunn v. Blumstein,* 405 U.S., at 344. And this power and responsibility of the State applies, not only to the qualifications of voters, but also to persons holding state elective or important nonelective executive, legislative, and judicial positions, for officers who 'participate directly in the formulation, execution, or review of broad public policy perform functions that go to the heart of representative government.' 413 U.S. 634, 647 (1973)." This language is far reaching and no limits on it were suggested by *Sugarman* itself: almost every governmental official can be understood as participating in the execution of broad public policies. The limits on this category within which citizenship is relevant to the political community are not easily defined, but our cases since *Sugarman* — *Foley v. Connelie,* 435 U.S. 291 (1978) and *Ambach v. Norwick,* 441 U.S. 68 (1979) — suggest that this Court will not look to the breadth of policy judgments required of a particular employee. Rather, the Court will look to the importance of the function as a factor giving substance to the concept of democratic self-government.

[9]It is worth noting, however, that of the categories mentioned by the District Court, toll service employees, inspectors of the Bureau of Livestock and cemetery sextons were all eliminated from

all, it could not stand. This is not the proper standard. Rather, the inquiry is whether the restriction reaches so far and is so broad and haphazard as to belie the state's claim that it is only attempting to ensure that an important function of government be in the hands of those having the "fundamental legal bond of citizenship." *Ambach v. Norwick,* 441 U.S. 68, 75 (1979). Under this standard, the classifications used need not be precise; there need only be a substantial fit. Our examination of the California scheme convinces us that it is sufficiently tailored to withstand a facial challenge.

The general requirements, including citizenship, for all California peace officers are found in Government Code § 1031. That section, however, does not designate any particular official as a peace officer; rather, Penal Code § 830 lists the specific occupations that fall within the general category of "peace officer." Even a casual reading of the Code makes clear that the unifying character of all categories of peace officers is their law enforcement function. Specific categories are defined by either their geographical jurisdiction or the specific substantive laws they have the responsibility to enforce. Thus, not surprisingly, the first categories listed include police officers at the county, city, and district levels. § 830.1. This is followed by various categories of police power authorized by the state: e.g., highway patrol officers, the state police and members of the California National Guard when ordered into active service. § 830.2. After this, the statute includes a long list of particular officers with responsibility for enforcement of different substantive areas of the law: e.g., individuals charged with enforcement of the alcoholic beverage laws, the food and drug laws, fire laws, and the horse racing laws. § 830.3. Finally, there are several catch-all provisions that include some officers with narrow geographic responsibilities — e.g., park rangers, San Francisco Bay Area Rapid Transit District police, harbor police, community college police, security officers of municipal utility districts, and security officers employed in government buildings — and some with narrow "clientele" — e.g., welfare fraud or child support investigators, correctional officers, parole and probation officers. §§ 830.31-830.6.

Although some of these categories may have only a tenuous connection to traditional police functions of law enforcement, the questionable classifications are comparatively few in number.[10] The general law enforcement character of all California "peace officers" is underscored by the fact that all have the power to make arrests, § 836, and all receive a course of training in the exercise of their respective arrest powers and in the use of firearms. § 832. *Foley, supra,* made clear that a state may limit the exercise of the sovereign's coercive police powers over the members of the community to citizens. The California statutes at issue here are an attempt to do just that. They are sufficiently tailored in light of that aim to pass the lower level of scrutiny we articulated as the appropriate equal protection standard for such an exercise of sovereign power in *Sugarman.*

---

coverage by amendments to Penal Code § 830.4, passed in 1980. Stats. 1980, c. 1340, p. —, § 12, effective September 30, 1980.

[10] The dissent specifically questions only four positions. Three of these — Dental Board Inspectors, Parks and Recreation Department employees, and voluntary fire wardens — are designated "peace officers" only when their "primary duty" is law enforcement. See Penal Code §§ 830.3(b), (c), (j).

IV

This District Court also held that the citizenship requirement was invalid as applied to the positions at issue here — deputy probation officers. In reaching this conclusion, it focused too narrowly on a comparison of the characteristics and functions of probation officers with those of the state troopers at issue in *Foley, supra,* and the teachers in *Ambach, supra. Foley* and *Ambach* did not describe the outer limits of permissible citizenship requirements. For example, although both of those cases emphasized the community-wide responsibilities of teachers and police, there was no suggestion that judges, who deal only with a narrow subclass of the community, cannot be subject to a citizenship requirement. See *Sugarman, supra,* at 647. Similarly, although both *Foley* and *Ambach* emphasized the unsupervised discretion that must be exercised by the teacher and the police officer in the performance of their duties, neither case suggested that jurors, who act under a very specific set of instructions, could not be required to be citizens. See *Perkins v. Smith,* 370 F. Supp. 134 (D. Md. 1974), *aff'd summarily* 426 U.S. 913 (1976). Definition of the important sovereign functions of the political community is necessarily the primary responsibility of the representative branches of government, subject to limited judicial review.[12]

Looking at the functions of California probation officers, we conclude that they, like the state troopers involved in *Foley,* sufficiently partake of the sovereign's power to exercise coercive force over the individual that they may be limited to citizens. Although the range of individuals over whom probation officers exercise supervisory authority is limited, the powers of the probation officer are broad with respect to those over whom they exercise that authority. The probation officer has the power both to arrest, Penal Code § 830.5, § 836, § 1203.2; Code of Civil Procedure § 131.4, and to release those over whom he has jurisdiction. Penal Code § 1203.1a. He has the power and the responsibility to supervise probationers and insure that all the conditions of probation are met and that the probationer accomplishes a successful reintegration into the community. Penal Code § 1203.1. With respect to juveniles, the probation officer has the responsibility to determine whether to release or detain offenders, Wel-

---

[12]Appellees also argue that the statute is facially invalid because it is impermissibly underinclusive. The District Court did not consider this contention and the only argument advanced by appellees in support of this claim is that California fails to impose a citizenship requirement upon its public school teachers. Brief for Appellees, at 29. At various points, the dissent also relies upon the alleged underinclusiveness of the statute.

Although there is some language in *Sugarman* indicating that such an argument is appropriate, 413 U.S., at 640, 642, and that a statutory exclusion of aliens from a particular form of public employment will be evaluated in light of the entire framework of public employment positions open and closed to aliens, clearly our subsequent cases have not adopted that position. Thus, in both *Foley* and *Ambach* only the specific governmental functions directly at issue were considered. Underinclusiveness arguments were relevant in *Sugarman* because there the classification involved — the competitive civil service — swept in a wide variety of governmental functions. Such a sweeping and apparently indiscriminate categorization raises legitimate questions of arbitrariness that are not raised when the state limits a particular and important governmental function — e.g., coercive police power — to citizens. When we deal with such a specific category, underinclusiveness arguments are relevant only within the category: Are there, for example, individuals who exercise the state's coercive police power that are not required to be citizens? In this respect, the California statutory scheme is not substantially underinclusive: Penal Code § 830.7 lists only two categories of positions which have the power to arrest but are not "peace officers" — and therefore are not subject to the citizenship requirement — security officers at institutions of higher education and certain individuals designated by a cemetery authority.

fare and Institutions Code § 628, and whether to institute judicial proceedings or take other supervisory steps over the minor. Welfare and Institutions Code §§ 630, 653-654. In carrying out these responsibilities the probation officer necessarily has a great deal of discretion that, just like that of the police officer and the teacher, must be exercised, in the first instance, without direct supervision:

> "Because the probation or parole officer's function is not so much to compel conformance to a strict code of behavior as to supervise a course of rehabilitation, he has been entrusted traditionally with broad discretion to judge the progress of rehabilitation in individual cases, and has been armed with the power to recommend or even to declare revocation." *Gagnon v. Scarpelli,* 411 U.S. 778, 784 (1973).

One need not take an overly idealistic view of the educational functions of the probation officer during this period to recognize that the probation officer acts as an extension of the judiciary's authority to set the conditions under which particular individuals will lead their lives and of the executive's authority to coerce obedience to those conditions. From the perspective of the probationer, his probation officer may personify the state's sovereign powers; from the perspective of the larger community, the probation officer may symbolize the political community's control over, and thus responsibility for, those who have been found to have violated the norms of social order. From both of these perspectives, a citizenship requirement may seem an appropriate limitation on those who would exercise and, therefore, symbolize this power of the political community over those who fall within its jurisdiction.

Therefore, the judgment of the District Court is reversed, and the case is remanded for further proceedings consistent with this opinion.

So ordered.

JUSTICE BLACKMUN, with whom JUSTICE BRENNAN, JUSTICE MARSHALL, and JUSTICE STEVENS join, dissenting....

The Court properly acknowledges that our decisions regarding state discrimination against permanent resident aliens have formed a pattern. Since *Yick Wo v. Hopkins,* 118 U.S. 356 (1886), this Court has recognized and honored the right of a lawfully admitted permanent resident alien to work for a living in the common occupations of the community. In *Truax v. Raich,* 239 U.S. 33, 41 (1915), the Court declared that right to be

> "the very essence of the personal freedom and opportunity that it was the purpose of the [Fourteenth] Amendment to secure.... If this could be refused solely upon the ground of race or nationality, the prohibition of the denial to any person of the equal protection of the laws would be a barren form of words."

In *Sugarman v. Dougall, supra,* we expressly refused to exempt public employment positions from this general rule. *Sugarman,* an 8-1 decision, struck down as facially inconsistent with the Equal Protection Clause a New York statute that excluded lawfully admitted aliens from all state civil service jobs offered on the basis of competitive examinations. *Sugarman* directed that permanent resident aliens may not be barred *as a class* from the common *public* occupations of the community. There, as here, the State had asserted its substantial interest in ensuring "that sovereign functions must be performed by members of the State." Brief for Appellants in *Sugarman v. Dougall,* O.T. 1972, No. 71-1222, p. 10. Without denying the weight of that interest, the Court concluded that, "judged in the context of the State's broad statutory framework and the justifications the State present[ed]," 413 U.S., at 640, the State's chosen means were insufficiently precise to uphold its broad exclusion of aliens from public employment.

Since *Sugarman,* the Court consistently has held that in each case where the State chooses to discriminate against permanent resident aliens, "the governmental interest claimed to justify the discrimination is to be carefully examined in order to determine whether that interest is legitimate and substantial, and inquiry must be made whether the means adopted to achieve the goal are necessary and precisely drawn." *Examining Board v. Flores de Otero,* 426 U.S. 572, 605 (1976)....

While *Sugarman* unambiguously proscribed blanket exclusion of aliens from state jobs, its dictum acknowledged a State's power to bar noncitizens as a class from a narrowly circumscribed range of important nonelective posts involving direct participation "in the formulation, execution, or review of broad public policy." 413 U.S., at 647. Under *Sugarman*'s exception, States may reserve certain public offices for their citizens if those offices "perform functions that go to the heart of representative government." *Ibid.*

As originally understood, the *Sugarman* exception was exceedingly narrow. Less demanding scrutiny was deemed appropriate only for statutes deriving from "a State's historical power to exclude aliens from participation in its democratic political institutions" or its "constitutional responsibility for the establishment and operation of its own government." *Id.,* at 648....

I read *Foley* and *Ambach* to require the State to show that it has historically reserved a particular executive position for its citizens as a matter of its "constitutional prerogativ[e]." *Sugarman,* 413 U.S., at 648. Furthermore, the State must demonstrate that the public employee in that position exercises plenary coercive authority and control over a substantial portion of the citizen population. The public employee must exercise this authority over his clientele without intervening judicial or executive supervision. Even then, the State must prove that citizenship "'bears some rational relationship to the special demands of the particular position.'" *Id.,* at 647, citing *Dougall v. Sugarman,* 339 F. Supp. 906, 911 (S.D.N.Y. 1971) (Lumbard, J., concurring)....

In the end, the State has identified no characteristic of permanent resident aliens *as a class* which disables them from performing the job of deputy probation officer. Cf. *Foley v. Connelie,* 435 U.S., at 308 (STEVENS, J., dissenting). The State does not dispute that these appellees possess the qualifications and educational background to perform the duties that job entails. Indeed, the State advances no rational reason why these appellees, native Spanish-speakers with graduate academic degrees, are not superbly qualified to act as probation officers for Spanish-speaking probationers, some of whom themselves may not be citizens. Cf. *Ambach v. Norwick,* 441 U.S., at 84, 87-88 (dissenting opinion)....

I only can conclude that California's exclusion of these appellees from the position of deputy probation officer stems solely from state parochialism and hostility toward foreigners who have come to this country lawfully. I find it ironic that the Court invokes the principle of democratic self-government to exclude from the law enforcement process individuals who have not only resided here lawfully, but who now desire merely to help the State enforce its laws. Section 1031(a) violates appellees' rights to equal treatment and an individualized determination of fitness....

NOTES

1. In *Ambach v. Norwick,* 441 U.S. 68 (1979), discussed in *Cabell,* a closely divided Supreme Court sustained the constitutionality of N.Y. Education Law § 3001(3), precluding the certification as school teacher of any person who is not a citizen and who has not manifested an intention to apply for citizenship:

Within the public school system, teachers play a critical part in developing students' attitude toward government and understanding of the role of citizens in our society. Alone among employees of the system, teachers are in direct, day-to-day contact with students both in the classrooms and in the other varied activities of a modern school. In shaping the students' experience to achieve educational goals, teachers by necessity have wide discretion over the way the course material is communicated to students. They are responsible for presenting and explaining the subject matter in a way that is both comprehensible and inspiring. No amount of standardization of teaching materials or lesson plans can eliminate the personal qualities a teacher brings to bear in achieving these goals. Further, a teacher serves as a role model for his students, exerting a subtle but important influence over their perceptions and values. Thus, through both the presentation of course materials and the example he sets, a teacher has an opportunity to influence the attitudes of students toward government, the political process, and a citizen's social responsibilities. This influence is crucial to the continued good health of a democracy.

Furthermore, it is clear that all public school teachers, and not just those responsible for teaching the courses most directly related to government, history, and civic duties, should help fulfill the broader function of the public school system. Teachers, regardless of their specialty, may be called upon to teach other subjects, including those expressly dedicated to political and social subjects. More importantly, a State properly may regard all teachers as having an obligation to promote civic virtues and understanding in their classes, regardless of the subject taught. Certainly a State also may take account of a teacher's function as an example for students, which exists independently of particular classroom subjects. In light of the foregoing considerations, we think it clear that public school teachers come well within the "governmental function" principle recognized in *Sugarman* and *Foley.* Accordingly, the Constitution requires only that a citizenship requirement applicable to teaching in the public schools bears a rational relationship to a legitimate state interest. See *Massachusetts Board of Retirement v. Murgia,* 427 U.S. 307, 314 (1976).

As the legitimacy of the State's interest in furthering the educational goals outlined above is undoubted, it remains only to consider whether § 3001 (3) bears a rational relationship to this interest. The restriction is carefully framed to serve its purpose, as it bars from teaching only those aliens who have demonstrated their unwillingness to obtain United States citizenship. Appellees, and aliens similarly situated, in effect have chosen to classify themselves. They prefer to retain citizenship in a foreign country with the obligations it entails of primary duty and loyalty. They have rejected the open invitation extended to qualify for eligibility to teach by applying for citizenship in this country. The people of New York, acting through their elected representatives, have made a judgment that citizenship should be a qualification for teaching the young of the State in the public schools, and § 3001 (3) furthers that judgment.

[Justices Blackmun, Brennan, Marshall, and Stevens dissented.] Compare *Bernal v. Fainter,* 104 S. Ct. 2312 (1984), wherein the Court struck down a Texas statute that required notaries public to be U.S. citizens, since the eight-member majority found no indication that Texas notaries are invested with policymaking responsibility or exercise broad discretion with respect to the application of public policy. The state's desire to ensure that prospective notaries will be familiar with state law could more appropriately be satisfied through the use of a testing procedure, instead of the blanket exclusion of all aliens. See generally Note, *Alienage and Public Employment: The Need for an Intermediate Standard in Equal Protection,* 32 Hastings L.J. 163 (1980).

2. *Hampton v. Mow Sun Wong,* 426 U.S. 88 (1976), found that a U.S. Civil Service Commission regulation that generally barred resident aliens from civil service employment deprived aliens of liberty without due process of law.

[T]he federal power over aliens is [not] so plenary that any agent of the National Government may arbitrarily subject all resident aliens to different substantive rules from those applied to citizens....

The rule enforced by the Commission has its impact on an identifiable class of persons who ... are already subject to disadvantages not shared by the remainder of the community.... The added disadvantage resulting from ... ineligibility for employment in a major sector of the economy is of sufficient significance to be characterized as a deprivation of an interest in liberty.... It follows that some judicial scrutiny of the deprivation is mandated by the Constitution....

When the Federal Government asserts an overriding national interest as justification for a discriminatory rule which would violate the Equal Protection Clause if adopted by a State, due process requires that there be a legitimate basis for presuming that the rule was actually intended to serve that interest. If the agency which promulgates the rule has direct responsibility for fostering or protecting that interest, it may reasonably be presumed that the asserted interest was the actual predicate for the rule.... Alternatively, if the rule were expressly mandated by the Congress or the President, we might presume that any interest which might rationally be served by the rule did in fact give rise to its adoption.

[We] may assume with the [Government] that if the Congress or the President had expressly imposed the citizenship requirement, it would be justified by the national interest in providing an incentive for aliens to become naturalized, or possibly even as providing the President with an expendable token for treaty negotiating purposes; but we are not willing to presume that the Chairman of the Civil Service Commission [was] deliberately fostering an interest so far removed from his normal responsibilities.

Since the challenged regulation had not been approved by either the Congress or the President, the Court concluded that it had been impermissibly adopted.

Following the *Mow Sun Wong* decision, President Ford issued Executive Order 11,935, 41 Fed. Reg. 37,301 (1976), barring lawfully admitted aliens from federal service positions. In *Vergara v. Hampton,* 581 F.2d 1281 (7th Cir.

1978), *cert. denied,* 441 U.S. 905 (1979), the propriety of this order was sustained on the basis of the dicta in the *Mow Sun Wong* opinion. Accord *Mow Sun Wong v. Campbell,* 626 F.2d 739 (9th Cir. 1980), *cert. denied,* 450 U.S. 959 (1981).

Yuen v. IRS, 649 F.2d 163 (2d Cir.), *cert. denied,* 454 U.S. 1053 (1981), involved an appropriations act provision forbidding the employment of most aliens in federal civil service positions in the continental United States. Although the statute precluded the employment of aliens from most countries, it did permit the hiring of permanent resident aliens from countries such as Cuba, Poland, South Vietnam, and the Baltic countries. Nonetheless, since the challenged exclusion was found to further important government interests, its constitutionality was sustained.

6. VETERANS' PREFERENCE

PERSONNEL ADMINISTRATOR v. FEENEY

442 U.S. 256, 99 S. Ct. 2282, 60 L. Ed. 2d 870 (1979)

JUSTICE STEWART delivered the opinion of the Court.

This case presents a challenge to the constitutionality of the Massachusetts Veterans Preference Statute, Mass. Gen. Laws, ch. 31, § 23, on the ground that it discriminates against women in violation of the Equal Protection Clause of the Fourteenth Amendment. Under ch. 31, § 23, all veterans who qualify for state civil service positions must be considered for appointment ahead of any qualifying nonveterans. The preference operates overwhelmingly to the advantage of males.

The appellee Helen B. Feeney is not a veteran. She brought this action pursuant to 42 U.S.C. § 1983, alleging that the absolute preference formula established in ch. 31, § 23, inevitably operates to exclude women from consideration for the best Massachusetts civil service jobs and thus unconstitutionally denies them the equal protection of the laws.[2] The three-judge District Court agreed, one judge dissenting....

I

A. The Federal Government and virtually all of the States grant some sort of hiring preference to veterans.[6] The Massachusetts preference, which is loosely

---

[2] No statutory claim was brought under Title VII of the Civil Rights Act of 1964, 42 U.S.C. § 2000e et seq. Section 712 of the Act, 42 U.S.C. § 2000e-11, provides that "nothing in the subchapter shall be construed to repeal or modify any federal, State, territorial or local law creating special rights or preference for veterans." The parties have evidently assumed that this provision precludes a Title VII challenge.

[6] The first comprehensive federal veterans' statute was enacted in 1944. Veterans' Preference Act of 1944, ch. 287, 58 Stat. 387. The Federal Government has, however, engaged in preferential hiring of veterans, through official policies and various special laws, since the Civil War. *See, e.g.,* Res. of March 3, 1865, No. 27, 13 Stat. 571 (hiring preference for disabled veterans). *See generally,* The Provision of Federal Benefits for Veterans, An Historical Analysis of Major Veterans' Legislation, 1862-1954, Committee Print No. 171, 84th Cong., 1st Sess. (House Comm. on Vets. Affairs, Dec. 28, 1955) 258-265. For surveys of state veterans' preference laws, many of which also date back to the late 19th century, *see* State Veterans' Laws, Digest of State Laws Regarding Rights, Benefits and Privileges of Veterans and Their Dependents, House Committee on Veterans' Affairs, 91st Cong., 1st Sess. (1969): Fleming & Shanor, *Veterans Preferences in Public Employment; Unconstitutional Gender Discrimination?,* 26 Emory L.J. 13 (1977).

termed an "absolute lifetime" preference, is among the most generous.[7] It applies to all positions in the State's classified civil service, which constitute approximately 60% of the public jobs in the State. It is available to "any person, male or female, including a nurse," who was honorably discharged from the United States Armed Forces after at least 90 days of active service, at least one day of which was during "wartime."[8] Persons who are deemed veterans and who are otherwise qualified for a particular civil service job may exercise the preference at any time and as many times as they wish.

Civil service positions in Massachusetts fall into two general categories, labor and official. For jobs in the official service, with which the proofs in this action were concerned, the preference mechanics are uncomplicated. All applicants for employment must take competitive examinations. Grades are based on a formula that gives weight both to objective test results and to training and experience. Candidates who pass are then ranked in the order of their respective scores on an "eligible list." Chapter 31, § 23, requires, however, that disabled veterans, veterans, and surviving spouses and surviving parents of veterans be ranked — in the order of their respective scores — above all other candidates.[10]

---

[7] The forms of veterans' hiring preferences vary widely. The Federal Government and approximately 41 States grant veterans a point advantage on civil service examinations, usually 10 points for a disabled veteran and 5 for one who is not disabled. See Fleming & Shanor, supra n. 6, 26 Emory L.J., at 17, and n. 12 (citing statutes). A few offer only tiebreaking preferences. Id., at n. 14 (citing statutes). A very few States, like Massachusetts, extend absolute hiring or positional preferences to qualified veterans. Id., at n. 13. See, e.g., N.J. Stat. Ann. § 11:27-4 (West 1976); S.D. Comp. Laws Ann. § 3-3-1 (1974); Utah Code Ann. § 34-30-11 (1953); Wash. Rev. Code §§ 41.04.010, 73.16.010 (1976).

[8] Mass. Gen. Laws Ann., ch. 4, § 7, Forty-third (West 1976), which supplies the general definition of the term "veteran," reads in pertinent part: "Veteran" shall mean any person male or female, including a nurse, (a) whose last discharge or release from his wartime service, as defined herein, was under honorable conditions and who (b) served in the army, navy, marine corps, coast guard, or air force of the United States for not less than ninety days active service, at least one day of which was for wartime service ...."

Persons awarded the Purple Heart, ch. 4, § 7, Forty-third, or one of a number of specified campaign badges or the Congressional Medal of Honor are also deemed veterans. Mass. Gen. Laws Ann., ch. 31, § 26 (West 1979).

"Wartime service" is defined as service performed by a "Spanish War veteran," a "World War I veteran," a "World War II veteran," a "Korean veteran," a "Vietnam veteran," or a member of the "WAAC." Mass. Gen. Laws Ann., ch. 4, § 7, Forty-third (West 1976). Each of these terms is further defined to specify a period of service. The statutory definitions, taken together, cover the entire period from September 16, 1940 to May 7, 1975. See ibid.

"WAAC" is defined as follows: "any woman who was discharged and so served in any corps or unit of the United States established for the purpose of enabling women to serve with, or as auxiliary to, the armed forces of the United States and such woman shall be deemed to be a veteran. Ibid.

[10] Ch. 131, § 23 provides in full:

"The names of persons who pass examination for appointment to any position classified under the civil service shall be placed upon the eligible lists in the following order:

"(1) Disabled veterans ... in the order of their respective standing; (2) veterans in the order of their respective standing; (3) persons described in section 23 B [the widow or widowed mother of a veteran killed in action or who died from a service-connected disability incurred in wartime service and who has not remarried] in the order of their respective standing; (4) other applicants in the order of their respective standing. Upon receipt of a requisition, names shall be certified from such lists according to the method of certification prescribed by the civil service rules. A disabled veteran shall be retained in employment in preference to all other persons, including veterans."

Rank on the eligible list and availability for employment are the sole factors that determine which candidates are considered for appointment to an official civil service position. When a public agency has a vacancy, it requisitions a list of "certified eligibles" from the state personnel division. Under formulas prescribed by civil service rules, a small number of candidates from the top of an appropriate list, three if there is only one vacancy, are certified. The appointing agency is then required to choose from among these candidates. Although the veterans' preference thus does not guarantee that a veteran will be appointed, it is obvious that the preference gives to veterans who achieve passing scores a well-nigh absolute advantage.

B. The appellee has lived in Dracut, Mass., most of her life. She entered the workforce in 1948, and for the next 14 years worked at a variety of jobs in the private sector. She first entered the state civil service system in 1963, having competed successfully for a position as Senior Clerk Stenographer in the Massachusetts Civil Defense Agency. There she worked for four years. In 1967, she was promoted to the position of Federal Funds and Personnel Coordinator in the same agency. The agency, and with it her job, was eliminated in 1975.

During her 12-year tenure as a public employee, Ms. Feeney took and passed a number of open competitive civil service examinations. On several she did quite well, receiving in 1971 the second highest score on an examination for a job with the Board of Dental Examiners, and in 1973 the third highest on a test for an Administrative Assistant position with a mental health center. Her high scores, however, did not win her a place on the certified eligible list. Because of the veterans' preference, she was ranked sixth behind five male veterans on the Dental Examiner list. She was not certified, and a lower scoring veteran was eventually appointed. On the 1973 examination, she was placed in a position on the list behind 12 male veterans, 11 of whom had lower scores. Following the other examinations that she took, her name was similarly ranked below those of veterans who had achieved passing grades.

Ms. Feeney's interest in securing a better job in state government did not wane. Having been consistently eclipsed by veterans, however, she eventually concluded that further competition for civil service positions of interest to veterans would be futile. In 1975, shortly after her civil defense job was abolished, she commenced this litigation.

C. The veterans' hiring preference in Massachusetts, as in other jurisdictions, has traditionally been justified as a measure designed to reward veterans for the sacrifice of military service, to ease the transition from military to civilian life, to encourage patriotic service, and to attract loyal and well-disciplined people to civil service occupations.[12] See, e.g., *Hutcheson v. Director of Civil Service*, 361 Mass. 480, 281 N.E.2d 53 (1972)....

A 1977 amendment extended the dependents' preference to "surviving spouses," and "surviving parents." 1977 Mass. Acts, ch. 815.

[12] Veterans' preference laws have been challenged so often that the rationale in their support has become essentially standardized. See, e.g., *Koelfgen v. Jackson*, 355 F. Supp. 243 (Minn. 1972), *summarily aff'd*, 410 U.S. 976; *August v. Bronstein, supra; Rios v. Dillman*, 499 F. 2d 329 (CA5 1974); cf. *Mitchell v. Cohen*, 333 U.S. 411, 419 n. 12. See generally Blumberg, *De Facto and De Jure Sex Discrimination Under the Equal Protection Clause: A Reconsideration of the Veterans' Prefer-*

D. The first Massachusetts veterans' preference statute defined the term "veterans" in gender-neutral language. See 1896 Mass. Acts, ch. 517, § 1 ("a person" who served in the United States Army or Navy), and subsequent amendments have followed this pattern, see, e.g., 1919 Mass. Acts, ch. 150, § 1 ("any person who has served ..."); 1954 Mass. Acts, ch. 627, § 1 ("any person, male or female, including a nurse"). Women who have served in official United States military units during wartime, then, have always been entitled to the benefit of the preference. In addition, Massachusetts, through a 1943 amendment to the definition of "wartime service," extended the preference to women who served in unofficial auxiliary woman's units. 1943 Mass. Acts, ch. 194.

When the first general veterans' preference statute was adopted in 1896, there were no women veterans.[18] The statute, however, covered only Civil War veterans. Most of them were beyond middle age, and relatively few were actively competing for public employment. Thus, the impact of the preference upon the employment opportunities of nonveterans as a group and women in particular was slight.

Notwithstanding the apparent attempts by Massachusetts to include as many military women as possible within the scope of the preference, the statute today benefits an overwhelmingly male class. This is attributable in some measure to the variety of federal statutes, regulations, and polices that have restricted the numbers of women who could enlist in the United States Armed Forces,[21] and

---

ence in Public Employment, 26 Buffalo L. Rev. 3 (1977). For a collection of early cases, see Annot., Veterans' Preference Laws, 161 A.L.R. 494 (1946).

[18] Small numbers of women served in combat roles in every war before the 20th century in which the United States was involved, but usually unofficially or disguised as men. See M. Binkin & S. Bach, Women and the Military 5 (1977) (hereinafter Binkin and Bach). Among the better-known are Molly Pitcher (Revolutionary War), Deborah Sampson (Revolutionary War), and Lucy Brewer (War of 1812). Passing as one "George Baker," Brewer served for three years as a gunner on the U.S.S. Constitution ("Old Ironsides") and distinguished herself in several major naval battles in the War of 1812. See J. Laffin, Women in Battle 116-122 (1967).

[21] The Army Nurse Corps, created by Congress in 1901, was the first official military unit for women, but its members were not granted full military rank until 1944. See Binkin and Bach, 4-21 (1977); M. Treadwell, The Women's Army Corps 6 (Dept. of Army 1954) (hereinafter Treadwell). During World War I, a variety of proposals were made to enlist women for work as doctors, telephone operators and clerks, but all were rejected by the War Department. See ibid. The Navy, however, interpreted its own authority broadly to include a power to enlist women as Yeoman F's and Marine F's. About 13,000 women served in this rank, working primarily at clerical jobs. These women were the first in the United States to be admitted to full military rank and status. See id., at 10.

Official military corps for women were established in response to the massive personnel needs of the Second World War. See generally Binkin and Bach; Treadwell. The Women's Army Auxiliary Corps (WAAC) — the unofficial predecessor of the Women's Army Corps (WAC) — was created on May 14, 1942, followed two months later by the WAVES (Women Accepted for Voluntary Emergency Service). See Binkin and Bach 7. Not long after, the United States Marine Corps Women's Reserve and the Coast Guard Women's Reserve (SPAR) were established. See ibid. Some 350,000 women served in the four services; some 800 women also served as Women's Airforce Service Pilots (WASPS). Ibid. Most worked in health care, administration, and communications; they were also employed as airplane mechanics, parachute riggers, gunnery instructors, air traffic controllers, and the like.

The authorizations for the women's units during World War II were temporary. The Women's Armed Services Integration Act of 1948, 62 Stat. 356, established the women's services on a permanent basis. Under the Act, women were given regular military status. However, quotas were placed on the numbers who could enlist; 62 Stat. 357, 360-361 (no more than 2% of total enlisted strength); eligibility requirements were more stringent than those for men, and career opportunities were limited. Binkin and Bach 11-12. During the 1950's and 1960's, enlisted women constituted little

largely to the simple fact that women have never been subjected to a military draft. See generally, Binkin and Bach 4-21 (1977).

When this litigation was commenced, then, over 98% of the veterans in Massachusetts were male; only 1.8% were female. And over one-quarter of the Massachusetts population were veterans. During the decade between 1963 and 1973 when the appellee was actively participating in the State's merit selection system, 47,005 new permanent appointments were made in the classified official service. Forty-three percent of those hired were women, and, 57% were men. Of the women appointed, 1.8% were veterans, while 54% of the men had veteran status. A large unspecified percentage of the female appointees were serving in lower paying positions for which males traditionally had not applied. On each of 50 sample eligible lists that are part of the record in this case, one or more women who would have been certified as eligible for appointment on the basis of test results were displaced by veterans whose test scores were lower.

At the outset of this litigation the State conceded that for "many of the permanent positions for which males and females have competed" the veterans' preference has "resulted in a substantially greater proportion of female eligibles than male eligibles" not being certified for consideration. The impact of the veterans' preference law upon the public employment opportunities of women has thus been severe. This impact lies at the heart of the appellee's federal constitutional claim.

II

The sole question for decision on this appeal is whether Massachusetts, in granting an absolute lifetime preference to veterans, has discriminated against women in violation of the Equal Protection Clause of the Fourteenth Amendment.

A. The equal protection guarantee of the Fourteenth Amendment does not take from the States all power of classification. *Massachusetts Bd. of Retirement v. Murgia,* 427 U.S. 307, 314. Most laws classify, and many affect certain groups unevenly, even though the law itself treats them no differently from all other members of the class described by the law. When the basic classification is rationally based, uneven effects upon particular groups within a class are ordinarily of no constitutional concern. *New York Transit Authority v. Beazer,* 440 U.S. 568; *Jefferson v. Hackney,* 406 U.S. 535, 548. Cf. *James v. Valtierra,* 402 U.S. 137. The calculus of effects, the manner in which a particular law reverberates in a society, is a legislative and not a judicial responsibility. *Dandridge v. Williams,* 397 U.S. 471; *San Antonio School Dist. v. Rodriguez,* 411 U.S. 1. In assessing an equal protection challenge, a court is called upon only to measure the basic validity of the legislative classification. *Barrett v. Indiana,* 229 U.S. 26, 29-30; *Railway Express Agency v. New York,* 336 U.S. 106. When some other independent right is not at stake, see, e.g., *Shapiro v. Thompson,* 394 U.S. 618, and when there is no "reason to infer antipathy,"

more than 1% of the total force. In 1967, the 2% quota was lifted, § 1(9)(E), 81 Stat. 375, 10 U.S.C. § 3209(b), and in the 1970's many restrictive polices concerning women's participation in the military have been eliminated or modified. See generally Binkin and Bach. In 1972, women still constituted less than 2% of the enlisted strength. *Id.,* at 14. By 1975, when this litigation was commenced, the percentage had risen to 4.0%. *Ibid.*

Vance v. Bradley, 440 U.S. 93, 97, it is presumed that "even improvident decisions will eventually be rectified by the democratic process ...." *Ibid.*

Certain classifications, however, in themselves supply a reason to infer antipathy. Race is the paradigm. A racial classification, regardless of purported motivation, is presumptively invalid and can be upheld only upon an extraordinary justification. *Brown v. Board of Education,* 347 U.S. 483; *McLaughlin v. Florida,* 379 U.S. 184. This rule applies as well to a classification that is ostensibly neutral but is an obvious pretext for racial discrimination. *Yick Wo v. Hopkins,* 118 U.S. 356; *Guinn v. United States,* 238 U.S. 347; cf. *Lane v. Wilson,* 307 U.S. 268; *Gomillion v. Lightfoot,* 364 U.S. 339. But, as was made clear in *Washington v. Davis,* 426 U.S. 229, and *Arlington Heights v. Metropolitan Housing Dev. Corp.,* 429 U.S. 252, even if a neutral law has a disproportionately adverse effect upon a racial minority, it is unconstitutional under the Equal Protection Clause only if that impact can be traced to a discriminatory purpose.

Classifications based upon gender, not unlike those based upon race, have traditionally been the touchstone for pervasive and often subtle discrimination. *Caban v. Mohammed,* 441 U.S. 380, 398 (STEWART, J., dissenting). This Court's recent cases teach that such classifications must bear a "close and substantial relationship to important governmental objectives." *Craig v. Boren,* 429 U.S. 190, 197, and are in many settings unconstitutional. *Reed v. Reed,* 404 U.S. 71; *Frontiero v. Richardson,* 411 U.S. 677; *Weinberger v. Wiesenfeld,* 420 U.S. 636; *Craig v. Boren, supra; Califano v. Goldfarb,* 430 U.S. 199; *Orr v. Orr,* 440 U.S. 268; *Caban v. Mohammed, supra.* Although public employment is not a constitutional right, *Massachusetts Bd. of Retirement v. Murgia, supra,* and the States have wide discretion in framing employee qualifications, see, e.g., *New York Transit Authority v. Beazer, supra,* these precedents dictate that any state law overtly or covertly designed to prefer males over females in public employment would require an exceedingly persuasive justification to withstand a constitutional challenge under the Equal Protection Clause of the Fourteenth Amendment.

B. The cases of *Washington v. Davis, supra,* and *Arlington Heights v. Metropolitan Housing Dev. Corp., supra,* recognize that when a neutral law has a disparate impact upon a group that has historically been the victim of discrimination, an unconstitutional purpose may still be at work. But those cases signalled no departure from the settled rule that the Fourteenth Amendment guarantees equal laws, not equal results. *Davis* upheld a job-related employment test that white people passed in proportionately greater numbers than Negroes, for there had been no showing that racial discrimination entered into the establishment or formulation of the test. *Arlington Heights* upheld a zoning board decision that tended to perpetuate racially segregated housing patterns, since, apart from its effect, the board's decision was shown to be nothing more than an application of constitutionally neutral zoning policy. Those principles apply with equal force to a case involving alleged gender discrimination.

When a statute gender-neutral on its face is challenged on the ground that its effects upon women are disproportionably adverse, a two-fold inquiry is thus appropriate. The first question is whether the statutory classification is indeed neutral in the sense that it is not gender-based. If the classification itself, covert or overt, is not based upon gender, the second question is whether the adverse effect reflects invidious gender-based discrimination. See *Arlington Heights v. Metropolitan Housing Dev. Corp., supra.* In this second inquiry, impact provides an "important starting point," 429 U.S., at 266, but purposeful discrimination is "the condition that offends the Constitution." *Swann v. Charlotte-Mecklenburg Board of Education,* 402 U.S. 1, 16.

It is against this background of precedent that we consider the merits of the case before us.

III

A. The question whether ch. 31, § 23, establishes a classification that is overtly or covertly based upon gender must first be considered. The appellee has conceded that ch. 31, § 23, is neutral on its face. She has also acknowledged that state hiring preferences for veterans are not *per se* invalid, for she has limited her challenge to the absolute lifetime preference that Massachusetts provides to veterans. The District Court made two central findings that are relevant here: first, that ch. 31, § 23, serves legitimate and worthy purposes; second, that the absolute preference was not established for the purpose of discriminating against women. The appellee has thus acknowledged and the District Court has thus found that the distinction between veterans and nonveterans drawn by ch. 31, § 23, is not a pretext for gender discrimination. The appellee's concession and the District Court's finding are clearly correct.

If the impact of this statute could not be plausibly explained on a neutral ground, impact itself would signal that the real classification made by the law was in fact not neutral. See *Washington v. Davis,* 426 U.S., at 242; *Arlington Heights v. Metropolitan Housing Dev. Corp., supra,* at 266. But there can be but one answer to the question whether this veteran preference excludes significant numbers of women from preferred state jobs because they are women or because they are nonveterans. Apart from the fact that the definition of "veterans" in the statute has always been neutral as to gender and that Massachusetts has consistently defined veteran status in a way that has been inclusive of women who have served in the military, this is not a law that can plausibly be explained only as a gender-based classification. Indeed, it is not a law that can rationally be explained on that ground. Veteran status is not uniquely made. Although few women benefit from the preference, the nonveteran class is not substantially all-female. To the contrary, significant numbers of nonveterans are men, and all nonveterans — male as well as female — are placed at a disadvantage. Too many men are affected by ch. 31, § 23, to permit the inference that the statute is but a pretext for preferring men over women.

Moreover, as the District Court implicitly found, the purposes of the statute provide the surest explanation for its impact. Just as there are cases in which impact alone can unmask an invidious classification, cf. *Yick Wo v. Hopkins,* 118 U.S. 356, there are others, in which — notwithstanding impact — the legitimate noninvidious purposes of a law cannot be missed. This is one. The distinction made by ch. 31, § 23, is, as it seems to be, quite simply between veterans and nonveterans, not between men and women.

B. The dispositive question, then, is whether the appellee has shown that a gender-based discriminatory purpose has, at least in some measure, shaped the Massachusetts veterans' preference legislation. As did the District Court, she points to two basic factors which in her view distinguish ch. 31, § 23, from the neutral rules at issue in the *Washington v. Davis* and *Arlington Heights* cases. The first is the nature of the preference, which is said to be demonstrably gender-biased in the sense that it favors a status reserved under federal military policy primarily to men. The second concerns the impact of the absolute life-time preference upon the employment opportunities of women, an impact claimed to be too inevitable to have been unintended. The appellee contends that these factors, coupled with the fact that the preference itself has little if any relevance to actual job performance, more than suffice to prove the discrimina-tory intent required to establish a constitutional violation.

1. The contention that this veterans' preference is "inherently non-neutral" or "gender-biased" presumes that the State, by favoring veterans, intentionally incorporated into its public employment policies the panoply of sex-based and assertedly discriminatory federal laws that have prevented all but a handful of women from becoming veterans. There are two serious difficulties with this argument. First, it is wholly at odds with the District Court's central finding that Massachusetts has not offered a preference to veterans for the purpose of discriminating against women. Second, it cannot be reconciled with the assump-tion made by both the appellee and the District Court that a more limited hiring preference for veterans could be sustained. Taken together, these difficulties are fatal.

To the extent that the status of veteran is one that few women have been enabled to achieve, every hiring preference for veterans, however modest or extreme, is inherently gender-biased. If Massachusetts by offering such a pref-erence can be said intentionally to have incorporated into its state employment policies the historical gender-based federal military personnel practices, the degree of the preference would or should make no constitutional difference. Invidious discrimination does not become less so because the discrimination accomplished is of a lesser magnitude.[23] Discriminatory intent is simply not amenable to calibration. It either is a factor that has influenced the legislative choice or it is not. The District Court's conclusion that the absolute veterans' preference was not originally enacted or subsequently reaffirmed for the pur-pose of giving an advantage to males as such necessarily compels the conclusion that the State intended nothing more than to prefer "veterans." Given this finding, simple logic suggests that an intent to exclude women from significant public jobs was not at work in this law. To reason that it was, by describing the preference as "inherently non-neutral" or "gender-biased," is merely to restate the fact of impact, not to answer the question of intent.

To be sure, this case is unusual in that it involves a law that by design is not neutral. The law overtly prefers veterans as such. As opposed to the written test at issue in *Davis,* it does not purport to define a job related characteristic. To the contrary, it confers upon a specifically described group — perceived to be particularly deserving — a competitive head start. But the District Court found, and the appellee has not disputed, that this legislative choice was legitimate. The

---

[23] This is not to say that the degree of impact is irrelevant to the question of intent. But it is to say that a more modest preference, while it might well lessen impact and, as the State argues, might lessen the effectiveness of the statute in helping veterans, would not be any more or less "neutral" in the constitutional sense.

basic distinction between veterans and nonveterans, having been found not gender-based, and the goals of the preference having been found worthy, ch. 31 must be analyzed as is any other neutral law that casts a greater burden upon women as a group than upon men as a group. The enlistment policies of the armed services may well have discriminated on the basis of sex. See *Frontiero v. Richardson,* 411 U.S. 677; cf. *Schlesinger v. Ballard,* 419 U.S. 498. But the history of discrimination against women in the military is not on trial in this case.

2. The appellee's ultimate argument rests upon the presumption, common to the criminal and civil law, that a person intends the natural and foreseeable consequences of his voluntary actions....

... The decision to grant a preference to veterans was of course "intentional." So, necessarily, did an adverse impact upon nonveterans follow from that decision. And it cannot seriously be argued that the legislature of Massachusetts could have been unaware that most veterans are men. It would thus be disingenuous to say that the adverse consequences of this legislation for women were unintended, in the sense that they were not volitional or in the sense that they were not foreseeable.

"Discriminatory purpose," however, implies more than intent as volition or intent as awareness of consequences. See *United Jewish Organizations v. Carey,* 430 U.S. 144, 179 (concurring opinion).[24] It implies that the decisionmaker, in this case a state legislature, selected or reaffirmed a particular course of action at least in part "because of," not merely "in spite of," its adverse effects upon an identifiable group.[25] Yet nothing in the record demonstrates that this preference for veterans was originally devised or subsequently re-enacted because it would accomplish the collateral goal of keeping women in a stereotypic and predefined place in the Massachusetts Civil Service.

To the contrary, the statutory history shows that the benefit of the preference was consistently offered to "any person" who was a veteran. That benefit has been extended to women under a very broad statutory definition of the term veteran. The preference formula itself, which is the focal point of this challenge, was first adopted — so it appears from this record — out of a perceived need to help a small group of older Civil War veterans. It has since been reaffirmed and extended only to cover new veterans.[27] When the totality of

---

[24] Proof of discriminatory intent must necessarily usually rely on objective factors, several of which were outlined in *Arlington Heights v. Metropolitan Housing Dev. Corp.,* 429 U.S. 252, 266. The inquiry is practical. What a legislature or any official entity is "up to" may be plain from the results its actions achieve, or the results they avoid. Often it is made clear from what has been called, in a different context, "the give and take of the situation." *Cramer v. United States,* 325 U.S. 1, 32-33. (Jackson, J.).

[25] This is not to say that the inevitability or foreseeability of consequences of a neutral rule has no bearing upon the existence of discriminatory intent. Certainly, when the adverse consequences of a law upon an identifiable group are as inevitable as the gender-based consequences of ch. 31, § 23, a strong inference that the adverse effects were desired can reasonably be drawn. But in this inquiry — made as it is under the Constitution — an inference is a working tool, not a synonym for proof. When as here, the impact is essentially an unavoidable consequence of a legislative policy that has in itself always been deemed to be legitimate, and when, as here, the statutory history and all of the available evidence affirmatively demonstrate the opposite, the inference simply fails to ripen into proof.

[27] The appellee has suggested that the former statutory exception for "women's requisitions" supplies evidence that Massachusetts, when it established and subsequently reaffirmed the absolute

legislative actions establishing and extending the Massachusetts veterans' preference are considered, see *Washington v. Davis*, 426 U.S., at 242, the law remains what it purports to be: a preference for veterans of either sex over nonveterans of either sex, not for men over women.

IV

Veterans' hiring preferences represent an awkward — and, many argue, unfair — exception to the widely shared view that merit and merit alone should prevail in the employment policies of government. After a war, such laws have been enacted virtually without opposition. During peacetime they inevitably have come to be viewed in many quarters as undemocratic and unwise. Absolute and permanent preferences, as the troubled history of this law demonstrates, have always been subject to the objection that they give the veteran more than a square deal. But the Fourteenth Amendment "cannot be made a refuge from ill-advised ... laws." *District of Columbia v. Brooke*, 214 U.S. 138, 150. The substantial edge granted to veterans by ch. 31, § 23, may reflect unwise policy. The appellee, however, has simply failed to demonstrate that the law in any way reflects a purpose to discriminate on the basis of sex.

The judgment is reversed, and the case is remanded for further proceedings consistent with this opinion.

It is so ordered.

JUSTICE STEVENS, with whom JUSTICE WHITE joins, concurring.

While I concur in the Court's opinion, I confess that I am not at all sure that there is any difference between the two questions posed. If a classification is not overtly based on gender, I am inclined to believe the question whether it is covertly gender-based is the same as the question whether its adverse effects reflect invidious gender-based discrimination. However the question is phrased, for me the answer is largely provided by the fact that the number of males disadvantaged by Massachusetts' Veterans Preference (1,867,000) is sufficiently large — and sufficiently close to the number of disadvantaged females (2,954,000) — to refute the claim that the rule was intended to benefit males as a class over females as a class.

JUSTICE MARSHALL, with whom JUSTICE BRENNAN joins, dissenting.

Although acknowledging that in some circumstances, discriminatory intent may be inferred from the inevitable or foreseeable impact of a statute, the Court concludes that no such intent has been established here. I cannot agree. In my judgment, Massachusetts' choice of an absolute veterans' preference system evinces purposeful gender-based discrimination. And because the statutory scheme bears no substantial relationship to a legitimate governmental objective, it cannot withstand scrutiny under the Equal Protection Clause.

---

preference legislation, assumed that women would not or should not compete with men. She has further suggested that the former provision extending the preference to certain female dependents of veterans, see n. 10, *supra*, demonstrates that ch. 31, § 23, is laced with "old notions" about the proper roles and needs of the sexes. See *Califano v. Goldfarb*, 430 U.S. 199; *Weinberger v. Wiesenfeld*, 420 U.S. 636. But the first suggestion is totally belied by the statutory history, and the second fails to account for the consistent statutory recognition of the contribution of women to this Nation's military efforts.

I

The District Court found that the "prime objective" of the Massachusetts Veterans Preference Statute, Mass. Gen. Laws, ch. 31, § 23, was to benefit individuals with prior military service. *Anthony v. Commonwealth,* 415 F. Supp. 485, 497 (Mass. 1976). See *Feeney v. Massachusetts,* 451 F. Supp. 143, 145 (Mass. 1978). Under the Court's analysis, this factual determination "necessarily compels the conclusion that the state intended nothing more than to prefer 'veterans.' Given this finding, simple logic suggests that an intent to exclude women from significant public jobs was not at work in this law." I find the Court's logic neither simple nor compelling.

That a legislature seeks to advantage one group does not, as a matter of logic or of common sense, exclude the possibility that it also intends to disadvantage another. Individuals in general and lawmakers in particular frequently act for a variety of reasons. As this Court recognized in *Arlington Heights v. Metropolitan Housing Dev. Corp.,* 429 U.S. 252, 265 (1977), "[r]arely can it be said that a legislature or administrative body operating under a broad mandate made a decision motivated by a single concern." Absent an omniscience not commonly attributed to the judiciary, it will often be impossible to ascertain the sole or even dominant purpose of a given statute. See *McGinnis v. Royster,* 410 U.S. 263, 276-277 (1973); Ely, Legislative and Administrative Motivation in Constitutional Law, 79 Yale L.J. 1205, 1214 (1970). Thus, the critical constitutional inquiry is not whether an illicit consideration was the primary or but-for cause of a decision, but rather whether it had an appreciable role in shaping a given legislative enactment. Where there is "proof that a discriminatory purpose has been *a* motivating factor in the decision, ... judicial deference is no longer justified." *Arlington Heights v. Metropolitan Housing Dev. Corp., supra,* at 265-266 (emphasis added).

Moreover, since reliable evidence of subjective intentions is seldom obtainable, resort to inference based on objective factors is generally unavoidable. See *Beer v. United States,* 425 U.S. 130, 148-149, n. 4 (1976) (MARSHALL, J., dissenting); cf. *Palmer v. Thompson,* 403 U.S. 217, 224-225 (1971); *United States v. O'Brien,* 391 U.S. 367, 383-384 (1968). To discern the purposes underlying facially neutral policies, this Court has therefore considered the degree, inevitability, and foreseeability of any disproportionate impact as well as the alternatives reasonably available. See *Monroe v. Board of Commissioners,* 391 U.S. 450, 459 (1968); *Goss v. Board of Education,* 373 U.S. 683, 688-689 (1963); *Gomillion v. Lightfoot,* 364 U.S. 339 (1960); *Griffin v. Illinois,* 351 U.S. 12, 17 n. 11 (1956). Cf. *Albemarle Paper Co. v. Moody,* 422 U.S. 405, 425 (1975).

In the instant case, the impact of the Massachusetts statute on women is undisputed. Any veteran with a passing grade on the civil service exam must be placed ahead of a nonveteran, regardless of their respective scores....

As the District Court recognized, this consequence followed foreseeably, indeed inexorably, from the long history of policies severely limiting women's participation in the military.[1] Although neutral in form, the statute is anything

---

[1]See *Anthony v. Massachusetts,* 415 F. Supp. 485, 490, 495-499 (Mass. 1976); *Feeney v. Massachusetts,* 451 F. Supp. 143, 145, 148 (Mass. 1978). In addition to the 2% quota on women's participation in the armed forces, enlistment and appointment requirements have been more stringent for

but neutral in application. It inescapably reserves a major sector of public employment to "an already established class which, as a matter of historical fact, is 98% male." *Ibid.* Where the foreseeable impact of a facially neutral policy is so disproportionate, the burden should rest on the State to establish that sex-based considerations played no part in the choice of the particular legislative scheme. Cf. *Castaneda v. Partida,* 430 U.S. 482 (1977); *Washington v. Davis,* 426 U.S. 229, 241 (1976); *Alexander v. Louisiana,* 405 U.S. 625, 632 (1972); see generally Brest, *Palmer v. Thompson: An Approach to the Problem of Unconstitutional Legislative Motive,* 1971 Sup. Ct. Rev. 95, 123.

Clearly, that burden was not sustained here. The legislative history of the statute reflects the Commonwealth's patent appreciation of the impact the preference system would have on women, and an equally evident desire to mitigate that impact only with respect to certain traditionally female occupations. Until 1971, the statute and implementing civil service regulations exempted from operation of the preference any job requisitions "especially calling for women." 1954 Mass. Acts, ch. 627, § 5. See also 1896 Mass. Acts, ch. 517, § 6; 1919 Mass. Acts, ch. 150, § 2; 1945 Mass. Acts, ch. 725, § 2(e); 1965 Mass. Acts, ch. 53. In practice, this exemption, coupled with the absolute preference for veterans, has created a gender-based civil service hierarchy, with women occupying low-grade clerical and secretarial jobs and men holding more responsible and remunerative positions. See 415 F. Supp., at 488; 451 F. Supp., at 148 n. 9.

Thus, for over 70 years, the Commonwealth has maintained, as an integral part of its veteran's preference system, an exemption relegating female civil service applicants to occupations traditionally filled by women. Such a statutory scheme both reflects and perpetuates precisely the kind of archaic assumptions about women's roles which we have previously held invalid. See *Orr v. Orr,* 440 U.S. 268 (1979); *Califano v. Goldfarb,* 430 U.S. 199, 210-211 (1977); *Stanton v. Stanton,* 421 U.S. 7, 14 (1975); *Weinberger v. Wiesenfeld,* 420 U.S. 636, 645 (1975). Particularly when viewed against the range of less discriminatory alternatives available to assist veterans,[2] Massachusetts' choice of a formula that so severely restricts public employment opportunities for women cannot reasonably be thought gender-neutral. Cf. *Albemarle Paper Co. v. Moody, supra,* at 425. The Court's conclusion to the contrary — that "nothing in the record"

---

females than males with respect to age, mental and physical aptitude, parental consent, and educational attainment. M. Binkin & S. Bach, Women and the Military (1977) (hereinafter Binkin and Bach); Note, *The Equal Rights Amendment and the Military,* 82 Yale L.J. 1533, 1539 (1973). Until the 1970's, the armed forces precluded enlistment and appointment of women, but not men, who were married or had dependent children. See 415 F. Supp., at 490; App. 85; Exs. 98, 99, 103, 104. Sex-based restrictions on advancement and training opportunities also diminished the incentives for qualified women to enlist. See Binkin and Bach 10-17; Beane, *Sex Discrimination in the Military,* 67 Mil. L. Rev. 19, 59-83 (1979). Cf. *Schlesinger v. Ballard,* 419 U.S. 498, 508 (1975).

Thus, unlike the employment examination in *Washington v. Davis,* 426 U.S. 229 (1976), which the Court found to be demonstrably job-related, the Massachusetts preference statute incorporates the results of sex-based military policies irrelevant to women's current fitness for civilian public employment. See 415 F. Supp., at 498-499.

[2]Only four States afford a preference comparable in scope to that of Massachusetts. See Fleming and Shanor, *Veterans' Preferences and Public Employment: Unconstitutional Gender Discrimination?,* 26 Emory L.J. 13, 17 n. 13 (1977) (citing statutes). Other States and the Federal Government grant point or tie-breaking preferences that do not foreclose opportunities for women. See *id.,* at 13, and nn. 13, 14; *ante,* n. 7; Hearings before the Subcommittee on Civil Service of the House Committee on Post Office and Civil Service, 95th Cong., 1st Sess., 4 (1977) (statement of Alan Campbell, Chairman, U. S. Civil Service Commission).

evinces a "collateral goal of keeping women in a stereotypic and predefined place in the Massachusetts Civil Service," — displays a singularly myopic view of the facts established below.[3]

II

To survive challenge under the Equal Protection Clause, statutes reflecting gender-based discrimination must be substantially related to the achievement of important governmental objectives. See *Califano v. Webster*, 430 U.S. 313, 316-317 (1977); *Craig v. Boren*, 429 U.S. 190, 197 (1976); *Reed v. Reed*, 404 U.S. 71, 76 (1971). Appellants here advance three interests in support of the absolute preference system: (1) assisting veterans in their readjustment to civilian life; (2) encouraging military enlistment; and (3) rewarding those who have served their country. Brief for Appellants 24. Although each of those goals is unquestionably legitimate, the "mere recitation of a benign compensatory purpose" cannot of itself insulate legislative classifications from constitutional scrutiny. *Weinberger v. Wiesenfeld, supra,* at 648. And in this case, the Commonwealth has failed to establish a sufficient relationship between its objectives and the means chosen to effectuate them....

... Here, there are a wide variety of less discriminatory means by which Massachusetts could effect its compensatory purposes. For example, a point preference system, such as that maintained by many States and the Federal Government, see n. 2, *supra,* or an absolute preference for a limited duration, would reward veterans without excluding all qualified women from upper level civil service positions. Apart from public employment, the Commonwealth, can, and does, afford assistance to veterans in various ways, including tax abatements, educational subsidies, and special programs for needy veterans. See Mass. Gen. Laws Ann., ch. 59, § 5, Fifth (West Supp. 1979); Mass. Gen. Laws Ann., ch. 69, §§ 7, 7B (West Supp. 1979); and Mass. Gen. Laws Ann., chs. 115, 115A (West 1969 and Supp. 1978). Unlike these and similar benefits, the costs of which are distributed across the taxpaying public generally, the Massachusetts statute exacts a substantial price from a discrete group of individuals who have long been subject to employment discrimination, and who, "because of circumstances totally beyond their control, have [had] little if any chance of becoming members in the preferred class." 415 F. Supp., at 499. See n. 1, *supra....*

NOTE

The New York Constitution and Civil Service Law grant a points-added employment preference to those veterans who were New York State residents at the time they entered the military service. In *Attorney General of New York v. Soto-Lopez,* 476 U.S. 898 (1986), the Supreme Court invalidated this preference. Justices Brennan, Marshall, Blackmun, and Powell found that the New

---

[3]Although it is relevant that the preference statute also disadvantages a substantial group of men, see *ante,* at 281 (STEVENS, J., concurring), it is equally pertinent that 47% of Massachusetts men over 18 are veterans, as compared to 0.8% of Massachusetts women. App. 83. Given this disparity, and the indicia of intent noted *supra,* the absolute number of men denied preference cannot be dispositive, especially since they have not faced the barriers to achieving veteran status confronted by women. See n. 1, *supra.*

York preference impermissibly infringed the constitutionally protected right to travel, since the stated desire of New York to encourage people to join the Armed Forces and to assist discharged veterans to reestablish themselves could have been accomplished without penalizing the right to travel by awarding the special credits to all veterans. Chief Justice Burger and Justice White concluded that the New York prior residence requirement failed to satisfy the rational-basis test mandated by the equal protection clause of the fourteenth amendment. Justices O'Connor, Rehnquist and Stevens dissented.

E. PUBLIC EMPLOYER IMMUNITY FROM SUIT

CITY OF ST. LOUIS v. PRAPROTNIK

485 U.S. 112, 108 S. Ct. 915, 99 L. Ed. 2d 107 (1988)

JUSTICE O'CONNOR announced the judgment of the Court and delivered an opinion, in which CHIEF JUSTICE REHNQUIST, JUSTICE WHITE, and JUSTICE SCALIA join.

This case calls upon us to define the proper legal standard for determining when isolated decisions by municipal officials or employees may expose the municipality itself to liability under 42 U.S.C. § 1983.

I

The principal facts are not in dispute. Respondent James H. Praprotnik is an architect who began working for petitioner of St. Louis in 1968. For several years, respondent consistently received favorable evaluations of his job performance, uncommonly quick promotions, and significant increases in salary. By 1980, he was serving in a management-level city planning position at petitioner's Community Development Agency (CDA).

The Director of CDA, Donald Spaid, had instituted a requirement that the agency's professional employees, including architects, obtain advance approval before taking on private clients. Respondent and other CDA employees objected to the requirement. In April 1980, respondent was suspended for 15 days by CDA's Director of Urban Design, Charles Kindleberger, for having accepted outside employment without prior approval. Respondent appealed to the city's Civil Service Commission, a body charged with reviewing employee grievances. Finding the penalty too harsh, the Commission reversed the suspension, awarded respondent back pay, and directed that he be reprimanded for having failed to secure a clear understanding of the rule.

The Commission's decision was not well received by respondent's supervisors at CDA. Kindleberger later testified that he believed respondent had lied to the Commission, and that Spaid was angry with respondent.

Respondent's next two annual job performance evaluations were markedly less favorable than those in previous years. In discussing one of these evaluations with respondent, Kindleberger apparently mentioned his displeasure with respondent's 1980 appeal to the Civil Service Commission. Respondent appealed both evaluations to the Department of Personnel. In each case, the Department ordered partial relief and was upheld by the city's Director of Personnel or the Civil Service Commission.

In April 1981, a new mayor came into office, and Donald Spaid was replaced as Director of CDA by Frank Hamsher. As a result of budget cuts, a number of layoffs and transfers significantly reduced the size of CDA and of the planning section in which respondent worked. Respondent, however, was retained.

In the spring of 1982, a second round of layoffs and transfers occurred at CDA. At that time, the city's Heritage and Urban Design Division (Heritage) was seeking approval to hire someone who was qualified in architecture and urban planning. Hamsher arranged with the Director of Heritage, Henry Jackson, for certain functions to be transferred from CDA to Heritage. This arrangement, which made it possible for Heritage to employ a relatively high-level "city planning manager," was approved by Jackson's supervisor, Thomas Nash. Hamsher then transferred respondent to Heritage to fill this position.

Respondent objected to the transfer, and appealed to the Civil Service Commission. The Commission declined to hear the appeal because respondent had not suffered a reduction in his pay or grade. Respondent then filed suit in federal district court, alleging that the transfer was unconstitutional. The city was named as a defendant, along with Kindleberger, Hamsher, Jackson (whom respondent deleted from the list before trial), and Deborah Patterson, who had succeeded Hamsher at CDA.

At Heritage, respondent became embroiled in a series of disputes with Jackson and Jackson's successor, Robert Killen. Respondent was dissatisfied with the work he was assigned, which consisted of unchallenging clerical functions far below the level of responsibilities that he had previously enjoyed. At least one adverse personnel decision was taken against respondent, and he obtained partial relief after appealing that decision.

In December 1983, respondent was laid off from Heritage. The lay off was attributed to a lack of funds, and this apparently meant that respondent's supervisors had concluded that they could create two lower-level positions with the funds that were being used to pay respondent's salary. Respondent then amended the complaint in his lawsuit to include a challenge to the layoff. He also appealed to the Civil Service Commission, but proceedings in that forum were postponed because of the pending lawsuit and have never been completed.

The case went to trial on two theories: (1) that respondent's First Amendment rights had been violated through retaliatory actions taken in response to his appeal of his 1980 suspension; and (2) that respondent's layoff from Heritage was carried out for pretextual reasons in violation of due process. The jury returned special verdicts exonerating each of the three individual defendants, but finding the city liable under both theories. Judgment was entered on the verdicts, and the city appealed.

A panel of the Court of Appeals for the Eighth Circuit found that the due process claim had been submitted to the jury on an erroneous legal theory and vacated that portion of the judgment. With one judge dissenting, however, the panel affirmed the verdict holding the city liable for violating respondent's First Amendment rights. 798 F.2d 1168 (1986). Only the second of these holdings is challenged here.

The Court of Appeals found that the jury had implicitly determined that respondent's layoff from Heritage was brought about by an unconstitutional city policy. *Id.,* at 1173. Applying a test under which a "policymaker" is one whose employment decisions are "final" in the sense that they are not subjected to *de novo* review by higher-ranking officials, the Court of Appeals concluded that the city could be held liable for adverse personnel decisions taken by respondent's supervisors. *Id.,* at 1173-1175. In response to petitioner's contention that the city's personnel policies are actually set by the Civil Service Commission, the Court of Appeals concluded that the scope of review before that body was too "highly circumscribed" to allow it fairly to be said that the Commission, rather than the officials who initiated the actions leading to respondent's injury, were the "final authority" responsible for setting city policy. *Id.,* at 1175.

Turning to the question of whether a rational jury could have concluded that respondent had been injured by an unconstitutional policy, the Court of Appeals found that respondent's transfer from CDA to Heritage had been "orchestrated" by Hamsher, that the transfer had amounted to a "constructive discharge," and that the injury had reached fruition when respondent was eventually laid off by Nash and Killen. *Id.,* at 1175-1176, and n. 8. The court held that the jury's verdict exonerating Hamsher and the other individual defendants could be reconciled with a finding of liability against the city because "the named defendants were not the supervisors directly causing the lay off, when the actual damages arose." *Id.,* at 1173, n. 3. Cf. *Los Angeles v. Heller,* 475 U.S. 796 (1986).

The dissenting judge relied on our decision in *Pembaur v. Cincinnati,* 475 U.S. 469 (1986). He found that the power to set employment policy for petitioner city of St. Louis lay with the mayor and aldermen, who were authorized to enact ordinances, and with the Civil Service Commission, whose function was to hear appeals from city employees who believed that their rights under the city's Charter, or under applicable rules and ordinances, had not been properly respected. 798 F.2d, at 1180. The dissent concluded that respondent had submitted no evidence proving that the mayor and aldermen, or the Commission, had established a policy of retaliating against employees for appealing from adverse personnel decisions. *Id.,* at 1179-1181. The dissenting judge also concluded that, even if there were such a policy, the record evidence would not support a finding that respondent was in fact transferred or laid off in retaliation for the 1980 appeal from his suspension. *Id.,* at 1181-1182.

We granted certiorari, 479 U.S. — (1987), and we now reverse.

II

We begin by addressing a threshold procedural issue....

III

A. Section 1 of the Ku Klux Klan Act of 1871, Rev. Stat. § 1979, as amended, 42 U.S.C. § 1983, provides:

"Every person who, under color of any statute, ordinance, regulation, custom, or usage, of any State ..., subjects, or causes to be subjected, any citizen of the United States or other person within the jurisdiction thereof to the deprivation of any rights, privileges, or immunities secured by the Constitution and laws, shall be liable to the party injured in an action at law, suit in equity, or other proper proceeding for redress...."

Ten years ago, this Court held that municipalities and other bodies of local government are "persons" within the meaning of this statute. Such a body may therefore be sued directly if it is alleged to have caused a constitutional tort through "a policy statement, ordinance, regulation, or decision officially adopted and promulgated by that body's officers." *Monell v. New York City Dept. of Social Services,* 436 U.S. 658, 690 (1978). The Court pointed out that § 1983 also authorizes suit "for constitutional deprivations visited pursuant to governmental 'custom' even though such a custom has not received formal approval through the body's official decisionmaking channels." *Id.,* at 690-691. At the same time, the Court rejected the use of the doctrine of *respondeat superior* and concluded that municipalities could be held liable only when an injury was inflicted by a government's "lawmakers or by those whose edicts or acts may fairly be said to represent official policy." *Id.,* at 694.

Monell's rejection of *respondeat superior,* and its insistence that local governments could be held liable only for the results of unconstitutional governmental "policies," arose from the language and history of § 1983. For our purposes here, the crucial terms of the statute are those that provide for liability when a government "subjects [a person], or causes [that person] to be subjected," to a deprivation of constitutional rights. Aware that governmental bodies can act only through natural persons, the Court concluded that these governments should be held responsible when, and only when, their official policies cause their employees to violate another person's constitutional rights. Reading the statute's language in the light of its legislative history, the Court found that vicarious liability would be incompatible with the causation requirement set out on the face of § 1983. See *id.,* at 691. That conclusion, like decisions that have widened the scope of § 1983 by recognizing constitutional rights that were unheard of in 1871, has been repeatedly reaffirmed. See, e.g., *Owen v. City of Independence,* 445 U.S. 622, 633, 655, n. 39 (1980); *Polk County v. Dodson,* 454 U.S. 312, 325 (1981); *Tuttle,* 471 U.S., at 818, and n. 5 (plurality opinion); *id.,* at 828 (BRENNAN, J., concurring in part and concurring in judgment); *Pembaur v. Cincinnati,* 475 U.S., at 478-480, and nn. 7-8. Cf. *Newport v. Fact Concerts, Inc.,* [453 U.S.,] at 259 ("[B]ecause the 1871 Act was designed to expose state and local officials to a new form of liability, it would defeat the promise of the statute to recognize any preexisting immunity without determining both the policies that it serves and its compatibility with the purposes of § 1983").

In *Monell* itself, it was undisputed that there had been an official policy requiring city employees to take actions that were unconstitutional under this Court's decisions. Without attempting to draw the line between actions taken pursuant to official policy and the independent actions of employees and agents, the *Monell* Court left the "full contours" of municipal liability under § 1983 to be developed further on "another day." 436 U.S., at 695.

In the years since *Monell* was decided, the Court has considered several cases involving isolated acts by government officials and employees. We have assumed that an unconstitutional governmental policy could be inferred from a single decision taken by the highest officials responsible for setting policy in that area of the government's business. See, e.g., *Owen v. City of Independence, supra; Newport v. Fact Concerts, Inc., supra.* Cf. *Pembaur, supra,* at 480. At the other end of the spectrum, we have held that an unjustified shooting by a police officer cannot, without more, be thought to result from official policy. *Tuttle,* 471 U.S., at 821 (plurality opinion); *id.,* at 830-831, and n. 5 (BRENNAN, J., concurring in part and concurring in judgment). Cf. *Kibbe,* 480 U.S., at — (dissenting opinion).

Two terms ago, in *Pembaur, supra,* we undertook to define more precisely when a decision on a single occasion may be enough to establish an unconstitutional municipal policy. Although the Court was unable to settle on a general formulation, JUSTICE BRENNAN's plurality opinion articulated several guiding principles. First, a majority of the Court agreed that municipalities may be held liable under § 1983 only for acts for which the municipality itself is actually responsible, "that is, acts which the municipality has officially sanctioned or ordered." 475 U.S., at 480. Second, only those municipal officials who have "final policymaking authority" may by their actions subject the government to § 1983 liability. *Id.,* at 483. Third, whether a particular official has "final policymaking authority" is a question of *state law. Ibid.* Fourth, the challenged action must have been taken pursuant to a policy adopted by the official or officials responsible under state law for making policy in *that area* of the city's business. *Id.,* at 482-483, and n. 12.

The Courts of Appeals have already diverged in their interpretations of these principles. Compare, for example, *Williams v. Butler,* 802 F.2d 296, 299-302 (CA8 1986) (en banc), cert. pending *sub nom. City of Little Rock v. Williams,* No. 86-1049, with *Jett v. Dallas Independent School Dist.,* 798 F.2d 748, 759-760 (CA5 1986) (dictum). Today, we set out again to clarify the issue that we last addressed in *Pembaur.*

B. We begin by reiterating that the identification of policymaking officials is a question of state law. "Authority to make municipal policy may be granted directly by a legislative enactment or may be delegated by an official who possesses such authority, and of course, whether an official had final policymaking authority is a question of state law." *Pembaur v. Cincinnati,* 475 U.S., at 483 (plurality opinion).[1] Thus the identification of policymaking officials is not a question of federal law and it is not a question of fact in the usual sense. The States have extremely wide latitude in determining the form that local government takes, and local preferences have led to a profusion of distinct forms. Among the many kinds of municipal corporations, political subdivisions, and special districts of all sorts, one may expect to find a rich variety of ways in which the power of government is distributed among a host of different officials

---

[1]Unlike JUSTICE BRENNAN, we would not replace this standard with a new approach in which state law becomes merely "an appropriate starting point" for an "assessment of a municipality's actual power structure." Municipalities cannot be expected to predict how courts or juries will assess their "actual power structures," and this uncertainty could easily lead to results that would be hard in practice to distinguish from the results of a regime governed by the doctrine of *respondeat superior.* It is one thing to charge a municipality with responsibility for the decisions of officials invested by law, or by a "custom or usage" having the force of law, with policymaking authority. It would be something else, and something inevitably more capricious, to hold a municipality responsible for every decision that is perceived as "final" through the lens of a particular factfinder's evaluation of the city's "actual power structure."

and official bodies. See generally C. Rhyne, The Law of Local Government Operations §§ 1.3-1.7 (1980). Without attempting to canvass the numberless factual scenarios that may come to light in litigation, we can be confident that state law (which may include valid local ordinances and regulations) will always direct a court to some official or body that has the responsibility for making law or setting policy in any given area of a local government's business.[2]

We are not, of course, predicting that state law will always speak with perfect clarity. We have no reason to suppose, however, that federal courts will face greater difficulties here than those that they routinely address in other contexts. We are also aware that there will be cases in which policymaking responsibility is shared among more than one official or body. In the case before us, for example, it appears that the mayor and aldermen are authorized to adopt such ordinances relating to personnel administration as are compatible with the City Charter. See St. Louis City Charter, art. XVIII, § 7(b), App. 62-63. The Civil Service Commission, for its part, is required to "prescribe ... rules for the administration and enforcement of the provisions of this article, and of any ordinance adopted in pursuance thereof, and not inconsistent therewith." § 7(a), App. 62. Assuming that applicable law does not make the decisions of the Commission reviewable by the mayor and aldermen, or vice versa, one would have to conclude that policy decisions made either by the mayor and aldermen or by the Commission would be attributable to the city itself. In any event, however, a federal court would not be justified in assuming that municipal policymaking authority lies somewhere other than where the applicable law purports to put it. And certainly there can be no justification for giving a jury the discretion to determine which officials are high enough in the government that their actions can be said to represent a decision of the government itself.

As the plurality in *Pembaur* recognized, special difficulties can arise when it is contended that a municipal policymaker has delegated his policymaking authority to another official. 475 U.S., at 482-483, and n. 12. If the mere exercise of discretion by an employee could give rise to a constitutional violation, the result would be indistinguishable from *respondeat superior* liability. If, however, a city's lawful policymakers could insulate the government from liability simply by

---

[2] JUSTICE STEVENS, who believes that *Monell* incorrectly rejected the doctrine of *respondeat superior,* suggests a new theory that reflects his perceptions of the congressional purposes underlying § 1983. This theory would apparently ignore state law, and distinguish between "high" officials and "low" officials on the basis of an independent evaluation of the extent to which a particular official's actions have "the potential of controlling governmental decisionmaking," or are "perceived as the actions of the city itself." Whether this evaluation would be conducted by judges or juries, we think the legal test is too imprecise to hold much promise of consistent adjudication or principled analysis. We can see no reason, except perhaps a desire to come as close as possible to *respondeat superior* without expressly adopting that doctrine, that could justify introducing such unpredictability into a body of law that is already so difficult.

As JUSTICE STEVENS acknowledges, this Court has repeatedly rejected his interpretation of Congress' intent. We have held that Congress intended to hold municipalities responsible under § 1983 only for the execution of official policies and customs, and not for injuries inflicted solely by employees or agents. See, e.g., *Monell,* 436 U.S., at 694; *Pembaur v. Cincinnati,* 475 U.S. 469, 478-480 (1986). Like the *Pembaur* plurality, we think it is self-evident that official policies can only be adopted by those legally charged with doing so. We are aware of nothing in § 1983 or its legislative history, and JUSTICE STEVENS points to nothing, that would support the notion that unauthorized acts of subordinate employees *are* official policies because they may have the "potential" to become official policies or may be "perceived as" official policies. Accordingly, we conclude that JUSTICE STEVENS' proposal is without a basis in the law.

delegating their policymaking authority to others, § 1983 could not serve its intended purpose. It may not be possible to draw an elegant line that will resolve this conundrum, but certain principles should provide useful guidance.

First, whatever analysis is used to identify municipal policymakers, egregious attempts by local government to insulate themselves from liability for unconstitutional policies are precluded by a separate doctrine. Relying on the language of § 1983, the Court has long recognized that a plaintiff may be able to prove the existence of a widespread practice that, although not authorized by written law or express municipal policy, is "so permanent and well settled as to constitute a 'custom or usage' with the force of law." *Adickes v. S. H. Kress & Co.,* 398 U.S. 144, 167-168 (1970). That principle, which has not been affected by *Monell* or subsequent cases, ensures that most deliberate municipal evasions of the Constitution will be sharply limited.

Second, as the *Pembaur* plurality recognized, the authority to make municipal policy is necessarily the authority to make *final* policy. 475 U.S., at 481-484. When an official's discretionary decisions are constrained by policies not of that official's making, those policies, rather than the subordinate's departures from them, are the act of the municipality. Similarly, when a subordinate's decision is subject to review by the municipality's authorized policymakers, they have retained the authority to measure the official's conduct for conformance with *their* policies. If the authorized policymakers approve a subordinate's decision and the basis for it, their ratification would be chargeable to the municipality because their decision is final.

C. Whatever refinements of these principles may be suggested in the future, we have little difficulty concluding that the Court of Appeals applied an incorrect legal standard in this case. In reaching this conclusion, we do not decide whether the First Amendment forbade the city from retaliating against respondent for having taken advantage of the grievance mechanism in 1980. Nor do we decide whether there was evidence in this record from which a rational jury could conclude either that such retaliation actually occurred or that respondent suffered any compensable injury from whatever retaliatory action may have been taken. Finally, we do not address petitioner's contention that the jury verdict exonerating the individual defendants cannot be reconciled with the verdict against the city. Even assuming that all these issues were properly resolved in respondent's favor, we would not be able to affirm the decision of the Court of Appeals.

The city cannot be held liable under § 1983 unless respondent proved the existence of an unconstitutional municipal policy. Respondent does not contend that anyone in city government ever promulgated, or even articulated, such a policy. Nor did he attempt to prove that such retaliation was ever directed against anyone other than himself. Respondent contends that the record can be read to establish that his supervisors were angered by his 1980 appeal to the Civil Service Commission; that new supervisors in a new administration chose, for reasons passed on through some informal means, to retaliate against respondent two years later by transferring him to another agency; and that this transfer was part of a scheme that led, another year and a half later, to his lay off. Even if one assumes that all this was true, it says nothing about the actions of those whom the law established as the makers of municipal policy in matters of personnel administration. The mayor and aldermen enacted no ordinance designed to retaliate against respondent or against similarly situated employees. On the contrary, the city established an independent Civil Service Commission and empowered it to review and correct improper personnel actions. Respondent does not deny that his repeated appeals from adverse personnel decisions repeatedly brought him at least partial relief, and the Civil Service Commission never so much as hinted that retaliatory transfers or lay offs were permissible. Respondent points to no evidence indicating that the Commission delegated to anyone its final authority to interpret and enforce the following policy set out in article XVIII of the city's Charter, § 2(a), App. 49:

> "Merit and fitness. All appointments and promotions to positions in the service of the city and all measures for the control and regulation of employment in such positions, and separation therefrom, shall be on the sole basis of merit and fitness ...."

The Court of Appeals concluded that "appointing authorities," like Hamsher and Killen, who had the authority to initiate transfers and layoffs, were municipal "policymakers." The court based this conclusion on its findings (1) that the decisions of these employees were not individually reviewed for "substantive propriety" by higher supervisory officials; and (2) that the Civil Service Commission decided appeals from such decisions, if at all, in a circumscribed manner that gave substantial deference to the original decisionmaker. 798 F.2d, at 1174-1175. We find these propositions insufficient to support the conclusion that Hamsher and Killen were authorized to establish employment policy for the city with respect to transfers and layoffs. To the contrary, the City Charter expressly states that the Civil Service Commission has the power and the duty:

> "To consider and determine any matter involved in the administration and enforcement of this [Civil Service] article and the rules and ordinances adopted in accordance therewith that may be referred to it for decision by the director [of personnel], or on appeal by any appointing authority, employe, or taxpayer of the city, from any act of the director or of any appointing authority. The decision of the commission in all such matters shall be final, subject, however, to any right of action under any law of the state or of the United States." St. Louis City Charter, art. XVIII, § 7(d), App. 63.

This case therefore resembles the hypothetical example in *Pembaur:* "[I]f [city] employment policy was set by the [mayor and aldermen and by the Civil Service Commission], only [those] bod[ies'] decisions would provide a basis for [city] liability. This would be true even if the [mayor and aldermen and the Commission] left the [appointing authorities] discretion to hire and fire employees and [they] exercised that discretion in an unconstitutional manner ...." 475 U.S., at 483, n. 12. A majority of the Court of Appeals panel determined that the Civil Service Commission's review of individual employment actions gave too much deference to the decisions of appointing authorities like Hamsher and Killen. Simply going along with discretionary decisions made by one's subordinates, however, is not a delegation to them of the authority to make policy. It is equally consistent with a presumption that the subordinates are faithfully attempting to comply with the policies that are supposed to guide them. It would be a different matter if a particular decision by a subordinate was cast in the form of a policy statement and expressly approved by the supervising policymaker. It would also be a different matter if a series of decisions by a subordinate official manifested a "custom or usage" of which the supervisor must have been aware. See *supra,* at 13. In both those cases, the supervisor could realistically be deemed to have adopted a policy that happened to have been formulated or initiated by a lower-ranking official. But the mere failure to investigate the basis of a subordinate's discretionary decisions does not amount to a delegation of policymaking authority, especially where (as here) the wrongfulness of the subordinate's decision arises from a retaliatory motive or other unstated rationale. In such circumstances, the purposes of § 1983 would not be served by treating a subordinate employee's decision as if it were a reflection of municipal policy.

JUSTICE BRENNAN's opinion, concurring in the judgment, finds implications in our discussion that we do not think necessary or correct. We nowhere say or imply, for example, that "a municipal charter's precatory admonition against discrimination or any other employment practice not based on merit and fitness effectively insulates the municipality from any liability based on acts inconsistent with that policy." Rather, we would respect the decisions, embodied in state and local law, that allocate policymaking authority among particular individuals and bodies. Refusals to carry out stated policies could obviously help to show that a municipality's actual policies were different from the ones that had been announced. If such a showing were made, we would be confronted with a different case than the one we decide today.

Nor do we believe that we have left a "gaping hole" in § 1983 that needs to be filled with the vague concept of *"de facto* final policymaking authority." Except perhaps as a step towards overruling *Monell* and adopting the doctrine of *respondeat superior,* ad hoc searches for officials possessing such *"de facto"* authority would serve primarily to foster needless unpredictability in the application of § 1983.

IV

We cannot accept either the Court of Appeals' broad definition of municipal policymakers or respondent's suggestion that a jury should be entitled to define for itself which officials' decisions should expose a municipality to liability. Respondent has suggested that the record will support an inference that policymaking authority was in fact delegated to individuals who took retaliatory action against him and who were not exonerated by the jury. Respondent's arguments appear to depend on a legal standard similar to the one suggested in JUSTICE STEVENS' dissenting opinion, which we do not accept. Our examination of the record and state law, however, suggests that further review of this case may be warranted in light of the principles we have discussed. That task is best left to the Court of Appeals, which will be free to invite additional briefing and argument if necessary. Accordingly, the decision of the Court of Appeals is reversed, and the case is remanded for further proceedings consistent with this opinion.

It is so ordered.

JUSTICE KENNEDY took no part in the consideration or decision of this case.

JUSTICE BRENNAN, with whom JUSTICE MARSHALL and JUSTICE BLACKMUN join, concurring.

Despite its somewhat confusing procedural background, this case at bottom presents a relatively straightforward question: whether respondent's supervisor at the Community Development Agency, Frank Hamsher, possessed the authority to establish final employment policy for the city of St. Louis such that the city can be held liable under 42 U.S.C. § 1983 for Hamsher's allegedly unlawful decision to transfer respondent to a dead-end job. Applying the test set out two Terms ago by the plurality in *Pembaur v. Cincinnati,* 475 U.S. 469 (1986), I conclude that Hamsher did not possess such authority and I therefore concur in the Court's judgment reversing the decision below. I write separately, however, because I believe that the commendable desire of today's plurality to "define more precisely when a decision on a single occasion may be enough" to subject a municipality to § 1983 liability, *ante,* has led it to embrace a theory of municipal liability that is both unduly narrow and unrealistic, and one that ultimately would permit municipalities to insulate themselves from liability for the acts of all but a small minority of actual city policymakers.

I

....

The District Court instructed the jury that generally a city is not liable under § 1983 for the acts of its employees, but that it may be held to answer for constitutional wrongs "committed by an official high enough in the government so that his or her actions can be said to represent a government decision." In a lengthy and involved instruction, the court further advised the jury that it must find in favor of respondent, and against the individual defendants, if it found six facts to be true, one of which was that "Hamsher and Kindleberger were personally involved in causing [respondent's] transfer and/or layoff." The jury exonerated the three individual defendants, but awarded respondent $15,000 on each of his constitutional claims against petitioner.

The Court of Appeals for the Eighth Circuit vacated the judgment entered on respondent's Due Process claim (a ruling not at issue here) but affirmed the judgment as to the First Amendment claim. 798 F.2d 1168 (1986). With respect to this latter claim, the court reasoned that the city could be held accountable for an improperly motivated transfer and layoff if it had delegated to the responsible officials, either directly or indirectly, the authority to act on behalf of the city, and if the decisions made within the scope of this delegated authority were essentially final. Applying this test, the court noted that under the City Charter, "appointing authorities," or department heads, such as Hamsher could undertake transfers and layoffs subject only to the approval of the Director of Personnel, who undertook no substantive review of such decisions and simply conditioned his approval on formal compliance with city procedures. Moreover, because the CSC engaged in highly circumscribed and deferential review of layoffs and, at least so far as this case reveals, no review whatever of lateral transfers, the court concluded that an appointing authority's transfer and layoff decisions were final. *Id.,* at 1174-1175.

Having found that Hamsher was a final policymaker whose acts could subject petitioner to § 1983 liability, the court determined that the jury had ample evidence from which it could find that Hamsher transferred respondent in retaliation for the latter's exercise of his First Amendment rights, and that the transfer in turn precipitated respondent's layoff. This constructive discharge theory, the majority found, also reconciled the jury's apparently inconsistent verdicts: the jury could have viewed Hamsher's unlawful motivation as the proximate cause of respondent's dismissal but, because Nash and Killen administered the final blows, it could have concluded that Hamsher, Kindleberger, and Patterson were not "personally involved" in the layoff as required by the instructions; accordingly, the jury could have reasonably exonerated the individual defendants while finding the city liable. *Id.,* at 1176, and n. 8.

II

In light of the jury instructions below, the central question before us is whether the city delegated to CDA Director Frank Hamsher the authority to establish final employment policy for the city respecting transfers. For if it did not, then his allegedly unlawful decision to move respondent to an unfulfilling, dead-end position is simply not an act for which the city can be held responsible under § 1983. I am constrained to conclude that Hamsher possessed no such policymaking power here, and that, on the contrary, his allegedly retaliatory act simply constituted an abuse of the discretionary authority the city had entrusted to him.

The scope of Hamsher's authority with respect to transfers derives its significance from our determination in *Monell v. New York City Dept. of Social Services,* 436 U.S. 658 (1978), that a municipality is not liable under § 1983 for each and every wrong committed by its employees. In rejecting the concept of vicarious municipal liability, we emphasized that "the touchstone of the § 1983 action against a government body is an allegation that official policy is responsible for the deprivation of rights protected by the Constitution." *Id.,* at 690. More recently we have explained that the touchstone of "official policy" is designed "to distinguish acts of the *municipality* from acts of *employees* of the municipality, and thereby make clear that municipal liability is limited to action for which the municipality is actually responsible." *Pembaur v. Cincinnati,* 475 U.S., at 479-480 (emphasis in original).

Municipalities, of course, conduct much of the business of governing through human agents. Where those agents act in accordance with formal policies, or pursuant to informal practices "so permanent and well settled as to constitute a 'custom or usage' with the force of law," *Adickes v. S. H. Kress & Co.,* 398 U.S. 144, 167-168 (1970), we naturally ascribe their acts to the municipalities themselves and hold the latter responsible for any resulting constitutional deprivations. *Monell,* which involved a challenge to a city-wide policy requiring all pregnant employees to take unpaid leave after their fifth month of pregnancy, was just such a case. Nor have we ever doubted that a single decision of a city's properly constituted legislative body is a municipal act capable of subjecting the city to liability. See, e.g., *Newport v. Fact Concerts, Inc.,* 453 U.S. 247 (1981) (city council canceled concert permit for content-based reasons); *Owen v. City of Independence,* 445 U.S. 622 (1980) (city council passed resolution firing police chief without any pretermination hearing). In these cases we neither required nor, as the plurality suggests, assumed that these decisions reflected generally applicable "policies" as that term is commonly understood, because it was perfectly obvious that the actions of the municipalities' policymaking organs, whether isolated or not, were properly charged to the municipalities themselves.[3] And, in *Pembaur* we recognized that "the power to establish policy is no more the exclusive province of the legislature at the local level than at the state or national level," 475 U.S., at 480, and that the isolated decision of an executive municipal policymaker, therefore, could likewise give rise to municipal liability under § 1983.

In concluding that Frank Hamsher was a policymaker, the Court of Appeals relied on the fact that the City had delegated to him "the authority, either directly or indirectly, to act on [its] behalf," and that his decisions within the scope of this delegated authority were effectively final. 798 F.2d, at 1174. In *Pembaur,* however, we made clear that a municipality is not liable merely because the official who inflicted the constitutional injury had the final authority to *act* on its behalf; rather, as four of us explained, the official in question must possess "final authority to establish municipal policy with respect to the [challenged] action." 475 U.S., at 481. Thus, we noted, "[t]he fact that a particular official — even a policymaking official — has discretion in the exercise of particular functions does not, without more, give rise to municipal liability based on an exercise of that discretion." *Id.,* at 481-482. By way of illustration, we explained that if, in a given county, the Board of County Commissioners established county employment policy and delegated to the County Sheriff alone the discretion to hire and fire employees, the county itself would not be liable if the Sheriff exercised this authority in an unconstitutional manner, because "the decision to act unlawfully would not be a decision of the Board." *Id.,* at 483, n. 12. We pointed out, however, that in that same county the Sheriff could be the final policymaker in other areas, such as law enforcement practices, and that if so, his or her decisions in such matters *could* give rise to municipal liability. *Ibid.* In short, just as in *Owen* and *Fact Concerts* we deemed it fair to hold municipalities liable for the isolated, unconstitutional acts of their legislative bodies, regardless of whether those acts were meant to establish generally applicable "policies," so too in *Pembaur* four of us concluded that it is equally appropriate to hold municipalities accountable for the isolated constitutional injury inflicted by an executive final municipal policymaker, even though the decision giving rise to the injury is not intended to govern future situations. In either case, as long as the contested decision is made in an area over which the official or legislative body *could* establish a final policy capable of governing future municipal conduct, it is both fair and consistent with the purposes of § 1983 to treat

---

[3] The plurality's suggestion that in *Owen* and *Fact Concerts* we "*assumed* that an unconstitutional governmental policy could be *inferred* from a single decision," see *ante* (emphasis added), elevates the identification of municipal policy from touchstone to talisman. Section 1983 imposes liability where a municipality "subjects [a person], or causes [a person] to be subjected ... to the deprivation of any rights, privileges, or immunities secured by the Constitution and laws ...." 42 U.S.C. § 1983. Our decision in *Monell,* interpreting the statute to require a showing that such deprivations arise from municipal policy, did not employ the policy requirement as an end in itself, but rather as a means of determining which acts by municipal employees are properly attributed to the municipality. Congress, we held, did not intend to subject cities to liability simply because they employ tortfeasors. But where a municipality's governing legislative body inflicts the constitutional injury, the municipal policy inquiry is essentially superfluous: the city is liable under the statute whether its decision reflects a considered policy judgment or nothing more than the bare desire to inflict harm.

the decision as that of the municipality itself, and to hold it liable for the resulting constitutional deprivation.

In my view, *Pembaur* controls this case. As an "appointing authority," Hamsher was empowered under the City Charter to initiate lateral transfers such as the one challenged here, subject to the approval of both the Director of Personnel and the appointing authority of the transferee agency. The Charter, however, nowhere confers upon agency heads any authority to establish city *policy*, final or otherwise, with respect to such transfers. Thus, for example, Hamsher was not authorized to promulgate binding guidelines or criteria governing how or when lateral transfers were to be accomplished. Nor does the record reveal that he in fact sought to exercise any such authority in these matters. There is no indication, for example, that Hamsher ever purported to institute or announce a practice of general applicability concerning transfers. Instead, the evidence discloses but one transfer decision — the one involving respondent — which Hamsher ostensibly undertook pursuant to a city-wide program of fiscal restraint and budgetary reductions. At most, then, the record demonstrates that Hamsher had the authority to determine how best to *effectuate* a policy announced by his superiors, rather than the power to *establish* that policy. Like the hypothetical Sheriff in *Pembaur*'s footnote 12, Hamsher had discretionary authority to transfer CDA employees laterally; that he may have used his authority to punish respondent for the exercise of his First Amendment rights does not, without more, render the city liable for respondent's resulting constitutional injury.[4] The court below did not suggest that either Killen or Nash, who together orchestrated respondent's ultimate layoff, shared Hamsher's constitutionally impermissible animus. Because the court identified only one unlawfully motivated municipal employee involved in respondent's transfer and layoff, and because that employee did not possess final policymaking authority with respect to the contested decision,[5] the city may not be held accountable for any constitutional wrong respondent may have suffered.

[4] While the Court of Appeals erred to the extent it equated the authority to act on behalf of a city with the power to establish municipal policy, in my view the lower court quite correctly concluded that the CSC's highly circumscribed and deferential review of Hamsher's decisions in no way rendered those decisions less than final. We of course generally accord great deference to the interpretation and application of state law by the courts of appeals, see *Brockett v. Spokane Arcades, Inc.*, 472 U.S. 491, 500 (1985); *United States v. S.A. Empresa de Viacao Aerea Rio Grandense*, 467 U.S. 797, 815, n. 12 (1984), and that deference is certainly applicable to the Court of Appeals' assessment of the scope of CSC review. Moreover, the facts of this case reveal that CSC believed it lacked the authority to review lateral transfers. Accordingly, had Frank Hamsher actually possessed policymaking authority with respect to such decisions, I would have little difficulty concluding that such authority was final.

[5] I am unable to agree with JUSTICE STEVENS that the record provides sufficient evidence of complicity on the part of other municipal policymakers such that we may sustain the jury's verdict against petitioner on a conspiracy theory neither espoused nor addressed by the court below. JUSTICE STEVENS' dissent relies to a large extent on respondent's controversial public testimony about the Serra sculpture, and the unwelcome reception that testimony drew in the mayor's office. Whatever else may be said about the strength of this evidence, however, the dissent's reliance on it is flawed in one crucial respect: the jury instructions concerning respondent's First Amendment claim refer exclusively to the exercise of his appellate rights before the CSC and make no mention whatever of his public testimony. Under these circumstances, the jury was simply not at liberty to impose liability against petitioner based on the allegedly retaliatory actions of the mayor and his close associates[;] thus we may not sustain its verdict on the basis of such evidence.

III

These determinations, it seems to me, are sufficient to dispose of this case, and I therefore think it unnecessary to decide, as the plurality does, who the actual policymakers in St. Louis are. I question more than the mere necessity of these determinations, however, for I believe that in the course of passing on issues not before us, the plurality announces legal principles that are inconsistent with our earlier cases and unduly restrict the reach of § 1983 in cases involving municipalities.

The plurality begins its assessment of St. Louis' power structure by asserting that the identification of policymaking officials is a question of state law, by which it means that the question is neither one of federal law nor of fact, at least "not in the usual sense." Instead, the plurality explains, courts are to identify municipal policymakers by referring exclusively to applicable state statutory law. Not surprisingly, the plurality cites no authority for this startling proposition, nor could it, for we have never suggested that municipal liability should be determined in so formulaic and unrealistic a fashion. In any case in which the policymaking authority of a municipal tortfeasor is in doubt, state law will naturally be the appropriate starting point, but ultimately the factfinder must determine where such policymaking authority actually resides, and not simply "where the applicable law purports to put it." As the plurality itself acknowledges, local governing bodies may take myriad forms. We in no way slight the dignity of municipalities by recognizing that in not a few of them real and apparent authority may diverge, and that in still others state statutory law will simply fail to disclose where such authority ultimately rests. Indeed, in upholding the Court of Appeals' determination in *Pembaur* that the County Prosecutor was a policymaking official with respect to county law enforcement practices, a majority of this Court relied on testimony which revealed that the County Sheriff's office routinely forwarded certain matters to the Prosecutor and followed his instructions in those areas. See 475 U.S., at 485; *ibid.* (WHITE, J., concurring); *id.,* at 491 (O'CONNOR, J., concurring). While the majority splintered into three separate camps on the ultimate theory of municipal liability, and the case generated five opinions in all, not a single member of the Court suggested that reliance on such extra-statutory evidence of the county's actual allocation of policymaking authority was in any way improper. Thus, although I agree with the plurality that juries should not be given open-ended "*discretion* to determine which officials are high enough in the government that their actions can be said to represent a decision of the government itself," *ante,* at 13 (emphasis added), juries can and must find the predicate facts necessary to a determination of whether a given official possesses final policymaking authority. While the jury instructions in this case were regrettably vague, the plurality's solution tosses the baby out with the bath water. The identification of municipal policymakers is an essentially factual determination "in the usual sense," and is therefore rightly entrusted to a properly instructed jury.

Nor does the "custom or usage" doctrine adequately compensate for the inherent inflexibility of a rule that leaves the identification of policymakers exclusively to state statutory law. That doctrine, under which municipalities and States can be held liable for unconstitutional practices so well settled and permanent that they have the force of law, see *Adickes v. Kress & Co.,* 398 U.S., at

167, has little if any bearing on the question whether a city has delegated *de facto* final policymaking authority to a given official. A city practice of delegating final policymaking authority to a subordinate or mid-level official would not be unconstitutional in and of itself, and an isolated unconstitutional act by an official entrusted with such authority would obviously not amount to a municipal "custom or usage." Under *Pembaur,* of course, such an isolated act *should* give rise to municipal liability. Yet a case such as this would fall through the gaping hole the plurality's construction leaves in § 1983, because state statutory law would not identify the municipal actor as a policymaking official, and a single constitutional deprivation, by definition, is not a well settled and permanent municipal practice carrying the force of law.[6]

For these same reasons, I cannot subscribe to the plurality's narrow and overly rigid view of when a municipal official's policymaking authority is "final." Attempting to place a gloss on *Pembaur's* finality requirement, the plurality suggests that whenever the decisions of an official are subject to some form of review — however limited — that official's decisions are nonfinal. Under the plurality's theory, therefore, even where an official wields policymaking authority with respect to a challenged decision, the city would not be liable for that official's policy decision unless *reviewing* officials affirmatively approved both the "decision and the basis for it." Reviewing officials, however, may as a matter of practice never invoke their plenary oversight authority, or their review powers may be highly circumscribed. See n. 4, *supra.* Under such circumstances, the subordinate's decision is in effect the final municipal pronouncement on the subject. Certainly a § 1983 plaintiff is entitled to place such considerations before the jury, for the law is concerned not with the niceties of legislative draftsmanship but with the realities of municipal decisionmaking, and any assessment of a municipality's actual power structure is necessarily a factual and practical one.[7]

Accordingly, I cannot endorse the plurality's determination, based on nothing more than its own review of the City Charter, that the mayor, the aldermen, and the CSC are the only policymakers for the city of St. Louis. While these officials may well have policymaking authority, that hardly ends the matter; the question before us is whether the officials responsible for respondent's allegedly

[6] Indeed, the plurality appears to acknowledge as much when it explains that the "custom or usage" doctrine will forestall *"egregious* attempts by local government to insulate themselves from liability for unconstitutional policies," and that *"most* deliberate municipal evasions of the Constitution will be sharply limited." (emphases added). Congress, however, did not enact § 1983 simply to provide redress for "most" constitutional deprivations, nor did it limit the statute's reach only to those deprivations that are truly "egregious."

[7] The plurality also asserts that "[w]hen an official's discretionary decisions are constrained by policies not of that official's making, those policies, rather than the subordinate's departures from them, are the act of the municipality." While I have no quarrel with such a proposition in the abstract, I cannot accept the plurality's apparent view that a municipal charter's precatory admonition against discrimination or any other employment practice not based on merit and fitness effectively insulates the municipality from any liability based on acts inconsistent with that policy. Again, the relevant inquiry is whether the policy in question is actually and effectively enforced through the city's review mechanisms. Thus in this case, a policy prohibiting lateral transfers for unconstitutional or discriminatory reasons would not shield the city from liability if an official possessing final policymaking authority over such transfers acted in violation of the prohibition, because the CSC would lack jurisdiction to review the decision and thus could not enforce the city policy. Where as here, however, the official merely possesses discretionary authority over transfers, the city policy is irrelevant, because the official's actions cannot subject the city to liability in any event.

unlawful transfer were final policymakers. As I have previously indicated, I do not believe that CDA Director Frank Hamsher possessed any policymaking authority with respect to lateral transfers and thus I do not believe that his allegedly improper decision to transfer respondent could, without more, give rise to municipal liability. Although the plurality reaches the same result, it does so by reasoning that because others could have reviewed the decisions of Hamsher and Killen, the latter officials simply could not have been final policymakers.

This analysis, however, turns a blind eye to reality, for it ignores not only the lower court's determination, nowhere disputed, that CSC review was highly circumscribed and deferential, but that in this very case the Commission *refused* to judge the propriety of Hamsher's transfer decision because a lateral transfer was not an "adverse" employment action falling within its jurisdiction. Nor does the plurality account for the fact that Hamsher's predecessor, Donald Spaid, promulgated what the city readily acknowledges was a binding policy regarding secondary employment; although the CSC ultimately modified the sanctions respondent suffered as a result of his apparent failure to comply with that policy, the record is devoid of any suggestion that the Commission reviewed the substance or validity of the policy itself. Under the plurality's analysis, therefore, even the hollowest promise of review is sufficient to divest all city officials save the mayor and governing legislative body of final policymaking authority. While clarity and ease of application may commend such a rule, we have remained steadfast in our conviction that Congress intended to hold municipalities accountable for those constitutional injuries inflicted not only by their lawmakers, but "by those whose edicts or acts may fairly be said to represent official policy." *Monell,* 436 U.S., at 694. Because the plurality's mechanical "finality" test is fundamentally at odds with the pragmatic and factual inquiry contemplated by *Monell,* I cannot join what I perceive to be its unwarranted abandonment of the traditional factfinding process in § 1983 actions involving municipalities.

Finally, I think it necessary to emphasize that despite certain language in the plurality opinion suggesting otherwise, the Court today need not and therefore does not decide that a city can only be held liable under § 1983 where the plaintiff "prove[s] the existence of an unconstitutional municipal policy." See *ante,* at 926. Just last Term, we left open for the second time the question whether a city can be subjected to liability for a policy that, while not unconstitutional in and of itself, may give rise to constitutional deprivations. See *Springfield v. Kibbe,* 480 U.S. — (1987); see also *Oklahoma City v. Tuttle,* 471 U.S. 808 (1985). That question is certainly not presented by this case, and nothing we say today forecloses its future consideration.

IV

For the reasons stated above, I concur in the judgment of the Court reversing the decision below and remanding the case so that the Court of Appeals may determine whether respondent's layoff resulted from the actions of any improperly motivated final policymakers.

JUSTICE STEVENS, dissenting.

If this case involved nothing more than a personal vendetta between a municipal employee and his superiors, it would be quite wrong to impose liability on the City of St. Louis. In fact, however, the jury found that top officials in the City administration, relying on pretextual grounds, had taken a series of retaliatory actions against respondent because he had testified truthfully on two occasions, one relating to personnel policy and the other involving a public controversy of importance to the Mayor and the members of his cabinet. No matter how narrowly the Court may define the standards for imposing liability upon municipalities in § 1983 litigation, the judgment entered by the District Court in this case should be affirmed....

I

....

In 1981 respondent testified before the Heritage and Urban Design Commission (HUD) in connection with a proposal to acquire a controversial rusting steel sculpture by Richard Serra. In his testimony he revealed the previously undisclosed fact that an earlier City administration had rejected an offer to acquire the same sculpture, and also explained that the erection of the sculpture would require the removal of structures on which the City had recently expended about $250,000. This testimony offended top officials of the City government, possibly including the Mayor, who supported the acquisition of the Serra sculpture, as well as respondent's agency superiors. They made it perfectly clear that they believed that respondent had violated a duty of loyalty to the Mayor by expressing his personal opinion about the sculpture. Thus, defendant Hamsher testified:

> "I'm not fond of the sculpture and wasn't then. But the mayor was elected by the people and he made the decision. He was going to support the installation of the sculpture.
> "Therefore, it was my responsibility and the responsibility of others who worked for my agency to do so as well and not to express personal opinions in public forums about what that sculpture was going to be and what it would look like."

Defendant Kindleberger made the same point:

> "Well, I think the obligation for a senior management individual is to represent fairly the position of his boss which, in our case, happens to be the mayor. And I would — I just think that is something that is appropriate for senior management to do."

After this testimony respondent was the recipient of a series of adverse personnel actions that culminated in his transfer from an important management level professional position to a rather menial assignment for which he was "grossly over qualified," and his eventual layoff. In preparing respondent's service ratings after the Serra sculpture incident, his superiors followed a "highly unusual" procedure that may have violated the City's personnel regulations. Moreover, management officials who were involved in implementing the decision to transfer respondent to a menial assignment made it clear that "there was no reason" for the transfer — except, it would seem, for the possible connection with "the Serra sculpture incident." It is equally clear that the City's asserted basis for respondent's ultimate layoff in 1983 — a lack of funds — was pretextual.

Thus, evidence in the record amply supports the conclusion that respondent was first transferred and then laid off, not for fiscal and administrative reasons, but in retaliation for his public testimony before the CSC and HUD. It is undisputed that respondent's right to testify in support of his civil service appeal and his right to testify in opposition to the City's acquisition of the Serra sculpture were protected by the First Amendment to the Federal Constitution. Given the jury's verdict, the case is therefore one in which a municipal employee's federal constitutional rights were violated by officials of the City government. There is, however, a dispute over the identity of the persons who were responsible for that violation. At trial, respondent relied on alternate theories: Either his immediate superiors at CDA (who were named as individual defendants) should be held accountable, or, if the decisions were made at a higher level of government, the City should be held responsible.

The record contains a good deal of evidence of participation in the constitutional tort by respondent's superiors at CDA, by those directly under the Mayor, and perhaps by the Mayor himself. Moreover, in closing argument, defense counsel attempted to exonerate the three individual defendants by referring to the actions of higher officials who were not named as defendants.

Thus, we have a case in which, after a full trial, a jury reasonably concluded that top officials in a City's administration, possibly including the Mayor, acting under color of law, took retaliatory action against a gifted but freethinking municipal employee for exercising rights protected by the First Amendment to the Federal Constitution. The legal question is whether the City itself is liable for such conduct under § 1983.

II

In the trial court there was little, if any, dispute over the governing rules of law. In advance of trial, the City filed a motion for summary judgment that the District Court ultimately denied because the record contained an affidavit stating that respondent "was transferred due to 'connivance' of the mayor, the mayor's chief of staff, and the city's personnel director." No one appears to have questioned the proposition that if such facts could be proved at trial, the City could be held liable....

Finally, the ultimate instruction to the jury on the issue of municipal liability was in fact proposed by the City's attorney, as the plurality acknowledges; see Brief for Respondent 48; Reply Brief for Petitioner 6:

"As a general principle, a municipality is not liable under 42 U.S.C. § 1983 for the actions of its employees. However, a municipality may be held liable under 12 U.S.C. § 1983 if the allegedly unconstitutional act was committed by an official high enough in the government so that his or her actions can be said to represent a government decision." Instruction No. 15, App. 113.[15]

....

---

[15] Proposing this instruction made good sense as litigation strategy, for respondent had sued not only the City but also three individual City officials, Frank Hamsher, Charles Kindleberger, and Deborah Patterson. Presumably the City's attorney, who was representing both the City and the

III

In *Monell v. New York City Department of Social Services,* 436 U.S. 658 (1978), we held that municipal corporations are "persons" within the meaning of 42 U.S.C. § 1983. Since a corporation is incapable of doing anything except through the agency of human beings, that holding necessarily gave rise to the question of what human activity undertaken by agents of the corporation may create municipal liability in § 1983 litigation.

The first case dealing with this question was, of course, *Monell,* in which female employees of the Department of Social Services and the Board of Education of New York City challenged the constitutionality of a City-wide policy concerning pregnancy leave. Once it was decided that the City was a "person," it obviously followed that the City had to assume responsibility for that policy. Even if some departments had followed a lawful policy, I have no doubt that the City would nevertheless have been responsible for the decisions made by either of the two major departments that were directly involved in the litigation.

In *Owen v. City of Independence,* 445 U.S. 622 (1980), the Court held that municipalities are not entitled to qualified immunity based on the good faith of their officials. As a premise to this decision, we agreed with the Court of Appeals that the City "was responsible for the deprivation of petitioner's constitutional rights." *Id.,* at 633; see also *id.,* at 655, n. 39. Petitioner had been fired as City Chief of Police without a notice of reasons and without a hearing, after the City Council and the City Manager had publicly reprimanded him for his administration of the Police Department property room. This isolated personnel action was clearly *not* taken pursuant to a rule of general applicability; nonetheless, we had no problem with the Court of Appeals' conclusion that the action of the City Council and City Manager was binding on the City.[20]

---

officials, hoped that the jury would focus on the individual defendants, exonerate them, and, having focused on these defendants, hold the City innocent as well by concluding that higher-ups were not implicated. As we know from the verdict — judgment for the individual defendants but against the City — this strategy partially failed. Although petitioner argues that the verdicts were inconsistent, they actually make perfect sense in light of the evidence that officials in the Mayor's office, possibly including the Mayor himself, and various agency heads participated in a deliberate plan to deprive respondent of his job in violation of his First Amendment rights.

[20]Since *Owen,* Members of the Court have offered varying explanations for that conclusion: "[T]he release of the information was an official action — that is, a policy or custom — of the city," *Oklahoma City v. Tuttle,* 471 U.S., at 832 (BRENNAN, J., concurring in the judgment); "[A] municipality may be liable under § 1983 for a single decision by its properly constituted legislative body — whether or not that body had taken similar action in the past or intended to do so in the future — because even a single decision by such a body unquestionably constitutes an act of official government policy," *Pembaur v. Cincinnati,* 475 U.S., at 480 (BRENNAN, J.); "Formal procedures that involve, for example, voting by elected officials, prepared reports, extended deliberation, or official records indicate that the resulting decisions taken 'may fairly be said to represent official policy.'" *Id.,* at 500 (POWELL, J., dissenting). Today, the plurality offers an explanation for *Owen* similar to that offered by JUSTICE POWELL in his *Pembaur* dissent: "We have assumed that an unconstitutional governmental policy could be inferred from a single decision taken by the highest officials responsible for setting policy in that area of the government's business." For its part, the concurrence's explanation of *Owen* resembles that offered by JUSTICE BRENNAN in *Pembaur:* "Nor have we ever doubted that a single decision of a city's properly constituted legislative body is a municipal act capable of subjecting the city to liability." But neither opinion explains *why* a single personnel decision by a legislature ought [to] bind a municipality any differently than any other duly authorized personnel decision.

In the next municipal liability case, the Court held that an isolated unconstitutional seizure by a sole police officer did not bind the municipality. *Oklahoma City v. Tuttle,* 471 U.S. 808 (1985). Thus, that holding rejected the common law doctrine of *respondeat superior* as the standard for measuring municipal liability under § 1983. It did not, of course, reject the possibility that liability might be predicated on the conduct of management level personnel with policymaking authority.

Finally, in *Pembaur v. Cincinnati,* 475 U.S., at 471, we definitively held that a "decision by municipal policymakers on a single occasion" was sufficient to support an award of damages against the municipality. In *Pembaur,* a County Prosecutor had advised County sheriffs at the doorstep of a recalcitrant doctor to "go in and get [the witnesses]" to alleged charges of fraud by the doctor. *Id.,* at 473. Because the sheriffs possessed only arrest warrants for the witnesses and not a search warrant for the doctor's office as well, the advice was unconstitutional, see *Steagald v. United States,* 451 U.S. 204 (1981), and the question was whether the County Prosecutor's isolated act could subject the County to damages under § 1983 in a suit by the doctor. In the part of his opinion that commanded a majority of the Court, JUSTICE BRENNAN wrote:

> "[A] government frequently chooses a course of action tailored to a particular situation and not intended to control decisions in later situations. If the decision to adopt that particular course of action is properly made by that government's authorized decisionmakers, it surely represents an act of official government 'policy' as that term is commonly understood. More importantly, where action is directed by those who establish governmental policy, the municipality is equally responsible whether that action is to be taken only once or to be taken repeatedly." *Pembaur v. Cincinnati, supra,* at 481 (footnote omitted).

Since the County Prosecutor was authorized to establish law enforcement policy, his decision in that area could be attributed to the County for purposes of § 1983 liability. As Justice Powell correctly pointed out in his dissent, "the Court ... focus[ed] almost exclusively on the status of the decisionmaker." *Id.,* at 498.

Thus, the Court has permitted a municipality to be held liable for the unconstitutional actions of its agents when those agents: enforced a rule of general applicability (*Monell*); were of sufficiently high stature and acted through a formal process (*Owen*); or were authorized to establish policy in the particular area of city government in which the tort was committed (*Pembaur*). Under this precedents, the City of St. Louis should be held liable in this case....

Every act of a high official constitutes a kind of "statement" about how similar decisions will be carried out; the assumption is that the same decision would have been made, and would again be made, across a class of cases. Lower officials do not control others in the same way. Since their actions do not dictate the responses of various subordinates, those actions lack the potential of controlling governmental decisionmaking; they are not perceived as the actions of the city itself. If a County police officer had broken down Dr. Pembaur's door on the officer's own initiative, this would have been seen as the action of an overanxious officer, and would not have sent a message to other officers that similar actions would be countenanced. One reason for this is that the County Prosecutor himself could step forward and say "that was wrong"; when the

County Prosecutor authorized the action himself, only a self-correction would accomplish the same task, and until such time his action would have County-wide ramifications. Here, the Mayor, those working for him, and the agency heads are high-ranking officials; accordingly, we must assume that their actions have City-wide ramifications, both through their similar response to a like class of situations, and through the response of subordinates who follow their lead....

[I]f the Court is willing to recognize the existence of municipal policy in a non-rule case as long as high enough officials engaged in a formal enough process, it should not deny the existence of such a policy merely because those same officials act "underground," as it were. It would be a truly remarkable doctrine for this Court to recognize municipal liability in an employee discharge case when high officials are foolish enough to act through a "formal process," but not when similarly high officials attempt to avoid liability by acting on the pretext of budgetary concerns, which is what this jury found based on the evidence presented at trial.

Thus, holding St. Louis liable in this case is supported by both *Pembaur* and *Owen*. We hold a municipality liable for the decisions of its high officials in large part because those decisions, by definition, would be applied across a class of cases. Just as we assume in *Pembaur* that the County Prosecutor (or his subordinates) would issue the same break-down-the-door order in similar cases, and just as we assume in *Owen* that the City Council (or those following its lead) would fire an employee without notice of reasons or opportunity to be heard in similar cases, so too must we assume that whistleblowers like respondent would be dealt with in similar retaliatory fashion if they offend the Mayor, his staff, and relevant agency heads, or if they offend those lower-ranking officials who follow the example of their superiors. Furthermore, just as we hold a municipality liable for discharging an employee without due process when its city council acts formally — for a due process violation is precisely the *type* of constitutional tort that a city council might commit when it acts formally — so too must we hold a municipality liable for discharging an employee in retaliation against his public speech when similarly high officials act informally — for a first amendment retaliation tort is precisely the *type* of constitutional tort that high officials might commit when they act in concert and informally.

Whatever difficulties the Court may have with binding municipalities on the basis of the unconstitutional conduct of individuals, it should have no such difficulties binding a city when many of its high officials — including officials directly under the mayor, agency heads, and possibly the mayor himself — cooperate to retaliate against a whistleblower for the exercise of his First Amendment rights.[23]

---

[23] The plurality incorrectly claims that I have suggested "a new theory" for determining when a municipality should be bound by the acts of its agents. As both the plurality and the concurrence recognize, a municipality, like any institution, can only act through the agency of human beings. By holding that isolated actions of high officials may give rise to municipal liability, see, e.g., *Owen v. City of Independence; Pembaur v. Cincinnati*, the Court has indicated that the mere status of City officials matters in determining whether the City may be held liable for the officials' actions. The argument of both the plurality and the concurrence that this principle should be applied only in the particular area of government that the erring official controls is unpersuasive, given the multifarious ways in which government agents may inflict constitutional harm. This case is a perfect example of why the "area-by-area" approach will not do; personnel actions may be taken in response to an employee's protected speech by a number of high officials, none of whom possesses specific author-

I would affirm the judgment of the Court of Appeals.

WILL v. MICHIGAN DEPARTMENT OF STATE POLICE

491 U.S. 58, 109 S. Ct. 2304, 105 L. Ed. 2d 45 (1989)

JUSTICE WHITE delivered the opinion of the Court.

This case presents the question whether a State, or an official of the State while acting in his or her official capacity, is a "person" within the meaning of 42 U.S.C. § 1983.

Petitioner Ray Will filed suit in Michigan Circuit Court alleging various violations of the United States and Michigan Constitutions as grounds for a claim under § 1983. He alleged that he had been denied a promotion to a data systems analyst position with the Department of State Police for an improper reason, that is, because his brother had been a student activist and the subject of a "red squad" file maintained by respondent. Named as defendants were the Department of State Police and the Director of State Police in his official capacity, also a respondent here.

The Circuit Court remanded the case to the Michigan Civil Service Commission for a grievance hearing. While the grievance was pending, petitioner filed suit in the Michigan Court of Claims raising an essentially identical § 1983 claim. The Civil Service Commission ultimately found in petitioner's favor, ruling that respondents had refused to promote petitioner because of "partisan considerations." On the basis of that finding, the state court judge, acting in both the Circuit Court and the Court of Claims cases, concluded that petitioner had established a violation of the United States Constitution. The judge held that the Circuit Court action was barred under state law but that the Claims Court action could go forward. The judge also ruled that respondents were persons for purposes of § 1983.

The Michigan Court of Appeals vacated the judgment against the Department of State Police, holding that a State is not a person under § 1983, but remanded the case for determination of the possible immunity of the Director of State Police from liability for damages. The Michigan Supreme Court granted discretionary review and affirmed the Court of Appeals in part and reversed in part. The Supreme Court agreed that the State itself is not a person under § 1983, but held that a State official acting in his or her official capacity also is not such a person.

The Michigan Supreme Court's holding that a State is not a person under § 1983 conflicts with a number of state and federal court cases that hold to the contrary. We granted certiorari to resolve the conflict. 485 U.S. 1005 (1988).

Prior to *Monell v. New York City Dept. of Social Services*, 436 U.S. 658 (1978), the question whether a State is a person within the meaning of § 1983

---

ity over "personnel" policy. Nevertheless, simply by virtue of their high rank, their actions may influence the actions of other municipal officials. It is that kind of influence that provides the common thread binding *Monell* and the later § 1983 municipal liability cases. In short, what the Court has characterized as "a new theory" is actually a way of understanding our precedents that will permit a judge to explain to a jury that "policy" means nothing if not "influence," and that while the isolated gunshot of an errant police officer would not influence his colleagues, see *Oklahoma City v. Tuttle*, adverse personnel actions taken by a City's highest officials in response to an employee's Civil Service Commission appeals and his public testimony would set an example for other, lower officials to follow.

had been answered by this Court in the negative. In *Monroe v. Pape*, 365 U.S. 167, 187-191 (1961), the Court had held that a municipality was not a person under § 1983. "[T]hat being the case," we reasoned, § 1983 "could not have been intended to include States as parties defendant." *Fitzpatrick v. Bitzer*, 427 U.S. 445, 452 (1976).

But in *Monell*, the Court overruled *Monroe*, holding that a municipality was a person under § 1983. 436 U.S., at 690. Since then, various members of the Court have debated whether a State is a person within the meaning of § 1983, see *Hutto v. Finney*, 437 U.S. 678, 700-704 (1978) (BRENNAN, J., concurring); *id.*, at 708, n. 6 (POWELL, J., concurring in part and dissenting in part), but this Court has never expressly dealt with that issue.[4]

Some courts, including the Michigan Supreme Court here, have construed our decision in *Quern v. Jordan*, 440 U.S. 332 (1979), as holding by implication that a State is not a person under § 1983. See *Smith v. Department of Pub. Health*, 428 Mich. 540, 581, 410 N.W.2d 749, 767 (1987). See also, e.g., *State v. Green*, 633 P.2d 1381, 1382 (Alaska 1981); *Woodbridge v. Worcester State Hospital*, 384 Mass. 38, 44-45, n. 7, 423 N.E.2d 782, 786, n. 7 (1981); *Edgar v. State*, 92 Wash. 2d 217, 221, 595 P.2d 534, 537 (1979), *cert. denied*, 444 U.S. 1077 (1980). *Quern* held that § 1983 does not override a State's Eleventh Amendment immunity, a holding that the concurrence suggested was "patently dicta" to the effect that a State is not a person, 440 U.S., at 351 (BRENNAN, J., concurring in judgment).

Petitioner filed the present § 1983 action in Michigan state court, which places the question whether a State is a person under § 1983 squarely before us since the Eleventh Amendment does not apply in state courts. *Maine v. Thiboutot*, 448 U.S. 1, 9, n. 7 (1980). For the reasons that follow, we reaffirm today what we had concluded prior to *Monell* and what some have considered implicit in *Quern*: that a State is not a person within the meaning of § 1983.

We observe initially that if a State is a "person" within the meaning of § 1983, the section is to be read as saying that "every person, including a State, who, under color of any statute, ordinance, regulation, custom, or usage, of any State or Territory or the District of Columbia, subjects ...." That would be a decidedly awkward way of expressing an intent to subject the States to liability. At the very least, reading the statute in this way is not so clearly indicated that it provides reason to depart from the often-expressed understanding that "'in common usage, the term 'person' does not include the sovereign, [and] statutes employing the [word] are ordinarily construed to exclude it.'" *Wilson v. Omaha*

---

[4] Petitioner cites [a] number of cases from this Court that he asserts have "assumed" that a State is a person. Those cases include ones in which a State has been sued by name under § 1983, see, e.g., *Maine v. Thiboutot*, 448 U.S. 1 (1980); *Martinez v. California*, 444 U.S. 277 (1980), various cases awarding attorney's fees against a State or a State agency, *Maine v. Thiboutot, supra; Hutto v. Finney*, 437 U.S. 678 (1978), and various cases discussing the waiver of Eleventh Amendment immunity by States, see, e.g., *Kentucky v. Graham*, 473 U.S. 159, 167, n. 14 (1985); *Edelman v. Jordan*, 415 U.S. 651 (1974). But the Court did not address the meaning of person in any of those cases, and in none of the cases was resolution of that issue necessary to the decision. Petitioner's argument evidently rests on the proposition that whether a State is a person under § 1983 is "jurisdictional" and "thus could have been raised by the Court on its own motion" in those cases. Even assuming that petitioner's premise and characterization of the cases is correct, "this Court has never considered itself bound [by prior *sub silentio* holdings] when a subsequent case finally brings the jurisdictional issue before us." *Hagins v. Lavine*, 415 U.S. 528, 535, n. 5 (1974).

Indian Tribe, 442 U.S. 653, 667 (1979) (quoting *United States v. Cooper Corp.,* 312 U.S. 600, 604 (1941)). See also *United States v. Mine Workers,* 330 U.S. 258, 275 (1947).

This approach is particularly applicable where it is claimed that Congress has subjected the States to liability to which they had not been subject before. In *Wilson v. Omaha Indian Tribe, supra,* we followed this rule in construing the phrase "white person" contained in 25 U.S.C. § 194, enacted as Act of June 30, 1834, 4 Stat. 729, as not including the "sovereign States of the Union." 442 U.S., at 667. This common usage of the term "person" provides a strong indication that person as used in § 1983 likewise does not include a State.

The language of § 1983 also falls far short of satisfying the ordinary rule of statutory construction that if Congress intends to alter the "usual constitutional balance between the States and the Federal Government," it must make its intention to do so "unmistakably clear in the language of the statute." *Atascadero State Hospital v. Scanlon,* 473 U.S. 234, 242 (1985); see also *Pennhurst State School and Hospital v. Halderman,* 465 U.S. 89, 99 (1984)....

Our conclusion that a State is not a person within the meaning of § 1983 is reinforced by Congress' purpose in enacting the statute. Congress enacted § 1 of the Civil Rights Act of 1871, 17 Stat. 13, the precursor to § 1983, shortly after the end of the Civil War "in response to the widespread deprivations of civil rights in the Southern States and the inability or unwillingness of authorities in those States to protect those rights or punish wrongdoers." *Felder v. Casey,* 487 U.S. —, — (1988). Although Congress did not establish federal courts as the exclusive forum to remedy these deprivations, *ibid.,* it is plain that "Congress assigned to the federal courts a paramount role" in this endeavor, *Patsy v. Board of Regents of Florida,* 457 U.S. 496, 503 (1982).

Section 1983 provides a federal forum to remedy many deprivations of civil liberties, but it does not provide a federal forum for litigants who seek a remedy against a State for alleged deprivations of civil liberties. The Eleventh Amendment bars such suits unless the State has waived its immunity, *Welch v. Texas Dept. of Highways and Public Transportation,* 483 U.S. 468, — (1987) (plurality opinion), or unless Congress has exercised its undoubted power under § 5 of the Fourteenth Amendment to override that immunity. That Congress, in passing § 1983, had no intention to disturb the States' Eleventh Amendment immunity and so to alter the Federal-State balance in that respect was made clear in our decision in *Quern.* Given that a principal purpose behind the enactment of § 1983 was to provide a federal forum for civil rights claims, and that Congress did not provide such a federal forum for civil rights claims against States, we cannot accept petitioner's argument that Congress intended nevertheless to create a cause of action against States to be brought in state courts, which are precisely the courts Congress sought to allow civil rights claimants to avoid through § 1983....

Our conclusion is further supported by our holdings that in enacting § 1983, Congress did not intend to override well-established immunities or defenses under the common law. "One important assumption underlying the Court's decisions in this area is that members of the 42d Congress were familiar with common-law principles, including defenses previously recognized in ordinary tort litigation, and that they likely intended these common-law principles to obtain, absent specific provisions to the contrary." *Newport v. Fact Concerts, Inc.,* 453 U.S. 247, 258 (1981). *Stump v. Sparkman,* 435 U.S. 349, 356 (1978); *Scheuer v. Rhodes,* 416 U.S. 232, 247 (1974); *Pierson v. Ray,* 386 U.S. 547, 554 (1967); and *Tenney v. Brandhove,* 341 U.S. 367, 376 (1951), are also to this effect. The doctrine of sovereign immunity was a familiar doctrine at common law. "The principle is elementary that a State cannot be sued in its own courts without consent." *Railroad Co. v. Tennessee,* 101 U.S. 337, 339 (1881). It is an "established principle of jurisprudence" that the sovereign cannot be sued in its own courts without its consent. *Beers v. Arkansas,* 20 How. 527, 529 (1858). We cannot conclude that § 1983 was intended to disregard the well-established immunity of a State from being sued without its consent.[7]

The legislative history of § 1983 does not suggest a different conclusion. Petitioner contends that the congressional debates on § 1 of the 1871 Act indicate that § 1983 was intended to extend to the full reach of the Fourteenth Amendment and thereby to provide a remedy "'against all forms of official violation of federally protected rights.'" Brief for Petitioner 16 (quoting *Monell,* 436 U.S., at 700-701). He refers us to various parts of the vigorous debates accompanying the passage of § 1983 and revealing that it was the failure of the States to take appropriate action that was undoubtedly the motivating force behind § 1983. The inference must be drawn, it is urged, that Congress must have intended to subject the States themselves to liability. But the intent of Congress to provide a remedy for unconstitutional state action does not without more include the sovereign States among those persons against whom § 1983 actions would lie. Construing § 1983 as a remedy for "official violation of federally protected rights" does no more than confirm that the section is directed against state action — action "under color of" state law. It does not suggest that the State itself was a person that Congress intended to be subject to liability.

Although there were sharp and heated debates, the discussion of § 1 of the Bill, which contained the present § 1983, was not extended. And although in other respects the impact on State sovereignty was much talked about, no one suggested that § 1 would subject the States themselves to a damages suit under Federal law. *Quern,* 440 U.S., at 343. There was complaint that § 1 would subject State officers to damages liability, but no suggestion that it would also expose the States themselves. Cong. Globe, 42d Cong., 1st Sess. 366, 385 (1871). We find nothing substantial in the legislative history that leads us to believe that Congress intended that the word "person" in § 1983 included the States of the Union. And surely nothing in the debates rises to the clearly expressed legislative intent necessary to permit that construction.

---

[7]Our recognition in *Monell v. New York City Dept. of Social Services,* 436 U.S. 658 (1978), that a municipality is a person under § 1983, is fully consistent with this reasoning. In *Owen v. City of Independence,* 445 U.S. 622 (1980), we noted that by the time of the enactment of § 1983, municipalities no longer retained the sovereign immunity they had previously shared with the States. "[B]y the end of the 19th century, courts regularly held that in imposing a specific duty on the municipality either in its charter or by statute, the State had impliedly withdrawn the city's immunity from liability for the nonperformance or misperformance of its obligation," *id.,* at 646, and, as a result, municipalities had been held liable for damages "in a multitude of cases" involving previously immune activities, *id.,* at 646-647.

Likewise, the Act of Feb. 25, 1871, § 2, 16 Stat. 431 (the "Dictionary Act")[8] on which we relied in *Monell,* 436 U.S., at 688-689, does not counsel a contrary conclusion here. As we noted in *Quern,* that Act, while adopted prior to § 1 of the Civil Rights Act of 1871, was adopted after § 2 of the Civil Rights Act of 1866, from which § 1 of the 1871 Act was derived. 440 U.S., at 341, n. 11. Moreover, we disagree with JUSTICE BRENNAN that at the time the Dictionary Act was passed "the phrase 'bodies politic and corporate' was understood to include the States." Post, at 8. Rather, an examination of authorities of the era suggests that the phrase was used to mean corporations, both private and public (municipal), and not to include the States.[9] In our view, the Dictionary Act, like § 1983 itself and its legislative history, fails to evidence a clear congressional intent that States be held liable.

Finally, *Monell* itself is not to the contrary. True, prior to *Monell* the Court had reasoned that if municipalities were not persons then surely States also were not. *Fitzpatrick v. Bitzer,* 427 U.S., at 452. And *Monell* overruled *Monroe,* undercutting that logic. But it does not follow that if municipalities are persons then so are States. States are protected by the Eleventh Amendment while municipalities are not, *Monell,* 436 U.S., at 690, n. 54, and we consequently limited our holding in *Monell* "to local government units which are not considered part of the State for Eleventh Amendment purposes," *ibid.* Conversely, our holding here does not cast any doubt on *Monell,* and applies only to States or governmental entities that are considered "arms of the State" for Eleventh Amendment purposes. See, e.g., *Mt. Healthy City School Dist. Bd. of Ed. v. Doyle,* 429 U.S. 274, 280 (1977).

Petitioner asserts, alternatively, that state officials should be considered "persons" under § 1983 even though acting in their official capacities. In this case, petitioner named as defendant not only the Michigan Department of State Police but also the Director of State Police in his official capacity.

Obviously, state officials literally are persons. But a suit against a state official in his or her official capacity is not a suit against the official but rather is a suit against the official's office. *Brandon v. Holt,* 469 U.S. 464, 471 (1985). As such, it is no different from a suit against the State itself. See, e.g., *Kentucky v. Graham,* 473 U.S. 159, 165-166 (1985); *Monell, supra,* at 690, n. 55. We see no reason to adopt a different rule in the present context, particularly when such a

---

[8] The Dictionary Act provided that

"in all acts hereafter passed ... the word 'person' may extend and be applied to bodies politic and corporate ... unless the context shows that such words were intended to be used in a more limited sense." Act of Feb. 25, 1871, § 2, 16 Stat. 431.

[9] See *United States v. Fox,* 94 U.S. 315, 321 (1877); 1 B. Abbott, Dictionary of Terms and Phrases Used in American or English Jurisprudence 155 (1879) ("most exact expression" for "public corporation"); W. Anderson, A Dictionary of Law 127 (1893) ("most exact expression for a public corporation or corporation having powers of government"); Black's Law Dictionary 143 (1891) ("body politic" is "term applied to a corporation, which is usually designated as a 'body corporate and politic'" and "is particularly appropriate to a *public* corporation invested with powers and duties of government"); 1 A. Burrill, A Law Dictionary and Glossary 212 (2d ed. 1871) ("body politic" is "term applied to a corporation, which is usually designated as a *body corporate and politic*"). A public corporation, in ordinary usage, was another term for a municipal corporation, and included towns, cities, and counties, but not States. See 2 Abbott, *supra,* at 347; Anderson, *supra,* at 264-265; Black, *supra,* at 278; 2 Burrill, *supra,* at 352.

...

rule would allow petitioner to circumvent congressional intent by a mere pleading device.[10]

We hold that neither a State nor its officials acting in their official capacities are "persons" under § 1983. The judgment of the Michigan Supreme Court is affirmed.

It is so ordered.

JUSTICE BRENNAN, with whom JUSTICE MARSHALL, JUSTICE BLACKMUN, and JUSTICE STEVENS join, dissenting.

. . . .

I

Section 1 of the Civil Rights of Act of 1871, 42 U.S.C. § 1983, renders certain "persons" liable for deprivations of constitutional rights. The question presented is whether the word "persons" in this statute includes the States and state officials acting in their official capacities.

One might expect that this statutory question would generate a careful and thorough analysis of the language, legislative history, and general background of § 1983. If this is what one expects, however, one will be disappointed by today's decision. For this case is not decided on the basis of our ordinary method of statutory construction; instead, the Court disposes of it by means of various rules of statutory interpretation that it summons to its aid each time the question looks close. Specifically, the Court invokes the following interpretative principles: the word "persons" is ordinarily construed to exclude the sovereign; congressional intent to affect the federal-state balance must be "clear and manifest"; and intent to abrogate States' Eleventh Amendment immunity must appear in the language of the statute itself. The Court apparently believes that each of these rules obviates the need for close analysis of a statute's language and history. Properly applied, however, only the last of these interpretative principles has this effect, and that principle is not pertinent to the case before us.

The Court invokes, first, the "often-expressed understanding" that "'in common usage, the term "person" does not include the sovereign, [and] statutes employing the [word] are ordinarily construed to exclude it.'" *Ante,* quoting *Wilson v. Omaha Indian Tribe,* 442 U.S. 653, 667 (1979). This rule is used both to refute the argument that the language of § 1983 demonstrates an intent that States be included as defendants, *ante,* and to overcome the argument based on

---

[10]Of course a State official in his or her official capacity, when sued for injunctive relief, would be a person under § 1983 because "official-capacity actions for prospective relief are not treated as actions against the State." *Kentucky v. Graham,* 473 U.S., at 167, n. 14; *Ex parte Young,* 209 U.S. 123, 159-160 (1908). This distinction is "commonplace in sovereign immunity doctrine," L. Tribe, American Constitutional Law § 3-27, p. 190, n. 3 (2d ed. 1988), and would not have been foreign to the 19th-century Congress that enacted § 1983, see, e.g., *In re Ayers,* 123 U.S. 443, 506-507 (1887); *United States v. Lee,* 106 U.S. 196, 219-222 (1882); *Board of Liquidation v. McComb,* 92 U.S. 531, 541 (1876); *Osborn v. Bank of United States,* 9 Wheat. 738 (1824). *City of Kenosha v. Bruno,* 412 U.S. 507, 513 (1973), on which JUSTICE STEVENS relies, see post, is not to the contrary. That case involved municipal liability under § 1983, and the fact that nothing in § 1983 suggests its "bifurcated application to municipal corporations depending on the nature of the relief sought against them," 412 U.S., at 513, is not surprising since by the time of the enactment of § 1983 municipalities were no longer protected by sovereign immunity.

the Dictionary Act's definition of "persons" to include bodies politic and corporate, *ante*. It is ironic, to say the least, that the Court chooses this interpretive rule in explaining why the Dictionary Act is not decisive, since the rule is relevant only when the word "persons" has no statutory definition. When one considers the origins and content of this interpretive guideline, moreover, one realizes that it is inapplicable here and, even if applied, would defeat rather than support the Court's approach and result....

The second interpretative principle that the Court invokes comes from cases such as *Rice v. Sante Fe Elevator Corp.,* 331 U.S. 218, 230 (1947); *Pennhurst State School and Hospital v. Halderman,* 451 U.S. 1, 16 (1981); *South Dakota v. Dole,* 483 U.S. 203, 207-208 (1987); and *United States v. Bass,* 404 U.S. 336, 349 (1971), which require a "clear and manifest" expression of congressional intent to change some aspect of federal-state relations. *Ante.* These cases do not, however, permit substitution of an absolutist rule of statutory construction for thorough statutory analysis. Indeed, in each of these decisions the Court undertook a careful and detailed analysis of the statutory language and history under consideration. *Rice* is a particularly inapposite source for the interpretative method that the Court today employs, since it observes that, according to conventional pre-emption analysis, a "clear and manifest" intent to pre-empt state legislation may appear in the "scheme" or "purpose" of the federal statute. See 331 U.S., at 230.

The only principle of statutory construction employed by the Court that would justify a perfunctory and inconclusive analysis of a statute's language and history is one that is irrelevant to this case. This is the notion "that if Congress intends to alter the 'usual constitutional balance between the States and the Federal Government,' it must make its intention to do so 'unmistakably clear in the language of the statute.'" *Ante,* quoting *Atascadero State Hospital v. Scanlon,* 473 U.S. 234, 242 (1985). As the Court notes, *Atascadero* was an Eleventh Amendment case; the "constitutional balance" to which *Atascadero* refers is that struck by the Eleventh Amendment as this Court has come to interpret it. Although the Court apparently wishes it were otherwise, the principle of interpretation that *Atascadero* announced is unique to cases involving the Eleventh Amendment.... Since this case was brought in state court, however, this strict drafting requirement has no application here. The Eleventh Amendment can hardly be "a consideration," *ante,* in a suit to which it does not apply.

That this Court has generated a uniquely daunting requirement of clarity in Eleventh Amendment cases explains why *Quern v. Jordan,* 440 U.S. 332 (1979), did not decide the question before us today. Because only the Eleventh Amendment permits use of this clear-statement principle, the holding of *Quern v. Jordan* that § 1983 does not abrogate States' Eleventh Amendment immunity tells us nothing about the meaning of the term "persons" in § 1983 as a matter of ordinary statutory construction. *Quern's* conclusion thus does not compel, or even suggest, a particular result today....

II

....

Although § 1983 itself does not define the term "person," we are not without a statutory definition of this word. "Any analysis of the meaning of the word 'person' in § 1983 ... must begin ... with the Dictionary Act." *Monell v. New York City Dept. of Social Services,* 436 U.S. 658, 719 (1978) (REHNQUIST, J., dissenting). Passed just two months before § 1983, and designed to "suppl[y] rules of construction for all legislation," *ibid.,* the Dictionary Act provided:

> "That in all acts hereafter passed ... the word 'person' may extend and be applied to bodies politic and corporate ... unless the context shows that such words were intended to be used in a more limited sense ...." Act of Feb. 25, 1871, § 2, 16 Stat. 431.

In *Monell,* we held this definition to be not merely allowable but mandatory, requiring that the word "person" be construed to include "bodies politic and corporate" unless the statute under consideration "by its terms called for a deviation from this practice." 436 U.S., at 689-690, n. 53. Thus, we concluded, where nothing in the "context" of a particular statute "call[s] for a restricted interpretation of the word 'person,' the language of that [statute] should prima facie be construed to include 'bodies politic' among the entities that could be sued." *Ibid.*

Both before and after the time when the Dictionary Act and § 1983 were passed, the phrase "bodies politic and corporate" was understood to include the States. See, e.g., J. Bouvier, 1 A Law Dictionary Adapted to the Constitution and Laws of the United States of America 185 (11th ed. 1866); W. Shumaker & G. Longsdorf, Cyclopedic Dictionary of Law 104 (1901); *Chisholm v. Georgia,* 2 Dall. 419, 447 (1793) (Iredell, J.); *id.,* at 468 (Cushing, J.); ...

The reason why States are "bodies politic and corporate" is simple: just as a corporation is an entity that can act only through its agents, "[t]he State is a political corporate body, can act only through agents, and can command only by laws." *Poindexter v. Greenhow, supra,* at 288. See also Black's Law Dictionary 159 (5th ed. 1979) ("body politic or corporate": "[a] social compact by which the whole people covenants with each citizen, and each citizen with the whole people, that all shall be governed by certain laws for the common good"). As a "body politic and corporate," a State falls squarely within the Dictionary Act's definition of a "person."

While it is certainly true that the phrase "bodies politic and corporate" referred to private and public corporations, see *ante,* this fact does not draw into question the conclusion that this phrase also applied to the States. Phrases may, of course, have multiple referents....

[T]he question before us is whether the presumption that the word "persons" in § 1 of the Civil Rights Act of 1871 included bodies politic and corporate — and hence the States — is overcome by anything in the statute's language and history. Certainly nothing in the statutory language overrides this presumption. The statute is explicitly directed at action taken "under color of" state law, and thus supports rather than refutes the idea that the "persons" mentioned in the statute include the States. Indeed, for almost a century — until *Monroe v. Pape,* 365 U.S. 167 (1961) — it was unclear whether the statute applied at all to action not authorized by the State, and the enduring significance of the first cases construing the Fourteenth Amendment, pursuant to which § 1 was passed, lies in their conclusion that the prohibitions of this Amendment do not reach private action. See *Civil Rights Cases,* 109 U.S. 3 (1883). In such a setting, one cannot reasonably deny the significance of § 1983's explicit focus on state action.

Unimpressed by such arguments, the Court simply asserts that reading "States" where the statute mentions "persons" would be "decidedly awkward." *Ante.* The Court does not describe the awkwardness that it perceives, but I take it that its objection is that the under-color-of-law requirement would be redundant if States were included in the statute because States necessarily act under color of state law. But § 1983 extends as well to natural persons, who do not necessarily so act; in order to ensure that *they* would be liable only when they did so, the statute needed the under-color-of-law requirement. The only way to remove the redundancy that the Court sees would have been to eliminate the catch-all phrase "persons" altogether, and separately describe each category of possible defendants and the circumstances under which they might be liable. I cannot think of a situation not involving the Eleventh Amendment, however, in which we have imposed such an unforgiving drafting requirement on Congress.

Taking the example closest to this case, we might have observed in *Monell* that § 1983 was clumsily written if it included municipalities, since these, too, may act only under color of state authority. Nevertheless, we held there that the statute does apply to municipalities. 436 U.S., at 690.

    ....

III

To describe the breadth of the Court's holding is to demonstrate its unwisdom. If States are not "persons" within the meaning of § 1983, then they may not be sued under that statute regardless of whether they have consented to suit. Even if, in other words, a State formally and explicitly consented to suits against it in federal or state court, no § 1983 plaintiff could proceed against it because States are not within the statute's category of possible defendants.

This is indeed an exceptional holding. Not only does it depart from our suggestion in *Alabama v. Pugh,* 438 U.S. 781, 782 (1978), that a State could be a defendant under § 1983 if it consented to suit, see also *Quern v. Jordan,* 440 U.S. at 340, but it also renders ineffective the choices some States have made to permit such suits against them. See, e.g., *Della Grotta v. Rhode Island,* 781 F.2d 343 (CA1 1986). I do not understand what purpose is served, what principle of federalism or comity is promoted, by refusing to give force to a State's explicit consent to suit.

The Court appears to be driven to this peculiar result in part by its view that "in enacting § 1983, Congress did not intend to override well-established immunities or defenses under the common law." *Ante.* But the question whether States are "persons" under § 1983 is separate and distinct from the question whether they may assert a defense of common-law sovereign immunity. In our prior decisions involving common-law immunities, we have not held that the existence of an immunity defense excluded the relevant state actor from the category of "persons" liable under § 1983, see, e.g., *Forrester v. White,* 484 U.S. 219 (1988), and it is a mistake to do so today. Such an approach entrenches the effect of common-law immunity even where the immunity itself has been waived....

JUSTICE STEVENS, dissenting.

Legal doctrines often flourish long after the *raison d'être* has perished. The doctrine of sovereign immunity rests on the fictional premise that the "King can do no wrong." Even though the plot to assassinate James I in 1605, the execution of Charles I in 1649, and the Colonists' reaction to George III's stamp tax made rather clear the fictional character of the doctrine's underpinnings, British subjects found a gracious means of compelling the King to obey the law rather than simply repudiating the doctrine itself. They held his advisors and his agents responsible.

In our administration of § 1983, we have also relied on fictions to protect the illusion that a sovereign State, absent consent, may not be held accountable for its delicts in federal court. Under a settled course of decision, in contexts ranging from school desegregation to the provision of public assistance benefits to the administration of prison systems and other state facilities, we have held the States liable under § 1983 for their constitutional violations through the artifice of naming a public officer as a nominal party. Once one strips away the Eleventh Amendment overlay applied to actions in federal court, it is apparent that the Court in these cases has treated the State as the real party in interest both for the purposes of granting prospective and ancillary relief and of denying retroactive relief. When suit is brought in state court, where the Eleventh Amendment is inapplicable, it follows that the State can be named directly as a party under § 1983.

An official-capacity suit is the typical way in which we have held States responsible for their duties under federal law. Such a suit, we have explained, "'generally represent[s] only another way of pleading an action against an entity of which an officer is an agent.'" *Kentucky v. Graham,* 473 U.S. 159, 165 (1985) (quoting *Monell v. New York City Dept. of Social Services,* 436 U.S. 658, 690, n. 55 (1978)); see also *Pennhurst State School and Hospital v. Halderman,* 465 U.S. 89, 101 (1984). In the peculiar Eleventh Amendment analysis we have applied to such cases, we have recognized that an official-capacity action is in reality always against the State and balanced interests to determine whether a particular type of relief is available. The Court has held that when a suit seeks equitable relief or money damages from a state officer for injuries suffered in the past, the interests in compensation and deterrence are insufficiently weighty to override the State's sovereign immunity. See *Papasan v. Allain,* 478 U.S. 265, 278 (1986); *Green v. Mansour,* 474 U.S. 64, 68 (1985); *Edelman v. Jordan,* 415 U.S. 651, 668 (1974). On the other hand, although prospective relief awarded against a state officer also "implicate[s] Eleventh Amendment concerns," *Mansour,* 474 U.S., at 68, the interests in "end[ing] a continuing violation of federal law," *ibid.,* outweigh the interests in state sovereignty and justify an award under § 1983 of an injunction that operates against the State's officers or even directly against the State itself. See, e.g., *Papasan, supra,* at 282; *Quern v. Jordan,* 440 U.S. 332, 337 (1979); *Milliken v. Bradley,* 433 U.S. 267, 289 (1977)....

The Civil Rights Act of 1871 was "intended to provide a remedy, to be broadly construed, against all forms of official violation of federally protected rights." *Monell v. New York City Dept. of Social Services, supra,* at 700-701. Our holdings that a § 1983 action can be brought against state officials in their official capacity for constitutional violations properly recognize and are faithful to that profound mandate. If prospective relief can be awarded against state officials under § 1983 and the State is the real party in interest in such suits, the State must be a "person" which can be held liable under § 1983. No other conclusion is available. Eleventh Amendment principles may limit the State's capacity to be sued as such in federal court. See *Alabama v. Pugh,* 438 U.S. 781 (1978). But since those principles are not applicable to suits in state court, see *Thiboutot, supra,* at 9, n. 7; *Nevada v. Hall,* 440 U.S. 410 (1979), there is no need to resort to the fiction of an official-capacity suit and the State may and should be named directly as a defendant in a § 1983 action....

NOTES

1. The eleventh amendment provides that the federal judicial power shall not extend to lawsuits prosecuted by individuals against states. In *Edelman v. Jordan,* 415 U.S. 651 (1974), the Court held that while that amendment did not preclude federal courts from granting prospective injunctive relief against state officials (*Ex parte Young,* 209 U.S. 123 (1908)), it did prevent any federal court order requiring the direct disbursement of state funds. In *Quern v. Jordan,* 440 U.S. 332 (1979), the Court reaffirmed the *Edelman* rule, expressly indicating that the eleventh amendment immunity enjoyed by the states was not abrogated by its decision in *Monell v. Department of Social Servs.,* 436 U.S. 658 (1978).

In *Pennhurst State Sch. & Hosp. v. Halderman,* 465 U.S. 89 (1984), the Supreme Court recognized that the eleventh amendment prohibits a federal district court from issuing an injunctive order requiring state officials to conform their conduct to *state* law. The *Ex parte Young* exception was found inapplicable, since the Court was not acting to vindicate the supreme authority of federal law. The Supreme Court thus concluded that where a federal court instructs state officials regarding their obligations under state law, this action conflicts directly with the principles of federalism that underlie the eleventh amendment.

2. *Forrester v. White,* 484 U.S. 219 (1988), involved a probation officer who claimed that a state circuit judge had demoted and discharged her because of her gender. The Supreme Court ruled that while judges enjoy absolute immunity with respect to their performance of "judicial" or "adjudicative" acts, they do not enjoy such expansive immunity with respect to the administrative, legislative, or executive functions they are occasionally required to perform. Since the Court determined that the state judge's allegedly discriminatory demotion and discharge decisions constituted "administrative," rather than "judicial," acts, it ruled that he was not entitled to absolute immunity. The Court indicated that qualified immunity might be available with respect to such personnel decisions, but it did not decide this issue.

3. In 1966, Congress approved a compact involving Maryland, Virginia, and the District of Columbia which created the Washington Metropolitan Area Transit Authority. That compact provides that WMATA "shall not be liable for any torts occurring in the performance of a governmental function." As a result of this specific provision, the eleventh amendment was found to prevent a federal court from entertaining a suit under 42 U.S.C. § 1983 and the Constitution by an individual who claimed that he had been discharged by WMATA in retaliation against his opposition to discriminatory employment practices. *Morris v. WMATA,* 781 F.2d 218 (D.C. Cir. 1986). See also *Sanders v. WMATA,* 819 F.2d 1151 (D.C. Cir. 1987).

4. In a section 1983 suit against a public official whose position might entitle him to qualified immunity, the plaintiff need only allege that the official deprived him of a federal right while acting under the color of state law. The burden is then upon the defendant to plead good faith as an affirmative defense, since a qualified immunity claim generally depends upon the establishment of facts peculiarly within the defendant's knowledge and control. See *Gomez v. City of Toledo,* 446 U.S. 635 (1980).

5. In *Daniels v. Williams,* 474 U.S. 327 (1986), the Supreme Court expressly ruled that the due process clause is not implicated by a state official's negligent act which inadvertently causes an unintended loss of or injury to someone's life, liberty, or property. It found that the due process clause was intended to protect individuals from an abuse of power by government officials. Mere negligence suggests no more than a failure to measure up to the conduct of a reasonable person — something far below an abuse of official power. "To hold that injury caused by [negligent] conduct is a deprivation within the meaning of the Fourteenth Amendment would trivialize the centuries-old principle of due process of law." Accord *Davidson v. Cannon,* 474 U.S. 344 (1986).

6. *Davis v. Scherer,* 468 U.S. 183 (1984), involved a former highway patrol worker who claimed in a section 1983 suit that his employment had been terminated in violation of his due process rights because of the absence of a formal pre-termination or a prompt post-termination hearing. Although the trial court had ultimately found that the plaintiff's alleged hearing right had not been "clearly established" at the time of his discharge in 1977, it awarded him damages against the responsible state officials. It found that the officials had forfeited their qualified immunity, since they had not complied with explicit departmental regulations that had the force of law. This contravention of departmental rules was found to render the officials' conduct unreasonable. The Supreme Court, however, rejected this analysis. It held that plaintiffs who seek damages for violation of their constitutional or statutory rights may overcome defendant-officials' qualified immunity defense only by showing that the infringed rights were "clearly established" at the time of the action in dispute.

> Under *Harlow* [*v. Fitzgerald,* 457 U.S. 800 (1982)], officials "are shielded from liability for civil damages insofar as their conduct does not violate clearly established statutory or constitutional rights of which a reasonable person would have known." 457 U.S., at 818. Whether an official may prevail in his qualified immunity defense depends upon the "objective reasonableness of [his] conduct as measured by reference to clearly established law." *Id.* No other "circumstances" are relevant to the issue of qualified immunity.

The *Davis* majority refused to hold that the violation of applicable state regulations would cause a loss of qualified immunity, since public officials are generally subject to a plethora of rules that are "so voluminous, ambiguous, and contradictory, and in such flux that officials can comply with them only selectively." See also *Auriemma v. Rice,* 895 F.2d 338 (7th Cir. 1990); *Hedge v. County of Tippecanoe,* 890 F.2d 4 (7th Cir. 1989).

7. The Supreme Court has held that neither U.S. Territories nor Territorial officers acting in their official capacities constitute "persons" under section 1983. *Ngiraingas v. Sanchez,* 110 S. Ct. 1737 (1990).

8. *Gurmankin v. Costanzo,* 626 F.2d 1115 (3d Cir. 1980), *cert. denied,* 450 U.S. 923 (1981), held that where a school board unconstitutionally deprives an individual of an employment opportunity, backpay will usually be presumptively awardable under section 1983. However, in *City of Newport v. Fact Con-*

certs, Inc., 453 U.S. 247 (1981), the Supreme Court recognized that punitive damages may not be awarded in section 1983 suits against municipalities for even malicious or reckless conduct by their officials. Only compensatory damages may be obtained from such governmental entities. Nonetheless, where a government official's conduct involves reckless or callous indifference to the plaintiff's federally protected rights, or is actually motivated by an evil intent, punitive damages may be recovered against that individual public servant. See *Smith v. Wade,* 461 U.S. 30 (1983).

9. In *Howlett v. Rose,* 110 S. Ct. 2430 (1990), the Supreme Court held that while state courts have jurisdiction to entertain actions under section 1983, they must apply federal substantive law to determine immunity questions. The Court thus held that state courts may not employ state law immunity theories to preclude section 1983 suits that could be prosecuted against school districts or municipalities under federal law.

10. See generally Mead, *42 U.S.C. § 1983 Municipal Liability: The Monell Sketch Becomes a Distorted Picture,* 65 N.C.L. Rev. 517 (1987); Whitman, *Government Responsibility for Constitutional Torts,* 85 Mich. L. Rev. 225 (1986); Kinports, *Qualified Immunity in Section 1983 Cases: The Unanswered Questions,* 23 Ga. L. Rev. 597 (1989).

HARLOW v. FITZGERALD

457 U.S. 800, 102 S. Ct. 2727, 73 L. Ed. 2d 396 (1982)

[During 1968, A. Ernest Fitzgerald, a management analyst with the Department of the Air Force, testified before a congressional subcommittee regarding substantial cost overruns associated with the development of a particular military airplane. In January of 1970, Fitzgerald's federal employment was terminated during a departmental reorganization. Claiming that his dismissal constituted unlawful retaliation for his previous congressional testimony, Fitzgerald ultimately sued former President Richard Nixon and two of his presidential aides, Bryce Harlow and Alexander Butterfield. Fitzgerald alleged that the defendants had unconstitutionally conspired to deprive him of his First Amendment freedom of speech and other statutory rights.]

JUSTICE POWELL delivered the opinion of the Court.

The issue in this case is the scope of the immunity available to the senior aides and advisers of the President of the United States in a suit for damages based upon their official acts.

I

In this suit for civil damages petitioners Bryce Harlow and Alexander Butterfield are alleged to have participated in a conspiracy to violate the constitutional and statutory rights of the respondent A. Ernest Fitzgerald. Respondent avers that petitioners entered the conspiracy in their capacities as senior White House aides to former President Richard M. Nixon....

Together with their codefendant Richard Nixon, petitioners Harlow and Butterfield moved for summary judgment on February 12, 1980. In denying the motion the District Court upheld the legal sufficiency of Fitzgerald's *Bivens (Bivens v. Six Unknown Fed. Narcotics Agents,* 403 U.S. 388 (1971)) claim under the First Amendment and his "inferred" statutory causes of action under

5 U.S.C. § 7211 (1976 ed., Supp. IV) and 18 U.S.C. § 1505.[10] The court found that genuine issues of disputed fact remained for resolution at trial. It also ruled that petitioners were not entitled to absolute immunity.

Independently of former President Nixon, petitioners invoked the collateral order doctrine and appealed the denial of their immunity defense to the Court of Appeals for the District of Columbia Circuit. The Court of Appeals dismissed the appeal without opinion. Never having determined the immunity available to the senior aides and advisers of the President of the United States, we granted certiorari. 452 U.S. 959 (1981).

II

As we reiterated today in *Nixon v. Fitzgerald,* our decisions consistently have held that government officials are entitled to some form of immunity from suits for damages. As recognized at common law, public officers require this protection to shield them from undue interference with their duties and from potentially disabling threats of liability.

Our decisions have recognized immunity defenses of two kinds. For officials whose special functions or constitutional status requires complete protection from suit, we have recognized the defense of "absolute immunity." The absolute immunity of legislators, in their legislative functions, see, e.g., *Eastland v. United States Servicemen's Fund,* 421 U.S. 491 (1975), and of judges, in their judicial functions, see, e.g., *Stump v. Sparkman,* 435 U.S. 349 (1978), now is well settled. Our decisions also have extended absolute immunity to certain officials of the Executive Branch. These include prosecutors and similar officials, see *Butz v. Economou,* 438 U.S. 478, 508-512 (1978), executive officers engaged in adjudicative functions, *id.,* at 513-517, and the President of the United States, see *Nixon v. Fitzgerald, ante,* p. 731.

For executive officials in general, however, our cases make plain that qualified immunity represents the norm. In *Scheuer v. Rhodes,* 416 U.S. 232 (1974), we acknowledged that high officials require greater protection than those with less complex discretionary responsibilities. Nonetheless, we held that a governor and his aides could receive the requisite protection from qualified or good-faith immunity. *Id.,* at 247-248. In *Butz v. Economou, supra,* we extended the approach of *Scheuer* to high federal officials of the Executive Branch. Discussing in detail the considerations that also had underlain our decision in *Scheuer,* we explained that the recognition of a qualified immunity defense for high executives reflected an attempt to balance competing values: not only the importance of a damages remedy to protect the rights of citizens, 438 U.S., at 504-505, but also "the need to protect officials who are required to exercise their discretion

---

[10] The first of these statutes, 5 U.S.C. § 7211 (Supp. III 1979), provides generally that "[t]he right of employees ... to ... furnish information to either House of Congress, or to a committee or a Member thereof, may not be interfered with or denied." The second, 18 U.S.C. § 1505, is a criminal statute making it a crime to obstruct congressional testimony. Neither expressly creates a private right to sue for damages. Petitioners argue that the District Court erred in finding that a private cause of action could be inferred under either statute, and that "special factors" present in the context of the federal employer-employee relationship preclude the recognition of respondent's *Bivens* action under the First Amendment. The legal sufficiency of respondent's asserted causes of action is not, however, a question that we view as properly presented for our decision in the present posture of this case.

and the related public interest in encouraging the vigorous exercise of official authority." *Id.,* at 506. Without discounting the adverse consequences of denying high officials an absolute immunity from private lawsuits alleging constitutional violations — consequences found sufficient in *Spalding v. Vilas,* 161 U.S. 483 (1896), and *Barr v. Matteo,* 360 U.S. 564 (1959), to warrant extension to such officials of absolute immunity from suits at common law — we emphasized our expectation that insubstantial suits need not proceed to trial:

> "Insubstantial lawsuits can be quickly terminated by federal courts alert to the possibilities of artful pleading. Unless the complaint states a compensable claim for relief ... , it should not survive a motion to dismiss. Moreover, the Court recognized in *Scheuer* that damages suits concerning constitutional violations need not proceed to trial, but can be terminated on a properly supported motion for summary judgment based on the defense of immunity.... In responding to such a motion, plaintiffs may not play dog in the manger; and firm application of the Federal Rules of Civil Procedure will ensure that federal officials are not harassed by frivolous lawsuits." 438 U.S., at 507-508 (citations omitted).

Butz continued to acknowledge that the special functions of some officials might require absolute immunity. But the Court held that "federal officials who seek absolute exemption from personal liability for unconstitutional conduct must bear the burden of showing that public policy requires an exemption of that scope." *Id.,* at 506. This we reaffirmed today in *Nixon v. Fitzgerald, ante,* at 747.

III

A. Petitioners argue that they are entitled to a blanket protection of absolute immunity as an incident of their offices as Presidential aides. In deciding this claim we do not write on an empty page. In *Butz v. Economou, supra,* the Secretary of Agriculture — a Cabinet official directly accountable to the President — asserted a defense of absolute official immunity from suit for civil damages. We rejected his claim. In so doing we did not question the power or the importance of the Secretary's office. Nor did we doubt the importance to the President of loyal and efficient subordinates in executing his duties of office. Yet we found these factors, alone, to be insuffficient to justify absolute immunity. "[T]he greater power of [high] officials," we reasoned, "affords a greater potential for a regime of lawless conduct." 438 U.S., at 506. Damages actions against high officials were therefore "an important means of vindicating constitutional guarantees." *Ibid.* Moreover, we concluded that it would be "untenable to draw a distinction for purposes of immunity law between suits brought against state officials under [42 U.S.C.] § 1983 and suits brought directly under the Constitution against federal officials." *Id.,* at 504.

Having decided in *Butz* that Members of the Cabinet ordinarily enjoy only qualified immunity from suit, we conclude today that it would be equally untenable to hold absolute immunity an incident of the office of every Presidential subordinate based in the White House. Members of the Cabinet are direct subordinates of the President, frequently with greater responsibilities, both to the President and to the Nation, than White House staff. The considerations that supported our decision in *Butz* apply with equal force to this case. It is no disparagement of the offices held by petitioners to hold that Presidential aides, like Members of the Cabinet, generally are entitled only to a qualified immunity.

B. In disputing the controlling authority of *Butz,* petitioners rely on the principles developed in *Gravel v. United States,* 408 U.S. 606 (1972).[12] In *Gravel* we endorsed the view that "it is literally impossible ... for Members of Congress to perform their legislative tasks without the help of aides and assistants" and that "the day-to-day work of such aides is so critical to the Members' performance that they must be treated as the latter's alter egos ...." *Id.,* at 616-617. Having done so, we held the Speech and Debate Clause derivately applicable to the "legislative acts" of a Senator's aide that would have been privileged if performed by the Senator himself. *Id.,* at 621-622.

Petitioners contend that the rationale of *Gravel* mandates a similar "derivative" immunity for the chief aides of the President of the United States. Emphasizing that the President must delegate a large measure of authority to execute the duties of his office, they argue that recognition of derivative absolute immunity is made essential by all the considerations that support absolute immunity for the President himself.

Petitioners' argument is not without force. Ultimately, however, it sweeps too far. If the President's aides are derivately immune because essential to the functioning of the Presidency, so should the members of the Cabinet — Presidential subordinates some of whose essential roles are acknowledged by the Constitution itself[13] — be absolutely immune. Yet we implicitly rejected such derivative immunity in *Butz.*[14] Moreover, in general our cases have followed a "functional" approach to immunity law. We have recognized that the judicial, prosecutorial, and legislative functions require absolute immunity. But this protection has extended no further than its justification would warrant. In *Gravel,* for example, we emphasized that Senators and their aides were absolutely immune only when performing "acts legislative in nature," and not when taking other acts even "in their official capacity." 408 U.S., at 625. See *Hutchinson v. Proxmire,* 443 U.S. 111, 125-133 (1979). Our cases involving judges[15] and prosecutors[16] have followed a similar line. The undifferentiated extension of

---

[12] Petitioners also claim support from other cases that have followed *Gravel* in holding that Congressional employees are derivatively entitled to the legislative immunity provided to United States Senators and Representatives under the Speech and Debate Clause. See *Eastland v. United States Servicemen's Fund,* 421 U.S. 491 (1975); *Doe v. McMillan,* 412 U.S. 306 (1973).

[13] See U.S. Const., Art. 2, § 2 ("The President ... may require the Opinion, in writing, of the principal Officer in each of the executive Departments, upon any Subject relating to the duties of their respective Offices ...").

[14] THE CHIEF JUSTICE, *post,* at 828, argues that senior Presidential aides work "more intimately on a daily basis with the President than does a Cabinet officer," and that *Butz* therefore is not controlling. In recent years, however, such men as Henry Kissinger and James Schlesinger have served in both Presidential advisory and Cabinet positions. Kissinger held both posts simultaneously. In our view it is impossible to generalize about the role of "offices" in an individual President's administration without reference to the functions that particular officeholders are assigned by the President. *Butz v. Economou* cannot be distinguished on this basis.

[15] See, e.g., *Supreme Court of Virginia v. Consumers Union of United States,* 446 U.S. 719, 731-737 (1980); *Stump v. Sparkman,* 435 U.S. 349, 362 (1978).

[16] In *Imbler v. Pachtman,* 424 U.S. 409, 430-431 (1973), this Court reserved the question whether absolute immunity would extend to "those aspects of the prosecutor's responsibility that cast him in the role of an administrator or investigative officer." Since that time the courts of

absolute "derivative" immunity to the President's aides therefore could not be reconciled with the "functional" approach that has characterized the immunity decisions of this Court, indeed including *Gravel* itself.[17]

C. Petitioners also assert an entitlement to immunity based on the "special functions" of White House aides. This form of argument accords with the analytical approach of our cases. For aides entrusted with discretionary authority in such sensitive areas as national security or foreign policy, absolute immunity might well be justified to protect the unhesitating performance of functions vital to the national interest. But a "special functions" rationale does not warrant a blanket recognition of absolute immunity for all Presidential aides in the performance of all their duties. This conclusion too follows from our decision in *Butz*, which establishes that an executive official's claim to absolute immunity must be justified by reference to the public interest in the special functions of his office, not the mere fact of high station.[19]

Butz also identifies the location of the burden of proof. The burden of justifying absolute immunity rests on the official asserting the claim. 438 U. S., at 506. We have not of course had occasion to identify how a Presidential aide might carry this burden. But the general requisites are familiar in our cases. In order to establish entitlement to absolute immunity a Presidential aide first must show that the responsibilities of his office embraced a function so sensitive as to require a total shield from liability.[20] He then must demonstrate that he was discharging the protected function when performing the act for which liability is asserted.[21]

Applying these standards to the claims advanced by petitioners Harlow and Butterfield, we cannot conclude on the record before us that either has shown that "public policy requires [for any of the functions of his office] an exemption of [absolute] scope." *Butz*, 438 U.S., at 506. Nor, assuming that petitioners did

---

appeals generally have ruled prosecutors do not enjoy absolute immunity for acts taken in those capacities. See, e.g., *Mancini v. Lester*, 630 F.2d 990, 992 (CA3 1980); *Forsyth v. Kleindeinst*, 599 F.2d 1203, 1213-1214 (CA3 1979). This Court at least implicitly has drawn the same distinction in extending absolute immunity to executive officials when they are engaged in quasi-prosecutorial functions. See *Butz v. Economou*, 438 U.S., at 515-517.

[17] Our decision today in *Nixon v. Fitzgerald* in no way abrogates this general rule. As we explained in that opinion, the recognition of absolute immunity for all of a President's acts in office derives in principal part from factors unique to his constitutional responsibilities and station. Suits against other officials — including Presidential aides — generally do not invoke separation-of-powers considerations to the same extent as suits against the President himself.

[19] *Gravel v. United States*, 408 U.S. 606 (1972), points to a similar conclusion. We fairly may assume that some aides are assigned to act as Presidential "alter egos," id., at 616-617, in the exercise of functions for which absolute immunity is "essential for the conduct of the public business," *Butz*, supra, at 507. Cf. *Gravel, supra*, at 620 (derivative immunity extends only to acts within the "central role" of the Speech and Debate Clause in permitting free legislative speech and debate). By analogy to *Gravel*, a derivative claim to Presidential immunity would be strongest in such "central" Presidential domains as foreign policy and national security, in which the President could not discharge his singularly vital mandate without delegating functions nearly as sensitive as his own.

[20] Here as elsewhere the relevant judicial inquiries would encompass considerations of public policy, the importance of which should be confirmed either by reference to the common law or, more likely, our constitutional heritage and structure. See *Nixon v. Fitzgerald*.

[21] The need for such an inquiry is implicit in *Butz v. Economou, supra*, at 508-517; see *Imbler v. Pachtman, supra*, at 430-431 (1976). Cases involving immunity under the Speech and Debate Clause have inquired explicitly into whether particular acts and activities qualified for the protection of the Clause. See, e.g., *Hutchinson v. Proxmire*, 443 U.S. 111; *Doe v. McMillan*, 412 U.S. 306 (1973); *Gravel v. United States, supra*.

have functions for which absolute immunity would be warranted, could we now conclude that the acts charged in this lawsuit — if taken at all — would lie within the protected area. We do not, however, foreclose the possibility that petitioners, on remand, could satisfy the standards properly applicable to their claims.

IV

Even if they cannot establish that their official functions require absolute immunity, petitioners assert that public policy at least mandates an application of the qualified immunity standard that would permit the defeat of insubstantial claims without resort to trial. We agree.

A. The resolution of immunity questions inherently requires a balance between the evils inevitable in any available alternative. In situations of abuse of office, an action for damages may offer the only realistic avenue for vindication of constitutional guarantees. *Butz v. Economou, supra,* at 506; see *Bivens v. Six Unknown Fed. Narcotics Agents,* 403 U.S., at 410 (1971) ("For people in Bivens' shoes, it is damages or nothing"). It is this recognition that has required the denial of absolute immunity to most public officers. At the same time, however, it cannot be disputed seriously that claims frequently run against the innocent as well as the guilty — at a cost not only to the defendant officials, but to the society as a whole. These social costs include the expenses of litigation, the diversion of official energy from pressing public issues, and the deterrence of able citizens from acceptance of public office. Finally, there is the danger that fear of being sued will "dampen the ardor of all but the most resolute, or the most irresponsible [public officials], in the unflinching discharge of their duties." *Gregoire v. Biddle,* 177 F. 2d 579, 581 (CA2 1949), *cert. denied,* 339 U.S. 949 (1950).

In identifying qualified immunity as the best attainable accommodation of competing values, in *Butz, supra,* at 507-508, as in *Scheuer,* 416 U.S., at 245-248, we relied on the assumption that this standard would permit "[i]nsubstantial lawsuits [to] be quickly terminated." 438 U.S., at 507-508; see *Hanrahan v. Hampton,* 446 U.S. 754, 765 (1980) (POWELL, J., concurring in part and dissenting in part). Yet petitioners advance persuasive arguments that the dismissal of insubstantial lawsuits without trial — a factor presupposed in the balance of competing interests struck by our prior cases — requires an adjustment of the "good faith" standard established by our decisions.

B. Qualified or "good faith" immunity is an affirmative defense that must be pleaded by a defendant official. *Gomez v. Toledo,* 446 U.S. 635 (1980). Decisions of this Court have established that the "good faith" defense has both an "objective" and a "subjective" aspect. The objective element involves a presumptive knowledge of and respect for "basic, unquestioned constitutional rights." *Wood v. Strickland,* 420 U.S. 308, 320 (1975). The subjective component refers to "permissible intentions." *Ibid.* Characteristically the Court has defined these elements by identifying the circumstances in which qualified immunity would *not* be available. Referring both to the objective and subjective elements, we have held that qualified immunity would be defeated if an official *"knew or reasonably should have known* that the action he took within his sphere of official responsibility would violate the constitutional rights of the [plaintiff], *or* if he took the action *with malicious intention* to cause a deprivation of constitutional rights or other injury ...." *Ibid.* (emphasis added).

The subjective element of the good-faith defense frequently has proved incompatible with our admonition in *Butz* that insubstantial claims should not proceed to trial. Rule 56 of the Federal Rules of Civil Procedure provides that disputed questions of fact ordinarily may not be decided on motions for summary judgment. And an official's subjective good faith has been considered to be a question of fact that some courts have regarded as inherently requiring resolution by a jury.

In the context of *Butz*'s attempted balancing of competing values, it now is clear that substantial costs attend the litigation of the subjective good faith of government officials. Not only are there the general costs of subjecting officials to the risks of trial — distraction of officials from their governmental duties, inhibition of discretionary action, and deterrence of able people from public service. There are special costs to "subjective" inquiries of this kind. Immunity generally is available only to officials performing discretionary functions. In contrast with the thought processes accompanying "ministerial" tasks, the judgments surrounding discretionary action almost inevitably are influenced by the decisionmaker's experiences, values, and emotions. These variables explain in part why questions of subjective intent so rarely can be decided by summary judgment. Yet they also frame a background in which there often is no clear end to the relevant evidence. Judicial inquiry into subjective motivation therefore may entail broad-ranging discovery and the deposing of numerous persons, including an official's professional colleagues. Inquiries of this kind can be peculiarly disruptive of effective government.

Consistently with the balance at which we aimed in *Butz*, we conclude today that bare allegations of malice should not suffice to subject government officials either to the costs of trial or to the burdens of broad-reaching discovery. We therefore hold that government officials performing discretionary functions generally are shielded from liability for civil damages insofar as their conduct does not violate clearly established statutory or constitutional rights of which a reasonable person would have known. See *Procunier v. Navarette,* 434 U.S. 555, 565 (1978); *Wood v. Strickland,* 420 U.S., at 321.[30]

Reliance on the objective reasonableness of an official's conduct, as measured by reference to clearly established law,[31] should avoid excessive disruption of government and permit the resolution of many insubstantial claims on summary judgment. On summary judgment, the judge appropriately may determine, not only the currently applicable law, but whether that law was clearly established at the time an action occurred. If the law at that time was not clearly established, an official could not reasonably be expected to anticipate subse-

---

[30] This case involves no issue concerning the elements of the immunity available to state officials sued for constitutional violations under 42 U.S.C. § 1983. We have found previously, however, that it would be "untenable to draw a distinction for purposes of immunity law between suits brought against state officials under § 1983 and suits brought directly under the Constitution against federal officials." *Butz v. Economou,* 438 U.S., at 504.

Our decision in no way diminishes the absolute immunity currently available to officials whose functions have been held to require a protection of this scope.

[31] This case involves no claim that Congress has expressed its intent to impose "no fault" tort liability on high federal officials for violations of particular statutes or the Constitution.

quent legal developments, nor could he fairly be said to "know" that the law forbade conduct not previously identified as unlawful. Until this threshold immunity question is resolved, discovery should not be allowed. If the law was clearly established, the immunity defense ordinarily should fail, since a reasonably competent public official should know the law governing his conduct. Nevertheless, if the official pleading the defense claims extraordinary circumstances and can prove that he neither knew nor should have known of the relevant legal standard, the defense should be sustained. But again, the defense would turn primarily on objective factors.

By defining the limits of qualified immunity essentially in objective terms, we provide no license to lawless conduct. The public interest in deterrence of unlawful conduct and in compensation of victims remains protected by a test that focuses on the objective legal reasonableness of an official's acts. Where an official could be expected to know that certain conduct would violate statutory or constitutional rights, he should be made to hesitate; and a person who suffers injury caused by such conduct may have a cause of action.[33] But where an official's duties legitimately require action in which clearly established rights are not implicated, the public interest may be better served by action taken "with independence and without fear of consequences." *Pierson v. Ray,* 386 U.S. 547, 554 (1967).[34]

C. In this case petitioners have asked us to hold that the respondent's pretrial showings were insufficient to survive their motion for summary judgment.[35] We think it appropriate, however, to remand the case to the District Court, for its reconsideration of this issue in light of this opinion. The trial court is more familiar with the record so far developed and also is better situated to make any such further findings as may be necessary.

V

The judgment of the Court of Appeals is vacated, and the case remanded for further action consistent with this opinion.

So ordered.

Justice Brennan, with whom Justice Marshall and Justice Blackmun join, concurring in the opinion of the Court.

I agree with the substantive standard announced by the Court today, imposing liability when a public-official defendant "knew or should have known" of the constitutionally violative effect of his actions. This standard would not allow the official who *actually knows* that he was violating the law to escape liability

---

[33] Cf. *Procunier v. Navarette, supra,* at 565 (footnote omitted) ("Because they could not reasonably have been expected to be aware of a constitutional right that had not yet been declared, petitioners did not act with such disregard for established law that their conduct 'cannot reasonably be characterized as being in good faith.'").

[34] We emphasize that our decision applies only to suits for civil *damages* arising from actions within the scope of an official's duties and in "objective" good faith. We express no view as to the conditions in which injunctive or declaratory relief might be available.

[35] In *Butz,* we admonished that "insubstantial" suits against high public officials should not be allowed to proceed to trial. 438 U.S., at 438. See *Schuck, supra,* 1980 Sup. Ct. Rev., at 324-327. We reiterate this admonition. Insubstantial lawsuits undermine the effectiveness of Government as contemplated by our constitutional structure, and "firm application of the Federal Rules of Civil Procedure" is fully warranted in such cases. *Id.,* at 508.

for his actions, even if he could not "reasonably have been expected" to know what he actually did know. Thus the clever and unusually well-informed violator of constitutional rights will not evade just punishment for his crimes. I also agree that this standard applies "across the board," to all "government officials performing discretionary functions.". . .

CHIEF JUSTICE BURGER, dissenting. . . .

In this case the Court decides that senior aides of a President do not have derivative immunity from the President. I am at a loss, however, to reconcile this conclusion with our holding in *Gravel v. United States,* 408 U.S. 606 (1972). The Court reads *Butz v. Economou,* 438 U.S. 478 (1978), as resolving that question; I do not. *Butz* is clearly distinguishable.

In *Gravel* we held that it is implicit in the Constitution that aides of Members of Congress have absolute immunity for acts performed for Members in relation to their legislative function. We viewed the aides' immunity as deriving from the Speech or Debate Clause, which provides that "for any Speech or Debate *in either House,* [Senators and Representatives] shall not be questioned in any other Place." Art. I, § 6, cl. 1 (emphasis added). Read literally, the Clause would, of course, limit absolute immunity only to the Member and only to speech and debate within the Chamber. But we have read much more into this plain language. The Clause says nothing about "legislative acts" outside the Chambers, but we concluded that the Constitution grants absolute immunity for legislative acts not only "in either House" but in committees and conferences and in reports on legislative activities.

Nor does the Clause mention immunity for congressional aides. Yet, going far beyond any words found in the Constitution itself, we held that a Member's aides who implement policies and decisions of the Member are entitled to the same absolute immunity as a Member. . . .

. . . How can we conceivably hold that a President of the United States, who represents a vastly larger constituency than does any Member of Congress, should not have "alter egos" with comparable immunity? . . .

NOTES

1. In *Nixon v. Fitzgerald,* 457 U.S. 731 (1982), the Supreme Court dismissed Fitzgerald's action against Richard Nixon, holding that a former President is entitled to absolute immunity from damage liability predicated upon his official acts while in office. The Court determined that a President's absolute immunity is "a functionally mandated incident of the President's unique office, rooted in the constitutional tradition of the separation of powers and supported by [this Nation's] history." This unqualified immunity extends to all acts performed within the "outer perimeter" of the President's duties in office, to ensure no judicial interference with the unique authority vested in the President.

2. *Army & Air Force Exch. Serv. v. Sheehan,* 456 U.S. 728 (1982), concerned a federal employee who held an appointive position that did not involve any express employment contract. When he was discharged as a result of off-duty conduct, Sheehan sued the Army and Air Force Exchange Service under the Tucker Act, 28 U.S.C. § 1346(a)(2), alleging that his termination violated applicable personnel regulations that provided him with implied contractual rights cognizable under that enactment. However, the Supreme Court rejected his

claim, holding that governmental regulations and personnel statutes do not establish contractual rights enforceable under the Tucker Act.

3. In *Dretar v. Smith,* 752 F.2d 1015 (5th Cir. 1985), the court relied on *Barr v. Matteo,* 360 U.S. 564 (1959), and *Bush v. Lucas,* 462 U.S. 367 (1983), to support its finding that sovereign immunity shielded a federal supervisor from tort liability arising from an alleged assault committed upon an employee during a heated, work-related confrontation where only minor injuries were inflicted. "A slight battery such as that suffered by [the employee] is the price that we all must pay to free our public officials from the fear of defending vindictive and ill-founded damage suits in performing their official duties." Had more severe injuries been inflicted, the supervisor would have forfeited his immunity. See *McIntosh v. Turner,* 861 F.2d 524 (8th Cir. 1988). See also *Schweiker v. Chilicky,* 487 U.S. 412 (1988).

4. In *Nietert v. Overby,* 816 F.2d 1464 (10th Cir. 1987), the court held that a clerk with the Army and Air Force Exchange Service who used a government "hotline" to report alleged wrongdoing by her supervisor was immune from defamation liability since it found that: (1) she was acting within the scope of her official duties when she made the report in question; (2) although her clerical job involved "very minimal discretion," her use of the government hotline required the exercise of judgment and discretion; and (3) the extension of immunity to people like her would advance the basic policies underlying the immunity doctrine. See also *Westfall v. Erwin,* 484 U.S. 292 (1988), indicating that federal officials only enjoy absolute immunity from state-law tort liability where they act within the scope of their employment *and* exercise some independent (i.e., "discretionary") judgment.

Table of Cases

References are to pages. Principal cases and the pages where they appear are in italics.

Index

A

T

U

V

W